PHILIP'S ROAD

GW01375550

2020 BIG ATLAS BRITAIN & IRELAND

CONTENTS

II Key to map symbols

III Motorway sevice areas

IV Restricted motorway junctions

VI **UK Truckstops – gourmet or gruesome?** Are Truckstops an option for the motorist?

VIII Route planning maps

XIV Road map of Ireland

XVI Distances and journey times

1 Road maps of Britain

97 **Urban approach maps**

- 97 Bristol *approaches*
- 98 Birmingham *approaches*
- 100 Cardiff *approaches*
- 101 Edinburgh *approaches*
- 102 Glasgow *approaches*
- 103 Leeds *approaches*
- 104 London *approaches*
- 108 Liverpool *approaches*
- 109 Manchester *approaches*
- 110 Newcastle *approaches*
- 111 Nottingham *approaches*
- 112 Sheffield *approaches*

113 **Town plans**

- 113 Aberdeen, Bath, Birmingham, Blackpool
- 114 Bournemouth, Bradford, Brighton, Bristol, Cambridge
- 115 Canterbury, Cardiff, Cheltenham, Chester, Chichester, Colchester
- 116 Coventry, Derby, Dundee, Durham, Edinburgh
- 117 Exeter, Glasgow, Gloucester, Harrogate, Hull
- 118 Ipswich, Lancaster, Leeds, Leicester, Lincoln
- 119 Liverpool, Luton, Manchester, Middlesbrough
- 120 London
- 122 Milton Keynes, Newcastle upon Tyne, Newport, Northampton, Norwich, Nottingham
- 123 Oxford, Peterborough, Plymouth, Poole, Portsmouth, Preston
- 124 Reading, Salisbury, Scarborough, Sheffield, Southampton
- 125 Southend-on-Sea, Stoke-on-Trent (Hanley), Stratford-upon-Avon, Sunderland, Swansea, Swindon
- 126 Telford, Torquay, Winchester, Windsor, Worcester, York

127 **Index to town plans**

137 **Index to road maps of Britain**

Inside back cover: **County and unitary authority boundaries**

www.philips-maps.co.uk

First published in 2009 by Philip's
a division of Octopus Publishing Group Ltd
www.octopusbooks.co.uk
Carmelite House, 50 Victoria Embankment
London EC4Y 0DZ
An Hachette UK Company
www.hachette.co.uk

Eleventh edition 2019
First impression 2019

ISBN 978-1-84907-504-6

Cartography by Philip's

Information for National Parks, Areas of Outstanding Natural Beauty, National Trails and Country Parks in Wales supplied by the Countryside Council for Wales.

Information for National Parks, Areas of Outstanding Natural Beauty, National Trails and Country Parks in England supplied by Natural England. Data for Regional Parks, Long Distance Footpaths and Country Parks in Scotland provided by Scottish Natural Heritage.

Gaelic name forms used in the Western Isles provided by Comhairle nan Eilean.

Data for the National Nature Reserves in England provided by Natural England. Data for the National Nature Reserves in Wales provided by Countryside Council for Wales. Darparwyd data'n ymwneud â Gwarchodfeydd Natur Cenedlaethol Cymru gan Gyngor Cefn Gwlad Cymru.

Information on the location of National Nature Reserves in Scotland was provided by Scottish Natural Heritage.

Data for National Scenic Areas in Scotland provided by the Scottish Executive Office. Crown copyright material is reproduced with the permission of the Controller of HMSO and the Queen's Printer for Scotland. Licence number C02W0003960.

Printed in China

*Data from Nielsen Total Consumer Market 2016 weeks 1–52

Road map symbols

M6	Motorway, toll motorway
4 5	Motorway junction – full, restricted access
S S	Motorway service area – full, restricted access
	Motorway under construction
A453	Primary route – dual, single carriageway
S	Service area, roundabout, multi-level junction
4 5	Numbered junction – full, restricted access
	Primary route under construction
	Narrow primary route
Derby	Primary destination
A34	A road – dual, single carriageway
	A road under construction, narrow A road
B2135	B road – dual, single carriageway
	B road under construction, narrow B road
	Minor road – over 4 metres, under 4 metres wide
	Minor road with restricted access
2	Distance in miles
	Scenic route
TOLL	Toll, steep gradient – arrow points downhill
	Tunnel
	National trail – England and Wales
	Long distance footpath – Scotland
	Railway with station
	Level crossing, tunnel
	Preserved railway with station
	National boundary
	County / unitary authority boundary
	Car ferry, catamaran
	Passenger ferry, catamaran
	Hovercraft
CALAIS	Ferry destination
Ferry	Car ferry – river crossing
	Principal airport, other airport
	National park
	Area of Outstanding Natural Beauty – England and Wales
	National Scenic Area – Scotland
	forest park / regional park / national forest
	Woodland
	Beach
	Linear antiquity
	Roman road
1066	Hillfort, battlefield – with date
795	Viewpoint, nature reserve, spot height – in metres
	Golf course, youth hostel, sporting venue
P&R	Camp site, caravan site, camping and caravan site
	Shopping village, park and ride
29	Adjoining page number – road maps

Relief

Feet	metres
3000	914
2600	792
2200	671
1800	549
1400	427
1000	305
0	0

Road map scale
1 : 200 000 • 1 cm = 2 km • 1 inch = 3·15 miles

0 1 2 3 4 5 6 7 8 9 10 km
0 1 2 3 4 5 6 miles

Parts of Scotland
1 : 250 000 • 1 cm = 2.5 km • 1 inch = 3.94 miles

0 1 2 3 4 5 6 7 8 9 10 11 12 km
0 1 2 3 4 5 6 7 8 miles

Orkney and Shetland Islands
1 : 340 000 • 1 cm = 3.4 km • 1 inch = 5.37 miles

0 2 4 6 8 10 12 km
0 1 2 3 4 5 6 7 8 miles

Approach map symbols

M6	Motorway
	Toll motorway
6 5	Motorway junction – full, restricted access
S	Service area
	Under construction
A6	Primary route – dual, single carriageway
S	Service area
	Multi-level junction
	Roundabout
	Under construction
A195	A road – dual, single carriageway
B1288	B road – dual, single carriageway
	Minor road – dual, single carriageway
	Ring road
3	Distance in miles
COSELEY	Railway with station
LOXDALE	Tramway with station
M	Underground or metro station
	Congestion charge area

Town plan symbols

	Motorway
	Primary route – dual, single carriageway
	A road – dual, single carriageway
	B road – dual, single carriageway
	Minor through road
	One-way street
	Pedestrian roads
	Shopping streets
	Railway with station
City Hall	Tramway with station
	Bus or railway station building
	Shopping precinct or retail park
	Park
	Building of public interest
	Theatre, cinema
P	Parking, shopmobility
Bank	Underground station
West St	Metro station
H	Hospital, Police station
PO	Post office

Tourist information

✝ Abbey, cathedral or priory	Church	House and garden	Safari park
Ancient monument	Country park England and Wales Scotland	Motor racing circuit	Theme park
Aquarium		Museum	Tourist information centre
Art gallery	Farm park	Picnic area	open all year
Bird collection or aviary	Garden	Preserved railway	open seasonally
	Historic ship	Race course	Zoo
Castle	House	Roman antiquity	Other place of interest

Motorway service areas

Motorway service area
Kinross
M90
M9
Stirling
M80
M9
Old Inns
M8
Bothwell
Heart of Scotland
Hamilton
M74
Happendon
Abington
A74(M)
Annandale Water
Gretna Green
Todhills
Southwaite
Washington
Durham
A1(M)
M6
Tebay
Scotch Corner
Killington Lake
Burton-in-Kendal
A1(M)
Wetherby
Lancaster
M6
M55
M65
Hartshead Moor
Blackburn with Darwen
Ferrybridge
Charnock Richard
M62
M62
Doncaster North
Birch
Rivington
Woolley Edge
M180
M1
Burtonwood
Blyth
Knutsford
Woodall
M56
Chester
Sandbach
Tibshelf
M1
Trowell
Keele
Stafford
Donington Park
M6
Telford
Norton Canes
Leicester
M54
Hilton Park
Leicester Forest East
Tamworth
Peterborough
Corley
M1
A1(M)
Frankley
M6
Watford Gap
Hopwood Park
Northampton
Warwick
M5
Strensham
M40
Newport Pagnell
Baldock
M50
M1
M11
Ross Spur
Cherwell Valley
Toddington
A1(M)
Birchanger Green
Gloucester
M5
Pont Abraham
Oxford
Swansea
Michaelwood
M25
South Mimms
M25
M4
Cardiff Gate
Magor
Beaconsfield
London Gateway
Sarn Park
Severn View
M4
Membury
Heston
Thurrock
Cardiff West
M4
Reading
Gordano
Leigh Delamere
Chieveley
Medway
M5
Cobham
Sedgemoor
M3
Fleet
M2
M25
Clacket Lane
Maidstone
M20
Stop 24
Bridgwater
Winchester
M23
Pease Pottage
M5
Taunton Deane
Tiverton
M27
Rownhams
M27
Cullompton
Exeter

Restricted motorway junctions

M1 Junction 34

M1 Leeds
Barnsley
34
A6109
Rotherham
A6178
Rotherham
A6109 Sheffield
34
A6178 Sheffield
A631
A6102
M1 Nottingham
London

M1 Junctions 6, 6A
M25 Junctions 21, 21A

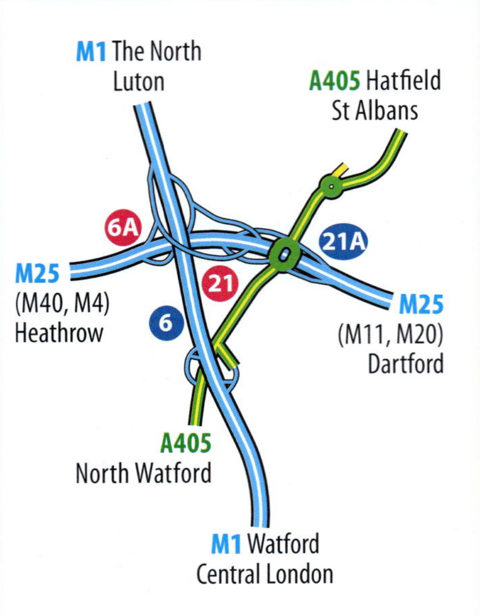
M1 The North
Luton
A405 Hatfield
St Albans
6A
21A
M25
(M40, M4)
Heathrow
21
6
M25
(M11, M20)
Dartford
A405
North Watford
M1 Watford
Central London

M4 Junctions 25, 25A, 26

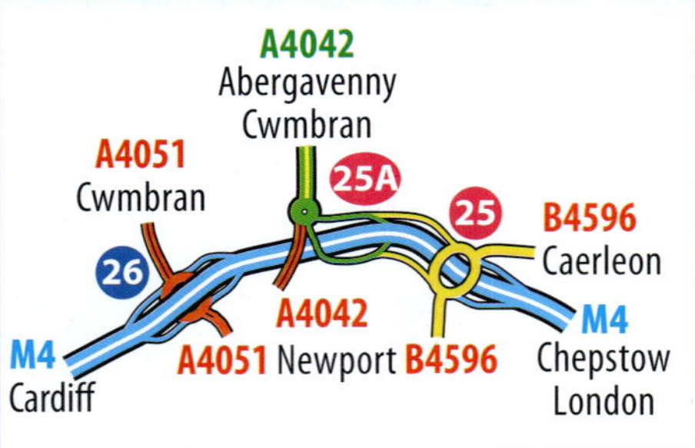
A4042
Abergavenny
Cwmbran
A4051
Cwmbran
25A
25
B4596
Caerleon
26
A4042
M4
M4
Cardiff
A4051 Newport B4596
Chepstow
London

M5 Junction 11A

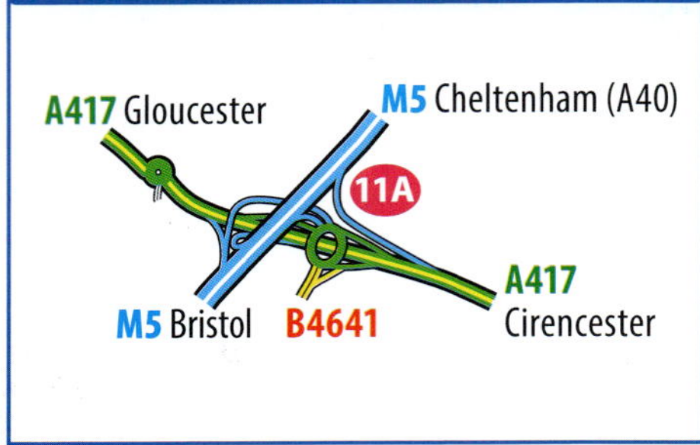
A417 Gloucester
M5 Cheltenham (A40)
11A
A417
Cirencester
M5 Bristol
B4641

M1	Northbound	Southbound
2	No exit	No access
4	No exit	No access
6A	No exit. Access from M25 only	No access. Exit to M25 only
7	No exit. Access from A414 only	No access. Exit to A414 only
17	No access. Exit to M45 only	No exit. Access from M45 only
19	No exit to A14	No access from A14
21A	No access	No exit
23A		Exit to A42 only
24A	No exit	No access
35A	No access	No exit
43	No access. Exit to M621 only	No exit. Access from M621 only
48	No exit to A1(M) southbound	

M3	Eastbound	Westbound
8	No exit	No access
10	No access	No exit
13	No access to M27 eastbound	
14	No exit	No access

M4	Eastbound	Westbound
1	Exit to A4 eastbound only	Access from A4 westbound only
2	Access from A4 eastbound only	Access to A4 westbound only
21	No exit	No access
23	No access	No exit
25	No exit	No access
25A	No exit	No access
29	No exit	No access
38		No access
39	No exit or access	No exit
41	No access	No exit
41A	No exit	No access
42	Access from A483 only	Exit to A483 only

M5	Northbound	Southbound
10	No exit	No access
11A	No access from A417 eastbound	No exit to A417 westbound

M6	Northbound	Southbound
3A	No access.	No exit. Access from M6 eastbound only
4A	No exit. Access from M42 southbound only	No access. Exit to M42 only
5	No access	No exit
10A	No access. Exit to M54 only	No exit. Access from M54 only
11A	No exit. Access from M6 Toll only	No access. Exit to M6 Toll only
20	No exit to M56 eastbound	No access from M56 westbound
24	No exit	No access
25	No access	No exit
30	No exit. Access from M61 northbound only	No access. Exit to M61 southbound only
31A	No access	No exit
45	No access	No exit

M6 Toll	Northbound	Southbound
T1		No exit
T2	No exit, no access	No access
T5	No exit	No access
T7	No access	No exit
T8	No access	No exit

M8	Eastbound	Westbound
6	No exit	No access
6A	No access	No exit
7	No Access	No exit
7A	No exit. Access from A725 northbound only	No access. Exit to A725 southbound only
8	No exit to M73 northbound	No access from M73 southbound
9	No access	No exit
13	No exit southbound	Access from M73 southbound only
14	No access	No exit
16	No exit	No access
17	No exit	
18		No exit
19	No exit to A814 eastbound	No access from A814 westbound
20	No exit	No access
21	No access from M74	No exit
22	No exit. Access from M77 only	No access. Exit to M77 only
23	No exit	No access
25	Exit to A739 northbound only. Access from A739 southbound only	
25A	No exit	No access
28	No exit	No access
28A	No exit	No access

M9	Eastbound	Westbound
2	No access	No exit
3	No exit	No access
6	No access	No exit
8	No exit	No access

M11	Northbound	Southbound
4	No exit	No access
5	No access	No exit
8A	No access	No exit
9	No access	No exit
13	No access	No exit
14	No exit to A428 westbound	No exit. Access from A14 westbound only

M20	Eastbound	Westbound
2	No access	No exit
3	No exit Access from M26 eastbound only	No access Exit to M26 westbound only
11A	No access	No exit

M23	Northbound	Southbound
7	No exit to A23 southbound	No access from A23 northbound
10A	No exit	No access

M25	Clockwise	Anticlockwise
5	No exit to M26 eastbound	No access from M26 westbound
19	No access	No exit
21	No exit to M1 southbound. Access from M1 southbound only	No exit to M1 southbound. Access from M1 southbound only
31	No exit	No access

M27	Eastbound	Westbound
10	No exit	No access
12	No access	No exit

M40	Eastbound	Westbound
3	No exit	No access
7	No exit	No access
8	No exit	No access
13	No exit	No access
14	No access	No exit
16	No access	No exit

M42	Northbound	Southbound
1	No exit	No access
7	No access Exit to M6 northbound only	No exit. Access from M6 northbound only
7A	No access. Exit to M6 southbound only	No exit
8	No exit. Access from M6 southbound only	Exit to M6 northbound only. Access from M6 southbound only

M45	Eastbound	Westbound
M1 J17	Access to M1 southbound only	No access from M1 southbound
With A45	No access	No exit

M48	Eastbound	Westbound
M4 J21	No exit to M4 westbound	No access from M4 eastbound
M4 J23	No access from M4 westbound	No exit to M4 eastbound

M8 Junctions 8, 9 · M73 Junctions 1, 2 · M74 Junctions 2A, 3, 3A, 4

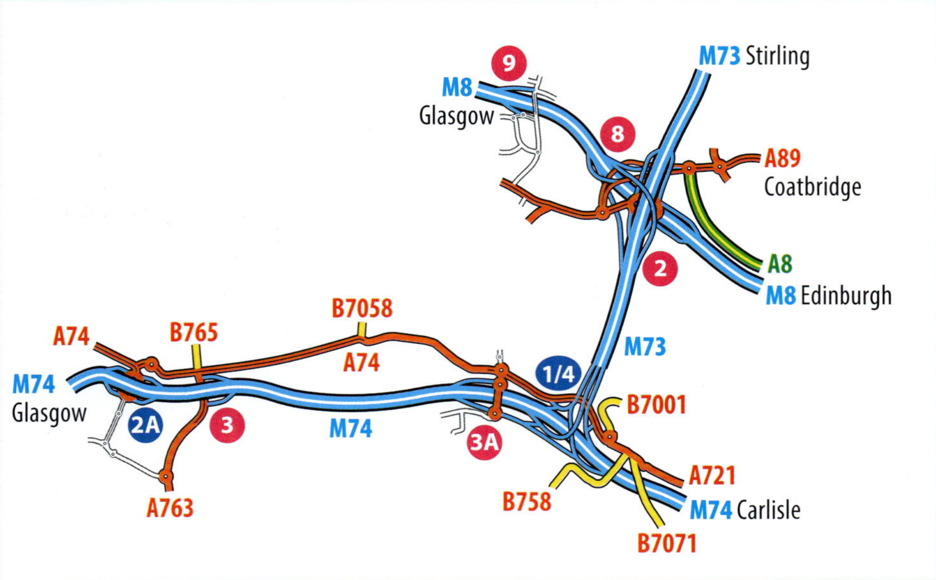
9
M8
Glasgow
M73 Stirling
8
A89
Coatbridge
2
A8
M8 Edinburgh
B7058
A74
B765
A74
M73
1/4
M74
Glasgow
2A
3
M74
3A
B7001
A721
A763
B758
M74 Carlisle
B7071

M11 Junctions 13, 14

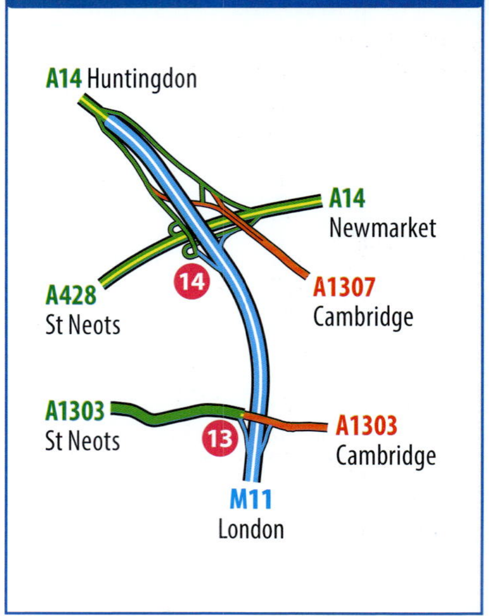
A14 Huntingdon
A14
Newmarket
A428
St Neots
14
A1307
Cambridge
A1303
St Neots
13
A1303
Cambridge
M11
London

M49	Southbound	Northbound
18A	No exit to M5 northbound	No access from M5 southbound

M53	Northbound	Southbound
11	Exit to M56 eastbound only. Access from M56 westbound only	Exit to M56 eastbnd only. Access from M56 westbound only

M56	Eastbound	Westbound
2	No exit	No access
3	No access	No exit
4	No exit	No access
7		No access
8	No exit or access	No exit
9	No access from M6 northbound	No access to M6 southbound
15	No exit to M53	No access from M53 northbound

M57	Northbound	Southbound
3	No exit	No access
5	No exit	No access

M58	Eastbound	Westbound
1	No exit	No access

M60	Clockwise	Anticlockwise
2	No exit	No access
3	No exit to A34 northbound	No exit to A34 northbound
4	No access from M56	No exit to M56
5	No exit to A5103 southbound	No exit to A5103 northbound
14	No exit	No access
16	No exit	No access
20	No access	No exit
22		No access
25	No access	
26		No exit or access
27	No exit	No access

M61	Northbound	Southbound
2	No access from A580 eastbound	No exit to A580 westbound
3	No access from A580 eastbound. No access from A666 southbound	No exit to A580 westbound
M6 J30	No exit to M6 southbound	No access from M6 northbound

M62	Eastbound	Westbound
23	No access	No exit

M65	Eastbound	Westbound
9	No access	No exit
11	No exit	No access

M66	Northbound	Southbound
1	No access	No exit

M6 Junction 20 · M56 Junction 9

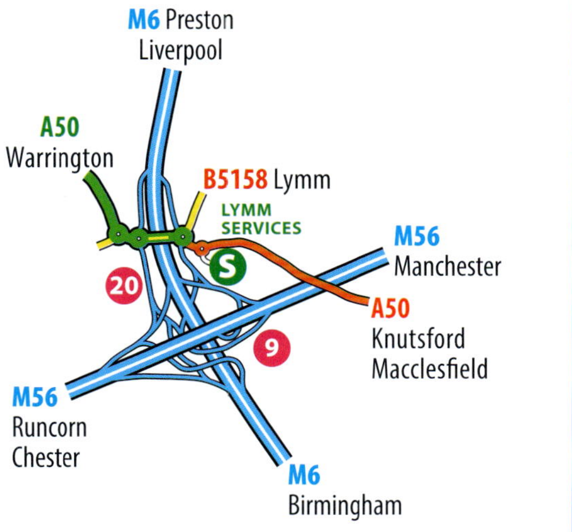
M6 Preston
Liverpool
A50
Warrington
B5158 Lymm
LYMM
SERVICES
M56
Manchester
20
9
A50
Knutsford
Macclesfield
M56
Runcorn
Chester
M6
Birmingham

M67	Eastbound	Westbound
1A	No access	No exit
2	No exit	No access

M69	Northbound	Southbound
2	No exit	No access

M73	Northbound	Southbound
2	No access from M8 eastbound	No exit to M8 westbound

M74	Northbound	Southbound
3	No access	No exit
3A	No exit	No access
7	No exit	No access
9	No exit or access	No access
10		No exit
11	No exit	No access
12	No access	No exit

M77	Northbound	Southbound
4	No exit	No access
6	No exit	No access
7	No exit	
8	No access	No access

M80	Northbound	Southbound
4A	No access	No exit
6A	No exit	No access
8	Exit to M876 northbound only. No access	Access from M876 southbound only. No exit

M90	Northbound	Southbound
1	Access from A90 northbound only	No access. Exit to A90 southbound only
2A	No access	No exit
7	No exit	No access
8	No access	No exit
10	No access from A912	No exit to A912

M180	Eastbound	Westbound
1	No access	No exit

M621	Eastbound	Westbound
2A	No exit	No access
4	No exit	
5	No exit	No access
6	No access	No exit

M876	Northbound	Southbound
2	No access	No exit

A1(M)	Northbound	Southbound
2	No access	No exit
3		No access
5	No exit	No exit, no access
14	No exit	No access
40	No access	No exit
43	No exit. Access from M1 only	No access. Exit to M1 only
57	No access	No exit
65	No access	No exit

M3 Junctions 13, 14 · M27 Junction 4

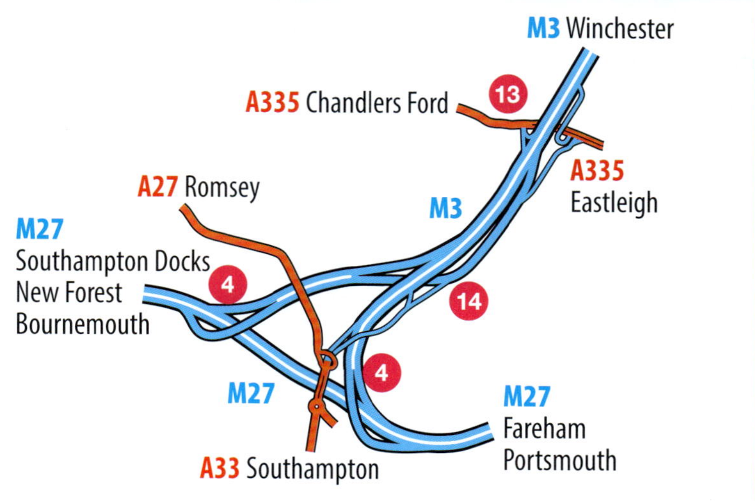
M3 Winchester
A335 Chandlers Ford
13
A335
Eastleigh
A27 Romsey
M3
M27
Southampton Docks
New Forest
Bournemouth
4
14
4
M27
M27
Fareham
Portsmouth
A33 Southampton

M6 Junctions 3A, 4A · M42 Junctions 7, 7A, 8, 9
M6 Toll Junctions T1, T2

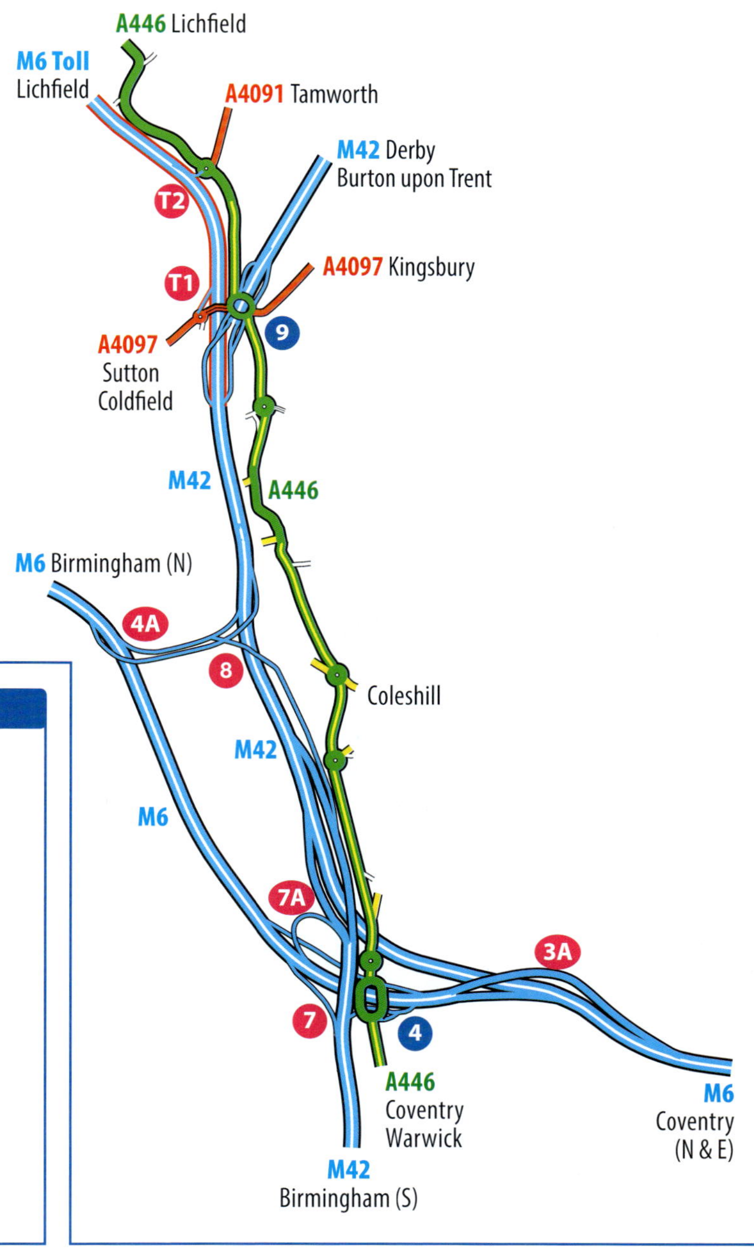
A446 Lichfield
M6 Toll
Lichfield
A4091 Tamworth
M42 Derby
Burton upon Trent
T2
T1
A4097 Kingsbury
A4097
Sutton
Coldfield
9
M42
A446
M6 Birmingham (N)
4A
8
Coleshill
M42
M6
7A
3A
7
4
A446
Coventry
Warwick
M6
Coventry
(N & E)
M42
Birmingham (S)

A3(M)	Northbound	Southbound
1	No exit	No access
4	No access	No exit

A38(M) with Victoria Rd, (Park Circus) Birmingham	
Northbound	No exit
Southbound	No access

A48(M)	Northbound	Southbound
M4 Junc 29	Exit to M4 eastbound only	Access from M4 westbound only
29A	Access from A48 eastbound only	Exit to A48 westbound only

A57(M)	Eastbound	Westbound
With A5103	No access	No exit
With A34	No access	No exit

A58(M)	Southbound
With Park Lane and Westgate, Leeds	No access

A64(M)	Eastbound	Westbound
With A58 Clay Pit Lane, Leeds	No access from A58	No exit to A58

A74(M)	Northbound	Southbound
18	No access	No exit
22		No exit to A75

A194(M)	Northbound	Southbound
A1(M) J65 Gateshead Western Bypass	Access from A1(M) northbound only	Exit to A1(M) southbound only

M62 Junctions 32A, 33 · A1(M) Junctions 40, 41

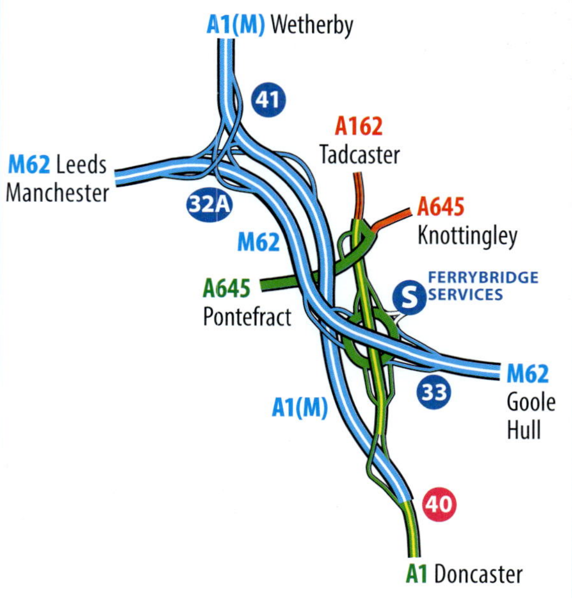
A1(M) Wetherby
41
A162
Tadcaster
M62 Leeds
Manchester
32A
A645
Knottingley
M62
A645
Pontefract
FERRYBRIDGE
SERVICES
M62
Goole
Hull
33
A1(M)
40
A1 Doncaster

UK Truckstops – gourmet or gruesome?

Are Truckstops an option for the motorist?

By Stephen Mesquita,
Philip's On the Road Correspondent

Transport picture library / Alamy • Winston Link / Alamy

Can there be a better way to spend a day than eating 10 All-day Full English Breakfasts at 10 truckstops around the Midlands? We've just done it and the answer is 'yes'. Two years ago, Philip's brought you our survey of the UK's Mobile Layby Cafes (also known as Butty Vans). One of our kind readers posted a customer review on a well-known online bookshop saying that 'at least it showed that the publisher has a sense of humour'. On this latest assignment, the publisher's sense of humour wore thin. Truckstops – not just for food

It was 6.30 on a dreary Thursday morning in early June when Philip's Sales Supremo, Stuart, and I met up just off the M1 at our first truckstop. Nine hours later, we went our separate ways having sampled ten Full English breakfasts. We could be traced by the trail of quarter-eaten breakfasts left deserted on café tables throughout the Midlands.

There were two questions we wanted to answer on this fearless exploration of roadside eateries. What is the food like in truckstops compared with other roadside eating options? And are truckstops only good for truckers – or should the rest of us give them a try?

Five things you need to know about truckstops (if you're not a trucker)

1 How do you find a truckstop?

If you're not a trucker and you're looking for something different, take a look in our ***Trucker's Navigator Atlas*** for our very useful location map of some selected UK truckstops. All those which we sampled in our 'breakfastathon' are listed there. The list is not exhaustive. There are plenty of suggestions online (search UK truckstops or transport cafés). Or there are apps with mapping to download: we tried *Iveco Hi-Stop UK Truckstops Directory* (free) and *Truckstop UK* (£1.99)

2 Is a truckstop just another name for a café?

Truckstops are for truckers and they're not just for food. The main purpose of a truckstop is for truckers to park up and rest. Food is part of the deal but it's not the main part. Not surprisingly, you'll find lots of trucks parked up – and many truckstops offer accommodation, showers and even a shop to go with the café.

3 Are truckstops always open?

There are plenty of 24-hour truckstops – or, at least, ones open from early in the morning till late at night. Not all the cafes are open for as long as this, although most open around 6am and close as late as 10pm. If in doubt, check in advance.

4 Will I be welcome if I'm not a trucker?

Now we get to the crunch. If you're not a trucker, will you be welcomed – and feel comfortable – eating in a truckstop? After eating at ten of them, we're pleased to report that at no stage were we made to feel unwanted.

It's true that the welcome varied from enthusiastic to peremptory. The highlight was being sent on our way with a cheerful 'Turrah, luv' in best Brummie. The lowlights were a couple of truckstops where we were served by people who gave the impression that they couldn't really be bothered. So you'll be unlucky if you're made to feel unwelcome.

But here's the crunch – could we recommend most truckstops to non-truckers? As I sampled each one, I asked myself the question – would I be happy taking my family here? Well, I have taken my family to a truckstop – and it was fine. But, after this experience, I feel I must have been lucky to choose an exceptional truckstop. Because – with the exception of the two truckstops that we have named and praised, I could not put my hand on my heart and say that truckstops are suitable family eating places. Most of the truckstops we sampled looked uninviting from the outside and, while they passed the test inside (mainly clean, reasonably comfortable if a bit basic), the overall impression of the ambiance was depressing.

Perhaps we hit a bad day – but the customers gave the impression that they were only there because they had no choice.There seemed to be none of the banter and chatty roadside welcome that was such a pleasant surprise when we tested the Butty Vans.

5 The fare

Let's start with the positives. Generally (not always) the breakfasts were cooked to order and hot. One up to truckstops over motorway service areas. And the price. If cheap is the name of the game, then truckstops come out winners.

But that's where the good news ends. Because

From the team's notebook

Prices sometimes included a cup of tea or coffee

Truckstop 1 £4.95

• ***egg*** *overcooked* • **bacon** *very salty but it had been grilled* • **hash browns** *from the freezer – like wet paper* • ***fried bread*** *tasted good, as it was mainly fat*

Truckstop 2 £3.99

• ***bacon*** *– old leather with salt* • *four canned* ***tomatoes*** *seems a crowd* • ***sausages*** *– not much meat* • ***egg*** *was decent*

Truckstop 3 £5.25

• ***egg*** *overcooked and like rubber* • ***chips*** *(chips for breakfast??) soggy* • ***tomatoes*** *not just canned but chopped* • ***bacon*** *far too salty and quite tough* • ***fried bread*** *was the nicest thing*

Truckstop 4 £5.50

• ***egg*** *decently cooked* • ***bacon*** *mainly salty and very rubbery with it* • ***sausage*** *artificial but quite tasty* • ***fried bread*** *ok*

Truckstop 5 £3.95

• ***bacon*** *like old boots with added salt* • ***sausage*** *ok taste but not much meat* • ***everything else*** *passable*

Truckstop 7 £5.95

• ***bacon*** *cold and tasteless* • *sausage a pig hasn't bothered it with its presence* • ***egg*** *mainly water* • ***fried bread*** *was the crust taking economy to its ultimate*

Truckstop 8 £5.45

• ***sausages*** *not great (signs of fatigue starting to surface among the team by now)* • ***bacon*** *a bit tough and salty but tasted ok-ish* • ***fried bread*** *tasteless* • ***eggs*** *ok* • ***fresh tomatoes*** *– at last*

Truckstop 9 £5.49

• ***edible*** *but unexciting*

cheap isn't the same as good value. Most (not all) of the truckstop breakfasts we sampled were made from the cheapest possible ingredients. There was almost no variety in the components. Sausages were mainly artificial. Bacon was beyond salty and tough. Tomatoes were tinned. All in all it was unappetising fare (except for the fried bread – but I have to confess a cholesterol-laden soft spot for fried bread).

Many of the breakfasts came with baked beans and/or hash browns (sometimes offered as an alternative to fried bread). It's not our place to argue whether these are authentic ingredients of the Full English. All the teas were teabags (usually dangled in the cup in front of you) and all the coffee was instant (except at the *Super Sausage*).

Because there was so little to choose between most of the breakfasts we sampled, we've taken the unusual step of only naming those truckstops (2 out of 10) where we felt that the breakfasts were out of the ordinary. And the ordinary was very ordinary. The proprietors would argue that they are not in the market for non-truckers and that, while non-trucking visitors are welcome, they are not the target market. And they might say that the truckers who eat there are perfectly happy with the fare. We'd say that it's a captive market. We'd say that it's possible to offer something a little more appetising (and healthy) than this and still make a decent profit. In fact, we'd say *'Truckers – you deserve better than this'*.

So well done to the two truckstops that did offer something more appetising!

Truckstop 6 £4.95

Why is the picture of a half-eaten breakfast? Because your Philip's team was so amazed at stumbling upon something edible that they set upon the food and were half way through when they realised they hadn't taken a pic. Highly unprofessional – but it shows the level of desperation to which we had sunk. So well done ***PJ's Transport Café***, Sudbury Derbyshire! It may have a rather unpromising exterior but, for £4.95 including a cuppa, we got a very decent breakfast.

• ***sausages*** *herby and by far the best yet* • ***bacon*** *salty but tasty 'piping hot* ***fried bread*** *nice and crisp* • ***mushrooms*** *– YES!!!* • ***no canned tomatoes*** *and* ***baked beans*** *were optional* • ***egg*** *– decent*

Truckstop 10 £5.50 (plus drinks)

Well done ***Super Sausage*** café, Towcester! But we have to add a proviso. This was on a different level because it aimed higher – as a truckstop and a family café. It was the most expensive – but it showed that if you offer quality, you can appeal to your traditional haulier's market – and to the family market.

• ***bacon*** *tasted of bacon* • *nice* ***sausages*** *– bravo!* • ***egg*** *nicely cooked* • ***tea*** *with tea leaves* • *real* ***coffee***

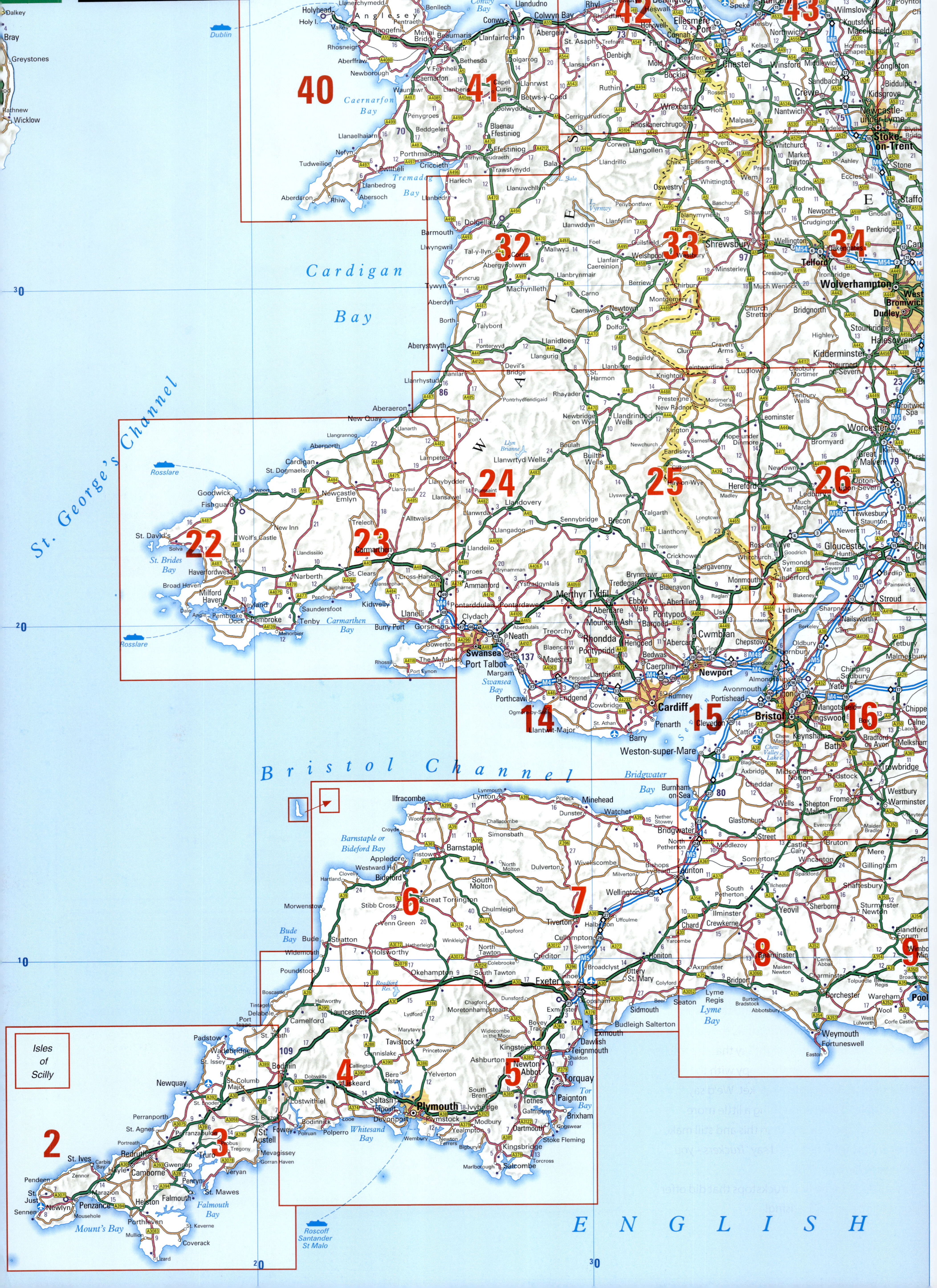
Cardigan
Bay
St. George's Channel
Bristol Channel
ENGLISH
Caernarfon Bay
Tremadog Bay
Carmarthen Bay
Swansea Bay
St. Brides Bay
Bridgwater Bay
Barnstaple or Bideford Bay
Bude Bay
Whitesand Bay
Falmouth Bay
Mount's Bay
Lyme Bay
Isles of Scilly
Dublin
Rosslare
Roscoff Santander St Malo
W A L E S
2
3
4
5
6
7
8
9
14
15
16
22
23
24
25
26
32
33
34
40
41
42
43
Holyhead
Anglesey
Bangor
Caernarfon
Llandudno
Conwy
Colwyn Bay
Rhyl
Liverpool
Birkenhead
Chester
Wrexham
Crewe
Stoke-on-Trent
Shrewsbury
Telford
Wolverhampton
Aberystwyth
Dolgellau
Machynlleth
Newtown
Cardigan
Fishguard
St. David's
Haverfordwest
Milford Haven
Pembroke
Tenby
Carmarthen
Llanelli
Swansea
Port Talbot
Neath
Merthyr Tydfil
Rhondda
Pontypridd
Bridgend
Cardiff
Barry
Newport
Cwmbran
Abergavenny
Monmouth
Brecon
Hereford
Leominster
Worcester
Gloucester
Chepstow
Bristol
Bath
Weston-super-Mare
Taunton
Bridgwater
Minehead
Ilfracombe
Barnstaple
Bideford
Tiverton
Exeter
Exmouth
Torquay
Paignton
Plymouth
Newquay
Bodmin
Truro
Falmouth
Penzance
St. Ives
Launceston
Okehampton
Yeovil
Dorchester
Weymouth
Bridport
Honiton

Motorway
junctions - full,restricted
Toll motorway
Services
Primary route
single/dual carriageway
A Road
B Road
Ferry route
Distances - in miles
major
minor
Railway
National boundary
Airport
Scale 1:1000000 1cm = 10km 1 inch = 15.78 miles
0 5 10 15 20 25 30 35 40 45 50 miles
0 10 20 30 40 50 60 70 80 km
CHANNEL
LONDON
BIRMINGHAM
Guernsey
Jersey
Alderney

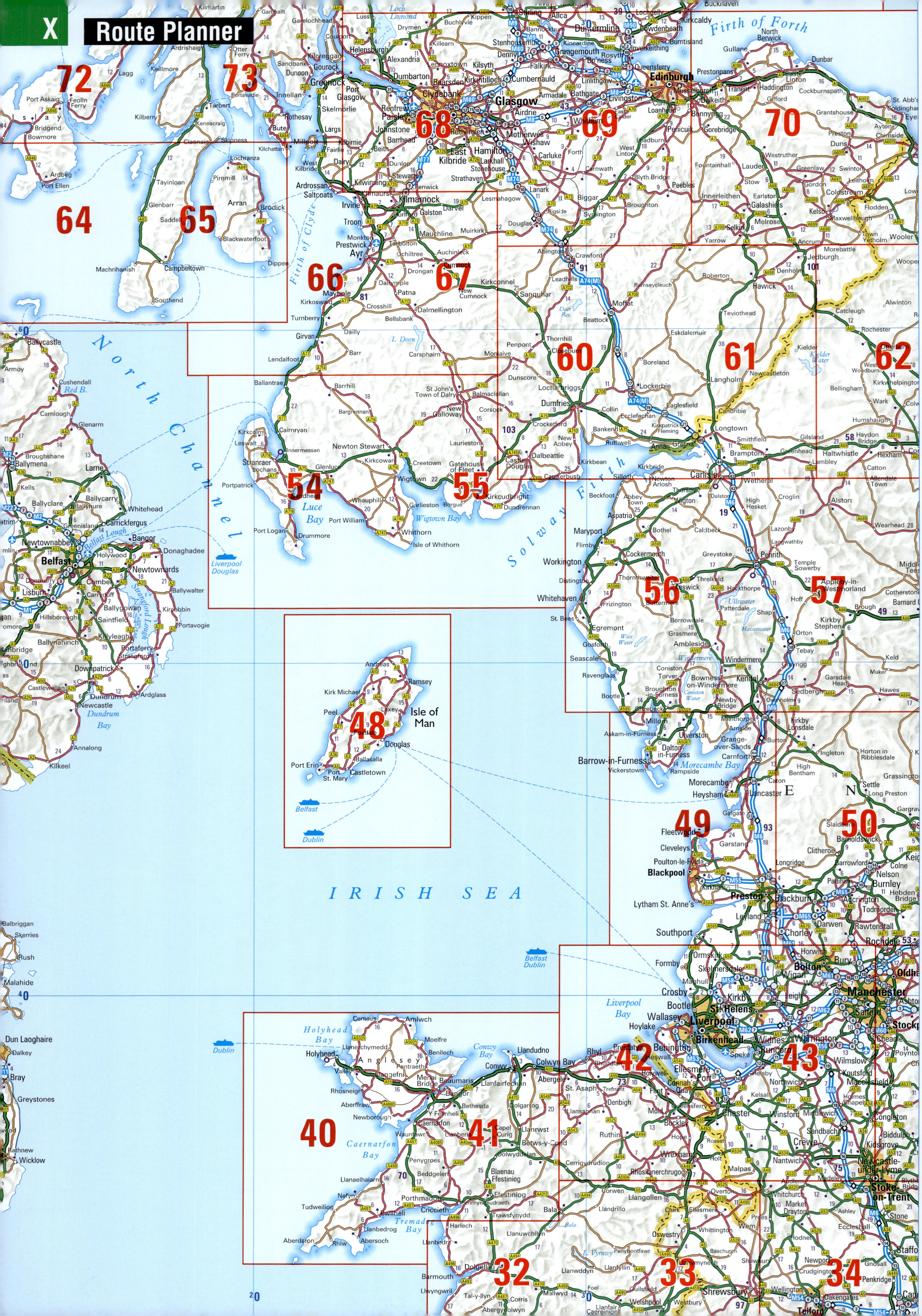

72
73
64
65
66
67
68
69
70
60
61
62
54
55
56
57
48
49
50
40
41
42
43
32
33
34
Firth of Forth
Firth of Clyde
North Channel
Solway Firth
IRISH SEA
Isle of Man
Morecambe Bay
Liverpool Bay
Caernarfon Bay
Holyhead Bay
Luce Bay
Wigtown Bay
Tremadog Bay
Glasgow
Edinburgh
Belfast
Carlisle
Douglas
Blackpool
Preston
Liverpool
Manchester
Stoke-on-Trent
Shrewsbury
Kilmarnock
Ayr
Dumfries
Stranraer
Lancaster
Kendal
Bangor
Holyhead
Chester
Wrexham

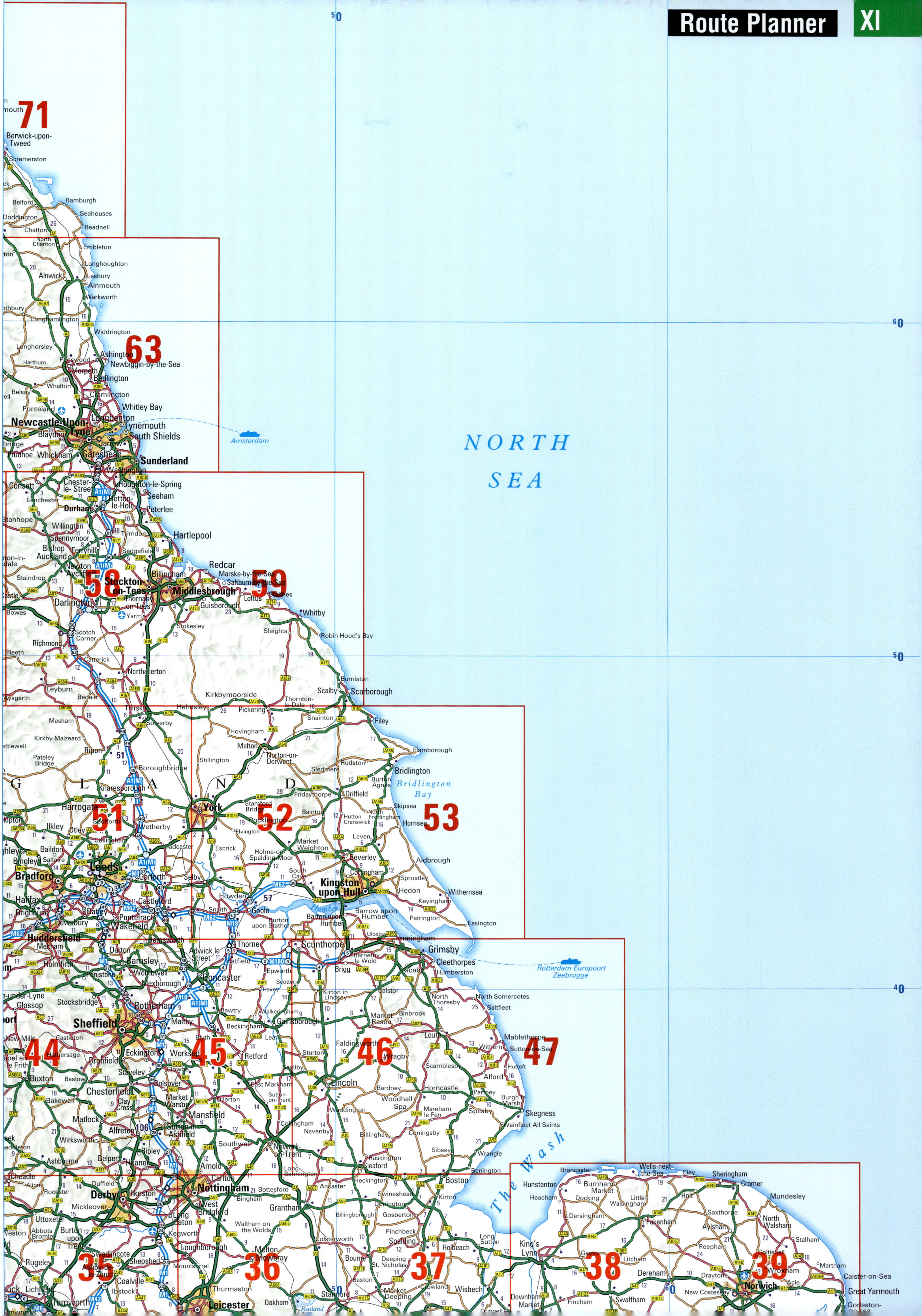
NORTH SEA
The Wash
Bridlington Bay
Amsterdam
Rotterdam Europoort Zeebrugge
71
63
59
58
53
52
51
47
46
45
44
39
38
37
36
35
Berwick-upon-Tweed
Bamburgh
Seahouses
Alnwick
Morpeth
Ashington
Newbiggin-by-the-Sea
Whitley Bay
Newcastle-upon-Tyne
Tynemouth
South Shields
Gateshead
Sunderland
Houghton-le-Spring
Seaham
Durham
Peterlee
Hartlepool
Redcar
Saltburn-by-the-Sea
Stockton-on-Tees
Middlesbrough
Darlington
Guisborough
Whitby
Robin Hood's Bay
Scarborough
Filey
Flamborough
Bridlington
Northallerton
Thirsk
Ripon
Malton
Pickering
Kirkbymoorside
Harrogate
Knaresborough
York
Driffield
Hornsea
Beverley
Kingston upon Hull
Withernsea
Leeds
Bradford
Halifax
Huddersfield
Wakefield
Selby
Goole
Scunthorpe
Grimsby
Cleethorpes
Barnsley
Doncaster
Sheffield
Rotherham
Gainsborough
Lincoln
Mablethorpe
Sutton-on-Sea
Skegness
Chesterfield
Mansfield
Newark-on-Trent
Boston
Nottingham
Derby
Grantham
Loughborough
Melton Mowbray
Spalding
King's Lynn
Hunstanton
Wells-next-the-Sea
Sheringham
Cromer
Fakenham
Dereham
Norwich
Great Yarmouth
Leicester
Wisbech

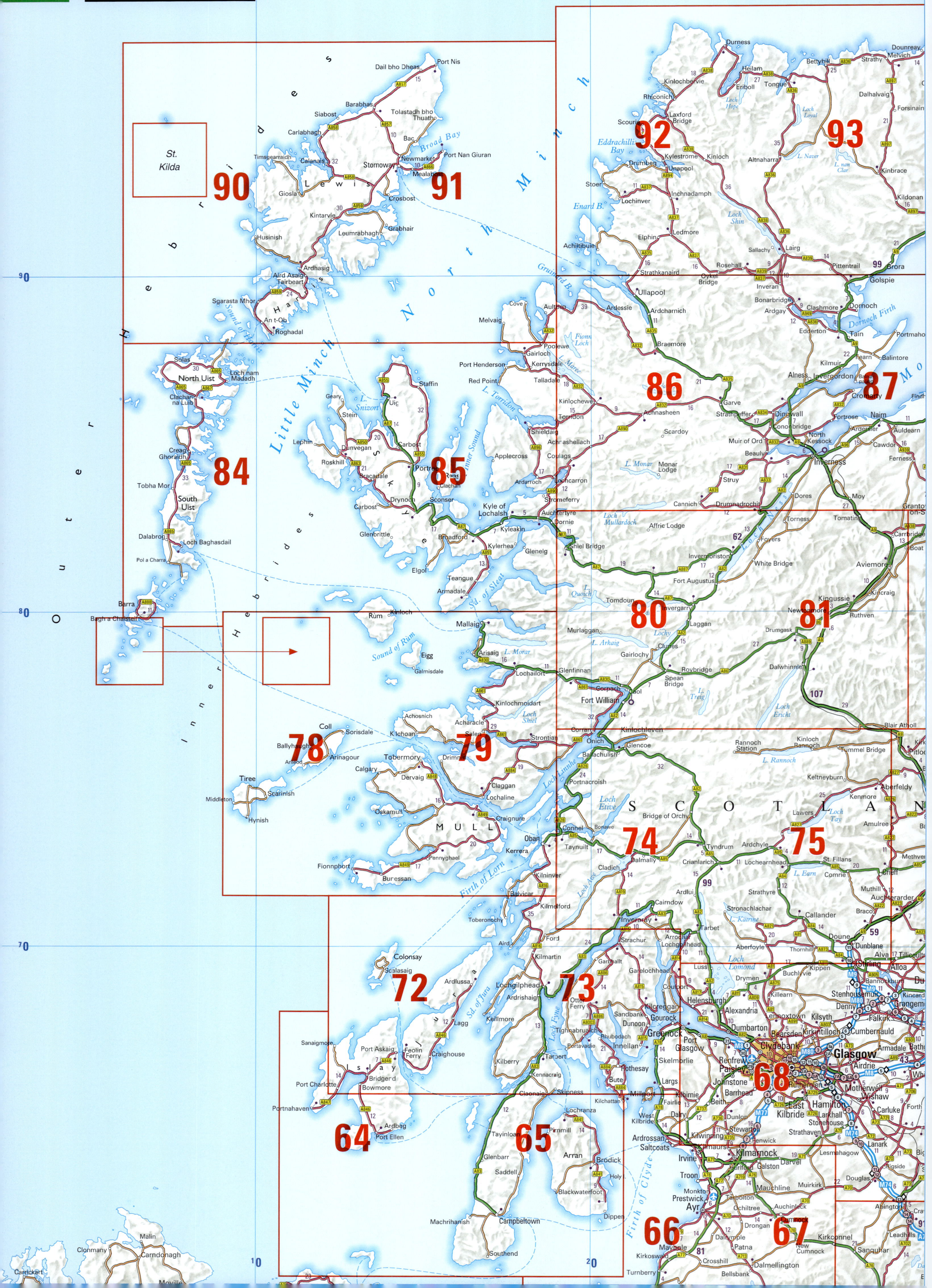

90
91
92
93
84
85
86
87
78
79
80
81
74
75
72
73
68
64
65
66
67
St. Kilda
Outer Hebrides
Inner Hebrides
North Minch
Little Minch
Lewis
Harris
North Uist
South Uist
Barra
Skye
Rum
Eigg
Coll
Tiree
Mull
Colonsay
Jura
Islay
Arran
Stornoway
Ullapool
Inverness
Fort William
Oban
Glasgow
Clydebank
Paisley
Kilmarnock
Ayr
Campbeltown
Mallaig
Portree
Kyle of Lochalsh
Aviemore
Stirling
Dingwall
Dornoch Firth
Firth of Lorn
Firth of Clyde
Sound of Harris
Sound of Sleat
Sound of Rum
Loch Lomond
Loch Rannoch
SCOTLAND

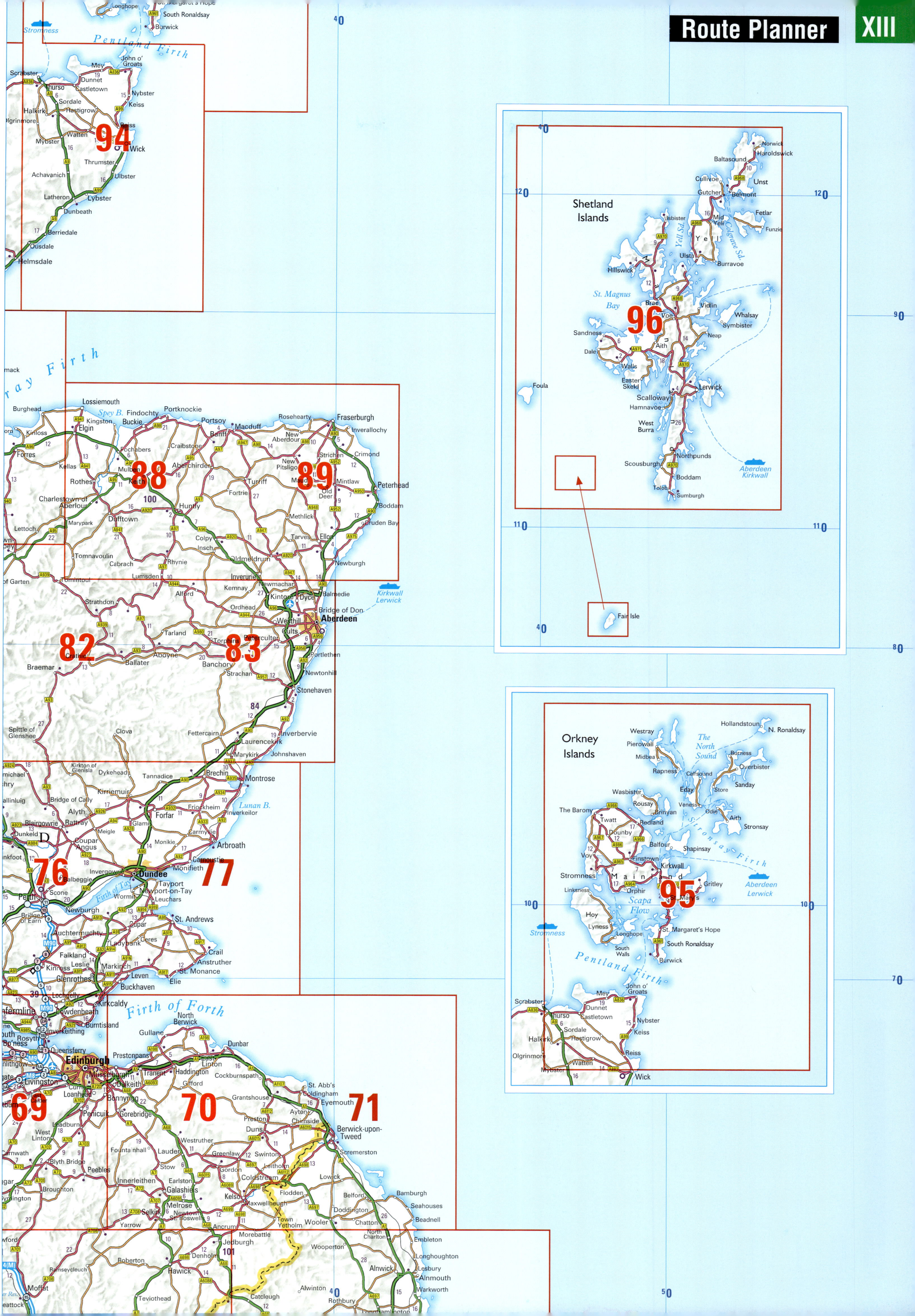
Shetland Islands
96
Norwick
Haroldswick
Baltasound
Unst
Cullivoe
Gutcher
Belmont
Fetlar
Funzie
Mid Yell
Yell
Yell Sd.
Colgrave Sd.
Isbister
Ulsta
Burravoe
Hillswick
St. Magnus Bay
Brae
Voe
Vidlin
Whalsay
Symbister
Sandness
Aith
Neap
Dale
Walls
Easter Skeld
Lerwick
Foula
Scalloway
Hamnavoe
West Burra
Scousburgh
Northpunds
Boddam
Toab
Sumburgh
Aberdeen Kirkwall
Fair Isle
Orkney Islands
95
Westray
Pierowall
Midbea
Hollandstoun
N. Ronaldsay
The North Sound
Burness
Overbister
Rapness
Calfsound
Sanday
Eday
Store
Wasbister
Rousay
The Barony
Brinyan
Veness
Odie
Aith
Twatt
Redland
Dounby
Stronsay
Stronsay Firth
Balfour
Shapinsay
Voy
Finstown
Kirkwall
Stromness
Mainland
Gritley
Linksness
Orphir
Aberdeen Lerwick
Scapa Flow
St. Mary's
Hoy
Lyness
Longhope
St. Margaret's Hope
South Ronaldsay
South Walls
Burwick
Pentland Firth
John o' Groats
Mey
Dunnet
Castletown
Nybster
Keiss
Reiss
Scrabster
Thurso
Sordale
Halkirk
Hastigrow
Olgrinmore
Watten
Mybster
Wick
94
Ulbster
Thrumster
Achavanich
Latheron
Lybster
Dunbeath
Berriedale
Ousdale
Helmsdale
Moray Firth
Burghead
Lossiemouth
Spey B.
Findochty
Portknockie
Kingston
Buckie
Portsoy
Macduff
Rosehearty
Fraserburgh
Inverallochy
Kinloss
Elgin
Banff
New Aberdour
Forres
Fochabers
Craibstone
Strichen
Crimond
Kellas
Mulben
88
Aberchirder
New Pitsligo
89
Rothes
Keith
Turriff
Maud
Mintlaw
Peterhead
Charlestown of Aberlour
100
Fortrie
Old Deer
Boddam
Huntly
Marypark
Dufftown
Methlick
Cruden Bay
Lettoch
Colpy
Tarves
Ellon
Insch
Tomnavoulin
Cabrach
Rhynie
Oldmeldrum
Newburgh
Lumsden
Inverurie
Tomintoul
Kemnay
Newmachar
Balmedie
Alford
Kintore
Dyce
Kirkwall Lerwick
Strathdon
Ordhead
Bridge of Don
Westhill
Aberdeen
Tarland
Cults
82
Peterculter
83
Torphins
Portlethen
Crathie
Aboyne
Ballater
Banchory
Braemar
Newtonhill
Strachan
Stonehaven
84
Spittle of Glenshee
Clova
Fettercairn
Inverbervie
Laurencekirk
Johnshaven
Marykirk
Kirkton of Glenisla
Dykehead
Tannadice
Brechin
Montrose
Kirriemuir
Bridge of Cally
Alyth
Friockheim
Lunan B.
Inverkeilor
Forfar
Blairgowrie
Rattray
Glamis
Dunkeld
Coupar Angus
Meigle
Carmyllie
Monikie
Arbroath
Carnoustie
76
Invergowrie
Dundee
Monifieth
77
Balbeggie
Scone
Perth
Tayport
Newport-on-Tay
Leuchars
Firth of Tay
Newburgh
Bridge of Earn
St. Andrews
Cupar
Auchtermuchty
Ladybank
Ceres
Falkland
Crail
Kinross
Leslie
Markinch
Anstruther
Glenrothes
St. Monance
Leven
Elie
Buckhaven
Lochgelly
Kirkcaldy
Dunfermline
Cowdenbeath
Firth of Forth
North Berwick
Burntisland
Inverkeithing
Gullane
Rosyth
Bo'ness
Queensferry
Dunbar
Prestonpans
East Linton
Edinburgh
Musselburgh
Tranent
Haddington
Livingston
Dalkeith
Gifford
Cockburnspath
Currie
Loanhead
Bonnyrigg
St. Abb's
Coldingham
Eyemouth
69
Penicuik
70
Gorebridge
Grantshouse
71
Leadburn
Ayton
Chirnside
Preston
Duns
Berwick-upon-Tweed
West Linton
Westruther
Scremerston
Carnwath
Fountainhall
Lauder
Greenlaw
Swinton
Blyth Bridge
Stow
Gordon
Peebles
Leitholm
Earlston
Coldstream
Lowick
Innerleithen
Galashiels
Kelso
Flodden
Belford
Bamburgh
Broughton
Melrose
Maxwellheugh
Seahouses
Newtown St. Boswells
Doddington
Selkirk
Town Yetholm
Wooler
Chatton
Beadnell
Yarrow
Ancrum
Morebattle
North Charlton
Embleton
Jedburgh
101
Wooperton
Denholm
Longhoughton
Roberton
Lesbury
Hawick
Alnwick
Alnmouth
Ramseycleuch
Moffat
Alwinton
Warkworth
Teviothead
Catcleugh
Rothbury
Stromness
South Ronaldsay
Burwick
Longhope
Pentland Firth
John o' Groats
Mey
Dunnet
Castletown
Nybster
Keiss
Scrabster
Thurso
Sordale
Halkirk
Hastigrow
Olgrinmore
Reiss
Watten
Wick

Legend
Motorway
junctions – full, restricted
Toll motorway - toll barrier
Services, tunnel, under construction
Primary route
single / dual carriageway
tunnel, under construction
A road (GB), National secondary road (IRL)
B road (GB), Regional road (IRL)
Scenic route
M25 A135 Motorway number, road number
Gradient – arrow points uphill
Distances – in miles
143 major
28 minor
Principal railway
tunnel
Liverpool Ferry route
Short ferry route
International boundary
Dublin Town of tourist interest
National park
AONB
Forest park
NORTHERN IRELAND
IRELAND
North Channel
Donegal Bay
Galway Bay
Dundalk Bay
Clew Bay
Sligo Bay
Lough Neagh
Lough Foyle
Mountains of Antrim
Mourne Mts.
Derryveagh Mts.
Nephin Beg Range
Maumturk Mts.
Sperrin
Belfast
Dublin
Derry/Londonderry
Galway
Sligo
Athlone
Dundalk
Drogheda
Enniskillen
Newry
Armagh
Omagh
Coleraine
Bangor
Larne
Carrickfergus
Lisburn
Portadown
Castlebar
Westport
Mullingar
Tullamore
Longford
Roscommon
Donegal
Letterkenny
Liverpool Douglas
Douglas Holyhead Liverpool
Cairnryan
Aran Is.
Achill I.
Clare I.
Inishmore
Rathlin Island

Index to Ireland

A

Abbey C3
Abbeydorney D2
Abbeyfeale D2
Abbeyleix D4
Adare D3
Adrigole E2
Aghalee B5
Ahoghill B5
Allihies E1
Anascaul D1
Annalong B6
Annestown D4
Antrim B5
Ardagh D2
Ardara B3
Ardee C5
Ardfert D2
Ardglass B6
Ardgroom E2
Ardkearagh E1
Arklow D5
Armagh B5
Armoy A5
Arthurstown D5
Ashbourne C5
Askeaton D3
Athboy C5
Athea D2
Athenry C3
Athleague C3
Athlone C4
Athy D5
Augher B4
Aughnacloy B5
Aughrim D5

B

Bailieborough C5
Balbriggan C5
Balla C2
Ballaghaderreen C3
Ballina B2
Ballinalack C4
Ballinamore B4
Ballinascarty E3
Ballinasloe C3
Ballindine C3
Ballingarry, *Limerick* D3
Ballingarry, *Tipperary* D4
Ballingeary E2
Ballinhassig E3
Ballinrobe C2
Ballinskellings E1
Ballinspittle E3
Ballintra B3
Ballivor C5
Ballon D5
Ballybay B5
Ballybofey B4
Ballybunion D2
Ballycanew D5
Ballycarry B6
Ballycastle, *Antrim* A5
Ballycastle, *Mayo* B2
Ballyclare B6
Ballyconneely C1
Ballycotton E3
Ballycroy B2
Ballydehob E2
Ballyferriter D1
Ballygawley B4
Ballygowan B6
Ballyhaunis C3
Ballyheige D2
Ballyjamesduff C4
Ballylanders D3
Ballylynan D4
Ballymahon C4
Ballymena B5
Ballymoe C3
Ballymoney A5
Ballymore C4
Ballymote B3
Ballynacorra E3
Ballynagore C4
Ballynahinch B6
Ballynure B6
Ballyragget D4
Ballysadare B3
Ballyshannon B3
Ballyvaughan C2
Ballyvourney E2
Ballywalter B6
Baltimore E2
Baltinglass D5
Banbridge B5
Bandon E3
Bangor, *Down* B6
Bangor, *Mayo* B2
Banteer D3
Bantry E2
Beaufort D2
Belcoo B4
Belfast B6
Belgooly E3
Bellananagh C4
Bellavary C2
Belleek B3
Belmullet B2
Beltra C2
Belturbet B4
Beragh B4
Birr C4
Blackwater D5
Blarney E3
Blessington C5
Borris D5
Borris-in-Ossory D4
Borrisokane D3
Borrisoleigh D4
Boyle C3
Bracklin C5
Bray C5
Broadford D3
Broughshane B5
Bruff D3
Bunahowen B2
Bunbeg A3
Bunclody D5
Buncrana A4
Bundoran B3
Bunmahon D4
Bunnyconnellan B2
Bunratty D3
Bushmills A5
Butler's Bridge B4
Buttevant D3

C

Caher D4
Caherciveen E1
Caherdaniel E1
Caledon B5
Callan D4
Camp D2
Cappamore D3
Cappoquin D4
Carlingford B5
Carlow D5
Carndonagh A4
Carnew D5
Carnlough B6
Carraroe C2
Carrick B3
Carrick-on-Shannon C3
Carrick-on-Suir D4
Carrickart A4
Carrickfergus B6
Carrickmacross C5
Carrigallen C4
Carryduff B6
Cashel D4
Castlebar C2
Castlebellingham C5
Castleblaney B5
Castlebridge D5
Castlecomer D4
Castlederg B4
Castledermot D5
Castleisland D2
Castlemaine D2
Castlemartyr E3
Castlepollard C4
Castlerea C3
Castletown Bearhaven E2
Castletownroche D3
Castlewellan B6
Cavan C4
Celbridge C5
Charlestown C3
Charleville D3
Clarecastle D3
Claregalway C3
Claremorris C2
Clarinbridge C3
Clashmore D4
Claudy B4
Clifden C1
Clogh D4
Cloghan, *Donegal* B4
Cloghan, *Offaly* C4
Clogheen D4
Clogher B4
Cloghjordan D3
Clonakilty E3
Clonaslee C4
Clondalkin C5
Clones B4
Clonmany A4
Clonmel D4
Clonmellon C4
Clonord C4
Clonroche D5
Cloone C4
Clough B6
Cloyne E3
Coachford E3
Coagh B5
Coalisland B5
Cóbh E3
Coleraine A5
Collon C5
Collooney B3
Comber B6
Cong C2
Conna D3
Connaugh D3
Cookstown B5
Coolgreany D5
Cooneen B4
Cootehill B4
Cork E3
Craughwell C3
Creeslough A4
Creeve B5
Crolly A3
Crookhaven E2
Crookstown E3
Croom D3
Crossakiel C4
Crosshaven E3
Crossmolina B2
Crumlin B5
Crusheen D3
Cullaville B5
Cushendall A5

D

Daingean C4
Darragh D2
Delvin C4
Derry/Londonderry B4
Derrygonnelly B4
Derrylin B4
Dervock A5
Dingle D1
Donaghadee B6
Donegal B3
Doonbeg D2
Downhill A5
Downpatrick B6
Dowra B3
Draperstown B5
Drimoleague E2
Drogheda C5
Dromahair B3
Dromcolliher D3
Dromore, *Down* B5
Dromore, *Tyrone* B4
Dromore West B3
Drumcliff B3
Drumkeeran B3
Drumquin B4
Drumshanbo B3
Drumsna C4
Dublin C5
Duleek C5
Dun Laoghaire C5
Dunboyne C5
Dundalk B5
Dundrum B6
Dunfanaghy A4
Dungannon B5
Dungarvan D4
Dungiven B5
Dunglow B3
Dungourney E3
Dunkineely B3
Dunlavin C5
Dunleer C5
Dunloy A5
Dunmanway E2
Dunmore C3
Dunmore East D5
Dunmurry B5
Dunshaughlin C5
Durrow D4
Durrus E2

E

Easky B3
Edenderry C4
Edgeworthstown C4
Eglinton A4
Emyvale B5
Enfield C5
Ennis D3
Enniscorthy D5
Enniskean E3
Enniskillen B4
Ennistimon D2

F

Falcarragh A3
Farranfore D2
Feeny B4
Fenagh B4
Fenit D2
Ferbane C4
Fermoy D3
Ferns D5
Fethard, *Tipperary* D4
Fethard, *Wexford* D5
Finnea C4
Fintona B4
Fivemiletown B4
Fontstown C5
Foxford C2
Foynes D2
Freshford D4

G

Galway C2
Garrison B3
Garvagh B5
Gilford B5
Glenamoy B2
Glenarm B6
Glenavy B5
Glenbeigh D2
Glencolumbkille B3
Glendalough C5
Glenealy D5
Glengarriff E2
Glennamaddy C3
Glenties B3
Glin D2
Glinsk C2
Gorey D5
Gort C3
Gortin B4
Gowran D4
Graiguenamanagh D5
Granard C4
Grange B3
Greencastle A5
Greenisland B6
Greystones C5

H

Hacketstown D5
Headford C2
Herbertstown D3
Hillsborough B5
Holycross D4
Holywood B6
Hospital D3

I

Inagh D2
Inishannon E3
Inishcrone B2
Inveran C2
Irvinestown B4

J

Johnstown D4
Julianstown C5

K

Kanturk D3
Keadew B3
Keady B5
Keel C1
Keenagh C4
Kells, *Antrim* B5
Kells, *Meath* C5
Kenmare E2
Kesh B4
Kilbaha D2
Kilbeggan C4
Kilcock C5
Kilconnell C3
Kilcormac C4
Kilcullen C5
Kilcurry B5
Kildare C5
Kildorrery D3
Kilgarvan E2
Kilkee D2
Kilkeel B6
Kilkelly C3
Kilkenny D4
Kilkieran C2
Kilkinlea D2
Kill D4
Killadysert D2
Killala B2
Killaloe D3
Killarney D2
Killashandra B4
Killashee C4
Killeigh C4
Killenaule D4
Killimor C3
Killinaboy D2
Killinick D5
Killorglin D2
Killucan C4
Killybegs B3
Killyleagh B6
Kilmacrenan A4
Kilmacthomas D4
Kilmaine C2
Kilmallock D3
Kilmeadan D4
Kilmeedy D3
Kilmore Quay D5
Kilnaleck C4
Kilrea B5
Kilrush D2
Kiltoom C3
Kingarrow B3
Kingscourt C5
Kinlough B3
Kinnegad C4
Kinnitty C4
Kinsale E3
Kinvarra C3
Kircubbin B6
Knock C3
Knocktopher D4

L

Laban C3
Lanesborough C4
Laragh C5
Larne B6
Lauragh E2
Laurencetown C3
Leap E2
Leenaun C2
Leighlinbridge D5
Leitrim C3
Letterfrack C2
Letterkenny B4
Lettermacaward B3
Lifford B4
Limavady A5
Limerick D3
Lisbellaw B4
Lisburn B5
Liscannor D2
Lisdoonvarna C2
Lismore D4
Lisnaskea B4
Lissycasey D2
Listowel D2
Littleton D4
Longford C4
Loughbrickland B5
Loughrea C3
Louisburgh C2
Lucan C5
Lurgan B5

M

Macroom E3
Maghera B5
Magherafelt B5
Magilligan A5
Maguiresbridge B4
Malahide C5
Malin A4
Mallaranny C2
Mallow D3
Manorhamilton B3
Markethill B5
Maum C2
Middletown B5
Midleton E3
Milford A4
Millstreet, *Cork* D2
Millstreet, *Waterford* D4
Milltown, *Galway* C3
Milltown, *Kerry* D1
Milltown Malbay D2
Mitchelstown D3
Moate C4
Mohill C4
Monaghan B5
Monasterevin C4
Moneygall D4
Moneymore B5
Mountbellew C3
Mountfield B4
Mountmellick C4
Mountrath D4
Moville A4
Moy B5
Moycullen C2
Moylough C3
Muckross D2
Muff A4
Muine Bheag D5
Mullanys Cross B3
Mullinavat D4
Mullingar C4

N

Naas C5
Naul C5
Navan C5
Nenagh D3
New Ross D5
Newbliss B4
Newbridge C5
Newcastle B6
Newcastle West D2
Newinn D4
Newmarket D3
Newmarket-on-Fergus D3
Newport, *Mayo* C2
Newport, *Tipperary* D3
Newry B5
Newtown Cunningham B4
Newtown Sands D2
Newtownabbey B6
Newtownards B6
Newtownbutler B4
Newtownhamilton B5
Newtown-mountkennedy C5
Newtownshandrum D3
Newtownstewart B4
Ninemilehouse D4

O

Oilgate D5
Oldcastle C4
Omagh B4
Oranmore C3
Oughterard C2

P

Pallas Green D3
Parknasilla E2
Passage East D5
Passage West E3
Patrickswell D3
Paulstown D4
Peterswell C3
Pettigo B4
Plumbridge B4
Pomeroy B5
Pontoon C2
Portacloy B2
Portadown B5
Portaferry B6
Portarlington C4
Portavogie B6
Portglenone B5
Portlaoise C4
Portmagne E1
Portroe D3
Portrush A5
Portstewart A5
Portumna C3
Poyntz Pass B5

R

Randalstown B5
Rathangan C5
Rathcoole C5
Rathcormack D3
Rathdrum D5
Rathfriland B5
Rathkeale D3
Rathmelton A4
Rathmolyon C5
Rathmore D2
Rathmullan A4
Rathnew D5
Rathvilly D5
Ratoath C5
Recess C2
Ringaskiddy E3
Roosky C4
Roscommon C3
Roscrea D4
Rosmult D4
Rosslare D5
Rosslare Harbour D5
Rosslea B4
Roundwood C5
Rush C5

S

Saint Johnstown B4
Saintfield B6
Sallins C5
Scarriff D3
Screeb C2
Seskinore B4
Shanagolden D2
Shercock C5
Shillelagh D5
Silvermines D3
Sion Mills B4
Skerries C5
Skibbereen E2
Slane C5
Sligo B3
Sneem E2
Spiddle C2
Strabane B4
Stradbally D1
Strandhill B3
Strangford B6
Stranorlar B4
Strokestown C3
Swanlinbar B4
Swatragh B5
Swinford C3
Swords C5

T

Tallaght C5
Tallow D4
Tarbert D2
Templederry D3
Templemore D4
Termonfeckin C5
Thomas Street C3
Thomastown D4
Thurles D4
Timoleague E3
Timolin D5
Tipperary D3
Tobermore B5
Toomyvara D3
Toormore E2
Tralee D2
Tramore D4
Trim C5
Tuam C3
Tubbercory B3
Tulla D3
Tullamore C4
Tullow D5
Tulsk C3
Tyrrellspass C4

U

Urlingford D4

V

Virginia C4

W

Warrenpoint B5
Waterford D4
Watergrasshill D3
Waterville E1
Wellingtonbridge D5
Westport C2
Wexford D5
Whitegate E3
Whitehead B6
Wicklow D5

Y

Youghal E4

Distance table

How to use this table

Distances are shown in miles and kilometres with estimated journey times in hours and minutes.

For example: the distance between Dover and Fishguard is 331 miles or 533 kilometres with an estimated journey time of 6 hours, 20 minutes.

Estimated driving times are based on an average speed of 60mph on Motorways and 40mph on other roads. Drivers should allow extra time when driving at peak periods or through areas likely to be congested.

	Fishguard	Exeter	Edinburgh	Dundee	Dover
Dundee					523 / 842 / 9:10
Edinburgh				56 / 90 / 1:30	462 / 744 / 8:10
Exeter			450 / 724 / 8:00	518 / 834 / 9:10	248 / 399 / 4:40
Fishguard		230 / 370 / 4:30	399 / 642 / 7:30	460 / 740 / 8:30	331 / 533 / 6:20
Fort William	486 / 782 / 9:30	560 / 901 / 10:20	144 / 232 / 3:30	127 / 204 / 3:10	596 / 959 / 11:00

	Swansea	Stranraer	Southampton	Shrewsbury	Sheffield	Portsmouth	Plymouth	Oxford	Oban	Nottingham	Norwich	Newcastle upon Tyne	Manchester	Liverpool	Lincoln	Leicester	Leeds	Land's End	Kyle of Lochalsh	Kingston upon Hull	John o' Groats	Inverness	Holyhead	Harwich	Great Yarmouth	Gloucester	Glasgow	Fort William	Fishguard	Exeter	Edinburgh	Dundee	Dover	Doncaster	Carlisle	Cardiff	Cambridge	Bristol	Brighton	Braemar	Bournemouth	Blackpool	Birmingham	Berwick-upon-Tweed	Ayr	Aberystwyth	Aberdeen	London
Aberdeen																																																517 / 832 / 11:20
Aberystwyth																																															445 / 716 / 8:40	211 / 340 / 4:40
Ayr																																														317 / 510 / 6:10	183 / 295 / 4:20	394 / 634 / 7:20
Berwick-upon-Tweed																																													134 / 216 / 3:00	311 / 501 / 6:20	182 / 293 / 4:40	352 / 567 / 7:30
Birmingham																																												274 / 441 / 5:30	289 / 465 / 5:30	114 / 183 / 2:50	420 / 676 / 8:30	117 / 188 / 2:50
Blackpool																																											123 / 198 / 2:40	181 / 291 / 3:50	180 / 290 / 3:30	153 / 246 / 3:20	308 / 496 / 6:20	226 / 364 / 4:30
Bournemouth																																										270 / 435 / 5:00	147 / 237 / 3:10	412 / 663 / 7:50	436 / 702 / 8:00	207 / 333 / 4:30	564 / 908 / 10:20	107 / 172 / 2:40
Braemar																																									524 / 843 / 9:30	281 / 452 / 5:20	385 / 620 / 7:10	148 / 238 / 3:20	143 / 230 / 3:00	405 / 652 / 7:50	59 / 95 / 1:30	482 / 776 / 10:30
Brighton																																								534 / 859 / 9:40	92 / 148 / 2:10	286 / 460 / 5:20	163 / 262 / 3:20	409 / 658 / 7:40	446 / 718 / 8:00	253 / 407 / 5:10	573 / 922 / 10:30	52 / 84 / 1:50
Bristol																																							147 / 237 / 4:10	477 / 768 / 8:40	82 / 132 / 2:30	204 / 328 / 3:50	81 / 130 / 2:00	362 / 583 / 6:50	370 / 595 / 6:40	125 / 201 / 3:00	493 / 793 / 9:10	122 / 196 / 2:50
Cambridge																																						169 / 272 / 3:10	116 / 187 / 2:20	438 / 705 / 7:50	154 / 248 / 3:00	208 / 335 / 3:50	100 / 161 / 2:10	306 / 493 / 5:40	357 / 575 / 6:20	214 / 344 / 4:20	471 / 758 / 10:00	54 / 87 / 1:30
Cardiff																																					190 / 306 / 3:30	45 / 72 / 1:20	182 / 293 / 3:40	483 / 778 / 8:40	117 / 188 / 3:00	209 / 336 / 4:00	103 / 166 / 2:20	368 / 592 / 7:00	382 / 615 / 7:00	105 / 169 / 2:40	505 / 813 / 9:20	157 / 253 / 3:20
Carlisle																																				289 / 465 / 5:20	264 / 425 / 4:40	277 / 446 / 5:00	370 / 596 / 6:40	196 / 316 / 3:50	343 / 552 / 6:20	87 / 140 / 1:50	196 / 315 / 3:50	87 / 140 / 2:10	93 / 150 / 2:00	224 / 360 / 4:30	221 / 356 / 4:30	301 / 484 / 5:40
Doncaster																																			142 / 229 / 3:00	209 / 336 / 4:00	116 / 187 / 2:10	175 / 282 / 3:20	236 / 380 / 4:30	310 / 499 / 5:40	235 / 378 / 4:20	94 / 151 / 1:50	94 / 151 / 2:00	184 / 296 / 3:50	235 / 378 / 4:20	176 / 283 / 3:40	344 / 554 / 6:50	171 / 275 / 3:30
Dover																																		242 / 390 / 4:30	389 / 626 / 7:00	238 / 383 / 4:30	125 / 201 / 2:30	202 / 325 / 3:50	82 / 132 / 2:20	553 / 890 / 9:50	174 / 280 / 4:30	312 / 502 / 5:40	194 / 312 / 3:50	424 / 683 / 7:50	478 / 769 / 8:30	297 / 478 / 5:50	588 / 947 / 10:40	71 / 114 / 2:00
Dundee																																	523 / 842 / 9:10	275 / 443 / 5:00	152 / 245 / 3:00	441 / 710 / 8:00	406 / 654 / 7:10	430 / 692 / 7:40	517 / 832 / 9:10	52 / 84 / 1:20	495 / 797 / 8:50	239 / 385 / 4:30	349 / 562 / 6:20	113 / 182 / 2:40	117 / 188 / 2:30	376 / 605 / 7:10	67 / 108 / 1:50	448 / 721 / 8:40
Edinburgh																																56 / 90 / 1:30	462 / 744 / 8:10	219 / 352 / 4:00	96 / 154 / 2:00	385 / 620 / 7:00	345 / 555 / 6:10	373 / 600 / 6:50	456 / 734 / 8:20	91 / 146 / 2:10	439 / 707 / 8:00	183 / 295 / 3:30	292 / 470 / 5:30	57 / 92 / 1:40	73 / 117 / 1:50	320 / 515 / 6:20	125 / 201 / 3:10	390 / 628 / 7:20
Exeter																															450 / 724 / 8:00	518 / 834 / 9:10	248 / 399 / 4:40	251 / 404 / 4:30	353 / 568 / 6:20	121 / 195 / 2:30	249 / 401 / 4:30	76 / 122 / 1:40	184 / 296 / 5:00	550 / 885 / 9:40	82 / 132 / 2:20	282 / 454 / 5:10	157 / 253 / 3:10	428 / 689 / 7:50	446 / 718 / 7:50	201 / 323 / 4:10	569 / 916 / 10:20	181 / 291 / 3:40
Fishguard																														230 / 370 / 4:30	399 / 642 / 7:30	460 / 740 / 8:30	331 / 533 / 6:20	247 / 398 / 4:50	297 / 478 / 5:40	112 / 180 / 2:40	270 / 435 / 5:10	154 / 248 / 3:20	291 / 468 / 5:40	493 / 794 / 9:10	222 / 357 / 4:40	209 / 336 / 4:10	170 / 274 / 3:40	371 / 597 / 7:20	373 / 600 / 7:00	56 / 90 / 1:30	504 / 811 / 10:10	260 / 418 / 5:20
Fort William																													486 / 782 / 9:30	560 / 901 / 10:20	144 / 232 / 3:30	127 / 204 / 3:10	596 / 959 / 11:00	357 / 575 / 7:00	206 / 332 / 4:30	485 / 781 / 9:10	479 / 771 / 9:00	486 / 782 / 9:10	575 / 926 / 10:50	125 / 201 / 3:10	539 / 867 / 10:10	296 / 476 / 6:00	392 / 631 / 7:40	190 / 306 / 4:40	133 / 214 / 3:20	430 / 692 / 8:40	149 / 240 / 3:50	510 / 821 / 9:50
Glasgow																												101 / 163 / 2:50	376 / 605 / 7:10	449 / 723 / 8:00	44 / 71 / 1:20	83 / 134 / 2:00	488 / 786 / 8:40	249 / 401 / 4:40	96 / 154 / 2:10	385 / 620 / 7:00	372 / 599 / 6:40	373 / 600 / 6:50	468 / 753 / 8:30	110 / 177 / 2:30	439 / 707 / 8:00	183 / 295 / 3:40	292 / 470 / 5:30	101 / 163 / 2:40	33 / 53 / 1:10	320 / 515 / 6:20	145 / 233 / 3:30	397 / 639 / 7:30
Gloucester																											346 / 557 / 6:10	454 / 731 / 8:30	153 / 246 / 3:10	111 / 179 / 2:10	349 / 562 / 6:10	410 / 660 / 7:10	191 / 307 / 3:30	150 / 241 / 2:50	247 / 398 / 4:20	56 / 90 / 1:20	123 / 198 / 2:20	35 / 56 / 1:00	159 / 256 / 3:10	443 / 713 / 8:00	99 / 159 / 2:40	174 / 280 / 3:10	56 / 90 / 1:20	318 / 512 / 6:00	330 / 531 / 5:50	102 / 164 / 2:30	468 / 753 / 8:30	109 / 175 / 2:30
Great Yarmouth																										225 / 362 / 4:40	419 / 674 / 8:00	527 / 848 / 10:20	366 / 589 / 7:20	335 / 539 / 6:30	386 / 621 / 7:30	484 / 779 / 9:00	185 / 298 / 4:00	167 / 269 / 3:40	320 / 515 / 6:20	284 / 457 / 5:50	82 / 132 / 2:10	275 / 443 / 5:40	180 / 290 / 4:10	477 / 768 / 9:10	240 / 386 / 5:00	252 / 406 / 5:10	180 / 290 / 4:10	345 / 555 / 7:00	402 / 647 / 7:40	294 / 473 / 6:20	517 / 832 / 10:50	128 / 206 / 3:40
Harwich																									82 / 132 / 2:10	196 / 316 / 4:00	432 / 695 / 8:10	543 / 874 / 10:30	337 / 542 / 6:40	279 / 449 / 5:20	413 / 665 / 7:40	469 / 755 / 8:40	125 / 201 / 2:50	194 / 312 / 4:00	336 / 541 / 6:20	246 / 396 / 5:00	67 / 108 / 1:50	217 / 349 / 4:30	128 / 206 / 3:00	504 / 811 / 9:20	187 / 301 / 4:00	275 / 443 / 5:20	167 / 269 / 3:40	372 / 599 / 7:20	425 / 684 / 8:00	281 / 452 / 5:50	535 / 861 / 11:20	76 / 122 / 2:20
Holyhead																								349 / 562 / 7:10	334 / 538 / 7:00	191 / 307 / 4:00	330 / 531 / 6:40	438 / 705 / 8:50	167 / 269 / 4:00	282 / 454 / 5:40	333 / 536 / 6:40	394 / 634 / 7:30	360 / 580 / 7:00	181 / 291 / 3:50	231 / 372 / 4:50	216 / 348 / 5:40	270 / 435 / 5:20	206 / 332 / 4:30	334 / 538 / 6:40	426 / 686 / 8:20	288 / 463 / 5:50	141 / 227 / 3:20	148 / 238 / 3:30	311 / 501 / 6:30	305 / 491 / 6:10	111 / 179 / 2:50	439 / 707 / 8:40	269 / 433 / 5:40
Inverness																							474 / 763 / 9:40	569 / 916 / 11:00	553 / 890 / 11:00	504 / 811 / 9:30	166 / 267 / 4:00	66 / 106 / 1:40	542 / 872 / 10:30	618 / 995 / 11:30	158 / 254 / 3:50	132 / 212 / 3:20	622 / 1001 / 11:30	383 / 617 / 7:30	262 / 422 / 5:30	549 / 884 / 10:20	505 / 813 / 9:30	539 / 867 / 10:10	617 / 993 / 11:30	75 / 121 / 2:00	597 / 961 / 11:20	348 / 560 / 7:00	458 / 737 / 9:00	215 / 346 / 5:10	199 / 320 / 4:30	486 / 782 / 9:40	105 / 169 / 2:50	550 / 885 / 10:40
John o' Groats																						129 / 208 / 3:20	603 / 970 / 12:40	693 / 1116 / 14:00	677 / 1090 / 14:00	628 / 1011 / 12:30	295 / 475 / 7:10	195 / 314 / 5:00	671 / 1080 / 13:40	744 / 1197 / 14:30	285 / 459 / 7:00	259 / 417 / 6:30	746 / 1201 / 14:40	507 / 816 / 10:30	391 / 629 / 8:40	680 / 1094 / 13:30	630 / 1014 / 12:30	668 / 1075 / 13:20	741 / 1193 / 14:40	202 / 325 / 5:00	724 / 1165 / 14:20	478 / 769 / 10:00	574 / 924 / 11:50	342 / 550 / 8:10	328 / 528 / 7:40	601 / 967 / 12:40	232 / 373 / 5:50	663 / 1067 / 13:30
Kingston upon Hull																					518 / 834 / 10:50	394 / 634 / 7:50	231 / 372 / 4:50	196 / 316 / 4:10	207 / 333 / 5:20	169 / 272 / 3:10	254 / 409 / 4:50	369 / 594 / 7:20	280 / 451 / 5:30	309 / 497 / 5:40	234 / 377 / 4:30	295 / 475 / 5:30	256 / 412 / 4:50	47 / 76 / 1:10	158 / 254 / 3:00	244 / 393 / 4:40	139 / 224 / 3:10	233 / 375 / 4:20	245 / 394 / 4:40	327 / 526 / 6:10	264 / 425 / 5:00	127 / 204 / 2:30	134 / 216 / 2:50	185 / 298 / 3:50	251 / 404 / 4:40	223 / 359 / 4:40	364 / 586 / 7:20	184 / 296 / 3:50
Kyle of Lochalsh																				445 / 716 / 9:00	189 / 304 / 4:40	84 / 135 / 2:10	514 / 827 / 10:40	611 / 983 / 12:10	602 / 969 / 12:10	528 / 850 / 10:20	179 / 288 / 4:40	76 / 122 / 1:50	567 / 913 / 11:20	628 / 1011 / 12:00	216 / 348 / 5:20	186 / 299 / 4:40	671 / 1080 / 12:50	432 / 695 / 8:40	275 / 443 / 6:10	564 / 908 / 11:10	555 / 893 / 10:50	552 / 888 / 10:50	651 / 1048 / 12:40	159 / 256 / 4:00	618 / 995 / 12:10	372 / 599 / 7:50	471 / 758 / 9:40	263 / 423 / 6:20	212 / 341 / 5:10	499 / 803 / 10:20	189 / 304 / 4:50	586 / 943 / 11:40
Land's End																			763 / 1228 / 15:10	421 / 678 / 8:20	868 / 1397 / 17:20	741 / 1193 / 14:20	405 / 652 / 8:30	390 / 628 / 8:00	446 / 718 / 9:10	235 / 378 / 5:00	573 / 922 / 10:50	686 / 1104 / 13:20	353 / 568 / 7:20	123 / 198 / 3:20	574 / 924 / 10:50	642 / 1033 / 12:00	381 / 613 / 7:40	374 / 602 / 7:20	477 / 768 / 9:10	245 / 394 / 5:20	374 / 602 / 7:20	200 / 322 / 4:40	308 / 496 / 7:50	665 / 1070 / 12:30	205 / 330 / 5:20	405 / 652 / 8:00	281 / 452 / 6:00	552 / 888 / 10:40	570 / 917 / 10:50	313 / 504 / 6:50	692 / 1114 / 13:10	297 / 478 / 6:30
Leeds																		405 / 652 / 8:30	394 / 634 / 8:20	55 / 89 / 1:30	487 / 784 / 10:20	360 / 579 / 7:10	176 / 283 / 4:00	223 / 359 / 4:30	196 / 315 / 4:20	174 / 280 / 3:20	215 / 346 / 4:10	329 / 530 / 6:40	237 / 381 / 4:40	270 / 435 / 5:00	202 / 325 / 4:00	258 / 415 / 4:50	260 / 418 / 4:50	29 / 47 / 0:50	119 / 192 / 2:30	232 / 373 / 4:20	145 / 233 / 2:50	194 / 312 / 3:50	260 / 419 / 5:00	293 / 472 / 5:30	255 / 410 / 4:50	72 / 116 / 1:40	113 / 182 / 2:30	156 / 251 / 3:20	212 / 341 / 4:00	169 / 272 / 3:40	327 / 526 / 6:50	189 / 304 / 3:50
Leicester																	95 / 153 / 2:00	320 / 515 / 6:30	500 / 805 / 9:50	102 / 164 / 2:10	588 / 947 / 11:50	461 / 742 / 8:50	190 / 306 / 4:00	147 / 237 / 3:10	140 / 225 / 3:20	85 / 137 / 1:40	314 / 505 / 5:40	422 / 679 / 8:00	209 / 336 / 4:10	196 / 315 / 3:40	296 / 476 / 5:20	349 / 562 / 6:20	185 / 298 / 3:30	74 / 119 / 1:30	206 / 332 / 3:50	154 / 248 / 3:00	68 / 109 / 1:20	120 / 193 / 2:30	166 / 267 / 3:20	389 / 626 / 7:00	158 / 254 / 3:10	140 / 225 / 2:40	39 / 63 / 1:10	252 / 406 / 5:00	299 / 481 / 5:20	153 / 246 / 3:20	414 / 666 / 7:40	97 / 156 / 2:20
Lincoln																51 / 82 / 1:20	68 / 109 / 1:50	371 / 597 / 7:30	476 / 766 / 9:40	44 / 71 / 1:20	554 / 892 / 11:30	427 / 687 / 8:30	216 / 348 / 4:40	155 / 249 / 3:30	128 / 206 / 3:20	159 / 256 / 3:10	291 / 468 / 5:30	399 / 642 / 7:50	272 / 438 / 5:30	247 / 398 / 4:40	258 / 415 / 5:00	314 / 505 / 5:50	202 / 325 / 4:00	39 / 63 / 1:10	191 / 307 / 3:40	208 / 335 / 4:10	85 / 137 / 2:20	183 / 295 / 3:40	197 / 317 / 4:00	357 / 575 / 6:40	209 / 336 / 4:10	128 / 206 / 2:40	90 / 145 / 2:10	224 / 360 / 4:40	274 / 441 / 5:10	199 / 320 / 4:20	383 / 616 / 7:20	131 / 211 / 3:10
Liverpool															129 / 208 / 2:50	130 / 209 / 2:40	75 / 121 / 1:50	361 / 581 / 7:20	407 / 655 / 8:30	130 / 209 / 2:40	511 / 822 / 10:40	382 / 615 / 7:40	102 / 164 / 2:40	265 / 427 / 5:20	240 / 386 / 5:00	140 / 225 / 2:40	216 / 348 / 4:10	329 / 530 / 6:40	160 / 257 / 3:30	237 / 381 / 4:30	216 / 348 / 4:10	286 / 460 / 5:20	299 / 481 / 5:30	86 / 138 / 1:50	120 / 193 / 2:30	169 / 272 / 3:20	194 / 312 / 3:40	161 / 259 / 3:10	272 / 438 / 5:10	318 / 512 / 6:00	234 / 377 / 4:30	49 / 79 / 1:20	93 / 150 / 2:10	219 / 352 / 4:30	213 / 343 / 4:10	104 / 167 / 2:40	341 / 549 / 6:40	202 / 325 / 4:10
Manchester														35 / 56 / 1:10	84 / 135 / 2:00	92 / 148 / 2:00	40 / 64 / 1:10	361 / 581 / 7:20	406 / 654 / 8:30	95 / 153 / 2:10	500 / 805 / 10:30	373 / 600 / 7:30	124 / 200 / 3:00	228 / 367 / 4:40	212 / 341 / 4:30	126 / 203 / 2:30	215 / 346 / 4:10	329 / 530 / 6:40	197 / 317 / 4:00	236 / 380 / 4:20	215 / 346 / 4:10	285 / 459 / 5:20	276 / 444 / 5:10	61 / 98 / 1:30	119 / 192 / 2:30	183 / 295 / 3:40	165 / 266 / 3:10	161 / 259 / 3:10	257 / 414 / 4:50	318 / 512 / 6:00	227 / 365 / 4:20	48 / 77 / 1:20	80 / 129 / 2:00	196 / 315 / 4:00	212 / 341 / 4:00	129 / 208 / 3:00	340 / 547 / 6:30	185 / 298 / 3:50
Newcastle upon Tyne													132 / 212 / 2:50	168 / 270 / 3:20	159 / 256 / 3:20	187 / 301 / 3:40	92 / 148 / 2:10	498 / 802 / 9:40	318 / 512 / 7:00	132 / 212 / 2:50	395 / 636 / 8:50	268 / 431 / 5:40	272 / 438 / 5:40	308 / 496 / 6:00	281 / 452 / 5:40	266 / 428 / 4:50	148 / 238 / 3:10	253 / 407 / 5:20	329 / 529 / 6:20	364 / 586 / 6:30	110 / 177 / 2:20	166 / 267 / 3:20	358 / 576 / 6:30	114 / 183 / 2:20	57 / 92 / 1:50	325 / 523 / 6:00	241 / 388 / 4:20	299 / 481 / 5:30	352 / 567 / 6:30	201 / 323 / 4:00	347 / 558 / 6:30	129 / 208 / 2:40	207 / 333 / 4:10	64 / 103 / 1:50	149 / 240 / 3:00	257 / 414 / 5:20	235 / 378 / 4:50	286 / 460 / 5:40
Norwich												264 / 425 / 5:20	185 / 298 / 4:30	220 / 354 / 4:40	105 / 169 / 2:50	119 / 192 / 3:20	176 / 283 / 3:50	421 / 678 / 8:40	582 / 937 / 11:50	149 / 240 / 4:00	654 / 1053 / 13:30	529 / 852 / 10:30	311 / 501 / 6:40	73 / 117 / 2:00	20 / 32 / 0:40	204 / 328 / 4:10	385 / 620 / 9:00	504 / 811 / 10:00	343 / 552 / 7:00	308 / 496 / 6:00	366 / 589 / 7:00	422 / 679 / 8:00	174 / 280 / 3:50	147 / 237 / 3:20	289 / 465 / 5:40	262 / 422 / 5:20	62 / 100 / 1:50	252 / 406 / 5:10	175 / 282 / 4:00	457 / 735 / 8:40	214 / 344 / 4:40	232 / 373 / 4:50	166 / 267 / 3:50	328 / 528 / 6:40	382 / 615 / 7:20	276 / 444 / 6:00	496 / 798 / 9:40	114 / 183 / 3:30
Nottingham											130 / 209 / 3:40	157 / 253 / 3:10	73 / 118 / 1:40	98 / 158 / 2:10	35 / 56 / 1:10	25 / 40 / 0:50	70 / 113 / 1:40	345 / 555 / 7:00	479 / 771 / 9:40	90 / 145 / 2:00	557 / 896 / 11:30	430 / 692 / 8:20	185 / 298 / 4:00	150 / 241 / 3:20	153 / 246 / 3:30	110 / 177 / 2:10	293 / 472 / 5:30	401 / 646 / 7:50	220 / 354 / 4:30	221 / 356 / 4:10	262 / 422 / 4:50	328 / 528 / 6:00	205 / 330 / 3:50	43 / 69 / 1:10	194 / 312 / 3:40	172 / 277 / 3:20	83 / 134 / 1:40	145 / 233 / 3:00	193 / 311 / 3:50	353 / 568 / 6:30	183 / 295 / 3:40	111 / 179 / 2:20	50 / 80 / 1:20	221 / 356 / 4:30	274 / 441 / 5:10	164 / 264 / 3:40	393 / 633 / 7:30	122 / 196 / 2:40
Oban										390 / 628 / 7:30	492 / 792 / 9:40	233 / 375 / 4:50	307 / 494 / 6:00	308 / 496 / 6:10	387 / 623 / 7:30	419 / 674 / 7:50	307 / 494 / 6:00	665 / 1070 / 12:50	128 / 206 / 3:10	346 / 557 / 6:40	244 / 393 / 6:10	117 / 188 / 3:00	427 / 687 / 8:30	524 / 843 / 10:00	515 / 829 / 10:00	441 / 710 / 8:10	92 / 148 / 2:30	49 / 79 / 1:20	481 / 774 / 9:10	549 / 884 / 10:00	123 / 198 / 3:00	117 / 188 / 2:50	585 / 942 / 10:40	346 / 557 / 6:40	188 / 303 / 4:00	477 / 768 / 9:00	468 / 753 / 8:40	465 / 748 / 8:40	565 / 910 / 10:30	141 / 227 / 3:30	530 / 853 / 9:50	285 / 459 / 5:40	384 / 618 / 7:30	180 / 290 / 4:20	94 / 151 / 2:20	412 / 663 / 8:10	178 / 286 / 4:20	499 / 803 / 9:30
Oxford									462 / 744 / 8:30	109 / 175 / 2:10	145 / 233 / 3:50	260 / 418 / 4:50	144 / 232 / 2:50	172 / 277 / 3:20	137 / 221 / 2:50	73 / 117 / 1:30	168 / 270 / 3:10	274 / 441 / 5:40	550 / 885 / 10:40	192 / 309 / 3:40	656 / 1056 / 13:00	532 / 856 / 10:00	238 / 383 / 4:50	145 / 233 / 3:10	200 / 322 / 4:20	52 / 84 / 1:30	356 / 573 / 6:30	472 / 760 / 9:00	205 / 330 / 4:10	156 / 251 / 3:00	372 / 599 / 6:40	433 / 697 / 7:40	141 / 227 / 2:50	145 / 233 / 2:40	260 / 418 / 4:40	108 / 174 / 2:20	83 / 134 / 1:40	74 / 119 / 1:40	108 / 174 / 2:20	465 / 749 / 8:20	90 / 145 / 2:00	187 / 301 / 3:30	64 / 103 / 1:30	324 / 521 / 6:10	353 / 568 / 6:20	154 / 248 / 3:20	483 / 777 / 8:50	57 / 92 / 1:40
Plymouth								199 / 320 / 4:00	587 / 945 / 11:00	267 / 430 / 5:10	343 / 552 / 7:00	410 / 660 / 7:40	283 / 455 / 5:30	283 / 455 / 5:30	293 / 472 / 5:50	242 / 389 / 4:40	316 / 509 / 6:00	89 / 143 / 2:20	674 / 1085 / 13:10	355 / 571 / 6:40	790 / 1271 / 15:40	664 / 1069 / 12:30	328 / 528 / 6:40	309 / 497 / 6:10	365 / 588 / 7:20	157 / 253 / 3:20	495 / 797 / 9:10	595 / 958 / 11:20	264 / 425 / 5:30	46 / 74 / 1:30	496 / 798 / 9:00	552 / 888 / 10:00	300 / 483 / 5:50	297 / 478 / 5:40	399 / 642 / 7:20	167 / 269 / 3:40	293 / 472 / 5:30	122 / 196 / 2:50	224 / 361 / 6:00	587 / 945 / 10:40	128 / 206 / 3:30	328 / 528 / 6:10	203 / 327 / 4:20	474 / 763 / 9:00	492 / 792 / 9:00	237 / 382 / 5:10	615 / 990 / 11:20	218 / 351 / 4:40
Portsmouth							176 / 283 / 4:50	77 / 124 / 1:40	545 / 877 / 10:00	191 / 307 / 3:40	207 / 333 / 4:20	337 / 542 / 6:10	236 / 380 / 4:30	254 / 409 / 4:50	201 / 323 / 4:00	162 / 261 / 3:10	257 / 414 / 4:50	259 / 417 / 5:40	633 / 1019 / 12:10	269 / 433 / 5:00	737 / 1186 / 14:30	613 / 987 / 11:30	311 / 501 / 6:10	166 / 267 / 3:40	221 / 356 / 4:40	119 / 192 / 3:00	448 / 721 / 8:10	555 / 893 / 10:20	251 / 404 / 5:00	135 / 217 / 2:40	453 / 729 / 8:10	514 / 827 / 9:00	130 / 209 / 2:50	234 / 377 / 4:20	348 / 560 / 6:10	142 / 229 / 3:00	144 / 232 / 2:50	97 / 156 / 2:10	48 / 77 / 1:40	547 / 881 / 9:50	52 / 84 / 1:30	264 / 425 / 4:50	141 / 227 / 3:00	401 / 645 / 7:30	430 / 692 / 7:40	222 / 357 / 4:40	560 / 901 / 10:10	70 / 113 / 2:00
Sheffield						230 / 370 / 4:20	283 / 455 / 5:30	135 / 217 / 2:40	339 / 546 / 6:30	37 / 60 / 1:00	146 / 235 / 3:20	125 / 201 / 2:40	38 / 61 / 1:00	72 / 116 / 1:40	46 / 74 / 1:20	62 / 100 / 1:20	33 / 53 / 1:00	361 / 581 / 7:10	427 / 687 / 8:40	65 / 105 / 1:30	520 / 837 / 10:50	393 / 632 / 7:40	168 / 270 / 3:40	187 / 301 / 3:50	166 / 267 / 3:40	126 / 203 / 2:20	248 / 399 / 4:40	348 / 560 / 6:50	215 / 346 / 4:20	237 / 381 / 4:20	235 / 378 / 4:20	291 / 468 / 5:20	245 / 394 / 4:30	18 / 29 / 0:40	152 / 245 / 3:00	194 / 312 / 3:40	120 / 193 / 2:20	161 / 259 / 3:10	226 / 364 / 4:20	320 / 515 / 6:00	216 / 348 / 4:10	86 / 138 / 1:50	76 / 122 / 1:50	190 / 306 / 4:00	245 / 394 / 4:30	159 / 256 / 3:30	360 / 579 / 6:50	159 / 256 / 3:20
Shrewsbury					82 / 132 / 2:10	207 / 333 / 3:50	225 / 362 / 4:40	106 / 171 / 2:10	364 / 586 / 7:00	93 / 150 / 2:00	205 / 330 / 4:20	201 / 323 / 3:50	69 / 111 / 1:40	58 / 93 / 1:50	133 / 214 / 2:50	84 / 135 / 1:40	109 / 175 / 2:20	303 / 488 / 6:10	451 / 726 / 9:00	169 / 272 / 3:10	567 / 912 / 11:30	438 / 705 / 8:20	113 / 182 / 2:50	240 / 386 / 4:40	225 / 362 / 4:40	77 / 124 / 1:30	272 / 438 / 5:00	382 / 615 / 7:20	145 / 233 / 3:10	179 / 288 / 3:20	274 / 441 / 5:00	330 / 531 / 6:00	251 / 404 / 4:30	109 / 175 / 2:10	176 / 283 / 3:20	111 / 179 / 2:20	159 / 256 / 3:00	103 / 166 / 2:50	226 / 364 / 4:20	371 / 597 / 6:50	185 / 298 / 3:40	98 / 158 / 2:00	45 / 72 / 1:20	265 / 426 / 5:10	269 / 433 / 5:00	77 / 124 / 2:10	399 / 642 / 7:30	160 / 258 / 3:20
Southampton				185 / 298 / 4:10	199 / 320 / 3:40	21 / 34 / 0:50	151 / 243 / 4:10	64 / 103 / 1:30	530 / 853 / 9:40	176 / 283 / 3:20	206 / 332 / 4:20	324 / 521 / 5:50	221 / 356 / 4:10	239 / 385 / 4:30	204 / 328 / 4:00	137 / 220 / 2:40	232 / 373 / 4:20	228 / 367 / 5:00	618 / 995 / 12:00	256 / 412 / 4:40	723 / 1164 / 14:10	598 / 963 / 11:10	293 / 472 / 5:50	164 / 264 / 3:30	220 / 354 / 4:40	105 / 169 / 2:40	433 / 697 / 7:40	541 / 871 / 10:00	233 / 375 / 4:40	105 / 169 / 3:00	438 / 705 / 7:50	500 / 805 / 8:50	143 / 230 / 2:50	209 / 336 / 3:50	324 / 521 / 5:50	121 / 195 / 2:30	148 / 238 / 2:50	76 / 122 / 2:20	61 / 98 / 1:50	532 / 856 / 9:30	31 / 50 / 1:00	251 / 404 / 4:40	128 / 206 / 2:40	388 / 624 / 7:10	417 / 671 / 7:30	201 / 323 / 4:10	547 / 880 / 10:00	77 / 124 / 2:00
Stranraer			445 / 716 / 8:20	277 / 446 / 5:30	263 / 423 / 5:20	461 / 742 / 8:40	500 / 805 / 9:40	379 / 610 / 7:10	148 / 238 / 3:40	290 / 467 / 5:50	403 / 649 / 8:10	158 / 254 / 3:40	220 / 354 / 4:40	221 / 356 / 4:40	298 / 480 / 6:00	330 / 531 / 6:20	220 / 354 / 4:40	585 / 942 / 11:30	263 / 423 / 6:30	259 / 417 / 5:20	379 / 610 / 9:00	262 / 422 / 6:00	338 / 544 / 7:00	410 / 660 / 8:10	426 / 686 / 8:40	343 / 552 / 6:30	84 / 135 / 2:30	195 / 314 / 4:50	392 / 631 / 7:50	454 / 731 / 8:30	124 / 200 / 3:00	167 / 269 / 3:40	496 / 798 / 9:10	257 / 414 / 5:10	101 / 163 / 2:40	390 / 628 / 7:30	379 / 610 / 7:10	378 / 608 / 7:20	475 / 765 / 9:00	194 / 312 / 4:20	444 / 715 / 8:30	188 / 303 / 4:00	297 / 478 / 6:00	170 / 274 / 4:10	51 / 82 / 1:20	325 / 523 / 6:50	228 / 367 / 5:10	402 / 647 / 7:50
Swansea		417 / 671 / 7:50	161 / 259 / 3:00	118 / 190 / 2:20	217 / 349 / 4:00	182 / 293 / 3:30	206 / 332 / 4:10	141 / 227 / 2:40	506 / 815 / 9:20	192 / 309 / 3:40	301 / 485 / 6:00	347 / 559 / 6:20	187 / 301 / 3:30	195 / 314 / 3:40	233 / 375 / 4:30	177 / 285 / 3:20	248 / 399 / 4:40	285 / 459 / 6:00	594 / 956 / 11:30	264 / 425 / 4:50	696 / 1120 / 13:40	572 / 921 / 10:40	184 / 296 / 4:50	267 / 430 / 5:10	329 / 530 / 6:30	89 / 143 / 1:50	409 / 658 / 7:20	496 / 798 / 9:20	67 / 108 / 1:50	161 / 259 / 3:00	412 / 663 / 7:20	473 / 761 / 8:20	274 / 441 / 5:00	232 / 373 / 4:10	309 / 497 / 5:30	41 / 66 / 1:10	227 / 365 / 4:10	85 / 137 / 1:50	222 / 357 / 4:20	505 / 813 / 9:00	167 / 269 / 3:20	216 / 348 / 4:00	119 / 192 / 2:30	383 / 616 / 7:10	379 / 610 / 6:50	73 / 117 / 2:00	507 / 816 / 9:20	194 / 312 / 4:00
York	272 / 438 / 5:10	222 / 357 / 4:40	258 / 415 / 5:10	133 / 214 / 2:40	52 / 84 / 1:20	278 / 448 / 5:10	333 / 536 / 6:20	181 / 291 / 3:20	309 / 497 / 6:00	77 / 124 / 1:40	181 / 291 / 4:20	84 / 135 / 2:20	64 / 103 / 1:30	99 / 159 / 2:10	75 / 121 / 1:50	108 / 174 / 2:10	24 / 39 / 0:50	411 / 661 / 8:00	407 / 655 / 8:20	37 / 60 / 1:10	479 / 771 / 10:10	352 / 566 / 7:00	204 / 328 / 4:20	228 / 367 / 4:40	201 / 323 / 4:20	189 / 304 / 3:30	217 / 349 / 4:10	330 / 531 / 6:30	261 / 420 / 5:10	287 / 462 / 5:10	194 / 312 / 3:40	250 / 402 / 4:40	282 / 454 / 5:10	34 / 55 / 1:00	121 / 195 / 2:30	244 / 393 / 4:40	165 / 266 / 3:10	222 / 357 / 4:10	275 / 443 / 5:10	285 / 459 / 5:20	269 / 433 / 5:00	96 / 154 / 2:00	130 / 209 / 2:40	148 / 238 / 3:10	214 / 344 / 4:00	195 / 314 / 4:10	319 / 513 / 6:10	207 / 333 / 4:10

Key to road map pages

56	Map pages at 1:200000 — 1 cm = 2 km • 1 inch = 3·15 miles
78	Map pages at 1:250000 — 1 cm = 2.5 km • 1 inch = 3.94 miles
96	Map pages at 1:340000 — 1 cm = 3.4 km • 1 inch = 5.37 miles

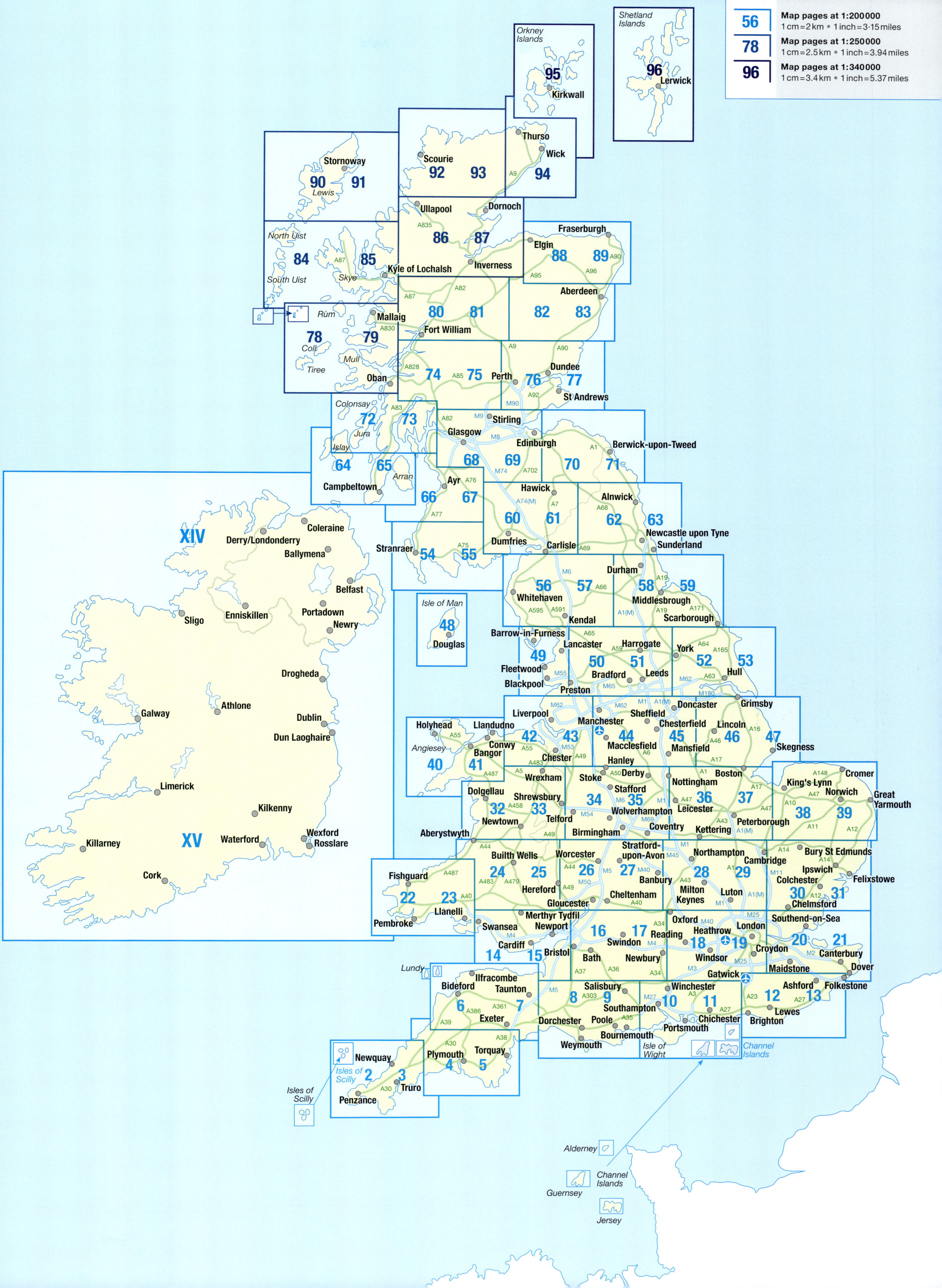

Isles of Scilly
SV
White Island
St Helens
St Martin's
King Charles Castle
Bryher
Cromwell's Castle
New Grimsby
Higher Town
Tresco
Bryher
Tresco Abbey Gardens
Crow Sound
Eastern Isles
Samson
Bant's Carn
The Road
North West Passage
Newford
Innisidgen Cairns
Maypole
Longstone Heritage Centre
St Mary's
Hugh Town
Crim Rocks
Garrison Walls
Old Town
St Mary's
Broad Sound
Annet
Smith Sound
St Mary's Sound
Penzance (Mar-Nov)
St Agnes
Gugh
St Agnes
Bishop Rock
SW
CORNWALL
Penhale
Ligger or Perran Bay
Perranporth
South West Coast Path
St Agnes Hd.
St Agnes
Trevellas
Mithian
Goonbell
Porthtowan
Mount Hawke
Three Burrows
Blackwater
Portreath
Mawla
Scorrier
Navax Pt.
Godrevy Island
Godrevy Pt.
Portreath
Tehidy
Illogan
Cornish Gold Tolgus Mill
Cornish Mines & Engines
St Day
Roscroggan
Redruth
The Carracks
Clodgy Pt.
Tate St Ives
The Island
St Ives Bay
Barbara Hepworth Museum
St Ives
South West Coast Path
Gwithian
Kehelland
Pool
Carnkie
Cambrea
Carharrack
Gwennap Pit
Gwennap
Tuckingmill
Camborne
Lanner
Gurnard's Head
Zennor
Halsetown
Carbis Bay
Phillack
Roseworthy
Trevithick Cottage
Connor Downs
Shire Horse Farm
Troon
Four Lanes
Porthmeor
Wayside Folk Museum
Towednack
Lelant
Copperhouse
Barripper
Carnhell Green
Penhalvaen
Stithians
South West Coast Path
Cripplesease
Paradise Park
Hayle
Praze-an-Beeble
Penmarth
Stithians Res.
Morvah
Chysauster Ancient Village
Nancledra
Canon's Town
Fraddam
Burras
Crowan
Carnkie
Longdowns
Geevor Tin Mine Museum
Pendeen
Bojewyan
Higher Boscaswell
St Erth
Leedstown
Trewellard
Newmill
Drym
Releath
Porkellis
Rame
Botallack
Carnyorth
Crowlas
Townshend
Cape Cornwall
Ludgvan
Relubbus
Godolphin House
Godolphin Cross
Nancegollan
Poldark Mine
Seworgan
The Brisons
St Just
Trengwainton
Madron
Gulval
P&R
St Hilary
Trescowe
Wendron
Ballowall Barrow
Land's End
Newbridge
Heamoor
Penzance
Chyandour
Marazion
Goldsithney
Crowntown
Helston Railway
Bosavern
St Michael's Mount
Perranuthnoe
Germoe
Kelynack
Sancreed
Penzance
Ashton
Sithney
Constantine
Carn Euny Ancient Village
Res.
Tredavoe
Breage
Trewennack
Land's End
Lower Drift
Newlyn
Newlyn Art Gallery
Praa Sands
Brane
Catchall
Paul
South West Coast Path
Helston
Whitesand Bay
Crows-an-wra
Kerris
Mousehole
Cudden Pt.
Rinsey
Gweek
Sennen Cove
St Buryan
St Clement's Island
Trewavas Hd.
Porthleven
Flambards Experience
National Seal Sanctuary
Longships
Sennen
Trewoofe
South West Coast Path
The Loe
Mawgan
Land's End
Polgigga
Lamorna
Porthleven Sands
Garras
St Martins
Boskenna
Tregiffian Burial Chamber
Halliggye Fogou
Trelowarren
Porthcurno
Treen
Lamorna Cove
Mount's Bay
Gunwalloe
Berepper
Newtown
Telegraph Museum Porthcurno
St Levan
Minack Open Air Theatre
Cury
Cross Lanes
Gwennap Hd.
Traboe
Runnel Stone
Goonhilly Downs
Mullion
Penhale
The Lizard
Trelan
Mullion Cove
Mullion Cove
Gwenter
Mullion Island
Kuggar
Predannack Wollas
Isles of Scilly (Mar-Nov)
Vellan Hd.
St Ruan
Ruan Minor
Cadgwith
Grade
South West Coast Path
Kynance Cove
Lizard
Hot Pt.
Lizard Point
Lizard
A30
A394
A3047
A3083
A3074
A3071
B3306
B3311
B3318
B3315
B3283
B3301
B3280
B3297
B3302
B3303
B3304
B3296
B3293
0 1 2 3 4 5 6 miles
0 1 2 3 4 5 6 7 8 9 10 km

6
7
8
9
10
11
SX
C o r n w a l l
C O R N W A L L
B O D M I N M O O R
Camelford
Delabole
Port Isaac
Port Isaac Bay
Port Quin
Pentire Pt.
Gulland Rock
Gunver Hd.
TREVOSE HEAD
Constantine Bay
Padstow
Padstow Bay
Wadebridge
Bodmin
Bodmin Forest
Liskeard
Lostwithiel
St Austell
ST. AUSTELL BAY
Newquay
Newquay Bay
Watergate Bay
Fistral Bay
Towan Hd.
Kelsey Hd.
Perranporth
St Columb Major
Indian Queens
Truro
Falmouth
Falmouth Bay
Penryn
St Mawes
Carrick Roads
Zone Pt.
Pendennis Pt.
Mevagissey
Mevagissey Bay
Gorran Haven
Dodman Pt.
Veryan Bay
Gerrans Bay
Nare Hd.
Greeb Pt.
Chapel Pt.
Black Hd.
Gribbin Hd.
Fowey
Polruan
Pencarrow Hd.
Polperro
Looe
Looe Bay
Talland Bay
St George's or Looe I.
Helford River
Rosemullion Hd.
St Anthony-in-Meneage
Nare Pt.
Manacle Pt.
The Manacles
Porthallow
Porthoustock
St Keverne
Lowland Pt.
Coverack
Chynhalls Pt.
Black Hd.
Trevose Head
Park Hd.
Berryl's Pt.
High Moor
Dozmary Pool
Colliford Lake
Siblyback Lake
A30
A38
A39
A390
A391
A392
A3058
A3059
A3078
A3082
A389
A394
B3274
B3275
B3314
B3266
B3268
B3269
B3273
B3287
B3289
B3284
B3285
NATIONAL MARITIME
PENDENNIS CASTLE
EDEN PROJECT
WORLD OF MODEL RAILWAYS
THE LOST GARDENS OF HELIGAN
RESTORMEL CASTLE
LANHYDROCK HOUSE
BODMIN AND WENFORD RAILWAY
NEWQUAY ZOO
BLUE REEF AQUARIUM
TRERICE
LAPPA VALLEY STEAM RAILWAY
CARNGLAZE SLATE CAVERNS
THE HURLERS STONE CIRCLES
MUSEUM OF SMUGGLING
SOUTH WEST COAST PATH
NATIONAL LOBSTER HATCHERY
PRIDEAUX PLACE
ST AUSTELL BREWERY
CHARLESTOWN SHIPWRECK & HERITAGE CENTRE
ST CATHERINE'S CASTLE
GLENDURGAN
TREBAH
TRELISSICK
ROYAL CORNWALL MUS
CATHEDRAL

BUDE BAY
CORNWALL
Widemouth Bay
Widemouth Sand
Marhamchurch
Bridgerule
Pyworthy
Derril
Derriton
Holsworthy
Chasty
Whimble
Hollacombe
Brandis Corner
Chilla
Graddon Moor
Winsford Walled Garden
Halwill Junction
Halwill
Beaworthy
Northlew
Oak Cross
Ashbury
Patchacott
BROADBURY
Quoditch
Clawton
Leworthy
Coppathorne
Budd's Titson
Millook
Dizzard Pt.
Poundstock
South West Coast Path
Treskinnick Cross
Whitstone
North Tamerton
Tetcott
Lana
Luffincott
Ashwater
Henford
Virginstow
Germansweek
Ewworthy
Boasley Cross
Thorndon Cross
Sourton Cross Services
Roadford Res.
Gnnacombe Moor
Bratton Clovelly
Tregole
Trewint
St Gennys
Week St Mary
Penhallam
Jacobstow
Wainhouse Corner
Crackington Haven
Rosecare
Cambeak
Fire Beacon Pt.
Tresparrett Posts
Tresparrett
Beeny
Boscastle
Marshgate
Otterham
Trelash
Lesnewth
Canworthy Water
Warbstow
South Wheatley
West Curry
Maxworthy
Bennacott
Brazacott
Boyton
Northcott
Chapmans Well
East Panson
St Giles on the Hth.
Gridley Corner
Tamar Otter & Wildlife Centre
Langdon
Trevalga
Tintagel Hd.
Old Post Office Tintagel
Bossiney
Tintagel
Trewarmett
Treknow
Start Pt.
Trebarwith
Trewassa
Davidstow
Tremail
Hallworthy
Treneglos
Tremaine
North Petherwin
Yeolmbridge
Bridgetown
Werrington
Broadwoodwidger
Cross Green
Thrushelton
Stowford
Lewdown
Bridestowe
Shortacombe
Lewtrenchard
Portgate
Lydford
Lydford Gorge
Dingle's Fairground Heritage Centre
The Arthurian Centre
Cornwall at War
Cold Northcott
Tresmeer
Tregeare
Egloskerry
Langore
St Stephen's
Launceston
Launceston Steam Railway
Dutson
Liftondown
Lifton
Tinhay
Coryton
Trelligga
South West Coast Path
Port Isaac Bay
Delabole
Valley Truckle
Camelford
Crowdy Res.
Davidstow Moor
St Clether
Laneast
Piper's Pool
Hidden Valley Discovery Park
Trethorne Leisure Farm
Tregadillett
Castle
Trewen
Dan's House
South Petherwin
Polyphant
Lawhitton
Kelly
Bradstone
Chillaton
North Brentor
Black Down
Willsworthy
Port Gaverne
Pendoggett
Helstone
St Teath
Treveighan
Trelill
Michaelstow
High Moor
Rough Tor
Brown Willy
Garrow Tor
Codda
Altarnun
Trewint
Lewannick
Congdon's Shop
Trebartha
Lezant
Trekenner
Rezare
Dunterton
Milton Abbot
SX
Mary Tavy
Horndon
Cudliptown
Peter Tavy
St Kew
St Tudy
St Breward
Row
Museum of Smuggling
Bolventor
BODMIN MOOR
Trebullett
Coad's Green
Treburley
Sydenham Damerel
Lamerton
Wilminstone
North Hill
Bray Shop
Stoke Climsland
Horsebridge
Merrivale
St Kew Highway
Wenfordbridge
Bradford
Dozmary Pool
Kilmar Tor
Henwood
Bathpool
Tavistock
St Mabyn
Blisland
Temple
Colliford Lake
Rilla Mill
Linkinhorne
South Hill
Downgate
Luckett
Latchley
Chilsworthy
Gunnislake
Whitchurch
Grenofen
Sampford Spiney
Pencarrow House
Egloshayle
Helland
Maidenwell
Millpool
Upton Cross
The Hurlers Stone Circles
Minions
Caradon Hill
Siblyback Lake
Golberdon
Haye
Kelly Bray
Kit Hill
St Ann's Chapel
Albaston
Drakewalls
Gulworthy
Higher Walreddon
Horrabridge
Walkhampton
Dousland
Burlawn
Washaway
Bodmin Forest
Bodmin
Bodmin Town Museum
Bodmin and Wenford Railway
Warleggan
Cardinham
Commonmoor
Golitha Falls
Darite
Trethevy Quoit
Tremar
King Doniert's Stone
Pensilva
Trevigro
Callington
Harrowbarrow
Dupath Well House
Cotehele House
St Dominick
Calstock
Monachorum
Buckland
The Garden House
Crapstone
Yelverton
Meavy
Nanstallon
St Lawrence
Mount
St Neot
Carnglaze Slate Caverns
St Cleer
Gang
St Ive
Newbridge
TAMAR VALLEY
Bere Alston
Buckland Abbey
Milton Combe
Clearbrook
Lanivet
Lanhydrock House
West Taphouse
East Taphouse
Fowey
Doublebois
Dobwalls
Ley
Merrymeet
Pengover Green
Quethiock
St Mellion
Weir Quay
Lopwell
Shaugh Prior
Trebyan
Restormel Castle
Sweetshouse
Redmoor
Braddock
St Pinnock
Liskeard
Menheniot
Pillaton
Blunts
Hatt
Cargreen
Landulph
Bere Ferrers
Tamerton Foliot
Roborough
Bickleigh
Lockengate
Bilberry
Lostwithiel
Herodsfoot
St Keyne
Tideford Cross
Landrake
Botusfleming
Saltash Services
Crownhill Fort
Plym
Forest
Bugle
Lanlivery
Couch's Mill
Trewidland
Duloe
Treruletoot
Widegates
Hessenford
Tideford
Trematon
Saltash
St Erney
St Stephens
Mary Newman's Cottage
St Budeaux
Crownhill
Plymouth
Eggbuckland
Plym Valley
Plympton
Stenalees
Penwithick
Luxulyan
Milltown
Lerryn
Boconnoc
Folk & Farm Museum
Lanreath
Sandplace
Morval
Polbathic
St Germans
Sheviock
Antony House
Torpoint
Devonport
Merchant's House
Trethurgy
Eden Project
St Blazey
Penpillick
Golant
St Veep
Penpoll
Muchlarnick
Pelynt
St Martin
Monkey Sanctuary
Seaton
Downderry
Portwrinkle
Crafthole
Antony
St John
Cremyll
Mount Edgcumbe
Royal Citadel
Plymstock
Elburton
Saltram
Carclaze
Boscoppa
St. Austell
Tywardreath
Par
Lanteglos Highway
Trenewan
Looe
East Looe
West Looe
Old Guildhall
Looe Bay
Holmbush
Shipwreck & Heritage Centre
Charlestown
St Austell Brewery
Polkerris
Menabilly
Fowey
St Catherine's Castle
Polruan
Bodinnick
Lansallos
Porthallow
Polperro
Heritage Museum
Talland Bay
St George's or Looe I.
South West Coast Path
Whitsand Bay
Freathy
Millbrook
Kingsand
Cawsand
Rame
Drake's I.
The Sound
Bovisand Bay
Hooe
Staddiscombe
Down Thomas
Knighton
Heybrook Bay
Wembury
Wembury Bay
Worswell
Great Mew Stone
Polgooth
Porthpean
ST. AUSTELL BAY
Pencarrow Hd.
Gribbin Hd.
Trenarren
Black Hd.
Pentewan
Penlee Pt.
Rame Hd.
World of Model Railways
Mevagissey
Chapel Pt.
Gorran Churchtown
Gorran Haven
Bosinger
Penare
Dodman Pt.
Roscoff Santander (Mar-Nov) St Malo (Nov-Mar)
A30
A39
A395
A388
A386
A390
A38
A391
A374
A387
A3079
A3072
A379
B3263
B3266
B3314
B3262
B3254
B3257
B3362
B3357
B3253
B3252
B3359
B3269
B3268
B3247
B3273
B3413
0 1 2 3 4 5 6 miles
0 1 2 3 4 5 6 7 8 9 10km

Okehampton
EXETER
Crediton
Exmouth
Budleigh Salterton
Topsham
Dawlish
Teignmouth
NEWTON ABBOT
Kingsteignton
Torquay
Paignton
TORBAY
Brixham
Dartmouth
Totnes
Ashburton
Buckfastleigh
Ivybridge
Kingsbridge
Salcombe
Moretonhampstead
Chagford
Bovey Tracey
Princetown
DARTMOOR
D A R T M O O R
N A T I O N A L
F O R E S T
P A R K
D e v o n
T o r b a y
S O U T H
D E V O N
BABBACOMBE BAY
TOR BAY
START BAY
BIGBURY BAY
START POINT
Bolt Tail
Bolt Hd.
Prawle Pt.
Stoke Pt.
Straight Pt.
Hope's Nose
Berry Head
Sharkham Pt.
Scabbacombe Hd.
Mew Stone
Slapton Sands
Lannacombe Bay
Burrator Res.
River Exe
Teign
Dart
A30
A38
A380
A385
A381
A379
A377
A376
A3052
A3122
A382
A383
A384
A386
M5
B3212
B3357
B3387
Whiteworks
Sheepstor
Yealmpton
Modbury
Holbeton
Newton Ferrers
Noss Mayo
Bigbury on Sea
Thurlestone
Hope
Malborough
East Portlemouth
Chillington
Torcross
Stokenham
Strete
Blackpool
Stoke Fleming
Kingswear
Galmpton
Churston Ferrers
Goodrington
Marldon
Cockington
Shiphay
Kingskerswell
Abbotskerswell
Ipplepen
Denbury
Dartington
Staverton
Landscove
Harbertonford
Halwell
Ugborough
South Brent
Cornwood
Lee Mill
Sparkwell
Harford
Wotter
Lee Moor
Shaugh Prior
Dean Prior
Holne
Poundsgate
Widecombe in the Moor
Manaton
Lustleigh
North Bovey
Haytor Vale
Ilsington
Liverton
Chudleigh
Chudleigh Knighton
Ideford
Luton
Bishopsteignton
Shaldon
Stokeinteignhead
Combeinteignhead
Maidencombe
Watcombe
Babbacombe
Wellswood
Holcombe
Cockwood
Starcross
Kenton
Powderham
Kenn
Kennford
Exminster
Alphington
Countess Wear
Heavitree
Whipton
Pinhoe
Sowton
Clyst St Mary
Clyst St George
Woodbury
Woodbury Salterton
Lympstone
Exton
Ebford
Littleham
Withycombe Raleigh
Knowle
East Budleigh
Otterton
Colaton Raleigh
Hawkerland
Newton Poppleford
Harpford
Venn Ottery
Aylesbeare
Farringdon
Marsh Green
Rockbeare
Whimple
Clyst Honiton
Broadclyst
Killerton House
Silverton
Bradninch
Stoke Canon
Rewe
Upton Pyne
Cowley
Newton St Cyres
Sweetham
Shobrooke
Sandford
Copplestone
Coleford
Colebrooke
Yeoford
Hittisleigh
Spreyton
Cheriton Bishop
Tedburn St Mary
Whitestone
Longdown
Dunsford
Doddiscombsleigh
Christow
Bridford
Trusham
Hennock
Ashcombe
Drewsteignton
Sandypark
Throwleigh
South Zeal
Sticklepath
Belstone
South Tawton
Whiddon Down
North Tawton
Bow
Zeal Monachorum
Honeychurch
Exbourne
Jacobstowe
Sampford Courtenay
Inwardleigh
Folly Gate
Hatherleigh
Meldon
Okehampton Camp
Taw Green
Gidleigh
Murchington
Teigncombe
Frenchbeer
Lettaford
Two Bridges
Postbridge
Bellever
Hexworthy
Dartmeet
Ponsworthy
Buckland in the Moor
Rundlestone
Sigford
Bickington
Highweek
Wolborough
Coffinswell
North Whilborough
Compton
Collaton St Mary
Berry Pomeroy
Blagdon
Tuckenhay
Cornworthy
Dittisham
Ashprington
Capton
Allaleigh
Blackawton
Woodford
Millcombe
East Allington
Moreleigh
Diptford
Avonwick
North Huish
Loddiswell
Woodleigh
Goveton
Harleston
Sherford
Frogmore
Charleton
West Alvington
South Milton
Churchstow
Aveton Gifford
Bigbury
St Ann's Chapel
Kingston
Ringmore
Bantham
Galmpton
Soar
South Pool
Kellaton
South Allington
East Prawle
Beeson
Beesands
Hallsands
Kernborough
Slapton
Frittiscombe
SOUTH WEST COAST PATH
DARTMOUTH CASTLE
BERRY HEAD
COLETON FISHACRE
OVERBECKS MUSEUM AND GARDEN
SALCOMBE
KENT'S CAVERN PREHISTORIC CAVES
MODEL VILLAGE
LIVING COASTS
TORRE ABBEY
COMPTON CASTLE
DARTINGTON HALL
BERRY POMEROY CASTLE
SOUTH DEVON RAILWAY
DARTMOUTH STEAM RAILWAY
PENNYWELL FARM & WILDLIFE CENTRE
BUCKFAST ABBEY
BUCKFAST BUTTERFLIES & DARTMOOR OTTER SANCTUARY
RIVER DART ADVENTURES
DARTMOOR ZOOLOGICAL PARK
UPPER PLYM VALLEY
HIGH MOORLAND VISITOR CENTRE
POSTBRIDGE INFORMATION CENTRE
HAYTOR INFORMATION CENTRE
STOVER
TRAGO MILLS
CANONTEIGN FALLS
CASTLE DROGO
POWDERHAM CASTLE
A LA RONDE
WORLD OF COUNTRY LIFE
EXMOUTH MODEL RAILWAY
DAWLISH WARREN
CRE ALY GREAT ADVENTURE PARK
EXETER INTERNATIONAL
EXETER SERVICES
CATHEDRAL
SHALDON WILDLIFE TRUST
WOODLANDS LEISURE PARK
NEWCOMEN ENGINE HOUSE
BAYARDS COVE FORT
GOLDEN HIND
GREENWAY
ZOO
FAIRLYNCH ARTS CENTRE AND MUSEUM
BICTON PARK
OTTERTON MILL
ESCOT PARK
THE COLLEGIATE CHURCH OF THE HOLY CROSS
OKEHAMPTON (Dartmoor)
DARTMOOR RAILWAY
FINCH FOUNDRY
WHITEHOUSE SERVICES
YES TOR
HIGH WILLHAYS
COSDON HILL
OKEMENT HILL
HANGINGSTONE HILL
CUT HILL
SITTAFORD TOR
HAMELDOWN TOR
ROUGH TOR
GT. MIS TOR
RIPPON TOR
RYDER'S HILL
SHELL TOP
UGBOROUGH BEACON
Ugborough Moor
WISTMAN'S WOOD
DENDLES WOOD
GRIMSPOUND
BRACKEN TOR
HOUND TOR
EAST DARTMOOR WOODS & HEATHS
THE MINIATURE PONY CENTRE
DARTINGTON CIDER PRESS CENTRE
PRICKLY BALL FARM
DECOY
PLANT WORLD
SOUTH WEST COAST PATH

LUNDY
North West Point
North East Point
South West Point
Surf Point
LUNDY MARINE NATURE RESERVE
ILFRACOMBE BIDEFORD (Mar-Oct)
LUNDY (Mar-Oct)
Ilfracombe
Combe Martin
Lynton
Barbrook
Highveer Pt.
Woody Bay
Rillage Pt.
Hele
Berrynarbor
Sterridge
Girt Down
Trentishoe
Martinhoe
Heale
Parracombe
Kentisbury
Blackmoor Gate
Challacombe Common
Challacombe
Shoulsbarrow Common
EXMOOR ZOO
WATERMOUTH CASTLE
WILDLIFE & DINOSAUR PARK
LYNTON AND BARNSTAPLE RLY
HELE CORN MILL
Bull Pt.
Rockham Bay
Morte Point
Mortehoe
Lee
Whitestone
Slade
Woolacombe
MORTE BAY
Woolacombe Sand
SOUTH WEST COAST PATH
Baggy Pt.
Putsborough
Pickwell
Croyde Bay
Georgeham
Croyde
Saunton
Lobb
Trimstone
Cheglinch
Dean
West Down
North Buckland
Nethercott
Darracott
Knowle
Braunton
Berry Down
Bittadon
East Down
Churchill
Arlington
ARLINGTON COURT
Loxhore
Knightacott
Milltown
Muddiford
Halsinger
Marwood
Guineaford
Kingsheanton
Shirwell
Shirwell Cross
Pippacott
Heanton Punchardon
MARWOOD HILL GARDENS
Prixford
ELLIOTT GALLERY
Wrafton
Saunton Sands
Braunton Burrows
Chivenor
Ashford
Burridge
Goodleigh
Stoke Rivers
Bratton Fleming
Benton
Lydcott
Brayford
High Bray
Charles
Barnstaple
MUSEUM OF BARNSTAPLE & NORTH DEVON
Pilton
Newport
Westacott
Fremington
Bickington
Yelland
Instow
Landkey
Swimbridge
Newland
West Buckland
East Buckland
Gunn
Filleigh
NORTH DEVON
BIDEFORD BAY
NORTHAM BURROWS
NORTH DEVON MARITIME MUSEUM
Appledore
Westward Ho!
Northam
TAPELEY PARK GDNS
Westleigh
Tawstock
Bishops Tawton
Orchard Hill
THE BIG SHEEP
Bideford
Eastleigh
Horwood
Newton Tracey
HARTLAND POINT
Windbury Pt.
Titchberry
HARTLAND ABBEY
Hartland Quay
Stoke
Hartland
SOUTH WEST COAST PATH
Milford
DOCTON MILL
Philham
ELMSCOTT
Elmscott
Eddistone
Tosberry
CLOVELLY VILLAGE
Clovelly
Higher Clovelly
Buck's Mills
Horns Cross
Buck's Cross
Fairy Cross
Abbotsham
Handy Cross
ATLANTIC VILLAGE
Landcross
East-the-Water
Woodtown
Ford
Littleham
Goldworthy
Parkham
THE MILKY WAY ADVENTURE PARK
Hiscott
Ensis
Chapelton
Fishleigh Barton
Woodtown
Alverdiscott
Herner
Cobbaton
COBBATON COMBAT COLLECTION
East Stowford
Chittlehampton
South Molton
QUINCE HONEY FARM
Umberleigh
Clapworthy
George Nympton
Warkleigh
Satterleigh
Chittlehamholt
Yarnscombe
Atherington
Langridge Ford
Sherwood Green
High Bickington
High Bullen
Weare Giffard
Monkleigh
Buckland Brewer
Woolfardisworthy
Hartland Forest
Alminstone Cross
Parkham Ash
South Hole
Knaps Longpeak
Welcombe
Meddon
Ashmansworthy
DARTINGTON CRYSTAL
Frithelstock
Frithelstock Stone
Great Torrington
Taddiport
St Giles in the Wood
King's Nympton
Kingscott
Roborough
Burrington
Cadbury Barton
Elstone
Chulmleigh
Little Torrington
R.H.S. GARDEN ROSEMOOR
Tythecott
Gooseham
Morwenstow
Eastcott
Woolley
Youlstone
Higher Sharpnose Pt.
Shop
Woodford
Lower Sharpnose Pt.
Dinworthy
West Putford
East Putford
GNOME RESERVE & GARDEN
Langtree
Bulkworthy
Stibb Cross
Peters Marland
Woollaton
Beaford
Riddlecombe
Ashreigney
Chawleigh
Kilkhampton
Coombe
Stibb
Bradworthy
Bradworthy Cross
Alfardisworthy
Sutcombe
Venn Green
Abbots Bickington
Newton St Petrock
Milton Damerel
Winswell
Merton
Huish
Dolton
Dowland
Ashley
Hollocombe
Wembworthy
Soldon Cross
Buckland Filleigh
Petrockstow
Meeth
Iddesleigh
Winkleigh
Brushford
Coldridge
Nymet Rowland
Flexbury
Poughill
Bude Haven
Stratton
Hersham
Grimscott
DUNSDON
Holsworthy Beacon
Chilsworthy
Shebbear
Thornbury
Bradford
Woodacott
Cookbury
Sheepwash
Black Torrington
Holemoor
Monkokehampton
Broadwood Kelly
Bondleigh
West Leigh
East Leigh
Zeal Monachorum
Bude
Upton
Launcells
Pancrasweek
Derril
Holsworthy
Whimble
Brandis Corner
Highampton
Hatherleigh
Widemouth Bay
Marhamchurch
Bridgerule
Pyworthy
Derriton
Chasty
Hollacombe
Chilla
Graddon Moor
WINSFORD WALLED GARDEN
Halwill Junction
Jacobstowe
Exbourne
Honeychurch
Sampford Courtenay
North Tawton
Bow
Millook
Coppathorne
Lewtorthy
Poundstock
Tregole
Treskinnick Cross
Week St Mary
PENHALLAM
Whitestone
North Tamerton
Clawton
Halwill
Beaworthy
Northlew
Inwardleigh
Oak Cross
Folly Gate
DARTMOOR RAILWAY
Taw Green
Spreyton
Jacobstow
Wainhouse Corner
Tetcott
Lana
Luffincott
Quoditch
BROADBURY
Ashbury
Patchacott
Ashwater
Henford
Eworthy
Germansweek
Boasley Cross
Okehampton
WHITEHOUSE SERVICES
Sticklepath
FINCH FOUNDRY
Belstone
South Tawton
South Zeal
Whiddon Down
South Wheatley
West Curry
Maxworthy
Chapmans Well
Virginstow
Roadford Res.
Thorndon Cross
SOURTON CROSS SERVICES
CASTLE
Okehampton Camp
OKEHAMPTON (Dartmoor)
BRACKEN TOR
Okehampton Common
Meldon
COSDON HILL
Throwleigh
YES TOR
Canworthy Water
Bennacott
Brazacott
Northcott
St Giles on the Hth.
East Panson
Gnnacombe Moor
Bratton Clovelly
Sourton
Warbstow
TAMAR OTTER & WILDLIFE CENTRE
Langdon
Gridley Corner
Broadwoodwidger
Bridestowe
BLACK-A-TOR COPSE
HIGH WILLHAYS
Bridestowe and Sourton Common
Wonson
Sandypark
Gidleigh
Easton
Murchington
Chagford
Teigncombe
Tremaine
Treneglos
North Petherwin
Bridgetown
Werrington
Cross Green
Thrushelton
Hallworthy
Tresmeer
Yeolmbridge
Eglosherry
Langore
Stowford
DINGLE'S FAIRGROUND HERITAGE CENTRE
Lewdown
Shortacombe
OKEMENT HILL
HANGINGSTONE HILL
Frenchbeer
Tregeare
Cold Northcott
St Stephen's
Dutson
LAUNCESTON STEAM RAILWAY
Liftondown
Lifton
Tinhay
Portgate
Lewtrenchard
Lydford
LYDFORD
LYDFORD GORGE
THE MINIATURE PONY CENTRE
Lettaford
HIDDEN VALLEY DISCOVERY PARK
TRETHORNE LEISURE
Piper's Pool
Tregadillett
Launceston
CASTLE
Coryton
DARTMOOR
DARTMOOR FOREST
CUT HILL
SITTAFORD TOR
Lawhitton
South Petherwin
Kelly
Chillaton
North Brentor
Black Down
Willsworthy
GRIMSPOUND
0 1 2 3 4 5 6 miles
0 1 2 3 4 5 6 7 8 9 10 km
SS
SX

Foreland Pt.
Lynmouth Bay
Countisbury
Lynmouth
Brendon
Malmsmead
Oare
Hurlstone Pt.
Porlock Bay
Porlock
Porlock Weir
Bossington
Allerford
Selworthy
Minehead
WEST SOMERSET RAILWAY
BUTLINS
Alcombe
Blue Anchor Bay
Dunster
Carhampton
Blue Anchor
Old Cleeve
Washford
Watchet
West Quantoxhead
Williton
BRIDGWATER BAY
EXMOOR FOREST
EXMOOR NATIONAL PARK
Brendon Common
Exe Plain
Simonsbath
Exford
Withypool
Withypool Common
Winsford
Exton
Luxborough
Wheddon Cross
BRENDON HILLS
Somerset
Elworthy
Monksilver
Stogumber
Crowcombe
QUANTOCK FOREST
QUANTOCK HILLS
Wimbleball Lake
Clatworthy Res.
Brompton Regis
Dulverton
Tarr Steps
Hawkridge
Molland Common
Anstey Common
Molland
Bampton
Morebath
Exebridge
Oakfordbridge
Wiveliscombe
Milverton
Vale of Taunton Deane
Taunton
Bishops Lydeard
Norton Fitzwarren
Wellington
Sampford Arundel
BLACKDOWN HILLS
Stapley
Churchinford
Hemyock
Culmstock
Uffculme
Willand
Tiverton
Bolham
Halberton
Sampford Peverell
Cullompton
Bickleigh
Thorverton
Silverton
Crediton
Exeter
Topsham
Exmouth
Budleigh Salterton
Otterton
Sidmouth
Sidford
Ottery St Mary
Honiton
Feniton
Seaton
Beer
Beer Hd.
Axmouth
Colyton
Colyford
Branscombe
Ladram Bay
Seaton Bay
East Devon
Devon
Moretonhampstead
Doddiscombsleigh
Kenton
Starcross
Exminster
Kennford
Woodbury
Clyst St George
Whipton
Heavitree
Alphington
Cheriton Bishop
Copplestone
Morchard Bishop
Witheridge
Rackenford
Knowstone
Bishops Nympton
Chulmleigh
Yeo Mill
North Molton
Danger Pt.
DORSET & EAST DEVON COAST WORLD HERITAGE SITE

Somerset
Dorset
East Devon
Blackdown Hills
Blackmoor Vale
Polden Hills
King's Sedge Moor
West Sedge Moor
Lyme Bay
ST
SY
Bridgwater
Taunton
Glastonbury
Street
Somerton
Langport
Ilminster
Chard
Crewkerne
South Petherton
Martock
Yeovil
Sherborne
Castle Cary
Wincanton
Bruton
Evercreech
Milborne Port
Stalbridge
Axminster
Seaton
Beer
Lyme Regis
Charmouth
Bridport
Beaminster
Dorchester
Weymouth
Portland
Fortuneswell
Easton
Bill of Portland
Chesil Beach
Portland Harbour
Cerne Abbas
Abbotsbury
West Bay
Merriott
Ilchester
Wellington
Ryme Intrinseca
Maiden Newton
Broadwindsor
Chideock
Honiton
Seaton Bay
Charlton Bay
Beer Hd.
West Bexington
Burton Bradstock
Preston
Osmington
Upwey
Broadmayne
Charminster
Puddletown
15
16
7
A30
A303
A35
A37
A39
A358
A372
A3088
A354
A352
A356
A359
A371
A3066
A3052
A378
M5
0 1 2 3 4 5 6 miles
0 1 2 3 4 5 6 7 8 9 10 km

CRANBORNE
CHASE
WEST
WILTSHIRE
DOWNS
Dorset
SU
SZ
NEW
FOREST
NATIONAL
PARK
ISLE OF PURBECK
POOLE BAY
Poole Harbour
Christchurch Bay
Swanage Bay
Studland Bay
Worbarrow Bay
Kimmeridge Bay
Lulworth Cove
Salisbury
Ringwood
Blandford Forum
Poole
Bournemouth
Swanage
Wareham
Wimborne Minster
Christchurch
Shaftesbury
Gillingham
Mere
Sturminster Newton
Fordingbridge
Verwood
Ferndown
Hamworthy
Corfe Mullen
Highcliffe
New Milton
Milford on Sea
Barton on Sea
Brockenhurst
Wilton
Tisbury
Wool
Corfe Castle
Studland
Sandbanks
Durlston Head
St Alban's Head
The Foreland
The Needles
Hengistbury Head
Durdle Door
Vale of Wardour
Great Ridge
Purbeck Hills
Nine Barrow Down
A30
A31
A35
A36
A338
A348
A350
A354
A303
A351
A352
16
17
10
GUERNSEY (April-Oct) ST. MALO (May-Sept) JERSEY
CHERBOURG
6
7
8
9
10
11
A
B
C
D
E
F
G
H

Hampshire
Winchester
Southampton
SOUTHAMPTON
EASTLEIGH
Romsey
Totton
Lyndhurst
Brockenhurst
LYMINGTON
New Milton
Barton on Sea
Milford on Sea
Hythe
Fawley
Fareham
Portsmouth
PORTSMOUTH
GOSPORT
Southsea
HAVANT
Emsworth
Waterlooville
Horndean
Wickham
Bishop's Waltham
New Alresford
Alton
Isle of Wight
NEWPORT
Cowes
East Cowes
RYDE
Bembridge
Sandown
Shanklin
Ventnor
Yarmouth
Totland
Freshwater
THE SOLENT
SPITHEAD
SOUTHAMPTON WATER
NEW FOREST NATIONAL PARK
FOREST OF BERE
South Hayling
HAYLING ISLAND
The Needles
St Catherine's Point
Christchurch Bay
Sandown Bay
Brighstone Bay
Chale Bay
Whitecliff Bay
BILBAO SANTANDER
GUERNSEY JERSEY
M27
M271
M275
M3
A3(M)
SU
SZ
0 1 2 3 4 5 6 miles
0 1 2 3 4 5 6 7 8 9 10 km

SOUTH DOWNS NATIONAL PARK
West Sussex
SOUTH DOWNS
Petersfield
Haslemere
Liphook
Bordon
Midhurst
Petworth
Pulborough
Billingshurst
Horsham
Crawley
Burgess Hill
Henfield
Storrington
Steyning
Arundel
Chichester
Bosham
Bognor Regis
Littlehampton
Rustington
Angmering
Worthing
Lancing
Shoreham-by-Sea
Southwick
Portslade-by-Sea
Hove
Brighton and Hove
Selsey
Selsey Bill
East Wittering
West Wittering
Chichester Harbour
Middleton-on-Sea
Pagham
Emsworth
Southbourne
Cranleigh
Grayshott
Hindhead
Chiddingfold
Fernhurst
Lodsworth
Upwaltham
Slindon
Fontwell
Amberley
Washington
Findon
Ferring
Goring-by-Sea
Selsey
TQ
TV
Alderney
3½ miles to 1 inch
Braye
St Anne
Quesnard Pt.
Longis Bay
Clonque Bay
Telegraph Bay
Brehou
ALDERNEY
DIELETTE ST. PETER PORT (Apr-Sept)
CAEN LE HAVRE ST. MALO
CHERBOURG (April-Sept)
Guernsey
3½ miles to 1 inch
GUERNSEY
St Peter Port
Herm
Jethou
L'Islet
St Sampson
Le Villocq
Mont Saint
Cobo Bay
Vazon Bay
Rocquaine Bay
Lihou I.
Pleinmont Pt.
Le Planel
Pointe de la Moye
Icart Pt.
St Martin's Pt.
Fort George
Carmel
Mouilpied
La Planque
Le Plomb
La Fontenelle
L'Ancresse Bay
Grand Havre
Belle Greve Bay
POOLE (Apr-Oct)
PORTSMOUTH
SARK
ST. HELIER
ST. HELIER ST. MALO
DIELETTE CARTERET ALDERNEY GRANVILLE (Apr-Sept)
Jersey
3½ miles to 1 inch
JERSEY
St Helier
St Aubin
St Ouens
St Ouen's Bay
St Mary's
St John's
St Peter's
Carrefour Selous
Trinity
St Martin's
Five Oaks
Grouville
Gorey
St Clements
Red Houses
Brelade
St Brelades Bay
St Aubin's Bay
Grosnez Pt.
Plémont Pt.
Sorel Pt.
Ronez Pt.
Belle Hougue Pt.
Bouley Bay
Tour de Rozel
Rozel
La Coupe Pt.
St Catherine's Bay
Royal Bay of Grouville
La Rocque Pt.
Le Nez Pt.
St Clements Bay
Noirmont Pt.
Corbière Pt.
CARTERET SARK
SARK (Apr-Sept)
ST. PETER PORT POOLE
ST. PETER PORT PORTSMOUTH
ST. MALO
GRANVILLE ST. PETER PORT CARTERET (Apr-Sept)

Merstham
Redhill
Reigate
Salfords
Horley
GATWICK AIRPORT
Crawley
Three Bridges
Copthorne
East Grinstead
Lingfield
Oxted
Limpsfield
Westerham
Edenbridge
Hever
Chiddingstone
Penshurst
TONBRIDGE
Southborough
ROYAL TUNBRIDGE WELLS
Pembury
Paddock Wood
Forest Row
Hartfield
Crowborough
ASHDOWN FOREST
Wadhurst
Mayfield
Heathfield
Uckfield
Maresfield
Nutley
Haywards Heath
Lindfield
Cuckfield
BURGESS HILL
Hurstpierpoint
Keymer
Ditchling
Lewes
Newhaven
Peacehaven
Seaford
Hailsham
Polegate
Willingdon
Eastbourne
BEACHY HEAD
Pevensey
Pevensey Bay
BEXHILL
Battle
Brighton and Hove
HOVE
BRIGHTON
SHOREHAM-BY-SEA
Southwick
Portslade-by-Sea
Rottingdean
Saltdean
Alfriston
East Dean
Birling Gap
DIEPPE
High Weald
East Sussex
South Downs
TQ
TV
0 1 2 3 4 5 6 miles
0 1 2 3 4 5 6 7 8 9 10km

Kent
Downs
ROMNEY MARSH
ROTHER LEVELS
ISLE OF OXNEY
Walland Marsh
Denge Marsh
DUNGENESS
ENGLISH CHANNEL
TR
Rye Bay
Romney Sands
CHANNEL TUNNEL
Ashford
Folkestone
Hastings
Charing
Headcorn
Staplehurst
Cranbrook
Hawkhurst
Tenterden
Kennington
Willesborough
Wye
Hythe
Saltwood
Sandgate
Dymchurch
St Mary's Bay
Littlestone on Sea
New Romney
Greatstone on Sea
Lydd
Lydd on Sea
Rye
Winchelsea
Winchelsea Beach
Camber
Hollington
St Leonards
Ore
Fairlight
Fairlight Cove
Cliff End
Pett
Icklesham
Udimore
Peasmarsh
Northiam
Bodiam
Sandhurst
Newenden
Wittersham
Appledore
Brookland
Old Romney
Snargate
Brenzett
Ivychurch
Hamstreet
Ruckinge
Orlestone
Kenardington
Warehorne
Bilsington
Burmarsh
Newchurch
Lympne
West Hythe
Sellindge
Stanford
Postling
Etchinghill
Lyminge
Elham
Densole
Hawkinge
Capel le Ferne
Biddenden
Smarden
Pluckley
Lenham
Harrietsham
Leeds
Sutton Valence
Langley
Linton
Marden
Goudhurst
Sissinghurst
Rolvenden
Benenden
Sedlescombe
Westfield
Three Oaks
Guestling Thorn
Baldslow
Crowhurst
Bulverhythe
West Marina
Silverhill
Mersham
Aldington
Smeeth
Brabourne
Godmersham
Crundale
Waltham
Chilham
Molash
Challock
Westwell
Egerton
Warren Street
Stalisfield Green
Barham
Denton
Wootton
Lydden
Swingfield Minnis
Alkham
M20
A20
A28
A259
A2070
A21
A229
20
21

SN
SS
Swansea
Neath
Port Talbot
(Castell-Nedd Port Talbot)
Rhondda Cynon Taff
(Rhondda Cynon Taf)
Bridgend
(Pen-y-bont ar Ogwr)
Vale of Glamorgan
(Bro Morgannwg)
SWANSEA BAY
BAE ABERTAWE
MÔR HAFREN
BRISTOL CHANNEL
EXMOOR
EXMOOR FOREST
NATIONAL PARK
BRENDON HILLS
Swansea (Abertawe)
Neath (Castell-Nedd)
Port Talbot
Bridgend (Pen-y-bont ar Ogwr)
Merthyr Tydfil (Merthyr Tudful)
Aberdare (Aberdâr)
Mountain Ash (Aberpennar)
Pontypridd
Maesteg
Porthcawl
The Mumbles (Y Mwmbwls)
Mumbles Hd. Trwyn yr Mwmbwls
Pwlldu Hd. Pen Pwlldu
Llantwit Major (Llanilltud Fawr)
Cowbridge (Y Bont-Faen)
Rhoose (Y Rhws)
Breaksea Pt. Trwyn Breaksea
Nash Pt. Trwyn yr As
Tusker Rock
Foreland Pt.
Hurlstone Pt.
Highveer Pt.
Lynton
Lynmouth
Minehead
Porlock
Dunster
Watchet
Williton
Combe Martin
Barnstaple
Exford
Simonsbath
Dulverton
Pontardawe
Pontarddulais
Gorseinon
Clydach
Skewen
Baglan
Margam
Pyle (Y Pîl)
Pencoed
Llantrisant
Tonypandy
Treorchy (Treorci)
Ferndale
Porth
Tonyrefail
Beddau
Ystradowen
St Athan
Barry
6
7
23
24
M4
0 1 2 3 4 5 6 miles
0 1 2 3 4 5 6 7 8 9 10 km

Monmouthshire
(Sir Fynwy)
Torfaen
(Tor-faen)
Caerphilly
(Caerffili)
Newport
(Casnewydd)
Cardiff
(Caerdydd)
North Somerset
Bristol
Somerset
MOUTH OF THE SEVERN
ABER HAFREN
ST
Blaenavon
Blaina
Rhymney
(Rhymni)
New Tredegar
(Tredegar Newydd)
Abertillery
(Abertyleri)
Abersychan
Pontypool
(Pont-y-pwl)
Griffithstown
Cwmbran
(Cwmbrân)
Usk
(Brynbuga)
Crumlin
(Crymlyn)
Blackwood
(Coed Duon)
Oakdale
Bargoed
(Bargod)
Gelligaer
Hengoed
Pontnewydd
Abercarn
Risca
(Rhisga)
Machen
Bedwas
Caerleon
(Caerllion)
Caerphilly
(Caerffili)
Chepstow
(Cas-gwent)
Caldicot
Magor
Lydney
Sedbury
Thornbury
Pilning
Severn Beach
Patchway
Bradley Stoke
Filton
Avonmouth
Portishead
Redcliff Bay
Clevedon
Nailsea
Long Ashton
Bristol
Keynsham
Whitchurch
Penarth
Barry
(Y Barri)
Barry Island
Sully Island
Ynys Sili
Lavernock Pt.
Trwyn Larnog
Flat Holm
Steep Holm
Sand Pt.
Sand Bay
Weston-super-Mare
Brean Down
Yatton
Congresbury
Wrington
Cheddar
Axbridge
Burnham-on-Sea
Highbridge
Bridgwater
Wells
Shepton Mallet
Glastonbury
Street
Wedmore
Mendip
Polden Hills
King's Sedge Moor
Bridgwater Bay
Quantock Hills
Berrow Flats
Stert Flats
M4
M5
M48
M49
M32
A48
A38
A39
A37
A361
A370
A371
A4042
A449
A470
A4232
A403
A4174
25
16
7
8
9
10
11
12

Gloucestershire
South Gloucestershire
Bristol
Bath and N.E. Somerset
Wiltshire
Mendip Hills
Cotswolds
Cranborne Chase
Chepstow
Stroud
Dursley
Wotton-under-Edge
Tetbury
Malmesbury
Nailsworth
Thornbury
Yate
Chipping Sodbury
Filton
Mangotsfield
Kingswood
BRISTOL
Keynsham
Bath
Portishead
Avonmouth
Nailsea
Long Ashton
Chippenham
Corsham
Melksham
Bradford-on-Avon
Trowbridge
Westbury
Warminster
Frome
Radstock
Midsomer Norton
Wells
Shepton Mallet
Glastonbury
Street
Cheddar
Bruton
Castle Cary
Mere
Caldicot
Lydney
Severn Beach
0 1 2 3 4 5 6 miles
0 1 2 3 4 5 6 7 8 9 10 km

Cirencester
Fairford
Lechlade-on-Thames
Carterton
Oxford
Abingdon-on-Thames
Didcot
Faringdon
Highworth
Cricklade
Swindon
Stratton St Margaret
Royal Wootton Bassett
Wantage
Calne
Marlborough
Hungerford
Newbury
Thatcham
Devizes
Pewsey
Tidworth
Ludgershall
Andover
Amesbury
Durrington
Whitchurch
Overton
Kings Worthy
Wilton
Vale of White Horse
Lambourn Downs
Marlborough Downs
Savernake Forest
Vale of Pewsey
Collingbourne Forest
Harewood Forest
North Wessex Downs
Berkshire
Hampshire
Wiltshire
Salisbury Plain
M4
A34
A303
A338
A346
A4
A419
A420

Oxford
Headington
Wheatley
Thame
Cowley
Abingdon-on-Thames
Didcot
Wallingford
Princes Risborough
Chinnor
High Wycombe
Amersham
Chesham
Berkhamsted
Beaconsfield
Marlow
Henley-on-Thames
Maidenhead
Slough
Windsor
Eton
Reading
Caversham
Woodley
Twyford
Wokingham
Bracknell
Crowthorne
Sandhurst
Camberley
Frimley
Farnborough
Fleet
Aldershot
Farnham
Guildford
Godalming
Haslemere
Hindhead
Grayshott
Bordon
Alton
Basingstoke
Hook
Overton
Whitchurch
Thatcham
Newbury
Goring
West Berkshire
Hampshire
Surrey
Windsor and Maidenhead
Wokingham
Bracknell Forest
Chiltern
0 1 2 3 4 5 6 miles
0 1 2 3 4 5 6 7 8 9 10 km

St Albans
Hatfield
Hemel Hempstead
Watford
RICKMANSWORTH
BOREHAMWOOD
BARNET
ENFIELD
CHESHUNT
WALTHAM ABBEY
POTTERS BAR
Loughton
Epping
Chigwell
Edmonton
Tottenham
Walthamstow
Harrow
Wembley
Uxbridge
Ruislip
Hayes
Southall
EALING
Acton
Hendon
Finchley
Hornsey
Hampstead
Willesden
Camden
Islington
Hackney
Stoke Newington
Leyton
Wanstead
Ilford
Barking
Romford
Dagenham
Woodford
City
Westminster
Kensington
Chelsea
Hammersmith
Fulham
Chiswick
Brentford
Kew Br.
Richmond
Twickenham
HOUNSLOW
HEATHROW AIRPORT
Staines-upon-Thames
EGHAM
Feltham
Sunbury-on-Thames
Teddington
Kingston upon Thames
Surbiton
Wimbledon
Merton
Wandsworth
Battersea
LAMBETH
Southwark
Bermondsey
Deptford
Greenwich
Lewisham
Camberwell
Brixton
Streatham
Catford
Woolwich
Woolwich Ferry
Blackwall Tunnel
Poplar
Bexley
DARTFORD
Erith
Sidcup
Orpington
BROMLEY
Beckenham
Croydon
Sutton
Cheam
Mitcham
Morden
New Malden
Epsom
Ewell
Esher
CHERTSEY
WEYBRIDGE
Addlestone
Byfleet
Cobham
WOKING
Leatherhead
Ashtead
Dorking
Reigate
Redhill
Banstead
Coulsdon
Purley
Caterham
Oxted
Westerham
Sevenoaks
Swanley
Biggin Hill
Warlingham
Godstone
Edenbridge
Lingfield
East Grinstead
Horley
GATWICK AIRPORT
Crawley
Three Bridges
Horsham
Cranleigh
Shalford
Greater London
Surrey
London
TL
TQ

Chelmsford
Maldon
Great Baddow
Danbury
Blackwater
Bradwell Waterside
Southminster
Burnham-on-Crouch
Chipping Ongar
Brentwood
Billericay
Wickford
Basildon
Rayleigh
Rochford
Southend-on-Sea
Shoeburyness
Canvey Island
South Benfleet
Hadleigh
Leigh-on-Sea
Westcliff-on-Sea
Foulness Island
Romford
Hornchurch
Upminster
Dagenham
Rainham
Thurrock
Stanford-le-Hope
Corringham
Grays
Tilbury
Purfleet
Erith
Dartford
Dartford Crossing
Bexley
Sidcup
Swanley
Orpington
Northfleet
Gravesend
Thames Estuary
Medway
Isle of Grain
Sheerness
Isle of Sheppey
Minster
Strood
Rochester
Chatham
Gillingham
Rainham
Sittingbourne
Walderslade
Snodland
West Malling
Maidstone
Bearsted
Sevenoaks
Kemsing
Borough Green
Tonbridge
Southborough
Royal Tunbridge Wells
Paddock Wood
Staplehurst
Marden
Headcorn
Cranbrook
Goudhurst
Lamberhurst
Charing
Lenham
Tenterden
Wadhurst
Crowborough
Hawkhurst
North Downs
Essex
Kent
Medway
0 1 2 3 4 5 6 miles
0 1 2 3 4 5 6 7 8 9 10 km

TM
TR
31
13
A
B
C
D
E
F
G
H
7
8
9
10
11
12
ST PETERS ON THE WALL
Bradwell on Sea
DENGIE
Ray Sand
Montsale
Deal Hall
Foulness Sand
Foulness Pt.
Courtsend
Churchend
MAPLIN SANDS
Warden Pt.
Warden
Leysdown-on-Sea
Isle of Harty
THE SWALE
Shell Ness
WHITSTABLE
HERNE BAY
Tankerton
Swalecliffe
Seasalter
Chestfield
Greenhill
Herne
South Street
Yorkletts
Graveney
Faversham
Goodnestone
Dargate
Hernhill
CHART GUNPOWDER MILLS
FLEUR DE LIS HERITAGE CENTRE
MOUNT EPHRAIM
BLEAN WOODS
Blean
Rough Common
Boughton Street
Dunkirk
Harbledown
Canterbury
Fordwich
Sturry
Calcott
Broadoak
Tyler Hill
Hales Place
Honey Hill
Hersden
Westbere
Upstreet
Chislet
Hoath
Boyden Gate
Sarre
St Nicholas at Wade
Reculver
RECULVER
RECULVER TOWERS AND ROMAN FORT
Minnis Bay
Hillborough
Beltinge
Broomfield
Birchington
Westgate on Sea
Margate
TURNER CONTEMPORARY
THE SHELL GROTTO
Cliftonville
DREAMLAND
Foreness Pt.
Kingsgate
NORTH FORELAND
LIGHTHOUSE
Northdown
St Peter's
BROADSTAIRS
BLEAK HOUSE
DICKENS HOUSE MUSEUM
Dumpton
Ramsgate
MARITIME MUSEUM
Newington
Manston
Northwood
QUEX HOUSE
Isle of Thanet
SPITFIRE AND HURRICANE MEM
Acol
Monkton
Minster
WINDMILL
Cliffsend
Pegwell
PEGWELL BAY
SANDWICH & PEGWELL BAY
ST AUGUSTINE'S CROSS
Pegwell Bay
Stour
West Stourmouth
East Stourmouth
Westmarsh
Ware
Grove
STODMARSH
Stodmarsh
Preston
Elmstone
Hoaden
RICHBOROUGH CASTLE
AMPHITHEATRE
Great Stonar
Sandwich
Sandwich Bay
ROYAL ST. GEORGE'S
Wickhambreaux
WINGHAM WILDLIFE PARK
Ickham
Wingham
Littlebourne
Guilton
Ash
Marshborough
Woodnesborough
Stone Cross
TOLL
Worth
HOWLETTS WILD ANIMAL PARK
Bekesbourne
Bramling
Staple
Gore
Patrixbourne
Goodnestone
GOODNESTONE PARK
Eastry
Knowlton
Ham
Finglesham
BETTESHANGER
Betteshanger
Northbourne
Sholden
DEAL
MARITIME AND LOCAL HISTORY MUSEUM
DEAL CASTLE
THE DOWNS
Walmer
WALMER CASTLE AND GARDENS
Great Mongeham
Ripple
Sutton
East Studdal
Ringwould
Kingsdown
Martin
Martin Mill
East Langdon
West Langdon
Whitfield
Guston
St Margaret's at Cliffe
THE BAY MUSEUM
West Cliffe
THE PINES GARDEN
St Margaret's Bay
SOUTH FORELAND
WHITE CLIFFS
CASTLE & HELLFIRE CORNER
CALAIS DUNKERQUE
DOVER
Maxton
Aycliff
DE BRADELEI WHARF
SAMPHIRE HOE
CHANNEL TUNNEL
Adisham
Aylesham
Nonington
Snowdown
Chillenden
Easole Street
Tilmanstone
Elvington
Womenswold
Barfrestone
EAST KENT RLY
Eythorne
Shepherdswell
Coldred
Woolage Green
Coxhill
Barham
Derringstone
Kingston
Bishopsbourne
Bridge
Lower Hardres
Upper Hardres Court
Nackington
Street End
Thanington
CANTERBURY TALES
ROMAN MUS
ST AUGUSTINE'S ABBEY
CANTERBURY
P&R
Chartham
Chartham Hatch
South Street
Oversland
GATE SERVICES
Old Wives Lees
Shalmsford Street
Garlinge Green
Petham
Waltham
Bossingham
ELHAM VALLEY VINEYARD
Stelling Minnis
Lyminge Forest
Denton
Wingmore
LYDDEN
Wootton
Selsted
ST JOHN'S COMMANDERY
Swingfield Street
Swingfield Minnis
Lydden
LYDDEN TEMPLE EWELL
Ewell Minnis
Temple Ewell
CRABBLE CORN MILL
Buckland
ROMAN PAINTED HOUSE
Alkham
Drellingore
West Hougham
Farthingloe
Hawkinge
Densole
KENT BATTLE OF BRITAIN MUSEUM
Paddlesworth
Capel le Ferne
EAST CLIFF & WARREN
East Wear Bay
Folkestone
ROTUNDA
CLIFF LIFT
Cheriton
Sandgate
Saltwood
ELHAM VALLEY RLY MUS
Newington
Peene
Etchinghill
Lyminge
Ottinge
Elham
Rhodes Minnis
Postling
Beachborough
Stanford
Pedlinge
Hythe
Palmarsh
BROCKHILL
Lympne
PORT LYMPNE WILD ANIMAL PARK AND GARDENS
West Hythe
Burmarsh
Newchurch
ROMNEY, HYTHE AND DYMCHURCH RAILWAY
Royal Military Canal
Bilsington
Ruckinge
Hamstreet
HAM STREET WOODS
Bonnington
Aldington
Court-at-Street
Newingreen
Aldington Frith
Clap Hill
Cheeseman's Green
Mersham
Kingsnorth
Sevington
Willesborough
Willesborough Lees
Smeeth
Sellindge
Sellindge Lees
STOP 24 SERVICES
E. Stour
Brabourne Lees
Brabourne
Stowting
Lymbridge Green
Elmsted
Bodsham
Hastingleigh
Hinxhill
Ashford
Kennington
Brook
CONNINGBROOK LAKES
Wye
WYE
WYE CROWN
Hassell Street
Crundale
Boughton Lees
Boughton Aluph
Goat Lees
Bilting
Sole Street
Godmersham
NORTH DOWNS WAY
Challock
Molash
Chilham
Shottenden
Badlesmere
Leaveland
Sheldwich
Selling
North Street
Ospringe
Preston
Oare
KENT
DOWNS
CHANNEL TUNNEL
M2
M20
A2
A20
A28
A256
A257
A258
A259
A260
A2070
A299
A253
A255
A254
A290
A291
A2050
A251
A252
A261
B2231
B2052
B2190
B2050
B2068
B2046
B2011
B2067

SM
SR
PEMBROKESHIRE COAST
ARFORDIR PENFRO
Pembrokeshire
(Sir Benfro)
ST. BRIDES
BAY
BAE SAIN FFRAID
MYNYDD PRESELI
ROSSLARE
Strumble Head
Pen Caer
Dinas Head
Cemaes Head
Pen Cemaes
Cardigan I.
Ynys
Aberteifi
Newport
Bay
Bae
Trefdraeth
Fishguard
Bay
Bae
Abergwaun
ST. DAVID'S
HEAD
PENMAEN DEWI
Whitesand Bay
Porth-mawr
Ramsey
Island
Ynys Dewi
Ramsey Sound
Tower Point
Trwyn Twr
Wooltack Point
Trwyn Woolteck
Skomer
Island
Ynys Skomer
Broad Sound
Gateholm
Island
Ynys Gateholm
Skokholm
Island
Ynys Skokholm
St Ann's Hd.
Pentir St. Ann
Sheep
Island
Ynys y Defaid
MILFORD HAVEN
ABERDAUGLEDDYF
Angle
Bay
Bae Angle
Freshwater
West
Linney
Hd.
Pentir Linney
The Wash
Stackpole Hd.
Pen Stackpole
St Govan's Hd.
Pen St Gofan
Trewent
Pt.
Trwyn Trewent
Old Castle
Hd.
Caldey Sound
Caldey
Island
Ynys Bŷr
Chapel Pt.
Trwyn Capel
Giltar Pt.
Cardigan
(Aberteifi)
Fishguard
(Abergwaun)
Haverfordwest
(Hwlffordd)
Milford Haven
(Aberdaugleddau)
Pembroke Dock
(Doc Penfro)
Pembroke
(Penfro)
Tenby
(Dinbych-
y-Pysgod)
St David's
(Tyddewi)
Newport
(Trefdraeth)
Narberth
(Arberth)
Goodwick
(Wdig)
Neyland
Poppit Sands
St Dogmaels
Moylgrove
Nevern
Felindre Farchog
Crosswell
Pontyglasier
Eglwyswrw
Crymych
Pentre-galar
Mynachlog-ddu
Rosebush
New Inn
Maenclochog
Llangolman
Efailwen
Llanycefn
New Moat
Henry's Moat
Puncheston
Castlebythe
Tufton
Woodstock
Llys-y-fran
Walton East
Clarbeston
Clarbeston Road
Bletherston
Llandissilio
Clunderwen
Llanfallteg
Gelli
Bethesda
Llawhaden
Robeston Wathen
Wiston
Crundale
Tangiers
Rudbaxton
Spittal
Triffleton
Ambleston
Wallis
Rinaston
Treffgarne
Brimaston
Wolf's Castle
St Dogwells
Welsh Hook
Letterston
Little Newcastle
Trecwn
Scleddau
Llanychaer
Pontfaen
Dinas Cross
Brynhenllan
Lower Town
Dyffryn
Manorowen
St Nicholas
Trefasser
Penbwchdy
Tresinwen
Llanwnda
Granston
Abercastle
Trefin
Porthgain
Mathry
Castlemorris
Newbridge
Llanrhian
Penparc
Abereiddy
Croes-goch
Tretio
Carnhedryn
Rhodiad
Treleddyd-fawr
Caerfarchell
Whitchurch
Middle Mill
Nine Wells
Solva
Rhosson
Treffynnon
Treglemais
Llanreithan
Llandeloy
Trefgarn Owen
Hayscastle
Hayscastle Cross
Mountain Water
Pont-yr-hafod
Treddiog
Penycwm
Newgale
Roch
Roch Gate
Wolfsdale
Camrose
Keeston
Nolton Haven
Nolton
Simpson Cross
Pelcomb Cross
Pelcomb Bridge
Lambston
Druidston
Portfield Gate
Haroldston West
Broad Haven
Little Haven
Walton West
Broadway
Dreenhill
Talbenny
St Bride's
Hasguard
Marloes
St Ishmael's
Sandy Haven
Dale
Herbrandston
Walwyn's Castle
Robeston Cross
Thornton
Tiers Cross
Johnston
North Johnston
Pope Hill
Merlin's Bridge
Freystrop
Hook
Uzmaston
Millin Cross
Boulston
Rosemarket
Steynton
Hakin
Waterston
Llanstadwell
Honeyborough
Llangwm
Hill Mountain
Port Lion
Houghton
Burton
Lawrenny
Black Tar
Landshipping
Landshipping Quay
Minwear
The Rhos
Blackpool
Martletwy
Yerbeston
Cresswell Quay
Cresselly
West Williamston
Carew Newton
Carew
Cosheston
Milton
Carew Cheriton
Sageston
Redberth
East Williamston
Jeffreyston
Broadmoor
Loveston
Begelly
Kilgetty
Reynalton
Thomas Chapel
Stepaside
Amroth
Saundersfoot
New Hedges
Penally
Lydstep
Manorbier
Jameston
Hodgeston
Freshwater East
Lamphey
St Florence
Gumfreston
Angle
Pwllcrochan
Rhoscrowther
Pennar
Monkton
Hundleton
Maiden Wells
St Twynnells
Castlemartin
Warren
Merrion
St Petrox
Stackpole
Chenton or Stackpole Elidor
Bosherston
Templeton
Cross Hands
Crinow
Cold Blow
Princes Gate
Ludchurch
Longstone
Lanteg
Tavernspite
Lampeter Velfrey
Llanddewi Velfrey
Whitland
Trevaughan
Llwyny-brain
Cwmfelin Boeth
Henllan Amgoed
Hiraeth
Login
Cross-hands
Cefn-y-pant
Llanglydwen
Pant-y-Caws
Glandy Cross
Hebron
Glandwr
Penygroes
Eglwyswen
Llanfair-Nant-Gwyn
Blaenffos
Pontgareg
Glanrhyd
Croft
Monington
Pen-y-bryn
Bridell
Cilgerran
Llantood
Rhos-hill
Gwbert
Y Ferwig
Bridgend
Cilgwyn
Brynberian
Parrog
Berry Hill
Dinas Cross
Afon Nevern
Ynysduellyn
Penclegyr
Newport Bay
A40
A487
A477
A478
A4076
A4075
A4115
A4139
B4313
B4329
B4330
B4331
B4341
B4327
B4320
B4319
B4322
B4325
B4584
B4585
B4582
B4546
B4548
B4316
B4314
B4318
B4328
0 1 2 3 4 5 6 miles
0 1 2 3 4 5 6 7 8 9 10km

Ceredigion
Carmarthenshire
(Sir Gaerfyrddin)
Swansea
(Abertawe)
CARMARTHEN
BAY
BAE CAERFYRDDIN
SWANSEA BAY
BAE ABERTAWE
SN
SS
BLACK
MOUNTAIN
Y MYNYDD DU
Brechfa Forest
Mynydd Pencarreg
Caeo Forest
New Quay
(Ceinewydd)
Aberporth
Cardigan
Newcastle
Emlyn
(Castell Newydd
Emlyn)
Lampeter
(Llanbedr Pont
Steffan)
Tregaron
Llandysul
Llandeilo
Carmarthen
(Caerfyrddin)
St Clears
(Sanclêr)
Kidwelly
(Cydweli)
Burry Port
(Porth Tywyn)
Llanelli
Ammanford
(Rhydaman)
Pontarddulais
Gorseinon
Clydach
Pontardawe
Brynamman
Swansea
(Abertawe)
The Mumbles
(Y Mwmbwls)
Llansawel
Llanwrda
Talley
Edwinsford
Abergorlech
Felindre
Pencader
Alltwalis
Cynwyl Elfed
Tanerdy
Abergwili
Nantgaredig
Llangathen
Golden Grove
Trapp
Llandybie
Cross Hands
Tumble
Pontyberem
Meinciau
Llangyndeyrn
Idole
Johnstown
Pensarn
Llangain
Llansteffan
Laugharne
Pendine
Marros
Red Roses
Whitland
Pwll-trap
Meidrim
Llangynin
Bancyfelin
Trelech
Hermon
Dinas
Talog
Abernant
Newchurch
Bronwydd
Arms
Ferryside
Llansaint
Mynyddygarreg
Pinged
Pembrey
Pembrey Forest
Pwll
Furnace
Dafen
Llangennech
Penclawdd
Crofty
Llanrhidian
Reynoldston
Llangennith
Rhossili
Middleton
Port Eynon
Port-Eynon
Horton
Oxwich
Penrice
Knelston
Nicholaston
Penmaen
Parkmill
Southgate
Bishopston
Killay
Upper Killay
Dunvant
Three Crosses
Blue Anchor
Gowerton
Waunarlwydd
Loughor
Morriston
Skewen
Llansamlet
Mayals
Black Pill
West Cross
Mumbles Hd.
Trwyn yr
Mwmbwls
Worms Head
Penrhyn-Gŵyr
Burry Holms
Whiteford Pt.
Trwyn
Whiteford
Llanrhidian Sands
Traeth Llanrhidian
Oxwich Bay
Bae Oxwich
Port Eynon Bay
Pwlldu Hd.
Pen Pwlldu
Rhossili Bay
Bae Rhossili
Pendine Sands
Traeth Pentywyn
East Marsh
GOWER
Afon Tywi
Afon Cothi
Afon Teifi
Afon Taf
Afon Gwili
Afon Aman
A40
A48
A483
A484
A485
A486
A487
A475
A482
A476
A477
A4138
A4069
A474
M4
24
14

Ceredigion
(Sir Ceredigion)
Carmarthenshire
(Sir Gaerfyrddin)
SN
Aberaeron
Aberarth
Llanon
Llansantffraed
Llanrhystud
Nebo
Cross Inn
Pennant
Monachty
Ciliau Aeron
Ystrad Aeron
Felinfach
Temple Bar
Dihewyd
Cribyn
Gorsgoch
Lampeter
(Llanbedr Pont Steffan)
Cwmann
Pencarreg
Llanybydder
Alltyblaca
Llanwenog
Cwmsychpant
Llanwnnen
Cellan
Llanfair Clydogau
Betws Bledrws
Llangybi
Olmarch
Llanddewi-Brefi
Tregaron
Llangeitho
Bwlch-Llan
Capel Betws Lleucu
Penuwch
Blaenpennal
Tyncelyn
Ty'n-yr-eithin
Bethania
Trefenter
Lledrod
Bronnant
Swydd-ffynnon
Ystradmeurig
Ffair-Rhos
Pontrhydfendigaid
Strata Florida Abbey
Tynygraig
Mynydd Bach
Ysbyty Ystwyth
Pont-rhyd-y-groes
Hafod Estate
Cwmystwyth
Blaenycwm
Devil's Bridge
Trisant
Ysbyty Cynfyn
Ystumtuen
Aberffrwd
Pisgah
Llanfihangel-y-Creuddyn
Cnwch-coch
New Cross
Gors
Capel Seion
Llanfarian
Chancery
Blaenplwyf
Llanilar
Abermagwr
Crosswood
Wenallt
Llanafan
Rhos-y-garth
Llangwyryfon
Llanddeiniol
Rhyd-Rosser
Rhydfudr
Cors Caron
Welsh Gold Centre
Fantasy Farm Park
Llanerchaeron
Cilcennin
Lundain-fach
Gartheli
Commins Capel Betws
Abermeurig
Llwyn-y-groes
Felindre
Ffynnon-oer
Silian
Maestir
Olwen
Pentrefelin
Llanycrwys
Ffarmers
Ffaldybrenin
Harford
Esgairdawe
Mynydd Pencarreg
Pumsaint
Dolaucothi Gold Mines
Caio
Crugybar
Llansawel
Edwinsford
Talley
Talley Abbey
Cwm-byr
Cwmdu
Abergorlech
Brechfa Forest
Brechfa
Rhydcymerau
Llidiad Nenog
Aber-Giâr
Llanllwni
New Inn
Gwyddgrug
Gwernogle
Nant-y-ffin
Pen-y-garn
Llanllawddog
Horeb
Llanfynydd
Capel Isaac
Pant-glas
Salem
Pantgwyn
Pentrefelin
Cwmifor
Manordeilo
Llandeilo
Ffairfach
Dinefwr Park
Aberglasney
Llangathen
Broad Oak
Court Henry
Felindre
Dryslwyn
Pont-ar-gothi
Nantgaredig
Llanegwad
Llanarthne
Capel Dewi
Nantycaws
National Botanic Garden of Wales
Penrhiwgoch
Golden Grove
Trapp
Carreg Cennen Castle & Farm
Llandyfan
Milo
Temple Bar
Carmel
Maesybont
Llanddarog
Porthyrhyd
Foelgastell
Cefneithin
Gorslas
Pentregwenlais
Llandybie
Dre-fach
Tir-y-dail
Ammanford
Betws (Rhydaman)
Pantyffynnon
Glanaman
Pontamman
Garnant
Gwaun-Cae-Gurwen
Brynamman
Rhosaman
Tycroes
Cross Hands
Tumble
Cwmgwili
Capel Hendre
Pentre
Pontyberem
Bancffosfelen
Drefach
Meinciau
Pont-Henri
Pontyates
Cynheidre
Sylen
Llannon
Llwyn-teg
Garnswllt
Mynydd y Gwair
Llanedi
Hendy
Pentrebach
Pontarddulais
Cwm-Dulais
Felindre
Rhyd-y-pandy
Craig-cefn-parc
Clydach
Trebanos
Pontardawe
Alltwen
Gellinudd
Rhos
Rhyd-y-fro
Cilybebyll
Godre'r-graig
Ystalyfera
Ystradgynlais
Gurnos
Cwmgiedd
Abercraf
Penrhos
Craig-y-nos
Penwyllt
Glyntawe
Dan-yr-Ogof
The National Showcaves for Wales
Wales Ape & Monkey Sanctuary
Coelbren
Caehopkin
Onllwyn
Dyffryn Cellwen
Seven Sisters
Nant-y-cafn
Crynant
Glyn-neath (Glynedd)
Morfa Glas
Pontneddfechan
Blaengwrach
Cwmgwrach
Resolven
Melincourt
Vale of Neath
Cwm Nedd
Hirwaun
Rhigos
Cwm-hwnt
Penderyn
Pontbren Llwyd
Aberdare (Aberdâr)
Dare Valley
Cwmdare
Trecynon
Llwydcoed
Penywaun
Tre-Gibbon
Swansea Valley
Cwm Abertawe
Mynydd March-Hywel
Cefn Coed Colliery Mus
Black Mountain
Y Mynydd Du
Brecon Beacons (Bannau Brycheiniog)
Fforest Fawr
Fan Brycheiniog
Fan Gihirych
Fan Fawr
Foel Fraith
Trichrug
Glas Fynydd Forest
Usk Reservoir
Llanddeusant
Twynllanan
Talsarn
Myddfai
Cilgwyn
Myrtle Hill
Halfway
Llandovery (Llanymddyfri)
Llanwrda
Cwmdwr
Waunclunda
Llansadwrn
Halfway
Ashfield
Hermon
Soar
Llangadog
Felindre
Dyffryn Ceidrych
Bethlehem
Pont-ar-llechau
Capel Gwynfe
Neuadd
Pontbren Araeth
Rhosmaen
Pont Aber
Twynmynydd
Gwaun-Leision
Tairgwaith
Cwmllynfell
Ystradowen
Upper Cwm-twrch
Lower Cwm-twrch
Cwmgors
Cynghordy
Llanfair-ar-y-bryn
Rhandirmwyn
Ystradffin
Nant-y-Bai
Cilycwm
Divlyn
Porthyrhyd
Siloh
Cwrt-y-cadno
Mynydd Mallaen
Crychan Forest
Cabo Forest
Tywi Forest
Llyn Brianne Res.
Mynydd Trawsnant
Soar-y-Mynydd
Tyncornel
Dolgoch
Nant Irfon
Abergwesyn
Beulah
Cwm Irfon
Llanwrtyd
Llanwrtyd Wells (Llanwrtud)
Llangammarch Wells
Cefn-gorwydd
Tirabad
Mynydd Epynt
Llanfechan
Garth
Pentre-llwyn-llwyd
Troed-rhiwdalar
Llanafan-fawr
Pentre Dolau-Honddu
Merthyr Cynog
Blaendyryn
Llanfihangel Nant Bran
Pont-faen
Llandeilo'r Fan
Pentre-bach
Mynydd Bwlch-y-groes
Babel
Pentre-ty-gwyn
Llywel
Trecastle
Pentre'r-felin
Sennybridge (Pont Senni)
Defynnog
Trallong
Aberyscir
Pentpont
Mynydd Illtyd
Tai'r-Bull
Libanus
Mountain Centre
Heol Senni
Felin-Crai
Crai
Pont ar Hydfer
Cwmwysg
Craig Cerrig-gleisiad a Fan Frynych
Llwyn y Celyn
Ystradfellte
Ystradfellte Res.
Beacons Res.
Cantref Res.
Llwyn-on Res.
Garwnant
Rhayader (Rhaeadr Gwy)
Llansantffraed Cwmdeuddwr
Gaufron
Welsh Royal Crystal
The Gigrin Farm Red Kite Feeding Centre
Nant-glas
Llanwrthwl
Elan Village
Caban-coch Res.
Garreg-ddu Res.
Penygarreg Res.
Craig-goch Res.
Claerwen
Claerwen Reservoir
Afon Claerwen
St Harmon
Pant-y-dwr
Nantgwyn
Wye (Gwy)
Irfon
Tywi
Teifi
Afon Aeron
Afon Cothi
Afon Twrch
Afon Tywi
Afon Aman
Usk (Wysg)
Neath
Mellte
Hepste
Loughor (Llwchwr)
Gwendraeth Fach
Lliedi Resrs.
Wales Coast Path
Mynydd Bach
Mynydd Llanllwni
Mynydd Rhos-wen
Drygarn Fawr
Drum-ddu
Bryn Crwn
Y Drum
Esgair Cerrig
Bryn Brawd
Trawsallt
Geifas
Pen y Garn
Dibyn Du
Esgair Ferchon
Bryn Du
Resolven Mtn.
Gwaun-Clawdd
Allt Rhyd y Groes
Nant Irfon
Coed Rheidol
Llanddeusant
Cynros
Porth-y-rhyd
Fiver Roads
Carway
Ffos Las
Horeb
Crwbin
Pont-Henri
Cwmisfael
Lliedi
A40
A44
A470
A482
A483
A485
A487
A48
A474
A4069
A4067
A4059
A4109
A465
A4221
A4061
A4215
A4120
A4086
B4343
B4337
B4342
B4576
B4577
B4340
B4575
B4574
B4302
B4310
B4300
B4297
B4556
B4306
B4310
B4519
B4518
B4358
B4338
23
32
14
M4
0 1 2 3 4 5 6 miles
0 1 2 3 4 5 6 7 8 9 10 km

Herefordshire
Monmouthshire (Sir Fynwy)
Torfaen (Tor-faen)
Ludlow
Knighton (Tref-y-Clawdd)
Presteigne (Llanandras)
Llandrindod Wells (Llandrindod)
Builth Wells (Llanfair-ym-Muallt)
Kington
Leominster
Hay-on-Wye (Y Gelli Gandryll)
Hereford
Brecon (Aberhonddu)
Abergavenny (Y Fenni)
Monmouth (Trefynwy)
Merthyr Tydfil (Merthyr Tudful)
Tredegar
Ebbw Vale (Glyn Ebwy)
Brynmawr
Blaenavon
Nantyglo
Blaina
Abertillery (Abertyleri)
Abersychan
New Tredegar (Tredegar Newydd)
Rhymney (Rhymni)
Talgarth
Crickhowell
Usk
Radnor Forest
Black Mountains
Y Mynyddoedd Duon
Brecon Beacons
Hergest Ridge
Golden Valley
Llangorse Lake
Talybont Res.
Pontsticill Reservoir
Neuadd Reservoirs
Wye
Lugg
Arrow
Teme
Usk
Monnow
A44
A49
A438
A465
A470
A479
A483
A4103
A40
A449
A4042
A4059
A4112
A4113
A480
A466
A4047
A4060
A481
A479
33
26
15
SO

Herefordshire
Worcestershire
Gloucestershire
Ludlow
Leominster
Hereford
Ross-on-Wye
Monmouth (Trefynwy)
Kidderminster
Bewdley
Stourport on Severn
Bromsgrove
Droitwich Spa
Worcester
Great Malvern
Malvern Link
Tenbury Wells
Bromyard
Ledbury
Tewkesbury
Pershore
Cheltenham
Charlton Kings
Gloucester
Stroud
Stonehouse
Newent
Cinderford
Coleford
Lydney
Upton upon Severn
Malvern Hills
Forest of Dean
River Severn
Wye
Teme
Frome
Leadon
M5
M50
A49
A44
A38
A40
A417
A449
A4103
A456
A443
SO
0 1 2 3 4 5 6 miles
0 1 2 3 4 5 6 7 8 9 10 km

Coventry
Kenilworth
Royal Leamington Spa
Warwick
Rugby
Redditch
Studley
Alcester
Stratford-upon-Avon
Henley-in-Arden
Southam
Evesham
Banbury
Shipston-on-Stour
Moreton-in-Marsh
Stow-on-the-Wold
Chipping Norton
Chipping Campden
Broadway
Charlbury
Woodstock
Kidlington
Witney
Burford
Carterton
Oxford
Headington
Cirencester
Winchcombe
Middleton Cheney
Warwick
VALE OF EVESHAM
Oxford
Cotswolds
SP
M40
M42
M45
A44
A46
A429
A34
A40
A361
A422
A423
A435
Grand Union Canal
Oxford Canal

N o r t h a m p t o n
B u c k i n g h a m
M i l t o n   K e y n e s
B e
SP
36
27
18
Rugby
Kettering
Wellingborough
Rushden
Higham Ferrers
Irthlingborough
Northampton
Daventry
Milton Keynes
Bletchley
Newport Pagnell
Olney
Towcester
Brackley
Buckingham
Banbury
Bicester
Winslow
Leighton Buzzard
Aylesbury
Tring
Berkhamsted
Wendover
Princes Risborough
Thame
Oxford
Kidlington
Headington
Cowley
Wheatley
Chesham
Stony Stratford
Wolverton
Middleton Cheney
Burton Latimer
Raunds
Finedon
Thrapston
Clifton upon Dunsmore
Hillmorton
Dunchurch
Crick
West Haddon
Long Buckby
Watford
Braunston
Welton
Norton
Weedon Bec
Bugbrooke
Kislingbury
Nether Heyford
Upper Heyford
Flore
Harpole
Duston
New Duston
Dallington
Kingsthorpe
Boughton
Moulton
Brixworth
Pitsford
Spratton
Creaton
Guilsborough
Cottesbrooke
Naseby
Maidwell
Haselbech
Draughton
Lamport
Old
Scaldwell
Walgrave
Hannington
Holcot
Sywell
Mears Ashby
Wilby
Earls Barton
Great Doddington
Wollaston
Bozeat
Strixton
Grendon
Easton Maudit
Yardley Hastings
Denton
Castle Ashby
Whiston
Cogenhoe
Brafield-on-the-Green
Great Houghton
Hardingstone
Collingtree
Wootton
Quinton
Piddington
Hackleton
Horton
Salcey Forest
Roade
Hartwell
Ashton
Grafton Regis
Hanslope
Castlethorpe
Haversham
Cosgrove
Potterspury
Yardley Gobion
Paulerspury
Pury End
Alderton
Stoke Bruerne
Shutlanger
Tiffield
Caldecote
Blisworth
Milton Malsor
Gayton
Rothersthorpe
Pattishall
Eastcote
Astcote
Cold Higham
Duncote
Greens Norton
Bradden
Abthorpe
Slapton
Wappenham
Silverstone
Whittlebury
Syresham
Biddlesden
Whitfield
Turweston
Evenley
Mixbury
Westbury
Shalstone
Dadford
Lillingstone Dayrell
Lillingstone Lovell
Akeley
Leckhampstead
Maids Moreton
Thornton
Deanshanger
Wicken
Passenham
Calverton
Upper Weald
Beachampton
Nash
Thornborough
Singleborough
Great Horwood
Little Horwood
Newton Longville
Drayton Parslow
Mursley
Swanbourne
Stewkley
Hoggeston
Dunton
Granborough
North Marston
Oving
Whitchurch
Cublington
Creslow
Aston Abbotts
Hardwick
Weedon
Rowsham
Hulcott
Bierton
Wingrave
Mentmore
Cheddington
Marsworth
Ivinghoe
Pitstone
Aldbury
Wigginton
Hastoe
Halton
Weston Turville
Aston Clinton
Buckland
Stoke Mandeville
Bishopstone
Dinton
Cuddington
Haddenham
Chearsley
Long Crendon
Shabbington
Ickford
Worminghall
Oakley
Brill
Boarstall
Dorton
Ashendon
Upper Winchendon
Lower Winchendon
Waddesdon
Westcott
Quainton
Pitchcott
Edgcott
Grendon Underwood
Marsh Gibbon
Twyford
Poundon
Charndon
Calvert
Steeple Claydon
Middle Claydon
East Claydon
Botolph Claydon
Addington
Adstock
Padbury
Gawcott
Tingewick
Barton Hartshorn
Preston Bissett
Chetwode
Hillesden
Fringford
Stratton Audley
Launton
Ambrosden
Blackthorn
Arncott
Piddington
Ludgershall
Kingswood
Wotton Underwood
Merton
Wendlebury
Chesterton
Kirtlington
Weston-on-the-Green
Bletchingdon
Islip
Noke
Beckley
Horton-cum-Studley
Stanton St John
Forest Hill
Holton
Waterstock
Tiddington
Great Milton
Garsington
Great Haseley
Tetsworth
Moreton
Towersey
Kingsey
Longwick
Ilmer
Owlswick
Kimble Wick
Meadle
Askett
Great Kimble
Little Kimble
Ellesborough
Butler's Cross
Dunsmore
Little Hampden
Great Hampden
Lee Clump
Ballinger Common
Cholesbury
Buckland Common
Bellingdon
Ashley Green
Wing
Ledburn
Slapton
Linslade
Soulbury
Stoke Hammond
Great Brickhill
Little Brickhill
Bow Brickhill
Woburn
Woburn Sands
Aspley Guise
Aspley Heath
Husborne Crawley
Ridgmont
Wavendon
Walton
Simpson
Fenny Stratford
Far Bletchley
Tattenhoe
Whaddon
Shenley Brook End
Shenley Church End
Loughton
Woughton on the Green
Broughton
Milton Keynes Village
Woolstone
Great Linford
Willen
Bradwell
New Bradwell
Moulsoe
Cranfield
Salford
Hulcote
Brogborough
Lidlington
Marston Moretaine
Broad Green
Lower Shelton
Upper Shelton
North Crawley
Chicheley
Sherington
Astwood
Hardmead
Stagsden
Gayhurst
Lathbury
Tathall End
Filgrave
Tyringham
Emberton
Clifton Reynes
Newton Blossomville
Turvey
Lavendon
Cold Brayfield
Warrington
Weston Underwood
Ravenstone
Stoke Goldington
Eakley Lanes
Courteenhall
Harrold
Odell
Carlton
Chellington
Felmersham
Pavenham
Sharnbrook
Souldrop
Podington
Hinwick
Farndish
Irchester
Little Irchester
Knuston
Wymington
Newton Bromswold
Chelveston
Caldecott
Stanwick
Ringstead
Denford
Woodford
Great Addington
Little Addington
Isham
Pytchley
Orlingbury
Little Harrowden
Great Harrowden
Broughton
Mawsley
Great Cransley
Loddington
Thorpe Malsor
Barton Seagrave
Cranford St Andrew
Cranford St John
Ecton
Great Billing
Little Billing
Weston Favell
Kingsley Park
Boothville
Overstone
Little Houghton
Little Harrowden
Ashby St Ledgers
Barby
Kilsby
Yelvertoft
Lilbourne
Clay Coton
Catthorpe
Winwick
Thornby
Cold Ashby
Coton
Ravensthorpe
Teeton
Hollowell
Holdenby
East Haddon
Chapel Brampton
Church Brampton
Harlestone
Whilton
Great Brington
Little Brington
Nobottle
Brockhall
Dodford
Badby
Newnham
Everdon
Church Stowe
Upper Stowe
Farthingstone
Litchborough
Maidford
Adstone
Blakesley
Woodend
Moreton Pinkney
Canons Ashby
Woodford Halse
Hinton
Byfield
Preston Capes
Charwelton
Hellidon
Catesby
Staverton
Priors Marston
Upper Boddington
Lower Boddington
Aston le Walls
Chipping Warden
Eydon
Culworth
Sulgrave
Weston
Weedon Lois
Helmdon
Greatworth
Thorpe Mandeville
Marston St Lawrence
Thenford
Halse
Radstone
Crowfield
Farthinghoe
Upper Astrop
Astrop
Newbottle
Charlton
Kings Sutton
Hinton-in-the-Hedges
Croughton
Aynho
Souldern
Cottisford
Hardwick
Hethe
Newton Purcell
Stoke Lyne
Fewcott
Ardley
Bucknell
Caversfield
Upper Heyford
Lower Heyford
Middleton Stoney
Steeple Aston
Middle Aston
North Aston
Somerton
Fritwell
Deddington
Clifton
Wardington
Upper Wardington
Williamscott
Chacombe
Overthorpe
Warkworth
Rugby
Napton on the Hill
Flecknoe
Lower Shuckburgh
Sawbridge
Grandborough
Willoughby
Woolscott
Kites Hardwick
Thurlaston
Draycote Water
Newton
Bilton
New Bilton
Northampton Services
Watford Gap Services
Newport Pagnell Services
Cherwell Valley Services
Oxford Services
Bicester Village
Silverstone
Yardley Chase
Whittlewood Forest
Grand Union Canal
Great Ouse
River Nene
Pitsford Reservoir
Sywell Reservoir
Daventry Res.
Boddington Reservoir
Stowe School and Gardens
Claydon House
Waddesdon Manor
Buckinghamshire Railway Centre
Quainton Windmill
Brill Windmill
Boarstall Tower
Nether Winchendon House
Rycote Chapel
Waterperry Gardens
Shotover
Woburn Safari Park
Woburn Abbey
Stockgrove Park
Leighton Buzzard Railway
Ascott
Mead Open Farm
Ashridge Estate
Santa Pod Raceway
Chicheley Hall
Gulliver's Land
Stoke Park Pavilions
Canal Museum
Old Dairy Farm Country Shopping & Craft Centre
Northamptonshire Ironstone Railway Trust
Hunsbury Hill
Billing Aquadrome
Castle Ashby
Harrold-Odell Country Park
Stevington Windmill
Holdenby House and Falconry Centre
Althorp
Cottesbrooke Hall and Gdns
Lamport Hall
Coton Manor
Brixworth
Daventry Mus
Canons Ashby House
Sulgrave Manor
Catanger Llama Trekking
Chipping Warden
Rousham House
Ashmolean Museum
Oxford Story
University Botanic Garden
Silverstone
Naseby Res.
M1
M40
M45
A14
A43
A45
A5
A508
A428
A509
A6
A422
A421
A413
A418
A41
A4146
A40
A34
A44
A361
A4500
A5123
A5076
A4010
A4009
A4129
A4142
A505
A4260
1 2 3 4 5 6 miles
1 2 3 4 5 6 7 8 9 10 km

Cambridge
Bedford
Huntingdon
St Ives
St Neots
Eynesbury
Sandy
Biggleswade
Royston
Baldock
Letchworth
Hitchin
Stevenage
Luton
Dunstable
Harpenden
St Albans
Hatfield
Welwyn Garden City
Welwyn
Hertford
Ware
Hoddesdon
Harlow
Bishop's Stortford
Sawbridgeworth
Cheshunt
Hemel Hempstead
Kempston
Shefford
Ampthill
Flitwick
Stotfold
Cambourne
Godmanchester
Brampton
Buntingford
Sawston
Great Shelford
Potters Bar
Cambridgeshire
Bedfordshire
Central
Hertfordshire
Grafham Water
TL
A14
A1
A1(M)
A428
A505
A10
A120
A414
A421
A6
M1
M11
M25
37
30
19

Isleham
Soham
Mildenhall
Newmarket
Bury St Edmunds
Cambridge
Burwell
Haverhill
Saffron Walden
Sudbury
Halstead
Braintree
Coggeshall
Kelvedon
Witham
Maldon
Chelmsford
Great Dunmow
Stansted Mountfitchet
STANSTED AIRPORT
BISHOP'S STORTFORD
Sawbridgeworth
Harlow
Tiptree
Lavenham
Clare
Long Melford
Great Shelford
Sawston
Linton
Thaxted
Danbury
Great Baddow
Kentford
Lakenheath
Barton Mills
Fordham
Cottenham
Histon
Waterbeach
Fulbourn
Ickleton
Great Chesterford
Newport
Elsenham
Takeley
Finchingfield
Wethersfield
Steeple Bumpstead
Kedington
Cavendish
Glemsford
Hadleigh
Boxford
Bures
Nayland
Dedham
Earls Colne
Great Leighs
Hatfield Peverel
Heybridge
Tollesbury
Goldhanger
Bradwell Waterside
Blackwater
Osea I.
Northey I.
Ramsey Island
St Lawrence
The Forest
TL
S u f f
E s s e x
THE RODINGS
A11
A14
A120
A12
A130
A131
A134
A143
A1307
A1092
A505
M11
29
38
20
0 1 2 3 4 5 6 miles
0 1 2 3 4 5 6 7 8 9 10 km

Halesworth
Southwold
Southwold Museum
Blythburgh
Walberswick
Wenhaston
Blyford
Holton
Wangford
Reydon
Hen Reedbed Nature Reserve
Dunwich
Dunwich Forest
Dunwich Underwater Exploration Exhibition
Suffolk Coast
Westleton
Westleton Heath
Minsmere RSPB Nature Reserve
Yoxford
Middleton
Theberton
Eastbridge
Leiston
Leiston Abbey
Long Shop Mus
Sizewell
Aldringham
Knodishall
Saxmundham
Kelsale
Carlton
Sternfield
Benhall Green
Friston
Thorpeness
Aldeburgh
Aldeburgh Bay
North Warren RSPB Nature Reserve
Snape
Snape Maltings
Iken
Tunstall
Tunstall Forest
Sudbourne
Orford
Orford Castle
Orford Ness
Orfordness-Havergate
Chillesford
Butley
Rendlesham
Rendlesham Forest
Capel St Andrew
Boyton
Hollesley
Hollesley Bay
Shingle Street
Alderton
Bawdsey
Sutton
Sutton Hoo
Woodbridge
Melton
Ufford
Wickham Market
Framlingham
Saxtead Green Post Mill
Easton Farm Park
Debenham
Eye
Stowmarket
Museum of East Anglian Life
Needham Market
Needham Lake
Mid Suffolk Light Rly Mus
Helmingham Hall Gardens
Wattisham Station Heritage
Haughley Park
Hadleigh
Wolves Wood RSPB Reserve
Ipswich
Christchurch Mansion
Ipswichmus
Whitton
Kesgrave
Martlesham
Martlesham Heath Control Tower
Orwell
Felixstowe
Felixstowe Ferry
Old Felixstowe
Walton
Trimley Marshes Nature Reserve
Charles Mannings Amusement Park
Harwich
Harwich Redoubt Fort
Dovercourt
Hoek van Holland
East Bergholt
Capel St Mary
Flatford
Bridge Cottage
Sir Alfred Munnings Art Museum
Dedham
Stour Valley
Mistley Towers
Mistley
Manningtree
Lawford
Colchester
Bourne Mill
Wivenhoe
Beth Chatto Gdns
Brightlingsea
St Osyth Priory
St Osyth
Point Clear
Clacton-on-Sea
Clacton Village
Great Clacton
Jaywick
Holland-on-Sea
Holland Haven
Frinton-on-Sea
Walton-on-the-Naze
Maritime Museum
The Naze
Hamford Water
Horsey Island
Kirby-le-Soken
Thorpe-le-Soken
Mersea Island
West Mersea
Mersea Island Museum
Cudmore Grove
Colne Estuary
Colne Pt.
Virley Channel
Sales Pt.
St Peters on the Wall
Bradwell on Sea
Dengie
Billingford Windmill
Thelnetham Windmill
Wingfield Old College
Suffolk
Coast and Heaths
TM
A12
A14
A140
A120
A133
A1214
A1071
A137
A143
A1120
A144
A1094
A1152
A1156
39
21
7 8 9 10 11 12
A B C D E F G H

Beddgelert
Blaenau Ffestiniog
Bethania
Llan Ffestiniog
Penrhyndeudraeth
Porthmadog
Criccieth
Tremadog
Penmorfa
Minffordd
Portmeirion
Borth-y-Gest
Morfa Bychan
Maentwrog
Gellilydan
Trawsfynydd
Bronaber
Llyn Trawsfynydd
Talsarnau
Ynys
Harlech
Tremadog Bay
Bae Tremadog
Llanfair
Llandanwg
Llanbedr
Morfa Dyffryn
Dyffryn Ardudwy
Tal-y-bont
Llanaber
Barmouth (Abermaw)
Barmouth Bay
Bae Bermo
Fairbourne
Arthog
Llwyngwril
Llangelynin
Rhoslefain
Llanfendigaid
Tonfanau
Bryncrug
Tywyn
Aberdovey
Aberdovey Bar
Bae Aberdyfi
Ynyslas
Borth
Upper Borth
Llandre
Bow Street
Clarach
Aberystwyth
Comins Coch
Capel Dewi
Llanbadarn Fawr
Penparcau
Southgate
Rhydyfelin
Chancery
Blaenplwyf
Llanfarian
Gors
New Cross
Llanilar
Pentre-llyn
Crosswood
Wenallt
Abermagwr
Llanafan
Ystrad Meurig
Rhydyfelin
Capel Seion
Aberffrwd
Pisgah
Mynydd Bach
Devil's Bridge
Ysbyty Ystwyth
Pont-rhyd-y-groes
Cwmystwyth
Ponterwyd
Goginan
Penrhyn-coch
Tal-y-bont
Tre'r-ddôl
Tre-Taliesin
Eglwys Fach
Glandyfi
Derwenlas
Machynlleth
Penegoes
Forge
Pennal
Corris
Corris Uchaf
Aberllefenni
Abergynolwyn
Llanfihangel-y-pennant
Tal-y-llyn
Minffordd
Dolgellau
Penmaenpool
Llanelltyd
Bontddu
Brithdir
Bont Newydd
Rhydymain
Llanfachreth
Ganllwyd
Coed y Brenin Forest
Dinas-Mawddwy
Mallwyd
Aberangell
Cemmaes
Cemmaes Road
Darowen
Tafolwern
Llanbrynmair
Talerddig
Carno
Staylittle
Dylife
Llanidloes
Llangurig
Old Hall
Tan Hinon
Hafren Forest
Pant Mawr
Glyn Brochan
Cwmbelan
Tylwch
Llyn Clywedog
Trefeglwys
Caersws
Llanwnog
Clatter
Llanerfyl
Foel
Llangadfan
Llanwddyn
Lake Vyrnwy
Bala (Y Bala)
Llanycil
Llanuwchllyn
Llyn Tegid or Bala Lake
Frongoch
Llandderfel
Llandrillo
Ffestiniog
Trawsfynydd
Gwynedd
Powys
Snowdonia
Afon Mawddach
Afon Dyfi
Dyfi Forest
Pumlumon Fawr
Nant-y-moch Reservoir
Source of R. Severn Blaen Hafren
Source of R. Wye Blaen Gwy
A470
A487
A493
A494
A44
A458
A489
A496
A4212
A4120
A485
0 1 2 3 4 5 6 miles
0 1 2 3 4 5 6 7 8 9 10 km

Wrexham
(Wrecsam)
Rhostyllen
Ruabon
(Rhiwabon)
Cefn-mawr
Llangollen
Corwen
Chirk
(Y Waun)
Oswestry
Ellesmere
Whitchurch
Wem
Shropshire
Shrewsbury
Welshpool
(Y Trallwng)
Llanfyllin
Llanfair Caereinion
Montgomery
(Trefaldwyn)
Newtown
(Y Drenewydd)
Bishop's Castle
Church Stretton
Craven Arms
Clun
Ludlow
Knighton
(Tref-y-Clawdd)
Baschurch
Shawbury
Bayston Hill
Minsterley
Pontesbury
Condover
Lydbury North
Clun Forest
The Long Mynd
Stiperstones
Wenlock Edge
Cynwyd Forest
Malpas
Overton
Penley
Prees
Hodnet
Powys
Llanymynech
Four Crosses
Chirbury
Kerry
Abermule
Onibury
Bromfield
Dee
Severn
Vyrnwy
Teme
42
43
34
25

Whitchurch
Market Drayton
Newcastle-under-Lyme
Stoke-on-Trent
Stoke
Hanley
Trent
Stone
Stafford
Eccleshall
S t a f f o r
Newport
Telford and Wrekin
Telford
Shrewsbury
Wellington
Oakengates
Dawley
Madeley
Much Wenlock
Bridgnorth
Shropshire
Wolverhampton
Cannock
Rugeley
Cannock Chase
Walsall
Wednesfield
Willenhall
Bilston
Darlaston
Wednesbury
Sedgley
Coseley
Tipton
West Bromwich
Dudley
Oldbury
Rowley Regis
Smethwick
Halesowen
Brierley Hill
Stourbridge
Kidderminster
Bewdley
Stourport on Severn
Bromsgrove
Brownhills
Kinver
W e s t M i
M6
M54
M5
Scale: 0 1 2 3 4 5 6 miles; 0 1 2 3 4 5 6 7 8 9 10 km

Ashbourne
Belper
Derby
Derby City
Nottingham
Nottingham City
Uttoxeter
Burton upon Trent
Swadlincote
Ashby-de-la-Zouch
Coalville
Loughborough
Shepshed
Lichfield
Tamworth
Atherstone
Nuneaton
Hinckley
Bedworth
Coventry
Rugby
Solihull
Birmingham
Sutton Coldfield
Leicester
Long Eaton
Ilkeston
Heanor
Eastwood
Beeston
Stapleford
West Bridgford
Arnold
Kimberley
Castle Donington
Melbourne
Kegworth
Lutterworth
Kenilworth
Market Bosworth
Measham
Tutbury
Repton
Mickleover
Allestree
Chaddesden
Duffield
Kilburn
Ruddington
Whitwick
Birstall
Anstey
Earl Shilton
Burbage
Coleshill
Castle Bromwich
Erdington
Dorridge
Shirley
THE NATIONAL FOREST
Leicester FOREST
Midlands
SK
SP
M1
M6
M6 Toll
M42
M69
M45
A38
A50
A52
A42
A5
A444
A46
A45
A47
A6
A453
A511
A515

Nottingham
City
ARNOLD
Carlton
Radcliffe on Trent
Bingham
BEESTON
WEST BRIDGFORD
Cotgrave
Ruddington
Keyworth
Clifton
Bottesford
Sedgebrook
Grantham
Great Gonerby
Barkston
Claypole
Long Bennington
Caythorpe
Vale of Belvoir
Belvoir
Harlaxton
Little Ponton
Great Ponton
Colsterworth
SK
Melton Mowbray
Waltham on the Wolds
Loughborough
Barrow upon Soar
Sileby
Mountsorrel
Syston
Birstall
Thurmaston
Anstey
Leicester
City
Oadby
Wigston
Rutland
Oakham
Uppingham
Rutland Water
Stamford
Empingham
Corby
Kettering
Market Harborough
Desborough
Rothwell
Burton Latimer
Oundle
Thrapston
Lutterworth
Rugby
Northampton
SP
Leicester
Wymondham
Cottesmore
Great Casterton
A1
A6
A46
A47
A52
A606
A607
A6003
A14
A43
M1
35
45
46
28
0 1 2 3 4 5 6 miles
0 1 2 3 4 5 6 7 8 9 10 km

Leasingham
Evedon
Ewerby
Ewerby Thorpe
South Kyme Fen
Amber Hill
Langrick
Anton's Gowt
Frith Bank
Hill Dyke
Boston Long Hedges
Leverton Outgate
Leverton Highgate
Leverton
Leverton Lucasgate
Benington
Holdingham
Kirkby la Thorpe
Howell
46
HOLLAND FEN
Brothertoft
Cowbridge
Boston West
Boston
Haltoft End
47
BOSTON DEEPS
LYNN DEEPS
Sleaford
Quarrington
Asgarby
East Heckington
Swineshead Bridge
Guildhall
Butterwick
Freiston
Silk Willoughby
Heckington
The Pearoom Centre
Heckington Windmill
Great Hale
Little Hale
Hubbert's Bridge
Chain Bridge
Skirbeck
Skirbeck Quarter
Wyberton
Fishtoft
Burton Pedwardine
North End
Kirton Holme
Frampton West End
Scrane End
Northbeck
Helpringham
Fenhouses
Scredington
Swineshead
THE WASH
Aswarby
Osbournby
Spanby
Drayton
Kirton End
Kirton
Frampton
Swaton
Bicker
Asperton
Sandholme
Skeldyke
Seadyke
Bucklegate
Threekingham
Bridge End
Northorpe
Donington
Wigtoft
Sutterton
Algarkirk
Walcot
Stow
Horbling
Billingborough
Donington South Ing
Church End
Quadring
Bicker Haven
Folkingham
Birthorpe
Fosdyke
Lynn Channel
Pointon
Westhorpe
Gosberton
Holbeach St Matthew
Laughton
Holbeach St Marks
Aslackby
Millthorpe
Dowsby
Gosberton Clough
Dawsmere
Risegate
Surfleet Seas End
HOLBEACH MARSH
Gedney Marsh
Gedney Drove End
Kirkby Underwood
Graby
Rippingale
Surfleet
Moulton Seas End
Saracen's Head
Holbeach Hurn
THE WASH
Bulby
Dunsby
Northgate
Crossgate
Pinchbeck
Pinchbeck Bars
Halesgate
Holbeach Bank
Holbeach Clough
Gedney Dyke
Guy's Head
Stainfield
Haconby
Baytree Owl Centre
Lutton
Hanthorpe
Morton
TF
Pinchbeck West
Weston
Whaplode
Holbeach
Fleet Hargate
Gedney Fleet
Chapelgate
Little London
Terrington Marsh
Ongar Hill
Elsthorpe
Springfields
Moulton
Moulton Mill
Long Sutton
Cawthorpe
Dyke
Spalding
Low Fulney
Austendike
Gedney Broadgate
Edenham
Pode Hole
Scottlethorpe
Little London
Clay Lake
Ayscoughfee Hall
Weston Hills
Sutton Bridge
Orange Row
Clenchwarton
Bourne
Twenty
Whaplode St Catherine
Sutton Crosses
Walpole Cross Keys
Terrington St Clement
Lound
Tongue End
Moulton Chapel
Tydd St Mary
Hay Green
Tilney High End
Tilney All Saints
Witham on the Hill
Northorpe
Cowbit
Holbeach St Johns
Sutton St James
Tydd Gote
Walpole St Andrew
Toft
Thurlby
Deeping Fen
Moulton Eaugate
Four Gotes
Walpole Marsh
Walpole St Peter
Manthorpe
Thetford
Deeping St Nicholas
Tydd St Giles
Ingleborough
St John's Highway
Terrington St John
Saddle Bow
Obthorpe
Brotherhouse Bar
Newton
West Walton
Tilney St Lawrence
Carlby
Wilsthorpe
Baston
Hop Pole
Whaplode Drove
Tydd St Giles Fen
Fitton End
Walpole Highway
Wiggenhall St Mary the Virgin
Braceborough
Langtoft
Shepeau Stow
Holbeach Drove
Sutton St Edmund
West Walton Highway
Marshland
Greatford
Gedney Hill
Gorefield
St John's Fen End
Wiggenhall St Mary Magdalen
Barholm
Towngate
Market Deeping
Frognall
Crowland Abbey
Dowsdale
Throckenholt
Church End
Leverington
Walsoken
Fenland & West Norfolk Aviation Museum
Tallington
West Deeping
Deeping Gate
Deeping St James
Crowland
North Fen
Peckover House
Wisbech
Marshland St James
Uffington
Maxey
Northborough
Nene Terrace
Morris Fen
Parson Drove
Wisbech & Fenland Mus
New Walsoken
Marshland Fen
Burghley
Etton
Peakirk
Newborough
Murrow
Wisbech St Mary
Emneth
Emneth Hungate
Stowbridge
Pilsgate
Bainton
Glinton
Rogue's Alley
Tholomas Drove
Elm
Holly End
Barnack
Ufford
Helpston
Bedford Level (North)
Thorney Toll
Friday Bridge
Outwell
West Head
Barnack Hills and Holes
Southorpe
Werrington
Eye Green
Thorney
Guyhirn Gull
Waldersey
Stow Bardolph Fen
Barroway Drove
Wittering
Peterborough
Gunthorpe
Eye
Guyhirn
Ring's End
Coldham
Laddus Fens
Upwell
Marholm
Walton
Dogsthorpe
Newark
Stone Bridge Corner
Three Holes
Nordelph
Sacrewell Farm & Country Centre
Castor Hanglands
Upton
Chainbridge
Thornhaugh
Longthorpe Tower
Nene (Old Course)
Euximoor Fen
Upwell Fen
Wansford
Stibbington
Ailsworth
Ferry Meadows
Fengate
North Side
Eldernell
West Fen
Westry
Euximoor Drove
South District
Sutton
Castor
Railworld
Flag Fen Bronze Age Excavations
Coates
Norwoodside
Ten Mile Bank
Yarwell
Nene Valley Railway
Old Fletton
Eastrea
March
Binnimoor Fen
Christchurch
Sibson
Water Newton
Longueville
Stanground
Whittlesey
Inham's End
Turves
Upwell Fen
Lakesend
Hilgay Fen
Nassington
Alwalton
Orton Waterville
Farcet
King's Delph
Town End
Tipsend
Old Bedford River
Chesterton
Crown Lakes
Twenty Foot River
BEDFORD LEVEL (MIDDLE)
Flood's Ferry
Ranson Moor
Wimblington
Welney
Fotheringhay
Elton
Peterborough Services
Wildfowl Trust Welney
Elton Hall
Haddon
Farcet Fen
Whittlesey Mere
Pondersbridge
White Fen
Doddington
Gold Hill
Eaglethorpe
Warmington
Morborne
Yaxley
Benwick
Sixteen Foot Drain
Manea
Apes Hall
Tansor
Folksworth
Norman Cross
Nene
Castle Site
Stilton
Holme Fen
Middle Moor
Ramsey Mereside
Wimblington Fen
Ashton
Caldecote
Holme
Ramsey St Mary's
Forty Foot Drain
Vermuden's Drain
Fodder Fen
Mare Fen
Polebrook
Luton
Denton
Ramsey Forty Foot
Chatteris
Purls Bridge
Horseway
Welches Dam
Littleport
Conington
Ramsey Heights
Ramsey Hollow
Pymoor
Glatton
Woodwalton Fen
TL
Ramsey
Ramsey Rural Museum
New Bedford River
BEDFORD LEVEL (SOUTH)
Hemington
Sawtry
Langwood Fen
Little Downham
Luddington in the Brook
Bury
Tick Fen
Ferry Hill
Great Gidding
Church End
Upwood Meadows
Chettisham
Thurning
Little Gidding
Upwood
Chapel Head
Horseley Fen
Wardy Hill
West Fen
Prickwillow
Steeple Gidding
Hamerton Zoo Park
Wood Walton
Wistow
Great Raveley
Mepal
Coveney
Queen Adelaide
Clopton
Winwick
Coppingford
Monks Wood
Little Raveley
Warboys
Pidley Fen
Witcham
Oliver Cromwell's House
Ely
Cathedral and Mus
Hamerton
Wennington
Fenton
Chatteris Fen
Sutton
Wentworth
Middle Fen
Upton
Abbots Ripton
Broughton
Pidley
Somersham
Witchford
Stuntney
Old Weston
Alconbury Weston
Little Stukeley
King's Ripton
Old Hurst
Colne
Hill Row Doles
North Hill
Little Thetford
Brington
Buckworth
Alconbury
Great Stukeley
Woodhurst
Bluntisham
Haddenham
Barway
Bythorn
Molesworth
Barham
Leighton Bromswold
Earith
Wilburton
Stretham
Soham Cotes
Soham
Woolley
Sapley
Hartford
Wyton
Aldreth
Soham Mere
Catworth
Spaldwick
Huntingdon
Houghton
Ouse Fen Nature Reserve
Great Ouse
Easton
Ellington
Brampton Hut Services
Hinchingbrooke
Cromwell Mus
Hemingford Abbots
Houghton Mill
St Ives
Needingworth
Holywell
Over
Willingham
Wicken
Down Fen Windmill
Stow
Covington
Lincolnshire
Peterborough
Cambridgeshire
29
38
A B C D E F G H

BRANCASTER ROADS
NORFOLK COAST
THE WASH
LYNN DEEPS
Lynn Channel
Blakeney Point
Holkham Bay
Brancaster Bay
SCOLT HEAD ISLAND
HOLME DUNES
HOLME BIRD OBSERVATORY
Holme next the Sea
Old Hunstanton
Hunstanton
SEA LIFE SANCTUARY
Ringstead
Titchwell
Thornham
Brancaster
Brancaster Staithe
Burnham Deepdale
Burnham Norton
Burnham Market
Burnham Overy Staithe
Burnham Overy Town
Burnham Thorpe
Holkham
HOLKHAM HALL
New Holkham
Wells-next-the-Sea
WELLS AND WALSINGHAM LIGHT RAILWAY
PEDDARS WAY & NORFOLK COAST PATH
Stiffkey
Morston
Blakeney
Cley next the Sea
Wiveton
Cockthorpe
Langham
Glandford
Warham
Westgate
Binham
Wighton
Saxlingham
Field Dalling
Copy's Green
Sharrington
Thornage
Brinton
Gunthorpe
Briningham
Melton Constable
Swanton Novers
Barney
Thursford
THURSFORD COLLECTION
Kettlestone
Fulmodestone
Great Walsingham
Little Walsingham
SHIREHALL MUS
Houghton St Giles
Great Snoring
Little Snoring
East Barsham
West Barsham
North Barsham
Waterden
North Creake
South Creake
CREAKE ABBEY
Summerfield
Docking
Stanhoe
Heacham
NORFOLK LAVENDER
Sedgeford
Fring
Bircham Newton
Great Bircham
Bircham Tofts
BIRCHAM MILL
Barmer
Syderstone
Blenheim Park
Wicken Green Village
Sculthorpe
Bagthorpe
Snettisham
SNETTISHAM PARK
SNETTISHAM NATURE RESERVE
Shepherd's Port
Ingoldisthorpe
Shernborne
Dersingham
DERSINGHAM BOG
Anmer
HOUGHTON HALL
West Rudham
East Rudham
Tattersett
Coxford
Shereford
Dunton
Tatterford
Hempton
Toftrees
Fakenham
PENSTHORPE NATURE RESERVE & GARDENS
Little Ryburgh
Great Ryburgh
Stibbard
Hindolveston
Wood Norton
Sandringham
Wolferton
West Newton
Flitcham
New Houghton
Harpley
Helhoughton
West Raynham
East Raynham
South Raynham
Colkirk
Oxwick
Hamrow
Horningtoft
Gateley
Guist
Twyford
Foulsham
Broom Green
Bintree
FOXLEY WOOD
Foxley
Castle Rising
Hillington
Little Massingham
Great Massingham
Weasenham St Peter
Weasenham All Saints
Wellingham
Whissonsett
Brisley
North Elmham
Billingford
Bawdeswell
Terrington Marsh
Ongar Hill
North Wootton
South Wootton
Roydon
ROYDON COMMON
Congham
CONGHAM HALL HERB GARDEN
Grimston
Pott Row
Massingham Heath
MARITIME EXHIBITION
Gaywood
King's Lynn
Clenchwarton
Terrington St Clement
Walpole Cross Keys
Orange Row
Walpole St Andrew
Walpole St Peter
West Lynn
Fairstead
Hardwick
Gayton
Ashwicken
Leziate
Gayton Thorpe
Rougham
EXTREME ADVENTURE
Tittleshall
Stanfield
East Bilney
Worthing
Tilney All Saints
Tilney High End
Hay Green
Fair Green
Tower End
Middleton
West Lexham
East Lexham
Litcham
Mileham
Beetley
Bittering
GRESSENHALL FARM & WORKHOUSE
Gressenhall
Swanton Morley
Hoe
Woodgate
Saddle Bow
West Winch
North Runcton
East Winch
East Walton
West Acre
Castle Acre
CASTLE ACRE PRIORY
Newton
Beeston
Longham
Sparrow Green
Etling Green
North Tuddenham
St John's Highway
Terrington St John
Tilney St Lawrence
Wiggenhall St Germans
Wiggenhall St Mary the Virgin
Wiggenhall St Mary Magdalen
Tottenhill Row
Setchey
Blackborough End
West Bilney
Pentney
Narborough
South Acre
Great Dunham
Little Dunham
Drury Square
Crane's Corner
Dereham
Walpole Highway
Marshland
St John's Fen End
Watlington
Tottenhill
Wormegay
Great Palgrave
Sporle
Great Fransham
Little Fransham
Wendling
Scarning
MID-NORFOLK RAILWAY
Toftwood
Clint Green
Yaxham
Daffy Green
Marshland St James
Marshland Fen
Runcton Holme
South Runcton
Shouldham
Shouldham Thorpe
Marham
Beachamwell Warren
Swaffham
Necton
West End
North Pickenham
Holme Hale
Bradenham
Westfield
Whinburgh
Garvestone
Thuxton
Emneth Hungate
Holly End
Stowbridge
West Head
Stow Bardolph
Fincham
Barton Bendish
Shipdham
Letton Green
Crowshill
Reymerston
Southburgh
Outwell
Wimbotsham
Downham Market
Broomhill
Stradsett
Crimplesham
Beachamwell
Shingham
Cockley Cley
ICENI VILLAGE AND MUSEUMS
South Pickenham
Ashill
Cranworth
Hardingham
Stow Bardolph Fen
Barroway Drove
Bexwell
Eastmoor
GOODERSTONE WATER GARDENS
Gooderstone
Saham Hills
Saham Toney
Ovington
Woodrising
Carbrooke
Upwell
Nordelph
Denver
Wereham
Boughton
Oxborough
OXBURGH HALL GARDEN & ESTATE
Hilborough
Great Cressingham
Caudlesprings
Hingham
Scoulton
Three Holes
West Dereham
Fordham
Wretton
Stoke Ferry
Whittington
Foulden
Bodney
Little Cressingham
Merton
Watton
Griston
Little Ellingham
Deopham Green
Upwell Fen
South District
Hilgay
Wissey
Northwold
The Arms
Northacre
Rockland St Peter
Great Ellingham
Lakesend
Ten Mile Bank
Brookville
Caston
Stow Bedon
Rockland All Saints
Thompson
WILDLIFE TRUST WELNEY
Welney
Old Bedford River
Hilgay Fen
Southery
Methwold Hythe
Methwold
Cranwich
Ickburgh
LYNFORD ARBORETUM AND LAKES
Mundford
Lower Stow Bedon
Shropham
Methwold Fens
Southery Fens
Queen's Ground
West Tofts
THETFORD BRECKLAND
Great Hockham
OLD BUCKENHAM
Gold Hill
Brandon Creek
Apes Hall
Feltwell
Wretham
Ecclés Road
Wilby
Brandon Bank
Feltwell Fens
Hockwold cum Wilton
Weeting
WEETING CASTLE
GRIMES GRAVES
FOREST
SNETTERTON
Larling
Quidenham
Mare Fen
Burnt Fen
Fodder Fen
Hockwold Fens
WEETING HEATH
Brandon
Santon Downham
Croxton
Little Ouse
Littleport
BEDFORD LEVEL (SOUTH)
Bridgham
East Harling
Kenninghall
Little Downham
Kenninghall Heath
Chettisham
Shippea Hill Sta.
Lakenheath
BRANDON PARK
HIGH LODGE FOREST CENTRE
THETFORD WARREN LODGE
PARK
Thetford Warren
Thetford
Brettenham
Shadwell
North Lopham
South Lopham
West Fen
Prickwillow
Great Ouse
Wangford Warren
ANCIENT HOUSE MUS
Rushford
Gasthorpe
Garboldisham
Queen Adelaide
Ely
OLIVER CROMWELL'S HOUSE
CATHEDRAL AND MUS
Kenny Hill
Lakenheath Warren
THETFORD HEATH
Knettishall
KNETTISHALL HEATH
Blo' Norton
REDGRAVE & LOPHAM FEN
Witchford
Middle Fen
Stuntney
Great Fen
Mildenhall Fen
Eriswell
Elveden
Barnham
Euston
EUSTON HALL
Coney Weston
Hopton
Market Weston
THELNETHAM WINDMILL
Thelnetham
Redgrave
Little Thetford
Broad Hill
Holywell Row
Beck Row
Fakenham Magna
Barningham
Hinderclay
Botesdale
Rickinghall
Barway
Soham Cotes
NORTHFIELD WINDMILL
Isleham Fen
Thistley Green
West Row
PRIORY CHURCH
Stretham
Isleham
Mildenhall
Worlington
Barton Mills
BARTON MILLS
Freckenham
CAVENHAM HEATH
Tuddenham
Icklingham
The King's Forest
WEST STOW
West Stow
Ingham
Ampton
Great Livermere
Troston
Ixworth Thorpe
Bardwell
Sapiston
Honington
Stanton
Upthorpe
Walsham le Willows
Hepworth
Wattisfield
Allwood Green
Cranmer Green
Wickham
0 1 2 3 4 5 6 miles
0 1 2 3 4 5 6 7 8 9 10 km
A149 A148 A1065 A47 A17 A10 A1122 A134 A11 A1066 A143 A1101 A142 A1075

6
7
8
9
10
11
A
B
C
D
E
F
G
H
Sheringham
Cromer
Mundesley
North Walsham
Aylsham
Holt
Reepham
Coltishall
Wroxham
Hoveton
Acle
Drayton
NORWICH
Thorpe St Andrew
Sprowston
Earlham
Cringleford
Wymondham
Attleborough
Brundall
Great Yarmouth
Caister-on-Sea
Gorleston-on-Sea
Lowestoft
Beccles
Bungay
Loddon
Harleston
Diss
Eye
Halesworth
Southwold
Hemsby
Belton
NORFOLK COAST
THE BROADS
Halvergate Marshes
PEDDARS WAY AND NORFOLK COAST PATH
NORTH NORFOLK RAILWAY (THE POPPY LINE)
CROMER MUSEUM
AMAZONIA ZOO
ENGLAND COAST PATH
STOW WINDMILL
BURE VALLEY RAILWAY
MUSEUM OF THE BROADS
WINTERTON DUNES
CAISTER ROMAN TOWN
PLEASURE BEACH
SEA LIFE GREAT YARMOUTH
PLEASUREWOOD HILLS LEISURE PARK
SOUTHWOLD MUSEUM
100TH BOMB GROUP MEMORIAL MUS
NORFOLK AND SUFFOLK AVIATION MUSEUM
BANHAM ZOO
A140
A47
A11
A146
A143
A12
A149
A148
A1074
A1117
A144
A145
31
TG
TM

2
3
4
5
6
A
B
C
D
E
F
G
H
The Skerries
Ynysoedd y Moelrhoniaid
Carmel Head
Pen Carmel
Wilfa Head
Pen Wilfa
Cemaes Bay
Bae Cemaes
Cemlyn Bay
Bae Cemlyn
Bull Bay
Porth Llechog
Point Lynas
Trwyn Eilian
Llanbadrig
Porthllechog
Burwen
Amlwch Port
Amlwch
Cemaes
Tregele
Llaneilian
Penygorffwysfa
Rhosbeirio
Llanfechell
Bodewryd
Penysarn
Nebo
Llanfairynghornwy
Isle of Anglesey
Llanfflewyn
Rhosgoch
Carreglefn
Rhosybol
Dulas
Church Bay
Porth Swtan
Rhydwyn
Llanrhyddlad
Tyn-y-pwll
City Dulas
Brynrefail
DUBLIN
Llanfaethlu
Llanbabo
Alaw Res.
Gwredog
Ty-mawr
LLYNON WINDMILL
Llanddeusant
Llandyfrydog
HOLYHEAD BAY
BAE CAERGYBI
Elim
Hebron
Mynydd Bodafon
Anglesey
North Stack
BREAKWATER
Llantwrog
Llanerchymedd
Bachau
Maenaddwyn
HOLYHEAD MOUNTAIN
Llaingoch
Holyhead
(Caergybi)
Llantrisant
Llanfachraeth
Carmel
Capel Coch
Brynteg
Goferydd
South Stack
ELLINS TOWER RSPB RESERVE
PENRHOS FEILW STANDING STONES
Kingsland
Pen-llyn
Llanynghenedl
Llechcynfarwy
CORS ERDDREINIOG
Newlands Park
(Sir Ynys Môn)
Penrhosfeilw
ANGLESEY
Bodedern
Trefor
Tregaian
CORS GOCH
Penrhyn Mawr
Valley
Llangwyllog
Trearddur
Glan-traeth
Llynfaes
Four Mile Bridge
Caergeiliog
A55
Bryngwran
Glan Gors
Rhosmeirch
Holy Island
Ynys Gybi
Llanfihangel yn Nhowyn
Gwalchmai
Bodffordd
ORIEL YNYS MÔN
Talwrn
Llanfairyneubwll
Heneglwys
Rhoscolyn
Capel-gwyn
Llangefni
Ceint
Cymyran Bay
Bae Cymyran
Pencarnisiog
Ddrydwy
Cerrigceinwen
Llangristiolus
HENBLAS COUNTRY PARK
Rhosneigr
Llanfaelog
Bryn Du
Soar
Capel Mawr
Pentre Berw
Gaerwen
WALES COAST PATH
Bethel
Trefdraeth
Afon Cefni
Llanddaniel Fab
Llangwyfan-isaf
Llangadwaladr
Aberffraw
Hermon
Malltraeth
Llangaffo
Brynsiencyn
TACLA TAID TRANSPORT MUSEUM
Bodorgan
Dwyran
SEA ZOO
NEWBOROUGH WARREN AND YNYS LLANDDWYN
Newborough
Pen-lôn
MODEL VILLAGE
FOEL FARM PARK
MENAI STRAIT
Malltraeth Bay
Bae Malltraeth
Newborough Forest
Waterloo Port
Llanddwyn I.
Ynys Llanddwyn
CASTLE & REGIMENTAL MUS
Caernarfon
The Bar
Abermenai Pt.
Trwyn Abermenai
WELSH HIGHLAND RAILWAY
Llanfaglan
Bontnewydd
CAERNARFON AIR MUSEUM
Saron
Glan-rhyd
Morfa Dinlle
Llanwnda
Rhostryfan
CAERNARFON BAY
BAE CAERNARFON
Dinas Dinlle
Ffrwd
Llandwrog
INIGO JONES TUDOR SLATEWORKS
GLYNLLIFON
Groeslon
Carmel
Cilgwyn
Penygroes
Talysarn
Pontllyfni
Tan-yr-allt
Llanllyfni
Aberdesach
Nebo
Clynnog-fawr
Tainlon
Nasareth
Gyrn-goch
Capel Uchaf
A487
Bryn-yr-eryr
Pant-glas
509 BWLCH MAWR
522 GYRN DDU
Upper Clynnog
Dafarn Faig
Trefor
564 YR EIFL
Llanaelhaearn
Cenin
Pen-sarn
Garndolbenmaen
Llecheiddior
Dwyfach
Llithfaen
Carreg Ddu
Porth Dinllaen
Pistyll
Llwyndyrys
Rhoslan
Pencaenewydd
Morfa Nefyn
Nefyn
LLEYN MARITIME MUSEUM
Llangybi
Edern
Fron
Llanarmon
Porth Ysgadan
Glanrhyd
Tan-y-graig
Rhos-fawr
Y Ffôr
Chwilog
Llanystumdwy
Criccieth
PENARTH FAWR MEDIEVAL HOUSE
Rhos-y-llan
Boduan
Llannor
LLOYD GEORGE MEMORIAL MUSEUM
CORS GEIRCH
Tudweiliog
Abererch
HAVEN
Dinas
Efailnewydd
PENRHYN LLŶN
Rhyd-y-clafdy
Denio
Pwllheli
Garnfadryn
Porth Golmon
Carreg yr Imbill
Bryn-mawr
Llaniestyn
South Beach
Penrhos
Pen-y-graig
Llangwnnadl
Rhedyn
Sarn Meyllteyrn
Llanbedrog
Penrhyn Mawr
Pen-y-groeslon
Ty-hen
Botwnnog
Nanhoron
Mynytho
Trwyn Llanbedrog
Bryncroes
Methlem
Rhydlios
Llandegwning
304 MYNYDD RHIW
PLAS-YN-RHIW
St Tudwal's Road
Angorfa St Tudwal
Capel Carmel
Rhoshirwaun
Llawrdref Bellaf
Llangian
Rhiw
Abersoch
Porth Neigwl or Hell's Mouth
Uwchmynydd
Llanfaelrhys
Llanengan
Sarn Bach
St Tudwal's Island East
Ynys St Tudwal Dwyrain
Aberdaron
Bwlchtocyn
Marchroes
Bodermid
St Tudwal's Island West
Ynys St Tudwal Gorllewin
Bardsey Sound
Swnt Enlli
Pen-y-cil
Cilan Uchaf
Trwyn Cilan
YNYS ENLLI
167
Bardsey Island
Ynys Enlli
ANGLESEY
YNYS MÔN
LLEYN
LLŶN
0 1 2 3 4 5 6 miles
0 1 2 3 4 5 6 7 8 9 10 km

7
8
9
10
11
A
B
C
D
E
F
G
H
12
ANGLESEY
YNYS MÔN
Moelfre
Marianglas
Tynygongl
Benllech
Red Wharf Bay
Traeth-coch
Red Wharf Bay
Llanbedrgoch
Llanddyfnan
Pentraeth
Tan-y-graig
Pen-y-garnedd
Llansadwrn
Rhoscefnhir
Penmynydd
Llandegfan
Menai Bridge
(Porthaethwy)
Bangor
Llandegai
Beaumaris
Llangoed
Penmon
Puffin Island
Ynys Seiriol
CONWY BAY
BAE CONWY
Lavan Sands
Traeth Lafan
Great Ormes Head
Pen-y-Gogarth
Llandudno
Penrhyn Bay
Rhos-on-Sea
Conwy Sands
Traeth Conwy
Deganwy
Llandudno Junction
(Cyffordd Llandudno)
Mochdre
COLWYN BAY
(BAE COLWYN)
Old Colwyn
Abergele Roads
Angorfa Abergele
Abergele
Llanddulas
Kinmel Bay
Towyn
Pensarn
RHYL
(Y RHYL)
Rhuddlan
Bodelwyddan
St George
Conwy
Dwygyfylchi
Penmaenmawr
Llanfairfechan
Abergwyngregyn
Aber Falls
Rhaeadr Aber
Bethesda
Gerlan
Rachub
Llanllechid
Tregarth
Y Felinheli
Llanfairpwll
Caernarfon
Llanrug
Deiniolen
Dinorwic
Llanberis
Pass of Llanberis
Nant Peris
Capel Curig
Betws-y-Coed
Llanrwst
Trefriw
Dolgarrog
Tal-y-Bont
Tal-y-cafn
Eglwysbach
Pentrefelin
Glan Conwy
Dolwen
Llanfair Talhaiarn
Llansannan
Denbigh
(Dinbych)
Pentrefoelas
Cerrigydrudion
Glasfryn
Llyn Brenig
Llyn Alwen
Clocaenog Forest
Nebo
Padog
Ysbyty Ifan
Dolwyddelan
Blaenau Ffestiniog
Tanygrisiau
Llan Ffestiniog
Maentwrog
Gellilydan
Penrhyndeudraeth
Porthmadog
Tremadog
Minffordd
Portmeirion
Beddgelert
Rhyd-Ddu
Betws-Garmon
Waunfawr
Nantlle
Snowdon
Yr Wyddfa
1085
Pen-y-Gwryd
Hotel
Llyn Cwellyn
Llyn Gwynant
Llyn Ogwen
Carnedd Llywelyn
Carnedd Dafydd
Llyn Celyn
Bala
(Y Bala)
Llanuwchllyn
Llangower
Llanycil
Rhos-y-gwaliau
Trawsfynydd
Llyn Trawsfynydd
Harlech
Talsarnau
Ynys
Morfa Harlech
Llanbedr
Llanfair
Llandanwg
Pentre Gwynfryn
Dyffryn Ardudwy
Morfa Dyffryn
TREMADOG BAY
BAE TREMADOG
Traeth Bach
Coed y Brenin Forest
Ganllwyd
Llanfachreth
Rhydymain
Pont Fronwydd
Cwm Cynllwyd
Bronaber
Migneint
Arenig Fawr
Arenig Fach
Llyn Arenig Fawr
Frongoch
Llidiardau
Parc
Gwynedd
Conwy
SNOWDONIA
PARC CENEDLAETHOL ERYRI
GWYDYR FOREST
Gwydyr Forest
VALE OF CONWY
DYFFRYN CONWY
A5
A55
A470
A487
A494
A4212
A4086
A498
A496
A497
B4407
B4391
42
32
SH
Lake Vyrnwy

IRISH SEA
LIVERPOOL BAY
SC
SH
49
41
32
33
Southport
Ainsdale
Formby
Formby Pt.
Hightown
Little Crosby
Crosby Channel
BELFAST
DOUGLAS (Nov-March) DUBLIN
DOUGLAS (March-Nov)
LITHERLAND
Bootle
Waterloo
Seaforth
New Brighton
Mockbeggar Wharf
Wallasey
HOYLAKE
Birkenhead
West Kirby
Hilbre I.
West Hoyle Bank
Welsh Channel
Point of Ayr
Yr Parlwr Du
River Dee
Afon Dyfrdwy
BEBINGTON
Heswall
Dawpool Bank
Holywell Bank
Gayton Sands
Neston
Willaston
Ellesmere Port
Talacre
Prestatyn
RHYL (Y RHYL)
Kinmel Bay
Abergele Roads
Angorfa
Abergele
Penrhyn Bay
Rhos-on-Sea
COLWYN BAY (BAE COLWYN)
Old Colwyn
Llanddulas
Rhuddlan
Dyserth
Mostyn Quay
Mostyn
Greenfield
Holywell (Treffynnon)
St Asaph (Llanelwy)
Flint (Y Fflint)
Connah's Quay
Shotton
Queensferry
Hawarden (Penarlâg)
Buckley (Bwcle)
Mold (Yr Wyddgrug)
Flintshire (Sir Y Fflint)
Denbigh (Dinbych)
Conwy
Ruthin (Rhuthun)
Denbighshire (Sir Ddinbych)
Clocaenog Forest
Llyn Brenig
Alwen Reservoir
Caergwrle
Hope (Yr Hôb)
Gresford
Wrexham (Wrecsam)
Rhosllanerchrugog
Ruabon (Rhiwabon)
Llangollen
Corwen
Cynwyd Forest
Glyndyfrdwy
Cerrigydrudion
Pentrefoelas
Llanfihangel Glyn Myfyr
Bryneglwys
Llandegla
Pen-y-stryt
Maerdy
Druid
Carrog
0 1 2 3 4 5 6miles
0 1 2 3 4 5 6 7 8 9 10km

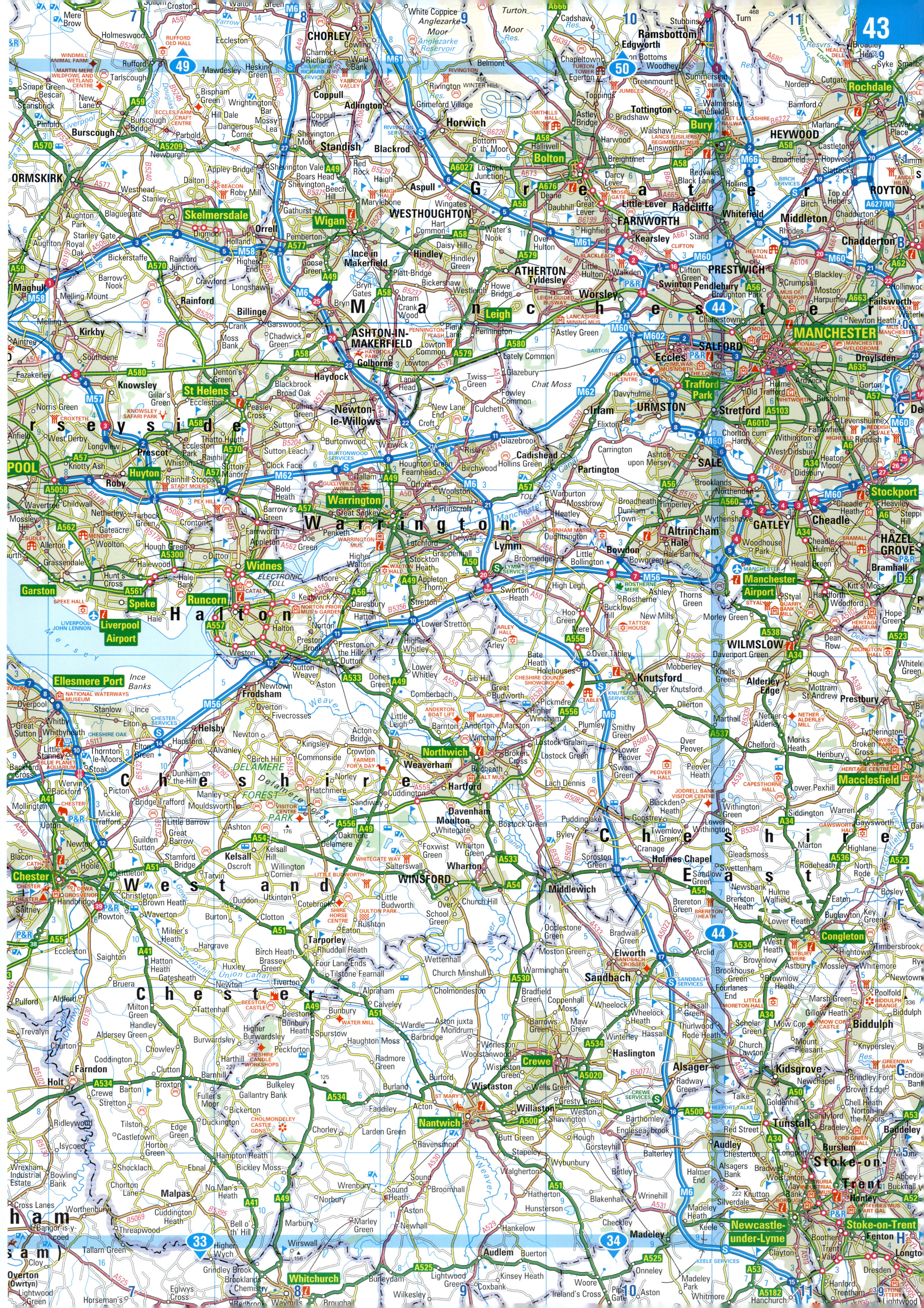
Greater Manchester
Merseyside
Warrington
Halton
Cheshire West and Chester
Cheshire East
SD
SJ
CHORLEY
ORMSKIRK
Skelmersdale
Wigan
WESTHOUGHTON
Bolton
Bury
Rochdale
HEYWOOD
ROYTON
Middleton
Chadderton
Oldham
FARNWORTH
Radcliffe
Whitefield
PRESTWICH
Leigh
ATHERTON
Tyldesley
Worsley
Swinton
Pendlebury
SALFORD
MANCHESTER
Eccles
Trafford Park
URMSTON
Stretford
Droylsden
St Helens
Knowsley
Huyton
Prescot
Kirkby
Maghull
Newton-le-Willows
ASHTON-IN-MAKERFIELD
Golborne
Haydock
Irlam
Cadishead
SALE
Altrincham
Hale
GATLEY
Cheadle
Stockport
HAZEL GROVE
Bramhall
Manchester Airport
WILMSLOW
Knutsford
Widnes
Runcorn
Speke
Liverpool Airport
Garston
Ellesmere Port
Frodsham
Helsby
Lymm
Northwich
Winsford
Middlewich
Sandbach
Congleton
Macclesfield
Biddulph
Kidsgrove
Alsager
Crewe
Nantwich
Chester
Tarporley
Malpas
Whitchurch
Holmes Chapel
Tunstall
Burslem
Stoke-on-Trent
Newcastle-under-Lyme
Audley
Madeley
Audlem
Farndon
Holt
Wrexham Industrial Estate
Overton (Owrtyn)
M6
M56
M62
M60
M61
M58
M57
M53
M65
M66
M602
A49
A556
A34
A51
A41
A500
A530
A54
A533

Rochdale
Littleborough
Wardle
Whitworth
Milnrow
HEYWOOD
Bury
Radcliffe
Whitefield
PRESTWICH
Middleton
ROYTON
Chadderton
Oldham
Shaw
MANCHESTER
SALFORD
Eccles
Trafford Park
URMSTON
Stretford
SALE
Ashton-under-Lyne
STALYBRIDGE
Dukinfield
Denton
Hyde
Droylsden
Failsworth
Stockport
Cheadle
GATLEY
Altrincham
Hale
Manchester Airport
HAZEL GROVE
Bramhall
Marple
Romiley
Bredbury
GLOSSOP
Hadfield
Charlesworth
New Mills
Whaley Bridge
Chapel-en-le-Frith
Buxton
Burbage
Poynton
WILMSLOW
Knutsford
Alderley Edge
Prestbury
Bollington
Macclesfield
Cheshire
East
Congleton
Biddulph
Kidsgrove
Alsager
Tunstall
Burslem
Stoke-on-Trent
Newcastle-under-Lyme
Fenton
Longton
Leek
Cheddleton
Stafford
Cheadle
Ashbourne
Matlock
Wirksworth
Cromford
Bakewell
Youlgreave
Hartington
Tideswell
Castleton
Hathersage
Bamford
Edale
Hope
Baslow
Ashford in the Water
Stocksbridge
Penistone
HOLMFIRTH
Meltham
Marsden
Slaithwaite
Huddersfield
Denby Dale
Skelmanthorpe
Clayton West
Kirkburton
Yorkshire
West
PEAK DISTRICT NATIONAL PARK
HOPE FOREST
HIGH PEAK
Saddleworth Moor
Wessenden Moor
Howden Moors
Midhope Moors
Broomhead Moor
Bradfield Moors
Ladybower Res.
Derwent Res.
Howden Res.
Dane
Dove
D
e
43
44
50
51
34
35
M60
M62
M66
M67
M56
M6
A6
A628
A616
A623
A515
A53
A52
A54
A537
A523
A34
A57
A635
A62
A629
A642
A6020
A619
0 1 2 3 4 5 6 miles
0 1 2 3 4 5 6 7 8 9 10 km

Barnsley
Doncaster
Rotherham
Sheffield
Chesterfield
Worksop
Mansfield
Gainsborough
Newark-on-Trent
RETFORD
Bolsover
ECKINGTON
Dronfield
Mexborough
Conisbrough
Maltby
Tickhill
Bawtry
Harworth
Thorne
Hatfield
Epworth
Hemsworth
Wombwell
Staveley
Clowne
Shirebrook
Market Warsop
Ollerton
Tuxford
MANSFIELD WOODHOUSE
SUTTON IN ASHFIELD
KIRKBY IN ASHFIELD
ALFRETON
RIPLEY
HEANOR
HUCKNALL
ARNOLD
Eastwood
Kimberley
ILKESTON
Belper
Southwell
SHERWOOD PINES FOREST PARK
Nottingham City
Nottingham
Yorkshire
South Yorkshire
Derbyshire
SE
SK
M1
M18
M180
A1(M)
A1
A57
A60
A614
A619
A631
A38

North Lincolnshire
North East Lincolnshire
LINCOLNSHIRE
SE
SK
Scunthorpe
Grimsby
Immingham
Lincoln
Gainsborough
Newark-on-Trent
Sleaford
Brigg
Market Rasen
Caistor
Horncastle
Woodhall Spa
Coningsby
Billinghay
Heckington
Leasingham
Ruskington
Metheringham
Bardney
Wragby
Saxilby
North Hykeham
Waddington
Navenby
Leadenham
Caythorpe
Claypole
Balderton
Collingham
Bassingham
Nettleham
Washingborough
Faldingworth
Kirton in Lindsey
Hibaldstow
Messingham
Scotter
Broughton
Barnetby le Wold
Laceby
Healing
Waltham
Binbrook
Keelby
Epworth
ISLE OF AXHOLME
Laughton Woods
Torksey
Sutton on Trent
Holton le Clay
North Thoresby
Ludford
Tealby
North Willingham
Humberside
HOLLAND FEN
South Kyme Fen
Wildmore Fen
Scale: 0 1 2 3 4 5 6 miles; 0 1 2 3 4 5 6 7 8 9 10 km

7
8
9
10
11
A
B
C
D
E
F
G
H
53
38
37
TA
TF
Easington
Kilnsea
SPURN DISCOVERY CENTRE
SPURN
SPURN HEAD
ROTTERDAM EUROPOORT ZEEBRUGGE
CLEETHORPES
MOUTH OF THE HUMBER
CLEETHORPES COAST LIGHT RAILWAY
Humberston
Tetney Lock
North Cotes
Tetney
N O R T H
S E A
Donna Nook
Marshchapel
Eskham
Wragholme
Grainthorpe
Fulstow
LINCOLNSHIRE WOLDS RLY
North Somercotes
DONNA NOOK
Skidbrooke North End
Covenham St Bartholomew
Conisholme
South Somercotes
Saltfleet
Covenham St Mary
Utterby
Yarburgh
Skidbrooke
Fotherby
Little Grimsby
Alvingham
North Cockerington
Saltfleetby St Clements
SALTFLEETBY THEDDLETHORPE
RUSHMOOR
Saltfleetby All Saints
Theddlethorpe St Helen
South Cockerington
Saltfleetby St Peter
Louth
Keddington
Grimoldby
Theddlethorpe All Saints
SEAL SANCTUARY & NATURE CENTRE
Stewton
ST JAMES
Manby
Meers Bridge
Hallington
Little Carlton
Great Carlton
Mablethorpe
Legbourne
Raithby
South Reston
Gayton le Marsh
Trusthorpe
Little Cawthorpe
North Reston
Tathwell
Strubby
Sutton on Sea
Haugham
Mucknton
Tothill
Withern
Thorpe
Maltby le Marsh
Authorpe
Beesby
Sandilands
Maidenwell
Burwell
Woodthorpe
WOODY'S TOP
Hannah
Farforth
Ruckland
Belleau
CLAYTHORPE WATER MILL AND WILDFOWL GARDENS
Saleby
Markby
White Pit
Swaby
Aby
Oxcombe
Asserby
ALFORD WINDMILL
Ketsby
South Thoresby
ALFORD MANOR HOUSE
Bilsby
Huttoft
South Ormsby
Haugh
Rigsby
Alford
Calceby
Anderby
ON YOUR MARQUES
Tetford
Farlesthorpe
Mumby
Authorpe Row
Driby
Well
Brinkhill
Cumberworth
Salmonby
Somersby
Ulceby
Helsey
Chapel St Leonards
Bonthorpe
Hogsthorpe
Sutterby
Bag Enderby
Harrington
Willoughby
Ashby Puerorum
Langton
Claxby
Sloothby
HARDY'S ANIMAL FARM
Greetham
Aswardby
Skendleby
Ingoldmells
Hagworthingham
Sausthorpe
FANTASY ISLAND
Scrafield
SNIPE DALES
Partney
Addlethorpe
Lusby
Welton le Marsh
Hameringham
Raithby
Scremby
FUNCOAST WORLD
Mavis Enderby
Candlesby
Orby Marsh
Asgarby
Ashby by Partney
GUNBY HALL
Orby
Winthorpe
Hareby
Old Bolingbroke
Spilsby
Hundleby
Bratoft
Burgh le Marsh
Seathorne
NORTHCOTE HEAVY HORSE CENTRE
Great Steeping
BOLINGBROKE
Toynton All Saints
Halton Holegate
NATURELAND SEAL SANCTUARY
Miningsby
West Keal
East Keal
Irby in the Marsh
BURGH LE MARSH WINDMILL
THE VILLAGE CHURCH FARM
Skegness
Firsby
Toynton St Peter
THE LIFEBOAT STATION
East Kirkby
Toynton Fen Side
Little Steeping
LINCOLNSHIRE AVIATION HERITAGE CENTRE
Keal Cotes
Thorpe Culvert
Thorpe St Peter
Croft
Revesby Bridge
Thorpe Fendykes
Seacroft
Croft Marsh
Stickford
Wainfleet All Saints
New Bolingbroke
Fen Side
Wainfleet Bank
MAGDALEN MUSEUM
GIBRALTAR POINT
Midville
New Leake
Wainfleet Tofts
Wainfleet St Mary
Stickney
Eastville
Friskney Eaudike
Wainfleet Sand
Medlam
LINCOLNSHIRE WILDLIFE PARK
East Fen
Friskney
Carrington
Lade Bank
Wrangle Bank
Friskney Tofts
Northlands
Leake Commonside
SIBSEY TRADER MILL
Sibsey
Old Leake
Wrangle Lowgate
Friskney Flats
Frithville
Wrangle
Fishtoft Drove
Hurn's End
Hill Dyke
Boston Long Hedges
Leverton Outgate
Frith Bank
Leverton
Leverton Highgate
Cowbridge
Leverton Lucasgate
Benington
BOSTON DEEPS
LYNN DEEPS
Haltoft End
Boston
GUILDHALL
Butterwick
Freiston
Chain Bridge
Skirbeck
Skirbeck Quarter
Fishtoft
Wyberton
Scrane End
THE WASH
BRANCASTER ROADS
Brancaster Bay
SCOLT HEAD ISLAND
HOLME DUNES
HOLME BIRD OBSERVATORY
Holme next the Sea
Titchwell
Brancaster Staithe
Burnham Deepdale
Brancaster
Burnham Norton
Thornham
Old Hunstanton
Hunstanton
Westgate
Burnham Market
A16
A158
A1028
A52
A157
A1104
A1031
A1111
A155
A149
B1200
B1201
B1195
B1184
B1183
B1196
B1373
B1449
B1153
WOLDS

NX
IRISH SEA
Isle of Man
SC
POINT OF AYRE
The Ayres
Rue Pt.
Glentruan
Cranstal
Dhowin
Bride
The Lhen
Andreas
MANX CROSSES
JURBY SOUTH
Jurby Head
Jurby East
Sandygate
Ballasalla
Jurby West
Regaby
MANX CROSSES
The Cronk
St Judes
Dhoor
RAMSEY BAY
CURRAGHS WILDLIFE PARK
GROVE MUS OF VICTORIAN LIFE
Ramsey
Orrisdale
Ballaugh
Sulby
Churchtown
MANX ELECTRIC RAILWAY
Port e Vullen
T.T. Course
Glen Auldyn
Maughold
Rhencullen
Ravensdale
Dreemskerry
Maughold Head
MANX CROSSES
Kirk Michael
565 NORTH BARRULE
Ballajora
MANX CROSSES
CELTIC CRAFT CENTRE
Corrany
Cornaa
Ballaleigh
SNAEFELL 621
Glen Mona
Barregarrow
Druidale
Dhoon
MURRAYS MOTORCYCLE MUSEUM
Agneash
LAXEY WHEEL AND MINES
Bulgham Bay
MANX TRANSPORT MUSEUM
Knocksharry
SNAEFELL MOUNTAIN RAILWAY
Laxey
Ballaquine
Cronk-y-Voddy
St Patrick's I.
PEEL
487 COLDEN
LAXEY WOOLLEN MILLS
Peel
Res.
Old Laxey
HOUSE OF MANANNAN
BALLALHEANNAGH GARDENS
Laxey Head
Contrary Head
TYNWALD CRAFT CENTRE
Fairy Cottage
KIPPER MUSEUM
TYNWALD HILL
Laxey Bay
Creg-ny-Baa
Patrick
St John's
Greeba
Baldwin
Ballacannel
Glenmaye
333
Baldrine
Clay Head
Lower Foxdale
Crosby
MANX CROSSES
Dalby Pt.
Glen Vine
Strang
Onchan
GROUDLE GLEN RAILWAY
HEYSHAM
Dalby
Union Mills
Tromode
Niarbyl
Foxdale
ONCHAN PLEASURE PARK
Eairy
LARNE (TT race period only)
Niarbyl Bay
Braaid
Spring Valley
Douglas
483 SOUTH BARRULE
222
Cooil
Douglas Bay
Close Clark
Ellenbrook
Douglas Head
Ballamodha
St Mark's
Newtown
Ballaveare
CAMERA OBSCURA
LIVERPOOL (March-Nov)
Lingague
Ronague
Little Ness
Fleshwick Bay
Grenaby
ISLE OF MAN STEAM RAILWAY
BIRKENHEAD (Nov-March)
Surby
Ballabeg
Bradda
Colby
RUSHEN ABBEY
Santon Head
Bradda Head
Ballasalla
Port Greenaugh
Port Erin
BILLOWN
ISLE OF MAN
RAILWAY MUS
Four Roads
The Howe
Castletown
Derbyhaven
Cregneash
CASTLE RUSHEN
NAUTICAL MUS
St Michael's I.
Port St Mary
SCARLETT VISITOR CENTRE
OLD HOUSE OF KEYS
CREGNEASH VILLAGE FOLK MUSEUM
128
Calf of Man
Spanish Head
Scarlett Point
Dreswick Pt.
BELFAST (April-Sept)
DUBLIN (April-Sept, & Christmas)
Chicken Rock
0 1 2 3 4 5 6 miles
0 1 2 3 4 5 6 7 8 9 10 km

Cumbria
Lancashire
IRISH SEA
MORECAMBE BAY
SD
Barrow-in-Furness
Morecambe
Heysham
Lancaster
Fleetwood
Blackpool
Southport
Preston
Ulverston
Millom
Dalton-in-Furness
Askam in Furness
Broughton in Furness
Grange-over-Sands
Carnforth
Milnthorpe
Kirkby-in-Furness
Cartmel
Flookburgh
Silverdale
Arnside
Bolton-le-Sands
Hest Bank
Isle of Walney
Walney Island
Roa Island
Piel Island
Foulney Island
South End Point
Rampside
Biggar
Vickerstown
Duddon Sands
Black Combe
Humphrey Head Pt.
Sunderland Pt.
Shoulder of Lune
Cockerham Sands
Knott End-on-Sea
Rossall Point
Cleveleys
Thornton
Poulton-le-Fylde
Lytham St Anne's
Salters Bank
Banks Sands
Great Bank
Horse Bank
Kirkham
Freckleton
Garstang
Cockerham
Galgate
Fulwood
Ribbleton
Bamber Bridge
Leyland
Chorley
Ainsdale
Birkdale
Burscough
Tarleton
Hesketh Bank
Longton
Warton
Wrea Green
Broughton
Barton
Carleton
Great Eccleston
St Michael's on Wyre
Hambleton
Preesall
Pilling
Carlisle
Halton
Caton
Hornby
Kirkby Lonsdale
Heversham
Levens
Sedgwick
Hincaster
Beetham
Holme
Burton-in-Kendal
Yealand Redmayne
Warton
DOUGLAS
M6
M55
A590
A595
A6
A583
A585
A565
A59
56
50
42
43
0 1 2 3 4 5 6 miles
0 1 2 3 4 5 6 7 8 9 10 km

Y O R K S H I R E
D A L E S
N A T I O N A L
P A R K
F O R E S T
O F
B O W L A N D
L a n c a s h i r e
SD
57
49
43
44
Kirkby Lonsdale
Ingleton
High Bentham
Settle
Skipton
Clitheroe
Keighley
Burnley
Blackburn
Preston
Rochdale
Bury
COLNE
NELSON
ACCRINGTON
RAWTENSTALL
Haslingden
Oswaldtwistle
Great Harwood
Padiham
Whalley
Barnoldswick
Earby
Gargrave
Grassington
Kettlewell
Malham
Giggleswick
Clapham
Horton in Ribblesdale
Dent
Sedbergh
Gawthrop
Cowgill
Hawes
Gayle
Askrigg
Aysgarth
Kidstones
Buckden
Starbotton
Arncliffe
Litton
Kilnsey
Conistone
Threshfield
Linton
Hebden
Burnsall
Hellifield
Long Preston
Slaidburn
Newton
Dunsop Bridge
Whitewell
Chipping
Ribchester
Longridge
Grimsargh
Fulwood
Ribbleton
Samlesbury
Wilpshire
Rishton
Clayton-le-Moors
Church
Darwen
Todmorden
Hebden Bridge
Mytholmroyd
Bacup
Whitworth
Wardle
Littleborough
Milnrow
Ramsbottom
Edenfield
Horwich
CHORLEY
LEYLAND
Bamber Bridge
Walton-le-Dale
Higher Walton
Hoghton
Brindle
Withnell
Whittle-le-Woods
Euxton
Heskin Green
Belmont
Edgworth
Tottington
HEYWOOD
Bamford
Norden
Trawden
Foulridge
Barrowford
Brierfield
Fence
Sabden
Worston
Downham
Chatburn
Sawley
Gisburn
Bolton-by-Bowland
Holden
Tosside
Wigglesworth
Rathmell
Austwick
Wennington
Low Bentham
Burton in Lonsdale
Tunstall
Arkholme
Whittington
Cowan Bridge
Casterton
Barbon
Mansergh
Old Town
Hutton Roof
Clawthorpe
Burton-in-Kendal
Holme
Farleton
Lupton
Gressingham
Hornby
Wray
Caton
Caton Green
Brookhouse
Halton
Crossgill
Quernmore
Abbeystead
Marshaw
Tarnbrook
Dolphinholme
Street
Oakenclough
Calder Vale
Bleasdale
Claughton
Whitechapel
Inglewhite
Goosnargh
Broughton
Knowle Green
Hurst Green
Great Mitton
Billington
Langho
Balderstone
Mellor
Salesbury
Copster Green
Wiswell
Pendleton
Barley
Roughlee
Newchurch
Higham
Worsthorne
Hurstwood
Cliviger
Holme Chapel
Portsmouth
Cornholme
Walsden
Lydgate
Shore
Lumbutts
Mankinholes
Heptonstall
Colden
Blackshaw Head
Chiserley
Wainstalls
Midgley
Luddenden
Luddenden Foot
Oxenhope
Haworth
Stanbury
Oakworth
Laycock
Goose Eye
Exley Head
Steeton
Utley
Silsden
Sutton-in-Craven
Glusburn
Cowling
Lothersdale
Elslack
Carleton
Thornton-in-Craven
Kelbrook
Salterforth
Bracewell
West Marton
East Marton
Broughton
Thorlby
Embsay
Eastby
Halton East
Draughton
Flasby
Rylstone
Cracoe
Hetton
Winterburn
Calton
Airton
Kirkby Malham
Hanlith
Bell Busk
Otterburn
Coniston Cold
Bank Newton
Eshton
Nappa
Halton West
Paythorne
Newsholme
Horton
Stainforth
Langcliffe
Stackhouse
Little Stainforth
Feizor
Lawkland
Eldroth
Keasden
Mewith Head
Lowgill
Wham
Mearbeck
Helwith Bridge
Wharfe
Newby
Ribblehead
Chapel-le-Dale
Selside
High Birkwith
New Houses
Halton Gill
Foxup
Hubberholme
Yockenthwaite
Cray
Walden
Walden Head
Horsehouse
Braidley
Woodale
Carlton
Carlton Moor
West Burton
Newbiggin
Thoralby
Thornton Rust
Carpley Green
Stalling Busk
Marsett
Burtersett
Countersett
Semer Water
Stone House
Gawthrop
Deepdale
Dentdale
Kearstwick
Leck
Ireby
Masongill
Westhouse
Nether Burrow
Cantsfield
Wrayton
Melling
Tatham
Salter
Goodber Common
Tatham Fells
Burn Moor
Catlow Fell
Haylot Fell
Clougha
Mallowdale Fell
Croasdale Fell
Tarnbrook Fell
Lee Fell
Sykes Fell
Hareden
Easington Fell
Lane Ends
Grindleton
West Bradford
Waddington
Bashall Eaves
Walker Fold
Low Moor
Hesketh Lane
Gisburn Forest
Stocks Reservoir
Whernside
Ingleborough
Pen-y-ghent
Scales Moor
Ingleborough Common
Simon Fell
Blea Moor
Gayle Moor
Cam Fell
Oughtershaw
Cragdale Moor
Langstrothdale Chase
Middle Tongue
Buckden Pike
Little Whernside
Great Whernside
Darnbrook Fell
Fountains Fell
Malham Tarn
Upper Barden Res.
Lower Barden Res.
Riggs Moor
Conistone Moor
Hebden Moor
Ribblesdale
Keighley Moor
The Forest of Trawden
Boulsworth Hill
Widdop Res.
Walshaw Dean Res.
Heptonstall Moor
Wadsworth Moor
Haworth Moor
Warley Moor Res.
Forest of Rossendale
Anglezarke Moor
Anglezarke Reservoir
White Coppice
Turton Moor
Turton Bottoms
Chapeltown
Cadshaw
Whittlestone Head
Hoddlesden
Belthorn
Guide
Lower Darwen
Ewood
Feniscowles
Pleasington
Cherry Tree
Mellor Brook
Beardwood
Shadsworth
Knuzden
Huncoat
Baxenden
Rising Bridge
Acre
Goodshaw
Crawshawbooth
Love Clough
Dunnockshaw
Clow Bridge
Loveclough
Water
Whitewell Bottom
Weir
Stacksteads
Britannia
Shawforth
Facit
Healey
Syke
Smallbridge
Newhey
Cutgate
Rake Head
Cowpe
Waterfoot
Edgeside
Helmshore
Stubbins
Summerseat
Greenmount
Walmersley
Affetside
Ashworth
Egerton
Harwood
Bradshaw
Walshaw
Tottington
Rivington
Winter Hill
Stalybridge
Blackrod
Adlington
Heath Charnock
Cowling
Wheelton
Brinscall
Abbey Village
Riley Green
Gregson Lane
Coupe Green
Higher Wheelton
Clayton-le-Woods
Clayton Green
Lostock Hall
Middleforth Green
Penwortham
Hutton
Walton Summit
Whittle-le-Woods
Buckshaw Village
Shaw Green
Runshaw Moor
Skipton Moor
Bishopdale
Widdale Fell
Dodd Fell
Ingleborough Show Cave
White Scar Caves
Gaping Gill
Settle Loop
Malham Cove
Kilnsey Park
Bentham Pottery
Watershed Mill Visitor Centre
Giggleswick School Chapel
Sawley Abbey
Whalley Abbey
Clitheroe Castle Museum
Pendle Heritage Centre
British in India Mus
Wycoller
Towneley Hall
Gawthorpe Hall
Haworth Bronte Parsonage Museum
Keighley and Worth Valley Railway
Rossendale Museum
East Lancashire Railway
Lancs Fusiliers Regimental Mus
Rochdale
Bolton

Bedale
Ripon
Thirsk
Sowerby
Masham
Harrogate
Knaresborough
Boroughbridge
Easingwold
Wetherby
York
Tadcaster
Otley
Ilkley
Addingham
Pateley Bridge
N I D D E R D A L E
Bingley
Shipley
Baildon
Bradford
Leeds
Pudsey
Horsforth
Guiseley
Yeadon
Garforth
Kippax
Rothwell
Morley
Batley
Dewsbury
Ossett
Wakefield
Normanton
Castleford
Pontefract
Featherstone
Knottingley
Sherburn in Elmet
Selby
Halifax
Brighouse
Elland
Huddersfield
Cleckheaton
Heckmondwike
Mirfield
Hemsworth
Queensbury
Sowerby Bridge
Spofforth
Collingham
Bramham
Boston Spa
MARSTON MOOR
Ilkley Moor
Masham Moor
Dallowgill Moor
Heathfield Moor
Pateley Moor
Pockstones Moor
Barden Fell
Stean Moor
Leighton Res.
Roundhill Res.
Grimwith Res.
Thruscross Res.
Fewston Res.
Swinsty Res.
Lindley Wood Res.
Eccup Res.
A1(M)
A1
A59
A61
A64
A65
A658
A660
A168
A170
A19
M1
M62
M621
M606
A629
A644
A642
A638
A639
A645
A650
58
52
45
44
North Yorkshire
West Yorkshire
SE

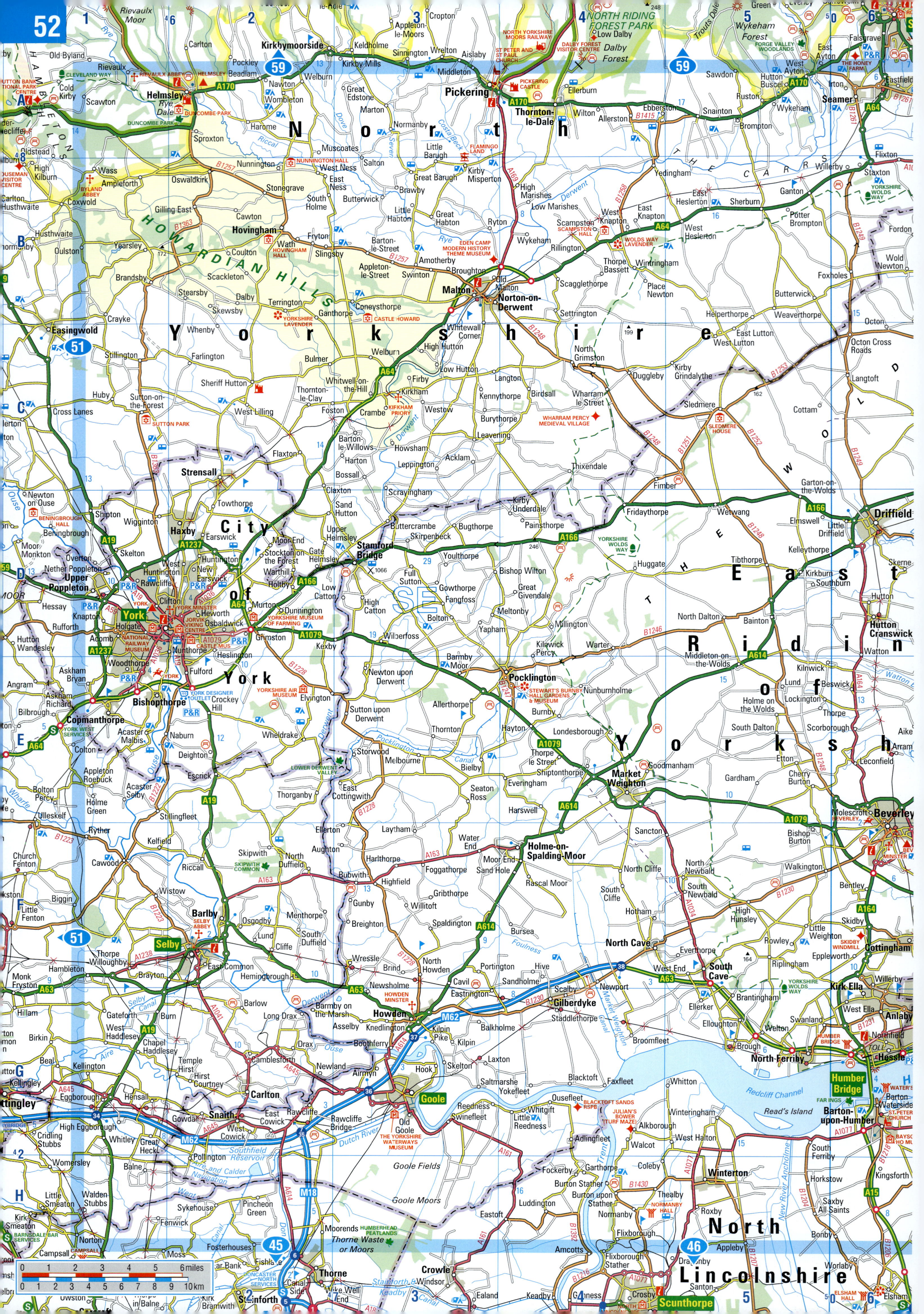

North Yorkshire
City of York
East Riding of Yorkshire
North Lincolnshire
Howardian Hills
The Wolds
North Riding Forest Park
Dalby Forest
Wykeham Forest
Helmsley
Kirkbymoorside
Pickering
Thornton-le-Dale
Malton
Norton-on-Derwent
Easingwold
Strensall
Haxby
York
Stamford Bridge
Pocklington
Market Weighton
Driffield
Beverley
Cottingham
Holme-on-Spalding-Moor
Selby
Howden
Goole
Snaith
North Cave
South Cave
Gilberdyke
North Ferriby
Hessle
Humber Bridge
Barton-upon-Humber
Winterton
Scunthorpe
Seamer
Thorne
Castle Howard
Eden Camp Modern History Theme Museum
Flamingo Land
Sledmere House
Wharram Percy Medieval Village
Kirkham Priory
Sutton Park
Beningbrough Hall
National Railway Museum
Yorkshire Air Museum
Blacktoft Sands RSPB
The Yorkshire Waterways Museum
Goole Fields
Goole Moors
Thorne Waste or Moors
0 1 2 3 4 5 6 miles
0 1 2 3 4 5 6 7 8 9 10 km

SCARBOROUGH CASTLE
ROTUNDA MUSEUM
Scarborough
South Bay
Osgodby
Cayton Bay
Yons Nab
CLEVELAND WAY
A165
Cayton
Lebberston
Gristhorpe
A1039
Filey Brigg
PLAYDALE FARM PARK
Filey
Folkton
Muston
Filey Bay
Primrose Valley
Hunmanby
Hunmanby Moor
Reighton Sands
Reighton Gap
Reighton
Speeton
Burton Fleming
B1229
Buckton
Bempton
B1255
FLAMBOROUGH HEAD
Grindale
Flamborough
B1259
Thwing
Boynton
SEWERBY HALL AND GARDENS
Sewerby
BONDVILLE MODEL VILLAGE
PRIORY
Rudston
B1253
BAYLE MUSEUM
Bridlington
Bessingby
West Hill
OLD PENNY MEMORIES
Hilderthorpe
Carnaby
Haisthorpe
A614
BURTON AGNES HALL
Thornholme
BRIDLINGTON BIRDS OF PREY & ANIMAL PARK
BRIDLINGTON BAY
Kilham
BURTON AGNES MANOR HOUSE
Burton Agnes
Ruston Parva
Harpham
Fraisthorpe
N O R T H
Lowthorpe
Gransmoor
Nafferton
Barmston
Great Kelk
Lissett
Gembling
Ulrome
Wansford
B1249
Foston on the Wolds
SKIPSEA CASTLE
Skipsea
Church End
Beeford
Skipsea Brough
S E A
Brigham
North Frodingham
B1242
TA
Rotsea
Dunnington
Hempholme
Bewholme
Atwick
North Cliff
Burshill
Hornsea
Hornsea Mere
Baswick Steer
Brandesburton
HORNSEA MUSEUM
Seaton
HORNSEA FREEPORT
Hornsea Bridge
B1244
Leven
Leven Canal
Sigglesthorne
Rolston
Catwick
Goxhill
Mappleton
Little Hatfield
Eske
Routh
A1035
Long Riston
B1243
Rise
Great Hatfield
Great Cowden
Tickton
Arnold
Withernwick
Weel
Meaux
New Ellerby
Aldbrough
Skirlaugh
Marton
West Newton
East Newton
Woodmansey
Wawne
Old Ellerby
BURTON CONSTABLE HALL
Flinton
Thearne
Swine
Coniston
Garton
Grimston
Dunswell
A1033
Bransholme
Thirtleby
Sproatley
Humbleton
Fitling
Hilston
Kingston-upon-Hull
Sutton on Hull
Ganstead
B1238
Lelley
Owstwick
Tunstall
Sutton Ings
Bilton
Elstronwick
Newland
Stoneferry
B1239
B1240
Burton Pidsea
North End
Sculcoates
Summergangs
Preston
Roos
A165
WILBERFORCE HOUSE
West End
Waxholme
East Ella
Marfleet
Salt End
Owthorne
STREETLIFE
THE DEEP
Hedon
Rimswell
Withernsea
KINGSTON UPON HULL
Haven Side
Burstwick
B1362
FERENS ART GALLERY
Halsham
East End
A63
Paull
Thorngumbald
Camerton
Keyingham
FORT PAULL
Ryehill
HUMBER
Ottringham
Hollym
Goxhill Haven
Winestead
New Holland
Little Humber
Holmpton
Thorney Crofts
Patrington
Barrow Haven
B1445
Out Newton
Goxhill
Welwick
Weeton
Cherry Cob Sands
Barrow upon Humber
South End
East Halton
Easington
Skeffling
Sunk Island
THORNTON ABBEY
Burnham
Thornton Curtis
North Killingholme
Wootton
A160
Immingham
Kilnsea
South Killingholme
SPURN DISCOVERY CENTRE
Ulceby
Ulceby Skitter
46
47
MUSEUM
Habrough
A180
B1211
SPURN
ROTTERDAM EUROPOORT ZEEBRUGGE
Croxton
BARNETBY SERVICES
Melton Ross
Kirmington
Brocklesby
Stallingborough
Keelby
Aylesby
Pyewipe
6 7 8 9 10 11
A B C D E F G H

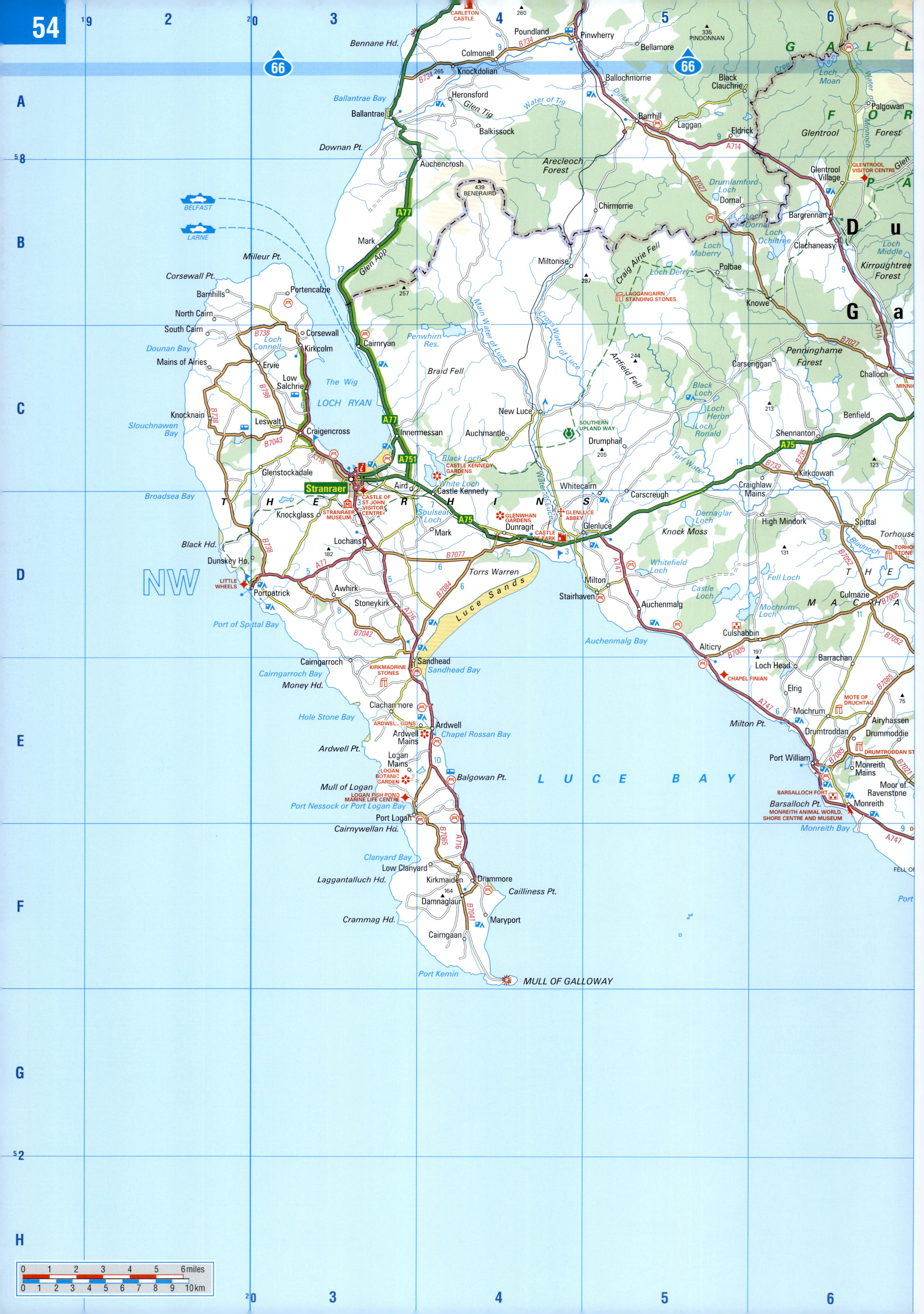

Bennane Hd.
Carleton Castle
Poundland
Pinwherry
Bellamore
335 Pindonnan
Colmonell
Knockdolian
Ballochmorrie
Black Clauchrie
Ballantrae Bay
Heronsford
Glen Tig
Water of Tig
Ballantrae
Barrhill
Laggan
Eldrick
Glentrool
Palgowan
Forest
Loch Moan
Downan Pt.
Balkissock
Auchencrosh
Arecleoch Forest
Glentrool Village
Glentrool Visitor Centre
Drumlamford Loch
Dornal
439 Beneraird
Chirmorrie
Belfast
Larne
Bargrennan
Mark
Glen App
Clachaneasy
Milleur Pt.
Miltonise
Loch Maberry
Polbae
Craig Airie Fell
Loch Derry
Kirroughtree Forest
Corsewall Pt.
Barnhills
Portencalzie
Laggangairn Standing Stones
Knowe
North Cairn
South Cairn
Corsewall
Cairnryan
Penwhirn Res.
Loch Connell
Kirkcolm
Dounan Bay
Mains of Airies
Ervie
Main Water of Luce
Cross Water of Luce
Artfield Fell
Carseriggan
Penninghame Forest
Challoch
Braid Fell
Low Salchrie
The Wig
Loch Ryan
Black Loch
Knocknain
Loch Heron
New Luce
Benfield
Slouchnawen Bay
Leswalt
Auchmantle
Loch Ronald
Shennanton
Craigencross
Innermessan
Southern Upland Way
Drumphail
Black Loch
Castle Kennedy Gardens
Glenstockadale
Tarf Water
Kirkcowan
Craighlaw Mains
Stranraer
Aird
White Loch
Castle Kennedy
Whitecairn
Carscreugh
Broadsea Bay
The Rhins
Castle of St. John Visitor Centre
Stranraer Museum
Knockglass
Soulseat Loch
Glenwhan Gardens
Glenluce Abbey
Dunragit
Castle of Park
Glenluce
Dernaglar Loch
High Mindork
Spittal
Torhouse
Knock Moss
Black Hd.
Lochans
Mark
Dunskey Ho.
Torrs Warren
Whitefield Loch
Fell Loch
Little Wheels
Portpatrick
Awhirk
Luce Sands
Milton
Stairhaven
Castle Loch
Culmazie
The Machars
Stoneykirk
Auchenmalg
Mochrum Loch
Port of Spittal Bay
Culshabbin
Auchenmalg Bay
Cairngarroch
Sandhead
Alticry
Loch Head
Barrachan
Kirkmadrine Stones
Sandhead Bay
Chapel Finian
Cairngarroch Bay
Money Hd.
Elrig
Mote of Druchtag
Clachanmore
Mochrum
Airyhassen
Hole Stone Bay
Milton Pt.
Drumtroddan
Drummoddie
Ardwell Gdns
Ardwell
Ardwell Mains
Chapel Rossan Bay
Drumtroddan Standing Stones
Ardwell Pt.
Logan Mains
Port William
Monreith Mains
Logan Botanic Garden
Balgowan Pt.
Luce Bay
Moor of Ravenstone
Mull of Logan
Logan Fish Pond Marine Life Centre
Barsalloch Fort
Barsalloch Pt.
Monreith
Port Nessock or Port Logan Bay
Monreith Animal World, Shore Centre and Museum
Port Logan
Monreith Bay
Cairnywellan Hd.
Clanyard Bay
Low Clanyard
Laggantalluch Hd.
Kirkmaiden
Drummore
164
Cailliness Pt.
Damnaglaur
Crammag Hd.
Maryport
Cairngaan
Port Kemin
Mull of Galloway
NW
Galloway Forest Park
Dumfries and Galloway
A77
A751
A75
A714
A747
A716
B7027
B7077
B7084
B7042
B7065
B7041
B7005
B7052
B7085
B7043
B738
B798
B734
B733
B735
66
0 1 2 3 4 5 6 miles
0 1 2 3 4 5 6 7 8 9 10 km

7
8
9
10
11
12
A
B
C
D
E
F
G
H
NX
67
60
56
Castlemaddy
Dundeugh
Kendoon
Glenhoul
KENDOON
Carsfad Loch
Lochinvar
Castlefairn
WETHER HILL
Holmhead
Dalmacallan Forest
Stroan
Wallaceton
Glenmidge
Auldgirth
Dalswinton
ELLISLAND FARM
Gall
CORSERINE 814
Loch Harrow
Forrest Lodge
MULLWHARCHAR
MERRICK
Loch Enoch
Loch Dungeon
Lochurr
BOGRIE HILL
Loch Urr
Sundaywell
Dunscore
Milton
Cairn Water
Loch Neldricken
Loch Valley
SILVER FLOWE
RHINNS OF KELLS
Millquarter
St John's Town of Dalry
Earlstoun Loch
Bogue
Corriedoo Forest
Drumbuie
BRUCE'S STONE
Trool
Glen Trool Lodge
Loch Trool
Clatteringshaws Forest
Clatteringshaws Loch
Loch Dee
Garroch
Glenlee
Blackcraig
Knocklearn
Drumpark
Newtonairds
Holywood
Irongray
Newbridge
Glenkiln Res.
Glenkiln
Terregles Banks
Lincluden
New Galloway
Balmaclellan
Gibbshill
LAMACHAN HILL
Glen
Shawhead
Maxwelltown
Ironmacannie
Craig
Corsock
CLATTERINGSHAWS FOREST VISITOR CENTRE
Dumfries and Galloway
RAIDERS ROAD FOREST DRIVE
Merkland
Urr Water
Brooklands
Brae
Lochfoot
Cargenbridge
Lochrutton Loch
Bennan Forest
Cairn Edward Hill
Crocketford or Ninemile Bar
Milton Loch
Auchenreoch Loch
Drumrash
WILD GOAT PARK
Loch Grannoch
FELL OF FLEET
Mossdale
Loch Ken
Parton
Kirkpatrick Durham
Milton
Mabie Forest
Springholm
Stroan Loch
Loch Skerrow
Beeswing
Loch Arthur
Lochaber Loch
DRUMCOLTRAN TOWER
Penkiln Burn
Palnure Burn
CAIRNSMORE OF FLEET
CAIRNSMORE OF FLEET
Woodhall Loch
Crossmichael
Old Bridge of Urr
Kirkgunzeon
Minnigaff
Creebridge
Newton Stewart
KIRROUGHTREE VISITOR CENTRE
Fleet Forest
Lochenbreck Loch
Haugh of Urr
Clarebrand
Townhead of Greenlaw
New Abbey
Clints of Dromore
Laurieston
MOTE OF URR
LONG FELL
Palnure
Laurieston Forest
THREAVE CASTLE
Loch Glentoo
Castle Douglas
OLD BUITTLE TOWER
Barhill
Dalbeattie
Baltersan
Cree
Big Water of Fleet
Loch Whinyeon
Loch Mannoch
Loch Bargatton
KELTON MAINS OPEN FARM
THREAVE GARDENS
Carlingwark Loch
Causeway End
Glengap Forest
BENGRAY
Glengap
Bridge of Dee
Rhonehouse or Kelton Hill
Carsegowan
GEM ROCK MUSEUM
Creetown
Gelston
Dalbeattie Forest
Drumstinchall
Caulkerbush
Preston
Mainsriddle
Wigtown Sands
Glen
FLEET
Ringford
Dee
Airieland
Palnackie
Barnbarroch
Wigtown
CAIRNHARROW
Anwoth
CARDONESS CASTLE
Gatehouse of Fleet
Valleyfield
ORCHARDTON TOWER
Sandyhills
Bladnoch
SCOTLAND'S BOOK TOWN
Carsluith
CARSLUITH CASTLE
VALLEY
Girthon
Twynholm
GALLOWAY HYDRO VISITOR CENTRE
BENGAIRN
Kippford or Scaur
MOTE OF MARK
Colvend
Rockcliffe
Portling
Mersehead Sands
VISITOR CENTRE
CAIRNHOLY CAIRNS
Tongland
BROUGHTON HOUSE AND GARDEN
EAST STEWARTRY COAST
ROUGH ISLAND
Rough I.
Castlehill Pt.
Braehead
Kirkinner
Baldoon Sands
Ravenshall Pt.
Fleet Bay
Sandgreen
Barharrow
Whinnieliggate
Ringdoo Pt.
STEWARTRY MUSEUM
Kirkcudbright
Auchencairn
Auchencairn Bay
Hestan I.
Whauphill
Islands of Fleet
Knockbrex
Kirkcarswell
Balcary Pt.
Kirkandrews
Borgue
St Mary's Isle
Mutehill
Rascarrel
Dundrennan
Rascarrel Bay
Sorbie
Garlieston
WIGTOWN BAY
Eggerness Pt.
Borness
Townhead
Orroland
DUNDRENNAN ABBEY
GALLOWAY HOUSE GARDENS
Ross
Kirkcudbright Bay
Netherlaw
Port Mary
Balmae
Borness Pt.
Abbey Hd.
Cults
Little Ross
CRUGGLETON CHURCH AND CASTLE
SOLWAY FIRTH
Bishopton
Whithorn
PRIORY AND MUSEUM
WHITHORN TRUST DISCOVERY CENTRE
Port Allen
Portyerrock Bay
Glasserton
Cairn Hd.
CARLETON
ST NINIAN'S CHAPEL
ST NINIAN'S CAVE
Isle of Whithorn
Castle Bay
Cutcloy
BURROW HEAD
Saltom Bay
ST BEES HEAD
A75
A76
A712
A713
A762
A711
A714
A746
A745
B7000
B7075
B794
B795
B796
B727
B736
B793
B7004
B7052
B7063
B7005
B733
B729

SOLWAY FIRTH
SOLWAY COAST
LAKE DISTRICT NATIONAL PARK
CUMBRIAN MOUNTAINS
Carlisle
Wigton
Silloth
Maryport
Workington
Whitehaven
Cockermouth
Keswick
Egremont
St Bees
Seascale
Ambleside
Windermere
Bowness-on-Windermere
Coniston
Broughton in Furness
Aspatria
Allonby
Cleator Moor
Frizington
Distington
Ravenglass
Grasmere
Thursby
Dalston
Staveley
GRIZEDALE FOREST PARK
WHINLATTER FOREST PARK
SKIDDAW FOREST
ENNERDALE FOREST
COPELAND FOREST
FURNESS FELLS
Derwent Water
Bassenthwaite Lake
Crummock Water
Buttermere
Loweswater
Ennerdale Water
Wast Water
Thirlmere
Ullswater
Coniston Water
Esthwaite Water
Windermere
Devoke Water
Seathwaite Tarn
Whinlatter Pass
Honister Pass
Hardknott Pass
Wrynose Pass
Kirkstone Pass
SCAFELL PIKE
HELVELLYN
SKIDDAW
GREAT GABLE
PILLAR
BLACK SAIL
NX
SC
0 1 2 3 4 5 6 miles
0 1 2 3 4 5 6 7 8 9 10 km

Newby East
Hayton
Farlam
Talkin
Tindale Fells
Tindale Tarn
Forest Head
Halton Lea Gate
Lambley
Stonehouse
Whitfield
Bearsbridge
Catton
Dye House
Dalton
Whitley Chapel
Slaley
Warwick Bridge
How
Heads Nook
Faugh
Castle Carrock
61
621 COLD FELL
Glendue Fell
Eals
Allendale Town
62
Slaley Forest
Broadwell House
Great Corby
King's Forest of Geltsdale
Knarsdale
Whitfield Moor
Ninebanks
Hexhamshire Common
Blanchland Moor
Cumwhitton
Slaggyford
Sinderhope
Allendale Common
Blanchland
Edmundbyers
Geltsdale Middle
Cumrew
Hornsby
Newbiggin
Ayle
Spartylea
Hunstanwerth
Holmwrangle
Croglin
Blagill
Carrshield
Nookton Fell
Aiketgate
Ainstable
South Tynedale Railway
Gossipgate Gallery
Alston
Nenthall
Dirt Pot
Allenheads
Armathwaite
Scale Houses
Raise
Coalcleugh
High Hesket
Watch Hill
Gilderdale Forest
Bayles
Middle Fell
Bolt's Law
Old Town
Ruckcroft
Renwick
Leadgate
Nenthead
Nenthead Mines
North of England Lead Mining Museum
Rookhope
Stanhope Common
Staffield
Hareseugh
High Bankhill
Middlehope Moor
Kirkoswald
Garrigill
Lanehead
Collier Law
Unthank
Cowshill
Crawleyside
Durham Dales Centre
Stanhope
Lazonby Fell
Townhead
Lazonby
Gamblesby
Alston Moor
Burnhope Reservoir
Wearhead
Weardale
Eastgate
Westgate
Glassonby
Maiden Way
Ireshopeburn
St John's Chapel
Daddry Shield
58
Plumpton
Brockleymoor
Great Salkeld
Little Salkeld
Melmerby
Melmerby Fell
Pennine Way
Burnhope Seat
Plumpton Head
Hunsonby
Round Hill
Ireshope Moor
North Pennines
Winskill
Ousby
Cross Fell
Harwood
Westernhope Moor
Bollihope Common
Langwathby
Edenhall
Skirwith
Kirkland
Milburn Forest
Moor House-Upper Teesdale
Langdon Common
Chapelfell Top
Catterlen
Viewing Hill
Pawlaw Pike
Newton Reigny
Fair Hill
Penrith
Blencarn
Crowdundle Beck
Langdon Beck
Newbiggin Common
Middleton Common
Carleton
Mayburgh Henge
Brougham Castle
Culgaith
Milburn
Widdybank Fell
Forest
Ettersgill
Bowlees Visitor Centre
Eamont Bridge
Acorn Bank
Newbiggin
Cow Green Reservoir
Cauldron Snout
High Force
Stainton
Sockbridge
Lilliput Lane
Clifton Hall
Clifton
Temple Sowerby
Dufton Fell
Cronkley Fell
Holwick
Middleton-in-Teesdale
Tirril
Knock
Lowmoor Row
Cliburn Moss
Teesdale
Lakeland Bird of Prey Centre
Melkinthorpe
Cliburn
Kirkby Thore
Dufton
NY
Hill Top
Eggleston
Askham
Lowther
Long Marton
Murton Fell
Mickle Fell
Bowbank
Mickleton
Eggleston Hall
Hackthorpe
Brampton
Lune Moor
Thringarth
Helton
Great Strickland
Morland
Bolton
Crackenthorpe
Lune Forest
Romaldkirk
Grassholme Reservoir
Grassholme
Whale
Newby
King's Meaburn
Murton
Hunderthwaite
Little Strickland
Colby
Appleby-in-Westmorland
Hilton
Warcop Fell
Selset Reservoir
Hury
Cotherstone
Bampton Grange
Sleagill
Burrells
Dow Crag
Hunderthwaite Moor
Hury Reservoir
Bampton
Reagill
Hoff
Eden Valley Railway
Great Ormside
Balder
Balderhead Reservoir
Clove Lodge
Baldersdale
Lartington
Bampton Common
Rosgill
Mauld's Meaburn
Sandford
Stainmore Common
Cotherstone Moor
Shap Abbey
Shap
Crosby Ravensworth
Drybeck
Warcop
Hillbeck
North Stainmore
Deep Dale
Deepdale Beck
Keld
Oddendale
Brough Castle
Brough
South Stainmore
Bowes
Bowes Castle
Gilmonby
Ralfland Forest
Great Asby
Bleatarn
Little Musgrave
Great Musgrave
Brough Sowerby
Kaber
Barras
Moudy Mea
Bowes Moor
Stainmore Forest
Soulby
Winton
Heggerscales
Sleightholme
Crosby Ravensworth Fell
Great Asby Scar
Crosby Garrett
Hartley
Scargill High Moor
Shap Fells
Little Asby
Kirkby Stephen
Winton Fell
Sleightholme Moor
Orton
Raisbeck
Smardale
Waitby
Cleasby Hill
Tebay Services
Smardale Gill
Nateby
Arkengarthdale Moor
Sadgill
Greenholme
Bretherdale Head
Gaisgill
Kelleth
Newbiggin-on-Lune
Ash Fell
Whaw
Tebay
J38 Truckstop Services
Bowderdale
Coldbeck
Stonesdale Moor
Weasdale
Ravenstonedale
Ravenseat
Rogan's Seat
Langthwaite
Arkle Town
Long Sleddale
Borrowdale
Birkdale
West Stonesdale
Great Pinseat
Common
Outhgill
Melbecks Moor
Lowbridge House
Forest Hall
Langdale Fell
Ravenstonedale Common
Keld
Angram
Healaugh
Garnett Bridge
The Pennine Bridleway
Mallerstang
Angram Common
Thwaite
Gunnerside
Feetham
Kearton
Watchgate
Howgill Fell
Muker
Satron
Low Row
Bowston
Garth Row
Patton Bridge
Lowgill
The Calf
Great Shunner Fell
Buttertubs Pass
Crackpot
Swaledale
Grayrigg
Beck Foot
Brant Fell
SD
Yorkshire Dales National Park
Burneside
Meal Bank
Abbotside Common
Lakeland Climbing Centre
Lambrigg Fell
Cautley
Cotterdale
Askrigg Common
East Bolton Moor
Kendal
Sedbergh
Farfield Mill Arts & Heritage Centre
Baugh Fell
Garsdale Head
High Shaw
Askrigg
Castle Bolton
New Hutton
Millthrop
Hardrow
Sedbusk
Newbiggin
Dales Countryside Museum
Low Mill Outdoor Centre
K Village
K Village Heritage Centre
Killington Services (Southbound Only)
Mossdale Moor
Appersett
Wensleydale Pottery
Hawes
Bainbridge
Worton
Woodhall
Carperby
Brigsteer
Natland
Millholme
Oxenholme
Killington
Garsdale
Gayle
Burtersett
Hawes
Wensleydale Creamery
Cubeck
Thornton Rust
Aysgarth
Sizergh
Middleshaw
Barrows Green
Old Hutton
Rise Hill
Widdale Fell
Countersett
Semer Water
Wether Fell
Carpley Green
Thoralby
Bishopdale Valley
Cotes
Sedgwick
Gawthrop
Dent
Dentdale
Cowgill
Stainton
Gatebeck
Levens
Middleton
Stone House
Wold Fell
Dodd Fell
Marsett
Stalling Busk
Newbiggin
Hincaster
Endmoor
Calf Top
Deepdale
Levens Hall
Crooklands
Leasgill
Heversham
Old Town
Crag Hill
Gayle Moor
Cragdale Moor
Walden
Milnthorpe
Lupton
Mansergh
Barbon
Whernside
Blea Moor
Cam Fell
Oughtershaw
Middle Tongue
Kidstones
50
M6
A66
A6
A686
A689
A685
A684
A683
A65
A591
B6277
B6276
B6270
B6259
B6260
B6261
B6255
B6160
B6278
Eden
Tees
Lune
Dee
Rawthey
Sprint
Kent

Sunderland
WASHINGTON
STANLEY
Consett
CHESTER-LE-STREET
HOUGHTON-LE-SPRING
SEAHAM
Durham
Easington Colliery
PETERLEE
Spennymoor
Crook
Willington
Bishop Auckland
Shildon
NEWTON AYCLIFFE
Hartlepool
BILLINGHAM
Stockton-on-Tees
Middlesbrough
Darlington
Barnard Castle
Staindrop
Stanhope
Wolsingham
Richmond
Scotch Corner
Catterick Garrison
Leyburn
Bedale
Northallerton
Thirsk
Yarm
Thornaby-on-Tees
Sedgefield
Ferryhill
Brompton
Middleham
Lanchester
Sacriston
Langley Park
Brandon
Ushaw Moor
Esh Winning
Wolsingham Park Moor
Pikeston Fell
Hamsterley Forest
Woodland Fell
Muggleswick Common
SWALE DALE
Beacon Pt.
0 1 2 3 4 5 6 miles
0 1 2 3 4 5 6 7 8 9 10 km

NZ
SE
ST HILDA'S PARISH CHURCH
Hartlepool Bay
Seaton Carew
Tees Bay
TEESMOUTH
Salt Scar
REDCAR
Coatham
Dormanstown
Marske-by-the-Sea
KIRKLEATHAM OLD HALL MUSEUM
Kirkleatham
South Bank
Grangetown
Yearby
New Marske
MINIATURE RAILWAY
Saltburn-by-the-Sea
SALTBURN VALLEY
CHRIS BIRKBECK INTERNATIONAL RALLY SCHOOL
Lazenby
Wilton
Upleatham
Brotton
Skinningrove
ENGLAND COAST PATH
Boulby
Eston
Dunsdale
TOCKETTS WATER MILL
Skelton
Carlin How
Loftus
Staithes
Normanby
Redcar and Cleveland
North Skelton
Kilton Thorpe
Easington
Port Mulgrave
Ormesby
PLATTS LANE WOODLAND
Guisborough
GUISBOROUGH PRIORY
Boosbeck
Lingdale
Hinderwell
Runswick Bay
ORMESBY HALL
Margrove Park
Stanghow
Liverton
Roxby
Runswick Bay
Kettleness
GUISBOROUGH FOREST
Hutton Gate
Charltons
Newton Mulgrave
Goldsborough
Nunthorpe
Moorsholm
Ellerby
Hutton Village
Gisborough Moor
Scaling
Lythe
Newton under Roseberry
Mickleby
East Barnby
Sandsend
Sandsend Wyke
West Barnby
East Row
SUTCLIFFE GALLERY
Whitby
Saltwick Bay
Commondale Moor
Scaling Dam Res.
Dunsley
Great Ayton
Little Ayton
New Row
Commondale
Danby Low Moor
Ugthorpe
Newholm
P&R
WHITBY ABBEY
WHITBY
CAPTAIN COOK MEMORIAL MUSEUM
Lealholm Moor
Easby
Kildale
Danby
THE MOORS CENTRE
Stonegate
Ruswarp
Stainsacre
Stokesley
Kildale Moor
Castleton
Ainthorpe
Houlsyke
Lealholm
Aislaby
Briggswath
Sleights
Sneaton
High Hawsker
Battersby
Ugglebarnby
Ness Pt.
CLEVELAND WAY
Kirkby
Great Broughton
Ingleby Greenhow
Westerdale
Low Garth
Street
Glaisdale
Egton
Grosmont
Sneatonthorpe
Raw
Robin Hood's Bay
OLD COASTGUARD STATION
BOGGLE HOLE
MUSEUM OF VICTORIAN SCIENCE
Egton Bridge
Esk Valley
Littlebeck
Fylingthorpe
Robin Hood's Bay
CLEVELAND WAY
Westerdale Moor
Glaisdale
Old Peak
Glaisdale Moor
Egton High Moor
Beck Hole
Goathland
Ravenscar
Urra
Seave Green
Farndale Moor
Wake Lady Green
Rosedale Moor
Flask Inn
Fylingdales Moor
Chop Gate
COCKAYNE RIDGE
Cockayne
WHEELDALE MOOR ROMAN ROAD
Staintondale
NORTH YORK MOORS
NATIONAL PARK
Church Houses
Wheeldale Moor
Goathland Moor
Harwood Dale Forest
CLEVELAND WAY
Bilsdale West Moor
Bilsdale East Moor
Thorgill
Rosedale Abbey
Harwood Dale
Cloughton Newlands
Cloughton Wyke
PICKERING MOOR
Pickering Forest
Saltergate
Cloughton
Fangdale Beck
Low Mill
ROSEDALE
Langdale Forest
Broxa Forest
Burniston
Bransdale
Rudland Rigg
Blakey Ridge
Spaunton Moor
Cropton
Hartoft End
Forest
Stape
Cromer Pt.
Scalby Ness Rocks
East Moors
Silpho
Suffield
Helmsley Moor
Skiplam Moor
RYEDALE FOLK MUSEUM
Lastingham
Newton Dale
Levisham
Langdale End
Broxa
Hackness
Scalby
SCARBOROUGH
SEA LIFE CENTRE
Gillamoor
Newton-on-Rawcliffe
Lockton
LOCKTON
North Bay
Hawnby
Fadmoor
Hutton-le-Hole
Spaunton
Staindale Forest
Wrench Green
Everley
Barrowcliff
Newby
Rievaulx Moor
Appleton-le-Moors
Cropton
NORTH RIDING FOREST PARK
Trouts Dale
Wykeham Forest
Scarborough
SCARBOROUGH CASTLE
ROTUNDA MUS.
Carlton
Kirkbymoorside
Keldholme
NORTH YORKSHIRE MOORS RAILWAY
Low Dalby
FORGE VALLEY WOODLANDS
Falsgrave
Old Byland
Pockley
Sinnington
Wrelton
Aislaby
ST PETER AND ST PAUL CHURCH
DALBY FOREST VISITOR CENTRE
Dalby Forest
East Ayton
Rievaulx
Beadlam
Kirkby Mills
Middleton
West Ayton
THE HONEY FARM
P&R
CLEVELAND WAY
RIEVAULX ABBEY
HELMSLEY
Welburn
PICKERING CASTLE
Sawdon
Hutton Buscel
Irton
Osgodby
Cold Kirby
Scawton
Helmsley
Rye Dale
DUNCOMBE PARK
Wombleton
Great Edstone
Pickering
Ellerburn
Ruston
Seamer
Eastfield
Cayton
Thornton-le-Dale
Wilton
Allerston
Ebberston
Snainton
Wykeham
Lebberston
DUNCOMBE PARK
Nawton
Marton
Normanby
PLAYDALE FARM PARK
Sproxton
HILLS
A66
A1053
A174
A171
A1043
A172
A173
A1085
A1042
B1269
B1380
B1292
B1257
B1366
A174
B1266
A171
B1410
B1416
B1447
A169
A171
A170
A170
A170
A64
A165
B1261
B1415
52
52
Res.
166
242
299
329
404
401
420
432
433
435
454
299
248
A
B
C
D
E
F
G
H
6
7
8
9
10
11

East Ayrshire
Dumfries and
Sorn
Airds Moss
Back Rogerton
Cronberry
Auchinleck
Lugar
Glenmuir
Holmhead
Logan
Glenmuirshaw
KEIR HARDIE STATUE
Cumnock
Netherthird
Craigens
Dalblair
Glenmuir Water
Netherwood
Smallburn
Muirkirk
Kames
593 CAIRN TABLE
497 WARDLAW HILL
Glespin
392 AUCHENSAUGH HILL
Middle Muir
Roberton Law
Roberton
Glentaggart
Crawfordjohn
Duneaton Water
Cowgill Upper Reservoir
Culter Waterhead Reservoir
COULTER FELL
GLENWHAPPEN RIG
Tweedsmuir
ABINGTON SERVICES
Abington
569 TEWSGILL HILL
Camps Water
Camps Reservoir
DRAKE LAW
Kirkton
Crawford
Glenbreck
478 MOUNT STUART
Fingland
494 RAKE LAW
553 WELLGRAIN DOD
Elvanfoot
553 CRAIGMAID
CLYDE LAW
LOWTHER HILLS
NS
509 KIRKLAND HILL
Kirkland
Pathhead
Mansfield
Connel Park
Bankglen
New Cumnock
Kirkconnel
Kelloholm
Nith
Burnside
Dalleagles
THE KNIPE 575
Crawick
Sanquhar
TOLBOOTH MUSEUM
SANQUHAR POST OFFICE
485 CONRIG HILL
Crawick Water
MUSEUM OF LEAD MINING
Leadhills
LEADHILLS & WANLOCKHEAD RLY
WANLOCKHEAD BEAM ENGINE
Wanlockhead
LOTUS LODGE
GREEN LOWTHER
LOWTHER HILL
Mennock Pass
Elvan Water
Watermeetings
March
Source of River Tweed
Nether Howecleuch
DEVIL'S BEEF TUB
Ericstane
Granton
Howslack
Kello Water
Mennock
SOUTHERN UPLAND WAY
Potrail Water
Daer Reservoir
569 ENOCH HILL
Afton Water
700 BLACKCRAIG HILL
Afton Reservoir
Euchan Water
449 CAIRN HILL
Enterkinfoot
Durisdeermill
Durisdeer
DURISDEER PARISH CHURCH
691 BALLENCLEUCH LAW
Coatsgate
Moffat
407
Easter Earshaig
Beattock
Kinnelhead
Scar Water
554 CAIRNKINNA HILL
Enoch
668 GANA HILL
Carsphairn Forest
Holestane
MORTON CASTLE
512 QUEENSBERRY
DRUMLANRIG CASTLE
Carronbridge
797 CAIRNSMORE OF CARSPHAIRN
Corlae
580 BENBRACK
Benbuie
Auchenbrack
Shinnel Water
Auchenbainzie
Gatelawbridge
Locherben
Burnhead
Penpont
Thornhill
Loch Ettrick
Lochwood
St Ann's
Carsphairn
Bardennoch
Dundeugh Forest
Water of Ken
Dalwhat Water
Tynron
Keir Mill
Closeburn
Forest of Ae
Johnstonebridge
Chapelhill
Knowehead
Craigdarroch
Moniaive
Kirkland
Park
Blackacre
Courance
Kendoon Loch
Glencrosh
Straith
Wallaceton
Ae Village
Water of Ae
Dundeugh
KENDOON
Glenhoul
Kendoon
Black Water
385 WETHER HILL
Castlefairn
Dalmacallan Forest
Glenmidge
Auldgirth
Parkgate
Nethermill
Templand
Carsfad Loch
Holmhead
Lochinvar
Lochurr
432 BOGRIE HILL
Dalswinton
Auchencairn
Shieldhill
Loch Urr
Dunscore
ELLISLAND FARM
Duncow
Marjoriebanks
Lochmaben
Millquarter
Earlstoun Loch
Sundaywell
Milton
Amisfield
Drumbuie
St John's Town of Dalry
Bogue
Corriedoo Forest
Cairn Water
Gallaberry
Tinwald
Garroch
Kirkton
LOCHMABEN CASTLE
Glenlee
Blackcraig
Newtonairds
Holywood
Locharbriggs
Heathhall
New Galloway
Balmaclellan
Knocklearn
Gibbshill
Drumpark
Irongray
Glenkiln Res.
DUMFRIES AND GALLOWAY AVIATION MUS
Newbridge
LINCLUDEN COLLEGE
The Grove
Torthorwald
Hightae
CLATTERINGSHAWS FOREST VISITOR CENTRE
Ironmacannie
Craig
Corsock
Glenkiln
Glen
Terregles Banks
Lincluden
OLD BRIDGE HOUSE MUS
Dumfries
Maxwelltown
Greystone
RAMMERSCALES HOUSE
Collin
Shawhead
Cargenbridge
BURNS HOUSE
ROBERT BURNS CENTRE
Greenlea
NX
Merkland
Urr Water
Brooklands
Brae
Lochfoot
Lochrutton Loch
DUMFRIES MUSEUM & CAMERA OBSCURA
Racks
Cleughbrae
RAIDERS ROAD FOREST DRIVE
Loch Ken
Bennan Forest
Cairn Edward Hill
Crocketford or Ninemile Bar
Auchenreoch Loch
Milton Loch
Islesteps
Kingholm Quay
Mouswald
Lochar Moss
Kelton
470 FELL OF FLEET
Mossdale
Drumrash
Parton
Kirkpatrick Durham
Milton
Mabie Forest
Mabie
KIRKCONNELL FLOW
Stroan Loch
Springholm
Beeswing
Loch Arthur
Lochaber Loch
Glencaple
Bankend
Clarencefield
Loch Skerrow
Old Bridge of Urr
MCOLTRAN TOWER
Kirkconnell
Ruthwell
Woodhall Loch
Craig
Crossmichael
Kirkgunzeon
Haugh of Urr
New Abbey Pow
New Abbey
SWEETHEART ABBEY
NEW ABBEY CORN MILL
Shearington
Blackshaw
CAERLAVEROCK CASTLE
Eastpark
Bowhouse
WILDFOWL AND WETLAND CENTRE
CAERLAVEROCK
Fleet Forest
Lochenbreck Loch
Townhead of Greenlaw
Clarebrand
MOTE OF URR
383 LONG FELL
Overton
Loch Kindar
NITH ESTUARY
Blackshaw Bank
Laurieston
Laurieston Forest
343
Big Water of Fleet
THREAVE CASTLE
Loch Glentoo
Castle Douglas
Carlingwark Loch
OLD BUITTLE TOWER
182
Barhill
Dalbeattie
Drumburn
Loch Whinyeon
Loch Mannoch
Glengap
KELTON MAINS OPEN FARM
THREAVE GARDENS
569 CRIFFELL
Carsethorn
366 BENGRAY
Forest
Glengap
Bridge of Dee
Rhonehouse or Kelton Hill
Gelston
Dalbeattie Forest
Drumstinchall
Kirkbean
ARBIGLAND GARDENS
Caulkerbush
Prestonmill
Mainsriddle
JOHN PAUL JONES COTTAGE MUSEUM
FLEET VALLEY
Ringford
Palnackie
Barnbarroch
Anwoth
CARDONESS CASTLE
Gatehouse of Fleet
Valleyfield
Airieland
ORCHARDTON TOWER
Sandyhills
GALLOWAY HYDRO VISITOR CENTRE
Twynholm
391 BENGAIRN
Kippford or Scaur
MOTE OF MARK
Colvend
Rockcliffe
Portling
Southerness
Southerness Pt.
Mersehead Sands
ROUGH ISLAND
Rough I.
Tongland
BROUGHTON HOUSE AND GARDEN
EAST STEWARTRY COAST
Castlehill Pt.
Whinnieliggate
STEWARTRY
Kirkcudbright
Auchencairn
Auchencairn Bay
Girthon
0 1 2 3 4 5 6 miles
0 1 2 3 4 5 6 7 8 9 10km
A76
A70
A702
A74(M)
M74
A701
A75
A710
A711
A712
A713
A762
A709
A745
B729
B797
B740
B7078
B7040
B725
B794
67
68
69
55
56

Scottish Borders
Dumfries and Galloway
Cumbria
NT
NY
Selkirk
Philiphaugh
Bowhill
Yarrow
Yarrow Feus
Mountbenger
Dryhope
Cappercleuch
St. Mary's Loch
Megget Reservoir
Talla Reservoir
Talla
Linnfoots
Fruid Reservoir
Crookhaugh
Hearthstane
Meggethead
Loch Skeen
Grey Mare's Tail Waterfalls
White Coomb
Hart Fell
Saddle Yoke
Birkhill
Ettrick Forest
Ettrickbridge
Kirkhope
Sundhope
Gilmanscleuch
Newburgh
Crosslee
Tushielaw
Loch of the Lowes
Ramsey Knowe
Wardlaw
Ettrick
Ettrickhill
Ramseycleuch
James Hogg Monument
Redfordgreen
Buccleuch
Glenkerry
Nether Dalgleish
Craik Forest
Craik
Howpasley
Riddell Monument
Akermoor Loch
Shaws Under Loch
Hellmoor Loch
Todrig
Woll
Ashkirk
Clerklands
Lilliesleaf
Hassendean
Horsleyhill
Clarilaw
Appletreehall
Minto
Denholm
Ashybank
Burnfoot
Hawick
Wilton
Museum and Scott Gallery
Drumlanrig's Tower
Cauldmill
Kirkton
Hallrule
Bonchester Bridge
Hobkirk
Rubers Law
Roberton
Borthwickshiels
Borthwickbrae
Burnfoot
Deanburnhaugh
Branxholm Park
Branxholme
Newmill
Teviotdale
Broadhaugh
Northhouse
Dodburn
Teviothead
Castleweary
Priesthaugh
Caldcleuch Head
Waverley Route
Wisp Hill
Tudhope Hill
Gorrenberry
Hermitage Castle
Hermitage
Newlands
Larriston
Steele Road
Dinlabyre
Saughtree
Deadwater
Peel Fell
Kielder
Kielder Forest Park
Larriston Fells
Old Castleton
Newcastleton
Newcastleton Forest
Newcastleton or Copshaw Holm
Glendhu Hill
Kershopefoot
Kershope Forest
Kershope Burn
Liddesdale
Bewcastle Fells
Sighty Crag
Whitelyne Common
Paddaburn Moor
Baileyhead
The Flatt
Blackpool Gate
Roughsike
Roadhead
Bewcastle
White Preston
Spadeadam Forest
Spadeadam Farm
Wiley Sike
Gilsland Spa
Gilsland
Birdoswald
Upper Denton
Denton Fell
Longnewton
Belses
Bloomfield
Ancrum
Greenhouse
Chesters
Lanton
Jedburgh Abbey
Mary Queen of Scots House
Newton
Bedrule
Hundalee
Bairnkine
Chesters
Cleuch Head
Southdean
Cragbank Wood
Wauchope Forest
Langburnshiels
Fanna Hill
Singdean
Roundstonefoot
Capplegill
Capel Fell
Ettrick Pen
Loch Fell
Black Knowe
Redcleuch Edge
Pike Hill
Dumcrieff
Davington
Kagyu Samye Ling Tibetan Centre
Eskdalemuir Forest
Eskdalemuir
Laverhay
Black Esk Reservoir
Jamestown
Castle O'er Forest
Castle O'er
Waterhead
Sandyford
Newton
Annandale Water Services
Dinwoodie Mains
Boreland
Hart Fell
Eskdale
Georgefield
Bentpath
Ewes
Arkleton
Pike Fell
Roan Fell
Black Edge
Calkin Rig
Potholm
Langholm
Malcolm Monument
Sibbaldbie
Corrie Common
Millhousebridge
Applegarthtown
Lockerbie
Paddockhole
Bankshill
Kirtleton
Tinnisburn Forest
Caulside
Burnswark
Burnswark Hillfort
Birkshaw Forest
Castlemilk
Kettleholm
Middleshaw
Waterbeck
Middlebie
Kirkconnel Churchyard
Birrens Fort
Springkell
Ecclefechan
Thomas Carlyle's Birthplace
Eaglesfield
Hoddomcross
Dalton
Carrutherstown
Hoddom Mains
Kirtlebridge
Merkland Cross
Chapelknowe
Evertown
Milltown
Woodhouselees
Gilnockie Tower
Claygate
Rowanburn
Canonbie
Riddings
Catlowdy
Crossings
Haggbeck
Moat
Scots Dyke
Netherby
Easton
Stapleton
Kirkpatrick-Fleming
Newton
Creca
Brydekirk
Charlesfield
Ruthwell Cross
Hollee
Gretna Green Services
Old Blacksmiths Shop Centre
Gretna Green
Springfield
Gretna
Gretna Gateway
Rigg
Longtown
Boltonfellend
Kirkcambeck
Hethersgill
Kirklinton
West Hall
Annan
Duncan Savings Bank Museum
Cummertrees
Powfoot
Welldale
Shawhill
Dornock
Eastriggs
Browhouses
Bowness-on-Solway
Port Carlisle
Solway Coast
Sandysike
Westlinton
Smithfield
Scaleby Hill
Scaleby
Walton
Newtown
Lanercost
Lanercost Priory
Vallum
Banks
Low Row
Hadrian's Wall Path
Todhills
Todhills Rest Area
Blackford
Rockcliffe
Harker
Laversdale
Irthington
Brampton
Milton
Course of Hadrian's Wall
Walby Farm Park
Carlisle Airport
Glasson
Drumburgh
Bowness Common
Cardurnock
Anthorn
Easton
Drumburgh Moss
Burgh by Sands
Beaumont
Cargo
Kingstown
Houghton
Linstock
Low Crosby
Newby East
Hayton
Talkin Tarn
Farlam
Talkin
Hallbankgate
Tindale
Tindale Tarn
Tindale Fells
Forest Head
Halton Lea Gate
Midgeholme
Whitrigg
Boustead Hill
Kirkandrews upon Eden
Grinsdale
Edentown
Stanwix
Carlisle
Warwick on Eden
Warwick Bridge
Castle Carrock
Heads Nook
How
Faugh
Cold Fell
Glendue Fell
Skinburness
Kirkbride
Newton Arlosh
Fingland
Finglandrigg Woods
Thurstonfield
Moorhouse
Kirkbampton
Oughterby
Little Orton
Tullie House Museum & Gallery
Carlisle Castle
Botcherby
Scotby
Harraby
Wetheral
Great Corby
Wetheral Priory Gatehouse
Silloth
Calvo
Seaville
Causewayhead
Greenrow
Blitterlees
Kingside Hill
Wedholme Flow
South Solway Mosses
Little Bampton
Aikton
Great Orton
Newby West
Wiggonby
Baldwinholme
Upperby
Cummersdale
Carleton
Cumwhinton
Cumwhitton
Brisco
Durdar
Oulton
Cumrew
King's Forest of Geltsdale
Geltsdale Middle
Smasha Hill
Black Knowe Head
Caver's Hill
Fastheugh Hill
Dollar Law
Black Law
Broad Law
Lochcraig Head
The Wiss
Southern Upland Way
Dryhope Tower
Halliwell's House Museum
Sir Walter Scott's Courtroom
Bowhill House & Country Park
The Pike
Dumfries and Galloway

NT
NY
THE CHEVIOT HILLS
NORTHUMBERLAND NATIONAL PARK
KIELDER FOREST PARK
Northumber
Wauchope Forest
Redesdale Forest
Kielder Forest
Wark Forest
Harwood Forest
Kidland Forest
Leithope Forest
Spadeadam Forest
Slaley Forest
REDESDALE
ROTHBURY FOREST
KIELDER WATER
Jedburgh
Wooler
Rothbury
Bellingham
Otterburn
Haltwhistle
Hexham
Corbridge
Haydon Bridge
Prudhoe
Shotley Bridge
Allendale Town
Kelso
Ancrum
Bonjedward
Crailing
Oxnam
Camptown
Byrness
Catcleugh
Rochester
Redesdale Camp
Elsdon
Alwinton
Harbottle
Kielder
Falstone
Greenhaugh
Wark
Simonburn
Chollerford
Humshaugh
Gilsland
Greenhead
Bardon Mill
Alnham
Ingram
Powburn
Whittingham
Hepple
Thropton
Great Tosson
Cambo
Kirkwhelpington
Ridsdale
West Woodburn
Birtley
Stonehaugh
Whitfield
Catton
Dilston
Riding Mill
Slaley
A68
A697
A696
A69
A6088
A698
61
70
71
57
HADRIAN'S WALL PATH
PENNINE WAY
COURSE OF HADRIAN'S WALL
THE CHEVIOT
815
0 1 2 3 4 5 6 miles
0 1 2 3 4 5 6 7 8 9 10km

NORTHUMBERLAND COAST
NU
NZ
Beadnell Bay
High Newton-by-the-Sea
Low Newton-by-the-Sea
Embleton Bay
Embleton
Dunstan Steads
Castle Point
DUNSTANBURGH CASTLE
Craster
Dunstan
Howick
Howick Haven
Longhoughton
Boulmer
Boulmer Haven
Alnwick
Alnmouth
Alnmouth Bay
Warkworth
Amble
Coquet I.
Hauxley
Radcliffe
DRUIDGE BAY
ENGLAND COAST PATH
Druridge Bay
Widdrington
The Scars
Cresswell
Lynemouth
Beacon Pt.
Ashington
Newbiggin-by-the-Sea
Morpeth
Bedlington
BLYTH
Cambois
Seaton Sluice
ST MARY'S LIGHTHOUSE
St Mary's or Bait I.
Cramlington
Seaton Delaval
WHITLEY BAY
AMSTERDAM
Cullercoats
BLUE REEF AQUARIUM
TYNEMOUTH CASTLE & PRIORY
Tynemouth
South Shields
Tyne Tunnel
NEWCASTLE UPON TYNE
Gateshead
WALLSEND
Jarrow
Hebburn
Marsden Bay
SOUTER LIGHTHOUSE
Whitburn Colliery
Whitburn
Gosforth
Longbenton
Ponteland
BLAYDON
Whickham
Felling
Boldon
WASHINGTON
Sunderland
Ryhope
STANLEY
CHESTER-LE-STREET
Tyne and Wear
Northumberland
A1
A189
A1068
A19
A697
A696
A69
A194(M)
58
71
A
B
C
D
E
F
G
H
7
8
9
10
11
12

ISLAY
RHINNS OF ISLAY
JURA
Argyll
NR
NORTH CHANNEL
SOUND OF ISLAY
LOCH INDAAL
LAGGAN BAY
THE OA
JURA FOREST
Rubha Bholsa
Rubha a'Mhail
COLONSAY
Nave Island
Ardnave Pt.
Ardnave
Carraig Bhan
An Clachan
Sanaigmore
Gortantaoid
Killinallan
Loch Gruinart
Bunnahabhain
BUNNAHABHAIN DISTILLERY
364 SGARBH BREAC
316
Loch an Aircill
785
755
PAPS OF JURA
Loch a Chnuic Bhric
Corran
Leargybreck
Gleann Astaile
561
Loch
72
Caol Ila
CAOL ILA DISTILLERY
Port Askaig
Feolin Ferry
FINLAGGAN CENTRE
Keills
Loch Finlaggan
Loch Ballygrant
Ballygrant
Kilmeny
Leckgruinart
Braigo
Ballinaby
Carnduncan
LOCH GRUINART NATURE RESERVE VISITORS CENTRE
Aoradh
Craigens
Loch Cam
Saligo Bay
Loch Gorm
Coul Pt.
Coull
Sunderland
Machir Bay
Kilchoman
Blackrock
Redhouses
Sorn
Daill
267 BEINN DUBH
Bridgend
Conisby
Bruichladdich
Keils
Craighouse
ISLE OF JURA DISTILLERY
Gleann Ullibh
342 BRAT BHEINN
Cabrach
Sm
Am Fraoch Eilean
Brosdale I.
Rubha na Tràil
McArthur's Hd.
Kilchiaran
Kilchiaran Bay
Tormisdale
ISLAY LIFE MUSEUM
ISLAY
Port Charlotte
Bowmore
BOWMORE ROUND CHURCH
Mulindry
Kilennan
232
Lossit
Lossit Pt.
Nerabus
Laggan
Laggan Pt.
471 BEINN BHAN
491 BEINN BHEIGEIR
Carraig Mhór
Ardtalla
Duich
Loch Beinn Uraraidh
Claggain Bay
Rubha na Faing
Portnahaven
Port Wemyss
Orsay
Rinns Pt.
Glenegedale
Kintour
Ardmore Pt.
KILDALTON CHURCH AND CROSSES
Eilean Craobhach
Eilean a'Chuirn
347 BEINN SHOLUM
Port Alsaig
Rubha Mòr
Kintra
Leorin
Eilean Bhride
ARDBEG DISTILLERY
Cornabus
Imeraval
Port Ellen
Lagavulin
Ardbeg
Eilean Imersay
Lower Cragabus
LAGAVULIN DISTILLERY
Laphroaig
LAPHROAIG DISTILLERY
Texa
Dùn Mór Ghil
152
Risabus
Lower Killeyan
Inerval
AMERICAN MONUMENT
Mull of Oa
202
Rubha nan Leacan
BALLYCASTLE
Rathlin Island
A847
A846
B8018
B8017
B8016
0 1 2 3 4 5 6 miles
0 1 2 3 4 5 6 7 8 9 10 km

Argyll and Bute
KNAPDALE
KINTYRE
ISLE OF ARRAN
NORTH ARRAN
ISLAND OF BUTE
KYLES OF BUTE
NS
SOUND OF BUTE
KILBRANNAN SOUND
SOUND OF GIGHA
Lagg
Loch Lesgamaill
Island of Danna
Lochead
Achahoish
St Columba's Cave
Eilean Mòr
St Cormac's Chapel
Kilmory
Kilmory Bay
Ellary
Clachbreck
Baile Boidheach
An Dùnan
Knockrome
Lowlandman's Bay
Pt. of Knap
Ormsary
Loch Caolisport
Druimdrishaig
Loch nan Torran
Miller's Bay
Cretshengan
Cruach Lagain
Coulaghailtro
Kilberry Hd.
Kilberry
Sculptured Stones
Carse Ho.
Dunmore
Loch Stornoway
Ardpatrick
Ardpatrick Ho.
Ardpatrick Pt.
Portachoillan
Eilean Traighe
Ronachan Pt.
Clachan
Loch Ciaran
Kilchamaig
Torinturk
Dun
Rhu
West Loch Tarbert
Erines
Stob Odhar
Loch Chaorain
Barfad
Tarbert
West Tarbert
East Loch Tarbert
Corranbuie
Kennacraig
Redhouse
Whitehouse
Gartnagrenach
Cnoc a'Bhaileshios
Glenreasdell Mains
Skipness
Skipness Castle
Skipness Pt.
Skipness Bay
Claonaig
Claonaig Bay
Cruach Nam Fiadh
Rubha Leathan
Kilfinan Bay
Kilfinan
Drum
Melldalloch
Auchalick Bay
Ardmarnock Bay
Barmore I.
Glenan Bay
Portavadie
Asgog Loch
Asgog Bay
Kilbride Bay
Ardlamont Ho.
Ardlamont Pt.
Auchenlochan
Kames
Millhouse
Blair's Ferry
Tighnabruaich
Port Driseach
Kyles of Bute
Beinn Bhreac
Ardentraive
Colintraive
Algaltraig
Loch Striven
Glen More
Windy Hill
Port Lamont
Ardyne Pt.
Kames B.
St Colmac
Port Bannatyne
Rothesay
Rothesay Castle
Rothesay Bay
Ettrick Bay
Straad
Loch Fad
Inchmarnock
Scalpsie
Loch Quien
Scalpsie Bay
Ardscalpsie Pt.
Stravanan Bay
Garroch Hd.
Eilean Garbh
West Tarbert Bay
East Tarbert Bay
Tarbert
Gigha Island
Druimyeon More
Ardminish
Ardminish Bay
Achamore Gardens
Gigalum Island
Cara Island
Balochroy
Crossaig Glen
Crossaig
Loch Garasdale
Cruach Mhic Gougan
Rhunahaorine
Cour Bay
Cour
Beinn Bhreac
Tayinloan
Cnoc nan Craobh
Killean
Beacharr
Cruach Mhic-an t-Saoir
Cruach nan Gabhar
Carradale Water
Grogport
Brackley
Clachaig Water
Muasdale
Carradale
Port Righ
Glenacardoch Pt.
Amod
Belloch
Barr Water
Glenbarr
Clan Macalister Centre
Bridgend
Torrisdale-Square
Beinn an Tuirc
Carradale Pt.
Carradale Bay
Cleongart
Saddell Glen
Saddell
Saddell Abbey
A'Chruach
Saddell Bay
Bellochantuy Bay
Bellochantuy
Killocraw
Lussa Loch
Tangy Loch
Sgreadan Hill
Ugadale
Westport
Skeroblingarry
Black Bay
Kilchenzie
Glenlussa Water
Peninver
Ardnacross Bay
West Darlochan
Kilmichael
Low Smerby
Machrihanish Bay
Campbeltown
Machrihanish
Trodigal
Campbeltown Heritage Centre
Campbeltown Loch
Island Davaar
Davaar Island Cave Painting
Drumlemble
Stewarton
Campbeltown Buckhouse
Kilkerran
Kildalloig
Knocknaha
Beinn Ghuilean
Achinhoan Hd.
Eararale Pt.
The Slate
Woodbank
Cnoc Moy
Feochaig
Rubh'a' Mharaiche
Glen Breackerie
Cnoc Odhar
Conie Glen
Johnston's Pt.
North Carrine
Kepigan
Strone Glen
Machariocn
Polliwilline Bay
Southend
Carskiey
Brunerican Bay
Cove Pt.
Port Mean
Mull of Kintyre
Rubha Chlachan
Sheep I.
Sanda Island
Ardrossan (May-Sept) Brodick (May-Sept, Sat only)
Ballycastle
(April-Oct)
(Oct-Mar)
Cock of Arran
Loch Ranza
Lochranza Castle
Lochranza
Millstone Pt.
Catacol Bay
Catacol
Isle of Arran Distillery
Meall nan Damh
Thundergay
Sannox
Sannox Bay
Glen Sannox
Loch Tanna
Pirnmill
Cìr Mhòr
Whitefarland
Beinn Bharrain
Beinn Tarsuinn
Goat Fell
Corrie
Imachar
Glen Iorsa
Glen Rosa
Brodick Castle
Dougarie
Ardrossan Campbeltown (May-Sept Sat only)
Machrie Water
Isle of Arran Heritage Museum
Brodick Bay
Brodick
Strathwhillan
Auchagallon
Glenloig
A'Chruach
Glen Cloy
Machrie Bay
Machrie Moor Standing Stones
Tormore
Clauchlands Pt.
King's Cave
Balmichael
Blairbeg
Margnaheglish
Lamlash
Lamlash Bay
Holy Island
Drumadoon Pt.
Torbeg
Shiskine
Cordon
Blackwaterfoot
Drumadoon Bay
Kilpatrick
Kilpatrick Dun
Tighvein
Auchencairn
Kingscross Pt.
Kingscross
Sliddery Water
Knockenkelly
Whiting Bay
North Kiscadale
South Kiscadale
Glenree
Largymore
Brown Hd.
Carn Ban
Corriecravie
Glenashdale Falls
Kilmory Water
Largybeg
Sliddery
Lagg
Levencorroch
Dippin
Dippin Head
Torrylinn Cairn
Kilmory
Bennan
Bennan Hd.
Kildonan
Sound of Pladda
Pladda
A83
A841
A844
A886
A8003
B8000
B8024
B8001
B842
B843
B880
B875
B878
B881
72
66
6
7
8
9
10
11
A
B
C
D
E
F
G
H

SOUND OF BUTE
Inchmarnock
Ardscalpsie Pt.
Great Cumbrae Island
Millport
Fairlie
Kilbirnie
Beith
Glenreasdell Mains
Skipness
SKIPNESS CASTLE
Skipness Pt.
Skipness Bay
Claonaig
Claonaig Bay
TARBERT (Oct-Mar)
(April-Oct)
CRUACH NAM FIADH
Crossaig Glen
Crossaig
Cock of Arran
LOCHRANZA CASTLE
Lochranza
Loch Ranza
Catacol
Catacol Bay
ISLE OF ARRAN DISTILLERY
Millstone Pt.
Garroch Hd.
Little Cumbrae Island
Portencross
Farland Hd.
West Kilbride
Seamill
Cour Bay
Cour
Grogport
Whitefarland
Pirnmill
Thundergay
MEALL NAN DAMH
North Ayrshire
NORTH
Loch Tanna
CIR MHÒR
BEINN BHARRAIN
BEINN TARSUINN
GOAT FELL
Glen Sannox
Sannox
Sannox Bay
Corrie
Imachar
ISLE OF ARRAN
Glen Rosa
BRODICK CASTLE
Glen Iorsa
Carradale
Port Righ
Carradale Pt.
Carradale Bay
Dougarie
Machrie Water
ISLE OF ARRAN HERITAGE MUSEUM
Brodick
Brodick Bay
Strathwhillan
Auchagallon
Glenloig
A'CHRUACH
Glen Cloy
Machrie Bay
Clauchlands Pt.
Tormore
MACHRIE MOOR STANDING STONES
Balmichael
KING'S CAVE
Blairbeg
Margnaheglish
Lamlash
Lamlash Bay
Cordon
Holy Island
CAMPBELTOWN (May-Sept)
CAMPBELTOWN (May-Sept) Sat only
Torbeg
Shiskine
Drumadoon Pt.
Blackwaterfoot
Drumadoon Bay
Kilpatrick
KILPATRICK DUN
Kingscross Pt.
Kingscross
Auchencairn
TIGHVEIN
Knockenkelly
Sliddery Water
Whiting Bay
North Kiscadale
South Kiscadale
Largymore
GLENASHDALE FALLS
Glenree
Brown Hd.
CARN BAN
Corriecravie
Kilmory Water
Largybeg
Dippin
Dippin Head
Sliddery
Lagg
Levencorroch
Kilmory
Bennan
Bennan Hd.
Kildonan
Sound of Pladda
Pladda
TORRYLINN CAIRN
KILBRANNAN SOUND
FIRTH OF CLYDE
NR
NW
Lady Isle
Horse Isle
Ardrossan
NORTH AYRSHIRE MUSEUM
Saltcoats
Stevenston
Kilwinning
Dalry
Irvine
SCOTTISH MARITIME MUSEUM
Irvine Bay
Troon
North Bay
South Bay
Barassie
Prestwick
Ayr
Heads of Ayr
Doonfoot
Alloway
Dunure
ELECTRIC BRAE
Culzean Bay
CULZEAN CASTLE
Maidenhead Bay
Maidens
Kirkoswald
Maybole
Turnberry
Turnberry Bay
Brest Rocks
Ailsa Craig
Girvan
Woodland Bay
Kennedy's Pass
Lendalfoot
CARLETON CASTLE
Bennane Hd.
Ballantrae Bay
Ballantrae
Pinwherry
Barr
Dailly
Old Dailly
Pinmore
Colmonell
Knockdolian
Ballochmorrie
Barrhill
Changue Forest
0 1 2 3 4 5 6 miles
0 1 2 3 4 5 6 7 8 9 10 km

East Renfrewshire
South Lanarkshire
East Ayrshire
Ayrshire
Dumfries and Galloway
Galloway Forest Park
The Glenkens
Rhinns of Kells
Lowther Hills
Nithsdale
Clydesdale
Barrhead
Neilston
Newton Mearns
Eaglesham
East Kilbride
Hamilton
Motherwell
Wishaw
Bothwell
Larkhall
Stonehouse
Strathaven
Carluke
Lanark
Lesmahagow
Coalburn
Douglas
Stewarton
Kilmarnock
Kilmaurs
Galston
Newmilns
Darvel
Hurlford
Riccarton
Dreghorn
Tarbolton
Mauchline
Catrine
Sorn
Muirkirk
Auchinleck
Cumnock
Drongan
Dalrymple
Patna
Dalmellington
New Cumnock
Kirkconnel
Sanquhar
Wanlockhead
Carsphairn
Moniaive
Thornhill
St John's Town of Dalry
Carrick Forest
Dalmacallan Forest
Carsphairn Forest
Dundeugh Forest
Tairlaw Forest
Loch Doon
Glengavel Reservoir
Afton Reservoir
Loch Spallander Reservoir
NS
NX

LOCH LOMOND AND THE TROSSACHS NATIONAL PARK
West Dunbartonshire
East Dunbartonshire
Inverclyde
Renfrewshire
East Renfrewshire
North Lanarkshire
South Lanarkshire
East Ayrshire
CLYDE MUIRSHIEL REGIONAL PARK
CUNNINGHAME
CAMPSIE FELLS
KILPATRICK HILLS
Glasgow
GLASGOW
Helensburgh
ALEXANDRIA
DUMBARTON
Greenock
PORT GLASGOW
Erskine Bridge
CLYDEBANK
BEARSDEN
Milngavie
RENFREW
Paisley
JOHNSTONE
Bridge of Weir
Kilmacolm
Lochwinnoch
Kilbirnie
Beith
Barrhead
Neilston
Newton Mearns
Rutherglen
Cambuslang
East Kilbride
Uddingston
Bothwell
HAMILTON
MOTHERWELL
WISHAW
Larkhall
Strathaven
COATBRIDGE
AIRDRIE
KIRKINTILLOCH
Kilsyth
CUMBERNAULD
Bishopbriggs
Lennoxtown
Strathblane
Killearn
Drymen
Balmaha
Luss
Arden
Aberfoyle
Gartmore
Buchlyvie
Kippen
Fintry
Balfron
Stewarton
Kilmarnock
Kilmaurs
Fenwick
Galston
Newmilns
Darvel
Irvine
Kilwinning
Stevenston
Dreghorn
Troon
Prestwick
Monkton
Tarbolton
Mauchline
Catrine
Auchinleck
Eaglesham
Dalry
Flow Moss
Whitelee Forest
Irvine Bay
Lady Isle
M8
M73
M74
M77
M80
M898
A82
A8
A737
A71
A77
A76
A726
A725
73
75
67

Clackmannanshire
Fife
Falkirk
West Lothian
Midlothian
Edinburgh
Scottish Borders
FIRTH OF FORTH
Stirling
ALLOA
Tillicoultry
Dollar
Menstrie
Alva
Tullibody
Cambus
Clackmannan
Bannockburn
Kincardine
Kincardine Bridge
Culross
Stenhousemuir
DENNY
Larbert
GRANGEMOUTH
FALKIRK
Bonnybridge
Polmont
Bo'ness
Linlithgow
Kirkcaldy
Kinghorn
Burntisland
Cowdenbeath
Lochgelly
Kelty
Lochore
Cardenden
DUNFERMLINE
Rosyth
Inverkeithing
Dalgety Bay
Aberdour
North Queensferry
Queensferry
Queensferry Crossing
Kirkliston
Winchburgh
Broxburn
Uphall
Bathgate
Armadale
LIVINGSTON
Whitburn
Blackburn
West Calder
Mid Calder
East Calder
Currie
Balerno
EDINBURGH
Leith
Musselburgh
Dalkeith
Loanhead
Penicuik
Roslin
Bonnyrigg and Lasswade
Shotts
Harthill
Fauldhouse
Carluke
Lanark
Forth
Carnwath
Biggar
Symington
Douglas
Abington
Crawford
Peebles
West Linton
Carlops
Leadburn
Eddleston
Stobo
Broughton
Tweedsmuir
PENTLAND HILLS REGIONAL PARK
TINTO HILLS
UPPER TWEEDDALE
MOORFOOT HILLS
Inchkeith
Inchcolm
Inchmickery
Cramond I.

Buckhaven
East Wemyss
Coaltown of Wemyss
West Wemyss
Dysart
Kirkcaldy
Linktown
Kinghorn
Pettycur
Inchkeith
Isle of May
FIRTH OF FORTH
Fidra
Craigleith
Bass Rock
Eyebroughy
North Berwick
Tantallon Castle
Auldhame
Scoughall
Dirleton
Gullane
Gullane Bay
Aberlady Bay
Aberlady
Kingston
Whitekirk
St. Baldred's Cradle
Tyne Mouth
Dunbar
Belhaven
West Barns
Tyninghame
East Linton
Preston
Drem
Athelstaneford
Ballencrieff
Craigielaw
Gosford Bay
Spittal
Longniddry
Cockenzie and Port Seton
Prestonpans
Musselburgh
Edinburgh
Leith
Portobello
Joppa
Haddington
Gladsmuir
Tranent
Macmerry
Penston
Elphinstone
Samuelston
Bolton
Traprain
Pitcox
Stenton
Spott
Broxburn
Barns Ness
East Barns
Skateraw
Thorntonloch
Innerwick
Reed Pt.
Cove
Cockburnspath
Oldhamstocks
Dunbar Common
Garvald
Pappl
Halls
East Lothian
Dalkeith
Bonnyrigg and Lasswade
Newtongrange
Gorebridge
Loanhead
Roslin
Pathhead
Crichton
Humbie
Fala
Fala Moor
Gifford
Danskine
Longyester
Long Newton
Stobshiel
Blegbie
Lammermuir Hills
Whiteadder Reservoir
Hopes Reservoir
Cranshaws
Ellemford
Abbey St. Bathans
Midlothian
Temple
Middleton
Heriot
Moorfoot Hills
Gilston
Hillhouse
Kirktonhill
Oxton
Addinston
Longformacus
Watch Water Reservoir
Duns
Preston
Clockmill
Cheeklaw
Gavinton
Choicelee
Polwarth
Wedderlie
Westruther
Lauder
Thirlestane
Houndslow
Greenlaw
Fogo
Sisterpath
Bogend
Halliburton
Leitholm
Eccles
Gordon
Legerwood
Stow
Torquhan
Fountainhall
Killochyett
Bow
Caitha Bowland
Galashiels
Earlston
Langshaw
Peebles
Innerleithen
Walkerburn
Traquair
Cardrona
Tweed Valley Forest Park
Elibank and Traquair Forest
Yair Hill Forest
Minch Moor
Melrose
Newstead
Darnick
Gattonside
Clovenfords
Caddonfoot
Boleside
Lindean
Selkirk
Philiphaugh
Bowhill
Yarrow
Ettrickbridge
St. Boswells
Newtown St. Boswells
Dryburgh
Bemersyde
Clintmains
Smailholm
Kelso
Maxwellheugh
Sprouston
Hadden
Kerchesters
Roxburgh
Rutherford
Maxton
Muirhouselaw
Nisbet
Eckford
Kalemouth
Crailing
Ancrum
Bonjedward
Jedburgh
Lilliesleaf
Midlem
Belses
Bloomfield
Chesters
Ashkirk
Woll
Morebattle
Cessford
Linton
Frogden
Heiton
Scottish Borders
0 1 2 3 4 5 6 miles
0 1 2 3 4 5 6 7 8 9 10 km

NORTH SEA
NU
NORTHUMBERLAND COAST
Siccar Pt.
Wheat Stack
FAST CASTLE
ST ABB'S HEAD
St. Abb's Head
Lumsdaine
Coldingham Moor
Northfield
St Abbs
St. Abb's Haven
Coldingham Bay
Grantshouse
Huxton
Coldingham
COLDINGHAM PRIORY
Houndwood
Cairncross
EYEMOUTH MUSEUM
Eyemouth
Auchencrow
Reston
AYTON CASTLE
Ayton
Burnmouth
Prenderguest
Lamberton Beach
Lintlaw
Lamberton
Chirnside
Chirnsidebridge
Edrom
Foulden
Clappers
FOULDEN TITHE BARN
Whiteadder Water
Buxley
MANDERSTON
Allanton
Hutton
Highfields
Berwick-upon-Tweed
BERWICK-UPON-TWEED BARRACKS & MAIN GUARD
Blackadder West
Paxton
PAXTON HOUSE
East Ord
Tweedmouth
Spittal
Sinclair's Hill
Whitsome
Fishwick
UNION SUSPENSION BRIDGE
Loanend
Redshin Cove
Horndean
Horncliffe
Thornton Park
NORHAM CASTLE
Murton
Thornton
Scremerston
Ladykirk
Swinton
SWINTON KIRK
Swintonmill
Simprim
Norham
West Allerdean
Cheswick
Shoreswood
Shoresdean
Goswick
Grindon
Ancroft
Haggerston
Felkington
Berrington
LINDISFARNE
Emmanuel Hd.
Holy Island (Lindisfarne)
LINDISFARNE CASTLE
Castle Pt.
Shellacres
Beal
Causeway
Holy Island Sands
Holy Island
LINDISFARNE PRIORY
HERITAGE CENTRE
Fenham
Castle Heaton
Duddo
Bowsden
Guile Pt.
Lennel
Coldstream
HIRSEL
Cornhill-on-Tweed
HEATHERSLAW LIGHT-RAILWAY
ERROL HUT SMITHY AND WOOD WORKSHOP
HEATHERSLAW CORNMILL
Etal
Barmoor Castle
Barmoor Lane End
Lowick
West Kyloe
East Kyloe
Fenwick
Kyloe Hills
Buckton
Farne Islands
Staple Sound
FARNE ISLANDS
Inner Sound
Carham
Wark
West Learmouth
East Learmouth
Crookham
Branxton
LADY WATERFORD HALL
Ford
Elwick
Ross
Budle Bay
BAMBURGH CASTLE
Bamburgh
Budle
Pressen
Holefield
Flodden
Kimmerston
Holburn
Detchant
Middleton
Hetton Steads
North Hazelrigg
Belford
Easington
Waren Mill
Glororum
Burton
Downham
Howtel
Milfield
Fenton Town
Nesbit
Spindlestone
Bradford
Mousen
Seahouses
Mindrum
Hoselaw
Pawston
Kilham
Doddington
South Hazelrigg
West Horton
East Horton
Bellshill
Adderstone
ADDERSTONE
Elford
North Sunderland
Shotton
Westnewton
Lanton
Coupland
Newtown
Weetwood Hall
Warenton
Lucker
Newham Hall
Swinhoe
Beadnell
Kirknewton
Akeld
Chatton
Greendikes
Warenford
Newham
Fleetham
Benthall
Beadnell Bay
KIRK YETHOLM
Town Yetholm
Kirk Yetholm
Hethpool
Humbleton
Wooler
WOOLER
Earle
Middleton Hall
Haugh Head
CHILLINGHAM CASTLE
Chillingham
WILD CATTLE OF CHILLINGHAM
Rosebrough
Newstead
Chathill
Ellingham
Preston
High Newton-by-the-Sea
PRESTON TOWER
Brunton
Low Newton-by-the-Sea
Embleton Bay
PENNINE WAY
COLD LAW
North Middleton
Lilburn Tower
East Lilburn
Hepburn
Brownyside
North Charlton
Christon Bank
Embleton
Dunstan Steads
Castle Point
DUNSTANBURGH CASTLE
Cliftoncote
South Middleton
Ilderton
Roseden
Old Bewick
MOUNTHOOLEY
THE SCHIL
Mowhaugh
Langleeford
West Ditchburn
South
Roddam
College Burn
Bowmont Water
Leet Water
Eye Water
Ale Water
Tweed
Glen
North Low
South Low
DEVIL'S CAUSEWAY
A1
A1107
A6105
A6112
A697
A698
B6355
B6437
B6438
B6460
B6461
B6470
B6351
B6352
B6353
B6354
B6525
B6348
B6349
B6347
B1340
B1341
B1342
B1339
62
63
7
8
9
10
11
12
A
B
C
D
E
F
G
H

ARDMEANACH
Aird of Kinloch
Kilfinichen Bay
MACLEAN'S CROSS
Eilean Annraidh
IONA ABBEY AND CATHEDRAL
IONA HERITAGE CENTRE
ST COLUMBA EXHIBITION & WELCOME CENTRE
Rubha nan Cearc
Kintra
Baile Mor
Iona
Fionnphort
Aridhglas
Fidden
Tiraghoil
Eorabus
Bunessan
Lee
Loch Assapol
THE BURG
LOCH SCRIDAIN
Pennycross
Torrans
BROLASS
CRUACHAN MIN
Leidle
Carsaig
Carsaig Bay
CARSAIG ARCHES
Malcolm's Pt.
Erraid
ROSS OF MULL
Ardalanish
Uisken
Ardchiavaig
Scoor
Rubha nam Braithrean
Eilean a'Chalmain
Rubh Ardalanish
Torran Rocks
Loch Fuaron
BEN BUIE
BEINN NA CROISE
Lochbuie
Loch Buie
Rubha Dubh
Loch Airdeglais
CREACH BEINN
Kinlochspelve
Loch Spelve
Barachandroman
Loch Uisg
Laggan Deer Forest
DRUIM FADA
LORD LOVAT'S CAVE
Frank Lockwood's Island
Croggan
Rubha nan Sailthean
Ardmore
Bach I.
Rubha Seanach
FIRTH OF LORN
Insh I.
Sound of Insh
Clachan-Seil
Clachan
CLACHAN BRIDGE
Seil
AN CALA GARDENS
Easdale
EASDALE ISLAND FOLK MUSEUM
Balvicar
Dubh-fheith
Cuan
Cullipool
Torsa
Kilchoan
Luing
Achafolla
ARDUAINE GARDEN
Arduaine
Sound of Luing
Toberonochy
Shuna Sound
Craobh Haven
Shuna
Lunga
Shuna Pt.
Rubha Aird Luing
NM
Garbh Eileach
Garvellachs
SCARBA, LUNGA AND THE GARVELLACHS
Eilean Dubh Mor
Eileach an Naoimh
CRUACH SCARBA
Scarba
Gulf of Corryvreckan
OBAN
Aird
Rèisa an t-Sruith
Craignish Pt.
Island Macaskin
Loch Craignish
Rubh'a'Geadha
Balnahard
Kiloran Bay
KILORAN GARDENS
Kiloran
Kilchattan
COLONSAY
Scalasaig
Loch Staosnaig
Garvard
Rubha Dubh
PRIORY
Dubh Eilean
Oronsay
Eilean nan Ron
Kinuachdrachd
Kinuachdrachd Harbour
CRUACH NA SEILCHEIG
Glengarrisdale Bay
Glendebadel Bay
BEN GARRISDALE
Loch Crinan
Crinan
Kilmahumaig
Bellanoch
Corpach Bay
BEINN BHREAC
Lealt
Gleann Aoistail
Ardlussa
Ardlussa Bay
Inverlussa
Lussagiven
Shian Bay
RAINBERG MOR
Loch Righ Mòr
Gallachoille
KNAPD
Carsaig
Tayvallich
Achanamara
Kilmichael of Inverlussa
Barrahormid
TAYNISH
Taynish
Loch Sween
CRUACH LUSACH
Dunrostan
Rubh'an t-Sàilein
Loch Tarbert
Tarbert
KEILLS CHAPEL
Keillmore
New Ulva
Island of Danna
CASTLE SWEEN
Lochead
ST COLUMBA'S CAVE
Achahoish
Rubha Lang-aoinidh
Rubha a'Mhail
Rubha Bholsa
Lagg
Loch Lesgamaill
Loch an Aircill
SGARBH BREAC
Nave Island
Ardnave Pt.
JURA
PAPS OF JURA
Loch a Chnuic Bhric
Corran
JURA FOREST
An Dùnan
Knockrome
Lowlandman's Bay
Leargybreck
Gleann Astaile
Loch na Mile
Eilean Môr
ST CORMAC'S CHAPEL
CHAPEL
Kilmory
Kilmory Bay
Ellary
Clachbreck
Baile Boidheach
Ormsary
Pt. of Knap
Loch Caolisport
Druimdrishaig
Ardnave
Gortantaoid
Bunnahabhain
BUNNAHABHAIN DISTILLERY
Killinallan
Caol Ila
CAOL ILA DISTILLERY
Port Askaig
Feolin Ferry
FINLAGGAN CENTRE
Loch Finlaggan
Keills
Loch Gruinart
LOCH GRUINART NATURE RESERVE VISITORS CENTRE
Leckgruinart
Aoradh
Craigens
Loch Cam
Ballygrant
Loch Ballygrant
Kilmeny
Gleann Ullibh
Craighouse
ISLE OF JURA DISTILLERY
Small Isles
BRAT BHEINN
Cabrach
Miller's Bay
Cretshengan
CRUACH LAGAIN
Coulaghailtro
Loch nan Torran
Kilberry Hd.
SCULPTURED STONES
Kilberry
ISLAY
NR
Blackrock
Redhouses
Bridgend
Daill
BEINN DUBH
Rubha na Tràille
Brosdale I.
Am Fraoch Eilean
SOUND OF JURA
SOUND OF ISLAY
Carse Ho.
Dunmore
Loch Stornoway
Ardpatrick
Gartnagrenach
Ardpatrick Ho.
Bowmore
BOWMORE ROUND CHURCH
Mulindry
Port Charlotte
Kilennan
McArthur's Hd.
LOCH INDAAL
Laggan
Laggan Pt.
Duich
BEINN BHAN
BEINN BHEIGEIR
Carraig Mhór
Ardtalla
Ardpatrick Pt.
Eilean Traighe
Portachoillan
WEST LOCH
Ronachan Pt.
Clachan
Loch Beinn Uraraidh
Claggain Bay
Eilean Garbh
West Tarbert Bay
PORT ELLEN
Gigha Island
East Tarbert Bay
Tarbert
Balochroy
Loch Ciaran
Loch Garasdale
Ardmore Pt.
0 1 2 3 4 5 6 miles
0 1 2 3 4 5 6 7 8 9 10 km
78
79
64
65

Argyll and Bute
Oban
Kilmore
Glen Lonan
Glenamachrie
Gallanach
Kilbride
Barran
Am Buth
Glen Feochan
Loch Feochan
Kilninver
Musdale
Barochreal
Glen Euchar
Bragleenmore
Loch Scamadale
Braes of Lorn
Blaran
Loch Tralaig
Melfort
Ardanstur
Kilmelford
Glenmore
Kames
Lagalochan
Garraron
Barravullin
Kintraw
Ardfern
Arichamish
Torran
Ford
Ederline
Finchairn
Finchairn Castle
Carnassarie Castle
Eilean Righ
Kilmartin
Kilmartin House Museum
Glebe Cairn
Slockavullin
Poltalloch
Kilmichael Glassary
Bridgend
Moine Mhor
Dunadd Fort
Cairnbaan
Lochgair
Asknish
Lochgilphead
Ardrishaig
Kilmory Castle Gardens
Kilmory Woodland Park
Carrick
Port Ann
Achnaba
Otter Ferry
Castleton
Eilean Mòr
Ballimore
Auchnaha
Achabraid
Inverneill
Kilfinan Bay
Kilfinan
Drum
Melldalloch
Erines
Auchalick Bay
Ardmarnock Bay
Barmore I.
Tarbert
West Tarbert
Barfad
East Loch Tarbert
Glenan Bay
Portavadie
Blair's Ferry
Millhouse
Kames
Auchenlochan
Tighnabruaich
Port Driseach
Kyles of Bute
Asgog Bay
Kilbride Bay
Ardlamont Ho.
Ardlamont Pt.
Rubha Leathan
Corranbuie
Rhu
Kennacraig
Redhouse
Whitehouse
Kilchamaig
Torinturk
Glenreasdell Mains
Skipness
Skipness Castle
Skipness Pt.
Skipness Bay
Claonaig
Claonaig Bay
Crossaig Glen
Crossaig
Cock of Arran
Loch Ranza
Sound of Bute
Inchmarnock
Ardscalpsie Pt.
Scalpsie Bay
Stravanan Bay
Kingarth
Kilchattan Bay
St Blane's Chapel
Garroch Hd.
Little Cumbrae Island
Great Cumbrae Island
Millport
Island of Bute
Rothesay
Rothesay Castle
Port Bannatyne
Ardyne Pt.
Kames B.
St Colmac
Ettrick Bay
Straad
Ascog
Montford
Craigmore
Ardencraig Gardens
Victorian Fernery
Kerrycroy
Scoulag
Mount Stuart House and Garden
Loch Fad
Loch Quien
Toward
Toward Pt.
Port Lamont
Newton Park
Innellan
Wemyss Bay
Skelmorlie
Upper Skelmorlie
Meigle
Routenburn
Largs
Largs Bay
Tomont End
Fairlie
Kilbirnie
Beith
Lochwinnoch
Inverclyde
Clyde-Muirshiel Regional Park
Gourock
Greenock
Port Glasgow
Inverkip
Dunoon
Kirn
Hunter's Quay
Sandbank
Holy Loch
Ardnadam
Kilmun
Strone
Strone Pt.
Kilcreggan
Rosneath
Rhu
Helensburgh
Craigendoran
Cardross
Garelochhead
Whistlefield
Portincaple
Loch Long
Loch Goil
Lochgoilhead
Carrick Castle
Ardgoil Forest
Arrochar
Tarbet
Succoth
Ardgartan
Glen Croe
Rest and Be Thankful
Glen Kinglas
Cairndow
Clachan
Ardno
St Catherine's
Inveraray
Inveraray Castle
Inveraray Jail
Newtown
Dalchenna
Auchindrain
Creggans
Strachur
Furnace
Glen Sluain
Newton
Crarae
Minard
Tullochgorm
Lephinmore
Lephinchapel
Strathlachlan Forest
Lachlan Castle
Dunans
Glendaruel Forest
Clachan of Glendaruel
Glenbranter
Loch Eck
Whistlefield
Benmore
Benmore Botanic Garden
Glenfinart
Ardentinny
Argyll Forest Park
Loch Lomond and The Trossachs National Park
Loch Awe
Loch Fyne
Loch Striven
Portonnisherrich
Eredine
Eredine Forest
Inverliever Forest
Kilmaha
Durran
Dalavich
Kilmun
Lochavich Ho
Drissaig
Inverinan
Ballimeanoch
Blarghour
Portsonachan
South Port
North Port
Annat
Kilchrenan
Ardanaiseig
Innis Chonain
Lochawe
Kilchurn Castle
Pass of Brander
Dalmally
Strath of Orchy
Inverlochy
Achnafalnich
Ben Lui
Inverarnan
Ardlui
Glenfyne Lodge
Ben Vorlich
Inveruglas
Arrochar
Inverbeg
Glen Luss
Glen Fruin
Shandon
Faslane Port
Gare Loch
Clynder
Cove
Portkil
Rosneath Pt.
Kilcreggan
NN
NS
74
68
66

Highland
Argyll and Bute
LOCH LINNHE
LYNN OF LORN
MAMORE FOREST
BEN NEVIS AND GLEN COE
BLACK MOUNT
BLACKWATER RESERVOIR
LOCH LOMOND AND THE TROSSACHS NATIONAL PARK
Ardgour
Glen Scaddle
Inverscaddle Bay
Corrana
Conaglen
Ardgour
Clovullin
Corran
Inchree
Glenrigh Forest
Keppanach
Onich
North Ballachulish
South Ballachulish
Ballachulish
Glencoe
Kinlochleven
Kinlochmore
ALUMINIUM STORY VISITOR CENTRE
GLENCOE AND NORTH LORN FOLK MUSEUM
GLENCOE VISITOR CENTRE
Loch Leven
Glen Coe
Altnafeadh
Kingshouse Hotel
GLENCOE SKI CENTRE
Black Corries Lodge
Loch Laidon
Royal Forest
Blair a'Chaorainn
Achriabhach
Glen Nevis
Lodge
LOCH OSSIAN
Loch Eilde Mor
Loch Eil
Glen Tarbert
Sallachan
Sallachan Pt.
Inversanda Bay
Inversanda
Kentallen
Glenduror Forest
Duror
Rubha Mor
Cuil Bay
Keil
Eilean Balnagowan
Kilmalieu
Camasnacroise
Shuna I.
Appin House
Glen Stockdale
Salachan Glen
Portnacroish
KINLOCHLAICH HOUSE GARDENS
Appin
Strath of Appin
Port Appin
Port Ramsay
Eriska
North Shian
South Shian
Creagan
South Creagan
Loch Creran
Barcaldine
Barcaldine Forest
Fasnacloich
Invercreran
Elleric
Glen Creran
Glen Ure
GLASDRUM WOOD
Glasdrum
Druimavuic
Gualachulain
Dalness
Glen Etive
Alltchaorunn
Inverchan
Glenceitlein
Loch Etive
Forest Lodge
Black Mount
Loch Tulla
Achallader
Inveroran Hotel
Loch Dochard
Bridge of Orchy
Glen Orchy
Arichastlich
Benderloch
Ledaig
Achnaba
Ferlochan
Kiel Crofts
Ardmucknish Bay
ARDCHATTAN PRIORY GARDENS
ARDCHATTAN PRIORY
North Connel
Connel
Black Crofts
FALLS OF LORA
Achnacloich
ACHNACLOICH GARDEN
Eilean Mor
Dunbeg
DUNSTAFFNAGE CASTLE
Oban
McCAIG'S TOWER
OBAN DISTILLERY
Bonawe
BONAWE IRON FURNACE
INVERAWE FISHERIES AND SMOKERIES EXHIBITION
Brochroy
Fearnoch Forest
Taynuilt
Ichrachan
Bridge of Awe
Pass of Brander
Cruachan Reservoir
Glen Kinglass
Glen Liver
Glen Noe
Glen Strae
Glen Lochy
Arrivain
Clifton
Tyndrum
Strath Fillan
Crianlarich
Inverherive
Stronmilchan
Dalmally
Strath of Orchy
Achnafalnich
Inverlochy
KILCHURN CASTLE
Lochawe
Falls of Cruachan
MCINTYRE MONUMENT
Teatle Water
CRUACHAN DAM VISITOR CENTRE
Loch Tromlee
ARDANAISEIG GARDENS
Ardanaiseig
Innis Chonain
INISHAIL CHAPEL
Inishail
BARGUILLEAN GARDENS
GLEN NANT
Glen Nant
Glenamachrie
Glen Lonan
Loch Nell
Barran
Kilbride
Glen Feochan
GLENFEOCHAN HOUSE GARDENS
Musdale
Sior Loch
Kilchrenan
Annat
North Port
South Port
Portsonachan
Cladich
Glen Fyne
Glen Falloch
Falls of Falloch
Inverarnan
Ardlui
Glen Euchar
Bragleenmore
Loch Scamadale
Braes of Lorn
Blarian
Loch Tralaig
Lochavich
Drissaig
Kilmun
Loch Avich
Dalavich
Kilmelford
Inverinan
Ballimeanoch
Tullich
Glen Aray
Glen Shira
Blarghour
ARDCHONNELL CASTLE
Portinnisherrich
Lagalochan
Inverliever Forest
Kilmaha
Eredine
Durran
Arichamish
Eredine Forest
Torran
Ford
Finchairn
FINCHAIRN CASTLE
Ederline
Loch Awe
Loch Leacann
Loch Gaineamhach
Auchindrain
AUCHINDRAIN OPEN AIR MUSEUM
Dalchenna
Inveraray
INVERARAY CASTLE
INVERARAY JAIL
MARITIME MUSEUM
BELL TOWER
Newtown
Dubh Loch
Clachan
Drishaig
Cairndow
ARDKINGLAS WOODLAND GARDEN
Ardno
St Catherine's
Glen Kinglas
Rest and Be Thankful
Hell's Glen
Mhonevechadan
Glen Croe
Ardgartan
Arrochar
Tarbet
Succoth
Inveruglas
Inversnaid Hotel
ROB ROY'S CAVE
Loch Sloy
Stuckgowan
Ardmay
Loch Arklet
Creggans
Clachan Strachur
Strachur
Strachur Bay
Furnace
Glen Sluain
Newton
Crarae
CRARAE GLEN GARDENS
Minard
Garbhallt
LACHLAN CASTLE
Lachlan Bay
Tullochgorm
Invernoaden
Glenbranter
Glenbranter Forest
Loch Eck
Whistlefield
Strathlachlan Forest
Caol Ghleann
Drimsynie
Lochgoilhead
Corrow
Blairmore
Ardgoil Forest
Loch Goil
Carrick Castle
CARRICK CASTLE
Portincaple
Glenmallan
Loch Long
Garelochhead
Edentaggart
Glen Luss
Glen Douglas
Inverbeg
INVERBEG GALLERY
Rowardennan
Rowardennan Forest
Ptarmigan Lodge
Inchlonaig
Luss
THISTLE BAGPIPE WORKS
NAT PARK CENTRE
Aldochlay
Asknish
Dunans
Bernice
CUP AND RING MARKS
ROCK MARKINGS
WEST HIGHLAND WAY
0 1 2 3 4 5 6 miles
0 1 2 3 4 5 6 7 8 9 10 km

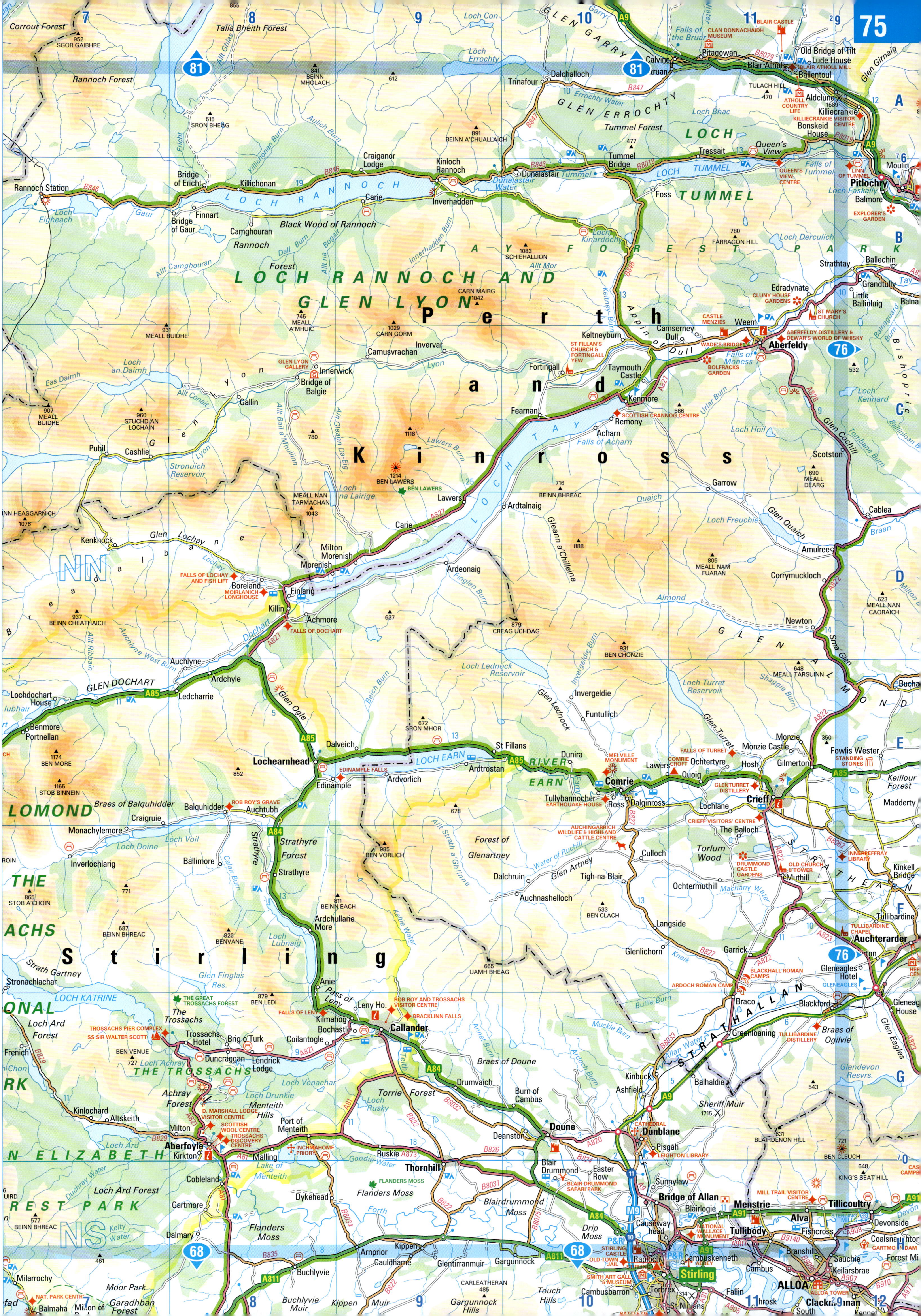

Corrour Forest
Talla Bheith Forest
Rannoch Forest
Loch Errochty
Dalchalloch
Trinafour
Glen Garry
Calvine
Blair Atholl
Blair Castle
Old Bridge of Tilt
Glen Errochty
Tummel Forest
Killiecrankie
Loch Tummel
Tummel Bridge
Tressait
Queen's View
Pitlochry
Moulin
Rannoch Station
Bridge of Ericht
Killichonan
Loch Rannoch
Kinloch Rannoch
Dunalastair
Craiganour Lodge
Carie
Inverhadden
Bridge of Gaur
Finnart
Camghouran
Black Wood of Rannoch
Rannoch
Foss
Schiehallion
Tay Forest Park
Farragon Hill
Strathtay
Ballechin
Grandtully
Loch Rannoch and Glen Lyon
Perth and Kinross
Carn Mairg
Carn Gorm
Meall Buidhe
Camusvrachan
Invervar
Glen Lyon
Innerwick
Bridge of Balgie
Gallin
Keltneyburn
Coshieville
Dull
Weem
Aberfeldy
Fortingall
Taymouth Castle
Kenmore
Fearnan
Acharn
Loch Tay
Pubil
Cashlie
Stronuich Reservoir
Ben Lawers
Lawers
Ardtalnaig
Glen Quaich
Scotston
Garrow
Amulree
Cablea
Kenknock
Glen Lochay
Carie
Milton Morenish
Morenish
Boreland
Finlarig
Killin
Achmore
Ardeonaig
Creag Uchdag
Newton
Glen Almond
Auchlyne
Glen Dochart
Ardchyle
Ledcharrie
Lochdochart House
Ben More
Portnellan
Stob Binnein
Lochearnhead
Dalveich
Loch Earn
St Fillans
Edinample
Ardvorlich
Ardtrostan
Dunira
Comrie
Glen Lednock
Invergeldie
Funtullich
Ben Chonzie
Monzie Castle
Monzie
Gilmerton
Fowlis Wester
Crieff
Lomond
Braes of Balquhidder
Balquhidder
Auchtubh
Craigruie
Monachylemore
Loch Voil
Loch Doine
Inverlochlarig
Ballimore
Strathyre Forest
Strathyre
Ben Vorlich
Forest of Glenartney
Dalchruin
Auchnashelloch
Glen Artney
Tigh-na-Blair
Culloch
Torlum Wood
Ochtermuthill
Muthill
Kinkell Bridge
The Trossachs
Stirling
Ben Each
Ardchullarie More
Benvane
Loch Lubnaig
Strath Gartney
Stronachlachar
Loch Katrine
Ben Ledi
Anie
Pass of Leny
Leny Ho.
Kilmahog
Bochastle
Callander
Uamh Bheag
Glenlichorn
Langside
Auchterarder
Garrick
Gleneagles Hotel
Strathallan
Blackford
Braco
Greenloaning
Braes of Ogilvie
Loch Ard Forest
Trossachs Hotel
Brig o' Turk
Coilantogle
Duncraggan
Lendrick Lodge
Ben Venue
Loch Achray
Loch Venachar
Braes of Doune
Drumvaich
Burn of Cambus
Torrie Forest
Kinbuck
Ashfield
Balhaldie
Sheriff Muir
Kinlochard
Altskeith
Milton
Aberfoyle
Kirkton
Menteith Hills
Port of Menteith
Lake of Menteith
Ruskie
Thornhill
Deanston
Doune
Dunblane
Blairdenon Hill
Ben Cleuch
Cobleland
Gartmore
Dykehead
Flanders Moss
Blair Drummond
Easter Row
Sunnyhaw
Bridge of Allan
Menstrie
Tillicoultry
Tullibody
Alva
Dalmary
Kippen
Arnprior
Gargunnock
Drip Moss
Causewayhead
Stirling
Cambus
Alloa
Buchlyvie
Cauldhame
Glentirranmuir
Cambusbarron
St Ninians
Balmaha
Garadhban Forest
Queen Elizabeth Forest Park

82
75
69
Perth
Dundee
Kirkcaldy
Pitlochry
Blair Atholl
Killiecrankie
Aberfeldy
Dunkeld
Birnam
Blairgowrie
Rattray
Coupar Angus
Alyth
Kirriemuir
Meigle
Forfar
Stanley
Scone
Methven
Crieff
Auchterarder
Bridge of Earn
Abernethy
Newburgh
Cupar
Ladybank
Auchtermuchty
Falkland
Glenrothes
Leslie
Markinch
Leven
Methil
Buckhaven
East Wemyss
Kinross
Milnathort
Kelty
Lochgelly
Cowdenbeath
Cardenden
Dollar
Tillicoultry
Alva
Menstrie
Invergowrie
Newport-
Errol
Kinfauns
Dunning
Muthill
Comrie
Kirkmichael
Bridge of Cally
Glenisla Forest
Forest of Alyth
Forest of Clunie
Craigvinean Forest
Glen Shee
Strathardle
River Tay
Perth and Kinross
Clackmannanshire
Sidlaw Hills
Braes of the Carse
Carse of Gowrie
Firth of Tay
Lomond Hills Regional Park
Loch Leven
Lochore Meadows Country Park
Glen Eagles
Glen Devon
Strathearn
Glen Almond
Loch Faskally
Ben Vrackie
Tay Rail Bridge
0 1 2 3 4 5 6 miles
0 1 2 3 4 5 6 7 8 9 10 km

Edzell
Luthermuir
Dykelands
Johnshaven
Mill of Benholm
Bridgend
Dunlappie
Brown Caterthun
White Caterthun
Tillyarblet
Auld Darkney
Glenmoy
Auchnacree
North Water Bridge
Inchbare
Newtonmill
Marykirk
Pert
Craigo
Logie
Ecclesgreig
Lochside
St Cyrus
Morphie
Milton Ness
Pathhead
Kirkton of Menmuir
Tigerton
Balhall
Mains of Balhall
Lochty
Little Brechin
Keithock
Logie Pert
Muirton of Ballochy
Glenogil
Ogil
Fern
Glenquiech
Hornieheugh
Newmill of Inshewan
Trinity
West Muir
Hillside
Kirkhill
Brechin
Brechin Castle Centre
Cathedral & Round Tower
Caledonian Railway
House of Dun
Dun
Noran Water
Careston Castle
Memus
Tannadice
South Esk
Inverquharity
Shielhill
Murthill
Finavon
Oathlaw
Aldbar Castle
Netherton
Mains of Melgund
Kinnaird Castle
Middle Drums
Bridge of Dun
Barnhead
Montrose Basin
Montrose
Museum and Art Gallery
Scurdie Ness
William Lamb Memorial Studio
Inchbraoch
Montrose Basin Visitor Centre
Ferryden
Aberlemno Sculptured Stones
Aberlemno
Farnell
Bonnyton
Maryton
Kirkton of Craig
Pitkennedy
Montreathmont Forest
Carcary
Long Craig
Fishtown of Usan
Carse Gray
Montreathmont Moor
Rossie Moor
Westerton
Dunninald
Boddin Pt.
Mosside
Lunanhead
Restenneth Priory
Rescobie
Turin
Dubton
Braehead of Lunan
Mains of Ballindarg
Padanaram
Forfar
Reswallie
Balgavies
Glasterlaw
Bolshan
Lunan
Forfar Loch
Burnside
Milldens
Guthrie
Kinnell
Lunan Bay
Redcastle
Drumgley
Kingsmuir
Dunnichen
Letham
Pitmuies
House of Pitmuies Garden
Friockheim
Boysack
Inverkeilor
Lunan Water
Caldhame
Lownie Moor
Chapelton
Lang Craig
Ethie Mains
Douglastown
Craichie
Idvies
Leysmill
Cauldcots
Red Head
Ethie Castle
Thornton
Kirkton
Tulloes
Drunkendub
Foffarty
Mosston
Colliston
Letham Grange
Auchmithie
Gateside
Inverarity
Whigstreet
Greystone
Redford
Marywell
Meg's Craig
St Vigeans
St Vigeans Museum
Kirkbuddo
Gallowfauld
Hayshead
Cliffburn
The Deil's Heid
Arbroath Abbey
Hayhillock
Carmyllie
Denhead of Arbirlot
Arbirlot
Arbroath
Signal Tower Museum
Crombie
Tealing
Newbigging
Monikie
Kirkton of Monikie
Balmirmer
Elliot
Salmond's Muir
Inveraldie
East March
Wellbank
Craigton
Carlungie Souterrain
Monikie Burn
Muirdrum
Muir of Pert
Bucklerheads
Drumsturdy
Newbigging
East Haven
Burnside of Duntrune
Kellas
Barry Mill
Panbride
Fintry
Souterrain Ardestie
Mains of Ardestie
Barry
Carnoustie
Baldovie
Douglas & Angus
Craigie
West Ferry
Monifieth
Barry Links
Broughty Ferry
Stannergate
Barnhill
Broughty Castle Museum
V&A Dundee
Discovery Point
Buddon Ness
Tay Bridge
Tayport
Scotscraig
Tentsmuir
Woodhaven
Tentsmuir Forest
Pickletillem
Rhynd
Carrick
Lucklawhill
Leuchars
Leuchars Norman Church
Balmullo
Logie
Guardbridge
Eden Mouth
Eden Estuary Centre
St Andrews Bay
Kincaple
St Andrews
St Andrews Aquarium
Dairsie or Osnaburgh
British Golf Mus
Cath & St Rule's Tower
Strathkinness
Newpark
Buddo Ness
Kemback
Blebocraigs
Balone
Craigtoun
Brownhills
Boarhills
Babbet Ness
St Andrews Botanic Garden
Denhead
Pitscottie
Prior Muir
Kingsbarns
Cameron Res.
Cameron Burn
Stravithie
Cambo Ness
Cambo Gardens
Carr Brigs
Tullybothy Craigs
Ceres
Baldinnie
Dunino
Balcomie
Craighead
Fife Folk Museum
Peat Inn
Fife Ness
Radernie
Kingsmuir
Crail Tolbooth
Woodside
Lathones
Lochty
Scotland's Secret Bunker
New Gilston
Crail
Crail Museum and Heritage Centre
Largoward
Carnbee
Pitcorthie
Pitkierie
West Ness
Wester Newburn
Kellie Castle and Garden
Arncroach
Kilrenny
Fife Coastal Path
Kirkton of Largo
Anstruther Easter
Scottish Fisheries Museum
Lundin Links
Drumeldrie
Colinsburgh
Pittenweem
Anstruther Wester
Robinson Crusoe Statue
Abercrombie
Kilconquhar
St Fillan's Cave
St Monan's Windmill
Lower Largo
Balchrystie
St Monans
St Monan's Church
Ardross
Largo Bay
Ruddons Pt.
Earlsferry
Elie
Chapel Ness
Sauchar Pt.
Isle of May
NO
NT
A90
A92
A93
A94
A917
A915
A91
A930
A932
A933
A934
A935
A937
A926
A928
A914
B9134
B9113
B9127
B961
B965
B978
B9128
B940
B939
B9131
B9171
B941
B942
B945
B946
B957
B966
B974
B9120
83
70
7
8
9
10
11
12
A
B
C
D
E
F
G
H

NF
NL
Canna
A'Chill
Garrisdale Pt.
Canna Harbour
Sanday
Sound of Canna
Guirdil Bay
Rubha Shamhnan Insir
Kilmory
Kilmory Glen
Kinloch Glen
Rubha na Roinne
388
84
85
MALLAIG (Sun only)
A'Bhrideanach
571 ORVAL
RÙM
Kinloch
KINLOCH CASTLE
Loch Scresort
Rubha Port na Caranean
Schooner Pt.
Harris
Glen Harris
812 ASKIVAL
781 AINSHVAL
Oigh-sgeir
Rubha Sgorr an t-Snidhe
Rubha nam Meirleach
THE SMALL ISLES
SOUND OF RÙM
Bay of Laig
Cleadale
Rubha an Fhasaidh
Eigg
Kildonnan
393 AN SGURR
Galmisdale
Eilean nan Each
SOUND OF EIGG
137
Port Mor
Muck
Bhatarsaigh (Vatersay)
Uidh
Bagh Bhatarsaigh
Bhatarsaigh
Caolas Shanndraigh
Flodaigh (Flodday)
207
Sanndraigh (Sandray)
Lingeigh (Lingay)
Greanamul
Caolas Phabaigh
Theisgeir (Heiskers)
171
Pabaidh (Pabbay)
Caolas Mhiui Laigh
273
Miùgh Laigh (Mingulay)
Bearnaraigh (Berneray)
Caolas Bhearnaraigh
Barra Hd.
Sanna Point
Sanna Bay
Sanna
Portuairk
Achnaha
Point of Ardnamurchan
ARDNAMURCHAN LIGHTHOUSE
Achosnich
B8007
Ormsaigmore
Ormsaigbeg
Kilchoan
Kilchoan Bay
An Acairseid
Cairns of Coll
Eilean Mor
Rubha Mor
Bousd
Sorisdale
Cliad Bay
Arnabost
Gallanach
Grishipoll
B8072
B8071
73
COLL
Ballyhaugh
Hogh Bay
104
Loch Cliad
Arinagour
Loch Eatharna
B8070
Totronald
Acha
Feall Bay
Arileod
Eilean Ornsay
Breachacha Castle
Friesland
Calgary Pt.
Gunna
Crossapol Bay
Soa
Loch Breachacha
OBAN
TIREE
Vaul Bay
Salum
Caolas
Rubha Dubh
Balephetrish Bay
Vaul
B8069
Ruaig
Hough Skerries
Balevullin
B8068
Gott Bay
Soa
R. Chraiginis
Kenovay
Kilkenneth
Moss
TIREE
Scarinish
B8065
Heylipol
Middleton
Port Mor
Crossapol
Heanish
Rubha Traigh an Duin
Loch a'Phuill
Barrapol
B8067
Hynish Bay
Balemartine
Rinn Thorbhais
Balephuil
141
B8066
Mannal
Balephuil Bay
Port Snoig
Hynish
Ardmore Bay
Ardmore Pt.
Bloody Bay
Quinish Pt.
Glengorm Castle
MULL MUSEUM
Mishnish
Caliach Pt.
Rubha an Aird
Sunipol
Quinish
Mornish
Penmore Mill
MULL THEATRE
292
Calgary
Calgary Bay
Dervaig
Achnadrish
THE OLD BYRE HERITAGE CENTRE
Treshnish Pt.
Ensay
342 CARN MOR
Lettermore
Haunn
B8073
Rubh a'Chaoil
Burg
Kilninian
Achnacraig
Achleck
Fanmore 390
Treshnish Isles
Fladda
LOCH TUATH
Ballygown
EAS FORS WATERFALL
424 BEINN NA DRISE
Eilean Dioghlum
Lunga
Gometra
Laggan Bay
Lagganulva
Bearnus 313
Oskamull
Ulva
Ulva House
Killiemor
Bac Mor
LOCH NA KEAL
Eorsa
Little Colonsay
ISLE OF
Staffa
STAFFA
FINGAL'S CAVE
INCH KENNETH CHAPEL
Inch Kenneth
Derryguaig
Balnahard
MACKINNON'S CAVE
561
Erisgeir
519 BEINN NA SREINE
Glen Seilisdeir
ARDMEANACH
Killiemore House
Kilfinichen Bay
THE BURG
Eilean Annraidh
MACLEAN'S CROSS
IONA ABBEY AND CATHEDRAL
100
Rubha nan Cearc
LOCH SCRIDAIN
Torrans
IONA HERITAGE CENTRE
Iona
Baile Mor
ST COLUMBA EXHIBITION & WELCOME CENTRE
Kintra
Aridhglas
Loch na Lathaich
Eorabus
Stac an Aoineidh
Fionnphort
A849
Fidden
Tiraghoil
Lee
376 CRUACHAN MIN
Sound of Iona
Bunessan
Loch Assapol
Erraid
ROSS OF MULL
Ardalanish
Uisken
Scoor
Soa I.
Ardchiavaig
Malcolm's Pt.
Rubha nam Braithrean
125
Eilean a'Chalmain
Rubh Ardalanish
72
Torran Rocks
Scale : 1:250 000
(approx 4 miles to 1 inch)
0 1 2 3 4 5 6 miles
0 1 2 3 4 5 6 7 8 9 10 km

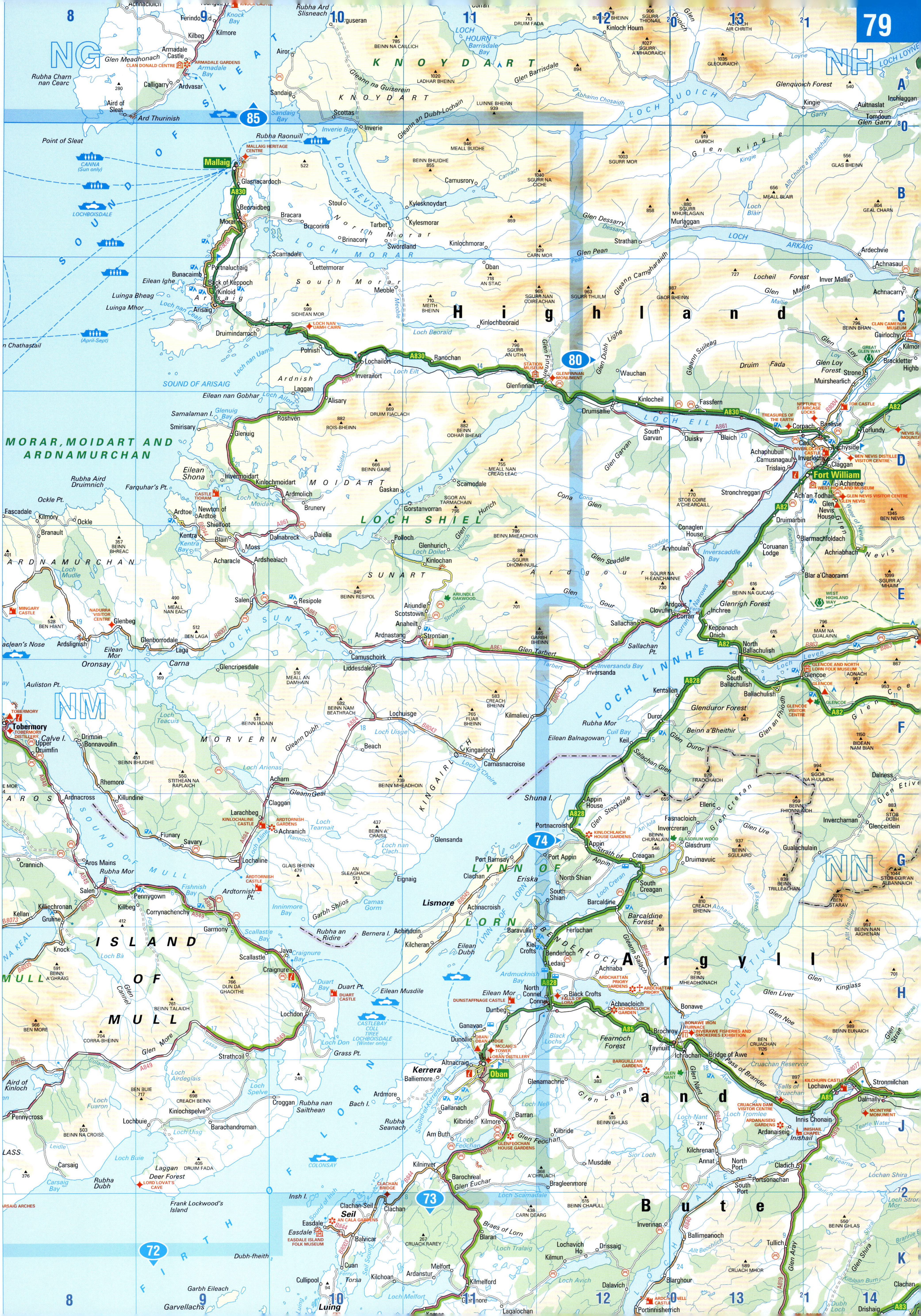
NG
NH
NM
NN
KNOYDART
Mallaig
SOUND OF SLEAT
Loch Nevis
Loch Morar
Highland
Loch Arkaig
Loch Eil
Fort William
Glenfinnan
Lochailort
Arisaig
SOUND OF ARISAIG
MORAR, MOIDART AND ARDNAMURCHAN
MOIDART
LOCH SHIEL
ARDNAMURCHAN
SUNART
Loch Sunart
Strontian
Glencoe
LOCH LINNHE
MORVERN
Tobermory
SOUND OF MULL
ISLAND OF MULL
Craignure
Lismore
LYNN OF LORN
Oban
Kerrera
Argyll and Bute
Loch Awe
Loch Etive
Inveraray
Seil
FIRTH OF LORN
Luing
Kilmelford
Appin
Ballachulish
Kinlochleven
Lochaline
Salen
Dalmally
Taynuilt
Connel

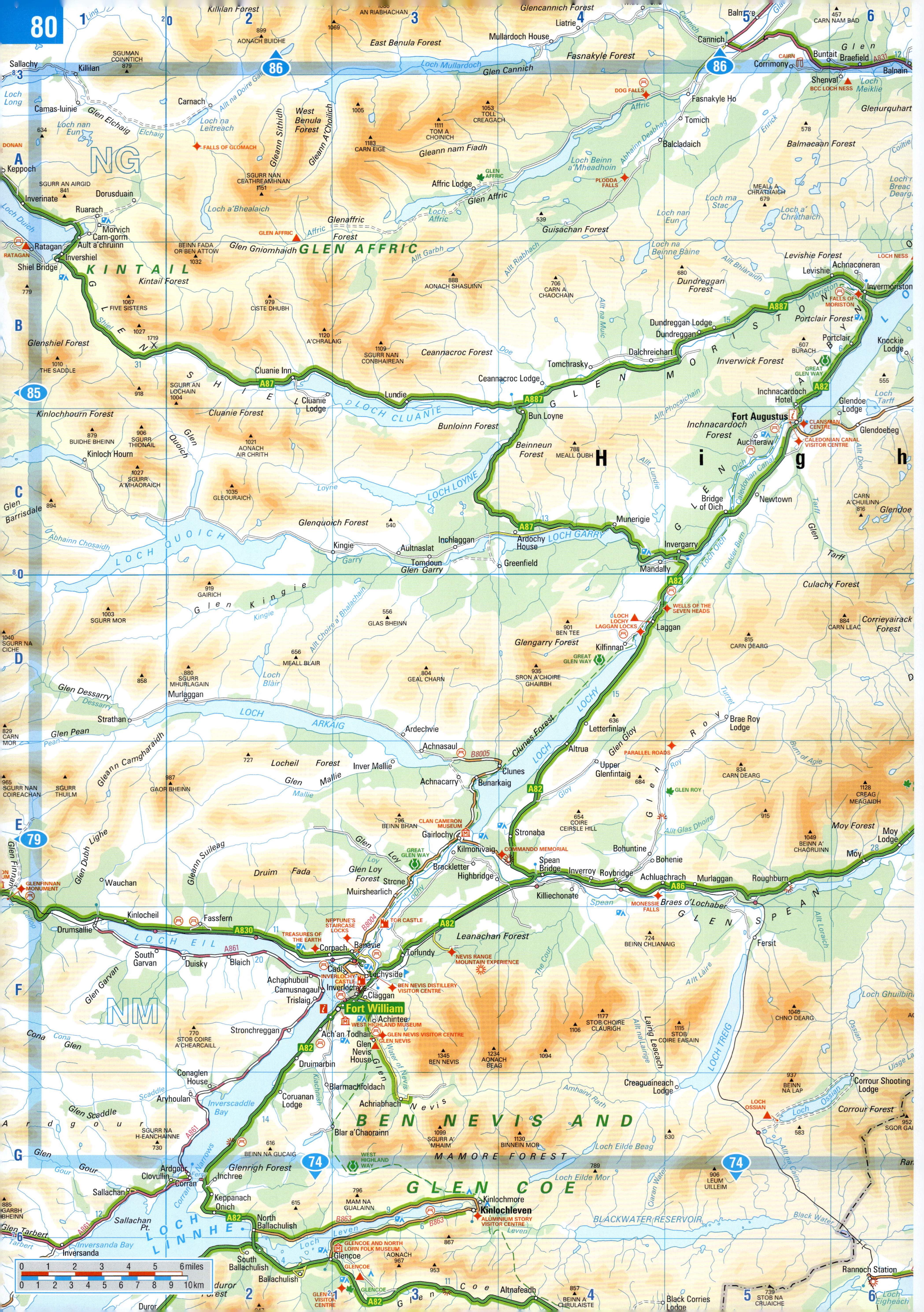

Kintail Forest
KINTAIL
GLEN AFFRIC
Glen Gniomhaidh
Glen Affric
Affric Lodge
Glen Cannich
Loch Mullardoch
Mullardoch House
Fasnakyle Forest
Cannich
Corrimony
Glen Urquhart
Balnain
Buntait
Braefield
Shenval
BCC LOCH NESS
Loch Meiklie
Glenurquhart
Fasnakyle Ho
Tomich
Balcladaich
Plodda Falls
Dog Falls
Guisachan Forest
Balmacaan Forest
Levishie Forest
Levishie
Achnaconeran
Invermoriston
Falls of Moriston
Dundreggan Forest
Dundreggan Lodge
Dundreggan
Dalchreichart
Tomchrasky
Ceannacroc Forest
Ceannacroc Lodge
Portclair Forest
Portclair
Inverwick Forest
Knockie Lodge
Inchnacardoch Hotel
Fort Augustus
Clansman Centre
Caledonian Canal Visitor Centre
Inchnacardoch Forest
Auchteraw
Glendoe Lodge
Glendoebeg
Glendoe
Newtown
Bridge of Oich
Bun Loyne
Bunloinn Forest
Beinneun Forest
Highlands
Cluanie Inn
Cluanie Lodge
Loch Cluanie
Lundie
Cluanie Forest
Glen Shiel
Glenshiel Forest
Shiel Bridge
Ratagan
Invershiel
Ault a'chruinn
Carn-gorm
Morvich
Ruarach
Dorusduain
Invershiel
Inverinate
Keppoch
Loch Duich
Camas-luinie
Glen Elchaig
Killilan
Sallachy
Killilan Forest
Carnach
Falls of Glomach
West Benula Forest
East Benula Forest
Kinloch Hourn
Kinlochhourn Forest
Glen Quoich
Loch Quoich
Glenquoich Forest
Kingie
Aultnaslat
Tomdoun
Glen Garry
Inchlaggan
Ardochy House
Loch Garry
Greenfield
Munerigie
Invergarry
Mandally
Loch Loyne
Glen Kingie
Glengarry Forest
Wells of the Seven Heads
Loch Lochy
Laggan Locks
Laggan
Kilfinnan
Great Glen Way
Culachy Forest
Corrieyairack Forest
Brae Roy Lodge
Glen Roy
Parallel Roads
Letterfinlay
Altrua
Upper Glenfintaig
Loch Arkaig
Murlaggan
Strathan
Glen Dessarry
Glen Pean
Achnasaul
Ardechvie
Clunes Forest
Clunes
Inver Mallie
Locheil Forest
Glen Mallie
Achnacarry
Bunarkaig
Clan Cameron Museum
Gairlochy
Stronaba
Commando Memorial
Kilmonivaig
Spean Bridge
Inverroy
Roybridge
Achluachrach
Murlaggan
Roughburn
Bohuntine
Bohenie
Killiechonate
Braes o'Lochaber
Monessie Falls
Glen Spean
Fersit
Moy Forest
Moy Lodge
Moy
Highbridge
Brackletter
Glen Loy Forest
Strone
Muirshearlich
Druim Fada
Wauchan
Glenfinnan Monument
Kinlocheil
Fassfern
Drumsallie
Loch Eil
South Garvan
Duisky
Blaich
Corpach
Banavie
Tor Castle
Neptune's Staircase Locks
Treasures of the Earth
Caol
Lochyside
Tórlundy
Leanachan Forest
Nevis Range Mountain Experience
Ben Nevis Distillery Visitor Centre
Inverlochy Castle
Achaphubuil
Camusnagaul
Trislaig
Inverlochy
Claggan
Fort William
Achintee
West Highland Museum
Glen Nevis Visitor Centre
Ach'an Todhair
Glen Nevis House
Stronchreggan
Druimarbin
Blarmachfoldach
Conaglen House
Aryhoulan
Inverscaddle Bay
Coruanan Lodge
Achriabhach
Blar a'Chaorainn
BEN NEVIS AND MAMORE FOREST
GLEN COE
Loch Eilde Mor
Loch Eilde Beag
Kinlochmore
Kinlochleven
Aluminium Story Visitor Centre
Blackwater Reservoir
Loch Treig
Creaguaineach Lodge
Corrour Shooting Lodge
Corrour Forest
Loch Ossian
Rannoch Station
Black Corries Lodge
Altnafeadh
Glencoe
Glencoe and North Lorn Folk Museum
Glen Coe
North Ballachulish
South Ballachulish
Ballachulish
Onich
Keppanach
Inchree
Corran
Ardgour
Clovullin
Sallachan
Sallachan Pt.
Glenrigh Forest
Loch Linnhe
Inversanda
Glen Tarbert
Glen Gour
Glen Scaddle
Ardgour
Glen Garvan
Cona Glen
Lochan
NG
NM
86
85
79
74
A87
A887
A82
A830
A861
A86
B8004
B8005
B863
A831
0 1 2 3 4 5 6 miles
0 1 2 3 4 5 6 7 8 9 10 km

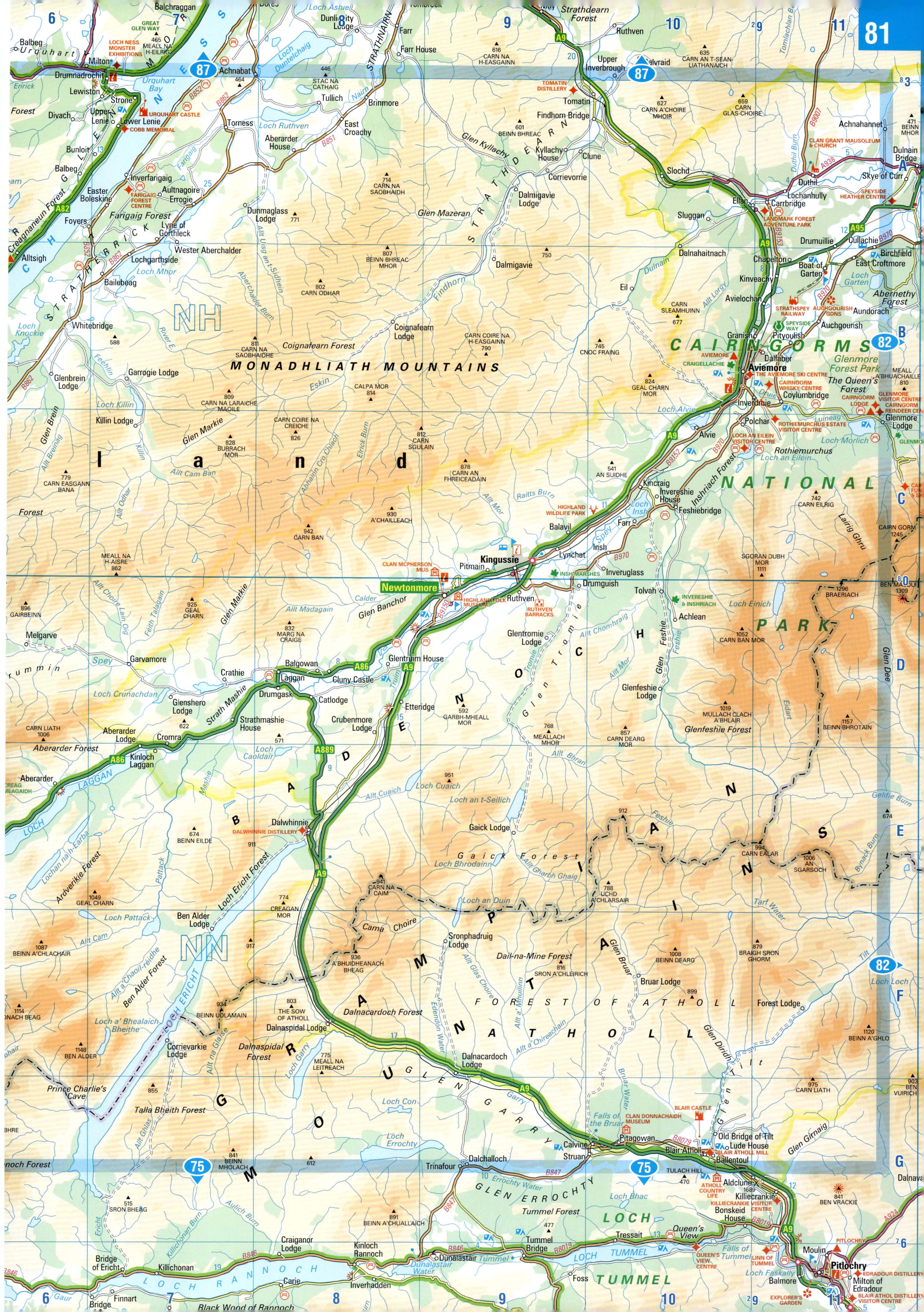

Strathdearn Forest
Ruthven
Upper Inverbrough
Alvraid
Dunlichity Lodge
Farr
Farr House
STRATHNAIRN
Balchraggan
Balbeg
Urquhart
Milton
Drumnadrochit
Achnabat
Lewiston
Strone
Upper Lenie
Lower Lenie
Divach
Forest
Bunloit
Balbeg
Easter Boleskine
Foyers
Alltsigh
Creagnaneun Forest
Inverfarigaig
Aultnagoire
Errogie
Farigaig Forest
Lyne of Gorthleck
Wester Aberchalder
Lochgarthside
Loch Mhor
Bailebeag
Whitebridge
Garrogie Lodge
Glenbrein Lodge
Killin Lodge
Loch Killin
Torness
Loch Ruthven
Aberarder House
East Croachy
Tullich
Brinmore
Dunmaglass Lodge
Glen Kyllachy
Tomatin
Findhorn Bridge
Kyllachy House
Clune
Corrievorrie
Dalmigavie Lodge
Dalmigavie
Glen Mazeran
STRATHDEARN
Coignafearn Lodge
Coignafearn Forest
MONADHLIATH MOUNTAINS
Slochd
Sluggan
Ellan
Carrbridge
Dalnahaitnach
Chapelton
Boat of Garten
Kinveachy
Avielochan
Eil
Granish
Pityoulish
Dalfaber
Aviemore
Inverdruie
Coylumbridge
Polchar
Alvie
Rothiemurchus
Glenmore Lodge
Loch Morlich
Loch Garten
Aundorach
Auchgourish
Abernethy Forest
Glenmore Forest Park
The Queen's Forest
Achnahannet
Duthil
Dulnain Bridge
Skye of Curr
Lochanhully
Drumuillie
Cullachie
Birchfield
East Croftmore
CAIRNGORMS
NATIONAL
PARK
Kincraig
Invereshie House
Feshiebridge
Loch Insh
Farr
Insh
Balavil
Lynchat
Kingussie
Inverglass
Drumguish
Tolvah
Achlean
Loch Einich
Pitmain
Newtonmore
Ruthven
Glen Banchor
Glentromie Lodge
Glenfeshie Lodge
Glenfeshie Forest
Glen Feshie
Glen Tromie
Gaick Lodge
Gaick Forest
Loch an t-Seilich
Loch Cuaich
Loch Bhrodainn
Glentruim House
Etteridge
Crubenmore Lodge
Catlodge
Cluny Castle
Balgowan
Laggan
Crathie
Drumgask
Glenshero Lodge
Strathmashie House
Strath Mashie
Garvamore
Melgarve
Loch Crunachdan
Aberarder Lodge
Aberarder Forest
Aberarder
Cromra
Kinloch Laggan
Loch Laggan
Loch Caoldair
Dalwhinnie
Ardverikie Forest
Ben Alder Lodge
Loch Ericht Forest
Loch Pattack
Ben Alder Forest
Loch a' Bhealaich Bheithe
Corrievarkie Lodge
Dalnaspidal Lodge
Dalnaspidal Forest
Loch Garry
Dalnacardoch Forest
Dalnacardoch Lodge
Sronphadruig Lodge
Dail-na-Mine Forest
FOREST OF ATHOLL
Bruar Lodge
Forest Lodge
Glen Bruar
Glen Tilt
Prince Charlie's Cave
Talla Bheith Forest
Loch Con
Loch Errochty
Glen Garry
Calvine
Struan
Pitagowan
Blair Atholl
Old Bridge of Tilt
Lude House
Baillentoul
Glen Girnaig
Trinafour
Dalchalloch
Glen Errochty
Tummel Forest
Tummel Bridge
Tressait
Queen's View
Loch Tummel
Aldclune
Killiecrankie
Bonskeid House
Moulin
Pitlochry
Milton of Edradour
Balmore
Foss
Craiganor Lodge
Kinloch Rannoch
Dunalastair
Bridge of Ericht
Killichonan
Carie
Inverhadden
Finnart
Bridge
Loch Rannoch
Black Wood of Rannoch
NH
NN
A9
A86
A889
A82
A95
B846
B847
B8019
B8079
B970
87
75
82
Cairn Gorm 1245
Braeriach 1296
Carn Ban Mor 1052
Sgoran Dubh Mor 1111
Mullach Clach a' Bhlair 1019
Beinn Bhrotain 1157
Carn Dearg Mor 857
Carn na Caim 941
A' Bhuidheanach Bheag 936
Beinn Udlamain 1011
Ben Alder 1148
Geal Charn 1049
Beinn Dearg 1008
Carn an Fhreiceadain 878
A' Chailleach 930
Carn Ban 942
Carn Dearg 1034
Carn Sgulain 812
Beinn Vrackie 841
Carn Liath 975
Beinn a' Ghlo 1120
Braigh Sron Ghorm 879
Carn Ealar 994
An Sgarsoch 1006

Moray
CAIRNGORMS
NATIONAL
PARK
CAIRNGORM
MOUNTAINS
THE CAIRNGORM MOUNTAINS
GRAMPIAN MOUNTAINS
DEESIDE AND
LOCHNAGAR
Angus
NJ
NO
Grantown-on-Spey
Cromdale
Anagach
Speybridge
Congash
Craggan
Dulnain Bridge
Skye of Curr
Nethy Bridge
Dell Lodge
Lettoch
Boat of Garten
Aundorach
Forest Lodge
Abernethy Forest
Braes of Abernethy
Glenmore Lodge
Glenmore
Loch Morlich
Tomintoul
Delnabo
Fodderletter
Bridge of Brown
Dirdhu
Lynemore
Glenlivet
Shenval
Auchbreck
Tomnavoulin
Knockandhu
Clashnoir
Chapeltown
Braes of Glenlivet
Glenlivet Forest
Strath Avon
HILLS OF CROMDALE
Haughs of Cromdale
Ballcorach
Drumin
Dalchirach
Upper Derraid
Auchnagallin
Lettoch
Dellefure
Mains of Dalvey
Glaschoil
Camerory
Cottartown
Glenbeg
Achnahannet
Blackwater Forest
Glenfiddich Forest
Bridgend
Tomnaven
Coynachie
Clashindarroch Forest
Clashindarroch
Milton of Lesmore
Auchmair
Cabrach
Aldunie
Belhinnie
Rhynie
Wheedlemont
Craig Castle
Clova
Lumsden
Mossat
Kildrummy
Rinmore
Milltown of Kildrummy
Glenbuchat Lodge
Badenyon
Belnacraig
Kirkton of Glenbuchat
LADDER HILLS
Blairnamarrow
Conglass Water
Bellabeg
Forbestown
Strathdon
Glen Ernan
Inverernan Ho.
Candacraig Ho.
Heugh-head
Tornashean Forest
Hillockhead
Boultenstone
Glenkindie
Towie
Milltown of Towie
Sinnahard
Hillockhead
Colnabaichin
Corgarff
Tornahaish
Cock Bridge
Delnadamph
Allt Tuileach
Easter Davoch
Migvie
Coynach
Doune
Logie Coldstone
Tarland
Milton of Logie
Glendavan Ho.
Ordie
Loch Davan
Loch Kinord
Dinnet
Muir of Dinnet
Glascorrie
Ballater
Bridge of Gairn
Milton of Tullich
Culsh
Littlemill
Coilacriech
Crathie
Easter Balmoral
Invergelder
Inver
Bush Crathie
Gairnshiel Lodge
Lary
Glen Gairn
Glen Fenzie
Glen Tanar House
House of Glenmuick
Birkhall
Mill of Sterin
Aucholzie
Glen Muick
Spittal of Glenmuick
Loch Muick
Glas-allt Shiel
Dubh Loch
Balmoral Forest
Ballochbuie Forest
Braemar
Invercauld House
Auchallater
Allanaquoich
Mar Lodge
Claybokie
Inverey
Muir
Forest of Mar
Glen Lui
Glen Dee
Glen Ey
Glen Callater
Loch Callater
Baddoch
Glen Clunie
Devil's Elbow
Caenlochan Forest
Glen Doll
Glendoll Lodge
Glendoll Forest
Braedownie
Clova
Glen Clova
Wheen
Rottal
Kilburn
Glenprosen Lodge
Balnaboth
Glenprosen Village
Glen Prosen
Clachnabrain
Glenmoy
Auchavan
Glenshee
Spittal of Glenshee
Glenlochsie
Dalnaglar Castle
Meikle Forter
Folda
Glenisla Forest
Cray
Ashintully Castle
Enochdhu
Straloch
Tarvie
Dalnavaid
Glen Brerachan
Kirkmichael
Brewlands Bridge
Freuchies
Kirkton of Glenisla
Blacklunans
Bellaty
Dykends
Balintore
Glenhead Farm
Backwater Res.
Easter Lednathie
Pearsie
Cortachy
Dykehead
Hornieshaugh
Glenquiech
Ogil
Fern
Glenogil
Auchnacree
Newmill of Inshewan
Memus
Tannadice
Inverquharity
Murthill
Shielhill
Oathlaw
Finavon
Balloch
Forest of Alyth
Glen Mark
Water of Mark
Invermark Lodge
Auchronie
Tarfside
Loch Lee
Glen Lee
Inchgrundle
Glen Effock
Water of Saughs
Loch Brandy
Hunthill Lodge
Loch Etchachan
Loch Avon
Loch Builg
Loch Vrotachan
Loch nan Eun
Loch Loch
Lochnagar 1150
Ben Macdui 1309
Cairn Gorm 1245
Beinn Mheadhoin 1182
Ben Avon 1171
Carn Eas 1089
Beinn a' Bhuird
Cairn Bannoch 1012
Broad Cairn 998
Glas Maol 1068
Cairnwell 933
Carn an Tuirc 1019
Tolmount 958
Glas Tulaichean 1051
Beinn Iutharn Mhor 1045
Carn a' Gheoidh
Mount Keen 939
Morven 871
Brown Cow Hill 823
Carn Liath 818
Carn Ealasaid 792
Carn Mor 804
Derry Cairngorm 1155
Beinn Bhreac 931
Carn na Drochaide 818
Conachcraig 850
Culardoch 900
Geallaig Hill 743
Driesh 947
Finalty Hill 905
Mayar
Ben Gulabin 806
Ben Vuirich 903
Ben Earb 801
Meall Uaine 794
Duchray Hill 702
Badendun Hill 740
Monamenach 808
Mount Blair 744
Cairn Gibbs 523
Creag Dhubh 641
Meall Reamhar
Knock of Balmyle
Cat Law 668
Creigh Hill 497
Mile Hill 409
Auld Darkney 545
Finbracks 756
White Hill 778
Cruys 741
West Knock 691
Muckle Cairn 826
Monawee 696
Lair of Aldararie 832
Cock Cairn 727
Hill of Cat 742
Clachan Yell 526
Fasheilach 721
Carn an t-Suidhe 732
Carn Daimh 569
Creggan a' Chaise 722
Hill of Three Stones 632
Round Hill 571
The Buck 721
The Socach 718
Craig of Bunzeach 531
Big Garvoun 742
The Bruach 715
Geal Charn 821
Meall a' Bhuachaille 810
Baddoch 568
Beinn Mhor 471
Forest of Glenavon
Glen Avon
Glen Tanar
Forest of Glen Tanar
Muir of Dinnet
Balmoral Castle and Gardens
Braemar Castle
Kindrochit Castle
Royal Lochnagar Distillery Visitor Centre
Crathie Church
Corgarff Castle
Lecht Ski Centre
Tomintoul Museum
Glenlivet Estate Visitor Centre
Glenlivet Distillery
Glenshee Ski Centre
Cairngorm Chairlift, Funicular Rly & Ski Centre
Glenmore Visitor Centre
Cairngorm Reindeer Centre
Linn of Dee
Linn of Muick Waterfall
Spittal of Glenmuick Visitor Centre
Corrie Fee
Glen Tanar
Glen Tanar Visitor Centre
Burn o Vat
Muir of Dinnet
Tomnaverie Stone Circle
Kildrummy Castle & Garden
Scottish Sculpture Workshop
St Mary's Church
Captain Scott & Dr Wilson Cairn
Prosen
Museum & Heritage Trust
Revack Estate
Speyside Heather Centre
Speyside Way
Abernethy Centre
Mar Lodge Estate
McEwan Gallery
Inverey
A95
A939
A93
A97
A941
A944
A924
A926
B9102
B9008
B9136
B970
B976
B9119
B955
B951
B950
B9002
81
88
76
0 1 2 3 4 5 6 miles
0 1 2 3 4 5 6 7 8 9 10 km

Aberdeenshire
Aberdeen City
Aberdeen
FORMARTINE
GARIOCH
KINCARDINE AND MEARNS
ANGUS
NK
NP
Culdrain
Blackburn
Glens of Foudland
Kirkton of Culsalmond
Rothmaise
Newseat
Folla Rule
St Katherine's
Cross of Jackston
Earlsford
Vedderlairs
Hilton
Mains of Birness
Kirkney
Gartly
Clashindarroch Forest
Cults
Knockandy Hill
Colpy
Largie
Wrangham
Cairnhill
Tocher
Bonnyton
Meikle Wartle
Kirkton of Rayne
Jackstown
Balgove
Tulloch
Craigdam
Tarves
Ythsie
West Kinharrachie
Esslemont
Ellon
Broomfield
Artrochie
Auchmacoy
Kennethmont
Milton of Noth
Oldtown
Ardlair
Insch
Ardoyne
Newton Ho.
Old Rayne
Pitmachie
Durno
Mounie Castle
Daviot
Fingask
Meldrum Ho.
Auquhorthies
Tolquhon Castle
Pitmedden Gardens
Pitmedden
Tipperty
Kirkton of Logie Buchan
Meikle Tarty
Waterside
Forvie
Sands of Forvie
Hackley Hd.
Cottown
Clatt
Duncanstone
Leslie
Kirkton
Oyne
Westhall
Whiteford
Pitcaple
Barra Castle
Oldmeldrum
Cairnbrogie
Udny Green
Tarty Burn
Newburgh
Knockespock Ho.
Coldwells Croft
Whitehaugh Forest
Auchleven
Bennachie
Kirkton of Oyne
Pittodrie
Chapel of Garioch
Harlaw Ho.
Balhalgardy
Kirkton of Bourtie
Hillbrae
Mill of Kingoodie
Hattoncrook
Pettymuick
Culterculllen
Foveran
Newburgh Bar
Muckletown
Correen Hills
Battle of Harlaw Memorial
Brandsbutt Stone
Burgh Muir
Carnegie Inverurie Museum
Inverurie
Whiterashes
Affleck
Udny Station
Minnes
Rashiereive
Drums
Tillycorthie
Tillygreig
Nether Crimond
Tillykerrie
Straloch
Arnage Ho.
Middlemuir
Delfrigs
Lord Arthur's Cairn
Tullynessle
Glenton
Keig
Manar Ho.
Port Elphinstone
Castle Forbes
Upper Woodend
Bograxie
Burnhervie
Aquhythie
Kinmuck
Middleton
Balbithan Ho.
Newmachar
Craigie
Causeyend
Whitecairns
Belhelvie
Bridge of Alford
Montgarrie
Alford Valley Railway
Haughton
Grampian Transport Mus
Rorandle
Pitfichie Forest
Blairdaff
Dalmadilly
Clovenstone
Kinkell Church
Balbithan
Wester Fintray
Cairnpark
Kinmundy
Balmedie
Auchintoul
Alford
Heritage Museum
Gateside
Pitfichie
Monymusk Arts Centre
Grantlodge
Kemnay
Cottown
Kintore
Hatton of Fintray
Old Church
Cothall
Drumligair
Potterton
Blackdog
Asloun
Whitehouse
Pitmunie
Todlachie
Monymusk
Craigearn
Leylodge
Parkhill Ho.
Corby Loch
Mundurno
Ley
Little Lynturk
Kirkton of Tough
Tillyfourie
Lauchintilly
Castle Fraser
Overton
Dyce
Aberdeen Airport
Muir of Fowlis
Bridgend
Correnie Forest
Ordhead
Sauchen
Achath
Lyne of Skene
Blackburn
Haughs of Clinterty
Stoneywood
Denmore
Milton of Cushnie
Tillyfour
Corrennie Moor
Bankhead
Kirkwall Lerwick
Leochel Cushnie
Craigievar Castle
Kintocher
Milton of Corsindae
Old Kinnernie
Dunecht
East Auchronie
Skene Ho.
Bucksburn
Hayton
Bridge of Don
Brig o' Balgownie
Cruickshank Botanic Garden
St Machar's Cathedral
Benaquhallie
Corsindae
Kirkton of Skene
Woodside
Kittybrewster
Old Aberdeen
King's College Visitor Centre
Midmar
Stone Circle
Loch of Skene
Westhill
Northfield
Mastrick
Craskins
Comers
Tillybirloch
Marionburgh
Echt
Garlogie
Cairnie
Elrick
Kingswells
Aberdeen Science Centre
Marischal Museum
Culsh Souterrain
Tornaveen
Findrack Ho.
Drumlasie
South Kirkton
Gordon Highlanders Museum
Mannofield
Ferryhill
Torry
Girdle Ness
Lumphanan
Midmar Forest
Redhill
Easter Ord
Blacktop
Cults
Ruthrieston
Kincorth
David Welch Winter Gardens
Nigg Bay
Greg Ness
Peel Ring of Lumphanan
Landerberry
Hill of Fare
Benthoul
Contlaw
Milton of Murtle
Bieldside
Garthdee
Doonies Farm
Milton of Auchinhove
Coull
Burn of Corrichie
West Cullery
Hardgate
Craigton
Banchory-Devenick
Nigg
Auchlossan
Slug of Dess Falls
Torphins
Milton of Campfield
Drum Castle
Milltimber
Charlestown
Cove Bay
Mid Beltie
Hirn
Peterculter
Aboyne
Kincardine O'Neil
Tillydrine
Brathens
Myrebird
Mains of Drum
Auchlunies
Hare Ness
Backhill of Trustach
Bridge of Canny
East Mains
Upper Lochton
The Neuk
Crathes Castle and Gardens
Drumoak
Kirkton of Maryculter
Maywell
Hillside
Findon Ness
Findon
Birsemore
Birse
Dee
Banchory Museum
Woodside of Arbeadie
Crathes
Woodlands
Muirskie
Auchlee
Portlethen
Marywell
Burn of Cattie
Arbeadie
Deebank
Banchory
Royal Deeside Rly
Kirkton of Durris
Denside
Upper Burnhaugh
Downies
Cammachmore Bay
Tom's Cairn
Blackhall Forest
Auchattie
Bridge of Feugh
Crossroads
Borrowfield
Cammachmore
Chapelton of Elsick
Cookney
Newtonhill
Carnferg
Tillygarmond
Finzean
Belts of Collonach
Strachan
Durris Forest
Cairn-mon-Earn
Netherley
Muchalls
Forest of Birse
Percie
Lochton
Raedykes Roman Camp
Bridge of Muchalls
Ballochan
Water of Feugh
Union Cottage
Garrol Hill
Mongour
Mergie
Rickarton
Water of Aven
Mount Shade
Kerloch
Cowie Water
Garron Pt.
Cowie
Glendye Lodge
Bridge of Dye
Kirktown of Fetteresso
Tewel
Stonehaven
Tolbooth Museum
Fetteresso Forest
Castle Haven
Dunnottar Castle
Thornyhive Bay
Burn of Tennet
Mount Battock
Glen Dye
Tannachie
New Mill
Carmont
Drumtochty Forest
Mains of Dellavaird
Burns Family Memorials
Drumlithie
Melun Cairn
Glenfarquhar Lodge
Glenbervie
Fiddes
Barras
Mill of Uras
Crawton
Cairn o' Mount
Drumtochty Castle
Strath Finella
Pitforthie
Roadside of Catterline
Crawton Bay
Catterline
The Retreat Glen Esk Folk Mus
Millden Lodge
Clatterin Bridge
Glensaugh
Auchenblae
Monboddo House
Mondynes
Braidon Bay
Todhead Point
East Cairnbeg
Brownmuir
Fordoun
Parkneuk
Roadside of Kinneff
Arbuthnott
Kinneff
Grassic Gibbon Centre
Arbuthnott Church
Arbuthnott House Gardens
Mains of Allardice
Little John's Haven
Hill of Wirren
Auchmull
Mains of Balnakettle
Thainston
Fettercairn Distillery Visitor Centre
Fettercairn
Howe of the Mearns
Scotston
Bent
Inverbervie
Bervie Bay
Mains of Thornton
Laurencekirk
Tulloch
Gourdon
Dalbog
Inch of Arnhall
Meikle Strath
Garvock
Garvock Hill
Redford
Witton
Gannochy
Edzell Castle and Gardens
Edzell
Sauchieburn
Luthermuir
Luther Water
Dykelands
Benholm
Mill of Benholm
Bridgend
Balfield
West Water
Dunlappie
Johnshaven
Tillyarblet
Brown Caterthun
White Caterthun
North Water Bridge
Inchbare
Newtonmill
Pert
Marykirk
Ecclesgreig
Kirkton of Menmuir
Tigerton
Craigo
Lochside
St Cyrus
Milton Ness
Mains of Balhall
Lochty
Bellie hill
Little Brechin
Keithock
Logie Pert
Muirton of Ballochy
Logie
Morphie
Pathhead
Trinity
West Muir
Hillside
Kirkhill
Brechin Castle Centre
Brechin
House of Dun
Caledonian Railway
Dun
Careston Castle
Cathedral & Round Tower
South Esk
Bridge of Dun
Montrose Basin
Montrose
Museum and Art Gallery
Scurdie Ness
William Lamb Memorial Studio
Aldbar Castle
Kinnaird Castle
Barnhead
Inchbraoch
Nethertown
Mains of Melgund
Middle Drums
Farnell
Bonnyton
Ferryden
Montrose Basin Visitor Centre
Aberlemno
A90
A92
A93
A96
A944
A920
A947
A956
A957
A980
A975
A935
89
77
7
8
9
10
11
12
A
B
C
D
E
F
G
80
76

Western Isles
UIBHIST A TUATH (NORTH UIST)
BEINN NA FAOGHLA (BENBECULA)
UIBHIST A DEAS (SOUTH UIST)
SOUTH UIST MACHAIR
EILEAN BHARRAIGH (BARRA)
Eilean Bhearnaraigh (Berneray)
Na h-eileanan Monach (Heisker or Monach Islands)
AN CAOLAS MHONACH
CAOLAS NA HEARADH
Baile Sear (Baleshare)
Griomasaigh (Grimsay)
Fuidhaigh (Wiay)
Eiriosgaigh (Eriskay)
Fuideigh (Fuday)
Bhatarsaigh (Vatersay)
Sanndraigh (Sandray)
Fiaraigh (Fiaray)
Lingeigh (Lingay)
Flodaigh (Flodday)
Vallay
Oronsay
Boreray
Kirkibost Island
Loch nam Madadh (Lochmaddy)
Loch Baghasdail (Lochboisdale)
Bagh a Chaisteil (Castlebay)
Baile Mhartainn
Solas
Cairinis
Baile a Mhanaich
Lionacleit
Tobha Mor
Dalabrog
Cille Bhrighde
Eolaigearraidh
Bruairnis
Tangasdal
Earsairidh
Loch Dunvegan
Dunvegan Head
Dunvegan
Neist Point
Waternish Point
Macleod's Tables
MACLEOD'S MAIDENS
Canna
Garrisdale Pt.
Oigh-sgeir
UIG
TARBERT
LOCHMADDY
MALLAIG OBAN (Winter only)
OBAN
NF
90
78
Scale : 1:250 000
(approx 4 miles to 1 inch)
0 1 2 3 4 5 6 miles
0 1 2 3 4 5 6 7 8 9 10 km

Fladda-chùain
Eilean Trodday
Rubha Hunish
Rubha na h-Aiseig
Duntulm
Balmacqueen
Kilmaluag
Hunglader
Borneskeitaig
Kilmuir
Flodigarry
Eilean Flodigarry
Staffin I.
Digg
Glashvin
Brogaig
Stenscholl
Staffin
Kilvaxter
Balgown
Linicro
TROTTERNISH
Kilt Rock
Kilbride Point
Totscore
Maligar
Elishader
Ascrib Islands
Idrigill
Uig
Uig Bay
Marishader
Valtos
Rubha nam Brathairean
Garros
Culnaknock
Ru Chorachan
Balnaknock
Earlish
Brekrey
Lealt
Lower Tote
Upper Tote
LOCH SNIZORT
Peinlich
Island of Rona
Greshornish Pt.
Lyndale Pt.
Kingsburgh
Lusta
Greshornish
Lyndale Ho.
Eilean Garbh
Flashader
Treaslane
Suladale
Edinbane
Eyre
TROTTERNISH
Eilean Tigh
Garbh Eilean
An Caol
The Aird
Kensaleyre
Bernisdale
Blackhill
Holm I.
Eilean Fladday
Glen Bernisdale
Tote
Borve
Skeabost
Carbost
Manish Pt.
Torran
Arnish
Uigshader
Drumuie
Achachork
Roskhill
Glengrasco
Roag
Torvaig
Vatten
Shulishadermor
Portree
Harlosh
Heatherfield
Penifiler
Ose
Balmore
Glenmore
Camastianavaig
ISLAND OF RAASAY
Glame
Balmeanach
Balachuirn
Rubha na'Leac
Mugeary
Bracadale
Tarner I.
Ullinish
Struan
Coillore
Conordan
Lower Ollach
Raasay Ho
Clachan
Oskaig
Inverarish
North Fearns
Eyre Point
Wiay
Oronsay
Portnalong
Upper Ollach
Gedintailor
The Braes
East Suisnish
Peinchorran
Rubha nan Clach
Fiskavaig
Fernilea
Carbost
Drynoch
Crossal
Merkadale
Sconser
Moll
Scalpay
Longay
Crowlin Islands
Eilean Mòr
Talisker Bay
Gleann Oraid
Talisker
Sligachan Hotel
Scalpay Ho.
Guillamon I.
Pabay
Eynort
Glen Brittle Forest
Grula
Luib
Dunan
RED HILLS
THE CUILLIN HILLS
CUILLIN HILLS
Glenbrittle House
Broadford
Waterloo
Lower Breakish
Upper Breakish
Harrapool
Skulamus
Corry
Bualintur
Soay
Torrin
Kilbride
Camasunary
Kirkibost
Kilmarie
Heast
Rubh an Dunain
Soay Sound
Strathaird
Rubha Suisnish
Kinloch
Drumfearn
Mol-chlach
Elgol
Glasnakille
Rubha na h-Easgainne
Eilean na h-Airde
Ord
Tokavaig
Duisdalemore
Ornsay
Isleornsay
Tarskavaig
Tarskavaig Pt.
Achnacloich
Camuscross
Teangue
Ferindonald
Kilbeg
Kilmore
Rubha Ard Slisneach
Knock Bay
Armadale Castle
Glen Meadhonach
Rubha Charn nan Cearc
Calligarry
Ardvasar
Aird of Sleat
Ard Thurinish
Point of Sleat
Rubha Shamhnan Insir
Canna Harbour
Kilmory
Kinloch Glen
Rubha na Roinne
Kinloch
Rubha Port na Caranean
Schooner Pt.
RÙM
SMALL ISLES
Harris
Glen Harris
Rubha Sgorr an t-Snidhe
Rubha nam Meirleach
SOUND OF RÙM
SOUND OF SLEAT
INNER SOUND
SOUND OF RAASAY
ISLE OF SKYE
Cleadale
Bay of Laig
Mallaig
Glasnacardoch
Beoraidbeg
Morar
Portnaluchaig
Back of Keppoch
Bunacaimb
Eilean Ighe
Bracara
Bracorina
Brinacory
Swordland
Stoul
Tarbet
Kinlochmorar
Meoble
Oban
LOCH MORAR
LOCH NEVIS
KNOYDART
Inverie
Scottas
Sandaig
Airor
Inverguseran
Glen Barrisdale
Gleann an Dubh-Lochain
Camusrory
Kylesknoydart
Kylesmorar
Arnisdale
Glen Arnisdale
Corran
LOCH HOURN
Kinlochhourn Forest
Sandaig Is.
Upper Sandaig
Glenelg
Eilanreach
Balvraid
Glen More
Bernera
Galltair
Kylerhea
Glen Arroch
Kyleakin
Kyle of Lochalsh
Balmacara
Balmacara Square
Reraig
Kirkton
Nostie
Auchertyre
Ardelve
Dornie
Totaig
Letterfearn
Keppoch
Invertinate
Ratagan
Shiel Bridge
Glenshiel Forest
Loch Duich
Ardintoul Pt.
Glas Eilean
LOCH ALSH
Erbusaig
Badicaul
Black Is.
Drumbuie
Duirinish
Port Cam
Plockton
Achmore
Stromeferry
Stromemore
Ardaneaskan
LOCH CARRON
An Dubh-aird
Uags
Toscaig
Kishorn I.
Ardarroch
Achintraid
Slumbay
Lochcarron
Ardnarff
Attadale
Attadale Ho.
Sanachan
Kirkton
New Kelso
Strathcarron
Achintee
Camusteel
Camusterrach
Culduie
Ard-dhubh
Applecross
Applecross Ho.
Applecross Bay
Applecross Forest
Eilean na Bà
Sallachy
Alit-nan-sùgh
Gleann Udalain
Bundalloch
Camas-luinie
Glenshieldaig Forest
Ben-damph Forest
Annat
Torridon
Torridon Forest
Glen Torridon
Fasag
Balgy
Shieldaig
Torridon Ho.
Inveralligin
Alligin Shuas
Rechullin
Upper Loch Torridon
Loch Shieldaig
Ardheslaig
Kenmore
Arinacrinachd
Fearnbeg
Fearnmore
Rubha na Fearn
Cuaig
Callakille
Lonbain
Lower Diabaig
Loch Torridon
WESTER ROSS
Flowerdale Forest
Baosbheinn Forest
Shieldaig
Redpoint
South Erradale
Opinan
Port Henderson
Badachro
Aird
Shieldaig
Kerrysdale
Charlestown
Gairloch
Smithstown
Strath
Big Sand
North Erradale
Longa Island
Rubha Bàn
Port Erradale
LOCH GAIRLOCH
Peterburn
Seana Chamas
Naast
Brae
Midtown
Rubha 'Ard na Bà
Tournaig
Londubh
Poolewe
Aird Dubh
Eilean Subhainn
Talladale
Loch Maree

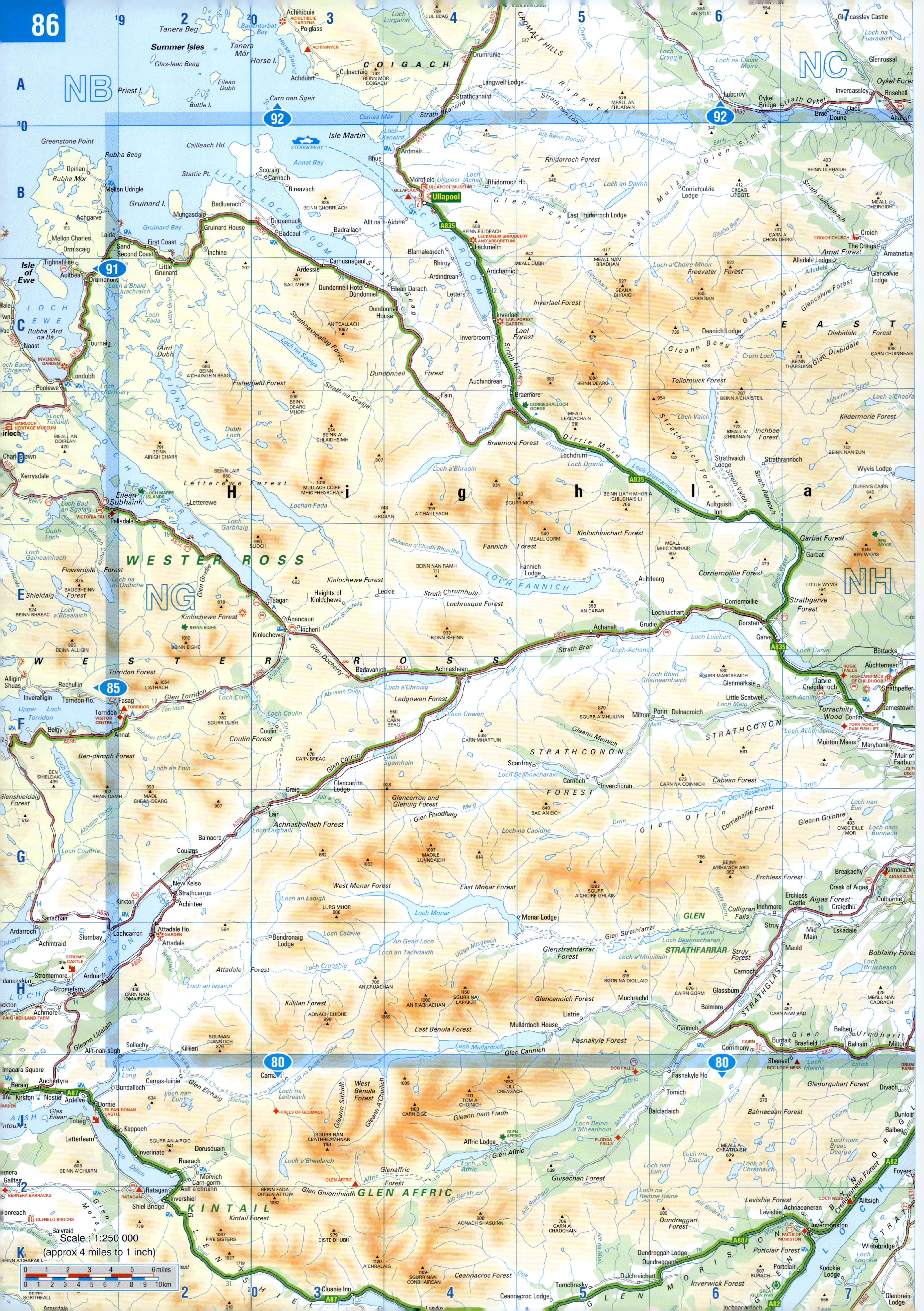
NB
NC
NG
NH
Summer Isles
Tanera Beg
Tanera Mór
Priest I.
Horse I.
Isle Martin
Achiltibuie
Polglass
COIGACH
Drumrunie
Ullapool
Loch Broom
Little Loch Broom
Gruinard I.
Gruinard Bay
Greenstone Point
Rubha Mor
Isle of Ewe
Loch Ewe
Poolewe
Aultbea
Laide
Dundonnell
Strath More
Braemore
Lael Forest
Inverlael
Fisherfield Forest
Letterewe Forest
Loch Maree
Kinlochewe
Talladale
Gairloch
Loch Fannich
Fannich Forest
Dirrie More
Loch Glascarnoch
Loch Droma
Braemore Forest
Aultguish Inn
Garbat Forest
Garve
Loch Garve
Loch Luichart
Lochluichart
Achanalt
Achnasheen
Strath Bran
WESTER ROSS
Highland
Torridon Forest
Torridon
Upper Loch Torridon
Shieldaig
Glen Torridon
Coulin Forest
Ben-damph Forest
Glen Carron
Achnashellach Forest
Lochcarron
Loch Carron
Plockton
Stromeferry
Strathcarron
West Monar Forest
East Monar Forest
Loch Monar
STRATHCONON
STRATHCONON FOREST
Glen Orrin
Orrin Reservoir
GLEN STRATHFARRAR
Strathglass
Cannich
Loch Mullardoch
Glen Cannich
GLEN AFFRIC
Loch Affric
Loch Beinn a' Mheadhoin
KINTAIL
Kintail Forest
Five Sisters
Glen Shiel
Shiel Bridge
Loch Duich
Dornie
Kyle of Lochalsh
Loch Alsh
Glenmoriston
Invermoriston
Dundreggan Forest
Ceannacroc Forest
Cluanie Inn
Balnain
Drumnadrochit
Loch Ness
Muir of Ord
Marybank
Contin
Strathpeffer
A835
A832
A890
A896
A87
A887
A831
A82
Scale : 1:250 000
(approx 4 miles to 1 inch)
miles
km

ND
NJ
93
88
81
MORAY FIRTH
DORNOCH FIRTH
CROMARTY FIRTH
BEAULY FIRTH
BLACK ISLE
Moray
CAIRNGORMS
NATIONAL PARK
MONADHLIATH MOUNTAINS
STRATHDEARN
HILLS OF CROMDALE
Inverness
Golspie
Brora
Dornoch
Tain
Balintore
Portmahomack
Tarbat Ness
Alness
Invergordon
Cromarty
Dingwall
Conon Bridge
Muir of Ord
Beauly
Fortrose
Nairn
Forres
Burghead
Grantown-on-Spey
Aviemore
Carrbridge
Bonar Bridge
Drumnadrochit
Culbin Forest
Burghead Bay
Nigg Bay
Rosemarkie
Ardersier
Fort George
Dallas
Tomintoul
Nethy Bridge
Boat of Garten
Dulnain Bridge
Tomatin
Kinveachy
Lairg
Rogart
Ardgay
Edderton
Evanton
Strathpeffer
Kiltarlity
Dores
Daviot
Croy
Cawdor
Auldearn
Dava

SPEY BAY
Burghead
Hopeman
Covesea
Covesea Skerries
Halliman Skerries
Stotfield
Branderburgh
Lossiemouth
Duffus
Gordonstoun
Cummingston
Roseisle
Roseisle Forest
Lossie Forest
Kingston
Spey Bay
Portknockie
Findochty
Cullen Bay
Logie Hd.
Cullen
Sandend
Portsoy
Redhythe Pt.
Buckie
Gordonsburgh
Portessie
Buckpool
Rathven
Portgordon
Lower Hempriggs
Quarrywood
Spynie
Bishopmill
Elgin
Newton
Miltonhill
Coltfield
Alves
Pittendreich
New Elgin
Moss of Barmuckity
Leuchars Ho.
Lochhill
Urquhart
Lhanbryde
Garmouth
Bogmoor
Upper Dallachy
Nether Dallachy
Porttannachy
Slackhead
Cairnfield Ho.
Drybridge
Lintmill
Milton
Fordyce
Kirktown of Deskford
Ardiecow
Berryhillock
Shiel Muir
Clochan
Broadley
Lochs Crofts
Mosstodloch
Auchenhalrig
Newlands of Tynet
Fochabers
Braes of Enzie
Miltonduff
Mains of Burgie
Monaughty Forest
Auchtertyre
Barnhill
Foresterseat
Paddockhaugh
Longmorn
Blackhills
Thomshill
Dipple
Orbliston
Speymouth Forest
Ordiequish
Teindland Forest
Inchberry
Wood of Ordiequish
Forgie
Broadrashes
Aultmore
Newmill
Craibstone
Little Toux
Newmills of Boyne
Oldtown of Ord
Cornhill
Mains of Edingight
Deerhill
Grange Crossroads
Edingight Ho.
Gordonstown
Knock Hill
Finnygaud
Crannoch
Sillyearn
Bracobrae
Knock
Knowes of Elrick
Davoch of Grange
Drumnagorrach
Farmtown
Aberchirder
Old Crombie
Knauchland
Marnoch
Califer
Briach
Branchill
Dallas Forest
Kellas
Glenlatterach
Dallas
Moray
Auchinroath
Newlands
Craigroy
Cairn Uish
Rothes
Glen of Rothes
Mulben
Keith
Rosarie Forest
Isla
Balloch Wood
Milltown of Rothiemay
Mains of Mayen
Hillbrae
Yonder Bognie
Bogniebrae
Fourman Hill
Burn of Rothes
Elchies Forest
Cairn na Cailliche
Whiteacen
Ben Aigan
Dandaleith
Maggieknockater
Towiemore
Edintore
Little Pitlurg
Coachford
Glen of Coachford
Ruthven
Cairnie
Archiestown
Craigellachie
Kininvie Ho.
Drummuir Castle
Drummuir
Upper Knockando
Cardow
Ringorm
Knockando Ho.
Knockando
Carron
Speyview
Charlestown of Aberlour
Milltown of Edinvillie
Daugh of Kinermony
Midtown of Buchromb
Milltown of Auchindoun
Dufftown
Daugh of Cairnborrow
Cairnborrow
Torry
The Bin
The Bin Forest
Corse of Kinnoir
Huntly
Lessendrum
Drumblade
Corse
Brideswell
Sliach
Larig Hill
Marypark
Bellehiglash
Kirktown of Mortlach
Haugh of Glass
Deveron
Strathbogie
Meikle Conval
The Scalp
Baileisward
Bridgend
Thomastown
Denend
Hillhead
Bainshole
Advie
Bridge of Avon
Dalchirach
Ben Rinnes
Glen Rinnes
Dullan Water
Favillar
Glen Fiddich
Ballochford
Succoth
Tillathrowie
Coynachie
Kirkstile
Shanquhar
Blackburn
Glens of Foudland
Lettoch
Mains of Dalvey
Kirkhill
Tomnaven
Clashindarroch Forest
Clashindarroch
Kirkney
Gartly
Cults
Knockandy Hill
Hill of Foudland
Largie
Drumin
Glenlivet
Shenval
Auchbreck
Glenfiddich Forest
Inverharroch
Bridgend
Black Water
Milton of Lesmore
Kennethmont
Milton of Noth
Oldtown
Ardlair
Aulton
The Shevock
Cromdale
Hills of Cromdale
Ballcorach
Tomnavoulin
Carn Daimh
Strath Avon
Auchmair
Cabrach
Round Hill
Blackwater Forest
Aldunie
Carn an t-Suidhe
Belhinnie
Rhynie
Cottown
Wheedlemont
Craig Castle
Clatt
Duncanstone
Leslie
Creggan a'Chaise
Knockandhu
Livet
The Buck
Knockespock Ho.
Coldwells Croft
Whitehaugh Forest
Glenlivet Forest
Clashnoir
Braes of Glenlivet
Chapeltown
Hill of Three Stones
Clova
Lumsden
Correen Hills
Muckletown
Dirdhu
Bridge of Brown
Fodderletter
Ladder Hills
Badenyon
Aberdeen
Tullynessle
Keig
Tomintoul
Delnabo
Carn Meadhonach
Carn Mor
Glenbuchat Lodge
Water of Buchat
Mossat
Lord Arthur's Cairn
Bridge of Alford
Montgarrie
Castle Forbes
Dorback Lodge
Conglass Water
Belnacraig
Rinmore
Kildrummy
Milltown of Kildrummy
Auchintoul
Alford
Gateside
Whitehouse
Blairnamarrow
Water of Nochty
Kirkton of Glenbuchat
Asloun
The Socach
Bellabeg
Forbestown
Strathdon
Glenkindie
Towie
Milltown of Towie
Sinnahard
Hillockhead
Ley
Little Lynturk
Geal Charn
Cairngorms National Park
Glen Ernan
Ernan Water
Inverernan Ho.
Candacraig Ho.
Heugh-head
Boultenstone
Muir of Fowlis
Bridgend
Kirkton of Tough
Tillyfour
Corrennie Moor
Carn Ealasaid
Tornashean Forest
Craig of Bunzeach
Hillockhead
Milton of Cushnie
Leochel Cushnie
Kintocher
Big Garvoun
Colnabaichin
Delnadamph
Cock Bridge
Corgarff
Tornahaish
Easter Davoch
Glen Avon
Migvie
Douneside
Craskins
Tornaveen
Findrack Ho.
The Bruach
Forest of Glenavon
Brown Cow Hill
Coynach
Logie Coldstone
Tarland
Lumphanan
Cromar
Morven
Milton of Logie
Glendavan Ho.
Coull
Milton of Auchinhove
Auchlossan
Torphins
Ben Avon
Gairnshiel
Glen Fenzie
Ordie
Lossiemouth Fisheries & Community Museum
Burghead Visitor Centre
Duffus Castle
Palace of Spynie
Elgin Museum
Cathedral
Cashmere Visitor Centre
Old Mills
Moray Motor Museum
Pluscarden Abbey
Birnie Church
Millbuies
Coxton Tower
Tugnet Ice House
Dolphin Centre
Baxters Highland Village
Fochabers Folk Museum Heritage Centre
St. Gregory's Chapel
Findlater Castle
Joiner's Workshop
Deskford Church
Strathisla Distillery
Keith and Dufftown Rly
Glen Grant Distillery
Macallan Distillery
Cardhu Distillery
Speyside Way Visitor Centre
Speyside Cooperage Visitor Centre
Balvenie Castle
Glenfiddich Distillery
Auchindoun Castle
Huntly Castle
Nordic Ski Centre
Brander Museum
Glenfarclas Distillery
Cragganmore Distillery
Speyside Way
Leith Hall
Glenlivet Distillery
St Mary's Church
Scottish Sculpture Workshop
Tomintoul Museum
Glenlivet Estate Visitor Centre
Lecht Ski Centre
Kildrummy Castle & Garden
Alford Valley Railway
Grampian Transport Museum
Haughton
Heritage Museum
Craigievar Castle
Corgarff Castle
Culsh Souterrain
Peel Ring of Lumphanan
Tomnaverie Stone Circle
A96
A95
A941
A920
A97
A98
A939
A944
A980
B9040
B9012
B9013
B9089
B9010
B9103
B9015
B9014
B9016
B9018
B9022
B9023
B9117
B9138
B9136
B9008
B9009
B9002
B9119
87
82
0 1 2 3 4 5 6 miles
0 1 2 3 4 5 6 7 8 9 10 km

Fraserburgh
Kinnaird Head
Rosehearty
Sandhaven
Pittulie
Broadsea
Inverallochy
Cairnbulg Pt.
Fraserburgh Bay
Macduff
Banff
Whitehills
Knock Hd.
Boyndie Bay
Head of Garness
Gamrie Bay
Gardenstown
Crovie
Troup Hd.
Pennan Hd.
Pennan
Quarry Hd.
New Aberdour
Strichen
New Pitsligo
Crimond
Rattray Head
St Fergus
Scotstown Hd.
Kirkton Hd.
Peterhead
Buchanhaven
Boddam
Buchan Ness
Longhaven
Cruden Bay
Port Erroll
Bay of Cruden
Whinnyfold
Collieston
Hackley Hd. or Forvie Ness
Newburgh
Newburgh Bar
Turriff
Cuminestown
Maud
Mintlaw
Longside
Old Deer
New Deer
Fyvie
Methlick
Ellon
Tarves
Oldmeldrum
Pitmedden
Inverurie
Kintore
Kemnay
Newmachar
Dyce
Balmedie
Blackdog
Bridge of Don
Aberdeen
Old Aberdeen
Westhill
Cults
Girdle Ness
Nigg Bay
Greg Ness
Cove Bay
Insch
Monymusk
Loch of Skene
Midmar Forest
B U C H A N
F O R M A R T I N E
G A R I O C H
A b e r d e e n s h i r e
A b e r d e e n   C i t y
NK
A90
A96
A947
A948
A950
A952
A981
A920
A975
KIRKWALL
LERWICK

NA
NF
St. Kilda
Boreray
Soay
ST KILDA
St Kilda or Hirta
(Hiort)
Dun
Bagh a Bhaile
Loch a' Ghlinne
CONACHAIR
MULLACH BI
Na h-Eileanan Flannach
Western Isles
Eilean Siar
Siabost bho Thuath
Siabost bho Dheas
Bàgh Dhail Beag
Dail Beag
Dail Mor
GEARRANNAN BLACKHOUSE VILLAGE
Na Gearrannan
Borghastan
Carlabhagh
Campay
Floday
Harsgeir
Little Bernera
DUN CARLOWAY BROCH
Dun Charlabhaigh
An Galan Uigeach
AN CAOLAS
Pabay Mor
Tobson
Crothair
IRON AGE HOUSE
Tolastadh a Chaolais
Aird Uig
Bhaltos
Vacsay
Breacleit
Great Bernera
Breascleit
Loch Rog an Ear
Loch Lacasabhat Ard
Bàgh Fhiabhaig
Cliobh
Miabhig
Timsgearraidh
Riof
Vuia Mor
Tacleit
Barraglom
Circebost
Tobhtarol
Keava
Eilean Kearstay
Calanais
CALANAIS VISITOR CENTRE
CALANAIS SMALL STONE CIRCLES
CALANAIS STANDING STONES
Gearraidh na h-Aibhne
Linsiader
Cradhlastadh
Uigen
Loch Rog
Vuia Beag
Crulabhig
Ard More Mangersta
Mangurstadh
Cairisiadar
Floday
Càrnais
Eadar Dha Fhadhail
SUAINAVAL
Geisiadar
Loch Smuaiseabhat
Loch Suainabhal
Aird Fenish
Loch Tungabhat
Einacleite
Aird Brenish
Islibhig
MEALISVAL
Breanais
Loch Grunabhat
Giosla
Loch Chaolartan
Loch Fuaroil
BEINN MHEADHONACH
Loch Airigh na h-Airde
Mealasta Island
Caolas an Eilein
Loch Morsgail
Loch Cro Criosdaig
Loch Coirigerod
Loch Tamanabhaigh
Loch Tealasabhaigh
Loch Bodabhat
Loch Beinisiabhat
Morsgail Forest
LOCH LANGABHAT
Loch Strandabhat
Kearstay
Scarp
Bràighe Mòr
Ceann Tarabhaigh
Airidh a Bhruaich
Aird an Troim
Loch a' Ghlinne
STULAVAL
Huisinis
Caolas an Scarp
SOUTH LEWIS,
HARRIS AND
NORTH UIST
TIRGA MOR
ULLAVAL
Aline Lodge
Seaforth I.
Gaisgeir
Hushinish Pt.
Aird a' Mhulaidh
Bàgh Huisinis
Gobhaig
Forest of Harris
UISGNAVAL MORE
Horsanish
Arda Mòra
Abhainn Suidhe
CLISHAM
CEANN A TUATH NA HEARADH
BEINN MHOR
Loch Shiphoirt
Taransay Glorigs
Soay Beag
Cliasmol
Miabhag
Maraig
Soay Mòr
Bun Abhainn Eadarra
LOCH A SIAR
Camus an t-suithean
OLD WHALING STATION
Aird Asaig
RHENIGIDALE
Reinigeadal
Tarasaigh
(Taransay)
Isay
Lochan Lacasdail
Loch Trollamarig
Paible
BEN LUSKENTYRE
Losgaintir
Tairbeart
(Tarbert)
Urgha
Carragraich
Rubha Sgeirigin
LUSKENTYRE BEACH
Caolas Tharasaigh
South Harris Forest
Caolas Scalpaigh
Carnach
Rudha Crago
Seilebost
Loch Ceann Dibig
Sgeotasaigh
Miabhag
Scalpay
Eilean Scalpay
Toe Head
Borve Lodge
Buirgh
NA HEARADH
(HARRIS)
Drinisiadar
Loch an Tairbeart
SCARISTA STANDING STONE
Kennacley
Plocropol Pt.
Coppay
CHAIPAVAL
Aird Mhighe
Greosabhagh
Plocrapol
Sgarasta Mhor
Liceasto
Leac a Li
Scadabhagh
Shillay
Little Shillay
Rubha'an Teampuill
BLEAVAL
Geocrab
Cluthar
Rubha Bhocaig
Sound of Shillay
Loch Langabhat
Beacrabhaic
Caolas Stocinis
Loch Greosabhagh
Brenish Pt.
Taobh Tuath
SEALLAM!
Stockinish I.
Fleoideabhagh
Manais
Pabaidh
(Pabbay)
Loch Steiseabhat
Aird Mhighe
Loch Fleoideabhagh
Quinish
Ensay
An t-Ob (Leverburgh)
Fionnsbhagh
ROINEABHAL
Cuidhtinis
Sound of Spuir
Caolas Phabaidh
Carminish Is.
Cairminis
Srannda
Borsam
Lingreabhagh
Loch Fionnsbhagh
Spuir
Killegray
Lingarabay I.
Ruisigearraidh
BERNERAY
Roghadal
ST CLEMENT'S CHURCH
Eilean Bhearnaraigh
(Berneray)
Baile
Langay
Vallay
Renish Pt.
Haskeir I.
Haskeir Eagach
Borgh
CAOLAS NA HEARADH
Caolas a' Mhorain
Boreray
Aird a'Mhòrain
Caolas Bhearnaraigh
Torogay
Groay
Gilsay
Lingay
Scaravay
Veilish Pt.
Lingay
Port nan Long
Vallay
Baile Mhic Phail
Griminish Pt.
Oronsay
Sursay
Tahay
Opsay
Scolpaig
TOWER
Vallay Strand
Greinetobht
Solas
Trumaisgearraidh
Loch Aimhsaraigh
Baile Mhartainn
Malacleit
Hermetray
UIG
84
Scale : 1:250 000
(approx 4 miles to 1 inch)
0 1 2 3 4 5 6 miles
0 1 2 3 4 5 6 7 8 9 10 km

RUBHA ROBHANAIS
(BUTT OF LEWIS)
CHURCH OF ST MOULAG
HARBOUR VIEW GALLERY
Eòropaidh
Port Nis
Cross Sands
Aird Dhail
Dail bho Dheas
Dail bho Thuath
Sgiogarstaigh
Cuiashader
Cellar Head
Gabhsann bho Thuath
Gabhsann bho Dheas
Mealabost Bhuirgh
Bail Àrd Bhuirgh
Coig Peighinnean Bhuirgh
Siadar
Rubha Leathann
Aird Barvas
TRUSHAL STONE
Siadar Iarach
Siadar Uarach
Baile an Truiseil
BLACK HOUSE MUSEUM
Labost
Bragar
Arnol
Brù
Barabhas Iarach
Barabhas Uarach
Barabhas
Loch Langabhat
Loch Mòr Shanndabhat
Abhainn Ghearadha
248 MUIRNEAG
Baile Ùr Tholastaidh
Tolastadh bho Thuath
Tolsta Head
Loch Sgeireach Mòr
Gleann Tholàstaidh
Port Bun a'Ghlinne
Griais
Creag Fhraoch
Bac
Col
Col Uarach
Vatisker Pt.
Breibhig
Coll Sands
Aird Thunga
Tunga
Sròn Ruadh
BROAD BAY OR LOCH A TUATH
Port Nan Giùran
Rubha an t-Siumpain
Port Mholair
Aird
Sulaisiadar
Seisiadar
Garrabost
EYE PENINSULA
Pabail Uarach
Pabail Iarach
Bàgh Phabail
Suardail
An Cnoc
A'Chearc
Mealabost
Aiginis
ST COLUMBA'S
Stornoway
Sanndabhaig
Tolm
Holm I.
BONNIE PRINCE CHARLIE'S MONUMENT
AN LANNTAIR GALLERY
LEWIS LOOM CENTRE
LEWIS CASTLE & MUS NAN EILEAN
Griannan
An Gleann Ur
Newmarket
Lacasdal
Loch Urabhal
Loch a' Ghainmhich
Acha Mor
ACHMORE STONE CIRCLE
Arnish Moor
Loch Orasaigh
Loch Tobhta Bridein
Liurbost
Griomsidar
Ben Casgro
Raerinish Pt.
Ranais
Crosbost
Soval Lodge
Barkin Is.
Tabhaidh Mhor
Lacasaidh
Ceos
Eilean Chaluim Chille
Eilean Orasaidh
Cromor
Eilean Thoraidh
Gearraidh Bhaird
Cabharstadh
Cearsiadair
Tabost
KERSHADER
Marbhig
Calbost
Ceann Shiphoirt
Taobh a' Ghlinne
Grabhair
Loch Odhairn
Kebock Head
Loch Shanndabhat
PARK OR PAIRC
Orasaigh
Eisgean
Leumrabhagh
Loch Shell or Loch Sealg
Srianach
Eilean Iubhard
470 CRIONAIG
Mol Truisg
Gob Rubh'Uisenis
Rubha Bhrollum
Rubha a'Bhaird
CAOLAS NAN EILEAN
Garbh Eilean
Eilean Mhuire
Na h-Eileanan Mòra (Shiant Islands)
Eilean an Tighe
ULLAPOOL
LEWIS
NB
NG
Fladda-chùain
Eilean Trodday
Rubha Hunish
Rubha na h-Aiseig
DUNTULM CASTLE
Duntulm
Kilmaluag
Eilean Mullagrach
Glas-leac Mòr
Glas-leac Beag
Priest I.
Bottle I.
Greenstone Point
Rubha Beag
Opinan
Rubha Mor
Mellon Udrigle
Gruinard I.
Gruinard Bay
Achgarve
Laide
Mellon Charles
Sand
First Coast
Second Coast
Ormiscaig
Tighnafiline
Aultbea
Drumchork
Little Gruinard
Loch a' Bhaid-luachraich
Isle of Ewe
LOCH EWE
Sròn a' Gheodha Dhuibh
Eilean Furadh Mór
Rubha Reidh
Camas Mòr
Loch an Draing
Cove
296 AN CUAIDH
Loch Sguod
Melvaig
Aultgrishan
Seana Chamas
Inverasdale
Midtown
Brae
Rubha 'Ard na Bà
Naast
Peterburn
Tournaig
INVEREWE GARDEN
Loch Bad a' Chreamh
Port Erradale
North Erradale
Londubh
Poolewe
Rubha Bàn
Big Sand
CARN DEARG
Longa Island
Caolas Beag
Strath
Smithstown
Gairloch
GAIRLOCH HERITAGE MUSEUM
Loch Tollaidh
LOCH GAIRLOCH
MEALL AN DOIREAN 420
Charlestown
Port Henderson
Aird
Badachro
Kerrysdale
791 BEINN AIRIGH CHARR
FIONN LOCH
Loch Fada
Aird Dubh
92
86
85
A
B
C
D
E
F
G
H
J
8
9
10
11
12
13

CAPE WRATH
Kearvaig
Faraid Head
Geodha Ruadh na Fola
Bay of Keisgaig
Loch Keisgaig
Inshore
Balnakeil Bay
Balnakeil
Durness
DURNESS VISITOR CENTRE
SMOO CAVE
Achiemore
Sangomore
Leirinmore
Keoldale
Eilean Hoan
Geodh'a' Bhrideoin
Eilean Clùimhrig
Sangobeg
Rispond
Geodha Ruadh
Am Balg
Sandwood Loch
Loch Airigh na Beinne
Kyle of Durness
Grudie
Sarsgrum
Rubh'an Fhir Léithe
Loch na Gainimh
Strath Shinary
Sheigra
Balchrick
Droman
Oldshore Beg
Oldshoremore
Eilean Roin Mor
Portnancon
Heilam
Hope
Lochside
Eilean Choraidh
Eriboll
LOCH ERIBOLL
Loch Hope
Loch Clash
Kinlochbervie
Badcall
Achriesgill
Gualin Ho.
Strath Dionard
Strath Beag
Polla
Bagh Loch an Roin
Loch Dughaill
Achlyness
Ceathramh Garbh
Rhiconich
Loch na Claise Carnaich
Ardmore Pt.
Rubha Ruadh
Ardmore
Foinaven
Handa Island
Fanagmore
Tarbet
Foindle
NORTH-WEST SUTHERLAND
Loch Dionard
Loch Crocach
BEN HOPE
Loch a'Garbh-bhaid Mòr
Laxford Bridge
Loch an Easain Uaine
ARKLE
Sound of Handa
Loch nam Brac
Scourie Bay
Scourie More
Scourie
Rubh'Aird an t-Sionnaich
Gorm Loch
Lochstack Lodge
Altnacaillich
DUN DORNAIGIL BROCH
Glen Golly
Strathmore
Upper Badcall
Lower Badcall
Badcall Bay
Loch Stack
BEN STACK
Strath Stack
Gobernuisgach Lodge
Eil. a'Bhreitheimh
Achfary
REAY FOREST
Lochmore Lodge
Rubha a'Mhucard
Meall Mòr
Calbha Mòr
Calbha Beag
Eddrachillis Bay
Duartmore Forest
Loch na Creige Duibhe
Loch More
Aultanrynie
Loch Coire na Saidhe Duibhe
Point of Stoer
Oldany Island
Cirean Geardail
R. nan Còsan
Eilean Chrona
Culkein
Culkein Drumbeg
Loch Nedd
Kylestrome
Kylesku
Glendhu
Forest
Kinloch
BEN HEE
Loch a'Ghorm-choire
Cluas Deas
Clashnessie Bay
Oldany
Drumbeg
Nedd
Loch Glendhu
Gleann Dubh
Unapool
Newton
Achnacarnin
Clashmore
Balchladich
Clashnessie
Rienachait
Stoer
Gleann Leireag
Loch an Leothaid
Loch Glencoul
Glen Coul
Loch Merkland
Merkland Lodge
Loch Fiag
Rubh'a' Mhill Dheirg
Bay of Stoer
Clachtoll
Loch Poll
QUINAG
BEINN LEOID
Loch an Eircill
Loch Dubh a'Chuail
Loch a'Ghriama
EAS COUL AULIN WATERFALL
Loch Beannach
Loch Crocach
Lochessynt Lodge
R. Leumair
Achmelvich Bay
Rhicarn
Achmelvich
Little Assynt
LOCH ASSYNT
Skiag Bridge
ARDVRECK CASTLE
BEINN UIDHE
Gorm Loch Mòr
Corrykinloch
Fionn Loch Mor
Overscaig Hotel
Glen Fiag
Fiag Plantation
Rubha Rodha
ASSYNT VISITOR CENTRE
Baddidarach
Lochinver
Brackloch
Glencanisp Lodge
Loch Feith an Leothaid
Inchnadamph
Inchnadamph Forest
Soyea I.
Loch Inver
Kirkaig Pt.
A'Chleit
Badnaban
Strathan
ASSYNT-
MAOVALLY
Fiag Bridge
Loch Kirkaig
Inverkirkaig
Glencanisp
Forest
Stronchrubie
BEN MORE ASSYNT
Rubha Coigeach
Rubha na Breige
Eilean Mòr
SUILVEN
Fionn Loch
Loch na Gainimh
CANISP
BREABAG
MEALL AN AONAICH
Duchally
Strath an Loin
ENARD BAY
Falls
COIGACH
Benmore Forest
Camas Eilean Ghlais
Rubha Mòr
Reiff
Rubh'a' Choin
Inverpolly Lodge
Loch Awe
Cam Loch
Loch Veyatie
Loch Sionascaig
Brae of Achnahaird
Altandhu
SUMMER ISLES SMOKEHOUSE
Ledmore
Altnacealgach Hotel
Loch Ailsh
Benmore Lodge
BEINN SGEIREACH
Eilean Mullagrach
Aird of Coigach
Inverpolly Forest
CUL MOR
Drumrunie Forest
Loch an Doire Dhuibh
HIGHLAND RARE BREEDS FARM
Elphin
Isle Ristol
Polbain
Loch Osgaig
STAC POLLAIDH
Knockan
Loch Urigill
Glas-leac Mòr
Loch Bad a'Ghaill
CUL BEAG
KNOCKAN CRAG
AN STUC
Glen Oykel
BEINN AN EOIN
Glencassley Castle
Achiltibuie
ACHILTIBUIE GARDENS
Tanera Beg
Badentarbat Bay
Polglass
Loch Lurgainn
CROMALT HILLS
Oykel
Loch na Fuaralaich
Summer Isles
Tanera Mòr
Horse Sound
ACHININVER
Drumrunie
Loch Craggie
Loch na Claise Moire
Glenrossal
Glas-leac Beag
Horse I.
COIGACH
Achduart
Culnacraig
BEINN MOR COIGACH
Langwell Lodge
Rappach
Priest I.
Eilean Dubh
Bottle I.
Carn nan Sgeir
Strathcanaird
Strath nan Lon
MEALL AN FHUARAIN
Lubcroy
Oykel Bridge
Strath Oykel
Invercassley
Rosehall
Camas Mòr
Strath
Kanaird
Brae
Doune
Altass
Greenstone Point
Isle Martin
Loch Kanaird
Allt Beinn Donuill
Rappach Water
Rubha Beag
Cailleach Hd.
STORNOWAY
Ardmair
Rhidorroch Forest
Glen Einig
BEINN ULBHAIDH
Opinan
NG
Annat Bay
Rhue
Stattic Pt.
Scoraig
Camach
Rireavach
LITTLE LOCH BROOM
Morefield
Ullapool
ULLAPOOL MUSEUM
Loch Achall
Rhidorroch Ho.
Loch an Daimh
Strath Mulzie
Corriemulzie Lodge
CREAG LOISGTE
Strath Cuileannach
MEALL DHEIRGIDH
Badluarach
BEINN GHOBHLACH
Glen Achall
East Rhidorroch Lodge
Gruinard House
Dundonnell
Badcaul
Badrallach
Allt na h-Airbhe
LOCH BROOM
BEINN EILIDEACH
LECKMELM SHRUBBERY AND ARBORETUM
Glasha Burn
CARN A' CHOIN DEIRG
Croich
CROICH CHURCH
Mellon Charles
Laide
Sand
First Coast
NB
Scale 1:250 000
(approx 4 miles to 1 inch)
miles
km

NC
ND
NH
NJ
87
94
Strathy Point
Totegan
Armadale Bay
Brawl
Strathy Bay
Melvich Bay
Red Pt.
Fresgoe
Sandside Bay
Brims Ness
Spear Hd.
Holborn Hd.
Clardon Hd.
Scrabster
Crosskirk
ST MARY'S CHAPEL
STROMNESS
Dunnet Hd.
Briga Hd.
The Thirl
Head
Rubha Thormaid
Eilean nan Ron
Ardmore Pt.
Kirtomy Pt.
Farr Pt.
Neave I. or Coombe I.
Port Vasgo
Caol Raineach
Rabbit Is.
Torrisdale Bay
Tongue Bay
Strathan
Midfield
West Strathan
Talmine
Skinnet
Midtown
Skerray
Achtoty
Airdtorrisdale
Torrisdale
Skullomie
Coldbackie
Borgie
Invernaver
Bettyhill
Achina
Farr
Swordly
Kirtomy
Armadale
Lednagullin
Aultiphurst
Baligill
Strathy
Melvich
Portskerra
Bighouse
Sandside Ho.
Reay
Isauld
Dounreay
Buldoo
Achvarasdal
Achreamie
Bridge of Forss
Shebster
Westfield
Thurso
THURSO CASTLE
CAITHNESS HORIZONS MUS
Thurso East
Millbank
Murkle
Castletown
Clardon
Haimer
Olrig Ho.
Newlands of Geise
Geise
Weydale
Achingills
Lieurary
Buckies
Sordale
Knockdee
Broubster
Calder Mains
Braal Castle
Roadside
Clayock
Halkirk
Banniskirk Ho.
Shurrery
Shurrery Lodge
Brawlbin
Scotscalder Station
Harpsdale
Olgrinmore
Dorrery
Spittal
Westerdale
Mybster
A'Mhoine
Achuvoldrach
TONGUE
Kirkiboll
Tongue
CASTLE VARRICH
KYLE OF TONGUE
Ribigill
Kinloch Lodge
Drum nan Clar
Loch Craggie
Borgie Forest
Leckfurin
Skelpick
ACHANLOCHY CLEARANCE VILLAGE
Achagary
STRATHNAVER MUSEUM
Loch Meadie
Strathy Forest
Loch Meala
Bowside Lodge
Golval
Loch Akran
Loch na Seilge
Achiemore
Upper Bighouse
Craigtown
Dalhalvaig
Trantlemore
Trantlebeg
STRATH HALLADALE
Forsinain
Loch Mor na Caorach
Loch nan Clach
Carnachy
Rhifail
527 BEINN STUMANADH
764 BEN LOYAL
Loch Loyal Lodge
557 CNOC NAN CULLEAN
Loch Loyal
Loch an Dherue
Loch Haluim
Loch Coulside
Inchkinloch
STRATHNAVER
Skail
Langdale
Syre
Loch Syre
Dalvina Lo.
ROSAL CLEARANCE TRAIL
Loch Strathy
Loch nam Breac
Loch na Saobhaidhe
280 SLETILL HILL
Loch Sletill
Forsinard
Forsinard Station
FORSINARD FLOWS
Loch Crocach
Loch Druim a'Chliabhain
580 BEN GRIAM BEG
Altnabreac Station
Lochdhu
Loch Dubh nan Geodh
Loch Gaineimh
Loch Eileanach
Strathmore Lodge
Lochmore Cottage
Loch More
Loch Ruard
Loch Thulachan
Loch Sand
Loch Rangag
Loch a'Mhuilinn
Dalnawillan Lodge
Rumsdale Water
Loch Meadie
Loch Eileanach
294 POLE HILL
Rimsdale Burn
Garvault Hotel
509 BEN GRIAM MORE
Achentoul Forest
373
348 BEN ALISKY
Loch Breac
Loch Dubh
Glutt Lodge
269 CNOCAN CONACHREAG
Braehungie
Houstry
Smerral
Mudale
Altnaharra
Loch Naver
Naver Forest
Loch Rimsdale
Loch nan Clàr
Badanloch Forest
Loch Badanloch
Loch an Ruathair
Loch Arichlinie
Lochside
438
Knockfin Heights
Clebrig
Loch Truderscaig
Loch an Alltan Fhearna
Badanloch Lodge
Strath Beg
Kinbrace
Achentoul
318 CNOC LOCH MHADADH
Dunbeath Water
Latheronwheel Ho.
Braemore
Berriedale Water
Strath Vagastie
721 BEN KLIBRECK
961 MEALL NAN CON
Loch Choire Forest
Loch Choire Lodge
Loch Choire
Highland
Borrobol Forest
Kinbrace Burn
438 CNOC COIRE NA PEARNA
705 MORVEN
626 SCARABEN
Balnabruich
Dunbeath
DUNBEATH CASTLE
Dunbeath Bay
Knockally
Ramscraigs
Crask Inn
542
Loch a'Bhealaich
581 MEALL A'BHATA
704 BEN ARMINE
Gorm-loch Beag
Gorm-loch Mor
713 CREAG MHÒR
Altanduin
365
Borrobol Lodge
387 CREAG NAM FIADH
Suisgill Burn
517 CNOC AN EIREANNAICH
555 CREAG SCALABSDALE
Wag
Langwell Forest
Aultibea
Borgue
Newport
Ceann Leathad nam Bò
Berriedale
Langwell Ho.
BADBEA CLEARANCE VILLAGE
Loch Gaineamhach
486
BEN ARMINE FOREST
Strath Skinsdale
Skinsdale
Kildonan Lodge
BAILE AN OR GOLDRUSH SITE
414 BEINN DUBHAIN
Tuarie Burn
STRATH OF KILDONAN
422
Ousdale
Strath Tirry
Glas-loch Mor
Ben Armine Lodge
Strath na Seilge
Craggie
Craggie Burn
Helmsdale
Torrish
Kilphedir
ELDRABLE HILL 417
Marrel
West Helmsdale
HELMSDALE
TIMESPAN HERITAGE CENTRE
Navidale
Ord Point
Helmsdale
461 MEALLAN LIATH MOR
345
Black Water
628 BEINN DHORAIN
592
Glen Loth
Glen Sletdale
Gartymore
Portgower
Rhian
Shinness
Dalnessie
LOCH SHIN
Achnairn
Loch Beannach
Balnacoil
538 COL-BHEINN
Lothmore
Lothbeg
Lothbeg Pt.
Dalchork
Dalchork Wood
Colaboll
Achnaluachrach
West Langwell
Strath Brora
Gordonbush
Sallachy
Saval
Lairg Lodge
Lairg Muir
Lairg
FERRYCROFT VISITOR CENTRE
Loch Craggie
323
Dalreavoch
Rhilochan
East Langwell
Loch Brora
BEN HORN 521
Loch Horn
Farlary
Achrimsdale
East Clyne
West Clyne
Clynelish
CLYNELISH DISTILLERY
Dalchalm
Brora
Claonel
Gruids
Torroble
Strath Fleet
Muie
Ardachu
Loch Cracail Mor
336
Rogart
Pittentrail
HECTOR MACDONALD MONUMENT
Rogart Station
377 CAGAR FEOSAIG
466 BEINN LUNNDAIDH
Backies
Doll
Achany
Shin Forest
Achinduich
Morvich
DUNROBIN CASTLE MUSEUM & GARDENS
Golspie
Linsidemore
FALLS OF SHIN VISITOR CENTRE
Torboll Farm
Culmaily
Achnahanat
Loch Laro
Loch Buidhe
Little Torboll
Kirkton
Cambusmore Lodge
Invercan
Invershin
Craigton
349 BEINN DOMHNAILL
LOCH FLEET
Loch Fleet
Cambusavie Farm
Littleferry
CARBISDALE CASTLE
Culrain
Balblair
297
Achvaich
Badninish
Skelbo
SKELBO CASTLE
Fourpenny
Braelangwell Lodge
Airdens
Clashcoig
Rearquhar
Poles
Embo
Embo Street
Pronсy
Migdale
Bonar Bridge
Western Gruinards
Soyal
Lower
Gablon
Pitgrudy
A836
A838
A897
B871
B873
A839
A9
B874
B870
A882
A99

HOY
Pegal Burn
Rack Wick
KNAP OF TROWIEGLEN
Rysa Little
Fara
Calf of Flotta
Roan Hd.
Hunda
FOSSIL AND VINTAGE CENTRE
Echnaloch Bay
Northtown
Burray
Burray Ness
Rose Ness
Sneuk Hd.
SCAPA FLOW VISITOR CENTRE
Lyness
Rinnigill
Weddel Sd.
Pan Hope
Pan
Bow
Flotta
Uppertown
Water Sound
Hillside
Burray Village
Southtown
St. Margaret's Hope
Rumley Pt.
Grimness
Grim Ness
Heldale Water
Burn of Ore
Little Rack Wick
Little Ayre
Crockness
Switha Sound
Hoxa
Herston
Herston Hd.
Quindry
Papley
Hoglinns Water
Wyng
Hackness
MARTELLO TOWERS
Longhope
Kirk Hope
Switha
Widewall
Aikers
Newark Bay
Melsetter
Hurliness
Brims
Aith Hope
Cantick Hd.
SOUTH WALLS
Garth Hd.
Sandwick
Sand Wick
Lythes
SOUTH RONALDSAY
Tor Ness
Brims Ness
Suckquoy
Wind Wick
Linklater
North Hd.
Barth Hd.
Dundas Ho.
Halcro Hd.
Swona
Burwick
Cleat
TOMB OF THE EAGLES AND BRONZE AGE HOUSE
Old Hd.
Liddel
Brough Ness
PENTLAND FIRTH
95
Langaton Point
Nethertown
Muckle Skerry
Red Head
Island of Stroma
(May-Sept)
Pentland Skerries
Mell Head
Uppertown
DUNNET HEAD
Men of Mey
St John's Pt.
Briga Hd.
Scarfskerry Pt.
Scarfskerry
East Mey
Boars of Duncansby
Gills Bay
STROMNESS
Brough
Ham
CASTLE OF MEY
Gills
Kirkstyle
Huna
DUNCANSBY HEAD
The Thirl
Hunspow
Rattar
Mey
Canisbay
John o' Groats
MARY ANN'S COTTAGE
St John's Loch
Stacks of Duncansby
Brims Ness
Spear Hd.
Holborn Hd.
Corsback
Barrock
Thurso Bay
Clardon Hd.
NATURAL HISTORY VISITOR CENTRE
Dunnet
DUNNET BAY
Inkstack
ST MARY'S CHAPEL
Crosskirk
Scrabster
THURSO CASTLE
CAITHNESS HORIZONS MUS
FLAGSTONE INTERPRETATIVE TRAIL
Castlehill
Loch Heilen
Brabster
Skirza
Clardon
Murkle
Gill Burn
Tofts
Skirza Head
Bridge of Forss
Thurso
Greenland
Lochend
Freswick
Freswick Bay
Dounreay
Buldoo
Achreamie
Millbank
Thurso East
Haimer
Castletown
Fresgoe
Newlands of Geise
Olrig Ho.
CASTLETOWN
Tain
Slickly
Ness Head
Sandside Bay
Isauld
Achvarasdal
CNOC FREKEDAIN CHAMBERED CAIRN
Geise
Hilliclay
Durran
Reaster
BUCHOLLY CASTLE
Reay
Westfield
Weydale
Bowermadden
Alterwall
CAITHNESS BROCH CENTRE
Shebster
Achingills
Lyth
Barrock Ho.
LYTH ARTS CENTRE
Sortat
Auckengill
Nybster
Lieurary
Buckies
Stemster
Bowertower
Howe
Brough Head
Loch Saorach
Sordale
Knockdee
Stemster Ho.
Keiss
KEISS CASTLE
Broubster
Calder Mains
Braal Castle
Roadside
Halcro
Hastigrow
Mireland
Loch Thormaid
Loch Calder
Claycock
Loch Scarmclate
Gillock
Kirk
Loch of Wester
Shurrery
Halkirk
North Watten
Myrelandhorn
SINCLAIR'S BAY
Brawlbin
Loch Olginey
Scotscalder Station
Harpsdale
Banniskirk Ho.
Mains of Watten
Killimster
Shurrery Lodge
Loch Shurrery
Olgrinmore
Loch Watten
Dorrery
Spittal
Backlass
Watten
Reiss
CASTLE SINCLAIR
CASTLE GIRNIGOE
Noss Head
NC
BEINN NAM BAD MOR
Loch Scye
Mybster
Loch of Toftingall
Bilbster
Winless
Ackergill
Sealky Head
ND
Staxigoe
Loch Tuim Ghlais
Strath
Wick
WICK HERITAGE MUS
Papigoe
Loch Caluim
Westerdale
Acharole
Burn of Acharole
Stirkoke Ho.
Milton
Broadhaven
Wick Bay
Old Wick
Loch Meadie
Newton
South Hd.
CASTLE OF OLD WICK
Highland
Loch Dubh nan Geodh
Badlipster
Whiterow
Gote O'Tram
Loch Eileanach
Strathmore Lodge
Little River
Tannach
Hempriggs House
Loch Gaineimh
Loch Hempriggs
Helman Hd.
Loch Sletill
Altnabreac Station
Lochmore Cottage
HILL OF OLICLETT
Thrumster
Lochdhu
Loch More
Rangag
GREY CAIRNS OF CAMSTER
Gansclet
Loch of Yarrows
Sarclet
93
Achavanich
Loch Ruard
Sarclet Hd.
Loch Thulachan
Loch Rangag
STEMSTER HILL
Camster
Loch a' Mhuilinn
Loch Sand
CAIRN OF GET
Ulbster
Whaligoe
Rumsdale Water
Dalnawillan Lodge
Roster
Bruan
Crofts of Benachielt
HILL O' MANY STANES
BEN ALISKY
Loch Breac
Braehungie
Rumster Forest
Upper Lybster
Mid Clyth
Glutt Lodge
Loch Dubh
West Clyth
CNOCAN CONACHREAG
Forse Ho.
Swiney
Lybster
Houstry
WAG OF FORSE
Smerral
Latheron
Forse
CLAN GUNN HERITAGE CENTRE
Dunbeath Water
CNOC LOCH MHADADH
Latheronwheel Ho.
Latheronwheel
LAIDHAY CROFT MUSEUM
Berriedale Water
Braemore
Balnabruich
DUNBEATH HERITAGE CENTRE
CNOC COIRE NA FEARNA
Dunbeath
Dunbeath Bay
MORVEN
Knockally
DUNBEATH CASTLE
CNOC AN EIREANNAICH
Ramscraigs
Wag
SCARABEN
Langwell Forest
Borgue
CREAG SCALABSDALE
Newport
Ceann Leathad nam Bò
Aultibea
Langwell Water
Langwell Ho.
Berriedale
BADBEA CLEARANCE VILLAGE
GOLDRUSH SITE
BEINN DUBHAIN
Ousdale
Torrish
Kilphedir
Ord Point
ELDRABLE HILL
Marrel
HELMSDALE
West Helmsdale
Navidale
TIMESPAN HERITAGE CENTRE
Glen Loth
Gartymore
Helmsdale
Portgower
Lothmore
Lothbeg Pt.
Scale : 1:250 000
(approx 4 miles to 1 inch)
0 1 2 3 4 5 6 miles
0 1 2 3 4 5 6 7 8 9 10 km

Orkney
HY
ND
Papa Westray
Holm of Papa
Westray
Holland
Aikerness
Backaskaill
Rackwick
Gayfield
Pierowall
Broughton
Braehead
NOUP HEAD
PIEROWALL CHURCH
NOLTLAND CASTLE
WESTRAY
FITTY HILL
Midbea
Skelwick
Langskaill
WESTSIDE CHURCH
Rapness
Sulland
THE NORTH SOUND
KIRKWALL
North Ronaldsay
Hollandstoun
BROCH OF BURRIAN
NORTH RONALDSAY FIRTH
Scar
Burness
Sellibister
Lettan
START PT.
Newark
Broughtown
Lady
Overbister
SANDAY
Kettletoft
Laminess
QUOYNESS CHAMBERED CAIRN
Stove
SANDAY SOUND
Calf of Eday
Carrick Ho.
CARRICK HOUSE
Calfsound
Braeswick
Millbounds
Guith
Loth
EDAY
Backaland
Veness
Faray
WESTRAY FIRTH
Wasbister
ROUSAY
Sourin
MIDHOWE BROCH
Eynhallow
EYNHALLOW CHURCH
Westness
KNOWE OF YARSO CAIRN
Frotoft
Brinian
CUBBIE'S ROO'S CASTLE AND ST MARY'S CHAPEL
Wyre
Egilsay
ST MAGNUS CHURCH
Muckle Green Holm
Linga Holm
Odie
Papa Stronsay
Whitehall Village
STRONSAY
Wardhill
Everbay
Grobister
Rothiesholm
Kirbister
Dishes
Holland
STRONSAY
Gairsay
Shapinsay
Edmonstone
Balfour
Newlot
FIRTH
Auskerry
ABERDEEN LERWICK
BROUGH HEAD
BROUGH OF BIRSAY
EARL'S PALACE
MARWICK HEAD NATURE RESERVE
Marwick
Abune-the-Hill
The Barony
Costa
Burgar
Kirbuster
Stenso
BROCH OF GURNESS
Redland
Twatt
Isbister
Beaquoy
Click Mill
CLICK MILL
Tingwall
Scarwell
Northdyke
Quoyloo
Skeabrae
Dounby
Hackland
Mirbister
Gorseness
Skaill
SKAILL HOUSE
Kierfiold Ho
CORRIGALL FARM MUSEUM
Brough
Isbister
Settiscarth
Breck of Cruan
Aith
Hestwall
Tenston
Netherbrough
Bimbister
Yesnaby
Voy
Arion
Finstown
STANDING STONES
RING OF BRODGAR
Quholm
Bridge of Waith
TORMISTON MILL
MAES HOWE
Heddle
Grimbister
WIRELESS MUSEUM
ORKNEY MUSEUM
Kirkwall
Work
Craigiefield
Nisthouse
Clouston
Outertown
ST MAGNUS CATHEDRAL
BISHOP'S & EARL'S PALACE
HIGHLAND PARK DISTILLERY
Berstane
Hall of Tankerness
PIER ARTS CENTRE
Stromness
STROMNESS MUSEUM
Ireland
Kirbister
Scapa
Tradespark
Whiteclet
North Halley
HOY AND WEST MAINLAND
Breckan
Clestrain
Cairnton
Hobbister
Smoogro
Greenigoe
Waulkmill Lodge
Deerness
Skaill
Grindigar
Murra
Graemsay
Petertown
Orphir
Swanbister
Gyre
Toab
Grittley
NORTH HOY NATURE RESERVE
Linksness
Houton
ST NICHOLAS CHURCH
Foubister
Quoyness
Hoy
WARD HILL
North Dawn
Upper Sanday
SCRABSTER
SCAPA FLOW
St Mary's
Braehead
ITALIAN CHAPEL
Copinsay
OLD MAN OF HOY
DWARFIE STANE
Rackwick
Cava
Cornquoy
RORA HEAD
KNAP OF TROWIEGLEN
Rysa Little
FOSSIL AND VINTAGE CENTRE
Northtown
Burray
Hunda
Hillside
HOY
Fara
SCAPA FLOW VISITOR CENTRE
Burray Village
Southtown
Lyness
Rinnigill
Bow
Pan
Flotta
Uppertown
St. Margaret's Hope
Grimness
Little Ayre
Crockness
Herston
Quindry
Wyng
Hackness
Papley
MARTELLO TOWERS
Widewall
Aikers
Longhope
Switha
Melsetter
Hurliness
Brims
SOUTH WALLS
Sandwick
Suckquoy
Lythes
SOUTH RONALDSAY
Linklater
Swona
Dundas Ho.
Cleat
Burwick
TOMB OF THE EAGLES AND BRONZE AGE HOUSE
Liddel
PENTLAND FIRTH
94
Island of Stroma
Nethertown
Uppertown
(May-Sept)
DUNNET HEAD
STROMNESS
Scarfskerry
East Mey
Brough
Ham
Rattar
CASTLE OF MEY
Gills
Kirkstyle
Huna
DUNCANSBY HEAD
Hunspow
MARY-ANN'S COTTAGE
Mey
Canisbay
John o' Groats
Corsback
Barrock
Dunnet
DUNNET BAY
NATURAL HISTORY VISITOR CENTRE
Brims Ness
ST MARY'S CHAPEL
Scrabster
THURSO CASTLE
CAITHNESS HORIZONS MUS.
INTERPRETATIVE TRAIL
Castlehill
Inkstack
Brabster
Crosskirk
Bridge of Forss
Thurso
Clardon
Murkle
Greenland
Lochend
Tofts
Skirza
Millbank
Thurso East
Hamer
Castletown
CASTLETOWN
Newlands of Geise
Geise
Olrig Ho.
Tain
Slickly
Freswick
Westfield
Weydale
Hilliclay
Reaster
BUCHOLLY CASTLE
CAITHNESS BROCH CENTRE
Shebster
Lieurary
Buckies
Achingills
Durran
Bowermadden
Alterwall
Auckengill
Sordale
Knockdee
Bowertower
Barrock Ho.
Lyth
LYTH ARTS CENTRE
Sortat
Nybster
Broubster
Calder Mains
Braal Castle
Stemster Ho.
Halcro
Hastigrow
Howe
Keiss
KEISS CASTLE
Roadside
Gillock
Mireland
Shurrery
Halkirk
Clayock
North Watten
Kirk
Myrelandhorn
SINCLAIR'S BAY
Shurrery Lodge
Brawlbin
Banniskirk Ho.
Mains of Watten
Killimster
Scotscalder Station
Harpsdale
Dorrery
Olgrinmore
CASTLE SINCLAIR
CASTLE GIRNIGOE
Spittal
Backlass
Watten
Winless
Reiss
Mybster
Ackergill
Staxigoe
Bilbster
Achavrole
Strath
WICK HERITAGE MUS.
Wick
Papigoe
Westerdale
Stirkoke Ho.
Milton
Broadhaven
Newton
Old Wick
Badlipster
Whiterow
CASTLE OF OLD WICK
Hempriggs House
Strathmore Lodge
Tannach
Lochmore Cottage
HILL OF OLICLETT
Gansclet
Thrumster
GREY CAIRNS OF CAMSTER
Rangag
Sarclet
Achavanich
Scale : 1:340 000
(approx 5¼ miles to 1 inch)
0 5 10 miles
0 5 10 15 km

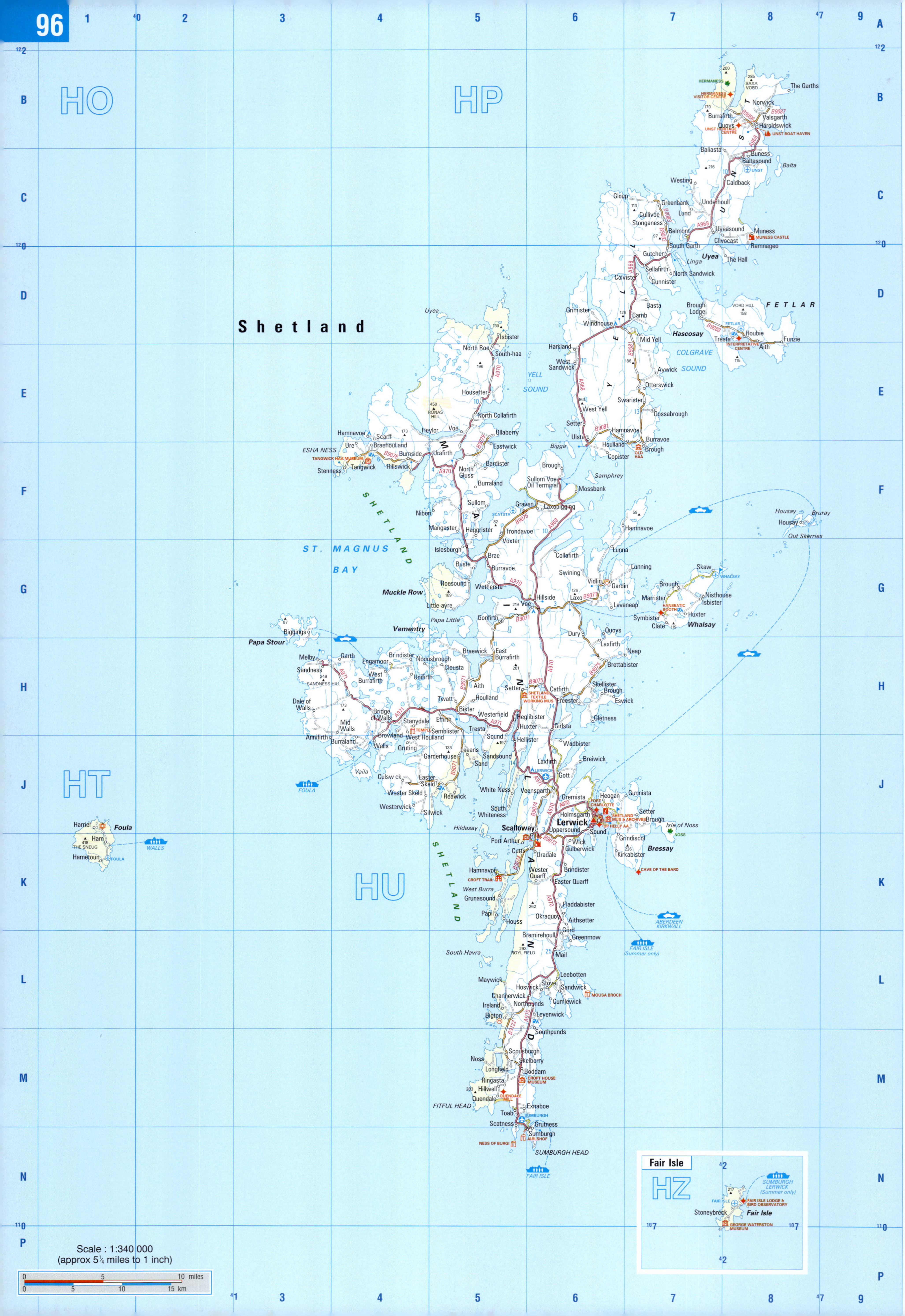
Shetland
HO
HP
HT
HU
HZ
Herma Ness
Hermaness Visitor Centre
Saxa Vord
The Garths
Norwick
Burrafirth
Valsgarth
Haroldswick
Quoys
Unst Heritage Centre
Unst Boat Haven
Baliasta
Buness
Baltasound
Balta
Unst
Westing
Caldback
Gloup
Greenbank
Underhoull
Cullivoe
Lund
Stonganess
Belmont
Uyeasound
Muness
Muness Castle
Clivocast
South Garth
Ramnageo
Gutcher
Linga
Uyea
The Hall
Sellafirth
North Sandwick
Colvister
Cunnister
Basta
Brough Lodge
Vord Hill
Fetlar
Gremister
Camb
Windhouse
Hascosay
Fetlar Interpretative Centre
Houbie
Tresta
Aith
Funzie
Mid Yell
Harkland
West Sandwick
Colgrave Sound
Aywick
Yell
Otterswick
Yell Sound
Swarister
West Yell
Gossabrough
Setter
Ulsta
Hamnavoe
Burravoe
Houlland
Brough
Copister
Old Haa
Bigga
Samphrey
Uyea
Isbister
North Roe
South-haa
Housetter
Ronas Hill
North Collafirth
Hamnavoe
Scarff
Heylor
Voe
Ollaberry
Esha Ness
Ure
Braehoulland
Tangwick Haa Museum
Burnside
Urafirth
Eastwick
Stenness
Tangwick
Hillswick
North Gluss
Bardister
Brough
Burraland
Sullom Voe Oil Terminal
Mossbank
Sullom
Graven
Laxobigging
Scatsta
Nibon
Mangaster
Haggrister
Trondavoe
Voxter
Housay
Bruray
Out Skerries
Hamnavoe
Lunna
Collafirth
Islesburgh
Brae
St. Magnus Bay
Swining
Busta
Burravoe
Lunning
Skaw
Whalsay
Vidlin
Gardin
Brough
Nisthouse
Roesound
Wethersta
Muckle Row
Hillside
Laxo
Marrister
Isbister
Little-ayre
Voe
Levaneap
Hanseatic Booth
Symbister
Hxuter
Clate
Whalsay
Papa Little
Gonfirth
Vementry
Biggings
Papa Stour
Dury
Quoys
Laxfirth
Neap
Melby
Garth
Brindister
Noonsbrough
Braewick
East Burrafirth
Brettabister
Sandness
Engamoor
West Burrafirth
Clousta
Unifirth
Sandness Hill
Aith
Setter
Shetland Textile Working Museum
Catfirth
Skellister
Brough
Dale of Walls
Twatt
Houlland
Freester
Eswick
Bridge of Walls
Bixter
Westerfield
Stanydale
Effirth
Heglibister
Mid Walls
Temple
Semblister
Tresta
Huxter
Girlsta
Gletness
Annirfirth
Browland
West Houlland
Sound
Burraland
Walls
Gruting
Hellister
Wadbister
Leeans
Sandsound
Garderhouse
Sand
Breiwick
Laxfirth
Vaila
Gott
Lerwick
Foula
Culswick
Easter Skeld
Wester Skeld
Reawick
White Ness
Veensgarth
Gremista
Heogan
Gunnista
Fort Charlotte
Westerwick
Silwick
South Whiteness
Holmsgarth
Setter
Shetland Museum & Archives
Brough
Up Helly Aa
Lerwick
Harrier
Foula
Ham
The Sneug
Hametoun
Walls
Foula
Hildasay
Scalloway
Uppersound
Sound
Isle of Noss
Noss
Port Arthur
Cutts
Wick
Gulberwick
Grindiscol
Bressay
Uradale
Kirkabister
Hamnavoe
Brindister
Cave of the Bard
Croft Trail
Wester Quarff
Easter Quarff
West Burra
Grunasound
Fladdabister
Papil
Okraquoy
Aithsetter
Aberdeen Kirkwall
Houss
Gord
Bremirehoull
Greenmow
South Havra
Royl Field
Mail
Fair Isle (Summer only)
Leebotten
Maywick
Hoswick
Stove
Sandwick
Channerwick
Mousa Broch
Ireland
Northouns
Cumlewick
Bigton
Levenwick
Southpunds
Scousburgh
Noss
Skelberry
Longfield
Boddam
Ringasta
Croft House Museum
Hillwell
Quendale
Quendale Mill
Fitful Head
Exnaboe
Toab
Sumburgh
Scatness
Grutness
Sumburgh
Jarlshof
Ness of Burgi
Sumburgh Head
Fair Isle
Fair Isle
HZ
Sumburgh Lerwick (Summer only)
Fair Isle Lodge & Bird Observatory
Stoneybreck
Fair Isle
George Waterston Museum
A970
A968
A971
B9081
B9082
B9071
B9074
B9075
B9073
B9087
B9088
Scale : 1:340 000
(approx 5¼ miles to 1 inch)
miles
km

BRISTOL
KINGSWOOD
FILTON
AVONMOUTH
Frampton End
Coalpit Heath
Mayshill
Winterbourne
Winterbourne Down
Watley's End
Whiteshill
Kendleshire
Henfield
Ram Hill
Lyde Green
Emersons Green
Mangotsfield
Shortwood
Siston
Siston Common
Goose Green
Webb's Heath
Warmley
Bridge Yate
North Common
Oldland
Cadbury Heath
Bitton
Longwell Green
Hanham
Hanham Green
Keynsham
Downend
Bromley Heath
Soundwell
Staple Hill
Hillfields
Fishponds
Speedwell
St. George
Crew's Hole
Conham
Frenchay
Broomhill
Stapleton
Eastville
Lockleaze
Clay Hill
St. Anne's Park
Broom Hill
Brislington
Stockwood
Flowers Hill
Arno's Vale
Knowle
Hengrove
Filwood Park
Lower Knowle
Windmill Hill
Bedminster
Bedminster Down
Novers Park
Hartcliffe
Headley Park
Highridge
Ashton Vale
Bower Ashton
Long Ashton
Barrow Wood
Bradley Stoke
Little Stoke
Great Stoke
Stoke Gifford
Harry Stoke
Patchway
Broad Mead
Cribbs Causeway
Catbrain
Compton Greenfield
Berwick
Hallen
Brentry
Southmead
Horfield
Henleaze
Golden Hill
Bishopston
Ashley Down
Montpelier
Cotham
Redland
Westbury Park
Eastfield
Westbury on Trym
Henbury
Lawrence Weston
Shirehampton
Sea Mills
Stoke Bishop
Sneyd Park
Clifton Down
Clifton
Hotwells
Leigh Woods
Avon Gorge
Abbots Leigh
Ham Green
Pill
Easton-in-Gordano
Portbury
Lower Failand
Failand
Tyntesfield
Tyntesfield Plantation
Ashton Hill Plantation
Cambridge Batch
Flax Bourton
River Avon
River Frome
Avonmouth Docks
The Royal Portbury Dock
AEROSPACE BRISTOL MUSEUM
MEMORIAL STADIUM (BRISTOL ROVERS FC)
COUNTY CRICKET GD
BRISTOL ZOO GARDENS
CLIFTON SUSPENSION BRIDGE
CABOT TOWER
SS GREAT BRITAIN
M SHED
ARNOLFINI GALLERY
ASHTON GATE (BRISTOL CITY FC & BRISTOL RUGBY)
ASHTON COURT ESTATE
BLAISE CASTLE
BLAISE CASTLE HOUSE
ROMAN VILLA
AVON VALLEY RAILWAY
GORDANO SERVICES
AVON RING ROAD
M4
M5
M32
M49
A4174
A4
A38
A37
A432
A420
A431
A4175
A4018
A4032
A369
A370
A403
A3029
0
1
2 miles
0
1
2
3 km

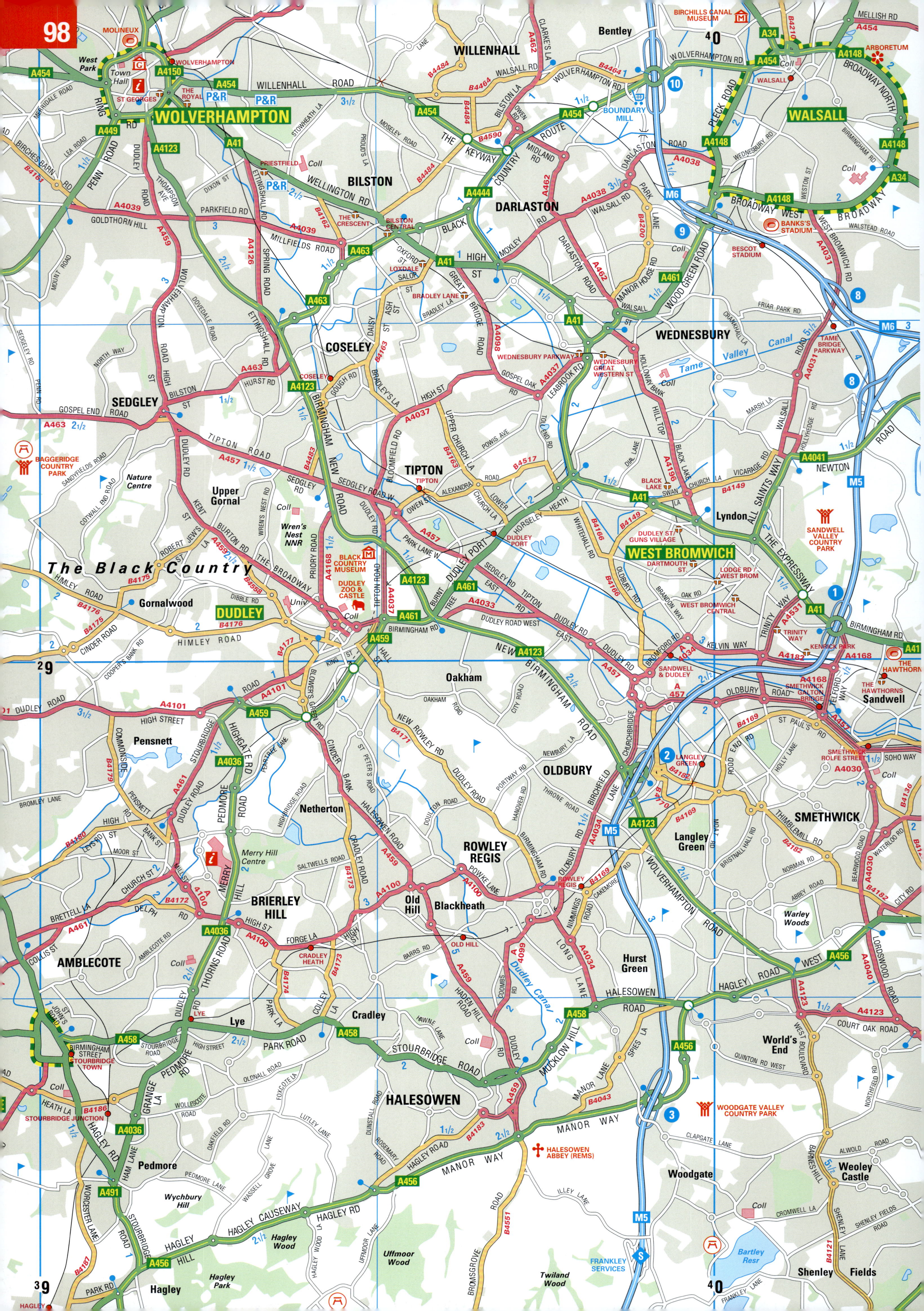
MOLINEUX
West Park
Town Hall
WOLVERHAMPTON
ST GEORGES
THE ROYAL
P&R
WILLENHALL
WILLENHALL ROAD
Bentley
BIRCHILLS CANAL MUSEUM
MELLISH RD
ARBORETUM
WALSALL
BROADWAY NORTH
BOUNDARY MILL
BILSTON
DARLASTON
BILSTON CENTRAL
THE CRESCENT
PRIESTFIELD
WELLINGTON RD
THE KEYWAY
BLACK COUNTRY ROUTE
BANKS'S STADIUM
BESCOT STADIUM
LOXDALE
BRADLEY LANE
COSELEY
WEDNESBURY
WEDNESBURY PARKWAY
WEDNESBURY GREAT WESTERN ST
TAME BRIDGE PARKWAY
Tame Valley Canal
SEDGLEY
GOSPEL END ROAD
BAGGERIDGE COUNTRY PARK
Nature Centre
Upper Gornal
TIPTON
Wren's Nest NNR
BLACK COUNTRY MUSEUM
DUDLEY ZOO & CASTLE
DUDLEY PORT
NEWTON
SANDWELL VALLEY COUNTRY PARK
Lyndon
BLACK LAKE
DUDLEY ST GUINS VILLAGE
WEST BROMWICH
DARTMOUTH ST
LODGE RD / WEST BROM
WEST BROMWICH CENTRAL
TRINITY WAY
KENRICK PARK
THE HAWTHORNS
Sandwell
SANDWELL & DUDLEY
SMETHWICK GALTON BRIDGE
SMETHWICK ROLFE STREET
The Black Country
Gornalwood
DUDLEY
HIMLEY ROAD
Oakham
Pensnett
Netherton
OLDBURY
LANGLEY GREEN
Langley Green
SMETHWICK
Merry Hill Centre
ROWLEY REGIS
BRIERLEY HILL
Old Hill
Blackheath
Warley Woods
AMBLECOTE
CRADLEY HEATH
OLD HILL
Hurst Green
Dudley Canal
World's End
Lye
Cradley
HALESOWEN
STOURBRIDGE TOWN
STOURBRIDGE JUNCTION
WOODGATE VALLEY COUNTRY PARK
HALESOWEN ABBEY (REMS)
MANOR WAY
Woodgate
Weoley Castle
Pedmore
Wychbury Hill
HAGLEY CAUSEWAY
Hagley Wood
Uffmoor Wood
FRANKLEY SERVICES
Bartley Resr
Shenley
Fields
Hagley
Hagley Park
Twiland Wood
HAGLEY
M5
M6
A41
A454
A4123
A459
A461
A463
A4036
A456
A458
A4034

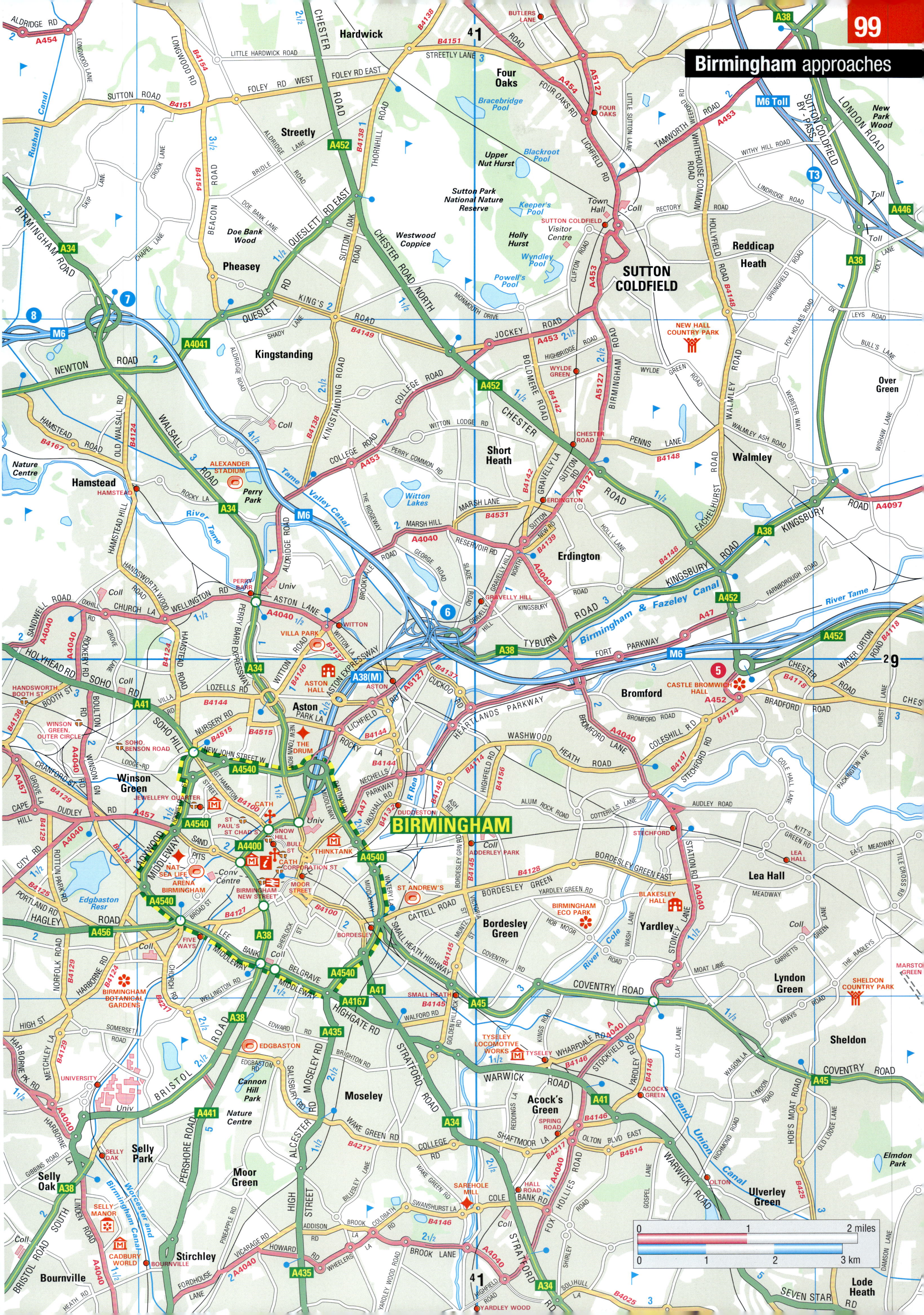
Hardwick
Four Oaks
Bracebridge Pool
Streetly
Upper Nut Hurst
Blackroot Pool
Sutton Park National Nature Reserve
Keeper's Pool
Town Hall
Doe Bank Wood
Westwood Coppice
Holly Hurst
Wyndley Pool
Powell's Pool
Pheasey
SUTTON COLDFIELD
Reddicap Heath
Kingstanding
NEW HALL COUNTRY PARK
Over Green
Short Heath
Walmley
Hamstead
Nature Centre
ALEXANDER STADIUM
Perry Park
Witton Lakes
Tame Valley Canal
River Tame
Erdington
Birmingham & Fazeley Canal
River Tame
Bromford
CASTLE BROMWICH HALL
Aston
ASTON HALL
VILLA PARK
THE DRUM
Winson Green
JEWELLERY QUARTER
BIRMINGHAM
THINKTANK
ST ANDREW'S
Edgbaston Resr
NAT SEA LIFE
ARENA BIRMINGHAM
Conv Centre
BIRMINGHAM NEW STREET
MOOR STREET
Bordesley Green
BIRMINGHAM ECO PARK
BLAKESLEY HALL
Yardley
Lea Hall
Lyndon Green
SHELDON COUNTRY PARK
Sheldon
FIVE WAYS
BIRMINGHAM BOTANICAL GARDENS
EDGBASTON
Cannon Hill Park
Nature Centre
TYSELEY LOCOMOTIVE WORKS
Acock's Green
Moseley
Grand Union Canal
Selly Park
Selly Oak
Moor Green
SARESHOLE MILL
Ulverley Green
Elmdon Park
SELLY MANOR
CADBURY WORLD
Worcester and Birmingham Canal
Stirchley
Bournville
Lode Heath
M6
M6 Toll
A38(M)
A38
A34
A452
A45
A41
A4540
0 1 2 miles
0 1 2 3 km

CARDIFF
(CAERDYDD)
Marshfield
Castleton
Blacktown
Peterstone Wentlooge (Llanbedr Gwynllŵg)
St. Mellons (Llaneirwg)
Trowbridge
Newton
Rumney (Rhymni)
Pwll-Mawr
Llanrumney
Llanedeyrn
Pentwyn
Begàn
Michaelston-y-Fedw
Park Wood
Cefn Mably Woods
Llwyncelyn
Coed Coesau-Whips
Lisvane (Llys Faen)
Llanishen Reservoir
Cyncoed
Roath Park
Roath
Splott
Tremorfa
Cathays
Maindy
Heath
Llanishen
Thornhill
Birchgrove
Gabalfa
Llandaff (Llandaf)
Llandaff North
Whitchurch
Rhiwbina
Pantmawr
Tongwynlais
Taff's Well (Ffynnon-Taf)
Nantgarw
Watford
Caerphilly Common
The Warren
Coed-y-Wenallt
Glan-y-llyn
Gwaelod-y-garth
Coed y Gedrys
Garth Wood
Morganstown
Radyr
Pentyrch
Grath Hill
Soar
Church Village
Taff vale
Pontcanna
Canton
Riverside
Butetown
Grangetown
Saltmead
Fairwater
Ely (Trelái)
Caerau
St Fagans (Sain Ffagan)
Michaelston-super-Ely
Culverhouse Cross
Wenvoe (Gwenfô)
Downs
Twyn-yr-odyn
Wallston
Leckwith
Michaelston-le-Pit
Llandough
St Nicholas (Sain Nicolas)
St Lythans
Drope
St Brides-super-Ely (Llansanffraid-ar-Elái)
St George's
PINEWOOD STUDIOS WALES
WALES MILLENNIUM CENTRE
NATIONAL ASSEMBLY
BBC ROATH LOCK STUDIOS
TECHNIQUEST
ICE ARENA
CARDIFF INTERNATIONAL POOL
CARDIFF CASTLE
CATHAYS NATIONAL MUSEUM CARDIFF
SSE SWALEC STAD
CARDIFF CITY
CARDIFF INTERNATIONAL SPORTS STAD
ST FAGANS NATIONAL HISTORY MUSEUM
LLANDAFF CATHEDRAL
CASTELL COCH
PARC CEFN ONN
FOREST FARM
TINKINSWOOD BURIAL CHAMBER
CARDIFF GATE SERVICES
CARDIFF WEST SERVICES
Cardiff Gate Retail Park
Valegate Retail Park
Cardiff Bay Barrage
River Taff
River Ely
Rhymney River
The Lake
Bute E Dock
Roath Dock
Qn Alexandra Dock
M4
A48(M)
A48
A469
A470
A4232
A4054
A4119
A4161
A4160
A4055
A4050
A4234
A4261
B4562
B4239
B4487
B4267
B4488
B4262
B4263
29
29A
30
32
33
P&R

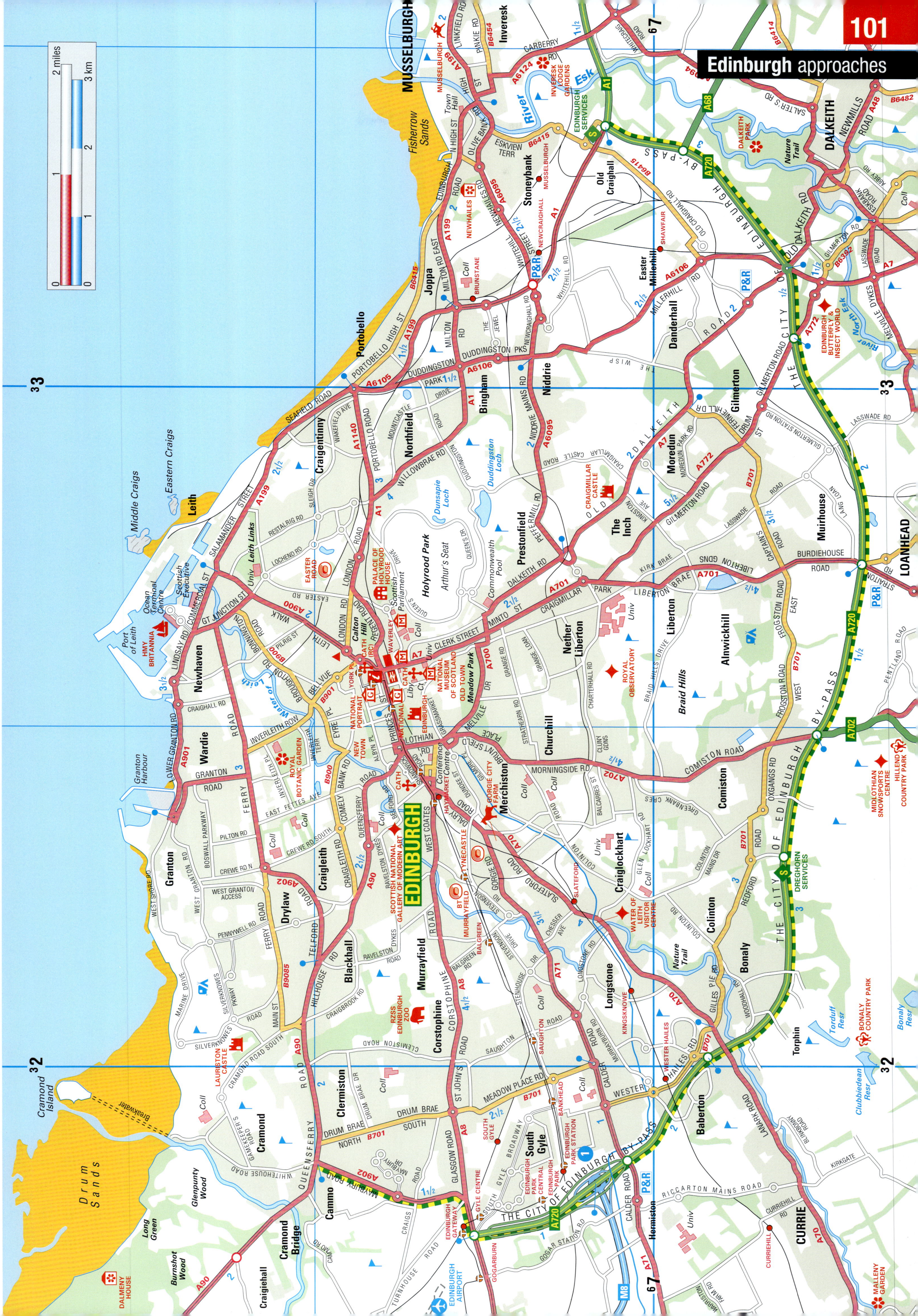
EDINBURGH
Musselburgh
Inveresk
Dalkeith
Portobello
Joppa
Leith
Newhaven
Granton
Wardie
Craigleith
Drylaw
Blackhall
Murrayfield
Corstorphine
Clermiston
Cramond
Cramond Bridge
Cammo
South Gyle
Merchiston
Churchill
Morningside
Craiglockhart
Longstone
Colinton
Bonaly
Comiston
Liberton
Nether Liberton
Alnwickhill
Braid Hills
Prestonfield
Niddrie
Bingham
Northfield
Craigentinny
Moredun
Gilmerton
Danderhall
Stoneybank
Old Craighall
Muirhouse
Loanhead
Baberton
Currie
Hermiston
Torphin
The Inch
Holyrood Park
Arthur's Seat
Drum Sands
Cramond Island
Fisherrow Sands
Middle Craigs
Eastern Craigs
Granton Harbour
Edinburgh Airport
Dalmeny House
Craigiehall
Burnshot Wood
Long Green
Glenpunty Wood
Duddingston Loch
Dunsapie Loch
Water of Leith
River Esk
Royal Botanic Garden
Royal Observatory
Craigmillar Castle
Lauriston Castle
Palace of Holyroodhouse
Scottish Parliament
HMY Britannia
Edinburgh Zoo
Meadow Park
Hillend Country Park
Midlothian Snowsports Centre
Bonaly Country Park
Malleny Garden
Dalkeith Park
Inveresk Lodge Gardens
Edinburgh Butterfly & Insect World
Edinburgh Services
Dreghorn Services
The City of Edinburgh By-Pass
2 miles
3 km

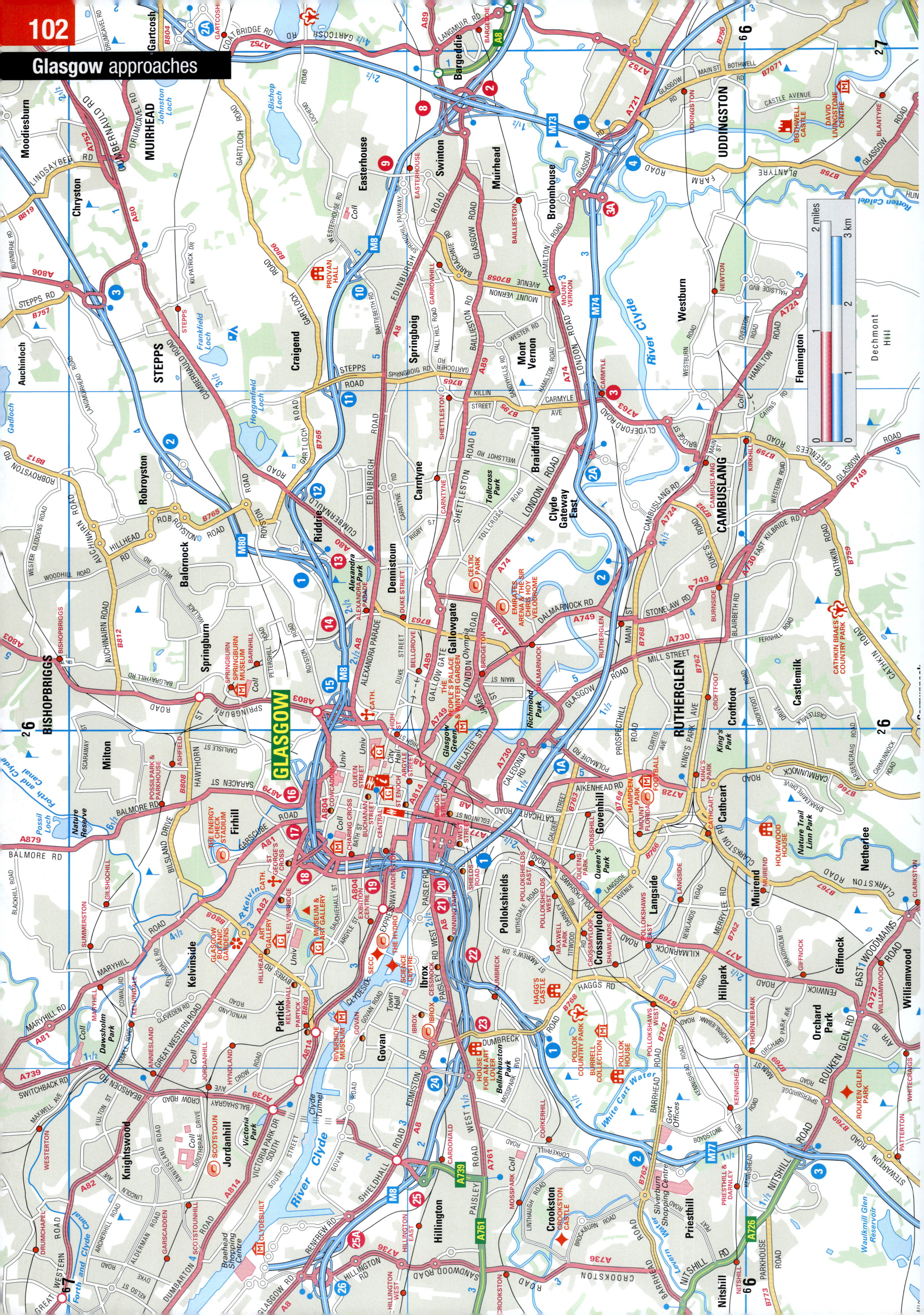
GLASGOW
Moodiesburn
Muirhead
Chryston
Stepps
Auchinloch
Craigend
Robroyston
Balornock
Springburn
Bishopbriggs
Milton
Firhill
Kelvinside
Partick
Dawsholm Park
Knightswood
Jordanhill
Victoria Park
Govan
Ibrox
Hillington
Pollokshields
Crossmyloof
Queen's Park
Langside
Govanhill
Cathcart
Rutherglen
Cambuslang
Croftfoot
Castlemilk
Netherlee
Muirend
Giffnock
Hillpark
Orchard Park
Williamwood
Crookston
Priesthill
Nitshill
Carntyne
Dennistoun
Riddrie
Springboig
Swinton
Easterhouse
Bargeddie
Baillieston
Mount Vernon
Broomhouse
Braidfauld
Clyde Gateway East
Uddingston
Westburn
Flemington
Dechmont Hill
Gallowgate
River Clyde
White Cart Water
Hogganfield Loch
Frankfield Loch
Bishop Loch
Johnston Loch
Tollcross Park
Bellahouston Park
Richmond Park
Glasgow Green
Forth and Clyde Canal
2 miles
3 km

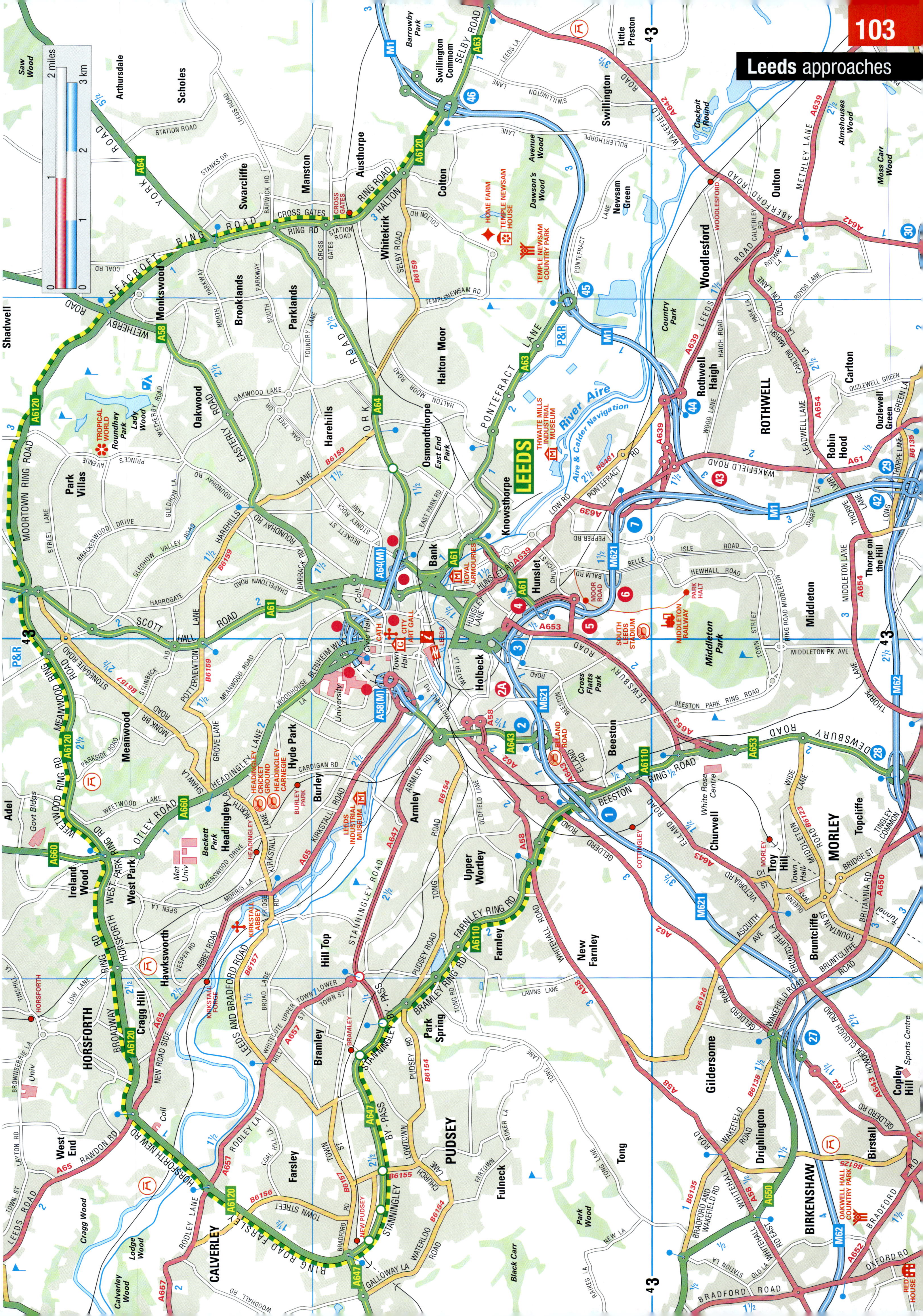
LEEDS
Shadwell
Scholes
Swarcliffe
Manston
Austhorpe
Colton
Whitkirk
Swillington
Swillington Common
Barrowby Park
Little Preston
Woodlesford
Oulton
Rothwell
Rothwell Haigh
ROTHWELL
Carlton
Oulzewell Green
Robin Hood
Thorpe on the Hill
Middleton
Middleton Park
Newsam Green
Temple Newsam House
Temple Newsam Country Park
Halton Moor
Osmondthorpe
Knowsthorpe
Hunslet
Holbeck
Beeston
Cross Flatts Park
Churwell
MORLEY
Topcliffe
Bruntcliffe
Gildersome
Drighlington
BIRKENSHAW
Birstall
Tong
Fulneck
PUDSEY
Farsley
CALVERLEY
Bramley
Hill Top
Armley
Upper Wortley
Farnley
New Farnley
Park Spring
Stanningley
Horsforth
HORSFORTH
Cragg Hill
Hawksworth
West Park
Ireland Wood
Adel
Meanwood
Headingley
Hyde Park
Burley
Kirkstall Abbey
Oakwood
Harehills
Brooklands
Parklands
Monkswood
Park Villas
Roundhay Park
Tropical World
Moortown Ring Road
Outer Ring Road
River Aire
Aire & Calder Navigation
Thwaite Mills Industrial Museum
Royal Armouries
Middleton Railway
South Leeds Stadium
Elland Road
Headingley Cricket Ground
Leeds Industrial Museum
University
Town Hall
City Art Gall
Cath
Civic Hall
Oakwell Hall Country Park
White Rose Centre
Cockpit Round
M1
M62
M621
A58(M)
A64(M)
A6120
A6110
A61
A62
A63
A64
A65
A643
A647
A650
A653
A654
A657
A660
A639
43

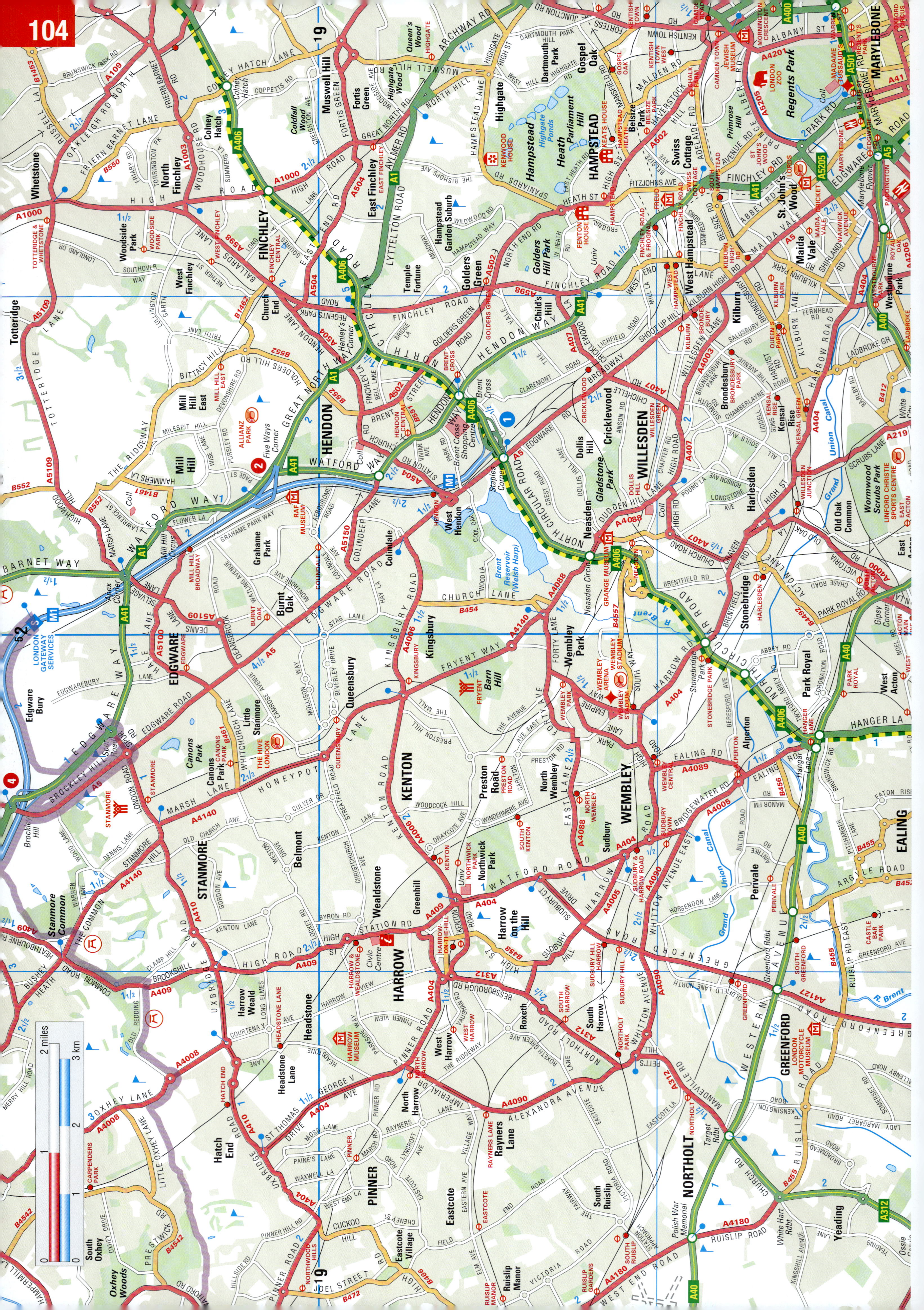
Whetstone
North Finchley
Woodside Park
West Finchley
FINCHLEY
Church End
Totteridge
Mill Hill
Mill Hill East
HENDON
Colindale
West Hendon
Burnt Oak
Grahame Park
EDGWARE
Edgware Bury
Canons Park
Little Stanmore
STANMORE
Stanmore Common
Belmont
Queensbury
Kingsbury
KENTON
Preston Road
North Wembley
WEMBLEY
Wembley Park
Sudbury
HARROW
Harrow on the Hill
Wealdstone
Greenhill
Harrow Weald
Headstone
Headstone Lane
Hatch End
North Harrow
West Harrow
Roxeth
South Harrow
Rayners Lane
Eastcote
PINNER
Ruislip Manor
South Ruislip
NORTHOLT
GREENFORD
Perivale
Alperton
Stonebridge
Park Royal
West Acton
EALING
Harlesden
WILLESDEN
Neasden
Dollis Hill
Cricklewood
Kilburn
Brondesbury
Kensal Rise
West Hampstead
HAMPSTEAD
Golders Green
Golders Hill Park
Temple Fortune
Hampstead Garden Suburb
East Finchley
Fortis Green
Muswell Hill
Highgate
Dartmouth Park
Gospel Oak
Belsize Park
Swiss Cottage
Primrose Hill
St John's Wood
Maida Vale
Regents Park
MARYLEBONE
Westbourne Park
Old Oak Common
Yeading
Oxhey Woods
South Oxhey
Colney Hatch
Brent Cross
Brent Reservoir (Welsh Harp)
NORTH CIRCULAR ROAD
WATFORD WAY
EDGWARE ROAD
FINCHLEY ROAD
HARROW ROAD
WESTERN AVENUE
BARNET WAY
Union Canal

PADDINGTON
Bayswater
Hyde Park
Kensington Gardens
CHELSEA
Knightsbridge
BATTERSEA
Battersea Park
Pimlico
Mayfair
Clapham Common
Balham
Tooting Bec
Upper Tooting
Tooting
Collier's Wood
Wandsworth Common
Earlsfield
WANDSWORTH
Wandsworth Park
Hurlingham Park
Parsons Green
FULHAM
Holland Park
Notting Hill
HAMMERSMITH
Shepherd's Bush
River Thames
BARNES
PUTNEY
Putney Heath
West Hill
Southfields
Wimbledon Park
WIMBLEDON
MERTON
MORDEN
Morden Hall Park
Wimbledon Common
Putney Vale
Roehampton
Richmond Park
Kingston Vale
Coombe
NEW MALDEN
Norbiton
KINGSTON UPON THAMES
SURBITON
ACTON
South Acton
Bedford Park
CHISWICK
Grove Park
Mortlake
East Sheen
North Sheen
Kew
RICHMOND
Richmond Hill
Petersham
Ham
Gunnersbury Park
West Ealing
Northfields
HANWELL
BRENTFORD
Syon Park
Old Deer Park
ISLEWORTH
St Margarets
TWICKENHAM
TEDDINGTON
Hampton Wick
Hampton Court Park
Bushy Park
Drayton Green
Osterley Park
Norwood Green
HESTON
HOUNSLOW
Whitton
Hounslow Heath
HANWORTH
Hampton
SOUTHALL
Dormer's Wells
North Hyde
Hounslow West
FELTHAM
SUNBURY
Hayes Town
Cranford
Low Emission Zone
River Wandle
River Brent
River Crane

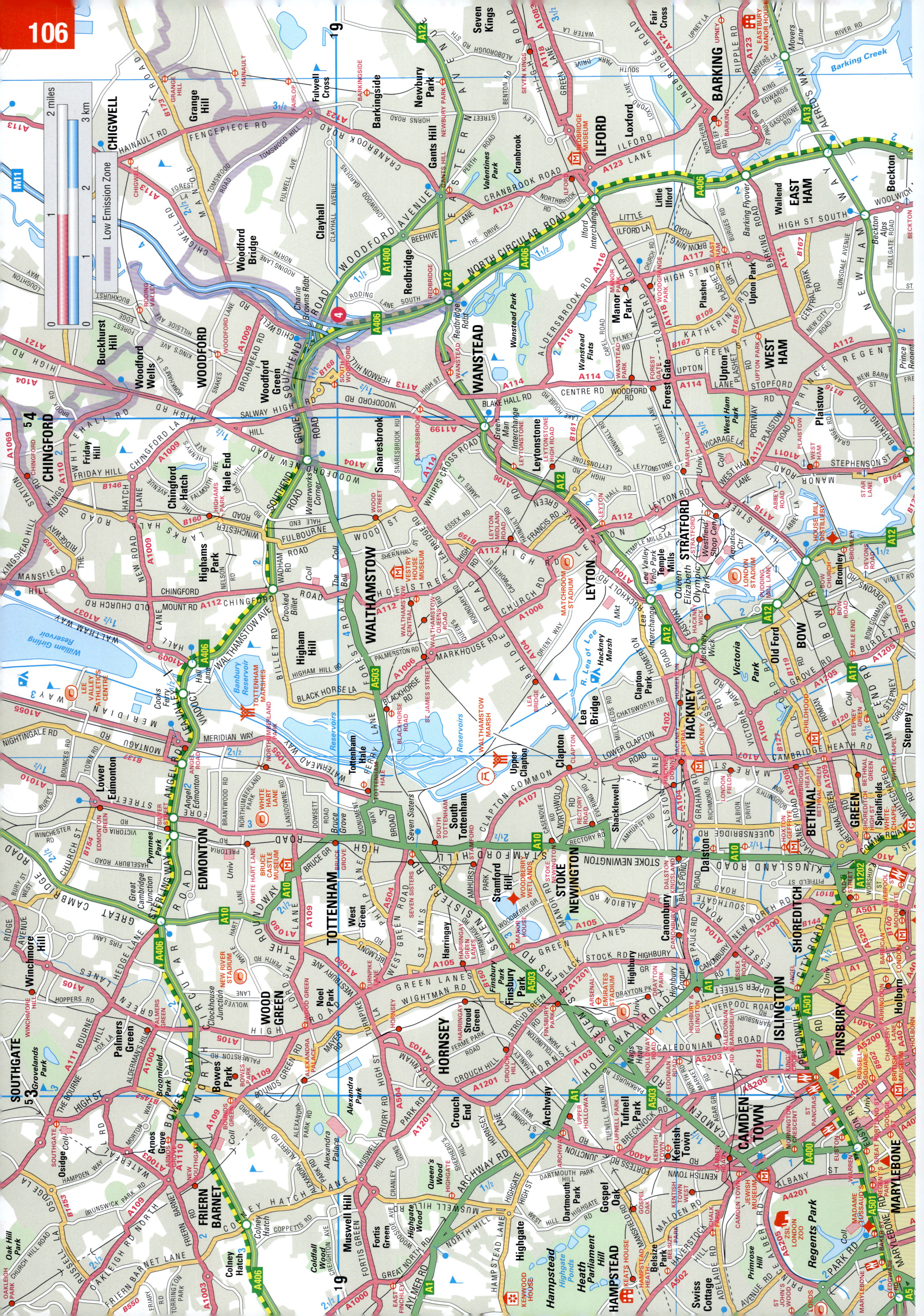
Low Emission Zone
2 miles
3 km
CHIGWELL
Grange Hill
Buckhurst Hill
WOODFORD
Woodford Wells
Woodford Green
Woodford Bridge
CHINGFORD
Chingford Hatch
Friday Hill
Hale End
Highams Park
Clayhall
Barkingside
Fullwell Cross
Newbury Park
Gants Hill
Seven Kings
ILFORD
Loxford
BARKING
Barking Creek
Valentines Park
Cranbrook
Redbridge
WANSTEAD
Wanstead Park
Wanstead Flats
Little Ilford
Manor Park
Plashet
Upton Park
EAST HAM
Wallend
Beckton
WEST HAM
Upton Lane
Forest Gate
Plaistow
West Ham Park
Leytonstone
LEYTON
STRATFORD
Queen Elizabeth Olympic Park
Bromley
BOW
Old Ford
Victoria Park
Stepney
HACKNEY
Hackney Marsh
Hackney Wick
Clapton Park
Lea Bridge
Upper Clapton
Clapton
Shacklewell
Dalston
BETHNAL GREEN
Spitalfields
SHOREDITCH
Walthamstow Marsh
WALTHAMSTOW
Snaresbrook
Higham Hill
William Girling Reservoir
Banbury Reservoir
Reservoirs
Tottenham Hale
South Tottenham
Stamford Hill
STOKE NEWINGTON
Seven Sisters
TOTTENHAM
West Green
EDMONTON
Lower Edmonton
Pymmes Park
Great Cambridge Junction
Winchmore Hill
Palmers Green
SOUTHGATE
Grovelands Park
Bowes Park
Arnos Grove
Broomfield Park
WOOD GREEN
Noel Park
Harringay
Finsbury Park
Canonbury
Highbury
HORNSEY
Stroud Green
Crouch End
Alexandra Park
Alexandra Palace
Muswell Hill
FRIERN BARNET
Colney Hatch
Coldfall Wood
Fortis Green
Highgate Wood
Queen's Wood
Highgate
Archway
Tufnell Park
Kentish Town
Dartmouth Park
Gospel Oak
Hampstead Heath
Parliament Hill
HAMPSTEAD
Belsize Park
Swiss Cottage
Primrose Hill
Regents Park
CAMDEN TOWN
ISLINGTON
FINSBURY
Holborn
MARYLEBONE
NORTH CIRCULAR ROAD
A406
A12
A13
A10
A1
M11

River Thames
North Woolwich
Woolwich Ferry
WOOLWICH
Plumstead
Charlton
Kidbrooke
Eltham Common
ELTHAM
New Eltham
CHISLEHURST
Chislehurst Common
Petts Wood
Mottingham
Grove Park
BROMLEY
Bickley
Widmore
Sundridge Park
Elmstead Wood
Plaistow
Downham
Shortlands
Lee
Hither Green
LEWISHAM
BLACKHEATH
GREENWICH
North Greenwich
Blackwall Tunnel
Blackwall
Canning Town
Silvertown
Custom House
POPLAR
ISLE OF DOGS
Canary Wharf
Millwall
Limehouse
Rotherhithe
Wapping
BERMONDSEY
DEPTFORD
New Cross
Brockley
Ladywell
CATFORD
Bellingham
Bell Green
Beckenham Place Park
BECKENHAM
Eden Park
Elmers End
PENGE
Anerley
Forest Hill
Sydenham
Honor Oak
Nunhead
Peckham
East Dulwich
Dulwich
West Dulwich
CAMBERWELL
Camberwell Green
Walworth
Elephant & Castle
Kennington
LAMBETH
BRIXTON
Brockwell Park
Tulse Hill
STREATHAM
Streatham Common
Streatham Vale
West Norwood
South Norwood
Norbury
CLAPHAM
Clapham Common
BATTERSEA
Battersea Park
CHELSEA
Pimlico
Vauxhall
Mayfair
Hyde Park
Green Park
Wandsworth Common
Balham
Upper Tooting
Tooting Bec Common
Furzedown
Collier's Wood
MITCHAM
Mitcham Common
Grange Mills

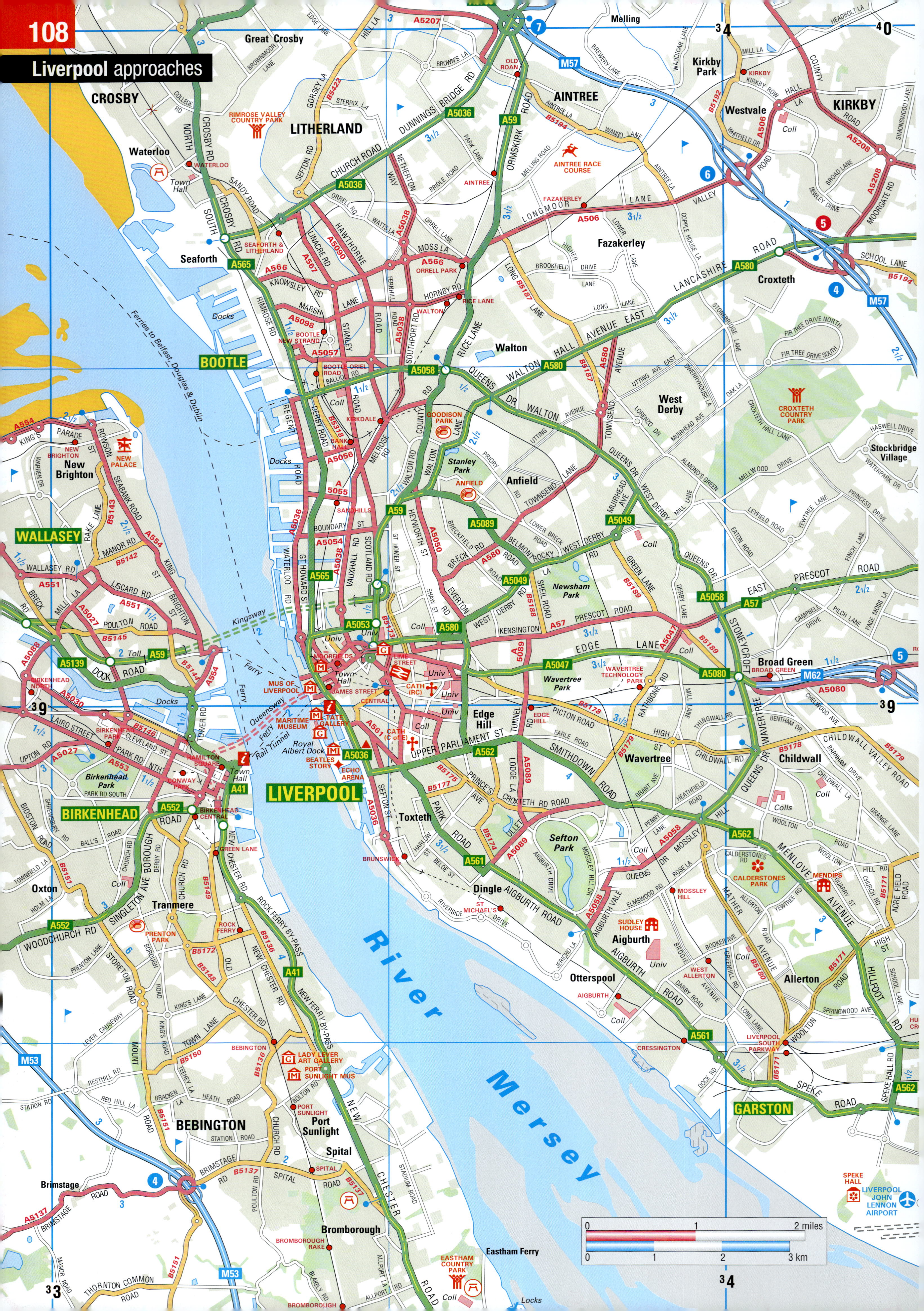
Great Crosby
CROSBY
Waterloo
Town Hall
LITHERLAND
RIMROSE VALLEY COUNTRY PARK
Melling
AINTREE
Kirkby Park
KIRKBY
Westvale
AINTREE RACE COURSE
Fazakerley
Croxteth
Seaforth
SEAFORTH & LITHERLAND
BOOTLE
Docks
Ferries to Belfast, Douglas & Dublin
Walton
West Derby
CROXTETH COUNTRY PARK
Stockbridge Village
GOODISON PARK
Stanley Park
ANFIELD
Anfield
New Brighton
NEW PALACE
NEW BRIGHTON
WALLASEY
Newsham Park
Broad Green
BROAD GREEN
Wavertree Park
WAVERTREE TECHNOLOGY PARK
MOORFIELDS
LIME STREET
JAMES STREET
CENTRAL
MUS OF LIVERPOOL
MARITIME MUSEUM
TATE GALLERY
Royal Albert Dock
BEATLES STORY
ECHO ARENA
CATH (RC)
CATH (C of E)
Edge Hill
EDGE HILL
LIVERPOOL
Kingsway
Queensway
Ferry
Rail Tunnel
Birkenhead Park
BIRKENHEAD PARK
BIRKENHEAD NORTH
HAMILTON SQUARE
CONWAY PARK
BIRKENHEAD CENTRAL
BIRKENHEAD
GREEN LANE
Wavertree
Childwall
Toxteth
Sefton Park
Dingle
ST MICHAEL'S
BRUNSWICK
CALDERSTONES PARK
MENDIPS
MOSSLEY HILL
SUDLEY HOUSE
Aigburth
AIGBURTH
WEST ALLERTON
Allerton
Otterspool
Oxton
Tranmere
PRENTON PARK
ROCK FERRY
LADY LEVER ART GALLERY
PORT SUNLIGHT MUS
PORT SUNLIGHT
Port Sunlight
BEBINGTON
Spital
SPITAL
BEBINGTON
Brimstage
Bromborough
BROMBOROUGH RAKE
BROMBOROUGH
EASTHAM COUNTRY PARK
Eastham Ferry
Locks
CRESSINGTON
LIVERPOOL SOUTH PARKWAY
GARSTON
SPEKE HALL
LIVERPOOL JOHN LENNON AIRPORT
River Mersey
M57
M62
M53
A59
A565
A5036
A580
A5058
A5080
A562
A561
A41
A552
A5139
A5047
A5049
A5089
A57
0 1 2 miles
0 1 2 3 km
39
34
33
40

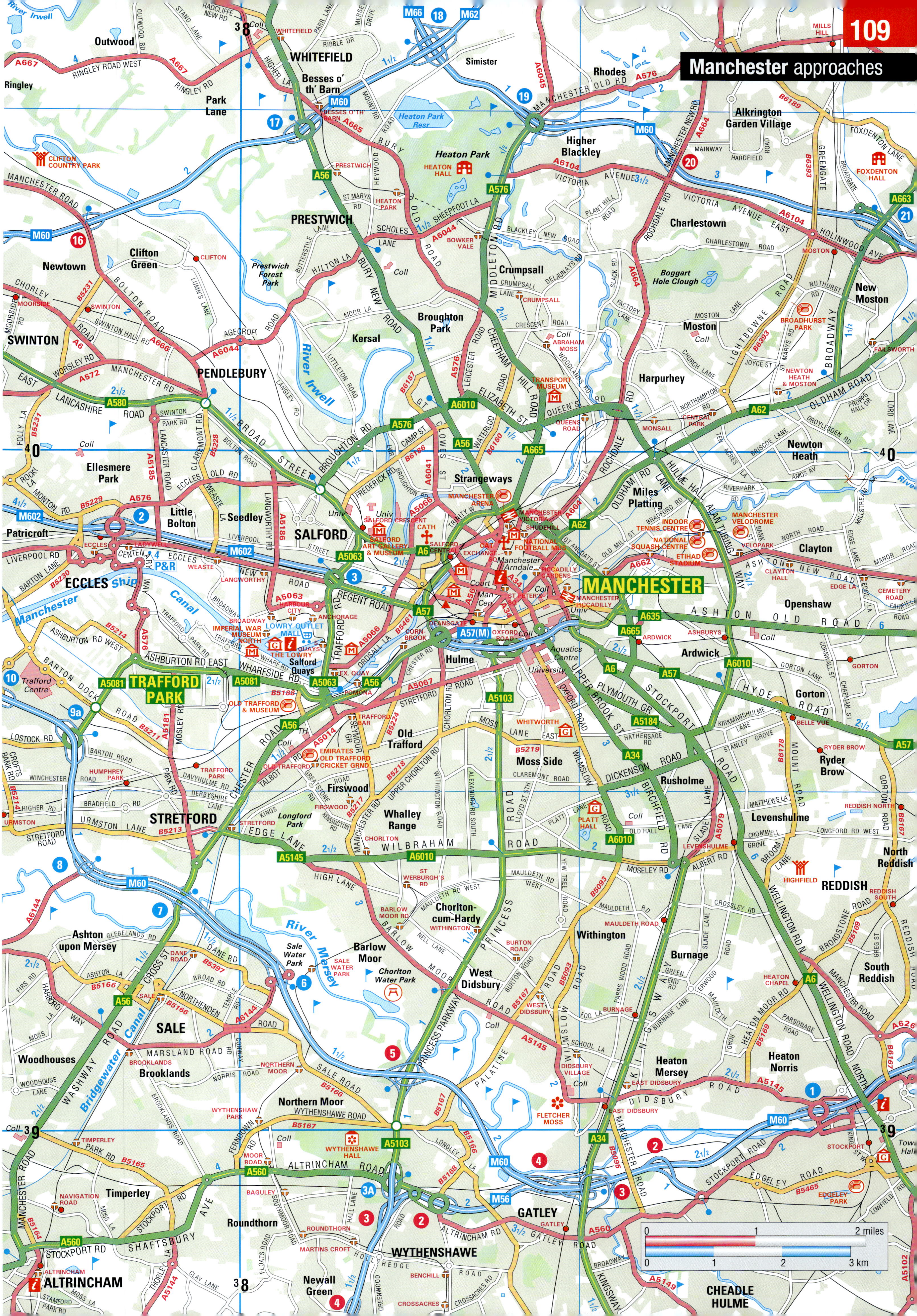
MANCHESTER
SALFORD
TRAFFORD PARK
ECCLES
SWINTON
PENDLEBURY
PRESTWICH
WHITEFIELD
Besses o' th' Barn
Heaton Park
Higher Blackley
Rhodes
Alkrington Garden Village
Charlestown
Crumpsall
Broughton Park
Kersal
Clifton Green
Newtown
Moston
New Moston
Harpurhey
Newton Heath
Miles Platting
Strangeways
Ellesmere Park
Little Bolton
Seedley
Patricroft
Clayton
Openshaw
Ardwick
Hulme
Old Trafford
Moss Side
Rusholme
Gorton
Ryder Brow
Levenshulme
North Reddish
REDDISH
South Reddish
Whalley Range
Firswood
STRETFORD
Chorlton-cum-Hardy
Withington
Burnage
West Didsbury
Heaton Mersey
Heaton Norris
Barlow Moor
Ashton upon Mersey
SALE
Woodhouses
Brooklands
Northern Moor
Timperley
Roundthorn
WYTHENSHAWE
GATLEY
ALTRINCHAM
Newall Green
CHEADLE HULME
Outwood
Ringley
Park Lane
Simister
River Irwell
River Mersey
Manchester Ship Canal
Bridgewater Canal
M60
M602
M56
M62
M66
A57(M)
1
2 miles
0
1
2
3 km

NEWCASTLE UPON TYNE
GATESHEAD
Brunswick Village
WIDE OPEN
Hazlerigg
NEWCASTLE INTERNATIONAL AIRPORT
Camperdown
Killingworth
Killingworth Centre
Backworth
SHIREMOOR
NEWCASTLE
Gosforth Wood
Gosforth Lake
BOUNDARY MILL NEWCASTLE
Woolsington
KINGSTON PARK
Fawdon
Gosforth
LONGBENTON
RISING SUN COUNTRY PARK
STEPHENSON RAILWAY MUSEUM
Govt Blds
Willington
WALLSEND
Blakelaw
Jesmond
Heaton
Town Hall
HOWDON
Fenham
MILITARY VEHICLE MUSEUM
SEGEDUNUM ROMAN FORT
Pedestrian Tunnel
River Tyne
DENTON HALL TURRET
Benwell
Scotswood
Elswick
ST. JAMES PARK
Univ
Civic Centre
Byker
Walker
HEBBURN
DISCOVERY
THE SAGE
BALTIC CENTRE
METRO RADIO ARENA
GATESHEAD INTERNATIONAL STADIUM
METROCENTRE
METROLAND
Metro Centre
Dunston
GATESHEAD STADIUM
Felling
Wardley
WHICKHAM THORNS CENTRE
SHIPLEY ART GALL
Bensham
LOBLEY HILL
Wrekenton
Sunniside
Hill Head Wood
Lyndhurst
Chowdene
Springwell
High Park Wood
Usworth
ANGEL OF THE NORTH
BOWES RAILWAY
WASHINGTON
ANDREWS HOUSE
TANFIELD RAILWAY
Kibblesworth
BIRTLEY
WASHINGTON OLD HALL
CAUSEY ARCH
Biddock
Lampton
WASHINGTON BIRTLEY SERVICES
Govt Offices
BEAMISH OPEN AIR MUSEUM
URPETH
OUSTON
Fatfield
Harraton
0 1 2 miles
0 1 2 3 km

Dobpark
HUCKNALL
Misk Hill
Watnall Coppice
Long Hill
Beauvale
Ruffs
Hazelgrove
Westville
Broomhill
Butler's Hill
Raceground Hill
Cobbler's Hill
Bestwood Park
Bestwood Village
BESTWOOD
The Warren
Gaunt's Hill
Bonner Hill
Woodborough
Rise Park
Top Valley
Redhill
TUMBLE TOWN
ARNOLD
Bestwood
Hunger Hill
Lambley
Wicketwood Hill
GEDLING
Crocket Beck
Nuthall
Kimberley
Bulwell
Highbury Vale
Old Basford
Cinderhill
Broxtowe
Aspley
Whitemoor
Strelley
Bilborough
Catstone Hill
Trowell Moor
Wodthorpe
Mapperley
Sherwood
Porchester
Gedling
CARLTON
New Basford
Carrington
Mapperley Park
Thorneywood
NOTTINGHAM
St. Ann's
Radford
Netherfield
Wollaton
Martin's Pond
Wollaton Park
WOLLATON HALL
The Lake
New Lenton
Sneinton
Colwick
HOLME PIERREPONT
Holme Pierrepont
NATIONAL WATER SPORTS CENTRE
River Trent
Nottingham Canal
Meadows
THE CITY GROUND
TRENT BRIDGE
Bramcore Hills
Nottingham University
UNIVERSITY OF NOTTINGHAM
Bramcote
Gamston
Bassingfield
NOTTINGHAM CITY AIRPORT
Grantham Canal
Wilford
WEST BRIDGFORD
Rylands
Chilwell
BEESTON
Beeston Canal
Clifton Grove
Wilford Hill
Edwalton
Sharp Hill
Tollerton
Clipston
Hoe Hill
ATTENBOROUGH
ATTENBOROUGH NATURE RESERVE
CLIFTON
Mill Hill
Brook Hill
Manor Park
FRAMEWORK KNITTERS' MUSEUM
RUDDINGTON
Barton in Fabis
Clifton Pasture
Fairham Brook
Ruddington Fields
RUSHCLIFFE
GREAT CENTRAL RAILWAY (NOTTINGHAM)
Plumtree
Normanton-on-the-Wolds
Plumtree Park
Normanton Wolds
KEYWORTH
Bradmore
Bradmore Moor
Ruddington Moor
Gotham Hill
Gotham Moor
Thrumpton
THRUMPTON HALL
M1
A60
A610
A6514
A52
A453
A606
A6011
A612
A6211
A611
A609
A6002
A6005
A6200
A6130
A6464
B6386
B684
B6009
B6004
B682
B683
B690
B686
0 1 2 miles
0 1 2 3 km

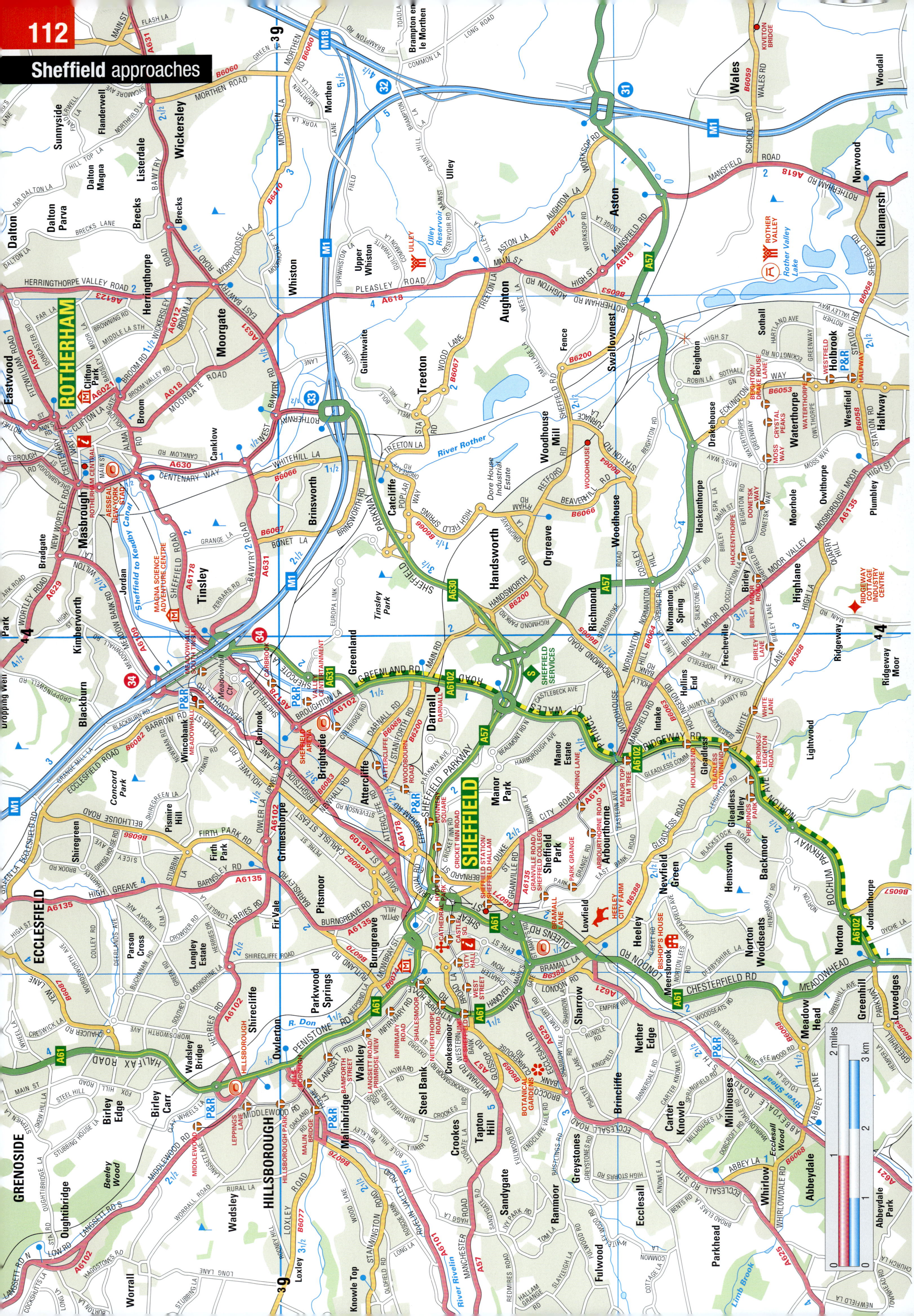

ROTHERHAM
SHEFFIELD
Wickersley
Sunnyside
Flanderwell
Listerdale
Dalton Magna
Dalton Parva
Dalton
Brecks
Herringthorpe
Moorgate
Whiston
Morthen
Ulley
Upper Whiston
Treeton
Aughton
Aston
Swallownest
Fence
Wales
Norwood
Killamarsh
Woodall
Beighton
Sothall
Holbrook
Halfway
Westfield
Waterthorpe
Drakehouse
Owlthorpe
Plumbley
Moorhole
Hackenthorpe
Birley
Highlane
Ridgeway
Ridgeway Moor
Frecheville
Normanton Spring
Intake
Hollins End
Gleadless
Gleadless Valley
Hemsworth
Backmoor
Norton
Jordanthorpe
Lowedges
Greenhill
Meadow Head
Norton Woodseats
Meersbrook
Heeley
Newfield Green
Arbourthorne
Lowfield
Sheffield Park
Manor Park
Manor Estate
Woodhouse
Woodhouse Mill
Orgreave
Richmond
Handsworth
Darnall
Catcliffe
Brinsworth
Canklow
Broom
Clifton Park
Eastwood
Masbrough
Bradgate
Kimberworth
Jordan
Tinsley
Tinsley Park
Greenland
Attercliffe
Brightside
Carbrook
Wincobank
Blackburn
Concord Park
Shiregreen
Pismire Hill
Firth Park
Grimesthorpe
Pitsmoor
Burngreave
Fir Vale
Longley Estate
Parson Cross
ECCLESFIELD
Shirecliffe
Parkwood Springs
Owlerton
Wadsley Bridge
Birley Carr
Birley Edge
Walkley
Malin Bridge
Hillsborough
Wadsley
Beeley Wood
Oughtibridge
GRENOSIDE
Worrall
Loxley
Knowle Top
Steel Bank
Crookesmoor
Crookes
Tapton Hill
Sandygate
Ranmoor
Greystones
Sharrow
Nether Edge
Brincliffe
Carter Knowle
Millhouses
Ecclesall
Fulwood
Parkhead
Whirlow
Abbeydale
Abbeydale Park
Ecclesall Wood
Lightwood
River Rother
River Don
River Sheaf
River Rivelin
Limb Brook
Ulley Reservoir
Rother Valley
Rother Valley Lake
Sheffield to Keadby Canal
Dore House Industrial Estate
Magna Science Adventure Centre
Meadowhall
Meadowhall Ctr
Sheffield Arena
Valley Centertainment
Sheffield Station/Sheffield Hallam
Cathedral
Castle Sq
City Hall
Botanical Gardens
Heeley City Farm
Bishop's House
Ridgeway Cottage Industry Centre
Sheffield Services
M1
M18
A57
A61
A630
A631
A6102
A6135
A6178
A618
A621
A625
A629
A6109
A6101
A6123
B6060
B6066
B6067
B6200
B6053
B6054
B6058
B6059
B6063
B6064
B6068
B6070
B6079
B6082
B6083
B6085
B6086
B6087
B6388
B6200
B6057
B6076
B6077
31
32
33
34
35
36
2 miles
3 km

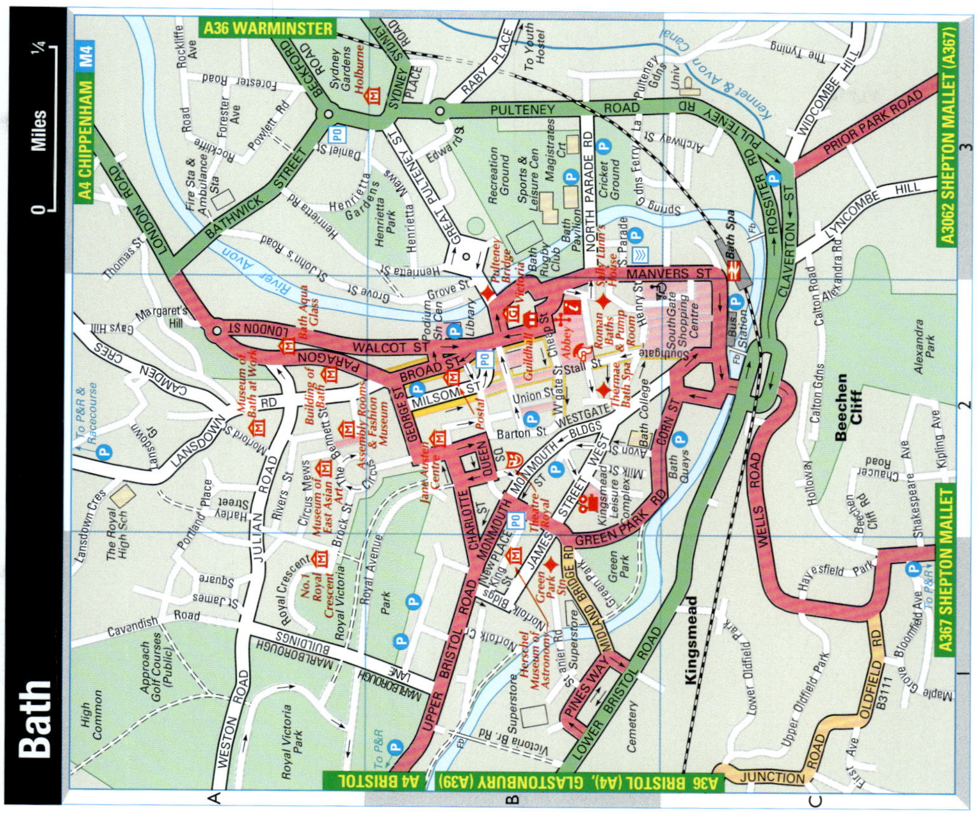
Bath
Miles
0
¼

Blackpool
Miles
0
¼

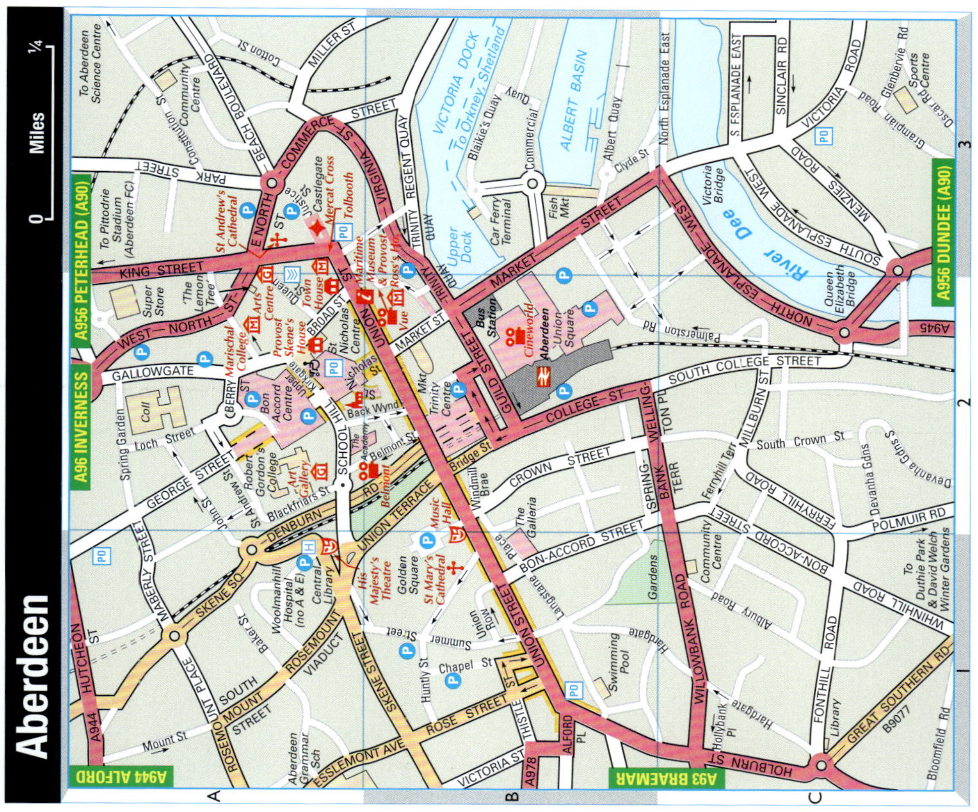
Aberdeen
Miles
0
¼

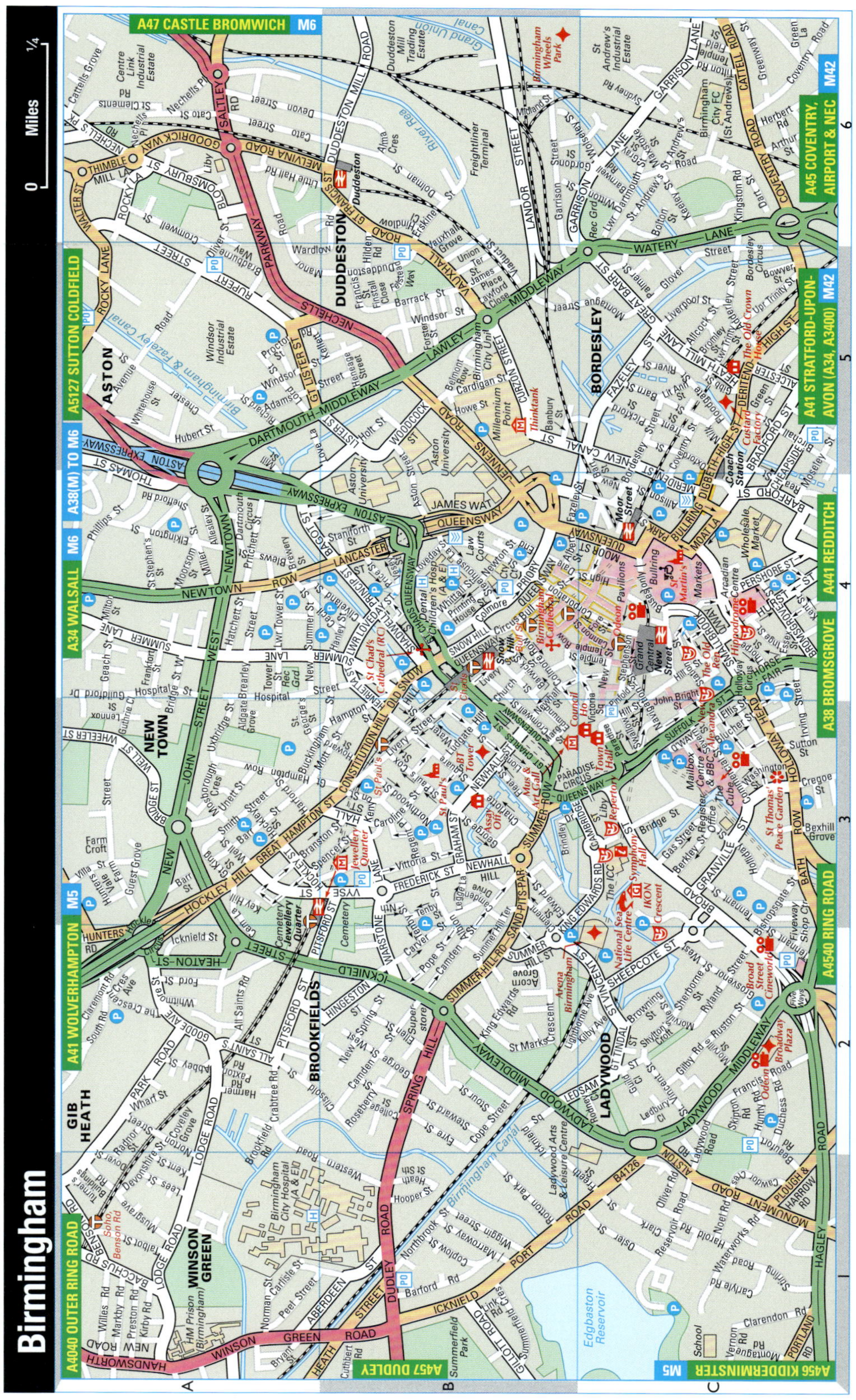
Birmingham
Miles
0
¼

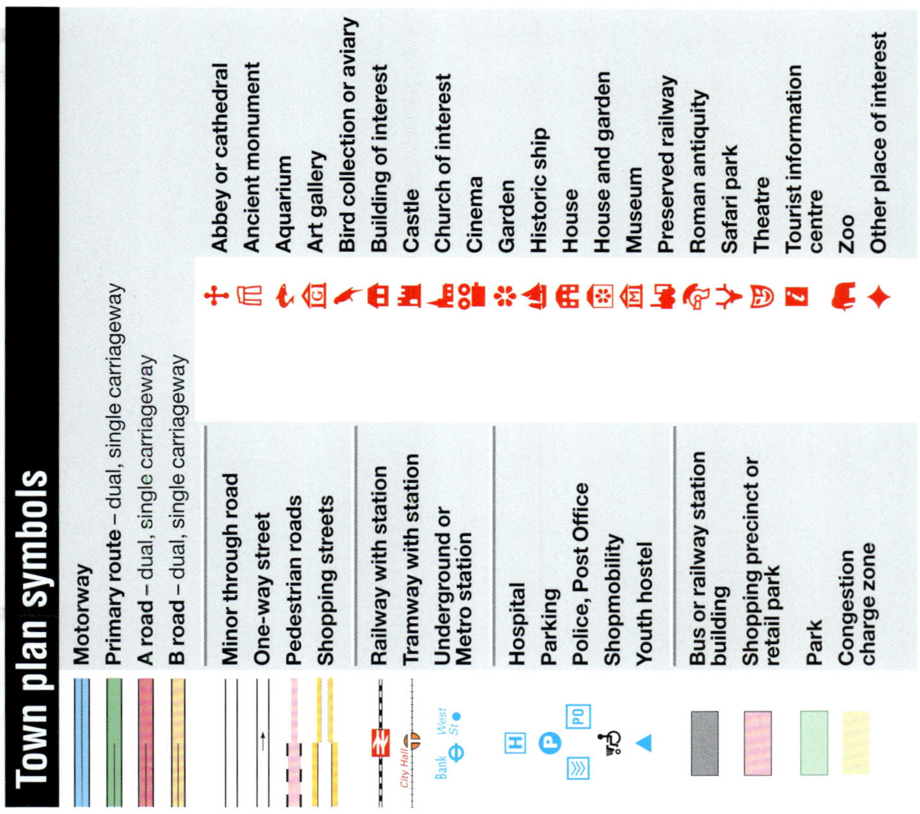
Town plan symbols
Motorway
Primary route – dual, single carriageway
A road – dual, single carriageway
B road – dual, single carriageway
Minor through road
One-way street
Pedestrian roads
Shopping streets
Railway with station
Tramway with station
Underground or Metro station
Hospital
Parking
Police, Post Office
Shopmobility
Youth hostel
Bus or railway station building
Shopping precinct or retail park
Park
Congestion charge zone
Abbey or cathedral
Ancient monument
Aquarium
Art gallery
Bird collection or aviary
Building of interest
Castle
Church of interest
Cinema
Garden
Historic ship
House
House and garden
Museum
Preserved railway
Roman antiquity
Safari park
Theatre
Tourist information centre
Zoo
Other place of interest

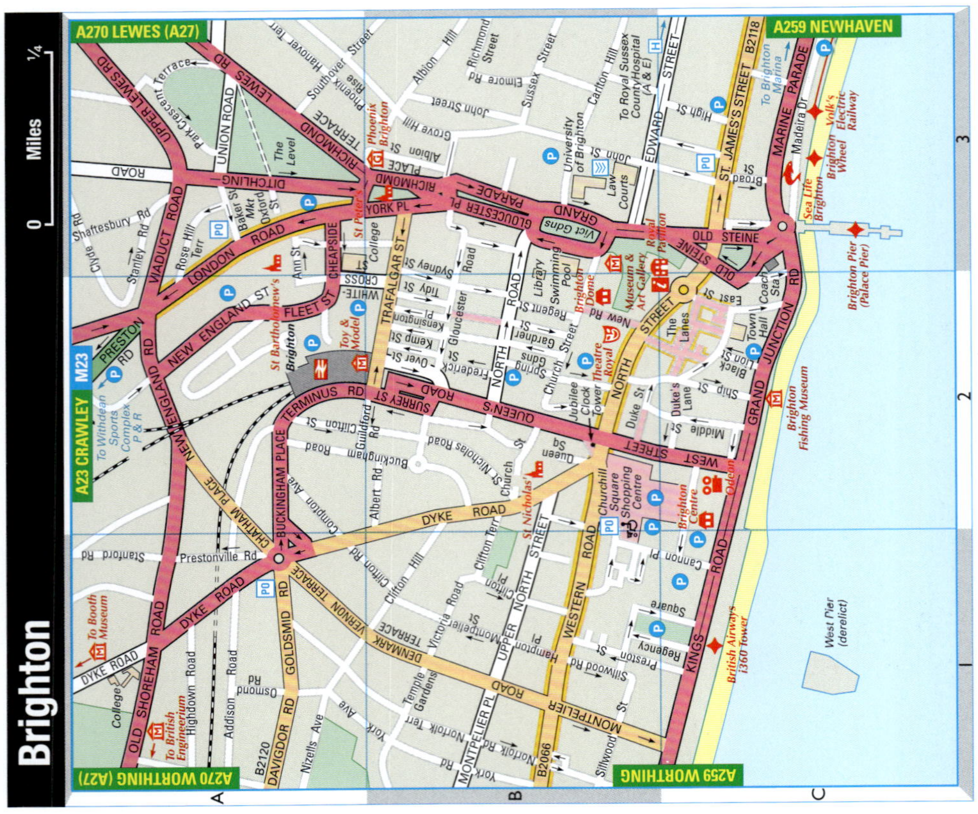
Brighton

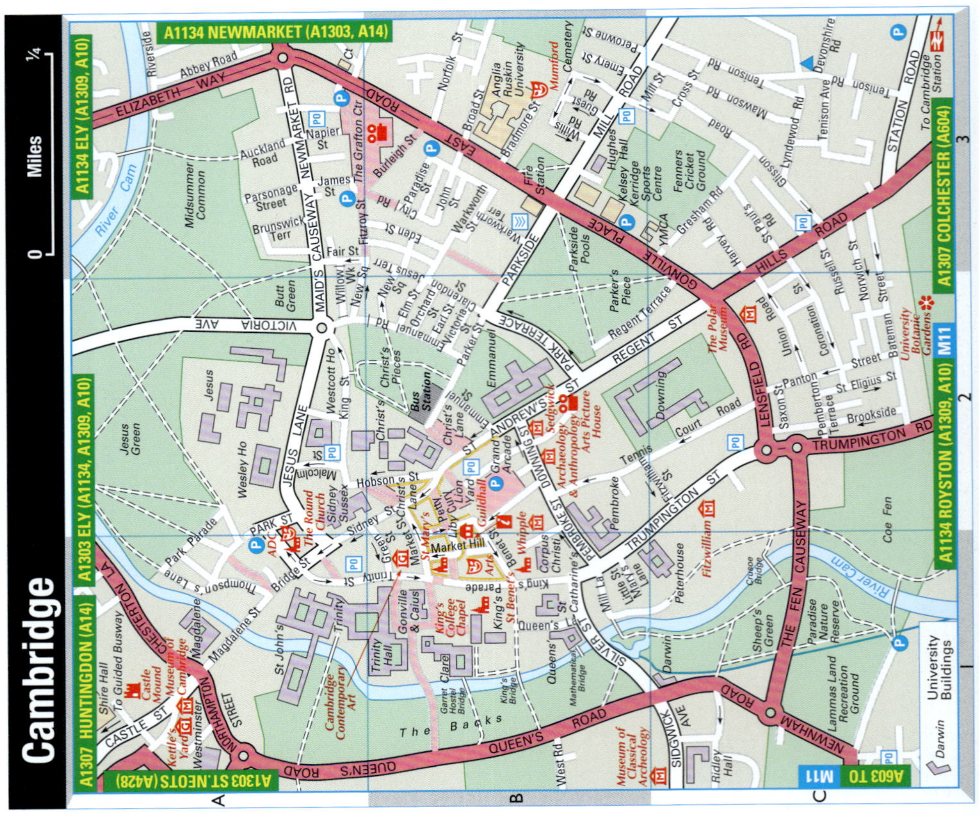
Cambridge

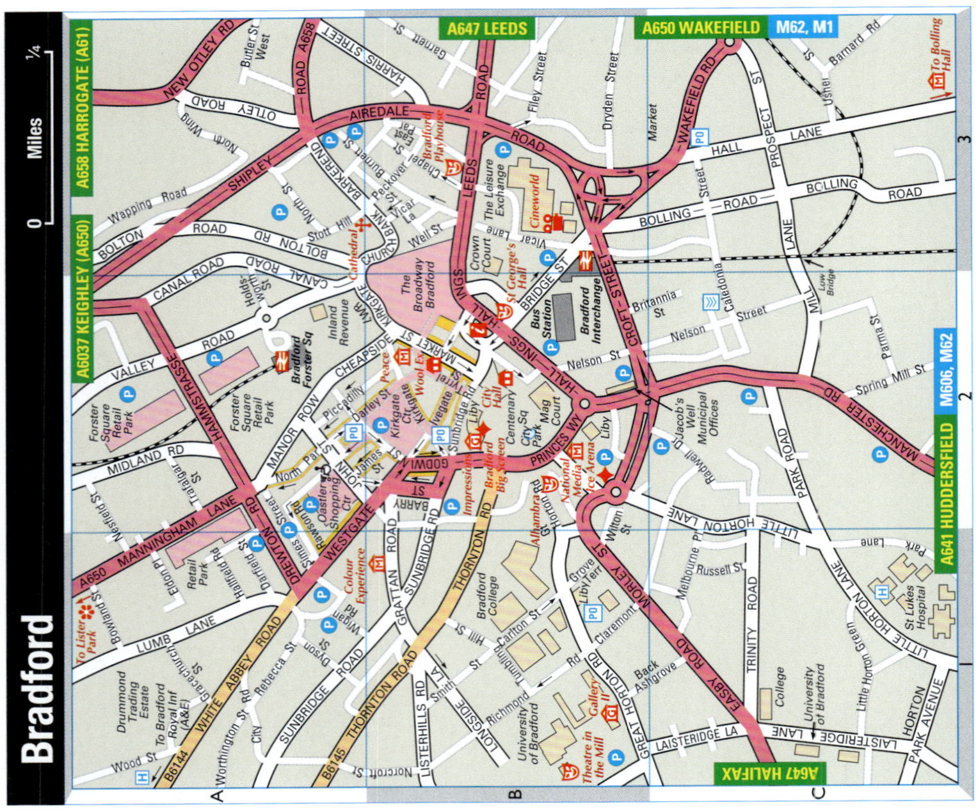
Bradford

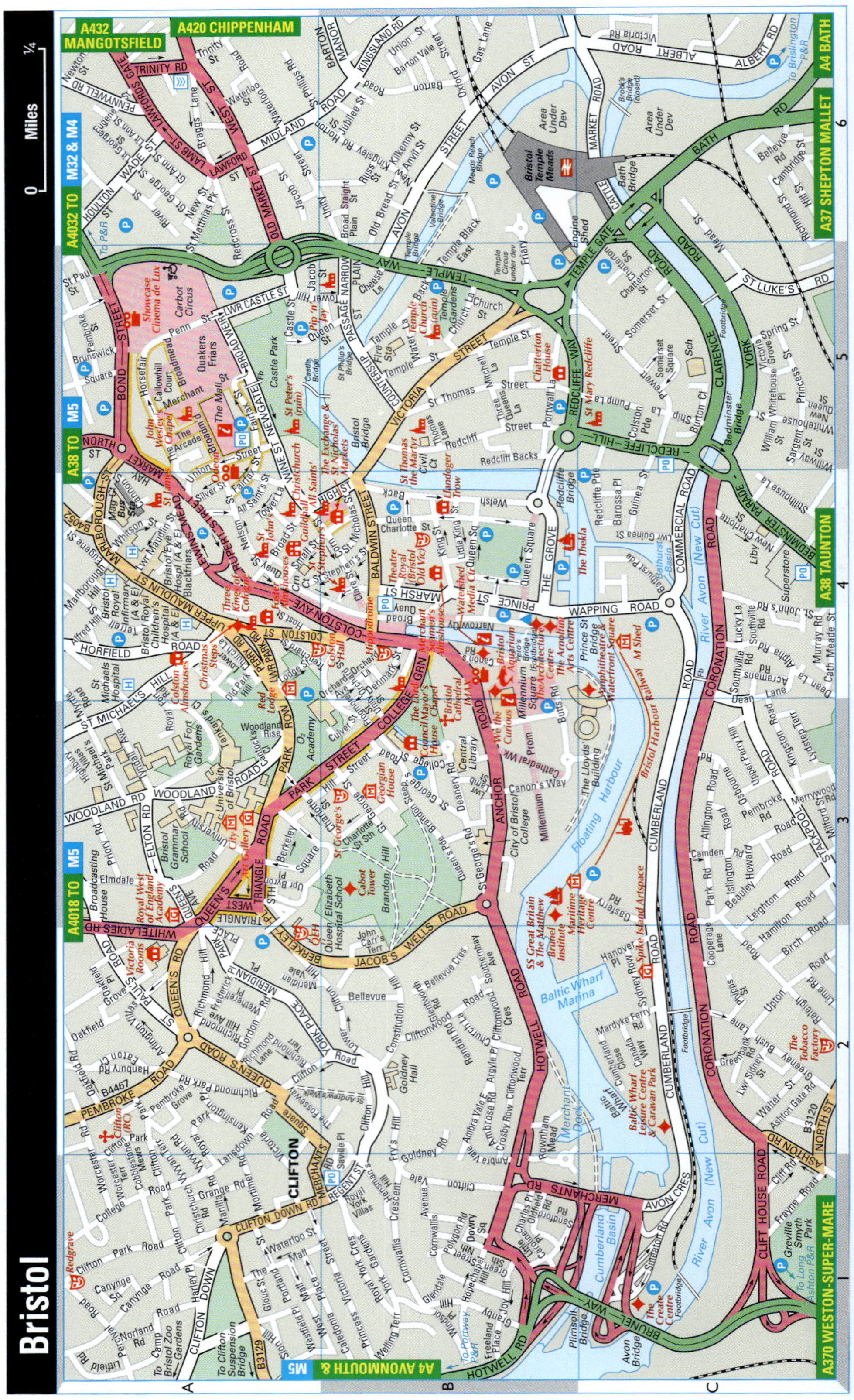
Bristol

Bournemouth

Cheltenham

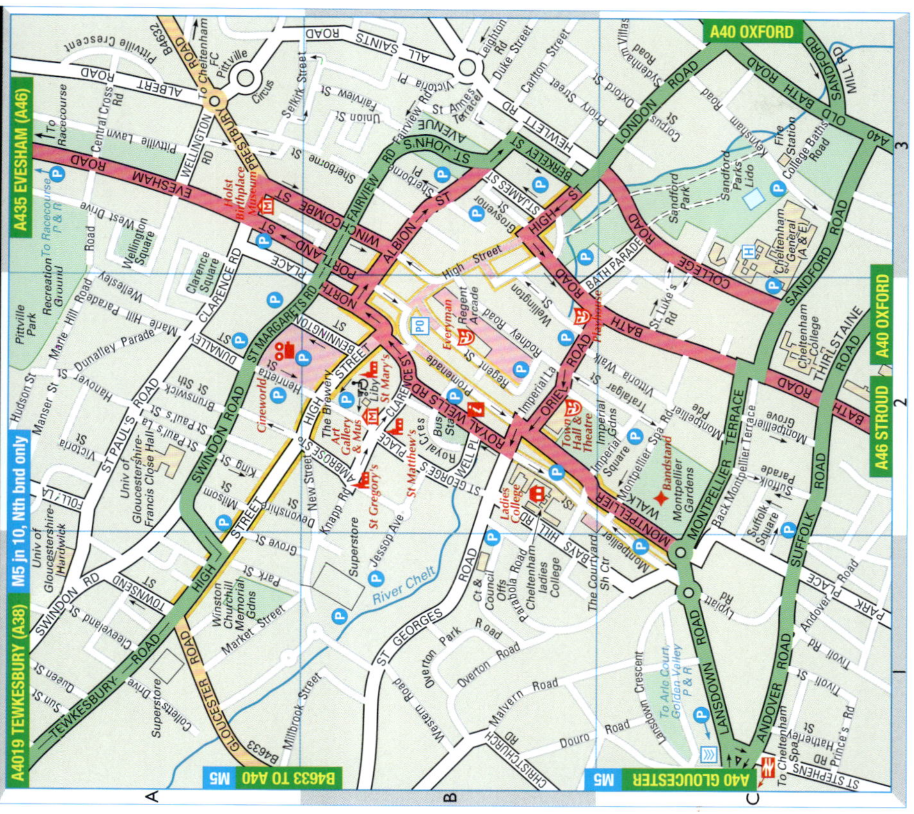

Colchester

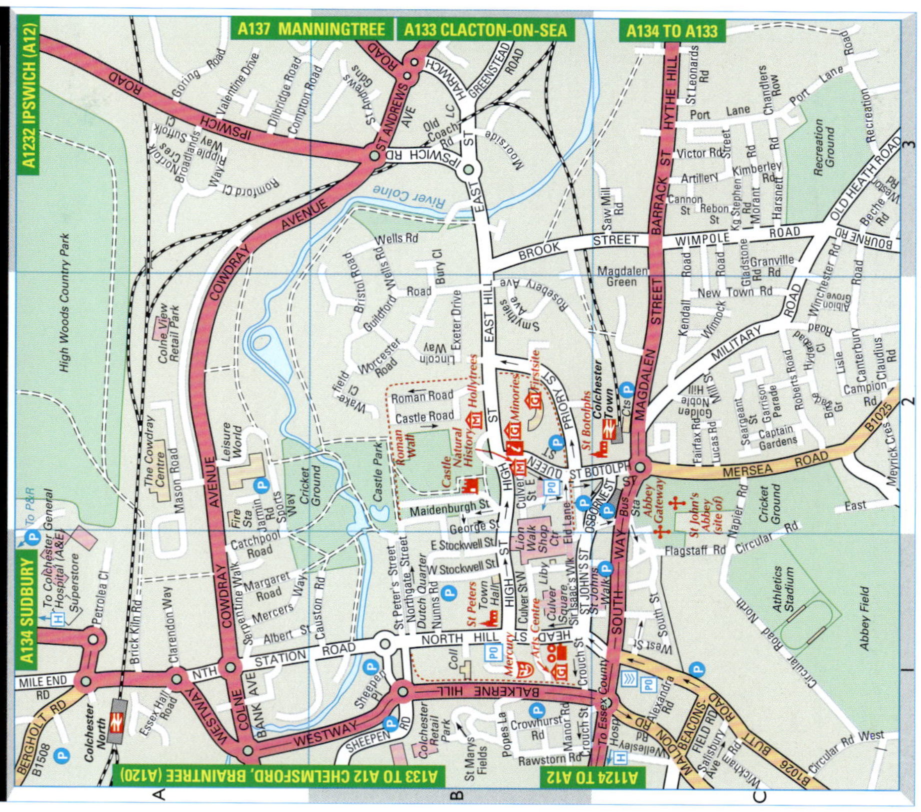

Cardiff / Caerdydd

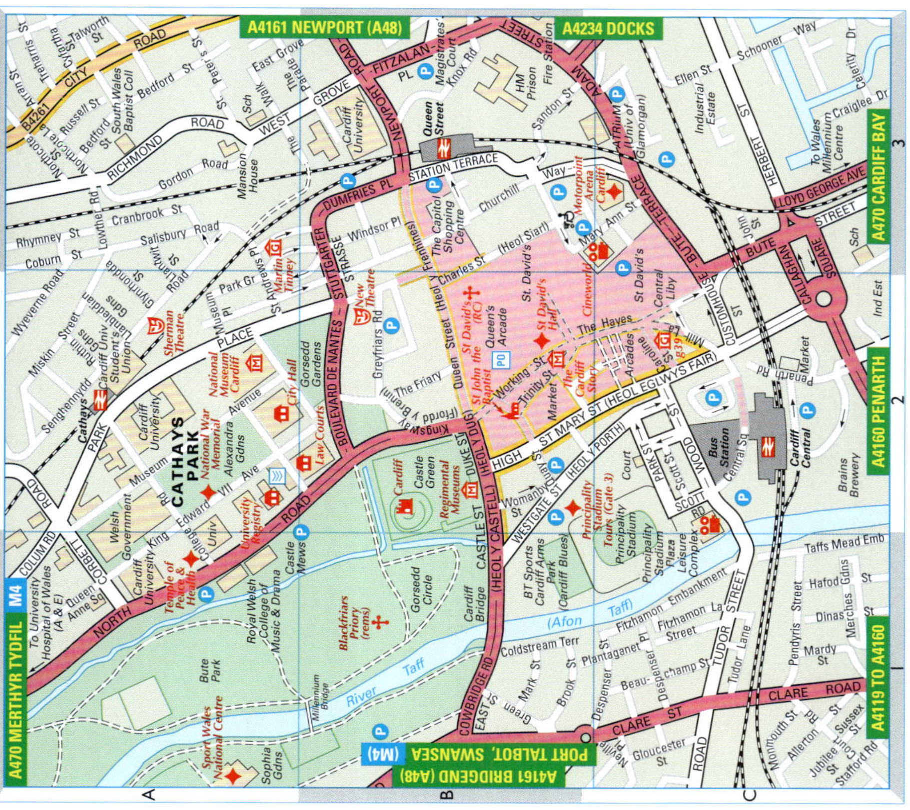

Chichester

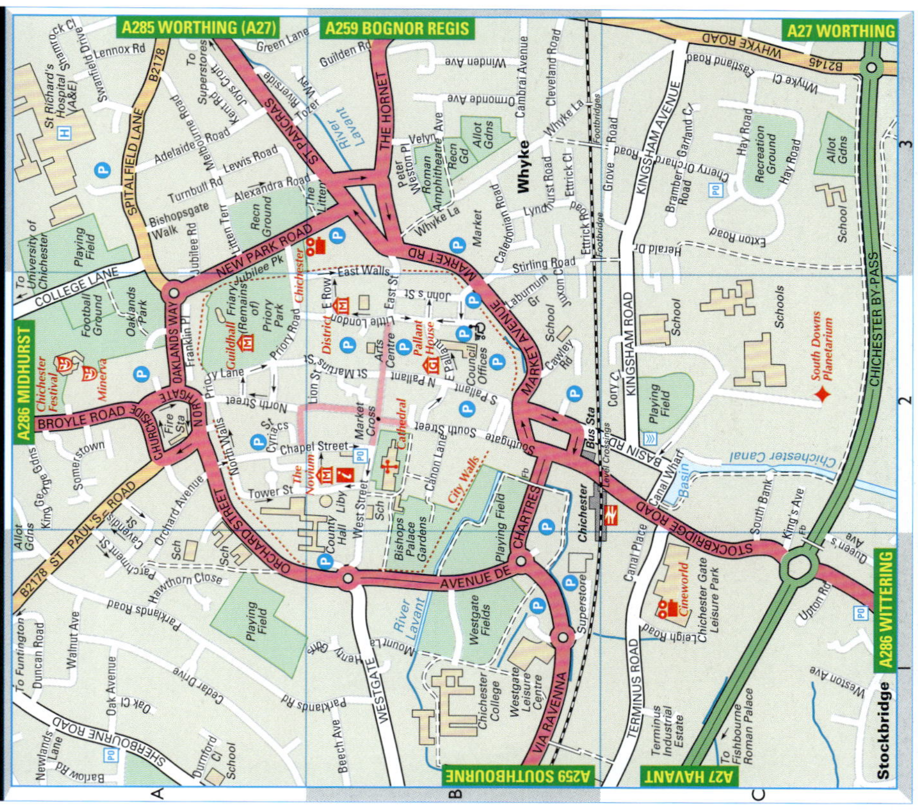

Canterbury

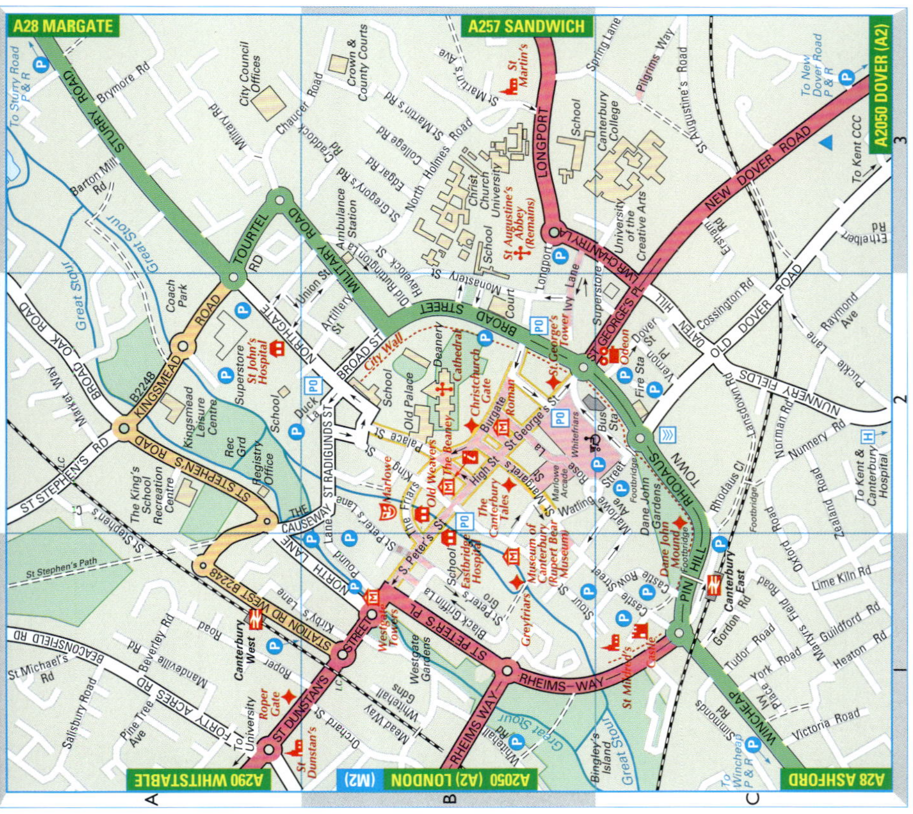

Chester

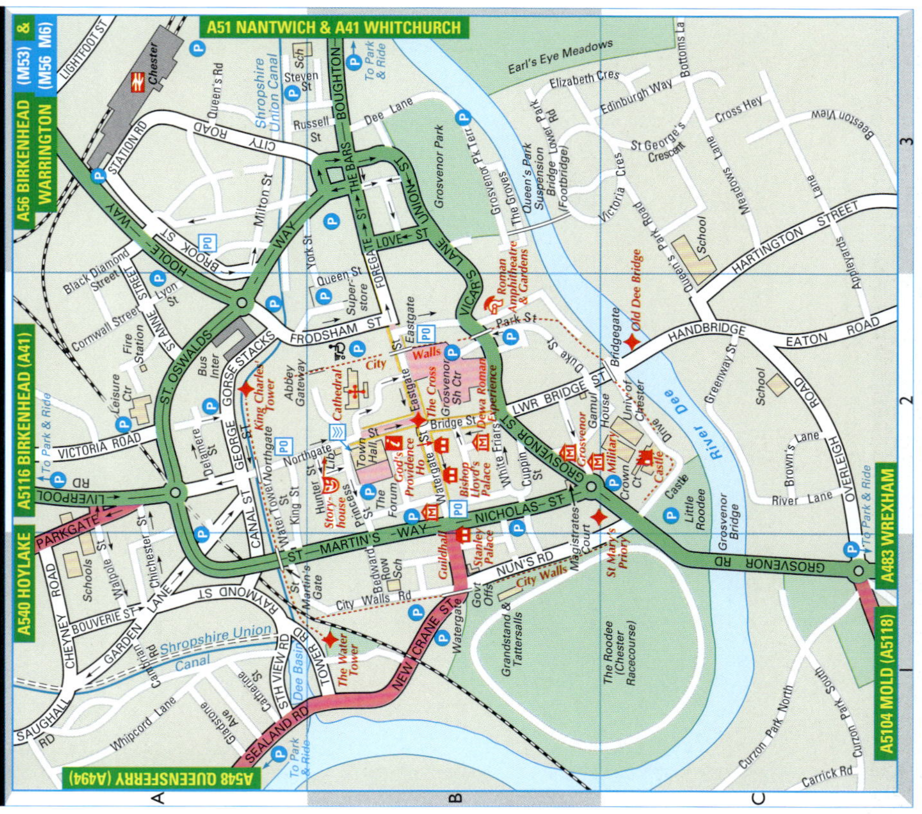

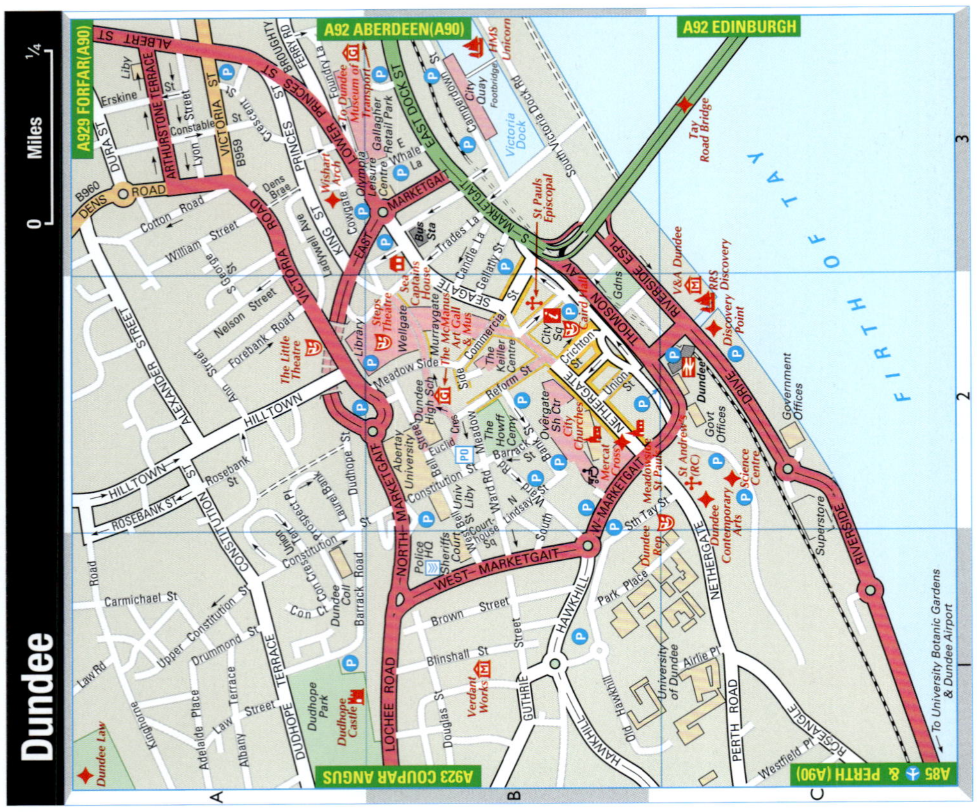
Dundee
Miles 0 ¼
A92 ABERDEEN (A90)
A92 EDINBURGH
A929 FORFAR (A90)
A923 COUPAR ANGUS
A85 & PERTH (A90)
FIRTH OF TAY
Tay Road Bridge

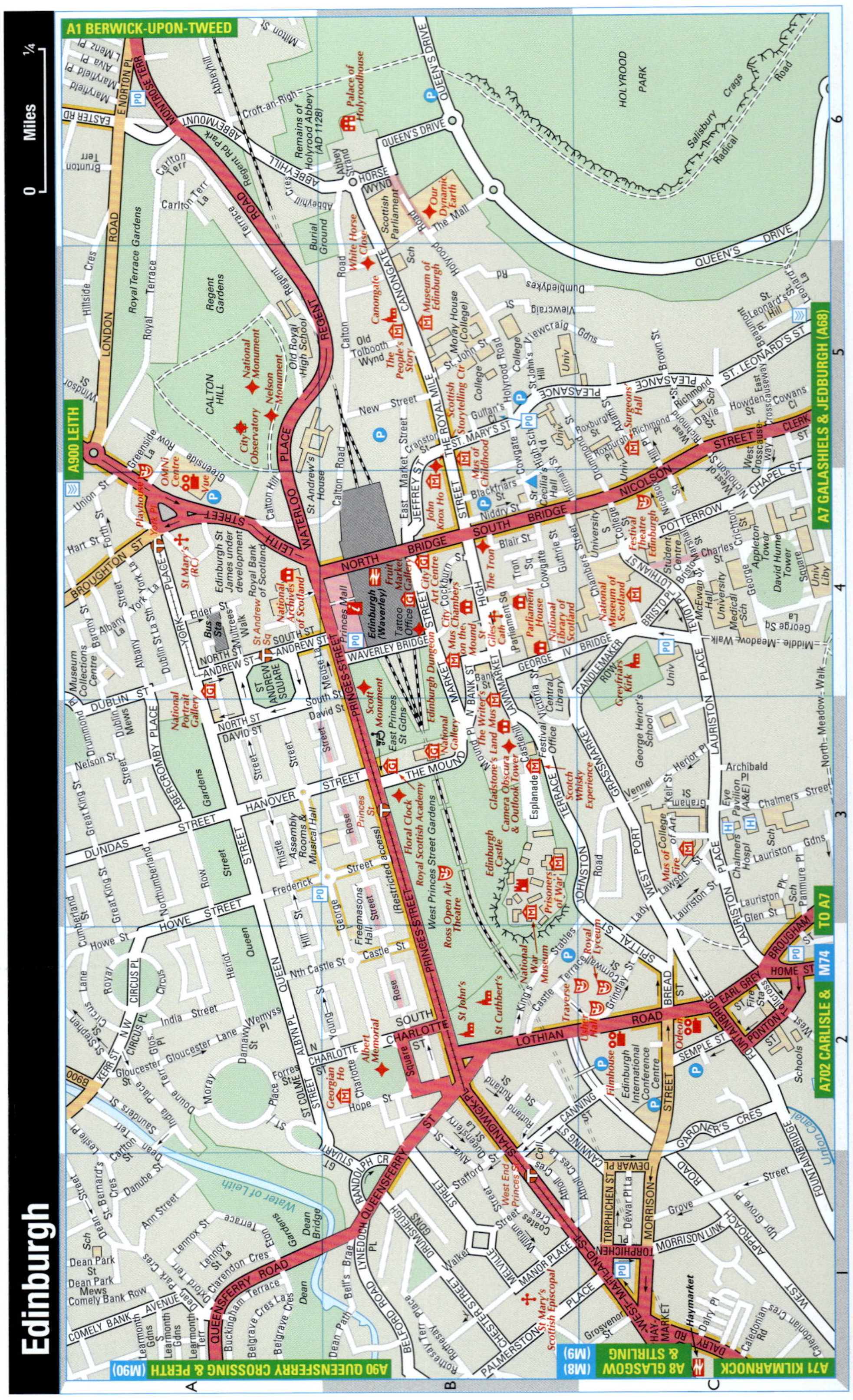
Edinburgh
Miles 0 ¼
A1 BERWICK-UPON-TWEED
A900 LEITH
A7 GALASHIELS & JEDBURGH (A68)
A702 CARLISLE & M74 TO A7
A71 KILMARNOCK
A8 GLASGOW (M8) & STIRLING (M9)
A90 QUEENSFERRY CROSSING & PERTH (M90)
HOLYROOD PARK
CALTON HILL

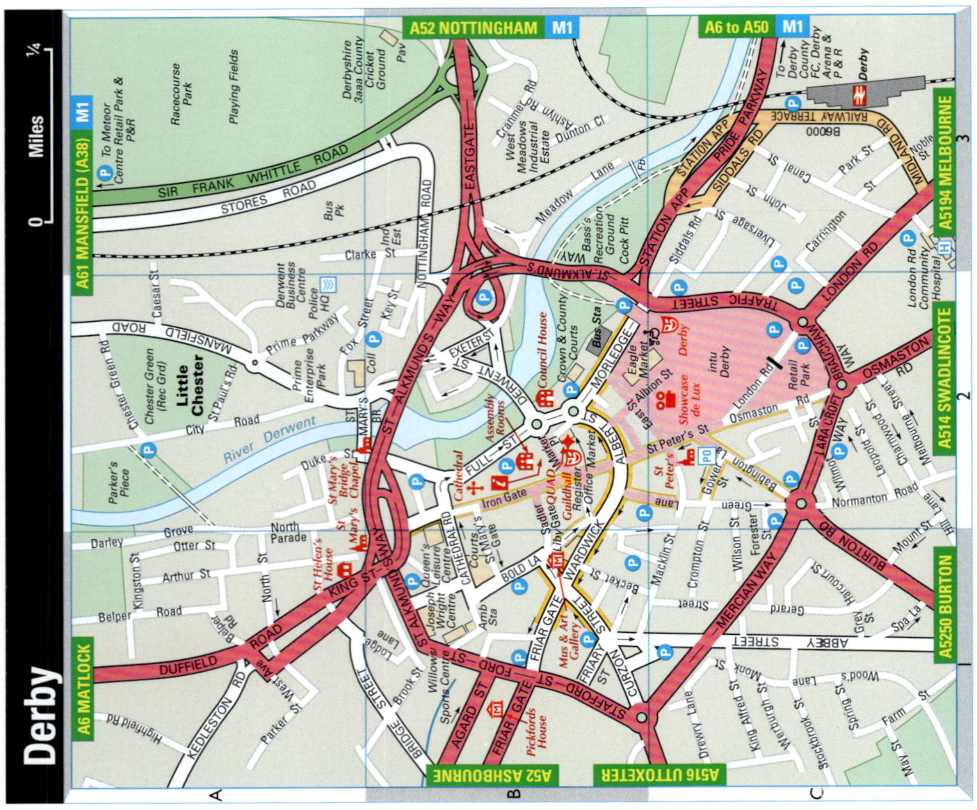
Derby
Miles 0 ¼
A52 NOTTINGHAM M1
A6 to A50 M1
A61 MANSFIELD (A38) M1
A5194 MELBOURNE
A514 SWADLINCOTE
A5250 BURTON
A516 UTTOXETER
A52 ASHBOURNE
A6 MATLOCK
River Derwent

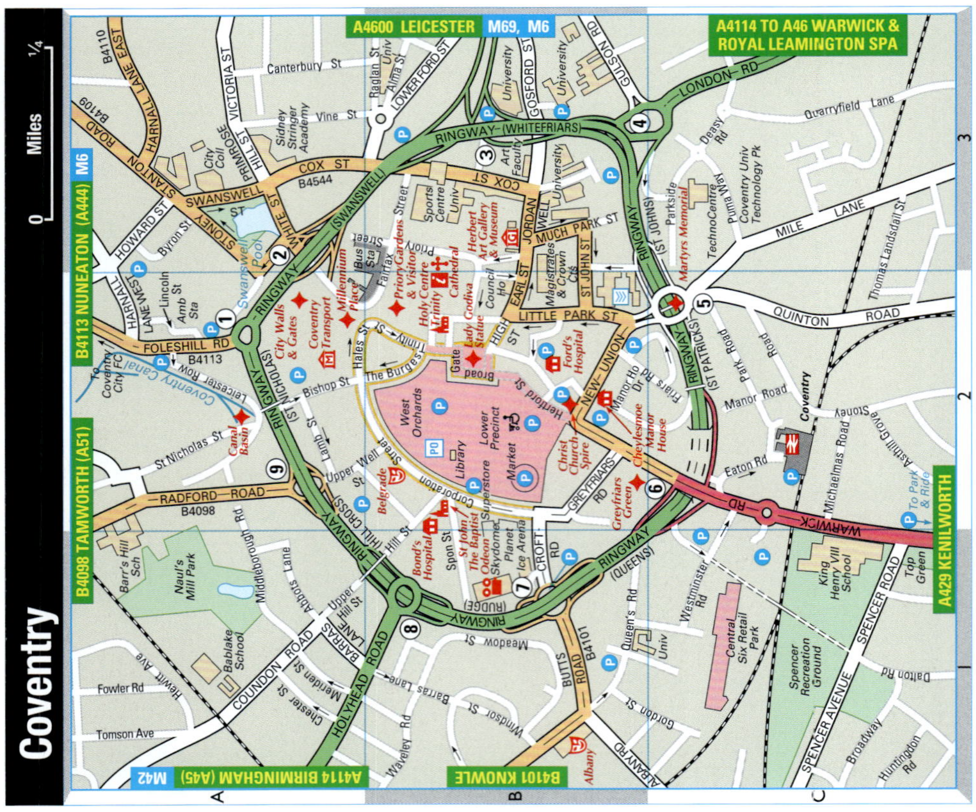
Coventry
Miles 0 ¼
A4600 LEICESTER M69, M6
A4114 TO A46 WARWICK & ROYAL LEAMINGTON SPA
B4113 NUNEATON (A444) M6
B4098 TAMWORTH (A51)
A4114 BIRMINGHAM (A45) M42
B4101 KNOWLE
A429 KENILWORTH
RINGWAY

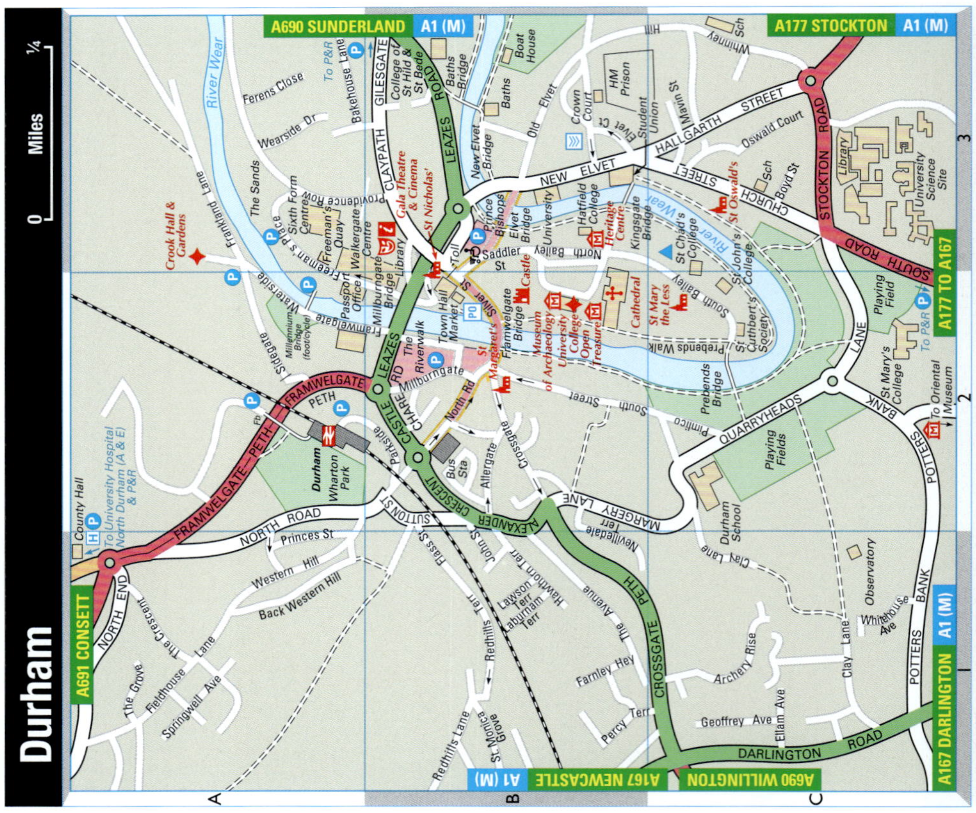
Durham
Miles 0 ¼
A690 SUNDERLAND A1 (M)
A177 STOCKTON A1 (M)
A691 CONSETT
A167 NEWCASTLE A1 (M)
A690 WILLINGTON
A167 DARLINGTON A1 (M)
River Wear

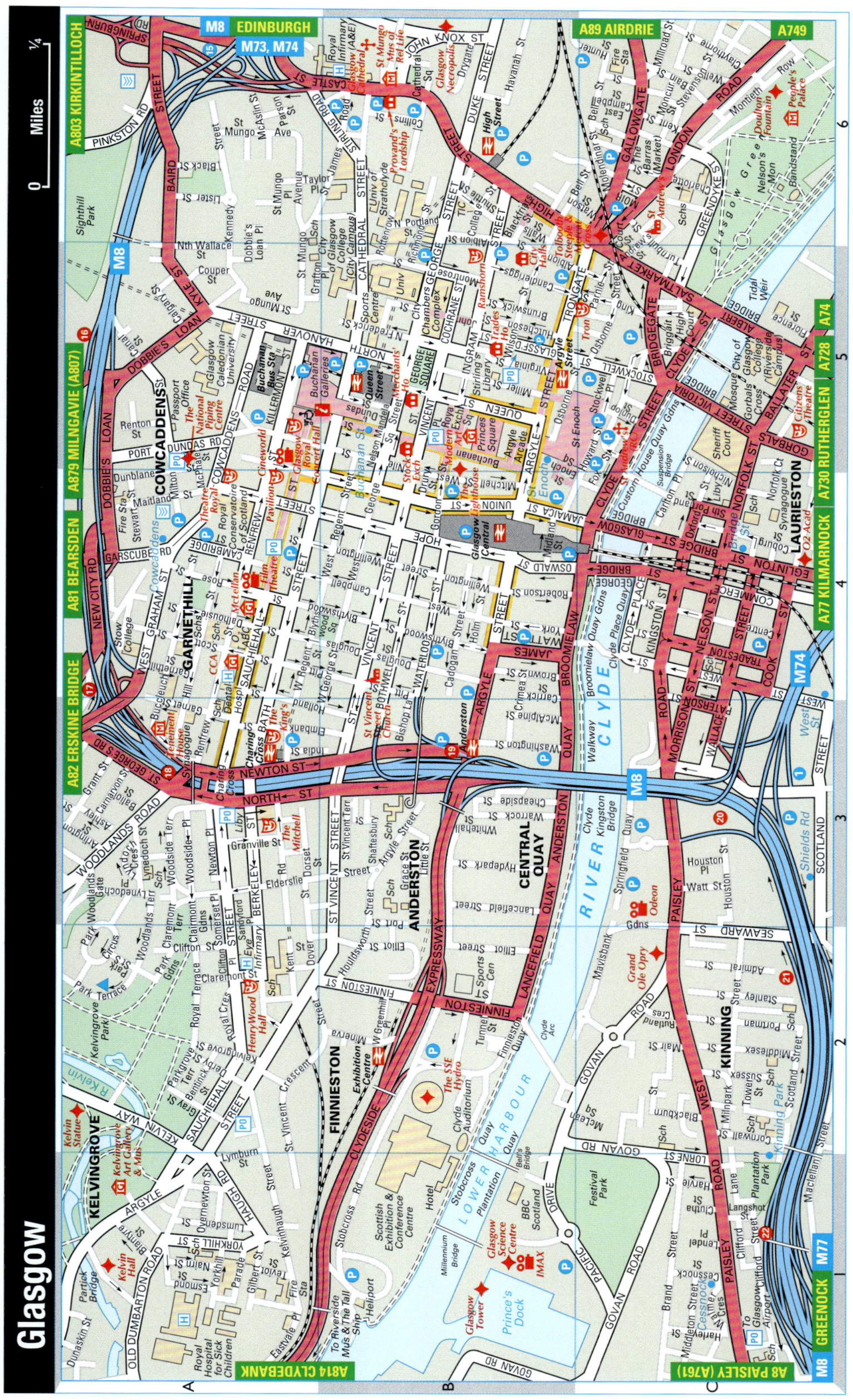
Glasgow
Miles
M8 EDINBURGH
M73, M74
A89 AIRDRIE
A749
A80 KIRKINTILLOCH
A879 MILNGAVIE (A807)
A81 BEARSDEN
A82 ERSKINE BRIDGE
A814 CLYDEBANK
A8 PAISLEY (A761)
M8 GREENOCK
M77
A77 KILMARNOCK
A730 RUTHERGLEN
A728
A74
M74
KELVINGROVE
FINNIESTON
ANDERSTON
CENTRAL QUAY
GARNETHILL
COWCADDENS
LAURIESTON
KINNING
RIVER CLYDE

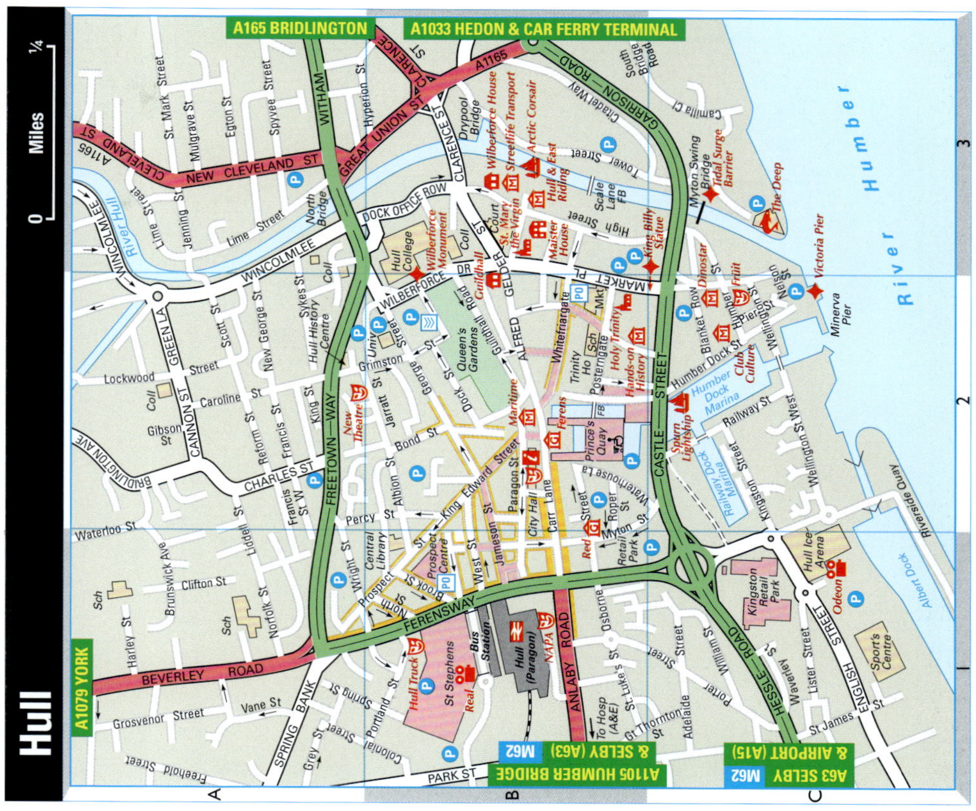
Hull
Miles
A165 BRIDLINGTON
A1033 HEDON & CAR FERRY TERMINAL
A1079 YORK
A1105 HUMBER BRIDGE & SELBY (A63) M62
A63 SELBY & AIRPORT (A15) M62
River Humber

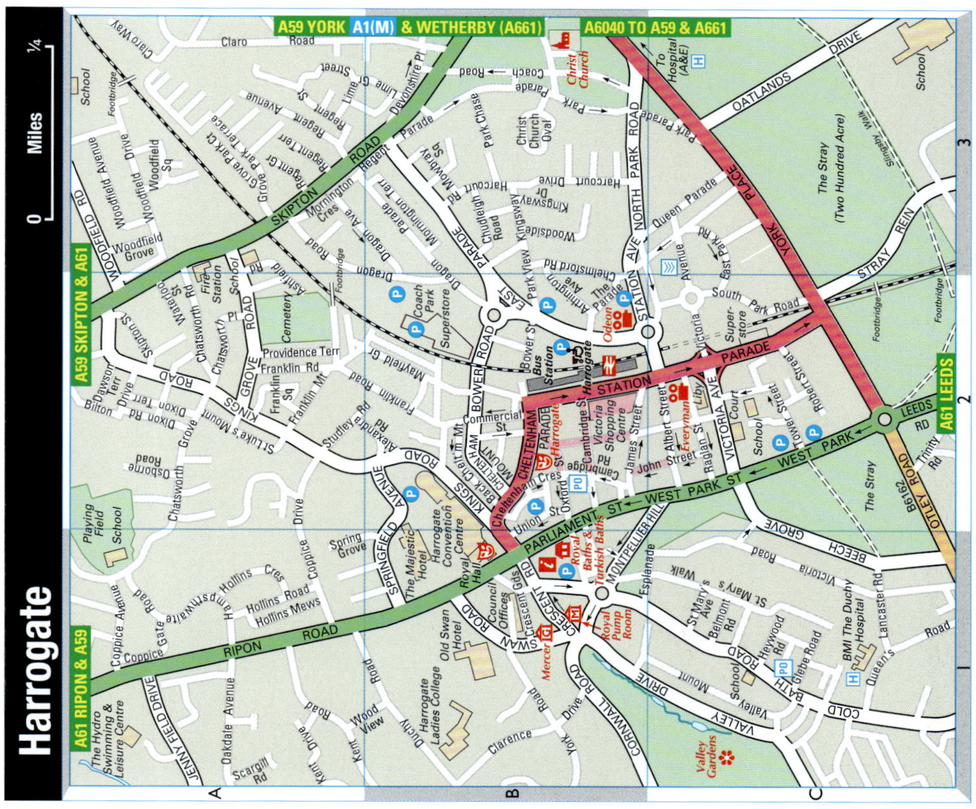
Harrogate
Miles
A59 YORK A1(M) & WETHERBY (A661)
A6040 TO A59 & A661
A59 SKIPTON & A61
A61 RIPON & A59
A61 LEEDS
The Stray (Two Hundred Acre)

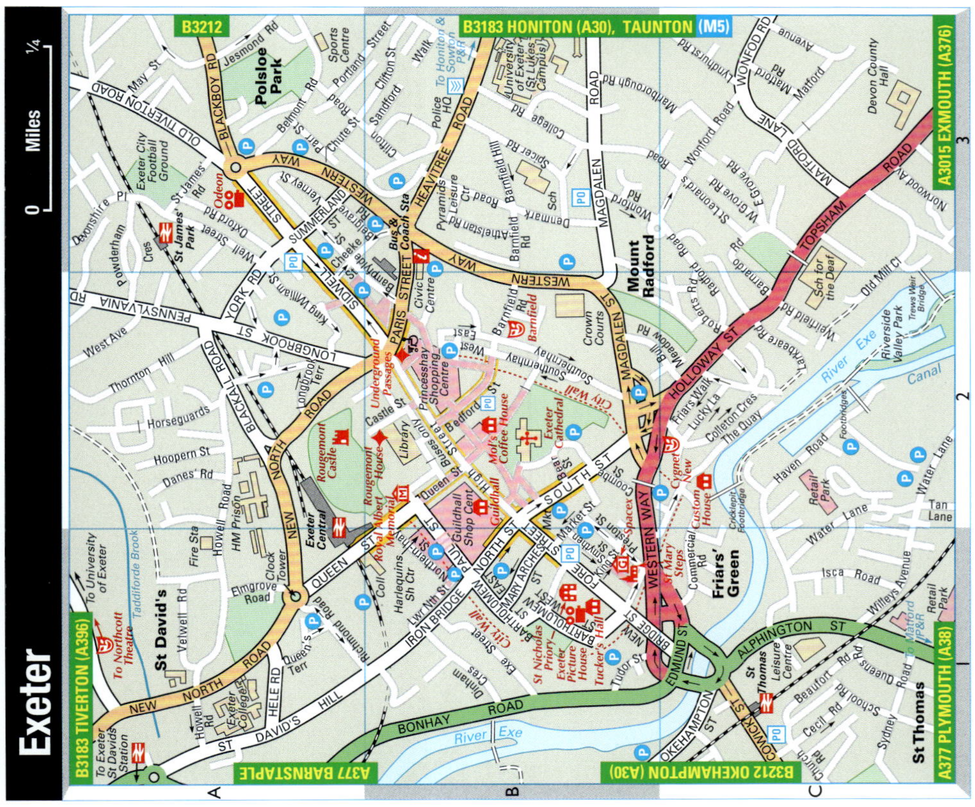
Exeter
Miles
B3212
B3183 HONITON (A30), TAUNTON (M5)
A3015 EXMOUTH (A376)
A377 PLYMOUTH (A38)
B3212 OKEHAMPTON (A30)
A377 BARNSTAPLE
B3183 TIVERTON (A396)
Polsloe Park
Mount Radford
Friars' Green
St David's
St Thomas
River Exe

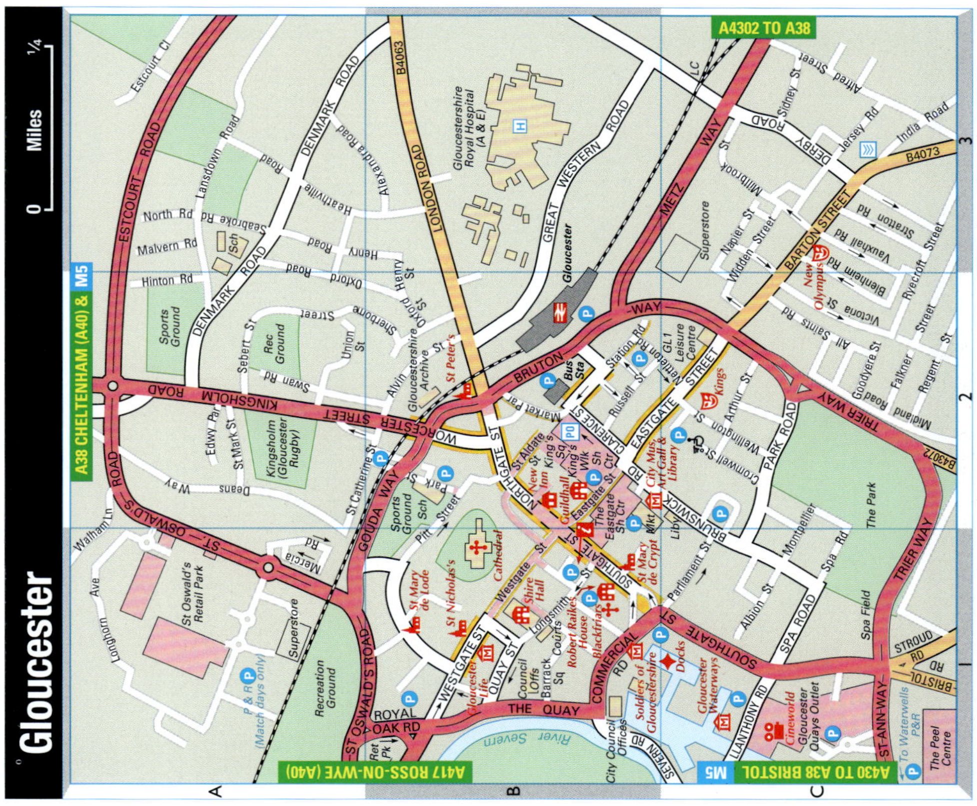
Gloucester
Miles
A4302 TO A38
A38 CHELTENHAM (A40) & M5
A40 ROSS-ON-WYE (A40)
M5 A430 TO A38 BRISTOL
Gloucester
River Severn

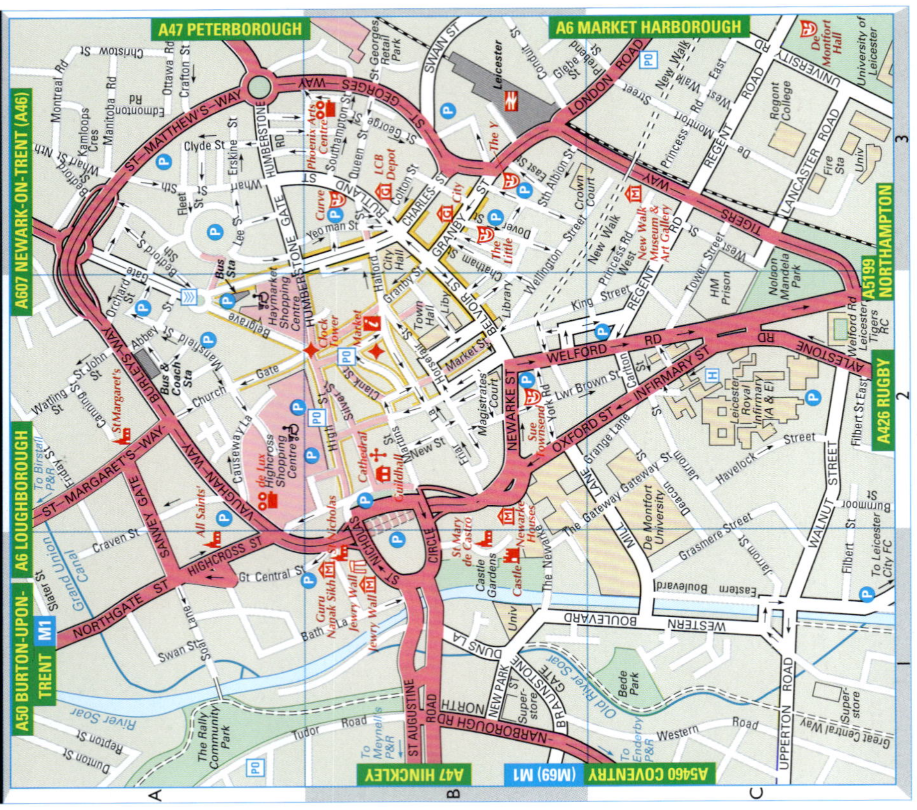

Leicester

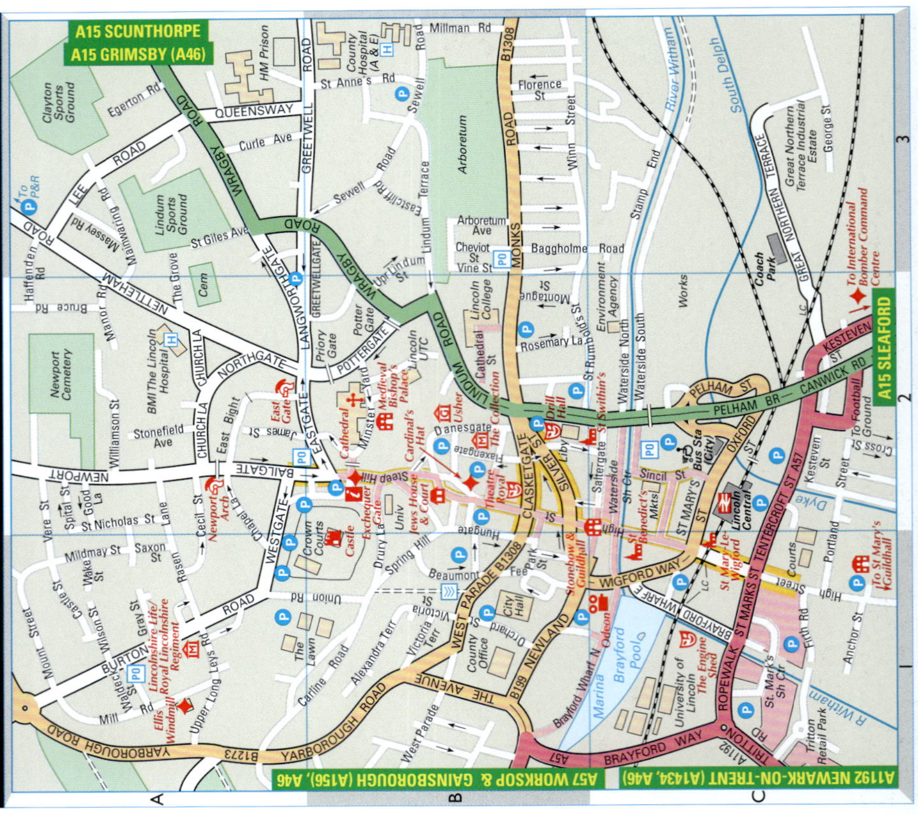

Lincoln

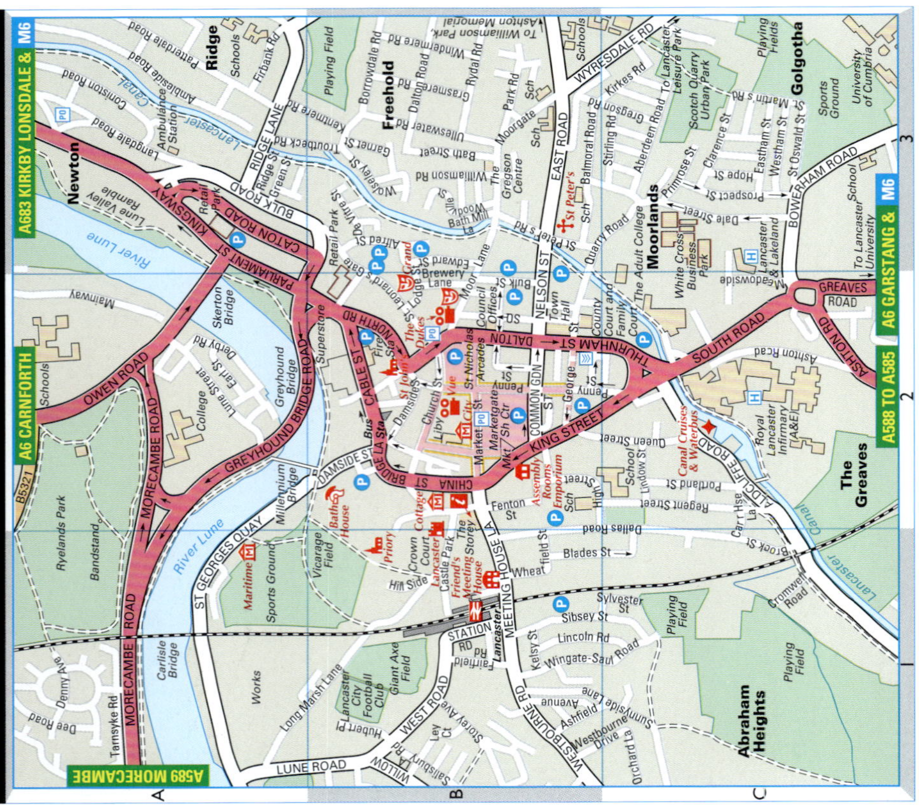

Lancaster

Ipswich

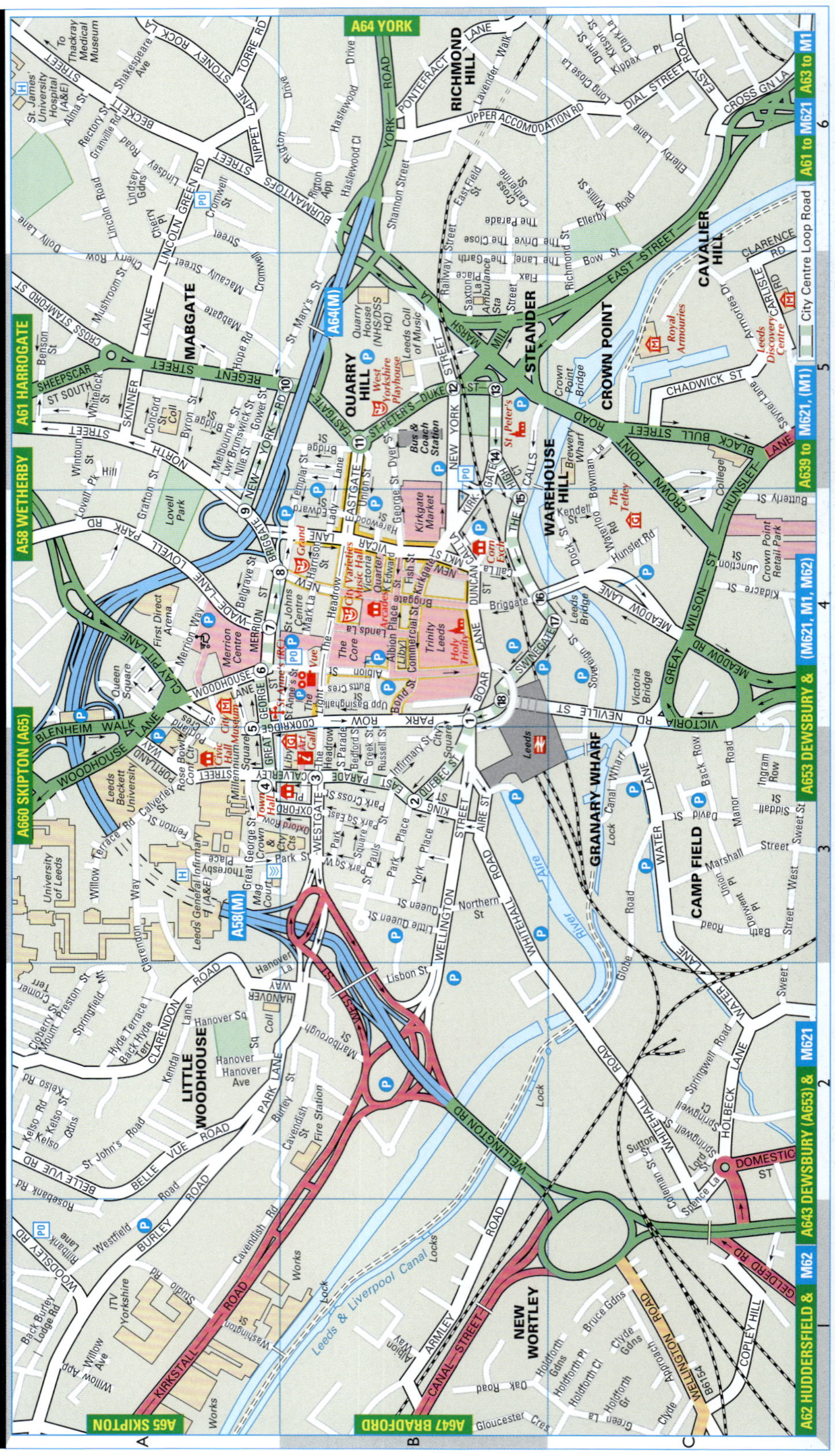

Leeds

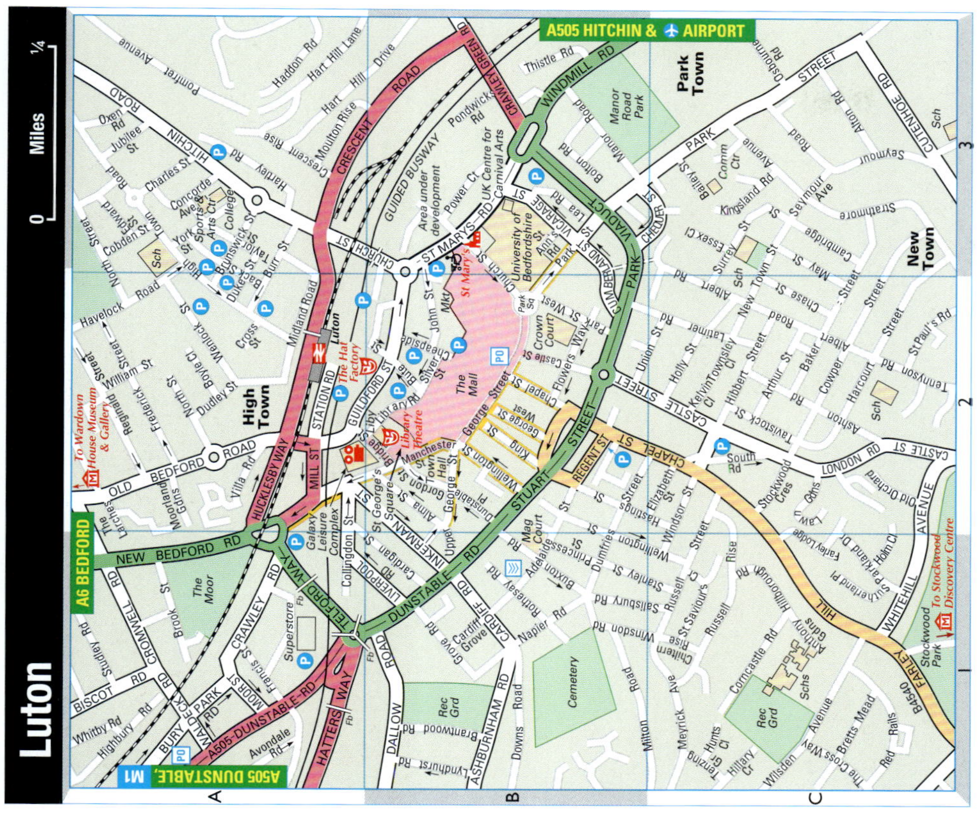
Luton

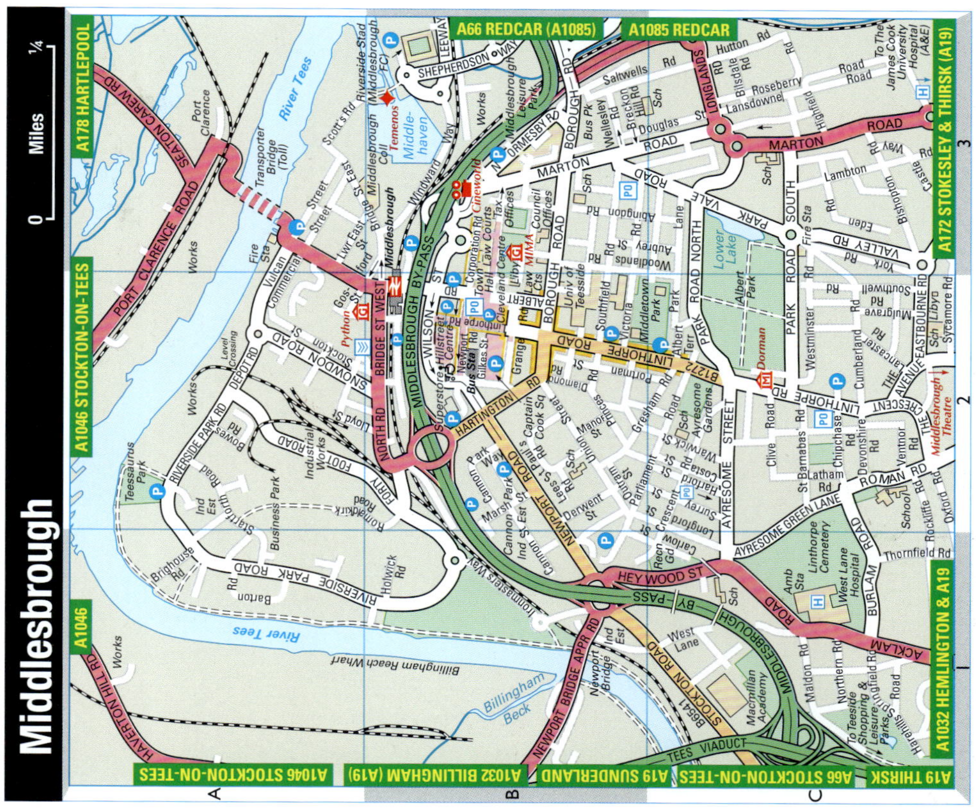
Middlesbrough

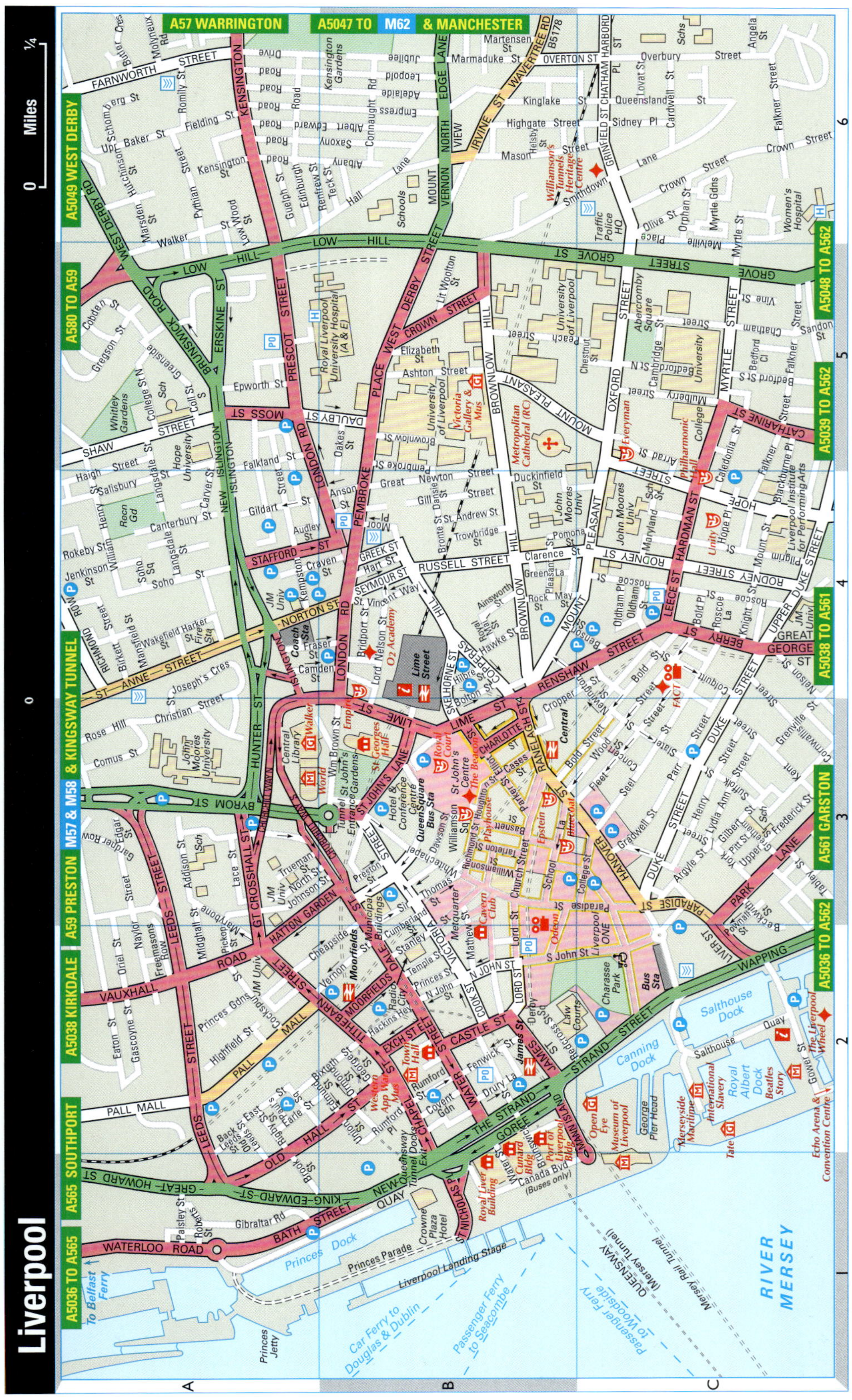
Liverpool

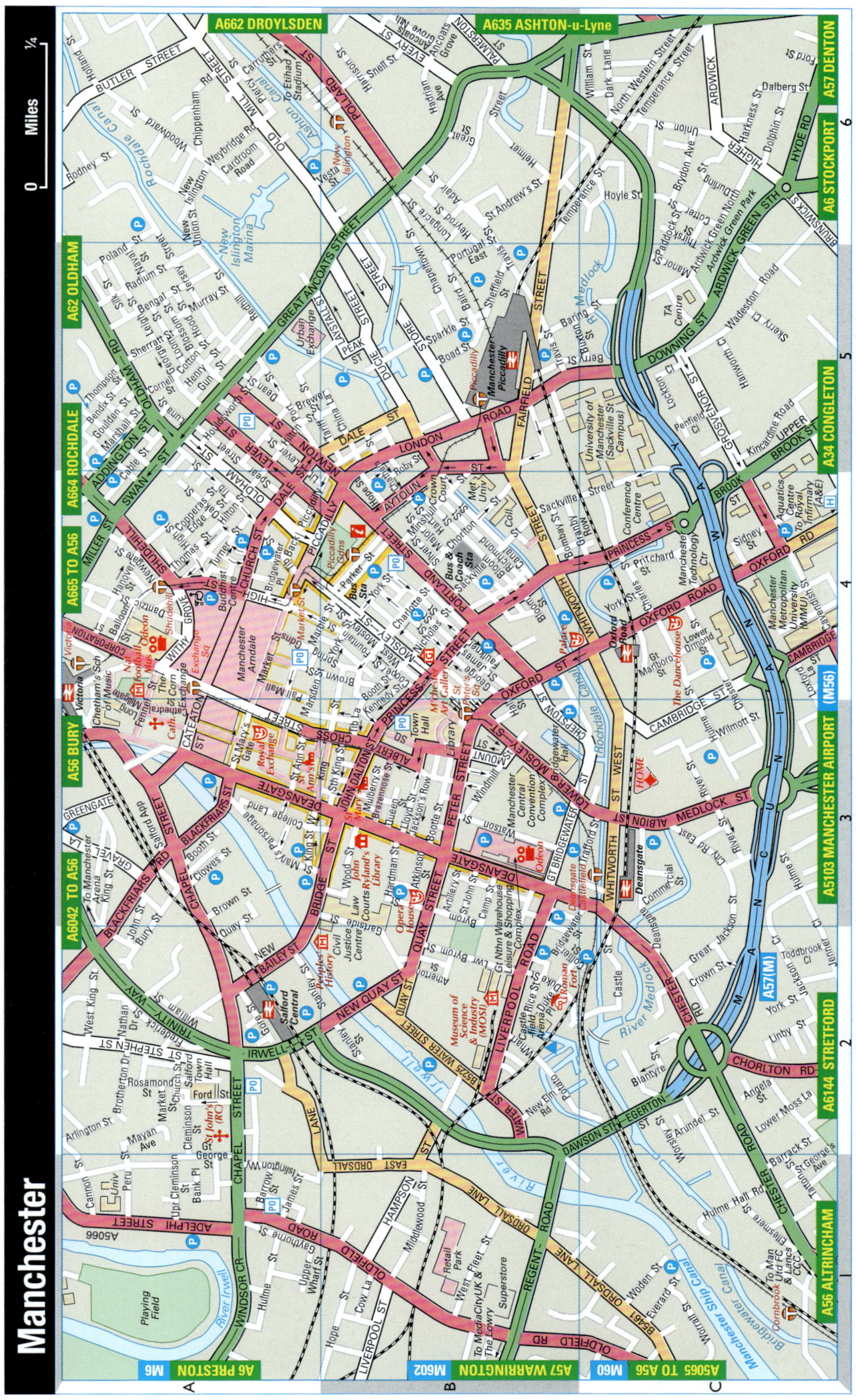
Manchester

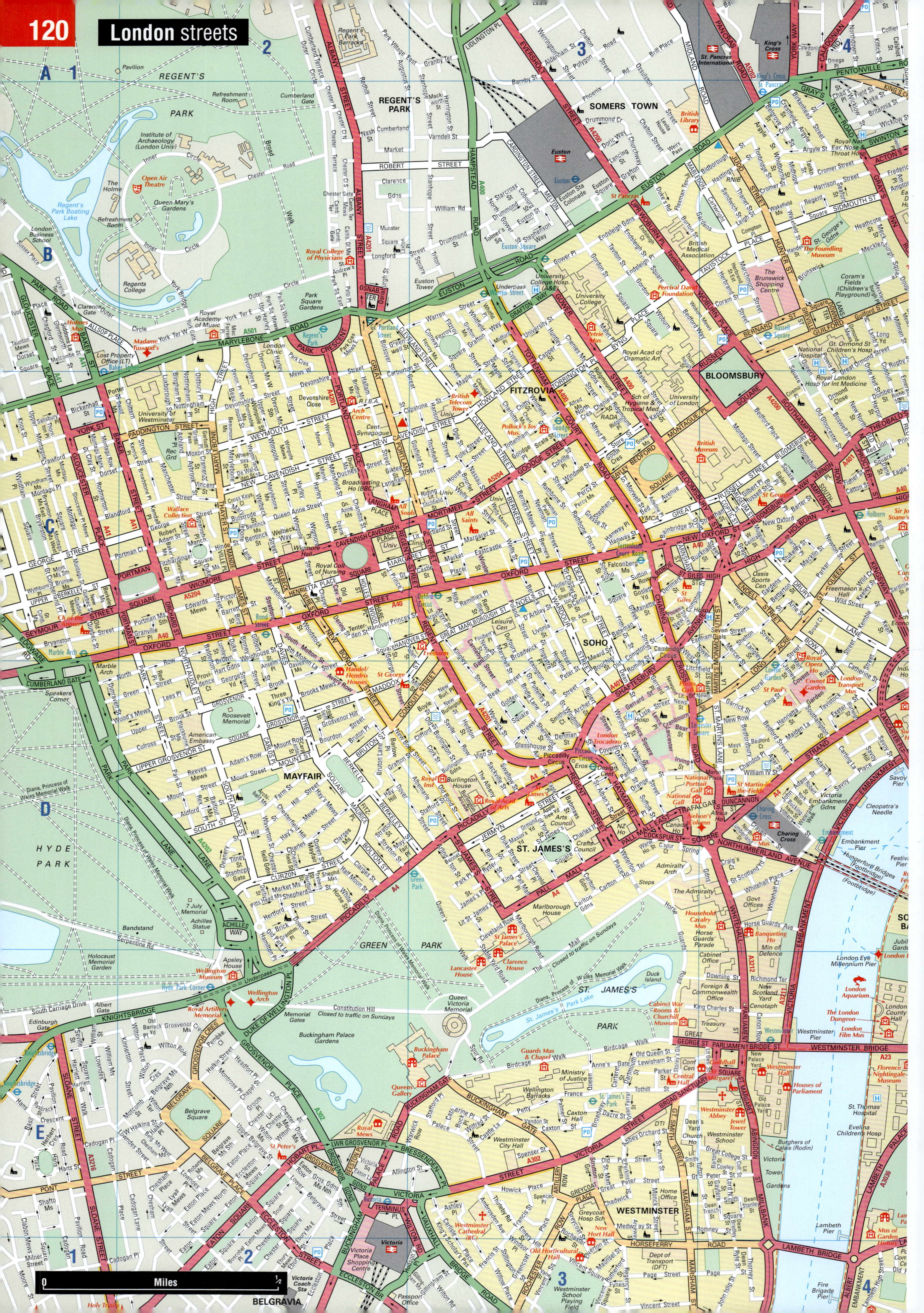
REGENT'S PARK
REGENT'S PARK
SOMERS TOWN
Euston
St. Pancras International
King's Cross
EUSTON ROAD
MARYLEBONE ROAD
BLOOMSBURY
FITZROVIA
British Museum
British Library
University College
University of London
University of Westminster
Wallace Collection
OXFORD STREET
OXFORD CIRCUS
SOHO
MAYFAIR
Piccadilly Circus
PICCADILLY
ST. JAMES'S
Trafalgar Square
Charing Cross
Covent Garden
Royal Opera Ho
STRAND
HYDE PARK
Marble Arch
GREEN PARK
ST. JAMES'S PARK
Buckingham Palace
KNIGHTSBRIDGE
BELGRAVIA
Victoria
WESTMINSTER
Westminster Abbey
Houses of Parliament
London Eye Millennium Pier
WESTMINSTER BRIDGE
LAMBETH BRIDGE
Cleopatra's Needle
Embankment
Waterloo Bridge
Miles
0
1/2

London Docklands
Congestion Charging Zone
Miles
FINSBURY
CLERKENWELL
HOLBORN
HOXTON
SHOREDITCH
THE CITY
SOUTHWARK
LAMBETH
RIVER THAMES
STEPNEY
POPLAR
WAPPING
BERMONDSEY
ROTHERHITHE
MILLWALL
ISLE OF DOGS
DEPTFORD
GREENWICH
CANNING TOWN
PENTONVILLE ROAD
CITY ROAD
OLD STREET
CLERKENWELL ROAD
FARRINGDON ROAD
LONDON WALL
CHEAPSIDE
VICTORIA EMBANKMENT
BLACKFRIARS BRIDGE
LONDON BRIDGE
TOWER BRIDGE
WATERLOO BRIDGE
BISHOPSGATE
The Barbican
St Paul's Cathedral
Tate Modern
Liverpool Street
Waterloo
Tower of London
Imperial War Museum
The O2 Arena (Millennium Dome)

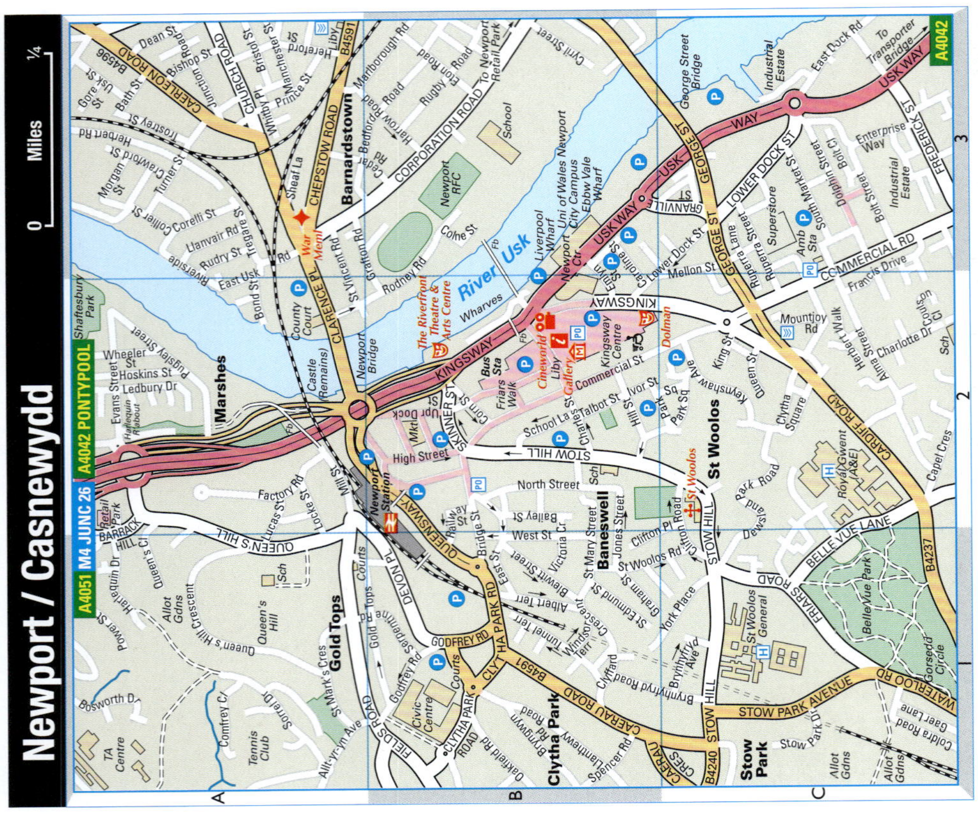
Newport / Casnewydd
A4051 M4 JUNC 26
A4042 PONTYPOOL
A4042

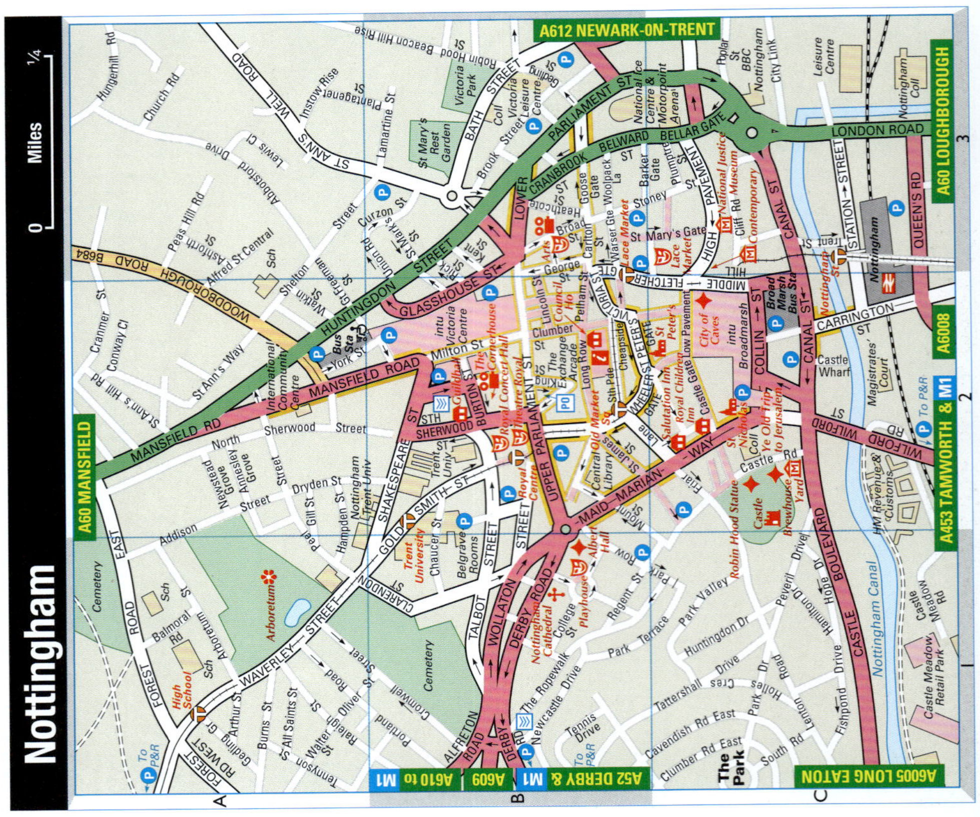
Nottingham
A612 NEWARK-ON-TRENT
A60 LOUGHBOROUGH
A453 TAMWORTH & M1
A6005 LONG EATON
A52 DERBY & M1
A609
A610 to M1
A60 MANSFIELD

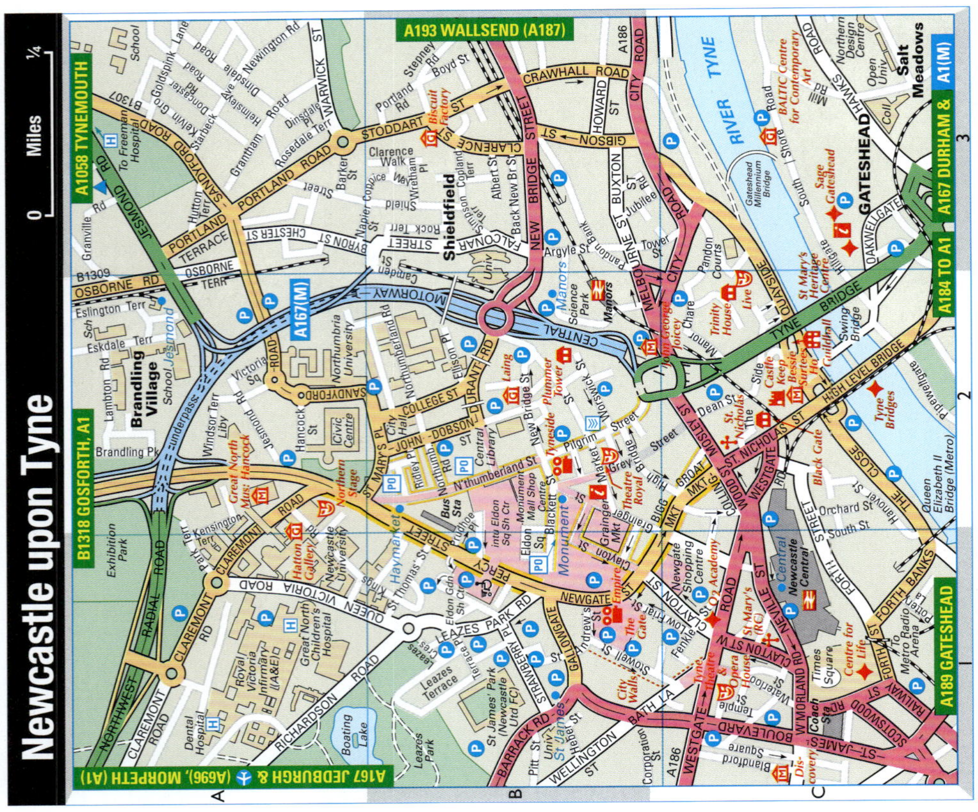
Newcastle upon Tyne
A193 WALLSEND (A187)
A1058 TYNEMOUTH
B1318 GOSFORTH A1
A167 DURHAM & A1(M)
A184 TO A1
A189 GATESHEAD
A167 JEDBURGH & A696, MORPETH (A1)

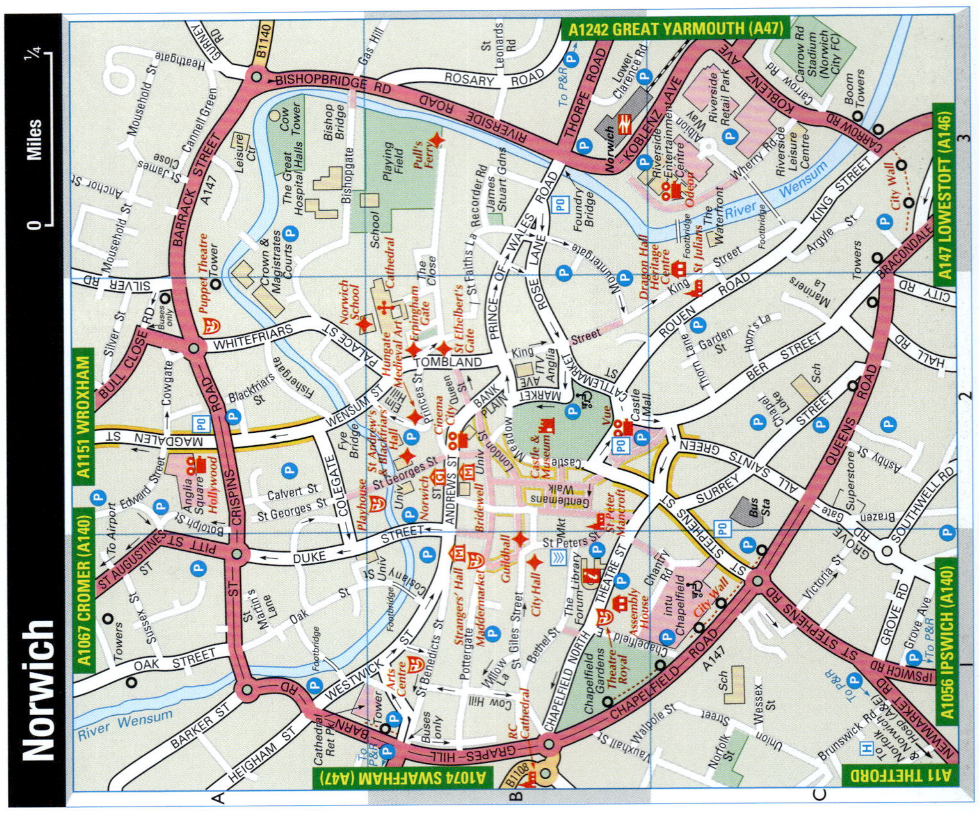
Norwich
A1242 GREAT YARMOUTH (A47)
A147 LOWESTOFT (A146)
A1056 IPSWICH (A140)
A11 THETFORD
A1074 SWAFFHAM (A47)
A1067 CROMER (A140)
A1151 WROXHAM

Milton Keynes
A509 NEWPORT PAGNELL & M1
A422 BEDFORD
A5 DUNSTABLE
A5 NORTHAMPTON (A508)
A422 TO A5

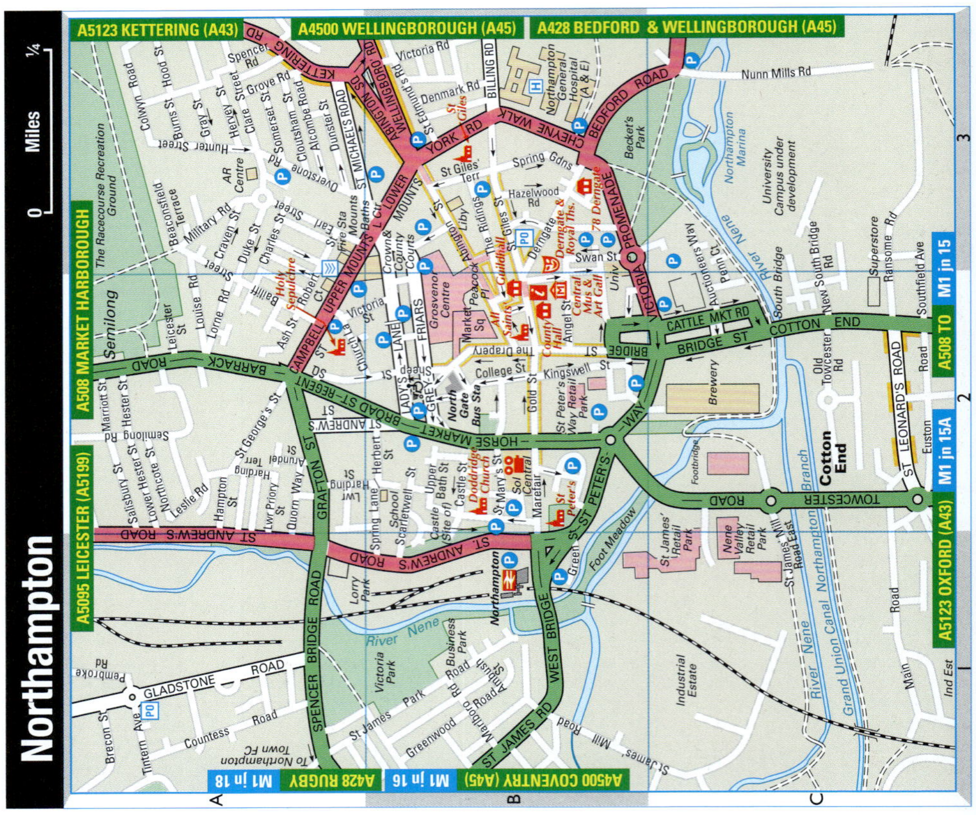
Northampton
A5123 KETTERING (A43)
A4500 WELLINGBOROUGH (A45)
A428 BEDFORD & WELLINGBOROUGH (A45)
A508 TO M1 in 15
A5123 OXFORD (A43)
M1 in 15A
A4500 COVENTRY (A45)
M1 in 16
A428 RUGBY
M1 in 18
A5095 LEICESTER (A5199)
A508 MARKET HARBOROUGH

Plymouth

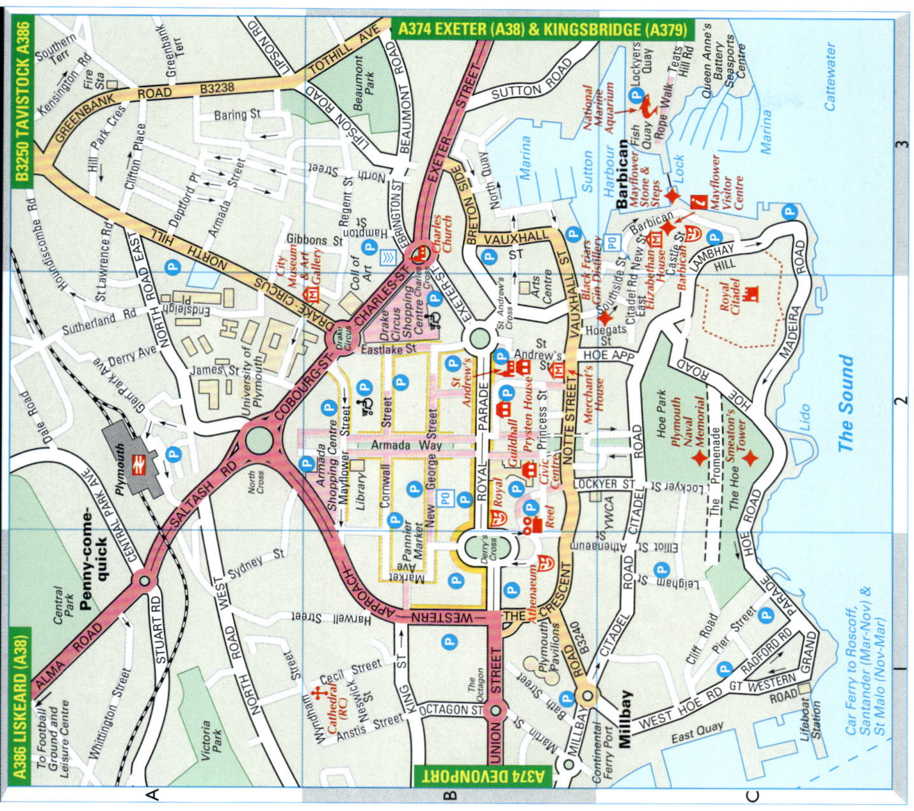

Preston

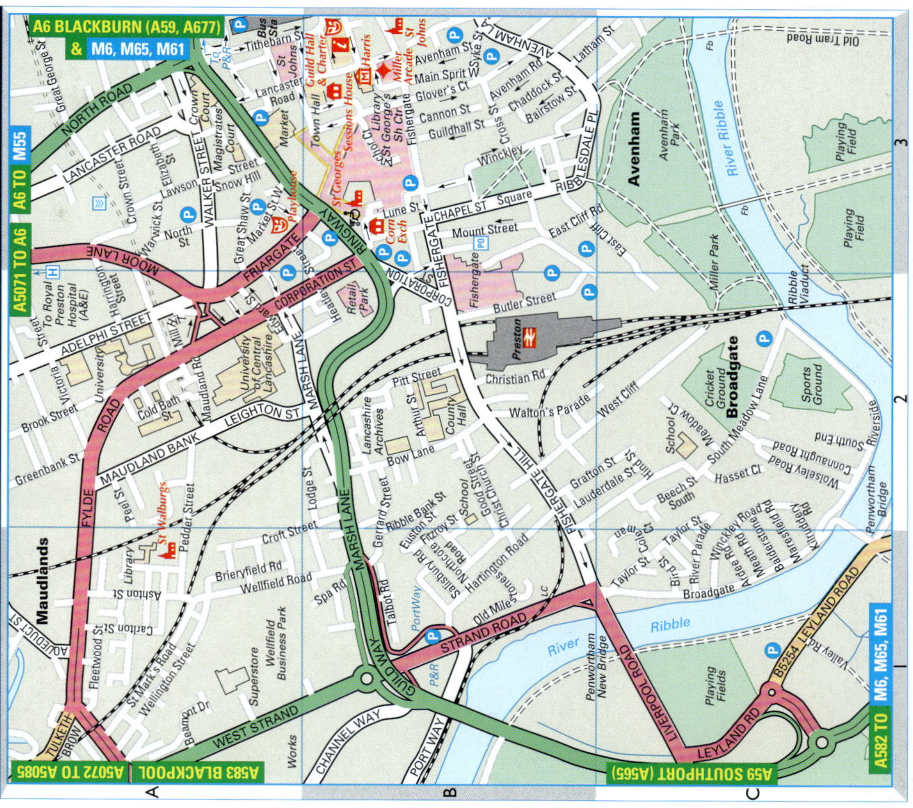

Peterborough

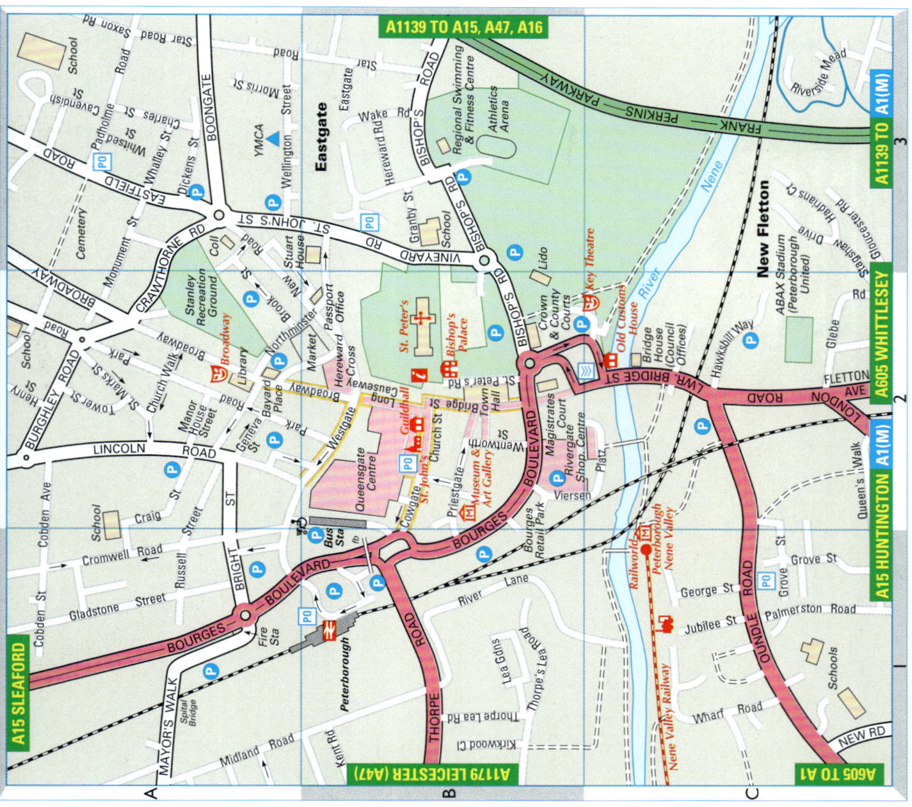

Portsmouth

Oxford

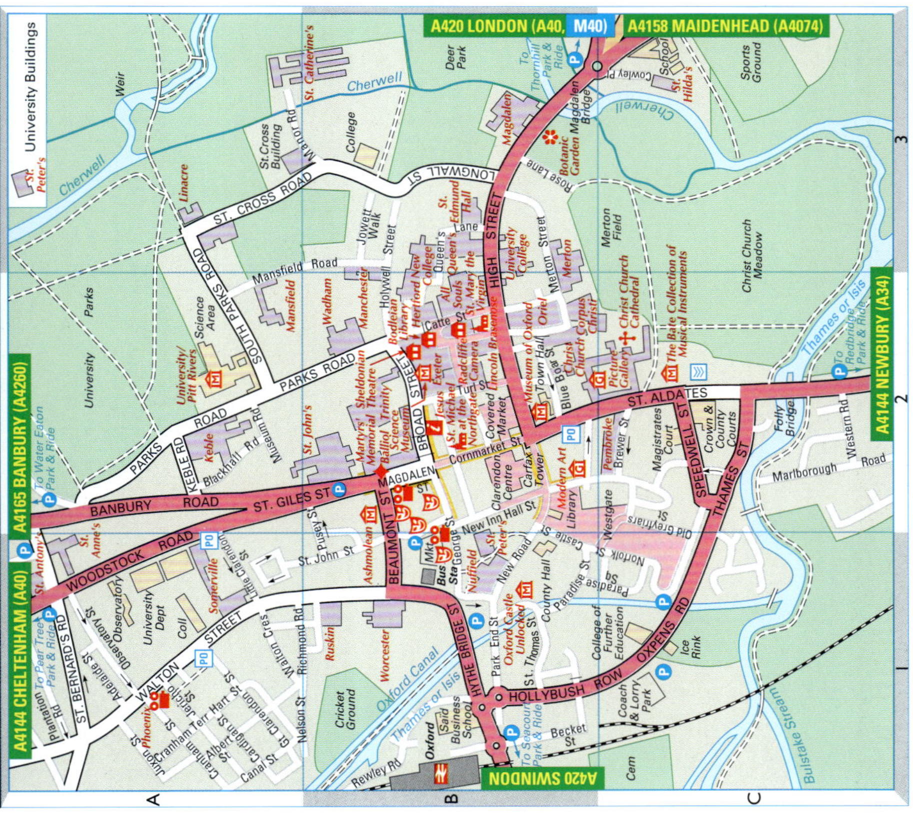

Poole

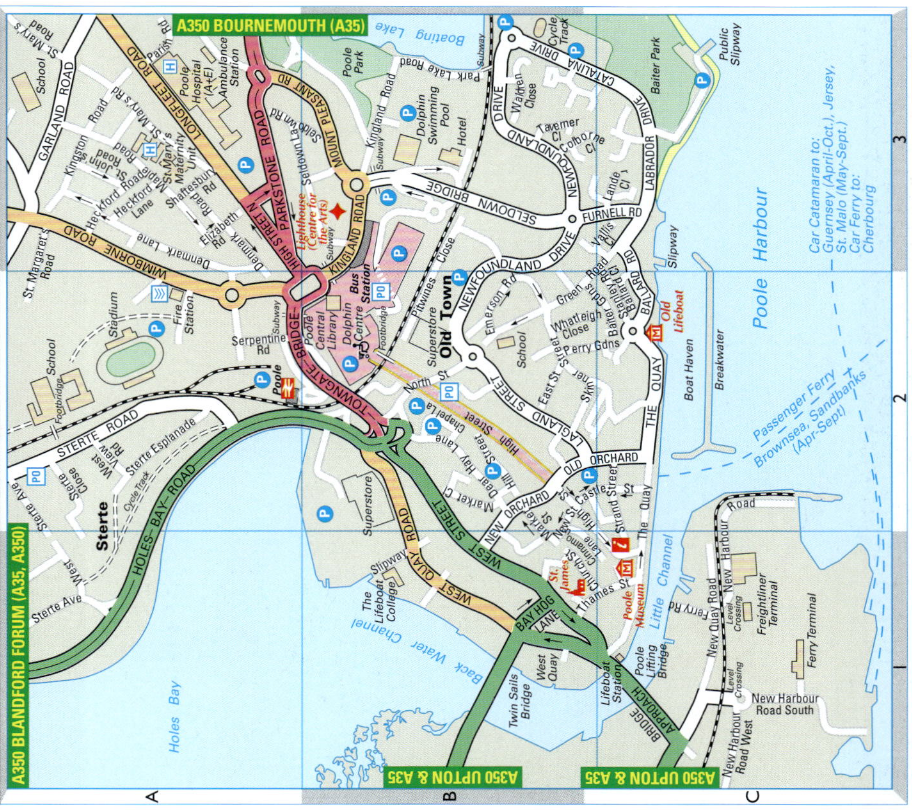

Scarborough
A165 WHITBY (A171)
A64 YORK, THIRSK (A170)
A165 BRIDLINGTON, FILEY
NORTH BAY
SOUTH BAY
Miles

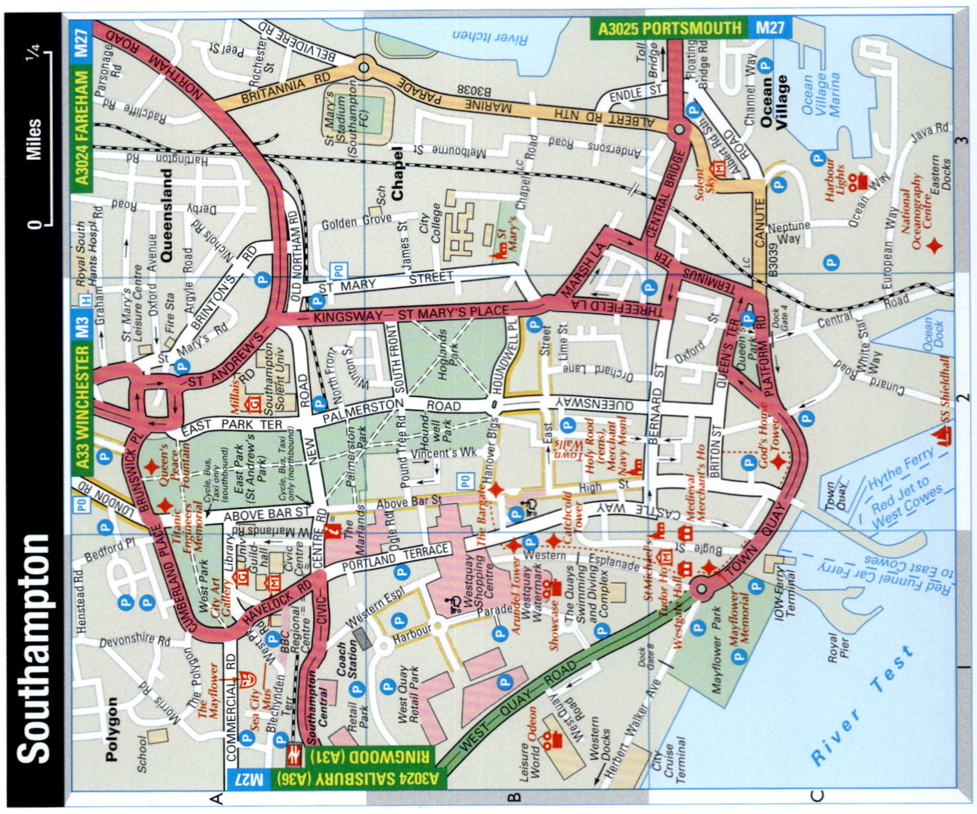
Southampton
A3025 PORTSMOUTH M27
A3024 FAREHAM M27
A33 WINCHESTER M3
A3024 SALISBURY (A36) RINGWOOD (A31) M27
River Test
Miles

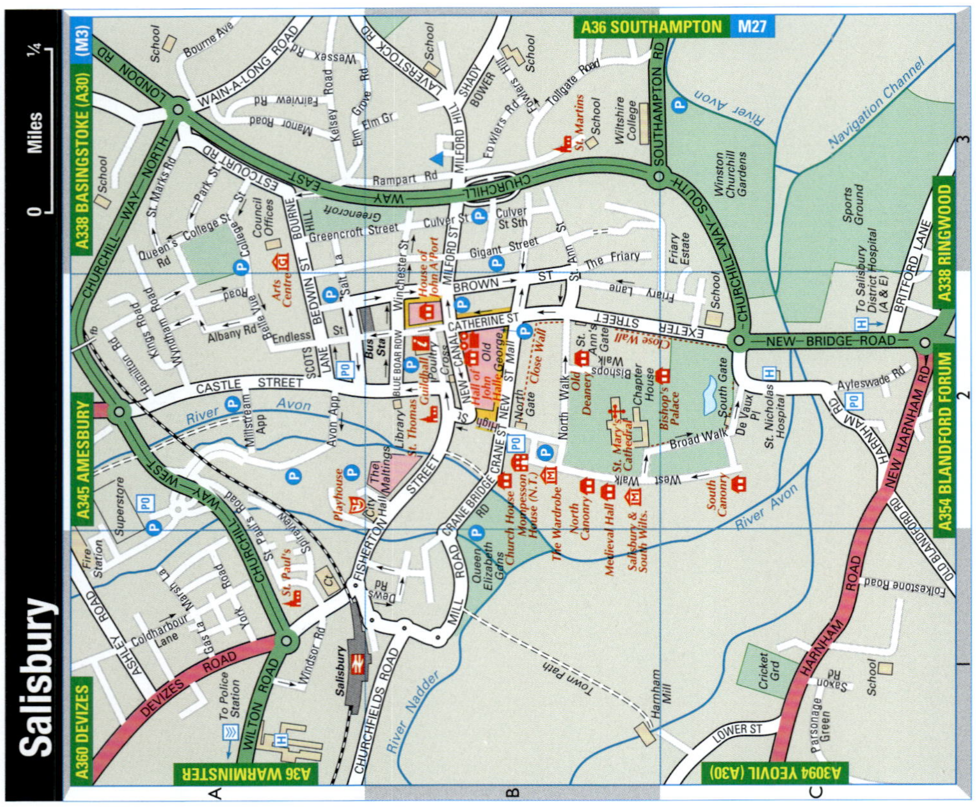
Salisbury
A36 SOUTHAMPTON M27
A338 BASINGSTOKE (A30) (M3)
A345 AMESBURY
A360 DEVIZES
A36 WARMINSTER
A3094 YEOVIL (A30)
A354 BLANDFORD FORUM
A338 RINGWOOD
Miles

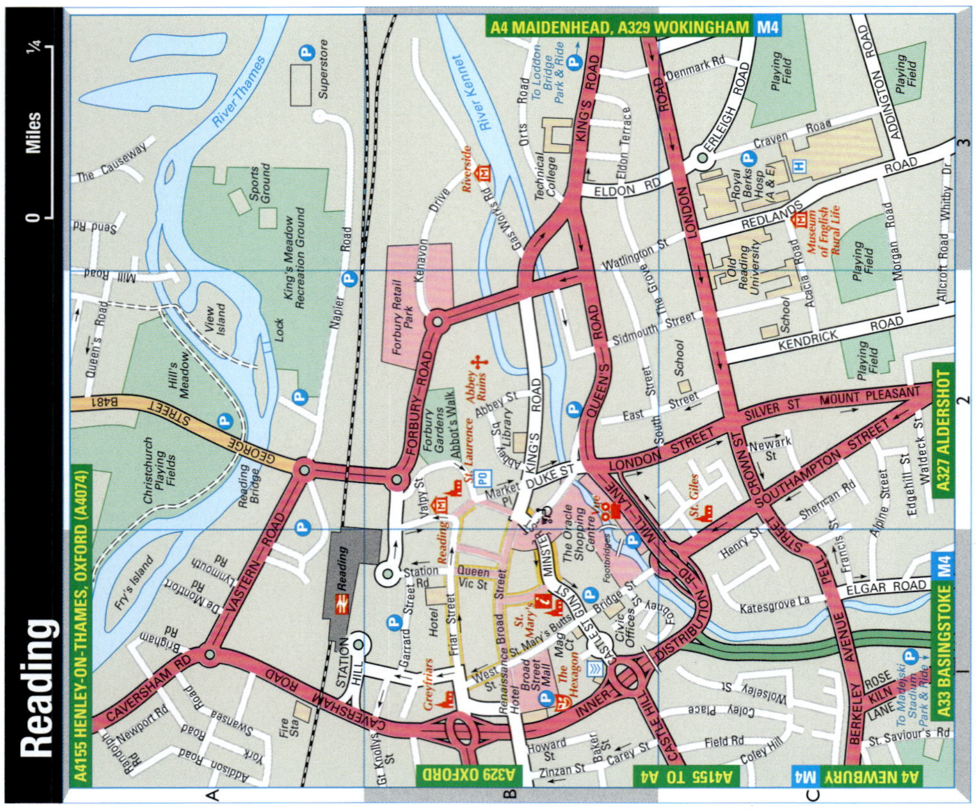
Reading
A4 MAIDENHEAD, A329 WOKINGHAM M4
A4155 HENLEY-ON-THAMES, OXFORD (A4074)
A329 OXFORD
A4155 TO A4
A4 NEWBURY M4
A33 BASINGSTOKE M4
A327 ALDERSHOT
Miles

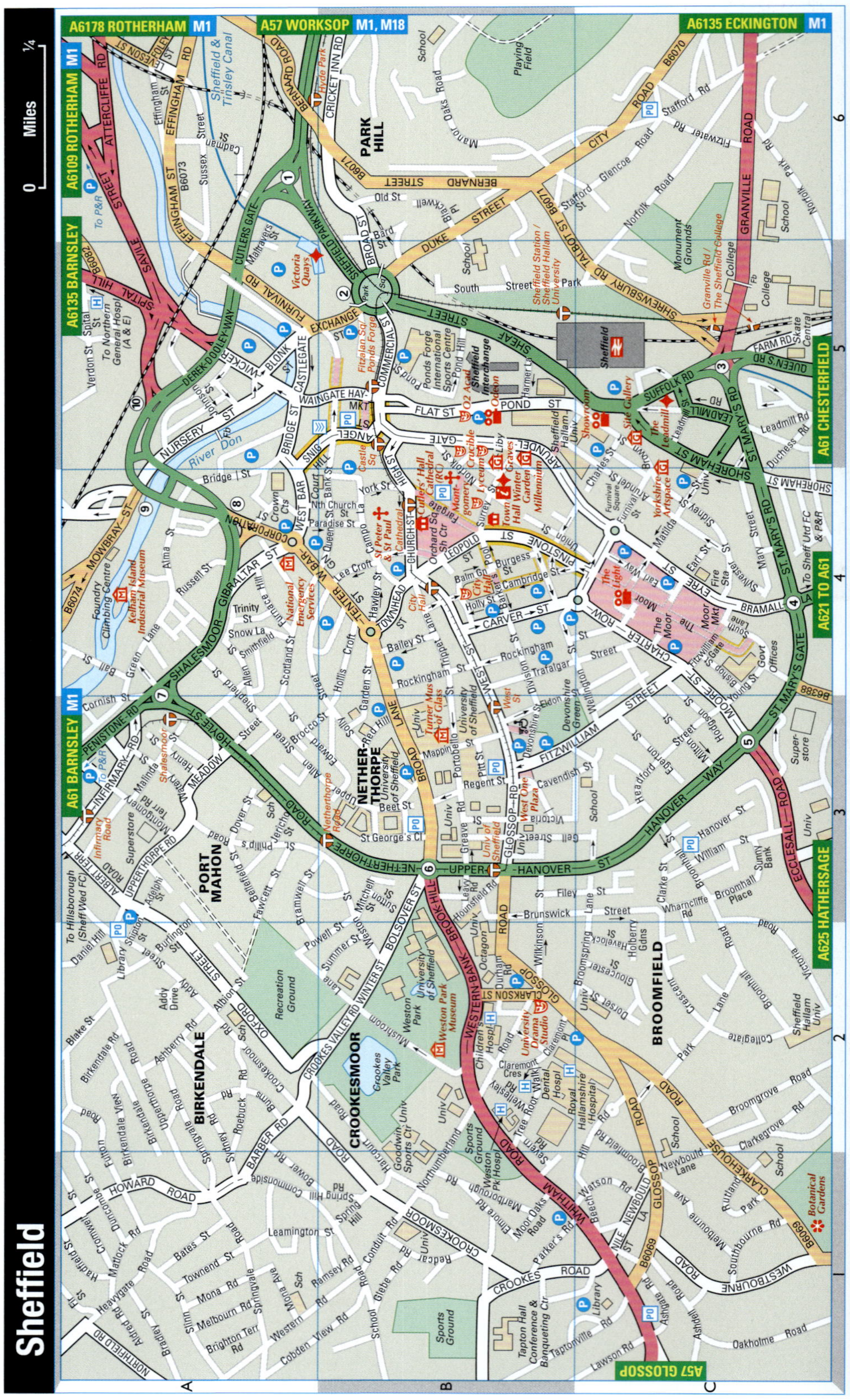
Sheffield
A6178 ROTHERHAM M1
A57 WORKSOP M1, M18
A6135 ECKINGTON M1
A6109 ROTHERHAM M1
A6135 BARNSLEY
A61 BARNSLEY M1
A61 CHESTERFIELD
A621 TO A61
A625 HATHERSAGE
A57 GLOSSOP
Miles

Stratford-upon-Avon
A439 WARWICK (A46)
M40
A422 BANBURY
A3400 OXFORD (A44)
A4390 TO A3400
A3400 BIRMINGHAM
M40,M42
A422 TO A46 WORCESTER (A422)
B439 EVESHAM (A46)

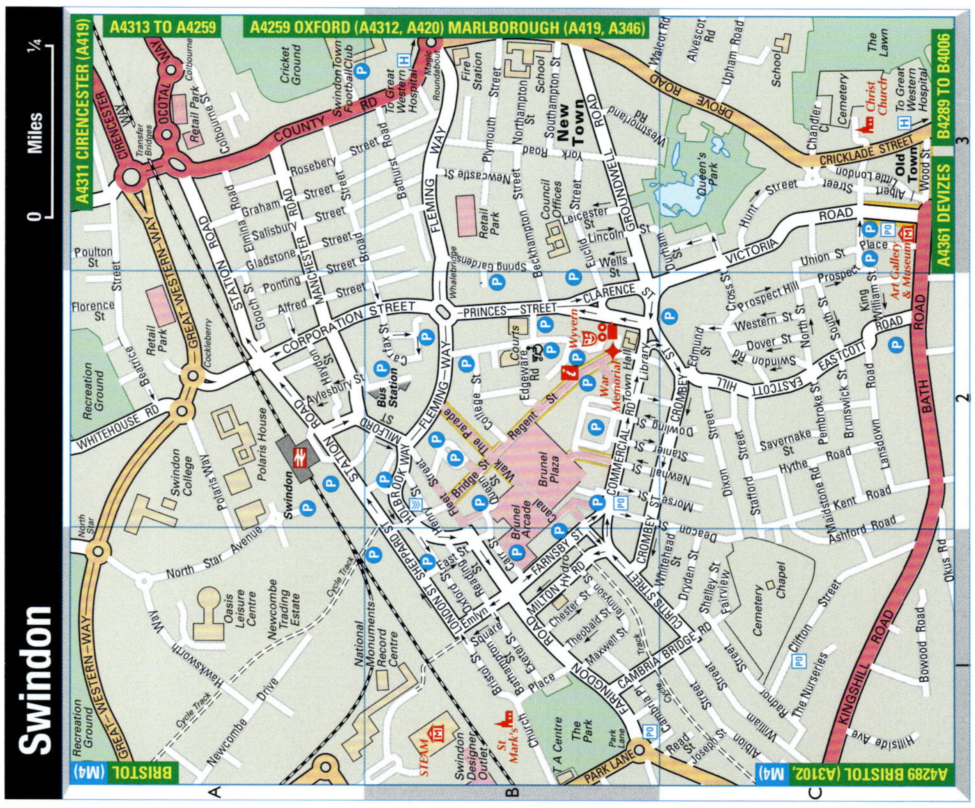
Swindon
A4313 TO A4259
A4259 OXFORD (A4312, A420) MARLBOROUGH (A419, A346)
A4311 CIRENCESTER (A419)
B4289 TO B4006
A4361 DEVIZES
BRISTOL (M4)
A4289 BRISTOL (A3102, M4)

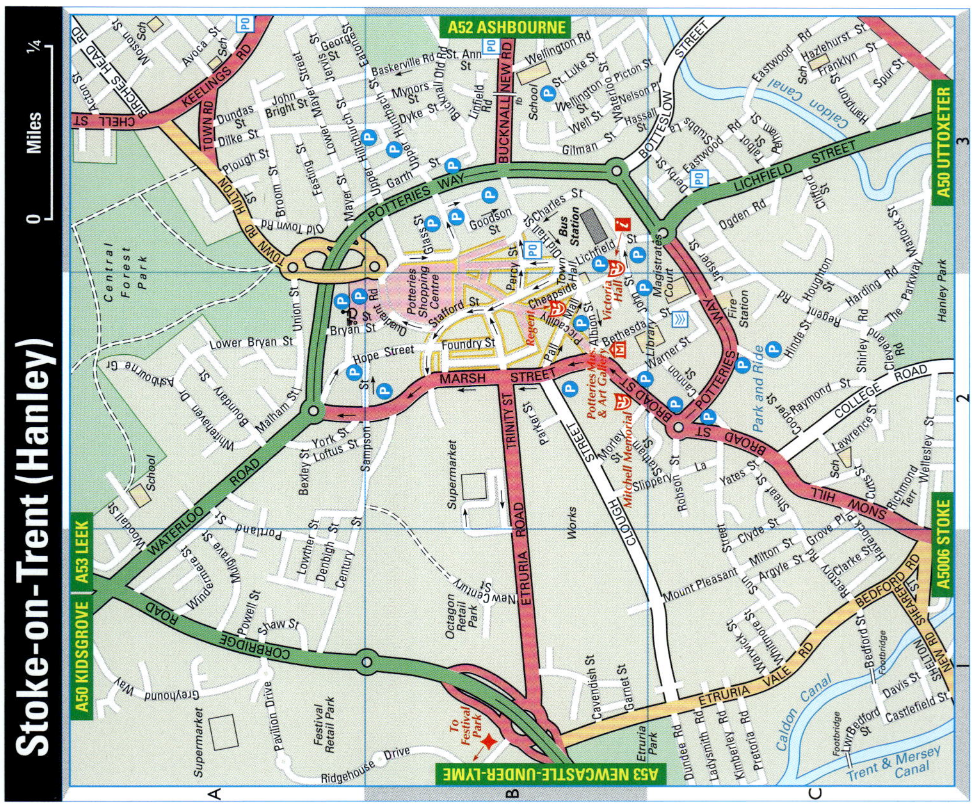
Stoke-on-Trent (Hanley)
A52 ASHBOURNE
A50 UTTOXETER
A5006 STOKE
A53 LEEK
A50 KIDSGROVE
A53 NEWCASTLE-UNDER-LYME

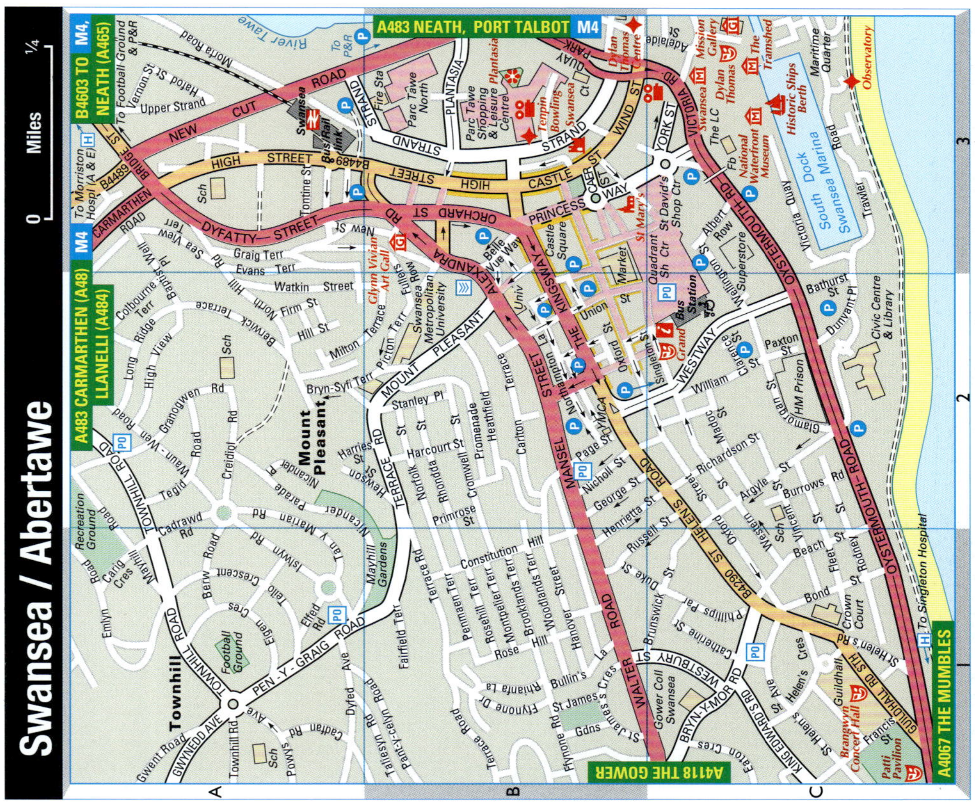
Swansea / Abertawe
A483 NEATH, PORT TALBOT
M4
B4603 TO M4, NEATH (A465)
A483 CARMARTHEN (A48) LLANELLI (A484)
A4067 THE MUMBLES
A4118 THE GOWER

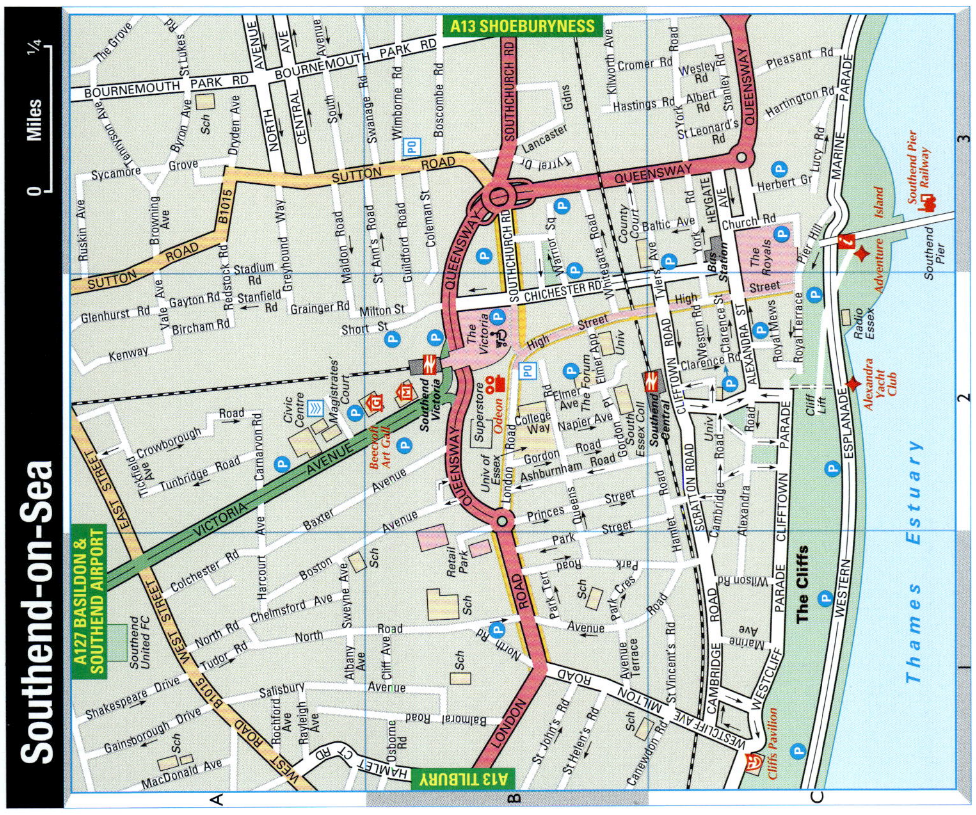
Southend-on-Sea
A13 SHOEBURYNESS
A127 BASILDON & SOUTHEND AIRPORT
A13 TILBURY
Thames Estuary

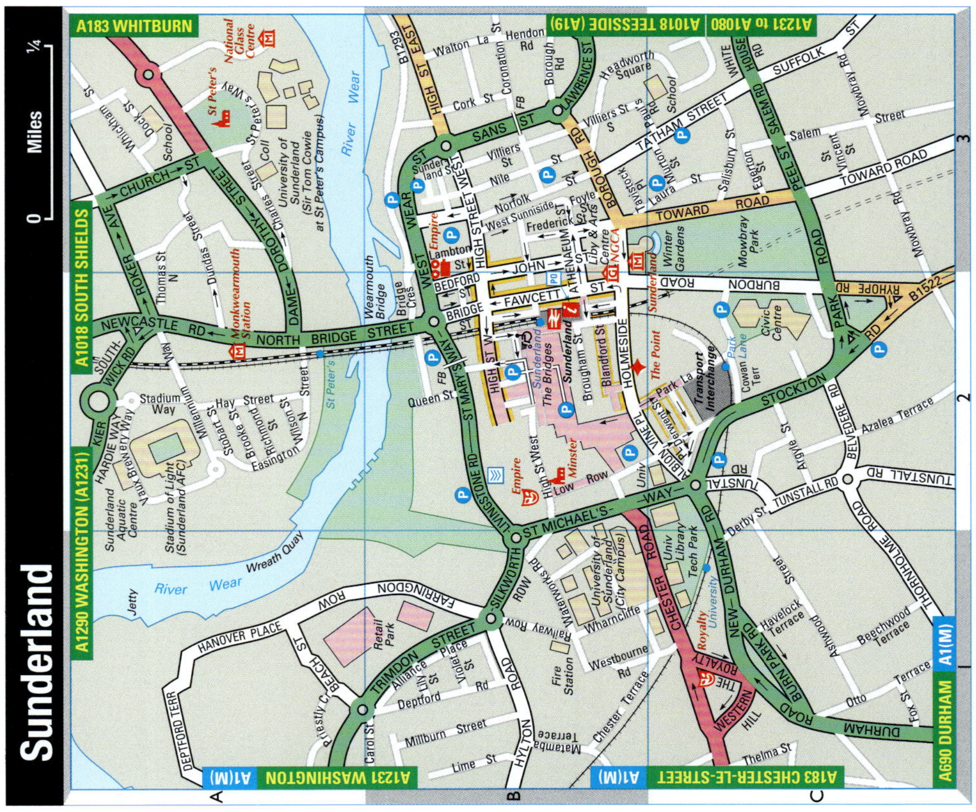
Sunderland
A183 WHITBURN
A1018 TEESSIDE (A19)
A1018 SOUTH SHIELDS
A1290 WASHINGTON (A1231)
A690 DURHAM
A1(M)
A1231 WASHINGTON
A183 CHESTER-LE-STREET

Winchester
TO M3
B3404 ALTON (A31)
M3 Sthbnd
B3330 TO M3
B3335 TO M3
B3040 ROMSEY (A3090)
B3049 STOCKBRIDGE
B3420 NEWBURY (A34)
B3047 BASINGSTOKE (A33)
0 Miles ¼

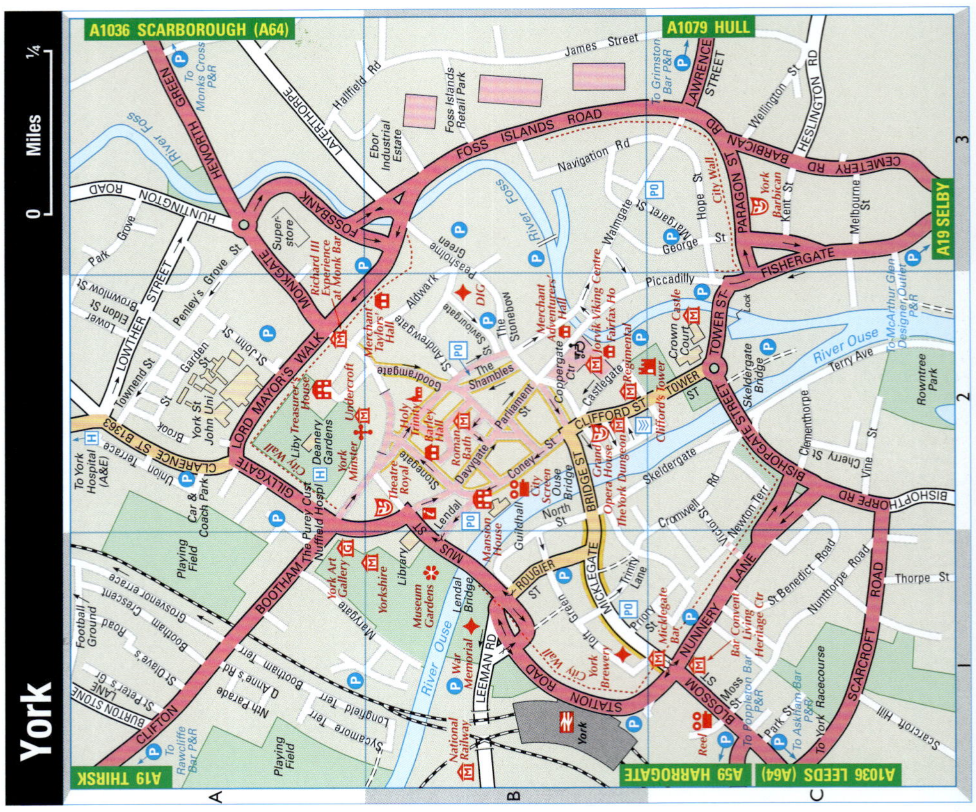
York
A1036 SCARBOROUGH (A64)
A1079 HULL
A19 SELBY
A1036 LEEDS (A64)
A59 HARROGATE
A19 THIRSK
0 Miles ¼

Torquay
A379 TEIGNMOUTH
A3022 PLYMOUTH (A385, A38)
A3022 EXETER (A380, A38) M5
TOR BAY
0 Miles ¼

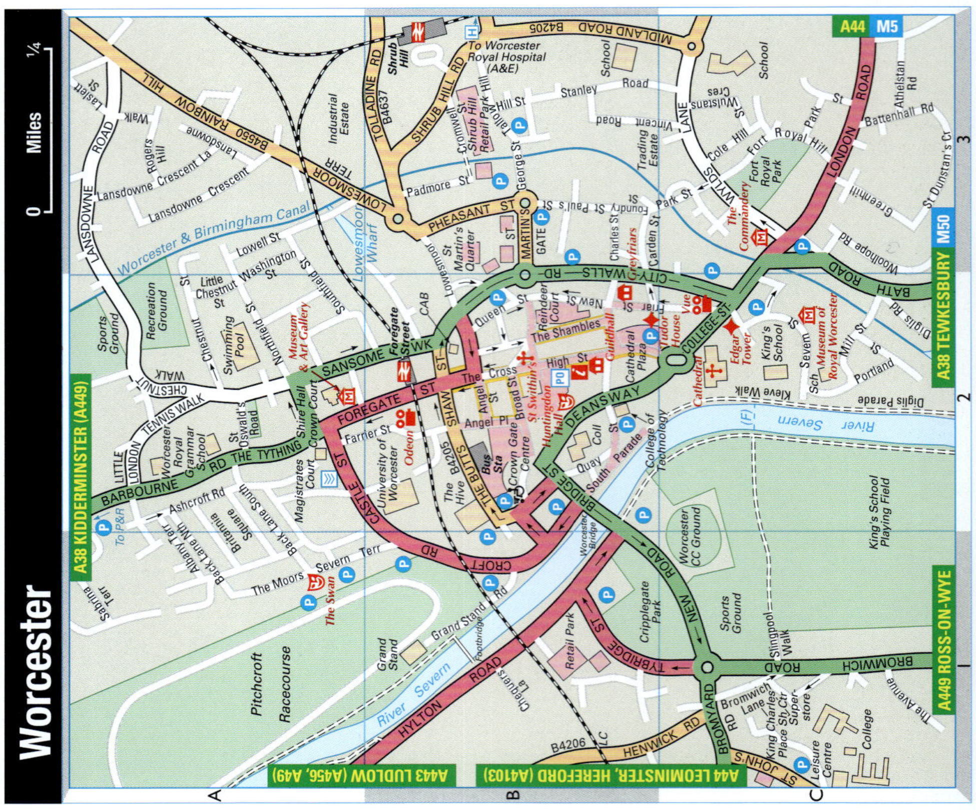
Worcester
A44 M5
A38 TEWKESBURY M50
A449 ROSS-ON-WYE
A44 LEOMINSTER, HEREFORD (A4103)
A443 LUDLOW (A456, A49)
A38 KIDDERMINSTER (A449)
0 Miles ¼

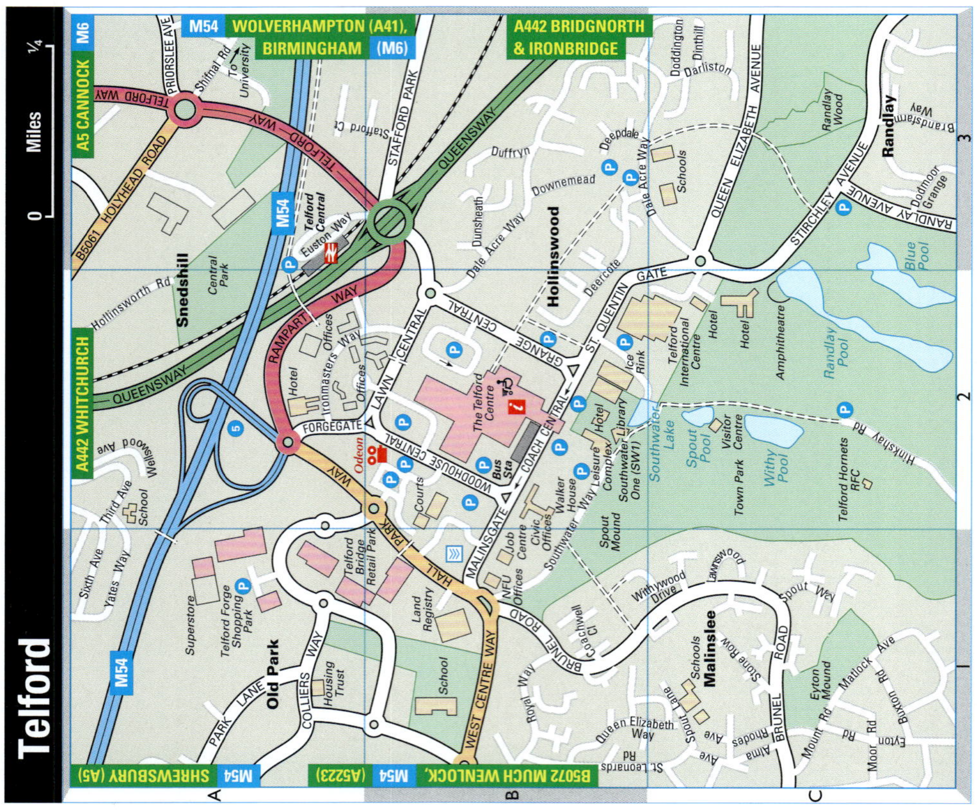
Telford
M54 WOLVERHAMPTON (A41), BIRMINGHAM (M6)
A442 BRIDGNORTH & IRONBRIDGE
B5072 MUCH WENLOCK M54 (A5223)
M54 SHREWSBURY (A5)
A442 WHITCHURCH
A5 CANNOCK M6
0 Miles ¼

Windsor
B470 TO A4 M4
M25
A308 STAINES
A308 MAIDENHEAD
A332 SLOUGH HEATHROW AIRPORT M4 (M4)
0 Miles ¼

Town plan indexes

Aberdeen 113
Aberdeen B2
Aberdeen Grammar School A1
Academy, The B2
Albert Basin B3
Albert Quay B3
Albury Rd C1
Alford Pl B1
Art Gallery A2
Arts Centre A2
Back Wynd A2
Baker St A1
Beach Blvd A3
Belmont B2
Belmont St B2
Berry St A2
Blackfriars St A2
Blaikie's Quay B3
Bloomfield Rd C1
Bon Accord Centre A2
Bon-Accord St B1/C1
Bridge St B2
Broad St A2
Bus Station B2
Car Ferry Terminal B3
Castlegate A3
Central Library A1
Chapel St B1
Cineworld B2
Clyde St B3
College A2
College St B2
Commerce St A3
Commercial Quay B3
Com Centre A3/C1
Constitution St A3
Cotton St A3
Crown St B2
Denburn Rd A2
Devanha Gdns C2
Devanha Gdns South C2
East North St A3
Esslemont Ave A1
Ferryhill Rd C2
Ferryhill Terr C2
Fish Market B3
Fonthill Rd C1
Galleria, The B1
Gallowgate A2
George St A2
Glenbervie Rd C3
Golden Sq B1
Grampian Rd C3
Great Southern Rd C1
Guild St B2
Hardgate B1/C1
His Majesty's Theatre A1
Holburn St C1
Hollybank Pl C1
Huntly St B1
Hutcheon St A1
Information Ctr B2
John St A2
Justice St A3
King St A2
Langstane Pl B1
Lemon Tree, The A2
Library C1
Loch St A2
Maberly St A1
Marischal Coll A2
Maritime Museum & Provost Ross's House B2
Market B2
Market St B2/B3
Menzies Rd C3
Mercat Cross A3
Millburn St C2
Miller St A3
Mount St A1
Music Hall B1
North Esp East C3
North Esp West C2
Oscar Rd C3
Palmerston Rd C2
Park St A3
Police Station A2
Polmuir Rd C2
Post Office A1/A2/A3/B1/C3
Provost Skene's House A2
Queen Elizabeth Br C2
Queen St A2
Regent Quay B3
Regent Road B3
Robert Gordon's College A2
Rose St B1
Rosemount Pl A1
Rosemount Viaduct A1
St Andrew St A2
St Andrew's Cath A3
St Mary's Cath B1
St Nicholas Centre A2
St Nicholas St A2
School Hill A2
Sinclair Rd C3
Skene Sq A1
Skene St B1
South College St C2
South Crown St C2
South Esp East C3
South Esp West C3
South Mount St A1
Sports Centre C3
Spring Garden A2
Springbank Terr C2
Summer St B1
Superstore A2
Swimming Pool B1
Thistle St B1
Tolbooth A3
Town House A2
Trinity Centre B2
Trinity Quay B3
Union Row B1
Union Square B2
Union St B1/B2
Upper Dock B3
Upper Kirkgate A2
Victoria Bridge C3
Victoria Dock B3
Victoria Rd C3
Victoria St B2
Virginia St A3
Vue B2
Wellington Pl B2
West North St A2
Whinhill Rd C1
Willowbank Rd C1
Windmill Brae B2
Woolmanhill Hospital A1

Bath 113
Alexandra Park C2
Alexandra Rd C2
Ambulance Station A3
Approach Golf Courses (Public) A1
Archway St C3
Assembly Rooms & Fashion Mus A2
Avon St B2
Barton St B2
Bath Abbey B2
Bath Aqua Glass A2
Bath College B2
Bath Rugby Club B3
Bath Spa Station C3
Bathwick St A3
Beckford Road A3
Beechen Cliff Rd C2
Bennett St A2
Bloomfield Ave C1
Broad Quay C2
Broad St B2
Brock St A1
Building of Bath Museum A2
Bus Station C2
Calton Gdns C2
Calton Rd C2
Camden Cr A2
Cavendish Rd A1
Cemetery B1
Charlotte St B2
Chaucer Rd C2
Cheap St B2
Circus Mews A2
Claverton St C2
Corn St C2
Cricket Ground B3
Daniel St A3
Edward St B3
Ferry La B3
Fire Station A3
First Ave C1
Forester Ave A3
Forester Rd A3
Gays Hill A2
George St B2
Great Pulteney St B3
Green Park B1
Green Park Rd B2
Gn Park Station B1
Grove St B2
Guildhall B2
Harley St A2
Hayesfield Park C1
Henrietta Gdns A3
Henrietta Mews B3
Henrietta Park B3
Henrietta Rd A3
Henrietta St B3
Henry St B2
Herschel Museum of Astronomy B1
High Common A1
Holburne Mus B3
Holloway C2
Information Ctr B2
James St West B1/B2
Jane Austen Ctr B2
Julian Rd A1
Junction Rd C1
Kingsmead Leisure Complex B2
Kipling Ave C2
Lansdown Cr A1
Lansdown Gr A2
Lansdown Rd A2
Library B2
London Rd A3
London St A2
Lower Bristol Rd B1
Lower Oldfield Pk C1
Lyncombe Hill C3
Magistrates' Court B3
Manvers St B3
Maple Gr C1
Margaret's Hill A2
Marlborough Bldgs A1
Marlborough La B1
Midland Bridge Rd B1
Milk St B2
Milsom St B2
Monmouth St B2
Morford St A2
Museum of Bath at Work A2
Museum of East Asian Art A2
New King St B1
No 1 Royal Cres A1
Norfolk Bldgs B1
Norfolk Cr B1
North Parade Rd B3
Oldfield Rd C1
Paragon A2
Pines Way B1
Podium Shopping Centre B2
Police Station B3
Post Office A3/B2/C2
Postal Museum B2
Powlett Rd A3
Prior Park Rd C3
Pulteney Bridge B2
Pulteney Gdns B3
Pulteney Rd B3/C3
Queen Sq B2
Raby Pl B3
Recreation Ground B3
Rivers St A2
Rockliffe Ave A3
Rockliffe Rd A3
Roman Baths & Pump Room B2
Rossiter Rd C3
Royal Ave A1
Royal Cr A1
Royal High School, The A2
Royal Victoria Park A1
St James Sq A1
St John's Rd A3
Sally Lunn's Ho B2
Shakespeare Ave C2
Shopmobility B2
South Pde B3
SouthGate Shopping Centre C2
Sports & Leisure Centre B3
Spring Gdns C3
Stall St B2
Stanier Rd B1
Superstore B1
Sydney Gdns A3
Sydney Pl B3
Sydney Rd B3
Theatre Royal B2
Thermae Bath Spa B2
Thomas St A3
Tyning, The C3
Union St B2
University C3
Upper Bristol Rd B1
Upper Oldfield Park C1
Victoria Art Gallery B2
Victoria Bridge Rd B1
Walcot St B2
Wells Rd C1
Westgate Buildings B2
Westgate St B2
Weston Rd A1
Widcombe Hill C3

Birmingham 113
Abbey St A2
Aberdeen St A1
Acorn Gr B2
Adams St A5
Adderley St C5
Albert St B4
Albion St B2
Alcester St C5
Aldgate Gr A3
All Saint's St A2
All Saints Rd A2
Allcock St C5
Allesley St A4
Allison St C4
Alma Cr B6
Alston Rd C1
Arcadian Centre C4
Arena Birmingham C2
Arthur St C6
Assay Office B3
Aston Expressway A5
Aston St B4
Aston Univ B4/B5
Avenue Rd A5
Bacchus Rd A1
Bagot St B4
Banbury St B5
Barford Rd B1
Barford St C4
Barn St C5
Barnwell Rd C6
Barr St A3
Barrack St B5
Barwick St B4
Bath Row C3
Beaufort Rd C1
Belmont Row B5
Benson Rd A1
Berkley St C3
Bexhill Gr C3
Birchall St C5
Birmingham City FC C6
Birmingham City Hospital (A&E) A1
Birmingham City Univ. B3
Birmingham Wheels Park B6
Bishopsgate St C3
Blews St A4
Bloomsbury St A6
Blucher St C3
Bordesley St C4
Bowyer St C5
Bradburne Way A5
Bradford St C5
Branston St A3
Brearley St A4
Brewery St A4
Bridge St A3
Bridge St C3
Bridge St West A4
Brindley Dr B3
Broad St C3
Broad Street Cineworld C2
Broadway Plaza C2
Bromley St C5
Bromsgrove St C4
Brookfield Rd A2
Browning St C2
Bryant St A1
BT Tower B3
Buckingham St A3
Bull St B4
Bull St B3
Bullring C4
Cambridge St C3
Camden Dr B3
Camden St B2
Cannon St C4
Cardigan St B5
Carlisle St A1
Carlyle Rd C1
Caroline St B3
Carver St B2
Cato St A6
Cattell Rd C6
Cattells Gr A6
Cawdor Cr C1
Cecil St B4
Cemetery A2/B2
Cemetery La A2
Ctr Link Ind Est A6
Charlotte St B3
Cheapside C4
Chester St A5
Children's Hospital (A&E) B4
Church St B4
Claremont Rd A2
Clarendon Rd C1
Clark St C1
Clement St B3
Clissold St B2
Cliveland St B4
Coach Station C5
College St B2
Colmore Circus B4
Colmore Row B4
Commercial St C3
Constitution Hill B3
Convention Ctr, The C3
Cope St B2
Coplow St B1
Corporation St C4
Council House B3
County Court B4
Coveley Gr A2
Coventry Rd C6
Coventry St C5
Cox St B3
Crabtree Rd A2
Cregoe St C3
Crescent Ave A2
Crescent Theatre C3
Crescent, The A2
Cromwell St A6
Cromwell St B3
Cube, The C3
Curzon St B5
Custard Factory C5
Cuthbert Rd B1
Dale End B4
Dart St C6
Dartmouth Circus A4
Dartmouth Middleway A5
Dental Hospital B4
Deritend C5
Devon St A6
Devonshire St A1
Digbeth High St C4
Dolman St B6
Dover St A1
Duchess Rd C2
Duddeston B6
Duddeston Manor Rd B5
Duddeston Mill Rd B6
Duddeston Mill Trading Estate B6
Dudley Rd B1
Edmund St B3
Edward St B3
Elkington St A4
Ellen St B2
Ellis St C3
Erskine St B6
Essex St C4
Eyre St B2
Farm Croft A3
Farm St A3
Fazeley St B4/C5
Felstead Way B5
Finstall Cl B5
Five Ways C2
Fiveway Shopping Centre C2
Fleet St B3
Floodgate St C5
Ford St A2
Fore St C4
Forster St B5
Francis Rd C2
Francis St B5
Frankfort St A4
Frederick St B3
Freeth St C1
Freightliner Terminal B6
Garrison La C6
Garrison St B6
Gas St C3
Geach St A4
George St B3
George St West B2
Gibb St C5
Gilby Rd C2
Gillott Rd B1
Glover St C5
Goode Ave A2
Goodrick Way A6
Gordon St B6
Graham St B3
Grand Central C4
Granville St C3
Gray St C6
Great Barr St C5
Great Charles St Queensway B3
Great Francis St B6
Great Hampton Row A3
Great Hampton St A3
Great King St A3
Great Lister St A5
Great Tindal St C2
Green La C6
Green St C5
Greenway St C6
Grosvenor St West C2
Guest Gr A3
Guild Cl C2
Guildford Dr A4
Guthrie Cl A3
Hagley Rd C1
Hall St B3
Hampton St A3
Handsworth New Rd A1
Hanley St B4
Harford St A3
Harmer Rd A2
Harold Rd C1
Hatchett St A4
Heath Mill La C5
Heath St B1
Heath St South B1
Heaton St A2
Heneage St B5
Henrietta St B4
Herbert Rd C6
High St C4
High St C5
Hilden Rd B5
Hill St C3/C4
Hindlow Cl B6
Hingeston St B2
Hippodrome Theatre C4
HM Prison A1
Hockley Circus A2
Hockley Hill A3
Hockley St A3
Holliday St C3
Holloway Circus C4
Holloway Head C3
Holt St B5
Hooper St B1
Horse Fair C4
Hospital St A4
Howard St B3
Howe St B5
Hubert St A5
Hunters Rd A2
Hunters Vale A3
Huntly Rd C2
Hurst St C4
Icknield Port Rd B1
Icknield Sq B2
Icknield St A2/B2
IKON C3
Information Ctr C3
Inge St C4
Irving St C3
James Watt Queensway B4
Jennens Rd B5
Jewellery Quarter A3
Jewellery Quarter Museum B3
John Bright St C4
Keeley St C6
Kellett Rd B5
Kent St C4
Kenyon St B3
Key Hill A3
Kilby Ave C2
King Edwards Rd B2
King Edwards Rd C3
Kingston Rd C6
Kirby Rd A1
Ladywood Arts & Leisure Centre B1
Ladywood Middleway C2/C3
Ladywood Rd C1
Lancaster St B4
Landor St B6
Law Courts B4
Lawford Cl B5
Lawley Middleway B5
Ledbury Cl C2
Ledsam St B2
Lees St A1
Legge La B3
Lennox St A3
Library A6/C3
Lighthorne Ave B2
Link Rd B1
Lionel St B3
Lister St B5
Little Ann St C5
Little Hall Rd A6
Liverpool St C5
Livery St B3/B4
Lodge Rd A1
Lord St A5
Love La A5
Loveday St B4
Lower Dartmouth St C6
Lower Loveday St B4
Lower Tower St A4
Lower Trinty St C5
Ludgate Hill B3
Mailbox Ctr & BBC C3
Margaret St B3
Markby Rd A1
Marroway St B1
Maxstoke St C6
Melvina Rd A6
Meriden St C4
Metropolitan (RC) B4
Midland St B6
Milk St C5
Mill St A5
Millennium Point B5
Miller St A4
Milton St A4
Moat La C4
Montague Rd C1
Montague St C5
Monument Rd C1
Moor St Queensway C4
Moor Street C4
Moorsom St A4
Morville St C2
Mosborough Cr A3
Moseley St C4
Mott St B3
Museum & Art Gallery B3
Musgrave Rd A1
National Sea Life Centre C3
Navigation St C3
Nechell's Park Rd A6
Nechells Parkway B5
Nechells Pl A6
New Alexandra C3
New Bartholomew St C4
New Canal St C5
New John St West A3
New Spring St B2
New St C4
New Street C4
New Summer St A4
New Town Row A4
Newhall Hill B3
Newhall St B3
Newton St B4
Newtown A4
Noel Rd C1
Norman St A1
Northbrook St B1
Northwood St B3
Norton St A2
Odeon C2
Old Crown Ho C5
Old Rep Theatre, The C4
Old Snow Hill B4
Oliver Rd C1
Oliver St A5
Osler St C1
Oxford St C5
Palmer St C5
Paradise Circus Queensway C3
Paradise St C3
Park Rd A2
Park St C4
Pavilions C4
Paxton Rd A2
Peel St A1
Pershore St C4
Phillips St A4
Pickford St C5
Pinfold St C4
Pitsford St A2
Plough & Harrow Rd C1
Police Station A4/B4/C2/C4
Pope St B2
Portland Rd C1
Post Office A5/B1/B3/B4/B5/C2/C3/C5
Preston Rd A1
Price St B4
Princip St B4
Printing House St B4
Priory Queensway B4
Pritchett St A4
Proctor St A5
Radnor St A2
Rea St C4
Regent Pl B3
Register Office C3
Repertory Theatre C3
Reservoir Rd C1
Richard St A5
River St C5
Rocky La A5/A6
Rodney Cl C2
Roseberry St B2
Rotton Park St B1
Rupert St A5
Ruston St C2
Ryland St C2
St Andrew's Ind Est C6
St Andrew's Rd C6
St Andrew's St C6
St Bolton St C6
St Chads B4
St Chads Queensway B4
St Clements Rd A6
St George's St A3
St James Pl B5
St Marks Cr B2
St Martin's C4
St Paul's B3
St Paul's B3
St Paul's Sq B3
St Philip's B4
St Stephen's St A4
St Thomas' Peace Garden C3
St Vincent St C2
Saltley Rd A6
Sand Pits Pde B3
Severn St C3
Shadwell St B4
Sheepcote St C2
Shefford Rd A4
Sherborne St C2
Shylton's Croft C2
Skipton Rd C2
Smallbrook Queensway C4
Smith St A3
Snow Hill B4
Snow Hill Queensway B4
Soho, Benson Rd A1
South Rd A2
Spencer St B3
Spring Hill B2
Staniforth St B4
Station St C4
Steelhouse La B4
Stephenson St C4
Steward St B2
Stirling Rd C1
Stour St B2
Suffolk St Queensway C3
Summer Hill Rd B2
Summer Hill St B2
Summer Hill Terr B2
Summer La A4
Summer Row B3
Summerfield Cr B1
Summerfield Park B1
Superstore B2
Sutton St C3
Swallow St C3
Sydney Rd C6
Symphony Hall C3
Talbot St A1
Temple Row C4
Temple St C4
Templefield St C6
Tenby St B3
Tenby St North B2
Tennant St C2/C3
Thimble Mill La A6
Thinktank (Science & Discovery) B5
Thomas St A4
Thorpe St C4
Tilton Rd C6
Tower St A4
Town Hall C3
Trent St C5
Turner's Buildings A1
Unett St A3
Union Terr B5
Upper Trinity St C5
Uxbridge St A3
Vauxhall Gr B5
Vauxhall Rd B5
Vernon Rd C1
Vesey St B4
Viaduct St B5
Victoria Sq C3
Villa St A3
Vittoria St B3
Vyse St B3
Walter St A6
Wardlow Rd A5
Warstone La B2
Washington St C3
Water St B3
Waterworks Rd C1
Watery La C5
Well St A3
Western Rd B1
Wharf St A2
Wheeler St A3
Whitehouse St A5
Whitmore St A2
Whittall St B4
Wholesale Market C4
Wiggin St B1
Willes Rd A1
Windsor Ind Est A5
Windsor St A5
Windsor St B5
Winson Green Rd A1
Witton St C6
Wolseley St C6
Woodcock St B5

Blackpool 113
Abingdon St A1
Addison Cr A3
Adelaide St B1
Albert Rd B2
Alfred St B2
Ascot Rd A3
Ashton Rd C2
Auburn Gr C3
Bank Hey St B1
Banks St A1
Beech Ave A3
Bela Gr C2
Belmont Ave B2
Birley St A1
Blackpool & Fleetwood Tram B1
Blackpool & the Fylde College B2
Blackpool FC C2
Blackpool North A2
Blackpool Tower B1
Blundell St C1
Bonny St B1
Breck Rd B3
Bryan Rd A3
Buchanan St A2
Bus Station A2
Cambridge Rd A3
Caunce St A2/A3
Central Dr B1/C2
Central Pier C1
Central Pier C1
Central Pier Theatre C1
Chapel St C1
Charles St A2
Charnley Rd B2
Church St A1/A2
Clinton Ave B2
Coach Station A2/C1
Cocker St A1
Coleridge Rd A3
Collingwood Ave A3
Comedy Carpet B1
Condor Gr C3
Cookson St A2
Coronation St B1
Corporation St A1
Courts B1
Cumberland Ave B3
Cunliffe Rd C3
Dale St C1
Devonshire Rd A3
Devonshire Sq A3
Dickson Rd A1
Elizabeth St A2
Ferguson Rd C3
Forest Gate B3
Foxhall Rd C1
Freckleton St C2
George St A2
Gloucester Ave B3
Golden Mile, The C1
Gorse Rd B3
Gorton St A2
Grand Theatre, The B1
Granville Rd A2
Grasmere Rd C2
Grosvenor St A2
Grundy Art Gallery A1
Harvey Rd B3
Hornby Rd B2
Houndshill Shopping Centre B1
Hull Rd B1
Ibbison Ct C2
Information Ctr A1
Kent Rd C2
Keswick Rd C2
King St A2
Knox Gr C3
Laycock Gate A3
Layton Rd A3
Leamington Rd B2
Leeds Rd B3
Leicester Rd B2
Levens Gr C2
Library A1
Lifeboat Station B1
Lincoln Rd B2
Liverpool Rd B3
Livingstone Rd B2
London Rd A3
Lune Gr C2
Lytham Rd C1
Madame Tussaud's Blackpool B1
Manchester Sq C1
Manor Rd B3
Maple Ave B3
Market St A1
Marlboro Rd B3
Mere Rd B3
Milbourne St A2
Newcastle Ave B3
Newton Dr A3
North Pier A1
North Pier A1
North Pier Theatre A1
Odeon C2
Olive Gr B3
Palatine Rd B2
Park Rd B2/C3
Peter St A2
Police Station B1
Post Office A1/A3/B1/B2
Princess Pde A1
Princess St C1/C2
Promenade A1/C1
Queen St A1
Queen Victoria Rd C2
Raikes Pde B2
Reads Ave B2
Regent Rd B2
Register Office B2
Ribble Rd B2
Rigby Rd C1/C2
Ripon Rd B3
St Albans Rd B3
St Ives Ave C3
St John's Square A1
St Vincent Ave C3
Salisbury Rd B3
Salthouse Ave C2
Salvation Army Ctr A2
Sands Way C2
Sea Life Centre B1
Seasiders Way C1
Selbourne Rd A2
Sharrow Gr C3
Somerset Ave C3
South King St B2
Springfield Rd A1
Sutton Pl B2
Talbot Rd A1/A2
Thornber Gr C2
Topping St A1
Tower B1
Town Hall A1
Tram Depot C1
Tyldesley Rd C1
Vance Rd B1
Victoria St B1
Victory Rd A2
Wayman Rd A3
Westmorland Ave C2/C3
Whitegate Dr B3
Winter Gardens Theatre B1
Woodland Gr B3
Woolman Rd B2

Bournemouth 114
Ascham Rd A3
Avenue Rd B1
Ave Shopping Ctr B1
Bath Rd C2
Beacon Rd C1
Beechey Rd A3
Bodorgan Rd B1
Bourne Ave B1
Bournemouth A3
Bournemouth & Poole College B3
Bournemouth International Ctr C1
Bournemouth Pier C2
Bournemouth Station B3
Braidley Rd A1
Cavendish Place A2
Cavendish Rd A2
Central Drive A1
Central Gdns B1
Christchurch Rd B3
Cliff Lift C1/C3
Coach House Pl A3
Coach Station A3
Commercial Rd B1
Cotlands Rd B3
Cranborne Rd C1
Cricket Ground A2
Cumnor Rd B2
Dean Park A2
Dean Park Cr B2
Dean Park Rd A2
Durrant Rd B1
East Overcliff Dr C3
Exeter Cr C1
Exeter La C2
Exeter Rd C1
Gervis Place B1
Gervis Rd B3
Glen Fern Rd B2
Golf Club B1
Grove Rd B3
Hinton Rd C2
Holdenhurst Rd B3
Horseshoe Comm B2
Information Ctr B2
Lansdowne B3
Lansdowne Rd A2
Lorne Park Rd B2
Lower Gdns B1/C2
Madeira Rd B2
Methuen Rd A3
Meyrick Park A1
Meyrick Rd B3
Milton Rd A2
Nuffield Health Bournemouth Hosp (private) A2
Oceanarium C2
Odeon Cinema C1
Old Christchurch Rd B2
Ophir Rd A3
Oxford Rd B3
Park Rd A3
Parsonage Rd B2
Pavilion C2
Pier Approach C2
Pier Theatre C2
Police Sta A3/B3
Portchester Rd A3
Post Office B1/B3
Priory Rd C1
Quadrant, The B2
Recreation Ground A1
Richmond Gardens Shopping Centre B2
Richmond Hill Rd B1
Russell-Cotes Art Gallery & Mus C2
Russell Cotes Rd C2
St Anthony's Rd A1
St Michael's Rd C1
St Paul's A3
St Paul's La B3
St Paul's Rd A3
St Peter's B2
St Peter's B2
St Peter's Rd B2
St Stephen's Rd B1/B2
St Swithun's B3
St Swithun's Rd B3
St Swithun's Rd South B3
St Valerie Rd A2
St Winifred's Rd A2
Square, The B1
Stafford Rd B3
Terrace Rd B1
Town Hall B1
Tregonwell Rd C1
Triangle, The B1
Trinity Rd B2
Undercliff Drive C3
Upper Hinton Rd B2
Upper Terr Rd C1
Wellington Rd A2/A3
Wessex Way A3/B1/B2
West Cliff Prom C1
West Hill Rd C1
West Undercliff Promenade C1
Westover Rd B2
Wimborne Rd A2
Wootton Mount B2
Wychwood Dr A1
Yelverton Rd B2
York Rd B3
Zig-Zag Walks C1/C3

Bradford 114
Alhambra B2
Back Ashgrove B1
Barkerend Rd A3
Barnard Rd C3
Barry St B2
Bolling Rd C3
Bolton Rd A3
Bowland St A1
Bradford Big Screen B2
Bradford College B1
Bradford Forster Sq A2
Bradford Interchange B3
Bradford Playhouse B3
Bridge St B2
Britannia St B2
Broadway Bradford, The B2
Burnett St B3
Bus Station B2
Butler St West A3
Caledonia St C2
Canal Rd A2
Carlton St B1
Cathedral A3
Centenary Sq B2
Chapel St B3
Cheapside A2
Church Bank B3
Cineworld B3
City Hall B2
City Rd A1
Claremont B1
Colour Experience B1
Croft St B2
Crown Court B3
Darfield St A1
Darley St A2
Drewton Rd A1
Drummond Trading Estate A1
Dryden St B3
Dyson St A1
Easby Rd C1
East Parade B3
Eldon Pl A1
Filey St B3
Forster Square Retail Park A2
Gallery II B1
Garnett St B3
Godwin St B2
Gracechurch St A1
Grattan Rd B1
Great Horton Rd B1/B2
Grove Terr B1
Hall Ings B2
Hall La C3
Hallfield Rd A1
Hammstrasse A2
Harris St B3
Holdsworth St A2
Ice Arena B2
Impressions B2
Information Ctr B2
Inland Revenue A2
Ivegate B2
Jacob's Well Municipal Offices B2
James St A2
John St A2
Kirkgate B2
Kirkgate Centre B2
Laisteridge La C1
Leeds Rd B3
Leisure Exchange, The B3
Library B1/B2
Listerhills Rd B1
Little Horton Gn C1
Little Horton La C1
Longside La B1
Lower Kirkgate B2
Lumb La A1
Magistrates Court B2
Manchester Rd C2
Manningham La A1
Manor Row A2
Market C3
Market St B2
Melbourne Place C1
Midland Rd A2
Mill La C2
Morley St B1
National Media B2
Nelson St B2/C2
Nesfield St A2
New Otley Rd A3
Norcroft St B1
North Parade A2
North St A3
North Wing A3
Oastler Shopping Centre A2
Otley Rd A3
Park Ave C1
Park La C1
Park Rd C2
Parma St C2
Peace Museum B2
Peckover St B3
Piccadilly A2
Police Station C2
Post Office A2/B1/B2/C3
Princes Way B2
Prospect St C3
Radwell Drive C2
Rawson Rd A1
Rebecca St A1
Richmond Rd B1
Russell St C1
St George's Hall B2
St Lukes Hosp C1
Shipley Airedale Rd A3/B3
Shopmobility A2
Simes St A1
Smith St B1
Spring Mill St C2
Stott Hill A3
Sunbridge Rd A1/B1/B2
Theatre in the Mill B1
Thornton Rd A1/B1
Trafalgar St A2
Trinity Rd C1
Tumbling Hill St B1
Tyrrel St B2
University of Bradford B1/C1
Usher St C3
Valley Rd A2
Vicar La B3
Wakefield Rd C3
Wapping Rd A3
Well St B3
Westgate A1
White Abbey Rd A1
Wigan Rd A1
Wilton St B1
Wood St A1
Wool Exchange B2
Worthington St A1

Brighton 114
Addison Rd A1
Albert Rd B2
Albion Hill B3
Albion St B3
Ann St A3
Baker St A3
Black Lion St C2
Brighton A2
Brighton Centre C2
Brighton Fishing Museum C2
Brighton Pier (Palace Pier) C3
Brighton Wheel C3
British Airways i360 Tower C1
Broad St C3
Buckingham Pl A2
Buckingham Rd B2
Cannon Pl C1

Carlton Hill B3
Chatham Pl A1
Cheapside A3
Church St B2
Churchill Square Shopping Ctr B2
Clifton Hill B1
Clifton Pl B1
Clifton Rd B1
Clifton St A3
Clifton Terr B1
Clyde Rd A3
Coach Station C3
Compton Ave A2
Davigdor Rd A1
Denmark Terr B1
Ditchling Rd A3
Dome B2
Duke St B2
Duke's La C2
Dyke Rd A1/B2
East St C2
Edward St B3
Elmore Rd B3
Fleet St A2
Frederick St B2
Gardner St B2
Gloucester Pl B3
Gloucester Rd B2
Goldsmid Rd A1
Grand Junction Rd C2
Grand Parade B3
Grove Hill B3
Guildford St A2
Hampton Pl B1
Hanover Terr A3
High St C3
Highdown Rd A1
Information Ctr C2
John St B3
Jubilee Clock Tower B2
Kemp St B2
Kensington Pl B2
Kings Rd C1
Lanes, The C2
Law Courts B3
Lewes Rd A3
Library B2
London Rd A3
Madeira Dr C3
Marine Pde C3
Middle St C2
Montpelier Pl B1
Montpelier Rd B1
Montpelier St B1
Museum & Art Gallery B3
New England Rd A2
New England St A2
New Rd B2
Nizells Ave A1
Norfolk Rd B1
Norfolk Terr B1
North Rd B2
North St B2
Odeon C2
Old Shoreham Rd A1
Old Steine C3
Osmond Rd A1
Over St B2
Oxford St A3
Park Crescent Terr A3
Phoenix Brighton B3
Phoenix Rise A3
Police Station B3
Post Office A1/A3/C3
Preston Rd A2
Preston St B1
Prestonville Rd A1
Queen's Rd B2
Queen Sq B2
Regency Sq C1
Regent St B2
Richmond Pl B3
Richmond St B3
Richmond Terr A3
Rose Hill Terr A3
Royal Pavilion B2
St Bartholomew's A3
St James's St C3
St Nicholas Rd B2
St Nicholas' B2
St Peter's A3
Sea Life Brighton C3
Shaftesbury Rd A3
Ship St C2
Silwood Rd B1
Silwood St B1
Southover St A3
Spring Gdns B2
Stanford Rd A1
Stanley Rd A3
Surrey St B2
Sussex St B3
Swimming Pool B3
Sydney St B3
Temple Gdns B1
Terminus Rd A2
Theatre Royal B2
Tidy St B2
Town Hall C2
Toy & Model Museum A2
Trafalgar St B2
Union Rd A3
Univ of Brighton B3
Upper Lewes Rd A3
Upper North St B1
Viaduct Rd A3
Victoria Gdns B3
Victoria Rd B1
Volk's Electric Railway C3
West Pier (derelict) C1
West St C2
Western Rd B1
Whitecross St B2
York Ave B1
York Pl B3
York Rd B1

Bristol 114

Acramans Rd C4
Albert Rd C6
Alfred Hill A4
All Saint's St A4
All Saints' B4
Allington Rd C3
Alpha Rd C4
Ambra Vale B1
Ambra Vale East B2
Ambrose Rd B2
Amphitheatre & Waterfront Sq C4
Anchor Rd B3
Anvil St B6
Arcade, The A5
Architecture Centre, The B4
Argyle Pl B2
Arlington Villas A2
Arnolfini Arts Centre, The B4
Art Gallery A3
Ashton Gate Rd C2
Ashton Rd C1
Avon Bridge C1
Avon Cr C1
Avon St B6
Baldwin St B4
Baltic Wharf C2
Baltic Wharf Leisure Centre & Caravan Park C2
Baltic Wharf Marina C2
Barossa Pl C4
Barton Manor B6
Barton Rd B6
Barton Vale B6
Bath Rd C6
Bathurst Basin C4
Bathurst Parade C4
Beauley Rd C3
Bedminster Bridge C5
Bedminster Parade C4
Bellevue B2
Bellevue Cr B2
Bellevue Rd C6
Berkeley Pl A2
Berkeley Sq A3
Birch Rd C2
Blackfriars A4
Bond St A5
Braggs La A6
Brandon Hill B3
Brandon Steep B3
Bristol Aquarium B4
Bristol Bridge B5
Bristol Cath (CE) B3
Bristol Eye Hospital (A&E) A4
Bristol Grammar School A3
Bristol Harbour Railway C3
Bristol Royal Children's Hospital A4
Bristol Royal Infirmary (A&E) A4
Bristol Temple Meads Station B6
Broad Plain B6
Broad Quay B4
Broad St A4
Broad Weir A5
Broadcasting Ho A3
Broadmead A5
Brunel Institute B3
Brunel Way C1
Brunswick Sq A5
Burton Cl C5
Bus Station A4
Butts Rd B3
Cabot Circus A5
Cabot Tower B3
Caledonia Pl B1
Callowhill Ct A5
Cambridge St C6
Camden Rd C3
Camp Rd A1
Canada Way C2
Cannon St A4
Canon's Way B3
Cantock's Cl A3
Canynge Rd A1
Canynge Sq A1
Castle Park A5
Castle St A5
Cathedral Walk B3
Catherine Meade St C4
Cattle Market Rd C6
Central Library B3
Charles Pl B1
Charlotte St B3
Charlotte St South B3
Chatterton Ho B5
Chatterton Sq C5
Chatterton St C5
Cheese La B5
Christchurch A4
Christchurch Rd A1
Christmas Steps A4
Church La B2/B5
Church St B5
City Museum A3
City of Bristol Coll B3
Civil and Family Justice Centre B5
Clare St B4
Clarence Rd C5
Cliff Rd C1
Clift House Rd C1
Clifton Cath (RC) A2
Clifton Down A1
Clifton Down Rd A1
Clifton Hill B2
Clifton Park A1/A2
Clifton Park Rd A1
Clifton Rd A2
Clifton Vale B1
Cliftonwood Cr B2
Cliftonwood Rd B2
Cliftonwood Terr B2
Cobblestone Mews A1
College Green B3
College Rd A1
College St B3
Colston Almshouses A4
Colston Ave B4
Colston Hall B4
Colston Parade C5
Colston St A4
Commercial Rd C4
Constitution Hill B2
Cooperage La C2
Corn St B4
Cornwallis Ave B1
Cornwallis Cr B1
Coronation Rd C2/C4
Council House B3
Counterslip B5
Create Ctr, The C1
Crosby Row B2
Crown Court A4
Culver St B3
Cumberland Basin C1
Cumberland Cl C2
Cumberland Rd C2/C3
Dean La C4
Deanery Rd B3
Denmark St B4
Dowry Sq B1
Eaton Cr A2
Elmdale Rd A3
Elton Rd A3
Eugene St A4/A6
Exchange and St Nicholas' Mkts, The B4
Fairfax St A4
Fire Station B5
Floating Harbour C3
Fosseway, The A2
Foster Almshouses A4
Frayne Rd C1
Frederick Pl A2
Freeland Pl B1
Friary B5
Frogmore St B3
Fry's Hill B2
Gas La B6
Gasferry Rd C3
Georgian House B3
Glendale B1
Glentworth Rd B2
Gloucester St A1
Goldney Hall B2
Goldney Rd B1
Gordon Rd A2
Granby Hill B1
Grange Rd A1
Great Ann St A6
Great George Rd B3
Great George St A6/B3
Green St North B1
Green St South B1
Greenay Bush La C2
Greenbank Rd C2
Greville Smyth Pk C1
Grove, The B4
Guildhall A4
Guinea St C4
Hamilton Rd C3
Hanbury Rd A2
Hanover Pl C2
Harley Pl A1
Haymarket A5
Hensman's Hill B1
High St B4
Highbury Villas A3
Hill St B3
Hill St C6
Hippodrome B4
Hopechapel Hill B1
Horfield Rd A4
Horsefair, The A5
Horton St B6
Host St A4
Hotwell Rd B1/B2
Houlton St A6
Howard Rd C3
IMAX Cinema B4
Information Ctr B4
Islington Rd C3
Jacob St A5/A6
Jacob's Wells Rd B2
John Carr's Terr B2
John Wesley's Chapel A5
Joy Hill B1
Jubilee St B6
Kensington Pl A2
Kilkenny St B6
King St B4
Kingsland Rd B6
Kingston Rd C3
Lamb St A6
Lansdown Rd A2
Lawford St A6
Lawfords Gate A6
Leighton Rd C3
Lewins Mead A4
Lime Rd C2
Litfield Rd A1
Little Ann St A6
Little Caroline Pl B1
Little George St A6
Little King St B4
Llandoger Trow B4
Lloyds' Building, The C3
Lodge St A4
Lord Mayor's Chapel, The B4
Lower Castle St A5
Lower Church La A4
Lower Clifton Hill B2
Lower Guinea St C4
Lower Lamb St B3
Lower Maudlin St A4
Lower Park Rd A4
Lower Sidney St C2
Lucky La C4
Lydstep Terr C3
M Shed C4
Magistrates' Court A4
Mall (Galleries Shopping Centre), The A5
Mall, The A1
Manilla Rd A1
Mardyke Ferry Rd C2
Maritime Heritage Centre B3
Marlborough Hill A4
Marlborough St A4
Marsh St B4
Mead St C5
Merchant Dock B2
Merchant Seamen's Almshouses B4
Merchant St A5
Merchants Rd A1
Merchants Rd C1
Meridian Pl A2
Meridian Vale A2
Merrywood Rd C3
Midland Rd A6
Milford St C3
Millennium Prom B3
Millennium Sq B3
Mitchell La B5
Mortimer Rd A1
Murray Rd C4
Myrtle Rd A3
Narrow Plain B5
Narrow Quay B4
Nelson St A4
New Charlotte St C4
New Kingsley Rd B6
New Queen St C5
New St A6
Newgate A5
Newton St A6
Norland Rd A1
North St C2
O2 Academy B3
Oakfield Gr A2
Oakfield Pl A2
Oakfield Rd A2
Old Bread St B6
Old Market St A6
Old Park Hill A4
Oldfield Rd B1
Orchard Ave B4
Orchard La B4
Orchard St B4
Osbourne Rd C3
Oxford St B6
Park Pl A2
Park Rd C3
Park Row A3
Park St A3
Passage St B5
Pembroke Gr A2
Pembroke Rd A2
Pembroke Rd C3
Pembroke St A5
Penn St A5
Pennywell Rd A6
Percival Rd A1
Pero's Bridge B4
Perry Rd A4
Phipps St C2
Pip 'n' Jay B5
Plimsoll Bridge B1
Police Sta A6
Polygon Rd B1
Portland St A1
Portwall La B5
Post Office A1/A3/A5/B1/B4/C4/C5
Prewett St C5
Prince St B4
Prince St Bridge C4
Princess St C5
Princess Victoria St B1
Priory Rd A3
Pump La C5
QEH Theatre A2
Quakers Friars A5
Quay St A4
Queen Charlotte St B4
Queen Elizabeth Hospital School B2
Queen Sq B4
Queen St A5
Queen's Ave A3
Queen's Parade B3
Queen's Rd A2/A3
Raleigh Rd C2
Randall Rd B2
Red Lodge A4
Redcliffe Backs B5
Redcliffe Bridge B4
Redcliffe Hill C5
Redcliffe Parade C4
Redcliffe St B5
Redcliffe Way B5
Redcross St A6
Redgrave Theatre A1
Regent St B1
Richmond Hill A2
Richmond Hill Ave A2
Richmond La A2
Richmond Park Rd A2
Richmond St C6
Richmond Terr A2
River St A6
Rownham Mead B2
Royal Fort Rd A3
Royal Park A2
Royal West of England Academy A3
Royal York Cr B1
Royal York Villas B1
Rupert St A4
Russ St B6
St Andrew's Walk B2
St George's B3
St George's Rd B3
St James A5
St John's A4
St John's Rd C4
St Luke's Rd C5
St Mary Redcliffe C5
St Matthias Park A6
St Michael's Hill A3
St Michael's Hospital A4
St Michael's Park A3
St Nicholas St B4
St Paul St A5
St Paul's Rd A2
St Peter's (ruin) A5
St Philip's Bridge B5
St Philips Rd A6
St Stephen's B4
St Stephen's St B4
St Thomas St B5
St Thomas the Martyr B5
Sandford Rd B1
Sargent St C5
Saville Pl B1
Ship La C5
Shopmobility A5
Showcase Cinema de Lux A5
Silver St A4
Sion Hill A1
Small St A4
Smeaton Rd C1
Somerset Sq C5
Somerset St C5
Southernhay Ave B2
Southville Rd C4
Spike Island Artspace C2
Spring St C5
Superstore C4
SS Great Britain and the Matthew B2
Stackpool Rd C3
Staight St B6
Stillhouse La C4
Sydney Row C2
Tankard's Cl A3
Temple Back B5
Temple Back East B5
Temple Bridge B5
Temple Church B5
Temple Circus B5
Temple Gate C5
Temple St B5
Temple Way B5
Terrell St A4
Theatre Royal (Bristol Old Vic) B4
Thekla B4
Thomas La B5
Three Kings of Cologne A4
Three Queens La B5
Tobacco Factory, The C2
Tower Hill B5
Tower La A4
Trenchard St A4
Triangle South A3
Triangle West A3
Trinity Rd A6
Trinity St A6
Tyndall Ave A3
Union St A5
Union St B6
Unity St A6
Unity St B3
University of Bristol A3
University Rd A3
Upper Byron Pl A3
Upper Maudlin St A4
Upper Perry Hill C3
Upton Rd C2
Valentine Bridge B6
Victoria Gr C5
Victoria Rd C6
Victoria Rooms A2
Victoria Sq A2
Victoria St B5
Vyvyan Rd A1
Vyvyan Terr A1
Wade St A6
Walter St C2
Wapping Rd C4
Water La B5
Waterloo Rd A6
Waterloo St A1
Waterloo St A6
Watershed Media Centre B4
We the Curious B3
Welling Terr B1
Welsh Back B4
West Mall A1
West St A6
Westfield Pl A1
Wetherell Pl A2
Whitehouse Pl C5
Whitehouse St C5
Whiteladies Rd A2
Whitson St A4
William St C5
Willway St C5
Windsor Pl B1
Wine St A4
Woodland Rd A3
Woodland Rise A3
Worcester Rd A1
Worcester Terr A1
YHA B4
York Gdns B1
York Pl A2
York Rd C5

Cambridge 114

Abbey Rd A3
ADC A2
Anglia Ruskin Univ B3
Archaeology & Anthropology B2
Arts Picture Ho B2
Arts Theatre B1
Auckland Rd A3
Backs, The B1
Bateman St C2
Benet St B1
Bradmore St B3
Bridge St A1
Broad St B3
Brookside C2
Brunswick Terr A3
Burleigh St B3
Bus Station B2
Butt Green A2
Cambridge Contemporary Art Gallery B1
Castle Mound A1
Castle St A1
Cemetery B3
Chesterton La A1
Christ's (Coll) B2
Christ's Lane B2
Christ's Pieces B2
City Rd B3
Clare (Coll) B1
Clarendon St B2
Coe Fen C2
Coronation St C2
Corpus Christi (Coll) B1
Court A3
Cross St C3
Crusoe Bridge C1
Darwin (Coll) C1
Devonshire Rd C3
Downing (Coll) C2
Downing St B2
Earl St B2
East Rd B3
Eden St B3
Elizabeth Way A3
Elm St B2
Emery St B3
Emmanuel (Coll) B2
Emmanuel Rd B2
Emmanuel St B2
Fair St A3
Fen Causeway, The C1
Fenner's Cricket Gd C3
Fire Station B3
Fitzroy St A3
Fitzwilliam Mus C2
Fitzwilliam St C2
Garrett Hostel Bridge B1
Glisson Rd C3
Gonville & Caius (Coll) B1
Gonville Place C2
Grafton Centre, The A3
Grand Arcade B2
Green St B1
Gresham Rd C3
Guest Rd B3
Guildhall B2
Harvey Rd C3
Hills Rd C3
Hobson St B2
Hughes Hall (Coll) B3
Information Ctr B2
James St A3
Jesus (Coll) A2
Jesus Green A2
Jesus La A2
Jesus Terr B3
John St B3
Kelsey Kerridge Sports Centre B3
Kettle's Yard A1
King's Bridge B1
King St A2
King's (Coll) B1
King's College Chapel B1
King's Parade B1
Lammas Land Rec Gd C1
Lensfield Rd C2
Library B2
Lion Yard B2
Little St Mary's La B1
Lyndewod Rd C3
Magdalene (Coll) A1
Magdalene St A1
Maid's Causeway A3
Malcolm St A2
Market Hill B1
Market St B1
Mathematical Bridge B1
Mawson Rd C3
Midsummer Comm A3
Mill La B1
Mill Rd B3
Mill St C3
Mumford B3
Museum of Cambridge A1
Museum of Classical Archeology C1
Napier St A3
New Square A3
Newmarket Rd A3
Newnham Rd C1
Norfolk St B3
Northampton St A1
Norwich St C2
Orchard St B2
Panton St C2
Paradise Nature Reserve C1
Paradise St B3
Park Parade A1
Park St A2
Park Terr B2
Parker St B2
Parker's Piece B2
Parkside B3
Parkside Pools B3
Parsonage St A3
Pemberton Terr C2
Pembroke (Coll) B2
Pembroke St B1
Perowne St B3
Peterhouse (Coll) C1
Petty Cury B2
Polar Mus, The C2
Police Station B3
Post Office A1/A3/B2/B3/C1/C2/C3
Queen's La B1
Queen's Rd B1
Queens' (Coll) B1
Regent St B2
Regent Terr B2
Ridley Hall (Coll) C1
Riverside A3
Round Church, The A1
Russell St C2
St Andrew's St B2
St Benet's B1
St Catharine's (Coll) B1
St Eligius St C2
St John's (Coll) A1
St Mary's B1
St Paul's Rd C3
Saxon St C2
Sedgwick Mus B2
Sheep's Green C1
Shire Hall A1
Sidgwick Ave C1
Sidney St A2
Sidney Sussex (Coll) A2
Silver St B1
Station Rd C3
Tenison Ave C3
Tenison Rd C3
Tennis Court Rd B2
Thompson's La A1
Trinity (Coll) A1
Trinity Hall (Coll) B1
Trinity St B1
Trumpington Rd C2
Trumpington St B1
Union Rd C2
University Botanic Gardens C2
Victoria Ave A2
Victoria St B2
Warkworth St B3
Warkworth Terr B3
Wesley Ho (Coll) A2
West Rd B1
Westcott Ho (Coll) A2
Westminster (Coll) A1
Whipple B2
Willis Rd B3
Willow Walk A2
YMCA C3

Canterbury 115

Artillery St B2
Barton Mill Rd A3
Beaconsfield Rd A1
Beaney, The B2
Beverley Rd A1
Bingley's Island B1
Black Griffin La B1
Broad Oak Rd A2
Broad St B2
Brymore Rd A3
Burgate B2
Bus Station C2
Canterbury College C3
Canterbury East C1
Canterbury Tales, The B2
Canterbury West A1
Castle C1
Castle Row C1
Castle St C1
Cathedral B2
Causeway, The A2
Chaucer Rd A3
Christ Church Univ B3
Christchurch Gate B2
City Council Offices A3
City Wall B2
Coach Park A2
College Rd B3
Cossington Rd C2
Court B2
Craddock Rd A3
Crown & County Courts B3
Dane John Gdns C2
Dane John Mound C1
Deanery B2
Dover St C2
Duck La B2
Eastbridge Hospital B1
Edgar Rd B3
Ersham Rd C3
Ethelbert Rd C3
Fire Station C2
Forty Acres Rd A1
Friars, The B2
Gordon Rd C1
Greyfriars B1
Guildford Rd C1
Havelock St B2
Heaton Rd C1
High St B2
Information Ctr A2/B2
Ivy La B2
Ivy Pl C1
King St B2
King's School B2/B3
King's School Rec Ctr, The A2
Kingsmead Leisure Centre A2
Kingsmead Rd A2
Kirby's La B1
Lansdown Rd C2
Lime Kiln Rd C1
Longport B3
Lower Chantry La C3
Mandeville Rd A1
Market Way A2
Marlowe Arcade B2
Marlowe Ave C2
Marlowe Theatre B2
Martyrs Field Rd C1
Mead Way B1
Military Rd B2
Monastery St B2
Museum of Canterbury (Rupert Bear Museum) B1
New Dover Rd C3
Norman Rd C2
North Holmes Rd B3
North La B1
Northgate A2
Nunnery Fields C2
Nunnery Rd C2
Oaten Hill C2
Odeon Cinema C2
Old Dover Rd C2
Old Palace B2
Old Ruttington La B2
Old Weavers B2
Orchard St B1
Oxford Rd C1
Palace St B2
Pilgrims Way C3
Pin Hill C1
Pine Tree Ave A1
Police Station C2
Post Office B2
Pound La B1
Puckle La C2
Raymond Ave C2
Recreation Ground A2
Registry Office A2
Rheims Way B1
Rhodaus Cl C2
Rhodaus Town C2
Roman Museum B2
Roper Gateway A1
Roper Rd A1
Rose La B2
Shopmobility B2
St Augustine's Abbey (remains) B3
St Augustine's Rd C3
St Dunstan's A1
St Dunstan's St A1
St George's Pl C2
St George's St B2
St George's Tower B2
St Gregory's Rd B3
St John's Hosp A2
St Margaret's St B2
St Martin's B3
St Martin's Ave B3
St Martin's Rd B3
St Michael's Rd A1
St Mildred's C1
St Peter's Gr B1
St Peter's La B2
St Peter's Pl B1
St Peter's St B1
St Radigunds St B2
St Stephen's Ct A1
St Stephen's Path A1
St Stephen's Rd A2
Salisbury Rd A1
Simmonds Rd C1
Spring La C3
Station Rd West B1
Stour St B1
Sturry Rd A3
Tourtel Rd A3
Tudor Rd C1
Union St B2
University for the Creative Arts C3
Vernon Pl C2
Victoria Rd C1
Watling St B2
Westgate Gdns B1
Westgate Towers B1
Whitefriars B2
Whitehall Gdns B1
Whitehall Rd B1
Wincheap C1
York Rd C1
Zealand Rd C2

Cardiff Caerdydd 115

Adam St B3
Alexandra Gdns A2
Allerton St C1
Arran St A3
ATRiuM (Univ of Glamorgan) C3
Beauchamp St C1
Bedford St A3
Blackfriars Priory (rems) B1
Bvd De Nantes B2
Brains Brewery C2
Brook St B1
BT Sports Cardiff Arms Park (Cardiff Blues) B1
Bus Station C2
Bute Park A1
Bute St C2
Bute Terr C3
Callaghan Sq C2/C3
Capitol Shopping Centre, The B3
Cardiff Bridge B1
Cardiff Castle B2
Cardiff Central Station C2
Cardiff Story, The B2
Cardiff Univ A1/A2/B3
Cardiff University Student's Union A2
Caroline St C2
Castle Green B2
Castle Mews A1
Castle St (Heol y Castell) B1
Cathays Station A2
Celerity Drive C3
Central Library C2
Central Sq C2
Charles St (Heol Siarl) B3
Churchill Way B3
City Hall A2
City Rd A3
Clare Rd C1
Clare St C1
Coburn St A3
Coldstream Terr B1
College Rd A1
Colum Rd A1
Court C2
Court Rd C1
Craiglee Drive C3
Cranbrook St A3
Customhouse St C2
Cyfartha St A3
Despenser Place C1
Despenser St C1
Dinas St C1
Duke St (Heol y Dug) B2
Dumfries Place B3
East Grove A3
Ellen St C3
Fire Station B3
Fitzalan Place B3
Fitzhamon Emb C1
Fitzhamon La C1
Friary, The B2
g39 B2
Gloucester St C1
Glynrhondda St A2
Gordon Rd A3
Gorsedd Gdns B2
Green St B1
Greyfriars Rd B2
Hafod St C1
Hayes, The B2
Herbert St C3
High St B2
HM Prison B3
Industrial Estate C3
John St C3
Jubilee St C1
King Edward VII Ave A1
Kingsway (Ffordd y Brenin) B2
Knox Rd B3
Law Courts B2
Llanbleddian Gdns A2
Llantwit St A2
Lloyd George Ave C3
Lower Cathedral Rd B1
Lowther Rd A3
Magistrates Court B3
Mansion House A3
Mardy St C1
Mark St B1
Market B2
Mary Ann St C3
Merches Gdns C1
Mill La C2
Millennium Bridge B1
Miskin St A2
Monmouth St C1
Motorpoint Arena Cardiff C3
Museum Ave A2
Museum Place A2
National Museum Cardiff A2
National War Memorial A2
Neville Place C1
New Theatre B2
Newport Rd B3
Northcote La A3
Northcote St A3
Parade, The A3
Park Grove A4
Park Place A2
Park St C2
Penarth Rd C2
Pendyris St C1
Plantaganet St C1
Post Office B2
Principality Plaza Leisure Complex C1
Principality Stadium C1
Principality Stadium Tours (Gate 3) B2
Quay St B2
Queen's Arcade B2
Queen Anne Sq A1
Queen St (Heol y Frenhines) B2
Queen St Station B3
Regimental Museums B2
Rhymney St A3
Richmond Rd A3
Royal Welsh Coll of Music and Drama A1
Russell St A3
Ruthin Gdns A2
St Andrews Place A2
St David's B2
St David's B2/C2
St David's Hall B2
St John the Baptist B2
St Mary St (Heol Eglwys Fair) B2
St Peter's St A3
Salisbury Rd A3
Sandon St B3
Schooner Way C3
Scott Rd C2
Scott St C2
Senghennydd Rd A2
Sherman Theatre A2
Sophia Gardens A1
South Wales Baptist College A3
Sport Wales National Ctr A1
Stafford Rd C1
Station Terr B3
Stuttgarter Strasse B2
Sussex St C1
Taffs Mead Emb C1
Talworth St A3
Temple of Peace & Health A1
Treharris St A3
Trinity St B2
Tudor La C1
Tudor St C1
Walk, The A3
Welsh Government A1
West Grove A3
Westgate St (Heol y Porth) B2
Windsor Place B3
Womanby St B2
Wood St C2
Working St B2
Wyeverne Rd A2

Cheltenham 115

Albert Rd A3
Albion St B3
All Saints Rd B3
Ambrose St B2
Andover Rd C1
Art Gallery & Museum B2
Back Montpellier Terr C2
Bandstand C2
Bath Pde B2
Bath Rd C2
Bays Hill Rd C1
Bennington St B2
Berkeley St B3
Brewery, The A2
Brunswick St South A2
Bus Station B2
Carlton St B3
Central Cross Road A3
Cheltenham Coll C2
Cheltenham FC A3
Cheltenham General (A&E) C3
Cheltenham Ladies College B2
Christchurch Rd B1
Cineworld A2
Clarence Rd A2
Clarence Sq A2
Clarence St B2
Cleeveland St A1
College Baths Rd C3
College Rd C2
Colletts Dr A1
Corpus St C3
Council Office B1
Court B1
Devonshire St A2
Douro Rd B1
Duke St B3
Dunalley Pde A2
Dunalley St A2
Everyman B2
Evesham Rd A3
Fairview Rd B3
Fairview St B3
Fire Station C3
Folly La A2
Gloucester Rd A1
Grosvenor St B3
Grove St A1
Hanover St A2
Hatherley St C1
Henrietta St A2
Hewlett Rd B3
High St B2/B3
Holst Birthplace Museum A3
Hudson St A2
Imperial Gdns C2
Imperial La B2
Imperial Sq C2
Information Ctr B2
Keynsham Rd C3
King St A2
Knapp Rd B2
Ladies College B2
Lansdown Cr C1
Lansdown Rd C1
Leighton Rd B3
Library B2
London Rd C3
Lypiatt Rd C1
Malvern Rd B1
Manser St A2
Market St A1
Marle Hill Pde A2
Marle Hill Rd A2
Millbrook St A1
Milsom St A2
Montpellier Gdns C2
Montpellier Gr C2
Montpellier Pde C2
Montpellier Spa Rd C2
Montpellier St C1
Montpellier Terr C2
Montpellier Walk C2
New St B2
North Pl B2
Old Bath Rd C3
Oriel Rd B2
Overton Park Rd B1
Overton Rd B1
Oxford St C3
Parabola Rd B1
Park Pl C1
Park St A1
Pittville Circus A3
Pittville Cr A3
Pittville Lawn A3
Pittville Park A2
Playhouse B2
Police Station C1
Portland St B3
Prestbury Rd A3
Prince's Rd C1
Priory St B3
Promenade B2
Queen St A1
Recreation Ground A2
Regent Arcade B2
Regent St B2
Rodney Rd B2
Royal Cr B2
Royal Wells Rd B2
St George's Pl B2
St Georges Rd B1
St Gregory's B2
St James St B3
St John's Ave B3
St Luke's Rd C2
St Margarets Rd A2
St Mary's B2
St Matthew's B2
St Paul's La A2
St Paul's Rd A2

St Paul's St A2
St Stephen's Rd C1
Sandford Parks Lido C3
Sandford Mill Road C3
Sandford Park C3
Sandford Rd C2
Selkirk St A3
Sherborne Pl B3
Sherborne St A3
Shopmobility B2
Suffolk Pde C2
Suffolk Rd C1
Suffolk Sq C1
Sun St A1
Swindon Rd B2
Sydenham Villas Rd C3
Tewkesbury Rd A1
The Courtyard B1
Thirlstaine Rd C2
Tivoli Rd C1
Tivoli St C1
Town Hall & Theatre B2
Townsend St A1
Trafalgar St C2
Union St B3
University of Gloucestershire (Francis Close Hall) A2
University of Gloucestershire (Hardwick) A1
Victoria Pl B3
Victoria St A2
Vittoria Walk C2
Wel Pl B2
Wellesley Rd A2
Wellington Rd A3
Wellington Sq A3
Wellington St B2
West Drive A3
Western Rd B1
Winchcombe St B3
Winston Churchill Meml Gardens A1

Chester 115

Abbey Gateway A2
Appleyards La C3
Bars, The B3
Bedward Row B1
Beeston View C3
Bishop Lloyd's Palace B2
Black Diamond St A2
Bottoms La C3
Boughton B3
Bouverie St A1
Bus Interchange A2
Bridge St B2
Bridgegate C2
Brook St A3
Brown's La C2
Cambrian Rd A1
Canal St A2
Carrick Rd C1
Castle C2
Castle Dr C2
Cathedral B2
Catherine St A1
Chester A3
Cheyney Rd A1
Chichester St A1
City Rd A3
City Walls B1/B2
City Walls Rd B1
Cornwall St A2
Cross Hey C3
Cross, The B2
Crown Ct C2
Cuppin St B2
Curzon Park North C1
Curzon Park South C1
Dee Basin A1
Dee La B3
Delamere St A2
Dewa Roman Experience B2
Duke St B2
Eastgate B2
Eastgate St B2
Eaton Rd C2
Edinburgh Way C3
Elizabeth Cr B3
Fire Station A2
Foregate St B2
Forum, The B2
Frodsham St B2
Gamul House B2
Garden La A1
George St A2
Gladstone Ave A1
God's Providence House B2
Gorse Stacks A2
Greenway St C2
Grosvenor Bridge C1
Grosvenor Mus B2
Grosvenor Park B3
Grosvenor Pk Terr C1
Grosvenor Shopping Ctr B2
Grosvenor St B2
Groves Rd B3
Groves, The B3
Guildhall Mus B1
Handbridge C2
Hartington St C3
Hoole Way A2
Hunter St B2
Information Ctr B2
King Charles' Tower A2
King St A2
Leisure Centre A2
Library B2
Lightfoot St A3
Little Roodee C2
Liverpool Rd A2
Love St B3
Lower Bridge St B2
Lower Park Rd B3
Lyon St A2
Magistrates Court B2
Meadows La C3
Meadows, The B3
Military Mus C2
Milton St A3
New Crane St B1
Nicholas St B2
Northgate A2
Northgate St A2
Nun's Rd B1
Old Dee Bridge C2
Overleigh Rd C2
Park St B2
Police Station B2
Post Office A2/A3/B2
Princess St B2
Queen St B2
Queen's Park Rd C3
Queen's Rd A3
Race Course B1
Raymond St A1
River La C2
Roman Amphitheatre & Gardens B2
Roodee (Chester Racecourse), The B1
Russell St A3
St Anne St A2
St George's Cr C3
St Martin's Gate A1
St Martin's Way B1
St Mary's Priory B2
St Oswalds Way A2
Saughall Rd A1
Sealand Rd A1
South View Rd A1
Stanley Palace B1
Station Rd A3
Steven St A3
Storyhouse B2
Superstore B2
Tower Rd B1
Town Hall B2
Union St B3
Univ of Chester C2
Vicar's La B2
Victoria Cr C3
Victoria Rd A2
Walpole St A1
Water Tower St A1
Water Tower, The B1
Watergate B1
Watergate St B2
Whipcord La A1
White Friars B2
York St B3

Chichester 115

Adelaide Rd A3
Alexandra Rd A3
Arts Centre B2
Ave de Chartres B1/B2
Barlow Rd A1
Basin Rd C2
Beech Ave B1
Bishops Palace Gardens B2
Bishopsgate Walk A3
Bramber Rd C3
Broyle Rd A2
Bus Station B2
Caledonian Rd B3
Cambrai Ave B3
Canal Pl C2
Canal Wharf C2
Canon La B2
Cathedral B2
Cavendish St A1
Cawley Rd B2
Cedar Dr A1
Chapel St A2
Cherry Orchard Rd C3
Chichester B2
Chichester By-Pass C2/C3
Chichester Coll B1
Chichester Cinema B3
Chichester Festival A2
Chichester Gate Leisure Pk C1
Churchside A2
Cineworld C1
City Walls B2
Cleveland Rd B3
College La A2
Cory Cl C2
Council Offices B2
County Hall B2
District B2
Duncan Rd A1
Durnford Cl A1
East Pallant B2
East Row B2
East St B2
East Walls B3
Eastland Rd C3
Ettrick Cl B3
Ettrick Rd B3
Exton Rd C3
Fire Station A2
Football Ground A2
Franklin Pl A2
Friary (Rems of) B2
Garland Cl C3
Green La A3
Grove Rd C3
Guilden Rd B3
Guildhall A2
Hawthorn Cl A1
Hay Rd C3
Henty Gdns B1
Herald Dr C3
Hornet, The B3
Information Ctr B2
John's St B2
Joys Croft A3
Jubilee Pk A3
Jubilee Rd A3
Juxon Cl B1
Kent Rd A3
King George Gdns A2
King's Ave C2
Kingsham Ave C3
Kingsham Rd C2
Laburnum Gr B3
Leigh Rd C1
Lennox Rd A3
Lewis Rd A3
Library B2
Lion St B2
Litten Terr A3
Litten, The A3
Little London B2
Lyndhurst Rd B3
Market B3
Market Ave B2
Market Cross B2
Market Rd B3
Melbourne Rd A3
Minerva A2
Mount La B1
New Park Rd A3
Newlands La A1
North Pallant B2
North St A2
North Walls A2
Northgate A2
Novium, The B2
Oak Ave A1
Oak Cl A1
Oaklands Park A2
Oaklands Way A2
Orchard Ave A1
Orchard St A1
Ormonde Ave B3
Pallant House B2
Parchment St A1
Parklands Rd A1/B1
Peter Weston Pl B3
Police Station C2
Post Office A1/B2/C3
Priory La A2
Priory Park A2
Priory Rd A2
Queen's Ave C1
Riverside A3
Roman Amphitheatre B3
St Cyriacs A2
St Martins' St B2
St Pancras A3
St Paul's Rd A2
St Richard's Hospital (A&E) A3
Shamrock Cl A3
Sherbourne Rd A1
Somerstown A2
South Bank C2
South Downs Planetarium C2
South Pallant B2
South St B2
Southgate B2
Spitalfield La A3
Stirling Rd B3
Stockbridge Rd C1/C2
Swanfield Dr A3
Terminus Ind Est C1
Tower St A2
Tozer Way A3
Turnbull Rd A3
Upton Rd C1
Velyn Ave B3
Via Ravenna B1
Walnut Ave A1
West St B2
Westgate B1
Westgate Fields B1
Westgate Leisure Centre B1
Weston Ave C1
Whyke Cl C3
Whyke La B3
Whyke Rd C3
Winden Ave B3

Colchester 115

Abbey Gateway C2
Albert St A1
Albion Grove C2
Alexandra Rd C1
Artillery St C3
Arts Centre B1
Balkerne Hill B1
Barrack St C3
Beaconsfield Rd C1
Beche Rd C3
Bergholt Rd A1
Bourne Rd C3
Brick Kiln Rd A1
Brigade Gr C2
Bristol Rd B2
Broadlands Way A3
Brook St B3
Bury Cl B2
Bus Sta B2
Butt Rd C1
Campion Rd C2
Cannon St C3
Canterbury Rd C2
Captain Gardens C2
Castle B2
Castle Park B2
Castle Rd B2
Catchpool Rd A1
Causton Rd B1
Chandlers Row C3
Circular Rd East C2
Circular Rd North C1
Circular Rd West C1
Clarendon Way A1
Claudius Rd C2
Colchester A1
Colchester Camp Abbey Field C1
Colchester Retail Park B1
Colchester Town C2
Colne Bank Ave A1
Colne View Retail Park A2
Compton Rd A3
Cowdray Ave A1/A2
Cowdray Centre, The A2
Crouch St B1
Crowhurst Rd B1
Culver Square Shopping Centre B1
Culver St East B2
Culver St West B1
Dilbridge Rd A3
East Hill B2
East St B3
East Stockwell St B1
Essex Hall Rd A1
Exeter Dr B2
Fairfax Rd C2
Fire Station A2
Firstsite B2
Flagstaff Rd C1
Garrison Parade C2
George St B2
Gladstone Rd C2
Golden Noble Hill C2
Goring Rd A3
Granville Rd C3
Greenstead Rd B3
Guildford Rd B2
Harsnett Rd C3
Harwich Rd B3
Head St B1
High St B1/B2
High Woods Country Park A2
Hollytrees B2
Hyderabad Cl C2
Hythe Hill C3
Information Ctr B2
Jarmin Rd A2
Kendall Rd C2
Kimberley Rd C3
King Stephen Rd C3
Leisure World A2
Library B1
Lincoln Way B2
Lion Walk Shopping Centre B1
Lisle Rd C2
Lucas Rd C2
Magdalen Green C3
Magdalen St C2
Maidenburgh St B2
Maldon Rd C1
Manor Rd B1
Margaret Rd A1
Mason Rd A2
Mercers Way A1
Mercury B1
Mersea Rd C2
Meyrick Cr C2
Mile End Rd A1
Military Rd C2
Mill St C2
Minories B2
Moorside B3
Morant Rd C3
Napier Rd C2
Natural History B2
New Town Rd C2
Norfolk Cr A3
North Hill B1
North Station Rd A1
Northgate St B1
Nunns Rd B1
Odeon B1
Old Coach Rd B3
Old Heath Rd C3
Osborne St B2
Petrolea Cl A1
Police Station C1
Popes La B1
Port La C3
Post Office B2/C1
Priory St B2
Queen St B2
Rawstorn Rd B1
Rebon St C3
Recreation Rd C3
Ripple Way A3
Roberts Rd C2
Roman Rd B2
Roman Wall B2
Romford Cl A3
Rosebery Ave B2
St Andrews Ave B3
St Andrews Gdns B3
St Botolph St B2
St Botolphs B2
St John's Abbey (site of) C2
St John's St B1
St Johns Walk Shopping Centre B1
St Leonards Rd C3
St Marys Fields B1
St Peter's St B1
St Peters B1
Salisbury Ave C1
Saw Mill Rd C3
Sergeant St C2
Serpentine Walk A1
Sheepen Pl B1
Sheepen Rd B1
Sir Isaac's Walk B1
Smythies Ave B2
South St C1
South Way C1
Sports Way A2
Suffolk Cl A3
Superstore A1
Town Hall B1
Valentine Dr A3
Victor Rd C3
Wakefield Cl B2
Wellesley Rd C1
Wells Rd B2/B3
West St C1
West Stockwell St B1
Weston Rd C3
Westway A1
Wickham Rd C1
Wimpole Rd C3
Winchester Rd C2
Winnock Rd C2
Worcester Rd B2

Coventry 116

Abbots La A1
Albany B1
Albany Rd B1
Alma St B3
Ambulance Sta A2
Art Faculty B3
Asthill Grove C2
Bablake School A1
Barras La A1/B1
Barr's Hill School A1
Belgrade B2
Bishop St A2
Bond's Hospital B1
Broad Gate B2
Broadway C1
Burges, The B2
Bus Station A3
Butts Radial B1
Byron St A3
Canal Basin A2
Canterbury St A3
Cathedral B3
Central Six Retail Park C1
Chester St A1
Cheylesmore Manor House B2
Christ Church Spire B2
City Coll A3
City Walls & Gates A2
Corporation St B2
Council House B2
Coundon Rd A1
Coventry Station C2
Coventry Transport Museum A2
Coventry University Technology Park C3
Cox St A3
Croft Rd B1
Dalton Rd C1
Deasy Rd C3
Earl St B2
Eaton Rd C2
Fairfax St B2
Foleshill Rd A2
Ford's Hospital B2
Fowler Rd A1
Friars Rd C2
Gordon St C1
Gosford St B3
Greyfriars Green B2
Greyfriars Rd B2
Gulson Rd B3
Hales St A2
Harnall Lane East A3
Harnall Lane West A2
Herbert Art Gallery & Museum B3
Hertford St B2
Hewitt Ave A1
High St B2
Hill St B1
Holy Trinity B2
Holyhead Rd A1
Howard St A3
Huntingdon Rd C1
Information Ctr B2
Jordan Well B3
King Henry VIII School C1
Lady Godiva Statue B2
Lamb St A2
Leicester Row A2
Library B2
Lincoln St A2
Little Park St B2
London Rd C3
Lower Ford St B3
Lower Precinct Shopping Centre B2
Magistrates & Crown Courts B2
Manor House Drive B2
Manor Rd C2
Market B2
Martyrs Meml C2
Meadow St B1
Meriden St A1
Michaelmas Rd C2
Middleborough Rd A1
Mile La C3
Millennium Pl A2
Much Park St B3
Naul's Mill Park A1
New Union B2
Odeon B1
Park Rd C2
Parkside C3
Planet Ice Arena B1
Post Office B2
Primrose Hill St A3
Priory Gardens & Visitor Centre B2
Priory St B3
Puma Way C3
Quarryfield La C3
Queen's Rd B1
Quinton Rd C2
Radford Rd A2
Raglan St B3
Ringway (Hill Cross) A1
Ringway (Queens) B1
Ringway (Rudge) B1
Ringway (St Johns) B3
Ringway (St Nicholas) A2
Ringway (St Patricks) C2
Ringway (Swanswell) A2
Ringway (Whitefriars) B3
St John St B2
St John the Baptist B2
St Nicholas St A2
Sidney Stringer Academy A3
Skydome B1
Spencer Ave C1
Spencer Rec Gnd C1
Spencer Rd C1
Spon St B1
Sports Centre B3
Stoney Rd C2
Stoney Stanton Rd A3
Superstore B2
Swanswell Pool A3
Technocentre C3
Thomas Landsdail St C2
Tomson Ave A1
Top Green C1
Trinity St B2
University B3
Univ Sports Ctr B3
Upper Hill St A1
Upper Well St A2
Victoria St A3
Vine St A3
Warwick Rd C2
Waveley Rd B1
West Orchards Shopping Ctr B2
Westminster Rd C1
White St A3
Windsor St B1

Derby 116

Abbey St C1
Agard St B1
Albert St B2
Albion St B2
Ambulance Station B1
Arthur St A1
Ashlyn Rd B3
Assembly Rooms B2
Babington La C2
Becket St B1
Belper Rd A1
Bold La B1
Bradshaw Way C2
Bradshaw Way Retail Park C2
Bridge St B1
Brook St B1
Burton Rd C1
Bus Station B2
Business Park A3
Caesar St A2
Canal St C3
Carrington St C3
Cathedral B2
Cathedral Rd B1
Charnwood St C2
Chester Green Rd A2
City Rd A2
Clarke St A3
Cock Pitt B3
Council House B2
Courts B1
Cranmer Rd B3
Crompton St C1
Crown & County Courts B2
Curzon St B1
Darley Grove A1
Derby C3
Derby C2
Derbyshire 3aaa County Cricket Gd B3
Derwent Bsns Ctr A2
Derwent St B2
Drewry La C1
Duffield Rd A1
Duke St A2
Dunton Cl B3
Eagle Market C2
East St B2
Eastgate B3
Exeter St B2
Farm St C1
Ford St B1
Forester St C1
Fox St A2
Friar Gate B1
Friary St B1
Full St B2
Gerard St C1
Gower St C2
Green La C2
Grey St C1
Guildhall B2
Harcourt St C1
Highfield Rd A1
Hill La C2
Information Ctr B2
intu Derby C2
Iron Gate B2
John St C3
Joseph Wright Ctr B1
Kedleston Rd A1
Key St B2
King Alfred St C1
King St A1
Kingston St A1
Lara Croft Way C2
Leopold St C2
Library B1
Liversage St C3
Lodge La B1
London Rd C2
London Rd Community Hospital C2
Macklin St C1
Mansfield Rd A2
Market B2
Market Pl B2
May St C1
Meadow La B3
Melbourne St C2
Mercian Way C1
Midland Rd C3
Monk St C1
Morledge B2
Mount St C1
Museum & Art Gallery B1
Noble St C3
North Parade A1
North St A1
Nottingham Rd B3
Osmaston Rd C2
Otter St A1
Park St C3
Parker St A1
Pickfords House B1
Police HQ A2
Police Station B2
Post Office A1/A2/B1/C2/C3
Pride Parkway C3
Prime Enterprise Park A2
Prime Parkway A2
QUAD B2
Queens Leisure Ctr B1
Racecourse Park A3
Railway Terr C3
Register Office B2
Sadler Gate B1
St Alkmund's Way B1/B2
St Helens House A1
St Mary's A1
St Mary's Bridge A2
St Mary's Bridge Chapel A2
St Mary's Gate B1
St Paul's Rd A2
St Peter's C2
St Peter's St C2
Showcase De Lux C2
Siddals Rd C3
Sir Frank Whittle Rd A3
Spa La C1
Spring St C1
Stafford St B1
Station Approach C3
Stockbrook St C1
Stores Rd A3
Traffic St C2
Wardwick B1
Werburgh St C1
West Ave A1
West Meadows Industrial Estate B3
Wharf Rd A2
Wilmot St C2
Wilson St C1
Wood's La C1

Dundee 116

Abertay University B2
Adelaide Pl A1
Airlie Pl C1
Albany Terr A1
Albert St A3
Alexander St A2
Ann St A2
Arthurstone Terr A3
Bank St B2
Barrack Rd A1
Barrack St B2
Bell St B2
Blinshall St B1
Broughty Ferry Rd A3
Brown St B1
Bus Station B3
Caird Hall B2
Camperdown St B3
Candle La B3
Carmichael St A1
City Churches B2
City Quay B3
City Square B2
Commercial St B2
Constable St A3
Constitution Cres A1
Constitution Ct A1
Constitution St A1/B2
Cotton Rd A3
Courthouse Sq B1
Cowgate A3
Crescent St A3
Crichton St B2
Dens Brae A3
Dens Rd A3
Discovery Point C2
Douglas St B1
Drummond St A1
Dudhope Castle A1
Dudhope St A2
Dudhope Terr A1
Dundee C2
Dundee Contemporary Arts C2
Dundee High School B2
Dundee Law A1
Dundee Repertory C2
Dunhope Park A1
Dura St A3
East Dock St B3
East Marketgait B3
East Whale La B3
Erskine St A3
Euclid Cr B2
Forebank Rd A2
Foundry La A3
Gallagher Retail Pk B3
Gellatly St B3
Government Offices C2
Guthrie St B1
Hawkhill B1
Hilltown A2
HMS Unicorn B3
Howff Cemetery, The B2
Information Ctr B2
Keiller Shopping Centre B2
Keiller Ctr, The B2
King St A3
Kinghorne Rd A1
Ladywell Ave A3
Laurel Bank A2
Law Rd A1
Law St A1
Library A2/A3
Library and Steps Theatre A2
Little Theatre, The A2
Lochee Rd B1
Lower Princes St A3
Lyon St A3
McManus Art Gallery & Museum, The B2
Meadow Side B2
Meadowside St Pauls B2
Mercat Cross B2
Murraygate B2
Nelson St A2
Nethergate B2/C1
North Lindsay St B2
North Marketgait B2
Old Hawkhill B1
Olympia Leisure Ctr B3
Overgate Shopping Centre B2
Park Pl B1
Perth Rd C1
Police Station B1
Post Office B2
Princes St A3
Prospect Pl A2
Reform St B2
Riverside Dr C2
Riverside Esplanade C2
Roseangle C1
Rosebank St A2
RRS Discovery C2
St Andrew's C2
St Pauls Episcopal B3
Science Centre C2
Seagate B2
Sheriffs Court B1
Shopmobility B2
South George St A2
South Marketgait B3
South Tay St B2
South Victoria Dock Road B3
South Ward Rd B2
Tay Road Bridge C3
Thomson Ave B2
Trades La B3
Union St B2
Union Terr A1
University Library B2
Univ of Dundee B1
Upper Constitution St A1
Verdant Works B1
V&A Dundee C2
Victoria Dock B3
Victoria Rd A2
Victoria St A3
Ward Rd B1
Wellgate B2
West Bell St B1
West Marketgait B1/B2
Westfield Pl C1
William St A3
Wishart Arch A3

Durham 116

Alexander Cr B2
Allergate B2
Archery Rise C1
Avenue, The B1
Back Western Hill A1
Bakehouse La A3
Baths B3
Baths Bridge B3
Boat House B3
Bowling A2
Boyd St C3
Bus Station B2
Castle B2
Castle Chare B2
Cathedral B2
Church St C3
Clay La C1
Claypath B3
College of St Hild & St Bede B3
County Hall A1
County Hospital B1
Crescent, The A1
Crook Hall & Gardens A3
Crossgate B2
Crossgate Peth C1
Crown Court B3
Darlington Rd C1
Durham A2
Durham School C2
Durham University Science Site C3
Ellam Ave C1
Elvet Bridge B3
Elvet Court B3
Farnley Hey B1
Ferens Cl A3
Fieldhouse La A1
Flass St B1
Framwelgate Bridge B2
Framwelgate A2
Framwelgate Peth A2
Framwelgate Waterside A2
Frankland La A3
Freeman's Pl A3
Freeman's Quay Leisure Centre A3
Gala Theatre & Cinema B3
Geoffrey Ave C1
Gilesgate B3
Grey College C3
Grove, The A1
Hallgarth St C3
Hatfield College B3
Hawthorn Terr B1
Heritage Centre B3
HM Prison B3
Information Ctr B3
John St B1
Kingsgate Bridge B3
Laburnum Terr B1
Lawson Terr B1
Leazes Rd B2/B3
Library B2
Library C3
Margery La B2
Market B2
Mavin St C3
Millburngate B2
Millburngate Bridge B2
Millennium Bridge (foot/cycle) A2
Mountjoy Research Centre C3
Museum of Archaeology B2
Nevilledale Terr B1
New Elvet B3
New Elvet Bridge B3
North Bailey B3
North End A1
North Rd A1/B2
Observatory C1
Old Elvet B3
Open Treasure B2
Oriental Mus C2
Oswald Court C3
Parkside B2
Passport Office A2
Percy Terr B1
Pimlico C2
Police Station B3
Post Office A1/B2
Potters Bank C1/C2
Prebends Bridge C2
Prebends Walk C2
Prince Bishops Shopping Centre B3
Princes St A1
Providence Row A3
Quarryheads La C2
Redhills La B1
Redhills Terr B1
Riverwalk, The B2
Saddler St B3
St Chad's College C3
St Cuthbert's Society C2
St John's College C2
St Margaret's B2
St Mary the Less C2
St Mary's College C2
St Monica Grove B1
St Nicholas' B3
St Oswald's C3
Sands, The A3
Shopmobility B3
Sidegate A2
Silver St B2
Sixth Form College A3
South Bailey C2
South Rd C3
South St B2
Springwell Ave A1
Stockton Rd C3
Student Union B3
Sutton St B2
Town Hall B2
Univ Arts Block B3
University Coll B2
Walkergate Centre A3
Wearside Dr A3
Western Hill A1
Wharton Park A2
Whinney Hill C3
Whitehouse Ave C1
YHA C3

Edinburgh 116

Abbey Strand B6
Abbeyhill B6
Abbeyhill Cr B6
Abbeymount A6
Abercromby Pl A3
Adam St C5
Albany La A4
Albany St A4
Albert Memorial B2
Albyn Pl A2
Alva Pl A6
Alva St B1
Ann St A1
Appleton Tower C4
Archibald Pl C3
Assembly Rooms & Musical Hall A3
Atholl Cr B1
Atholl Crescent La C1
Bank St B4
Barony St A4
Beaumont Pl C5
Belford Rd B1
Belgrave Cr A1
Belgrave Cres La A1
Bell's Brae B1
Blackfriars St B4
Blair St B4
Bread St C2
Bristo Pl C4
Bristo St C4
Brougham St C2
Broughton St A4
Brown St C5
Brunton Terr A6
Buckingham Terr A1
Burial Ground A6
Bus Station A4
Caledonian Cr C1
Caledonian Rd C1
Calton Hill A4
Calton Hill A5
Calton Rd B4
Camera Obscura & Outlook Tower B3
Candlemaker Row C4
Canning St B2
Canongate B5
Canongate B5
Carlton St A1
Carlton Terr A6
Carlton Terrace La A6
Castle St B2
Castle Terr B2
Castlehill B3
Central Library B4
Chalmers Hosp C3
Chalmers St C3
Chambers St C4
Chapel St C4
Charles St C4
Charlotte Sq B2
Chester St B1
Circus La A2
Circus Pl A2
City Art Centre B4
City Chambers B4
City Observatory A5
Clarendon Cr A1
Clerk St C5
Coates Cr B1
Cockburn St B4
College of Art C3
Comely Bank Ave A1
Comely Bank Row A1
Cornwall St C2
Cowans Cl C5
Cowgate B4
Cranston St B5
Crichton St C4
Croft-An-Righ A6
Cumberland St A2
Dalry Pl C1
Dalry Rd C1
Danube St A1
Darnawy St A2
David Hume Tower C4
Davie St C5
Dean Bridge A1
Dean Gdns A1
Dean Park Cr A1
Dean Park Mews A1
Dean Park St A1
Dean Path B1
Dean St A1
Dean Terr A1
Dewar Pl C1
Dewar Place La C1
Doune Terr A2
Drummond Pl A3
Drummond St C5
Drumsheugh Gdns B1
Dublin Mews A3
Dublin St A4
Dublin St La South A4
Dumbiedykes Rd B5
Dundas St A3
Earl Grey St C2
East Crosscauseway C5
East Market St B4
East Norton Pl A6
East Princes St Gdns B3
Easter Rd A6
Edinburgh (Waverley) B4
Edinburgh Castle B3
Edinburgh Dungeon B4
Edinburgh Int Conference Ctr C2
Elder St A4
Esplanade B3
Eton Terr A1
Eye Pavilion C3
Festival Office B3
Festival Theatre Edinburgh C4
Filmhouse C2
Fire Station C2
Floral Clock B3
Forres St A2
Forth St A4
Fountainbridge C2
Frederick St A3
Freemasons' Hall B3
Fruit Market B4
Gardner's Cr C2
George Heriot's School C3
George IV Bridge B4
George Sq C4
George Sq La C4
George St B3
Georgian House B2
Gladstone's Land B3
Glen St C3
Gloucester La A2
Gloucester Pl A2
Gloucester St A2
Graham St C3
Grassmarket C3
Great King St A3
Great Stuart B1
Greenside La A5
Greenside Row A5
Greyfriars Kirk C4
Grindlay St C2
Grosvenor St C1
Grove St C1
Gullan's Cl B5
Guthrie St B4
Hanover St A3
Hart St A4
Haymarket C1
Haymarket Sta C1
Heriot Pl C3
Heriot Row A2
High School Yard B5
High St B4
Hill Pl C5
Hill St A2
Hillside Cr A5
Holyrood Park C6
Holyrood Rd B5
Home St C2
Hope St B2
Horse Wynd B6
Howden St C5
Howe St A2
India Pl A2
India St A2
Infirmary St B4
Information Ctr B4

Jeffrey St B4
John Knox Ho B4
Johnston Terr C3
Keir St C3
Kerr St A2
King's Stables Rd B2
Lady Lawson St C3
Lauriston Gdns C3
Lauriston Park C3
Lauriston Pl C3
Lauriston St C3
Lawnmarket B3
Learmonth Gdns A1
Learmonth Terr A1
Leith St A4
Lennox St A1
Lennox St La A1
Leslie Pl A2
London Rd A5
Lothian Rd B2
Lothian St C4
Lower Menz Pl A6
Lynedoch Pl B1
Mall,The B6
Manor Pl B1
Market St B4
Marshall St C4
Maryfield A6
Maryfield Pl A6
McEwan Hall C4
Medical School C4
Melville St B1
Meuse La B4
Middle Meadow Walk C4
Milton St A6
Montrose Terr A6
Moray House (Coll) B5
Moray Place A2
Morrison Link C1
Morrison St C1
Mound Pl B3
Mound,The B3
Multrees Walk A4
Mus Collections Ctr A4
Museum of Childhood B5
Museum of Edinburgh B5
Museum of Fire C3
Museum on the Mound B4
National Archives of Scotland A4
National Museum of Scotland C4
National Gallery B3
National Library of Scotland B4
National Monument A5
National Portrait Gallery B4
Nelson Monument A5
Nelson St A3
New St B5
Nicolson Sq C4
Nicolson St C4
Niddry St B4
North Bank St B3
North Bridge B4
North Castle St A2
North Charlotte St A2
North Mdw Walk C3
North St Andrew St A4
North St David St A3
North West Cir Pl A2
Northumberland St A3
Odeon C2
Old Royal High School A5
Old Tolbooth Wynd B5
OMNi Centre A4
Our Dynamic Earth B6
Oxford Terr A1
Palace of Holyroodhouse B6
Palmerston Pl B1
Panmure Pl C3
Parliament Ho B4
Parliament Sq B4
People's Story, The B5
Playhouse Theatre A4
Pleasance C5
Police Station A4
Ponton St C2
Post Office A3/B4/B5/C1/C2/C4
Potterrow C4
Princes Mall B4
Princes St B3
Princes St B3
Prisoners of War B3
Queen St A2
Queen Street Gdns A3
Queen's Dr B6/C6
Queensferry Rd A1
Queensferry St B1
Queensferry St La B2
Radical Rd C6
Randolph Cr B1
Regent Gdns A5
Regent Rd B5
Regent Rd Park A6
Regent Terr A5
Holyrood Abbey, remains of (AD 1128) A6
Richmond La C5
Richmond Pl C5
Rose St B2
Ross Open Air Theatre B3
Rothesay Pl B1
Rothesay Terr B1
Roxburgh Place C5
Roxburgh St C5
Royal Bank of Scotland A4
Royal Circus A2
Royal Lyceum C2
Royal Mile,The B5
Royal Scottish Academy B3
Royal Terr A5
Royal Terrace Gdns A5
Rutland Sq B2
Rutland St B2
St Andrew Sq A4
St Andrew Sq A4
St Andrew's House A4
St Bernard's Cr A1
St Cecilia's Hall B4
St Colme St A2
St Cuthbert's B2
St Giles' B4
St John St B5
St John's B2
St John's Hill B5
St Leonard's Hill C5
St Leonard's La C5
St Leonard's St C5
St Mary's A4
St Mary's Scottish Episcopal B1
St Mary's St B5
St Stephen St A2
Salisbury Crags C6
Saunders St A2
Scotch Whisky Experience B3
Scott Monument B4
Scottish Parliament B6
Scottish Storytelling Centre B5
Semple St C2
Shandwick Pl B2
South Bridge B4
South Charlotte St B2
South College St C4
South Learmonth Gdns A1
South St Andrew St A4
South St David St A3
Spittal St C2
Stafford St B1
Student Centre C4
Surgeons' Hall C5
Tattoo Office B4
Teviot Pl C4
Thistle St A3
Torphichen Pl C1
Torphichen St C1
Traverse Theatre B2
Tron Sq B4
Tron,The B4
Union St A4
University C4
University Library C4
Upper Grove Pl C1
Usher Hall C2
Vennel C3
Victoria St B3
Viewcraig Gdns B5
Viewcraig St B5
Vue A4
Walker St B1
Waterloo Pl A4
Waverley Bridge B4
Wemyss Pl A2
West Approach Rd C1
West Crosscauseway C5
West End Princess St B1
West Maitland St C1
West of Nicholson St C4
West Port C3
West Princes Street Gdns B3
West Richmond St C5
West Tollcross C2
White Horse Cl B5
William St B1
Windsor St A5
Writer's Museum, The B4
York La A4
York Pl A4
York Pl A4
Young St B2

Exeter 117

Alphington St C1
Athelstan Rd B3
Bampfylde St B2
Barnardo Rd C3
Barnfield Hill B3
Barnfield Rd B2/B3
Barnfield Theatre B2
Bartholomew St East B1
Bartholomew St West B1
Bear St B2
Beaufort Rd C1
Bedford St B2
Belgrave Rd A3
Belmont Rd A3
Blackall Rd A2
Blackboy Rd A3
Bonhay Rd B1
Bull Meadow Rd C2
Bus & Coach Sta B3
Castle St B2
Cecil Rd C1
Cheeke St A3
Church Rd C1
Chute St A3
City Wall B1/B2
Civic Centre B2
Clifton Rd B3
Clifton St B3
Clock Tower A1
College Rd B3
Colleton Cr C2
Commercial Rd C1
Coombe St B2
Cowick St C1
Crown Courts B2
Custom House C2
Cygnet New Theatre C2
Danes' Rd A2
Denmark Rd B3
Devon County Hall C3
Devonshire Pl A3
Dinham Cres B1
East Grove Rd C3
Edmund St C1
Elmgrove Rd A1
Exe St B1
Exeter Cathedral B2
Exeter Central Station A1
Exeter City Football Ground A3
Exeter College A1
Exeter Picture House B1
Fire Station A1
Fore St B1
Friars Walk C2
Guildhall B2
Guildhall Shopping Centre B2
Harlequins Shopping Centre B1
Haven Rd C2
Heavitree Rd B3
Hele Rd A1
High St B2
HM Prison A2
Holloway St C2
Hoopern St A2
Horseguards A2
Howell Rd A1
Information Ctr B3
Iron Bridge B1
Isca Rd C1
Jesmond Rd A3
King St B1
King William St A2
Larkbeare Rd C2
Leisure Centre C1
Library B2
Longbrook St A2
Longbrook Terr A2
Lower North St B1
Lucky La C2
Lyndhurst Rd C3
Magdalen Rd B3
Magdalen St B2
Market B2
Market St B2
Marlborough Rd C3
Mary Arches St B1
Matford Ave C3
Matford La C3
Matford Rd C3
May St A3
Mol's Coffee Ho B2
New Bridge St B1
New North Rd A1/A2
North St B1
Northernhay St B1
Norwood Ave C3
Odeon A3
Okehampton St C1
Old Mill Cl C2
Old Tiverton Rd A3
Oxford Rd A3
Paris St B2
Parr St A3
Paul St B1
Pennsylvania Rd A2
Police HQ B3
Portland Street A3
Post Office A3/B2/B3/C1
Powderham Cr A3
Preston St B1
Princesshay Shopping Centre B2
Pyramids Leisure Centre B3
Quay,The C2
Queen St A1
Queen's Terr A1
Queens Rd C1
Radford Rd C2
Richmond Rd A1
Roberts Rd C2
Rougemont Castle A2
Rougemont Ho B2
Royal Albert Memorial Mus B2
St David's Hill A1
St James' Pk Sta A3
St James' Rd A3
St Leonard's Rd C3
St Mary Steps C1
St Nicholas Priory B1
St Thomas Sta C1
Sandford Walk B3
School for the Deaf C2
School Rd C1
Sidwell St A2
Smythen St B1
South St B2
Southernhay East B2
Southernhay West B2
Spacex Gallery B1
Spicer Rd B3
Sports Centre A3
Summerland St A3
Sydney Rd C1
Tan La C2
Thornton Hill A2
Topsham Rd C3
Tucker's Hall B1
Tudor St B1
Underground Passages B2
Univ of Exeter (St Luke's Campus) B3
Velwell Rd A1
Verney St A3
Water La C1/C2
Weirfield Rd C2
Well St A3
West Ave A2
West Grove Rd C3
Western Way A3/B1/B2
Willeys Ave C1
Wonford Rd B3/C3
York Rd A2

Glasgow 117

Admiral St C2
Albert Bridge C5
Albion St B5
Anderston B3
Anderston Quay B3
Argyle Arcade B5
Argyle St A1/A2/B3/B4/B5
Argyle Street B5
Arlington St A3
Arts Centre B3
Ashley St A3
Bain St C6
Baird St A6
Baliol St A3
Ballater St C5
Barras (Mkt),The C6
Bath St A3
BBC Scotland B1
Bell St C6
Bell's Bridge B1
Bentinck St A2
Berkeley St A3
Bishop La B3
Black St A6
Blackburn St C2
Blackfriars St B6
Blantyre St A1
Blythswood Sq A4
Blythswood St B4
Bothwell St B4
Brand St C1
Breadalbane St A2
Bridge St C4
Bridge St C4
Bridgegate C5
Briggait C5
Broomielaw B4
Broomielaw Quay Gardens B3
Brown St B4
Brunswick St B5
Buccleuch St A3
Buchanan Bus Sta A5
Buchanan Galleries A5
Buchanan St B5
Buchanan St B5
Cadogan St B4
Caledonian Univ A5
Calgary St A5
Cambridge St A4
Canal St A5
Candleriggs B5
Carlton Pl C4
Carnarvon St A3
Carrick St B4
Castle St B6
Cathedral Sq B6
Cathedral St B5
Ctr for Contemporary Arts A4
Centre St C4
Cessnock C1
Cessnock St C1
Charing Cross A3
Charlotte St C6
Cheapside St B3
Cineworld A5
Citizens' Theatre C5
City Chambers Complex B5
City Halls B5
City of Glasgow Coll (City Campus) B5
City of Glasgow College (Riverside Campus) C5
Clairmont Gdns A2
Claremont St A2
Claremont Terr A2
Claythorne St C6
Cleveland St A3
Clifford La C1
Clifford St C1
Clifton Pl A2
Clifton St A2
Clutha St C1
Clyde Arc B2
Clyde Auditorium B2
Clyde Pl C4
Clyde Place Quay C4
Clyde St C5
Clyde Walkway C3
Clydeside Expressway B2
Coburg St C4
Cochrane St B5
College St B6
Collins St B6
Commerce St C4
Cook St C4
Cornwall St C2
Couper St A5
Cowcaddens A4
Cowcaddens Rd A4
Crimea St B3
Custom House Quay Gardens C4
Dalhousie St A4
Dental Hospital A4
Derby St A2
Dobbie's Loan A4/A5
Dobbie's Loan Pl A5
Dorset St A3
Douglas St B4
Doulton Fountain C6
Dover St A2
Drury St B4
Drygate B6
Duke St B6
Dunaskin St A1
Dunblane St A4
Dundas St B5
Dunlop St C5
East Campbell St C6
Eastvale Pl A1
Eglinton St C4
Elderslie St A3
Elliot St B2
Elmbank St A3
Esmond St A1
Exhibition Ctr B2
Eye Infirmary A2
Festival Park C1
Film Theatre A4
Finnieston Quay B2
Finnieston St B2
Fire Station C6
Florence St C5
Fox St C5
Gallowgate C6
Garnet St A3
Garnethill St A4
Garscube Rd A4
George Sq B5
George St B5
George V Bridge C4
Gilbert St A1
Glasgow Bridge C4
Glasgow Cathedral B6
Glasgow Central B4
Glasgow Green C6
Glasgow Necropolis B6
Glasgow Royal Concert Hall A5
Glasgow Science Centre B1
Glasgow Tower B1
Glassford St B5
Glebe St A6
Gorbals Cross C5
Gorbals St C5
Gordon St B4
Govan Rd B1/C1/C2
Grace St B3
Grafton Pl A5
Grand Ole Opry C2
Grant St A3
Granville St A3
Gray St A2
Greendyke St C6
Grey Eagle St B7
Harley St C1
Harvie St C1
Haugh Rd A1
Havanah St B6
Heliport B1
Henry Wood Hall A2
High Court C5
High St B6
High Street B6
Hill St A3
Holland St A3
Holm St B4
Hope St A5
Houldsworth St B2
Houston Pl C3
Houston St C3
Howard St C5
Hunter St C6
Hutcheson St B5
Hydepark St B3
Imax Cinema B1
India St A3
Information Ctr B5
Ingram St B5
Jamaica St B4
James Watt St B4
John Knox St B6
John St B5
Kelvin Hall A1
Kelvin Statue A2
Kelvin Way A2
Kelvingrove Art Gallery & Mus A1
Kelvingrove Park A2
Kelvingrove St A2
Kelvinhaugh St A1
Kennedy St A6
Kent Rd A2
Killermont St A5
King St B5
King's,The A3
Kingston Bridge C3
Kingston St C4
Kinning Park C2
Kyle St A5
Lancefield Quay B2
Lancefield St B3
Langshot St C1
Lendel Pl C1
Lighthouse,The B4
Lister St A6
Little St B3
London Rd C6
Lorne St C1
Lower Harbour B1
Lumsden St A1
Lymburn St A1
Lyndoch Cr A3
Lynedoch Pl A3
Lynedoch St A3
Maclellan St C1
Mair St C2
Maitland St A4
Mansell St C7
Mavisbank Gdns C2
Mcalpine St B3
Mcaslin St A6
McLean Sq C2
McLellan Gallery A4
McPhater St A4
Merchants' Ho B5
Middlesex St C2
Middleton St C1
Midland St B4
Miller St B5
Millennium Bridge B1
Millroad St C6
Milnpark St C2
Milton St A4
Minerva St B2
Mitchell Liby,The A3
Mitchell St West B4
Mitchell Theatre, The A3
Modern Art Gallery B5
Moir St C6
Molendinar St C6
Moncur St C6
Montieth Row C6
Montrose St B5
Morrison St C3
Mosque C5
Nairn St A1
National Piping Centre,The A5
Nelson Mandela Square B5
Nelson St C4
Nelson's Monument C6
New City Rd A4
Newton Pl A3
Newton St A3
Nicholson St C4
Nile St B5
Norfolk Court C4
Norfolk St C4
North Frederick St B5
North Hanover St B5
North Portland St B6
North St A3
North Wallace St A5
O2 ABC A4
O2 Academy C4
Odeon C3
Old Dumbarton Rd A1
Osborne St B5/C5
Oswald St B4
Overnewton St A1
Oxford St C4
Pacific Dr B1
Paisley Rd C3
Paisley Rd West C1
Park Circus A2
Park Gdns A2
Park St South A2
Park Terr A2
Parkgrove Terr A2
Parnie St C5
Parson St A6
Partick Bridge A1
Passport Office A5
Pavilion Theatre A4
Pembroke St A3
People's Palace C6
Pinkston Rd A6
Pitt St A4/B4
Plantation Park C1
Plantation Quay B1
Police Station A4/A6
Port Dundas Rd A5
Port St B2
Portman St C2
Prince's Dock B1
Princes Sq B5
Provand's Lordship B6
Queen St B5
Queen Street B5
Ramshorn B5
Renfrew St A3/A4
Renton St A5
Richmond St B5
Robertson St B4
Rose St A4
Rottenrow B5
Royal Concert Hall A5
Royal Conservatoire of Scotland A4
Royal Crescent A2
Royal Exchange Square B5
Royal Highland Fusiliers Mus A3
Royal Hospital For Sick Children A1
Royal Infirmary B6
Royal Terr A2
Rutland Cr C2
St Andrew's C6
St Andrew's (RC) C5
St Andrew's St C5
St Enoch B5
St Enoch Shopping Centre B5
St Enoch Sq B4
St George's Rd A3
St James Rd B6
St Kent St C6
St Mungo Ave A5/A6
St Mungo Museum of Religious Life B6
St Mungo Pl A6
St Vincent Cr A2
St Vincent Pl B5
St Vincent St B3/B4
St Vincent Street Church B4
St Vincent Terr B3
Saltmarket C5
Sandyford Pl A3
Sauchiehall St A2/A4
School of Art A4
Sclater St B7
Scotland St C2
Scott St A4
Scottish Ex & Conference Ctr B1
Seaward St C2
Shaftesbury St B3
Sheriff Court C5
Shields Rd C3
Shopmobility A5
Shuttle St B6
Sighthill Park A6
Somerset Pl A2
South Portland St C4
Springburn Rd A6
Springfield Quay C3
SSE Hydro The B2
Stanley St C2
Stevenson St C6
Stewart St A4
Stirling Rd B6
Stirling's Library B5
Stobcross Quay B1
Stobcross Rd B1
Stock Exchange B5
Stockwell Pl C5
Stockwell St B5
Stow College A4
Sussex St C2
Synagogues A3/C4
Taylor Pl A6
Tenement Ho A3
Teviot St A1
Theatre Royal A4
Tolbooth Steeple & Mercat Cross C6
Tower St C2
Trades House B5
Tradeston St C4
Transport Mus A1
Tron C5
Trongate B5
Tunnel St B2
Turnbull St C5
Union St B4
Univ of Strathclyde B6
Victoria Bridge C5
Virginia St B5
Wallace St C3
Walls St B6
Walmer Cr C1
Warrock St B3
Washington St B3
Waterloo St B4
Watson St B6
Watt St C3
Wellington St B4
West Campbell St B4
West George St B4
West Graham St A4
West Greenhill Pl B2
West Regent St A4
West Regent St B4
West St C4
West St C4
Whitehall St B3
Wilkes St C7
Wilson St B5
Woodlands Gate A3
Woodlands Rd A3
Woodlands Terr A2
Woodside Pl A3
Woodside Terr A3
York St B4
Yorkhill Parade A1
Yorkhill St A1

Gloucester 117

Albion St C1
Alexandra Rd B3
Alfred St C3
All Saints Rd C2
Alvin St B2
Arthur St C2
Barrack Square B1
Barton St C2
Blackfriars B1
Blenheim Rd C2
Bristol Rd C1
Brunswick Rd C2
Bruton Way B2
Bus Station B2
Cineworld C1
City Council Offices B1
City Mus, Art Gall & Library B2
Clarence St B2
Commercial Rd B1
Council Offices B1
Courts B1
Cromwell St C2
Deans Way A2
Denmark Rd A3
Derby Rd C3
Docks C1
Eastgate St B2
Eastgate,The B1
Edwy Pde A2
Estcourt Cl A3
Estcourt Rd A3
Falkner St C2
GL1 Leisure Centre C2
Gloucester Cath B1
Gloucester Life B1
Gloucester Quays Outlet C1
Gloucester Sta B2
Gloucester Waterways C1
Gloucestershire Archive B2
Gloucestershire Royal Hospital (A&E) B3
Goodyere St C2
Gouda Way A1
Great Western Rd B3
Guildhall B2
Heathville Rd A3
Henry Rd B3
Henry St B2
Hinton Rd A2
India Rd C3
Information Ctr B1
Jersey Rd C3
King's C2
King's Walk Shopping Centre B2
Kingsholm (Gloucester Rugby) A2
Kingsholm Rd A2
Lansdown Rd A3
Library C2
Llanthony Rd C1
London Rd B3
Longhorn Ave A1
Longsmith St B1
Malvern Rd A3
Market B2
Market Pde B2
Mercia Rd A1
Metz Way C3
Midland Rd C2
Millbrook St C3
Montpellier C1
Napier St C3
Nettleton Rd C2
New Inn B2
New Olympus C3
North Rd A3
Northgate St B2
Oxford Rd A2
Oxford St B2
Park & Ride Gloucester A1
Park Rd C2
Park St B2
Park,The C2
Parliament St C1
Peel Centre,The C1
Pitt St B1
Police Station C3
Post Office B2
Quay St B1
Quay,The B1
Recreation Gd A1/A2
Regent St C2
Robert Raikes Ho B1
Royal Oak Rd B1
Russell St B2
Ryecroft St C2
St Aldate St B2
St Ann Way C1
St Catherine St A2
St Mark St A2
St Mary de Crypt B1
St Mary de Lode B1
St Nicholas's B1
St Oswald's Rd A1
St Oswald's Retail Park A1
St Peter's B2
Seabroke Rd A3
Sebert St A2
Severn Rd C1
Sherborne St B2
Shire Hall B1
Sidney St C3
Soldiers of Gloucestershire B1
Southgate St B1/C1
Spa Field C1
Spa Rd C1
Sports Ground A2/B2
Station Rd B2
Stratton Rd C3
Stroud Rd C1
Superstore A1
Swan Rd A2
Trier Way C1/C2
Union St A2
Vauxhall Rd C3
Victoria St C2
Walham Lane A1
Wellington St C2
Westgate Retail Pk B1
Westgate St B1
Widden St C2
Worcester St B2

Harrogate 117

Albert St C2
Alexandra Rd B2
Arthington Ave B2
Ashfield Rd A2
Back Cheltenham Mount B2
Beech Grove C1
Belmont Rd C1
Bilton Dr A2
BMI The Duchy Hospital C1
Bower Rd B2
Bower St B2
Bus Station B2
Cambridge Rd B2
Cambridge St B2
Cemetery A2
Chatsworth Grove A2
Chatsworth Pl A2
Chatsworth Rd A2
Chelmsford Rd B3
Cheltenham Cr B2
Cheltenham Mt B2
Cheltenham Pde B2
Christ Church B3
Christ Church Oval B3
Chudleigh Rd B3
Clarence Dr B1
Claro Rd A3
Claro Way A3
Coach Park B2
Coach Rd B3
Cold Bath Rd C1
Commercial St B2
Coppice Ave A1
Coppice Dr A1
Coppice Gate A1
Cornwall Rd B1
Council Offices B1
Crescent Gdns B1
Crescent Rd B1
Dawson Terr A2
Devonshire Pl B3
Dixon Rd A2
Dixon Terr A2
Dragon Ave B3
Dragon Parade B2
Dragon Rd B2
Duchy Rd B1
East Parade B2
East Park Rd C3
Esplanade B1
Everyman B2
Fire Station A2
Franklin Mount A2
Franklin Rd B2
Franklin Square A2
Glebe Rd C1
Grove Park Ct A3
Grove Park Terr A3
Grove Rd A2
Hampsthwaite Rd A1
Harcourt Dr B3
Harcourt Rd B3
Harrogate B2
Harrogate Convention Centre B1
Harrogate Justice Ctr (Magistrates' and County Courts) C2
Harrogate Ladies College B1
Harrogate Theatre B2
Heywood Rd C1
Hollins Cr A1
Hollins Mews A1
Hollins Rd A1
Hydro Leisure Centre,The A1
Information Ctr B1
James St B2
Jenny Field Dr A1
John St B2
Kent Dr A1
Kent Rd A1
Kings Rd A2
Kingsway B3
Kingsway Dr B3
Lancaster Rd C1
Leeds Rd C2
Lime Grove B3
Lime St A3
Mayfield Grove B2
Mercer B1
Montpellier Hill B1
Mornington Cr A3
Mornington Terr B3
Mowbray Sq B3
North Park Rd B3
Oakdale Ave A1
Oatlands Dr C3
Odeon B2
Osborne Rd A2
Otley Rd C2
Oxford St B2
Parade,The B2
Park Chase B3
Park Parade B3
Park View B2
Parliament St B1
Police Station C3
Post Office B2/C1
Providence Terr A2
Queen Parade C3
Queen's Rd C1
Raglan St C2
Regent Ave A3
Regent Grove A3
Regent Parade A3
Regent St A3
Regent Terr A3
Ripon Rd A1
Robert St C2
Royal Baths & Turkish Baths B1
Royal Pump Room B1
St Luke's Mount A2
St Mary's Ave C1
St Mary's Walk C1
Scargill Rd A1
Skipton Rd A3
Skipton St A2
Slingsby Walk C3
South Park Rd C2
Spring Grove A1
Springfield Ave B1
Station Ave B2
Station Parade B2
Stray Rein C3
Stray,The C2/C3
Studley Rd A2
Superstore B2/C1
Swan Rd B1
Tower St C2
Trinity Rd C2
Union St B2
Valley Dr C1
Valley Gardens C1
Valley Mount C1
Victoria Ave C2
Victoria Rd C1
Victoria Shopping Centre B2
Waterloo St A2
West Park C2
West Park St C2
Wood View A1
Woodfield Ave A3
Woodfield Dr A3
Woodfield Grove A3
Woodfield Rd A3
Woodfield Square A3
Woodside B3
York Pl C3
York Rd B1

Hull 117

Adelaide St C1
Albert Dock C1
Albion St B2
Alfred Gelder St B2
Anlaby Rd B1
Arctic Corsair B3
Beverley Rd A1
Blanket Row C2
Bond St B2
Bridlington Ave A2
Brook St B1
Brunswick Ave A1
Bus Station B1
Camilla Cl C3
Cannon St A2
Caroline St A2
Carr La B2
Castle St C2
Central Library B1
Charles St A2
Citadel Way B3
City Hall B2
City Hall Theatre B2
Clarence St B3
Cleveland St A3
Clifton St A1
Club Culture C2
Colonial St B1
Court B2
Deep,The C3
Dinostar C2
Dock Office Row B3
Dock St B2
Drypool Bridge B3
Egton St A3
English St C1
Ferens Gallery B2
Ferensway B1
Francis St A2
Francis St West A2
Freehold St A1
Freetown Way A2
Früit Theatre C2
Garrison Rd B3
George St B2
Gibson St A2
Great Thornton St B1
Great Union St A3
Green La A2
Grey St A1
Grimston St B2
Grosvenor St A1
Guildhall B2
Guildhall Rd B2
Hands-on History B2
Harley St A1
Hessle Rd C1
High St B3
Holy Trinity B2
Hull (Paragon) Station B1
Hull & East Riding Museum B3
Hull Ice Arena C1
Hull College B2
Hull History Centre A2
Hull Truck Theatre B1
Humber Dock Marina C2
Humber Dock St C2
Humber St C2
Hyperion St A3
Information Ctr B2
Jameson St B1
Jarratt St B2
Jenning St A3
King Billy Statue C2
King Edward St B2
King St A2
Kingston Retail Pk C1
Kingston St C2
Liddell St A1
Lime St A3
Lister St C1
Lockwood St A2
Maister House B3
Maritime Mus B2
Market B2
Market Place B2
Minerva Pier C2
Mulgrave St A3
Myton Swing Bridge C3
Myton St B1
NAPA (Northern Acad of Performing Arts) B1
Nelson St C2
New Cleveland St A3
New George St A2
New Theatre A2
Norfolk St A1
North Bridge A3
North St B1
Odeon C1
Old Harbour C3
Osborne St B1
Paragon St B2
Park St B1
Percy St A2
Pier St C2
Police Station B2
Porter St C1
Portland St B1
Post Office B1/B2
Posterngate B2
Prince's Quay B2
Prospect Centre B1
Prospect St B1
Queen's Gdns B2
Railway Dock Marina C2
Railway St C2
Real B1
Red Gallery B1
Reform St A2
Retail Park B1
Riverside Quay C2
Roper St B2
St James St C1
St Luke's St B1
St Mark St A3
St Mary the Virgin B3
St Stephens Shopping Centre B1
Scale Lane Footbridge B3
Scott St A2
South Bridge Rd B3
Sport's Centre C1
Spring Bank A1
Spring St B1
Spurn Lightship C2
Spyvee St A3
Streetlife Transport Museum B3
Sykes St A2
Tidal Surge Barrier C3
Tower St B3
Trinity House B2
University B2
Vane St A1
Victoria Pier C2
Waterhouse La B2
Waterloo St A1
Waverley St C1
Wellington St C2
Wellington St West C2
West St B1
Whitefriargate B2
Wilberforce Dr B2
Wilberforce House B3
Wilberforce Monument B3
William St C1
Wincolmlee A3
Witham A3
Wright St A1

Ipswich 118

Alderman Rd B2
All Saints' Rd A1
Alpe St B2
Ancaster Rd C1
Ancient House B3
Anglesea Rd B2
Ann St B2
Arboretum A2
Austin St C2
Avenue, The A3
Belstead Rd C2
Berners St B2
Bibb Way B1
Birkfield Dr C1
Black Horse La B2
Bolton La B3
Bond St C3
Bowthorpe Cl B2
Bramford La A1
Bramford Rd A1
Bridge St C2
Brookfield Rd A1
Brooks Hall Rd A1
Broomhill Park A2
Broomhill Rd A1
Broughton Rd A2
Bulwer Rd B1
Burrell Rd C2
Bus Station C2
Butter Market B2
Buttermarket Shopping Ctr, The B3
Cardinal Park Leisure Park C2
Carr St B3
Cecil Rd B2
Cecilia St C2
Chancery Rd C2
Charles St B2
Chevallier St A1
Christchurch Mansion & Wolsey Art Gallery B3
Christchurch Park A3
Christchurch St B3
Cineworld C2
Civic Centre B2
Civic Dr B2
Clarkson St B1
Cobbold St B3
Commercial Rd C2
Constable Rd A3
Constantine Rd C1
Constitution Hill A2
Corder Rd A3
Corn Exchange B2
Cotswold Ave A2
Council Offices C2
County Hall B3
Crown Court C2
Crown St B2
Cullingham Rd B1
Cumberland St B2
Curriers La B2
Dale Hall La A2
Dales View Rd A1
Dalton Rd B2
Dillwyn St B1
Elliot St B1
Elm St B2
Elsmere Rd A3
Falcon St C2
Felaw St C3
Fire Station C2
Flint Wharf C3
Fonnereau Rd B2
Fore St C3
Foundation St C3
Franciscan Way C2
Friars St C2
Gainsborough Rd A3
Gatacre Rd B1
Geneva Rd B2
Gippeswyk Ave C1
Gippeswyk Park C1
Grafton Way C2
Graham Rd A1
Great Whip St C3
Grimwade St C3
Handford Cut B1
Handford Rd B1
Henley Rd A2
Hervey St B3
High St B2
Holly Rd A2
Information Ctr B3
Ipswich Haven Marina C3
Ipswich Museum & Art Gallery B2
Ipswich School A2
Ipswich Station C2
Ipswich Town FC (Portman Road) C2
Ivry St A2
Kensington Rd A1
Kesteven Rd C1
Key St C3
Kingsfield Ave A3
Kitchener Rd A1
Little's Cr C2
London Rd B1
Low Brook St C3
Lower Orwell St C3
Luther Rd C2
Magistrates Court B2
Manor Rd A3
Mornington Ave A1
Museum St B2
Neale St B3
New Cardinal St C2
New Cut East C3
New Cut West C3
New Wolsey B2
Newson St B2
Norwich Rd A1/B1
Oban St B2
Old Custom Ho C3
Old Foundry Rd B3
Old Merchant's House C3
Orford St B2
Paget Rd A2
Park Rd A3
Park View Rd A2
Peter's St C2
Philip Rd C2
Pine Ave A2
Pine View Rd A2
Police Station B2
Portman Rd B2
Portman Walk C1
Post Office B2
Princes St C2
Prospect St B1
Queen St B2
Ranelagh Rd C1
Recreation Ground B1
Rectory Rd C2
Regent Theatre B3
Retail Park C1
Retail Park C2
Richmond Rd A1
Rope Walk C3
Rose La C2
Russell Rd C2
St Edmund's Rd A2
St George's St B2
St Helen's St B3
Sherrington Rd A1
Shopmobility B2
Silent St C2
Sir Alf Ramsey Way C1
Sirdar Rd B1
Soane St B3
Springfield La A1
Star La C3
Stevenson Rd B1
Suffolk College C3
Suffolk Retail Park B1
Superstore B1
Surrey Rd B1
Tacket St C3
Tavern St B3
Tower Ramparts B2
Tower Ramparts Shopping Centre B2
Tower St B3
Town Hall B2
Tuddenham Rd A3
University C3
Upper Brook St B3
Upper Orwell St B3
Valley Rd A2
Vermont Cr B3
Vermont Rd B3
Vernon St C3
Warrington Rd A2
Waterloo Rd A1
Waterworks St C3
Wellington St B1
West End Rd B1
Westerfield Rd A3
Westgate St B2
Westholme Rd A1
Westwood Ave A1
Willoughby Rd C2
Withipoll St B3
Woodbridge Rd B3
Woodstone Ave A3
Yarmouth Rd B1

Lancaster 118

Aberdeen Rd C3
Adult College, The C3
Aldcliffe Rd C2
Alfred St B3
Ambleside Rd A3
Ambulance Sta A3
Ashfield Ave B1
Ashton Rd C2
Assembly Rooms Emporium B2
Balmoral Rd B3
Bath House B2
Bath Mill La B3
Bath St B3
Blades St B1
Borrowdale Rd B3
Bowerham Rd C3
Brewery La B2
Bridge La B2
Brook St C1
Bulk Rd A3
Bulk St B2
Bus Station B2
Cable St B2
Canal Cruises & Waterbus C2
Carlisle Bridge A1
Carr House La C2
Castle B1
Castle Park B1
Caton Rd A3
China St B2
Church St B2
City Museum B2
Clarence St C3
Common Gdn St B2
Coniston Rd A3
Cottage Museum B2
Council Offices B2
County College & Family Court B2
Cromwell Rd C1
Crown Court B1
Dale St C3
Dallas Rd B1/C1
Dalton Rd B3
Dalton Sq B2
Damside St B2
De Vitre St B3
Dee Rd A1
Denny Ave A1
Derby Rd A2
Dukes, The B2
Earl St B2
East Rd B3
Eastham St C3
Edward St B3
Fairfield Rd B1
Fenton St B2
Firbank Rd A3
Fire Station B2
Friend's Meeting House B1
Garnet St B3
George St B2
Giant Axe Field B1
Grand B2
Grasmere Rd B3
Greaves Rd C2
Green St A3
Gregson Ctr, The B3
Gregson Rd C3
Greyhound Bridge A2
Greyhound Bridge Rd A2
High St B2
Hill Side B1
Hope St C3
Hubert Pl B1
Information Ctr B2
Kelsy St B1
Kentmere Rd B3
King St B2
Kingsway A3
Kirkes Rd C3
Lancaster & Lakeland C3
Lancaster City Football Club B1
Lancaster Sta B1
Langdale Rd A3
Ley Ct B1
Library B2
Lincoln Rd B1
Lindow St C2
Lodge St B2
Long Marsh La B1
Lune Rd A1
Lune St A2
Lune Valley Ramble A3
Mainway A2
Maritime Mus A1
Marketgate Shopping Centre B2
Market St B2
Meadowside C2
Meeting House La B1
Millennium Bridge A2
Moor La B2
Moorgate B3
Morecambe Rd A1/A2
Nelson St B2
North Rd B2
Orchard La C1
Owen Rd A2
Park Rd B3
Parliament St A3
Patterdale Rd A3
Penny St B2
Police Station B2
Portland St C2
Post Office B2
Primrose St C3
Priory B1
Prospect St C3
Quarry Rd B3
Queen St C2
Regent St C2
Ridge La A3
Ridge St A3
Royal Lancaster Infirmary (A&E) C2
Rydal Rd B3
Ryelands Park A1
St Georges Quay A1
St John's B2
St Leonard's Gate B2
St Martin's Rd C3
St Nicholas Arcades Shopping Centre B2
St Oswald St C3
St Peter's B3
St Peter's Rd B3
Salisbury Rd B1
Scotch Quarry Urban Park C3
Sibsey St B1
Skerton Bridge A2
South Rd C2
Station Rd B1
Stirling Rd C3
Storey Ave B1
Sunnyside La C1
Sylvester St C1
Tarnsyke Rd A1
Thurnham St C2
Town Hall B2
Troutbeck Rd B3
Ulleswater Rd B3
Univ of Cumbria C3
Vicarage Field B1
Vue B2
West Rd B1
Westbourne Dr C1
Westbourne Rd B1
Westham St C3
Wheatfield St B1
White Cross Business Park C2
Williamson Rd B3
Willow La B1
Windermere Rd B3
Wingate-Saul Rd B1
Wolseley St B3
Woodville St B3
Wyresdale Rd C3

Leeds 118

Aire St B3
Albion Pl B4
Albion St B4
Albion Way B1
Alma St A6
Ambulance Sta B5
Arcades B4
Armley Rd B1
Armories Dr C5
Back Burley Lodge Rd A1
Back Hyde Terr A2
Back Row C3
Bath Rd C3
Beckett St A6
Bedford St B3
Belgrave St A4
Belle Vue Rd A2
Benson St A5
Black Bull St C5
Blenheim Walk A3
Boar La B4
Bond St B4
Bow St C5
Bowman La C4
Brewery C4
Brewery Wharf C5
Bridge St A5/B5
Briggate B4
Bruce Gdns C1
Burley Rd A1
Burley St B1
Burmantofs St B6
Bus & Coach Sta B5
Butterly St C4
Butts Cr B4
Byron St A5
Call La B4
Calls, The B5
Calverley St A3/B3
Canal St B1
Canal Wharf C3
Carlisle Rd C5
Cavendish Rd A1
Cavendish St A2
Chadwick St C5
Cherry Pl A6
Cherry Row A5
City Museum A4
City Varieties Music Hall B4
City Sq B3
Civic Hall A3
Clarence Road C5
Clarendon Rd A2
Clarendon Way A3
Clark La C6
Clay Pit La A4
Cloberry St A2
Close, The B6
Clyde Approach C1
Clyde Gdns C2
Coleman St C2
Commercial St B4
Concord St A5
Cookridge St A4
Copley Hill C1
Core, The B4
Corn Exchange B4
Cromer Terr A2
Cromwell St A5
Cross Catherine St B6
Cross Green La C6
Cross Stamford St A5
Crown & County Courts A3
Crown Point Bridge C5
Crown Point Rd C4
Crown Point Retail Park C4
David St C3
Dent St C6
Derwent Pl C3
Dial St C6
Dock St C4
Dolly La A6
Domestic St C2
Drive, The B6
Duke St B5
Duncan St B4
Dyer St B5
East Field St B6
East Parade B3
East St C5
Eastgate B5
Easy Rd C6
Edward St B4
Ellerby La C6
Ellerby Rd C6
Fenton St A3
Fire Station B2
First Direct Arena A4
Fish St B4
Flax Pl B6
Garth, The B5
Gelderd Rd C1
George St B4
Globe Rd C2
Gloucester Cr B1
Gower St A5
Grafton St A4
Grand Theatre B4
Granville Rd A6
Great George St A3
Great Wilson St C4
Greek St B3
Green La C1
Hanover Ave A2
Hanover La A2
Hanover Sq A2
Hanover Way A2
Harewood St B4
Harrison St B4
Haslewood Cl B6
Haslewood Drive B6
Headrow, The B3/B4
High Court B5
Holbeck La C2
Holdforth Cl C1
Holdforth Gdns B1
Holdforth Gr C1
Holdforth Pl C1
Holy Trinity B4
Hope Rd A5
Hunslet La C4
Hunslet Rd C4
Hyde Terr A2
Infirmary St B3
Information Ctr B3
Ingram Row C3
ITV Yorkshire A1
Junction St C4
Kelso Gdns A2
Kelso Rd A2
Kelso St A2
Kendal La A2
Kendell St C4
Kidacre St C4
King Edward St B4
King St B3
Kippax Place C6
Kirkgate B4
Kirkgate Market B4
Kirkstall Rd A1
Kitson St C6
Lady La B4
Lands La B4
Lane, The B5
Lavender Walk B6
Leeds Art Gallery B3
Leeds Beckett Univ A3
Leeds Bridge C4
Leeds Coll of Music B5
Leeds Discovery Centre C5
Leeds General Infirmary (A&E) A3
Leeds Station B3
Library B3/B4
Light, The B4
Lincoln Green Rd A6
Lincoln Rd A6
Lindsey Gdns A6
Lindsey Rd A6
Lisbon St B3
Little Queen St B3
Long Close La C6
Lord St C2
Lovell Park A4
Lovell Park Hill A4
Lovell Park Rd A4
Lower Brunswick St A5
Mabgate A5
Macaulay St A5
Magistrates Court A3
Manor Rd C3
Mark La B4
Marlborough St B2
Marsh La B5
Marshall St C3
Meadow La C4
Meadow Rd C4
Melbourne St A5
Merrion Centre A4
Merrion St A4
Merrion Way A4
Mill St B5
Millennium Sq A3
Mount Preston St A2
Mushroom St A5
Neville St C4
New Briggate A4/B4
New Market St B4
New York Rd A5
New York St B5
Nile St A5
Nippet La A6
North St A4
Northern St B3
Oak Rd B1
Oxford Pl B3
Oxford Row A3
Parade, The B6
Park Cross St B3
Park La A2
Park Pl B3
Park Row B4
Park Sq B3
Park Sq East B3
Park Sq West B3
Park St B3
Police Station B5
Pontefract La B6
Portland Cr A3
Portland Way A3
Post Office B4/B5
Quarry Ho (NHS/DSS HQ) B5
Quebec St B3
Queen St B3
Railway St B5
Rectory St A6
Regent St A5
Richmond St C5
Rigton Approach B6
Rigton Dr B6
Rillbank La A1
Rosebank Rd A1
Rose Bowl Conference Ctr A3
Royal Armouries C5
Russell St B3
St Anne's Cathedral (RC) A4
St Anne's St B4
St James' Hosp A6
St John's Rd A2
St Johns Centre B4
St Mary's St B5
St Pauls St B3
St Peter's B5
Saxton La B5
Sayner La C5
Shakespeare Ave A6
Shannon St B6
Sheepscar St South A5
Siddall St C3
Skinner La A5
South Pde B3
Sovereign St C4
Spence La C2
Springfield Mount A2
Springwell Ct C2
Springwell Rd C2
Springwell St C2
Stoney Rock La A6
Studio Rd A1
Sutton St C2
Sweet St C3
Sweet St West C3
Swinegate B4
Templar St B5
Tetley, The C4
Thoresby Pl A3
Torre Rd A6
Town Hall A3
Union Pl C3
Union St B5
University of Leeds A3
Upper Accomodation Rd B6
Upper Basinghall St B4
Vicar La B4
Victoria Bridge C4
Victoria Quarter B4
Victoria Rd C4
Vue B4
Wade La A4
Washington St A1
Water La C3
Waterloo Rd C4
Wellington Rd B2/C1
Wellington St B3
West St B2
West Yorkshire Playhouse B5
Westfield Rd A1
Westgate B3
Whitehall Rd B3/C2
Whitelock St A5
Willis St C6
Willow Approach A1
Willow Ave A1
Willow Terrace Rd A3
Wintoun St A5
Woodhouse La A3/A4
Woodsley Rd A1
York Pl B3
York Rd B6

Leicester 118

Abbey St A2
All Saints' A1
Aylestone Rd C2
Bath La A1
Bede Park C1
Bedford St A3
Bedford St South A3
Belgrave Gate A2
Belvoir St B2
Braunstone Gate B1
Burleys Way A2
Burnmoor St C2
Bus & Coach Sta A2
Canning St A2
Carlton St C2
Castle B1
Castle Gardens B1
Cathedral B2
Causeway La A2
Charles St B3
Chatham St B2
Christow St A3
Church Gate A2
City Gallery B3
City Hall B3
Clank St B2
Clock Tower B2
Clyde St A3
Colton St B3
Conduit St B3
Crafton St A3
Craven St A1
Crown Courts B3
Curve B3
De Lux A2
De Montfort Hall C3
De Montfort St C3
De Montfort Univ C1
Deacon St C2
Dover St B3
Duns La B1
Dunton St A1
East St B3
Eastern Boulevard C1
Edmonton Rd A3
Erskine St A3
Filbert St C1
Filbert St East C2
Fire Station C3
Fleet St A3
Friar La B2
Friday St A2
Gateway St C2
Gateway, The C2
Glebe St B3
Granby St B3
Grange La C2
Grasmere St C1
Great Central St A1
Guildhall B2
Guru Nanak Sikh Museum B1
Halford St B2
Havelock St C2
Haymarket Shopping Centre A2
High St A2
Highcross Shopping Centre A2
Highcross St A1
HM Prison C2
Horsefair St B2
Humberstone Gate B2
Humberstone Rd A3
Infirmary St C2
Information Ctr B2
Jarrom St C2
Jewry Wall B1
Kamloops Cr A3
King St B2
Lancaster Rd C3
LCB Depot B3
Lee St A3
Leicester Royal Infirmary (A&E) C2
Leicester Station B3
Library B2
London Rd C3
Lower Brown St B2
Magistrates' Court B2
Manitoba Rd A3
Mansfield St A2
Market B2
Market St B2
Mill La C2
Montreal Rd A3
Narborough Rd North B1
Nelson Mandela Pk C2
New Park St B1
New St B2
New Walk C3
New Walk Museum & Art Gallery C3
Newarke Houses B2
Newarke St B2
Newarke, The B1
Northgate St A1
Orchard St A2
Ottawa Rd A3
Oxford St C2
Phoenix Arts Ctr B3
Police Station A3
Post Office A1/B2/C3
Prebend St C3
Princess Rd East C3
Princess Rd West C3
Queen St B3
Rally Com Pk, The A2
Regent College C3
Regent Rd C2/C3
Repton St A1
Rutland St B3
St Augustine Rd B1
St Georges Retail Park B3
St George St B3
St Georges Way B3
St John St A2
St Margaret's A2
St Margaret's Way A2
St Martins B2
St Mary de Castro B1
St Matthew's Way A3
St Nicholas B1
St Nicholas Circle B1
Sanvey Gate A2
Silver St B2
Slater St A1
Soar La A1
South Albion St B3
Southampton St B3
Sue Townsend Theatre B2
Swain St B3
Swan St A1
Tigers Way C3
Tower St C3
Town Hall B2
Tudor Rd B1
Univ of Leicester C3
University Rd C3
Upper Brown St B2
Upperton Rd C1
Vaughan Way A2
Walnut St C2
Watling St A2
Welford Rd B2
Welford Rd Leicester Tigers RC C2
Wellington St B2
West St C3
West Walk C3
Western Boulevard C1
Western Rd C1
Wharf St North A3
Wharf St South A3
Y Theatre, The B3
Yeoman St B3
York Rd B2

Lincoln 118

Alexandra Terr B1
Anchor St C1
Arboretum B3
Arboretum Ave B3
Avenue, The B1
Baggholme Rd B3
Bailgate A2
Beaumont Fee B1
BMI The Lincoln Hospital A2
Brayford Way C1
Brayford Wharf East C1
Brayford Wharf North B1
Bruce Rd A2
Burton Rd A1
Bus Station (City) C2
Canwick Rd C2
Cardinal's Hat B2
Carline Rd B1
Castle B1
Castle St A1
Cathedral B2
Cathedral St B2
Cecil St A2
Chapel La A2
Cheviot St B3
Church La A2
City Hall B1
Clasketgate B2
Clayton Sports Gd A3
Coach Park C2
Collection, The B2
County Hospital (A&E) B3
County Office B1
Courts C1
Cross St C2
Crown Courts B1
Curle Ave A3
Danesgate B2
Drill Hall B2
Drury La B1
East Bight A2
East Gate A2
Eastcliff Rd B3
Eastgate B2
Egerton Rd A3
Ellis Windmill A1
Engine Shed, The C1
Environment Agency C2
Exchequer Gate B2
Firth Rd C1
Flaxengate B2
Florence St B3
George St C3
Good La A2
Gray St A1
Great Northern Terr C3
Great Northern Terrace Ind Est C3
Greetwell Rd B3
Greetwellgate B3
Grove, The A3
Haffenden Rd A2
High St B2/C1
HM Prison A3
Hungate B2
James St A2
Jews House & Ct B2
Kesteven St C2
Langworthgate A2
Lawn, The B1
Lee Rd A3
Library B2
Lincoln Central Station C2
Lincoln College B2
Lincolnshire Life/ Royal Lincolnshire Regiment Mus A1
Lincoln University Technical College (UTC) B2
Lindum Rd B2
Lindum Sports Gd A3
Lindum Terr B3
Mainwaring Rd A3
Manor Rd A2
Market C2
Massey Rd A3
Medieval Bishop's Palace B2
Mildmay St A1
Mill Rd A1
Millman Rd B3
Minster Yard B2
Monks Rd B3
Montague St B2
Mount St A1
Nettleham Rd A2
Newland B1
Newport A2
Newport Arch A2
Newport Cemetery A2
Northgate A2
Odeon C1
Orchard St B1
Oxford St C2
Park St B1
Pelham Bridge C2
Pelham St C2
Police Station B1
Portland St C2
Post Office A1/B3/C2
Potter Gate B2
Priory Gate B2
Queensway A3
Rasen La A1
Ropewalk C1
Rosemary La B2
St Anne's Rd B3
St Benedict's C1
St Giles Ave A3
St Mark's Shopping Centre C1
St Marks St C1
St Mary-le-Wigford C1
St Mary's St C2
St Nicholas St A2
St Rumbold's St B2
St Swithin's B2
Saltergate C1
Saxon St A1
Sewell Rd B3
Silver St B2
Sincil St C2
Spital St A2
Spring Hill B1
Stamp End C3
Steep Hill B2
Stonebow & Guildhall C2
Stonefield Ave A2
Tentercroft St C1
Theatre Royal B2
Tritton Rd C1
Tritton Retail Park C1
Union Rd B1
Univ of Lincoln C1
Upper Lindum St B3
Upper Long Leys Rd A1
Usher B2
Vere St A2
Victoria St B1
Victoria Terr B1
Vine St B3
Wake St A1
Waldeck St A1
Waterside North C2
Waterside Shopping Centre C2
Waterside South C2
West Pde B1
Westgate A2
Wigford Way C1
Williamson St A2
Wilson St A1
Winn St B3
Wragby Rd A3
Yarborough Rd A1

Liverpool 119

Abercromby Sq C5
Addison St A3
Adelaide Rd B6
Ainsworth St B4
Albany Rd B6
Albert Edward Rd B6
Angela St C6
Anson St B4
Argyle St C3
Arrad St C4
Ashton St B5
Audley St A4
Back Leeds St A2
Basnett St B3
Bath St A1
Beacon, The B3
Beatles Story C2
Beckwith St C3
Bedford Close C5
Bedford St North C5
Bedford St South C5
Benson St C4
Berry St C4
Birkett St A4
Bixteth St B2
Blackburne Place C4
Bluecoat B3
Bold Place C4
Bold St C4
Bolton St B3
Bridport St B4
Bronte St B4
Brook St A1
Brownlow Hill B4/B5
Brownlow St B5
Brunswick Rd A5
Brunswick St B1
Bus Station C2
Butler Cr A6
Byrom St A3
Caledonia St C4
Cambridge St C5
Camden St A4
Canada Blvd B1
Canning Dock C2
Canterbury St A4
Cardwell St C6
Carver St A4
Cases St B3
Castle St B2
Catherine St C5
Cavern Club B3
Central Library A3
Central Station B3
Chapel St B2
Charlotte St B3
Chatham Place C6
Chatham St C5
Cheapside B2
Cherasse Park C5
Chestnut St C5
Christian St A3
Church St B3
Churchill Way North A3
Churchill Way South B3
Clarence St B4
Coach Station A4
Cobden St A5
Cockspur St A2
College St C3
College St North A5
College St South A5
Colquitt St C4
Comus St A3
Concert St C3
Connaught Rd B6
Cook St B2
Copperas Hill B4
Cornwallis St C3
Covent Garden B2
Craven St A4
Cropper St B3
Crown St B5/C6
Cumberland St B2
Cunard Building B1
Dale St B2
Dansie St B4
Daulby St B5
Dawson St B3
Derby Sq B2
Drury La B2
Duckinfield St B4
Duke St C3
Earle St A2
East St A2
Eaton St A2
Echo Arena C2
Edgar St A3
Edge La B6
Edinburgh Rd A6
Edmund St B2
Elizabeth St B5
Elliot St B3
Empire Theatre B4
Empress Rd B6
Epstein Theatre B3
Epworth St A5
Erskine St A5
Everyman Theatre C5
Exchange St East B2
FACT C4
Falkland St A5
Falkner St C5/C6
Farnworth St A6
Fenwick St B2
Fielding St A6
Fire Sta A4
Fleet St C3
Fraser St A4
Freemasons Row A2
Gardner Row A3
Gascoyne St A2
George Pier Head C1
George St B2
Gibraltar Road A1
Gilbert St C3
Gildart St A4
Gill St B4
Goree B2
Gower St C2
Gradwell St C3
Great Crosshall St A3
Great George St C4
Great Howard St A1
Great Newton St B4
Greek St B4
Green La B4
Greenside A5
Greetham St C3
Gregson St A5
Grenville St C3
Grinfield St C6
Grove St C5
Guelph St A6
Hackins Hey B2
Haigh St A4
Hall La B6
Hanover St B3
Harbord St C6
Hardman St C4
Harker St A4
Hart St B4
Hatton Garden A2
Hawke St B4
Helsby St B6
Henry St C3
Highfield St A2
Highgate St B6
Hilbre St B4
HM Customs & Excise National Mus C2
Hope Place C4
Hope St C4
Hope University A5
Houghton St B3
Hunter St A3
Hutchinson St A6
Information Ctr B4/C2
Institute for the Performing Arts C4
Int Slavery C2
Irvine St B6
Irwell St B2
Islington A4
James St B2
James St Station B2
Jenkinson St A4
John Moores Univ A2/A3/A4/B4/C4
Johnson St A3
Jubilee Drive B6
Kempston St A4
Kensington A6
Kensington Gdns B6
Kensington St A6
Kent St C3
King Edward St A1
Kinglake St B6
Knight St C4
Lace St A3
Langsdale St A4
Law Courts C2
Leece St C4
Leeds St A2
Leopold Rd B6
Lime St B3
Lime St Station B4
Little Woolton St B5
Liver St C2
Liverpool Landing Stage B1
Liverpool Institute for Performing Arts C4
Liverpool ONE C2
Liverpool Wheel, The C2
London Rd A4/B4
Lord Nelson St B4
Lord St B2
Lovat St C6
Low Hill A5
Low Wood St A6
Lydia Ann St C3
Mansfield St A4
Marmaduke St B6
Marsden St A6
Martensen St B6
Marybone A3
Maryland St C4
Mason St B6
Mathew St B2
May St B4
Melville Place C6
Merseyside Maritime Museum C2
Metquarter B3
Metropolitan Cathedral (RC) B5
Midghall St A2
Molyneux Rd A6
Moor Place B4
Moorfields B2
Moorfields Sta B2
Moss St A5
Mount Pleasant B4/B5
Mount St C4
Mount Vernon B6
Mulberry St C5
Municipal Bldgs B2
Mus of Liverpool C2
Myrtle Gdns C6
Myrtle St C5
Naylor St A2
Nelson St C4
New Islington A4
New Quay B1
Newington St C3
North John St B2
North St A3
North View B6
Norton St A4
O2 Academy B4
Oakes St B5
Odeon B2
Old Hall St A1
Old Leeds St A2
Oldham Place C4
Oldham St C4
Olive St C6
Open Eye Gallery C2
Oriel St A2
Ormond St B2
Orphan St C6
Overbury St C6
Overton St B6
Oxford St C5
Paisley St A1
Pall Mall A2
Paradise St C3
Park La C3
Parker St B3
Parr St C3
Peach St B5
Pembroke Place B4
Pembroke St B5
Philharmonic Hall C5
Pickop St A2
Pilgrim St C4
Pitt St C3
Playhouse Theatre B3
Pleasant St B4
Police HQ C2
Police Station A4/A6/B4
Pomona St B4
Port of Liverpool Building B2
Post Office A2/A4/A5/B2/B3/B4/C4
Pownall St C2

Prescot St A5
Preston St B3
Princes Dock A1
Princes Gdns A2
Princes Jetty A1
Princes Pde B1
Princes St B2
Pythian St A6
Queen Sq Bus Sta B3
Queensland St C6
Queensway Tunnel (Docks exit) B1
Queensway Tunnel (Entrance) B3
Radio City B2
Ranelagh St B3
Redcross St B2
Renfrew St B6
Renshaw St B4
Richmond Row A4
Richmond St B3
Rigby St A2
Roberts St A1
Rock St B4
Rodney St C4
Rokeby St A4
Romily St A6
Roscoe La C4
Roscoe St C4
Rose Hill A3
Royal Albert Dock C2
Royal Ct Theatre B3
Royal Liver Building B1
Royal Liverpool Hospital (A&E) B5
Royal Mail St B4
Rumford Place B2
Rumford St B2
Russell St B4
St Andrew St B4
St Anne St A4
St Georges Hall B3
St John's Centre B3
St John's Gdns B3
St John's La B3
St Joseph's Cr A4
St Minishull St B5
St Nicholas Place B1
St Paul's Sq A2
St Vincent Way B4
Salisbury St A4
Salthouse Dock C2
Salthouse Quay C2
Sandon St C5
Saxony Rd B6
Schomberg St A6
School La B2
Seel St C3
Seymour St B4
Shaw St A5
Shopmobility C2
Sidney Place C6
Sir Thomas St B3
Skelhorne St B4
Slater St C3
Smithdown La B6
Soho Sq A4
Soho St A4
South John St B2
Springfield A4
Stafford St A4
Standish St A3
Stanley St B2
Strand St C2
Strand, The B2
Suffolk St C3
Tabley St C3
Tarleton St B3
Tate Gallery C2
Teck St B6
Temple St B2
Tithebarn St B2
Town Hall B2
Traffic Police HQ C6
Trowbridge St B4
Trueman St A3
Union St B2
Unity Theatre C4
University C5
Univ of Liverpool B5
Upper Baker St A6
Upper Duke St C4
Upper Frederick St C3
Vauxhall Rd A2
Vernon St B2
Victoria Gallery & Museum B5
Victoria St B2
Vine St C5
Wakefield St A4
Walker Art Gallery A3
Walker St A6
Wapping C2
Water St B1/B2
Waterloo Rd A1
Wavertree Rd B6
West Derby Rd A6
West Derby St B5
Western Approaches War Museum B2
Whitechapel B3
Whitley Gdns A5
William Brown St B3
William Henry St A4
Williamson Sq B3
Williamson St B3
Williamson's Tunnels Heritage Ctr C6
Women's Hosp C6
Wood St B3
World Museum, Liverpool A3
York St C3

London 120

Abbey Orchard St E3
Abchurch La D6
Abingdon St E4
Achilles Way D2
Acton St B4
Addington St E4
Air St D3
Albany St B2
Albemarle St D3
Albert Emb F4
Aldenham St A3
Aldersgate St C6
Aldford St D2
Aldgate C7
Aldgate High St C7
Aldwych C4
Allsop Pl B1
Amwell St B5
Andrew Borde St C3
Angel A5
Appold St C7
Argyle Sq B4
Argyle St B4
Argyll St C3
Arnold Circus B7
Artillery La C7
Artillery Row E3
Association of Photographers Gallery B6
Baker St B1
Baker St B1
Baldwin's Gdns C5
Baltic St B6
Bank C6
Bank Museum C6
Bank of England C6
Bankside D6
Bankside Gallery D5
Banner St B6
Barbican C6
Barbican Centre for Arts, The C6
Barbican Gallery C6
Basil St E1
Bastwick St B6
Bateman's Row B7
Bath St B6
Bayley St C3
Baylis Rd E5
Beak St D3
Bedford Row C4
Bedford Sq C3
Bedford St D4
Bedford Way B3
Beech St C6
Belgrave Pl E2
Belgrave Sq E2
Bell La C7
Belvedere Rd E4
Berkeley Sq D2
Berkeley St D2
Bernard St B4
Berners Pl C3
Berners St C3
Berwick St C3
Bethnal Green Rd B7
Bevenden St B6
Bevis Marks C7
BFI (British Film Institute) D4
BFI London IMAX Cinema D5
Bidborough St B4
Binney St C2
Birdcage Walk E3
Bishopsgate C7
Blackfriars D5
Blackfriars Bridge D5
Blackfriars Rd E5
Blandford St C1
Blomfield St C6
Bloomsbury St C3
Bloomsbury Way C4
Bolton St D2
Bond St C2
Borough High St E6
Boswell St C4
Bow St C4
Bowling Green La B5
Brad St D5
Bressenden Pl E3
Brewer St D3
Brick St D2
Bridge St E4
Britannia Walk B6
British Film Institute (BFI) D4
British Library B3
British Museum C4
Britton St B5
Broad Sanctuary E3
Broadway E3
Brook Dr F5
Brook St D2
Brunswick Pl B6
Brunswick Shopping Centre, The B4
Brunswick Sq B4
Brushfield St C7
Bruton St D2
Bryanston St C1
BT Centre C6
Buckingham Gate E3
Buckingham Palace E3
Buckingham Palace Rd F2
Bunhill Row B6
Byward St D7
Cabinet War Rooms & Churchill Mus E3
Cadogan La E2
Cadogan Pl E1
Cadogan Sq F1
Caledonian Rd A4
Calshot St A4
Calthorpe St B4
Calvert Ave B7
Cambridge Circus C3
Camomile St C7
Cannon St D6
Cannon St D6
Carey St C4
Carlisle La E4
Carlisle Pl E3
Carlton House Terr D3
Carmelite St D5
Carnaby St C3
Carter La C5
Carthusian St C6
Cartwright Gdns B4
Castle Baynard St D5
Cavendish Pl C2
Cavendish Sq C2
Caxton Hall E3
Caxton St E3
Central St B6
Chalton St B3
Chancery Lane C5
Chapel St E2
Charing Cross D4
Charing Cross Rd C3
Charles II St D3
Charles Sq B6
Charles St D2
Charlotte Rd B7
Charlotte St C3
Chart St B6
Charterhouse Sq C5
Charterhouse St C5
Cheapside C6
Chenies St C3
Chesham St E2
Chester Sq F2
Chesterfield Hill D2
Chiltern St C2
Chiswell St C6
City Garden Row A5
City Rd B6
City Thameslink C5
City University, The B5
Claremont Sq A5
Clarges St D2
Clerkenwell Cl B5
Clerkenwell Green B5
Clerkenwell Rd B5
Cleveland St C3
Clifford St D3
Clink Prison Museum D6
Clock Museum C6
Club Row B7
Cockspur St D3
Coleman St C6
Columbia Rd B7
Commercial St C7
Compton St B5
Conduit St D2
Constitution Hill E2
Copperfield St E5
Coptic St C4
Cornhill C6
Cornwall Rd D5
Coronet St B7
Courtauld Gallery D4
Covent Garden D4
Covent Garden D4
Cowcross St C5
Cowper St B6
Cranbourn St D3
Craven St D4
Crawford St C1
Creechurch La C7
Cremer St A7
Cromer St B4
Cumberland Gate D1
Cumberland Terr A2
Curtain Rd B7
Curzon St D2
Cut, The E5
D'arblay St C3
Davies St C2
Dean St C3
Deluxe Gallery B7
Denmark St C3
Dering St C2
Devonshire St C2
Diana, Princess of Wales Meml Wlk E3
Dingley Rd B6
Dorset St C1
Doughty St B4
Dover St D2
Downing St E4
Druid St E7
Drummond St B3
Drury La C4
Drysdale St B7
Duchess St C2
Dufferin St B6
Duke of Wellington Place E2
Duke St C2
Duke St D3
Duke St Hill D6
Duke's Pl C7
Duncannon St D4
East Rd B6
Eastcastle St C3
Eastcheap D7
Eastman Dental Hospital B4
Eaton Pl E2
Eaton Sq E2
Eccleston St E2
Edgware Rd C1
Eldon St C6
Embankment D4
Endell St C4
Endsleigh Pl B3
Euston B3
Euston Rd B3
Euston Square B3
Evelina Children's Hospital E4
Eversholt St A3
Exmouth Market B5
Fann St B6
Farringdon C5
Farringdon Rd C5
Farringdon St C5
Featherstone St B6
Fenchurch St D7
Fenchurch St D7
Fetter La C5
Finsbury Circus C6
Finsbury Pavement C6
Finsbury Sq B6
Fitzalan St F5
Fitzmaurice Pl D2
Fleet St C5
Floral St D4
Florence Nightingale Museum E4
Folgate St C7
Foot Hospital B3
Fore St C6
Foster La C6
Francis St F3
Frazier St E5
Freemason's Hall C4
Friday St C6
Gainsford St E7
Garden Row E5
Gee St B6
George St C1
Gerrard St D3
Giltspur St C5
Glasshouse St D3
Gloucester Pl C1
Golden Hinde D6
Golden La B6
Golden Sq D3
Goodge St C3
Goodge St C3
Gordon Sq B3
Goswell Rd B5
Gough St B4
Goulston St C7
Gower St B3
Gracechurch St D6
Grafton Way B3
Gray's Inn Rd B4
Great College St E4
Great Cumberland Place C1
Great Eastern St B7
Great Guildford St D6
Great Marlborough St C3
Great Ormond St B4
Great Ormond St Children's Hosp B4
Great Percy St B4
Great Peter St E3
Great Portland Street B2
Great Portland St C2
Great Queen St C4
Great Russell St C3
Great Scotland Yd D4
Great Smith St E3
Great Suffolk St D5
Great Titchfield St C3
Great Tower St D7
Great Windmill St D3
Greek St C3
Green Park D3
Green St D2
Greencoat Pl F3
Gresham St C6
Greville St B4/C5
Greycoat Hosp Sch E3
Greycoat Pl E3
Grosvenor Cres E2
Grosvenor Gdns E2
Grosvenor Pl E2
Grosvenor Sq D2
Grosvenor St D2
Guards Museum and Chapel E3
Guildhall Art Gallery C6
Guilford St B4
Guy's Hospital D6
Haberdasher St B6
Hackney Rd B7
Half Moon St D2
Halkin St E2
Hall St B5
Hallam St C2
Hampstead Rd B3
Hanover Sq C2
Hans Cres E1
Hanway St C3
Hardwick St B5
Harley St C2
Harrison St B4
Hastings St B4
Hatfields D5
Hay's Galleria D7
Hay's Mews D2
Hayles St F5
Haymarket D3
Hayne St C5
Hayward Gallery D4
Helmet Row B6
Herbrand St B4
Hercules Rd E4
Hertford St D2
High Holborn C4
Hill St D2
HMS Belfast D7
Hobart Pl E2
Holborn C4
Holborn C5
Holborn Viaduct C5
Holland St D5
Holmes Mus B1
Holywell La B7
Horse Guards' Rd D3
Houndsditch C7
Houses of Parliament E4
Howland St C3
Hoxton Sq B7
Hoxton St B7
Hunter St B4
Hunterian Mus C4
Hyde Park D1
Hyde Park Cnr E2
Imperial War Museum E5
Inner Circle B2
Inst of Archaeology (London Univ) B2
Ironmonger Row B6
James St C2
James St D4
Jermyn St D3
Jockey's Fields C4
John Carpenter St D5
John St B4
Judd St B4
Kennington Rd E5
King Charles St E4
King St D3
King St D4
King William St C6
King's Coll London D5
King's Cross A4
King's Cross Rd B4
King's Cross St Pancras A4
King's Rd E2
Kingley St C3
Kingsland Rd B7
Kingsway C4
Kinnerton St E2
Knightsbridge E1
Lamb St C7
Lamb's Conduit St C4
Lambeth Bridge F4
Lambeth High St F4
Lambeth North E5
Lambeth Palace E4
Lambeth Palace Rd E4
Lambeth Rd E5
Lambeth Walk F4
Lancaster Pl D4
Langham Pl C2
Leadenhall St C7
Leake St E4
Leather La C5
Leicester Sq D3
Leicester St D3
Leonard St B6
Lever St B6
Lexington St D3
Lidlington Pl A3
Lime St D7
Lincoln's Inn Fields C4
Lindsey St C5
Lisle St D3
Liverpool St C7
Liverpool St C7
Lloyd Baker St B5
Lloyd Sq B5
Lombard St C6
London Aquarium E4
London Bridge D6
London Bridge Hospital D6
London City Hall D7
London Dungeon, The E4
London Film Museum E4
London Guildhall University C6
London Rd E5
London Transport Museum D4
London Wall C6
London Eye E4
Long Acre D4
Long La C5
Longford St B2
Lower Belgrave St E2
Lower Grosvenor Pl E2
Lower Marsh E5
Lower Thames St D6
Lowndes St E2
Ludgate Circus C5
Ludgate Hill C5
Luxborough St C2
Lyall St E2
Macclesfield Rd B6
Madame Tussaud's B2
Maddox St D2
Malet St C3
Mall, The E3
Manchester Sq C2
Manchester St C2
Mandeville Pl C2
Mansell St D7
Mansion House C6
Mansion House D6
Maple St C3
Marble Arch C1
Marble Arch D1
Marchmont St B4
Margaret St C3
Margery St B5
Mark La D7
Marlborough Rd D3
Marshall St C3
Marsham St E3
Marylebone High St C2
Marylebone La C2
Marylebone Rd B2
Marylebone St C2
Mecklenburgh Sq B4
Middle Temple La C5
Middlesex St (Petticoat La) C7
Midland Rd A3
Migration Mus F5
Minories C7
Monck St E3
Monmouth St C4
Montagu Pl C1
Montagu Sq C1
Montagu St C4
Montague Pl C3
Monument D6
Monument St D6
Monument, The D6
Moor La C6
Moorfields C6
Moorfields Eye Hospital B6
Moorgate C6
Moorgate C6
Moreland St B5
Morley St E5
Mortimer St C3
Mount Pleasant B5
Mount St D2
Murray Gr A6
Museum of Garden History E4
Mus of London C6
Museum St C4
Myddelton Sq B5
Myddelton St B5
National Gallery D3
National Hosp B4
National Portrait Gallery D3
Neal St C4
Nelson's Column D4
New Bond St C2/D2
New Bridge St C5
New Cavendish St C2
New Change C6
New Fetter La C5
New Inn Yard B7
New North Rd A6
New Oxford St C3
New Scotland Yard E3
New Sq C4
Newgate St C5
Newton St C4
Nile St B6
Noble St C6
Noel St C3
North Audley St D2
North Cres C3
North Row D2
Northampton Sq B5
Northington St B4
Northumberland Ave D4
Norton Folgate C7
Nottingham Pl C2
Obstetric Hosp B3
Old Bailey C5
Old Broad St C6
Old Compton St C3
Old County Hall E4
Old Gloucester St C4
Old King Edward St C6
Old Nichol St B7
Old Paradise St F4
Old Spitalfields Market C7
Old St B6
Old St B6
Old Vic E5
Open Air Theatre B2
Operating Theatre Museum D6
Orange St D3
Orchard St C2
Ossulston St A3
Outer Circle B1
Oxford Circus C3
Oxford St C2/C3
Paddington St C2
Palace St E3
Pall Mall D3
Pall Mall East D3
Pancras Rd A4
Panton St D3
Paris Gdn D5
Park Cres B2
Park La D2
Park Rd B1
Park St D2
Park St D6
Parker St C4
Parliament Sq E4
Parliament St E4
Paternoster Sq C5
Paul St B6
Pear Tree St B5
Penton Rise B4
Penton St A5
Pentonville Rd A4/A5
Percival St B5
Petticoat La (Middlesex St) C7
Petty France E3
Phoenix Pl B4
Phoenix Rd A3
Photo Gallery D3
Piccadilly D2
Piccadilly Cir D3
Pitfield St B7
Pollock's Toy Museum C3
Polygon Rd A3
Pont St E1
Portland Pl C2
Portman Mews C2
Portman Sq C2
Portman St C1
Portugal St C4
Poultry C6
Primrose St C7
Princes St C6
Procter St C4
Provost St B6
Quaker St B7
Queen Anne St C2
Queen Elizabeth Hall D4
Queen Sq B4
Queen St D6
Queen Street Pl D6
Queen Victoria St D5
Queens Gallery E3
Radnor St B6
Rathbone Pl C3
Rawstorne St B5
Red Lion Sq C4
Red Lion St C4
Redchurch St B7
Redcross Way D6
Regency St F3
Regent Sq B4
Regent St C3
Regent's Park B2
Richmond Terr E4
Ridgmount St C3
Rivington St B7
Robert St B2
Rochester Row F3
Ropemaker St C6
Rosebery Ave B5
Roupell St D5
Royal Academy of Arts D3
Royal Academy of Dramatic Art B3
Royal Academy of Music B2
Royal Artillery Memorial E2
Royal College of Nursing C2
Royal College of Surgeons C4
Royal Festival Hall D4
Royal London Hosp for Integrated Medicine C4
Royal National Theatre D5
Royal National Throat, Nose and Ear Hospital B4
Royal Opera Ho D4
Russell Sq B3
Russell Square B4
Sackville St D3
Sadlers Wells B5
Saffron Hill C5
St Alban's St D3
St Andrew St C5
St Bartholomew's Hospital C5
St Botolph St C7
St Bride St C5
St George's Circus E5
St George's Rd E5
St Giles High St C3
St James's Pal D3
St James's Park E3
St James's St D3
St John St B5
St Margaret St E4
St Mark's Hosp B5
St Martin's La D4
St Martin's Le Grand C6
St Mary Axe C7
St Pancras Int A4
St Paul's C6
St Paul's Cath C6
St Paul's Churchyard C5
St Peter's Hosp D4
St Thomas St D6
St Thomas' Hosp E4
Savile Row D3
Savoy Pl D4
Savoy St D4
School of Hygiene & Tropical Medicine C3
Scrutton St B7
Sekforde St B5
Serpentine Rd D1
Seven Dials C4
Seward St B5
Seymour St C1
Shad Thames D7
Shaftesbury Ave D3
Shakespeare's Globe Theatre D6
Shepherd Market D2
Sherwood St D3
Shoe La C5
Shoreditch High St B7
Shoreditch High St B7
Shorts Gdns C4
Sidmouth St B4
Silk St C6
Sir John Soane's Museum C4
Skinner St B5
Sloane St E1
Snow Hill C5
Soho Sq C3
Somerset Ho D4
South Audley St D2
South Carriage Dr E1
South Molton St C2
South Pl C6
South St D2
Southampton Row C4
Southampton St D4
Southwark D5
Southwark Bridge D6
Southwark Bridge Rd D6
Southwark Cath D6
Southwark St D6
Speakers' Corner D1
Spencer St B5
Spital Sq C7
Stamford St D5
Stanhope St B3
Stephenson Way B3
Stock Exchange C5
Stoney St D6
Strand C5
Stratton St D2
Sumner St D5
Sutton's Way B6
Swanfield St B7
Swinton St B4
Tabernacle St B6
Tate Modern D6
Tavistock Pl B4
Tavistock Sq B3
Tea & Coffee Museum D6
Temple D5
Temple Ave D5
Temple Pl D4
Terminus Pl E2
Thayer St C2
Theobald's Rd C4
Thorney St F4
Threadneedle St C6
Throgmorton St C6
Tonbridge St B4
Tooley St D7
Torrington Pl B3
Tothill St E3
Tottenham Ct Rd B3
Tottenham Ct Rd C3
Tottenham St C3
Tower Bridge D7
Tower Bridge App D7
Tower Bridge Rd E7
Tower Hill D7
Tower Hill D7
Tower of London, The D7
Toynbee St C7
Trafalgar Square D3
Trinity Sq D7
Trocadero Centre D3
Tudor St D5
Turnmill St C5
Ufford St E5
Union St D5
Univ Coll Hosp B3
Univ of London C3
University of Westminster C2
University St B3
Upper Belgrave St E2
Upper Berkeley St C1
Upper Brook St D2
Upper Grosvenor St D2
Upper Ground D5
Upper Montague St C1
Upper St Martin's La D4
Upper Thames St D6
Upper Wimpole St C2
Upper Woburn Pl B3
Vere St C2
Vernon Pl C4
Vestry St B6
Victoria E2
Victoria Emb D4
Victoria Place Shopping Centre F2
Victoria St E3
Villiers St D4
Vincent Sq F3
Vinopolis City of Wine D6
Virginia Rd B7
Wakley St B5
Walbrook C6
Wallace Collection C2
Wardour St C3/D3
Warner St B5
Warren St B3
Warren St B3
Waterloo E5
Waterloo Bridge D4
Waterloo East D5
Waterloo Rd E5
Watling St C6
Webber St E5
Welbeck St C2
Wellington Arch E2
Wellington Mus E2
Wells St C3
Wenlock St A6
Wentworth St C7
West Smithfield C5
West Sq E5
Westminster E4
Westminster Abbey E4
Westminster Bridge E4
Westminster Bridge Rd E5
Westminster Cathedral (RC) E3
Westminster City Hall E3
Westminster Hall E4
Weymouth St C2
Wharf Rd A6
Wharton St B4
Whitcomb St D3
White Cube B7
White Lion Hill D5
White Lion St A5
Whitecross St B6
Whitefriars St C5
Whitehall D4
Whitehall Pl D4
Wigmore Hall C2
Wigmore St C2
William IV St D4
Wilmington Sq B5
Wilson St C6
Wilton Cres E2
Wimpole St C2
Windmill Walk D5
Woburn Pl B4
Woburn Sq B3
Women's Hosp C3
Wood St C6
Woodbridge St B5
Wootton St D5
Wormwood St C7
Worship St B6
Wren St B4
Wynyatt St B5
York Rd E4
York St C1
York Terrace East B2
York Terrace West B2
York Way A4

Luton 119

Adelaide St B1
Albert Rd C2
Alma St B2
Alton Rd C3
Anthony Gdns C1
Arthur St C2
Ashburnham Rd B1
Ashton Rd C2
Avondale Rd A1
Back St A2
Bailey St C3
Baker St C2
Biscot Rd A1
Bolton Rd B3
Boyle Close A2
Brantwood Rd B1
Bretts Mead C1
Bridge St B2
Brook St A1
Brunswick St A3
Burr St A3
Bury Park Rd A1
Bute St B2
Buxton Rd B2
Cambridge St C3
Cardiff Grove B1
Cardiff Rd B1
Cardigan St A2
Castle St B2/C2
Chapel St C2
Charles St A3
Chase St C2
Cheapside B2
Chequer St C3
Chiltern Rise C1
Church St B2/B3
Cinema A2
Cobden St A3
College A3
Collingdon St A1
Community Centre C3
Concorde Ave A3
Corncastle Rd C1
Cowper St C2
Crawley Green Rd B3
Crawley Rd A1
Crescent Rd A3
Crescent Rise A3
Cromwell Rd A1
Cross St A2
Cross Way, The C1
Crown Court B2
Cumberland St B2
Cutenhoe Rd C3
Dallow Rd B1
Downs Rd B1
Dudley St A2
Duke St A2
Dumfries St B1
Dunstable Place B2
Dunstable Rd A1/B1
Edward St A3
Elizabeth St C2
Essex Cl C3
Farley Hill C1
Farley Lodge C1
Flowers Way B2
Francis St A1
Frederick St A2
Galaxy Leisure Complex A2
George St B2
George St West B2
Gordon St B2
Grove Rd B1
Guildford St A2
Haddon Rd A3
Harcourt St C2
Hart Hill Drive A3
Hart Hill Lane A3
Hartley Rd A3
Hastings St B2
Hat Factory, The B2
Hatters Way A1
Havelock Rd A2
Hibbert St C2
High Town Rd A3
Highbury Rd A1
Hightown Community Sports & Arts Ctr A3
Hillary Cres C1
Hillborough Rd C1
Hitchin Rd A3
Holly St C2
Holm C1
Hucklesby Way A2
Hunts Cl C1
Inkerman St A2
John St B2
Jubilee St A3
Kelvin Cl C2
King St B2
Kingsland Rd C3
Larches, The A2
Latimer Rd C2
Lawn Gdns C2
Lea Rd B3
Library B2
Library Rd B2
Library Theatre B2
Liverpool Rd B1
London Rd C2
Luton Station A2
Lyndhurst Rd B1
Magistrates Court B2
Mall, The B2
Manchester St B2
Manor Rd B3
Manor Road Park B3
May St C3
Meyrick Ave C1
Midland Rd A2
Mill St A2
Milton Rd B1
Moor St A1
Moor, The A1
Moorland Gdns A2
Moulton Rise A3
Napier Rd B1
New Bedford Rd A1
New Town St C2
North St A3
Old Bedford Rd A2
Old Orchard C2
Osbourne Rd C3
Oxen Rd A3
Park Sq B2
Park St B3/C3
Park St West B2
Park Viaduct B3
Parkland Drive C1
Police Station B1
Pomfret Ave A3
Pondwicks Rd B3
Post Office A1/B2
Power Court B3
Princess St B1
Red Rails C1
Regent St B2
Reginald St A2
Rothesay Rd B1
Russell Rise C1
Russell St C1
St Ann's Rd B3
St George's Square B2
St Mary's B3
St Marys Rd B3
St Paul's Rd C2
St Saviour's Cres C1
Salisbury Rd B1
Seymour Ave C3
Seymour Rd C3
Silver St B2
South Rd C2
Stanley St B1
Station Rd A2
Stockwood Cres C2
Stockwood Park C1
Strathmore Ave C2
Stuart St B2
Studley Rd A1
Surrey St C3
Sutherland Place C1
Tavistock St C2
Taylor St A3
Telford Way A1
Tennyson Rd C2
Tenzing Grove C1
Thistle Rd B3
Town Hall B2
Townsley Cl C2
UK Centre for Carnival Arts B3
Union St B2
University of Bedfordshire B3
Upper George St B2
Vicarage St B3
Villa Rd A2
Waldeck Rd A1
Wardown Ho Mus & Gallery A2
Wellington St B1/B2
Wenlock St A2
Whitby Rd A1
Whitehill Ave C1
William St A2
Wilsden Ave C1
Windmill Rd B3
Windsor St C2
Winsdon Rd B1
York St A3

Manchester 119

Adair St B6
Addington St A5
Adelphi St A1
Albert Sq B3
Albion St C3
Ancoats Gr B6
Ancoats Gr North B6
Angela St C2
Aquatics Centre C4
Ardwick Gn North C5
Ardwick Gn Park C5
Ardwick Gn South C5
Arlington St A2
Artillery St B3
Arundel St C2
Atherton St B2
Atkinson St B3
Aytoun St B4
Back Piccadilly A4
Baird St B5
Balloon St A4
Bank Pl A1
Baring St B5
Barrack St C1
Barrow St A1
Bendix St A5
Bengal St A5
Berry St C5
Blackfriars Rd A3
Blackfriars St A3
Blantyre St C2
Bloom St B4
Blossom St A5
Boad St B5
Bombay St B4
Booth St A3
Booth St B4
Bootle St B3
Brazennose St B3
Brewer St A5
Bridge St A3
Bridgewater Hall B3
Bridgewater Pl A4
Bridgewater St B2
Brook St C4
Brotherton Dr A2
Brown St A3
Brown St B4
Brunswick St C6
Brydon Ave C6
Buddhist Centre A4
Bury St A2
Bus & Coach Sta B4
Bus Station B4
Butler St A6
Buxton St C5
Byrom St B3
Cable St A5
Cambridge St C3/C4
Camp St B3
Canal St B4
Cannon St A1
Cardroom Rd A6
Carruthers St A6
Castle St C2
Castlefield Arena B2
Cateaton St A3
Cathedral A3
Cathedral St A3
Cavendish St C4
Chapel St A1/A3
Chapeltown St B5
Charles St C4
Charlotte St B4
Chatham St B4
Chepstow St B3
Chester Rd C1/C2
Chester St C4
Chetham's School of Music A3
China La B5
Chippenham Rd A6
Chorlton Rd C2
Chorlton St B4
Church St A2
Church St A4
City Park A4
City Rd East C3
Civil Justice Centre B2
Cleminson St A2
Clowes St A3
College Land A3
Collier St B2
Commercial St C3
Conference Centre C4

Cooper St B4
Copperas St A4
Corn Exchange, The A4
Cornbrook C1
Cornell St A5
Corporation St A4
Cotter St C6
Cotton St A5
Cow La B1
Cross St B3
Crown Court B4
Crown St C2
Dalberg St C6
Dale St A4/B5
Dancehouse, The C4
Dantzic St A4
Dark La C6
Dawson St C2
Dean St A5
Deansgate A3/B3/C2
Deansgate Castlefield C3
Deansgate Sta C3
Dolphin St C6
Downing St C5
Ducie St B5
Duke Pl B2
Duke St B2
Durling St C6
East Ordsall La A2/B1
Edge St A4
Egerton St C2
Ellesmere St C1
Everard St C1
Every St B6
Exchange Sq A4
Fairfield St B5
Faulkner St B4
Fennel St A3
Ford St A2
Ford St C6
Fountain St B4
Frederick St A2
Gartside St B2
Gaythorne St A1
George Leigh St A5
George St B4
Gore St A2
Goulden St A5
Granby Row B4
Gravel La A3
Great St B6
Great Ancoats St A5
Great Bridgewater St B3
Great George St A1
Great Jackson St C2
Great Marlborough St C4
Great Northern Warehouse Leisure & Shopping Complex B3
Greengate A3
Grosvenor St C5
Gun St A5
Hadrian Ave B6
Hall St B3
Hampson St B1
Hanover St A4
Hanworth Cl C5
Hardman St B3
Harkness St C6
Harrison St B6
Hart St B4
Helmet St B6
Henry St A5
Heyrod St B6
High St A4
Higher Ardwick C6
Hilton St A4/A5
Holland St A6
HOME C3
Hood St A5
Hope St B1
Hope St B4
Houldsworth St A5
Hoyle St C6
Hulme Hall Rd C1
Hulme St A1
Hulme St C3
Hyde Rd C6
Islington Way A1
Information Ctr B4
Irwell St A2
Jackson Cr C2
Jackson's Row B3
James St A1
Jenner Cl C2
Jersey St A5
John Dalton St B3
John Ryland's Library B3
John St A2
Kennedy St B3
Kincardine Rd C5
King St A3
King St West A3
Law Courts B3
Laystall St B5
Lever St A5
Library B3
Linby St C2
Little Lever St A4
Liverpool Rd B2
Liverpool St B1
Lloyd St B3
Lockton Cl C5
London Rd B5
Long Millgate A3
Longacre St B6
Loom St A5
Lower Byrom St B2
Lower Mosley St B3
Lower Moss La C2
Lower Ormond St C4
Loxford La C4
Luna St A5
Major St B4
Manchester Arndale A4
Manchester Art Gallery B4
Manchester Central Convention Complex B3
Manchester Metropolitan Univ (MMU) B4/C4
Manchester Piccadilly Station B5
Manchester Technology Ctr C4
Mancunian Way C3
Manor St C5
Marble St A4
Market St A2
Market St A4
Market St A4
Marsden St A3
Marshall St A5
Mayan Ave A2
Medlock St C3
Middlewood St B1
Miller St A4
Minshull St B4
Mosley St A4
Mount St B3
Mulberry St B3
Murray St A5
Museum of Science & Industry (MOSI) B2
Nathan Dr A2
National Football Museum A4
Naval St A5
New Bailey St A2
New Elm Rd B2
New Islington A6
New Islington Station B6
New Quay St B2
New Union St A6
Newgate St A4
Newton St A5
Nicholas St B4
North Western St C6
Oak St A4
Odeon A4/B3
Old Mill St A6
Oldfield Rd A1/C1
Oldham Rd A5
Oldham St A4
Opera House B3
Ordsall La C1
Oxford Rd C4
Oxford Rd C4
Oxford St B4
Paddock St C6
Palace Theatre B4
Pall Mall A3
Palmerston St B6
Parker St B4
Peak St B5
Penfield Cl C5
Peoples' History Museum B2
Peru St A1
Peter St B3
Piccadilly A4
Piccadilly B5
Piccadilly Gdns B4
Piercy St A6
Poland St A5
Police Sta B3/B5
Pollard St B6
Port St A5
Portland St B4
Portugal St East B5
Post Office A1/A2/A4/A5/B3/B4
Potato Wharf B2
Princess St B3/C4
Pritchard St C4
Quay St A2
Quay St B2
Queen St B3
Radium St A5
Redhill St A5
Regent Rd B1
Retail Park A5
Rice St B2
Richmond St B4
River St C3
Roby St B5
Rodney St A6
Roman Fort B2
Rosamond St A2
Royal Exchange A3
Sackville St B4
St Andrew's St B6
St Ann St A3
St Ann's A3
St George's Ave C1
St James St B4
St John St B3
St John's Cathedral (RC) A2
St Mary's B3
St Mary's Gate A3
St Mary's Parsonage A3
St Peter's Sq B3
St Stephen St A2
Salford Approach A3
Salford Central A2
Sheffield St B5
Sherratt St A5
Shopmobility A4
Shudehill A4
Shudehill A4
Sidney St C4
Silk St A5
Silver St B4
Skerry Cl C5
Snell St B6
South King St B3
Sparkle St B5
Spear St A4
Spring Gdns A4
Stanley St A2/B2
Store St B5
Superstore B1
Swan St A4
Tariff St B5
Tatton St C1
Temperance St B6/C6
Thirsk St C6
Thomas St A4
Thompson St A5
Tib La B3
Tib St A4
Town Hall (Manchester) B3
Town Hall (Salford) A2
Trafford St C3
Travis St B5
Trinity Way A2
Turner St A4
Union St C6
Univ of Manchester (Sackville St Campus) C5
Univ of Salford A1
Upper Brook St C5
Upper Cleminson St A1
Upper Wharf St A1
Urban Exchange A5
Vesta St B6
Victoria A4
Victoria Station A4
Wadesdon Rd C5
Water St B2
Watson St B3
West Fleet St B1
West King St A2
West Mosley St B4
Weybridge Rd A6
Whitworth St B4
Whitworth St West C3
William St A2
William St C6
Wilmott St C3
Windmill St B3
Windsor Cr A1
Withy Gr A4
Woden St C1
Wood St B3
Woodward St A6
Worrall St C1
Worsley St C2
York St B4
York St C2
York St C4

Middlesbrough 119

Abingdon Rd C3
Acklam Rd C1
Albert Park C2
Albert Rd B2
Albert Terr C2
Ambulance Station C1
Aubrey St C3
Avenue, The C2
Ayresome Gdns C2
Ayresome Green La C1
Ayresome St C2
Barton Rd A1
Bilsdale Rd C3
Bishopton Rd C3
Borough Rd B2/B3
Bowes Rd A2
Breckon Hill Rd B3
Bridge St East B3
Bridge St West B2
Brighouse Rd A1
Burlam Rd C1
Bus Station B2
Cannon Park B1
Cannon Park Way B2
Cannon St B1
Captain Cook Sq B2
Carlow St C1
Castle Way C3
Chipchase Rd C2
Cineworld B3
Cleveland Centre B2
Clive Rd C2
Commercial St A2
Corporation Rd B2
Costa St C2
Council Offices B3
Crescent Rd C2
Crescent, The C2
Cumberland Rd C2
Depot Rd A2
Derwent St B2
Devonshire Rd C2
Diamond Rd B2
Dorman Mus C2
Douglas St B3
Eastbourne Rd C2
Eden Rd C3
Fire Sta A3
Forty Foot Rd A2
Gilkes St B2
Gosford St A2
Grange Rd B2
Gresham Rd B2
Harehills Rd C1
Harford St C2
Hartington Rd B2
Haverton Hill Rd A1
Hey Wood St B1
Highfield Rd C3
Hillstreet Centre B2
Holwick Rd B1
Hutton Rd C3
Ironmasters Way B1
Lambton Rd C3
Lancaster Rd C2
Lansdowne Rd C3
Latham Rd C2
Law Courts B2/B3
Lees Rd B2
Leeway B3
Library B2/C2
Linthorpe Cemetery C1
Linthorpe Rd B2
Lloyd St B2
Longford St C2
Longlands Rd C3
Lower East St A3
Lower Lake C3
Macmillan Acad C1
Maldon Rd C1
Manor St B2
Marsh St B2
Marton Rd B3
Middlehaven B3
Middlesbrough By-Pass B2/C1
Middlesbrough Coll B3
Middlesbrough Leisure Park B3
Middlesbrough Station B2
Middletown Park C2
MIMA B3
Mulgrave Rd C2
Newport Bridge B1
Newport Bridge Approach Rd B1
Newport Rd B2
North Ormesby Rd B3
North Rd B2
Northern Rd C1
Outram St B2
Oxford Rd C2
Park La C2
Park Rd North C2
Park Rd South C2
Park Vale Rd C3
Parliament Rd B1
Police Station A2
Port Clarence Rd A3
Portman St B2
Post Office B3/C1/C2
Princes Rd B2
Python A2
Riverside Park Rd A1
Riverside Stadium (Middlesbrough FC) B3
Rockliffe Rd C2
Romaldkirk Rd B1
Roman Rd C2
Roseberry Rd C3
St Barnabas' Rd C2
St Paul's Rd B2
Saltwells Rd B3
Scott's Rd A3
Seaton Carew Rd A3
Shepherdson Way B3
Shopmobility B2
Snowdon Rd A2
South West Ironmasters Park B1
Southfield Rd B2
Southwell Rd C2
Springfield Rd C1
Startforth Rd A2
Stockton Rd C1
Stockton St A2
Superstore B2
Surrey St C2
Sycamore Rd C2
Tax Offices B3
Tees Viaduct C1
Teessaurus Park A2
Teesside Tertiary College C3
Temenos B3
Thornfield Rd C1
Town Hall B2
Transporter Bridge (Toll) A3
Union St B2
Univ of Teesside B2
Upper Lake C2
Valley Rd C3
Ventnor Rd C2
Victoria Rd B2
Vulcan St A2
Warwick St C2
Wellesley Rd B3
West La C1
West Lane Hosp C1
Westminster Rd C2
Wilson St B2
Windward Way B3
Woodlands Rd B2
York Rd C3

Milton Keynes 122

Abbey Way A1
Arbrook Ave B1
Armourer Dr A3
Arncliffe Dr A1
Avebury C2
Avebury Blvd C2
Bankfield B3
Bayard Ave A2
Belvedere A2
Bishopstone A1
Blundells Rd A1
Boundary, The C3
Boycott Ave C2
Bradwell Common Blvd B1
Bradwell Rd C1
Bramble Ave A2
Brearley Ave C2
Breckland A1
Brill Place B1
Burnham Dr B1
Campbell Park B3
Cantle Ave A3
Central Retail Park C1
Century Ave C2
Chaffron Way C3
Childs Way C1
Christ the Cornerstone B2
Cineworld B2
Civic Offices B2
Cleavers Ave B2
Colesbourne Dr A3
Conniburrow Blvd B2
Currier Dr A2
Dansteed Way A2/A3/B1
Deltic Ave B1
Downs Barn A2
Downs Barn Blvd A3
Eaglestone C3
Eelbrook Ave B1
Elder Gate B1
Evans Gate C2
Fairford Cr A3
Falcon Ave B3
Fennel Dr A2
Fishermead Blvd C3
Food Centre B3
Fulwoods Dr C3
Glazier Dr A2
Glovers La A1
Grafton Gate C1
Grafton St A1/C2
Gurnards Ave B3
Harrier Dr C3
The Hub Leisure Quarter B2/C2
Ibstone Ave B1
intu Milton Keynes B2
Langcliffe Dr A1
Leisure Centre C3
Leisure Plaza C1
Leys Rd C1
Library B2
Linceslade Grove C1
Linford Wood A2
Magistrates Court B2
Marlborough Gate B3
Marlborough St A2/B3
Mercers Dr A1
Midsummer C2
Midsummer Blvd B2
Milton Keynes Central C1
Milton Keynes Hospital (A&E) C3
Monks Way A1
Mullen Ave A3
Mullion Pl C3
Neath Hill A3
North Elder C1
North Grafton B1
North Overgate A3
North Row B2
North Saxon B2
North Secklow B2
North Skeldon A3
North Witan B1
Oakley Gdns A3
Odeon B2
Oldbrook Blvd C2
Open-Air Theatre B3
Overgate A3
Overstreet A3
Patriot Dr B1
Pencarrow Pl B3
Penryn Ave B3
Perran Ave C3
Pitcher La C1
Place Retail Pk, The C1
Police Station B2
Portway B2
Post Office A2/B2/B3
Precedent Dr B1
Quinton Dr B1
Ramsons Ave B2
Retail Park C2
Rockingham Dr A2
Rooksley B1
Saxon Gate B2
Saxon St A1/C3
Secklow Gate B2
Shackleton Pl C2
Shopmobility B2
Silbury Blvd B2
Skeldon A3
South Enmore B3
South Grafton C2
South Row C2
South Saxon C2
South Secklow B3
South Witan C2
Springfield B3
Stainton Dr A1/B1
Stanton Wood A1
Stantonbury A1
Stantonbury Leisure Centre A1
Strudwick Dr C2
Sunrise Parkway A2
Superstore C1/C2
Theatre & Art Gallery B3
theCentre:mk B2
Tolcarne Ave C3
Towan Ave C3
Trueman Pl C2
Vauxhall A1
Winterhill Retail Pk C2
Witan Gate B2
Xscape B3

Newcastle upon Tyne 122

Albert St B3
Argyle St B3
Back New Bridge St B3
BALTIC Centre for Contemporary Art C3
Barker St A3
Barrack Rd B1
Bath La B1
Bessie Surtees House C2
Bigg Market C2
Biscuit Factory B3
Black Gate C2
Blackett St B2
Blandford Sq C1
Boating Lake A1
Boyd St B3
Brandling Park A2
Bus Station B2
Buxton St B3
Byron St A3
Camden St B2
Castle Keep C2
Central C1
Central Library B2
Central Motorway B2
Chester St A3
City Hall B2
City Rd B3/C3
City Walls C1
Civic Centre A2
Claremont Rd A1
Clarence St B3
Clarence Walk B3
Clayton St C1/B1
Clayton St West C1
Close, The C2
Coach Station C1
College St B2
Collingwood St C2
Copland Terr B3
Coppice Way B3
Corporation St B1
Courts C3
Crawhall Rd B3
Dean St C2
Dental Hospital A1
Dinsdale Pl A3
Dinsdale Rd A3
Discovery C1
Doncaster Rd A3
Durant Rd B2
Eldon Sq B1
Ellison Pl B2
Empire B1
Eskdale Terrace A2
Eslington Terrace A2
Exhibition Park A1
Falconar St B3
Fenkle St C1
Forth Banks C1
Forth St C1
Gallowgate B1
Gate, The B1
Gateshead Millennium Bridge C3
Gibson St B3
Goldspink La A3
Grainger Market B2
Grainger St B2
Grantham Rd A3
Granville Rd A3
Great North Children's Hosp A1
Great North Mus:Hancock A2
Grey St B2
Groat Market C2
Guildhall C2
Hancock St A2
Hanover St C2
Hatton Gallery A1
Hawks Rd C3
Haymarket B2
Heber St B1
Helmsley Rd A3
High Bridge B2
High Level Bridge C2
Hillgate C3
Howard St B3
Hutton Terr A3
Information Ctr C3
intu Eldon Sq Shopping Centre B2
Jesmond A2
Jesmond Rd A2/A3
John Dobson St B2
John George Joicey Museum C2
Jubilee Rd B3
Kelvin Gr A3
Kensington Terr A2
Laing Gallery B2
Lambton Rd A2
Leazes Cr B1
Leazes La B1
Leazes Park B1
Leazes Park Rd B1
Leazes Terr B1
Library A2
Live C2
Low Friar St C1
Manor Chare C2
Manors B2
Manors Station B2
Market St B2
Melbourne St B2
Mill Rd C3
Monument B2
Monument Mall Shopping Centre B2
Morpeth St A2
Mosley St C2
Napier St A3
New Bridge St B2/B3
Newcastle Central Station C1
Newcastle Univ A1
Newgate Shopping Centre C1
Newgate St B1
Newington Rd A3
Northern Design Centre C3
Northern Stage Theatre A2
Northumberland Rd B2
Northumberland St B2
Northumbria Univ A2
Northwest Radial Rd A1
O2 Academy C1
Oakwellgate C3
Open Univ C3
Orchard St C2
Osborne Rd A2
Osborne Terr A3
Pandon C3
Pandon Bank B3
Park Terr A1
Percy St B1
Pilgrim St B2
Pipewellgate C2
Pitt St B1
Plummer Tower A2
Police Station B2
Portland Rd A3/B3
Portland Terr A3
Post Office B1/B2
Pottery La C1
Prudhoe Pl B1
Prudhoe St B1
Quayside C2
Queen Elizabeth II Bridge C2
Queen Victoria Rd A1
Richardson Rd A1
Ridley Pl B2
Rock Terr B3
Rosedale Terr A3
Royal Victoria Infirmary A1
Sage Gateshead C3
St Andrew's St B1
St James B1
St James' Blvd C1
St James' Park (Newcastle Utd FC) B1
St Mary's Heritage Centre C3
St Mary's (RC) C1
St Mary's Place B2
St Nicholas C2
St Nicholas St C2
St Thomas' St B1
Sandyford Rd A2/A3
Science Park B2
Shield St B3
Shieldfield B3
Shopmobility B1
Side, The C2
Simpson Terr B3
South Shore Rd C3
South St C1
Starbeck Ave A3
Stepney Rd B3
Stoddart St B3
Stowell St B1
Strawberry Pl B1
Swing Bridge C2
Temple St C1
Terrace Pl B1
Theatre Royal B2
Times Sq C1
Tower St B3
Trinity House C2
Tyne Bridge C2
Tyne Bridges C2
Tyne Theatre & Opera House C1
Tyneside B2
Victoria Sq A2
Warwick St A3
Waterloo St C1
Wellington St B1
Westgate Rd C1/C2
Windsor Terr A2
Worswick St B2
Wretham Pl B3

Newport
Casnewydd 122

Albert Terr B1
Allt-yr-Yn Ave A1
Alma St C2
Ambulance Station C3
Bailey St B2
Barrack Hill A2
Bath St A3
Bedford Rd B3
Belle Vue La C1
Belle Vue Park C1
Bishop St A3
Blewitt St B1
Bolt Cl C3
Bolt St C3
Bond St A2
Bosworth Dr A1
Bridge St B1
Bristol St A3
Bryngwyn Rd B1
Brynhyfryd Ave C1
Brynhyfryd Rd C1
Bus Station B2
Caerau Cres C1
Caerau Rd B1
Caerleon Rd A3
Capel Cres C2
Cardiff Rd C2
Caroline St B3
Castle (Remains) A2
Cedar Rd B3
Charles St B2
Charlotte Dr C2
Chepstow Rd A3
Church Rd A3
Cineworld B2
Civic Centre B1
Clarence Pl A2
Clifton Pl B1
Clifton Rd C1
Clyffard Cres B1
Clytha Park Rd B1
Clytha Sq C2
Coldra Rd C1
Collier St A3
Colne St B3
Comfrey Cl A1
Commercial Rd C3
Commercial St B2
Corelli St A3
Corn St B2
Corporation Rd B3
Coulson Cl C2
County Court A2
Courts A1
Courts B1
Crawford St A3
Cyril St B3
Dean St A3
Devon Pl B1
Dewsland Park Rd C2
Dolman B2
Dolphin St C3
East Dock Rd C3
East St B1
East Usk Rd A3
Ebbw Vale Wharf B3
Emlyn St B2
Enterprise Way C3
Eton Rd B3
Evans St A2
Factory Rd A2
Fields Rd B1
Francis Dr C2
Frederick St C3
Friars Rd C1
Friars Walk B2
Gaer La C1
George St C3
George St Bridge C3
Godfrey Rd B1
Gold Tops B1
Gore St A3
Gorsedd Circle C1
Grafton Rd A3
Graham St B1
Granville St C3
Harlequin Dr A1
Harrow Rd B3
Herbert Rd A3
Herbert Walk C2
Hereford St A3
High St B2
Hill St B2
Hoskins St A2
Information Ctr B2
Ivor St B2
Jones St B1
Junction Rd A3
Keynshaw Ave C2
King St C2
Kingsway B2
Kingsway Centre B2
Ledbury Dr A2
Library A3
Library, Museum & Art Gallery B2
Liverpool Wharf B3
Llanthewy Rd B1
Llanvair Rd A3
Locke St A2
Lower Dock St C3
Lucas St A2
Manchester St A3
Market B2
Marlborough Rd B3
Mellon St C3
Mill St A2
Morgan St A3
Mountjoy Rd C2
Newport Bridge A2
Newport Ctr B2
Newport RFC B3
Newport Station B2
North St B2
Oakfield Rd B1
Park Sq C2
Police Sta A3/C2
Post Office B2/C3
Power St A1
Prince St A3
Pugsley St A2
Queen St C2
Queen's Cl A1
Queen's Hill A1
Queen's Hill Cres A1
Queensway B2
Railway St B2
Riverfront Theatre & Arts Ctr, The B2
Riverside A3
Rodney Rd B2
Royal Gwent (A&E) C2
Rudry St A3
Rugby Rd B3
Ruperra La C3
Ruperra St C3
St Edmund St B1
St Mark's Cres A1
St Mary St B1
St Vincent Rd A3
St Woolos C2
St Woolos General (no A&E) C1
St Woolos Rd B1
School La B2
Serpentine Rd B1
Shaftesbury Park A2
Sheaf La A3
Skinner St B2
Sorrel Dr A1
South Market St C3
Spencer Rd B1
Stow Hill B2/C1/C2
Stow Park Ave C1
Stow Park Dr C1
TA Centre A1
Talbot St B2
Tennis Club A1
Tregare St A3
Trostrey St A3
Tunnel Terr B1
Turner St A3
Univ of Wales Newport City Campus B3
Upper Dock St B2
Usk St A3
Usk Way B3/C3
Victoria Cr B1
War Memorial A3
Waterloo Rd C1
West St B1
Wharves B2
Wheeler St A2
Whitby Pl A3
Windsor Terr B1
York Pl C1

Northampton 122

78 Derngate B3
Abington Sq B3
Abington St B3
Alcombe St A3
All Saints' B2
Ambush St B1
Angel St B2
AR Centre A3
Arundel St A2
Ash St A2
Auctioneers Way C2
Bailiff St A2
Barrack Rd A2
Beaconsfield Terr A3
Becket's Park C3
Bedford Rd B3
Billing Rd B3
Brecon St A1
Brewery C2
Bridge St C2
Broad St B2
Burns St A3
Bus Station B2
Campbell St A2
Castle (Site of) B2
Castle St B2
Cattle Market Rd C2
Central Museum & Art Gallery B2
Charles St A3
Cheyne Walk B3
Church La A2
Clare St A3
Cloutsham St A3
College St B2
Colwyn Rd A3
Cotton End C2
Countess Rd A1
County Hall B2
Court A2
Craven St A3
Crown & County Courts B3
Denmark Rd B3
Derngate B3
Derngate & Royal Theatres B3
Doddridge Church B2
Drapery, The B2
Duke St A3
Dunster St A3
Earl St A3
Euston Rd C2
Fire Station A3
Foot Meadow B2
Gladstone Rd A1
Gold St B2
Grafton St A2
Gray St A3
Green St B1
Greenwood Rd B1
Greyfriars B2
Grosvenor Centre B2
Grove Rd A3
Guildhall B2
Hampton St A2
Harding Terr A2
Hazelwood Rd B3
Herbert St B2
Hervey St A3
Hester St A2
Holy Sepulchre A2
Hood St A3
Horse Market B2
Hunter St A3
Information Ctr B2
Kettering Rd A3
Kingswell St B2
Lady's La B2
Leicester St A2
Leslie Rd A2
Library B3
Lorne Rd A2
Lorry Park A1
Louise Rd A2
Lower Harding St A2
Lower Hester St A2
Lower Mounts B3
Lower Priory St A2
Main Rd C1
Marefair B2
Market Sq B2
Marlboro Rd B1
Marriott St A2
Military Rd A3
Mounts Baths Leisure Centre A3
Nene Valley Retail Park C1
New South Bridge Rd C2
Northampton General Hospital (A&E) B3
Northampton Marina C3
Northampton Station B1
Northcote St A2
Nunn Mills Rd C3
Old Towcester Rd C2
Overstone Rd A3
Peacock Pl B2
Pembroke Rd A1
Penn Court C2
Police Station B3
Post Office A1/B3
Quorn Way A2
Ransome Rd C3
Regent Sq A2
Ridings, The B3
Robert St A2
St Andrew's Rd B1
St Andrew's St A2
St Edmund's Rd B3
St George's St A2
St Giles B3
St Giles St B3
St Giles' Terr B3
St James Park Rd B1
St James Rd B1
St James Retail Pk C1
St James' Mill Rd B1
St James' Mill Rd East C1
St Leonard's Rd C2
St Mary's St B2
St Michael's Rd A3
St Peter's B2
St Peter's Way Shopping Prec B2
St Peter's Way B2
Salisbury St A2
Scarletwell St B2
Semilong Rd A2
Sheep St B2
Sol Central (Leisure Centre) B2
Somerset St A3
South Bridge C2
Southfield Ave C2
Spencer Bridge Rd A1
Spencer Rd A3
Spring Gdns B3
Spring La B2
Superstore C2
Swan St B3
Tintern Ave A1
Towcester Rd C2
Upper Bath St B2
Upper Mounts A2
Victoria Park A1
Victoria Prom B2
Victoria Rd B3
Victoria St A2
Wellingborough Rd B3
West Bridge B1
York Rd B3

Norwich 122

Albion Way C3
All Saints Green C2
Anchor St A3
Anglia Sq A2
Argyle St C3
Arts Centre B1
Ashby St C2
Assembly House B1
Bank Plain B2
Barker St A1
Barn Rd A1
Barrack St A3
Ber St C2
Bethel St B1
Bishop Bridge A3
Bishopbridge Rd A3
Bishopgate A3
Blackfriars St A2
Botolph St A2
Bracondale C3
Brazen Gate C2
Bridewell B2
Brunswick Rd C1
Bull Close Rd A2
Bus Station C2
Calvert St A2
Cannell Green A3
Carrow Rd C3
Castle & Mus B2
Castle Mall B2
Castle Meadow B2
Cathedral B2
Cath Retail Park A1
Cattlemarket St B2
Chantry Rd C1
Chapel Loke C2
Chapelfield East B1
Chapelfield Gdns B1
Chapelfield North B1
Chapelfield Rd B1
Cinema City B2
City Hall B1
City Rd C2
City Wall C1/C3
Close, The B2/B3
Colegate A2
Coslany St B1
Cow Hill B1
Cow Tower A3
Cowgate A2
Crown & Magistrates' Courts A2
Dragon Hall Heritage Ctr C3
Duke St A1
Edward St A2
Elm Hill B2
Erpingham Gate B2
Fishergate A2
Forum, The B1
Foundry Bridge B3
Fye Bridge A2
Garden St C2
Gas Hill B3
Gentlemans Walk B2
Grapes Hill B1
Great Hospital Halls, The A3
Grove Ave C1
Grove Rd C1
Guildhall B1
Gurney Rd A3
Hall Rd C2
Heathgate A3
Heigham St A1
Hollywood A2
Horn's La C2
Hungate Medieval Art B2
Information Ctr B1
intu Chapelfield C1
Ipswich Rd C1
ITV Anglia C3
James Stuart Gdns B3
King St B2
King St C3
Koblenz Ave C3
Leisure Centre A3
Library B1
London St B2
Lower Clarence Rd B3
Maddermarket B1
Magdalen St A2
Mariners La C2
Market B2
Market Ave B2
Mountergate B3
Mousehold St A3
Newmarket Rd C1
Norfolk St C1
Norwich City FC C3
Norwich Gallery B2
Norwich School B2
Norwich Station B3
Oak St A1
Odeon C3
Palace St A2
Pitt St A1
Playhouse B2
Police Station B1
Post Office A2/B2/B3/C1
Pottergate B1
Prince of Wales Rd B2
Princes St B2
Pull's Ferry B3
Puppet Theatre A2
Queen St B2
Queens Rd C2
RC Cathedral B1

Recorder Rd B3
Riverside Entertainment Ctr C3
Riverside Leisure Centre C3
Riverside Rd B3
Riverside Retail Pk C3
Rosary Rd B3
Rose La B2
Rouen Rd C2
St Andrews St B2
St Augustines St A1
St Benedicts St B1
St Ethelbert's Gate ✦ B2
St Faiths La B3
St Georges St A2
St Giles St B1
St James Cl A3
St Julians C2
St Leonards Rd B3
St Martin's La A1
St Peter Mancroft B2
St Peters St B1
St Stephens Rd C1
St Stephens St C1
Shopmobility C1
Silver Rd A2
Silver St A2
Southwell Rd C2
St. Andrew's & Blackfriars' Hall ✦ B2
Strangers' Hall B1
Superstore C2
Surrey St C2
Sussex St A1
Theatre Royal B1
Theatre St B1
Thorn La C2
Thorpe Rd B3
Tombland B2
Union St C1
Vauxhall St B1
Victoria St C1
Vue B2
Walpole St B1
Waterfront,The C3
Wensum St A2
Wessex St C1
Westwick St A1
Wherry Rd C3
Whitefriars A2
Willow La B1

Nottingham 122

Abbotsford Dr A3
Addison St A1
Albert Hall ✦ B1
Alfred St Central A3
Alfreton Rd B1
All Saints St A1
Annesley Gr A2
Arboretum A1
Arboretum St A1
Arthur St A1
Arts Theatre B3
Ashforth St A3
Balmoral Rd A1
Barker Gate B3
Bath St B3
BBC Nottingham C3
Beacon Hill Rise B3
Belgrave Rooms B1
Bellar Gate B3
Belward St B3
Brewhouse Yard C2
Broad Marsh Bus Station C2
Broad St B3
Brook St B3
Burns St A1
Burton St B2
Bus Station A2
Canal St C2
Carlton St B3
Carrington St C2
Castle C2
Castle Blvd C1
Castle Gate C2
Castle Meadow Rd C1
Castle Meadow Retail Park C1
Castle Rd C2
Castle Wharf C2
Cavendish Rd East C1
Cemetery A1/B1
Chaucer St B1
Cheapside B2
Church Rd A3
City Link C3
City of Caves ✦ C2
Clarendon St B1
Cliff Rd C3
Clumber Rd East C1
Clumber St B2
College St B1
Collin St C2
Contemporary C3
Conway Cl A2
Cornerhouse,The B2
Council House B2
Cranbrook St B3
Cranmer St A2
Cromwell St B1
Curzon St B3
Derby Rd B1
Dryden St A2
Exchange Ctr,The B2
Fishpond Dr C1
Fletcher Gate B3
Forest Rd East A1
Forest Rd West A1
Friar La C2
Gedling Gr A1
Gedling St B3
George St B3
Gill St A2
Glasshouse St B2
Goldsmith St B2
Goose Gate B3
Great Freeman St A2
Guildhall B2
Hamilton Dr C1
Hampden St A1
Heathcote St B3
High Pavement C3
High School A1
HM Revenue & Customs C2
Holles Cr C1
Hope Dr C1
Hungerhill Rd A3
Huntingdon Dr C1
Huntingdon St A2
Information Ctr B2
Instow Rise A3
Int Com Ctr A2
intu Broadmarsh C2
intu Victoria Ctr B2
Kent St B3
King St B2
Lace Market B3
Lace Mkt Theatre C3
Lamartine St B3
Leisure Ctr C3
Lenton Rd C1
Lewis Cl A3
Lincoln St B2
London Rd C3
Long Row B2
Low Pavement C2
Lower Parliament St B3
Magistrates' Court C2
Maid Marian Way B2
Mansfield Rd A2/B2
Middle Hill C2
Milton St B2
Mount St B2
National Ice Centre & Motorpoint Arena C3
National Justice Museum C3
Newcastle Dr B1
Newstead Gr A2
North Sherwood St A2
Nottingham Arena C3
Nottingham Cathedral ✝ B1
Nottingham Coll C3
Nottingham Station C3
Nottingham Station C3
Nottingham Trent University A2/B2
Old Mkt Square B2
Oliver St A1
Park Dr C1
Park Row C1
Park Terr B1
Park Valley C1
Park,The C1
Peas Hill Rd A3
Peel St A1
Pelham St B2
Peveril Dr C1
Plantagenet St A3
Playhouse Theatre B1
Plumptre St C3
Police Sta B1/B2
Poplar St C3
Portland Rd B1
Post Office B2
Queen's Rd C3
Raleigh St A1
Regent St B1
Rick St B3
Robin Hood St B3
Robin Hood Statue ✦ C2
Ropewalk,The B1
Royal Centre B2
Royal Children Inn C2
Royal Concert Hall B2
St Ann's Hill Rd A2
St Ann's Way A2
St Ann's Well Rd A3
St James' St B2
St Mark's St B3
St Mary's Rest Garden B3
St Mary's Gate B3
St Nicholas C2
St Peter's C2
St Peter's Gate B2
Salutation Inn C2
Shakespeare St B2
Shelton St A2
Shopmobility A2
South Pde B2
South Rd C1
South Sherwood St B2
Station Street C3
Stoney St B3
Talbot St B1
Tattershall Dr C1
Tennis Dr B1
Tennyson St A1
Theatre Royal B2
Trent St C3
Trent University B2
Union Rd B3
Upper Parliament St B2
Victoria Leisure Centre B3
Victoria Park B3
Victoria St B2
Walter St A1
Warser Gate B3
Watkin St A2
Waverley St A1
Wheeler Gate B2
Wilford Rd C2
Wilford St C2
Wollaton St B1
Woodborough Rd A2
Woolpack La B3
Ye Old Trip to Jerusalem ✦ C2
York St A2

Oxford 123

Adelaide St A1
Albert St A1
All Souls (Coll) B2
Ashmolean Museum B2
Balliol (Coll) B2
Banbury Rd A2
Bate Collection of Musical Instruments C2
Beaumont St B1
Becket St B1
Blackhall Rd A2
Blue Boar St B2
Bodleian Library B2
Botanic Garden B3
Brasenose (Coll) B2
Brewer St C2
Broad St B2
Burton-Taylor Theatre B2
Bus Station B1
Canal St A1
Cardigan St A1
Carfax Tower B2
Castle B1
Castle St B1
Catte St B2
Cemetery C1
Christ Church (Coll) B2
Christ Church Cathedral ✝ C2
Christ Church Meadow C2
Clarendon Centre B2
Coach & Lorry Park C1
College B3
Coll of Further Ed C1
Cornmarket St B2
Corpus Christi (Coll) B2
County Hall B1
Covered Market B2
Cowley Pl C3
Cranham St A1
Cranham Terr A1
Cricket Ground B1
Crown & County Courts C2
Deer Park B3
Exeter (Coll) B2
Folly Bridge C2
George St B1
Great Clarendon St A1
Hart St A1
Hertford (Coll) B2
High St B3
Hollybush Row B1
Holywell St B2
Hythe Bridge St B1
Ice Rink C1
Information Ctr B2
Jericho St A1
Jesus (Coll) B2
Jowett Walk B3
Juxon St A1
Keble (Coll) A2
Keble Rd A2
Library B2
Linacre (Coll) A3
Lincoln (Coll) B2
Little Clarendon St A1
Longwall St B3
Magdalen (Coll) B3
Magdalen Bridge B2
Magdalen St B2
Magistrate's Court C2
Manchester (Coll) B2
Manor Rd B3
Mansfield (Coll) A2
Mansfield Rd A3
Market B1
Marlborough Rd C2
Martyrs' Meml ✦ B2
Merton (Coll) B3
Merton Field B3
Merton St B2
Museum of Modern Art B2
Mus of Oxford B2
Museum Rd A2
New College (Coll) B3
New Inn Hall St B2
New Rd B1
New Theatre B2
Norfolk St C1
Nuffield (Coll) B1
Observatory A1
Observatory St A1
Odeon B1/B2
Old Fire Station B1
Old Greyfriars St C2
Oriel (Coll) B2
Oxford Station B1
Oxford University Research Centres A1
Oxpens Rd C1
Paradise Sq C1
Paradise St B1
Park End St B1
Parks Rd A2/B2
Pembroke (Coll) C2
Phoenix A1
Picture Gallery C2
Plantation Rd A1
Playhouse B2
Police Station C2
Post Office A1/B2
Pusey St B1
Queen's (Coll) B3
Queen's La B3
Radcliffe Camera B2
Rewley Rd B1
Richmond Rd A1
Rose La B3
Ruskin (Coll) B1
Said Business Sch B1
St Aldates C2
St Anne's (Coll) A1
St Antony's (Coll) A1
St Bernard's Rd A1
St Catherine's (Coll) B3
St Cross Building A3
St Cross Rd A3
St Edmund Hall (Coll) B3
St Giles St A2
St Hilda's (Coll) C3
St John St B2
St John's (Coll) B2
St Mary the Virgin B2
St Michael at the Northgate B2
St Peter's (Coll) B1
St Thomas St B1
Science Area A2
Science Mus B2
Sheldonian Theatre B2
Somerville (Coll) A1
South Parks Rd A2
Speedwell St C2
Sports Ground C3
Thames St C2
Town Hall C2
Trinity (Coll) B2
Turl St B2
Univ Coll (Coll) B3
Univ Mus & Pitt Rivers Mus A2
University Parks A2
Wadham (Coll) B2
Walton Cr A1
Walton St A1
Western Rd C2
Westgate C2
Woodstock Rd A1
Worcester (Coll) B1

Peterborough 123

ABAX Stadium (Peterborough United) C2
Athletics Arena B3
Bishop's Palace B2
Bishop's Rd B2/B3
Boongate A3
Bourges Boulevard A1
Bourges Retail Park B1/B2
Bridge House (Council Offices) C2
Bridge St B2
Bright St A1
Broadway A2
Broadway A2
Brook St A2
Burghley Rd A2
Bus Station B2
Cavendish St A3
Charles St A3
Church St B2
Church Walk A2
Cobden Ave A1
Cobden St A1
Cowgate B2
Craig St A2
Crawthorne Rd A2
Cromwell Rd A1
Dickens St A3
Eastfield Rd A3
Eastgate B3
Fire Station A1
Fletton Ave C2
Frank Perkins Parkway C3
Geneva St A2
George St C1
Gladstone St A1
Glebe Rd C2
Gloucester Rd C3
Granby St B3
Grove St C1
Guildhall B2
Hadrians Ct C3
Hawksbill Way C2
Henry St A2
Hereward Cross (shopping) B2
Hereward Rd B3
Information Ctr B2
Jubilee St C1
Kent Rd B1
Key Theatre C2
Kirkwood Cl B1
Lea Gdns B1
Library A2
Lincoln Rd A2
London Rd C2
Long Causeway B2
Lower Bridge St C2
Magistrates Court B2
Manor House St A2
Mayor's Walk A1
Midland Rd A1
Monument St A2
Morris St A3
Museum & Art Gallery B2
Nene Valley Railway C1
New Rd A2
New Rd C1
Northminster A2
Old Customs Ho C2
Oundle Rd C1
Padholme Rd A3
Palmerston Rd C1
Park Rd A2
Passport Office B2
Peterborough Nene Valley C1
Peterborough Station B1
Police Station B2
Post Office A3/B1/B2/B3/C1
Priestgate B2
Queen's Walk C2
Queensgate Centre B2
Railworld C1
Regional Swimming & Fitness Centre B3
River La B1
Rivergate Shopping Centre B2
Riverside Mead C3
Russell St A1
St John's B2
St John's St A3
St Marks St A2
St Peter's ✝ B2
St Peter's Rd B2
Saxon Rd A3
Spital Bridge A1
Stagshaw Dr C3
Star Rd B3
Thorpe Lea Rd B1
Thorpe Rd B1
Thorpe's Lea Rd B1
Tower St A2
Town Hall B2
Viersen Platz B2
Vineyard Rd B3
Wake Rd B3
Wellington St A3
Wentworth St B2
Westgate B2
Whalley St A3
Wharf Rd C1
Whitsed St A3
YMCA A3

Plymouth 123

Alma Rd A1
Anstis St B1
Armada Shop Ctr B2
Armada St A3
Armada Way B2
Arts Centre B2
Athenaeum B1
Athenaeum St C1
Barbican C3
Barbican C3
Baring St A3
Bath St B1
Beaumont Park B3
Beaumont Rd B3
Black Friars Gin Distillery ✦ C2
Breton Side B3
Castle St C3
Cathedral (RC) ✝ B1
Cecil St B1
Central Park A1
Central Park Ave A2
Charles Church B3
Charles Cross B3
Charles St B2
Citadel Rd C2
Citadel Rd East C2
City Museum & Art Gallery B2
Civic Centre B2
Cliff Rd C1
Clifton Pl A3
Cobourg St A2
College of Art B2
Continental Ferry Port B1
Cornwall St B2
Crescent,The B1
Dale Rd A2
Deptford Pl A3
Derry Ave A2
Derry's Cross B1
Drake Circus B2
Drake Circus Shopping Centre B2
Eastlake St B2
Ebrington St B3
Elizabethan Ho C3
Elliot St C1
Endsleigh Pl A2
Exeter St B3
Fire Station A3
Fish Quay C3
Gibbons St A3
Glen Park Ave A2
Grand Pde C1
Great Western Rd C1
Greenbank Rd A3
Greenbank Terr A3
Guildhall B2
Hampton St B3
Harwell St B1
Hill Park Cr A3
Hoe Approach B2
Hoe Rd C2
Hoe,The C2
Hoegate St C2
Houndiscombe Rd A2
Information Ctr C3
James St A2
Kensington Rd A3
King St B1
Lambhay Hill C3
Leigham St C1
Library B2
Lipson Rd A3/B3
Lockyer St C2
Lockyers Quay C3
Madeira Rd C2
Marina B3
Market Ave B1
Martin St B1
Mayflower St B2
Mayflower Stone & Steps ✦ C3
Mayflower Visitor Centre ✦ C3
Merchant's Ho B2
Millbay Rd B1
National Marine Aquarium C3
Neswick St B1
New George St B2
New St C3
North Cross A2
North Hill A3
North Quay B2
North Rd East A2
North Rd West A1
North St B3
Notte St B2
Octagon,The B1
Octagon St B1
Pannier Market B1
Pennycomequick A1
Pier St C1
Plymouth Naval Memorial ✦ C2
Plymouth Pavilions B1
Plymouth Sta A2
Police Station B3
Post Office C2
Princess St B2
Promenade,The C2
Prysten House B2
Queen Anne's Battery Seasports Centre C3
Radford Rd C1
Reel B2
Regent St B3
Rope Walk C3
Royal Citadel C2
Royal Pde B2
Royal Theatre B2
St Andrew's B2
St Andrew's Cross B2
St Andrew's St B2
St Lawrence Rd A2
Saltash Rd A2
Shopmobility B2
Smeaton's Tower ✦ C2
Southern Terr A3
Southside St C2
Stuart Rd A1
Sutherland Rd A2
Sutton Rd B3
Sydney St A1
Teats Hill Rd C3
Tothill Ave B3
Union St B1
Univ of Plymouth A2
Vauxhall St B2/3
Victoria Park A1
West Hoe Rd C1
Western Approach B1
Whittington St A1
Wyndham St B1
YMCA B2
YWCA C2

Poole 123

Ambulance Station A3
Baiater Gdns C2
Baiter Park C3
Ballard Cl C2
Ballard Rd C2
Bay Hog La B1
Bridge Approach C1
Bus Station B2
Castle St B2
Catalina Dr B3
Chapel La B2
Church St B1
Cinnamon La B1
Colborne Cl B3
Dear Hay La B2
Denmark La A3
Denmark Rd A3
Dolphin Ctr B2
East St B2
Elizabeth Rd A3
Emerson Rd B2
Ferry Rd C1
Ferry Terminal C1
Fire Station A2
Freightliner Terminal C1
Furnell Rd B3
Garland Rd A3
Green Rd B2
Heckford La A3
Heckford Rd A3
High St B2
High St North A3
Hill St B2
Holes Bay Rd A1
Hospital (A&E) A3
Information Ctr C2
Kingland Rd B3
Kingston Rd A3
Labrador Dr C3
Lagland St B2
Lander Cl C3
Lifeboat Coll,The B2
Lighthouse – Poole Centre for the Arts ✦ B3
Longfleet Rd A3
Maple Rd A3
Market Cl B2
Market St B2
Mount Pleasant Rd B3
New Harbour Rd C1
New Harbour Rd South C1
New Harbour Rd West C1
New Orchard B1
New Quay Rd C1
New St B2
Newfoundland Dr B2
North St B2
Old Lifeboat C2
Old Orchard B2
Parish Rd A3
Park Lake Rd B3
Parkstone Rd A3
Perry Gdns B2
Pitwines Cl B2
Police Station A2
Poole Central Liby B2
Poole Lifting Bridge C1
Poole Park B2
Poole Station A2
Poole Museum C1
Post Office A2/B2
Quay,The C2
St John's Rd A3
St Margaret's Rd A2
St Mary's Maternity Unit A3
St Mary's Rd A3
Seldown Bridge B3
Seldown La B3
Seldown Rd B3
Serpentine Rd A2
Shaftesbury Rd A3
Skinner St B2
Slipway B1
Stanley Rd C2
Sterte Ave A2
Sterte Ave West A1
Sterte Cl A2
Sterte Esplanade A2
Sterte Rd A2
Strand St C2
Swimming Pool B3
Taverner Cl B3
Thames St B1
Towngate Bridge B2
Vallis Cl C3
Waldren Cl B3
West Quay B1
West Quay Rd B1
West St B1
West View Rd A2
Whatleigh Cl B2
Wimborne Rd A3

Portsmouth 123

Action Stations ✦ C1
Admiralty Rd A1
Alfred Rd A2
Anglesea Rd B2
Arundel St B3
Aspex B1
Bishop St A2
Broad St C1
Buckingham Ho C2
Burnaby Rd B2
Bus Station B1
Camber Dock C1
Cambridge Rd B2
Car Ferry to Isle of Wight B1
Cascades Shopping Centre A3
Castle Rd C3
City Museum & Art Gallery B2
Civic Offices B3
Clarence Pier C2
College St B1
Commercial Rd A3
Cottage Gr B3
Cross St A1
Cumberland St A2
Duisburg Way C2
Durham St A3
East St B1
Edinburgh Rd A2
Elm Gr C3
Emirates Spinnaker Tower ✦ B1
Great Southsea St C3
Green Rd B3
Greetham St B3
Grosvenor St B3
Groundlings A2
Grove Rd North C3
Grove Rd South C3
Guildhall B3
Guildhall Walk B3
Gunwharf Quays Designer Outlet B1
Gunwharf Rd B1
Hambrook St C2
Hampshire Terr B2
Hanover St A1
Hard,The B1
High St C2
HM Naval Base A1
HMS Nelson (Royal Naval Barracks) A2
HMS Victory A1
HMS Warrior A1
Hovercraft Terminal C2
Hyde Park Rd B3
Information Ctr A1/B3
Isambard Brunel Rd B3
Isle of Wight Car Ferry Terminal B1
Kent Rd C3
Kent St A2
King St B3
King's Rd C3
King's Terr C2
Lake Rd A3
Law Courts B3
Library B3
Long Curtain Rd C2
Market Way A3
Marmion Rd C3
Mary Rose Mus A1
Middle St B3
Millennium Promenade B1/C1
Museum Rd B2
National Museum of the Royal Navy A1
Naval Rec Gd C2
Nightingale Rd C3
Norfolk St B3
North St A2
Osborne Rd C3
Park Rd B2
Passenger Catamaran to Isle of Wight B1
Passenger Ferry to Gosport B1
Pelham Rd C3
Pembroke Gdns C2
Pier Rd C2
Point Battery C1
Police Station B3
Portsmouth & Southsea Sta A3
Portsmouth Harbour Station B1
Portsmouth Historic Dockyard A1
Post Office A3/B1/B3
Queen St A1
Queen's Cr C3
Round Tower ✦ C1
Royal Garrison Church C1
St Edward's Rd C3
St George's Rd B2
St George's Sq B1
St George's Way B2
St James's Rd B3
St James's St A2
St John's Cathedral (RC) ✝ A3
St Thomas's Cath ✝ C1
St Thomas's St B2
Shopmobility A3/B1
Somers Rd B3
Southsea Common C2
Southsea Terr C2
Square Tower ✦ C1
Station St A3
Town Fortifications ✦ C1
Unicorn Rd A2
United Services Rec Gd B2
University of Portsmouth A2/B2
Univ of Portsmouth – Coll of Art, Design & Media B3
Upper Arundel St A3
Victoria Ave C2
Victoria Park A2
Victory Gate A1
Vue B1
Warblington St B1
Western Pde C2
White Hart Rd C1
Winston Churchill Ave B3

Preston 123

Adelphi St A2
Anchor Ct B3
Aqueduct St A1
Ardee Rd C1
Arthur St B2
Ashton St A1
Avenham La B3
Avenham Park C3
Avenham Rd B3
Avenham St B3
Bairstow St B3
Balderstone Rd C1
Beamont Dr A1
Beech St South C2
Bird St C1
Bow La B2
Brieryfield Rd C1
Broadgate C1
Brook St A2
Bus Station A3
Butler St B2
Cannon St B3
Carlton St A1
Chaddock St B3
Channel Way B1
Chapel St B3
Christ Church St B2
Christian Rd B2
Cold Bath St A2
Coleman Ct C1
Connaught Rd C2
Corn Exchange B3
Corporation St A2/B2
County Hall B2
Cricket Ground C2
Croft St A1
Cross St B3
Crown Court A3
Crown St A3
East Cliff C3
East Cliff Rd B3
Edward St A2
Elizabeth St A3
Euston St B1
Fishergate B2/B3
Fishergate Hill B2
Fishergate Shopping Centre B2
Fitzroy St B1
Fleetwood St A1
Friargate A3
Fylde Rd A1/A2
Gerrard St B2
Glover's Ct B3
Good St B2
Grafton St B2
Great George St A3
Great Shaw St A3
Greenbank St A2
Guild Way B1
Guild Hall & Charter B3
Guildhall St B3
Harrington St A2
Harris Museum B3
Hartington Rd B1
Hasset Cl C2
Heatley St B2
Hind St C2
Information Ctr B3
Kilruddery Rd C1
Lancashire Archives B2
Lancaster Rd A3/B3
Latham St B3
Lauderdale St C2
Lawson St A3
Leighton St A2
Leyland Rd C1
Library A1
Library B3
Liverpool Rd C1
Lodge St B2
Lune St B3
Magistrate's Court A3
Main Sprit West B3
Maresfield Rd C1
Market St West A3
Marsh La B1/B2
Maudland Bank A2
Maudland Rd A2
Meadow Ct C2
Meath Rd C1
Mill Hill A2
Miller Arcade ✦ B3
Miller Park C3
Moor La A3
Mount St B3
North Rd A3
North St A3
Northcote Rd B1
Old Milestones B1
Old Tram Rd C3
Pedder St A1/A2
Peel St A2
Penwortham Bridge C2
Penwortham New Bridge C1
Pitt St B2
Playhouse A3
Police Station A3
Port Way B1
Post Office B3
Preston Station B2
Ribble Bank St B2
Ribble Viaduct C2
Ribblesdale Pl B3
Ringway B3
River Parade C1
Riverside C2
St George's Shopping Centre B3
St Georges B3
St Johns B3
St Johns Shopping Centre A3
St Mark's Rd A1
St Walburges A1
Salisbury Rd B1
Sessions House B3
Snow Hill A3
South End C2
South Meadow La C2
Spa Rd B1
Sports Ground C2
Strand Rd B1
Syke St B3
Talbot Rd B1
Taylor St C1
Tithebarn St A3
Town Hall B3
Tulketh Brow A1
University of Central Lancashire A2
Valley Rd C1
Victoria St A2
Walker St A3
Walton's Parade B2
Warwick St A3
Wellfield Bsns Park A1
Wellfield Rd A1
Wellington St A1
West Cliff C2
West Strand A1
Winckley Rd C1
Winckley Square B3
Wolseley Rd C2

Reading 124

Abbey Ruins ✝ B2
Abbey Sq B2
Abbey St B2
Abbot's Walk B2
Acacia Rd C2
Addington Rd C3
Addison Rd A1
Allcroft Rd C3
Alpine St C2
Baker St B1
Berkeley Ave C1
Bridge St B1
Brigham Rd A1
Broad St B1
Broad Street Mall B1
Carey St B1
Castle Hill C1
Castle St B1
Causeway,The A3
Caversham Rd A1
Christchurch Playing Fields A2
Civic Offices B1
Coley Hill C1
Coley Pl C1
Craven Rd C3
Crown St C2
De Montfort Rd A1
Denmark Rd C3
Duke St B2
East St B2
Edgehill St C2
Eldon Rd B3
Eldon Terr B3
Elgar Rd C1
Erleigh Rd C3
Field Rd C1
Fire Station A1
Fobney St B1
Forbury Gdns B2
Forbury Rd B2
Forbury Retail Park B2
Francis St C1
Friar St B1
Garrard St B1
Gas Works Rd B3
George St A2
Great Knollys St B1
Greyfriars B1
Grove,The B2
Gun St B1
Henry St C1
Hexagon Theatre, The B1
Hill's Meadow A2
Howard St B1
Information Ctr B1
Inner Distribution Rd B1
Katesgrove La C1
Kenavon Dr B2
Kendrick Rd C2
King's Meadow Rec Gd A2
King's Rd B2
Library B2
London Rd C3
London St B2
Lynmouth Rd A1
Magistrate's Court B1
Market Pl B2
Mill La B2
Mill Rd A2
Minster St B1
Morgan Rd C3
Mount Pleasant C2
Museum of English Rural Life C3
Napier Rd A2
Newark St C2
Newport Rd A1
Old Reading Univ C3
Oracle Shopping Centre,The B1
Orts Rd B3
Pell St C1
Police Station B1
Post Office B2
Queen Victoria St B1
Queen's Rd A2
Queen's Rd B2
Randolph Rd A1
Reading Bridge A2
Reading Station A1
Redlands Rd C3
Renaissance Hotel B1
Riverside Mus B3
Rose Kiln La C1
Royal Berks Hospital (A&E) C3
St Giles C2
St Laurence B2
St Mary's B1
St Mary's Butts B1
St Saviour's Rd C1
Send Rd A3
Sherman Rd C2
Sidmouth St B2
Silver St C2
South St B2
Southampton St C2
Station Hill A1
Station Rd B1
Superstore A3
Swansea Rd A1
Technical College B3
Valpy St B2
Vastern Rd A1
Vue B2
Waldeck St C2
Watlington St B3
West St B1
Whitby Dr C3
Wolseley St C1
York Rd A1
Zinzan St B1

Salisbury 124

Albany Rd A2
Arts Centre A3
Ashley Rd A1
Avon Approach A2
Ayleswade Rd C2
Bedwin St A2
Belle Vue A2
Bishop's Palace C2
Bishops Walk B2
Blue Boar Row B2
Bourne Ave A3
Bourne Hill A3
Britford La C2
Broad Walk C2
Brown St B2
Bus Station B2
Castle St A2
Catherine St B2
Chapter House B2
Church House B2
Churchfields Rd B1
Churchill Way East B3
Churchill Way North A3
Churchill Way South C2
Churchill Way West A1
City Hall B2
Close Wall B2
Coldharbour La A1
College St A3
Council Offices A3
Court A1
Crane Bridge Rd B2
Crane St B2
Cricket Ground C1
Culver St South B3
De Vaux Pl C2
Devizes Rd A1
Dews Rd B1
Elm Grove B3
Elm Grove Rd A3
Endless St A2
Estcourt Rd A3
Exeter St C2
Fairview Rd A3
Fire Station A1
Fisherton St A1
Folkestone Rd C1
Fowlers Hill B3
Fowlers Rd B3
Friary Estate C3
Friary La B2
Friary,The B3
Gas La A1
Gigant St B3
Greencroft B3
Greencroft St A3
Guildhall B2
Hall of John Halle B2
Hamilton Rd A2
Harnham Mill B1
Harnham Rd C1/C2
High St B2
Hospital A1
House of John A'Port B2
Information Ctr B2
Kelsey Rd A3
King's Rd A3
Laverstock Rd B3
Library B2

London Rd A3
Lower St C1
Maltings, The B2
Manor Rd A3
Marsh La A1
Medieval Hall B2
Milford Hill B3
Milford St B3
Mill Rd B1
Millstream App A2
Mompesson House (NT) B2
New Bridge Rd C2
New Canal B2
New Harnham Rd C2
New St B2
North Canonry B2
North Gate B2
North Walk B2
Old Blandford Rd C1
Old Deanery B2
Old George Hall B2
Park St A3
Parsonage Green C1
Playhouse Theatre A2
Post Office A2/B2/C2
Poultry Cross B2
Queen Elizabeth Gdns B1
Queen's Rd A3
Rampart Rd B3
St Ann St B2
St Ann's Gate B2
St Marks Rd A3
St Martins B3
St Mary's Cath B2
St Nicholas Hosp C2
St Paul's A1
St Paul's Rd A1
St Thomas B2
Salisbury & South Wiltshire Mus B2
Salisbury Sta A1
Salt La A3
Saxon Rd C1
Scots La A2
Shady Bower B3
South Canonry C2
South Gate C2
Southampton Rd B2
Spire View A1
Sports Ground C3
Tollgate Rd B3
Town Path B1
Wain-a-Long Rd A3
Wardrobe, The B2
Wessex Rd A3
West Walk C2
Wilton Rd A1
Wiltshire College B3
Winchester St B3
Windsor Rd A1
Winston Churchill Gdns C3
Wyndham Rd A2
YHA B3
York Rd A1

Scarborough 124

Aberdeen Walk B2
Albert Rd A2
Albion Rd C2
Auborough St B2
Balmoral Ctr B2
Belle Vue St C1
Belmont Rd C2
Blenheim Terrace A2
Brunswick Shop Ctr B2
Castle Dykes B3
Castle Hill A3
Castle Rd B2
Castle Walls A3
Castlegate B3
Cemetery B1
Central Tramway B2
Coach Park B1
Columbus Ravine A1
Court B1
Crescent, The C2
Cricket Ground A1
Cross St B2
Crown Terr C2
Dean Rd B1
Devonshire Dr A1
East Harbour B3
East Pier B3
Eastborough B2
Elmville Ave B1
Esplanade C2
Falconers Rd B2
Falsgrave Rd C1
Fire Station B2
Foreshore Rd B2
Friargate B2
Gladstone Rd B1
Gladstone St B1
Hollywood Plaza A1
Holms, The A3
Hoxton Rd B1
King St B2
Library B2
Lifeboat Station B3
Londesborough Rd C1
Longwestgate B3
Marine Dr A3
Luna Park B3
Miniature Railway A1
Nelson St B1
Newborough B2
Nicolas St B2
North Marine Rd A1
North St B2
Northway B1
Old Harbour B3
Olympia Leisure B2
Peasholm Park A1
Peasholm Rd A1
Police Station B1
Post Office B2
Princess St B3
Prospect Rd B1
Queen St B2
Queen's Parade A2
Queen's Tower (Remains) A3
Ramshill Rd C2
Roman Signal Station A3
Roscoe St C1
Rotunda Mus C2
Royal Albert Dr A2
Royal Albert Park A2
St Martin-on-the-Hill C2
St Martin's Ave C2
St Mary's B3
St Thomas St B2
Sandside B3
Scarborough C1
Scarborough Art Gallery C2
Scarborough Bowls Centre A1
Scarborough Castle A3
Shopmobility C2
Somerset Terr C2
South Cliff Lift C2
Spa Theatre, The C2
Spa, The C2
Stephen Joseph Theatre C1
Tennyson Ave B1
Tollergate B2
Town Hall B2
Trafalgar Rd B1
Trafalgar Square A1
Trafalgar St West B1
Valley Bridge Par C2
Valley Rd C1
Vernon Rd C2
Victoria Pk Mount A1
Victoria Rd B1
West Pier B3
Westborough C1
Westover Rd C1
Westwood C1
Woodall Ave A1
YMCA Theatre B2
York Pl B2
Yorkshire Coast College (Westwood Campus) C1

Sheffield 124

Addy Dr A2
Addy St A2
Adelphi St A3
Albert Terrace Rd A3
Albion St A2
Aldred Rd A1
Allen St A4
Alma St A4
Angel St B5
Arundel Gate B5
Arundel St C4
Ashberry Rd A2
Ashdell Rd C1
Ashgate Rd C1
Athletics Centre B2
Attercliffe Rd A6
Bailey St B4
Ball St A4
Balm Green B4
Bank St B4
Barber Rd A2
Bard St B5
Barker's Pool B4
Bates St A1
Beech Hill Rd C1
Beet St B3
Bellefield St A3
Bernard Rd A6
Bernard St B6
Birkendale A2
Birkendale Rd A2
Birkendale View A1
Bishop St C4
Blackwell Pl B6
Blake St A2
Blonk St A5
Bolsover St B2
Botanical Gdns C1
Bower Rd A1
Bradley St A1
Bramall La C4
Bramwell St A3
Bridge St A4/A5
Brighton Terr Rd A1
Broad La B3
Broad St B6
Brocco St A3
Brook Hill B3
Broomfield Rd C1
Broomgrove Rd C2
Broomhall Pl C3
Broomhall Rd C2
Broomhall St C3
Broomspring La C2
Brown St C5
Brunswick St B3
Burgess St B4
Burlington St A2
Burns Rd A2
Cadman St A6
Cambridge St B4
Campo La B4
Carver St B4
Castle Square B5
Castlegate A5
Cathedral B4
Cathedral (RC) B4
Cavendish St B3
Charles St C4
Charter Row C4
Children's Hosp B2
Church St B4
City Hall B4
City Hall B4
City Rd C6
Claremont Cr B2
Claremont Pl B2
Clarke St C3
Clarkegrove Rd C2
Clarkehouse Rd C1
Clarkson St B2
Cobden View Rd A1
Collegiate Cr C2
Commercial St B5
Commonside A1
Conduit Rd B1
Cornish St A3
Corporation St A4
Court B4
Cricket Inn Rd B6
Cromwell St A1
Crookes Rd B1
Crookes Valley Park B2
Crookes Valley Rd B2
Crookesmoor Rd A2
Crown Court A4
Crucible Theatre B5
Cutlers' Hall B4
Cutlers Gate A6
Daniel Hill A2
Dental Hospital B2
Derek Dooley Way A5
Devonshire Green B3
Devonshire St B3
Division St B4
Dorset St C2
Dover St A3
Duchess Rd C5
Duke St B5
Duncombe St A1
Durham Rd B2
Earl St C4
Earl Way C4
Ecclesall Rd C3
Edward St B3
Effingham Rd A6
Effingham St A6
Egerton St C3
Eldon St B3
Elmore Rd B1
Exchange St B5
Eyre St C4
Fargate B4
Farm Rd C5
Fawcett St A3
Filey St B3
Fir St A1
Fire Station C4
Fitzalan Sq/Ponds Forge B5
Fitzwater Rd C6
Fitzwilliam Gate C4
Fitzwilliam St B3
Flat St B5
Foley St A6
Foundry Climbing Centre A4
Fulton Rd A1
Furnace Hill A4
Furnival Rd A5
Furnival Sq C4
Furnival St C4
Garden St B3
Gell St B3
Gibraltar St A4
Glebe Rd B1
Glencoe Rd C6
Glossop Rd B2/B3/C1
Gloucester St C2
Government Offices C4
Granville Rd C6
Granville Rd / The Sheffield Coll C5
Graves Gallery B5
Greave Rd B3
Green La A4
Hadfield St A1
Hanover St C3
Hanover Way C3
Harcourt Rd B1
Harmer La B5
Havelock St C2
Hawley St B4
Haymarket B5
Headford St C3
Heavygate Rd A1
Henry St A3
High St B4
Hodgson St C3
Holberry Gdns C2
Hollis Croft B4
Holly St B4
Hounsfield Rd B3
Howard Rd A1
Hoyle St A3
Hyde Park A6
Infirmary Rd A3
Infirmary Rd A3
Information Ctr B4
Jericho St A3
Johnson St A5
Kelham Island Industrial Mus A4
Lawson Rd C1
Leadmill Rd C5
Leadmill St C5
Leadmill, The C5
Leamington St A1
Leavy Rd B3
Lee Croft B4
Leopold St B4
Leveson St A6
Library A2/B5/C1
Light, The C4
Lyceum Theatre B5
Malinda St A3
Maltravers St A5
Manor Oaks Rd B6
Mappin St B3
Marlborough Rd B1
Mary St C4
Matilda St C4
Matlock Rd A1
Meadow St A3
Melbourn Rd A1
Melbourne Ave C1
Millennium Galleries B5
Milton St C3
Mitchell St B3
Mona Ave A1
Mona Rd A1
Montgomery Terrace Rd A3
Montgomery Theatre B4
Monument Grounds C6
Moor Oaks Rd B1
Moor, The C4
Moor, The C4
Moor Market C4
Moore St C3
Mowbray St A4
Mushroom La B2
National Emergency Service A4
Netherthorpe Rd B3
Netherthorpe Rd B3
Newbould La C1
Nile St C1
Norfolk Park Rd C6
Norfolk Rd C6
Norfolk St B4
North Church St B4
Northfield Rd A1
Northumberland Rd B1
Nursery St A5
O2 Academy B5
Oakholme Rd C1
Octagon B2
Odeon B5
Old St B6
Orchard Square B4
Orch Sq Shop Ctr B4
Oxford St A2
Paradise St B4
Park La C2
Park Sq B5
Parker's Rd B1
Pearson Building (Univ) C2
Penistone Rd A3
Pinstone St B4
Pitt St B3
Police Station B5
Pond Hill B5
Pond St B5
Ponds Forge Int Sports Ctr B5
Portobello St B3
Post Office A2/B3/B4/B5/C1/C3/C6
Powell St A2
Queen St B4
Queen's Rd C5
Ramsey Rd B1
Red Hill B3
Redcar Rd B1
Regent St B3
Rockingham St B4
Roebuck Rd A2
Royal Hallamshire Hospital C2
Russell St A4
Rutland Park C1
St George's Cl B3
St Mary's Gate C3
St Mary's Rd C4/C5
St Peter & St Paul Cathedral B4
St Philip's Rd A3
Savile St A5
School Rd B1
Scotland St A4
Severn Rd B1
Shalesmoor A4
Shalesmoor A3
Sheaf St B5
Sheffield Hallam University B5
Sheffield Ice Sports Centre – Skate Central C5
Sheffield Interchange B5
Sheffield Parkway A6
Sheffield Station C5
Sheffield Station/Sheffield Hallam University B5
Sheffield University B2
Shepherd St A3
Shipton St A2
Shopmobility B3
Shoreham St C4
Showroom C5
Shrewsbury Rd C5
Sidney St C4
Site Gallery C5
Slinn St A1
Smithfield A4
Snig Hill A5
Snow La A4
Solly St B3
South La C4
South Street Park B5
Southbourne Rd C1
Spital Hill A5
Spital St A5
Spring Hill B1
Spring Hill Rd B1
Springvale Rd A1
Stafford Rd C6
Stafford St B6
Suffolk Rd C5
Summer St B2
Sunny Bank C3
Superstore A3/C3
Surrey St B4
Sussex St A6
Sutton St B3
Sydney Rd A2
Sylvester St C4
Talbot St B5
Tapton Hall Conference & Banqueting Ctr B1
Taptonville Rd B1
Tenter St B4
Town Hall B4
Townend St A1
Townhead St B4
Trafalgar St B4
Tree Root Walk B2
Trinity St A4
Trippet La B4
Turner Museum of Glass B3
Union St B4
University Drama Studio B2
Univ of Sheffield B3
Upper Allen St A3
Upper Hanover St B3
Upperthorpe Rd A2/A3
Verdon St A5
Victoria Rd C2
Victoria St B3
Waingate B5
Watery St A3
Watson Rd C1
Wellesley Rd B2
Wellington St C3
West Bar A4
West Bar Green A4
West One Plaza B3
West St B3
West St B3
Westbourne Rd C1
Western Bank B2
Western Rd A1
Weston Park B2
Weston Pk Hosp B2
Weston Pk Mus B2
Weston St B2
Wharncliffe Rd C3
Whitham Rd B1
Wicker A5
Wilkinson St B2
William St C3
Winter Garden B4
Winter St B2
York St B4
Yorkshire Artspace C5
Young St C4

Southampton 124

Above Bar St A2
Albert Rd North B3
Albert Rd South C3
Andersons Rd B3
Argyle Rd A2
Arundel Tower B1
Bargate, The B2
BBC Regional Ctr A1
Bedford Pl A1
Belvidere Rd A3
Bernard St C2
Blechynden Terr A1
Brinton's Rd A2
Britannia Rd A3
Briton St C2
Brunswick Pl A2
Bugle St C1
Canute Rd C3
Castle Way C2
Catchcold Tower B1
Central Bridge C3
Central Rd C2
Channel Way C3
Chapel Rd B3
City Art Gallery A1
City College B3
City Cruise Terminal C1
Civic Centre A1
Civic Centre Rd A1
Coach Station B1
Commercial Rd A1
Cumberland Pl A1
Cunard Rd C2
Derby Rd A3
Devonshire Rd A1
Dock Gate 4 C2
Dock Gate 8 B1
East Park (Andrew's Park) A2
East Park Terr A2
East St B2
Endle St B3
European Way C2
Fire Station A2
Floating Bridge Rd C3
God's House Tower C2
Golden Grove A3
Graham Rd A2
Guildhall A1
Hanover Bldgs B2
Harbour Lights C3
Harbour Pde B1
Hartington Rd A3
Havelock Rd A1
Henstead Rd A1
Herbert Walker Ave B1
High St B2
Hoglands Park B2
Holy Rood (Rems), Merchant Navy Memorial B2
Houndwell Park B2
Houndwell Pl B2
Hythe Ferry C2
Information Ctr A1
Isle of Wight Ferry Terminal C1
James St B3
Kingsway A2
Leisure World B1
Library A1
Lime St B2
London Rd A2
Marine Parade B3
Marlands Shopping Ctr, The A1
Marsh La B2
Mayflower Meml C1
Mayflower Park C1
Mayflower Theatre, The A1
Medieval Merchant's House C1
Melbourne St B3
Millais A2
Morris Rd A1
National Oceanography Centre C3
Neptune Way C3
New Rd A2
Nichols Rd A3
North Front A2
Northam Rd A3
Ocean Dock C2
Ocean Village Marina C3
Ocean Way C3
Odeon B1
Ogle Rd B1
Old Northam Rd A2
Orchard La B2
Oxford Ave A2
Oxford St C2
Palmerston Park A2
Palmerston Rd A2
Parsonage Rd A3
Peel St A3
Platform Rd C2
Polygon, The A1
Portland Terr B1
Post Office A2/A3/B2
Pound Tree Rd B2
Quays Swimming & Diving Complex, The B1
Queen's Park C2
Queen's Peace Fountain A2
Queen's Terr C2
Queensway B2
Radcliffe Rd A3
Rochester St A3
Royal Pier C1
Royal South Hants Hospital A2
St Andrew's Rd A2
St Mary's B3
St Mary St A2
St Mary's Leisure Centre A2
St Mary's Pl B2
St Mary's Rd A2
St Mary's Stadium (Southampton FC) A3
St Michael's C1
Sea City Mus A1
Showcase Cinema de Lux B1
Solent Sky C3
South Front B2
Southampton Central Station A1
Southampton Solent University A2
SS Shieldhall C2
Terminus Terr C2
Threefield La B2
Titanic Engineers' Memorial A2
Town Quay C1
Town Walls B2
Tudor House C1
Vincent's Walk B2
Westgate Hall C1
West Marlands Rd A1
West Park A1
West Park Rd A1
West Quay Rd B1
West Quay Retail Pk B1
Western Esplanade B1
Westquay Shop Ctr B1
Westquay Watermark B1
White Star Way C2
Winton St A2

Southend-on-Sea 125

Adventure Island C3
Albany Ave A1
Albert Rd C3
Alexandra Rd C2
Alexandra St C2
Alexandra Yacht Club C2
Ashburnham Rd B2
Ave Rd B1
Avenue Terr B1
Balmoral Rd B1
Baltic Ave B3
Baxter Ave A2/B2
Beecroft Art Gallery B2
Bircham Rd A2
Boscombe Rd B3
Boston Ave A1/B2
Bournemouth Park Rd A3
Browning Ave A3
Bus Station C3
Byron Ave A3
Cambridge Rd C1/C2
Canewdon Rd B1
Carnarvon Rd A2
Central Ave A3
Chelmsford Ave A1
Chichester Rd B2
Church Rd C3
Civic Centre A2
Clarence Rd C2
Clarence St C2
Cliff Ave B1
Cliffs Pavilion C1
Clifftown Parade C2
Clifftown Rd C2
Colchester Rd A1
Coleman St B3
College Way B2
County Court B3
Cromer Rd B3
Crowborough Rd A2
Dryden Ave A3
East St A2
Elmer App B2
Elmer Ave B2
Forum, The B2
Gainsborough Dr A1
Gayton Rd A2
Glenhurst Rd A2
Gordon Pl B2
Gordon Rd B2
Grainger Rd A2
Greyhound Way A3
Grove, The A3
Guildford Rd B3
Hamlet Ct Rd B1
Hamlet Rd C1
Harcourt Ave A1
Hartington Rd C3
Hastings Rd B3
Herbert Gr C3
Heygate Ave C3
High St B2/C2
Information Ctr C3
Kenway A2
Kilworth Ave B3
Lancaster Gdns B3
London Rd B1
Lucy Rd C3
MacDonald Ave A1
Magistrates' Court A2
Maldon Rd A2
Marine Ave C1
Marine Parade C3
Marine Rd C1
Milton Rd B1
Milton St B2
Napier Ave B2
North Ave A3
North Rd A1/B1
Odeon B2
Osborne Rd B1
Park Cres B1
Park Rd B1
Park St B1
Park Terr B1
Pier Hill C3
Pleasant Rd C3
Police Station A2
Post Office B2/B3
Princes St B2
Queens Rd B2
Queensway B2/B3/C3
Radio Essex C2
Rayleigh Ave A1
Redstock Rd A2
Rochford Ave A1
Royal Mews C2
Royal Terr C2
Royals Shopping Centre, The C3
Ruskin Ave A3
St Ann's Rd B3
St Helen's Rd B1
St John's Rd B1
St Leonard's Rd C3
St Lukes Rd A3
St Vincent's Rd C1
Salisbury Ave A1/B1
Scratton Rd C2
Shakespeare Dr A1
Shopmobility B2
Short St A2
South Ave A3
Southchurch Rd B3
Southend Central B2
Southend Pier Railway C3
Southend United FC A1
Southend Victoria B2
Stanfield Rd A2
Stanley Rd C3
Sutton Rd A3/B3
Swanage Rd B3
Sweyne Ave A1
Sycamore Gr A3
Tennyson Ave A3
Tickfield Ave A2
Tudor Rd A1
Tunbridge Rd A2
Tylers Ave B3
Tyrrel Dr B3
Univ of Essex B2/C2
Vale Ave A2
Victoria Ave A2
Victoria Shopping Centre, The B2
Warrior Sq B3
Wesley Rd C3
West Rd A1
West St A1
Westcliff Ave C1
Westcliff Parade C1
Western Esplanade C1
Weston Rd C2
Whitegate Rd B3
Wilson Rd C1
Wimborne Rd B3
York Rd C3

Stoke-on-Trent (Hanley) 125

Acton St A3
Albion St B2
Argyle St C1
Ashbourne Gr A2
Avoca St A3
Baskerville Rd B3
Bedford Rd C1
Bedford St C1
Bethesda St B2
Bexley St A2
Birches Head Rd A3
Botteslow St C3
Boundary St A2
Broad St C2
Broom St A3
Bryan St A2
Bucknall New Rd B3
Bucknall Old Rd B3
Bus Station B3
Cannon St C2
Castlefield St C1
Cavendish St B1
Central Forest Pk A2
Charles St B3
Cheapside B2
Chell St A3
Clarke St C1
Cleveland Rd C2
Clifford St C3
Clough St B2
Clyde St C1
College Rd C2
Cooper St C2
Corbridge Rd A1
Cutts St C2
Davis St C1
Denbigh St A1
Derby St C3
Dilke St A3
Dundas St A3
Dundee Rd C1
Dyke St B3
Eastwood Rd C3
Eaton St A3
Etruria Park B1
Etruria Rd B1
Etruria Vale Rd C1
Festing St A3
Festival Retail Park A1
Fire Station C2
Foundry St B2
Franklyn St C3
Garnet St B1
Garth St B3
George St A3
Gilman St B3
Glass St B3
Goodson St B3
Greyhound Way A1
Grove Pl C1
Hampton St C3
Hanley Park C2
Hanley Park C2
Harding Rd C2
Hassall St B3
Havelock Pl C1
Hazlehurst St C3
Hinde St C2
Hope St B2
Houghton St C2
Hulton St A3
Information Ctr B3
Jasper St C2
Jervis St A3
John Bright St A3
John St B2
Keelings Rd A3
Kimberley Rd C1
Ladysmith Rd C1
Lawrence St C2
Leek Rd C3
Library C2
Lichfield St C3
Linfield Rd B3
Loftus St A2
Lower Bedford St C1
Lower Bryan St A2
Lower Mayer St A3
Lowther St A1
Magistrates Court C2
Malham St A2
Marsh St B2
Matlock St C3
Mayer St A3
Milton St C1
Mitchell Memorial Theatre B2
Morley St B2
Moston St A3
Mount Pleasant C1
Mulgrave St A1
Mynors St B3
Nelson Pl B3
New Century St B1
Octagon Retail Pk B1
Ogden Rd C3
Old Hall St B3
Old Town Rd A3
Pall Mall B2
Palmerston St C3
Park and Ride C2
Parker St B2
Parkway, The C2
Pavilion Dr A1
Pelham St C3
Percy St B2
Piccadilly B2
Picton St B3
Plough St A3
Police Station C2
Portland St A1
Post Office A3/B3/C3
Potteries Museum & Art Gallery B2
Potteries Shopping Centre B2
Potteries Way C2
Powell St A1
Pretoria Rd C1
Quadrant Rd B2
Ranelagh St C2
Raymond St C2
Rectory Rd C1
Regent Rd C2
Regent Theatre B2
Richmond Terr C2
Ridgehouse Dr A1
Robson St C2
St Ann St B3
St Luke St B3
Sampson St B2
Shaw St A1
Sheaf St C2
Shearer St C1
Shelton New Rd C1
Shirley Rd C2
Slippery La B2
Snow Hill C2
Spur St C3
Stafford St B2
Statham St B2
Stubbs La C3
Sun St C1
Supermarket A1/B2
Talbot St C3
Town Hall B2
Town Rd A3
Trinity St B2
Union St A2
Upper Hillchurch St A3
Upper Huntbach St B3
Victoria Hall Theatre B3
Warner St C2
Warwick St C1
Waterloo Rd A1
Waterloo St B3
Well St B3
Wellesley St C2
Wellington Rd B3
Wellington St B3
Whitehaven Dr A2
Whitmore St C1
Windermere St A1
Woodall St A1
Yates St C2
York St A2

Stratford-upon-Avon 125

Albany Rd B1
Alcester Rd B1
Ambulance Station B1
Arden St B2
Avenue Farm A1
Ave Farm Ind Est A1
Avenue Rd A3
Baker Ave A1
Bandstand C3
Benson Rd A3
Birmingham Rd A2
Boat Club B3
Borden Pl C1
Bridge St B2
Bridgetown Rd C3
Bridgeway B3
Broad St C2
Broad Walk C2
Brookvale Rd C1
Brunel Way B1
Bull St C2
Butterfly Farm C3
Cemetery C1
Chapel La B2
Cherry Orchard C1
Chestnut Walk B2
Children's Playground C3
Church St C2
Civic Hall B2
Clarence Rd B1
Clopton Bridge B3
Clopton Rd A2
College B1
College La C2
College St C2
Com Sports Centre B1
Council Offices (District) B2
Courtyard, The C2
Cox's Yard B3
Cricket Ground C3
Ely Gdns B2
Ely St B2
Evesham Rd C1
Fire Station B1
Foot Ferry C3
Fordham Ave A2
Garrick Way C1
Gower Memorial B3
Great William St B2
Greenhill St B2
Greenway, The C2
Grove Rd B2
Guild St B2
Guildhall & School B2
Hall's Croft C2
Harvard House B2
Henley St B2
Hertford Rd C1
High St B2
Holton St C2
Holy Trinity C2
Information Ctr B3
Jolyffe Park Rd A2
Kipling Rd C3
Library B2
Lodge Rd B1
Maidenhead Rd A3
Mansell St B2
Masons Court B2
Masons Rd A1
Maybird Shopping Park A2
Maybrook Retail Pk A2
Maybrook Rd A1
Mayfield Ave A2
Meer St B2
Mill La C2
Moat House Hotel B3
Narrow La C2
Nash's House & New Place B2
New St C2
Old Town C2
Orchard Way C1
Other Place, The C2
Paddock La C1
Park Rd A1
Payton St B2
Percy St A2
Police Station B2
Post Office B2
Recreation Ground C2
Regal Road A2
Rother St B2
Rowley Cr A3
Royal Shakespeare Theatre B3
Ryland St C2
Saffron Meadow C2
St Andrew's Cr B1
St Gregory's A3
St Gregory's Rd A3
St Mary's Rd A2
Sanctus Dr C2
Sanctus St C1
Sandfield Rd C2
Scholars La B2
Seven Meadows Rd C2
Shakespeare Inst C2
Shakespeare St B2
Shakespeare's Birthplace B2
Sheep St B2
Shelley Rd C3
Shipston Rd C3
Shottery Rd C1
Slingates Rd A2
Southern La C2
Station Rd B1
Stratford Healthcare B2
Stratford Hosp B2
Stratford Leisure Centre B3
Stratford Sports Club B1
Stratford-upon-Avon Station B1
Swan Theatre B3
Swan's Nest La B3
Talbot Rd A2
Tiddington Rd B3
Timothy's Bridge Industrial Estate A1
Timothy's Bridge Rd A1
Town Hall & Council Offices B2
Town Sq B2
Trinity Cl C2
Tyler St B2
War Memorial Gdns B3
Warwick Rd B3
Waterside B3
Welcombe Rd A3
West St C2
Western Rd A2
Wharf Rd A2
Willows North, The B1
Willows, The B1
Wood St B2

Sunderland 125

Albion Pl C2
Alliance Pl B1
Argyle St C2
Ashwood St C1
Athenaeum St B2
Azalea Terr C2
Beach St A1
Bedford St B2
Beechwood Terr C1
Belvedere Rd C2
Blandford St B2
Borough Rd B3
Bridge Cr B2
Bridge St B2
Bridges, The B2
Brooke St A2
Brougham St B2
Burdon Rd C2
Burn Park C1
Burn Park Rd C1
Burn Pk Tech Pk C1
Carol St B1
Charles St A3
Chester Rd C1
Chester Terr B1
Church St A3
Civic Centre C2
Cork St B3
Coronation St B3
Cowan Terr C2
Dame Dorothy St A2
Deptford Rd B1
Deptford Terr A1
Derby St C2
Derwent St C2
Dock St A3
Dundas St A2
Durham Rd C1
Easington St A2
Egerton St C3
Empire B3
Empire Theatre B2
Farringdon Row B1
Fawcett St B2
Fire Station B1
Fox St C1
Foyle St B3
Frederick St B3
Hanover Pl A1
Havelock Terr C1
Hay St A2
Headworth Sq B3
Hendon Rd B3
High St East B3
High St West B2/B3
Holmeside B2
Hylton Rd B1
Information Ctr B2
John St B3
Kier Hardie Way A2
Lambton St B3
Laura St C3
Lawrence St B3
Library & Arts Ctr B3
Lily St B1
Lime St B1
Livingstone Rd B2
Low Row B2
Matamba Terr B1
Millburn St B1
Millennium Way A2
Minster B2
Monkwearmouth Station Mus A2
Mowbray Park C3
Mowbray Rd C3
Murton St C3
National Glass Centre A3
New Durham Rd C1
Newcastle Rd A2
Nile St B3
Norfolk St B3
North Bridge St A2
Northern Gallery for Contemporary Art B3
Otto Terr C1
Park La C2
Park Lane C2
Park Rd C2
Paul's Rd B3
Peel St C3
Point, The B2
Police Station B2
Priestly Cr A1
Queen St B2

Railway Row B1
Retail Park B1
Richmond St A2
Roker Ave A2
Royalty Theatre C1
Royalty,The C1
Ryhope Rd C2
St Mary's Way B2
St Michael's Way B2
St Peter's A3
St Peter's A2
St Peter's Way A3
St Vincent St C3
Salem Rd C3
Salem St C3
Salisbury St C3
Sans St B3
Shopmobility B2
Silkworth Row B1
Southwick Rd A2
Stadium of Light (Sunderland AFC) A2
Stadium Way A2
Stobart St A2
Stockton Rd C2
Suffolk St C3
Sunderland B2
Sunderland Aquatic Centre A2
Sunderland Mus B3
Sunderland St B3
Sunderland Sta B2
Tatham St C3
Tavistock Pl B3
Thelma St C1
Thomas St North A2
Thornholme Rd C1
Toward Rd C3
Transport Interchange C2
Trimdon St Way B1
Tunstall Rd C2
University C1
University Library C1
Univ of Sunderland (City Campus) B1
Univ of Sunderland (Sir Tom Cowle at St Peter's Campus) A3
Vaux Brewery Way A2
Villiers St B3
Villiers St South B3
Vine Pl C2
Violet St B1
Walton La B3
Waterworks Rd B1
Wearmouth Bridge B2
West Sunniside B3
West Wear St B3
Westbourne Rd B1
Western Hill C1
Wharncliffe B1
Whickham St A3
White House Rd C3
Wilson St North A2
Winter Gdns C3
Wreath Quay A1

Swansea Abertawe 125

Adelaide St C3
Albert Row C3
Alexandra Rd B3
Argyle St C1
Baptist Well Pl A2
Beach St C1
Belle Vue Way B3
Berw Rd A1
Berwick Terr A2
Bond St C1
Brangwyn Concert Hall C1
Bridge St A3
Brookands Terr B1
Brunswick St C1
Bryn-Syfi Terr A2
Bryn-y-Mor Rd C1
Bullins La B1
Burrows Rd C1
Bus Station C2
Bus/Rail link A3
Cadfan Rd A1
Cadrawd Rd A1
Caer St B3
Carig Cr A1
Carlton Terr B2
Carmarthen Rd A3
Castle Square B3
Castle St B3
Catherine St C1
Cinema C3
Civic Ctr & Library C2
Clarence St C2
Colbourne Terr A2
Constitution Hill B1
Court B3
Creidiol Rd A2
Cromwell St B2
Crown Courts C1
Duke St B1
Dunvant Pl C2
Dyfatty Park A3
Dyfatty St A3
Dyfed Ave A1
Dylan Thomas Centre B3
Dylan Thomas Theatre C3
Eaton Cr C1
Eigen Cr A1
Elfed Rd A1
Emlyn Rd A1
Evans Terr A3
Fairfield Terr B1
Ffynone Dr B1
Ffynone Rd B1
Fire Station B3
Firm St A2
Fleet St C1
Francis St C1
Fullers Row B2
George St B2
Glamorgan St C2
Glynn Vivian Art Gallery B3
Gower College Swansea C1
Graig Terr A3
Grand Theatre C2
Granogwen Rd A2
Guildhall C1
Guildhall Rd South C1
Gwent Rd A1
Gwynedd Ave A1
Hafod St A3
Hanover St B1
Harcourt St B2
Harries St A2
Heathfield B2
Henrietta St B1
Hewson St B2
High St A3/B3
High View A2
Hill St A2
Historic Ships Berth C3
HM Prison C2
Information Ctr C2
Islwyn Rd A1
King Edward's Rd C1
Kingsway,The B2
LC,The C3
Long Ridge A2
Madoc St C2
Mansel St B2
Maritime Quarter C3
Market B3
Mayhill Gdns B1
Mayhill Rd A1
Milton Terr A2
Mission Gallery C3
Montpelier Terr B1
Morfa Rd A3
Mount Pleasant B2
National Waterfront Museum C3
New Cut Rd A3
New St A3
Nicander Pde A2
Nicander Pl A2
Nicholl St B2
Norfolk St B2
North Hill Rd A2
Northampton La B2
Observatory C3
Orchard St B3
Oxford St B2
Oystermouth Rd C1
Page St B2
Pant-y-Celyn Rd B1
Parc Tawe North B3
Parc Tawe Shopping & Leisure Centre B3
Patti Pavilion C1
Paxton St C2
Pen-y-Graig Rd A1
Penmaen Terr B1
Phillips Pde C1
Picton Terr B2
Plantasia B3
Plantasia B3
Police Station B2
Post Office A1/A2/C1/C2
Powys Ave A1
Primrose St B2
Princess Way B3
Promenade B2
Pryder Gdns A1
Quadrant Shop Ctr C2
Quay Park B3
Rhianfa La B1
Rhondda St B2
Richardson St C2
Rodney St C1
Rose Hill B1
Rosehill Terr B1
Russell St B1
St David's Shopping Centre C3
St Helen's Ave C1
St Helen's Cr C1
St Helen's Rd C1
St James Gdns B1
St James's Cr B1
St Mary's B3
Sea View Terr A1
Singleton St C2
South Dock C3
Stanley Pl B2
Strand B3
Swansea Castle B3
Swansea Metropolitan University B2
Swansea Mus C3
Swansea Station A3
Taliesyn Rd B1
Tan y Marian Rd A1
Tegid Rd A2
Teilo Cr A1
Tenpin Bowling B3
Terrace Rd B1/B2
Tontine St A3
Townhill Rd A1
Tramshed,The C3
Trawler Rd C3
Union St B2
Upper Strand A3
Vernon St A3
Victoria Quay C3
Victoria Rd B3
Vincent St C1
Walter Rd B1
Watkin St A2
Waun-Wen Rd A2
Wellington St C2
Westbury St C1
Western St C1
Westway C2
William St C2
Wind St B3
Woodlands Terrace B1
YMCA B2
York St C3

Swindon 125

Albert St C3
Albion St C1
Alfred St A2
Alvescot Rd C3
Art Gallery & Museum C3
Ashford Rd C1
Aylesbury St A2
Bath Rd C2
Bathampton St B1
Bathurst Rd B3
Beatrice St A2
Beckhampton St B3
Bowood Rd C1
Bristol St B1
Broad St A3
Brunel Arcade B2
Brunel Plaza B2
Brunswick St C2
Bus Station B2
Cambria Bridge Rd B1
Cambria Place B1
Canal Walk B2
Carfax St B2
Carr St B1
Cemetery C1/C3
Chandler Cl C3
Chapel C1
Chester St B1
Christ Church C3
Church Place B1
Cirencester Way A3
Clarence St B2
Clifton St C1
Cockleberry A2
Colbourne A3
Colbourne St A3
College St B2
Commercial Rd B2
Corporation St A2
Council Offices B3
County Rd A3
Courts B2
Cricket Ground A3
Cricklade Street C3
Crombey St B1/C2
Cross St C2
Curtis St B1
Deacon St C1
Designer Outlet (Great Western) B1
Dixon St C2
Dover St C2
Dowling St C2
Drove Rd C3
Dryden St C1
Durham St C3
East St B1
Eastcott Hill C2
Eastcott Rd C2
Edgeware Rd B2
Edmund St C2
Elmina Rd A3
Emlyn Square B1
Euclid St B3
Exeter St B1
Fairview C1
Faringdon Rd B1
Farnsby St B1
Fire Station B3
Fleet St B2
Fleming Way B2/B3
Florence St A2
Gladstone St A3
Gooch St A2
Graham St A3
Great Western Way A1/A2
Groundwell Rd B3
Hawksworth Way A1
Haydon St A2
Henry St B2
Hillside Ave C1
Holbrook Way B2
Hunt St C3
Hydro B1
Hythe Rd C2
Information Ctr B2
Joseph St C1
Kent Rd C2
King William St C2
Kingshill Rd C1
Lansdown Rd C2
Lawn,The C3
Leicester St B3
Library B2
Lincoln St B3
Little London C3
London St B1
Magic B3
Maidstone Rd C2
Manchester Rd A3
Maxwell St B1
Milford St B2
Milton Rd B1
Morse St C2
National Monuments Record Centre B1
Newcastle St B3
Newcombe Drive A1
Newcombe Trading Estate A1
Newhall St C2
North St C2
North Star A1
North Star Ave A1
Northampton St B3
Nurseries,The C1
Oasis Leisure Ctr A1
Ocotal Way A3
Okus Rd C1
Old Town C3
Oxford St B1
Parade,The B2
Park Lane B1
Park Lane B1
Park,The B1
Pembroke St C2
Plymouth St B3
Polaris House A2
Polaris Way A2
Police Station B2
Ponting St A2
Post Office B1/B2/C1/C3
Poulton St A3
Princes St B2
Prospect Hill C2
Prospect Place C2
Queen St B2
Queen's Park C3
Radnor St C1
Read St C1
Reading St B1
Regent St B2
Retail Park A2/A3/B3
Rosebery St A3
St Mark's B1
Salisbury St A3
Savernake St C2
Shelley St C1
Sheppard St B1
South St C2
Southampton St B3
Spring Gardens B3
Stafford Street C2
Stanier St C2
Station Road A2
STEAM B1
Swindon College A2
Swindon Rd C2
Swindon Station A2
Swindon Town Football Club A3
T A Centre B1
Tennyson St B1
Theobald St B1
Town Hall B2
Transfer Bridges A3
Union St C2
Upham Rd C3
Victoria Rd C3
Walcot Rd B3
War Memorial B2
Wells St B3
Western St C2
Westmorland Rd B3
Whalebridge B2
Whitehead St C1
Whitehouse Rd A2
William St C1
Wood St C3
Wyvern Theatre & Arts Centre B2
York Rd B3

Telford 126

Alma Ave C1
Amphitheatre C2
Bowling Alley B2
Brandsfarm Way C3
Brunel Rd B1
Bus Station B2
Buxton Rd C1
Central Park A2
Civic Offices B2
Coach Central B2
Coachwell Cl B1
Colliers Way A1
Courts B2
Dale Acre Way B3
Darliston C3
Deepdale B3
Deercote B2
Dinthill C3
Doddington C3
Dodmoor Grange C3
Downemead B3
Duffryn B3
Dunsheath B3
Euston Way A3
Eyton Mound C1
Eyton Rd C1
Forgegate A2
Grange Central B2
Hall Park Way B1
Hinkshay Rd C2
Hollinsworth Rd A2
Holyhead Rd A3
Housing Trust A1
Ice Rink B2
Information Ctr B2
Ironmasters Way A2
Job Centre B1
Land Registry B1
Lawn Central B2
Lawnswood C1
Library B2
Malinsgate B1
Matlock Ave C1
Moor Rd C1
Mount Rd C1
NFU Offices B1
Odeon B2
Park Lane A1
Police Station B2
Priorslee Ave A3
Queen Elizabeth Ave C3
Queen Elizabeth Way B1
Queensway A2/B3
Rampart Way A2
Randlay Ave C3
Randlay Wood C3
Rhodes Ave C1
Royal Way B1
St Leonards Rd B1
St Quentin Gate B2
Shifnal Rd A3
Sixth Ave A1
Southwater One (SW1) B2
Southwater Way B1
Spout Lane C1
Spout Mound B1
Spout Way C1
Stafford Court B3
Stafford Park B3
Stirchley Ave C3
Stone Row C1
Telford Bridge Retail Park A1
Telford Central Station A3
Telford Centre,The B2
Telford Forge Shopping Park A1
Telford Hornets RFC C2
Telford Int Ctr C2
Telford Way A3
Third Ave A2
Town Park C2
Town Pk Visitor Ctr B2
Walker House B2
Wellswood Ave A2
West Centre Way B1
Withywood Drive C1
Woodhouse Central B2
Yates Way A1

Torquay 126

Abbey Rd B2
Alexandra Rd A2
Alpine Rd B3
AMF Bowling C3
Ash Hill Rd A2
Babbacombe Rd B3
Bampfylde Rd B1
Barton Rd A1
Beacon Quay C2
Belgrave Rd A1/B1
Belmont Rd A3
Berea Rd A3
Braddons Hill Rd East B3
Brewery Park A3
Bronshill Rd A2
Castle Circus A2
Castle Rd A2
Cavern Rd A3
Central B2
Chatsworth Rd A2
Chestnut Ave B1
Church St A1
Civic Offices A2
Coach Station A1
Corbyn Head C1
Croft Hill B1
Croft Rd B1
East St A1
Egerton Rd A3
Ellacombe Church Rd A3
Ellacombe Rd A2
Falkland Rd B1
Fleet St B2
Fleet Walk Shopping Centre B2
Grafton Rd B3
Haldon Pier C2
Hatfield Rd A2
Highbury Rd A2
Higher Warberry Rd A3
Hillesdon Rd B3
Hoxton Rd A3
Hunsdon Rd B3
Information Ctr B2
Inner Harbour C3
Kenwyn Rd A3
King's Drive,The B1
Laburnum St A1
Law Courts A2
Library A2
Lime Ave B1
Living Coasts C3
Lower Warberry Rd B3
Lucius St B1
Lymington Rd A1
Magdalene Rd A1
Marina C2
Market Forum,The B2
Market St B2
Meadfoot Lane C3
Meadfoot Rd C3
Melville St B2
Middle Warberry Rd B3
Mill Lane A1
Montpellier Rd B3
Morgan Ave A1
Museum Rd B3
Newton Rd A1
Oakhill Rd A1
Outer Harbour C2
Parkhill Rd C3
Pavilion Shopping Centre C2
Pimlico B2
Police Station A1
Post Office A1/B2
Prince of Wales Steps C3
Princes Rd A3
Princes Rd East A3
Princes Rd West A3
Princess Gdns C2
Princess Pier C2
Princess Theatre C2
Rathmore Rd B1
Recreation Grd B1
Riviera Int Ctr B1
Rock End Ave C3
Rock Rd B2
Rock Walk B2
Rosehill Rd A3
South West Coast Path C3
St Efride's Rd A1
St John's B3
St Luke's Rd B2
St Luke's Rd North B2
St Luke's Rd South B2
St Marychurch Rd A2
Scarborough Rd B1
Shedden Hill B2
South Pier C2
South St A1
Spanish Barn B1
Stitchill Rd B3
Strand B3
Sutherland Rd B3
Teignmouth Rd A1
Temperance St B2
Terrace,The B3
Thurlow Rd A1
Tor Bay B1
Tor Church Rd A1
Tor Hill Rd A1
Torbay Rd B2
Torquay Mus B3
Torquay Station C1
Torre Abbey Mansion B1
Torre Abbey Meadows B1
Torre Abbey Sands B1
Torwood Gdns B3
Torwood St C3
Town Hall A2
Union Square Shopping Centre A2
Union St A1
Upton Hill A2
Upton Park A1
Upton Rd A1
Vanehill Rd C3
Vansittart Rd A1
Vaughan Parade C3
Victoria Parade C3
Victoria Rd A2
Warberry Rd West B2
Warren Rd B2
Windsor Rd A2/A3
Woodville Rd A3

Winchester 126

Andover Rd A2
Andover Road Retail Park A2
Archery La C2
Arthur Rd A2
Bar End Rd C3
Beaufort Rd C2
Beggar's La B3
Bereweeke Ave A1
Bereweeke Rd A1
Boscobel Rd A2
Brassey Rd A2
Broadway B3
Brooks Shopping Centre,The B3
Bus Station B3
Butter Cross B2
Canon St C2
Castle Wall C2/C3
Castle, King Arthur's Round Table B2
Cathedral C2
Cheriton Rd A1
Chesil St C3
Chesil Theatre C3
Christchurch Rd C1
City Mill B3
City Museum B2
City Rd B2
Clifton Rd B1
Clifton Terr B2
Close Wall C2/C3
Coach Park A2
Colebrook St C3
College St C2
College Walk C3
Compton Rd C2
Council Offices C3
County Council Offices B2
Cranworth Rd A2
Cromwell Rd C1
Culver Rd C2
Domum Rd C3
Durngate Pl B3
Eastgate St B3
Edgar Rd C2
Egbert Rd A2
Elm Rd B1
Everyman B2
Fairfield Rd A1
Fire Station B3
Fordington Ave B1
Fordington Rd A1
Friarsgate B3
Gordon Rd B3
Greenhill Rd B1
Guildhall B3
Hatherley Rd A1
High St B2
Hillier Way A3
HM Prison B1
Hyde Abbey (Remains) A2
Hyde Abbey Rd B2
Hyde Cl A2
Hyde St A2
Information Ctr B3
Jane Austen's House C2
Jewry St B2
King Alfred Pl A2
Kingsgate Arch C2
Kingsgate Park C2
Kingsgate Rd C2
Kingsgate St C2
Lankhills Rd A2
Law Courts B2
Library B2
Lower Brook St B3
Magdalen Hill B3
Market La B2
Mews La B1
Middle Brook St B3
Middle Rd B1
Military Museums B2
Milland Rd C3
Milverton Rd B1
Monks Rd A3
North Hill Cl A2
North Walls B2
North Walls Recreation Gnd A3
Nuns Rd A3
Oram's Arbour B1
Owens Rd A2
Parchment St B2
Park & Ride C3
Park Ave B3
Playing Field A1
Police HQ B1
Portal Rd C3
Post Office B2/C1
Quarry Rd C3
Ranelagh Rd C1
Regiment Mus B2
River Park Leisure Ctr B3
Romans' Rd C2
Romsey Rd B1
Royal Hampshire County Hospital (A&E) B1
St Cross Rd C2
St George's St B2
St Giles Hill C3
St James Villas C2
St James' La B1
St James' Terr B1
St John's B3
St John's St B3
St Michael's Rd C2
St Paul's Hill B1
St Peter St B2
St Swithun St C2
St Thomas St C2
Saxon Rd A2
School of Art B3
Sleepers Hill Rd C1
Southgate St B2
Sparkford Rd C1
Square,The B2
Staple Gdns B2
Station Rd B2
Step Terr B1
Stockbridge Rd A1
Stuart Cres C1
Sussex St B2
Swan Lane B2
Tanner St B3
Theatre Royal B2
Tower St B2
Union St B3
Univ of Southampton (Winchester School of Art) B3
University of Winchester (King Alfred Campus) C1
Upper Brook St B2
Wales St B3
Water Lane B3
Weirs,The C3
West End Terr B1
Western Rd B1
Westgate B2
Wharf Hill C3
Winchester College C2
Winchester Sta A2
Winnall Moors Wildlife Reserve A3
Wolvesey Castle C3
Worthy Lane A2
Worthy Rd A2

Windsor 126

Adelaide Sq C3
Albany Rd C2
Albert St B1
Alexandra Gdns B2
Alexandra Rd C2
Alma Rd B2
Ambulance Station B1
Arthur Rd B2
Bachelors Acre B3
Barry Ave B2
Beaumont Rd C2
Bexley St B1
Boat House B2
Brocas St B2
Brocas,The A2
Brook St C3
Bulkeley Ave C1
Castle Hill B3
Charles St B2
Claremont Rd C2
Clarence Cr B2
Clarence Rd B1
Clewer Court Rd B1
Coach Park B2
College Cr C1
Courts C2
Cricket Club A3
Cricket Ground C3
Dagmar Rd C2
Datchet Rd B3
Devereux Rd C2
Dorset Rd C2
Duke St B1
Elm Rd C1
Eton College A3
Eton Ct A2
Eton Sq A2
Eton Wick Rd A2
Farm Yard B3
Fire Station C2
Frances Rd C2
Frogmore Dr B3
Gloucester Pl C3
Goslar Way C1
Goswell Hill B2
Goswell Rd B2
Green La C1
Grove Rd C2
Guildhall B3
Helena Rd C2
Helston La B1
High St A2/B3
Holy Trinity C2
Home Park,The A3/C3
Hosp (Private) C2
Household Cavalry C2
Imperial Rd C1
Information Ctr B2/B3
Keats La A2
King Edward Ct B2
King Edward VII Ave A3
King Edward VII Hospital C2
King George V Memorial B3
King Stable St A2
King's Rd C3
Library C2
Long Walk,The C3
Maidenhead Rd B1
Meadow La A2
Municipal Offices C3
Nell Gwynne's House B3
Osborne Rd C2
Oxford Rd B1
Park St B3
Peascod St B2
Police Station C2
Post Office A2
Princess Margaret Hospital C2
Queen Victoria's Walk B3
Queen's Rd C2
River St B2
Romney Island A3
Romney Lock A3
Romney Lock Rd A3
Russell St C2
St John's B3
St John's Chapel A2
St Leonards Rd C2
St Mark's Rd C2
Sheet St C3
South Meadow A2
South Meadow La A2
Springfield Rd C1
Stovell Rd B1
Sunbury Rd A3
Tangier La A2
Tangier St A3
Temple Rd C2
Thames St B3
Theatre Royal B3
Trinity Pl C2
Vansittart Rd B1/C1
Vansittart Rd Gdns C1
Victoria Barracks C2
Victoria St C2
Ward Royal B2
Westmead C1
White Lilies Island A1
William St B2
Windsor & Eton Central B2
Windsor & Eton Riverside A3
Windsor Arts Centre C2
Windsor Bridge B3
Windsor Castle B3
Windsor Great Park C3
Windsor Leisure Ctr B1
Windsor Relief Rd A1
Windsor Royal Shopping B2
York Ave C1
York Rd C1

Worcester 126

Albany Terr A1
Angel Pl B2
Angel St B2
Ashcroft Rd A2
Athelstan Rd C3
Avenue,The C1
Back Lane North A1
Back Lane South A1
Barbourne Rd A2
Bath Rd C2
Battenhall Rd C3
Bridge St B2
Britannia Sq A1
Broad St B2
Bromwich La C1
Bromwich Rd C1
Bromyard Rd C1
Bus Station B2
Butts,The B2
Carden St B3
Castle St A2
Cathedral C2
Cathedral Plaza B2
Charles St B3
Chequers La B1
Chestnut St A2
Chestnut Walk A2
Citizens' Advice Bureau B2
City Walls Rd B2
Cole Hill C3
Coll of Technology B2
College St C2
Commandery,The C3
Cripplegate Park B1
Croft Rd B1
Cromwell St B3
Cross,The B2
CrownGate Ctr B2
Deansway B2
Diglis Pde C2
Diglis Rd C2
Edgar Tower C2
Farrier St A2
Foregate St B2
Foregate Street B2
Fort Royal Hill C3
Fort Royal Park C3
Foundry St B3
Friar St C2
George St B3
Grand Stand Rd B1
Greenhill C3
Greyfriars B2
Guildhall B2
Henwick Rd B1
High St B2
Hill St B3
Hive,The B2
Hylton Rd B1
Information Ctr B2
King Charles Place Shopping Centre C1
King's School C2
King's School Playing Field C2
Kleve Walk C2
Lansdowne Cr A3
Lansdowne Rd A3
Lansdowne Walk A3
Laslett St A3
Leisure Centre A3
Little Chestnut St A2
Little London A2
London Rd C3
Lowell St A3
Lowesmoor B2
Lowesmoor Terr A3
Lowesmoor Wharf A3
Magistrates Court A2
Midland Rd B3
Mill St C2
Moors Severn Terrace,The A1
Museum & Art Gallery A2
Museum of Royal Worcester C2
New Rd C1
New St B2
Northfield St A2
Odeon B2
Padmore St B3
Park St C3
Pheasant St B3
Pitchcroft Racecourse A1
Police Station A2
Portland St C2
Post Office B2
Quay St B2
Queen St B2
Rainbow Hill A3
Recreation Ground A2
Reindeer Court B2
Rogers Hill A3
Sabrina Terr A1
St Dunstan's Cr C3
St John's C1
St Martin's Gate B3
St Martin's Quarter B3
St Oswald's Rd A2
St Paul's St B3
St Swithin's Church B2
St Wulstans Cr C3
Sansome Walk A2
Severn St C2
Shambles,The B2
Shaw St B2
Shire Hall Crown Ct A2
Shrub Hill B3
Shrub Hill Rd B3
Shrub Hill Retail Pk B3
Slingpool Walk C1
South Quay B2
Southfield St A2
Sports Ground A2/C1
Stanley Rd B3
Swan,The A1
Swimming Pool A2
Tallow Hill B3
Tennis Walk A2
Tolladine Rd B3
Tudor House B2
Tybridge St B1
Tything,The A2
Univ of Worcester B2
Vincent Rd B3
Vue C2
Washington St A3
Woolhope Rd C3
Worcester Bridge B2
Worcester County Cricket Ground C1
Worcester Royal Grammar School A2
Wylds La C3

York 126

Aldwark B2
Barbican Rd C3
Bar Convent Living Heritage Ctr C1
Barley Hall B2
Bishopgate St C2
Bishopthorpe Rd C2
Blossom St C1
Bootham A1
Bootham Crescent A1
Bootham Terrace A1
Bridge St B2
Brook St A2
Brownlow St A2
Burton Stone La A1
Castle Museum C2
Castlegate B2
Cemetery Rd C3
Cherry St C2
City Screen B2
City Wall A2/B1/C3
Clarence St A2
Clementhorpe C2
Clifford St B2
Clifford's Tower B2
Clifton A1
Coach park A2
Coney St B2
Coppergate Ctr B2
Cromwell Rd C2
Crown Court C2
Davygate B2
Deanery Gdns A2
DIG B2
Ebor Industrial Est B3
Fairfax House B2
Fishergate C3
Foss Islands Rd B3
Foss Islands Retail Park B3
Fossbank A3
Garden St A2
George St C3
Gillygate A2
Goodramgate B2
Grand Opera Ho B2
Grosvenor Terr A1
Guildhall B2
Hallfield Rd A3
Heslington Rd C3
Heworth Green A3
Holy Trinity B2
Hope St C3
Huntington Rd A3
Information Ctr B2
James St B3
Jorvik Viking Ctr B2
Kent St C3
Lawrence St C3
Layerthorpe A3
Leeman Rd B1
Lendal B2
Lendal Bridge B1
Library A2/B1
Longfield Terr A1
Lord Mayor's Walk A2
Lower Eldon St A2
Lowther St A2
Mansion House B2
Margaret St C3
Marygate A1
Melbourne St C3
Merchant Adventurers' Hall B2
Merchant Taylors' Hall B2
Micklegate B1
Micklegate Bar C1
Monkgate A2
Moss St C1
Museum Gdns B1
Museum St B1
National Railway Museum B1
Navigation Rd B3
Newton Terr C2
North Parade A1
North St B2
Nunnery La C1
Nunthorpe Rd C1
Ouse Bridge B2
Paragon St C3
Park Gr A3
Park St C1
Parliament St B2
Peasholme Green B3
Penley's Grove St A2
Piccadilly B2
Police Station B2
Post Office B1/B2/C3
Priory St B1
Purey Cust Nuffield Hospital,The A2
Queen Anne's Rd A1
Reel C1
Regimental Mus B2
Richard III Experience at Monk Bar A2
Roman Bath B2
Rowntree Park C2
St Andrewgate B2
St Benedict Rd C1
St John St A2
St Olave's Rd A1
St Peter's Gr A1
St Saviourgate B2
Scarcroft Hill C1
Scarcroft Rd C1
Shambles,The B2
Shopmobility B2
Skeldergate C2
Skeldergate Bridge C2
Station Rd B1
Stonebow,The B2
Stonegate B2
Superstore A3
Sycamore Terr A1
Terry Ave C2
Theatre Royal B2
Thorpe St C1
Toft Green B1
Tower St C2
Townend St A2
Treasurer's Ho A2
Trinity La B1
Undercroft Mus A2
Union Terr A2
Victor St C2
Vine St C2
Walmgate B3
War Memorial B1
Wellington St C3
York Art Gallery A1
York Barbican C3
York Brewery B1
York Dungeon, The B2
York Minster A2
York St John University A2
York Station B1

Abbreviations used in the index

Aberdeen	Aberdeen City
Aberds	Aberdeenshire
Ald	Alderney
Anglesey	Isle of Anglesey
Angus	Angus
Argyll	Argyll and Bute
Bath	Bath and North East Somerset
Bedford	Bedford
Bl Gwent	Blaenau Gwent
Blackburn	Blackburn with Darwen
Blackpool	Blackpool
Bmouth	Bournemouth
Borders	Scottish Borders
Brack	Bracknell
Bridgend	Bridgend
Brighton	City of Brighton and Hove
Bristol	City and County of Bristol
Bucks	Buckinghamshire
C Beds	Central Bedfordshire
Caerph	Caerphilly
Cambs	Cambridgeshire
Cardiff	Cardiff
Carms	Carmarthenshire
Ceredig	Ceredigion
Ches E	Cheshire East
Ches W	Cheshire West and Chester
Clack	Clackmannanshire
Conwy	Conwy
Corn	Cornwall
Cumb	Cumbria
Darl	Darlington
Denb	Denbighshire
Derby	City of Derby
Derbys	Derbyshire
Devon	Devon
Dorset	Dorset
Dumfries	Dumfries and Galloway
Dundee	Dundee City
Durham	Durham
E Ayrs	East Ayrshire
E Dunb	East Dunbartonshire
E Loth	East Lothian
E Renf	East Renfrewshire
E Sus	East Sussex
E Yorks	East Riding of Yorkshire
Edin	City of Edinburgh
Essex	Essex
Falk	Falkirk
Fife	Fife
Flint	Flintshire
Glasgow	City of Glasgow
Glos	Gloucestershire
Gtr Man	Greater Manchester
Guern	Guernsey
Gwyn	Gwynedd
Halton	Halton
Hants	Hampshire
Hereford	Herefordshire
Herts	Hertfordshire
Highld	Highland
Hrtlpl	Hartlepool
Hull	Hull
IoM	Isle of Man
IoW	Isle of Wight
Invclyd	Inverclyde
Jersey	Jersey
Kent	Kent
Lancs	Lancashire
Leicester	City of Leicester
Leics	Leicestershire
Lincs	Lincolnshire
London	Greater London
Luton	Luton
M Keynes	Milton Keynes
M Tydf	Merthyr Tydfil
Mbro	Middlesbrough
Medway	Medway
Mers	Merseyside
Midloth	Midlothian
Mon	Monmouthshire
Moray	Moray
N Ayrs	North Ayrshire
N Lincs	North Lincolnshire
N Lanark	North Lanarkshire
N Som	North Somerset
N Yorks	North Yorkshire
NE Lincs	North East Lincolnshire
Neath	Neath Port Talbot
Newport	City and County of Newport
Norf	Norfolk
Northants	Northamptonshire
Northumb	Northumberland
Nottingham	City of Nottingham
Notts	Nottinghamshire
Orkney	Orkney
Oxon	Oxfordshire
Pboro	Peterborough
Pembs	Pembrokeshire
Perth	Perth and Kinross
Plym	Plymouth
Poole	Poole
Powys	Powys
Ptsmth	Portsmouth
Reading	Reading
Redcar	Redcar and Cleveland
Renfs	Renfrewshire
Rhondda	Rhondda Cynon Taff
Rutland	Rutland
S Ayrs	South Ayrshire
S Glos	South Gloucestershire
S Lanark	South Lanarkshire
S Yorks	South Yorkshire
Scilly	Scilly
Shetland	Shetland
Shrops	Shropshire
Slough	Slough
Som	Somerset
Soton	Southampton
Staffs	Staffordshire
Southend	Southend-on-Sea
Stirling	Stirling
Stockton	Stockton-on-Tees
Stoke	Stoke-on-Trent
Suff	Suffolk
Sur	Surrey
Swansea	Swansea
Swindon	Swindon
T&W	Tyne and Wear
Telford	Telford and Wrekin
Thurrock	Thurrock
Torbay	Torbay
Torf	Torfaen
V Glam	The Vale of Glamorgan
W Berks	West Berkshire
W Dunb	West Dunbartonshire
W Isles	Western Isles
W Loth	West Lothian
W Mid	West Midlands
W Sus	West Sussex
W Yorks	West Yorkshire
Warks	Warwickshire
Warr	Warrington
Wilts	Wiltshire
Windsor	Windsor and Maidenhead
Wokingham	Wokingham
Worcs	Worcestershire
Wrex	Wrexham
York	City of York

Index to road maps of Britain

How to use the index

Example **Thornton-le-Beans** N Yorks **58** G4

- G4 – grid square
- 58 – page number
- N Yorks – county or unitary authority

A

Ab Kettleby Leics 36 C3
Ab Lench Worcs 27 C7
Abbas Combe Som 8 B6
Abberley Worcs 26 B4
Abberton Essex 31 G7
Abberton Worcs 26 C6
Abberwick Northumb 63 B7
Abbess Roding Essex 30 G2
Abbey Devon 7 E10
Abbey-cwm-hir Powys 25 A7
Abbey Dore Hereford 25 E10
Abbey Field Essex 30 F6
Abbey Hulton Stoke 44 H3
Abbey St Bathans Borders 70 D6
Abbey Town Cumb 56 A3
Abbey Village Lancs 50 G2
Abbey Wood London 19 D11
Abbeydale S Yorks 45 D7
Abbeystead Lancs 50 D1
Abbots Bickington Devon 6 E2
Abbots Bromley Staffs 35 C6
Abbots Langley Herts 19 A7
Abbots Leigh N Som 15 D11
Abbots Morton Worcs 27 C7
Abbots Ripton Cambs 37 H8
Abbots Salford Warks 27 C7
Abbotsbury Dorset 8 F4
Abbotsham Devon 6 D3
Abbotskerswell Devon 5 E9
Abbotsley Cambs 29 C9
Abbotswood Hants 10 B2
Abbotts Ann Hants 17 G10
Abcott Shrops 33 H9
Abdon Shrops 34 G1
Aber Ceredig 23 B9
Aber-Arad Carms 23 C8
Aber-banc Ceredig 23 B8
Aber Cowarch Gwyn 32 D4
Aber-Giâr Carms 23 B10
Aber-gwynfi Neath 14 B4
Aber-Hirnant Gwyn 32 B5
Aber-nant Rhondda 14 A6
Aber-Rhiwlech Gwyn 32 C5
Aber-Village Powys 25 F8
Aberaeron Ceredig 24 B1
Aberaman Rhondda 14 A6
Aberangell Gwyn 32 D4
Aberarder Highld 81 E6
Aberarder House Highld 81 A8
Aberarder Lodge Highld 81 E7
Aberargie Perth 76 F4
Aberarth Ceredig 24 B1
Aberavon Neath 14 B3
Aberbeeg Bl Gwent 15 A8
Abercanaid M Tydf 14 A6
Abercarn Caerph 15 B8
Abercastle Pembs 22 C3
Abercegir Powys 32 E4
Aberchirder Aberds 88 C6
Abercraf Powys 24 G5
Abercrombie Fife 77 G8
Abercych Pembs 23 B7
Abercynafon Powys 25 G7
Abercynon Rhondda 14 B6
Aberdalgie Perth 76 E3
Aberdâr = Aberdare Rhondda 14 A5
Aberdare = Aberdâr Rhondda 14 A5
Aberdaron Gwyn 40 H3
Aberdaugleddau = Milford Haven Pembs 22 F4
Aberdeen Aberdeen 83 C11
Aberdesach Gwyn 40 E6
Aberdour Fife 69 B10
Aberdovey Gwyn 32 F2
Aberdulais Neath 14 A3
Aberedw Powys 25 D7
Abereiddy Pembs 22 C2
Abererch Gwyn 40 G5
Aberfan M Tydf 14 A6
Aberfeldy Perth 75 C11
Aberffraw Anglesey 40 D5
Aberffrwd Ceredig 32 H2
Aberford W Yorks 51 F10
Aberfoyle Stirling 75 G8
Abergavenny = Y Fenni Mon 25 G9
Abergele Conwy 42 E2
Abergorlech Carms 23 C10
Abergwaun = Fishguard Pembs 22 C4
Abergwesyn Powys 24 C5
Abergwili Carms 23 D9
Abergwynant Gwyn 32 D2
Abergwyngregyn Gwyn 41 C8
Abergynolwyn Gwyn 32 E2
Aberhonddu = Brecon Powys 25 F7
Aberhosan Powys 32 F4
Aberkenfig Bridgend 14 C4
Aberlady E Loth 70 B3
Aberlemno Angus 77 B8
Aberllefenni Gwyn 32 E3
Abermagwr Ceredig 24 A3
Abermaw = Barmouth Gwyn 32 D2
Abermeurig Ceredig 23 A10
Abermule Powys 33 F7
Abernaint Powys 33 C7
Abernant Carms 23 D8
Abernethy Perth 76 F4
Abernyte Perth 76 D5
Aberpennar = Mountain Ash Rhondda 14 B6
Aberporth Ceredig 23 A7
Abersoch Gwyn 40 H5
Abersychan Torf 15 A8
Abertawe = Swansea Swansea 14 B2
Aberteifi = Cardigan Ceredig 22 B6
Aberthin V Glam 14 D6
Abertillery = Abertyleri Bl Gwent 15 A8
Abertridwr Caerph 15 C7
Abertridwr Powys 32 D6
Abertyleri = Abertillery Bl Gwent 15 A8
Abertysswg Caerph 25 H8
Aberuthven Perth 76 F2
Aberyscir Powys 24 F6
Aberystwyth Ceredig 32 G1
Abhainn Suidhe W Isles 90 G5
Abingdon-on-Thames Oxon 17 B11
Abinger Common Sur 19 G8
Abinger Hammer Sur 19 G7
Abington S Lanark 60 A5
Abington Pigotts Cambs 29 D10
Ablington Glos 27 H8
Ablington Wilts 17 G8
Abney Derbys 44 E5
Aboyne Aberds 83 D7
Abram Gtr Man 43 B9
Abriachan Highld 87 H8
Abridge Essex 19 B11
Abronhill N Lanark 68 C6
Abson S Glos 16 D4
Abthorpe Northants 28 D3
Abune-the-Hill Orkney 95 F3
Aby Lincs 47 E8
Acaster Malbis York 52 E1
Acaster Selby N Yorks 52 E1
Accrington Lancs 50 G3
Acha Argyll 78 F4
Acha Mor W Isles 91 E8
Achabraid Argyll 73 E7
Achachork Highld 85 D9
Achafolla Argyll 72 B6
Achagary Highld 93 D10
Achahoish Argyll 72 F6
Achalader Perth 76 C4
Achallader Argyll 74 C6
Ach'an Todhair Highld 80 F2
Achanalt Highld 86 E5
Achanamara Argyll 72 E6
Achandunie Highld 87 D9
Achany Highld 93 J8
Achaphubuil Highld 80 F2
Acharacle Highld 79 E9
Acharn Highld 79 F10
Acharn Perth 75 C10
Acharole Highld 94 E4
Achath Aberds 83 B9
Achavanich Highld 94 F3
Achavraat Highld 87 G12
Achddu Carms 23 F9
Achduart Highld 92 J3
Achentoul Highld 93 F11
Achfary Highld 92 F5
Achgarve Highld 91 H13
Achiemore Highld 92 C6
Achiemore Highld 93 D11
A'Chill Highld 84 H7
Achiltibuie Highld 92 J3
Achina Highld 93 C10
Achinduich Highld 93 J8
Achinduin Argyll 79 H11
Achingills Highld 94 D3
Achintee Highld 80 F3
Achintee Highld 86 G2
Achintraid Highld 85 E13
Achlean Highld 81 D10
Achleck Argyll 78 G7
Achluachrach Highld 80 E4
Achlyness Highld 92 D5
Achmelvich Highld 92 G3
Achmore Highld 85 E13
Achmore Stirling 75 D8
Achnaba Argyll 73 E8
Achnaba Argyll 74 D2
Achnabat Highld 87 H8
Achnacarnin Highld 92 F3
Achnacarry Highld 80 E3
Achnacloich Argyll 74 D2
Achnacloich Highld 85 H10
Achnaconeran Highld 80 B6
Achnacraig Argyll 78 G7
Achnacroish Argyll 79 G11
Achnadrish Argyll 78 F7
Achnafalnich Argyll 74 E5
Achnagarron Highld 87 E9
Achnaha Highld 78 E7
Achnahanat Highld 87 B8
Achnahannet Highld 82 A1
Achnairn Highld 93 H8
Achnaluachrach Highld 93 J9
Achnasaul Highld 80 E3
Achnasheen Highld 86 F4
Achosnich Highld 78 E7
Achranich Highld 79 G10
Achreamie Highld 93 C13
Achriabhach Highld 80 G3
Achriesgill Highld 92 D5
Achrimsdale Highld 93 J12
Achtoty Highld 93 C9
Achurch Northants 36 G6
Achuvoldrach Highld 93 D8
Achvaich Highld 87 B10
Achvarasdal Highld 93 C12
Ackergill Highld 94 E5
Acklam Mbro 58 E5
Acklam N Yorks 52 C3
Ackleton Shrops 34 F3
Acklington Northumb 63 C8
Ackton W Yorks 51 G10
Ackworth Moor Top W Yorks 51 H10
Acle Norf 39 D10
Acock's Green W Mid 35 G7
Acol Kent 21 E10
Acomb Northumb 62 G5
Acomb York 52 D1
Aconbury Hereford 26 E2
Acre Lancs 50 G3
Acre Street W Sus 11 E6
Acrefair Wrex 33 A8
Acton Ches E 43 G9
Acton Dorset 9 G8
Acton London 19 C9
Acton Shrops 33 G9
Acton Suff 30 D5
Acton Wrex 42 G6
Acton Beauchamp Hereford 26 C3
Acton Bridge Ches W 43 E8
Acton Burnell Shrops 33 E11
Acton Green Hereford 26 C3
Acton Pigott Shrops 33 E11
Acton Round Shrops 34 F2
Acton Scott Shrops 33 G10
Acton Trussell Staffs 34 D5
Acton Turville S Glos 16 C5
Adbaston Staffs 34 C3
Adber Dorset 8 B4
Adderley Shrops 34 A2
Adderstone Northumb 71 G10
Addiewell W Loth 69 D8
Addingham W Yorks 51 E6
Addington Bucks 28 F4
Addington Kent 20 F3
Addington London 19 E10
Addinston Borders 70 E4
Addiscombe London 19 E10
Addlestone Sur 19 E7
Addlethorpe Lincs 47 F9
Adel W Yorks 51 F8
Adeney Telford 34 D3
Adfa Powys 33 E6
Adforton Hereford 25 A11
Adisham Kent 21 F9
Adlestrop Glos 27 F9
Adlingfleet E Yorks 52 G4
Adlington Lancs 43 A9
Admaston Staffs 34 C6
Admaston Telford 34 D2
Admington Warks 27 D9
Adstock Bucks 28 E4
Adstone Northants 28 C2
Adversane W Sus 11 B9
Advie Highld 88 E1
Adwalton W Yorks 51 G8
Adwell Oxon 18 B3
Adwick le Street S Yorks 45 B9
Adwick upon Dearne S Yorks 45 B8
Adziel Aberds 89 C9
Ae Village Dumfries 60 E5
Affleck Aberds 89 F8
Affpuddle Dorset 9 E7
Affric Lodge Highld 80 A3
Afon-wen Flint 42 E4
Afton IoW 10 F2
Agglethorpe N Yorks 58 H1
Agneash IoM 48 D4
Aigburth Mers 43 D6
Aiginis W Isles 91 D9
Aike E Yorks 52 E6
Aikerness Orkney 95 C5
Aikers Orkney 95 J5
Aiketgate Cumb 57 B6
Aikton Cumb 56 A4
Ailey Hereford 25 D10
Ailstone Warks 27 C9
Ailsworth Pboro 37 F7
Ainderby Quernhow N Yorks 51 A9
Ainderby Steeple N Yorks 58 G4
Aingers Green Essex 31 F8
Ainsdale Mers 42 A6
Ainsdale-on-Sea Mers 42 A6
Ainstable Cumb 57 B7
Ainsworth Gtr Man 43 A10
Ainthorpe N Yorks 59 F8
Aintree Mers 43 C6
Aird Argyll 72 C6
Aird Dumfries 54 C3
Aird Highld 85 A12
Aird W Isles 91 D10
Aird a Mhachair W Isles 84 D2
Aird a' Mhulaidh W Isles 90 F6
Aird Asaig W Isles 90 G6
Aird Dhail W Isles 91 A9
Aird Mhidhinis W Isles 84 H2
Aird Mhighe W Isles 90 H6
Aird Mhighe W Isles 90 J5
Aird Mhor W Isles 84 H2
Aird of Sleat Highld 85 H10
Aird Thunga W Isles 91 D9
Aird Uig W Isles 90 D5
Airdens Highld 87 B9
Airdrie N Lanark 68 D6
Airdtorrisdale Highld 93 C9
Airidh a Bhruaich W Isles 90 F7
Airieland Dumfries 55 D10
Airmyn E Yorks 52 G3
Airntully Perth 76 D3
Airor Highld 85 H12
Airth Falk 69 B7
Airton N Yorks 50 D5
Airyhassen Dumfries 54 E6
Aisby Lincs 36 B6
Aisby Lincs 46 C2
Aisgernis W Isles 84 F2
Aiskew N Yorks 58 H3
Aislaby N Yorks 59 F9
Aislaby N Yorks 59 H8
Aislaby Stockton 58 E5
Aisthorpe Lincs 46 D3
Aith Orkney 95 G3
Aith Shetland 96 D8
Aith Shetland 96 H5
Aithsetter Shetland 96 K6
Aitkenhead S Ayrs 66 F6
Aitnoch Highld 87 H12
Akeld Northumb 71 H8
Akeley Bucks 28 E4
Akenham Suff 31 D8
Albaston Corn 4 D5
Alberbury Shrops 33 D9
Albourne W Sus 12 E1
Albrighton Shrops 33 D10
Albrighton Shrops 34 E4
Alburgh Norf 39 G8
Albury Herts 29 F11
Albury Sur 19 G7
Albury End Herts 29 F11
Alby Hill Norf 39 B7
Alcaig Highld 87 F8
Alcaston Shrops 33 G10
Alcester Warks 27 C7
Alciston E Sus 12 F4
Alcombe Som 7 B8
Alcombe Wilts 16 E5
Alconbury Cambs 37 H7
Alconbury Weston Cambs 37 H7
Aldbar Castle Angus 77 B8
Aldborough N Yorks 51 C10
Aldborough Norf 39 B7
Aldbourne Wilts 17 D9
Aldbrough E Yorks 53 F8
Aldbrough St John N Yorks 58 E3
Aldbury Herts 28 G6
Aldcliffe Lancs 49 C4
Aldclune Perth 76 A2
Aldeburgh Suff 31 C11
Aldeby Norf 39 F10
Aldenham Herts 19 B8
Alderbury Wilts 9 B10
Aldercar Derbys 45 H8
Alderford Norf 39 D7
Alderholt Dorset 9 C10
Alderley Glos 16 B4
Alderley Edge Ches E 44 E2
Aldermaston W Berks 18 E2
Aldermaston Wharf W Berks 18 E3
Alderminster Warks 27 D9
Alder's End Hereford 26 D3
Aldersey Green Ches W 43 G7
Aldershot Hants 18 F5
Alderton Glos 27 E7
Alderton Northants 28 D4
Alderton Shrops 33 C10
Alderton Suff 31 D10
Alderton Wilts 16 C5
Alderwasley Derbys 45 G7
Aldfield N Yorks 51 C8
Aldford Ches W 43 G7
Aldham Essex 30 F6
Aldham Suff 31 D7
Aldie Highld 87 C10
Aldingbourne W Sus 11 D8
Aldingham Cumb 49 B2
Aldington Kent 13 C9
Aldington Worcs 27 D7
Aldington Frith Kent 13 C9
Aldochlay Argyll 68 A2
Aldreth Cambs 29 A11
Aldridge W Mid 35 E6
Aldringham Suff 31 B11
Aldsworth Glos 27 G8
Aldunie Moray 82 A5
Aldwark Derbys 44 G6
Aldwark N Yorks 51 C10
Aldwick W Sus 11 E8
Aldwincle Northants 36 G6
Aldworth W Berks 18 D2
Alexandria W Dunb 68 C2
Alfardisworthy Devon 6 E1
Alfington Devon 7 G10
Alfold Sur 11 A9
Alfold Bars W Sus 11 A9
Alfold Crossways Sur 19 H7
Alford Aberds 83 B7
Alford Lincs 47 E8
Alford Som 8 A5
Alfreton Derbys 45 G8
Alfrick Worcs 26 C4
Alfrick Pound Worcs 26 C4
Alfriston E Sus 12 F4
Algaltraig Argyll 73 F9
Algarkirk Lincs 37 B8
Alhampton Som 8 A5
Aline Lodge W Isles 90 F6
Alisary Highld 79 D10
Alkborough N Lincs 52 G4
Alkerton Oxon 27 D10
Alkham Kent 21 G9
Alkington Shrops 33 B11
Alkmonton Derbys 35 B7
All Cannings Wilts 17 E7
All Saints South Elmham Suff 39 G9
All Stretton Shrops 33 F10
Alladale Lodge Highld 86 C7
Allaleigh Devon 5 F9
Allanaquoich Aberds 82 D3
Allangrange Mains Highld 87 F9
Allanton Borders 71 E7
Allanton N Lanark 69 E7
Allathasdal W Isles 84 H1
Allendale Town Northumb 62 H4
Allenheads Northumb 57 B10
Allens Green Herts 29 G11
Allensford Durham 58 A1
Allensmore Hereford 25 E11
Allenton Derby 35 B9
Aller Som 8 B3
Allerby Cumb 56 C2
Allerford Som 7 B8
Allerston N Yorks 52 A4
Allerthorpe E Yorks 52 E3
Allerton Mers 43 D7
Allerton W Yorks 51 F7
Allerton Bywater W Yorks 51 G10
Allerton Mauleverer N Yorks 51 D10
Allesley W Mid 35 G9
Allestree Derby 35 B9
Allet Corn 3 E6
Allexton Leics 36 E4
Allgreave Ches E 44 F3
Allhallows Medway 20 D5
Allhallows-on-Sea Medway 20 D5
Alligin Shuas Highld 85 C13
Allimore Green Staffs 34 D4
Allington Lincs 36 A4
Allington Wilts 17 E7
Allington Wilts 17 H9
Allithwaite Cumb 49 B3
Alloa Clack 69 A7
Allonby Cumb 56 B2
Alloway S Ayrs 66 E6
Allt Carms 23 F10
Allt na h-Airbhe Highld 86 B4
Allt-nan-sùgh Highld 85 F14
Alltchaorunn Highld 74 B4
Alltforgan Powys 32 C5
Alltmawr Powys 25 D7
Alltnacaillich Highld 92 E7
Alltsigh Highld 81 B6
Alltwalis Carms 23 C9
Alltwen Neath 14 A3
Alltyblaca Ceredig 23 B10
Allwood Green Suff 31 A7
Almeley Hereford 25 C10
Almer Dorset 9 E8
Almholme S Yorks 45 B9
Almington Staffs 34 B3
Alminstone Cross Devon 6 D2
Almondbank Perth 76 E3
Almondbury W Yorks 51 H7
Almondsbury S Glos 16 C3
Alne N Yorks 51 C10
Alness Highld 87 E9
Alnham Northumb 62 B5
Alnmouth Northumb 63 B8
Alnwick Northumb 63 B7
Alperton London 19 C8
Alphamstone Essex 30 E5
Alpheton Suff 30 C5
Alphington Devon 7 G8
Alport Derbys 44 F6
Alpraham Ches E 43 G8
Alresford Essex 31 F7
Alrewas Staffs 35 D7
Alsager Ches E 43 G10
Alsagers Bank Staffs 44 H2
Alsop en le Dale Derbys 44 G5
Alston Cumb 57 B9
Alston Devon 8 D2
Alstone Glos 26 E6
Alstonefield Staffs 44 G5
Alswear Devon 7 D6
Altandhu Highld 92 H2
Altanduin Highld 93 G11
Altarnun Corn 4 C3
Altass Highld 92 J7
Alterwall Highld 94 D4
Altham Lancs 50 F3
Althorne Essex 20 B6
Althorpe N Lincs 46 B2
Alticry Dumfries 54 D5
Altnabreac Station Highld 93 E13
Altnacealgach Hotel Highld 92 H5
Altnacraig Argyll 79 J11
Altnafeadh Highld 74 B5
Altnaharra Highld 93 F8
Altofts W Yorks 51 G9
Alton Derbys 45 F7
Alton Hants 18 H4
Alton Staffs 35 A6
Alton Pancras Dorset 8 D6
Alton Priors Wilts 17 E8
Altrincham Gtr Man 43 D10
Altrua Highld 80 E4
Altskeith Stirling 75 G7
Altyre Ho. Moray 87 F13
Alva Clack 75 H11
Alvanley Ches W 43 E7
Alvaston Derby 35 B9
Alvechurch Worcs 27 A7
Alvecote Warks 35 E8
Alvediston Wilts 9 B8
Alveley Shrops 34 G3
Alverdiscott Devon 6 D4
Alverstoke Hants 10 E5
Alverstone IoW 10 F4
Alverton Notts 36 A3
Alves Moray 88 B1
Alvescot Oxon 17 A9
Alveston S Glos 16 C3
Alveston Warks 27 C9
Alvie Highld 81 C10
Alvingham Lincs 47 C7
Alvington Glos 16 A3
Alwalton Cambs 37 F7
Alweston Dorset 8 C5
Alwinton Northumb 62 C5
Alwoodley W Yorks 51 E8
Alyth Perth 76 C5
Am Baile W Isles 84 G2
Am Buth Argyll 79 J11
Amatnatua Highld 86 B7
Amber Hill Lincs 46 H6
Ambergate Derbys 45 G7
Amberley Glos 16 A5
Amberley W Sus 11 C9
Amble Northumb 63 C8
Amblecote W Mid 34 G4
Ambler Thorn W Yorks 51 G6
Ambleside Cumb 56 F5
Ambleston Pembs 22 D5
Ambrosden Oxon 28 G3
Amcotts N Lincs 46 A2
Amersham Bucks 18 B6
Amesbury Wilts 17 G8
Amington Staffs 35 E8
Amisfield Dumfries 60 E5
Amlwch Anglesey 40 A6
Amlwch Port Anglesey 40 A6
Ammanford = Rhydaman Carms 24 G3
Amod Argyll 65 E8
Amotherby N Yorks 52 B3
Ampfield Hants 10 B3
Ampleforth N Yorks 52 B1
Ampney Crucis Glos 17 A7
Ampney St Mary Glos 17 A7
Ampney St Peter Glos 17 A7
Amport Hants 17 G9
Ampthill C Beds 29 E7
Ampton Suff 30 A5
Amroth Pembs 22 F6
Amulree Perth 75 D11
An Caol Highld 85 C11
An Cnoc W Isles 91 D9
An Gleann Ur W Isles 91 D9
An t-Ob = Leverburgh W Isles 90 J5
Anagach Highld 82 A2
Anaheilt Highld 79 E11
Anancaun Highld 86 E3
Ancaster Lincs 36 A5
Anchor Shrops 33 G7
Anchorsholme Blackpool 49 E3
Ancroft Northumb 71 F8
Ancrum Borders 62 A2
Anderby Lincs 47 E9
Anderson Dorset 9 E7
Anderton Ches W 43 E9
Andover Hants 17 G10
Andover Down Hants 17 G10
Andoversford Glos 27 G7
Andreas IoM 48 C4
Anfield Mers 43 C6
Angersleigh Som 7 E10
Angle Pembs 22 F3
Angmering W Sus 11 D9
Angram N Yorks 51 E11
Angram N Yorks 57 G10
Anie Stirling 75 F8
Ankerville Highld 87 D11
Anlaby E Yorks 52 G6
Anmer Norf 38 C3
Anna Valley Hants 17 G10
Annan Dumfries 61 G7
Annat Argyll 74 E3
Annat Highld 85 C13
Annbank S Ayrs 67 D7
Annesley Notts 45 G9
Annesley Woodhouse Notts 45 G8
Annfield Plain Durham 58 A2
Annifirth Shetland 96 J3
Annitsford T&W 63 F8
Annscroft Shrops 33 E10
Ansdell Lancs 49 G3
Ansford Som 8 A5
Ansley Warks 35 F8
Anslow Staffs 35 C8
Anslow Gate Staffs 35 C7
Anstey Herts 29 E11
Anstey Leics 35 E11
Anstruther Easter Fife 77 G8
Anstruther Wester Fife 77 G8
Ansty Hants 18 G4
Ansty W Sus 12 D1
Ansty Warks 35 G9
Ansty Wilts 9 B8
Anthill Common Hants 10 C5
Anthorn Cumb 61 H7
Antingham Norf 39 B8
Anton's Gowt Lincs 46 H6
Antonshill Falk 69 B7
Antony Corn 4 F4
Anwick Lincs 46 G5
Anwoth Dumfries 55 D8
Aoradh Argyll 64 B3
Apes Hall Cambs 38 F1
Apethorpe Northants 36 F6
Apeton Staffs 34 D4
Apley Lincs 46 E5
Apperknowle Derbys 45 E7
Apperley Glos 26 F5
Apperley Bridge W Yorks 51 F7
Appersett N Yorks 57 G10
Appin Argyll 74 C2
Appin House Argyll 74 C2
Appleby N Lincs 46 A3
Appleby-in-Westmorland Cumb 57 D8
Appleby Magna Leics 35 E9
Appleby Parva Leics 35 E9
Applecross Highld 85 D12
Applecross Ho. Highld 85 D12
Appledore Devon 6 C3
Appledore Devon 7 E9
Appledore Kent 13 D8
Appledore Heath Kent 13 C8
Appleford Oxon 18 B2
Applegarthtown Dumfries 61 E7
Appleshaw Hants 17 G10
Applethwaite Cumb 56 D4
Appleton Halton 43 D8
Appleton Oxon 17 A11
Appleton-le-Moors N Yorks 59 H8
Appleton-le-Street N Yorks 52 B3
Appleton Roebuck N Yorks 52 E1
Appleton Thorn Warr 43 D9
Appleton Wiske N Yorks 58 F4
Appletreehall Borders 61 B11
Appletreewick N Yorks 51 C6
Appley Som 7 D9
Appley Bridge Lancs 43 B8
Apse Heath IoW 10 F4
Apsley End C Beds 29 E8
Apuldram W Sus 11 D7
Aquhythie Aberds 83 B9
Arabella Highld 87 D11
Arbeadie Aberds 83 D8
Arberth = Narberth Pembs 22 E6
Arbirlot Angus 77 C9
Arboll Highld 87 C11
Arborfield Wokingham 18 E4
Arborfield Cross Wokingham 18 E4
Arborfield Garrison Wokingham 18 E4
Arbour-thorne S Yorks 45 D7
Arbroath Angus 77 C9
Arbuthnott Aberds 83 F9
Archiestown Moray 88 D2
Arclid Ches E 43 F10
Ard-dhubh Highld 85 D12
Ardachu Highld 93 J9
Ardalanish Argyll 78 K6
Ardanaiseig Argyll 74 E3
Ardaneaskan Highld 85 E13
Ardanstur Argyll 73 B7
Ardargie House Hotel Perth 76 F3
Ardarroch Highld 85 E13
Ardbeg Argyll 64 D5
Ardbeg Argyll 73 E10
Ardcharnich Highld 86 C4
Ardchiavaig Argyll 78 K6
Ardchullarie More Stirling 75 F8
Ardchyle Stirling 75 E8
Arddleen Powys 33 D8
Ardechvie Highld 80 D3
Ardeley Herts 29 F10
Ardelve Highld 85 F13
Arden Argyll 68 B2
Ardens Grafton Warks 27 C8
Ardentinny Argyll 73 E10
Ardentraive Argyll 73 F9
Ardeonaig Stirling 75 D9
Ardersier Highld 87 F10
Ardessie Highld 86 C3
Ardfern Argyll 73 C7
Ardgartan Argyll 74 G5
Ardgay Highld 87 B8
Ardgour Highld 74 A3
Ardheslaig Highld 85 C12
Ardiecow Moray 88 B5
Ardindrean Highld 86 C4
Ardingly W Sus 12 D2
Ardington Oxon 17 C11
Ardlair Aberds 83 A7
Ardlamont Ho. Argyll 73 G8
Ardleigh Essex 31 F7
Ardler Perth 76 C5
Ardley Oxon 28 F2
Ardlui Argyll 74 F6
Ardlussa Argyll 72 E5
Ardmair Highld 86 B4
Ardmay Argyll 74 G5
Ardminish Argyll 65 D7
Ardmolich Highld 79 D10
Ardmore Argyll 79 J10
Ardmore Highld 87 C10
Ardmore Highld 92 D5
Ardnacross Argyll 79 G8
Ardnadam Argyll 73 F10
Ardnagrask Highld 87 G8
Ardnarff Highld 85 E13
Ardnastang Highld 79 E11
Ardnave Argyll 64 A3
Ardno Argyll 73 C10
Ardo Aberds 89 E8
Ardo Ho. Aberds 89 F9
Ardoch Perth 76 D3
Ardochy House Highld 80 C4
Ardoyne Aberds 83 A8
Ardpatrick Argyll 72 G6
Ardpatrick Ho. Argyll 72 H6
Ardpeaton Argyll 73 E11
Ardrishaig Argyll 73 E7
Ardross Fife 77 G8
Ardross Highld 87 D9
Ardross Castle Highld 87 D9
Ardrossan N Ayrs 66 B5
Ardshealach Highld 79 E9
Ardsley S Yorks 45 B7
Ardslignish Highld 79 E8
Ardtalla Argyll 64 C5
Ardtalnaig Perth 75 D10
Ardtoe Highld 79 D9
Ardtrostan Perth 75 E9
Arduaine Argyll 72 B6
Ardullie Highld 87 E8
Ardvasar Highld 85 H11
Ardvorlich Perth 75 E9
Ardwell Dumfries 54 E4
Ardwell Mains Dumfries 54 E4
Ardwick Gtr Man 44 C2
Areley Kings Worcs 26 A5
Arford Hants 18 H5
Argoed Caerph 15 B7
Argoed Powys 24 B6
Arichamish Argyll 73 C8
Arichastlich Argyll 74 D5
Aridhglas Argyll 78 J6
Arileod Argyll 78 F4
Arinacrinachd Highld 85 C12
Arinagour Argyll 78 F5
Arion Orkney 95 G3
Arisaig Highld 79 C9
Ariundle Highld 79 E11
Arkendale N Yorks 51 C9
Arkesden Essex 29 E11
Arkholme Lancs 50 B1
Arkle Town N Yorks 58 F1
Arkleton Dumfries 61 D9
Arkley London 19 B9
Arksey S Yorks 45 B9
Arkwright Town Derbys 45 E8
Arle Glos 26 F6
Arlecdon Cumb 56 E2
Arlesey C Beds 29 E8
Arleston Telford 34 D2
Arley Ches E 43 D9
Arlingham Glos 26 G4
Arlington Devon 6 B5
Arlington E Sus 12 F4
Arlington Glos 27 H8
Armadale Highld 93 C10
Armadale W Loth 69 D8
Armadale Castle Highld 85 H11
Armathwaite Cumb 57 B7
Arminghall Norf 39 E8
Armitage Staffs 35 D6
Armley W Yorks 51 F8
Armscote Warks 27 D9
Armthorpe S Yorks 45 B10
Arnabost Argyll 78 F5
Arncliffe N Yorks 50 B5
Arncroach Fife 77 G8
Arne Dorset 9 F8
Arnesby Leics 36 F2
Arngask Perth 76 F4
Arnisdale Highld 85 G13
Arnish Highld 85 D10
Arniston Engine Midloth 70 D2
Arnol W Isles 91 C8
Arnold E Yorks 53 E7
Arnold Notts 45 H9
Arnprior Stirling 68 A5
Arnside Cumb 49 B4
Aros Mains Argyll 79 G8
Arowry Wrex 33 B10
Arpafeelie Highld 87 F9
Arrad Foot Cumb 49 A3
Arram E Yorks 52 E6
Arrathorne N Yorks 58 G3
Arreton IoW 10 F4
Arrington Cambs 29 C10
Arrivain Argyll 74 D5
Arrochar Argyll 74 G5
Arrow Warks 27 C7
Arthington W Yorks 51 E8
Arthingworth Northants 36 G3
Arthog Gwyn 32 D2
Arthrath Aberds 89 E9
Arthurstone Perth 76 C5
Artrochie Aberds 89 E10
Arundel W Sus 11 D9
Aryhoulan Highld 80 G2
Asby Cumb 56 D2
Ascog Argyll 73 G10
Ascot Windsor 18 E6
Ascott Warks 27 E10
Ascott-under-Wychwood Oxon 27 G10
Asenby N Yorks 51 B9
Asfordby Leics 36 D3
Asfordby Hill Leics 36 D3
Asgarby Lincs 46 H5
Asgarby Lincs 47 F7
Ash Kent 20 E2
Ash Kent 21 F9
Ash Som 8 B3
Ash Sur 18 F5
Ash Bullayne Devon 7 F6
Ash Green Warks 35 G9
Ash Magna Shrops 34 B1
Ash Mill Devon 7 D6
Ash Priors Som 7 D10
Ash Street Suff 31 D7
Ash Thomas Devon 7 E9
Ash Vale Sur 18 F5
Ashampstead W Berks 18 D2
Ashbocking Suff 31 C8
Ashbourne Derbys 44 H5
Ashbrittle Som 7 D9
Ashburton Devon 5 E8
Ashbury Devon 6 G4
Ashbury Oxon 17 C9
Ashby N Lincs 46 B3
Ashby by Partney Lincs 47 F8
Ashby cum Fenby NE Lincs 46 B6
Ashby de la Launde Lincs 46 G4
Ashby-de-la-Zouch Leics 35 D9
Ashby Folville Leics 36 D3
Ashby Magna Leics 36 F1
Ashby Parva Leics 35 G11
Ashby Puerorum Lincs 47 E7
Ashby St Ledgers Northants 28 B2
Ashby St Mary Norf 39 E9
Ashchurch Glos 26 E6
Ashcombe Devon 5 D10
Ashcott Som 15 H10
Ashdon Essex 30 D2
Ashe Hants 18 G2
Asheldham Essex 20 A6
Ashen Essex 30 D4
Ashendon Bucks 28 G4
Ashfield Carms 24 F3
Ashfield Stirling 75 G10
Ashfield Suff 31 B9
Ashfield Green Suff 31 A9
Ashfold Crossways W Sus 11 B11
Ashford Devon 6 C4
Ashford Hants 9 C10
Ashford Kent 13 B9
Ashford Sur 19 D7
Ashford Bowdler Shrops 26 A2
Ashford Carbonell Shrops 26 A2
Ashford Hill Hants 18 E2
Ashford in the Water Derbys 44 F5
Ashgill S Lanark 68 F6
Ashill Devon 7 E9
Ashill Norf 38 E4
Ashill Som 8 C2
Ashingdon Essex 20 B5
Ashington Northumb 63 E8
Ashington Som 8 B4
Ashington W Sus 11 C10
Ashintully Castle Perth 76 A4
Ashkirk Borders 61 A10
Ashlett Hants 10 D3
Ashleworth Glos 26 F5
Ashley Cambs 30 B3
Ashley Ches E 43 D10
Ashley Devon 6 E5
Ashley Dorset 9 D10
Ashley Glos 16 B6
Ashley Hants 10 A2
Ashley Hants 10 E1
Ashley Northants 36 F3
Ashley Staffs 34 B3
Ashley Green Bucks 28 H6
Ashley Heath Dorset 9 D10
Ashley Heath Staffs 34 B3
Ashmanhaugh Norf 39 C9
Ashmansworth Hants 17 F11
Ashmansworthy Devon 6 E2
Ashmore Dorset 9 C8
Ashorne Warks 27 C10
Ashover Derbys 45 F7
Ashow Warks 27 A10
Ashprington Devon 5 F9
Ashreigney Devon 6 E5
Ashtead Sur 19 F8
Ashton Ches W 43 F8
Ashton Corn 2 G5
Ashton Hants 10 C4
Ashton Hereford 26 B2
Ashton Invclyd 73 F11
Ashton Northants 28 D4
Ashton Northants 37 G6
Ashton Common Wilts 16 F5
Ashton-In-Makerfield Gtr Man 43 C8
Ashton Keynes Wilts 17 B7
Ashton under Hill Worcs 26 E6
Ashton-under-Lyne Gtr Man 44 C3
Ashton upon Mersey Gtr Man 43 C10
Ashurst Hants 10 C2
Ashurst Kent 12 C4
Ashurst W Sus 11 C10
Ashurstwood W Sus 12 C3
Ashwater Devon 6 G2
Ashwell Herts 29 E9
Ashwell Rutland 36 D4
Ashwell Som 8 C2
Ashwellthorpe Norf 39 F7
Ashwick Som 16 G3
Ashwicken Norf 38 D3
Ashybank Borders 61 B11
Askam in Furness Cumb 49 B2
Askern S Yorks 45 A9
Askerswell Dorset 8 E4
Askett Bucks 28 H5
Askham Cumb 57 D7
Askham Notts 45 E11
Askham Bryan York 52 E1
Askham Richard York 51 E11
Asknish Argyll 73 D8
Askrigg N Yorks 57 G11
Askwith N Yorks 51 E7
Aslackby Lincs 37 B6
Aslacton Norf 39 F7
Aslockton Notts 36 B3
Asloun Aberds 83 B7
Aspatria Cumb 56 B3
Aspenden Herts 29 F10
Asperton Lincs 37 B8
Aspley Guise C Beds 28 E6
Aspley Heath C Beds 28 E6
Aspull Gtr Man 43 B9
Asselby E Yorks 52 G3
Asserby Lincs 47 E8
Assington Suff 30 E6
Assynt Ho. Highld 87 E8
Astbury Ches E 44 F2
Astcote Northants 28 C3
Asterley Shrops 33 E9
Asterton Shrops 33 F9
Asthall Oxon 27 G9
Asthall Leigh Oxon 27 G10
Astley Shrops 33 D11
Astley Warks 35 G9
Astley Worcs 26 B4
Astley Abbotts Shrops 34 F3
Astley Bridge Gtr Man 43 A10
Astley Cross Worcs 26 B5
Astley Green Gtr Man 43 C10
Aston Ches E 43 H9
Aston Ches W 43 E8
Aston Derbys 44 D5
Aston Hereford 25 A11
Aston Herts 29 F9
Aston Oxon 17 A10
Aston S Yorks 45 D8
Aston Shrops 33 C11
Aston Staffs 34 A3
Aston Telford 34 E2
Aston W Mid 35 G6
Aston Wokingham 18 C4
Aston Abbotts Bucks 28 F5
Aston Botterell Shrops 34 G2
Aston-By-Stone Staffs 34 B5
Aston Cantlow Warks 27 C8
Aston Clinton Bucks 28 G5
Aston Crews Hereford 26 F3
Aston Cross Glos 26 E6
Aston End Herts 29 F9
Aston Eyre Shrops 34 F2
Aston Fields Worcs 26 B6
Aston Flamville Leics 35 F10
Aston Ingham Hereford 26 F3
Aston juxta Mondrum Ches E 43 G9
Aston le Walls Northants 27 C11
Aston Magna Glos 27 E8
Aston Munslow Shrops 33 G11
Aston on Clun Shrops 33 G9
Aston-on-Trent Derbys 35 C10
Aston Rogers Shrops 33 E9
Aston Rowant Oxon 18 B4
Aston Sandford Bucks 28 H4
Aston Somerville Worcs 27 E7
Aston Subedge Glos 27 D8
Aston Tirrold Oxon 18 C2
Aston Upthorpe Oxon 18 C2
Astrop Northants 28 E2
Astwick C Beds 29 E9
Astwood M Keynes 28 D6
Astwood Worcs 26 C5
Astwood Bank Worcs 27 B7
Aswarby Lincs 37 B6
Aswardby Lincs 47 E7
Atch Lench Worcs 27 C7
Atcham Shrops 33 E11
Athelhampton Dorset 9 E6
Athelington Suff 31 A9
Athelney Som 8 B2
Athelstaneford E Loth 70 C4
Atherington Devon 6 D4
Atherstone Warks 35 F9
Atherstone on Stour Warks 27 C9
Atherton Gtr Man 43 B9
Atley Hill N Yorks 58 F3
Atlow Derbys 44 H6
Attadale Highld 86 H2
Attadale Ho. Highld 86 H2
Attenborough Notts 35 B11
Atterby Lincs 46 C3
Attercliffe S Yorks 45 D7
Attleborough Norf 38 F6
Attleborough Warks 35 F9
Attlebridge Norf 39 D7
Atwick E Yorks 53 D7
Atworth Wilts 16 E5
Aubourn Lincs 46 F3
Auchagallon N Ayrs 66 C1
Auchallater Aberds 82 E3
Aucharnie Aberds 89 D6
Auchattie Aberds 83 D8
Auchavan Angus 82 G3
Auchbreck Moray 82 A4
Auchenback E Renf 68 E4
Auchenbainzie Dumfries 60 D4
Auchenblae Aberds 83 F9
Auchenbrack Dumfries 60 D3
Auchenbreck Argyll 73 E9
Auchencairn Dumfries 55 D10
Auchencairn Dumfries 60 E5
Auchencairn N Ayrs 66 D3
Auchencrosh S Ayrs 54 B4
Auchencrow Borders 71 D7
Auchendinny Midloth 69 D11
Auchengray S Lanark 69 E8
Auchenhalrig Moray 88 B3
Auchenheath S Lanark 69 F7
Auchenlochan Argyll 73 F8
Auchenmalg Dumfries 54 D5
Auchensoul S Ayrs 66 G5
Auchentiber N Ayrs 67 B6
Auchertyre Highld 85 F13
Auchgourish Highld 81 B11
Auchincarroch W Dunb 68 B3
Auchindrain Argyll 73 C9
Auchindrean Highld 86 C4
Auchininna Aberds 89 D6
Auchinleck E Ayrs 67 D8
Auchinloch N Lanark 68 C5
Auchinroath Moray 88 C2
Auchintoul Aberds 83 B7
Auchiries Aberds 89 E10
Auchlee Aberds 83 D10
Auchleven Aberds 83 A8
Auchlochan S Lanark 69 G7
Auchlossan Aberds 83 C7
Auchlunies Aberds 83 D10
Auchlyne Stirling 75 E8
Auchmacoy Aberds 89 E9
Auchmair Moray 82 A5
Auchmantle Dumfries 54 C4
Auchmillan E Ayrs 67 D8
Auchmithie Angus 77 C9
Auchmuirbridge Fife 76 G5
Auchmull Angus 83 F7
Auchnacree Angus 77 A7
Auchnagallin Highld 87 H13
Auchnagatt Aberds 89 D9
Auchnaha Argyll 73 E8
Auchnashelloch Perth 75 F10
Aucholzie Aberds 82 D5
Auchrannie Angus 76 B5
Auchroisk Highld 82 A2
Auchronie Angus 82 E6
Auchterarder Perth 76 F2
Auchteraw Highld 80 C5
Auchterderran Fife 76 H5
Auchterhouse Angus 76 D6
Auchtermuchty Fife 76 F5
Auchterneed Highld 86 F7
Auchtertool Fife 69 A11
Auchtertyre Moray 88 C1
Auchtubh Stirling 75 E8
Auckengill Highld 94 D5
Auckley S Yorks 45 B10
Audenshaw Gtr Man 44 C3
Audlem Ches E 34 A2
Audley Staffs 43 G10
Audley End Essex 30 E5
Auds Aberds 89 B6
Aughton E Yorks 52 F3
Aughton Lancs 43 B6
Aughton Lancs 50 C1
Aughton S Yorks 45 D8
Aughton Wilts 17 F9
Aughton Park Lancs 43 B7
Auldearn Highld 87 F12
Aulden Hereford 25 C11
Auldgirth Dumfries 60 E5
Auldhame E Loth 70 B4
Auldhouse S Lanark 68 E5
Ault a'chruinn Highld 80 A1
Aultanrynie Highld 92 F6
Aultbea Highld 91 J13
Aultdearg Highld 86 E5
Aultgrishan Highld 91 J12
Aultguish Inn Highld 86 D6
Aultibea Highld 93 G13
Aultiphurst Highld 93 C11
Aultmore Moray 88 C4
Aultnagoire Highld 81 A7
Aultnamain Inn Highld 87 C9
Aultnaslat Highld 80 C3
Aulton Aberds 83 A8
Aundorach Highld 82 B1
Aunsby Lincs 36 B6
Auquhorthies Aberds 89 F8
Aust S Glos 16 C2
Austendike Lincs 37 C8
Austerfield S Yorks 45 C10

Austrey Warks 35 E8
Austwick N Yorks 50 C3
Authorpe Lincs 47 D8
Authorpe Row Lincs 47 E9
Avebury Wilts 17 E8
Aveley Thurrock 20 C2
Avening Glos 16 B5
Averham Notts 45 G11
Aveton Gifford Devon 5 G7
Avielochan Highld 81 B11
Aviemore Highld 81 B10
Avington Hants 10 A4
Avington W Berks 17 E10
Avoch Highld 87 F10
Avon Hants 9 E10
Avon Dassett Warks 27 D11
Avonbridge Falk 69 C8
Avonmouth Bristol 15 D11
Avonwick Devon 5 F8
Awbridge Hants 10 B2
Awhirk Dumfries 54 D3
Awkley S Glos 16 C2
Awliscombe Devon 7 F10
Awre Glos 26 H4
Awsworth Notts 35 A10
Axbridge Som 15 F10
Axford Hants 18 G3
Axford Wilts 17 D9
Axminster Devon 8 E1
Axmouth Devon 8 E1
Axton Flint 42 D4
Aycliff Kent 21 G10
Aycliffe Durham 58 D3
Aydon Northumb 62 G6
Aylburton Glos 16 A3
Ayle Northumb 57 B9
Aylesbeare Devon 7 G9
Aylesbury Bucks 28 G5
Aylesby NE Lincs 46 B6
Aylesford Kent 20 F4
Aylesham Kent 21 F9
Aylestone Leicester 36 E1
Aylmerton Norf 39 B7
Aylsham Norf 39 C7
Aylton Hereford 26 E3
Aymestrey Hereford 25 B11
Aynho Northants 28 E2
Ayot St Lawrence Herts 29 G8
Ayot St Peter Herts 29 G9
Ayr S Ayrs 66 D6
Aysgarth N Yorks 58 H1
Ayside Cumb 49 A3
Ayston Rutland 36 E4
Aythorpe Roding Essex 30 G2
Ayton Borders 71 D8
Aywick Shetland 96 E7
Azerley N Yorks 51 B8

B

Babbacombe Torbay 5 E10
Babbinswood Shrops 33 B9
Babcary Som 8 B4
Babel Carms 24 E5
Babell Flint 42 E4
Babraham Cambs 30 C2
Babworth Notts 45 D10
Bac W Isles 91 C9
Bachau Anglesey 40 B6
Back of Keppoch Highld 79 C9
Back Rogerton E Ayrs 67 D8
Backaland Orkney 95 E6
Backaskaill Orkney 95 C5
Backbarrow Cumb 49 A3
Backe Carms 23 E7
Backfolds Aberds 89 C10
Backford Ches W 43 E7
Backford Cross Ches W 43 E6
Backhill Aberds 89 E10
Backhill Aberds 89 E7
Backhill of Clackriach Aberds 89 D9
Backhill of Fortree Aberds 89 D9
Backhill of Trustach Aberds 83 D8
Backies Highld 93 J11
Backlass Highld 94 E4
Backwell N Som 15 E10
Backworth T&W 63 F9
Bacon End Essex 30 G3
Baconsthorpe Norf 39 B7
Bacton Hereford 25 E10
Bacton Norf 39 B9
Bacton Suff 31 B7
Bacton Green Suff 31 B7
Bacup Lancs 50 G4
Badachro Highld 85 A12
Badanloch Lodge Highld 93 F10
Badavanich Highld 86 F4
Badbury Swindon 17 C8
Badby Northants 28 C2
Badcall Highld 92 D5
Badcaul Highld 86 B3
Baddeley Green Stoke 44 G3
Baddesley Clinton Warks 27 A9
Baddesley Ensor Warks 35 F8
Baddidarach Highld 92 G3
Baddoch Aberds 82 E3
Baddock Highld 87 F10
Badenscoth Aberds 89 E7
Badenyon Aberds 82 B5
Badger Shrops 34 F3
Badger's Mount Kent 19 E11
Badgeworth Glos 26 G6
Badgworth Som 15 F9
Badicaul Highld 85 F12
Badingham Suff 31 B10
Badlesmere Kent 21 F7
Badlipster Highld 94 F4
Badluarach Highld 86 B2
Badminton S Glos 16 C5
Badnaban Highld 92 G3
Badninish Highld 87 B10
Badrallach Highld 86 B3
Badsey Worcs 27 D7
Badshot Lea Sur 18 G5
Badsworth W Yorks 45 A8
Badwell Ash Suff 30 B6
Bae Colwyn = Colwyn Bay Conwy 41 C10
Bag Enderby Lincs 47 E7
Bagby N Yorks 51 A10
Bagendon Glos 27 H7
Bagh a Chaisteil = Castlebay W Isles 84 J1
Bagh Mor W Isles 84 C3
Bagh Shiarabhagh W Isles 84 H2
Baghasdal W Isles 84 G2
Bagillt Flint 42 E5
Baginton Warks 27 A10
Baglan Neath 14 B3
Bagley Shrops 33 C10
Bagnall Staffs 44 G3
Bagnor W Berks 17 E11
Bagshot Sur 18 E6
Bagshot Wilts 17 E10
Bagthorpe Norf 38 B3
Bagthorpe Notts 45 G8
Bagworth Leics 35 E10
Bagwy Llydiart Hereford 25 F11
Bail àrd Bhuirgh W Isles 91 B9
Bail' lochdrach W Isles 84 C3
Bail Uachdraich W Isles 84 B3
Bail' Ur Tholastaidh W Isles 91 C10
Baildon W Yorks 51 F7
Baile W Isles 90 J4
Baile a Mhanaich W Isles 84 C2
Baile Ailein W Isles 91 E7
Baile an Truiseil W Isles 91 B8
Baile Boidheach Argyll 72 F6
Baile Glas W Isles 84 C3
Baile Mhartainn W Isles 84 A2
Baile Mhic Phail W Isles 84 A3
Baile Mor Argyll 78 J5
Baile Mor W Isles 84 B2
Baile na Creige W Isles 84 H1
Baile nan Cailleach W Isles 84 C2
Baile Raghaill W Isles 84 A2
Bailebeag Highld 81 B7
Baileyhead Cumb 61 F11
Bailiesward Aberds 88 E4
Baillieston Glasgow 68 D5
Bainbridge N Yorks 57 G11
Bainsford Falk 69 B7
Bainshole Aberds 88 E6
Bainton E Yorks 52 D5
Bainton Pboro 37 E6
Bairnkine Borders 62 B2
Baker Street Thurrock 20 C3
Baker's End Herts 29 G10
Bakewell Derbys 44 F6
Bala = Y Bala Gwyn 32 B5
Balachuirn Highld 85 D10
Balavil Highld 81 C9
Balbeg Highld 81 A6
Balbeg Highld 86 H7
Balbeggie Perth 76 E4
Balbithan Aberds 83 B9
Balbithan Ho. Aberds 83 B10
Balblair Highld 87 B8
Balblair Highld 87 E10
Balby S Yorks 45 B9
Balchladich Highld 92 F3
Balchraggan Highld 87 G8
Balchraggan Highld 87 H8
Balchrick Highld 92 D4
Balchrystie Fife 77 G7
Balcladaich Highld 80 A4
Balcombe W Sus 12 C2
Balcombe Lane W Sus 12 C2
Balcomie Fife 77 F9
Balcurvie Fife 76 G6
Baldersby N Yorks 51 B9
Baldersby St James N Yorks 51 B9
Balderstone Lancs 50 F2
Balderton Ches W 42 F6
Balderton Notts 46 G2
Baldhu Corn 3 E6
Baldinnie Fife 77 F7
Baldock Herts 29 E9
Baldovie Dundee 77 D7
Baldrine IoM 48 D4
Baldslow E Sus 13 E6
Baldwin IoM 48 D3
Baldwinholme Cumb 56 A5
Baldwin's Gate Staffs 34 A3
Bale Norf 38 B6
Balearn Aberds 89 C10
Balemartine Argyll 78 G2
Balephuil Argyll 78 G2
Balerno Edin 69 D10
Balevullin Argyll 78 G2
Balfield Angus 83 G7
Balfour Orkney 95 G5
Balfron Stirling 68 B4
Balfron Station Stirling 68 B4
Balgaveny Aberds 89 D6
Balgavies Angus 77 B8
Balgonar Fife 69 A9
Balgove Aberds 89 E8
Balgowan Highld 81 D8
Balgown Highld 85 B8
Balgrochan E Dunb 68 C5
Balgy Highld 85 C13
Balhaldie Stirling 75 G11
Balhalgardy Aberds 83 A9
Balham London 19 D9
Balhary Perth 76 C5
Baliasta Shetland 96 C8
Baligill Highld 93 C11
Balintore Angus 76 B5
Balintore Highld 87 D11
Balintraid Highld 87 D10
Balk N Yorks 51 A10
Balkeerie Angus 76 C6
Balkemback Angus 76 D6
Balkholme E Yorks 52 G3
Balkissock S Ayrs 54 A4
Ball Shrops 33 C9
Ball Haye Green Staffs 44 G3
Ball Hill Hants 17 E11
Ballabeg IoM 48 E2
Ballacannel IoM 48 D4
Ballachulish Highld 74 B3
Ballajora IoM 48 C4
Ballaleigh IoM 48 D3
Ballamodha IoM 48 E2
Ballantrae S Ayrs 54 A3
Ballaquine IoM 48 D4
Ballards Gore Essex 20 B6
Ballasalla IoM 48 C3
Ballasalla IoM 48 E2
Ballater Aberds 82 D5
Ballaugh IoM 48 C3
Ballaveare IoM 48 E3
Ballcorach Moray 82 A3
Ballechin Perth 76 B2
Balleigh Highld 87 C10
Ballencrieff E Loth 70 C3
Ballentoul Perth 81 G10
Ballidon Derbys 44 G6
Balliemore Argyll 73 E9
Balliemore Argyll 79 J11
Ballikinrain Stirling 68 B4
Ballimeanoch Argyll 73 B9
Ballimore Argyll 73 E8
Ballimore Stirling 75 F8
Ballinaby Argyll 64 B3
Ballindean Perth 76 E5
Ballingdon Suff 30 D5
Ballinger Common Bucks 18 A6
Ballingham Hereford 26 E2
Ballingry Fife 76 H4
Ballinlick Perth 76 C2
Ballinluig Perth 76 B2
Ballintuim Perth 76 B4
Balloch Angus 76 B6
Balloch Highld 87 G10
Balloch N Lanark 68 C6
Balloch W Dunb 68 B2
Ballochan Aberds 83 D7
Ballochford Moray 88 E3
Ballochmorrie S Ayrs 54 A5
Balls Cross W Sus 11 B8
Balls Green Essex 31 F7
Ballygown Argyll 78 G7
Ballygrant Argyll 64 B4
Ballyhaugh Argyll 78 F4
Balmacara Highld 85 F13
Balmacara Square Highld 85 F13
Balmaclellan Dumfries 55 B9
Balmacneil Perth 76 B2
Balmacqueen Highld 85 A9
Balmae Dumfries 55 E9
Balmaha Stirling 68 A3
Balmalcolm Fife 76 G6
Balmeanach Highld 85 D10
Balmedie Aberds 83 B11
Balmer Heath Shrops 33 B10
Balmerino Fife 76 E6
Balmerlawn Hants 10 D2
Balmichael N Ayrs 66 C2
Balmirmer Angus 77 D8
Balmore Highld 85 D7
Balmore Highld 86 H6
Balmore Highld 87 G11
Balmore Perth 76 B2
Balmule Fife 69 B11
Balmullo Fife 77 E7
Balmungie Highld 87 F10
Balnaboth Angus 82 G5
Balnabruaich Highld 87 E10
Balnabruich Highld 94 H3
Balnacoil Highld 93 H11
Balnacra Highld 86 G2
Balnafoich Highld 87 H9
Balnagall Highld 87 C11
Balnaguard Perth 76 B2
Balnahard Argyll 72 D3
Balnahard Argyll 78 H7
Balnain Highld 86 H7
Balnakeil Highld 92 C6
Balnaknock Highld 85 B9
Balnapaling Highld 87 E10
Balne N Yorks 52 H1
Balochroy Argyll 65 C8
Balone Fife 77 F7
Balornock Glasgow 68 D5
Balquharn Perth 76 D3
Balquhidder Stirling 75 E8
Balsall W Mid 35 H8
Balsall Common W Mid 35 H8
Balsall Hth. W Mid 35 G6
Balscott Oxon 27 D10
Balsham Cambs 30 C2
Baltasound Shetland 96 C8
Balterley Staffs 43 G10
Baltersan Dumfries 55 C7
Balthangie Aberds 89 C8
Baltonsborough Som 8 A4
Balvaird Highld 87 F8
Balvicar Argyll 72 B6
Balvraid Highld 85 G13
Balvraid Highld 87 H11
Bamber Bridge Lancs 50 G1
Bambers Green Essex 30 F2
Bamburgh Northumb 71 G10
Bamff Perth 76 B5
Bamford Derbys 44 D6
Bamford Gtr Man 44 A2
Bampton Cumb 57 E7
Bampton Devon 7 D8
Bampton Oxon 17 A10
Bampton Grange Cumb 57 E7
Banavie Highld 80 F3
Banbury Oxon 27 D11
Bancffosfelen Carms 23 E9
Banchory Aberds 83 D8
Banchory-Devenick Aberds 83 C11
Bancycapel Carms 23 E9
Bancyfelin Carms 23 E8
Bancyffordd Carms 23 C9
Bandirran Perth 76 D5
Banff Aberds 89 B6
Bangor Gwyn 41 C7
Bangor-is-y-coed Wrex 43 H6
Banham Norf 39 G6
Bank Hants 10 D1
Bank Newton N Yorks 50 D5
Bank Street Worcs 26 B3
Bankend Dumfries 60 G6
Bankfoot Perth 76 D3
Bankglen E Ayrs 67 E9
Bankhead Aberdeen 83 B10
Bankhead Aberds 83 C8
Banknock Falk 68 C6
Banks Cumb 61 G11
Banks Lancs 49 G3
Bankshill Dumfries 61 E7
Banningham Norf 39 C8
Banniskirk Ho. Highld 94 E3
Bannister Green Essex 30 F3
Bannockburn Stirling 69 A7
Banstead Sur 19 F9
Bantham Devon 5 G7
Banton N Lanark 68 C6
Banwell N Som 15 F9
Banyard's Green Suff 31 A9
Bapchild Kent 20 E6
Bar Hill Cambs 29 B10
Barabhas W Isles 91 C8
Barabhas Iarach W Isles 91 C8
Barabhas Uarach W Isles 91 B8
Barachandroman Argyll 79 J9
Barassie S Ayrs 66 C6
Baravullin Argyll 79 H11
Barbaraville Highld 87 D10
Barber Booth Derbys 44 D5
Barbieston S Ayrs 67 E7
Barbon Cumb 50 A2
Barbridge Ches E 43 G9
Barbrook Devon 6 B6
Barby Northants 28 A2
Barcaldine Argyll 74 C2
Barcheston Warks 27 E9
Barcombe E Sus 12 E3
Barcombe Cross E Sus 12 E3
Barden N Yorks 58 G2
Barden Scale N Yorks 51 D6
Bardennoch Dumfries 67 G8
Bardfield Saling Essex 30 F3
Bardister Shetland 96 F5
Bardney Lincs 46 F5
Bardon Leics 35 D10
Bardon Mill Northumb 62 G3
Bardowie E Dunb 68 C4
Bardrainney Invclyd 68 C2
Bardsea Cumb 49 B3
Bardsey W Yorks 51 E9
Bardwell Suff 30 A6
Bare Lancs 49 C4
Barfad Argyll 73 G7
Barford Norf 39 E7
Barford Warks 27 B9
Barford St John Oxon 27 E11
Barford St Martin Wilts 9 A9
Barford St Michael Oxon 27 E11
Barfrestone Kent 21 F9
Bargod = Bargoed Caerph 15 B7
Bargoed = Bargod Caerph 15 B7
Bargrennan Dumfries 54 B6
Barham Cambs 37 H7
Barham Kent 21 F9
Barham Suff 31 C8
Barharrow Dumfries 55 D9
Barhill Dumfries 55 C11
Barholm Lincs 37 D6
Barkby Leics 36 E2
Barkestone-le-Vale Leics 36 B3
Barkham Wokingham 18 E4
Barking London 19 C11
Barking Suff 31 C7
Barking Tye Suff 31 C7
Barkingside London 19 C11
Barkisland W Yorks 51 H6
Barkston Lincs 36 A5
Barkston N Yorks 51 F10
Barkway Herts 29 E10
Barlaston Staffs 34 B4
Barlavington W Sus 11 C8
Barlborough Derbys 45 E8
Barlby N Yorks 52 F2
Barlestone Leics 35 E10
Barley Herts 29 E10
Barley Lancs 50 E4
Barley Mow T&W 58 A3
Barleythorpe Rutland 36 E4
Barling Essex 20 C6
Barlow Derbys 45 E7
Barlow N Yorks 52 G2
Barlow T&W 63 G7
Barmby Moor E Yorks 52 E3
Barmby on the Marsh E Yorks 52 G2
Barmer Norf 38 B4
Barmoor Castle Northumb 71 G8
Barmoor Lane End Northumb 71 G9
Barmouth = Abermaw Gwyn 32 D2
Barmpton Darl 58 E4
Barmston E Yorks 53 D7
Barnack Pboro 37 E6
Barnacle Warks 35 G9
Barnard Castle Durham 58 E1
Barnard Gate Oxon 27 G11
Barnardiston Suff 30 D4
Barnbarroch Dumfries 55 D11
Barnburgh S Yorks 45 B8
Barnby Suff 39 G10
Barnby Dun S Yorks 45 B10
Barnby in the Willows Notts 46 G2
Barnby Moor Notts 45 D10
Barnes Street Kent 20 G3
Barnet London 19 B9
Barnetby le Wold N Lincs 46 B4
Barney Norf 38 B5
Barnham Suff 38 H4
Barnham W Sus 11 D8
Barnham Broom Norf 39 E6
Barnhead Angus 77 B9
Barnhill Ches W 43 G7
Barnhill Dundee 77 D7
Barnhill Moray 88 C1
Barnhills Dumfries 54 B2
Barningham Durham 58 E1
Barningham Suff 38 H5
Barnoldby le Beck NE Lincs 46 B6
Barnoldswick Lancs 50 E4
Barns Green W Sus 11 B10
Barnsley Glos 27 H7
Barnsley S Yorks 45 B7
Barnstaple Devon 6 C4
Barnston Essex 30 G3
Barnston Mers 42 D5
Barnstone Notts 36 B3
Barnt Green Worcs 27 A7
Barnton Ches W 43 E9
Barnton Edin 69 C10
Barnwell All Saints Northants 36 G6
Barnwell St Andrew Northants 36 G6
Barnwood Glos 26 G5
Barochreal Argyll 79 J11
Barons Cross Hereford 25 C11
Barr S Ayrs 66 G5
Barra Castle Aberds 83 A9
Barrachan Dumfries 54 E6
Barrack Aberds 89 D8
Barraglom W Isles 90 D6
Barrahormid Argyll 72 E6
Barran Argyll 79 J11
Barrapol Argyll 78 G2
Barras Aberds 83 E10
Barras Cumb 57 E10
Barrasford Northumb 62 F5
Barravullin Argyll 73 C7
Barregarrow IoM 48 D3
Barrhead E Renf 68 E3
Barrhill S Ayrs 54 A5
Barrington Cambs 29 D10
Barrington Som 8 C2
Barripper Corn 2 F5
Barrmill N Ayrs 67 A6
Barrock Highld 94 C4
Barrock Ho. Highld 94 D4
Barrow Lancs 50 F3
Barrow Rutland 36 D4
Barrow Suff 30 B4
Barrow Green Kent 20 E6
Barrow Gurney N Som 15 E11
Barrow Haven N Lincs 53 G6
Barrow-in-Furness Cumb 49 C2
Barrow Island Cumb 49 C1
Barrow Nook Lancs 43 B7
Barrow Street Wilts 9 A7
Barrow upon Humber N Lincs 53 G6
Barrow upon Soar Leics 36 D1
Barrow upon Trent Derbys 35 C9
Barroway Drove Norf 38 E1
Barrowburn Northumb 62 B4
Barrowby Lincs 36 B4
Barrowcliff N Yorks 59 H11
Barrowden Rutland 36 E5
Barrowford Lancs 50 F4
Barrows Green Ches E 43 G9
Barrows Green Cumb 57 H7
Barrow's Green Mers 43 D8
Barry Angus 77 D8
Barry = Y Barri V Glam 15 E7
Barry Island V Glam 15 E7
Barsby Leics 36 D2
Barsham Suff 39 G9
Barston W Mid 35 H8
Bartestree Hereford 26 D2
Barthol Chapel Aberds 89 E8
Barthomley Ches E 43 G10
Bartley Hants 10 C2
Bartley Green W Mid 34 G6
Bartlow Cambs 30 D2
Barton Cambs 29 C11
Barton Ches W 43 G7
Barton Glos 27 F8
Barton Lancs 42 B6
Barton Lancs 49 F5
Barton N Yorks 58 F3
Barton Oxon 28 H2
Barton Torbay 5 E10
Barton Warks 27 C8
Barton Bendish Norf 38 E3
Barton Hartshorn Bucks 28 E3
Barton in Fabis Notts 35 B11
Barton in the Beans Leics 35 E9
Barton-le-Clay C Beds 29 E7
Barton-le-Street N Yorks 52 B3
Barton-le-Willows N Yorks 52 C3
Barton Mills Suff 30 A4
Barton on Sea Hants 9 E11
Barton on the Heath Warks 27 E9
Barton St David Som 8 A4
Barton Seagrave Northants 36 H4
Barton Stacey Hants 17 G11
Barton Turf Norf 39 C9
Barton-under-Needwood Staffs 35 D7
Barton-upon-Humber N Lincs 52 G6
Barton Waterside N Lincs 52 G6
Barugh S Yorks 45 B7
Barway Cambs 37 H11
Barwell Leics 35 F10
Barwick Herts 29 G10
Barwick Som 8 C4
Barwick in Elmet W Yorks 51 F9
Baschurch Shrops 33 C10
Bascote Warks 27 B11
Basford Green Staffs 44 G3
Bashall Eaves Lancs 50 E2
Bashley Hants 9 E11
Basildon Essex 20 C4
Basingstoke Hants 18 F3
Baslow Derbys 44 E6
Bason Bridge Som 15 G9
Bassaleg Newport 15 C8
Bassenthwaite Cumb 56 C4
Bassett Soton 10 C3
Bassingbourn Cambs 29 D10
Bassingfield Notts 36 B2
Bassingham Lincs 46 F3
Bassingthorpe Lincs 36 C5
Basta Shetland 96 D7
Baston Lincs 37 D7
Bastwick Norf 39 D10
Baswick Steer E Yorks 53 E6
Batchworth Heath Herts 19 B7
Batcombe Dorset 8 D5
Batcombe Som 16 H3
Bate Heath Ches E 43 E9
Batford Herts 29 G8
Bath Bath 16 E4
Bathampton Bath 16 E4
Bathealton Som 7 D9
Batheaston Bath 16 E4
Bathford Bath 16 E4
Bathgate W Loth 69 D8
Bathley Notts 45 G11
Bathpool Corn 4 D3
Bathpool Som 8 B1
Bathville W Loth 69 D8
Batley W Yorks 51 G8
Batsford Glos 27 E8
Battersby N Yorks 59 F6
Battersea London 19 D9
Battisborough Cross Devon 5 G6
Battisford Suff 31 C7
Battisford Tye Suff 31 C7
Battle E Sus 12 E6
Battle Powys 25 E7
Battledown Glos 26 F6
Battlefield Shrops 33 D11
Battlesbridge Essex 20 B4
Battlesden C Beds 28 F6
Battlesea Green Suff 39 H8
Battleton Som 7 D8
Battram Leics 35 E10
Battramsley Hants 10 E2
Baughton Worcs 26 D5
Baughurst Hants 18 F2
Baulking Oxon 17 B10
Baumber Lincs 46 E6
Baunton Glos 17 A7
Baverstock Wilts 9 A9
Bawburgh Norf 39 E7
Bawdeswell Norf 38 C6
Bawdrip Som 15 H9
Bawdsey Suff 31 D10
Bawtry S Yorks 45 C10
Baxenden Lancs 50 G3
Baxterley Warks 35 F8
Baybridge Hants 10 B4
Baycliff Cumb 49 B2
Baydon Wilts 17 D9
Bayford Herts 29 H10
Bayford Som 8 B6
Bayles Cumb 57 B9
Baylham Suff 31 C8
Baynard's Green Oxon 28 F2
Bayston Hill Shrops 33 E10
Baythorn End Essex 30 D4
Bayton Worcs 26 A3
Beach Highld 79 F10
Beachampton Bucks 28 E4
Beachamwell Norf 38 E3
Beachans Moray 87 G13
Beacharr Argyll 65 D7
Beachborough Kent 21 H8
Beachley Glos 16 B2
Beacon Devon 7 F10
Beacon End Essex 30 F6
Beacon Hill Sur 18 H5
Beacon's Bottom Bucks 18 B4
Beaconsfield Bucks 18 C6
Beacrabhaic W Isles 90 H6
Beadlam N Yorks 52 A2
Beadlow C Beds 29 E8
Beadnell Northumb 71 H11
Beaford Devon 6 E4
Beal N Yorks 51 G11
Beal Northumb 71 F9
Beamhurst Staffs 35 B6
Beaminster Dorset 8 D3
Beamish Durham 58 A3
Beamsley N Yorks 51 D6
Bean Kent 20 D2
Beanacre Wilts 16 E6
Beanley Northumb 62 B6
Beaquoy Orkney 95 F4
Bear Cross Bmouth 9 E9
Beardwood Blackburn 50 G2
Beare Green Sur 19 G8
Bearley Warks 27 B8
Bearnus Argyll 78 G6
Bearpark Durham 58 B3
Bearsbridge Northumb 62 H3
Bearsden E Dunb 68 C4
Bearsted Kent 20 F4
Bearstone Shrops 34 B3
Bearwood Hereford 25 C10
Bearwood Poole 9 E9
Bearwood W Mid 34 G6
Beattock Dumfries 60 C6
Beauchamp Roding Essex 30 G2
Beauchief S Yorks 45 D7
Beaufort Bl Gwent 25 G8
Beaufort Castle Highld 87 G8
Beaulieu Hants 10 D2
Beauly Highld 87 G8
Beaumaris Anglesey 41 C8
Beaumont Cumb 61 H9
Beaumont Essex 31 F8
Beaumont Hill Darl 58 E3
Beausale Warks 27 A9
Beauworth Hants 10 B4
Beaworthy Devon 6 G3
Beazley End Essex 30 F4
Bebington Mers 42 D6
Bebside Northumb 63 E8
Beccles Suff 39 F10
Becconsall Lancs 49 G4
Beck Foot Cumb 57 G8
Beck Hole N Yorks 59 F9
Beck Row Suff 38 H2
Beck Side Cumb 49 A2
Beckbury Shrops 34 E3
Beckenham London 19 E10
Beckermet Cumb 56 F2
Beckfoot Cumb 56 B2
Beckfoot Cumb 56 F3
Beckford Worcs 26 E6
Beckhampton Wilts 17 E7
Beckingham Lincs 46 G2
Beckingham Notts 45 D11
Beckington Som 16 F5
Beckley E Sus 13 D7
Beckley Hants 9 E11
Beckley Oxon 28 G2
Beckton London 19 C11
Beckwithshaw N Yorks 51 D8
Becontree London 19 C11
Bed-y-coedwr Gwyn 32 C3
Bedale N Yorks 58 H3
Bedburn Durham 58 C2
Bedchester Dorset 9 C7
Beddau Rhondda 14 C6
Beddgelert Gwyn 41 F7
Beddingham E Sus 12 F3
Beddington London 19 E10
Bedfield Suff 31 B9
Bedford Bedford 29 C7
Bedham W Sus 11 B9
Bedhampton Hants 10 D6
Bedingfield Suff 31 B8
Bedlam N Yorks 51 C8
Bedlington Northumb 63 E8
Bedlington Station Northumb 63 E8
Bedlinog M Tydf 14 A6
Bedminster Bristol 16 D2
Bedmond Herts 19 A7
Bednall Staffs 34 D5
Bedrule Borders 62 B2
Bedstone Shrops 33 H9
Bedwas Caerph 15 C7
Bedworth Warks 35 G9
Bedworth Heath Warks 35 G9
Beeby Leics 36 E2
Beech Hants 18 H3
Beech Staffs 34 B4
Beech Hill Gtr Man 43 B8
Beech Hill W Berks 18 E3
Beechingstoke Wilts 17 F7
Beedon W Berks 17 D11
Beeford E Yorks 53 D7
Beeley Derbys 44 F6
Beelsby NE Lincs 46 B6
Beenham W Berks 18 E2
Beeny Corn 4 B2
Beer Devon 7 H11
Beer Hackett Dorset 8 C4
Beercrocombe Som 8 B2
Beesands Devon 5 G9
Beesby Lincs 47 D8
Beeson Devon 5 G9
Beeston C Beds 29 D8
Beeston Ches W 43 G8
Beeston Norf 38 D5
Beeston Notts 35 B11
Beeston W Yorks 51 F8
Beeston Regis Norf 39 A7
Beeswing Dumfries 55 C11
Beetham Cumb 49 B4
Beetley Norf 38 D5
Begbroke Oxon 27 G11
Begelly Pembs 22 F6
Beggar's Bush Powys 25 B9
Beguildy Powys 33 H7
Beighton Norf 39 E9
Beighton S Yorks 45 D8
Beighton Hill Derbys 44 G6
Beith N Ayrs 66 A6
Bekesbourne Kent 21 F8
Belaugh Norf 39 D8
Belbroughton Worcs 34 H5
Belchamp Otten Essex 30 D5
Belchamp St Paul Essex 30 D4
Belchamp Walter Essex 30 D5
Belchford Lincs 46 E6
Belford Northumb 71 G10
Belhaven E Loth 70 C5
Belhelvie Aberds 83 B11
Belhinnie Aberds 82 A6
Bell Bar Herts 29 H9
Bell Busk N Yorks 50 D5
Bell End Worcs 34 H5
Bell o' th' Hill Ches W 43 H8
Bellabeg Aberds 82 B5
Bellamore S Ayrs 66 H5
Bellanoch Argyll 72 D6
Bellaty Angus 76 B5
Belleau Lincs 47 E8
Bellehiglash Moray 88 E1
Bellerby N Yorks 58 G2
Bellever Devon 5 D7
Belliehill Angus 77 A8
Bellingdon Bucks 28 H6
Bellingham Northumb 62 E4
Belloch Argyll 65 E7
Bellochantuy Argyll 65 E7
Bells Yew Green E Sus 12 C5
Bellsbank E Ayrs 67 F7
Bellshill N Lanark 68 D6
Bellshill Northumb 71 G10
Bellspool Borders 69 G10
Bellsquarry W Loth 69 D9
Belmaduthy Highld 87 F9
Belmesthorpe Rutland 36 D6
Belmont Blackburn 50 H2
Belmont London 19 E9
Belmont S Ayrs 66 D6
Belmont Shetland 96 C7
Belnacraig Aberds 82 B5
Belowda Corn 3 C8
Belper Derbys 45 H7
Belper Lane End Derbys 45 H7
Belsay Northumb 63 F7
Belses Borders 70 H4
Belsford Devon 5 F8
Belstead Suff 31 D8
Belston S Ayrs 67 D6
Belstone Devon 6 G5
Belthorn Blackburn 50 G3
Beltinge Kent 21 E8
Beltoft N Lincs 46 B2
Belton Leics 35 C10
Belton Lincs 36 B5
Belton N Lincs 45 B11
Belton Norf 39 E10
Belton in Rutland Rutland 36 E4
Beltring Kent 20 G3
Belts of Collonach Aberds 83 D8
Belvedere London 19 D11
Belvoir Leics 36 B4
Bembridge IoW 10 F5
Bemersyde Borders 70 G4
Bemerton Wilts 9 A10
Bempton E Yorks 53 B7
Ben Alder Lodge Highld 81 F7
Ben Armine Lodge Highld 93 H10
Ben Casgro W Isles 91 E9
Benacre Suff 39 G11
Benbuie Dumfries 60 D3
Benderloch Argyll 74 D2
Bendronaig Lodge Highld 86 H3
Benenden Kent 13 C7
Benfield Dumfries 54 C6
Bengate Norf 39 C9
Bengeworth Worcs 27 D7
Benhall Green Suff 31 B10
Benhall Street Suff 31 B10
Benholm Aberds 83 G10
Beningbrough N Yorks 51 D11
Benington Herts 29 F9
Benington Lincs 47 H7
Benllech Anglesey 41 B7
Benmore Argyll 73 E10
Benmore Stirling 75 E7
Benmore Lodge Highld 92 H6
Bennacott Corn 6 G1
Bennan N Ayrs 66 D2
Benniworth Lincs 46 D6
Benover Kent 20 G4
Bensham T&W 63 G8
Benslie N Ayrs 66 B6
Benson Oxon 18 B3
Bent Aberds 83 F8
Bent Gate Lancs 50 G3
Benthall Northumb 71 H11
Benthall Shrops 34 E2
Bentham Glos 26 G6
Benthoul Aberdeen 83 C10
Bentlawnt Shrops 33 E9
Bentley E Yorks 52 F6
Bentley Hants 18 G4
Bentley S Yorks 45 B9
Bentley Suff 31 E8
Bentley Warks 35 F8
Bentley Worcs 26 B6
Bentley Heath W Mid 35 H7
Benton Devon 6 C5
Bentpath Dumfries 61 D9
Bents W Loth 69 D8
Bentworth Hants 18 G3
Benvie Dundee 76 D6
Benwick Cambs 37 F9
Beoley Worcs 27 B7
Beoraidbeg Highld 79 B9
Bepton W Sus 11 C7
Berden Essex 29 F11
Bere Alston Devon 4 E5
Bere Ferrers Devon 4 E5
Bere Regis Dorset 9 E7
Berepper Corn 2 G5
Bergh Apton Norf 39 E9
Berinsfield Oxon 18 B2
Berkeley Glos 16 B3
Berkhamsted Herts 28 H6
Berkley Som 16 G5
Berkswell W Mid 35 H8
Bermondsey London 19 D10
Bernera Highld 85 F13
Bernice Argyll 73 D10
Bernisdale Highld 85 C9
Berrick Salome Oxon 18 B3
Berriedale Highld 94 H3
Berrier Cumb 56 D5
Berriew Powys 33 E7
Berrington Northumb 71 F9
Berrington Shrops 33 E11
Berrow Som 15 F9
Berrow Green Worcs 26 C4
Berry Down Cross Devon 6 B4
Berry Hill Glos 26 G2
Berry Hill Pembs 22 B5
Berry Pomeroy Devon 5 E9
Berryfield Bucks 28 G4
Berryhillock Moray 88 B5
Berrynarbor Devon 6 B4
Bersham Wrex 42 H6
Berstane Orkney 95 G5
Berwick E Sus 12 F4
Berwick Bassett Wilts 17 D7
Berwick Hill Northumb 63 F7
Berwick St James Wilts 17 H7
Berwick St John Wilts 9 B8
Berwick St Leonard Wilts 9 A8
Berwick-upon-Tweed Northumb 71 E8
Bescar Lancs 43 A6
Besford Worcs 26 D6
Bessacarr S Yorks 45 B10
Bessels Leigh Oxon 17 A11
Bessingby E Yorks 53 C7
Bessingham Norf 39 B7
Bestbeech Hill E Sus 12 C5
Besthorpe Norf 39 F6
Besthorpe Notts 46 F2
Bestwood Nottingham 36 A1
Bestwood Village Notts 45 H9
Beswick E Yorks 52 E6
Betchworth Sur 19 G9
Bethania Ceredig 24 B2
Bethania Gwyn 41 E8
Bethania Gwyn 41 F9
Bethel Anglesey 40 C5
Bethel Gwyn 32 B5
Bethel Gwyn 41 D7
Bethersden Kent 13 B8
Bethesda Gwyn 41 D8
Bethesda Pembs 22 E5
Bethlehem Carms 24 F3
Bethnal Green London 19 C10
Betley Staffs 43 H10
Betsham Kent 20 D3
Betteshanger Kent 21 F10
Bettiscombe Dorset 8 E2
Bettisfield Wrex 33 B10
Betton Shrops 33 E9
Betton Shrops 34 B2
Bettws Bridgend 14 C5
Bettws Mon 25 G9
Bettws Newport 15 B8
Bettws Cedewain Powys 33 F7
Bettws Gwerfil Goch Denb 42 H3
Bettws Ifan Ceredig 23 B8
Bettws Newydd Mon 25 H10
Bettws-y-crwyn Shrops 33 G8
Bettyhill Highld 93 C10
Betws Carms 24 G3
Betws Bledrws Ceredig 23 A10
Betws-Garmon Gwyn 41 E7
Betws-y-Coed Conwy 41 E9
Betws-yn-Rhos Conwy 42 E2
Beulah Ceredig 23 B7
Beulah Powys 24 C6
Bevendean Brighton 12 F2
Bevercotes Notts 45 E10
Beverley E Yorks 52 F6
Beverston Glos 16 B5
Bevington Glos 16 B3
Bewaldeth Cumb 56 C4
Bewcastle Cumb 61 F11
Bewdley Worcs 34 H3
Bewerley N Yorks 51 C7
Bewholme E Yorks 53 D7
Bexhill E Sus 12 F6
Bexley London 19 D11
Bexleyheath London 19 D11
Bexwell Norf 38 E2
Beyton Suff 30 B6
Bhaltos W Isles 90 D5
Bhatarsaigh W Isles 84 J1
Bibury Glos 27 H8
Bicester Oxon 28 F2
Bickenhall Som 8 C1
Bickenhill W Mid 35 G7
Bicker Lincs 37 B8
Bickershaw Gtr Man 43 B9
Bickerstaffe Lancs 43 B7
Bickerton Ches E 43 G8
Bickerton N Yorks 51 D10
Bickington Devon 5 D8
Bickington Devon 6 C4
Bickleigh Devon 4 E6
Bickleigh Devon 7 F8
Bickleton Devon 6 C4
Bickley London 19 E11
Bickley Moss Ches W 43 H8
Bicknacre Essex 20 A4
Bicknoller Som 7 C10
Bicknor Kent 20 F5
Bickton Hants 9 C10
Bicton Shrops 33 D10
Bicton Shrops 33 G8
Bidborough Kent 12 B4
Biddenden Kent 13 C7
Biddenham Bedford 29 D7
Biddestone Wilts 16 D5
Biddisham Som 15 F9
Biddlesden Bucks 28 D3
Biddlestone Northumb 62 C5
Biddulph Staffs 44 G2
Biddulph Moor Staffs 44 G3
Bideford Devon 6 D3
Bidford-on-Avon Warks 27 C8
Bidston Mers 42 C5
Bielby E Yorks 52 E3
Bieldside Aberdeen 83 C10
Bierley IoW 10 G4
Bierley W Yorks 51 F7
Bierton Bucks 28 G5
Big Sand Highld 85 A12
Bigbury Devon 5 G7
Bigbury on Sea Devon 5 G7
Bigby Lincs 46 B4
Biggar Cumb 49 C1
Biggar S Lanark 69 G9
Biggin Derbys 44 G5
Biggin Derbys 44 H6
Biggin N Yorks 51 F11
Biggin Hill London 19 F11
Biggings Shetland 96 G3
Biggleswade C Beds 29 D8
Bighouse Highld 93 C11
Bighton Hants 10 A5
Bignor W Sus 11 C8
Bigton Shetland 96 L5
Bilberry Corn 3 C9
Bilborough Nottingham 35 A11
Bilbrook Som 7 B9
Bilbrough N Yorks 51 E11
Bilbster Highld 94 E4
Bildershaw Durham 58 D3
Bildeston Suff 30 D6
Billericay Essex 20 B3
Billesdon Leics 36 E3
Billesley Warks 27 C8
Billingborough Lincs 37 B7
Billinge Mers 43 B8
Billingford Norf 38 C6
Billingham Stockton 58 D5
Billinghay Lincs 46 G5
Billingley S Yorks 45 B8
Billingshurst W Sus 11 B9
Billingsley Shrops 34 G3
Billington C Beds 28 F6
Billington Lancs 50 F3
Billockby Norf 39 D10
Billy Row Durham 58 C2
Bilsborrow Lancs 49 F5
Bilsby Lincs 47 E8
Bilsham W Sus 11 D8
Bilsington Kent 13 C9
Bilson Green Glos 26 G3
Bilsthorpe Notts 45 F10
Bilsthorpe Moor Notts 45 G10
Bilston Midloth 69 D11
Bilston W Mid 34 F5
Bilstone Leics 35 E9
Bilting Kent 21 G7
Bilton E Yorks 53 F7
Bilton Northumb 63 B8
Bilton Warks 27 A11
Bilton in Ainsty N Yorks 51 E10
Bimbister Orkney 95 G4
Binbrook Lincs 46 C6
Binchester Blocks Durham 58 C3
Bincombe Dorset 8 F5
Bindal Highld 87 C12
Binegar Som 16 G3
Binfield Brack 18 D5
Binfield Hth. Oxon 18 D4
Bingfield Northumb 62 F5
Bingham Notts 36 B3
Bingley W Yorks 51 F7
Bings Heath Shrops 33 D11
Binham Norf 38 B5
Binley Hants 17 F11
Binley W Mid 35 H9
Binley Woods Warks 35 H9
Binniehill Falk 69 C7
Binsoe N Yorks 51 B8
Binstead IoW 10 E4
Binsted Hants 18 G4
Binton Warks 27 C8
Bintree Norf 38 C6
Binweston Shrops 33 E9
Birch Essex 30 G6
Birch Gtr Man 44 B2
Birch Green Essex 30 G6
Birch Heath Ches W 43 F8
Birch Hill Ches W 43 E8
Birch Vale Derbys 44 D4
Bircham Newton Norf 38 B3
Bircham Tofts Norf 38 B3
Birchanger Essex 30 F2
Birchencliffe W Yorks 51 H7
Bircher Hereford 25 B11
Birchgrove Cardiff 15 D7
Birchgrove Swansea 14 B3
Birchington Kent 21 E9
Birchmoor Warks 35 E8
Birchover Derbys 44 F6
Birchwood Lincs 46 F3
Birchwood Warr 43 C9
Bircotes Notts 45 C10
Birdbrook Essex 30 D4
Birdforth N Yorks 51 B10
Birdham W Sus 11 E7
Birdholme Derbys 45 F7
Birdingbury Warks 27 B11
Birdlip Glos 26 G6
Birds Edge W Yorks 44 B6
Birdsall N Yorks 52 C4
Birdsgreen Shrops 34 G3
Birdsmoor Gate Dorset 8 D2
Birdston E Dunb 68 C5
Birdwell S Yorks 45 B7
Birdwood Glos 26 G4
Birgham Borders 70 G6
Birkby N Yorks 58 F4
Birkdale Mers 49 H3
Birkenhead Mers 42 D6
Birkenhills Aberds 89 D7
Birkenshaw N Lanark 68 D5
Birkenshaw W Yorks 51 G8
Birkhall Aberds 82 D5
Birkhill Angus 76 D6
Birkhill Borders 61 B8
Birkholme Lincs 36 C5
Birkin N Yorks 51 G11
Birley Hereford 25 C11
Birling Kent 20 E3
Birling Northumb 63 C8
Birling Gap E Sus 12 G4
Birlingham Worcs 26 D6
Birmingham W Mid 35 G6
Birnam Perth 76 C3
Birse Aberds 83 D7
Birsemore Aberds 83 D7
Birstall Leics 36 E1
Birstall W Yorks 51 G8
Birstwith N Yorks 51 D8
Birthorpe Lincs 37 B7
Birtley Hereford 25 B10
Birtley Northumb 62 F4
Birtley T&W 63 H8
Birts Street Worcs 26 E4
Bisbrooke Rutland 36 F4
Biscathorpe Lincs 46 D6
Biscot Luton 29 F7
Bish Mill Devon 7 D6
Bisham Windsor 18 C5
Bishampton Worcs 26 C6
Bishop Auckland Durham 58 D3
Bishop Burton E Yorks 52 F5
Bishop Middleham Durham 58 C4
Bishop Monkton N Yorks 51 C9
Bishop Norton Lincs 46 C3
Bishop Sutton Bath 16 F2
Bishop Thornton N Yorks 51 C8
Bishop Wilton E Yorks 52 D3
Bishopbridge Lincs 46 C4
Bishopbriggs E Dunb 68 D5
Bishopmill Moray 88 B2
Bishops Cannings Wilts 17 E7
Bishop's Castle Shrops 33 G9
Bishop's Caundle Dorset 8 C5
Bishop's Cleeve Glos 26 F6
Bishops Frome Hereford 26 D3
Bishop's Green Essex 30 G3
Bishop's Hull Som 7 D11
Bishop's Itchington Warks 27 C10
Bishops Lydeard Som 7 D10
Bishops Nympton Devon 7 D6
Bishop's Offley Staffs 34 C3
Bishop'S Stortford Herts 29 F11
Bishop's Sutton Hants 10 A5
Bishop's Tachbrook Warks 27 B10
Bishops Tawton Devon 6 C4
Bishop's Waltham Hants 10 C4
Bishop's Wood Staffs 34 E4
Bishopsbourne Kent 21 F8
Bishopsteignton Devon 5 D10
Bishopstoke Hants 10 C3
Bishopston Swansea 23 H10
Bishopstone Bucks 28 G5
Bishopstone E Sus 12 F3
Bishopstone Hereford 25 D11
Bishopstone Swindon 17 C9
Bishopstone Wilts 9 B9
Bishopstrow Wilts 16 G5
Bishopswood Som 8 C1
Bishopsworth Bristol 16 E2
Bishopthorpe York 52 E1
Bishopton Darl 58 D4
Bishopton Dumfries 55 E7
Bishopton N Yorks 51 B9
Bishopton Renfs 68 C3
Bishopton Warks 27 C8
Bishton Newport 15 C9
Bisley Glos 26 H6
Bisley Sur 18 F6
Bispham Blackpool 49 E3
Bispham Green Lancs 43 A7
Bissoe Corn 3 E6
Bisterne Close Hants 9 D11
Bitchfield Lincs 36 C5
Bittadon Devon 6 B4
Bittaford Devon 5 F7
Bittering Norf 38 D5
Bitterley Shrops 34 H1
Bitterne Soton 10 C3
Bitteswell Leics 35 G11
Bitton S Glos 16 E3
Bix Oxon 18 C4
Bixter Shetland 96 H5
Blaby Leics 36 F1
Black Bourton Oxon 17 A9
Black Callerton T&W 63 G7
Black Clauchrie S Ayrs 54 A5
Black Corries Lodge Highld 74 B5
Black Crofts Argyll 74 D2
Black Dog Devon 7 F7
Black Heddon Northumb 62 F6
Black Lane Gtr Man 43 B10
Black Marsh Shrops 33 F9
Black Mount Argyll 74 C5
Black Notley Essex 30 F4
Black Pill Swansea 14 B2
Black Tar Pembs 22 F4
Black Torrington Devon 6 F3
Blackacre Dumfries 60 D6
Blackadder West Borders 71 E7
Blackawton Devon 5 F9
Blackborough Devon 7 F9
Blackborough End Norf 38 D2
Blackboys E Sus 12 D4
Blackbrook Derbys 45 H7
Blackbrook Mers 43 C8
Blackbrook Staffs 34 B3
Blackburn Aberds 83 B10
Blackburn Aberds 88 E5
Blackburn Blackburn 50 G2
Blackburn W Loth 69 D8
Blackcraig Dumfries 60 E3
Blackden Heath Ches E 43 E10
Blackdog Aberds 83 B11
Blackfell T&W 63 H8
Blackfield Hants 10 D3
Blackford Cumb 61 G9
Blackford Perth 75 G11
Blackford Som 8 B5
Blackford Som 15 G10
Blackfordby Leics 35 D9
Blackgang IoW 10 G3
Blackhall Colliery Durham 58 C5
Blackhall Mill T&W 63 H7
Blackhall Rocks Durham 58 C5
Blackham E Sus 12 C3
Blackhaugh Borders 70 G3
Blackheath Essex 31 F7
Blackheath Suff 31 A11
Blackheath Sur 19 G7
Blackheath W Mid 34 G5
Blackhill Aberds 89 C10
Blackhill Aberds 89 D10
Blackhill Highld 85 C8
Blackhills Highld 87 F12
Blackhills Moray 88 C2
Blackhorse S Glos 16 D3
Blackland Wilts 17 E7
Blacklaw Aberds 89 C6
Blackley Gtr Man 44 B2
Blacklunans Perth 76 A4
Blackmill Bridgend 14 C5
Blackmoor Hants 11 A6
Blackmoor Gate Devon 6 B5
Blackmore Essex 20 A3
Blackmore End Essex 30 E4
Blackmore End Herts 29 G8
Blackness Falk 69 C9
Blacknest Hants 18 G4
Blacko Lancs 50 E4
Blackpool Blackpool 49 F3
Blackpool Devon 5 G9
Blackpool Pembs 22 E5
Blackpool Gate Cumb 61 F11
Blackridge W Loth 69 D7
Blackrock Argyll 64 B4
Blackrock Mon 25 G9
Blackrod Gtr Man 43 A9
Blackshaw Dumfries 60 G6
Blackshaw Head W Yorks 50 G5
Blacksmith's Green Suff 31 B8
Blackstone W Sus 11 C11
Blackthorn Oxon 28 G3
Blackthorpe Suff 30 B6
Blacktoft E Yorks 52 G4
Blacktop Aberdeen 83 C10
Blacktown Newport 15 C8
Blackwall Tunnel London 19 C10
Blackwater Corn 2 E6
Blackwater Hants 18 F5
Blackwater IoW 10 F4
Blackwaterfoot N Ayrs 66 D1
Blackwell Darl 58 E3
Blackwell Derbys 44 E5
Blackwell Derbys 45 G8
Blackwell W Sus 12 C2
Blackwell Warks 27 D9
Blackwell Worcs 26 A6
Blackwood = Coed Duon Caerph 15 B7
Blackwood S Lanark 68 F6
Blackwood Hill Staffs 44 G3
Blacon Ches W 43 F6
Bladnoch Dumfries 55 D7
Bladon Oxon 27 G11
Blaen-gwynfi Neath 14 B4
Blaen-waun Carms 23 D7
Blaen-y-coed Carms 23 D8
Blaen-y-Cwm Denb 32 B6
Blaen-y-cwm Gwyn 32 C3
Blaen-y-cwm Powys 33 C6
Blaenannerch Ceredig 23 B7
Blaenau Ffestiniog Gwyn 41 F9
Blaenavon Torf 25 H9
Blaencelyn Ceredig 23 A8
Blaendyryn Powys 24 E6
Blaenffos Pembs 22 C6
Blaengarw Bridgend 14 B5
Blaengwrach Neath 24 H5
Blaenpennal Ceredig 24 B3
Blaenplwyf Ceredig 32 H1
Blaenporth Ceredig 23 B7
Blaenrhondda Rhondda 14 A5
Blaenycwm Ceredig 32 H4
Blagdon N Som 15 F11
Blagdon Torbay 5 E9
Blagdon Hill Som 7 E11
Blagill Cumb 57 B9
Blaguegate Lancs 43 B7
Blaich Highld 80 F2
Blain Highld 79 E9
Blaina Bl Gwent 25 H9
Blair Atholl Perth 81 G10
Blair Drummond Stirling 75 H10
Blairbeg N Ayrs 66 C3
Blairdaff Aberds 83 B8
Blairglas Argyll 68 B2
Blairgowrie Perth 76 C4
Blairhall Fife 69 B9
Blairingone Perth 76 H2
Blairland N Ayrs 66 B6
Blairlogie Stirling 75 H11
Blairlomond Argyll 74 H4
Blairmore Argyll 73 E10
Blairnamarrow Moray 82 B4
Blairquhosh Stirling 68 B4
Blair's Ferry Argyll 73 G8
Blairskaith E Dunb 68 C4
Blaisdon Glos 26 G4
Blakebrook Worcs 34 H4
Blakedown Worcs 34 H4
Blakelaw Borders 70 G6
Blakeley Staffs 34 F4
Blakeley Lane Staffs 44 H3
Blakemere Hereford 25 D10
Blakeney Glos 26 H3
Blakeney Norf 38 A6
Blakenhall Ches E 43 H10
Blakenhall W Mid 34 F5
Blakeshall Worcs 34 G4
Blakesley Northants 28 C3
Blanchland Northumb 57 A11
Bland Hill N Yorks 51 D8
Blandford Forum Dorset 9 D7
Blandford St Mary Dorset 9 D7
Blanefield Stirling 68 C4
Blankney Lincs 46 F4
Blantyre S Lanark 68 E5
Blar a'Chaorainn Highld 80 G3
Blaran Argyll 73 B7
Blarghour Argyll 73 B8
Blarmachfoldach Highld 80 G2
Blarnalearoch Highld 86 B4
Blashford Hants 9 D10
Blaston Leics 36 F4
Blatherwycke Northants 36 F5
Blawith Cumb 56 H4
Blaxhall Suff 31 C10
Blaxton S Yorks 45 B10
Blaydon T&W 63 G7
Bleadon N Som 15 F9
Bleak Hey Nook Gtr Man 44 B4
Blean Kent 21 E8
Bleasby Lincs 46 D5
Bleasby Notts 45 H11
Bleasdale Lancs 50 E1
Bleatarn Cumb 57 E9
Blebocraigs Fife 77 F7
Bleddfa Powys 25 B9
Bledington Glos 27 F9
Bledlow Bucks 18 A4
Bledlow Ridge Bucks 18 B4
Blegbie E Loth 70 D3
Blencarn Cumb 57 C8
Blencogo Cumb 56 B3
Blendworth Hants 10 C6
Blenheim Park Norf 38 B4
Blennerhasset Cumb 56 B3
Blervie Castle Moray 87 F13
Bletchingdon Oxon 28 G2
Bletchingley Sur 19 F10
Bletchley M Keynes 28 E5
Bletchley Shrops 34 B2
Bletherston Pembs 22 D5
Bletsoe Bedford 29 C7
Blewbury Oxon 18 C2
Blickling Norf 39 C7
Blidworth Notts 45 G9
Blindburn Northumb 62 B4
Blindcrake Cumb 56 C3
Blindley Heath Sur 19 G10
Blisland Corn 4 D2
Bliss Gate Worcs 26 A4
Blissford Hants 9 C10
Blisworth Northants 28 C4
Blithbury Staffs 35 C6
Blitterlees Cumb 56 A3
Blo' Norton Norf 38 H6
Blockley Glos 27 E8
Blofield Norf 39 E9
Blofield Heath Norf 39 D9
Bloomfield Borders 61 A11
Blore Staffs 44 H5
Blount's Green Staffs 35 B6
Blowick Mers 49 H3
Bloxham Oxon 27 E11
Bloxholm Lincs 46 G4
Bloxwich W Mid 34 E5
Bloxworth Dorset 9 E7
Blubberhouses N Yorks 51 D7
Blue Anchor Som 7 B9
Blue Anchor Swansea 23 G10
Blue Row Essex 31 G7
Blundeston Suff 39 F11
Blunham C Beds 29 C8
Blunsdon St Andrew Swindon 17 C8
Bluntington Worcs 26 A5
Bluntisham Cambs 29 A10
Blunts Corn 4 E4
Blyborough Lincs 46 C3
Blyford Suff 39 H10
Blymhill Staffs 34 D4
Blyth Northumb 63 E9
Blyth Notts 45 D10
Blyth Bridge Borders 69 F10
Blythburgh Suff 39 H10
Blythe Borders 70 F4
Blythe Bridge Staffs 34 A5
Blyton Lincs 46 C2
Boarhills Fife 77 F8
Boarhunt Hants 10 D5
Boars Head Gtr Man 43 B8
Boars Hill Oxon 17 A11
Boarshead E Sus 12 C4
Boarstall Bucks 28 G3
Boasley Cross Devon 6 G3
Boat of Garten Highld 81 B11
Boath Highld 87 D8
Bobbing Kent 20 E5
Bobbington Staffs 34 F4
Bobbingworth Essex 30 H2
Bocaddon Corn 4 F2
Bochastle Stirling 75 G9
Bocking Essex 30 F4
Bocking Churchstreet Essex 30 F4
Boddam Aberds 89 D11
Boddam Shetland 96 M5
Boddington Glos 26 F5
Bodedern Anglesey 40 B5
Bodelwyddan Denb 42 E3
Bodenham Hereford 26 C2
Bodenham Wilts 9 B10
Bodenham Moor Hereford 26 C2
Bodermid Gwyn 40 H3
Bodewryd Anglesey 40 A5
Bodfari Denb 42 E3
Bodffordd Anglesey 40 C6
Bodham Norf 39 A7
Bodiam E Sus 13 D6
Bodicote Oxon 27 E11
Bodieve Corn 3 B8
Bodinnick Corn 4 F2
Bodle Street Green E Sus 12 E5
Bodmin Corn 4 E1
Bodney Norf 38 F4
Bodorgan Anglesey 40 D5
Bodsham Kent 21 G8
Boduan Gwyn 40 G5
Bodymoor Heath Warks 35 F7
Bogallan Highld 87 F9
Bogbrae Aberds 89 E10
Bogend Borders 70 F6
Bogend S Ayrs 67 C6
Boghall W Loth 69 D8
Boghead S Lanark 68 F6
Bogmoor Moray 88 B3
Bogniebrae Aberds 88 D5
Bognor Regis W Sus 11 E8
Bograxie Aberds 83 B9
Bogside N Lanark 69 E7
Bogton Aberds 89 C6
Bogue Dumfries 55 A9
Bohenie Highld 80 E4
Bohortha Corn 3 F7
Bohuntine Highld 80 E4
Boirseam W Isles 90 J5
Bojewyan Corn 2 F2
Bolam Durham 58 D2
Bolam Northumb 62 E6
Bolberry Devon 5 H7
Bold Heath Mers 43 D8
Boldon T&W 63 G9
Boldon Colliery T&W 63 G9
Boldre Hants 10 E2
Boldron Durham 58 E1
Bole Notts 45 D11
Bolehill Derbys 44 G6
Boleside Borders 70 G3
Bolham Devon 7 E8
Bolham Water Devon 7 E10
Bolingey Corn 3 D6
Bollington Ches E 44 E3
Bollington Cross Ches E 44 E3
Bolney W Sus 12 D1
Bolnhurst Bedford 29 C7
Bolshan Angus 77 B9
Bolsover Derbys 45 E8
Bolsterstone S Yorks 44 C6
Bolstone Hereford 26 E2
Boltby N Yorks 58 H5
Bolter End Bucks 18 B4
Bolton Cumb 57 D8
Bolton E Loth 70 C4
Bolton E Yorks 52 D3
Bolton Gtr Man 43 B10
Bolton Northumb 63 B7
Bolton Abbey N Yorks 51 D6
Bolton Bridge N Yorks 51 D6
Bolton-by-Bowland Lancs 50 E3
Bolton-le-Sands Lancs 49 C4
Bolton Low Houses Cumb 56 B4
Bolton-on-Swale N Yorks 58 G3
Bolton Percy N Yorks 51 E11
Bolton Town End Lancs 49 C4
Bolton upon Dearne S Yorks 45 B8
Boltonfellend Cumb 61 G10
Boltongate Cumb 56 B4
Bolventor Corn 4 D2
Bomere Heath Shrops 33 D10
Bon-y-maen Swansea 14 B2
Bonar Bridge Highld 87 B9
Bonawe Argyll 74 D3
Bonby N Lincs 52 H6
Boncath Pembs 23 C7
Bonchester Bridge Borders 61 B11
Bonchurch IoW 10 G4
Bondleigh Devon 6 F5
Bonehill Devon 5 D8
Bonehill Staffs 35 E7
Bo'ness Falk 69 B8
Bonhill W Dunb 68 C2
Boningale Shrops 34 E4
Bonjedward Borders 62 A2
Bonkle N Lanark 69 E7
Bonnavoulin Highld 79 F8
Bonnington Edin 69 D10
Bonnington Kent 13 C9
Bonnybank Fife 76 G6
Bonnybridge Falk 69 B7
Bonnykelly Aberds 89 C8
Bonnyrigg and Lasswade Midloth 70 D2
Bonnyton Aberds 89 E6
Bonnyton Angus 76 D6
Bonnyton Angus 77 B9
Bonsall Derbys 44 G6
Bonskeid House Perth 75 A11
Bont Mon 25 G10
Bont-Dolgadfan Powys 32 E4
Bont-goch Ceredig 32 G2
Bont-newydd Conwy 42 E3
Bont Newydd Gwyn 32 C3
Bont Newydd Gwyn 41 F9
Bontddu Gwyn 32 D2
Bonthorpe Lincs 47 E8
Bontnewydd Ceredig 24 B3
Bontnewydd Gwyn 40 E6
Bontuchel Denb 42 G3
Bonvilston V Glam 14 D6
Booker Bucks 18 B5
Boon Borders 70 F4
Boosbeck Redcar 59 E7
Boot Cumb 56 F3
Boot Street Suff 31 D9
Booth W Yorks 50 G6
Booth Wood W Yorks 50 H6
Boothby Graffoe Lincs 46 G3
Boothby Pagnell Lincs 36 B5
Boothen Stoke 34 A4
Boothferry E Yorks 52 G3
Boothville Northants 28 B4
Bootle Cumb 56 H3
Bootle Mers 42 C6
Booton Norf 39 C7
Boquhan Stirling 68 B4
Boraston Shrops 26 A3
Borden Kent 20 E5
Borden W Sus 11 B7
Bordley N Yorks 50 C5
Bordon Hants 18 H5
Bordon Camp Hants 18 H4
Boreham Essex 30 H4
Boreham Wilts 16 G5
Boreham Street E Sus 12 E5
Borehamwood Herts 19 B8
Boreland Dumfries 61 D7
Boreland Stirling 75 D8
Borgh W Isles 84 H1
Borgh W Isles 90 J4
Borghastan W Isles 90 C7
Borgie Highld 93 D9
Borgue Dumfries 55 E9
Borgue Highld 94 H3
Borley Essex 30 D5
Bornais W Isles 84 F2
Bornesketaig Highld 85 A8
Borness Dumfries 55 E9
Borough Green Kent 20 F3
Boroughbridge N Yorks 51 C9
Borras Head Wrex 42 G6
Borreraig Highld 84 C6
Borrobol Lodge Highld 93 G11
Borrowash Derbys 35 B10
Borrowby N Yorks 58 H5
Borrowdale Cumb 56 E4
Borrowfield Aberds 83 D10
Borth Ceredig 32 F2
Borth-y-Gest Gwyn 41 G7
Borthwickbrae Borders 61 B10
Borthwickshiels Borders 61 B10
Borve Highld 85 D9
Borve Lodge W Isles 90 H5
Borwick Lancs 49 B5
Bosavern Corn 2 F2
Bosbury Hereford 26 D3
Boscastle Corn 4 B2
Boscombe Bmouth 9 E10
Boscombe Wilts 17 H9
Boscoppa Corn 3 D9
Bosham W Sus 11 D7
Bosherston Pembs 22 G4
Boskenna Corn 2 G3
Bosley Ches E 44 F3
Bossall N Yorks 52 C3
Bossiney Corn 4 C1
Bossingham Kent 21 G8
Bossington Som 7 B7
Bostock Green Ches W 43 F9
Boston Lincs 37 A9
Boston Long Hedges Lincs 47 H7
Boston Spa W Yorks 51 E10
Boston West Lincs 46 H6
Boswinger Corn 3 E8
Botallack Corn 2 F2
Botany Bay London 19 B9
Botcherby Cumb 61 H10
Botcheston Leics 35 E10
Botesdale Suff 38 H6
Bothal Northumb 63 E8
Bothamsall Notts 45 E10
Bothel Cumb 56 C3
Bothenhampton Dorset 8 E3
Bothwell S Lanark 68 E6
Botley Bucks 18 A6
Botley Hants 10 C4
Botley Oxon 27 H11
Botolph Claydon Bucks 28 F4
Botolphs W Sus 11 D10
Bottacks Highld 86 E7
Bottesford Leics 36 B4
Bottesford N Lincs 46 B2
Bottisham Cambs 30 B2
Bottlesford Wilts 17 F8
Bottom Boat W Yorks 51 G9
Bottom House Staffs 44 G4
Bottom o' th' Moor Gtr Man 43 A9
Bottom of Hutton Lancs 49 G4
Bottomcraig Fife 76 E6
Botusfleming Corn 4 E5
Botwnnog Gwyn 40 G4
Bough Beech Kent 19 G11
Boughrood Powys 25 E8
Boughspring Glos 16 B2
Boughton Norf 38 E2
Boughton Northants 28 B4
Boughton Notts 45 F10
Boughton Aluph Kent 21 G7
Boughton Lees Kent 21 G7
Boughton Malherbe Kent 20 G5
Boughton Monchelsea Kent 20 F4
Boughton Street Kent 21 F7
Boulby Redcar 59 E8
Boulden Shrops 33 G11
Boulmer Northumb 63 B8
Boulston Pembs 22 E4
Boultenstone Aberds 82 B6
Boultham Lincs 46 F3
Bourn Cambs 29 C10
Bourne Lincs 37 C6
Bourne End Bucks 18 C5
Bourne End C Beds 28 D6
Bourne End Herts 29 H7
Bournemouth Bmouth 9 E9
Bournes Green Glos 16 A6
Bournes Green Southend 20 C6
Bournheath Worcs 26 A6
Bournmoor Durham 58 A4
Bournville W Mid 34 G6
Bourton Dorset 9 A6
Bourton N Som 15 E9
Bourton Oxon 17 C9
Bourton Shrops 34 F1
Bourton on Dunsmore Warks 27 A11
Bourton on the Hill Glos 27 E8
Bourton-on-the-Water Glos 27 F8
Bousd Argyll 78 E5
Boustead Hill Cumb 61 H8
Bouth Cumb 56 H5
Bouthwaite N Yorks 51 B7
Boveney Bucks 18 D6
Boverton V Glam 14 E5
Bovey Tracey Devon 5 D9
Bovingdon Herts 19 A7
Bovingdon Green Bucks 18 C5
Bovingdon Green Herts 19 A7
Bovinger Essex 30 H2
Bovington Camp Dorset 9 F7
Bow Borders 70 F3
Bow Devon 6 F6
Bow Orkney 95 J4
Bow Brickhill M Keynes 28 E6
Bow of Fife Fife 76 F6
Bow Street Ceredig 32 G2
Bowbank Durham 57 D11
Bowburn Durham 58 C4
Bowcombe IoW 10 F3
Bowd Devon 7 G10
Bowden Borders 70 G4
Bowden Devon 5 G9
Bowden Hill Wilts 16 E6

Bowderdale Cumb 57 F8
Bowdon Gtr Man 43 D10
Bower Northumb 62 E3
Bower Hinton Som 8 C3
Bowerchalke Wilts 9 B9
Bowerhill Wilts 16 E6
Bowermadden Highld 94 D4
Bowers Gifford Essex 20 C4
Bowershall Fife 69 A9
Bowertower Highld 94 D4
Bowes Durham 57 E11
Bowgreave Lancs 49 E4
Bowgreen Gtr Man 43 D10
Bowhill Borders 70 H3
Bowhouse Dumfries 60 G6
Bowland Bridge Cumb 56 H6
Bowley Hereford 26 C2
Bowlhead Green Sur 18 H6
Bowling W Dunb 68 C3
Bowling W Yorks 51 F7
Bowling Bank Wrex 43 H6
Bowling Green Worcs 26 C5
Bowmanstead Cumb 56 G5
Bowmore Argyll 64 C4
Bowness-on-Solway Cumb 61 G8
Bowness-on-Windermere Cumb 56 G6
Bowsden Northumb 71 F8
Bowside Lodge Highld 93 C11
Bowston Cumb 57 G6
Bowthorpe Norf 39 E7
Box Glos 16 A5
Box Wilts 16 E5
Box End Bedford 29 D7
Boxbush Glos 26 G4
Boxford Suff 30 D6
Boxford W Berks 17 D11
Boxgrove W Sus 11 D8
Boxley Kent 20 F4
Boxmoor Herts 29 H7
Boxted Essex 30 E6
Boxted Suff 30 C5
Boxted Cross Essex 31 E7
Boxted Heath Essex 31 E7
Boxworth Cambs 29 B10
Boxworth End Cambs 29 B10
Boyden Gate Kent 21 E9
Boylestone Derbys 35 B7
Boyndie Aberds 89 B6
Boynton E Yorks 53 C7
Boysack Angus 77 C9
Boyton Corn 6 G2
Boyton Suff 31 D10
Boyton Wilts 16 H6
Boyton Cross Essex 30 H3
Boyton End Suff 30 D4
Bozeat Northants 28 C6
Brù W Isles 91 C8
Braaid IoM 48 E3
Braal Castle Highld 94 D3
Brabling Green Suff 31 B9
Brabourne Kent 13 B9
Brabourne Lees Kent 13 B9
Brabster Highld 94 D5
Bracadale Highld 85 E8
Bracara Highld 79 B10
Braceborough Lincs 37 D6
Bracebridge Lincs 46 F3
Bracebridge Heath Lincs 46 F3
Bracebridge Low Fields Lincs 46 F3
Braceby Lincs 36 B6
Bracewell Lancs 50 E4
Brackenfield Derbys 45 G7
Brackenthwaite Cumb 56 B4
Brackenthwaite N Yorks 51 D8
Bracklesham W Sus 11 E7
Brackletter Highld 80 E3
Brackley Argyll 65 D8
Brackley Northants 28 E2
Brackloch Highld 92 G4
Bracknell Brack 18 E5
Braco Perth 75 G11
Bracobrae Moray 88 C5
Bracon Ash Norf 39 F7
Bracorina Highld 79 B10
Bradbourne Derbys 44 G6
Bradbury Durham 58 D4
Bradda IoM 48 F1
Bradden Northants 28 D3
Braddock Corn 4 E2
Bradeley Stoke 44 G2
Bradenham Bucks 18 B5
Bradenham Norf 38 E5
Bradenstoke Wilts 17 D7
Bradfield Essex 31 E8
Bradfield Norf 39 B8
Bradfield W Berks 18 D3
Bradfield Combust Suff 30 C5
Bradfield Green Ches E 43 G9
Bradfield Heath Essex 31 F8
Bradfield St Clare Suff 30 C6
Bradfield St George Suff 30 B6
Bradford Corn 4 D2
Bradford Derbys 44 F6
Bradford Devon 6 F3
Bradford Northumb 71 G10
Bradford W Yorks 51 F7
Bradford Abbas Dorset 8 C4
Bradford Leigh Wilts 16 E5
Bradford-on-Avon Wilts 16 E5
Bradford-on-Tone Som 7 D10
Bradford Peverell Dorset 8 E5
Brading IoW 10 F5
Bradley Derbys 44 H6
Bradley Hants 18 G3
Bradley NE Lincs 46 B6
Bradley Staffs 34 D4
Bradley W Mid 34 F5
Bradley W Yorks 51 G7
Bradley Green Worcs 26 B6
Bradley in the Moors Staffs 35 A6
Bradley Stoke S Glos 16 C3
Bradlow Hereford 26 E4
Bradmore Notts 36 B1
Bradmore W Mid 34 F4
Bradninch Devon 7 F9
Bradnop Staffs 44 G4
Bradpole Dorset 8 E3
Bradshaw Gtr Man 43 A10
Bradshaw W Yorks 44 A4
Bradstone Devon 4 C4
Bradwall Green Ches E 43 F10
Bradway S Yorks 45 D7
Bradwell Derbys 44 D5
Bradwell Essex 30 F5
Bradwell M Keynes 28 E5
Bradwell Norf 39 E11
Bradwell Staffs 44 H2
Bradwell Grove Oxon 27 H9
Bradwell on Sea Essex 31 H7
Bradwell Waterside Essex 30 H6
Bradworthy Devon 6 E2
Bradworthy Cross Devon 6 E2
Brae Dumfries 60 F4
Brae Highld 91 J13
Brae Highld 92 J7
Brae Shetland 96 G5
Brae of Achnahaird Highld 92 H3
Brae Roy Lodge Highld 80 D5
Braeantra Highld 87 D8
Braedownie Angus 82 F4
Braefield Highld 86 H7
Braegrum Perth 76 E3
Braehead Dumfries 55 D7
Braehead Orkney 95 D5
Braehead Orkney 95 H6
Braehead S Lanark 69 E8
Braehead S Lanark 69 G7
Braehead of Lunan Angus 77 B9
Braehoulland Shetland 96 F4
Braehungie Highld 94 G3
Braelangwell Lodge Highld 87 B8
Braemar Aberds 82 D3
Braemore Highld 86 D4
Braemore Highld 94 G2
Braes of Enzie Moray 88 C3
Braeside Invclyd 73 F11
Braeswick Orkney 95 E7
Braewick Shetland 96 H5
Brafferton Darl 58 D3
Brafferton N Yorks 51 B10
Brafield-on-the-Green Northants 28 C5
Bragar W Isles 91 C7
Bragbury End Herts 29 F9
Bragleenmore Argyll 74 E2
Braichmelyn Gwyn 41 D8
Braid Edin 69 D11
Braides Lancs 49 D4
Braidley N Yorks 50 A6
Braidwood S Lanark 69 F7
Braigo Argyll 64 B3
Brailsford Derbys 35 A8
Brainshaugh Northumb 63 C8
Braintree Essex 30 F4
Braiseworth Suff 31 A8
Braishfield Hants 10 B2
Braithwaite Cumb 56 D4
Braithwaite S Yorks 45 A10
Braithwaite W Yorks 50 E6
Braithwell S Yorks 45 C9
Bramber W Sus 11 C10
Bramcote Notts 35 B11
Bramcote Warks 35 G10
Bramdean Hants 10 B5
Bramerton Norf 39 E8
Bramfield Herts 29 G9
Bramfield Suff 31 A10
Bramford Suff 31 D8
Bramhall Gtr Man 44 D2
Bramham W Yorks 51 E10
Bramhope W Yorks 51 E8
Bramley Hants 18 F3
Bramley S Yorks 45 C8
Bramley Sur 19 G7
Bramley W Yorks 51 F8
Bramling Kent 21 F9
Brampford Speke Devon 7 G8
Brampton Cambs 29 A9
Brampton Cumb 57 D8
Brampton Cumb 61 G11
Brampton Derbys 45 E7
Brampton Hereford 25 E11
Brampton Lincs 46 E2
Brampton Norf 39 C8
Brampton S Yorks 45 B8
Brampton Suff 39 G10
Brampton Abbotts Hereford 26 F3
Brampton Ash Northants 36 G3
Brampton Bryan Hereford 25 A10
Brampton en le Morthen S Yorks 45 D8
Bramshall Staffs 35 B6
Bramshaw Hants 10 C1
Bramshill Hants 18 E4
Bramshott Hants 11 A7
Bran End Essex 30 F3
Branault Highld 79 E8
Brancaster Norf 38 A3
Brancaster Staithe Norf 38 A3
Brancepeth Durham 58 C3
Branch End Northumb 62 G6
Branchill Moray 87 F13
Brand Green Glos 26 F4
Branderburgh Moray 88 A2
Brandesburton E Yorks 53 E7
Brandeston Suff 31 B9
Brandhill Shrops 33 H10
Brandis Corner Devon 6 F3
Brandiston Norf 39 C7
Brandon Durham 58 C3
Brandon Lincs 46 H3
Brandon Northumb 62 B6
Brandon Suff 38 G3
Brandon Warks 35 H10
Brandon Bank Cambs 38 G2
Brandon Creek Norf 38 F2
Brandon Parva Norf 39 E6
Brandsby N Yorks 52 B1
Brandy Wharf Lincs 46 C4
Brane Corn 2 G3
Branksome Poole 9 E9
Branksome Park Poole 9 E9
Bransby Lincs 46 E2
Branscombe Devon 7 H10
Bransford Worcs 26 C4
Bransgore Hants 9 E10
Branshill Clack 69 A7
Bransholme Hull 53 F7
Branson's Cross Worcs 27 A7
Branston Leics 36 C4
Branston Lincs 46 F4
Branston Staffs 35 C8
Branston Booths Lincs 46 F4
Branstone IoW 10 F4
Bransty Cumb 56 E1
Brant Broughton Lincs 46 G3
Brantham Suff 31 E8
Branthwaite Cumb 56 C4
Branthwaite Cumb 56 D2
Brantingham E Yorks 52 G5
Branton Northumb 62 B6
Branton S Yorks 45 B10
Branxholm Park Borders 61 B10
Branxholme Borders 61 B10
Branxton Northumb 71 G7
Brassey Green Ches W 43 F8
Brassington Derbys 44 G6
Brasted Kent 19 F11
Brasted Chart Kent 19 F11
Brathens Aberds 83 D8
Bratoft Lincs 47 F8
Brattleby Lincs 46 D3
Bratton Telford 34 D2
Bratton Wilts 16 F6
Bratton Clovelly Devon 6 G3
Bratton Fleming Devon 6 C5
Bratton Seymour Som 8 B5
Braughing Herts 29 F10
Braunston Northants 28 B2
Braunston-in-Rutland Rutland 36 E4
Braunstone Town Leicester 36 E1
Braunton Devon 6 C3
Brawby N Yorks 52 B3
Brawl Highld 93 C11
Brawlbin Highld 94 E2
Bray Windsor 18 D6
Bray Shop Corn 4 D4
Bray Wick Windsor 18 D5
Braybrooke Northants 36 G3
Braye Ald 11
Brayford Devon 6 C5
Braystones Cumb 56 F2
Braythorn N Yorks 51 E8
Brayton N Yorks 52 F2
Brazacott Corn 6 G1
Breach Kent 20 E5
Breachacha Castle Argyll 78 F4
Breachwood Green Herts 29 F8
Breacleit W Isles 90 D6
Breaden Heath Shrops 33 B10
Breadsall Derbys 35 B9
Breadstone Glos 16 A4
Breage Corn 2 G5
Breakachy Highld 86 G7
Bream Glos 26 H3
Breamore Hants 9 C10
Brean Som 15 F8
Breanais W Isles 90 E4
Brearton N Yorks 51 C9
Breascleit W Isles 90 D7
Breaston Derbys 35 B10
Brechfa Carms 23 C10
Brechin Angus 77 A8
Breck of Cruan Orkney 95 G4
Breckan Orkney 95 H3
Breckrey Highld 85 B10
Brecon = Aberhonddu Powys 25 F7
Bredbury Gtr Man 44 C3
Brede E Sus 13 E7
Bredenbury Hereford 26 C3
Bredfield Suff 31 C9
Bredgar Kent 20 E5
Bredhurst Kent 20 E4
Bredicot Worcs 26 C6
Bredon Worcs 26 E6
Bredon's Norton Worcs 26 E6
Bredwardine Hereford 25 D10
Breedon on the Hill Leics 35 C10
Breibhig W Isles 84 J1
Breibhig W Isles 91 D9
Breich W Loth 69 D8
Breightmet Gtr Man 43 B10
Breighton E Yorks 52 F3
Breinton Hereford 25 E11
Breinton Common Hereford 25 D11
Breiwick Shetland 96 J6
Bremhill Wilts 16 D6
Bremirehoull Shetland 96 L6
Brenchley Kent 12 B5
Brendon Devon 7 B6
Brenkley T&W 63 F8
Brent Eleigh Suff 30 D6
Brent Knoll Som 15 F9
Brent Pelham Herts 29 E11
Brentford London 19 D8
Brentingby Leics 36 D3
Brentwood Essex 20 B2
Brenzett Kent 13 D9
Brereton Staffs 35 D6
Brereton Green Ches E 43 F10
Brereton Heath Ches E 44 F2
Bressingham Norf 39 G6
Bretby Derbys 35 C8
Bretford Warks 35 H10
Bretforton Worcs 27 D7
Bretherdale Head Cumb 57 F7
Bretherton Lancs 49 G4
Brettabister Shetland 96 H6
Brettenham Norf 38 G5
Brettenham Suff 30 C6
Bretton Derbys 44 E6
Bretton Flint 42 F6
Brewer Street Sur 19 F10
Brewlands Bridge Angus 76 A4
Brewood Staffs 34 E4
Briach Moray 87 F13
Briants Puddle Dorset 9 E7
Brick End Essex 30 F2
Brickendon Herts 29 H10
Bricket Wood Herts 19 A8
Bricklehampton Worcs 26 D6
Bride IoM 48 B4
Bridekirk Cumb 56 C3
Bridell Pembs 22 B6
Bridestowe Devon 4 C6
Brideswell Aberds 88 E5
Bridford Devon 5 C9
Bridfordmills Devon 5 C9
Bridge Kent 21 F8
Bridge End Lincs 37 B7
Bridge Green Essex 29 E11
Bridge Hewick N Yorks 51 B9
Bridge of Alford Aberds 83 B7
Bridge of Allan Stirling 75 H10
Bridge of Avon Moray 88 E1
Bridge of Awe Argyll 74 E3
Bridge of Balgie Perth 75 C8
Bridge of Cally Perth 76 B4
Bridge of Canny Aberds 83 D8
Bridge of Craigisla Angus 76 B5
Bridge of Dee Dumfries 55 D10
Bridge of Don Aberdeen 83 B11
Bridge of Dun Angus 77 B9
Bridge of Dye Aberds 83 E8
Bridge of Earn Perth 76 F4
Bridge of Ericht Perth 75 B8
Bridge of Feugh Aberds 83 D9
Bridge of Forss Highld 93 C13
Bridge of Gairn Aberds 82 D5
Bridge of Gaur Perth 75 B8
Bridge of Muchalls Aberds 83 D10
Bridge of Oich Highld 80 C5
Bridge of Orchy Argyll 74 D5
Bridge of Waith Orkney 95 G3
Bridge of Walls Shetland 96 H4
Bridge of Weir Renfs 68 D2
Bridge Sollers Hereford 25 D11
Bridge Street Suff 30 D5
Bridge Trafford Ches W 43 E7
Bridge Yate S Glos 16 D3
Bridgefoot Angus 76 D6
Bridgefoot Cumb 56 D2
Bridgehampton Som 8 B4
Bridgehill Durham 58 A1
Bridgemary Hants 10 D4
Bridgemont Derbys 44 D4
Bridgend Aberds 83 B7
Bridgend Aberds 88 E5
Bridgend Angus 83 G7
Bridgend Argyll 64 B4
Bridgend Argyll 65 E8
Bridgend Argyll 73 D7
Bridgend = Pen-y-bont ar Ogwr Bridgend 14 D5
Bridgend Cumb 56 E5
Bridgend Fife 76 F6
Bridgend Moray 88 E3
Bridgend N Lanark 68 C5
Bridgend Pembs 22 B6
Bridgend W Loth 69 C9
Bridgend of Lintrathen Angus 76 B5
Bridgerule Devon 6 F1
Bridges Shrops 33 F9
Bridgeton Glasgow 68 D5
Bridgetown Corn 4 C4
Bridgetown Som 7 C8
Bridgham Norf 38 G5
Bridgnorth Shrops 34 F3
Bridgtown Staffs 34 E5
Bridgwater Som 15 H9
Bridlington E Yorks 53 C7
Bridport Dorset 8 E3
Bridstow Hereford 26 F2
Brierfield Lancs 50 F4
Brierley Glos 26 G3
Brierley Hereford 25 C11
Brierley S Yorks 45 A8
Brierley Hill W Mid 34 G5
Briery Hill Bl Gwent 25 H8
Brig o'Turk Stirling 75 G8
Brigg N Lincs 46 B4
Briggswath N Yorks 59 F9
Brigham Cumb 56 C2
Brigham E Yorks 53 D6
Brighouse W Yorks 51 G7
Brighstone IoW 10 F3
Brightgate Derbys 44 G6
Brighthampton Oxon 17 A10
Brightling E Sus 12 D5
Brightlingsea Essex 31 G7
Brighton Brighton 12 F2
Brighton Corn 3 D8
Brighton Hill Hants 18 G3
Brightons Falk 69 C8
Brightwalton W Berks 17 D11
Brightwell Suff 31 D9
Brightwell Baldwin Oxon 18 B3
Brightwell cum Sotwell Oxon 18 B2
Brignall Durham 58 E1
Brigsley NE Lincs 46 B6
Brigsteer Cumb 57 H6
Brigstock Northants 36 G5
Brill Bucks 28 G3
Brilley Hereford 25 D9
Brimaston Pembs 22 D4
Brimfield Hereford 26 B2
Brimington Derbys 45 E8
Brimley Devon 5 D8
Brimpsfield Glos 26 G6
Brimpton W Berks 18 E2
Brims Orkney 95 K3
Brimscombe Glos 16 A5
Brimstage Mers 42 D6
Brinacory Highld 79 B10
Brind E Yorks 52 F3
Brindister Shetland 96 H4
Brindister Shetland 96 K6
Brindle Lancs 50 G2
Brindley Ford Stoke 44 G2
Brineton Staffs 34 D4
Bringhurst Leics 36 F4
Brington Cambs 37 H6
Brinian Orkney 95 F5
Briningham Norf 38 B6
Brinkhill Lincs 47 E7
Brinkley Cambs 30 C3
Brinklow Warks 35 H10
Brinkworth Wilts 17 C7
Brinmore Highld 81 A8
Brinscall Lancs 50 G2
Brinsea N Som 15 E10
Brinsley Notts 45 H8
Brinsop Hereford 25 D11
Brinsworth S Yorks 45 D8
Brinton Norf 38 B6
Brisco Cumb 56 A6
Brisley Norf 38 C5
Brislington Bristol 16 D3
Bristol Bristol 16 D2
Briston Norf 39 B6
Britannia Lancs 50 G4
Britford Wilts 9 B10
Brithdir Gwyn 32 D3
British Legion Village Kent 20 F4
Briton Ferry Neath 14 B3
Britwell Salome Oxon 18 B3
Brixham Torbay 5 F10
Brixton Devon 5 F6
Brixton London 19 D10
Brixton Deverill Wilts 16 H5
Brixworth Northants 28 A4
Brize Norton Oxon 27 H10
Broad Blunsdon Swindon 17 B8
Broad Campden Glos 27 E8
Broad Chalke Wilts 9 B9
Broad Green C Beds 28 D6
Broad Green Essex 30 F5
Broad Green Worcs 26 C4
Broad Haven Pembs 22 E3
Broad Heath Worcs 26 B3
Broad Hill Cambs 38 H1
Broad Hinton Wilts 17 D8
Broad Laying Hants 17 E11
Broad Marston Worcs 27 D8
Broad Oak Carms 23 D10
Broad Oak Cumb 56 G3
Broad Oak Dorset 8 E3
Broad Oak Dorset 9 C6
Broad Oak E Sus 12 D5
Broad Oak E Sus 13 E7
Broad Oak Hereford 25 F11
Broad Oak Mers 43 C8
Broad Street Kent 20 F5
Broad Street Green Essex 30 H5
Broad Town Wilts 17 D7
Broadbottom Gtr Man 44 C3
Broadbridge W Sus 11 D7
Broadbridge Heath W Sus 11 A10
Broadclyst Devon 7 G8
Broadfield Gtr Man 44 A2
Broadfield Lancs 49 G5
Broadfield Pembs 22 F6
Broadfield W Sus 12 C1
Broadford Highld 85 F11
Broadford Bridge W Sus 11 B9
Broadhaugh Borders 61 C10
Broadhaven Highld 94 E5
Broadheath Gtr Man 43 D10
Broadhembury Devon 7 F10
Broadhempston Devon 5 E9
Broadholme Derbys 45 H7
Broadholme Lincs 46 E2
Broadland Row E Sus 13 E7
Broadlay Carms 23 F8
Broadley Lancs 50 H4
Broadley Moray 88 B3
Broadley Common Essex 29 H11
Broadmayne Dorset 8 F6
Broadmeadows Borders 70 G3
Broadmere Hants 18 G3
Broadmoor Pembs 22 F5
Broadoak Kent 21 E8
Broadrashes Moray 88 C4
Broadsea Aberds 89 B9
Broadstairs Kent 21 E10
Broadstone Poole 9 E9
Broadstone Shrops 33 G11
Broadtown Lane Wilts 17 D7
Broadwas Worcs 26 C4
Broadwater Herts 29 F9
Broadwater W Sus 11 D10
Broadway Carms 23 F7
Broadway Pembs 22 E3
Broadway Som 8 C2
Broadway Suff 39 H9
Broadway Worcs 27 E7
Broadwell Glos 26 G2
Broadwell Glos 27 F9
Broadwell Oxon 17 A9
Broadwell Warks 27 B11
Broadwell House Northumb 57 A11
Broadwey Dorset 8 F5
Broadwindsor Dorset 8 D3
Broadwood Kelly Devon 6 F5
Broadwoodwidger Devon 4 C5
Brobury Hereford 25 D10
Brochel Highld 85 D10
Brochloch Dumfries 67 G8
Brochroy Argyll 74 D3
Brockamin Worcs 26 C4
Brockbridge Hants 10 C5
Brockdam Northumb 63 A7
Brockdish Norf 39 H8
Brockenhurst Hants 10 D2
Brocketsbrae S Lanark 69 G7
Brockford Street Suff 31 B8
Brockhall Northants 28 B3
Brockham Sur 19 G8
Brockhampton Glos 27 F7
Brockhampton Hereford 26 E2
Brockholes W Yorks 44 A5
Brockhurst Derbys 45 F7
Brockhurst Hants 10 D5
Brocklebank Cumb 56 B5
Brocklesby Lincs 46 A5
Brockley N Som 15 E10
Brockley Green Suff 30 C5
Brockleymoor Cumb 57 C6
Brockton Shrops 33 E9
Brockton Shrops 33 G9
Brockton Shrops 34 E3
Brockton Shrops 34 F1
Brockton Telford 34 D3
Brockweir Glos 15 A11
Brockwood Hants 10 B5
Brockworth Glos 26 G5
Brocton Staffs 34 D5
Brodick N Ayrs 66 C3
Brodsworth S Yorks 45 B9
Brogaig Highld 85 B9
Brogborough C Beds 28 E6
Broken Cross Ches E 44 E2
Broken Cross Ches W 43 E9
Brokenborough Wilts 16 C6
Bromborough Mers 42 D6
Brome Suff 39 H7
Brome Street Suff 39 H7
Bromeswell Suff 31 C10
Bromfield Cumb 56 B3
Bromfield Shrops 33 H10
Bromham Bedford 29 C7
Bromham Wilts 16 E6
Bromley London 19 E11
Bromley W Mid 34 G5
Bromley Common London 19 E11
Bromley Green Kent 13 C8
Brompton Medway 20 E4
Brompton N Yorks 52 A5
Brompton N Yorks 58 G4
Brompton-on-Swale N Yorks 58 G3
Brompton Ralph Som 7 C9
Brompton Regis Som 7 C8
Bromsash Hereford 26 F3
Bromsberrow Hth. Glos 26 E4
Bromsgrove Worcs 26 A6
Bromyard Hereford 26 C3
Bromyard Downs Hereford 26 C3
Bronaber Gwyn 41 G9
Brongest Ceredig 23 B8
Bronington Wrex 33 B10
Bronllys Powys 25 E8
Bronnant Ceredig 24 B3
Bronwydd Arms Carms 23 D9
Bronydd Powys 25 D9
Bronygarth Shrops 33 B8
Brook Carms 23 F7
Brook Hants 10 B2
Brook Hants 10 C1
Brook IoW 10 F2
Brook Kent 13 B9
Brook Sur 18 H6
Brook Sur 19 G7
Brook End Bedford 29 B7
Brook Hill Hants 10 C1
Brook Street Kent 13 C8
Brook Street Kent 20 G2
Brook Street W Sus 12 D2
Brooke Norf 39 F8
Brooke Rutland 36 E4
Brookenby Lincs 46 C6
Brookend Glos 16 B2
Brookfield Renfs 68 D3
Brookhouse Lancs 49 C5
Brookhouse Green Ches E 44 F2
Brookland Kent 13 D8
Brooklands Dumfries 60 F4
Brooklands Gtr Man 43 C10
Brooklands Shrops 33 A11
Brookmans Park Herts 19 A9
Brooks Powys 33 F7
Brooks Green W Sus 11 B10
Brookthorpe Glos 26 G5
Brookville Norf 38 F3
Brookwood Sur 18 F6
Broom C Beds 29 D8
Broom S Yorks 45 C8
Broom Warks 27 C7
Broom Worcs 34 H5
Broom Green Norf 38 C5
Broom Hill Dorset 9 D9
Broome Norf 39 F9
Broome Shrops 33 G10
Broome Park Northumb 63 B7
Broomedge Warr 43 D10
Broomer's Corner W Sus 11 B10
Broomfield Aberds 89 E9
Broomfield Essex 30 G4
Broomfield Kent 20 F5
Broomfield Kent 21 E8
Broomfield Som 7 C11
Broomfleet E Yorks 52 G4
Broomhall Ches E 43 H9
Broomhall Windsor 18 E6
Broomhaugh Northumb 62 G6
Broomhill Norf 38 E2
Broomhill Northumb 63 C8
Broomhill S Yorks 45 B8
Broomholm Norf 39 B9
Broomley Northumb 62 G6
Broompark Durham 58 B3
Broom's Green Glos 26 E4
Broomy Lodge Hants 9 C11
Brora Highld 93 J12
Broseley Shrops 34 E2
Brotherhouse Bar Lincs 37 D8
Brotherstone Borders 70 G5
Brothertoft Lincs 46 H6
Brotherton N Yorks 51 G10
Brotton Redcar 59 E7
Broubster Highld 93 C13
Brough Cumb 57 E9
Brough Derbys 44 D5
Brough E Yorks 52 G5
Brough Highld 94 C4
Brough Notts 46 G2
Brough Orkney 95 G4
Brough Shetland 96 F7
Brough Shetland 96 F6
Brough Shetland 96 G7
Brough Shetland 96 H6
Brough Shetland 96 J7
Brough Lodge Shetland 96 D7
Brough Sowerby Cumb 57 E9
Broughall Shrops 34 A1
Broughton Borders 69 G10
Broughton Cambs 37 H8
Broughton Flint 42 F6
Broughton Hants 10 A2
Broughton Lancs 49 F5
Broughton M Keynes 28 D5
Broughton N Lincs 46 B3
Broughton N Yorks 50 D5
Broughton N Yorks 52 B3
Broughton Northants 36 H4
Broughton Orkney 95 D5
Broughton Oxon 27 E11
Broughton V Glam 14 D5
Broughton Astley Leics 35 F11
Broughton Beck Cumb 49 A2
Broughton Common Wilts 16 E5
Broughton Gifford Wilts 16 E5
Broughton Hackett Worcs 26 C6
Broughton in Furness Cumb 56 H4
Broughton Mills Cumb 56 G4
Broughton Moor Cumb 56 C2
Broughton Park Gtr Man 44 B2
Broughton Poggs Oxon 17 A9
Broughtown Orkney 95 D7
Broughty Ferry Dundee 77 D7
Browhouses Dumfries 61 G8
Browland Shetland 96 H4
Brown Candover Hants 18 H2
Brown Edge Lancs 42 A6
Brown Edge Staffs 44 G3
Brown Heath Ches W 43 F7
Brownhill Aberds 89 D8
Brownhill Aberds 89 D6
Brownhill Blackburn 50 F2
Brownhill Shrops 33 C10
Brownhills Fife 77 F8
Brownhills W Mid 34 E6
Brownlow Ches E 44 F2
Brownlow Heath Ches E 44 F2
Brownmuir Aberds 83 F9
Brown's End Glos 26 E4
Brownshill Glos 16 A5
Brownston Devon 5 F7
Brownyside Northumb 63 A7
Broxa N Yorks 59 G10
Broxbourne Herts 29 H10
Broxburn E Loth 70 C5
Broxburn W Loth 69 C9
Broxholme Lincs 46 E3
Broxted Essex 30 F2
Broxton Ches W 43 G7
Broxwood Hereford 25 C10
Broyle Side E Sus 12 E3
Bruairnis W Isles 84 H2
Bruan Highld 94 G5
Bruar Lodge Perth 81 F10
Brucehill W Dunb 68 C2
Bruera Ches W 43 F7
Bruern Abbey Oxon 27 F9
Bruichladdich Argyll 64 B3
Bruisyard Suff 31 B10
Brumby N Lincs 46 B2
Brund Staffs 44 F5
Brundall Norf 39 E9
Brundish Suff 31 B9
Brundish Street Suff 31 A9
Brunery Highld 79 D10
Brunshaw Lancs 50 F4
Brunswick Village T&W 63 F8
Bruntcliffe W Yorks 51 G8
Bruntingthorpe Leics 36 F2
Brunton Fife 76 E6
Brunton Northumb 63 A8
Brunton Wilts 17 F9
Brushford Devon 6 F5
Brushford Som 7 D8
Bruton Som 8 A5
Bryanston Dorset 9 D7
Brydekirk Dumfries 61 F7
Bryher Scilly 2 C2
Brymbo Wrex 42 G5
Brympton Som 8 C4
Bryn Carms 23 F10
Bryn Gtr Man 43 B8
Bryn Neath 14 B4
Bryn Shrops 33 G8
Bryn-coch Neath 14 B3
Bryn Du Anglesey 40 C5
Bryn Gates Gtr Man 43 B8
Bryn-glas Conwy 41 D10
Bryn Golau Rhondda 14 C5
Bryn-Iwan Carms 23 C8
Bryn-mawr Gwyn 40 G4
Bryn-nantllech Conwy 42 F2
Bryn-penarth Powys 33 E7
Bryn Rhyd-yr-Arian Conwy 42 F2
Bryn Saith Marchog Denb 42 G3
Bryn Sion Gwyn 32 D4
Bryn-y-gwenin Mon 25 G10
Bryn-y-maen Conwy 41 C10
Bryn-yr-eryr Gwyn 40 F5
Brynamman Carms 24 G4
Brynberian Pembs 22 C6
Brynbryddan Neath 14 B3
Brynbuga = Usk Mon 15 A9
Bryncae Rhondda 14 C5
Bryncethin Bridgend 14 C5
Bryncir Gwyn 40 F6
Bryncroes Gwyn 40 G4
Bryncrug Gwyn 32 E2
Bryneglwys Denb 42 H4
Brynford Flint 42 E4
Bryngwran Anglesey 40 C5
Bryngwyn Ceredig 23 B7
Bryngwyn Mon 25 H10
Bryngwyn Powys 25 D8
Brynhenllan Pembs 22 C5
Brynhoffnant Ceredig 23 A8
Brynithel Bl Gwent 15 A8
Brynmawr Bl Gwent 25 G8
Brynmenyn Bridgend 14 C5
Brynmill Swansea 14 B2
Brynna Rhondda 14 C5
Brynrefail Anglesey 40 B6
Brynrefail Gwyn 41 D7
Brynsadler Rhondda 14 C6
Brynsiencyn Anglesey 40 D6
Brynteg Anglesey 40 B6
Brynteg Ceredig 23 B9
Buaile nam Bodach W Isles 84 H2
Bualintur Highld 85 F9
Buarthmeini Gwyn 41 G10
Bubbenhall Warks 27 A10
Bubwith E Yorks 52 F3
Buccleuch Borders 61 B9
Buchanhaven Aberds 89 D11
Buchanty Perth 76 E2
Buchlyvie Stirling 68 A4
Buckabank Cumb 56 B5
Buckden Cambs 29 B8
Buckden N Yorks 50 B5
Buckenham Norf 39 E9
Buckerell Devon 7 F10
Buckfast Devon 5 E8
Buckfastleigh Devon 5 E8
Buckhaven Fife 76 H6
Buckholm Borders 70 G3
Buckholt Mon 26 G2
Buckhorn Weston Dorset 9 B6
Buckhurst Hill Essex 19 B11
Buckie Moray 88 B4
Buckies Highld 94 D3
Buckingham Bucks 28 E3
Buckland Bucks 28 G5
Buckland Devon 5 G7
Buckland Glos 27 E7
Buckland Hants 10 E2
Buckland Herts 29 E10
Buckland Kent 21 G10
Buckland Oxon 17 B10
Buckland Sur 19 F9
Buckland Brewer Devon 6 D3
Buckland Common Bucks 28 H6
Buckland Dinham Som 16 F4
Buckland Filleigh Devon 6 F3
Buckland in the Moor Devon 5 D8
Buckland Monachorum Devon 4 E5
Buckland Newton Dorset 8 D5
Buckland St Mary Som 8 C1
Bucklebury W Berks 18 D2
Bucklegate Lincs 37 B9
Bucklerheads Angus 77 D7
Bucklers Hard Hants 10 E3
Bucklesham Suff 31 D9
Buckley = Bwcle Flint 42 F5
Bucklow Hill Ches E 43 D10
Buckminster Leics 36 C4
Bucknall Lincs 46 F5
Bucknall Stoke 44 H3
Bucknell Oxon 28 F2
Bucknell Shrops 25 A10
Buckpool Moray 88 B4
Buck's Cross Devon 6 D2
Bucks Green W Sus 11 A9
Bucks Horn Oak Hants 18 G5
Buck's Mills Devon 6 D2
Bucksburn Aberdeen 83 C10
Buckshaw Village Lancs 50 G1
Buckskin Hants 18 F3
Buckton E Yorks 53 B7
Buckton Hereford 25 A10
Buckton Northumb 71 G9
Buckworth Cambs 37 H7
Budbrooke Warks 27 B9
Budby Notts 45 F10
Budd's Titson Corn 4 A3
Bude Corn 6 F1
Budlake Devon 7 G8
Budle Northumb 71 G10
Budleigh Salterton Devon 7 H9
Budock Water Corn 3 F6
Buerton Ches E 34 A2
Buffler's Holt Bucks 28 E3
Bugbrooke Northants 28 C3
Buglawton Ches E 44 F2
Bugle Corn 3 D9
Bugley Wilts 16 G5
Bugthorpe E Yorks 52 D3
Buildwas Shrops 34 E2
Builth Road Powys 25 C7
Builth Wells = Llanfair-ym-Muallt Powys 25 C7
Buirgh W Isles 90 H5
Bulby Lincs 37 C6
Bulcote Notts 36 A2
Buldoo Highld 93 C12
Bulford Wilts 17 G8
Bulford Camp Wilts 17 G8
Bulkeley Ches E 43 G8
Bulkington Warks 35 G9
Bulkington Wilts 16 F6
Bulkworthy Devon 6 E2
Bull Hill Hants 10 E2
Bullamoor N Yorks 58 G4
Bullbridge Derbys 45 G7
Bullbrook Brack 18 E5
Bulley Glos 26 G4
Bullgill Cumb 56 C2
Bullington Hants 17 G11
Bullington Lincs 46 E4
Bull's Green Herts 29 G9
Bullwood Argyll 73 F10
Bulmer Essex 30 D5
Bulmer N Yorks 52 C2
Bulmer Tye Essex 30 E5
Bulphan Thurrock 20 C3
Bulverhythe E Sus 13 F6
Bulwark Aberds 89 D9
Bulwell Nottingham 45 H9
Bulwick Northants 36 F5
Bumble's Green Essex 29 H11
Bun Abhainn Eadarra W Isles 90 G6
Bun a'Mhuillin W Isles 84 G2
Bun Loyne Highld 80 C4
Bunacaimb Highld 79 C9
Bunarkaig Highld 80 E3
Bunbury Ches E 43 G8
Bunbury Heath Ches E 43 G8
Bunchrew Highld 87 G9
Bundalloch Highld 85 F13
Buness Shetland 96 C8
Bunessan Argyll 78 J6
Bungay Suff 39 G9
Bunker's Hill Lincs 46 E3
Bunker's Hill Lincs 46 G6
Bunkers Hill Oxon 27 G11
Bunloit Highld 81 A7
Bunnahabhain Argyll 64 A5
Bunny Notts 36 C1
Buntait Highld 86 H6
Buntingford Herts 29 F10
Bunwell Norf 39 F7
Burbage Derbys 44 E4
Burbage Leics 35 F10
Burbage Wilts 17 E9
Burchett's Green Windsor 18 C5
Burcombe Wilts 9 A9
Burcot Oxon 18 B2
Burcott Bucks 28 F5
Burdon T&W 58 A4
Bures Suff 30 E6
Bures Green Suff 30 E6
Burford Ches E 43 G9
Burford Oxon 27 G9
Burford Shrops 26 B2
Burg Argyll 78 G6
Burgar Orkney 95 F4
Burgate Hants 9 C10
Burgate Suff 39 H6
Burgess Hill W Sus 12 E2
Burgh Suff 31 C9
Burgh by Sands Cumb 61 H9
Burgh Castle Norf 39 E10
Burgh Heath Sur 19 F9
Burgh le Marsh Lincs 47 F9
Burgh Muir Aberds 83 A9
Burgh next Aylsham Norf 39 C8
Burgh on Bain Lincs 46 D6
Burgh St Margaret Norf 39 D10
Burgh St Peter Norf 39 F10
Burghclere Hants 17 E11
Burghead Moray 87 E14
Burghfield W Berks 18 E3
Burghfield Common W Berks 18 E3
Burghfield Hill W Berks 18 E3
Burghill Hereford 25 D11
Burghwallis S Yorks 45 A9
Burham Kent 20 E4
Buriton Hants 10 B6
Burland Ches E 43 G9
Burlawn Corn 3 B8
Burleigh Brack 18 E5
Burlescombe Devon 7 E9
Burleston Dorset 9 E6
Burley Hants 9 D11
Burley Rutland 36 D4
Burley W Yorks 51 F8
Burley Gate Hereford 26 D2
Burley in Wharfedale W Yorks 51 E7
Burley Lodge Hants 9 D11
Burley Street Hants 9 D11
Burleydam Ches E 34 A2
Burlingjobb Powys 25 C9
Burlow E Sus 12 E4
Burlton Shrops 33 C10
Burmarsh Kent 13 C9
Burmington Warks 27 E9
Burn N Yorks 52 G1
Burn of Cambus Stirling 75 G10
Burnaston Derbys 35 B8
Burnbank S Lanark 68 E6
Burnby E Yorks 52 E4
Burncross S Yorks 45 C7
Burneside Cumb 57 G7
Burness Orkney 95 D7
Burneston N Yorks 58 H4
Burnett Bath 16 E3
Burnfoot Borders 61 B11
Burnfoot Borders 61 B10
Burnfoot E Ayrs 67 F7
Burnfoot Perth 76 G2
Burnham Bucks 18 C6
Burnham N Lincs 53 H6
Burnham Deepdale Norf 38 A4
Burnham Green Herts 29 G9
Burnham Market Norf 38 A4
Burnham Norton Norf 38 A4
Burnham-on-Crouch Essex 20 B6
Burnham-on-Sea Som 15 G9
Burnham Overy Staithe Norf 38 A4
Burnham Overy Town Norf 38 A4
Burnham Thorpe Norf 38 A4
Burnhead Dumfries 60 D4
Burnhead S Ayrs 66 F5
Burnhervie Aberds 83 B9
Burnhill Green Staffs 34 E3
Burnhope Durham 58 B2
Burnhouse N Ayrs 67 A6
Burniston N Yorks 59 G11
Burnlee W Yorks 44 B5
Burnley Lancs 50 F4
Burnley Lane Lancs 50 F4
Burnmouth Borders 71 D8
Burnopfield Durham 63 H7
Burnsall N Yorks 50 C6
Burnside Angus 77 B8
Burnside E Ayrs 67 E8
Burnside Fife 76 G4
Burnside S Lanark 68 D5
Burnside Shetland 96 F4
Burnside W Loth 69 C9
Burnside of Duntrune Angus 77 D7
Burnswark Dumfries 61 F7
Burnt Heath Derbys 44 E6
Burnt Houses Durham 58 D2
Burnt Yates N Yorks 51 C8
Burntcommon Sur 19 F7
Burnthouse Corn 3 F6
Burntisland Fife 69 B11
Burnton E Ayrs 67 F7
Burntwood Staffs 35 E6
Burnwynd Edin 69 D10
Burpham Sur 19 F7
Burpham W Sus 11 D9
Burradon Northumb 62 C5
Burradon T&W 63 F8
Burrafirth Shetland 96 B8
Burraland Shetland 96 F5
Burraland Shetland 96 J4
Burras Corn 2 F5
Burravoe Shetland 96 F7
Burravoe Shetland 96 G5
Burray Village Orkney 95 J5
Burrells Cumb 57 E8
Burrelton Perth 76 D5
Burridge Devon 6 C4
Burridge Hants 10 C4
Burrill N Yorks 58 H3
Burringham N Lincs 46 B2
Burrington Devon 6 E5
Burrington Hereford 25 A11
Burrington N Som 15 F10
Burrough Green Cambs 30 C3
Burrough on the Hill Leics 36 D3
Burrow-bridge Som 8 B2
Burrowhill Sur 18 E6
Burry Swansea 23 G9
Burry Green Swansea 23 G9
Burry Port = Porth Tywyn Carms 23 F9
Burscough Lancs 43 A7
Burscough Bridge Lancs 43 A7
Bursea E Yorks 52 F4
Burshill E Yorks 53 E6
Bursledon Hants 10 D3
Burslem Stoke 44 H2
Burstall Suff 31 D7
Burstock Dorset 8 D3
Burston Norf 39 G7
Burston Staffs 34 B5
Burstow Sur 12 B2
Burstwick E Yorks 53 G8
Burtersett N Yorks 57 H10
Burtle Som 15 G9
Burton Ches W 42 E6
Burton Ches W 43 F8
Burton Dorset 9 E10
Burton Lincs 46 E3
Burton Northumb 71 G10
Burton Pembs 22 F4
Burton Som 7 B10
Burton Wilts 16 D5
Burton Agnes E Yorks 53 C7
Burton Bradstock Dorset 8 F3
Burton Dassett Warks 27 C10
Burton Fleming E Yorks 53 B6
Burton Green W Mid 35 H8
Burton Green Wrex 42 G6
Burton Hastings Warks 35 F10
Burton-in-Kendal Cumb 49 B5
Burton in Lonsdale N Yorks 50 B2
Burton Joyce Notts 36 A2
Burton Latimer Northants 28 A6
Burton Lazars Leics 36 D3
Burton-le-Coggles Lincs 36 C5
Burton Leonard N Yorks 51 C9
Burton on the Wolds Leics 36 C1
Burton Overy Leics 36 F2
Burton Pedwardine Lincs 37 A7
Burton Pidsea E Yorks 53 F8
Burton Salmon N Yorks 51 G10
Burton Stather N Lincs 52 H4
Burton upon Stather N Lincs 52 H4
Burton upon Trent Staffs 35 C8
Burtonwood Warr 43 C8
Burwardsley Ches W 43 G8
Burwarton Shrops 34 G2
Burwash E Sus 12 D5
Burwash Common E Sus 12 D5
Burwash Weald E Sus 12 D5
Burwell Cambs 30 B2
Burwell Lincs 47 E7
Burwen Anglesey 40 A6
Burwick Orkney 95 K5
Bury Cambs 37 G8
Bury Gtr Man 44 A2
Bury Som 7 D8
Bury W Sus 11 C9
Bury Green Herts 29 F11
Bury St Edmunds Suff 30 B5
Burythorpe N Yorks 52 C3
Busby E Renf 68 E4
Buscot Oxon 17 B9
Bush Bank Hereford 25 C11
Bush Crathie Aberds 82 D4
Bush Green Norf 39 G8
Bushbury W Mid 34 E5
Bushby Leics 36 E2
Bushey Herts 19 B8
Bushey Heath Herts 19 B8
Bushley Worcs 26 E5
Bushton Wilts 17 D7
Buslingthorpe Lincs 46 D4
Busta Shetland 96 G5
Butcher's Cross E Sus 12 D4
Butcombe N Som 15 E11
Butetown Cardiff 15 D7
Butleigh Som 8 A4
Butleigh Wootton Som 15 H11
Butler's Cross Bucks 28 H5
Butler's End Warks 35 G8
Butlers Marston Warks 27 C11
Butley Suff 31 C10
Butley High Corner Suff 31 D10
Butt Green Ches E 43 G9
Butterburn Cumb 62 F2
Buttercrambe N Yorks 52 D3
Butterknowle Durham 58 D2
Butterleigh Devon 7 F8
Buttermere Cumb 56 E3
Buttermere Wilts 17 E10
Buttershaw W Yorks 51 G7
Butterstone Perth 76 C3
Butterton Staffs 44 G4
Butterwick Durham 58 D4
Butterwick Lincs 47 H7
Butterwick N Yorks 52 B5
Butterwick N Yorks 52 B3
Buttington Powys 33 E8
Buttonoak Worcs 34 H3
Butt's Green Hants 10 B2
Buttsash Hants 10 D3
Buxhall Suff 31 C7
Buxhall Fen Street Suff 31 C7
Buxley Borders 71 E7
Buxted E Sus 12 D3
Buxton Derbys 44 E4
Buxton Norf 39 C8
Buxworth Derbys 44 D4
Bwcle = Buckley Flint 42 F5
Bwlch Powys 25 F8
Bwlch-Llan Ceredig 23 A10
Bwlch-y-cibau Powys 33 D7
Bwlch-y-fadfa Ceredig 23 B9
Bwlch-y-ffridd Powys 33 F6
Bwlch-y-sarnau Powys 25 A7
Bwlchgwyn Wrex 42 G5
Bwlchnewydd Carms 23 D8
Bwlchtocyn Gwyn 40 H5
Bwlchyddar Powys 33 C7
Bwlchygroes Pembs 23 C7
Byermoor T&W 63 H7
Byers Green Durham 58 C3
Byfield Northants 28 C2
Byfleet Sur 19 E7
Byford Hereford 25 D10
Bygrave Herts 29 E9
Byker T&W 63 G8
Bylchau Conwy 42 F2
Byley Ches W 43 F10
Bynea Carms 23 G10
Byrness Northumb 62 C3
Bythorn Cambs 37 H6
Byton Hereford 25 B10
Byworth W Sus 11 B8

C

Cabharstadh W Isles 91 E8
Cablea Perth 76 D2
Cabourne Lincs 46 B5
Cabrach Argyll 72 G3
Cabrach Moray 82 A5
Cabrich Highld 87 G8
Cabus Lancs 49 E4
Cackle Street E Sus 12 D3
Cadbury Devon 7 F8
Cadbury Barton Devon 6 E5
Cadder E Dunb 68 C5
Caddington C Beds 29 G7
Caddonfoot Borders 70 G3
Cade Street E Sus 12 D5
Cadeby Leics 35 E10
Cadeby S Yorks 45 B9
Cadeleigh Devon 7 F8
Cadgwith Corn 2 H6
Cadham Fife 76 G5
Cadishead Gtr Man 43 C10
Cadle Swansea 14 B2
Cadley Lancs 49 F5
Cadley Wilts 17 E9
Cadley Wilts 17 F9
Cadmore End Bucks 18 B4
Cadnam Hants 10 C1
Cadney N Lincs 46 B4
Cadole Flint 42 F5
Cadoxton V Glam 15 E7
Cadoxton-Juxta-Neath Neath 14 B3
Cadshaw Blackburn 50 H3
Cadzow S Lanark 68 E6
Caeathro Gwyn 41 D7
Caehopkin Powys 24 G5
Caenby Lincs 46 D4
Caenby Corner Lincs 46 D3
Caér-bryn Carms 23 E10
Caer Llan Mon 25 H11
Caerau Bridgend 14 B4
Caerau Cardiff 15 D7
Caerdeon Gwyn 32 D2
Caerdydd = Cardiff Cardiff 15 D7
Caerfarchell Pembs 22 D2
Caerffili = Caerphilly Caerph 15 C7
Caerfyrddin = Carmarthen Carms 23 D9
Caergeiliog Anglesey 40 C5
Caergwrle Flint 42 G6
Caergybi = Holyhead Anglesey 40 B4
Caerleon = Caerllion Newport 15 B9
Caerllion = Caerleon Newport 15 B9
Caernarfon Gwyn 40 D6
Caerphilly = Caerffili Caerph 15 C7
Caersws Powys 32 F6
Caerwedros Ceredig 23 A8
Caerwent Mon 15 B10
Caerwych Gwyn 41 G8
Caerwys Flint 42 E4
Caethle Gwyn 32 F2
Caim Anglesey 41 B8
Caio Carms 24 E3
Cairinis W Isles 84 B3
Cairisiadar W Isles 90 D5
Cairminis W Isles 90 J5
Cairnbaan Argyll 73 D7
Cairnbanno Ho. Aberds 89 D8
Cairnborrow Aberds 88 D4
Cairnbrogie Aberds 89 F8
Cairnbulg Castle Aberds 89 B10
Cairncross Angus 82 F6
Cairncross Borders 71 D7
Cairndow Argyll 74 F4
Cairness Aberds 89 B10
Cairneyhill Fife 69 B9
Cairnfield Ho. Moray 88 B4
Cairngaan Dumfries 54 F4
Cairngarroch Dumfries 54 E3
Cairnhill Aberds 89 E6
Cairnie Aberds 83 C10
Cairnie Aberds 88 D4
Cairnorrie Aberds 89 D8
Cairnpark Aberds 83 B10
Cairnryan Dumfries 54 C3
Cairnton Orkney 95 H4
Caister-on-Sea Norf 39 D11
Caistor Lincs 46 B5
Caistor St Edmund Norf 39 E8
Caistron Northumb 62 C5
Caitha Bowland Borders 70 F3
Calais Street Suff 30 E6
Calanais W Isles 90 D7
Calbost W Isles 91 F9
Calbourne IoW 10 F3
Calceby Lincs 47 E7
Calcot Row W Berks 18 D3
Calcott Kent 21 E8
Caldback Shetland 96 C8
Caldbeck Cumb 56 C5
Caldbergh N Yorks 58 H1
Caldecote Cambs 29 C10
Caldecote Cambs 37 G7
Caldecote Herts 29 E9
Caldecote Northants 28 C3
Caldecott Northants 28 B6
Caldecott Oxon 17 B11
Caldecott Rutland 36 F4
Calder Bridge Cumb 56 F2
Calder Hall Cumb 56 F2
Calder Mains Highld 94 E2
Calder Vale Lancs 49 E5
Calderbank N Lanark 68 D6
Calderbrook Gtr Man 50 H5
Caldercruix N Lanark 69 D7
Caldermill S Lanark 68 F5
Calderwood S Lanark 68 E5
Caldhame Angus 77 C7
Caldicot Mon 15 C10
Caldwell Derbys 35 D8
Caldwell N Yorks 58 E2
Caldy Mers 42 D5
Caledrhydiau Ceredig 23 A9
Calfsound Orkney 95 E6
Calgary Argyll 78 F6
Califer Moray 87 F13
California Falk 69 C8
California Norf 39 D11
Calke Derbys 35 C9
Callakille Highld 85 C11
Callaly Northumb 62 C6
Callander Stirling 75 G9
Callaughton Shrops 34 F2
Callestick Corn 3 D6
Calligarry Highld 85 H11
Callington Corn 4 E4
Callow Hereford 25 E11
Callow End Worcs 26 D5
Callow Hill Wilts 17 C7
Callow Hill Worcs 26 A4
Callows Grave Worcs 26 B2
Calmore Hants 10 C2
Calmsden Glos 27 H7
Calne Wilts 17 D7
Calow Derbys 45 E8
Calshot Hants 10 D3
Calstock Corn 4 E5
Calstone Wellington Wilts 17 E7
Calthorpe Norf 39 B7
Calthwaite Cumb 56 B6
Calton N Yorks 50 D5
Calton Staffs 44 G5
Calveley Ches E 43 G8
Calver Derbys 44 E6
Calver Hill Hereford 25 D10
Calverhall Shrops 34 B2
Calverleigh Devon 7 E8
Calverley W Yorks 51 F8
Calvert Bucks 28 F3
Calverton M Keynes 28 E4
Calverton Notts 45 H10
Calvine Perth 81 G10
Calvo Cumb 56 A3
Cam Glos 16 B4
Camas-luinie Highld 80 A1
Camasnacroise Highld 79 F11
Camastianavaig Highld 85 E10
Camasunary Highld 85 G10
Camault Muir Highld 87 G8
Camb Shetland 96 D7
Camber E Sus 13 E8
Camberley Sur 18 E5
Camberwell London 19 D10
Camblesforth N Yorks 52 G2
Cambo Northumb 62 E6
Cambois Northumb 63 E9
Camborne Corn 2 E5
Cambourne Cambs 29 C10
Cambridge Cambs 29 C11
Cambridge Glos 16 A4
Cambridge Town Southend 20 C6
Cambus Clack 69 A7
Cambusavie Farm Highld 87 B10
Cambusbarron Stirling 68 A6
Cambuskenneth Stirling 69 A7
Cambuslang S Lanark 68 D5
Cambusmore Lodge Highld 87 B10
Camden London 19 C9
Camelford Corn 4 C2
Camelsdale Sur 11 A7
Camerory Highld 87 H13
Camer's Green Worcs 26 E4
Camerton Bath 16 F3
Camerton Cumb 56 C2
Camerton E Yorks 53 G8
Camghouran Perth 75 B8
Cammachmore Aberds 83 D11
Cammeringham Lincs 46 D3
Camore Highld 87 B10
Camp Hill Warks 35 F9
Campbeltown Argyll 65 F8
Camperdown T&W 63 F8
Campmuir Perth 76 D5
Campsall S Yorks 45 A9
Campsey Ash Suff 31 C10
Campton C Beds 29 E8
Camptown Borders 62 B2
Camrose Pembs 22 D4
Camserney Perth 75 C11
Camster Highld 94 F4
Camuschoirk Highld 79 E10
Camuscross Highld 85 G11
Camusnagaul Highld 80 F2
Camusnagaul Highld 86 C3
Camusrory Highld 79 B11
Camusteel Highld 85 D12
Camusterrach Highld 85 D12
Camusvrachan Perth 75 C9
Canada Hants 10 C1
Canadia E Sus 12 E6
Canal Side S Yorks 45 A10
Candacraig Ho. Aberds 82 B5
Candlesby Lincs 47 F8
Candy Mill S Lanark 69 F9
Cane End Oxon 18 D3
Canewdon Essex 20 B5
Canford Bottom Dorset 9 D9
Canford Cliffs Poole 9 F9
Canford Magna Poole 9 E9
Canham's Green Suff 31 B7
Canholes Derbys 44 E4
Canisbay Highld 94 C5
Cann Dorset 9 B7
Cann Common Dorset 9 B7
Cannard's Grave Som 16 G3
Cannich Highld 86 H6
Cannington Som 15 H8
Cannock Staffs 34 E5
Cannock Wood Staffs 34 D6
Canon Bridge Hereford 25 D11
Canon Frome Hereford 26 D3
Canon Pyon Hereford 25 D11
Canonbie Dumfries 61 F9
Canons Ashby Northants 28 C2
Canonstown Corn 2 F4
Canterbury Kent 21 F8
Cantley Norf 39 E9
Cantley S Yorks 45 B10
Cantlop Shrops 33 E11
Canton Cardiff 15 D7
Cantraybruich Highld 87 G10
Cantraydoune Highld 87 G10
Cantraywood Highld 87 G10
Cantsfield Lancs 50 B2
Canvey Island Essex 20 C4
Canwick Lincs 46 F3
Canworthy Water Corn 4 B3
Caol Highld 80 F3
Caol Ila Argyll 64 A5
Caolas Argyll 78 G3
Caolas Scalpaigh W Isles 90 H7
Caolas Stocinis W Isles 90 H6
Capel Sur 19 G8
Capel Bangor Ceredig 32 G2
Capel Betws Lleucu Ceredig 24 C3
Capel Carmel Gwyn 40 H3
Capel Coch Anglesey 40 B6
Capel Curig Conwy 41 E9
Capel Cynon Ceredig 23 B8
Capel Dewi Carms 23 D9
Capel Dewi Ceredig 23 B9
Capel Dewi Ceredig 32 G2
Capel Garmon Conwy 41 E10
Capel-gwyn Anglesey 40 C5
Capel Gwyn Carms 23 D9
Capel Gwynfe Carms 24 F4
Capel Hendre Carms 23 E10
Capel Hermon Gwyn 32 C3
Capel Isaac Carms 23 D10
Capel Iwan Carms 23 C7
Capel le Ferne Kent 21 H9
Capel Llanilltern Cardiff 14 C6
Capel Mawr Anglesey 40 C6
Capel St Andrew Suff 31 D10
Capel St Mary Suff 31 E7
Capel Seion Ceredig 32 H2
Capel Tygwydd Ceredig 23 B7
Capel Uchaf Gwyn 40 F6
Capel-y-graig Gwyn 41 D7
Capelulo Conwy 41 C9
Capenhurst Ches W 42 E6
Capernwray Lancs 49 B5
Capheaton Northumb 62 E6
Cappercleuch Borders 61 A8
Capplegill Dumfries 61 C7
Capton Devon 5 F9
Caputh Perth 76 D3
Car Colston Notts 36 A3
Carbis Bay Corn 2 F4
Carbost Highld 85 D9
Carbost Highld 85 E8
Carbrook S Yorks 45 D7
Carbrooke Norf 38 E5
Carburton Notts 45 E10
Carcant Borders 70 E2
Carcary Angus 77 B9
Carclaze Corn 3 D9
Carcroft S Yorks 45 A9
Cardenden Fife 69 A11
Cardeston Shrops 33 D9
Cardiff = Caerdydd Cardiff 15 D7
Cardigan = Aberteifi Ceredig 22 B6
Cardington Bedford 29 D7
Cardington Shrops 33 F11
Cardinham Corn 4 E2
Cardonald Glasgow 68 D4
Cardow Moray 88 D1
Cardrona Borders 70 G2
Cardross Argyll 68 C2
Cardurnock Cumb 61 H7
Careby Lincs 36 D6
Careston Castle Angus 77 B8
Carew Pembs 22 F5
Carew Cheriton Pembs 22 F5
Carew Newton Pembs 22 F5
Carey Hereford 26 E2
Carfrae E Loth 70 D4
Cargenbridge Dumfries 60 F5
Cargill Perth 76 D4
Cargo Cumb 61 H9
Cargreen Corn 4 E5
Carham Northumb 71 G7
Carhampton Som 7 B9
Carharrack Corn 2 E6
Carie Perth 75 B9
Carie Perth 75 D9
Carines Corn 3 D6
Carisbrooke IoW 10 F3
Cark Cumb 49 B3
Carlabhagh W Isles 90 C7
Carland Cross Corn 3 D7
Carlby Lincs 37 D6
Carlecotes S Yorks 44 B5
Carlesmoor N Yorks 51 B7
Carleton Cumb 56 A6
Carleton Cumb 57 D7
Carleton Lancs 49 F3
Carleton N Yorks 50 E5
Carleton Forehoe Norf 39 E6
Carleton Rode Norf 39 F7
Carlin How Redcar 59 E8
Carlingcott Bath 16 F3
Carlisle Cumb 61 H10
Carlops Borders 69 E10
Carlton Bedford 28 C6
Carlton Cambs 30 C3
Carlton Leics 35 E9
Carlton N Yorks 51 A6
Carlton N Yorks 52 G2
Carlton N Yorks 58 E2
Carlton N Yorks 59 H7
Carlton Notts 36 A2
Carlton S Yorks 45 A7
Carlton Stockton 58 D4
Carlton Suff 31 B10
Carlton W Yorks 51 G9
Carlton Colville Suff 39 G11
Carlton Curlieu Leics 36 F2
Carlton Husthwaite N Yorks 51 B10
Carlton in Cleveland N Yorks 58 F6
Carlton in Lindrick Notts 45 D9
Carlton le Moorland Lincs 46 G3
Carlton Miniott N Yorks 51 A9
Carlton on Trent Notts 45 F11
Carlton Scroop Lincs 36 A5
Carluke S Lanark 69 E7
Carmarthen = Caerfyrddin Carms 23 D9
Carmel Anglesey 40 B5
Carmel Carms 23 E10
Carmel Flint 42 E4
Carmel Guern 11
Carmel Gwyn 40 E6
Carmont Aberds 83 E10
Carmunnock Glasgow 68 E5
Carmyle Glasgow 68 D5
Carmyllie Angus 77 C8
Carn-gorm Highld 80 A1
Carnaby E Yorks 53 C7
Carnach Highld 80 A2
Carnach Highld 86 B3
Carnach W Isles 90 H7
Carnachy Highld 93 D10
Càrnais W Isles 90 D5
Carnbee Fife 77 G8
Carnbo Perth 76 G3
Carnbrea Corn 2 E5
Carnduff S Lanark 68 F5
Carnduncan Argyll 64 B3
Carne Corn 3 F8
Carnforth Lancs 49 B4
Carnhedryn Pembs 22 D3
Carnhell Green Corn 2 F5
Carnkie Corn 2 F5
Carnkie Corn 2 F6
Carno Powys 32 F5
Carnoch Highld 86 F5
Carnoch Highld 86 H6
Carnock Fife 69 B9
Carnon Downs Corn 3 E6
Carnousie Aberds 89 C6
Carnoustie Angus 77 D8
Carnwath S Lanark 69 F8
Carnyorth Corn 2 F2
Carperby N Yorks 58 H1
Carpley Green N Yorks 57 H11
Carr S Yorks 45 C9
Carr Hill T&W 63 G8
Carradale Argyll 65 E9
Carragraich W Isles 90 H6
Carrbridge Highld 81 A11
Carrefour Selous Jersey 11
Carreg-wen Pembs 23 B7
Carreglefn Anglesey 40 B5
Carrick Argyll 73 E8
Carrick Fife 77 E7
Carrick Castle Argyll 73 D10
Carrick Ho. Orkney 95 E6
Carriden Falk 69 B9
Carrington Gtr Man 43 C10
Carrington Lincs 47 G7
Carrington Midloth 70 D2
Carrog Conwy 41 F9
Carrog Denb 33 A7
Carron Falk 69 B7
Carron Moray 88 D2
Carron Bridge Stirling 68 B6
Carronbridge Dumfries 60 D4
Carronshore Falk 69 B7
Carrshield Northumb 57 B10
Carrutherstown Dumfries 61 F7
Carrville Durham 58 B4
Carsaig Argyll 72 E6
Carsaig Argyll 79 J8
Carscreugh Dumfries 54 D5
Carse Gray Angus 77 B7
Carse Ho. Argyll 72 G6
Carsegowan Dumfries 55 D7
Carseriggan Dumfries 54 C6
Carsethorn Dumfries 60 H5
Carshalton London 19 E9
Carsington Derbys 44 G6
Carskiey Argyll 65 H7
Carsluith Dumfries 55 D7
Carsphairn Dumfries 67 G8
Carstairs S Lanark 69 F8
Carstairs Junction S Lanark 69 F8
Carswell Marsh Oxon 17 B10
Carter's Clay Hants 10 B2
Carterton Oxon 27 H9
Carterway Heads Northumb 58 A1
Carthew Corn 3 D9
Carthorpe N Yorks 51 A9
Cartington Northumb 62 C6
Cartland S Lanark 69 F7
Cartmel Cumb 49 B3
Cartmel Fell Cumb 56 H6
Carway Carms 23 F9
Cary Fitzpaine Som 8 B4
Cas-gwent = Chepstow Mon 15 B11
Cascob Powys 25 B9
Cashlie Perth 75 C7
Cashmoor Dorset 9 C8
Casnewydd = Newport Newport 15 C9
Cassey Compton Glos 27 G7
Cassington Oxon 27 G11
Cassop Durham 58 C4
Castell Denb 42 F4
Castell-Howell Ceredig 23 B9

Castell-Nedd = Neath Neath 14 B3
Castell Newydd Emlyn = Newcastle Emlyn Carms 23 B8
Castell-y-bwch Torf 15 B8
Castellau Rhondda 14 C6
Casterton Cumb 50 B2
Castle Acre Norf 38 D4
Castle Ashby Northants 28 C5
Castle Bolton N Yorks 58 G1
Castle Bromwich W Mid 35 G7
Castle Bytham Lincs 36 D5
Castle Caereinion Powys 33 E7
Castle Camps Cambs 30 D3
Castle Carrock Cumb 61 H11
Castle Cary Som 8 A5
Castle Combe Wilts 16 D5
Castle Donington Leics 35 C10
Castle Douglas Dumfries 55 C10
Castle Eaton Swindon 17 B8
Castle Eden Durham 58 C5
Castle Forbes Aberds 83 B8
Castle Frome Hereford 26 D3
Castle Green Sur 18 E6
Castle Gresley Derbys 35 D8
Castle Heaton Northumb 71 F8
Castle Hedingham Essex 30 E4
Castle Hill Kent 12 B5
Castle Huntly Perth 76 E6
Castle Kennedy Dumfries 54 D4
Castle O'er Dumfries 61 D8
Castle Pulverbatch Shrops 33 E10
Castle Rising Norf 38 C2
Castle Stuart Highld 87 G10
Castlebay = Bagh a Chaisteil W Isles 84 J1
Castlebythe Pembs 22 D5
Castlecary N Lanark 68 C6
Castlecraig Highld 87 E11
Castlefairn Dumfries 60 E3
Castleford W Yorks 51 G10
Castlehill Borders 69 G11
Castlehill Highld 94 D3
Castlehill W Dunb 68 C2
Castlemaddy Dumfries 67 H8
Castlemartin Pembs 22 G4
Castlemilk Dumfries 61 F7
Castlemilk Glasgow 68 E5
Castlemorris Pembs 22 C4
Castlemorton Worcs 26 E4
Castleside Durham 58 B1
Castlethorpe M Keynes 28 D5
Castleton Angus 76 C6
Castleton Argyll 73 E7
Castleton Derbys 44 D5
Castleton Gtr Man 44 A2
Castleton N Yorks 59 F7
Castleton Newport 15 C8
Castletown Ches W 43 G7
Castletown Highld 87 G10
Castletown Highld 94 D3
Castletown IoM 48 F2
Castletown T&W 63 H9
Castleweary Borders 61 C10
Castley N Yorks 51 E8
Caston Norf 38 F5
Castor Pboro 37 F7
Catacol N Ayrs 66 B2
Catbrain S Glos 16 C2
Catbrook Mon 15 A11
Catchall Corn 2 G3
Catchems Corner W Mid 35 H8
Catchgate Durham 58 A2
Catcleugh Northumb 62 C3
Catcliffe S Yorks 45 D8
Catcott Som 15 H9
Caterham Sur 19 F10
Catfield Norf 39 C9
Catfirth Shetland 96 H6
Catford London 19 D10
Catforth Lancs 49 F4
Cathays Cardiff 15 D7
Cathcart Glasgow 68 D4
Cathedine Powys 25 F8
Catherington Hants 10 C5
Catherton Shrops 34 H2
Catlodge Highld 81 D8
Catlowdy Cumb 61 F10
Catmore W Berks 17 C11
Caton Lancs 49 C5
Caton Green Lancs 49 C5
Catrine E Ayrs 67 D8
Cat's Ash Newport 15 B9
Catsfield E Sus 12 E6
Catshill Worcs 26 A6
Cattal N Yorks 51 D10
Cattawade Suff 31 E8
Catterall Lancs 49 E4
Catterick N Yorks 58 G3
Catterick Bridge N Yorks 58 G3
Catterick Garrison N Yorks 58 G2
Catterlen Cumb 57 C6
Catterline Aberds 83 F10
Catterton N Yorks 51 E11
Catthorpe Leics 36 H1
Cattistock Dorset 8 E4
Catton N Yorks 51 B9
Catton Northumb 62 H4
Catwick E Yorks 53 E7
Catworth Cambs 29 A7
Caudlesprings Norf 38 E5
Caulcott Oxon 28 F2
Cauldcots Angus 77 C9
Cauldhame Stirling 68 A5
Cauldmill Borders 61 B11
Cauldon Staffs 44 H4
Caulkerbush Dumfries 60 H5
Caulside Dumfries 61 E10
Caunsall Worcs 34 G4
Caunton Notts 45 G11
Causeway End Dumfries 55 C7
Causeway Foot W Yorks 51 F6
Causeway-head Stirling 75 H10
Causewayend S Lanark 69 G9
Causewayhead Cumb 56 A3
Causey Park Bridge Northumb 63 D7
Causeyend Aberds 83 B11
Cautley Cumb 57 G8
Cavendish Suff 30 D5
Cavendish Bridge Leics 35 C10
Cavenham Suff 30 B4
Caversfield Oxon 28 F2
Caversham Reading 18 D4
Caverswall Staffs 34 A5
Cavil E Yorks 52 F3
Cawdor Highld 87 F11
Cawkwell Lincs 46 E6
Cawood N Yorks 52 F1
Cawsand Corn 4 F5
Cawston Norf 39 C7
Cawthorne S Yorks 44 B6
Cawthorpe Lincs 37 C6
Cawton N Yorks 52 B2
Caxton Cambs 29 C10
Caynham Shrops 26 A2
Caythorpe Lincs 46 H3
Caythorpe Notts 45 H10
Cayton N Yorks 53 A6
Ceann a Bhaigh W Isles 84 B2
Ceann a Deas Loch Baghasdail W Isles 84 G2
Ceann Shiphoirt W Isles 91 F7
Ceann Tarabhaigh W Isles 90 F7
Ceannacroc Lodge Highld 80 B4
Cearsiadair W Isles 91 E8
Cefn Berain Conwy 42 F2
Cefn-brith Conwy 42 G2
Cefn Canol Powys 33 B8
Cefn-coch Conwy 41 D10
Cefn Coch Powys 33 C7
Cefn-coed-y-cymmer M Tydf 25 H7
Cefn Cribbwr Bridgend 14 C4
Cefn Cross Bridgend 14 C4
Cefn-ddwysarn Gwyn 32 B5
Cefn Einion Shrops 33 G8
Cefn-gorwydd Powys 24 D6
Cefn-mawr Wrex 33 A8
Cefn-y-bedd Flint 42 G6
Cefn-y-pant Carms 22 D6
Cefneithin Carms 23 E10
Cei-bach Ceredig 23 A9
Ceinewydd = New Quay Ceredig 23 A8
Ceint Anglesey 40 C6
Cellan Ceredig 24 D3
Cellarhead Staffs 44 H3
Cemaes Anglesey 40 A5
Cemmaes Powys 32 E4
Cemmaes Road Powys 32 E4
Cenarth Carms 23 B7
Cenin Gwyn 40 F6
Central Invclyd 73 F11
Ceos W Isles 91 E8
Ceres Fife 77 F7
Cerne Abbas Dorset 8 D5
Cerney Wick Glos 17 B7
Cerrigceinwen Anglesey 40 C6
Cerrigydrudion Conwy 42 H2
Cessford Borders 62 A3
Ceunant Gwyn 41 D7
Chaceley Glos 26 E5
Chacewater Corn 3 E6
Chackmore Bucks 28 E3
Chacombe Northants 27 D11
Chad Valley W Mid 34 G6
Chadderton Gtr Man 44 B3
Chadderton Fold Gtr Man 44 B2
Chaddesden Derby 35 B9
Chaddesley Corbett Worcs 26 A5
Chaddleworth W Berks 17 D11
Chadlington Oxon 27 F10
Chadshunt Warks 27 C10
Chadwell Leics 36 C3
Chadwell St Mary Thurrock 20 D3
Chadwick End W Mid 27 A9
Chadwick Green Mers 43 C8
Chaffcombe Som 8 C2
Chagford Devon 5 C8
Chailey E Sus 12 E2
Chain Bridge Lincs 37 A9
Chainbridge Cambs 37 E10
Chainhurst Kent 20 G4
Chalbury Dorset 9 D9
Chalbury Common Dorset 9 D9
Chaldon Sur 19 F10
Chaldon Herring Dorset 9 F6
Chale IoW 10 G3
Chale Green IoW 10 G3
Chalfont Common Bucks 19 B7
Chalfont St Giles Bucks 18 B6
Chalfont St Peter Bucks 19 B7
Chalford Glos 16 A5
Chalgrove Oxon 18 B3
Chalk Kent 20 D3
Challacombe Devon 6 B5
Challoch Dumfries 54 C6
Challock Kent 21 F7
Chalton C Beds 29 F7
Chalton Hants 10 C6
Chalvington E Sus 12 F4
Chancery Ceredig 32 H1
Chandler's Ford Hants 10 B3
Channel Tunnel Kent 21 H8
Channerwick Shetland 96 L6
Chantry Som 16 G4
Chantry Suff 31 D8
Chapel Fife 69 A11
Chapel Allerton Som 15 F10
Chapel Allerton W Yorks 51 F9
Chapel Amble Corn 3 B8
Chapel Brampton Northants 28 B4
Chapel Choriton Staffs 34 B4
Chapel-en-le-Frith Derbys 44 D4
Chapel End Warks 35 F9
Chapel Green Warks 27 B11
Chapel Green Warks 35 G8
Chapel Haddlesey N Yorks 52 G1
Chapel Head Cambs 37 G9
Chapel Hill Aberds 89 E10
Chapel Hill Lincs 46 G6
Chapel Hill Mon 15 B11
Chapel Hill N Yorks 51 E9
Chapel Lawn Shrops 33 H9
Chapel-le-Dale N Yorks 50 B3
Chapel Milton Derbys 44 D4
Chapel of Garioch Aberds 83 A9
Chapel Row W Berks 18 E2
Chapel St Leonards Lincs 47 E9
Chapel Stile Cumb 56 F5
Chapelgate Lincs 37 C10
Chapelhall N Lanark 68 D6
Chapelhill Dumfries 60 D6
Chapelhill Highld 87 D11
Chapelhill N Ayrs 66 B5
Chapelhill Perth 76 D3
Chapelhill Perth 76 E5
Chapelknowe Dumfries 61 F9
Chapelton Angus 77 C9
Chapelton Devon 6 D4
Chapelton Highld 81 B11
Chapelton S Lanark 68 F5
Chapeltown Blackburn 50 H3
Chapeltown Moray 82 A4
Chapeltown S Yorks 45 C7
Chapmans Well Devon 4 C4
Chapmanslade Wilts 16 G5
Chapmore End Herts 29 G10
Chappel Essex 30 F5
Chard Som 8 D2
Chardstock Devon 8 D2
Charfield S Glos 16 B4
Charford Worcs 26 B6
Charing Kent 20 G6
Charing Cross Dorset 9 C10
Charing Heath Kent 20 G6
Charingworth Glos 27 E9
Charlbury Oxon 27 G10
Charlcombe Bath 16 E4
Charlecote Warks 27 C9
Charles Devon 6 C5
Charles Tye Suff 31 C7
Charlesfield Dumfries 61 G7
Charleston Angus 76 C6
Charleston Renfs 68 D3
Charlestown Aberdeen 83 C11
Charlestown Corn 3 D9
Charlestown Derbys 44 C4
Charlestown Dorset 8 G5
Charlestown Fife 69 B9
Charlestown Gtr Man 44 B2
Charlestown Highld 85 A13
Charlestown Highld 87 G9
Charlestown W Yorks 50 G5
Charlestown of Aberlour Moray 88 D2
Charlesworth Derbys 44 C4
Charleton Devon 5 G8
Charlton London 19 D11
Charlton Hants 17 G10
Charlton Herts 29 F8
Charlton Northants 28 E2
Charlton Northumb 62 E4
Charlton Som 16 F3
Charlton Telford 34 D1
Charlton W Sus 11 C7
Charlton Wilts 9 B8
Charlton Wilts 16 C6
Charlton Wilts 17 F8
Charlton Worcs 27 D7
Charlton Abbots Glos 27 F7
Charlton Adam Som 8 B4
Charlton-All-Saints Wilts 9 B10
Charlton Down Dorset 8 E5
Charlton Horethorne Som 8 B5
Charlton Kings Glos 26 F6
Charlton Mackerell Som 8 B4
Charlton Marshall Dorset 9 D7
Charlton Musgrove Som 8 B6
Charlton on Otmoor Oxon 28 G2
Charltons Redcar 59 E7
Charlwood Sur 19 G9
Charlynch Som 7 C11
Charminster Dorset 8 E5
Charmouth Dorset 8 E2
Charndon Bucks 28 F3
Charney Bassett Oxon 17 B10
Charnock Richard Lancs 50 H1
Charsfield Suff 31 C9
Chart Corner Kent 20 F4
Chart Sutton Kent 20 G5
Charter Alley Hants 18 F2
Charterhouse Som 15 F10
Charterville Allotments Oxon 27 G10
Chartham Kent 21 F8
Chartham Hatch Kent 21 F8
Chartridge Bucks 18 A6
Charvil Wokingham 18 D4
Charwelton Northants 28 C2
Chasetown Staffs 34 E6
Chastleton Oxon 27 F9
Chasty Devon 6 F2
Chatburn Lancs 50 E3
Chatcull Staffs 34 B3
Chatham Medway 20 E4
Chathill Northumb 71 H10
Chattenden Medway 20 D4
Chatteris Cambs 37 G9
Chattisham Suff 31 D7
Chatto Borders 62 B3
Chatton Northumb 71 H9
Chawleigh Devon 7 E6
Chawley Oxon 17 A11
Chawston Bedford 29 C8
Chawton Hants 18 H4
Cheadle Gtr Man 44 D2
Cheadle Staffs 34 A6
Cheadle Heath Gtr Man 44 D2
Cheadle Hulme Gtr Man 44 D2
Cheam London 19 E9
Cheapside Sur 19 F7
Chearsley Bucks 28 G4
Chebsey Staffs 34 C4
Checkendon Oxon 18 C3
Checkley Ches E 43 H10
Checkley Hereford 26 E2
Checkley Staffs 34 B6
Chedburgh Suff 30 C4
Cheddar Som 15 F10
Cheddington Bucks 28 G6
Cheddleton Staffs 44 G3
Cheddon Fitzpaine Som 8 B1
Chedglow Wilts 16 B6
Chedgrave Norf 39 F9
Chedington Dorset 8 D3
Chediston Suff 39 H9
Chedworth Glos 27 G7
Chedzoy Som 15 H9
Cheeklaw Borders 70 E6
Cheeseman's Green Kent 13 C9
Cheglinch Devon 6 B4
Cheldon Devon 7 E6
Chelford Ches E 44 E2
Chell Heath Stoke 44 G2
Chellaston Derby 35 B9
Chellington Bedford 28 C6
Chelmarsh Shrops 34 G3
Chelmer Village Essex 30 H4
Chelmondiston Suff 31 E9
Chelmorton Derbys 44 F5
Chelmsford Essex 30 H4
Chelsea London 19 D9
Chelsfield London 19 E11
Chelsworth Suff 30 D6
Cheltenham Glos 26 F6
Chelveston Northants 28 B6
Chelvey N Som 15 E10
Chelwood Bath 16 E3
Chelwood Common E Sus 12 D3
Chelwood Gate E Sus 12 D3
Chelworth Wilts 16 B6
Chelworth Green Wilts 17 B7
Chemistry Shrops 33 A11
Chenies Bucks 19 B7
Cheny Longville Shrops 33 G10
Chepstow = Cas-gwent Mon 15 B11
Chequerfield W Yorks 51 G10
Cherhill Wilts 17 D7
Cherington Glos 16 B6
Cherington Warks 27 E9
Cheriton Devon 7 B6
Cheriton Hants 10 B4
Cheriton Kent 21 H8
Cheriton Swansea 23 G9
Cheriton Bishop Devon 7 G6
Cheriton Fitzpaine Devon 7 F7
Cheriton or Stackpole Elidor Pembs 22 G4
Cherrington Telford 34 C2
Cherry Burton E Yorks 52 E5
Cherry Hinton Cambs 29 C11
Cherry Orchard Worcs 26 C5
Cherry Willingham Lincs 46 E4
Cherrybank Perth 76 E4
Chertsey Sur 19 E7
Cheselbourne Dorset 9 E6
Chesham Bucks 18 A6
Chesham Bois Bucks 18 B6
Cheshunt Herts 19 A10
Cheslyn Hay Staffs 34 E5
Chessington London 19 E8
Chester Ches W 43 F7
Chester-Le-Street Durham 58 A3
Chester Moor Durham 58 B3
Chesterblade Som 16 G3
Chesterfield Derbys 45 E7
Chesters Borders 62 A2
Chesters Borders 62 B2
Chesterton Cambs 29 B11
Chesterton Cambs 37 F7
Chesterton Glos 17 A7
Chesterton Oxon 28 F2
Chesterton Shrops 34 F3
Chesterton Staffs 44 H2
Chesterton Warks 27 C10
Chesterwood Northumb 62 G4
Chestfield Kent 21 E8
Cheston Devon 5 F7
Cheswardine Shrops 34 C3
Cheswick Northumb 71 F9
Chetnole Dorset 8 D5
Chettiscombe Devon 7 E8
Chettisham Cambs 37 G11
Chettle Dorset 9 C8
Chetton Shrops 34 F2
Chetwode Bucks 28 F3
Chetwynd Aston Telford 34 D3
Cheveley Cambs 30 B3
Chevening Kent 19 F11
Chevington Suff 30 C4
Chevithorne Devon 7 E8
Chew Magna Bath 16 E2
Chew Stoke Bath 16 E2
Chewton Keynsham Bath 16 E3
Chewton Mendip Som 16 F2
Chicheley M Keynes 28 D6
Chichester W Sus 11 D7
Chickerell Dorset 8 F5
Chicklade Wilts 9 A8
Chicksgrove Wilts 9 A8
Chidden Hants 10 C5
Chiddingfold Sur 18 H6
Chiddingly E Sus 12 E4
Chiddingstone Kent 19 G11
Chiddingstone Causeway Kent 20 G2
Chiddingstone Hoath Kent 12 B3
Chideock Dorset 8 E3
Chidham W Sus 11 D6
Chidswell W Yorks 51 G8
Chieveley W Berks 17 D11
Chignall St James Essex 30 H3
Chignall Smealy Essex 30 G3
Chigwell Essex 19 B11
Chigwell Row Essex 19 B11
Chilbolton Hants 17 H10
Chilcomb Hants 10 B4
Chilcombe Dorset 8 E4
Chilcompton Som 16 F3
Chilcote Leics 35 D8
Child Okeford Dorset 9 C7
Childer Thornton Ches W 42 E6
Childrey Oxon 17 C10
Child's Ercall Shrops 34 C2
Childswickham Worcs 27 E7
Childwall Mers 43 D7
Childwick Green Herts 29 G8
Chilfrome Dorset 8 E4
Chilgrove W Sus 11 C7
Chilham Kent 21 F7
Chilhampton Wilts 9 A9
Chilla Devon 6 F3
Chillaton Devon 4 C5
Chillenden Kent 21 F9
Chillerton IoW 10 F3
Chillesford Suff 31 C10
Chillingham Northumb 71 H9
Chillington Devon 5 G8
Chillington Som 8 C2
Chilmark Wilts 9 A8
Chilson Oxon 27 G10
Chilsworthy Corn 4 D5
Chilsworthy Devon 6 F2
Chilthorne Domer Som 8 C4
Chiltington E Sus 12 E2
Chilton Bucks 28 G3
Chilton Durham 58 D3
Chilton Oxon 17 C11
Chilton Cantelo Som 8 B4
Chilton Foliat Wilts 17 D10
Chilton Lane Durham 58 C4
Chilton Polden Som 15 H9
Chilton Street Suff 30 D4
Chilton Trinity Som 15 H8
Chilvers Coton Warks 35 F9
Chilwell Notts 35 B11
Chilworth Hants 10 C3
Chilworth Sur 19 G7
Chimney Oxon 17 A10
Chineham Hants 18 F3
Chingford London 19 B10
Chinley Derbys 44 D4
Chinley Head Derbys 44 D4
Chinnor Oxon 18 A4
Chipnall Shrops 34 B3
Chippenhall Green Suff 39 H8
Chippenham Cambs 30 B3
Chippenham Wilts 16 D6
Chipperfield Herts 19 A7
Chipping Herts 29 E10
Chipping Lancs 50 E2
Chipping Campden Glos 27 E8
Chipping Hill Essex 30 G5
Chipping Norton Oxon 27 F10
Chipping Ongar Essex 20 A2
Chipping Sodbury S Glos 16 C4
Chipping Warden Northants 27 D11
Chipstable Som 7 D9
Chipstead Kent 19 F11
Chipstead Sur 19 F9
Chirbury Shrops 33 F8
Chirk = Y Waun Wrex 33 B8
Chirk Bank Shrops 33 B8
Chirmorrie S Ayrs 54 B5
Chirnside Borders 71 E7
Chirnsidebridge Borders 71 E7
Chirton Wilts 17 F7
Chisbury Wilts 17 E9
Chiselborough Som 8 C3
Chiseldon Swindon 17 D8
Chiserley W Yorks 50 G6
Chislehampton Oxon 18 B2
Chislehurst London 19 D11
Chislet Kent 21 E9
Chiswell Green Herts 19 A8
Chiswick London 19 D9
Chiswick End Cambs 29 D10
Chisworth Derbys 44 C3
Chithurst W Sus 11 B7
Chittering Cambs 29 A11
Chitterne Wilts 16 G6
Chittlehamholt Devon 6 D5
Chittlehampton Devon 6 D5
Chittoe Wilts 16 E6
Chivenor Devon 6 C4
Chobham Sur 18 E6
Choicelee Borders 70 E6
Cholderton Wilts 17 G9
Cholesbury Bucks 28 H6
Chollerford Northumb 62 F5
Chollerton Northumb 62 F5
Cholmondeston Ches E 43 F9
Cholsey Oxon 18 C2
Cholstrey Hereford 25 C11
Chop Gate N Yorks 59 G6
Choppington Northumb 63 E8
Chopwell T&W 63 H7
Chorley Ches E 43 G8
Chorley Lancs 50 H1
Chorley Shrops 34 G2
Chorley Staffs 35 D6
Chorleywood Herts 19 B7
Chorlton cum Hardy Gtr Man 44 C2
Chorlton Lane Ches W 43 H7
Choulton Shrops 33 G9
Chowdene T&W 63 H8
Chowley Ches W 43 G7
Chrishall Essex 29 E11
Christchurch Cambs 37 F10
Christchurch Dorset 9 E10
Christchurch Glos 26 G2
Christchurch Newport 15 C9
Christian Malford Wilts 16 D6
Christleton Ches W 43 F7
Christmas Common Oxon 18 B4
Christon N Som 15 F9
Christon Bank Northumb 63 A8
Christow Devon 5 C9
Chryston N Lanark 68 C5
Chudleigh Devon 5 D9
Chudleigh Knighton Devon 5 D9
Chulmleigh Devon 6 E5
Chunal Derbys 44 C4
Church Lancs 50 G3
Church Aston Telford 34 D3
Church Brampton Northants 28 B4
Church Broughton Derbys 35 B8
Church Crookham Hants 18 F5
Church Eaton Staffs 34 D4
Church End C Beds 28 E6
Church End C Beds 28 F6
Church End C Beds 29 E8
Church End Cambs 37 E9
Church End Cambs 37 G8
Church End E Yorks 53 D6
Church End Essex 30 D2
Church End Essex 30 F4
Church End Hants 18 F3
Church End Lincs 37 B8
Church End Warks 35 F8
Church End Warks 35 F8
Church End Wilts 17 D7
Church Enstone Oxon 27 F10
Church Fenton N Yorks 51 F11
Church Green Devon 7 G10
Church Green Norf 39 F6
Church Gresley Derbys 35 D8
Church Hanborough Oxon 27 G11
Church Hill Ches W 43 F9
Church Houses N Yorks 59 G7
Church Knowle Dorset 9 F8
Church Laneham Notts 46 E2
Church Langton Leics 36 F3
Church Lawford Warks 35 H10
Church Lawton Ches E 44 G2
Church Leigh Staffs 34 B6
Church Lench Worcs 27 C7
Church Mayfield Staffs 35 A7
Church Minshull Ches E 43 F9
Church Norton W Sus 11 E7
Church Preen Shrops 33 F11
Church Pulverbatch Shrops 33 E10
Church Stoke Powys 33 F8
Church Stowe Northants 28 C3
Church Street Kent 20 D4
Church Stretton Shrops 33 F10
Church Town N Lincs 45 B11
Church Town Sur 19 F10
Church Village Rhondda 14 C6
Church Warsop Notts 45 F9
Churcham Glos 26 G4
Churchbank Shrops 33 H8
Churchbridge Staffs 34 E5
Churchdown Glos 26 G5
Churchend Essex 21 B7
Churchend Essex 30 F3
Churchend S Glos 16 B4
Churchfield W Mid 34 F6
Churchgate Street Essex 29 G11
Churchill Devon 6 B4
Churchill Devon 8 D2
Churchill N Som 15 F10
Churchill Oxon 27 F9
Churchill Worcs 26 C6
Churchill Worcs 34 H4
Churchinford Som 7 E11
Churchover Warks 35 G11
Churchstanton Som 7 E10
Churchstow Devon 5 G8
Churchtown Derbys 44 F6
Churchtown IoM 48 C4
Churchtown Lancs 49 E4
Churchtown Mers 49 H3
Chursnike Lodge Northumb 62 F2
Churston Ferrers Torbay 5 F10
Churt Sur 18 H5
Churton Ches W 43 G7
Churwell W Yorks 51 G8
Chute Standen Wilts 17 F10
Chwilog Gwyn 40 G6
Chyandour Corn 2 F3
Cilan Uchaf Gwyn 40 H4
Cilcain Flint 42 F4
Cilcennin Ceredig 24 B2
Cilfor Gwyn 41 G8
Cilfrew Neath 14 A3
Cilfynydd Rhondda 14 B6
Cilgerran Pembs 22 B6
Cilgwyn Carms 24 F4
Cilgwyn Gwyn 40 E6
Cilgwyn Pembs 22 C5
Ciliau Aeron Ceredig 23 A9
Cill Donnain W Isles 84 F2
Cille Bhrighde W Isles 84 G2
Cille Pheadair W Isles 84 G2
Cilmery Powys 25 C7
Cilsan Carms 23 D10
Ciltalgarth Gwyn 41 F10
Cilwendeg Pembs 23 C7
Cilybebyll Neath 14 A3
Cilycwm Carms 24 E4
Cimla Neath 14 B3
Cinderford Glos 26 G3
Cippyn Pembs 22 B6
Circebost W Isles 90 D6
Cirencester Glos 17 A7
Ciribhig W Isles 90 C6
City London 19 C10
City Powys 33 G8
City Dulas Anglesey 40 B6
Clachaig Argyll 73 E10
Clachan Argyll 65 D8
Clachan Argyll 72 B6
Clachan Argyll 74 F4
Clachan Argyll 79 G11
Clachan Highld 85 E10
Clachan W Isles 84 D2
Clachan na Luib W Isles 84 B3
Clachan of Campsie E Dunb 68 C5
Clachan of Glendaruel Argyll 73 E8
Clachan-Seil Argyll 72 B6
Clachan Strachur Argyll 73 C9
Clachaneasy Dumfries 54 B6
Clachanmore Dumfries 54 E3
Clachbreck Argyll 72 F6
Clachnabrain Angus 82 G5
Clachtoll Highld 92 G3
Clackmannan Clack 69 A8
Clacton-on-Sea Essex 31 G8
Cladach Chireboist W Isles 84 B2
Claddach-knockline W Isles 84 B2
Cladich Argyll 74 E3
Claggan Highld 79 G9
Claggan Highld 80 F3
Claigan Highld 84 C7
Claines Worcs 26 C5
Clandown Bath 16 F3
Clanfield Hants 10 C6
Clanfield Oxon 17 A9
Clanville Hants 17 G10
Claonaig Argyll 73 H7
Claonel Highld 93 J8
Clap Hill Kent 13 C9
Clapgate Dorset 9 D9
Clapgate Herts 29 F11
Clapham Bedford 29 C7
Clapham London 19 D9
Clapham N Yorks 50 C3
Clapham W Sus 11 D9
Clappers Borders 71 E8
Clappersgate Cumb 56 F5
Clapton Som 8 D3
Clapton-in-Gordano N Som 15 D10
Clapton-on-the-Hill Glos 27 G8
Clapworthy Devon 6 D5
Clara Vale T&W 63 G7
Clarach Ceredig 32 G2
Clarbeston Pembs 22 D5
Clarbeston Road Pembs 22 D5
Clarborough Notts 45 D11
Clardon Highld 94 D3
Clare Suff 30 D4
Clarebrand Dumfries 55 C10
Clarencefield Dumfries 60 G6
Clarilaw Borders 61 B11
Clark's Green Sur 19 H8
Clarkston E Renf 68 E4
Clashandorran Highld 87 G8
Clashcoig Highld 87 B9
Clashindarroch Aberds 88 E4
Clashmore Highld 87 C10
Clashmore Highld 92 F3
Clashnessie Highld 92 F3
Clashnoir Moray 82 A4
Clate Shetland 96 G7
Clathy Perth 76 F2
Clatt Aberds 83 A7
Clatter Powys 32 F5
Clatterford IoW 10 F3
Clatterin Bridge Aberds 83 F8
Clatworthy Som 7 C9
Claughton Lancs 49 E5
Claughton Lancs 50 C1
Claughton Mers 42 D6
Claverdon Warks 27 B8
Claverham N Som 15 E10
Clavering Essex 29 E11
Claverley Shrops 34 F3
Claverton Bath 16 E4
Clawdd-newydd Denb 42 G3
Clawthorpe Cumb 49 B5
Clawton Devon 6 G2
Claxby Lincs 46 C5
Claxby Lincs 47 E8
Claxton N Yorks 52 C2
Claxton Norf 39 E9
Clay Common Suff 39 G10
Clay Coton Northants 36 H1
Clay Cross Derbys 45 F7
Clay Hill W Berks 18 D2
Clay Lake Lincs 37 C8
Claybokie Aberds 82 D2
Claybrooke Magna Leics 35 G10
Claybrooke Parva Leics 35 G10
Claydon Oxon 27 C11
Claydon Suff 31 C8
Claygate Dumfries 61 F9
Claygate Kent 12 B6
Claygate Sur 19 E8
Claygate Cross Kent 20 F3
Clayhanger Devon 7 D9
Clayhanger W Mid 34 E6
Clayhidon Devon 7 E10
Clayhill E Sus 13 D7
Clayhill Hants 10 D2
Clayock Highld 94 E3
Claypole Lincs 46 H2
Clayton S Yorks 45 B8
Clayton Staffs 34 A4
Clayton W Sus 12 E1
Clayton W Yorks 51 F7
Clayton Green Lancs 50 G1
Clayton-le-Moors Lancs 50 F3
Clayton-le-Woods Lancs 50 G1
Clayton West W Yorks 44 A6
Clayworth Notts 45 D11
Cleadale Highld 78 C7
Cleadon T&W 63 G9
Clearbrook Devon 4 E6
Clearwell Glos 26 H2
Cleasby N Yorks 58 E3
Cleat Orkney 95 K5
Cleatlam Durham 58 E2
Cleator Cumb 56 E2
Cleator Moor Cumb 56 E2
Clebrig Highld 93 F8
Cleckheaton W Yorks 51 G7
Clee St Margaret Shrops 34 G1
Cleedownton Shrops 34 G1
Cleehill Shrops 34 H1
Cleethorpes NE Lincs 47 B7
Cleeton St Mary Shrops 34 H2
Cleeve N Som 15 E10
Cleeve Hill Glos 26 F6
Cleeve Prior Worcs 27 D7
Clegyrnant Powys 32 E5
Clehonger Hereford 25 E11
Cleish Perth 76 H3
Cleland N Lanark 69 E7
Clench Common Wilts 17 E8
Clenchwarton Norf 38 C1
Clent Worcs 34 H5
Cleobury Mortimer Shrops 34 H2
Cleobury North Shrops 34 G2
Cleongart Argyll 65 E7
Clephanton Highld 87 F11
Clerklands Borders 61 A11
Clestrain Orkney 95 H4
Cleuch Head Borders 61 B11
Cleughbrae Dumfries 60 F6
Clevancy Wilts 17 D7
Clevedon N Som 15 D10
Cleveley Oxon 27 F10
Cleveleys Lancs 49 E3
Cleverton Wilts 16 C6
Clevis Bridgend 14 D4
Clewer Som 15 F10
Cley next the Sea Norf 38 A6
Cliaid W Isles 84 H1
Cliasmol W Isles 90 G5
Cliburn Cumb 57 D7
Click Mill Orkney 95 F4
Cliddesden Hants 18 G3
Cliff End E Sus 13 E7
Cliffburn Angus 77 C9
Cliffe Medway 20 D4
Cliffe N Yorks 52 F2
Cliffe Woods Medway 20 D4
Clifford Hereford 25 D9
Clifford W Yorks 51 E10
Clifford Chambers Warks 27 C8
Clifford's Mesne Glos 26 F4
Cliffsend Kent 21 E10
Clifton Bristol 16 D2
Clifton C Beds 29 E8
Clifton Cumb 57 D7
Clifton Derbys 35 A7
Clifton Lancs 49 F4
Clifton N Yorks 51 E7
Clifton Northumb 63 E8
Clifton Nottingham 36 B1
Clifton Oxon 27 E11
Clifton S Yorks 45 C9
Clifton Stirling 74 D6
Clifton Worcs 26 D5
Clifton York 52 D1
Clifton Campville Staffs 35 D8
Clifton Green Gtr Man 43 B10
Clifton Hampden Oxon 18 B2
Clifton Reynes M Keynes 28 C6
Clifton upon Dunsmore Warks 35 H11
Clifton upon Teme Worcs 26 B4
Cliftoncote Borders 70 H7
Cliftonville Kent 21 D10
Climaen gwyn Neath 24 H4
Climping W Sus 11 D9
Climpy S Lanark 69 E8
Clink Som 16 G4
Clint N Yorks 51 D8
Clint Green Norf 38 D6
Clintmains Borders 70 G5
Cliobh W Isles 90 D5
Clippesby Norf 39 D10
Clipsham Rutland 36 D5
Clipston Northants 36 G3
Clipstone Notts 45 F9
Clitheroe Lancs 50 E3
Cliuthar W Isles 90 H6
Clive Shrops 33 C11
Clivocast Shetland 96 C8
Clixby Lincs 46 B5
Clocaenog Denb 42 G3
Clochan Moray 88 B4
Clock Face Mers 43 C8
Clockmill Borders 70 E6
Cloddiau Powys 33 E8
Clodock Hereford 25 F10
Clola Aberds 89 D10
Clophill C Beds 29 E7
Clopton Northants 37 G6
Clopton Suff 31 C9
Clopton Corner Suff 31 C9
Clopton Green Suff 30 C4
Close Clark IoM 48 E2
Closeburn Dumfries 60 D4
Closworth Som 8 C4
Clothall Herts 29 E9
Clotton Ches W 43 F8
Clough Foot W Yorks 50 G5
Cloughton N Yorks 59 G11
Cloughton Newlands N Yorks 59 G11
Clousta Shetland 96 H5
Clouston Orkney 95 G3
Clova Aberds 82 A6
Clova Angus 82 F5
Clove Lodge Durham 57 E11
Clovelly Devon 6 D2
Clovenfords Borders 70 G3
Clovenstone Aberds 83 B9
Clovullin Highld 74 A3
Clow Bridge Lancs 50 G4
Clowne Derbys 45 E8
Clows Top Worcs 26 A4
Cloy Wrex 33 A9
Cluanie Inn Highld 80 B2
Cluanie Lodge Highld 80 B2
Clun Shrops 33 G9
Clunbury Shrops 33 G9
Clunderwen Carms 22 E6
Clune Highld 81 A9
Clunes Highld 80 E4
Clungunford Shrops 33 H9
Clunie Aberds 89 C6
Clunie Perth 76 C4
Clunton Shrops 33 G9
Cluny Fife 76 H5
Cluny Castle Highld 81 D8
Clutton Bath 16 F3
Clutton Ches W 43 G7
Clwt-grugoer Conwy 42 F2
Clwt-y-bont Gwyn 41 D7
Clydach Mon 25 G9
Clydach Swansea 14 A2
Clydach Vale Rhondda 14 B5
Clydebank W Dunb 68 C3
Clydey Pembs 23 C7
Clyffe Pypard Wilts 17 D7
Clynder Argyll 73 E11
Clyne Neath 14 A4
Clynelish Highld 93 J11
Clynnog-fawr Gwyn 40 E6
Clyro Powys 25 D9
Clyst Honiton Devon 7 G8
Clyst Hydon Devon 7 F9
Clyst St George Devon 5 C10
Clyst St Lawrence Devon 7 F9
Clyst St Mary Devon 7 G8
Cnoc Amhlaigh W Isles 91 D10
Cnwch-coch Ceredig 32 H2
Coachford Aberds 88 D4
Coad's Green Corn 4 D3
Coal Aston Derbys 45 E7
Coalbrookdale Telford 34 E2
Coalbrookvale Bl Gwent 25 H8
Coalburn S Lanark 69 G7
Coalburns T&W 63 G7
Coalcleugh Northumb 57 B10
Coaley Glos 16 A4
Coalhall E Ayrs 67 E7
Coalhill Essex 20 B4
Coalpit Heath S Glos 16 C3
Coalport Telford 34 E2
Coalsnaughton Clack 76 H2
Coaltown of Balgonie Fife 76 H6
Coaltown of Wemyss Fife 76 H6
Coalville Leics 35 D10
Coalway Glos 26 G2
Coat Som 8 B3
Coatbridge N Lanark 68 D6
Coatdyke N Lanark 68 D6
Coate Swindon 17 C8
Coate Wilts 17 E7
Coates Cambs 37 F9
Coates Glos 16 A6
Coates Lancs 50 E4
Coates Notts 46 D2
Coates W Sus 11 C8
Coatham Redcar 59 D6
Coatham Mundeville Darl 58 D3
Coatsgate Dumfries 60 C6
Cobbaton Devon 6 D5
Cobbler's Green Norf 39 F8
Coberley Glos 26 G6
Cobham Kent 20 E3
Cobham Sur 19 E8
Cobholm Island Norf 39 E11
Cobleland Stirling 75 H8
Cobnash Hereford 25 B11
Coburty Aberds 89 B9
Cock Bank Wrex 42 H6
Cock Bridge Aberds 82 C4
Cock Clarks Essex 20 A5
Cock & End Suff 30 C4
Cock Green Essex 30 G4
Cock Marling E Sus 13 E7
Cockayne N Yorks 59 G7
Cockayne Hatley Cambs 29 D9
Cockburnspath Borders 70 C6
Cockenzie and Port Seton E Loth 70 C3
Cockerham Lancs 49 D4
Cockermouth Cumb 56 C3
Cockernhoe Green Herts 29 F8
Cockfield Durham 58 D2
Cockfield Suff 30 C6
Cockfosters London 19 B9
Cocking W Sus 11 C7
Cockington Torbay 5 E9
Cocklake Som 15 G10
Cockley Beck Cumb 56 F4
Cockley Cley Norf 38 E3
Cockshutt Shrops 33 C10
Cockthorpe Norf 38 A5
Cockwood Devon 5 C10
Cockyard Hereford 25 E11
Codda Corn 4 D2
Coddenham Suff 31 C8
Coddington Ches W 43 G7
Coddington Hereford 26 D4
Coddington Notts 46 G2
Codford St Mary Wilts 16 H6
Codford St Peter Wilts 16 H6
Codicote Herts 29 G9
Codmore Hill W Sus 11 B9
Codnor Derbys 45 H8
Codrington S Glos 16 D4
Codsall Staffs 34 E4
Codsall Wood Staffs 34 E4
Coed Duon = Blackwood Caerph 15 B7
Coed Mawr Gwyn 41 C7
Coed Morgan Mon 25 G10
Coed-Talon Flint 42 G5
Coed-y-bryn Ceredig 23 B8
Coed-y-paen Mon 15 B9
Coed-yr-ynys Powys 25 F8
Coed Ystumgwern Gwyn 32 C1
Coedely Rhondda 14 C6
Coedkernew Newport 15 C8
Coedpoeth Wrex 42 G5
Coedway Powys 33 D9
Coelbren Powys 24 G5
Coffinswell Devon 5 E9
Cofton Hackett Worcs 34 H6
Cogan V Glam 15 D7
Cogenhoe Northants 28 B5
Cogges Oxon 27 H10
Coggeshall Essex 30 F5
Coggeshall Hamlet Essex 30 F5
Coggins Mill E Sus 12 D4
Coig Peighinnean W Isles 91 A10
Coig Peighinnean Bhuirgh W Isles 91 B9
Coignafearn Lodge Highld 81 B8
Coilacriech Aberds 82 D5
Coilantogle Stirling 75 G8
Coilleag W Isles 84 G2
Coillore Highld 85 E8
Coity Bridgend 14 C5
Col W Isles 91 C9
Col Uarach W Isles 91 D9
Colaboll Highld 93 H8
Colan Corn 3 C7
Colaton Raleigh Devon 7 H9
Colbost Highld 84 D7
Colburn N Yorks 58 G2
Colby Cumb 57 D8
Colby IoM 48 E2
Colby Norf 39 B8
Colchester Essex 31 F7
Colcot V Glam 15 E7
Cold Ash W Berks 18 E2
Cold Ashby Northants 36 H2
Cold Ashton S Glos 16 D4
Cold Aston Glos 27 G8
Cold Blow Pembs 22 E6
Cold Brayfield M Keynes 28 C6
Cold Hanworth Lincs 46 D4
Cold Harbour Lincs 36 B5
Cold Hatton Telford 34 C2
Cold Hesledon Durham 58 B5
Cold Higham Northants 28 C3
Cold Kirby N Yorks 51 A11
Cold Newton Leics 36 E3
Cold Northcott Corn 4 C3
Cold Norton Essex 20 A5
Cold Overton Leics 36 D4
Coldbackie Highld 93 D9
Coldbeck Cumb 57 F9
Coldblow London 20 D2
Coldean Brighton 12 F2
Coldeast Devon 5 D9
Colden W Yorks 50 G5
Colden Common Hants 10 B3
Coldfair Green Suff 31 B11
Coldham Cambs 37 E10
Coldharbour Glos 16 A2
Coldharbour Kent 20 F2
Coldharbour Sur 19 G8
Coldingham Borders 71 D8
Coldrain Perth 76 G3
Coldred Kent 21 G9
Coldridge Devon 6 F5
Coldstream Angus 76 D6
Coldstream Borders 71 G7
Coldwaltham W Sus 11 C9
Coldwells Aberds 89 D11
Coldwells Croft Aberds 83 A7
Coldyeld Shrops 33 F9
Cole Som 8 A5
Cole Green Herts 29 G9
Cole Henley Hants 17 F11
Colebatch Shrops 33 G9
Colebrook Devon 7 F9
Colebrooke Devon 7 G6
Coleby Lincs 46 F3
Coleby N Lincs 52 H4
Coleford Devon 7 F6
Coleford Glos 26 G2
Coleford Som 16 G3
Colehill Dorset 9 D9
Coleman's Hatch E Sus 12 C3
Colemere Shrops 33 B10
Colemore Hants 10 A6
Coleorton Leics 35 D10
Colerne Wilts 16 D5
Cole's Green Suff 31 B9
Coles Green Suff 31 D7
Colesbourne Glos 26 G6
Colesden Bedford 29 C8
Coleshill Bucks 18 B6
Coleshill Oxon 17 B9
Coleshill Warks 35 G8
Colestocks Devon 7 F9
Colgate W Sus 11 A11
Colgrain Argyll 68 B2
Colinsburgh Fife 77 G7
Colinton Edin 69 D11
Colintraive Argyll 73 F9
Colkirk Norf 38 C5
Collace Perth 76 D5
Collafirth Shetland 96 G6
Collaton St Mary Torbay 5 F9
College Milton S Lanark 68 E5
Collessie Fife 76 F5
Collier Row London 20 B2
Collier Street Kent 20 G4
Collier's End Herts 29 F10
Collier's Green Kent 13 C6
Colliery Row T&W 58 B4
Collieston Aberds 89 F10
Collin Dumfries 60 F6
Collingbourne Ducis Wilts 17 F9
Collingbourne Kingston Wilts 17 F9
Collingham Notts 46 F2
Collingham W Yorks 51 E9
Collington Hereford 26 B3
Collingtree Northants 28 C4
Collins Green Warr 43 C8
Colliston Angus 77 C9
Collycroft Warks 35 G9
Collynie Aberds 89 E8
Collyweston Northants 36 E5
Colmonell S Ayrs 66 H4
Colmworth Bedford 29 C8
Coln Rogers Glos 27 H7
Coln St Aldwyn's Glos 27 H8
Coln St Dennis Glos 27 G7
Colnabaichin Aberds 82 C4
Colnbrook Slough 19 D7
Colne Cambs 37 H9
Colne Lancs 50 E4
Colne Edge Lancs 50 E4
Colne Engaine Essex 30 E5
Colney Norf 39 E7
Colney Heath Herts 29 H9
Colney Street Herts 19 A8
Colpy Aberds 89 E6
Colquhar Borders 70 F2
Colsterdale N Yorks 51 A7
Colsterworth Lincs 36 C5
Colston Bassett Notts 36 B3
Coltfield Moray 88 B1
Colthouse Cumb 56 G5
Coltishall Norf 39 D8
Coltness N Lanark 69 E7
Colton Cumb 56 H5
Colton N Yorks 51 E11
Colton Norf 39 E7
Colton Staffs 35 C6
Colton W Yorks 51 F9
Colva Powys 25 C9
Colvend Dumfries 55 D11
Colvister Shetland 96 D7
Colwall Green Hereford 26 D4
Colwall Stone Hereford 26 D4
Colwell Northumb 62 F5
Colwich Staffs 34 C6
Colwick Notts 36 A2
Colwinston V Glam 14 D5
Colworth W Sus 11 D8
Colwyn Bay = Bae Colwyn Conwy 41 C10
Colyford Devon 8 E1
Colyton Devon 8 E1
Combe Hereford 25 B10
Combe Oxon 27 G11
Combe W Berks 17 E10
Combe Common Sur 18 H6
Combe Down Bath 16 E4
Combe Florey Som 7 C10
Combe Hay Bath 16 F4
Combe Martin Devon 6 B4
Combe Moor Hereford 25 B10
Combe Raleigh Devon 7 F10
Combe St Nicholas Som 8 C2
Combeinteignhead Devon 5 D10
Comberbach Ches W 43 E9
Comberton Cambs 29 C10
Comberton Hereford 25 B11
Combpyne Devon 8 E1
Combridge Staffs 35 B6
Combrook Warks 27 C10
Combs Derbys 44 E4
Combs Suff 31 C7
Combs Ford Suff 31 C7
Combwich Som 15 G8
Comers Aberds 83 C8
Comins Coch Ceredig 32 G2
Commercial End Cambs 30 B2
Commins Capel Betws Ceredig 24 C3
Commins Coch Powys 32 E4
Common Edge Blackpool 49 F3
Common Side Derbys 45 E7
Commondale N Yorks 59 E7
Commonmoor Corn 4 E3
Commonside Ches W 43 E8
Compstall Gtr Man 44 C3
Compton Devon 5 E9
Compton Hants 10 B3
Compton Sur 18 G5
Compton Sur 18 G6
Compton W Berks 18 D2
Compton W Sus 11 C6
Compton Wilts 17 F8
Compton Abbas Dorset 9 C7
Compton Abdale Glos 27 G7
Compton Bassett Wilts 17 D7
Compton Beauchamp Oxon 17 C9
Compton Bishop Som 15 F9
Compton Chamberlayne Wilts 9 B9
Compton Dando Bath 16 E3
Compton Dundon Som 8 A3
Compton Martin Bath 15 F11
Compton Pauncefoot Som 8 B5
Compton Valence Dorset 8 E4
Comrie Fife 69 B9
Comrie Perth 75 E10
Conaglen House Highld 80 G2
Conchra Argyll 73 E9
Concraigie Perth 76 C4
Conder Green Lancs 49 D4
Conderton Worcs 26 E6
Condicote Glos 27 F8
Condorrat N Lanark 68 C6
Condover Shrops 33 E10
Coney Weston Suff 38 H5
Coneyhurst W Sus 11 B10
Coneysthorpe N Yorks 52 B3
Coneythorpe N Yorks 51 D9
Conford Hants 11 A7
Congash Highld 82 A2
Congdon's Shop Corn 4 D3
Congerstone Leics 35 E9
Congham Norf 38 C3
Congl-y-wal Gwyn 41 F9
Congleton Ches E 44 F2
Congresbury N Som 15 E10
Congreve Staffs 34 D5
Conicavel Moray 87 F12
Coningsby Lincs 46 G6
Conington Cambs 29 B10
Conington Cambs 37 G7
Conisbrough S Yorks 45 C9
Conisby Argyll 64 B3
Conisholme Lincs 47 C8
Coniston Cumb 56 G5
Coniston E Yorks 53 F7
Coniston Cold N Yorks 50 D5
Conistone N Yorks 50 C5
Connah's Quay Flint 42 F5
Connel Argyll 74 D2
Connel Park E Ayrs 67 E9
Connor Downs Corn 2 F4
Conon Bridge Highld 87 F8
Conon House Highld 87 F8
Cononley N Yorks 50 E5
Conordan Highld 85 E10
Consall Staffs 44 H3
Consett Durham 58 A2
Constable Burton N Yorks 58 G2
Constantine Corn 2 G6
Constantine Bay Corn 3 B7
Contin Highld 86 F7
Contlaw Aberdeen 83 C10
Conwy Conwy 41 C9
Conyer Kent 20 E6
Conyers Green Suff 30 B5
Cooden E Sus 12 F6
Cooil IoM 48 E3
Cookbury Devon 6 F3
Cookham Windsor 18 C5
Cookham Dean Windsor 18 C5
Cookham Rise Windsor 18 C5
Cookhill Worcs 27 C7
Cookley Suff 39 H9
Cookley Worcs 34 G4
Cookley Green Oxon 18 B3
Cookney Aberds 83 D10
Cookridge W Yorks 51 E8
Cooksbridge E Sus 12 E3
Cooksmill Green Essex 30 H3
Coolham W Sus 11 B10
Cooling Medway 20 D4
Coombe Corn 3 D8
Coombe Corn 4 F2
Coombe Hants 10 B5
Coombe Wilts 17 F8
Coombe Bissett Wilts 9 B10
Coombe Hill Glos 26 F5
Coombe Keynes Dorset 9 F7
Coombes W Sus 11 D10
Coopersale Common Essex 19 A11
Cootham W Sus 11 C9
Copdock Suff 31 D8
Copford Green Essex 30 F6
Copgrove N Yorks 51 C9
Copister Shetland 96 F6
Cople Bedford 29 D8
Copley Durham 58 D1
Coplow Dale Derbys 44 E5
Copmanthorpe York 52 E1
Coppathorne Corn 4 A3
Coppenhall Staffs 34 D5
Coppenhall Moss Ches E 43 G10
Copperhouse Corn 2 F4
Coppingford Cambs 37 G7
Copplestone Devon 7 F6
Coppull Lancs 43 A8
Coppull Moor Lancs 43 A8
Copsale W Sus 11 B10
Copster Green Lancs 50 F2
Copston Magna Warks 35 G10
Copt Heath W Mid 35 H7
Copt Hewick N Yorks 51 B9
Copt Oak Leics 35 D10
Copthorne Shrops 33 D10
Copthorne Sur 12 C2
Copy's Green Norf 38 B5
Copythorne Hants 10 C2
Corbets Tey London 20 C2
Corbridge Northumb 62 G5
Corby Northants 36 G4
Corby Glen Lincs 36 C5
Cordon N Ayrs 66 C3
Coreley Shrops 26 A3
Cores End Bucks 18 C6
Corfe Som 7 E11
Corfe Castle Dorset 9 F8
Corfe Mullen Dorset 9 E8
Corfton Shrops 33 G10
Corgarff Aberds 82 C4
Corhampton Hants 10 B5
Corlae Dumfries 67 G9
Corley Warks 35 G9
Corley Ash Warks 35 G8
Corley Moor Warks 35 G8
Cornaa IoM 48 D4
Cornabus Argyll 64 D4
Cornel Conwy 41 D9
Corner Row Lancs 49 F4
Corney Cumb 56 G3
Cornforth Durham 58 C4
Cornhill Aberds 88 C5
Cornhill-on-Tweed Northumb 71 G7
Cornholme W Yorks 50 G5
Cornish Hall End Essex 30 E3
Cornquoy Orkney 95 J6
Cornsay Durham 58 B2
Cornsay Colliery Durham 58 B2
Corntown Highld 87 F8
Corntown V Glam 14 D5
Cornwell Oxon 27 F9
Cornwood Devon 5 F7
Cornworthy Devon 5 F9
Corpach Highld 80 F2
Corpusty Norf 39 B7
Corran Highld 74 A3
Corran Highld 85 H13
Corranbuie Argyll 73 G7
Corrany IoM 48 D4
Corrie N Ayrs 66 B3
Corrie Common Dumfries 61 E8
Corriecravie N Ayrs 66 D2
Corriemoillie Highld 86 E6
Corriemulzie Lodge Highld 86 B6
Corrievarkie Lodge Perth 81 F7
Corrievorrie Highld 81 A9
Corrimony Highld 86 H6
Corringham Lincs 46 C2
Corringham Thurrock 20 C4
Corris Gwyn 32 E3
Corris Uchaf Gwyn 32 E3
Corrour Shooting Lodge Highld 80 G6
Corrow Argyll 74 G4
Corry Highld 85 F11
Corry of Ardnagrask Highld 87 G8
Corrykinloch Highld 92 G6
Corrymuckloch Perth 75 D11
Corrynachenchy Argyll 79 G9
Cors-y-Gedol Gwyn 32 C1
Corsback Highld 94 C4
Corscombe Dorset 8 D4
Corse Aberds 88 D6
Corse Glos 26 F4
Corse Lawn Worcs 26 E5
Corse of Kinnoir Aberds 88 D5
Corsewall Dumfries 54 C3
Corsham Wilts 16 D5
Corsindae Aberds 83 C8
Corsley Wilts 16 G5
Corsley Heath Wilts 16 G5
Corsock Dumfries 60 F3
Corston Bath 16 E3
Corston Wilts 16 C6
Corstorphine Edin 69 C10
Cortachy Angus 76 B6
Corton Suff 39 F11
Corton Wilts 16 G6
Corton Denham Som 8 B5
Coruanan Lodge Highld 80 G2
Corunna W Isles 84 B3
Corwen Denb 33 A6
Coryton Devon 4 C5
Coryton Thurrock 20 C4
Cosby Leics 35 F11
Coseley W Mid 34 F5
Cosgrove Northants 28 D4
Cosham Ptsmth 10 D5
Cosheston Pembs 22 F5
Cossall Notts 35 A10
Cossington Leics 36 D2
Cossington Som 15 G9
Costa Orkney 95 F4
Costessey Norf 39 D7
Costock Notts 36 C1
Coston Leics 36 C4
Cote Oxon 17 A10
Cotebrook Ches W 43 F8
Cotehill Cumb 56 A6
Cotes Cumb 56 H6
Cotes Leics 36 C1
Cotes Staffs 34 B4
Cotesbach Leics 35 G11
Cotgrave Notts 36 B2
Cothall Aberds 83 B10
Cotham Notts 45 H11
Cothelstone Som 7 C10
Cotherstone Durham 58 E1
Cothill Oxon 17 B11
Cotleigh Devon 7 F11
Cotmanhay Derbys 35 A10
Cotmaton Devon 7 H10
Coton Cambs 29 C11
Coton Northants 28 A3
Coton Staffs 34 B5
Coton Staffs 34 C4
Coton Staffs 35 E7
Coton Clanford Staffs 34 C4
Coton Hill Shrops 33 D10
Coton Hill Staffs 34 B5
Coton in the Elms Derbys 35 D8
Cott Devon 5 E8
Cottam E Yorks 52 C5
Cottam Lancs 49 F5
Cottam Notts 46 E2
Cottartown Highld 87 H13
Cottenham Cambs 29 B11
Cotterdale N Yorks 57 G10
Cottered Herts 29 F10
Cotteridge W Mid 34 H6
Cotterstock Northants 36 F6
Cottesbrooke Northants 28 A4
Cottesmore Rutland 36 D5
Cottevylands Devon 7 E8
Cottingham E Yorks 52 F6
Cottingham Northants 36 F4
Cottingley W Yorks 51 F7
Cottisford Oxon 28 E2
Cotton Staffs 44 H4
Cotton Suff 31 B7
Cotton End Bedford 29 D7
Cottown Aberds 83 A7
Cottown Aberds 83 B9
Cottown Aberds 89 D8
Cotwalton Staffs 34 B5
Couch's Mill Corn 4 F2
Coughton Hereford 26 F2
Coughton Warks 27 B7
Coulaghailtro Argyll 72 G6
Coulags Highld 86 G2
Coulby Newham Mbro 58 E6
Coulderton Cumb 56 F1
Coulin Highld 86 F3
Coull Aberds 83 C7
Coull Argyll 64 B3
Coulport Argyll 73 E11
Coulsdon London 19 F9
Coulston Wilts 16 F6
Coulter S Lanark 69 G9
Coulton N Yorks 52 B2
Cound Shrops 34 E1
Coundon Durham 58 D3
Coundon W Mid 35 G9
Coundon Grange Durham 58 D3
Countersett N Yorks 57 H11
Countess Wilts 17 G8
Countess Wear Devon 5 C10
Countesthorpe Leics 36 F1
Countisbury Devon 7 B6
County Oak W Sus 12 C1
Coup Green Lancs 50 G1
Coupar Angus Perth 76 C5
Coupland Northumb 71 G8
Cour Argyll 65 D9
Courance Dumfries 60 D6
Court-at-Street Kent 13 C9
Court Henry Carms 23 D10
Courteenhall Northants 28 C4
Courtsend Essex 21 B7
Courtway Som 7 C11
Cousland Midloth 70 D2
Cousley Wood E Sus 12 C5
Cove Argyll 73 E11
Cove Borders 70 C6
Cove Devon 7 E8
Cove Hants 18 F5
Cove Highld 91 H13
Cove Bay Aberdeen 83 C11
Cove Bottom Suff 39 H10
Covehithe Suff 39 G11
Coven Staffs 34 E5
Coveney Cambs 37 G10
Covenham St Bartholomew Lincs 47 C7
Covenham St Mary Lincs 47 C7
Coventry W Mid 35 H9
Coverack Corn 3 H6
Coverham N Yorks 58 H2
Covesea Moray 88 A1
Covington Cambs 29 A7
Covington S Lanark 69 G8
Cow Ark Lancs 50 E2
Cowan Bridge Lancs 50 B2
Cowbeech E Sus 12 E5
Cowbit Lincs 37 D8
Cowbridge Lincs 47 H7
Cowbridge Som 7 B8
Cowbridge = Y Bont-Faen V Glam 14 D5
Cowdale Derbys 44 E4
Cowden Kent 12 B3
Cowdenbeath Fife 69 A10
Cowdenburn Borders 69 E11
Cowers Lane Derbys 45 H7
Cowes IoW 10 E3
Cowesby N Yorks 58 H5
Cowfold W Sus 11 B11
Cowgill Cumb 57 H9
Cowie Aberds 83 E10
Cowie Stirling 69 B7
Cowley Devon 7 G8
Cowley Glos 26 G6
Cowley London 19 C7
Cowley Oxon 18 A2
Cowleymoor Devon 7 E8
Cowling N Yorks 50 E5
Cowling N Yorks 58 H3
Cowlinge Suff 30 C4
Cowpe Lancs 50 G4
Cowpen Northumb 63 E9
Cowpen Bewley Stockton 58 D5
Cowplain Hants 10 C5
Cowshill Durham 57 B10
Cowslip Green N Som 15 E10
Cowstrandburn Fife 69 A9
Cowthorpe N Yorks 51 D10
Cox Common Suff 39 G10
Cox Green Windsor 18 D5
Cox Moor Notts 45 G9
Coxbank Ches E 34 A2
Coxbench Derbys 35 A9
Coxford Norf 38 C4
Coxford Soton 10 C2
Coxheath Kent 20 F4
Coxhill Kent 21 G9
Coxhoe Durham 58 C4
Coxley Som 15 G11
Coxwold N Yorks 51 B11
Coychurch Bridgend 14 D5
Coylton S Ayrs 67 D7
Coylumbridge Highld 81 B11
Coynach Aberds 82 C6
Coynachie Aberds 88 E4
Coytrahen Bridgend 14 C4
Crabadon Devon 5 F8
Crabbs Cross Worcs 27 B7
Crabtree W Sus 11 B11
Crackenthorpe Cumb 57 D8
Crackington Haven Corn 4 B2
Crackley Warks 27 A9
Crackleybank Shrops 34 D3
Crackpot N Yorks 57 G11
Cracoe N Yorks 50 C5
Craddock Devon 7 E9
Cradhlastadh W Isles 90 D5
Cradley Hereford 26 D4
Cradley Heath W Mid 34 G5
Crafthole Corn 4 F4
Cragg Vale W Yorks 50 G6
Craggan Highld 82 A2
Craggie Highld 87 H10
Craggie Highld 93 H11
Craghead Durham 58 A3
Crai Powys 24 F5
Craibstone Moray 88 C4
Craichie Angus 77 C8
Craig Dumfries 55 B9
Craig Dumfries 55 C9
Craig Highld 86 G3
Craig Castle Aberds 82 A6
Craig-cefn-parc Swansea 14 A2
Craig Penllyn V Glam 14 D5
Craig-y-don Conwy 41 B9
Craig-y-nos Powys 24 G5
Craiganor Lodge Perth 75 B9
Craigdam Aberds 89 E8
Craigdarroch Dumfries 60 D3
Craigdarroch Highld 86 F7
Craigdhu Highld 86 G7
Craigearn Aberds 83 B9
Craigellachie Moray 88 D2
Craigencross Dumfries 54 C3
Craigend Perth 76 E4
Craigend Stirling 68 B6
Craigendive Argyll 73 E9
Craigendoran Argyll 68 B2
Craigends Renfs 68 D3
Craigens Argyll 64 B3
Craigens E Ayrs 67 E8
Craighat Stirling 68 B3
Craighead Fife 77 G9
Craighlaw Mains Dumfries 54 C6
Craighouse Argyll 72 G4
Craigie Aberds 83 B11
Craigie Dundee 77 D7
Craigie Perth 76 C4
Craigie Perth 76 E4
Craigie S Ayrs 67 C7
Craigiefield Orkney 95 G5
Craigielaw E Loth 70 C3
Craiglockhart Edin 69 C11
Craigmalloch E Ayrs 67 G7
Craigmaud Aberds 89 C8
Craigmillar Edin 69 C11
Craigmore Argyll 73 G10
Craignant Shrops 33 B8
Craigneuk N Lanark 68 D6
Craigneuk N Lanark 68 E6
Craignure Argyll 79 H10
Craigo Angus 77 A9
Craigow Perth 76 G3
Craigrothie Fife 76 F6
Craigroy Moray 87 F14
Craigruie Stirling 75 E7
Craigston Castle Aberds 89 C7
Craigton Aberdeen 83 C10
Craigton Angus 76 B6
Craigton Angus 77 D8
Craigton Highld 87 B9
Craigtown Highld 93 D11
Craik Borders 61 C9
Crail Fife 77 G9
Crailing Borders 62 A2
Crailinghall Borders 62 A2
Craiselound N Lincs 45 C11
Crakehill N Yorks 51 B10
Crakemarsh Staffs 35 B6
Crambe N Yorks 52 C3
Cramlington Northumb 63 F8
Cramond Edin 69 C10
Cramond Bridge Edin 69 C10
Cranage Ches E 43 F10
Cranberry Staffs 34 B4
Cranborne Dorset 9 C9
Cranbourne Brack 18 D6
Cranbrook Kent 13 C6
Cranbrook Common Kent 13 C6
Crane Moor S Yorks 45 B7
Crane's Corner Norf 38 D5
Cranfield C Beds 28 D6
Cranford London 19 D8
Cranford St Andrew Northants 36 H5
Cranford St John Northants 36 H5
Cranham Glos 26 G5
Cranham London 20 C2
Crank Mers 43 C8
Crank Wood Gtr Man 43 B9
Cranleigh Sur 19 H7
Cranley Suff 31 A8
Cranmer Green Suff 31 A7
Cranmore IoW 10 E2

Cranna Aberds 89 C6
Crannich Argyll 79 G8
Crannoch Moray 88 C4
Cranoe Leics 36 F3
Cransford Suff 31 B10
Cranshaws Borders 70 D5
Cranstal IoM 48 B4
Crantock Corn 3 C6
Cranwell Lincs 46 H4
Cranwich Norf 38 F3
Cranworth Norf 38 E5
Craobh Haven Argyll 72 C6
Crapstone Devon 4 E6
Crarae Argyll 73 D8
Crask Inn Highld 93 G8
Crask of Aigas Highld 86 G7
Craskins Aberds 83 C7
Craster Northumb 63 B8
Craswall Hereford 25 E9
Cratfield Suff 39 H9
Crathes Aberds 83 D9
Crathie Aberds 82 D4
Crathie Highld 81 D7
Crathorne N Yorks 58 F5
Craven Arms Shrops 33 G10
Crawcrook T&W 63 G7
Crawford Lancs 43 B7
Crawford S Lanark 60 A5
Crawfordjohn S Lanark 60 A4
Crawick Dumfries 60 B3
Crawley Hants 10 A3
Crawley Oxon 27 G10
Crawley W Sus 12 C1
Crawley Down W Sus 12 C2
Crawleyside Durham 57 B11
Crawshawbooth Lancs 50 G4
Crawton Aberds 83 F10
Cray N Yorks 50 B5
Cray Perth 76 A4
Crayford London 20 D2
Crayke N Yorks 52 B1
Crays Hill Essex 20 B4
Cray's Pond Oxon 18 C3
Creacombe Devon 7 E7
Creag Ghoraidh W Isles 84 D2
Creagan Argyll 74 C2
Creaguaineach Lodge Highld 80 G5
Creaksea Essex 20 B6
Creaton Northants 28 A4
Creca Dumfries 61 F8
Credenhill Hereford 25 D11
Crediton Devon 7 F7
Creebridge Dumfries 55 C7
Creech Heathfield Som 8 B1
Creech St Michael Som 8 B1
Creed Corn 3 E8
Creekmouth London 19 C11
Creeting Bottoms Suff 31 C8
Creeting St Mary Suff 31 C7
Creeton Lincs 36 C6
Creetown Dumfries 55 D7
Creg-ny-Baa IoM 48 D3
Creggans Argyll 73 C9
Cregneash IoM 48 F1
Cregrina Powys 25 C8
Creich Fife 76 E6
Creigiau Cardiff 14 C6
Cremyll Corn 4 F5
Creslow Bucks 28 F5
Cressage Shrops 34 E1
Cressbrook Derbys 44 E5
Cresselly Pembs 22 F5
Cressing Essex 30 F4
Cresswell Northumb 63 D8
Cresswell Staffs 34 B5
Cresswell Quay Pembs 22 F5
Creswell Derbys 45 E9
Cretingham Suff 31 B9
Cretshengan Argyll 72 G6
Crewe Ches E 43 G10
Crewe Ches W 43 G7
Crewgreen Powys 33 D9
Crewkerne Som 8 D3
Crianlarich Stirling 74 E6
Cribyn Ceredig 23 A10
Criccieth Gwyn 40 G6
Crich Derbys 45 G7
Crichie Aberds 89 D9
Crichton Midloth 70 D2
Crick Mon 15 B10
Crick Northants 28 A2
Crickadarn Powys 25 D7
Cricket Malherbie Som 8 C2
Cricket St Thomas Som 8 D2
Crickheath Shrops 33 C8
Crickhowell Powys 25 G9
Cricklade Wilts 17 B8
Cricklewood London 19 C9
Cridling Stubbs N Yorks 51 G11
Crieff Perth 75 E11
Criggion Powys 33 D8
Crigglestone W Yorks 51 H9
Crimond Aberds 89 C10
Crimonmogate Aberds 89 C10
Crimplesham Norf 38 E2
Crinan Argyll 72 D6
Cringleford Norf 39 E7
Cringles W Yorks 50 E6
Crinow Pembs 22 E6
Cripplesease Corn 2 F4
Cripplestyle Dorset 9 C9
Cripp's Corner E Sus 13 D6
Croasdale Cumb 56 E2
Crock Street Som 8 C2
Crockenhill Kent 20 E2
Crockernwell Devon 7 G6
Crockerton Wilts 16 G5
Crocketford or Ninemile Bar Dumfries 60 F4
Crockey Hill York 52 E2
Crockham Hill Kent 19 F11
Crockleford Heath Essex 31 F7
Crockness Orkney 95 J4
Croes-goch Pembs 22 C3
Croes-lan Ceredig 23 B8
Croes-y-mwyalch Torf 15 B9
Croeserw Neath 14 B4
Croesor Gwyn 41 F8
Croesyceiliog Carms 23 E9
Croesyceiliog Torf 15 B9
Croesywaun Gwyn 41 E7
Croft Leics 35 F11
Croft Lincs 47 F9
Croft Pembs 22 B6
Croft Warr 43 C9
Croft-on-Tees N Yorks 58 F3
Croftamie Stirling 68 B3
Croftmalloch W Loth 69 D8
Crofton W Yorks 51 H9
Crofton Wilts 17 E9
Crofts of Benachielt Highld 94 G3
Crofts of Haddo Aberds 89 E8
Crofts of Inverthernie Aberds 89 D7
Crofts of Meikle Ardo Aberds 89 D8
Crofty Swansea 23 G10
Croggan Argyll 79 J10
Croglin Cumb 57 B7
Croich Highld 86 B7
Crois Dughaill W Isles 84 F2
Cromarty Highld 87 E10
Cromblet Aberds 89 E7
Cromdale Highld 82 A2
Cromer Herts 29 F9
Cromer Norf 39 A8
Cromford Derbys 44 G6
Cromhall S Glos 16 B3
Cromhall Common S Glos 16 C3
Cromor W Isles 91 E9
Cromra Highld 81 D7
Cromwell Notts 45 F11
Cronberry E Ayrs 68 H5
Crondall Hants 18 G4
Cronk-y-Voddy IoM 48 D3
Cronton Mers 43 D7
Crook Cumb 56 G6
Crook Durham 58 C2
Crook of Devon Perth 76 G3
Crookedholm E Ayrs 67 C7
Crookes S Yorks 45 D7
Crookham Northumb 71 G8
Crookham W Berks 18 E2
Crookham Village Hants 18 F4
Crookhaugh Borders 69 H10
Crookhouse Borders 70 H6
Crooklands Cumb 49 A5
Cropredy Oxon 27 D11
Cropston Leics 36 D1
Cropthorne Worcs 26 D6
Cropton N Yorks 59 H8
Cropwell Bishop Notts 36 B2
Cropwell Butler Notts 36 B2
Cros W Isles 91 A10
Crosbost W Isles 91 E8
Crosby Cumb 56 C2
Crosby IoM 48 E3
Crosby N Lincs 46 A2
Crosby Garrett Cumb 57 F9
Crosby Ravensworth Cumb 57 E8
Crosby Villa Cumb 56 C2
Croscombe Som 16 G2
Cross Som 15 F10
Cross Ash Mon 25 G11
Cross-at-Hand Kent 20 G4
Cross Green Devon 4 C4
Cross Green Suff 30 C6
Cross Green Suff 30 C5
Cross Green Warks 27 C10
Cross-hands Carms 22 D6
Cross Hands Carms 23 E10
Cross Hands Pembs 22 E5
Cross Hill Derbys 45 H8
Cross Houses Shrops 33 E11
Cross in Hand E Sus 12 D4
Cross in Hand Leics 35 G11
Cross Inn Ceredig 23 A8
Cross Inn Ceredig 24 B2
Cross Inn Rhondda 14 C6
Cross Keys Kent 20 F2
Cross Lane Head Shrops 34 F3
Cross Lanes Corn 2 G5
Cross Lanes N Yorks 51 C11
Cross Lanes Wrex 43 H6
Cross o' th' hands Derbys 44 H6
Cross Oak Powys 25 F8
Cross of Jackston Aberds 89 E7
Cross Street Suff 39 H7
Cross Trickett's Dorset 9 D9
Crossaig Argyll 65 C9
Crossal Highld 85 E9
Crossapol Argyll 78 G2
Crossburn Falk 69 C7
Crossbush W Sus 11 D9
Crosscanonby Cumb 56 C2
Crossdale Street Norf 39 B8
Crossens Mers 49 H3
Crossflatts W Yorks 51 E7
Crossford Fife 69 B9
Crossford S Lanark 69 F7
Crossgate Lincs 37 C8
Crossgatehall E Loth 70 D2
Crossgates Fife 69 B10
Crossgates Powys 25 B7
Crossgill Lancs 50 C1
Crosshill E Ayrs 67 D7
Crosshill Fife 76 H4
Crosshill S Ayrs 66 F6
Crosshouse E Ayrs 67 C6
Crossings Cumb 61 F11
Crosskeys Caerph 15 B8
Crosskirk Highld 93 B13
Crosslanes Shrops 33 D9
Crosslee Borders 61 B9
Crosslee Renfs 68 D3
Crossmichael Dumfries 55 C10
Crossmoor Lancs 49 F4
Crossroads Aberds 83 D9
Crossroads E Ayrs 67 C7
Crossway Hereford 26 E3
Crossway Mon 25 G11
Crossway Powys 25 C7
Crossway Green Worcs 26 B5
Crossways Dorset 9 F6
Crosswell Pembs 22 C6
Crosswood Ceredig 24 A3
Crosthwaite Cumb 56 G6
Croston Lancs 49 H4
Crostwick Norf 39 D8
Crostwight Norf 39 C9
Crothair W Isles 90 D6
Crouch Kent 20 F3
Crouch Hill Dorset 8 C6
Crouch House Green Kent 19 G11
Croucheston Wilts 9 B9
Croughton Northants 28 E2
Crovie Aberds 89 B8
Crow Edge S Yorks 44 B5
Crow Hill Hereford 26 F3
Crowan Corn 2 F5
Crowborough E Sus 12 C4
Crowcombe Som 7 C10
Crowdecote Derbys 44 F5
Crowden Derbys 44 C4
Crowell Oxon 18 B4
Crowfield Northants 28 D3
Crowfield Suff 31 C8
Crowhurst E Sus 13 E6
Crowhurst Sur 19 G10
Crowhurst Lane End Sur 19 G10
Crowland Lincs 37 D8
Crowlas Corn 2 F4
Crowle N Lincs 45 A11
Crowle Worcs 26 C6
Crowmarsh Gifford Oxon 18 C3
Crown Corner Suff 31 A9
Crownhill Plym 4 F5
Crownland Suff 31 B7
Crownthorpe Norf 39 E6
Crowntown Corn 2 F5
Crows-an-wra Corn 2 G2
Crowshill Norf 38 E5
Crowsnest Shrops 33 E9
Crowthorne Brack 18 E5
Crowton Ches W 43 E8
Croxall Staffs 35 D7
Croxby Lincs 46 C5
Croxdale Durham 58 C3
Croxden Staffs 35 B6
Croxley Green Herts 19 B7
Croxton Cambs 29 B9
Croxton N Lincs 46 A4
Croxton Norf 38 G4
Croxton Staffs 34 B3
Croxton Kerrial Leics 36 C4
Croxtonbank Staffs 34 B3
Croy Highld 87 G10
Croy N Lanark 68 C6
Croyde Devon 6 C3
Croydon Cambs 29 D10
Croydon London 19 E10
Crubenmore Lodge Highld 81 D8
Cruckmeole Shrops 33 E10
Cruckton Shrops 33 D10
Cruden Bay Aberds 89 E10
Crudgington Telford 34 D2
Crudwell Wilts 16 B6
Crug Powys 25 A8
Crugmeer Corn 3 B8
Crugybar Carms 24 E3
Crulabhig W Isles 90 D6
Crumlin = Crymlyn Caerph 15 B8
Crumpsall Gtr Man 44 B2
Crundale Kent 21 G7
Crundale Pembs 22 E4
Cruwys Morchard Devon 7 E7
Crux Easton Hants 17 F11
Crwbin Carms 23 E9
Crya Orkney 95 H4
Cryers Hill Bucks 18 B5
Crymlyn = Crumlin Caerph 15 B8
Crymlyn Gwyn 41 C8
Crymych Pembs 22 C6
Crynant Neath 14 A3
Crynfryn Ceredig 24 B2
Cuaig Highld 85 C12
Cuan Argyll 72 B6
Cubbington Warks 27 B10
Cubeck N Yorks 57 H11
Cubert Corn 3 D6
Cubley S Yorks 44 B6
Cubley Common Derbys 35 B7
Cublington Bucks 28 F5
Cublington Hereford 25 E11
Cuckfield W Sus 12 D2
Cucklington Som 9 B6
Cuckney Notts 45 E9
Cuckoo Hill Notts 45 C11
Cuddesdon Oxon 18 A3
Cuddington Bucks 28 G4
Cuddington Ches W 43 E8
Cuddington Heath Ches W 43 H7
Cuddy Hill Lancs 49 F4
Cudham London 19 F11
Cudliptown Devon 4 D6
Cudworth S Yorks 45 B7
Cudworth Som 8 C2
Cuffley Herts 19 A10
Cuiashader W Isles 91 B10
Cuidhir W Isles 84 H1
Cuidhtinis W Isles 90 J5
Culbo Highld 87 E9
Culbokie Highld 87 F9
Culburnie Highld 86 G7
Culcabock Highld 87 G9
Culcairn Highld 87 E9
Culcharry Highld 87 F11
Culcheth Warr 43 C9
Culdrain Aberds 88 E5
Culduie Highld 85 D12
Culford Suff 30 A5
Culgaith Cumb 57 D8
Culham Oxon 18 B2
Culkein Highld 92 F3
Culkein Drumbeg Highld 92 F4
Culkerton Glos 16 B6
Cullachie Highld 81 A11
Cullen Moray 88 B5
Cullercoats T&W 63 F9
Cullicudden Highld 87 E9
Cullingworth W Yorks 51 F6
Cullipool Argyll 72 B6
Cullivoe Shetland 96 C7
Culloch Perth 75 F10
Culloden Highld 87 G10
Cullompton Devon 7 F9
Culmaily Highld 87 B11
Culmazie Dumfries 54 D6
Culmington Shrops 33 G10
Culmstock Devon 7 E10
Culnacraig Highld 92 J3
Culnaknock Highld 85 B10
Culpho Suff 31 D9
Culrain Highld 87 B8
Culross Fife 69 B8
Culroy S Ayrs 66 E6
Culsh Aberds 82 D5
Culsh Aberds 89 D8
Culshabbin Dumfries 54 D6
Culswick Shetland 96 J4
Cultercullen Aberds 89 F9
Cults Aberdeen 83 C10
Cults Aberds 88 E5
Cults Dumfries 55 E7
Culverstone Green Kent 20 E3
Culverthorpe Lincs 36 A6
Culworth Northants 28 D2
Culzie Lodge Highld 87 D8
Cumbernauld N Lanark 68 C6
Cumbernauld Village N Lanark 68 C6
Cumberworth Lincs 47 E9
Cuminestown Aberds 89 C8
Cumlewick Shetland 96 L6
Cummersdale Cumb 56 A5
Cummertrees Dumfries 61 G7
Cummingston Moray 88 B1
Cumnock E Ayrs 67 D8
Cumnor Oxon 17 A11
Cumrew Cumb 57 A7
Cumwhinton Cumb 56 A6
Cumwhitton Cumb 57 A7
Cundall N Yorks 51 B10
Cunninghamhead N Ayrs 67 B6
Cunnister Shetland 96 D7
Cupar Fife 76 F6
Cupar Muir Fife 76 F6
Cupernham Hants 10 B2
Curbar Derbys 44 E6
Curbridge Hants 10 C4
Curbridge Oxon 27 H10
Curdridge Hants 10 C4
Curdworth Warks 35 F7
Curland Som 8 C1
Curlew Green Suff 31 B10
Currarie S Ayrs 66 G4
Curridge W Berks 17 D11
Currie Edin 69 D10
Curry Mallet Som 8 B2
Curry Rivel Som 8 B2
Curtisden Green Kent 12 B6
Curtisknowle Devon 5 F8
Cury Corn 2 G5
Cushnie Aberds 89 B7
Cushuish Som 7 C11
Cusop Hereford 25 D9
Cutcloy Dumfries 55 F7
Cutcombe Som 7 C8
Cutgate Gtr Man 44 A2
Cutiau Gwyn 32 D2
Cutlers Green Essex 30 E2
Cutnall Green Worcs 26 B5
Cutsdean Glos 27 E7
Cutthorpe Derbys 45 E7
Cutts Shetland 96 K6
Cuxham Oxon 18 B3
Cuxton Medway 20 E4
Cuxwold Lincs 46 B5
Cwm Bl Gwent 25 H8
Cwm Denb 42 E3
Cwm Swansea 14 B2
Cwm-byr Carms 24 E3
Cwm-Cewydd Gwyn 32 D4
Cwm-cou Ceredig 23 B7
Cwm-Dulais Swansea 14 A2
Cwm-felin-fach Caerph 15 B7
Cwm Ffrwd-oer Torf 15 A8
Cwm-hesgen Gwyn 32 C3
Cwm-hwnt Rhondda 24 H6
Cwm Irfon Powys 24 D5
Cwm-Llinau Powys 32 E4
Cwm-mawr Carms 23 E10
Cwm-parc Rhondda 14 B5
Cwm Penmachno Conwy 41 F9
Cwm-y-glo Carms 23 E10
Cwm-y-glo Gwyn 41 D7
Cwmafan Neath 14 B3
Cwmaman Rhondda 14 B6
Cwmann Carms 23 B10
Cwmavon Torf 25 H9
Cwmbach Carms 23 D7
Cwmbach Carms 23 F9
Cwmbach Powys 25 C7
Cwmbach Powys 25 E8
Cwmbach Rhondda 14 A6
Cwmbelan Powys 32 G5
Cwmbran = Cwmbrân Torf 15 B8
Cwmbrân = Cwmbran Torf 15 B8
Cwmbrwyno Ceredig 32 G3
Cwmcarn Caerph 15 B8
Cwmcarvan Mon 25 H11
Cwmcych Carms 23 C7
Cwmdare Rhondda 14 A5
Cwmderwen Powys 32 E5
Cwmdu Carms 24 E3
Cwmdu Powys 25 F8
Cwmdu Swansea 14 B2
Cwmduad Carms 23 C8
Cwmdwr Carms 24 E4
Cwmfelin Bridgend 14 C4
Cwmfelin M Tydf 14 A6
Cwmfelin Boeth Carms 22 E6
Cwmfelin Mynach Carms 23 D7
Cwmffrwd Carms 23 E9
Cwmgiedd Powys 24 G4
Cwmgors Neath 24 G4
Cwmgwili Carms 23 E10
Cwmgwrach Neath 14 A4
Cwmhiraeth Carms 23 C8
Cwmifor Carms 24 F3
Cwmisfael Carms 23 E9
Cwmllynfell Neath 24 G4
Cwmorgan Pembs 23 C7
Cwmpengraig Carms 23 C8
Cwmrhos Powys 25 F8
Cwmsychpant Ceredig 23 B9
Cwmtillery Bl Gwent 25 H9
Cwmwysg Powys 24 F5
Cwmyoy Mon 25 F9
Cwmystwyth Ceredig 24 A4
Cwrt Gwyn 32 E2
Cwrt-newydd Ceredig 23 B9
Cwrt-y-cadno Carms 24 D3
Cwrt-y-gollen Powys 25 G9
Cydweli = Kidwelly Carms 23 F9
Cyffordd Llandudno = Llandudno Junction Conwy 41 C9
Cyffylliog Denb 42 G3
Cyfronydd Powys 33 E7
Cymer Neath 14 B4
Cyncoed Cardiff 15 C7
Cynghordy Carms 24 D5
Cynheidre Carms 23 F9
Cynwyd Denb 33 A6
Cynwyl Elfed Carms 23 D8
Cywarch Gwyn 32 D4

D

Dacre Cumb 56 D6
Dacre N Yorks 51 C7
Dacre Banks N Yorks 51 C7
Daddry Shield Durham 57 C10
Dadford Bucks 28 E3
Dadlington Leics 35 F10
Dafarn Faig Gwyn 40 F6
Dafen Carms 23 F10
Daffy Green Norf 38 E5
Dagenham London 19 C11
Daglingworth Glos 26 H6
Dagnall Bucks 28 G6
Dail Beag W Isles 90 C7
Dail bho Dheas W Isles 91 A9
Dail bho Thuath W Isles 91 A9
Dail Mor W Isles 90 C7
Daill Argyll 64 B4
Dailly S Ayrs 66 F5
Dairsie or Osnaburgh Fife 77 F7
Daisy Hill Gtr Man 43 B9
Dalabrog W Isles 84 F2
Dalavich Argyll 73 B8
Dalbeattie Dumfries 55 C11
Dalblair E Ayrs 67 E9
Dalbog Angus 83 F7
Dalbury Derbys 35 B8
Dalby IoM 48 E2
Dalby N Yorks 52 B2
Dalchalloch Perth 75 A10
Dalchalm Highld 93 J12
Dalchenna Argyll 73 C9
Dalchirach Moray 88 E1
Dalchork Highld 93 H8
Dalchreichart Highld 80 B4
Dalchruin Perth 75 F10
Dalderby Lincs 46 F6
Dale Pembs 22 F3
Dale Abbey Derbys 35 B10
Dale Head Cumb 56 E6
Dale of Walls Shetland 96 H3
Dalelia Highld 79 E10
Daless Highld 87 H11
Dalfaber Highld 81 B11
Dalgarven N Ayrs 66 B5
Dalgety Bay Fife 69 B10
Dalginross Perth 75 E10
Dalguise Perth 76 C2
Dalhalvaig Highld 93 D11
Dalham Suff 30 B4
Dalinlongart Argyll 73 E10
Dalkeith Midloth 70 D2
Dallam Warr 43 C8
Dallas Moray 87 F14
Dalleagles E Ayrs 67 E8
Dallinghoo Suff 31 C9
Dallington E Sus 12 E5
Dallington Northants 28 B4
Dallow N Yorks 51 B7
Dalmadilly Aberds 83 B9
Dalmally Argyll 74 E4
Dalmarnock Glasgow 68 D5
Dalmary Stirling 75 H8
Dalmellington E Ayrs 67 F7
Dalmeny Edin 69 C10
Dalmigavie Highld 81 B9
Dalmigavie Lodge Highld 81 A9
Dalmore Highld 87 E9
Dalmuir W Dunb 68 C3
Dalnabreck Highld 79 E9
Dalnacardoch Lodge Perth 81 F9
Dalnacroich Highld 86 F6
Dalnagiar Castle Perth 76 A4
Dalnahaitnach Highld 81 A10
Dalnaspidal Lodge Perth 81 F8
Dalnavaid Perth 76 A3
Dalnavie Highld 87 D9
Dalnawillan Lodge Highld 93 E13
Dalness Highld 74 B4
Dalnessie Highld 93 H9
Dalqueich Perth 76 G3
Dalreavoch Highld 93 J10
Dalry N Ayrs 66 B5
Dalrymple E Ayrs 67 E6
Dalserf S Lanark 69 E7
Dalston Cumb 56 A5
Dalswinton Dumfries 60 E5
Dalton Dumfries 61 F7
Dalton Lancs 43 B7
Dalton N Yorks 51 B10
Dalton N Yorks 58 F2
Dalton Northumb 62 H5
Dalton Northumb 63 F7
Dalton S Yorks 45 C8
Dalton-in-Furness Cumb 49 B2
Dalton-le-Dale Durham 58 B5
Dalton-on-Tees N Yorks 58 F3
Dalton Piercy Hrtlpl 58 C5
Dalveich Stirling 75 E9
Dalvina Lo. Highld 93 E10
Dalwhinnie Highld 81 E8
Dalwood Devon 8 D1
Dalwyne S Ayrs 66 G6
Dam Green Norf 39 G6
Dam Side Lancs 49 E4
Damerham Hants 9 C10
Damgate Norf 39 E10
Damnaglaur Dumfries 54 F4
Damside Borders 69 F10
Danbury Essex 30 H4
Danby N Yorks 59 F8
Danby Wiske N Yorks 58 G4
Dandaleith Moray 88 D2
Danderhall Midloth 70 D2
Dane End Herts 29 F10
Danebridge Ches E 44 F3
Danehill E Sus 12 D3
Danemoor Green Norf 39 E6
Danesford Shrops 34 F3
Daneshill Hants 18 F3
Dangerous Corner Lancs 43 A8
Dankirke Highld 87 F11
Danskine E Loth 70 D4
Darcy Lever Gtr Man 43 B10
Darenth Kent 20 D2
Daresbury Halton 43 D8
Darfield S Yorks 45 B8
Darfoulds Notts 45 E9
Dargate Kent 21 E7
Darite Corn 4 E3
Darlaston W Mid 34 F5
Darley N Yorks 51 D8
Darley Bridge Derbys 44 F6
Darley Head N Yorks 51 D7
Darlingscott Warks 27 D9
Darlington Darl 58 E3
Darliston Shrops 34 B1
Darlton Notts 45 E11
Darnall S Yorks 45 D7
Darnick Borders 70 G4
Darowen Powys 32 E4
Darra Aberds 89 D7
Darracott Devon 6 C3
Darras Hall Northumb 63 F7
Darrington W Yorks 51 G10
Darsham Suff 31 B11
Dartford Kent 20 D2
Dartford Crossing Kent 20 D2
Dartington Devon 5 E8
Dartmeet Devon 5 D7
Dartmouth Devon 5 F9
Darton S Yorks 45 B7
Darvel E Ayrs 68 G4
Darwell Hole E Sus 12 E5
Darwen Blackburn 50 G2
Datchet Windsor 18 D6
Datchworth Herts 29 G9
Datchworth Green Herts 29 G9
Daubhill Gtr Man 43 B10
Daugh of Kinermony Moray 88 D2
Dauntsey Wilts 16 C6
Dava Moray 87 H13
Davenham Ches W 43 E9
Davenport Green Ches E 44 E2
Daventry Northants 28 B2
David's Well Powys 33 H6
Davidson's Mains Edin 69 C11
Davidstow Corn 4 C2
Davington Dumfries 61 C8
Daviot Aberds 83 A9
Daviot Highld 87 H10
Davoch of Grange Moray 88 C4
Davyhulme Gtr Man 43 C10
Dawley Telford 34 E2
Dawlish Devon 5 D10
Dawlish Warren Devon 5 D10
Dawn Conwy 41 C10
Daws Heath Essex 20 C5
Daw's House Corn 4 C4
Dawsmere Lincs 37 B10
Dayhills Staffs 34 B5
Daylesford Glos 27 F9
Ddôl-Cownwy Powys 32 D6
Ddrydwy Anglesey 40 C5
Deadwater Northumb 62 D2
Deaf Hill Durham 58 C4
Deal Kent 21 F10
Deal Hall Essex 21 B7
Dean Cumb 56 D2
Dean Devon 5 E8
Dean Devon 6 B4
Dean Dorset 9 C8
Dean Hants 10 C4
Dean Som 16 G3
Dean Prior Devon 5 E8
Dean Row Ches E 44 D2
Deanburnhaugh Borders 61 B9
Deane Gtr Man 43 B9
Deane Hants 18 F2
Deanich Lodge Highld 86 C6
Deanland Dorset 9 C8
Deans W Loth 69 D9
Deanscales Cumb 56 D2
Deanshanger Northants 28 E4
Deanston Stirling 75 G10
Dearham Cumb 56 C2
Debach Suff 31 C9
Debden Essex 19 B11
Debden Essex 30 E2
Debden Cross Essex 30 E2
Debenham Suff 31 B8
Dechmont W Loth 69 C9
Deddington Oxon 27 E11
Dedham Essex 31 E7
Dedham Heath Essex 31 E7
Deebank Aberds 83 D8
Deene Northants 36 F5
Deenethorpe Northants 36 F5
Deepcar S Yorks 44 C6
Deepcut Sur 18 F6
Deepdale Cumb 50 A3
Deeping Gate Lincs 37 E7
Deeping St James Lincs 37 E7
Deeping St Nicholas Lincs 37 D8
Deerhill Moray 88 C4
Deerhurst Glos 26 F5
Deerness Orkney 95 H6
Defford Worcs 26 D6
Defynnog Powys 24 F6
Deganwy Conwy 41 C9
Deighton N Yorks 58 F4
Deighton W Yorks 51 H7
Deighton York 52 E2
Deiniolen Gwyn 41 D7
Delabole Corn 4 C1
Delamere Ches W 43 F8
Delfrigs Aberds 89 F9
Dell Lodge Highld 82 B2
Delliefure Highld 87 H13
Delnabo Moray 82 B3
Delnadamph Aberds 82 C4
Delph Gtr Man 44 B3
Delves Durham 58 B2
Delvine Perth 76 C4
Dembleby Lincs 36 B6
Denaby Main S Yorks 45 C8
Denbigh = Dinbych Denb 42 F3
Denbury Devon 5 E9
Denby Derbys 45 H7
Denby Dale W Yorks 44 B6
Denchworth Oxon 17 B10
Dendron Cumb 49 B2
Denel End C Beds 29 E7
Denend Aberds 88 E6
Denford Northants 28 A6
Dengie Essex 20 A6
Denham Bucks 19 C7
Denham Suff 30 B4
Denham Suff 31 A8
Denham Street Suff 31 A8
Denhead Aberds 89 C9
Denhead Fife 77 F7
Denhead of Arbilot Angus 77 C8
Denhead of Gray Dundee 76 D6
Denholm Borders 61 B11
Denholme W Yorks 51 F6
Denholme Clough W Yorks 51 F6
Denio Gwyn 40 G5
Denmead Hants 10 C5
Denmore Aberdeen 83 B11
Denmoss Aberds 89 D6
Dennington Suff 31 B9
Denny Falk 69 B7
Denny Lodge Hants 10 D2
Dennyloanhead Falk 69 B7
Denshaw Gtr Man 44 A3
Denside Aberds 83 D10
Densole Kent 21 G9
Denston Suff 30 C4
Denstone Staffs 35 A7
Dent Cumb 57 H9
Denton Cambs 37 G7
Denton Darl 58 E3
Denton E Sus 12 F3
Denton Gtr Man 44 C3
Denton Kent 21 G9
Denton Lincs 36 B4
Denton N Yorks 51 E7
Denton Norf 39 G8
Denton Northants 28 C5
Denton Oxon 18 A2
Denton's Green Mers 43 C7
Denver Norf 38 E2
Denwick Northumb 63 B8
Deopham Norf 39 E6
Deopham Green Norf 38 F6
Depden Suff 30 C4
Depden Green Suff 30 C4
Deptford London 19 D10
Deptford Wilts 17 H7
Derby Derby 35 B9
Derbyhaven IoM 48 F2
Dereham Norf 38 D5
Deri Caerph 15 A7
Derril Devon 6 F2
Derringstone Kent 21 G9
Derrington Staffs 34 C4
Derriton Devon 6 F2
Derry Hill Wilts 16 D6
Derryguaig Argyll 78 H7
Derrythorpe N Lincs 46 B2
Dersingham Norf 38 B2
Dervaig Argyll 78 F7
Derwen Denb 42 G3
Derwenlas Powys 32 F3
Desborough Northants 36 G4
Desford Leics 35 E10
Detchant Northumb 71 G9
Detling Kent 20 F4
Deuddwr Powys 33 D8
Devauden Mon 15 B10
Devil's Bridge Ceredig 32 H3
Devizes Wilts 17 E7
Devol Involyd 68 C2
Devonport Plym 4 F5
Devonside Clack 76 H2
Devoran Corn 3 F6
Dewar Borders 70 F2
Dewlish Dorset 9 E6
Dewsbury W Yorks 51 G8
Dewsbury Moor W Yorks 51 G8
Dewshall Court Hereford 25 E11
Dhoon IoM 48 D4
Dhoor IoM 48 C4
Dhowin IoM 48 B4
Dial Post W Sus 11 C10
Dibden Hants 10 D3
Dibden Purlieu Hants 10 D3
Dickleburgh Norf 39 G7
Didbrook Glos 27 E7
Didcot Oxon 18 C2
Diddington Cambs 29 B8
Diddlebury Shrops 33 G11
Didley Hereford 25 E11
Didling W Sus 11 C7
Didmarton Glos 16 C5
Didsbury Gtr Man 44 C2
Didworthy Devon 5 E7
Digby Lincs 46 G4
Digg Highld 85 B9
Diggle Gtr Man 44 B4
Digmoor Lancs 43 B7
Digswell Park Herts 29 G9
Dihewyd Ceredig 23 A9
Dilham Norf 39 C9
Dilhorne Staffs 34 A5
Dillarburn S Lanark 69 F7
Dillington Cambs 29 B8
Dilston Northumb 62 G5
Dilton Marsh Wilts 16 G5
Dilwyn Hereford 25 C11
Dinas Carms 23 C7
Dinas Gwyn 40 G4
Dinas Cross Pembs 22 C5
Dinas Dinlle Gwyn 40 E6
Dinas-Mawddwy Gwyn 32 D4
Dinas Powys V Glam 15 D7
Dinbych = Denbigh Denb 42 F3
Dinbych-y-Pysgod = Tenby Pembs 22 F6
Dinder Som 16 G2
Dinedor Hereford 26 E2
Dingestow Mon 25 G11
Dingle Mers 42 D6
Dingleden Kent 13 C7
Dingley Northants 36 G3
Dingwall Highld 87 F8
Dinlabyre Borders 61 D11
Dinmael Conwy 32 A6
Dinnet Aberds 82 D6
Dinnington S Yorks 45 D9
Dinnington Som 8 C3
Dinnington T&W 63 F8
Dinorwic Gwyn 41 D7
Dinton Bucks 28 G4
Dinton Wilts 9 A9
Dinwoodie Mains Dumfries 61 D7
Dinworthy Devon 6 E2
Dippen N Ayrs 66 D3
Dippenhall Sur 18 G5
Dipple Moray 88 C3
Dipple S Ayrs 66 F5
Diptford Devon 5 F8
Dipton Durham 58 A2
Dirdhu Highld 82 A2
Dirleton E Loth 70 B4
Dirt Pot Northumb 57 B10
Discoed Powys 25 B9
Diseworth Leics 35 C10
Dishes Orkney 95 F7
Dishforth N Yorks 51 B9
Disley Ches E 44 D3
Diss Norf 39 H7
Disserth Powys 25 C7
Distington Cumb 56 D2
Ditchampton Wilts 9 A9
Ditcheat Som 16 H3
Ditchingham Norf 39 F9
Ditchling E Sus 12 E2
Ditherington Shrops 33 D11
Dittisham Devon 5 F9
Ditton Halton 43 D7
Ditton Kent 20 F4
Ditton Green Cambs 30 C3
Ditton Priors Shrops 34 G2
Divach Highld 81 A6
Divlyn Carms 24 E4
Dixton Glos 26 E6
Dixton Mon 26 G2
Dobcross Gtr Man 44 B3
Dobwalls Corn 4 E3
Doc Penfro = Pembroke Dock Pembs 22 F4
Doccombe Devon 5 C8
Dochfour Ho. Highld 87 H9
Dochgarroch Highld 87 G9
Docking Norf 38 B3
Docklow Hereford 26 C2
Dockray Cumb 56 D5
Dockroyd W Yorks 50 F6
Dodburn Borders 61 C10
Doddinghurst Essex 20 B2
Doddington Cambs 37 F9
Doddington Kent 20 F6
Doddington Lincs 46 E3
Doddington Northumb 71 G8
Doddington Shrops 34 H2
Doddiscombsleigh Devon 5 C9
Dodford Northants 28 B3
Dodford Worcs 26 A6
Dodington S Glos 16 C4
Dodleston Ches W 43 F6
Dods Leigh Staffs 34 B6
Dodworth S Yorks 45 B7
Doe Green Warr 43 D8
Doe Lea Derbys 45 F8
Dog Village Devon 7 G8
Dogdyke Lincs 46 G6
Dogmersfield Hants 18 F4
Dogridge Wilts 17 C7
Dogsthorpe Pboro 37 E7
Dol-fôr Powys 32 E4
Dôl-y-Bont Ceredig 32 G2
Dol-y-cannau Powys 25 D9
Dolanog Powys 33 D6
Dolau Powys 25 B8
Dolau Rhondda 14 C5
Dolbenmaen Gwyn 41 F7
Dolfach Powys 32 E5
Dolfor Powys 33 G7
Dolgarrog Conwy 41 D9
Dolgellau Gwyn 32 D3
Dolgran Carms 23 C9
Dolhendre Gwyn 41 G10
Doll Highld 93 J11
Dollar Clack 76 H2
Dolley Green Powys 25 B9
Dollwen Ceredig 32 G2
Dolphin Flint 42 E4
Dolphinholme Lancs 49 D5
Dolphinton S Lanark 69 F10
Dolton Devon 6 E4
Dolwen Conwy 41 C10
Dolwen Powys 32 E5
Dolwyd Conwy 41 C10
Dolwyddelan Conwy 41 E9
Dolyhir Powys 25 C9
Doncaster S Yorks 45 B9
Dones Green Ches W 43 E9
Donhead St Andrew Wilts 9 B8
Donhead St Mary Wilts 9 B8
Donibristle Fife 69 B10
Donington Lincs 37 B8
Donington on Bain Lincs 46 D6
Donington South Ing Lincs 37 B8
Donisthorpe Leics 35 D9
Donkey Town Sur 18 E6
Donnington Glos 27 F8
Donnington Hereford 26 E4
Donnington Shrops 34 E1
Donnington Telford 34 D3
Donnington W Berks 17 E11
Donnington W Sus 11 D7
Donnington Wood Telford 34 D3
Donyatt Som 8 C2
Doonfoot S Ayrs 66 E6
Dorback Lodge Highld 82 B2
Dorchester Dorset 8 E5
Dorchester Oxon 18 B2
Dordon Warks 35 E8
Dore S Yorks 45 D7
Dores Highld 87 H8
Dorking Sur 19 G8
Dormansland Sur 12 B3
Dormanstown Redcar 59 D6
Dormington Hereford 26 D2
Dormston Worcs 26 C6
Dornal S Ayrs 54 B5
Dorney Bucks 18 D6
Dornie Highld 85 F13
Dornoch Highld 87 C10
Dornock Dumfries 61 G8
Dorrery Highld 94 E2
Dorridge W Mid 35 H7
Dorrington Lincs 46 G4
Dorrington Shrops 33 E10
Dorsington Warks 27 D8
Dorstone Hereford 25 D10
Dorton Bucks 28 G3
Dorusduain Highld 80 A1
Dosthill Staffs 35 F8
Dottery Dorset 8 E3
Doublebois Corn 4 E2
Dougarie N Ayrs 66 C1
Doughton Glos 16 B5
Douglas IoM 48 E3
Douglas S Lanark 69 G7
Douglas & Angus Dundee 77 D7
Douglas Water S Lanark 69 G7
Douglas West S Lanark 69 G7
Douglastown Angus 77 C7
Doulting Som 16 G3
Dounby Orkney 95 F3
Doune Highld 92 J7
Doune Stirling 75 G10
Doune Park Aberds 89 B7
Douneside Aberds 82 C6
Dounie Highld 87 B8
Dounreay Highld 93 C12
Dousland Devon 4 E6
Dovaston Shrops 33 C9
Dove Holes Derbys 44 E4
Dovenby Cumb 56 C2
Dover Kent 21 G10
Dovercourt Essex 31 E9
Doverdale Worcs 26 B5
Doveridge Derbys 35 B7
Doversgreen Sur 19 G9
Dowally Perth 76 C3
Dowbridge Lancs 49 F4
Dowdeswell Glos 27 G7
Dowlais M Tydf 25 H7
Dowland Devon 6 E4
Dowlish Wake Som 8 C2
Down Ampney Glos 17 B8
Down Hatherley Glos 26 F5
Down St Mary Devon 7 F6
Down Thomas Devon 4 F6
Downcraig Ferry N Ayrs 73 H10
Downderry Corn 4 F4
Downe London 19 E11
Downend IoW 10 F4
Downend S Glos 16 D3
Downend W Berks 17 D11
Downfield Dundee 76 D6
Downgate Corn 4 D4
Downham Essex 20 B4
Downham Lancs 50 E3
Downham Northumb 71 G7
Downham Market Norf 38 E2
Downhead Som 16 G3
Downhill Perth 76 D3
Downhill T&W 63 H9
Downholland Cross Lancs 42 B6
Downholme N Yorks 58 G2
Downies Aberds 83 D11
Downley Bucks 18 B5
Downside Som 16 G3
Downside Sur 19 F8
Downton Hants 10 E1
Downton Wilts 9 B10
Downton on the Rock Hereford 25 A11
Dowsby Lincs 37 C7
Dowsdale Lincs 37 D8
Dowthwaitehead Cumb 56 D5
Doxey Staffs 34 C5
Doxford Northumb 63 A7
Doxford Park T&W 58 A4
Doynton S Glos 16 D4
Draffan S Lanark 68 F6
Dragonby N Lincs 46 A3
Drakeland Corner Devon 5 F6
Drakemyre N Ayrs 66 A5
Drake's Broughton Worcs 26 D6
Drakes Cross Worcs 35 H6
Drakewalls Corn 4 D5
Draughton N Yorks 50 D6
Draughton Northants 28 A4
Drax N Yorks 52 G2
Draycote Warks 27 A11
Draycott Derbys 35 B10
Draycott Glos 27 E8
Draycott Som 15 F10
Draycott in the Clay Staffs 35 C7
Draycott in the Moors Staffs 34 A5
Drayford Devon 7 E6
Drayton Leics 36 F4
Drayton Lincs 37 B8
Drayton Norf 39 D7
Drayton Oxon 17 B11
Drayton Oxon 27 D11
Drayton Ptsmth 10 D5
Drayton Som 8 B3
Drayton Worcs 34 H5
Drayton Bassett Staffs 35 E7
Drayton Beauchamp Bucks 28 G6
Drayton Parslow Bucks 28 F5
Drayton St Leonard Oxon 18 B2
Dre-fach Carms 24 G3
Dre-fach Ceredig 23 B10
Drebley N Yorks 51 D6
Dreemskerry IoM 48 C4
Dreenhill Pembs 22 E4
Drefach Carms 23 C8
Drefach Carms 23 E10
Drefelin Carms 23 C8
Dreghorn N Ayrs 67 C6
Drellingore Kent 21 G9
Drem E Loth 70 C4
Dresden Stoke 34 A5
Dreumasdal W Isles 84 E2
Drewsteignton Devon 7 G6
Driby Lincs 47 E7
Driffield E Yorks 52 D6
Driffield Glos 17 B7
Drigg Cumb 56 G2
Drighlington W Yorks 51 G8
Drimnin Highld 79 F8
Drimpton Dorset 8 D3
Drimsynie Argyll 74 G4
Drinisiadar W Isles 90 H6
Drinkstone Suff 30 B6
Drinkstone Green Suff 30 B6
Drishaig Argyll 74 F4
Drissaig Argyll 73 B8
Drochil Borders 69 F10
Drointon Staffs 34 C6
Droitwich Spa Worcs 26 B5
Droman Highld 92 D4
Dron Perth 76 F4
Dronfield Derbys 45 E7
Dronfield Woodhouse Derbys 45 E7
Drongan E Ayrs 67 E7
Dronley Angus 76 D6
Droxford Hants 10 C5
Droylsden Gtr Man 44 C3
Druid Denb 32 A6
Druidston Pembs 22 E3
Druimarbin Highld 80 F2
Druimavuic Argyll 74 C3
Druimdrishaig Argyll 72 F6
Druimindarroch Highld 79 C9
Druimyeon More Argyll 65 C7
Drum Argyll 73 F8
Drum Perth 76 G3
Drumbeg Highld 92 F4
Drumblade Aberds 88 D5
Drumblair Aberds 89 D7
Drumbuie Dumfries 55 A8
Drumbuie Highld 85 E12
Drumburgh Cumb 61 H8
Drumburn Dumfries 60 G5
Drumchapel Glasgow 68 C4
Drumchardine Highld 87 G8
Drumchork Highld 91 J13
Drumclog S Lanark 68 G5
Drumderfit Highld 87 F9
Drumeldrie Fife 77 G7
Drumelzier Borders 69 G10
Drumfearn Highld 85 G11
Drumgask Highld 81 D8
Drumgley Angus 77 B7
Drumguish Highld 81 D9
Drumin Moray 88 E1
Drumlasie Aberds 83 C8
Drumlemble Argyll 65 G7
Drumligair Aberds 83 B11
Drumlithie Aberds 83 E9
Drummoddie Dumfries 54 E6
Drummond Highld 87 E9
Drummore Dumfries 54 F4
Drummuir Moray 88 D3
Drummuir Castle Moray 88 D3
Drumnadrochit Highld 81 A7
Drumnagorrach Moray 88 C5
Drumoak Aberds 83 D9
Drumpark Dumfries 60 E4
Drumphail Dumfries 54 C5
Drumrash Dumfries 55 B9
Drumrunie Highld 92 J4
Drums Aberds 89 F9
Drumsallie Highld 80 F1
Drumstinchall Dumfries 55 D11
Drumsturdy Angus 77 D7
Drumtochty Castle Aberds 83 F8
Drumtroddan Dumfries 54 E6
Drumuie Highld 85 D9
Drumuillie Highld 81 A11
Drumvaich Stirling 75 G9
Drumwhindle Aberds 89 E9
Drunkendub Angus 77 C9
Drury Flint 42 F5
Drury Square Norf 38 D5
Dry Doddington Lincs 46 H2
Dry Drayton Cambs 29 B10
Drybeck Cumb 57 E8
Drybridge Moray 88 B4
Drybridge N Ayrs 67 C6
Drybrook Glos 26 G3
Dryburgh Borders 70 G4
Dryhope Borders 61 A8
Drylaw Edin 69 C11
Drym Corn 2 F5
Drymen Stirling 68 B3
Drymuir Aberds 89 D9
Drynoch Highld 85 E9
Dryslwyn Carms 23 D10
Dryton Shrops 34 E1
Dubford Aberds 89 B8
Dubton Angus 77 B8
Duchally Highld 92 H6
Duchlage Argyll 68 B2
Duck Corner Suff 31 D10
Duckington Ches W 43 G7
Ducklington Oxon 27 H10
Duckmanton Derbys 45 E8
Duck's Cross Bedford 29 C8
Duddenhoe End Essex 29 E11
Duddingston Edin 69 C11
Duddington Northants 36 E5
Duddleswell E Sus 12 D3
Duddo Northumb 71 F8
Duddon Ches W 43 F8
Duddon Bridge Cumb 56 H4
Dudleston Shrops 33 B9
Dudleston Heath Shrops 33 B9
Dudley T&W 63 F8
Dudley W Mid 34 F5
Dudley Port W Mid 34 F5
Duffield Derbys 35 A9
Duffryn Neath 14 B4
Duffryn Newport 15 C8
Dufftown Moray 88 E3
Duffus Moray 88 B1
Dufton Cumb 57 D8
Duggleby N Yorks 52 C4
Duirinish Highld 85 E12
Duisdalemore Highld 85 G12
Duisky Highld 80 F2
Dukestown Bl Gwent 25 G8
Dukinfield Gtr Man 44 C3
Dulas Anglesey 40 B6
Dulcote Som 16 G2
Dulford Devon 7 F9
Dull Perth 75 C11
Dullatur N Lanark 68 C6
Dullingham Cambs 30 C3
Dulnain Bridge Highld 82 A1
Duloe Bedford 29 B8
Duloe Corn 4 F3
Dulsie Highld 87 G12
Dulverton Som 7 D8
Dulwich London 19 D10
Dumbarton W Dunb 68 C2
Dumbleton Glos 27 E7
Dumcrieff Dumfries 61 C7
Dumfries Dumfries 60 F5
Dumgoyne Stirling 68 B4
Dummer Hants 18 G2
Dumpford W Sus 11 B7
Dumpton Kent 21 E10
Dun Angus 77 B9
Dun Charlabhaigh W Isles 90 C6
Dunain Ho. Highld 87 G9
Dunalastair Perth 75 B10
Dunan Highld 85 F10
Dunans Argyll 73 D9
Dunball Som 15 G9
Dunbar E Loth 70 C5
Dunbeath Highld 94 H3
Dunbeg Argyll 79 H11
Dunblane Stirling 75 G10
Dunbog Fife 76 F5
Duncanston Aberds 83 A7
Duncanston Highld 87 F8
Dunchideock Devon 5 C9
Dunchurch Warks 27 A11
Duncote Northants 28 C3
Duncow Dumfries 60 E5
Duncraggan Stirling 75 G8
Duncrievie Perth 76 G4
Duncton W Sus 11 C8
Dundas Ho. Orkney 95 K5
Dundee Dundee 77 D7
Dundeugh Dumfries 67 H8
Dundon Som 8 A3
Dundonald S Ayrs 67 C6
Dundonnell Highld 86 C3
Dundonnell Hotel Highld 86 C3
Dundonnell House Highld 86 C4
Dundraw Cumb 56 B4
Dundreggan Highld 80 B5
Dundreggan Lodge Highld 80 B5
Dundrennan Dumfries 55 E10
Dundry N Som 16 E2
Dunecht Aberds 83 C9
Dunfermline Fife 69 B9
Dunfield Glos 17 B8
Dunford Bridge S Yorks 44 B5
Dungworth S Yorks 44 D6
Dunham Notts 46 E2
Dunham-on-the-Hill Ches W 43 E7
Dunham Town Gtr Man 43 D10
Dunhampton Worcs 26 B5
Dunholme Lincs 46 E4
Dunino Fife 77 F8
Dunipace Falk 69 B7
Dunira Perth 75 E10
Dunkeld Perth 76 C3
Dunkerton Bath 16 F4
Dunkeswell Devon 7 F10
Dunkeswick N Yorks 51 E9
Dunkirk Kent 21 F7
Dunkirk Norf 39 C8
Dunk's Green Kent 20 F3
Dunlappie Angus 83 G7
Dunley Hants 17 F11
Dunley Worcs 26 B4
Dunlichity Lodge Highld 87 H9
Dunlop E Ayrs 67 B7
Dunmaglass Lodge Highld 81 A7
Dunmore Argyll 72 G6
Dunmore Falk 69 B7
Dunnet Highld 94 C4
Dunnichen Angus 77 C8
Dunninald Angus 77 B10
Dunning Perth 76 F3
Dunnington E Yorks 53 D7
Dunnington Warks 27 C7
Dunnington York 52 D2
Dunnockshaw Lancs 50 G4
Dunollie Argyll 79 H11
Dunoon Argyll 73 F10
Dunragit Dumfries 54 D4
Dunrostan Argyll 72 E6
Duns Borders 70 E6
Duns Tew Oxon 27 F11
Dunsby Lincs 37 C7
Dunscore Dumfries 60 E4
Dunscroft S Yorks 45 B10
Dunsdale Redcar 59 E7
Dunsden Green Oxon 18 D4
Dunsfold Sur 19 H7
Dunsford Devon 5 C9
Dunshalt Fife 76 F5
Dunshillock Aberds 89 D9
Dunskey Ho. Dumfries 54 D3
Dunsley N Yorks 59 E9
Dunsmore Bucks 28 H5
Dunsop Bridge Lancs 50 D2
Dunstable C Beds 29 F7
Dunstall Staffs 35 C7
Dunstall Common Worcs 26 D5
Dunstall Green Suff 30 B4
Dunstan Northumb 63 B8
Dunstan Steads Northumb 63 A8
Dunster Som 7 B8
Duntisbourne Abbots Glos 26 H6
Duntisbourne Leer Glos 26 H6
Duntisbourne Rouse Glos 26 H6
Duntish Dorset 8 D5
Duntocher W Dunb 68 C3
Dunton Bucks 28 F5
Dunton C Beds 29 D9
Dunton Norf 38 B4
Dunton Bassett Leics 35 F11
Dunton Green Kent 20 F2
Dunton Wayletts Essex 20 B3
Duntulm Highld 85 A9
Dunure S Ayrs 66 E5
Dunvant Swansea 23 G10
Dunvegan Highld 84 D7
Dunwich Suff 31 A11
Dunwood Staffs 44 G3
Dupplin Castle Perth 76 F3
Durdar Cumb 56 A6
Durgates E Sus 12 C5
Durham Durham 58 B3
Durisdeer Dumfries 60 C4
Durisdeermill Dumfries 60 C4
Durkar W Yorks 51 H9
Durleigh Som 15 H8
Durley Hants 10 C4
Durley Wilts 17 E9
Durnamuck Highld 86 B3
Durness Highld 92 C7
Durno Aberds 83 A9
Duror Highld 74 B2
Durran Argyll 73 C8
Durran Highld 94 D3
Durrington W Sus 11 D10
Durrington Wilts 17 G8
Dursley Glos 16 B4
Durston Som 8 B1
Durweston Dorset 9 D7
Dury Shetland 96 G6
Duston Northants 28 B4
Duthil Highld 81 A11
Dutlas Powys 33 H8
Duton Hill Essex 30 F3
Dutson Corn 4 C4
Dutton Ches W 43 E8
Duxford Cambs 29 D11
Duxford Oxon 17 B10
Dwygyfylchi Conwy 41 C9
Dwyran Anglesey 40 D6
Dyce Aberdeen 83 B10
Dye House Northumb 62 H5
Dyffryn Bridgend 14 B4
Dyffryn Carms 23 D8
Dyffryn Pembs 22 C4
Dyffryn Ardudwy Gwyn 32 C1
Dyffryn Castell Ceredig 32 G3
Dyffryn Ceidrych Carms 24 F4
Dyffryn Cellwen Neath 24 H5
Dyke Lincs 37 C7
Dyke Moray 87 F12
Dykehead Angus 76 A6
Dykehead N Lanark 69 D7
Dykehead Stirling 75 H8
Dykelands Aberds 83 G9
Dykends Angus 76 B5
Dykeside Aberds 89 D7
Dykesmains N Ayrs 66 B5
Dylife Powys 32 F4
Dymchurch Kent 13 D9
Dymock Glos 26 E4
Dyrham S Glos 16 D4
Dysart Fife 70 A2
Dyserth Denb 42 E3

E

Eachwick Northumb 63 F7
Eadar Dha Fhadhail W Isles 90 D5
Eagland Hill Lancs 49 E4
Eagle Lincs 46 F2
Eagle Barnsdale Lincs 46 F2
Eagle Moor Lincs 46 F2
Eaglescliffe Stockton 58 E5
Eaglesfield Cumb 56 D2
Eaglesfield Dumfries 61 F8
Eaglesham E Renf 68 E4
Eaglethorpe Northants 37 F6
Eairy IoM 48 E2
Eakley Lanes M Keynes 28 C5
Eakring Notts 45 F10
Ealand N Lincs 45 A11
Ealing London 19 C8
Eals Northumb 62 H2
Eamont Bridge Cumb 57 D7
Earby Lancs 50 E5
Earcroft Blackburn 50 G2
Eardington Shrops 34 F3
Eardisland Hereford 25 C11
Eardisley Hereford 25 D10
Eardiston Shrops 33 C9
Eardiston Worcs 26 B3
Earith Cambs 29 A10
Earl Shilton Leics 35 F10
Earl Soham Suff 31 B9
Earl Sterndale Derbys 44 F4
Earl Stonham Suff 31 C8
Earle Northumb 71 H8
Earley Wokingham 18 D4
Earlham Norf 39 E8
Earlish Highld 85 B8
Earls Barton Northants 28 B5
Earls Colne Essex 30 F5
Earl's Croome Worcs 26 D5
Earl's Green Suff 31 B7
Earlsdon W Mid 35 H9
Earlsferry Fife 77 H7
Earlsfield Lincs 36 B5
Earlsford Aberds 89 E8
Earlsheaton W Yorks 51 G8
Earlsmill Moray 87 F12
Earlston Borders 70 G4
Earlston E Ayrs 67 C7
Earlswood Mon 15 B10
Earlswood Sur 19 G9
Earlswood Warks 27 A8
Earnley W Sus 11 E7
Earsairidh W Isles 84 J2
Earsdon T&W 63 F9
Earsham Norf 39 G9
Earswick York 52 D2
Eartham W Sus 11 D8
Easby N Yorks 58 F2
Easby N Yorks 59 F6
Easdale Argyll 72 B6
Easebourne W Sus 11 B7
Easenhall Warks 35 H10
Eashing Sur 18 G6
Easington Bucks 28 G3
Easington Durham 58 B5
Easington E Yorks 53 H9
Easington Northumb 71 G10
Easington Oxon 18 B3
Easington Oxon 27 E11
Easington Redcar 59 E8
Easington Colliery Durham 58 B5
Easington Lane T&W 58 B4
Easingwold N Yorks 51 C11
Easole Street Kent 21 F9
Eassie Angus 76 C6
East Aberthaw V Glam 14 E6
East Adderbury Oxon 27 E11
East Allington Devon 5 G8
East Anstey Devon 7 D7
East Appleton N Yorks 58 G3
East Ardsley W Yorks 51 G9
East Ashling W Sus 11 D7
East Auchronie Aberds 83 C10
East Ayton N Yorks 59 H10
East Bank Bl Gwent 25 H9
East Barkwith Lincs 46 D5
East Barming Kent 20 F4
East Barnby N Yorks 59 E9
East Barnet London 19 B9
East Barns E Loth 70 C6
East Barsham Norf 38 B5
East Beckham Norf 39 B7
East Bedfont London 19 D7
East Bergholt Suff 31 E7
East Bilney Norf 38 D5
East Blatchington E Sus 12 F3
East Boldre Hants 10 D2
East Brent Som 15 F9
East Bridge Suff 31 B11
East Bridgford Notts 36 A2
East Buckland Devon 6 C5
East Budleigh Devon 7 H9
East Burrafirth Shetland 96 H5
East Burton Dorset 9 F7
East Butsfield Durham 58 B2
East Butterwick N Lincs 46 B2
East Cairnbeg Aberds 83 F9
East Calder W Loth 69 D9
East Carleton Norf 39 E7
East Carlton Northants 36 G4
East Carlton W Yorks 51 E8
East Chaldon Dorset 9 F6
East Challow Oxon 17 C10
East Chiltington E Sus 12 E2
East Chinnock Som 8 C3
East Chisenbury Wilts 17 F8
East Clandon Sur 19 F7
East Claydon Bucks 28 F4
East Clyne Highld 93 J12
East Coker Som 8 C4
East Combe Som 7 C10
East Common N Yorks 52 F2
East Compton Som 16 G3
East Cottingwith E Yorks 52 E3
East Cowes IoW 10 E4
East Cowick E Yorks 52 G2
East Cowton N Yorks 58 F4
East Cramlington Northumb 63 F8
East Cranmore Som 16 G3
East Creech Dorset 9 F8
East Croachy Highld 81 A8
East Croftmore Highld 81 B11
East Curthwaite Cumb 56 B5
East Dean E Sus 12 G4
East Dean Hants 10 B1
East Dean W Sus 11 C8
East Down Devon 6 B5
East Drayton Notts 45 E11
East Ella Hull 53 G6
East End Dorset 9 E8
East End E Yorks 53 G8
East End Hants 10 E2
East End Hants 10 B5
East End Hants 17 E10
East End Herts 29 F11
East End Kent 13 C7
East End N Som 15 D10
East End Oxon 27 G10
East Farleigh Kent 20 F4
East Farndon Northants 36 G3
East Ferry Lincs 46 C2
East Fortune E Loth 70 C4
East Garston W Berks 17 D10
East Ginge Oxon 17 C11
East Goscote Leics 36 D2
East Grafton Wilts 17 E9
East Grimstead Wilts 9 B11
East Grinstead W Sus 12 C2
East Guldeford E Sus 13 D8
East Haddon Northants 28 B3
East Hagbourne Oxon 18 C2
East Halton N Lincs 53 H7
East Ham London 19 C11
East Hanney Oxon 17 B11
East Hanningfield Essex 20 A4
East Hardwick W Yorks 51 H10
East Harling Norf 38 G5
East Harlsey N Yorks 58 G5
East Harnham Wilts 9 B10
East Harptree Bath 16 F2
East Hartford Northumb 63 F8
East Harting W Sus 11 C6
East Hatley Cambs 29 C9
East Hauxwell N Yorks 58 G2
East Haven Angus 77 D8
East Heckington Lincs 37 A7
East Hedleyhope Durham 58 B2
East Hendred Oxon 17 C11
East Herrington T&W 58 A4
East Heslerton N Yorks 52 B5
East Hoathly E Sus 12 E4
East Horrington Som 16 G2
East Horsley Sur 19 F7
East Horton Northumb 71 G9
East Huntspill Som 15 G9
East Hyde C Beds 29 G8
East Ilkerton Devon 6 B6
East Ilsley W Berks 17 C11
East Keal Lincs 47 F7
East Kennett Wilts 17 E8
East Keswick W Yorks 51 E9
East Kilbride S Lanark 68 E5
East Kirkby Lincs 47 F7
East Knapton N Yorks 52 B4
East Knighton Dorset 9 F7
East Knoyle Wilts 9 A7
East Kyloe Northumb 71 G9
East Lambrook Som 8 C3
East Lamington Highld 87 D10
East Langdon Kent 21 G10
East Langton Leics 36 F3
East Langwell Highld 93 J10
East Lavant W Sus 11 D7
East Lavington W Sus 11 C8
East Layton N Yorks 58 F2
East Leake Notts 36 C1
East Learmouth Northumb 71 G7
East Leigh Devon 6 F5
East Lexham Norf 38 D4
East Lilburn Northumb 62 A6
East Linton E Loth 70 C4
East Liss Hants 11 B6
East Looe Corn 4 F3
East Lound N Lincs 45 C11
East Lulworth Dorset 9 F7
East Lutton N Yorks 52 C5
East Lydford Som 8 A4
East Mains Aberds 83 D8
East Malling Kent 20 F4
East March Angus 77 D7
East Marden W Sus 11 C7
East Markham Notts 45 E11
East Marton N Yorks 50 D5
East Meon Hants 10 B5
East Mere Devon 7 E8
East Mersea Essex 31 G7
East Mey Highld 94 C5
East Molesey Sur 19 E8
East Morden Dorset 9 E8
East Morton W Yorks 51 E6
East Ness N Yorks 52 B2
East Newton E Yorks 53 F8
East Norton Leics 36 E3
East Nynehead Som 7 D10
East Oakley Hants 18 F2
East Ogwell Devon 5 D9
East Orchard Dorset 9 C7
East Ord Northumb 71 E8
East Panson Devon 6 G2
East Peckham Kent 20 G3
East Pennard Som 16 H2
East Perry Cambs 29 B8
East Portlemouth Devon 5 H8
East Prawle Devon 5 H8
East Preston W Sus 11 D9
East Putford Devon 6 E2
East Quantoxhead Som 7 B10
East Rainton T&W 58 B4
East Ravendale NE Lincs 46 C6
East Raynham Norf 38 C4
East Rhidorroch Lodge Highld 86 B5
East Rigton W Yorks 51 E9
East Rounton N Yorks 58 F5
East Row N Yorks 59 E9
East Rudham Norf 38 C4
East Runton Norf 39 A7
East Ruston Norf 39 C9
East Saltoun E Loth 70 D3
East Sleekburn Northumb 63 E8
East Somerton Norf 39 D10
East Stockwith Lincs 45 C11
East Stoke Dorset 9 F7
East Stoke Notts 45 H11
East Stour Dorset 9 B7
East Stourmouth Kent 21 E9
East Stowford Devon 6 D5
East Stratton Hants 18 H2
East Studdal Kent 21 G10
East Suisnish Highld 85 E10
East Taphouse Corn 4 E2
East-the-Water Devon 6 D3
East Thirston Northumb 63 D7
East Tilbury Thurrock 20 D3
East Tisted Hants 10 A6
East Torrington Lincs 46 D5
East Tuddenham Norf 39 D6
East Tytherley Hants 10 B1
East Tytherton Wilts 16 D6
East Village Devon 7 F7
East Wall Shrops 33 F11
East Walton Norf 38 D3
East Wellow Hants 10 B2
East Wemyss Fife 76 H6
East Whitburn W Loth 69 D8
East Williamston Pembs 22 F5
East Winch Norf 38 D2
East Winterslow Wilts 9 A11
East Wittering W Sus 11 E6
East Witton N Yorks 58 H2
East Woodburn Northumb 62 E5
East Woodhay Hants 17 E11
East Worldham Hants 18 H4
East Worlington Devon 7 E6
East Worthing W Sus 11 D10
Eastbourne E Sus 12 G5
Eastbridge Suff 31 B11
Eastburn W Yorks 50 E6
Eastbury London 19 B7
Eastbury W Berks 17 D10
Eastby N Yorks 50 D6
Eastchurch Kent 20 D6
Eastcombe Glos 16 A5
Eastcote London 19 C8
Eastcote Northants 28 C3
Eastcote W Mid 35 H7
Eastcott Corn 6 E1
Eastcott Wilts 17 F7
Eastcourt Wilts 16 B6
Eastcourt Wilts 17 E9
Easter Ardross Highld 87 D9
Easter Balmoral Aberds 82 D4
Easter Boleskine Highld 81 A7
Easter Compton S Glos 16 C2
Easter Cringate Stirling 68 B6
Easter Davoch Aberds 82 C6
Easter Earshaig Dumfries 60 C6
Easter Fearn Highld 87 C9
Easter Galcantray Highld 87 G11
Easter Howgate Midloth 69 D11
Easter Howlaws Borders 70 F6
Easter Kinkell Highld 87 F8
Easter Lednathie Angus 76 A6
Easter Milton Highld 87 F12
Easter Moniack Highld 87 G8
Easter Ord Aberdeen 83 C10
Easter Quarff Shetland 96 K6
Easter Rhynd Perth 76 F4
Easter Row Stirling 75 H10
Easter Silverford Aberds 89 B7
Easter Skeld Shetland 96 J5
Easter Whyntie Aberds 88 B6
Eastergate W Sus 11 D8
Easterhouse Glasgow 68 D5
Eastern Green W Mid 35 G8

Easterton Wilts 17 F7
Eastertown Som 15 F9
Eastertown of Auchleuchries Aberds 89 E10
Eastfield N Lanark 69 D7
Eastfield N Yorks 52 A6
Eastfield Hall Northumb 63 C8
Eastgate Durham 57 C11
Eastgate Norf 39 C7
Eastham Mers 42 D6
Eastham Ferry Mers 42 D6
Easthampstead Brack 18 E5
Eastheath Wokingham 18 E5
Easthope Shrops 34 F1
Easthorpe Essex 30 F6
Easthorpe Leics 36 B4
Easthorpe Notts 45 G11
Easthouses Midloth 70 D2
Eastington Devon 7 F6
Eastington Glos 26 H4
Eastington Glos 27 G8
Eastleach Martin Glos 27 H9
Eastleach Turville Glos 27 H8
Eastleigh Devon 6 D3
Eastleigh Hants 10 C3
Eastling Kent 20 F6
Eastmoor Derbys 45 E7
Eastmoor Norf 38 E3
Eastney Ptsmth 10 E5
Eastnor Hereford 26 E4
Eastoft N Lincs 52 H4
Eastoke Hants 10 E6
Easton Cambs 29 A8
Easton Cumb 61 F10
Easton Cumb 61 H8
Easton Devon 5 C8
Easton Dorset 8 G5
Easton Hants 10 A4
Easton Lincs 36 C5
Easton Norf 39 D7
Easton Som 15 G11
Easton Suff 31 C9
Easton Wilts 16 D5
Easton Grey Wilts 16 C5
Easton-in-Gordano N Som 15 D11
Easton Maudit Northants 28 C5
Easton on the Hill Northants 36 E6
Easton Royal Wilts 17 E9
Eastpark Dumfries 60 G6
Eastrea Cambs 37 F8
Eastriggs Dumfries 61 G8
Eastrington E Yorks 52 G3
Eastry Kent 21 F10
Eastville Bristol 16 D3
Eastville Lincs 47 G8
Eastwell Leics 36 C3
Eastwick Herts 29 G11
Eastwick Shetland 96 F5
Eastwood Notts 45 H8
Eastwood Southend 20 C5
Eastwood W Yorks 50 G5
Eathorpe Warks 27 B10
Eaton Ches E 44 F2
Eaton Ches W 43 F8
Eaton Leics 36 C3
Eaton Norf 39 E8
Eaton Notts 45 E11
Eaton Oxon 17 A11
Eaton Shrops 33 G9
Eaton Shrops 33 G11
Eaton Bishop Hereford 25 E11
Eaton Bray C Beds 28 F6
Eaton Constantine Shrops 34 E1
Eaton Green C Beds 28 F6
Eaton Hastings Oxon 17 B9
Eaton on Tern Shrops 34 C2
Eaton Socon Cambs 29 C8
Eavestone N Yorks 51 C8
Ebberston N Yorks 52 A4
Ebbesbourne Wake Wilts 9 B8
Ebbw Vale = Glyn Ebwy Bl Gwent 25 H8
Ebchester Durham 63 H7
Ebford Devon 5 C10
Ebley Glos 26 H5
Ebnal Ches W 43 H7
Ebrington Glos 27 D8
Ecchinswell Hants 17 F11
Ecclaw Borders 70 D6
Ecclefechan Dumfries 61 F7
Eccles Borders 70 F6
Eccles Gtr Man 43 C10
Eccles Kent 20 E4
Eccles on Sea Norf 39 C10
Eccles Road Norf 38 F6
Ecclesall S Yorks 45 D7
Ecclesfield S Yorks 45 C7
Ecclesgreig Aberds 83 G9
Eccleshall Staffs 34 C4
Eccleshill W Yorks 51 F7
Ecclesmachan W Loth 69 C9
Eccleston Ches W 43 F7
Eccleston Lancs 49 H5
Eccleston Mers 43 C7
Eccleston Park Mers 43 C7
Eccup W Yorks 51 E8
Echt Aberds 83 C9
Eckford Borders 70 H6
Eckington Derbys 45 E8
Eckington Worcs 26 D6
Ecton Northants 28 B5
Edale Derbys 44 D5
Edburton W Sus 11 C11
Edderside Cumb 56 B2
Edderton Highld 87 C10
Eddistone Devon 6 D1
Eddleston Borders 69 F11
Eden Park London 19 E10
Edenbridge Kent 19 G11
Edenfield Lancs 50 H3
Edenhall Cumb 57 C7
Edenham Lincs 37 C6
Edensor Derbys 44 F6
Edentaggart Argyll 68 A2
Edenthorpe S Yorks 45 B10
Edentown Cumb 61 H9
Ederline Argyll 73 C7
Edern Gwyn 40 G4
Edgarley Som 15 H11
Edgbaston W Mid 35 G6
Edgcott Bucks 28 F3
Edgcott Som 7 C7
Edge Shrops 33 E9
Edge End Glos 26 G2
Edge Green Ches W 43 G7
Edge Hill Mers 42 C6
Edgebolton Shrops 34 C1
Edgefield Norf 39 B6
Edgefield Street Norf 39 B6
Edgeside Lancs 50 G4
Edgeworth Glos 26 H6
Edgmond Telford 34 D3
Edgmond Marsh Telford 34 C3
Edgton Shrops 33 G9
Edgware London 19 B8
Edgworth Blackburn 50 H3
Edinample Stirling 75 E8
Edinbane Highld 85 C8
Edinburgh Edin 69 C11
Edingale Staffs 35 D8
Edingight Ho. Moray 88 C5
Edingley Notts 45 G10
Edingthorpe Norf 39 B9
Edingthorpe Green Norf 39 B9
Edington Som 15 H9
Edington Wilts 16 F6
Edintore Moray 88 D4
Edith Weston Rutland 36 E5
Edithmead Som 15 G9
Edlesborough Bucks 28 G6
Edlingham Northumb 63 C7
Edlington Lincs 46 E6
Edmondsham Dorset 9 C9
Edmondsley Durham 58 B3
Edmondthorpe Leics 36 D4
Edmonstone Orkney 95 F6
Edmonton London 19 B10
Edmundbyers Durham 58 A1
Ednam Borders 70 G6
Ednaston Derbys 35 A8
Edradynate Perth 75 B11
Edrom Borders 71 E7
Edstaston Shrops 33 B11
Edstone Warks 27 B8
Edvin Loach Hereford 26 C3
Edwalton Notts 36 B1
Edwardstone Suff 30 D6
Edwinsford Carms 24 E3
Edwinstowe Notts 45 F10
Edworth C Beds 29 D9
Edwyn Ralph Hereford 26 C3
Edzell Angus 83 G7
Efail Isaf Rhondda 14 C6
Efailnewydd Gwyn 40 G5
Efailwen Carms 22 D6
Efenechtyd Denb 42 G4
Effingham Sur 19 F8
Effirth Shetland 96 H5
Efford Devon 7 F7
Egdon Worcs 26 C6
Egerton Gtr Man 43 A10
Egerton Kent 20 G6
Egerton Forstal Kent 20 G5
Eggborough N Yorks 52 G1
Eggbuckland Plym 4 F6
Eggington C Beds 28 F6
Egginton Derbys 35 C8
Egglescliffe Stockton 58 E5
Eggleston Durham 57 D11
Egham Sur 19 D7
Egleton Rutland 36 E4
Eglingham Northumb 63 B7
Egloshayle Corn 3 B8
Egloskerry Corn 4 C3
Eglwys-Brewis V Glam 14 E6
Eglwys Cross Wrex 33 A10
Eglwys Fach Ceredig 32 F2
Eglwysbach Conwy 41 C10
Eglwyswen Pembs 22 C6
Eglwyswrw Pembs 22 C6
Egmanton Notts 45 F11
Egremont Cumb 56 E2
Egremont Mers 42 C6
Egton N Yorks 59 F9
Egton Bridge N Yorks 59 F9
Eight Ash Green Essex 30 F6
Eignaig Highld 79 G10
Eil Highld 81 B10
Eilanreach Highld 85 G13
Eilean Darach Highld 86 C4
Eileanach Lodge Highld 87 E8
Einacleite W Isles 90 E6
Eisgean W Isles 91 F8
Eisingrug Gwyn 41 G8
Elan Village Powys 24 B6
Elberton S Glos 16 C3
Elburton Plym 4 F6
Elcho Perth 76 E4
Elcombe Swindon 17 C8
Eldernell Cambs 37 F9
Eldersfield Worcs 26 E5
Elderslie Renfs 68 D3
Eldon Durham 58 D3
Eldrick S Ayrs 54 A5
Eldroth N Yorks 50 C3
Eldwick W Yorks 51 E7
Elfhowe Cumb 56 G6
Elford Northumb 71 G10
Elford Staffs 35 D7
Elgin Moray 88 B2
Elgol Highld 85 G10
Elham Kent 21 G8
Elie Fife 77 G7
Elim Anglesey 40 B5
Eling Hants 10 C2
Elishader Highld 85 B10
Elishaw Northumb 62 D4
Elkesley Notts 45 E10
Elkstone Glos 26 G6
Ellan Highld 81 A10
Elland W Yorks 51 G7
Ellary Argyll 72 F6
Ellastone Staffs 35 A7
Ellemford Borders 70 D6
Ellenbrook IoM 48 E3
Ellenhall Staffs 34 C4
Ellen's Green Sur 19 H7
Ellerbeck N Yorks 58 G5
Ellerburn N Yorks 52 A4
Ellerby N Yorks 59 E8
Ellerdine Heath Telford 34 C2
Ellerhayes Devon 7 F8
Elleric Argyll 74 C3
Ellerker E Yorks 52 G5
Ellerton E Yorks 52 F3
Ellerton Shrops 34 C3
Ellesborough Bucks 28 H5
Ellesmere Shrops 33 B10
Ellesmere Port Ches W 43 E7
Ellingham Norf 39 F9
Ellingham Northumb 71 H10
Ellingstring N Yorks 51 A7
Ellington Cambs 29 A8
Ellington Northumb 63 D8
Elliot Angus 77 D9
Ellisfield Hants 18 G3
Ellistown Leics 35 D10
Ellon Aberds 89 E9
Ellonby Cumb 56 C6
Ellough Suff 39 G10
Elloughton E Yorks 52 G5
Ellwood Glos 26 H2
Elm Cambs 37 E10
Elm Hill Dorset 9 B7
Elm Park London 20 C2
Elmbridge Worcs 26 B6
Elmdon Essex 29 E11
Elmdon W Mid 35 G7
Elmdon Heath W Mid 35 G7
Elmers End London 19 E10
Elmesthorpe Leics 35 F10
Elmfield IoW 10 E5
Elmhurst Staffs 35 D7
Elmley Castle Worcs 26 D6
Elmley Lovett Worcs 26 B5
Elmore Glos 26 G4
Elmore Back Glos 26 G4
Elmscott Devon 6 D1
Elmsett Suff 31 D7
Elmstead Market Essex 31 F7
Elmsted Kent 13 B10
Elmstone Kent 21 E9
Elmstone Hardwicke Glos 26 F6
Elmswell E Yorks 52 D5
Elmswell Suff 30 B6
Elmton Derbys 45 E9
Elphin Highld 92 H5
Elphinstone E Loth 70 C2
Elrick Aberds 83 C10
Elrig Dumfries 54 E6
Elsdon Northumb 62 D5
Elsecar S Yorks 45 C7
Elsenham Essex 30 F2
Elsfield Oxon 28 G2
Elsham N Lincs 46 A4
Elsing Norf 39 D6
Elslack N Yorks 50 E5
Elson Shrops 33 B9
Elsrickle S Lanark 69 F9
Elstead Sur 18 G6
Elsted W Sus 11 C7
Elsthorpe Lincs 37 C6
Elstob Durham 58 D4
Elston Notts 45 H11
Elston Wilts 17 G7
Elstone Devon 6 E5
Elstow Bedford 29 D7
Elstree Herts 19 B8
Elstronwick E Yorks 53 F8
Elswick Lancs 49 F4
Elsworth Cambs 29 B10
Elterwater Cumb 56 F5
Eltham London 19 D11
Eltisley Cambs 29 C9
Elton Cambs 37 F6
Elton Ches W 43 E7
Elton Derbys 44 F6
Elton Glos 26 G4
Elton Hereford 25 A11
Elton Notts 36 B3
Elton Stockton 58 E5
Elton Green Ches W 43 E7
Elvanfoot S Lanark 60 B5
Elvaston Derbys 35 B10
Elveden Suff 38 H4
Elvingston E Loth 70 C3
Elvington Kent 21 F9
Elvington York 52 E2
Elwick Hrtlpl 58 C5
Elwick Northumb 71 G10
Elworth Ches E 43 F10
Elworthy Som 7 C9
Ely Cambs 37 G11
Ely Cardiff 15 D7
Emberton M Keynes 28 D5
Embleton Cumb 56 C3
Embleton Northumb 63 A8
Embo Highld 87 B11
Embo Street Highld 87 B11
Emborough Som 16 F3
Embsay N Yorks 50 D6
Emersons Green S Glos 16 D3
Emery Down Hants 10 D1
Emley W Yorks 44 A6
Emmbrook Wokingham 18 E4
Emmer Green Reading 18 D4
Emmington Oxon 18 A4
Emneth Norf 37 E10
Emneth Hungate Norf 37 E11
Empingham Rutland 36 E5
Empshott Hants 11 A6
Emstrey Shrops 33 D11
Emsworth Hants 10 D6
Enborne W Berks 17 E11
Enchmarsh Shrops 33 F11
Enderby Leics 35 F11
Endmoor Cumb 49 A5
Endon Staffs 44 G3
Endon Bank Staffs 44 G3
Enfield London 19 B10
Enfield Wash London 19 B10
Enford Wilts 17 F8
Engamoor Shetland 96 H4
Engine Common S Glos 16 C3
Englefield W Berks 18 D3
Englefield Green Sur 18 D6
Englesea-brook Ches E 43 G10
English Bicknor Glos 26 G2
English Frankton Shrops 33 C10
Englishcombe Bath 16 E4
Enham Alamein Hants 17 G10
Enmore Som 8 A1
Ennerdale Bridge Cumb 56 E2
Enoch Dumfries 60 C4
Enochdhu Perth 76 A3
Ensay Argyll 78 G6
Ensbury Bmouth 9 E9
Ensdon Shrops 33 D10
Ensis Devon 6 D4
Enstone Oxon 27 F10
Enterkinfoot Dumfries 60 C4
Enterpen N Yorks 58 F5
Enville Staffs 34 G4
Eolaigearraidh W Isles 84 H2
Eorabus Argyll 78 J6
Eòropaidh W Isles 91 A10
Epperstone Notts 45 H10
Epping Essex 19 A11
Epping Green Essex 29 H11
Epping Green Herts 29 H9
Epping Upland Essex 19 A11
Eppleby N Yorks 58 E2
Eppleworth E Yorks 52 F6
Epsom Sur 19 E9
Epwell Oxon 27 D10
Epworth N Lincs 45 B11
Epworth Turbary N Lincs 45 B11
Erbistock Wrex 33 A9
Erbusaig Highld 85 F12
Erchless Castle Highld 86 G7
Erdington W Mid 35 F7
Eredine Argyll 73 C8
Eriboll Highld 92 D7
Ericstane Dumfries 60 B6
Eridge Green E Sus 12 C4
Erines Argyll 73 F7
Eriswell Suff 38 H3
Erith London 20 D2
Erlestoke Wilts 16 F6
Ermine Lincs 46 E3
Ermington Devon 5 F7
Erpingham Norf 39 B7
Errogie Highld 81 A7
Errol Perth 76 E5
Erskine Renfs 68 C3
Erskine Bridge Renfs 68 C3
Ervie Dumfries 54 C3
Erwarton Suff 31 E9
Erwood Powys 25 D7
Eryholme N Yorks 58 F4
Eryrys Denb 42 G5
Escomb Durham 58 D2
Escrick N Yorks 52 E2
Esgairdawe Carms 24 D3
Esgairgeiliog Powys 32 E3
Esh Durham 58 B2
Esh Winning Durham 58 B2
Esher Sur 19 E8
Esholt W Yorks 51 E7
Eshott Northumb 63 D8
Eshton N Yorks 50 D5
Esk Valley N Yorks 59 F9
Eskadale Highld 86 H7
Eskbank Midloth 70 D2
Eskdale Green Cumb 56 F3
Eskdalemuir Dumfries 61 D8
Eske E Yorks 53 E6
Eskham Lincs 47 C7
Esprick Lancs 49 F4
Essendine Rutland 36 D6
Essendon Herts 29 H9
Essich Highld 87 H9
Essington Staffs 34 E5
Esslemont Aberds 89 F9
Eston Redcar 59 E6
Eswick Shetland 96 H6
Etal Northumb 71 G8
Etchilhampton Wilts 17 E7
Etchingham E Sus 12 D6
Etchinghill Kent 21 H8
Etchinghill Staffs 34 D6
Ethie Castle Angus 77 C9
Ethie Mains Angus 77 C9
Etling Green Norf 38 D6
Eton Windsor 18 D6
Eton Wick Windsor 18 D6
Etteridge Highld 81 D8
Ettersgill Durham 57 D10
Ettingshall W Mid 34 F5
Ettington Warks 27 D9
Etton E Yorks 52 E5
Etton Pboro 37 E7
Ettrick Borders 61 B8
Ettrickbridge Borders 61 A9
Ettrickhill Borders 61 B8
Etwall Derbys 35 B8
Euston Suff 38 H4
Euximoor Drove Cambs 37 F10
Euxton Lancs 50 H1
Evanstown Bridgend 14 C5
Evanton Highld 87 E9
Evedon Lincs 46 H4
Evelix Highld 87 B10
Evenjobb Powys 25 B9
Evenley Northants 28 E2
Evenlode Glos 27 F9
Evenwood Durham 58 D2
Evenwood Gate Durham 58 D2
Everbay Orkney 95 F7
Evercreech Som 16 H3
Everdon Northants 28 C2
Everingham E Yorks 52 E4
Everleigh Wilts 17 F9
Everley N Yorks 59 H10
Eversholt C Beds 28 E6
Evershot Dorset 8 D4
Eversley Hants 18 E4
Eversley Cross Hants 18 E4
Everthorpe E Yorks 52 F5
Everton C Beds 29 C9
Everton Hants 10 E1
Everton Mers 42 C6
Everton Notts 45 C10
Evertown Dumfries 61 F9
Evesbatch Hereford 26 D3
Evesham Worcs 27 D7
Evington Leicester 36 E2
Ewden Village S Yorks 44 C6
Ewell Sur 19 E9
Ewell Minnis Kent 21 G9
Ewelme Oxon 18 B3
Ewen Glos 17 B7
Ewenny V Glam 14 D5
Ewerby Lincs 46 H5
Ewerby Thorpe Lincs 46 H5
Ewes Dumfries 61 D9
Ewesley Northumb 62 D6
Ewhurst Sur 19 G7
Ewhurst Green E Sus 13 D6
Ewhurst Green Sur 19 H7
Ewloe Flint 42 F6
Ewloe Grn. Flint 42 F5
Ewood Blackburn 50 G2
Eworthy Devon 6 G3
Ewshot Hants 18 G5
Ewyas Harold Hereford 25 F10
Exbourne Devon 6 F5
Exbury Hants 10 E3
Exebridge Devon 7 D8
Exelby N Yorks 58 H3
Exeter Devon 7 G8
Exford Som 7 C7
Exhall Warks 27 C8
Exley Head W Yorks 50 F6
Exminster Devon 5 C10
Exmouth Devon 5 C11
Exnaboe Shetland 96 M5
Exning Suff 30 B3
Exton Devon 5 C10
Exton Hants 10 B5
Exton Rutland 36 D5
Exton Som 7 C8
Exwick Devon 7 G8
Eyam Derbys 44 E6
Eydon Northants 28 C2
Eye Hereford 25 B11
Eye Pboro 37 E8
Eye Suff 31 A8
Eye Green Pboro 37 E8
Eyemouth Borders 71 D8
Eyeworth C Beds 29 D9
Eyhorne Street Kent 20 F5
Eyke Suff 31 C10
Eynesbury Cambs 29 C8
Eynort Highld 85 F8
Eynsford Kent 20 E2
Eynsham Oxon 27 H11
Eype Dorset 8 E3
Eyre Highld 85 C9
Eyre Highld 85 E10
Eythorne Kent 21 G9
Eyton Hereford 25 B11
Eyton Shrops 33 G9
Eyton Wrex 33 A9
Eyton upon the Weald Moors Telford 34 D2

F

Faccombe Hants 17 F10
Faceby N Yorks 58 F5
Facit Lancs 50 H4
Faddiley Ches E 43 G8
Fadmoor N Yorks 59 H7
Faerdre Swansea 14 A2
Failand N Som 15 D11
Failford S Ayrs 67 D7
Failsworth Gtr Man 44 B2
Fain Highld 86 D4
Fair Green Norf 38 D2
Fair Hill Cumb 57 C7
Fair Oak Hants 10 C3
Fair Oak Green Hants 18 E3
Fairbourne Gwyn 32 D2
Fairburn N Yorks 51 G10
Fairfield Derbys 44 E4
Fairfield Stockton 58 E5
Fairfield Worcs 27 D7
Fairfield Worcs 34 H5
Fairford Glos 17 A8
Fairhaven Lancs 49 G3
Fairlie N Ayrs 73 H11
Fairlight E Sus 13 E7
Fairlight Cove E Sus 13 E7
Fairmile Devon 7 G9
Fairmilehead Edin 69 D11
Fairoak Staffs 34 B3
Fairseat Kent 20 E3
Fairstead Essex 30 G4
Fairstead Norf 38 D2
Fairwarp E Sus 12 D3
Fairy Cottage IoM 48 D4
Fairy Cross Devon 6 D3
Fakenham Norf 38 C5
Fakenham Magna Suff 38 H5
Fala Midloth 70 D3
Fala Dam Midloth 70 D3
Falahill Borders 70 E2
Falcon Hereford 26 E3
Faldingworth Lincs 46 D4
Falfield S Glos 16 B3
Falkenham Suff 31 E9
Falkirk Falk 69 C7
Falkland Fife 76 G5
Falla Borders 62 B3
Fallgate Derbys 45 F7
Fallin Stirling 69 A7
Fallowfield Gtr Man 44 C2
Fallsidehill Borders 70 F5
Falmer E Sus 12 F2
Falmouth Corn 3 F7
Falsgrave N Yorks 59 H11
Falstone Northumb 62 E3
Fanagmore Highld 92 E4
Fangdale Beck N Yorks 59 G6
Fangfoss E Yorks 52 D3
Fankerton Falk 68 B6
Fanmore Argyll 78 G7
Fannich Lodge Highld 86 E5
Fans Borders 70 F5
Far Bank S Yorks 45 A10
Far Bletchley M Keynes 28 E5
Far Cotton Northants 28 C4
Far Forest Worcs 26 A4
Far Laund Derbys 45 H7
Far Sawrey Cumb 56 G5
Farcet Cambs 37 F8
Farden Shrops 34 H1
Fareham Hants 10 D4
Farewell Staffs 35 D6
Farforth Lincs 47 E7
Faringdon Oxon 17 B9
Farington Lancs 49 G5
Farlam Cumb 61 H11
Farlary Highld 93 J10
Farleigh N Som 15 E10
Farleigh Sur 19 E10
Farleigh Hungerford Som 16 F5
Farleigh Wallop Hants 18 G3
Farlesthorpe Lincs 47 E8
Farleton Cumb 49 A5
Farleton Lancs 50 C1
Farley Shrops 33 E9
Farley Staffs 35 A6
Farley Wilts 9 B11
Farley Green Sur 19 G7
Farley Hill Luton 29 F7
Farley Hill Wokingham 18 E4
Farleys End Glos 26 G4
Farlington N Yorks 52 C2
Farlow Shrops 34 G2
Farmborough Bath 16 E3
Farmcote Glos 27 F7
Farmcote Shrops 34 F3
Farmington Glos 27 G8
Farmoor Oxon 27 H11
Farmtown Moray 88 C5
Farnborough Hants 18 F5
Farnborough London 19 E11
Farnborough W Berks 17 C11
Farnborough Warks 27 D11
Farnborough Green Hants 18 F5
Farncombe Sur 18 G6
Farndish Bedford 28 B6
Farndon Ches W 43 G7
Farndon Notts 45 G11
Farnell Angus 77 B9
Farnham Dorset 9 C8
Farnham Essex 29 F11
Farnham N Yorks 51 C9
Farnham Suff 31 B10
Farnham Sur 18 G5
Farnham Common Bucks 18 C6
Farnham Green Essex 29 F11
Farnham Royal Bucks 18 C6
Farnhill N Yorks 50 E6
Farningham Kent 20 E2
Farnley N Yorks 51 E8
Farnley W Yorks 51 F8
Farnley Tyas W Yorks 44 A5
Farnsfield Notts 45 G10
Farnworth Gtr Man 43 B10
Farnworth Halton 43 D8
Farr Highld 81 C10
Farr Highld 87 H9
Farr Highld 93 C10
Farr House Highld 87 H9
Farringdon Devon 7 G9
Farrington Gurney Bath 16 F3
Farsley W Yorks 51 F8
Farthinghoe Northants 28 E2
Farthingloe Kent 21 G9
Farthingstone Northants 28 C3
Fartown W Yorks 51 H7
Farway Devon 7 G10
Fasag Highld 85 C13
Fascadale Highld 79 D8
Faslane Port Argyll 73 E11
Fasnacloich Argyll 74 C3
Fasnakyle Ho Highld 80 A5
Fassfern Highld 80 F2
Fatfield T&W 58 A4
Fattahead Aberds 89 C6
Faugh Cumb 57 A7
Fauldhouse W Loth 69 D8
Faulkbourne Essex 30 G4
Faulkland Som 16 F4
Fauls Shrops 34 B1
Faversham Kent 21 E7
Favillar Moray 88 E2
Fawdington N Yorks 51 B10
Fawfieldhead Staffs 44 F4
Fawkham Green Kent 20 E2
Fawler Oxon 27 G10
Fawley Bucks 18 C4
Fawley Hants 10 D3
Fawley W Berks 17 C10
Fawley Chapel Hereford 26 F2
Faxfleet E Yorks 52 G4
Faygate W Sus 11 A11
Fazakerley Mers 43 C6
Fazeley Staffs 35 E8
Fearby N Yorks 51 A7
Fearn Highld 87 D11
Fearn Lodge Highld 87 C9
Fearn Station Highld 87 D11
Fearnan Perth 75 C10
Fearnbeg Highld 85 C12
Fearnhead Warr 43 C9
Fearnmore Highld 85 B12
Featherstone Staffs 34 E5
Featherstone W Yorks 51 G10
Featherwood Northumb 62 C4
Feckenham Worcs 27 B7
Feering Essex 30 F5
Feetham N Yorks 57 G11
Feizor N Yorks 50 C3
Felbridge Sur 12 C2
Felbrigg Norf 39 B8
Felcourt Sur 12 B2
Felden Herts 19 A7
Felin-Crai Powys 24 F5
Felindre Carms 23 C8
Felindre Carms 23 D10
Felindre Carms 24 E3
Felindre Carms 24 F4
Felindre Ceredig 23 A10
Felindre Powys 33 G7
Felindre Swansea 14 A2
Felindre Farchog Pembs 22 C6
Felinfach Ceredig 23 A10
Felinfach Powys 25 E7
Felinfoel Carms 23 F10
Felingwm isaf Carms 23 D10
Felingwm uchaf Carms 23 D10
Felinwynt Ceredig 23 A7
Felixkirk N Yorks 51 A10
Felixstowe Suff 31 E9
Felixstowe Ferry Suff 31 E10
Felkington Northumb 71 F8
Felkirk W Yorks 45 A7
Fell Side Cumb 56 C5
Felling T&W 63 G8
Felmersham Bedford 28 C6
Felmingham Norf 39 C8
Felpham W Sus 11 E8
Felsham Suff 30 C6
Felsted Essex 30 F3
Feltham London 19 D8
Felthorpe Norf 39 D7
Felton Hereford 26 D2
Felton N Som 15 E11
Felton Northumb 63 C7
Felton Butler Shrops 33 D9
Feltwell Norf 38 F3
Fen Ditton Cambs 29 B11
Fen Drayton Cambs 29 B10
Fen End W Mid 35 H8
Fen Side Lincs 47 G7
Fenay Bridge W Yorks 51 H7
Fence Lancs 50 F4
Fence Houses T&W 58 A4
Fengate Norf 39 C7
Fengate Pboro 37 F8
Fenham Northumb 71 F9
Fenhouses Lincs 37 A8
Feniscliffe Blackburn 50 G2
Feniscowles Blackburn 50 G2
Feniton Devon 7 G10
Fenlake Bedford 29 D7
Fenny Bentley Derbys 44 G5
Fenny Bridges Devon 7 G10
Fenny Compton Warks 27 C11
Fenny Drayton Leics 35 F9
Fenny Stratford M Keynes 28 E5
Fenrother Northumb 63 D7
Fenstanton Cambs 29 B10
Fenton Cambs 37 H9
Fenton Lincs 46 E2
Fenton Lincs 46 G2
Fenton Stoke 34 A4
Fenton Barns E Loth 70 B4
Fenton Town Northumb 71 G8
Fenwick E Ayrs 67 B7
Fenwick Northumb 62 F6
Fenwick Northumb 71 F9
Fenwick S Yorks 52 H1
Feochaig Argyll 65 G8
Feock Corn 3 F7
Feolin Ferry Argyll 72 G3
Ferindonald Highld 85 H11
Feriniquarrie Highld 84 C6
Ferlochan Argyll 74 C2
Fern Angus 77 A7
Ferndale Rhondda 14 B6
Ferndown Dorset 9 D9
Ferness Highld 87 G12
Ferney Green Cumb 56 G6
Fernham Oxon 17 B9
Fernhill Heath Worcs 26 C5
Fernhurst W Sus 11 B7
Fernie Fife 76 F6
Ferniegair S Lanark 68 E6
Fernilea Highld 85 E8
Fernilee Derbys 44 E4
Ferrensby N Yorks 51 C9
Ferring W Sus 11 D9
Ferry Hill Cambs 37 G9
Ferry Point Highld 87 C10
Ferrybridge W Yorks 51 G10
Ferryden Angus 77 B10
Ferryhill Aberdeen 83 C11
Ferryhill Durham 58 C3
Ferryhill Station Durham 58 C4
Ferryside Carms 23 E8
Fersfield Norf 39 G6
Fersit Highld 80 F5
Ferwig Ceredig 22 B6
Feshiebridge Highld 81 C10
Fetcham Sur 19 F8
Fetterangus Aberds 89 C9
Fettercairn Aberds 83 F8
Fettes Highld 87 F8
Fewcott Oxon 28 F2
Fewston N Yorks 51 D7
Ffair-Rhos Ceredig 24 B4
Ffairfach Carms 24 F3
Ffaldybrenin Carms 24 D3
Ffarmers Carms 24 D3
Ffawyddog Powys 25 G9
Fforest Carms 23 F10
Fforest-fâch Swansea 14 B2
Ffos-y-ffin Ceredig 24 B1
Ffostrasol Ceredig 23 B8
Ffridd-Uchaf Gwyn 41 E7
Ffrith Wrex 42 G5
Ffrwd Gwyn 40 E6
Ffynnon ddrain Carms 23 D9
Ffynnon-oer Ceredig 23 A10
Ffynnongroyw Flint 42 D4
Fidden Argyll 78 J6
Fiddes Aberds 83 E10
Fiddington Glos 26 E6
Fiddington Som 7 B11
Fiddleford Dorset 9 C7
Fiddlers Hamlet Essex 19 A11
Field Staffs 34 B6
Field Broughton Cumb 49 A3
Field Dalling Norf 38 B6
Field Head Leics 35 E10
Fifehead Magdalen Dorset 9 B6
Fifehead Neville Dorset 9 C6
Fifield Oxon 27 G9
Fifield Wilts 17 F8
Fifield Windsor 18 D6
Fifield Bavant Wilts 9 B9
Figheldean Wilts 17 G8
Filands Wilts 16 C6
Filby Norf 39 D10
Filey N Yorks 53 A7
Filgrave M Keynes 28 D5
Filkins Oxon 17 A9
Filleigh Devon 6 D5
Filleigh Devon 7 E6
Fillingham Lincs 46 D3
Fillongley Warks 35 G8
Filton S Glos 16 D3
Fimber E Yorks 52 C4
Finavon Angus 77 B7
Finchairn Argyll 73 C8
Fincham Norf 38 E2
Finchampstead Wokingham 18 E4
Finchdean Hants 10 C6
Finchingfield Essex 30 E3
Finchley London 19 B9
Findern Derbys 35 B9
Findhorn Moray 87 E13
Findhorn Bridge Highld 81 A10
Findo Gask Perth 76 E3
Findochty Moray 88 B4
Findon Aberds 83 D11
Findon W Sus 11 D10
Findon Mains Highld 87 E9
Findrack Ho. Aberds 83 C8
Finedon Northants 28 A6
Fingal Street Suff 31 B9
Fingask Aberds 83 A9
Fingerpost Worcs 26 A4
Fingest Bucks 18 B4
Finghall N Yorks 58 H2
Fingland Cumb 61 H8
Fingland Dumfries 60 B3
Finglesham Kent 21 F10
Fingringhoe Essex 31 F7
Finlarig Stirling 75 D8
Finmere Oxon 28 E3
Finnart Perth 75 B8
Finningham Suff 31 B7
Finningley S Yorks 45 C10
Finnygaud Aberds 88 C5
Finsbury London 19 C10
Finstall Worcs 26 B6
Finsthwaite Cumb 56 H5
Finstock Oxon 27 G10
Finstown Orkney 95 G4
Fintry Aberds 89 C7
Fintry Dundee 77 D7
Fintry Stirling 68 B5
Finzean Aberds 83 D8
Fionnphort Argyll 78 J6
Fionnsbhagh W Isles 90 J5
Fir Tree Durham 58 C2
Firbeck S Yorks 45 D9
Firby N Yorks 52 C3
Firby N Yorks 58 H3
Firgrove Gtr Man 44 A3
Firsby Lincs 47 F8
Firsdown Wilts 9 A11
First Coast Highld 86 B2
Fishbourne IoW 10 E4
Fishbourne W Sus 11 D7
Fishburn Durham 58 C4
Fishcross Clack 75 H11
Fisher Place Cumb 56 E5
Fisherford Aberds 89 E6
Fisher's Pond Hants 10 B3
Fisherstreet W Sus 11 A8
Fisherton Highld 87 F10
Fisherton S Ayrs 66 E5
Fishguard = Abergwaun Pembs 22 C4
Fishlake S Yorks 45 A10
Fishleigh Barton Devon 6 D4
Fishponds Bristol 16 D3
Fishpool Glos 26 F3
Fishtoft Lincs 37 A9
Fishtoft Drove Lincs 47 H7
Fishtown of Usan Angus 77 B10
Fishwick Borders 71 E8
Fiskavaig Highld 85 E8
Fiskerton Lincs 46 E4
Fiskerton Notts 45 G11
Fitling E Yorks 53 F8
Fittleton Wilts 17 G8
Fittleworth W Sus 11 C9
Fitton End Cambs 37 D10
Fitz Shrops 33 D10
Fitzhead Som 7 D10
Fitzwilliam W Yorks 51 H10
Fiunary Highld 79 G9
Five Acres Glos 26 G2
Five Ashes E Sus 12 D4
Five Oak Green Kent 20 G3
Five Oaks Jersey 11
Five Oaks W Sus 11 B9
Five Roads Carms 23 F9
Fivecrosses Ches W 43 E8
Fivehead Som 8 B2
Flack's Green Essex 30 G4
Flackwell Heath Bucks 18 C5
Fladbury Worcs 26 D6
Fladdabister Shetland 96 K6
Flagg Derbys 44 F5
Flamborough E Yorks 53 B8
Flamstead Herts 29 G7
Flamstead End Herts 19 A10
Flansham W Sus 11 D8
Flanshaw W Yorks 51 G9
Flasby N Yorks 50 D5
Flash Staffs 44 F4
Flashader Highld 85 C8
Flask Inn N Yorks 59 F10
Flaunden Herts 19 A7
Flawborough Notts 36 A3
Flawith N Yorks 51 C10
Flax Bourton N Som 15 E11
Flaxby N Yorks 51 D9
Flaxholme Derbys 35 A9
Flaxley Glos 26 G3
Flaxpool Som 7 C10
Flaxton N Yorks 52 C2
Fleckney Leics 36 F2
Flecknoe Warks 28 B2
Fledborough Notts 46 E2
Fleet Hants 10 D6
Fleet Hants 18 F5
Fleet Lincs 37 C9
Fleet Hargate Lincs 37 C9
Fleetham Northumb 71 H10
Fleetlands Hants 10 D4
Fleetville Herts 29 H8
Fleetwood Lancs 49 E3
Flemingston V Glam 14 D6
Flemington S Lanark 68 E5
Flempton Suff 30 B5
Fleoideabhagh W Isles 90 J5
Fletchertown Cumb 56 B4
Fletching E Sus 12 D3
Flexbury Corn 6 F1
Flexford Sur 18 G6
Flimby Cumb 56 C2
Flimwell E Sus 12 C6
Flint = Y Fflint Flint 42 E5
Flint Mountain Flint 42 E5
Flintham Notts 45 H11
Flinton E Yorks 53 F8
Flintsham Hereford 25 C10
Flitcham Norf 38 C3
Flitton C Beds 29 E7
Flitwick C Beds 29 E7
Flixborough N Lincs 52 H4
Flixborough Stather N Lincs 46 A2
Flixton Gtr Man 43 C10
Flixton N Yorks 52 B6
Flixton Suff 39 G9
Flockton W Yorks 44 A6
Flodaigh W Isles 84 C3
Flodden Northumb 71 G8
Flodigarry Highld 85 A9
Flood's Ferry Cambs 37 F9
Flookburgh Cumb 49 B3
Florden Norf 39 F7
Flore Northants 28 B3
Flotterton Northumb 62 C5
Flowton Suff 31 D7
Flush House W Yorks 44 B5
Flushing Aberds 89 D10
Flushing Corn 3 F7
Flyford Flavell Worcs 26 C6
Foals Green Suff 31 A9
Fobbing Thurrock 20 C4
Fochabers Moray 88 C3
Fochriw Caerph 25 H8
Fockerby N Lincs 52 H4
Fodderletter Moray 82 A3
Fodderty Highld 87 F8
Foel Powys 32 D5
Foel-gastell Carms 23 E10
Foffarty Angus 77 C7
Foggathorpe E Yorks 52 F3
Fogo Borders 70 F6
Fogorig Borders 70 F6
Foindle Highld 92 E4
Folda Angus 76 A4
Fole Staffs 34 B6
Foleshill W Mid 35 G9
Folke Dorset 8 C5
Folkestone Kent 21 H9
Folkingham Lincs 37 B6
Folkington E Sus 12 F4
Folksworth Cambs 37 G7
Folkton N Yorks 53 B6
Folla Rule Aberds 89 E7
Follifoot N Yorks 51 D9
Folly Gate Devon 6 G4
Fonthill Bishop Wilts 9 A8
Fonthill Gifford Wilts 9 A8
Fontmell Magna Dorset 9 C7
Fontwell W Sus 11 D8
Foolow Derbys 44 E5
Foots Cray London 19 D11
Forbestown Aberds 82 B5
Force Mills Cumb 56 G5
Forcett N Yorks 58 E2
Ford Argyll 73 C7
Ford Bucks 28 H4
Ford Devon 6 D3
Ford Glos 27 F7
Ford Northumb 71 G8
Ford Shrops 33 D10
Ford Staffs 44 G4
Ford W Sus 11 D8
Ford Wilts 16 D5
Ford End Essex 30 G3
Ford Street Som 7 E10
Fordcombe Kent 12 B4
Fordell Fife 69 B10
Forden Powys 33 E8
Forder Grn. Devon 5 E8
Fordham Cambs 30 A3
Fordham Essex 30 F6
Fordham Norf 38 F2
Fordhouses W Mid 34 E5
Fordingbridge Hants 9 C10
Fordon E Yorks 52 B6
Fordoun Aberds 83 F9
Ford's Green Suff 31 B7
Fordstreet Essex 30 F6
Fordwells Oxon 27 G10
Fordwich Kent 21 F8
Fordyce Aberds 88 B5
Forebridge Staffs 34 C5
Forest Durham 57 C10
Forest Becks Lancs 50 D3
Forest Gate London 19 C11
Forest Green Sur 19 G8
Forest Hall Cumb 57 F7
Forest Head Cumb 61 H11
Forest Hill Oxon 28 H2
Forest Lane Head N Yorks 51 D9
Forest Lodge Argyll 74 C5
Forest Lodge Highld 82 B2
Forest Lodge Perth 81 F11
Forest Mill Clack 69 A8
Forest Row E Sus 12 C3
Forest Town Notts 45 F9
Forestburn Gate Northumb 62 D6
Foresterseat Moray 88 C1
Forestside W Sus 11 C6
Forfar Angus 77 B7
Forgandenny Perth 76 F3
Forge Powys 32 F3
Forge Side Torf 25 H9
Forgewood N Lanark 68 E6
Forgie Moray 88 C3
Forglen Ho. Aberds 89 C6
Formby Mers 42 B6
Forncett End Norf 39 F7
Forncett St Mary Norf 39 F7
Forncett St Peter Norf 39 F7
Forneth Perth 76 C3
Fornham All Saints Suff 30 B5
Fornham St Martin Suff 30 B5
Forres Moray 87 F13
Forrest Lodge Dumfries 67 H8
Forrestfield N Lanark 69 D7
Forsbrook Staffs 34 A5
Forse Highld 94 G4
Forse Ho. Highld 94 G4
Forsinain Highld 93 E12
Forsinard Highld 93 E11
Forsinard Station Highld 93 E11
Forston Dorset 8 E5
Fort Augustus Highld 80 C5
Fort George Guern 11
Fort George Highld 87 F10
Fort William Highld 80 F3
Forteviot Perth 76 F3
Forth S Lanark 69 E8
Forth Road Bridge Edin 69 C10
Forthampton Glos 26 E5
Fortingall Perth 75 C10
Forton Hants 17 G11
Forton Lancs 49 D4
Forton Shrops 33 D10
Forton Som 8 D2
Forton Staffs 34 C3
Forton Heath Shrops 33 D10
Fortrie Aberds 89 D6
Fortrose Highld 87 F10
Fortuneswell Dorset 8 G5
Forty Green Bucks 18 B6
Forty Hill London 19 B10
Forward Green Suff 31 C7
Fosbury Wilts 17 F10
Fosdyke Lincs 37 B9
Foss Perth 75 B10
Foss Cross Glos 27 H7
Fossebridge Glos 27 G7
Foster Street Essex 29 H11
Fosterhouses S Yorks 45 A10
Foston Derbys 35 B7
Foston Lincs 36 A4
Foston N Yorks 52 C2
Foston on the Wolds E Yorks 53 D7
Fotherby Lincs 47 C7
Fotheringhay Northants 37 F6
Foubister Orkney 95 H6
Foul Mile E Sus 12 E5
Foulby W Yorks 51 H9
Foulden Borders 71 E8
Foulden Norf 38 F3
Foulis Castle Highld 87 E8
Foulridge Lancs 50 E4
Foulsham Norf 38 C6
Fountainhall Borders 70 F3
Four Ashes Staffs 34 G4
Four Ashes Suff 31 A7
Four Crosses Powys 33 D8
Four Crosses Powys 33 E6
Four Crosses Wrex 42 G5
Four Elms Kent 19 G11
Four Forks Som 7 C11
Four Gotes Cambs 37 D10
Four Lane Ends Ches W 43 F8
Four Lanes Corn 2 F5
Four Marks Hants 10 A5
Four Mile Bridge Anglesey 40 C4
Four Oaks E Sus 13 D7
Four Oaks W Mid 35 F7
Four Oaks W Mid 35 G8
Four Roads Carms 23 F9
Four Roads IoM 48 F2
Four Throws Kent 13 D6
Fourlane Ends Derbys 45 G7
Fourlanes End Ches E 44 G2
Fourpenny Highld 87 B11
Fourstones Northumb 62 G4
Fovant Wilts 9 B9
Foveran Aberds 89 F9
Fowey Corn 4 F2
Fowley Common Warr 43 C9
Fowlis Angus 76 D6
Fowlis Wester Perth 76 E2
Fowlmere Cambs 29 D11
Fownhope Hereford 26 E2
Fox Corner Sur 18 F6
Fox Lane Hants 18 F5
Fox Street Essex 31 F7
Foxbar Renfs 68 D3
Foxcombe Hill Oxon 17 A11
Foxdale IoM 48 E2
Foxearth Essex 30 D5
Foxfield Cumb 56 H4
Foxham Wilts 16 D6
Foxhole Corn 3 D8
Foxhole Swansea 14 B2
Foxholes N Yorks 52 B6
Foxhunt Green E Sus 12 E4
Foxley Norf 38 C6
Foxley Wilts 16 C5
Foxt Staffs 44 H4
Foxton Cambs 29 D11
Foxton Durham 58 D4
Foxton Leics 36 F3
Foxup N Yorks 50 B4
Foxwist Green Ches W 43 F9
Foxwood Shrops 34 H2
Foy Hereford 26 F2
Foyers Highld 81 A6
Fraddam Corn 2 F4
Fraddon Corn 3 D8
Fradley Staffs 35 D7
Fradswell Staffs 34 B5
Fraisthorpe E Yorks 53 C7
Framfield E Sus 12 D3
Framingham Earl Norf 39 E8
Framingham Pigot Norf 39 E8
Framlingham Suff 31 B9
Frampton Dorset 8 E5
Frampton Lincs 37 B9
Frampton Cotterell S Glos 16 C3
Frampton Mansell Glos 16 A6
Frampton on Severn Glos 26 H4
Frampton West End Lincs 37 A8
Framsden Suff 31 C8
Framwellgate Moor Durham 58 B3
Franche Worcs 34 H4
Frankby Mers 42 D5
Frankley Worcs 34 G5
Frank's Bridge Powys 25 C8
Frankton Warks 27 A11
Frant E Sus 12 C4
Fraserburgh Aberds 89 B9
Frating Green Essex 31 F7
Fratton Ptsmth 10 E5
Freathy Corn 4 F4
Freckenham Suff 30 A3
Freckleton Lancs 49 G4
Freeby Leics 36 C4
Freehay Staffs 34 A6
Freeland Oxon 27 G11
Freester Shetland 96 H6
Freethorpe Norf 39 E10
Freiston Lincs 37 A9
Fremington Devon 6 C4
Fremington N Yorks 58 G1
Frenchay S Glos 16 D3
Frenchbeer Devon 5 C7
Frenich Stirling 75 G7
Frensham Sur 18 G5
Fresgoe Highld 93 C12
Freshfield Mers 42 B5
Freshford Bath 16 E4
Freshwater IoW 10 F2
Freshwater Bay IoW 10 F2
Freshwater East Pembs 22 G5
Fressingfield Suff 39 H8
Freston Suff 31 E8
Freswick Highld 94 D5
Fretherne Glos 26 H4
Frettenham Norf 39 D8
Freuchie Fife 76 G5
Freuchies Angus 76 A5
Freystrop Pembs 22 E4
Friar's Gate E Sus 12 C3
Friarton Perth 76 E4
Friday Bridge Cambs 37 E10
Friday Street E Sus 12 F5
Fridaythorpe E Yorks 52 D4
Friern Barnet London 19 B9
Friesland Argyll 78 F4
Friesthorpe Lincs 46 D4
Frieston Lincs 46 H3
Frieth Bucks 18 B4
Frilford Oxon 17 B11
Frilsham W Berks 18 D2
Frimley Sur 18 F5
Frimley Green Sur 18 F5
Frindsbury Medway 20 D4
Fring Norf 38 B3
Fringford Oxon 28 F3
Frinsted Kent 20 F5
Frinton-on-Sea Essex 31 F9
Friockheim Angus 77 C8
Friog Gwyn 32 D2
Frisby on the Wreake Leics 36 D2
Friskney Lincs 47 G8
Friskney Eaudike Lincs 47 G8
Friskney Tofts Lincs 47 G8
Friston E Sus 12 G4
Friston Suff 31 B11
Fritchley Derbys 45 G7
Frith Bank Lincs 47 H7
Frith Common Worcs 26 B3
Fritham Hants 9 C11
Frithelstock Devon 6 E3
Frithelstock Stone Devon 6 E3
Frithville Lincs 47 G7
Frittenden Kent 13 B7
Frittiscombe Devon 5 G9
Fritton Norf 39 E10
Fritton Norf 39 F8
Fritwell Oxon 28 F2
Frizinghall W Yorks 51 F7
Frizington Cumb 56 E2
Frocester Glos 16 A4
Frodesley Shrops 33 E11
Frodingham N Lincs 46 A2
Frodsham Ches W 43 E8
Frogden Borders 70 H6
Froggatt Derbys 44 E6
Froghall Staffs 44 H4
Frogmore Devon 5 G8
Frogmore Hants 18 F5
Frognall Lincs 37 D7
Frogshail Norf 39 B8
Frolesworth Leics 35 F11
Frome Som 16 G4
Frome St Quintin Dorset 8 D4
Fromes Hill Hereford 26 D3
Fron Denb 42 F3
Fron Gwyn 40 G5
Fron Gwyn 41 E7
Fron Powys 25 B7
Fron Powys 33 E8
Fron Powys 33 F7
Froncysyllte Wrex 33 A8
Frongoch Gwyn 32 B5
Frostenden Suff 39 G10
Frosterley Durham 58 C1
Frotoft Orkney 95 F5
Froxfield Wilts 17 E9
Froxfield Green Hants 10 B6
Froyle Hants 18 G4
Fryerning Essex 20 A3
Fryton N Yorks 52 B2
Fulbeck Lincs 46 G3
Fulbourn Cambs 30 C2
Fulbrook Oxon 27 G9
Fulford Som 7 D11
Fulford Staffs 34 B5
Fulford York 52 E2
Fulham London 19 D9
Fulking W Sus 11 C11
Full Sutton E Yorks 52 D3
Fullarton Glasgow 68 D5
Fullarton N Ayrs 66 C6
Fuller Street Essex 30 G4
Fuller's Moor Ches W 43 G7
Fullerton Hants 17 H10
Fulletby Lincs 46 E6
Fullwood E Ayrs 67 A7
Fulmer Bucks 18 C6
Fulmodestone Norf 38 B5
Fulnetby Lincs 46 E4
Fulstow Lincs 47 C7
Fulwell T&W 63 H9
Fulwood Lancs 49 F5
Fulwood S Yorks 45 D7
Fundenhall Norf 39 F7
Fundenhall Street Norf 39 F7
Funtington W Sus 11 D6
Funtley Hants 10 D4
Funtullich Perth 75 E10
Funzie Shetland 96 D8
Furley Devon 8 D1
Furnace Argyll 73 C9
Furnace Carms 23 F10
Furnace End Warks 35 F8
Furneaux Pelham Herts 29 F11
Furness Vale Derbys 44 D4
Furze Platt Windsor 18 C5
Furzehill Devon 7 B6
Fyfett Som 7 E11
Fyfield Essex 30 H2
Fyfield Glos 17 A9
Fyfield Hants 17 G9
Fyfield Oxon 17 B11
Fyfield Wilts 17 E8
Fylingthorpe N Yorks 59 F10
Fyvie Aberds 89 E7

G

Gabhsann bho Dheas W Isles 91 B9
Gabhsann bho Thuath W Isles 91 B9
Gablon Highld 87 B10
Gabroc Hill E Ayrs 67 A7
Gaddesby Leics 36 D2
Gadebridge Herts 29 H7
Gaer Powys 25 F8
Gaerllwyd Mon 15 B10
Gaerwen Anglesey 40 C6
Gagingwell Oxon 27 F11
Gaick Lodge Highld 81 E9
Gailey Staffs 34 D5
Gainford Durham 58 E2
Gainsborough Lincs 46 C2
Gainsborough Suff 31 D8
Gainsford End Essex 30 E4
Gairloch Highld 85 A13
Gairlochy Highld 80 E3
Gairney Bank Perth 76 H4
Gairnshiel Lodge Aberds 82 C4
Gaisgill Cumb 57 F8
Gaitsgill Cumb 56 B5
Galashiels Borders 70 G3
Galgate Lancs 49 D4
Galhampton Som 8 B5
Gallaberry Dumfries 60 E5
Gallachoille Argyll 72 E6
Gallanach Argyll 78 E5
Gallanach Argyll 79 J11
Gallantry Bank Ches E 43 G8
Gallatown Fife 69 A11
Galley Common Warks 35 F9
Galley Hill Cambs 29 B10
Galleyend Essex 20 A4
Galleywood Essex 20 A4
Gallin Perth 75 C8
Gallowfauld Angus 77 C7
Gallows Green Staffs 35 A6
Galltair Highld 85 F13
Galmisdale Highld 78 C7
Galmpton Devon 5 G7
Galmpton Torbay 5 F9
Galphay N Yorks 51 B8
Galston E Ayrs 67 C8
Galtrigill Highld 84 C6
Gamblesby Cumb 57 C8
Gamesley Derbys 44 C4
Gamlingay Cambs 29 C9
Gammersgill N Yorks 51 A6
Gamston Notts 45 E11
Ganarew Hereford 26 G2
Ganavan Argyll 79 H11
Gang Corn 4 E4
Ganllwyd Gwyn 32 C3
Gannochy Angus 83 F7
Gannochy Perth 76 E4
Gansclet Highld 94 F5
Ganstead E Yorks 53 F7
Ganthorpe N Yorks 52 B2
Ganton N Yorks 52 B5
Garbat Highld 86 E7
Garbhallt Argyll 73 D9
Garboldisham Norf 38 G6
Garden City Flint 42 F6
Garden Village W Yorks 51 F10
Garden Village Wrex 42 G6
Gardenstown Aberds 89 B7
Garderhouse Shetland 96 J5
Gardham E Yorks 52 E5
Gardin Shetland 96 G6
Gare Hill Som 16 G4
Garelochhead Argyll 73 D11
Garford Oxon 17 B11
Garforth W Yorks 51 F10
Gargrave N Yorks 50 D5
Gargunnock Stirling 68 A6
Garlic Street Norf 39 G8
Garlieston Dumfries 55 E7
Garlinge Green Kent 21 F8
Garlogie Aberds 83 C9
Garmond Aberds 89 C8
Garmony Argyll 79 G9
Garmouth Moray 88 B3
Garn-yr-erw Torf 25 G9
Garnant Carms 24 G3
Garndiffaith Torf 15 A8
Garndolbenmaen Gwyn 40 F6
Garnedd Conwy 41 E9
Garnett Bridge Cumb 57 G7
Garnfadryn Gwyn 40 G4
Garnkirk N Lanark 68 D5
Garnlydan Bl Gwent 25 G8
Garnswllt Swansea 24 H3
Garrabost W Isles 91 D10
Garraron Argyll 73 C7
Garras Corn 2 G6
Garreg Gwyn 41 F8
Garrick Perth 75 F11
Garrigill Cumb 57 B9
Garriston N Yorks 58 G2
Garroch Dumfries 55 A8
Garrogie Lodge Highld 81 B7
Garros Highld 85 B9
Garrow Perth 75 C11
Garryhorn Dumfries 67 G8
Garsdale Cumb 57 H9
Garsdale Head Cumb 57 G9
Garsdon Wilts 16 C6
Garshall Green Staffs 34 B5
Garsington Oxon 18 A2
Garstang Lancs 49 E4
Garston Mers 43 D7
Garswood Mers 43 C8
Gartcosh N Lanark 68 D5
Garth Bridgend 14 B4
Garth Gwyn 41 C7
Garth Powys 24 D6
Garth Shetland 96 H4
Garth Wrex 33 A8
Garth Row Cumb 57 G7
Garthamlock Glasgow 68 D5
Garthbrengy Powys 25 E7
Garthdee Aberdeen 83 C11
Gartheli Ceredig 23 A10
Garthmyl Powys 33 F7
Garthorpe Leics 36 C4
Garthorpe N Lincs 52 H4
Gartly Aberds 88 E5
Gartmore Stirling 75 H8
Gartnagrenach Argyll 72 H6
Gartness N Lanark 68 D6
Gartness Stirling 68 B4
Gartocharn W Dunb 68 B3
Garton E Yorks 53 F8
Garton-on-the-Wolds E Yorks 52 D5
Gartsherrie N Lanark 68 D6
Gartymore Highld 93 H13
Garvald E Loth 70 C4
Garvamore Highld 81 D7
Garvard Argyll 72 D2
Garvault Hotel Highld 93 F10
Garve Highld 86 E6
Garvestone Norf 38 E6
Garvock Aberds 83 F9
Garvock Invclyd 73 F11
Garway Hereford 25 F11
Garway Hill Hereford 25 F11
Gaskan Highld 79 D10
Gastard Wilts 16 E5
Gasthorpe Norf 38 G5
Gatcombe IoW 10 F3
Gate Burton Lincs 46 D2
Gate Helmsley N Yorks 52 D2
Gateacre Mers 43 D7
Gatebeck Cumb 57 H7
Gateford Notts 45 D9
Gateforth N Yorks 52 G1
Gatehead E Ayrs 67 C6
Gatehouse Northumb 62 E3
Gatehouse of Fleet Dumfries 55 D9
Gatelawbridge Dumfries 60 D5
Gateley Norf 38 C5
Gatenby N Yorks 58 H4
Gateshead T&W 63 G8
Gatesheath Ches W 43 F7
Gateside Aberds 83 B8
Gateside Angus 77 C7
Gateside E Renf 68 E3
Gateside Fife 76 G4
Gateside N Ayrs 67 A6
Gathurst Gtr Man 43 B8
Gatley Gtr Man 44 D2
Gattonside Borders 70 G4
Gatwick Airport W Sus 12 B1
Gaufron Powys 24 B6
Gaulby Leics 36 E2
Gauldry Fife 76 E6
Gaunt's Common Dorset 9 D9
Gautby Lincs 46 E5
Gavinton Borders 70 E6
Gawber S Yorks 45 B7
Gawcott Bucks 28 E3
Gawsworth Ches E 44 F2
Gawthorpe W Yorks 51 G8
Gawthrop Cumb 57 H8
Gawthwaite Cumb 49 A2
Gay Street W Sus 11 B9
Gaydon Warks 27 C10
Gayfield Orkney 95 C5
Gayhurst M Keynes 28 D5
Gayle N Yorks 57 H10
Gayles N Yorks 58 F2
Gayton Mers 42 D5
Gayton Norf 38 D3
Gayton Northants 28 C4
Gayton Staffs 34 C5
Gayton le Marsh Lincs 47 D8
Gayton le Wold Lincs 46 D6
Gayton Thorpe Norf 38 D3
Gaywood Norf 38 C2
Gazeley Suff 30 B4
Geanies House Highld 87 D11
Gearraidh Bhailteas W Isles 84 F2
Gearraidh Bhaird W Isles 91 E8
Gearraidh na h-Aibhne W Isles 90 D7
Gearraidh na Monadh W Isles 84 G2
Geary Highld 84 B7
Geddes House Highld 87 F11
Gedding Suff 30 C6
Geddington Northants 36 G4
Gedintailor Highld 85 E10
Gedling Notts 36 A2
Gedney Lincs 37 C10
Gedney Broadgate Lincs 37 C10
Gedney Drove End Lincs 37 C10
Gedney Dyke Lincs 37 C10
Gedney Hill Lincs 37 D9
Gee Cross Gtr Man 44 C3
Geilston Argyll 68 C2
Geirinis W Isles 84 D2
Geise Highld 94 D3
Geisiadar W Isles 90 D6
Geldeston Norf 39 F9
Gell Conwy 41 D10
Gelli Pembs 22 E5
Gelli Rhondda 14 B5
Gellideg M Tydf 25 H7
Gellifor Denb 42 F4
Gelligaer Caerph 15 B7
Gellilydan Gwyn 41 G8
Gellinudd Neath 14 A3
Gellyburn Perth 76 D3
Gellywen Carms 23 D7
Gelston Dumfries 55 D10
Gelston Lincs 36 A5
Gembling E Yorks 53 D7
Gentleshaw Staffs 35 D6
Geocrab W Isles 90 H6
George Green Bucks 19 C7
George Nympton Devon 6 D6
Georgefield Dumfries 61 D8
Georgeham Devon 6 C3
Georgetown Bl Gwent 25 H8
Gerlan Gwyn 41 D8
Germansweek Devon 6 G3
Germoe Corn 2 G4
Gerrans Corn 3 F7
Gerrards Cross Bucks 19 C7
Gestingthorpe Essex 30 E5
Geuffordd Powys 33 D8
Gib Hill Ches W 43 E9
Gibbet Hill Warks 35 G11
Gibbshill Dumfries 60 F3
Gidea Park London 20 C2
Gidleigh Devon 5 C7
Giffnock E Renf 68 E4
Gifford E Loth 70 D4
Giffordland N Ayrs 66 B5
Giffordtown Fife 76 F5
Giggleswick N Yorks 50 C4
Gilberdyke E Yorks 52 G4
Gilchriston E Loth 70 D3
Gilcrux Cumb 56 C3
Gildersome W Yorks 51 G8
Gildingwells S Yorks 45 D9
Gileston V Glam 14 E6
Gilfach Caerph 15 B7
Gilfach Goch Rhondda 14 C5
Gilfachrheda Ceredig 23 A9
Gillamoor N Yorks 59 H7
Gillar's Green Mers 43 C7
Gillen Highld 84 C7
Gilling East N Yorks 52 B2
Gilling West N Yorks 58 F2
Gillingham Dorset 9 B7
Gillingham Medway 20 E4
Gillingham Norf 39 F10
Gillock Highld 94 E4
Gillow Heath Staffs 44 G2
Gills Highld 94 C5
Gill's Green Kent 13 C6
Gilmanscleuch Borders 61 A9
Gilmerton Edin 69 D11
Gilmerton Perth 75 E11
Gilmonby Durham 57 E11
Gilmorton Leics 36 G1
Gilmourton S Lanark 68 F5
Gilsland Northumb 62 G2
Gilsland Spa Cumb 62 G2
Gilston Borders 70 E3
Gilston Herts 29 G11
Gilwern Mon 25 G9
Gimingham Norf 39 B8
Giosla W Isles 90 E6
Gipping Suff 31 B7
Gipsey Bridge Lincs 46 H6
Girdle Toll N Ayrs 66 B6
Girlsta Shetland 96 H6
Girsby N Yorks 58 F4
Girtford C Beds 29 C8
Girthon Dumfries 55 D9
Girton Cambs 29 B11
Girton Notts 46 F2
Girvan S Ayrs 66 G4
Gisburn Lancs 50 E4
Gisleham Suff 39 G11
Gislingham Suff 31 A7
Gissing Norf 39 G7
Gittisham Devon 7 G10
Gladestry Powys 25 C9
Gladsmuir E Loth 70 C3
Glais Swansea 14 A3
Glaisdale N Yorks 59 F8
Glame Highld 85 D10
Glamis Angus 76 C6
Glan Adda Gwyn 41 C7
Glan Conwy Conwy 41 C10
Glan-Conwy Conwy 41 E10
Glan-Duar Carms 23 B10
Glan-Dwyfach Gwyn 40 F6
Glan Gors Anglesey 40 C6
Glan-rhyd Gwyn 40 E6
Glan-traeth Anglesey 40 C4
Glan-y-don Flint 42 E4
Glan-y-nant Powys 32 G5
Glan-y-wern Gwyn 41 G8
Glan-yr-afon Anglesey 41 B8
Glan-yr-afon Gwyn 32 A5
Glan-yr-afon Gwyn 32 A6
Glanaman Carms 24 G3
Glandford Norf 38 A6
Glandwr Pembs 22 D6
Glandy Cross Carms 22 D6
Glandyfi Ceredig 32 F2
Glangrwyney Powys 25 G9
Glanmule Powys 33 F7
Glanrafon Ceredig 32 G2
Glanrhyd Gwyn 40 G4
Glanrhyd Pembs 22 B6
Glanton Northumb 62 B6
Glanton Pike Northumb 62 B6
Glanvilles Wootton Dorset 8 D5
Glapthorn Northants 36 F6
Glapwell Derbys 45 F8
Glas-allt Shiel Aberds 82 E4
Glasbury Powys 25 E8
Glaschoil Highld 87 H13
Glascoed Denb 42 E2
Glascoed Mon 15 A9
Glascoed Powys 33 D7
Glascorrie Aberds 82 D5
Glascote Staffs 35 E8
Glascwm Powys 25 C8
Glasdrum Argyll 74 C3
Glasfryn Conwy 42 G2
Glasgow Glasgow 68 D4
Glashvin Highld 85 B9
Glasinfryn Gwyn 41 D7
Glasnacardoch Highld 79 B9
Glasnakille Highld 85 G10
Glasphein Highld 84 D6
Glaspwll Powys 32 F3
Glassburn Highld 86 H6
Glasserton Dumfries 55 F7
Glassford S Lanark 68 F6
Glasshouse Hill Glos 26 F4
Glasshouses N Yorks 51 C7
Glasslie Fife 76 G5
Glasson Cumb 61 G8
Glasson Lancs 49 D4
Glassonby Cumb 57 C7
Glasterlaw Angus 77 B8
Glaston Rutland 36 E4
Glastonbury Som 15 H11
Glatton Cambs 37 G7
Glazebrook Warr 43 C9
Glazebury Warr 43 C9
Glazeley Shrops 34 G3
Gleadless S Yorks 45 D7
Gleadsmoss Ches E 44 F2
Gleann Tholàstaidh W Isles 91 C10
Gleaston Cumb 49 B2
Gleiniant Powys 32 F5
Glemsford Suff 30 D5
Glen Dumfries 55 D8
Glen Dumfries 60 F4
Glen Auldyn IoM 48 C4
Glen Bernisdale Highld 85 D9
Glen Ho Borders 69 G11
Glen Mona IoM 48 D4
Glen Nevis House Highld 80 F3
Glen Parva Leics 36 F1
Glen Sluain Argyll 73 D9
Glen Tanar House Aberds 82 D6
Glen Trool Lodge Dumfries 55 A7
Glen Village Falk 69 C7
Glen Vine IoM 48 E3
Glenamachrie Argyll 74 E2
Glenbarr Argyll 65 E7
Glenbeg Highld 79 E8
Glenbeg Highld 82 A2
Glenbervie Aberds 83 E9
Glenboig N Lanark 68 D6
Glenborrodale Highld 79 E9
Glenbranter Argyll 73 D10
Glenbreck Borders 60 A6
Glenbrein Lodge Highld 81 B6
Glenbrittle House Highld 85 F9
Glenbuchat Lodge Aberds 82 B5
Glenbuck E Ayrs 68 H6
Glenburn Renfs 68 D3
Glencalvie Lodge Highld 86 C7
Glencanisp Lodge Highld 92 G4
Glencaple Dumfries 60 G5
Glencarron Lodge Highld 86 F3
Glencarse Perth 76 E4
Glencassley Castle Highld 92 J7
Glenceitlein Highld 74 C4
Glencoe Highld 74 B3
Glencraig Fife 76 H4
Glencripesdale Highld 79 F9
Glencrosh Dumfries 60 E3
Glendavan Ho. Aberds 82 C6
Glendevon Perth 76 G2
Glendoe Lodge Highld 80 C6
Glendoebeg Highld 80 C6
Glendoick Perth 76 E5
Glendoll Lodge Angus 82 F4
Glendoune S Ayrs 66 G4
Glenduckie Fife 76 F5
Glendye Lodge Aberds 83 E8
Gleneagles Hotel Perth 76 F2
Gleneagles House Perth 76 G2
Glenegedale Argyll 64 C4
Glenelg Highld 85 G13
Glenernie Moray 87 G13
Glenfarg Perth 76 F4
Glenfarquhar Lodge Aberds 83 E9
Glenferness House Highld 87 G12
Glenfeshie Lodge Highld 81 D10
Glenfield Leics 35 E11
Glenfinnan Highld 79 C11
Glenfoot Perth 76 F4
Glenfyne Lodge Argyll 74 F5
Glengap Dumfries 55 D9
Glengarnock N Ayrs 66 A6
Glengorm Castle Argyll 78 F7
Glengrasco Highld 85 D9
Glenhead Farm Angus 76 A5
Glenhoul Dumfries 67 H9

Glenhurich Highld 79 E11
Glenkerry Borders 61 B8
Glenkiln Dumfries 60 F4
Glenkindie Aberds 82 B6
Glenlatterach Moray 88 C1
Glenlee Dumfries 55 A9
Glenlichorn Perth 75 F10
Glenlivet Moray 82 A3
Glenlochsie Perth 82 F2
Glenloig N Ayrs 66 C2
Glenluce Dumfries 54 D5
Glenmallan Argyll 74 H5
Glenmarksie Highld 86 F6
Glenmassan Argyll 73 E10
Glenmavis N Lanark 68 D6
Glenmaye IoM 48 E2
Glenmidge Dumfries 60 E4
Glenmore Argyll 73 B7
Glenmore Highld 85 D9
Glenmore Lodge Highld 82 C1
Glenmoy Angus 77 A7
Glenogil Angus 77 A7
Glenprosen Lodge Angus 82 G4
Glenprosen Village Angus 82 G5
Glenquiech Angus 77 A7
Glenreasdell Mains Argyll 73 H7
Glenree N Ayrs 66 D2
Glenridding Cumb 56 E5
Glenrossal Highld 92 J7
Glenrothes Fife 76 G5
Glensanda Highld 79 G11
Glensaugh Aberds 83 F8
Glenshero Lodge Highld 81 D7
Glenstockadale Dumfries 54 C3
Glenstriven Argyll 73 F9
Glentaggart S Lanark 69 H7
Glentham Lincs 46 C4
Glentirranmuir Stirling 68 A5
Glenton Aberds 83 A8
Glentress Borders 69 G11
Glentromie Lodge Highld 81 D9
Glentrool Village Dumfries 54 B6
Glentruan IoM 48 B4
Glentruim House Highld 81 D8
Glentworth Lincs 46 D3
Glenuig Highld 79 D9
Glenurquhart Highld 87 E10
Glespin S Lanark 69 H7
Gletness Shetland 96 H6
Glewstone Hereford 26 F2
Glinton Pboro 37 E7
Glooston Leics 36 F3
Glororum Northumb 71 G10
Glossop Derbys 44 C4
Gloster Hill Northumb 63 C8
Gloucester Glos 26 G5
Gloup Shetland 96 C7
Glusburn N Yorks 50 E6
Glutt Lodge Highld 93 F12
Glutton Bridge Staffs 44 F4
Glympton Oxon 27 F11
Glyn-Ceiriog Wrex 33 B8
Glyn-cywarch Gwyn 41 G8
Glyn Ebwy = Ebbw Vale Bl Gwent 25 H8
Glyn-neath = Glynedd Neath 24 H5
Glynarthen Ceredig 23 B8
Glynbrochan Powys 32 G5
Glyncoch Rhondda 14 B6
Glyncorrwg Neath 14 B4
Glynde E Sus 12 F3
Glyndebourne E Sus 12 E3
Glyndyfrdwy Denb 33 A7
Glynedd = Glyn-neath Neath 24 H5
Glynogwr Bridgend 14 C5
Glyntaff Rhondda 14 C6
Glyntawe Powys 24 G5
Gnosall Staffs 34 C4
Gnosall Heath Staffs 34 C4
Goadby Leics 36 F3
Goadby Marwood Leics 36 C3
Goat Lees Kent 21 G7
Goatacre Wilts 17 D7
Goathill Dorset 8 C5
Goathland N Yorks 59 F9
Goathurst Som 8 A1
Gobernuisgach Lodge Highld 92 E7
Gobhaig W Isles 90 G5
Gobowen Shrops 33 B9
Godalming Sur 18 G6
Godley Gtr Man 44 C3
Godmanchester Cambs 29 A9
Godmanstone Dorset 8 E5
Godmersham Kent 21 F7
Godney Som 15 G10
Godolphin Cross Corn 2 F5
Godre'r-graig Neath 24 H4
Godshill Hants 9 C10
Godshill IoW 10 F4
Godstone Sur 19 F10
Godwinscroft Hants 9 E10
Goetre Mon 25 H10
Goferydd Anglesey 40 B4
Goff's Oak Herts 19 A10
Gogar Edin 69 C10
Goginan Ceredig 32 G2
Golan Gwyn 41 F7
Golant Corn 4 F2
Golberdon Corn 4 D4
Golborne Gtr Man 43 C9
Golcar W Yorks 51 H7
Gold Hill Norf 37 F11
Goldcliff Newport 15 C9
Golden Cross E Sus 12 E4
Golden Green Kent 20 G3
Golden Grove Carms 23 E10
Golden Hill Hants 10 E1
Golden Pot Hants 18 G4
Golden Valley Glos 26 F6
Goldenhill Stoke 44 G2
Golders Green London 19 C9
Goldhanger Essex 30 H6
Golding Shrops 33 E11
Goldington Bedford 29 C7
Goldsborough N Yorks 51 D9
Goldsborough N Yorks 59 E9
Goldsithney Corn 2 F4
Goldsworthy Devon 6 D2
Goldthorpe S Yorks 45 B8
Gollanfield Highld 87 F11
Golspie Highld 93 J11
Golval Highld 93 C11
Gomeldon Wilts 17 H8
Gomersal W Yorks 51 G8
Gomshall Sur 19 G7
Gonalston Notts 45 H10
Gonfirth Shetland 96 G5
Good Easter Essex 30 G3
Gooderstone Norf 38 E3
Goodleigh Devon 6 C5
Goodmanham E Yorks 52 E4
Goodnestone Kent 21 E7
Goodnestone Kent 21 F9
Goodrich Hereford 26 G2
Goodrington Torbay 5 F9
Goodshaw Lancs 50 G4
Goodwick = Wdig Pembs 22 C4
Goodworth Clatford Hants 17 G10
Goole E Yorks 52 G3
Goonbell Corn 2 E6
Goonhavern Corn 3 D6
Goose Eye W Yorks 50 E6
Goose Green Gtr Man 43 B8
Goose Green Norf 39 G7
Goose Green W Sus 11 C10
Gooseham Corn 6 E1
Goosey Oxon 17 B10
Goosnargh Lancs 50 F1
Goostrey Ches E 43 E10
Gorcott Hill Warks 27 B7
Gord Shetland 96 L6
Gordon Borders 70 F5
Gordonbush Highld 93 J11
Gordonsburgh Moray 88 B4
Gordonstoun Moray 88 B1
Gordonstown Aberds 88 C5
Gordonstown Aberds 89 E7
Gore Kent 21 F10
Gore Cross Wilts 17 F7
Gore Pit Essex 30 G5
Gorebridge Midloth 70 D2
Gorefield Cambs 37 D10
Gorey Jersey 11
Gorgie Edin 69 C11
Goring Oxon 18 C3
Goring-by-Sea W Sus 11 D10
Goring Heath Oxon 18 D3
Gorleston-on-Sea Norf 39 E11
Gornalwood W Mid 34 F5
Gorrachie Aberds 89 C7
Gorran Churchtown Corn 3 E8
Gorran Haven Corn 3 E9
Gorrenberry Borders 61 D10
Gors Ceredig 32 H2
Gorse Hill Swindon 17 C8
Gorsedd Flint 42 E4
Gorseinon Swansea 23 G10
Gorseness Orkney 95 G5
Gorsgoch Ceredig 23 A9
Gorslas Carms 23 E10
Gorsley Glos 26 F3
Gorstan Highld 86 E6
Gorstanvorran Highld 79 D11
Gorsteyhill Staffs 43 G10
Gorsty Hill Staffs 35 C7
Gortantaoid Argyll 64 A4
Gorton Gtr Man 44 C2
Gosbeck Suff 31 C8
Gosberton Lincs 37 B8
Gosberton Clough Lincs 37 C7
Gosfield Essex 30 F4
Gosford Hereford 26 B2
Gosforth Cumb 56 F2
Gosforth T&W 63 G8
Gosmore Herts 29 F8
Gosport Hants 10 E5
Gossabrough Shetland 96 E7
Gossington Glos 16 A4
Goswick Northumb 71 F9
Gotham Notts 35 B11
Gotherington Glos 26 F6
Gott Shetland 96 J6
Goudhurst Kent 12 C6
Goulceby Lincs 46 E6
Gourdas Aberds 89 D7
Gourdon Aberds 83 F10
Gourock Invclyd 73 F11
Govan Glasgow 68 D4
Govanhill Glasgow 68 D4
Goveton Devon 5 G8
Govilon Mon 25 G9
Gowanhill Aberds 89 B10
Gowdall E Yorks 52 G2
Gowerton Swansea 23 G10
Gowkhall Fife 69 B9
Gowthorpe E Yorks 52 D3
Goxhill E Yorks 53 E7
Goxhill N Lincs 53 G7
Goxhill Haven N Lincs 53 G7
Goytre Neath 14 C3
Grabhair W Isles 91 F8
Graby Lincs 37 C6
Grade Corn 2 H6
Graffham W Sus 11 C8
Grafham Cambs 29 B8
Grafham Sur 19 G7
Grafton Hereford 25 E11
Grafton N Yorks 51 C10
Grafton Oxon 17 A9
Grafton Shrops 33 D10
Grafton Worcs 26 B2
Grafton Flyford Worcs 26 C6
Grafton Regis Northants 28 D4
Grafton Underwood Northants 36 G5
Grafty Green Kent 20 G5
Graianrhyd Denb 42 G5
Graig Conwy 41 C10
Graig Denb 42 E3
Graig-fechan Denb 42 G4
Grain Medway 20 D5
Grainsby Lincs 46 C6
Grainthorpe Lincs 47 C7
Grampound Corn 3 E8
Grampound Road Corn 3 D8
Gramsdal W Isles 84 C3
Granborough Bucks 28 F4
Granby Notts 36 B3
Grandborough Warks 27 B11
Grandtully Perth 76 B2
Grange Cumb 56 E4
Grange E Ayrs 67 C7
Grange Medway 20 E4
Grange Mers 42 D5
Grange Perth 76 E5
Grange Crossroads Moray 88 C4
Grange Hall Moray 87 E13
Grange Hill Essex 19 B11
Grange Moor W Yorks 51 H8
Grange of Lindores Fife 76 F5
Grange-over-Sands Cumb 49 B4
Grange Villa Durham 58 A3
Grangemill Derbys 44 G6
Grangemouth Falk 69 B8
Grangepans Falk 69 B9
Grangetown Cardiff 15 D7
Grangetown Redcar 59 D6
Granish Highld 81 B11
Gransmoor E Yorks 53 D7
Granston Pembs 22 C3
Grantchester Cambs 29 C11
Grantham Lincs 36 B5
Grantley N Yorks 51 C8
Grantlodge Aberds 83 B9
Granton Dumfries 60 C6
Granton Edin 69 C11
Grantown-on-Spey Highld 82 A2
Grantshouse Borders 71 D7
Grappenhall Warr 43 D9
Grasby Lincs 46 B4
Grasmere Cumb 56 F5
Grasscroft Gtr Man 44 B3
Grassendale Mers 43 D6
Grassholme Durham 57 D11
Grassington N Yorks 50 C6
Grassmoor Derbys 45 F8
Grassthorpe Notts 45 F11
Grateley Hants 17 G9
Gratwich Staffs 34 B6
Graveley Cambs 29 B9
Graveley Herts 29 F9
Gravelly Hill W Mid 35 F7
Gravels Shrops 33 E9
Graven Shetland 96 F6
Graveney Kent 21 E7
Gravesend Herts 29 F11
Gravesend Kent 20 D3
Grayingham Lincs 46 C3
Grayrigg Cumb 57 G7
Grays Thurrock 20 D3
Grayshott Hants 18 H5
Grayswood Sur 11 A8
Graythorp Hrtlpl 58 D6
Grazeley Wokingham 18 E3
Greasbrough S Yorks 45 C8
Greasby Mers 42 D5
Great Abington Cambs 30 D2
Great Addington Northants 28 A6
Great Alne Warks 27 C8
Great Altcar Lancs 42 B6
Great Amwell Herts 29 G10
Great Asby Cumb 57 E8
Great Ashfield Suff 30 B6
Great Ayton N Yorks 59 E6
Great Baddow Essex 20 A4
Great Bardfield Essex 30 E3
Great Barford Bedford 29 C8
Great Barr W Mid 34 F6
Great Barrington Glos 27 G9
Great Barrow Ches W 43 F7
Great Barton Suff 30 B5
Great Barugh N Yorks 52 B3
Great Bavington Northumb 62 E5
Great Bealings Suff 31 D9
Great Bedwyn Wilts 17 E9
Great Bentley Essex 31 F8
Great Billing Northants 28 B5
Great Bircham Norf 38 B3
Great Blakenham Suff 31 C8
Great Blencow Cumb 56 C6
Great Bolas Telford 34 C2
Great Bookham Sur 19 F8
Great Bourton Oxon 27 D11
Great Bowden Leics 36 G3
Great Bradley Suff 30 C3
Great Braxted Essex 30 G5
Great Bricett Suff 31 C7
Great Brickhill Bucks 28 E6
Great Bridge W Mid 34 F5
Great Bridgeford Staffs 34 C4
Great Brington Northants 28 B3
Great Bromley Essex 31 F7
Great Broughton Cumb 56 C2
Great Broughton N Yorks 59 F6
Great Budworth Ches W 43 E9
Great Burdon Darl 58 E4
Great Burgh Sur 19 F9
Great Burstead Essex 20 B3
Great Busby N Yorks 58 F6
Great Canfield Essex 30 G2
Great Carlton Lincs 47 D8
Great Casterton Rutland 36 E6
Great Chart Kent 13 B8
Great Chatwell Staffs 34 D3
Great Chesterford Essex 30 D2
Great Cheverell Wilts 16 F6
Great Chishill Cambs 29 E11
Great Clacton Essex 31 G8
Great Cliff W Yorks 51 H9
Great Clifton Cumb 56 D2
Great Coates NE Lincs 46 B6
Great Comberton Worcs 26 D6
Great Corby Cumb 56 A6
Great Cornard Suff 30 D5
Great Cowden E Yorks 53 E8
Great Coxwell Oxon 17 B9
Great Crakehall N Yorks 58 G3
Great Cransley Northants 36 H4
Great Cressingham Norf 38 E4
Great Crosby Mers 42 C6
Great Cubley Derbys 35 B7
Great Dalby Leics 36 D3
Great Denham Bedford 29 D7
Great Doddington Northants 28 B5
Great Dunham Norf 38 D4
Great Dunmow Essex 30 F3
Great Durnford Wilts 17 H8
Great Easton Essex 30 F3
Great Easton Leics 36 F4
Great Eccleston Lancs 49 E4
Great Edstone N Yorks 52 A3
Great Ellingham Norf 38 F6
Great Elm Som 16 G4
Great Eversden Cambs 29 C10
Great Fencote N Yorks 58 G3
Great Finborough Suff 31 C7
Great Fransham Norf 38 D4
Great Gaddesden Herts 29 G7
Great Gidding Cambs 37 G7
Great Givendale E Yorks 52 D4
Great Glemham Suff 31 B10
Great Glen Leics 36 F2
Great Gonerby Lincs 36 B4
Great Gransden Cambs 29 C9
Great Green Norf 39 G8
Great Green Suff 30 C6
Great Habton N Yorks 52 B3
Great Hale Lincs 37 A7
Great Hallingbury Essex 30 G2
Great Hampden Bucks 18 A5
Great Harrowden Northants 28 A5
Great Harwood Lancs 50 F3
Great Haseley Oxon 18 A3
Great Hatfield E Yorks 53 E7
Great Haywood Staffs 34 C6
Great Heath W Mid 35 G9
Great Heck N Yorks 52 G1
Great Henny Essex 30 E5
Great Hinton Wilts 16 F6
Great Hockham Norf 38 F5
Great Holland Essex 31 G9
Great Horkesley Essex 30 E6
Great Hormead Herts 29 F10
Great Horton W Yorks 51 F7
Great Horwood Bucks 28 E4
Great Houghton Northants 28 C4
Great Houghton S Yorks 45 B8
Great Hucklow Derbys 44 E5
Great Kelk E Yorks 53 D7
Great Kimble Bucks 28 H5
Great Kingshill Bucks 18 B5
Great Langton N Yorks 58 G3
Great Leighs Essex 30 G4
Great Lever Gtr Man 43 B10
Great Limber Lincs 46 B5
Great Linford M Keynes 28 D5
Great Livermere Suff 30 A5
Great Longstone Derbys 44 E6
Great Lumley Durham 58 B3
Great Lyth Shrops 33 E10
Great Malvern Worcs 26 D4
Great Maplestead Essex 30 E5
Great Marton Blackpool 49 F3
Great Massingham Norf 38 C3
Great Melton Norf 39 E7
Great Milton Oxon 18 A3
Great Missenden Bucks 18 A5
Great Mitton Lancs 50 F3
Great Mongeham Kent 21 F10
Great Moulton Norf 39 F7
Great Munden Herts 29 F10
Great Musgrave Cumb 57 E9
Great Ness Shrops 33 D9
Great Notley Essex 30 F4
Great Oakley Essex 31 F8
Great Oakley Northants 36 G4
Great Offley Herts 29 F8
Great Ormside Cumb 57 E9
Great Orton Cumb 56 A5
Great Ouseburn N Yorks 51 C10
Great Oxendon Northants 36 G3
Great Oxney Green Essex 30 H3
Great Palgrave Norf 38 D4
Great Parndon Essex 29 H11
Great Paxton Cambs 29 B9
Great Plumpton Lancs 49 F3
Great Plumstead Norf 39 D9
Great Ponton Lincs 36 B5
Great Preston W Yorks 51 G10
Great Raveley Cambs 37 G8
Great Rissington Glos 27 G8
Great Rollright Oxon 27 E10
Great Ryburgh Norf 38 C5
Great Ryle Northumb 62 B6
Great Ryton Shrops 33 E10
Great Saling Essex 30 F4
Great Salkeld Cumb 57 C7
Great Sampford Essex 30 E3
Great Sankey Warr 43 D8
Great Saxham Suff 30 B4
Great Shefford W Berks 17 D10
Great Shelford Cambs 29 C11
Great Smeaton N Yorks 58 F4
Great Snoring Norf 38 B5
Great Somerford Wilts 16 C6
Great Stainton Darl 58 D4
Great Stambridge Essex 20 B5
Great Staughton Cambs 29 B8
Great Steeping Lincs 47 F8
Great Stonar Kent 21 F10
Great Strickland Cumb 57 D7
Great Stukeley Cambs 29 A9
Great Sturton Lincs 46 E6
Great Sutton Ches W 43 E6
Great Sutton Shrops 33 G11
Great Swinburne Northumb 62 F5
Great Tew Oxon 27 F10
Great Tey Essex 30 F5
Great Thurkleby N Yorks 51 B10
Great Thurlow Suff 30 C3
Great Torrington Devon 6 E3
Great Tosson Northumb 62 C6
Great Totham Essex 30 G5
Great Totham Essex 30 G5
Great Tows Lincs 46 C6
Great Urswick Cumb 49 B2
Great Wakering Essex 20 C6
Great Waldingfield Suff 30 D6
Great Walsingham Norf 38 B5
Great Waltham Essex 30 G3
Great Warley Essex 20 B2
Great Washbourne Glos 26 E6
Great Weldon Northants 36 G5
Great Welnetham Suff 30 C5
Great Wenham Suff 31 E7
Great Whittington Northumb 62 F6
Great Wigborough Essex 30 G6
Great Wilbraham Cambs 30 C2
Great Wishford Wilts 17 H7
Great Witcombe Glos 26 G6
Great Witley Worcs 26 B4
Great Wolford Warks 27 E9
Great Wratting Suff 30 D3
Great Wymondley Herts 29 F9
Great Wyrley Staffs 34 E5
Great Wytheford Shrops 34 D1
Great Yarmouth Norf 39 E11
Great Yeldham Essex 30 E4
Greater Doward Hereford 26 G2
Greatford Lincs 37 D6
Greatgate Staffs 35 A6
Greatham Hants 11 A6
Greatham Hrtlpl 58 D5
Greatham W Sus 11 C9
Greatstone on Sea Kent 13 D9
Greatworth Northants 28 D2
Greave Lancs 50 G4
Greeba IoM 48 D3
Green Denb 42 F3
Green End Bedford 29 C8
Green Hammerton N Yorks 51 D10
Green Lane Powys 33 F7
Green Ore Som 16 F2
Green St Green London 19 E11
Green Street Herts 19 B8
Greenbank Shetland 96 C7
Greenburn W Loth 69 D8
Greendikes Northumb 71 H9
Greenfield C Beds 29 E7
Greenfield Flint 42 E4
Greenfield Gtr Man 44 B3
Greenfield Highld 80 C4
Greenfield Oxon 18 B4
Greenford London 19 C8
Greengairs N Lanark 68 C6
Greenham W Berks 17 E11
Greenhaugh Northumb 62 E3
Greenhead Northumb 62 G2
Greenhill Falk 69 C7
Greenhill Kent 21 E8
Greenhill Leics 35 D10
Greenhill London 19 C8
Greenhills N Ayrs 67 A6
Greenhithe Kent 20 D2
Greenholm E Ayrs 67 C8
Greenholme Cumb 57 F7
Greenhouse Borders 61 A11
Greenhow Hill N Yorks 51 C7
Greenigoe Orkney 95 H5
Greenland Highld 94 D4
Greenlands Bucks 18 C4
Greenlaw Aberds 89 C6
Greenlaw Borders 70 F6
Greenlea Dumfries 60 F6
Greenloaning Perth 75 G11
Greenmount Gtr Man 43 A10
Greenmow Shetland 96 L6
Greenock Invclyd 73 F11
Greenock West Invclyd 73 F11
Greenodd Cumb 49 A3
Greenrow Cumb 56 A3
Greens Norton Northants 28 D3
Greenside T&W 63 G7
Greensidehill Northumb 62 B5
Greenstead Green Essex 30 F5
Greensted Essex 20 A2
Greenwich London 19 D10
Greet Glos 27 E7
Greete Shrops 26 A2
Greetham Lincs 47 E7
Greetham Rutland 36 D5
Greetland W Yorks 51 G6
Gregg Hall Cumb 56 G6
Gregson Lane Lancs 50 G1
Greinetobht W Isles 84 A3
Greinton Som 15 H10
Gremista Shetland 96 J6
Grenaby IoM 48 E2
Grendon Northants 28 B5
Grendon Warks 35 E8
Grendon Common Warks 35 F8
Grendon Green Hereford 26 C2
Grendon Underwood Bucks 28 F3
Grenofen Devon 4 D5
Grenoside S Yorks 45 C7
Greosabhagh W Isles 90 H6
Gresford Wrex 42 G6
Gresham Norf 39 B7
Greshornish Highld 85 C8
Gressenhall Norf 38 D5
Gressingham Lancs 50 C1
Gresty Green Ches E 43 G10
Greta Bridge Durham 58 E1
Gretna Dumfries 61 G9
Gretna Green Dumfries 61 G9
Gretton Glos 27 E7
Gretton Northants 36 F4
Gretton Shrops 33 F11
Grewelthorpe N Yorks 51 B8
Grey Green N Lincs 45 B11
Greygarth N Yorks 51 B7
Greynor Carms 23 F10
Greysouthen Cumb 56 D2
Greystoke Cumb 56 C6
Greystone Angus 77 C8
Greystone Dumfries 60 F5
Greywell Hants 18 F4
Griais W Isles 91 C9
Grianan W Isles 91 D9
Gribthorpe E Yorks 52 F3
Gridley Corner Devon 6 G2
Griff Warks 35 G9
Griffithstown Torf 15 B8
Grimbister Orkney 95 G4
Grimblethorpe Lincs 46 D6
Grimeford Village Lancs 43 A9
Grimethorpe S Yorks 45 B8
Griminis W Isles 84 C2
Grimister Shetland 96 D6
Grimley Worcs 26 B5
Grimness Orkney 95 J5
Grimoldby Lincs 47 D7
Grimpo Shrops 33 C9
Grimsargh Lancs 50 F1
Grimsbury Oxon 27 D11
Grimsby NE Lincs 46 A6
Grimscote Northants 28 C3
Grimscott Corn 6 F1
Grimsthorpe Lincs 36 C6
Grimston E Yorks 53 F8
Grimston Leics 36 C2
Grimston Norf 38 C3
Grimston York 52 D2
Grimstone Dorset 8 E5
Grinacombe Moor Devon 6 G3
Grindale E Yorks 53 B7
Grindigar Orkney 95 H6
Grindiscol Shetland 96 K6
Grindle Shrops 34 E3
Grindleford Derbys 44 E6
Grindleton Lancs 50 E3
Grindley Staffs 34 C6
Grindley Brook Shrops 33 A11
Grindlow Derbys 44 E5
Grindon Northumb 71 F8
Grindon Staffs 44 G4
Grindonmoor Gate Staffs 44 G4
Gringley on the Hill Notts 45 C11
Grinsdale Cumb 61 H9
Grinshill Shrops 33 C11
Grinton N Yorks 58 G1
Griomsidar W Isles 91 E8
Grishipoll Argyll 78 F4
Grisling Common E Sus 12 D3
Gristhorpe N Yorks 53 A6
Griston Norf 38 F5
Gritley Orkney 95 H6
Grittenham Wilts 17 C7
Grittleton Wilts 16 C5
Grizebeck Cumb 49 A2
Grizedale Cumb 56 G5
Grobister Orkney 95 F7
Groby Leics 35 E11
Groes Conwy 42 F3
Groes Neath 14 C3
Groes-faen Rhondda 14 C6
Groes-lwyd Powys 33 D8
Groesffordd Marli Denb 42 E3
Groeslon Gwyn 40 E6
Groeslon Gwyn 41 D7
Grogport Argyll 65 D9
Gromford Suff 31 C10
Gronant Flint 42 D3
Groombridge E Sus 12 C4
Grosmont Mon 25 F11
Grosmont N Yorks 59 F9
Groton Suff 30 D6
Grougfoot Falk 69 C9
Grouville Jersey 11
Grove Dorset 8 G6
Grove Kent 21 E9
Grove Notts 45 E11
Grove Oxon 17 B11
Grove Park London 19 D11
Grove Vale W Mid 34 F6
Grovesend Swansea 23 F10
Grudie Highld 86 E6
Gruids Highld 93 J8
Gruinard House Highld 86 B2
Grula Highld 85 F8
Gruline Argyll 79 G8
Grunasound Shetland 96 K5
Grundisburgh Suff 31 C9
Grunsagill Lancs 50 D3
Gruting Shetland 96 J4
Grutness Shetland 96 N6
Gualachulain Highld 74 C4
Gualin Ho. Highld 92 D6
Guardbridge Fife 77 F7
Guarlford Worcs 26 D5
Guay Perth 76 C3
Guestling Green E Sus 13 E7
Guestling Thorn E Sus 13 E7
Guestwick Norf 39 C6
Guestwick Green Norf 39 C6
Guide Blackburn 50 G3
Guide Post Northumb 63 E8
Guilden Morden Cambs 29 D9
Guilden Sutton Ches W 43 F7
Guildford Sur 18 G6
Guildtown Perth 76 D4
Guilsborough Northants 28 A3
Guilsfield Powys 33 D8
Guilton Kent 21 F9
Guineaford Devon 6 C4
Guisborough Redcar 59 E7
Guiseley W Yorks 51 E7
Guist Norf 38 C5
Guith Orkney 95 E6
Guiting Power Glos 27 F7
Gulberwick Shetland 96 K6
Gullane E Loth 70 B3
Gulval Corn 2 F3
Gulworthy Devon 4 D5
Gumfreston Pembs 22 F6
Gumley Leics 36 F2
Gummow's Shop Corn 3 D7
Gun Hill E Sus 12 E4
Gunby E Yorks 52 F3
Gunby Lincs 36 C5
Gundleton Hants 10 A5
Gunn Devon 6 C5
Gunnerside N Yorks 57 G11
Gunnerton Northumb 62 F5
Gunness N Lincs 46 A2
Gunnislake Corn 4 D5
Gunnista Shetland 96 J7
Gunthorpe Norf 38 B6
Gunthorpe Notts 36 A2
Gunthorpe Pboro 37 E7
Gunville IoW 10 F3
Gunwalloe Corn 2 G5
Gurnard IoW 10 E3
Gurnett Ches E 44 E3
Gurney Slade Som 16 G3
Gurnos Powys 24 H4
Gussage All Saints Dorset 9 C9
Gussage St Michael Dorset 9 C8
Guston Kent 21 G10
Gutcher Shetland 96 D7
Guthrie Angus 77 B8
Guyhirn Cambs 37 E9
Guyhirn Gull Cambs 37 E9
Guy's Head Lincs 37 C10
Guy's Marsh Dorset 9 B7
Guyzance Northumb 63 C8
Gwaenysgor Flint 42 D3
Gwalchmai Anglesey 40 C5
Gwaun-Cae-Gurwen Neath 24 G4
Gwaun-Leision Neath 24 G4
Gwbert Ceredig 22 B6
Gweek Corn 2 G6
Gwehelog Mon 15 A9
Gwenddwr Powys 25 D7
Gwennap Corn 2 F6
Gwenter Corn 2 H6
Gwernaffield Flint 42 F5
Gwernesney Mon 15 A10
Gwernogle Carms 23 C10
Gwernymynydd Flint 42 F5
Gwersyllt Wrex 42 G6
Gwespyr Flint 42 D4
Gwithian Corn 2 E4
Gwredog Anglesey 40 B6
Gwyddelwern Denb 42 H3
Gwyddgrug Carms 23 C9
Gwydyr Uchaf Conwy 41 D9
Gwynfryn Wrex 42 G5
Gwystre Powys 25 B7
Gwytherin Conwy 41 D10
Gyfelia Wrex 42 H6
Gyffin Conwy 41 C9
Gyre Orkney 95 H4
Gyrn-goch Gwyn 40 F6

H

Habberley Shrops 33 E9
Habergham Lancs 50 F4
Habrough NE Lincs 46 A5
Haceby Lincs 36 B6
Hacheston Suff 31 C10
Hackbridge London 19 E9
Hackenthorpe S Yorks 45 D8
Hackford Norf 39 E6
Hackforth N Yorks 58 G3
Hackland Orkney 95 F4
Hackleton Northants 28 C5
Hackness N Yorks 59 G10
Hackness Orkney 95 J4
Hackney London 19 C10
Hackthorn Lincs 46 D3
Hackthorpe Cumb 57 D7
Haconby Lincs 37 C7
Hacton London 20 C2
Hadden Borders 70 G6
Haddenham Bucks 28 H4
Haddenham Cambs 37 H10
Haddington E Loth 70 C4
Haddington Lincs 46 F3
Haddiscoe Norf 39 F10
Haddon Cambs 37 F7
Haddon Ches E 44 F3
Hade Edge W Yorks 44 B5
Hademore Staffs 35 E7
Hadfield Derbys 44 C4
Hadham Cross Herts 29 G11
Hadham Ford Herts 29 F11
Hadleigh Essex 20 C5
Hadleigh Suff 31 D7
Hadley Telford 34 D2
Hadley End Staffs 35 C7
Hadlow Kent 20 G3
Hadlow Down E Sus 12 D4
Hadnall Shrops 33 D11
Hadstock Essex 30 D2
Hady Derbys 45 E7
Hadzor Worcs 26 B6
Haffenden Quarter Kent 13 B7
Hafod-Dinbych Conwy 41 E10
Hafod-Iom Conwy 41 C10
Haggate Lancs 50 F4
Haggbeck Cumb 61 F10
Haggerston Northumb 71 F9
Haggrister Shetland 96 F5
Hagley Hereford 26 D2
Hagley Worcs 34 G5
Hagworthingham Lincs 47 F7
Haigh Gtr Man 43 B9
Haigh S Yorks 44 A6
Haigh Moor W Yorks 51 G8
Haighton Green Lancs 50 F1
Hail Weston Cambs 29 B8
Haile Cumb 56 F2
Hailes Glos 27 E7
Hailey Herts 29 G10
Hailey Oxon 27 G10
Hailsham E Sus 12 F4
Haimer Highld 94 D3
Hainault London 19 B11
Hainford Norf 39 D8
Hainton Lincs 46 D5
Hairmyres S Lanark 68 E5
Haisthorpe E Yorks 53 C7
Hakin Pembs 22 F3
Halam Notts 45 G10
Halbeath Fife 69 B10
Halberton Devon 7 E9
Halcro Highld 94 D4
Hale Gtr Man 43 D10
Hale Halton 43 D7
Hale Hants 9 C10
Hale Bank Halton 43 D7
Hale Street Kent 20 G3
Halebarns Gtr Man 43 D10
Hales Norf 39 F9
Hales Staffs 34 B3
Hales Place Kent 21 F8
Halesfield Telford 34 E3
Halesgate Lincs 37 C9
Halesowen W Mid 34 G5
Halesworth Suff 39 H9
Halewood Mers 43 D7
Halford Shrops 33 G10
Halford Warks 27 D9
Halfpenny Furze Carms 23 E7
Halfpenny Green Staffs 34 F4
Halfway Carms 24 E3
Halfway Carms 24 E5
Halfway W Berks 17 E11
Halfway Bridge W Sus 11 B8
Halfway House Shrops 33 D9
Halfway Houses Kent 20 D6
Halifax W Yorks 51 G6
Halket E Ayrs 67 A7
Halkirk Highld 94 E3
Halkyn Flint 42 E5
Hall Dunnerdale Cumb 56 G4
Hall Green W Mid 35 G7
Hall Green W Yorks 51 H9
Hall Grove Herts 29 G9
Hall of Tankerness Orkney 95 H6
Hall of the Forest Shrops 33 G8
Halland E Sus 12 E3
Hallaton Leics 36 F3
Hallatrow Bath 16 F3
Hallbankgate Cumb 61 H11
Hallen S Glos 15 C11
Halliburton Borders 70 F5
Hallin Highld 84 C7
Halling Medway 20 E4
Hallington Lincs 47 D7
Hallington Northumb 62 F5
Halliwell Gtr Man 43 A10
Halloughton Notts 45 G10
Hallow Worcs 26 C5
Hallrule Borders 61 B11
Halls E Loth 70 C5
Hall's Green Herts 29 F9
Hallsands Devon 5 H9
Hallthwaites Cumb 56 H3
Hallworthy Corn 4 C2
Hallyburton House Perth 76 D5
Hallyne Borders 69 F10
Halmer End Staffs 43 H10
Halmore Glos 16 A3
Halmyre Mains Borders 69 F10
Halnaker W Sus 11 D8
Halsall Lancs 42 A6
Halse Northants 28 D2
Halse Som 7 D10
Halsetown Corn 2 F4
Halsham E Yorks 53 G8
Halsinger Devon 6 C4
Halstead Essex 30 E5
Halstead Kent 19 E11
Halstead Leics 36 E3
Halstock Dorset 8 D4
Haltham Lincs 46 F6
Haltoft End Lincs 47 H7
Halton Bucks 28 G5
Halton Halton 43 D8
Halton Lancs 49 C5
Halton Northumb 62 G5
Halton W Yorks 51 F9
Halton Wrex 33 B9
Halton East N Yorks 50 D6
Halton Gill N Yorks 50 B4
Halton Holegate Lincs 47 F8
Halton Lea Gate Northumb 62 H2
Halton West N Yorks 50 D4
Haltwhistle Northumb 62 G3
Halvergate Norf 39 E10
Halwell Devon 5 F8
Halwill Devon 6 G3
Halwill Junction Devon 6 F3
Ham Devon 7 F11
Ham Glos 16 B3
Ham Highld 94 C4
Ham Kent 21 F10
Ham London 19 D8
Ham Shetland 96 K1
Ham Wilts 17 E10
Ham Common Dorset 9 B7
Ham Green Hereford 26 D4
Ham Green Kent 13 D7
Ham Green Kent 20 E5
Ham Green N Som 15 D11
Ham Green Worcs 27 B7
Ham Street Som 8 A4
Hamble-le-Rice Hants 10 D3
Hambleden Bucks 18 C4
Hambledon Hants 10 C5
Hambledon Sur 18 H6
Hambleton Lancs 49 E3
Hambleton N Yorks 52 F1
Hambridge Som 8 B2
Hambrook S Glos 16 D3
Hambrook W Sus 11 D6
Hameringham Lincs 47 F7
Hamerton Cambs 37 H7
Hametoun Shetland 96 K1
Hamilton S Lanark 68 E6
Hammer W Sus 11 A7
Hammerpot W Sus 11 D9
Hammersmith London 19 D9
Hammerwich Staffs 35 E6
Hammerwood E Sus 12 C3
Hammond Street Herts 19 A10
Hammoon Dorset 9 C7
Hamnavoe Shetland 96 E4
Hamnavoe Shetland 96 E6
Hamnavoe Shetland 96 F6
Hamnavoe Shetland 96 K5
Hampden Park E Sus 12 F5
Hamperden End Essex 30 E2
Hampnett Glos 27 G7
Hampole S Yorks 45 A9
Hampreston Dorset 9 E9
Hampstead London 19 C9
Hampstead Norreys W Berks 18 D2
Hampsthwaite N Yorks 51 D8
Hampton London 19 E8
Hampton Shrops 34 G3
Hampton Worcs 27 D7
Hampton Bishop Hereford 26 E2
Hampton Heath Ches W 43 H7
Hampton in Arden W Mid 35 G8
Hampton Loade Shrops 34 G3
Hampton Lovett Worcs 26 B5
Hampton Lucy Warks 27 C9
Hampton on the Hill Warks 27 B9
Hampton Poyle Oxon 28 G2
Hamrow Norf 38 C5
Hamsey E Sus 12 E3
Hamsey Green London 19 F10
Hamstall Ridware Staffs 35 D7
Hamstead IoW 10 E3
Hamstead W Mid 34 F6
Hamstead Marshall W Berks 17 E11
Hamsterley Durham 58 C2
Hamsterley Durham 63 H7
Hamstreet Kent 13 C9
Hamworthy Poole 9 E8
Hanbury Staffs 35 C7
Hanbury Worcs 26 B6
Hanbury Woodend Staffs 35 C7
Hanby Lincs 36 B6
Hanchurch Staffs 34 A4
Handbridge Ches W 43 F7
Handcross W Sus 12 D1
Handforth Ches E 44 D2
Handley Ches W 43 G7
Handsacre Staffs 35 D6
Handsworth S Yorks 45 D8
Handsworth W Mid 34 F6
Handy Cross Devon 6 D3
Hanford Stoke 34 A4
Hanging Langford Wilts 17 H7
Hangleton W Sus 11 D9
Hanham S Glos 16 D3
Hankelow Ches E 43 H9
Hankerton Wilts 16 B6
Hankham E Sus 12 F5
Hanley Stoke 44 H2
Hanley Castle Worcs 26 D5
Hanley Child Worcs 26 B3
Hanley Swan Worcs 26 D5
Hanley William Worcs 26 B3
Hanlith N Yorks 50 C5
Hanmer Wrex 33 B10
Hannah Lincs 47 E9
Hannington Hants 18 F2
Hannington Northants 28 A5
Hannington Swindon 17 B8
Hannington Wick Swindon 17 B8
Hansel Village S Ayrs 67 C6
Hanslope M Keynes 28 D5
Hanthorpe Lincs 37 C6
Hanwell London 19 C8
Hanwell Oxon 27 D11
Hanwood Shrops 33 E10
Hanworth London 19 D8
Hanworth Norf 39 B7
Happendon S Lanark 69 G7
Happisburgh Norf 39 B9
Happisburgh Common Norf 39 C9
Hapsford Ches W 43 E7
Hapton Lancs 50 F3
Hapton Norf 39 F7
Harberton Devon 5 F8
Harbertonford Devon 5 F8
Harbledown Kent 21 F8
Harborne W Mid 34 G6
Harborough Magna Warks 35 H10
Harbottle Northumb 62 C5
Harbury Warks 27 C10
Harby Leics 36 B3
Harby Notts 46 E2
Harcombe Devon 7 G10
Harden W Mid 34 E6
Harden W Yorks 51 F6
Hardenhuish Wilts 16 D6
Hardgate Aberds 83 C9
Hardham W Sus 11 C9
Hardingham Norf 38 E6
Hardingstone Northants 28 C4
Hardington Som 16 F4
Hardington Mandeville Som 8 C4
Hardington Marsh Som 8 D4
Hardley Hants 10 D3
Hardley Street Norf 39 E9
Hardmead M Keynes 28 D6
Hardrow N Yorks 57 G10
Hardstoft Derbys 45 F8
Hardway Hants 10 D5
Hardway Som 8 A6
Hardwick Bucks 28 G5
Hardwick Cambs 29 C10
Hardwick Norf 38 D2
Hardwick Norf 39 G8
Hardwick Northants 28 B5
Hardwick Notts 45 E10
Hardwick Oxon 27 H10
Hardwick Oxon 28 F2
Hardwick W Mid 35 F6
Hardwicke Glos 26 F6
Hardwicke Glos 26 G4
Hardwicke Hereford 25 D9
Hardy's Green Essex 30 F6
Hare Green Essex 31 F7
Hare Hatch Wokingham 18 D5
Hare Street Herts 29 F10
Hareby Lincs 47 F7
Hareden Lancs 50 D2
Harefield London 19 B7
Harehills W Yorks 51 F9
Harehope Northumb 62 A6
Haresceugh Cumb 57 B8
Harescombe Glos 26 G5
Haresfield Glos 26 G5
Hareshaw N Lanark 69 D7
Hareshaw Head Northumb 62 E4
Harewood W Yorks 51 E9
Harewood End Hereford 26 F2
Harford Carms 24 D3
Harford Devon 5 F7
Hargate Norf 39 F7
Hargatewall Derbys 44 E5
Hargrave Ches W 43 F7
Hargrave Northants 29 A7
Hargrave Suff 30 C4
Harker Cumb 61 G9
Harkland Shetland 96 E6
Harkstead Suff 31 E8
Harlaston Staffs 35 D8
Harlaw Ho. Aberds 83 A9
Harlaxton Lincs 36 B4
Harle Syke Lancs 50 F4
Harlech Gwyn 41 G7
Harlequin Notts 36 B2
Harlescott Shrops 33 D11
Harlesden London 19 C9
Harleston Devon 5 G8
Harleston Norf 39 G8
Harleston Suff 31 C7
Harlestone Northants 28 B4
Harley S Yorks 45 C7
Harley Shrops 34 E1
Harleyholm S Lanark 69 G8
Harlington C Beds 29 E7
Harlington London 19 D7
Harlington S Yorks 45 B8
Harlosh Highld 85 D7
Harlow Essex 29 G11
Harlow Hill N Yorks 51 D8
Harlow Hill Northumb 62 G6
Harlthorpe E Yorks 52 F3
Harlton Cambs 29 C10
Harman's Cross Dorset 9 F8
Harmby N Yorks 58 H2
Harmer Green Herts 29 G9
Harmer Hill Shrops 33 C10
Harmondsworth London 19 D7
Harmston Lincs 46 F3
Harnham Northumb 62 F6
Harnhill Glos 17 A7
Harold Hill London 20 B2
Harold Wood London 20 B2
Haroldston West Pembs 22 E3
Haroldswick Shetland 96 B8
Harome N Yorks 52 A2
Harpenden Herts 29 G8
Harpford Devon 7 G9
Harpham E Yorks 53 C6
Harpley Norf 38 C3
Harpley Worcs 26 B3
Harpole Northants 28 B3
Harpsdale Highld 94 E3
Harpsden Oxon 18 C4
Harpswell Lincs 46 D3
Harpur Hill Derbys 44 E4
Harpurhey Gtr Man 44 B2
Harraby Cumb 56 A6
Harrapool Highld 85 F11
Harrier Shetland 96 J1
Harrietfield Perth 76 E2
Harrietsham Kent 20 F5
Harrington Cumb 56 D1
Harrington Lincs 47 E7
Harrington Northants 36 G3
Harringworth Northants 36 F5
Harris Highld 78 B6
Harrogate N Yorks 51 D9
Harrold Bedford 28 C6
Harrow London 19 C8
Harrow on the Hill London 19 C8
Harrow Street Suff 30 E6
Harrow Weald London 19 B8
Harrowbarrow Corn 4 E4
Harrowden Bedford 29 D7
Harrowgate Hill Darl 58 E3
Harston Cambs 29 C11
Harston Leics 36 B4
Harswell E Yorks 52 E4
Hart Hrtlpl 58 C5
Hart Common Gtr Man 43 B9
Hart Hill Luton 29 F8
Hart Station Hrtlpl 58 C5
Hartburn Northumb 62 E6
Hartburn Stockton 58 E5
Hartest Suff 30 C5
Hartfield E Sus 12 C3
Hartford Cambs 29 A9
Hartford Ches W 43 E9
Hartford End Essex 30 G3
Hartfordbridge Hants 18 F4
Hartforth N Yorks 58 F2
Harthill Ches W 43 G8
Harthill N Lanark 69 D8
Harthill S Yorks 45 D8
Hartington Derbys 44 F5
Hartland Devon 6 D1
Hartlebury Worcs 26 A5
Hartlepool Hrtlpl 58 C6
Hartley Cumb 57 F9
Hartley Kent 13 C6
Hartley Kent 20 E3
Hartley Northumb 63 F9
Hartley Westpall Hants 18 F3
Hartley Wintney Hants 18 F4
Hartlip Kent 20 E5
Hartoft End N Yorks 59 G8
Harton N Yorks 52 C3
Harton Shrops 33 G10
Harton T&W 63 G9
Hartpury Glos 26 F4
Hartshead W Yorks 51 G7
Hartshill Warks 35 F9
Hartshorne Derbys 35 C9
Hartsop Cumb 56 E6
Hartwell Northants 28 C4
Hartwood N Lanark 69 E7
Harvieston Stirling 68 B4
Harvington Worcs 27 D7
Harvington Cross Worcs 27 D7
Harwell Oxon 17 C11
Harwich Essex 31 E9
Harwood Durham 57 C10
Harwood Gtr Man 43 A10
Harwood Dale N Yorks 59 G10
Harworth Notts 45 C10
Hasbury W Mid 34 G5
Hascombe Sur 18 G6
Haselbech Northants 36 H3
Haselbury Plucknett Som 8 C3
Haseley Warks 27 B9
Haselor Warks 27 C8
Hasfield Glos 26 F5
Hasguard Pembs 22 F3
Haskayne Lancs 42 B6
Hasketon Suff 31 C9
Hasland Derbys 45 F7
Haslemere Sur 11 A8
Haslingden Lancs 50 G3
Haslingfield Cambs 29 C11
Haslington Ches E 43 G10
Hassall Ches E 43 G10
Hassall Green Ches E 43 G10
Hassell Street Kent 21 G7
Hassendean Borders 61 A11
Hassingham Norf 39 E9
Hassocks W Sus 12 E1
Hassop Derbys 44 E6
Hastigrow Highld 94 D4
Hastingleigh Kent 13 B9
Hastings E Sus 13 F7
Hastingwood Essex 29 H11
Hastoe Herts 28 H6
Haswell Durham 58 B4
Haswell Plough Durham 58 B4
Hatch C Beds 29 D8
Hatch Hants 18 F3
Hatch Wilts 9 B8
Hatch Beauchamp Som 8 B2
Hatch End London 19 B8
Hatch Green Som 8 C2
Hatchet Gate Hants 10 D2
Hatching Green Herts 29 G8
Hatchmere Ches W 43 E8
Hatcliffe NE Lincs 46 B6
Hatfield Hereford 26 C2
Hatfield Herts 29 H9
Hatfield S Yorks 45 B10
Hatfield Worcs 26 C5
Hatfield Broad Oak Essex 30 G2
Hatfield Garden Village Herts 29 H9
Hatfield Heath Essex 30 G2
Hatfield Hyde Herts 29 G9
Hatfield Peverel Essex 30 G4
Hatfield Woodhouse S Yorks 45 B10
Hatford Oxon 17 B10
Hatherden Hants 17 F10
Hatherleigh Devon 6 F4
Hathern Leics 35 C10
Hatherop Glos 27 H8
Hathersage Derbys 44 D6
Hathershaw Gtr Man 44 B3
Hatherton Ches E 43 H9
Hatherton Staffs 34 D5
Hatley St George Cambs 29 C9
Hatt Corn 4 E4
Hattingley Hants 18 H3
Hatton Aberds 89 E10
Hatton Derbys 35 C8
Hatton Lincs 46 E5
Hatton Shrops 33 F10
Hatton Warks 27 B9
Hatton Warr 43 D8
Hatton Castle Aberds 89 D7
Hatton Heath Ches W 43 F7
Hatton of Fintray Aberds 83 B10
Hattoncrook Aberds 89 F8
Haugh E Ayrs 67 D7
Haugh Gtr Man 44 A3
Haugh Lincs 47 E8
Haugh Head Northumb 71 H9
Haugh of Glass Moray 88 E4
Haugh of Urr Dumfries 55 C11
Haugham Lincs 47 D7
Haughley Suff 31 B7
Haughley Green Suff 31 B7
Haughs of Clinterty Aberdeen 83 B10
Haughton Notts 45 E10
Haughton Shrops 33 C9
Haughton Shrops 34 D1
Haughton Shrops 34 E3
Haughton Shrops 34 F2
Haughton Staffs 34 C4
Haughton Castle Northumb 62 F5
Haughton Green Gtr Man 44 C3
Haughton Moss Ches E 43 G8
Haultwick Herts 29 F10
Haunn Argyll 78 G6
Haunn W Isles 84 G2
Haunton Staffs 35 D8
Hauxley Northumb 63 C8
Hauxton Cambs 29 C11
Havant Hants 10 D6
Haven Hereford 25 C11
Haven Bank Lincs 46 G6
Haven Side E Yorks 53 G7
Havenstreet IoW 10 E4
Havercroft W Yorks 45 A7
Haverfordwest = Hwlffordd Pembs 22 E4
Haverhill Suff 30 D3
Haverigg Cumb 49 B1
Havering-atte-Bower London 20 B2
Haveringland Norf 39 C7
Haversham M Keynes 28 D5
Haverthwaite Cumb 49 A3
Haverton Hill Stockton 58 D5
Hawarden = Penarlâg Flint 42 F6
Hawcoat Cumb 49 B2
Hawen Ceredig 23 B8
Hawes N Yorks 57 H10
Hawes' Green Norf 39 F8
Hawes Side Blackpool 49 F3
Hawford Worcs 26 B5
Hawick Borders 61 B11
Hawk Green Gtr Man 44 D3
Hawkchurch Devon 8 D2
Hawkedon Suff 30 C4
Hawkenbury Kent 12 C4
Hawkenbury Kent 13 B7
Hawkeridge Wilts 16 F5
Hawkerland Devon 7 H9
Hawkes End W Mid 35 G9
Hawkesbury S Glos 16 C4
Hawkesbury Warks 35 G9
Hawkesbury Upton S Glos 16 C4
Hawkhill Northumb 63 B8
Hawkhurst Kent 13 C6
Hawkinge Kent 21 H9
Hawkley Hants 10 B6
Hawkridge Som 7 C7
Hawkshead Cumb 56 G5
Hawkshead Hill Cumb 56 G5
Hawksland S Lanark 69 G7
Hawkswick N Yorks 50 B5
Hawksworth Notts 36 A3
Hawksworth W Yorks 51 E7
Hawksworth W Yorks 51 F8
Hawkwell Essex 20 B5
Hawley Hants 18 F5
Hawley Kent 20 D2
Hawling Glos 27 F7
Hawnby N Yorks 59 H6
Haworth W Yorks 50 F6
Hawstead Suff 30 C5
Hawthorn Durham 58 B5
Hawthorn Rhondda 15 C7
Hawthorn Wilts 16 E5
Hawthorn Hill Brack 18 D5
Hawthorn Hill Lincs 46 G6
Hawthorpe Lincs 36 C6
Hawton Notts 45 G11
Haxby York 52 D2
Haxey N Lincs 45 C11
Hay Green Norf 37 D11
Hay-on-Wye = Y Gelli Gandryll Powys 25 D9
Hay Street Herts 29 F10
Haydock Mers 43 C8
Haydon Dorset 8 C5
Haydon Bridge Northumb 62 G4
Haydon Wick Swindon 17 C8
Haye Corn 4 E4
Hayes London 19 C8
Hayes London 19 E11
Hayfield Derbys 44 D4
Hayfield Fife 69 A11
Hayhill E Ayrs 67 E7
Hayhillock Angus 77 C8
Hayle Corn 2 F4
Haynes C Beds 29 D7
Haynes Church End C Beds 29 D7
Hayscastle Pembs 22 D3
Hayscastle Cross Pembs 22 D4
Hayshead Angus 77 C9
Hayton Aberdeen 83 C11
Hayton Cumb 56 B3
Hayton Cumb 61 H11
Hayton E Yorks 52 E4
Hayton Notts 45 D11
Hayton's Bent Shrops 33 G11
Haytor Vale Devon 5 D8
Haywards Heath W Sus 12 D2
Haywood S Yorks 45 A9
Haywood Oaks Notts 45 G10
Hazel Grove Gtr Man 44 D3
Hazel Street Kent 12 C5
Hazelbank S Lanark 69 F7
Hazelbury Bryan Dorset 8 D6
Hazeley Hants 18 F4
Hazelhurst Gtr Man 44 B3
Hazelslade Staffs 34 D6
Hazelton Glos 27 G7
Hazelton Walls Fife 76 E6
Hazelwood Derbys 45 H7
Hazlemere Bucks 18 B5
Hazlerigg T&W 63 F8
Hazlewood N Yorks 51 D6
Hazon Northumb 63 C7
Heacham Norf 38 B2
Head of Muir Falk 69 B7
Headbourne Worthy Hants 10 A3
Headbrook Hereford 25 C10
Headcorn Kent 13 B7
Headingley W Yorks 51 F8
Headington Oxon 28 H2
Headlam Durham 58 E2
Headless Cross Worcs 27 B7
Headley Hants 18 E2
Headley Hants 18 H5
Headley Sur 19 F9
Headon Notts 45 E11
Heads S Lanark 68 F6
Heads Nook Cumb 61 H10
Heage Derbys 45 G7
Healaugh N Yorks 51 E10
Healaugh N Yorks 58 G1
Heald Green Gtr Man 44 D2
Heale Devon 6 B5
Heale Som 16 G3
Healey Gtr Man 50 H4
Healey N Yorks 51 A7
Healey Northumb 62 H6
Healing NE Lincs 46 A6
Heamoor Corn 2 F3
Heanish Argyll 78 G3
Heanor Derbys 45 H8
Heanton Punchardon Devon 6 C4
Heapham Lincs 46 D2
Hearthstane Borders 69 H10
Heasley Mill Devon 7 C6
Heast Highld 85 G11
Heath Cardiff 15 D7
Heath Derbys 45 F8
Heath and Reach C Beds 28 F6
Heath End Hants 18 E2
Heath End Sur 18 G5
Heath End Warks 27 B9
Heath Hayes Staffs 34 D6
Heath Hill Shrops 34 D3
Heath House Som 15 G10
Heath Town W Mid 34 F5
Heathcote Derbys 44 F5
Heather Leics 35 D9
Heatherfield Highld 85 D9
Heathfield Devon 5 D9
Heathfield E Sus 12 D4
Heathfield Som 7 D10
Heathhall Dumfries 60 F5
Heathrow Airport London 19 D7
Heathstock Devon 8 D1
Heathton Shrops 34 F4
Heatley Warr 43 D10
Heaton Lancs 49 C4
Heaton Staffs 44 F3
Heaton T&W 63 G8
Heaton W Yorks 51 F7
Heaton Moor Gtr Man 44 C2
Heaverham Kent 20 F2
Heaviley Gtr Man 44 D3
Heavitree Devon 7 G8
Hebburn T&W 63 G9
Hebden N Yorks 50 C6
Hebden Bridge W Yorks 50 G5
Hebron Anglesey 40 B6
Hebron Carms 22 D6
Hebron Northumb 63 E7
Heck Dumfries 60 E6
Heckfield Hants 18 E4
Heckfield Green Suff 39 H7
Heckfordbridge Essex 30 F6
Heckington Lincs 37 A7
Heckmondwike W Yorks 51 G8
Heddington Wilts 16 E6
Heddle Orkney 95 G4
Heddon-on-the-Wall Northumb 63 G7
Hedenham Norf 39 F9
Hedge End Hants 10 C3
Hedgerley Bucks 18 C6
Hedging Som 8 B2
Hedley on the Hill Northumb 62 H6
Hednesford Staffs 34 D6
Hedon E Yorks 53 G7
Hedsor Bucks 18 C6
Hedworth T&W 63 G9
Hegdon Hill Hereford 26 C2
Heggerscales Cumb 57 E10
Heglibister Shetland 96 H5
Heighington Darl 58 D3
Heighington Lincs 46 F4
Heights of Brae Highld 87 E8
Heights of Kinlochewe Highld 86 E3
Heilam Highld 92 C7
Heiton Borders 70 G6
Hele Devon 6 B4
Hele Devon 7 F8
Helensburgh Argyll 73 E11
Helford Corn 3 G6
Helford Passage Corn 3 G6
Helhoughton Norf 38 C4
Helions Bumpstead Essex 30 D3
Hellaby S Yorks 45 C9
Helland Corn 4 D1
Hellesdon Norf 39 D8
Hellidon Northants 28 C2
Hellifield N Yorks 50 D4
Hellingly E Sus 12 E4
Hellington Norf 39 E9
Hellister Shetland 96 J5
Helm Northumb 63 D7
Helmdon Northants 28 D2
Helmingham Suff 31 C8
Helmington Row Durham 58 C2
Helmsdale Highld 93 H13
Helmshore Lancs 50 G3
Helmsley N Yorks 52 A2
Helperby N Yorks 51 C10
Helperthorpe N Yorks 52 B5
Helpringham Lincs 37 A7
Helpston Pboro 37 E7
Helsby Ches W 43 E7
Helsey Lincs 47 E9
Helston Corn 2 G5
Helstone Corn 4 C1
Helton Cumb 57 D7
Helwith Bridge N Yorks 50 C4
Hemblington Norf 39 D9
Hemel Hempstead Herts 29 H7
Hemingbrough N Yorks 52 F2
Hemingby Lincs 46 E6
Hemingford Abbots Cambs 29 A9
Hemingford Grey Cambs 29 A9
Hemingstone Suff 31 C8
Hemington Leics 35 C10
Hemington Northants 37 G6
Hemington Som 16 F4
Hemley Suff 31 D9
Hemlington Mbro 58 E6
Hemp Green Suff 31 B10
Hempholme E Yorks 53 D6
Hempnall Norf 39 F8
Hempnall Green Norf 39 F8
Hempriggs House Highld 94 F5
Hempstead Essex 30 E3
Hempstead Medway 20 E4
Hempstead Norf 39 B7
Hempstead Norf 39 C10
Hempsted Glos 26 G5
Hempton Norf 38 C5
Hempton Oxon 27 E11
Hemsby Norf 39 D10
Hemswell Lincs 46 C3
Hemswell Cliff Lincs 46 D3
Hemsworth W Yorks 45 A8
Hemyock Devon 7 E10
Hen-feddau fawr Pembs 23 C7
Henbury Bristol 16 D2
Henbury Ches E 44 E2
Hendon London 19 C9
Hendon T&W 63 H10
Hendre Flint 42 F4
Hendre-ddu Conwy 41 D10
Hendreforgan Rhondda 14 C5
Hendy Carms 23 F10
Heneglwys Anglesey 40 C6
Henfield W Sus 11 C11
Henford Devon 6 G2
Henghurst Kent 13 C8
Hengoed Caerph 15 B7
Hengoed Powys 25 C9
Hengoed Shrops 33 B8
Hengrave Suff 30 B5
Henham Essex 30 F2
Heniarth Powys 33 E7
Henlade Som 8 B1
Henley Shrops 33 H11
Henley Som 8 A3
Henley Suff 31 C8
Henley W Sus 11 B7
Henley-in-Arden Warks 27 B8
Henley-on-Thames Oxon 18 C4
Henley's Down E Sus 12 E6
Henllan Ceredig 23 B8
Henllan Denb 42 F3
Henllan Amgoed Carms 22 D6
Henllys Torf 15 B8
Henlow C Beds 29 E8
Hennock Devon 5 C9
Henny Street Essex 30 E5
Henryd Conwy 41 C9
Henry's Moat Pembs 22 D5
Hensall N Yorks 52 G1
Henshaw Northumb 62 G3
Hensingham Cumb 56 E1
Henstead Suff 39 G10
Henstridge Som 8 C6
Henstridge Ash Som 8 B6
Henstridge Marsh Som 8 B6
Henton Oxon 18 A4
Henton Som 15 G10
Henwood Corn 4 D3
Heogan Shetland 96 J6
Heol-las Swansea 14 B2
Heol Senni Powys 24 F6
Heol-y-Cyw Bridgend 14 C5
Hepburn Northumb 62 A6
Hepple Northumb 62 C5
Hepscott Northumb 63 E8
Heptonstall W Yorks 50 G5
Hepworth Suff 30 A6
Hepworth W Yorks 44 B5
Herbrandston Pembs 22 F3
Hereford Hereford 26 D2
Heriot Borders 70 E2
Hermiston Edin 69 C10
Hermitage Borders 61 D11
Hermitage Dorset 8 D5
Hermitage W Berks 18 D2
Hermitage W Sus 11 D6
Hermon Anglesey 40 D5
Hermon Carms 23 C8
Hermon Carms 24 F3
Hermon Pembs 23 C7
Herne Kent 21 E8
Herne Bay Kent 21 E8
Herner Devon 6 D4
Hernhill Kent 21 E7
Herodsfoot Corn 4 E3
Herongate Essex 20 B3
Heronsford S Ayrs 54 A4
Herriard Hants 18 G3
Herringfleet Suff 39 F10
Herringswell Suff 30 A4
Hersden Kent 21 E9
Hersham Corn 6 F1
Hersham Sur 19 E8
Herstmonceux E Sus 12 E5
Herston Orkney 95 J5
Hertford Herts 29 G10
Hertford Heath Herts 29 G10
Hertingfordbury Herts 29 G10
Hesket Newmarket Cumb 56 C5
Hesketh Bank Lancs 49 G4
Hesketh Lane Lancs 50 E2
Heskin Green Lancs 49 H5
Hesleden Durham 58 C5
Hesleyside Northumb 62 E4
Heslington York 52 D2
Hessay York 51 D11
Hessenford Corn 4 F4
Hessett Suff 30 B6
Hessle E Yorks 52 G6
Hest Bank Lancs 49 C4
Heston London 19 D8
Hestwall Orkney 95 G3
Heswall Mers 42 D5
Hethe Oxon 28 F2
Hethersett Norf 39 E7
Hethersgill Cumb 61 G10
Hethpool Northumb 71 H7
Hett Durham 58 C3
Hetton N Yorks 50 D5
Hetton-le-Hole T&W 58 B4
Hetton Steads Northumb 71 G9
Heugh Northumb 62 F6
Heugh-head Aberds 82 B5
Heveningham Suff 31 A10
Hever Kent 12 B3
Heversham Cumb 49 A4
Hevingham Norf 39 C7
Hewas Water Corn 3 E8
Hewelsfield Glos 16 A2
Hewish N Som 15 E10
Hewish Som 8 D3
Heworth York 52 D2
Hexham Northumb 62 G5
Hextable Kent 20 D2
Hexton Herts 29 E8
Hexworthy Devon 5 D7
Hey Lancs 50 E4
Heybridge Essex 20 B3
Heybridge Essex 30 H5
Heybridge Basin Essex 30 H5
Heybrook Bay Devon 4 G6
Heydon Cambs 29 D11

Heydon Norf 39 C7
Heydour Lincs 36 B6
Heylipol Argyll 78 G2
Heylor Shetland 96 E4
Heysham Lancs 49 C4
Heyshott W Sus 11 C7
Heyside Gtr Man 44 B3
Heytesbury Wilts 16 G6
Heythrop Oxon 27 F10
Heywood Gtr Man 44 A2
Heywood Wilts 16 F5
Hibaldstow N Lincs 46 B3
Hickleton S Yorks 45 B8
Hickling Norf 39 C10
Hickling Notts 36 C2
Hickling Green Norf 39 C10
Hickling Heath Norf 39 C10
Hickstead W Sus 12 D1
Hidcote Boyce Glos 27 D8
High Ackworth W Yorks 51 H10
High Angerton Northumb 62 E6
High Bankhill Cumb 57 B7
High Barnes T&W 63 H9
High Beach Essex 19 B11
High Bentham N Yorks 50 C2
High Bickington Devon 6 D5
High Birkwith N Yorks 50 B3
High Blantyre S Lanark 68 E5
High Bonnybridge Falk 69 C7
High Bradfield S Yorks 44 C6
High Bray Devon 6 C5
High Brooms Kent 12 B4
High Bullen Devon 6 D4
High Buston Northumb 63 C8
High Callerton Northumb 63 F7
High Catton E Yorks 52 D3
High Cogges Oxon 27 H10
High Coniscliffe Darl 58 E3
High Cross Hants 10 B6
High Cross Herts 29 G10
High Easter Essex 30 G3
High Eggborough N Yorks 52 G1
High Ellington N Yorks 51 A7
High Ercall Telford 34 D1
High Etherley Durham 58 D2
High Garrett Essex 30 F4
High Grange Durham 58 C2
High Green Norf 39 E7
High Green S Yorks 45 C7
High Green Worcs 26 D5
High Halden Kent 13 C7
High Halstow Medway 20 D4
High Ham Som 8 A3
High Harrington Cumb 56 D2
High Hatton Shrops 34 C2
High Hawsker N Yorks 59 F10
High Hesket Cumb 57 B6
High Hesleden Durham 58 C5
High Hoyland S Yorks 44 A6
High Hunsley E Yorks 52 F5
High Hurstwood E Sus 12 D3
High Hutton N Yorks 52 C3
High Ireby Cumb 56 C4
High Kelling Norf 39 A7
High Kilburn N Yorks 51 B11
High Lands Durham 58 D2
High Lane Gtr Man 44 D3
High Lane Worcs 26 B3
High Laver Essex 30 H2
High Legh Ches E 43 D10
High Leven Stockton 58 E5
High Littleton Bath 16 F3
High Lorton Cumb 56 D3
High Marishes N Yorks 52 B4
High Marnham Notts 46 E2
High Melton S Yorks 45 B9
High Mickley Northumb 62 G6
High Mindork Dumfries 54 D6
High Newton Cumb 49 A4
High Newton-by-the-Sea Northumb 71 H11
High Nibthwaite Cumb 56 H4
High Offley Staffs 34 C3
High Ongar Essex 20 A2
High Onn Staffs 34 D4
High Roding Essex 30 G3
High Row Cumb 56 C5
High Salvington W Sus 11 D10
High Sellafield Cumb 56 F2
High Shaw N Yorks 57 G10
High Spen T&W 63 H7
High Stoop Durham 58 B2
High Street Corn 3 D8
High Street Kent 12 C6
High Street Suff 30 D5
High Street Suff 31 A11
High Street Suff 31 C11
High Street Green Suff 31 C7
High Throston Hrtlpl 58 C5
High Toynton Lincs 46 F6
High Trewhitt Northumb 62 C6
High Valleyfield Fife 69 B9
High Westwood Durham 63 H7
High Wray Cumb 56 F5
High Wych Herts 29 G11
High Wycombe Bucks 18 B5
Higham Derbys 45 G7
Higham Kent 20 D4
Higham Lancs 50 F4
Higham Suff 30 B4
Higham Suff 31 E7
Higham Dykes Northumb 63 F7
Higham Ferrers Northants 28 B6
Higham Gobion C Beds 29 E8
Higham on the Hill Leics 35 F9
Higham Wood Kent 20 G2
Highampton Devon 6 F3
Highbridge Highld 80 E3
Highbridge Som 15 G9
Highbrook W Sus 12 C2
Highburton W Yorks 44 A5
Highbury Som 16 G3
Highclere Hants 17 E11
Highcliffe Dorset 9 E11
Higher Ansty Dorset 9 D6
Higher Ashton Devon 5 C9
Higher Ballam Lancs 49 F3
Higher Bartle Lancs 49 F5
Higher Boscaswell Corn 2 F2
Higher Burwardsley Ches W 43 G8
Higher Clovelly Devon 6 D2
Higher End Gtr Man 43 B8
Higher Kinnerton Flint 42 F6
Higher Penwortham Lancs 49 G5
Higher Town Scilly 2 C3
Higher Walreddon Devon 4 D5
Higher Walton Lancs 50 G1
Higher Walton Warr 43 D8
Higher Wheelton Lancs 50 G2
Higher Whitley Ches W 43 D9
Higher Wincham Ches W 43 E9
Higher Wych Ches W 33 A10
Highfield E Yorks 52 F3
Highfield Gtr Man 43 B10
Highfield N Ayrs 66 A6
Highfield Oxon 28 F2
Highfield S Yorks 45 D7
Highfield T&W 63 H7
Highfields Cambs 29 C10
Highfields Northumb 71 E8
Highgate London 19 C9
Highlane Ches E 44 F2
Highlane Derbys 45 D8
Highlaws Cumb 56 B3
Highleadon Glos 26 F4
Highleigh W Sus 11 E7
Highley Shrops 34 G3
Highmoor Cross Oxon 18 C4
Highmoor Hill Mon 15 C10
Highnam Glos 26 G4
Highnam Green Glos 26 F4
Highsted Kent 20 E6
Highstreet Green Essex 30 E4
Hightae Dumfries 60 F6
Hightown Ches E 44 F2
Hightown Mers 42 B6
Hightown Green Suff 30 C6
Highway Wilts 17 D7
Highweek Devon 5 D9
Highworth Swindon 17 B9
Hilborough Norf 38 E4
Hilcote Derbys 45 G8
Hilcott Wilts 17 F8
Hilden Park Kent 20 G2
Hildenborough Kent 20 G2
Hildersham Cambs 30 D2
Hilderstone Staffs 34 B5
Hilderthorpe E Yorks 53 C7
Hilfield Dorset 8 D5
Hilgay Norf 38 F2
Hill Pembs 22 F6
Hill S Glos 16 B3
Hill W Mid 35 F7
Hill Brow W Sus 11 B6
Hill Dale Lancs 43 A7
Hill Dyke Lincs 47 H7
Hill End Durham 58 C1
Hill End Fife 76 H3
Hill End N Yorks 51 D6
Hill Head Hants 10 D4
Hill Head Northumb 62 G5
Hill Mountain Pembs 22 F4
Hill of Beath Fife 69 A10
Hill of Fearn Highld 87 D11
Hill of Mountblairy Aberds 89 C6
Hill Ridware Staffs 35 D6
Hill Top Durham 57 D11
Hill Top Hants 10 D3
Hill Top W Mid 34 F5
Hill Top W Yorks 51 H9
Hill View Dorset 9 E8
Hillam N Yorks 51 G11
Hillbeck Cumb 57 E9
Hillborough Kent 21 E9
Hillbrae Aberds 83 A9
Hillbrae Aberds 88 D6
Hillbutts Dorset 9 D8
Hillcliffane Derbys 44 H6
Hillcommon Som 7 D10
Hillend Fife 69 B10
Hillerton Devon 7 G6
Hillesden Bucks 28 F3
Hillesley Glos 16 C4
Hillfarance Som 7 D10
Hillhead Aberds 88 E5
Hillhead Devon 5 F10
Hillhead S Ayrs 67 E7
Hillhead of Auchentumb Aberds 89 C9
Hillhead of Cocklaw Aberds 89 D10
Hillhouse Borders 70 E4
Hilliclay Highld 94 D3
Hillingdon London 19 C7
Hillington Glasgow 68 D4
Hillington Norf 38 C3
Hillmorton Warks 28 A2
Hillockhead Aberds 82 B6
Hillockhead Aberds 82 C5
Hillside Aberds 83 D11
Hillside Angus 77 A10
Hillside Mers 42 A6
Hillside Orkney 95 J5
Hillside Shetland 96 G6
Hillswick Shetland 96 F4
Hillway IoW 10 F5
Hillwell Shetland 96 M5
Hilmarton Wilts 17 D7
Hilperton Wilts 16 F5
Hilsea Ptsmth 10 D5
Hilston E Yorks 53 F8
Hilton Aberds 89 E9
Hilton Cambs 29 B9
Hilton Cumb 57 D9
Hilton Derbys 35 B8
Hilton Dorset 9 D6
Hilton Durham 58 D2
Hilton Highld 87 C10
Hilton Shrops 34 F3
Hilton Stockton 58 E5
Hilton of Cadboll Highld 87 D11
Himbleton Worcs 26 C6
Himley Staffs 34 F4
Hincaster Cumb 49 A5
Hinckley Leics 35 F10
Hinderclay Suff 38 H6
Hinderton Ches W 42 E6
Hinderwell N Yorks 59 E8
Hindford Shrops 33 B9
Hindhead Sur 18 H5
Hindley Gtr Man 43 B9
Hindley Green Gtr Man 43 B9
Hindlip Worcs 26 C5
Hindolveston Norf 38 C6
Hindon Wilts 9 A8
Hindringham Norf 38 B5
Hingham Norf 38 E6
Hinstock Shrops 34 C2
Hintlesham Suff 31 D7
Hinton Hants 9 E11
Hinton Hereford 25 E10
Hinton Northants 28 C2
Hinton S Glos 16 D4
Hinton Shrops 33 E10
Hinton Ampner Hants 10 B4
Hinton Blewett Bath 16 F2
Hinton Charterhouse Bath 16 F4
Hinton-in-the-Hedges Northants 28 E2
Hinton Martell Dorset 9 D9
Hinton on the Green Worcs 27 D7
Hinton Parva Swindon 17 C9
Hinton St George Som 8 C3
Hinton St Mary Dorset 9 C6
Hinton Waldrist Oxon 17 B10
Hints Shrops 26 A3
Hints Staffs 35 E7
Hinwick Bedford 28 B6
Hinxhill Kent 13 B9
Hinxton Cambs 29 D11
Hinxworth Herts 29 D9
Hipperholme W Yorks 51 G7
Hipswell N Yorks 58 G2
Hirael Gwyn 41 C7
Hiraeth Carms 22 D6
Hirn Aberds 83 C9
Hirnant Powys 33 C6
Hirst N Lanark 69 D7
Hirst Northumb 63 E8
Hirst Courtney N Yorks 52 G2
Hirwaen Denb 42 F4
Hirwaun Rhondda 24 H6
Hiscott Devon 6 D4
Histon Cambs 29 B11
Hitcham Suff 30 C6
Hitchin Herts 29 F8
Hither Green London 19 D10
Hittisleigh Devon 7 G6
Hive E Yorks 52 F4
Hixon Staffs 34 C6
Hoaden Kent 21 F9
Hoaldalbert Mon 25 F10
Hoar Cross Staffs 35 C7
Hoarwithy Hereford 26 F2
Hoath Kent 21 E9
Hobarris Shrops 33 H9
Hobbister Orkney 95 H4
Hobkirk Borders 61 B11
Hobson Durham 63 H7
Hoby Leics 36 D2
Hockering Norf 39 D6
Hockerton Notts 45 G11
Hockley Essex 20 B5
Hockley Heath W Mid 27 A8
Hockliffe C Beds 28 F6
Hockwold cum Wilton Norf 38 G3
Hockworthy Devon 7 E9
Hoddesdon Herts 29 H10
Hoddlesden Blackburn 50 G3
Hoddom Mains Dumfries 61 F7
Hoddomcross Dumfries 61 F7
Hodgeston Pembs 22 G5
Hodley Powys 33 F7
Hodnet Shrops 34 C2
Hodthorpe Derbys 45 E9
Hoe Hants 10 C4
Hoe Norf 38 D5
Hoe Gate Hants 10 C5
Hoff Cumb 57 E8
Hog Patch Sur 18 G5
Hoggard's Green Suff 30 C5
Hoggeston Bucks 28 F5
Hogha Gearraidh W Isles 84 A2
Hoghton Lancs 50 G2
Hognaston Derbys 44 G6
Hogsthorpe Lincs 47 E9
Holbeach Lincs 37 C9
Holbeach Bank Lincs 37 C9
Holbeach Clough Lincs 37 C9
Holbeach Drove Lincs 37 D9
Holbeach Hurn Lincs 37 C9
Holbeach St Johns Lincs 37 D9
Holbeach St Marks Lincs 37 B9
Holbeach St Matthew Lincs 37 B10
Holbeck Notts 45 E9
Holbeck W Yorks 51 F8
Holbeck Woodhouse Notts 45 E9
Holberrow Green Worcs 27 C7
Holbeton Devon 5 F7
Holborn London 19 C10
Holbrook Derbys 35 A9
Holbrook S Yorks 45 D8
Holbrook Suff 31 E8
Holburn Northumb 71 G9
Holbury Hants 10 D3
Holcombe Devon 5 D10
Holcombe Som 16 G3
Holcombe Rogus Devon 7 E9
Holcot Northants 28 B4
Holden Lancs 50 E3
Holdenby Northants 28 B3
Holdenhurst Bmouth 9 E10
Holdgate Shrops 34 G1
Holdingham Lincs 46 H4
Holditch Dorset 8 D2
Hole-in-the-Wall Hereford 26 F3
Holefield Borders 71 G7
Holehouses Ches E 43 E10
Holemoor Devon 6 F3
Holestane Dumfries 60 D4
Holford Som 7 B10
Holgate York 52 D1
Holker Cumb 49 B3
Holkham Norf 38 A4
Hollacombe Devon 6 F2
Holland Orkney 95 C5
Holland Orkney 95 F7
Holland Fen Lincs 46 H6
Holland-on-Sea Essex 31 G9
Hollandstoun Orkney 95 C8
Hollee Dumfries 61 G8
Hollesley Suff 31 D10
Hollicombe Torbay 5 E9
Hollingbourne Kent 20 F5
Hollington Derbys 35 B8
Hollington E Sus 13 E6
Hollington Staffs 35 B6
Hollington Grove Derbys 35 B8
Hollingworth Gtr Man 44 C4
Hollins Gtr Man 44 B2
Hollins Green Warr 43 C9
Hollins Lane Lancs 49 D4
Hollinsclough Staffs 44 F4
Hollinwood Gtr Man 44 B3
Hollinwood Shrops 33 B11
Hollocombe Devon 6 E5
Hollow Meadows S Yorks 44 D6
Holloway Derbys 45 G7
Hollowell Northants 28 A3
Holly End Norf 37 E10
Holly Green Worcs 26 D5
Hollybush Caerph 15 A7
Hollybush E Ayrs 67 E6
Hollybush Worcs 26 E4
Hollym E Yorks 53 G9
Hollywood Worcs 35 H6
Holmbridge W Yorks 44 B5
Holmbury St Mary Sur 19 G8
Holmbush Corn 3 D9
Holmcroft Staffs 34 C5
Holme Cambs 37 G7
Holme Cumb 49 B5
Holme N Yorks 51 A9
Holme Notts 46 G2
Holme W Yorks 44 B5
Holme Chapel Lancs 50 G4
Holme Green N Yorks 52 E1
Holme Hale Norf 38 E4
Holme Lacy Hereford 26 E2
Holme Marsh Hereford 25 C10
Holme next the Sea Norf 38 A3
Holme-on-Spalding-Moor E Yorks 52 F4
Holme on the Wolds E Yorks 52 E5
Holme Pierrepont Notts 36 B2
Holme St Cuthbert Cumb 56 B3
Holme Wood W Yorks 51 F7
Holmer Hereford 26 D2
Holmer Green Bucks 18 B6
Holmes Chapel Ches E 43 F10
Holmesfield Derbys 45 E7
Holmeswood Lancs 49 H4
Holmewood Derbys 45 F8
Holmfirth W Yorks 44 B5
Holmhead Dumfries 60 E3
Holmhead E Ayrs 67 D8
Holmisdale Highld 84 D6
Holmpton E Yorks 53 G9
Holmrook Cumb 56 G2
Holmsgarth Shetland 96 J6
Holmwrangle Cumb 57 B7
Holne Devon 5 E8
Holnest Dorset 8 D5
Holsworthy Devon 6 F2
Holsworthy Beacon Devon 6 F2
Holt Dorset 9 D9
Holt Norf 39 B6
Holt Wilts 16 E5
Holt Worcs 26 B5
Holt Wrex 43 G7
Holt End Hants 18 H3
Holt End Worcs 27 B7
Holt Fleet Worcs 26 B5
Holt Heath Worcs 26 B5
Holt Park W Yorks 51 E8
Holtby York 52 D2
Holton Oxon 28 H3
Holton Som 8 B5
Holton Suff 39 H9
Holton cum Beckering Lincs 46 D5
Holton Heath Dorset 9 E8
Holton le Clay Lincs 46 B6
Holton le Moor Lincs 46 C4
Holton St Mary Suff 31 E7
Holwell Dorset 8 C6
Holwell Herts 29 E8
Holwell Leics 36 C3
Holwell Oxon 27 H9
Holwick Durham 57 D11
Holworth Dorset 9 F6
Holy Cross Worcs 34 H5
Holy Island Northumb 71 F10
Holybourne Hants 18 G4
Holyhead = Caergybi Anglesey 40 B4
Holymoorside Derbys 45 F7
Holyport Windsor 18 D5
Holystone Northumb 62 C5
Holytown N Lanark 68 D6
Holywell Cambs 29 A10
Holywell Corn 3 D6
Holywell Dorset 8 D4
Holywell E Sus 12 G4
Holywell = Treffynnon Flint 42 E4
Holywell Northumb 63 F9
Holywell Green W Yorks 51 H6
Holywell Lake Som 7 D10
Holywell Row Suff 38 H3
Holywood Dumfries 60 E5
Hom Green Hereford 26 F2
Homer Shrops 34 E2
Homersfield Suff 39 G8
Homington Wilts 9 B10
Honey Hill Kent 21 E8
Honey Street Wilts 17 E8
Honey Tye Suff 30 E6
Honeyborough Pembs 22 F4
Honeybourne Worcs 27 D8
Honeychurch Devon 6 F5
Honiley Warks 27 A9
Honing Norf 39 C9
Honingham Norf 39 D7
Honington Lincs 36 A5
Honington Suff 30 A6
Honington Warks 27 D9
Honiton Devon 7 F10
Honley W Yorks 44 A5
Hoo Green Ches E 43 D10
Hoo St. Werburgh Medway 20 D4
Hood Green S Yorks 45 B7
Hooe E Sus 12 F5
Hooe Plym 4 F6
Hooe Common E Sus 12 E5
Hook E Yorks 52 G3
Hook Hants 18 F4
Hook London 19 E8
Hook Pembs 22 E4
Hook Wilts 17 C7
Hook Green Kent 12 C5
Hook Green Kent 20 E3
Hook Norton Oxon 27 E10
Hooke Dorset 8 E4
Hookgate Staffs 34 B3
Hookway Devon 7 G7
Hookwood Sur 12 B1
Hoole Ches W 43 F7
Hooley Sur 19 F9
Hoop Mon 26 H2
Hooton Ches W 42 E6
Hooton Levitt S Yorks 45 C9
Hooton Pagnell S Yorks 45 B8
Hooton Roberts S Yorks 45 C8
Hop Pole Lincs 37 D7
Hope Derbys 44 D5
Hope Devon 5 H7
Hope = Yr Hôb Flint 42 G6
Hope Highld 92 C7
Hope Powys 33 E8
Hope Shrops 33 E9
Hope Staffs 44 G5
Hope Bagot Shrops 26 A2
Hope Bowdler Shrops 33 F10
Hope End Green Essex 30 F2
Hope Green Ches E 44 D3
Hope Mansell Hereford 26 G3
Hope under Dinmore Hereford 26 C2
Hopeman Moray 88 B1
Hope's Green Essex 20 C4
Hopesay Shrops 33 G9
Hopley's Green Hereford 25 C10
Hopperton N Yorks 51 D10
Hopstone Shrops 34 F3
Hopton Shrops 33 C9
Hopton Shrops 34 C1
Hopton Staffs 34 C5
Hopton Suff 38 H5
Hopton Cangeford Shrops 33 G11
Hopton Castle Shrops 33 H9
Hopton on Sea Norf 39 E11
Hopton Wafers Shrops 34 H2
Hoptonheath Shrops 33 H9
Hopwas Staffs 35 E7
Hopwood Gtr Man 44 B2
Hopwood Worcs 34 H6
Horam E Sus 12 E4
Horbling Lincs 37 B7
Horbury W Yorks 51 H8
Horcott Glos 17 A8
Horden Durham 58 B5
Horderley Shrops 33 G10
Hordle Hants 10 E1
Hordley Shrops 33 B9
Horeb Carms 23 D10
Horeb Carms 23 F9
Horeb Ceredig 23 B8
Horfield Bristol 16 D3
Horham Suff 31 A9
Horkesley Heath Essex 30 F6
Horkstow N Lincs 52 H5
Horley Oxon 27 D11
Horley Sur 12 B1
Hornblotton Green Som 8 A4
Hornby Lancs 50 C1
Hornby N Yorks 58 F4
Hornby N Yorks 58 G3
Horncastle Lincs 46 F6
Hornchurch London 20 C2
Horncliffe Northumb 71 F8
Horndean Borders 71 F7
Horndean Hants 10 C6
Horndon Devon 4 D6
Horndon on the Hill Thurrock 20 C3
Horne Sur 12 B2
Horniehaugh Angus 77 A7
Horning Norf 39 D9
Horninghold Leics 36 F4
Horninglow Staffs 35 C8
Horningsea Cambs 29 B11
Horningsham Wilts 16 G5
Horningtoft Norf 38 C5
Horns Corner Kent 12 D6
Horns Cross Devon 6 D2
Horns Cross E Sus 13 D7
Hornsby Cumb 57 A7
Hornsea E Yorks 53 E8
Hornsea Bridge E Yorks 53 E8
Hornsey London 19 C10
Hornton Oxon 27 D10
Horrabridge Devon 4 E6
Horringer Suff 30 B5
Horringford IoW 10 F4
Horse Bridge Staffs 44 G3
Horsebridge Devon 4 D5
Horsebridge Hants 10 A2
Horsebrook Staffs 34 D4
Horsehay Telford 34 E2
Horseheath Cambs 30 D3
Horsehouse N Yorks 50 A6
Horsell Sur 18 F6
Horseman's Green Wrex 33 A10
Horseway Cambs 37 G10
Horsey Norf 39 C10
Horsford Norf 39 D7
Horsforth W Yorks 51 F8
Horsham W Sus 11 A10
Horsham Worcs 26 C4
Horsham St Faith Norf 39 D8
Horsington Lincs 46 F5
Horsington Som 8 B6
Horsley Derbys 35 A9
Horsley Glos 16 B5
Horsley Northumb 62 D4
Horsley Northumb 62 G6
Horsley Cross Essex 31 F8
Horsley Woodhouse Derbys 35 A9
Horsleycross Street Essex 31 F8
Horsleyhill Borders 61 B11
Horsleyhope Durham 58 B1
Horsmonden Kent 12 B5
Horspath Oxon 18 A2
Horstead Norf 39 D8
Horsted Keynes W Sus 12 D2
Horton Bucks 28 G6
Horton Dorset 9 D9
Horton Lancs 50 D4
Horton Northants 28 C5
Horton S Glos 16 C4
Horton Shrops 33 C10
Horton Som 8 C2
Horton Staffs 44 G3
Horton Swansea 23 H9
Horton Wilts 17 E7
Horton Windsor 19 D7
Horton-cum-Studley Oxon 28 G2
Horton Green Ches W 43 H7
Horton Heath Hants 10 C3
Horton in Ribblesdale N Yorks 50 B4
Horton Kirby Kent 20 E2
Hortonlane Shrops 33 D10
Horwich Gtr Man 43 A9
Horwich End Derbys 44 D4
Horwood Devon 6 D4
Hose Leics 36 C3
Hoselaw Borders 71 G7
Hoses Cumb 56 G4
Hosh Perth 75 E11
Hosta W Isles 84 A2
Hoswick Shetland 96 L6
Hotham E Yorks 52 F4
Hothfield Kent 20 G6
Hoton Leics 36 C1
Houbie Shetland 96 D8
Houdston S Ayrs 66 G4
Hough Ches E 43 G10
Hough Ches E 44 E2
Hough Green Halton 43 D7
Hough-on-the-Hill Lincs 46 H3
Hougham Lincs 36 A4
Houghton Cambs 29 A9
Houghton Cumb 61 H10
Houghton Hants 10 A2
Houghton Pembs 22 F4
Houghton W Sus 11 C9
Houghton Conquest C Beds 29 D7
Houghton Green E Sus 13 D8
Houghton Green Warr 43 C9
Houghton-le-Side Darl 58 D3
Houghton-Le-Spring T&W 58 B4
Houghton on the Hill Leics 36 E2
Houghton Regis C Beds 29 F7
Houghton St Giles Norf 38 B5
Houlland Shetland 96 F7
Houlland Shetland 96 H5
Houlsyke N Yorks 59 F8
Hound Hants 10 D3
Hound Green Hants 18 F4
Houndslow Borders 70 F5
Houndwood Borders 71 D7
Hounslow London 19 D8
Hounslow Green Essex 30 G3
Housay Shetland 96 F8
House of Daviot Highld 87 G10
House of Glenmuick Aberds 82 D5
Housetter Shetland 96 E5
Houss Shetland 96 K5
Houston Renfs 68 D3
Houstry Highld 94 G3
Houton Orkney 95 H4
Hove Brighton 12 F1
Hoveringham Notts 45 H10
Hoveton Norf 39 D9
Hovingham N Yorks 52 B2
How Cumb 61 H11
How Caple Hereford 26 E3
How End C Beds 29 D7
How Green Kent 19 G11
Howbrook S Yorks 45 C7
Howden Borders 62 A2
Howden E Yorks 52 G3
Howden-le-Wear Durham 58 C2
Howe Highld 94 D5
Howe N Yorks 51 A9
Howe Norf 39 E8
Howe Bridge Gtr Man 43 B9
Howe Green Essex 20 A4
Howe of Teuchar Aberds 89 D7
Howe Street Essex 30 E3
Howe Street Essex 30 G3
Howell Lincs 46 H5
Howey Powys 25 C7
Howgate Midloth 69 E11
Howick Northumb 63 B8
Howle Durham 58 D1
Howle Telford 34 C2
Howlett End Essex 30 E2
Howley Som 8 D1
Hownam Borders 62 B3
Hownam Mains Borders 62 A3
Howpasley Borders 61 C9
Howsham N Lincs 46 B4
Howsham N Yorks 52 C3
Howslack Dumfries 60 C6
Howtel Northumb 71 G7
Howton Hereford 25 F11
Howtown Cumb 56 E6
Howwood Renfs 68 D2
Hoxne Suff 39 H7
Hoy Orkney 95 H3
Hoylake Mers 42 D5
Hoyland S Yorks 45 B7
Hoylandswaine S Yorks 44 B6
Hubberholme N Yorks 50 B5
Hubbert's Bridge Lincs 37 A8
Huby N Yorks 51 E8
Huby N Yorks 52 C1
Hucclecote Glos 26 G5
Hucking Kent 20 F5
Hucknall Notts 45 H9
Huddersfield W Yorks 51 H7
Huddington Worcs 26 C6
Hudswell N Yorks 58 F2
Huggate E Yorks 52 D4
Hugglescote Leics 35 D10
Hugh Town Scilly 2 C3
Hughenden Valley Bucks 18 B5
Hughley Shrops 34 F1
Huish Devon 6 E4
Huish Wilts 17 E8
Huish Champflower Som 7 D9
Huish Episcopi Som 8 B3
Huisinis W Isles 90 F4
Hulcott Bucks 28 G5
Hulland Derbys 44 H6
Hulland Ward Derbys 44 H6
Hullavington Wilts 16 C5
Hullbridge Essex 20 B5
Hulme Gtr Man 44 C2
Hulme End Staffs 44 G5
Hulme Walfield Ches E 44 F2
Hulver Street Suff 39 G10
Hulverstone IoW 10 F2
Humber Hereford 26 C2
Humber Bridge N Lincs 52 G6
Humberston NE Lincs 47 B7
Humbie E Loth 70 D3
Humbleton E Yorks 53 F8
Humbleton Northumb 71 H8
Humby Lincs 36 B6
Hume Borders 70 F6
Humshaugh Northumb 62 F5
Huna Highld 94 C5
Huncoat Lancs 50 F3
Huncote Leics 35 F11
Hundalee Borders 62 B2
Hunderthwaite Durham 57 D11
Hundle Houses Lincs 46 G6
Hundleby Lincs 47 F7
Hundleton Pembs 22 F4
Hundon Suff 30 D4
Hundred Acres Hants 10 C4
Hundred End Lancs 49 G4
Hundred House Powys 25 C8
Hungarton Leics 36 E2
Hungerford Hants 9 C10
Hungerford W Berks 17 E10
Hungerford Newtown W Berks 17 D10
Hungerton Lincs 36 C4
Hungladder Highld 85 A8
Hunmanby N Yorks 53 B6
Hunmanby Moor N Yorks 53 B7
Hunningham Warks 27 B10
Hunny Hill IoW 10 F3
Hunsdon Herts 29 G11
Hunsingore N Yorks 51 D10
Hunslet W Yorks 51 F9
Hunsonby Cumb 57 C7
Hunspow Highld 94 C4
Hunstanton Norf 38 A2
Hunstanworth Durham 57 B11
Hunsterson Ches E 43 H9
Hunston Suff 30 B6
Hunston W Sus 11 D7
Hunstrete Bath 16 E3
Hunt End Worcs 27 B7
Hunter's Quay Argyll 73 F10
Hunthill Lodge Angus 82 F6
Hunting-tower Perth 76 E3
Huntingdon Cambs 29 A9
Huntingfield Suff 31 A10
Huntingford Dorset 9 A7
Huntington E Loth 70 C3
Huntington Hereford 25 C9
Huntington Staffs 34 D5
Huntington York 52 D2
Huntley Glos 26 G4
Huntly Aberds 88 E5
Huntlywood Borders 70 F5
Hunton Kent 20 G4
Hunton N Yorks 58 G2
Hunt's Corner Norf 39 G6
Hunt's Cross Mers 43 D7
Huntsham Devon 7 D9
Huntspill Som 15 G9
Huntworth Som 8 A2
Hunwick Durham 58 C2
Hunworth Norf 39 B6
Hurdsfield Ches E 44 E3
Hurley Warks 35 F8
Hurley Windsor 18 C5
Hurlford E Ayrs 67 C7
Hurliness Orkney 95 K3
Hurn Dorset 9 E10
Hurn's End Lincs 47 H8
Hursley Hants 10 B3
Hurst N Yorks 58 F1
Hurst Som 8 C3
Hurst Wokingham 18 D4
Hurst Green E Sus 12 D6
Hurst Green Lancs 50 F2
Hurst Wickham W Sus 12 E1
Hurstbourne Priors Hants 17 G11
Hurstbourne Tarrant Hants 17 F10
Hurstpierpoint W Sus 12 E1
Hurstwood Lancs 50 F4
Hurtmore Sur 18 G6
Hurworth Place Darl 58 F3
Hury Durham 57 E11
Husabost Highld 84 C7
Husbands Bosworth Leics 36 G2
Husborne Crawley C Beds 28 E6
Husthwaite N Yorks 51 B11
Hutchwns Bridgend 14 D4
Huthwaite Notts 45 G8
Huttoft Lincs 47 E9
Hutton Borders 71 E8
Hutton Cumb 56 D6
Hutton E Yorks 52 D6
Hutton Essex 20 B3
Hutton Lancs 49 G4
Hutton N Som 15 F9
Hutton Buscel N Yorks 52 A5
Hutton Conyers N Yorks 51 B9
Hutton Cranswick E Yorks 52 D6
Hutton End Cumb 56 C6
Hutton Gate Redcar 59 E6
Hutton Henry Durham 58 C5
Hutton-le-Hole N Yorks 59 G8
Hutton Magna Durham 58 E2
Hutton Roof Cumb 50 B1
Hutton Roof Cumb 56 C5
Hutton Rudby N Yorks 58 F5
Hutton Sessay N Yorks 51 B10
Hutton Village Redcar 59 E6
Hutton Wandesley N Yorks 51 D11
Huxley Ches W 43 F8
Huxter Shetland 96 G7
Huxter Shetland 96 H5
Huxton Borders 71 D7
Huyton Mers 43 C7
Hwlffordd = Haverfordwest Pembs 22 E4
Hycemoor Cumb 56 H2
Hyde Glos 16 A5
Hyde Gtr Man 44 C3
Hyde Hants 9 C10
Hyde Heath Bucks 18 A6
Hyde Park S Yorks 45 B9
Hydestile Sur 18 G6
Hylton Castle T&W 63 H9
Hyndford Bridge S Lanark 69 F8
Hynish Argyll 78 H2
Hyssington Powys 33 F9
Hythe Hants 10 D3
Hythe Kent 21 H8
Hythe End Windsor 19 D7
Hythie Aberds 89 C10

I

Ibberton Dorset 9 D6
Ible Derbys 44 G6
Ibsley Hants 9 D10
Ibstock Leics 35 D10
Ibstone Bucks 18 B4
Ibthorpe Hants 17 F10
Ibworth Hants 18 F2
Ichrachan Argyll 74 D3
Ickburgh Norf 38 F4
Ickenham London 19 C7
Ickford Bucks 28 H3
Ickham Kent 21 F9
Ickleford Herts 29 E8
Icklesham E Sus 13 E7
Ickleton Cambs 29 D11
Icklingham Suff 30 A4
Ickwell Green C Beds 29 D8
Icomb Glos 27 F9
Idbury Oxon 27 G9
Iddesleigh Devon 6 F4
Ide Devon 7 G7
Ide Hill Kent 19 F11
Ideford Devon 5 D9
Iden E Sus 13 D8
Iden Green Kent 12 C6
Iden Green Kent 13 C7
Idle W Yorks 51 F7
Idlicote Warks 27 D9
Idmiston Wilts 17 H8
Idole Carms 23 E9
Idridgehay Derbys 44 H6
Idrigill Highld 85 B8
Idstone Oxon 17 C9
Idvies Angus 77 C8
Iffley Oxon 18 A2
Ifield W Sus 19 H9
Ifold W Sus 11 A9
Iford E Sus 12 F3
Ifton Heath Shrops 33 B9
Ightfield Shrops 34 B1
Ightham Kent 20 F2
Iken Suff 31 C11
Ilam Staffs 44 G5
Ilchester Som 8 B4
Ilderton Northumb 62 A6
Ilford London 19 C11
Ilfracombe Devon 6 B4
Ilkeston Derbys 35 A10
Ilketshall St Andrew Suff 39 G9
Ilketshall St Lawrence Suff 39 G9
Ilketshall St Margaret Suff 39 G9
Ilkley W Yorks 51 E7
Illey W Mid 34 G5
Illingworth W Yorks 51 G6
Illogan Corn 2 E5
Illston on the Hill Leics 36 F3
Ilmer Bucks 28 H4
Ilmington Warks 27 D9
Ilminster Som 8 C2
Ilsington Devon 5 D8
Ilston Swansea 23 G10
Ilton N Yorks 51 B7
Ilton Som 8 C2
Imachar N Ayrs 66 B1
Imeraval Argyll 64 D4
Immingham NE Lincs 46 A5
Impington Cambs 29 B11
Ince Ches W 43 E7
Ince Blundell Mers 42 B6
Ince in Makerfield Gtr Man 43 B8
Inch of Arnhall Aberds 83 F8
Inchbare Angus 83 G8
Inchberry Moray 88 C3
Inchbraoch Angus 77 B10
Incheril Highld 86 E3
Inchgrundle Angus 82 F6
Inchina Highld 86 B2
Inchinnan Renfs 68 D3
Inchkinloch Highld 93 E8
Inchlaggan Highld 80 C3
Inchlumpie Highld 87 D8
Inchmore Highld 86 G6
Inchnacardoch Hotel Highld 80 B5
Inchnadamph Highld 92 G5
Inchree Highld 74 A3
Inchture Perth 76 E5
Inchyra Perth 76 E4
Indian Queens Corn 3 D8
Inerval Argyll 64 D4
Ingatestone Essex 20 B3
Ingbirchworth S Yorks 44 B6
Ingestre Staffs 34 C5
Ingham Lincs 46 D3
Ingham Norf 39 C9
Ingham Suff 30 A5
Ingham Corner Norf 39 C9
Ingleborough Norf 37 D10
Ingleby Derbys 35 C9
Ingleby Lincs 46 E2
Ingleby Arncliffe N Yorks 58 F5
Ingleby Barwick Stockton 58 E5
Ingleby Greenhow N Yorks 59 F6
Inglemire Hull 53 F6
Inglesbatch Bath 16 E4
Inglesham Swindon 17 B9
Ingleton Durham 58 D2
Ingleton N Yorks 50 B2
Inglewhite Lancs 49 E5
Ingliston Edin 69 C10
Ingoe Northumb 62 F6
Ingol Lancs 49 F5
Ingoldisthorpe Norf 38 B2
Ingoldmells Lincs 47 F9
Ingoldsby Lincs 36 B6
Ingon Warks 27 C9
Ingram Northumb 62 B6
Ingrow W Yorks 51 F6
Ings Cumb 56 G6
Ingst S Glos 16 C2
Ingworth Norf 39 C7
Inham's End Cambs 37 F8
Inkberrow Worcs 27 C7
Inkpen W Berks 17 E10
Inkstack Highld 94 C4
Inn Cumb 56 F6
Innellan Argyll 73 F10
Innerleithen Borders 70 G2
Innerleven Fife 76 G6
Innermessan Dumfries 54 C3
Innerwick E Loth 70 C6
Innerwick Perth 75 C8
Innis Chonain Argyll 74 E4
Insch Aberds 83 A8
Insh Highld 81 C10
Inshore Highld 92 C6
Inskip Lancs 49 F4
Instoneville S Yorks 45 A9
Instow Devon 6 C3
Intake S Yorks 45 B9
Inver Aberds 82 D4
Inver Highld 87 C11
Inver Perth 76 C3
Inver Mallie Highld 80 E3
Inverailort Highld 79 C10
Inveraldie Angus 77 D7
Inveralligin Highld 85 C13
Inverallochy Aberds 89 B10
Inveran Highld 87 B8
Inveraray Argyll 73 C9
Inverarish Highld 85 E10
Inverarity Angus 77 C7
Inverarnan Stirling 74 F6
Inverasdale Highld 91 J13
Inverbeg Argyll 74 H6
Inverbervie Aberds 83 F10
Inverboyndie Aberds 89 B6
Inverbroom Highld 86 C4
Invercassley Highld 92 J7
Invercauld House Aberds 82 D3
Inverchaolain Argyll 73 F9
Invercharnan Highld 74 C4
Inverchoran Highld 86 F5
Invercreran Argyll 74 C3
Inverdruie Highld 81 B11
Inverebrie Aberds 89 E9
Invereck Argyll 73 E10
Inverernan Ho. Aberds 82 B5
Invereshie House Highld 81 C10
Inveresk E Loth 70 C2
Inverey Aberds 82 E2
Inverfarigaig Highld 81 A7
Invergarry Highld 80 C5
Invergelder Aberds 82 D4
Invergeldie Perth 75 E10
Invergordon Highld 87 E10
Invergowrie Perth 76 D6
Inverguseran Highld 85 H12
Inverhadden Perth 75 B9
Inverharroch Moray 88 E3
Inverherive Stirling 74 E6
Inverie Highld 79 B10
Inverinan Argyll 73 B8
Inverinate Highld 85 F14
Inverkeilor Angus 77 C9
Inverkeithing Fife 69 B10
Inverkeithny Aberds 89 D6
Inverkip Invclyd 73 F11
Inverkirkaig Highld 92 H3
Inverlael Highld 86 C4
Inverlochlarig Stirling 75 F7
Inverlochy Argyll 74 E4
Inverlochy Highld 80 F3
Inverlussa Argyll 72 E5
Invermark Lodge Angus 82 E6
Invermoidart Highld 79 D9
Invermoriston Highld 80 B6
Invernaver Highld 93 C10
Inverneill Argyll 73 E7
Inverness Highld 87 G9
Invernettie Aberds 89 D11
Invernoaden Argyll 73 D10
Inveroran Hotel Argyll 74 C5
Inverpolly Lodge Highld 92 H3
Inverquharity Angus 77 B7
Inverquhomery Aberds 89 D10
Inverroy Highld 80 E4
Inversanda Highld 74 B2
Invershiel Highld 80 B1
Invershin Highld 87 B8
Inversnaid Hotel Stirling 74 G6
Inverugie Aberds 89 D11
Inveruglas Argyll 74 G6
Inveruglass Highld 81 C10
Inverurie Aberds 83 A9
Invervar Perth 75 C9
Inverythan Aberds 89 D7
Inwardleigh Devon 6 G4
Inworth Essex 30 G5
Iochdar W Isles 84 D2
Iping W Sus 11 B7
Ipplepen Devon 5 E9
Ipsden Oxon 18 C3
Ipsley Worcs 27 B7
Ipstones Staffs 44 G4
Ipswich Suff 31 D8
Irby Mers 42 D5
Irby in the Marsh Lincs 47 F8
Irby upon Humber NE Lincs 46 B5
Irchester Northants 28 B6
Ireby Cumb 56 C4
Ireby Lancs 50 B2
Ireland Orkney 95 H4
Ireland Shetland 96 L5
Ireland's Cross Shrops 34 A3
Ireleth Cumb 49 B2
Ireshopeburn Durham 57 C10
Irlam Gtr Man 43 C10
Irnham Lincs 36 C6
Iron Acton S Glos 16 C3
Iron Cross Warks 27 C7
Ironbridge Telford 34 E2
Irongray Dumfries 60 F5
Ironmacannie Dumfries 55 B9
Ironside Aberds 89 C8
Ironville Derbys 45 G8
Irstead Norf 39 C9
Irthington Cumb 61 G10
Irthlingborough Northants 28 A6
Irton N Yorks 52 A6
Irvine N Ayrs 66 C6
Isauld Highld 93 C12
Isbister Orkney 95 F3
Isbister Orkney 95 G4
Isbister Shetland 96 D5
Isbister Shetland 96 G7
Isfield E Sus 12 E3
Isham Northants 28 A5
Isle Abbotts Som 8 B2
Isle Brewers Som 8 B2
Isle of Whithorn Dumfries 55 F7
Isleham Cambs 30 A3
Isleornsay Highld 85 G12
Islesburgh Shetland 96 G5
Islesteps Dumfries 60 F5
Isleworth London 19 D8
Isley Walton Leics 35 C10
Islibhig W Isles 90 E4
Islington London 19 C10
Islip Northants 36 H5
Islip Oxon 28 G2
Istead Rise Kent 20 E3
Isycoed Wrex 43 G7
Itchen Soton 10 C3
Itchen Abbas Hants 10 A4
Itchen Stoke Hants 10 A4
Itchingfield W Sus 11 B10
Itchington S Glos 16 C3
Itteringham Norf 39 B7
Itton Devon 6 G5
Itton Common Mon 15 B10
Ivegill Cumb 56 B6
Iver Bucks 19 C7
Iver Heath Bucks 19 C7
Iveston Durham 58 A2
Ivinghoe Bucks 28 G6
Ivinghoe Aston Bucks 28 G6
Ivington Hereford 25 C11
Ivington Green Hereford 25 C11
Ivy Chimneys Essex 19 A11
Ivy Cross Dorset 9 B7
Ivy Hatch Kent 20 F2
Ivybridge Devon 5 F7
Ivychurch Kent 13 D9
Iwade Kent 20 E6
Iwerne Courtney or Shroton Dorset 9 C7
Iwerne Minster Dorset 9 C7
Ixworth Suff 30 A6
Ixworth Thorpe Suff 30 A6

J

Jack Hill N Yorks 51 D8
Jack in the Green Devon 7 G9
Jacksdale Notts 45 G8
Jackstown Aberds 89 E7
Jacobstow Corn 4 B2
Jacobstowe Devon 6 F4
Jameston Pembs 22 G5
Jamestown Dumfries 61 D9
Jamestown Highld 86 F7
Jamestown W Dunb 68 B2
Jarrow T&W 63 G9
Jarvis Brook E Sus 12 D4
Jasper's Green Essex 30 F4
Java Argyll 79 H10
Jawcraig Falk 69 C7
Jaywick Essex 31 G8
Jealott's Hill Brack 18 D5
Jedburgh Borders 62 A2
Jeffreyston Pembs 22 F5
Jellyhill E Dunb 68 C5
Jemimaville Highld 87 E10
Jersey Farm Herts 29 H8
Jesmond T&W 63 G8
Jevington E Sus 12 F4
Jockey End Herts 29 G7
John o' Groats Highld 94 C5
Johnby Cumb 56 C6
John's Cross E Sus 12 D6
Johnshaven Aberds 83 G9
Johnston Pembs 22 E4
Johnstone Renfs 68 D3
Johnstonebridge Dumfries 60 D6
Johnstown Carms 23 E9
Johnstown Wrex 42 H6
Joppa Edin 70 C2
Joppa S Ayrs 67 E7
Jordans Bucks 18 B6
Jordanthorpe S Yorks 45 D7
Jump S Yorks 45 B7
Jumpers Green Dorset 9 E10
Juniper Green Edin 69 D10
Jurby East IoM 48 C3
Jurby West IoM 48 C3

K

Kaber Cumb 57 E9
Kaimend S Lanark 69 F8
Kaimes Edin 69 D11
Kalemouth Borders 70 H6
Kames Argyll 73 B7
Kames Argyll 73 F8
Kames E Ayrs 68 H5
Kea Corn 3 E7
Keadby N Lincs 46 A2
Keal Cotes Lincs 47 F7
Kearsley Gtr Man 43 B10
Kearstwick Cumb 50 A2
Kearton N Yorks 57 G11
Kearvaig Highld 92 B5
Keasden N Yorks 50 C3
Keckwick Halton 43 D8
Keddington Lincs 47 D7
Kedington Suff 30 D4
Kedleston Derbys 35 A9
Keelby Lincs 46 A5
Keele Staffs 44 H2
Keeley Green Bedford 29 D7
Keeston Pembs 22 E4
Keevil Wilts 16 F6
Kegworth Leics 35 C10
Kehelland Corn 2 E5
Keig Aberds 83 B8
Keighley W Yorks 51 E6
Keil Highld 74 B2
Keilarsbrae Clack 69 A7
Keilhill Aberds 89 C7
Keillmore Argyll 72 E5
Keillor Perth 76 C5
Keillour Perth 76 E2
Keills Argyll 64 B5
Keils Argyll 72 G4
Keinton Mandeville Som 8 A4
Keir Mill Dumfries 60 D4
Keisby Lincs 36 C6
Keiss Highld 94 D5
Keith Moray 88 C4
Keith Inch Aberds 89 D11
Keithock Angus 77 A9
Kelbrook Lancs 50 E5
Kelby Lincs 36 A6
Keld Cumb 57 E7
Keld N Yorks 57 F10
Keldholme N Yorks 59 H8
Kelfield N Lincs 46 B2
Kelfield N Yorks 52 F1
Kelham Notts 45 G11
Kellan Argyll 79 G8
Kellas Angus 77 D7
Kellas Moray 88 C1
Kellaton Devon 5 H9
Kelleth Cumb 57 F8
Kelleythorpe E Yorks 52 D5
Kelling Norf 39 A6
Kellingley N Yorks 51 G11
Kellington N Yorks 52 G1
Kelloe Durham 58 C4
Kelloholm Dumfries 60 B3
Kelly Devon 4 C4
Kelly Bray Corn 4 D4
Kelmarsh Northants 36 H3
Kelmscot Oxon 17 B9
Kelsale Suff 31 B10
Kelsall Ches W 43 F8
Kelsall Hill Ches W 43 F8
Kelshall Herts 29 E10
Kelsick Cumb 56 A3
Kelso Borders 70 G6
Kelstedge Derbys 45 F7
Kelstern Lincs 46 C6
Kelston Bath 16 E4
Keltneyburn Perth 75 C10
Kelton Dumfries 60 F5
Kelty Fife 69 A10
Kelvedon Essex 30 G5
Kelvedon Hatch Essex 20 B2
Kelvin S Lanark 68 E5
Kelvinside Glasgow 68 D4
Kelynack Corn 2 F2
Kemback Fife 77 F7
Kemberton Shrops 34 E3
Kemble Glos 16 B6
Kemerton Worcs 26 E6
Kemeys Commander Mon 15 A9
Kemnay Aberds 83 B9
Kemp Town Brighton 12 F2
Kempley Glos 26 F3
Kemps Green Warks 27 A8
Kempsey Worcs 26 D5
Kempsford Glos 17 B8
Kempshott Hants 18 F3
Kempston Bedford 29 D7
Kempston Hardwick Bedford 29 D7
Kempton Shrops 33 G9
Kemsing Kent 20 F2
Kemsley Kent 20 E6
Kenardington Kent 13 C8
Kenchester Hereford 25 D11
Kencot Oxon 17 A9
Kendal Cumb 57 G7
Kendoon Dumfries 67 H9
Kendray S Yorks 45 B7
Kenfig Bridgend 14 C4
Kenfig Hill Bridgend 14 C4
Kenilworth Warks 27 A9
Kenknock Stirling 75 D7
Kenley London 19 F10
Kenley Shrops 34 E1
Kenmore Highld 85 C12
Kenmore Perth 75 C10
Kenn Devon 5 C10
Kenn N Som 15 E10
Kennacley W Isles 90 H6
Kennacraig Argyll 73 G7
Kennerleigh Devon 7 F7
Kennet Clack 69 A8
Kennethmont Aberds 83 A7
Kennett Cambs 30 B3
Kennford Devon 5 C10
Kenninghall Norf 38 G6
Kenninghall Heath Norf 38 G6
Kennington Kent 13 B9
Kennington Oxon 18 A2
Kennoway Fife 76 G6
Kenny Hill Suff 38 H2
Kennythorpe N Yorks 52 C3
Kenovay Argyll 78 G2
Kensaleyre Highld 85 C9
Kensington London 19 D9
Kensworth C Beds 29 G7
Kensworth Common C Beds 29 G7
Kent Street E Sus 13 E6
Kent Street Kent 20 F3
Kent Street W Sus 11 B11
Kentallen Highld 74 B3
Kentchurch Hereford 25 F11
Kentford Suff 30 B4
Kentisbeare Devon 7 F9
Kentisbury Devon 6 B5
Kentisbury Ford Devon 6 B5
Kentmere Cumb 56 F6
Kenton Devon 5 C10
Kenton Suff 31 B8
Kenton T&W 63 G8
Kenton Bankfoot T&W 63 G8
Kentra Highld 79 E9
Kents Bank Cumb 49 B3
Kent's Green Glos 26 F4
Kent's Oak Hants 10 B2
Kenwick Shrops 33 B10
Kenwyn Corn 3 E7
Keoldale Highld 92 C6
Keppanach Highld 74 A3
Keppoch Highld 85 F14
Keprigan Argyll 65 G7
Kepwick N Yorks 58 G5
Kerchesters Borders 70 G6
Keresley W Mid 35 G9
Kernborough Devon 5 G8
Kerne Bridge Hereford 26 G2
Kerris Corn 2 G3
Kerry Powys 33 G7
Kerrycroy Argyll 73 G10
Kerry's Gate Hereford 25 E10
Kerrysdale Highld 85 A13
Kersall Notts 45 F11
Kersey Suff 31 D7
Kershopefoot Cumb 61 E10
Kersoe Worcs 26 E6
Kerswell Devon 7 F9
Kerswell Green Worcs 26 D5
Kesgrave Suff 31 D9
Kessingland Suff 39 G11
Kessingland Beach Suff 39 G11
Kessington E Dunb 68 C4
Kestle Corn 3 E8
Kestle Mill Corn 3 D7
Keston London 19 E11
Keswick Cumb 56 D4
Keswick Norf 39 B9
Keswick Norf 39 E8
Ketley Telford 34 D2
Ketley Bank Telford 34 D2
Ketsby Lincs 47 E7
Kettering Northants 36 H4
Ketteringham Norf 39 E7
Kettins Perth 76 D5
Kettlebaston Suff 30 C6
Kettlebridge Fife 76 G6
Kettleburgh Suff 31 B9
Kettlehill Fife 76 G6
Kettleholm Dumfries 61 F7
Kettleness N Yorks 59 E9
Kettleshume Ches E 44 E3
Kettlesing Bottom N Yorks 51 D8
Kettlesing Head N Yorks 51 D8
Kettlestone Norf 38 B5
Kettlethorpe Lincs 46 E2
Kettletoft Orkney 95 E7
Kettlewell N Yorks 50 B5
Ketton Rutland 36 E5
Kew London 19 D8
Kew Br. London 19 D8
Kewstoke N Som 15 E9
Kexbrough S Yorks 45 B7
Kexby Lincs 46 D2
Kexby York 52 D3
Key Green Ches E 44 F2
Keyham Leics 36 E2
Keyhaven Hants 10 E2
Keyingham E Yorks 53 G8
Keymer W Sus 12 E2
Keynsham Bath 16 E3
Keysoe Bedford 29 B7
Keysoe Row Bedford 29 B7
Keyston Cambs 36 H6
Keyworth Notts 36 B2
Kibblesworth T&W 63 H8
Kibworth Beauchamp Leics 36 F2
Kibworth Harcourt Leics 36 F2
Kidbrooke London 19 D11
Kiddemore Green Staffs 34 E4
Kidderminster Worcs 34 H4
Kiddington Oxon 27 F11
Kidlington Oxon 27 G11
Kidmore End Oxon 18 D3
Kidsgrove Staffs 44 G2
Kidstones N Yorks 50 A5
Kidwelly = Cydweli Carms 23 F9
Kiel Crofts Argyll 74 D2
Kielder Northumb 62 D2
Kierfiold Ho Orkney 95 G3
Kilbagie Fife 69 B8
Kilbarchan Renfs 68 D3
Kilbeg Highld 85 H11
Kilberry Argyll 72 G6
Kilbirnie N Ayrs 66 A6
Kilbride Argyll 74 E2
Kilbride Argyll 79 J11
Kilbride Highld 85 F10
Kilburn Angus 82 G5
Kilburn Derbys 45 H7
Kilburn London 19 C9
Kilburn N Yorks 51 B11
Kilby Leics 36 F2
Kilchamaig Argyll 73 G7
Kilchattan Argyll 72 D2
Kilchattan Bay Argyll 66 A4
Kilchenzie Argyll 65 F7
Kilcheran Argyll 79 H11
Kilchiaran Argyll 64 B3
Kilchoan Argyll 72 B6
Kilchoan Highld 78 E7
Kilchoman Argyll 64 B3
Kilchrenan Argyll 74 E3
Kilconquhar Fife 77 G7
Kilcot Glos 26 F3
Kilcoy Highld 87 F8
Kilcreggan Argyll 73 E11
Kildale N Yorks 59 F7
Kildalloig Argyll 65 G8
Kildary Highld 87 D10
Kildermorie Lodge Highld 87 D8
Kildonan N Ayrs 66 D3
Kildonan Lodge Highld 93 G12
Kildonnan Highld 78 C7
Kildrummy Aberds 82 B6
Kildwick N Yorks 50 E6
Kilfinan Argyll 73 F8
Kilfinnan Highld 80 D4
Kilgetty Pembs 22 F6
Kilgwrrwg Common Mon 15 B10
Kilham E Yorks 53 C6
Kilham Northumb 71 G7
Kilkenneth Argyll 78 G2
Kilkerran Argyll 65 G8
Kilkhampton Corn 6 E1
Killamarsh Derbys 45 D8
Killay Swansea 14 B2
Killbeg Argyll 79 G9
Killean Argyll 65 D7
Killearn Stirling 68 B4
Killen Highld 87 F9
Killerby Darl 58 E2
Killichonan Perth 75 B8
Killiechonate Highld 80 E4
Killiechronan Argyll 79 G8
Killiecrankie Perth 76 A2
Killiemor Argyll 78 H7
Killiemore House Argyll 78 J7
Killilan Highld 86 H2
Killimster Highld 94 E5
Killin Stirling 75 D8
Killin Lodge Highld 81 C7
Killinallan Argyll 64 A4
Killinghall N Yorks 51 D8
Killington Cumb 57 H8
Killingworth T&W 63 F8
Killmahumaig Argyll 72 D6
Killochyett Borders 70 F3
Killocraw Argyll 65 E7
Killundine Highld 79 G8
Kilmacolm Invclyd 68 D2
Kilmaha Argyll 73 C8
Kilmahog Stirling 75 G9
Kilmalieu Highld 79 F11
Kilmaluag Highld 85 A9
Kilmany Fife 76 E6
Kilmarie Highld 85 G10
Kilmarnock E Ayrs 67 C7
Kilmaron Castle Fife 76 F6
Kilmartin Argyll 73 D7
Kilmaurs E Ayrs 67 B7
Kilmelford Argyll 73 B7
Kilmeny Argyll 64 B4
Kilmersdon Som 16 F3
Kilmeston Hants 10 B4
Kilmichael Argyll 65 F7
Kilmichael Glassary Argyll 73 D7
Kilmichael of Inverlussa Argyll 72 E6
Kilmington Devon 8 E1
Kilmington Wilts 16 H4
Kilmonivaig Highld 80 E3
Kilmorack Highld 86 G7
Kilmore Argyll 79 J11
Kilmore Highld 85 H11
Kilmory Argyll 72 F6
Kilmory Highld 79 D8
Kilmory Highld 85 H8
Kilmory N Ayrs 66 D2
Kilmuir Highld 84 D7
Kilmuir Highld 85 A8
Kilmuir Highld 87 D10
Kilmuir Highld 87 G9
Kilmun Argyll 73 B8
Kilmun Argyll 73 E10
Kiln Pit Hill Northumb 58 A1
Kilncadzow S Lanark 69 F7
Kilndown Kent 12 C6
Kilnhurst S Yorks 45 C8
Kilninian Argyll 78 G6
Kilninver Argyll 79 J11
Kilnsea E Yorks 53 H10
Kilnsey N Yorks 50 C5
Kilnwick E Yorks 52 E5
Kilnwick Percy E Yorks 52 D4
Kiloran Argyll 72 D2
Kilpatrick N Ayrs 66 D2
Kilpeck Hereford 25 E11
Kilphedir Highld 93 H12
Kilpin E Yorks 52 G3
Kilpin Pike E Yorks 52 G3
Kilrenny Fife 77 G8
Kilsby Northants 28 A2
Kilspindie Perth 76 E5
Kilsyth N Lanark 68 C6
Kiltarlity Highld 87 G8
Kilton Notts 45 E9
Kilton Som 7 B10
Kilton Thorpe Redcar 59 E7
Kilvaxter Highld 85 B8
Kilve Som 7 B10
Kilvington Notts 36 A3
Kilwinning N Ayrs 66 B6
Kimber worth S Yorks 45 C8
Kimberley Norf 39 E6
Kimberley Notts 35 A11
Kimble Wick Bucks 28 H5
Kimblesworth Durham 58 B3
Kimbolton Cambs 29 B7
Kimbolton Hereford 26 B2
Kimcote Leics 36 G1
Kimmeridge Dorset 9 G8
Kimmerston Northumb 71 G8
Kimpton Hants 17 G9
Kimpton Herts 29 G8
Kinbrace Highld 93 F11
Kinbuck Stirling 75 G10
Kincaple Fife 77 F7
Kincardine Fife 69 B8
Kincardine Highld 87 C9
Kincardine Bridge Falk 69 B8
Kincardine O'Neil Aberds 83 D7
Kinclaven Perth 76 D4
Kincorth Aberdeen 83 C11
Kincorth Ho. Moray 87 E13
Kincraig Highld 81 C10
Kincraigie Perth 76 C2
Kindallachan Perth 76 C2
Kineton Glos 27 F7
Kineton Warks 27 C10
Kinfauns Perth 76 E4
King Edward Aberds 89 C7
King Sterndale Derbys 44 E4
Kingairloch Highld 79 F11
Kingarth Argyll 73 H9
Kingcoed Mon 25 H11
Kingerby Lincs 46 C4
Kingham Oxon 27 F9
Kingholm Quay Dumfries 60 F5
Kinghorn Fife 69 B11
Kingie Highld 80 C3
Kinglassie Fife 76 H5
Kingoodie Perth 76 E6
King's Acre Hereford 25 D11
King's Bromley Staffs 35 D7
King's Caple Hereford 26 F2
King's Cliffe Northants 36 F6
King's Coughton Warks 27 C7
King's Heath W Mid 35 G6
Kings Hedges Cambs 29 B11
King's Hill Kent 20 F3
Kings Langley Herts 19 A7
King's Lynn Norf 38 C2
King's Meaburn Cumb 57 D8
King's Mills Wrex 42 H6
Kings Muir Borders 69 G11
King's Newnham Warks 35 H10
King's Newton Derbys 35 C9
King's Norton Leics 36 E2
King's Norton W Mid 35 H6
King's Nympton Devon 6 E5
King's Pyon Hereford 25 C11
King's Ripton Cambs 37 H8
King's Somborne Hants 10 A2
King's Stag Dorset 8 C6
King's Stanley Glos 16 A5
King's Sutton Northants 27 E11
King's Thorn Hereford 26 E2
King's Walden Herts 29 F8
Kings Worthy Hants 10 A3
Kingsand Corn 4 F5
Kingsbarns Fife 77 F8
Kingsbridge Devon 5 G8
Kingsbridge Som 7 C8
Kingsburgh Highld 85 C8
Kingsbury London 19 C9
Kingsbury Warks 35 F8
Kingsbury Episcopi Som 8 B3
Kingsclere Hants 18 F2
Kingscote Glos 16 B5
Kingscott Devon 6 E4
Kingscross N Ayrs 66 D3
Kingsdon Som 8 B4
Kingsdown Kent 21 G10
Kingseat Fife 69 A10
Kingsey Bucks 28 H4
Kingsfold W Sus 19 H8
Kingsford E Ayrs 67 B7
Kingsford Worcs 34 G4
Kingsforth N Lincs 52 H6
Kingsgate Kent 21 D10
Kingsheanton Devon 6 C4
Kingshouse Hotel Highld 74 B5
Kingside Hill Cumb 56 A3
Kingskerswell Devon 5 E9
Kingskettle Fife 76 G6
Kingsland Anglesey 40 B4
Kingsland Hereford 25 B11
Kingsley Ches W 43 E8
Kingsley Hants 18 H4
Kingsley Staffs 44 H4
Kingsley Green W Sus 11 A7
Kingsley Holt Staffs 44 H4
Kingsley Park Northants 28 B4
Kingsmuir Angus 77 C7
Kingsmuir Fife 77 G8
Kingsnorth Kent 13 C9
Kingstanding W Mid 35 F6
Kingsteignton Devon 5 D9
Kingsthorpe Northants 28 B4
Kingston Cambs 29 C10
Kingston Devon 5 G7
Kingston Dorset 9 D6
Kingston Dorset 9 G8
Kingston E Loth 70 B4
Kingston Hants 9 D10
Kingston IoW 10 F3
Kingston Kent 21 F8
Kingston Moray 88 B3
Kingston Bagpuize Oxon 17 B11
Kingston Blount Oxon 18 B4
Kingston by Sea W Sus 11 D11
Kingston Deverill Wilts 16 H5
Kingston Gorse W Sus 11 D9
Kingston Lisle Oxon 17 C10
Kingston Maurward Dorset 8 E6
Kingston near Lewes E Sus 12 F2
Kingston on Soar Notts 35 C11
Kingston Russell Dorset 8 E4
Kingston St Mary Som 7 D11
Kingston Seymour N Som 15 E10
Kingston Upon Hull Hull 53 G6
Kingston upon Thames London 19 E8
Kingston Vale London 19 D9
Kingstone Hereford 25 E11
Kingstone Som 8 C2
Kingstone Staffs 35 C6
Kingstown Cumb 61 H9
Kingswear Devon 5 F9
Kingswells Aberdeen 83 C10
Kingswinford W Mid 34 G4
Kingswood Bucks 28 G3
Kingswood Glos 16 B4
Kingswood Hereford 25 C9
Kingswood Kent 20 F5
Kingswood Powys 33 E8
Kingswood S Glos 16 D3
Kingswood Sur 19 F9
Kingswood Warks 27 A8
Kingthorpe Lincs 46 E5
Kington Hereford 25 C9
Kington Worcs 26 C6
Kington Langley Wilts 16 D6
Kington Magna Dorset 9 B6
Kington St Michael Wilts 16 D6
Kingussie Highld 81 C9
Kingweston Som 8 A4
Kininvie Ho. Moray 88 D3
Kinkell Bridge Perth 76 F2
Kinknockie Aberds 89 D10
Kinlet Shrops 34 G3
Kinloch Fife 76 F5
Kinloch Highld 78 B6
Kinloch Highld 85 G11
Kinloch Highld 92 F6
Kinloch Perth 76 C5
Kinloch Perth 76 C4
Kinloch Hourn Highld 80 C1
Kinloch Laggan Highld 81 E7
Kinloch Lodge Highld 93 D8
Kinloch Rannoch Perth 75 B9
Kinlochan Highld 79 E11
Kinlochard Stirling 75 G7
Kinlochbeoraid Highld 79 C11
Kinlochbervie Highld 92 D5

Kinlocheil Highld 80 F1
Kinlochewe Highld 86 E3
Kinlochleven Highld 74 A4
Kinlochmoidart Highld 79 D10
Kinlochmorar Highld 79 B11
Kinlochmore Highld 74 A4
Kinlochspelve Argyll 79 J9
Kinloid Highld 79 C9
Kinloss Moray 87 E13
Kinmel Bay Conwy 42 D2
Kinmuck Aberds 83 B10
Kinmundy Aberds 83 B10
Kinnadie Aberds 89 D9
Kinnaird Perth 76 E5
Kinnaird Castle Angus 77 B9
Kinneff Aberds 83 F10
Kinnelhead Dumfries 60 C6
Kinnell Angus 77 B9
Kinnerley Shrops 33 C9
Kinnersley Hereford 25 D10
Kinnersley Worcs 26 D5
Kinnerton Powys 25 B9
Kinnesswood Perth 76 G4
Kinninvie Durham 58 D1
Kinnordy Angus 76 B6
Kinoulton Notts 36 B2
Kinross Perth 76 G4
Kinrossie Perth 76 D4
Kinsbourne Green Herts 29 G8
Kinsey Heath Ches E 34 A2
Kinsham Hereford 25 B10
Kinsham Worcs 26 E6
Kinsley W Yorks 45 A8
Kinson Bmouth 9 E9
Kintbury W Berks 17 E10
Kintessack Moray 87 E12
Kintillo Perth 76 F4
Kintocher Aberds 83 C7
Kinton Hereford 25 A11
Kinton Shrops 33 D9
Kintore Aberds 83 B9
Kintour Argyll 64 C5
Kintra Argyll 64 D4
Kintra Argyll 78 J6
Kintraw Argyll 73 C7
Kinuachdrachd Argyll 72 D6
Kinveachy Highld 81 B11
Kinver Staffs 34 G4
Kippax W Yorks 51 F10
Kippen Stirling 68 A5
Kippford or Scaur Dumfries 55 D11
Kirbister Orkney 95 F7
Kirbister Orkney 95 H4
Kirbuster Orkney 95 F3
Kirby Bedon Norf 39 E8
Kirby Bellars Leics 36 D3
Kirby Cane Norf 39 F9
Kirby Cross Essex 31 F9
Kirby Grindalythe N Yorks 52 C5
Kirby Hill N Yorks 51 C9
Kirby Hill N Yorks 58 F2
Kirby Knowle N Yorks 58 H5
Kirby-le-Soken Essex 31 F9
Kirby Misperton N Yorks 52 B3
Kirby Muxloe Leics 35 E11
Kirby Row Norf 39 F9
Kirby Sigston N Yorks 58 G5
Kirby Underdale E Yorks 52 D4
Kirby Wiske N Yorks 51 A9
Kirdford W Sus 11 B9
Kirk Highld 94 E4
Kirk Bramwith S Yorks 45 A10
Kirk Deighton N Yorks 51 D9
Kirk Ella E Yorks 52 G6
Kirk Hallam Derbys 35 A10
Kirk Hammerton N Yorks 51 D10
Kirk Ireton Derbys 44 G6
Kirk Langley Derbys 35 B8
Kirk Merrington Durham 58 C3
Kirk Michael IoM 48 C3
Kirk of Shotts N Lanark 69 D7
Kirk Sandall S Yorks 45 B10
Kirk Smeaton N Yorks 51 H11
Kirk Yetholm Borders 71 H7
Kirkabister Shetland 96 K6
Kirkandrews Dumfries 55 E9
Kirkandrews upon Eden Cumb 61 H9
Kirkbampton Cumb 61 H9
Kirkbean Dumfries 60 H5
Kirkbride Cumb 61 H8
Kirkbuddo Angus 77 C8
Kirkburn Borders 69 G11
Kirkburn E Yorks 52 D5
Kirkburton W Yorks 44 A5
Kirkby Lincs 46 C4
Kirkby Mers 43 C7
Kirkby N Yorks 59 F6
Kirkby Fleetham N Yorks 58 G3
Kirkby Green Lincs 46 G4
Kirkby In Ashfield Notts 45 G9
Kirkby-in-Furness Cumb 49 A2
Kirkby la Thorpe Lincs 46 H5
Kirkby Lonsdale Cumb 50 B2
Kirkby Malham N Yorks 50 C4
Kirkby Mallory Leics 35 E10
Kirkby Malzeard N Yorks 51 B8
Kirkby Mills N Yorks 59 H8
Kirkby on Bain Lincs 46 F6
Kirkby Overflow N Yorks 51 E9
Kirkby Stephen Cumb 57 F9
Kirkby Thore Cumb 57 D8
Kirkby Underwood Lincs 37 C6
Kirkby Wharfe N Yorks 51 E11
Kirkbymoorside N Yorks 59 H7
Kirkcaldy Fife 69 A11
Kirkcambeck Cumb 61 G11
Kirkcarswell Dumfries 55 E10
Kirkcolm Dumfries 54 C3
Kirkconnel Dumfries 60 B3
Kirkconnell Dumfries 60 G5
Kirkcowan Dumfries 54 C6
Kirkcudbright Dumfries 55 D9
Kirkdale Mers 42 C6
Kirkfieldbank S Lanark 69 F7
Kirkgunzeon Dumfries 55 C11
Kirkham Lancs 49 F4
Kirkham N Yorks 52 C3
Kirkhamgate W Yorks 51 G8
Kirkharle Northumb 62 E6
Kirkheaton Northumb 62 F6
Kirkheaton W Yorks 51 H7
Kirkhill Angus 77 A9
Kirkhill Highld 87 G8
Kirkhill Midloth 69 D11
Kirkhill Moray 88 E2
Kirkhope Borders 61 A9
Kirkhouse Borders 70 G2
Kirkiboll Highld 93 D8
Kirkibost Highld 85 G10
Kirkinch Angus 76 C6
Kirkinner Dumfries 55 D7
Kirkintilloch E Dunb 68 C5
Kirkland Cumb 56 E2
Kirkland Cumb 57 C8
Kirkland Dumfries 60 B3
Kirkland Dumfries 60 D4
Kirkleatham Redcar 59 D6
Kirklevington Stockton 58 F5
Kirkley Suff 39 F11
Kirklington N Yorks 51 A9
Kirklington Notts 45 G10
Kirklinton Cumb 61 G10
Kirkliston Edin 69 C10
Kirkmaiden Dumfries 54 F4
Kirkmichael Perth 76 B3
Kirkmichael S Ayrs 66 F6
Kirkmuirhill S Lanark 68 F6
Kirknewton Northumb 71 G8
Kirknewton W Loth 69 D10
Kirkney Aberds 88 E5
Kirkoswald Cumb 57 B7
Kirkoswald S Ayrs 66 F5
Kirkpatrick Durham Dumfries 60 F3
Kirkpatrick-Fleming Dumfries 61 F8
Kirksanton Cumb 49 A1
Kirkstall W Yorks 51 F8
Kirkstead Lincs 46 F5
Kirkstile Aberds 88 E5
Kirkstyle Highld 94 C5
Kirkton Aberds 83 A8
Kirkton Aberds 89 D6
Kirkton Angus 77 C7
Kirkton Angus 77 D7
Kirkton Borders 61 B11
Kirkton Dumfries 60 E5
Kirkton Fife 76 E6
Kirkton Highld 85 F13
Kirkton Highld 86 G2
Kirkton Highld 87 B10
Kirkton Highld 87 F10
Kirkton Perth 76 F2
Kirkton S Lanark 60 A5
Kirkton Stirling 75 G8
Kirkton Manor Borders 69 G11
Kirkton of Airlie Angus 76 B6
Kirkton of Auchterhouse Angus 76 D6
Kirkton of Auchterless Aberds 89 D7
Kirkton of Barevan Highld 87 G11
Kirkton of Bourtie Aberds 89 F8
Kirkton of Collace Perth 76 D4
Kirkton of Craig Angus 77 B10
Kirkton of Culsalmond Aberds 89 E6
Kirkton of Durris Aberds 83 D9
Kirkton of Glenbuchat Aberds 82 B5
Kirkton of Glenisla Angus 76 A5
Kirkton of Kingoldrum Angus 76 B6
Kirkton of Largo Fife 77 G7
Kirkton of Lethendy Perth 76 C4
Kirkton of Logie Buchan Aberds 89 F9
Kirkton of Maryculter Aberds 83 D10
Kirkton of Menmuir Angus 77 A8
Kirkton of Monikie Angus 77 D8
Kirkton of Oyne Aberds 83 A8
Kirkton of Rayne Aberds 83 A8
Kirkton of Skene Aberds 83 C10
Kirkton of Tough Aberds 83 B8
Kirktonhill Borders 70 E3
Kirktown Aberds 89 C10
Kirktown of Alvah Aberds 89 B6
Kirktown of Deskford Moray 88 B5
Kirktown of Fetteresso Aberds 83 E10
Kirktown of Mortlach Moray 88 E3
Kirktown of Slains Aberds 89 F10
Kirkurd Borders 69 F10
Kirkwall Orkney 95 G5
Kirkwhelpington Northumb 62 E5
Kirmington N Lincs 46 A5
Kirmond le Mire Lincs 46 C5
Kirn Argyll 73 F10
Kirriemuir Angus 76 B6
Kirstead Green Norf 39 F8
Kirtlebridge Dumfries 61 F8
Kirtleton Dumfries 61 E8
Kirtling Cambs 30 C3
Kirtling Green Cambs 30 C3
Kirtlington Oxon 27 G11
Kirtomy Highld 93 C10
Kirton Lincs 37 B9
Kirton Notts 45 F10
Kirton Suff 31 E9
Kirton End Lincs 37 A8
Kirton Holme Lincs 37 A8
Kirton in Lindsey N Lincs 46 C3
Kislingbury Northants 28 C3
Kites Hardwick Warks 27 B11
Kittisford Som 7 D9
Kittle Swansea 23 H10
Kitt's Green W Mid 35 G7
Kitt's Moss Gtr Man 44 D2
Kittybrewster Aberdeen 83 C11
Kitwood Hants 10 A5
Kivernoll Hereford 25 E11
Kiveton Park S Yorks 45 D8
Knaith Lincs 46 D2
Knaith Park Lincs 46 D2
Knap Corner Dorset 9 B7
Knaphill Sur 18 F6
Knapp Perth 76 D5
Knapp Som 8 B2
Knapthorpe Notts 45 G11
Knapton Norf 39 B9
Knapton York 52 D1
Knapton Green Hereford 25 C11
Knapwell Cambs 29 B10
Knaresborough N Yorks 51 D9
Knarsdale Northumb 57 A8
Knauchland Moray 88 C5
Knaven Aberds 89 D8
Knayton N Yorks 58 H5
Knebworth Herts 29 F9
Knedlington E Yorks 52 G3
Kneesall Notts 45 F11
Kneesworth Cambs 29 D10
Kneeton Notts 45 H11
Knelston Swansea 23 H9
Knenhall Staffs 34 B5
Knettishall Suff 38 G5
Knightacott Devon 6 C5
Knightcote Warks 27 C10
Knightley Dale Staffs 34 C4
Knighton Devon 4 G6
Knighton Leicester 36 E1
Knighton = Tref-y Clawdd Powys 25 A9
Knighton Staffs 34 A3
Knighton Staffs 34 C3
Knightswood Glasgow 68 D4
Knightwick Worcs 26 C4
Knill Hereford 25 B9
Knipton Leics 36 B4
Knitsley Durham 58 B2
Kniveton Derbys 44 G6
Knock Argyll 79 H8
Knock Cumb 57 D8
Knock Moray 88 C5
Knockally Highld 94 H3
Knockan Highld 92 H5
Knockandhu Moray 82 A4
Knockando Moray 88 D1
Knockando Ho. Moray 88 D2
Knockbain Highld 87 F9
Knockbreck Highld 84 B7
Knockbrex Dumfries 55 E8
Knockdee Highld 94 D3
Knockdolian S Ayrs 66 H4
Knockenkelly N Ayrs 66 D3
Knockentiber E Ayrs 67 C6
Knockespock Ho. Aberds 83 A7
Knockfarrel Highld 87 F8
Knockglass Dumfries 54 D3
Knockholt Kent 19 F11
Knockholt Pound Kent 19 F11
Knockie Lodge Highld 80 B6
Knockin Shrops 33 C9
Knockinlaw E Ayrs 67 C7
Knocklearn Dumfries 60 F3
Knocknaha Argyll 65 G7
Knocknain Dumfries 54 C2
Knockrome Argyll 72 F4
Knocksharry IoM 48 D2
Knodishall Suff 31 B11
Knolls Green Ches E 44 E2
Knolton Wrex 33 B9
Knolton Bryn Wrex 33 B9
Knook Wilts 16 G6
Knossington Leics 36 E4
Knott End-on-Sea Lancs 49 E3
Knotting Bedford 29 B7
Knotting Green Bedford 29 B7
Knottingley W Yorks 51 G11
Knotts Cumb 56 D6
Knotts Lancs 50 D3
Knotty Ash Mers 43 C7
Knotty Green Bucks 18 B6
Knowbury Shrops 26 A2
Knowe Dumfries 54 B6
Knowehead Dumfries 67 G9
Knowes of Elrick Aberds 88 C6
Knowesgate Northumb 62 E5
Knoweton N Lanark 68 E6
Knowhead Aberds 89 C9
Knowl Hill Windsor 18 D5
Knowle Bristol 16 D3
Knowle Devon 6 C3
Knowle Devon 7 F6
Knowle Devon 7 H9
Knowle Shrops 26 A2
Knowle W Mid 35 H7
Knowle Green Lancs 50 F2
Knowle Park W Yorks 51 E6
Knowlton Dorset 9 C9
Knowlton Kent 21 F9
Knowsley Mers 43 C7
Knowstone Devon 7 D7
Knox Bridge Kent 13 B6
Knucklas Powys 25 A9
Knuston Northants 28 B6
Knutsford Ches E 43 E10
Knutton Staffs 44 H2
Knypersley Staffs 44 G2
Kuggar Corn 2 H6
Kyle of Lochalsh Highld 85 F12
Kyleakin Highld 85 F12
Kylerhea Highld 85 F12
Kylesknoydart Highld 79 B11
Kylesku Highld 92 F5
Kylesmorar Highld 79 B11
Kylestrome Highld 92 F5
Kyllachy House Highld 81 A9
Kynaston Shrops 33 C9
Kynnersley Telford 34 D2
Kyre Magna Worcs 26 B3

L

La Fontenelle Guern 11
La Planque Guern 11
Labost W Isles 91 C7
Lacasaidh W Isles 91 E8
Lacasdal W Isles 91 D9
Laceby NE Lincs 46 B6
Lacey Green Bucks 18 B5
Lach Dennis Ches W 43 E10
Lackford Suff 30 A4
Lacock Wilts 16 E6
Ladbroke Warks 27 C11
Laddingford Kent 20 G3
Lade Bank Lincs 47 G7
Ladock Corn 3 D7
Lady Orkney 95 D7
Ladybank Fife 76 F6
Ladykirk Borders 71 F7
Ladysford Aberds 89 B9
Laga Highld 79 E9
Lagalochan Argyll 73 B7
Lagavulin Argyll 64 D5
Lagg Argyll 72 F4
Lagg N Ayrs 66 D2
Laggan Argyll 64 C3
Laggan Highld 79 D10
Laggan Highld 80 D4
Laggan Highld 81 D8
Laggan S Ayrs 54 A5
Lagganulva Argyll 78 G7
Laide Highld 91 H13
Laigh Fenwick E Ayrs 67 B7
Laigh Glengall S Ayrs 66 E6
Laighmuir E Ayrs 67 B7
Laindon Essex 20 C3
Lair Highld 86 G3
Lairg Highld 93 J8
Lairg Lodge Highld 93 J8
Lairg Muir Highld 93 J8
Lairgmore Highld 87 H8
Laisterdyke W Yorks 51 F7
Laithes Cumb 56 C6
Lake IoW 10 F4
Lake Wilts 17 H8
Lakenham Norf 39 E8
Lakenheath Suff 38 G3
Lakesend Norf 37 F11
Lakeside Cumb 56 H5
Laleham Sur 19 E7
Laleston Bridgend 14 D4
Lamarsh Essex 30 E5
Lamas Norf 39 C8
Lambden Borders 70 F6
Lamberhurst Kent 12 C5
Lamberhurst Quarter Kent 12 C5
Lamberton Borders 71 E8
Lambeth London 19 D10
Lambhill Glasgow 68 D4
Lambley Northumb 62 H2
Lambley Notts 45 H10
Lamborough Hill Oxon 17 A11
Lambourn W Berks 17 D10
Lambourne End Essex 19 B11
Lambs Green W Sus 19 H9
Lambston Pembs 22 E4
Lambton T&W 58 A3
Lamerton Devon 4 D5
Lamesley T&W 63 H8
Laminess Orkney 95 E7
Lamington Highld 87 D10
Lamington S Lanark 69 G8
Lamlash N Ayrs 66 C3
Lamloch Dumfries 67 G8
Lamonby Cumb 56 C6
Lamorna Corn 2 G3
Lamorran Corn 3 E7
Lampardbrook Suff 31 B9
Lampeter = Llanbedr Pont Steffan Ceredig 23 B10
Lampeter Velfrey Pembs 22 E6
Lamphey Pembs 22 F5
Lamplugh Cumb 56 D2
Lamport Northants 28 A4
Lamyatt Som 16 H3
Lana Devon 6 G2
Lanark S Lanark 69 F7
Lancaster Lancs 49 C4
Lanchester Durham 58 B2
Lancing W Sus 11 D10
Landbeach Cambs 29 B11
Landcross Devon 6 D3
Landerberry Aberds 83 C9
Landford Wilts 10 C1
Landford Manor Wilts 10 B1
Landimore Swansea 23 G9
Landkey Devon 6 C4
Landore Swansea 14 B2
Landrake Corn 4 E4
Landscove Devon 5 E8
Landshipping Pembs 22 E5
Landshipping Quay Pembs 22 E5
Landulph Corn 4 E5
Landwade Suff 30 B3
Lane Corn 3 C7
Lane End Bucks 18 B5
Lane End Cumb 56 G3
Lane End Dorset 9 E7
Lane End Hants 10 B4
Lane End IoW 10 F5
Lane End Lancs 50 E4
Lane Ends Lancs 50 D3
Lane Ends Lancs 50 F3
Lane Ends N Yorks 50 E5
Lane Head Derbys 44 E5
Lane Head Durham 58 E2
Lane Head Gtr Man 43 C9
Lane Head W Yorks 44 B5
Lane Side Lancs 50 G3
Laneast Corn 4 C3
Laneham Notts 46 E2
Lanehead Durham 57 B10
Lanehead Northumb 62 E3
Lanercost Cumb 61 G11
Laneshaw Bridge Lancs 50 E5
Lanfach Caerph 15 B8
Langar Notts 36 B3
Langbank Renfs 68 C2
Langbar N Yorks 51 D6
Langburnshiels Borders 61 C11
Langcliffe N Yorks 50 C4
Langdale Highld 93 E9
Langdale End N Yorks 59 G10
Langdon Corn 4 C4
Langdon Beck Durham 57 C10
Langdon Hills Essex 20 C3
Langdyke Fife 76 G6
Langenhoe Essex 31 G7
Langford C Beds 29 D8
Langford Devon 7 F9
Langford Essex 30 H5
Langford Notts 46 G2
Langford Oxon 17 A9
Langford Budville Som 7 D10
Langham Essex 31 E7
Langham Norf 38 A6
Langham Rutland 36 D4
Langham Suff 30 B6
Langhaugh Borders 69 G11
Langho Lancs 50 F3
Langholm Dumfries 61 E9
Langleeford Northumb 62 A5
Langley Ches E 44 E3
Langley Hants 10 D3
Langley Herts 29 F9
Langley Kent 20 F5
Langley Northumb 62 G4
Langley Slough 19 D7
Langley W Sus 11 B7
Langley Warks 27 B8
Langley Burrell Wilts 16 D6
Langley Common Derbys 35 B8
Langley Heath Kent 20 F5
Langley Lower Green Essex 29 E11
Langley Marsh Som 7 D9
Langley Park Durham 58 B3
Langley Street Norf 39 E9
Langley Upper Green Essex 29 E11
Langney E Sus 12 F5
Langold Notts 45 D9
Langore Corn 4 C4
Langport Som 8 B3
Langrick Lincs 46 H6
Langridge Bath 16 E4
Langridge Ford Devon 6 D4
Langrigg Cumb 56 B3
Langrish Hants 10 B6
Langsett S Yorks 44 B6
Langshaw Borders 70 G4
Langside Perth 75 F10
Langskaill Orkney 95 D5
Langstone Hants 10 D6
Langstone Newport 15 B9
Langthorne N Yorks 58 G3
Langthorpe N Yorks 51 C9
Langthwaite N Yorks 58 F1
Langtoft E Yorks 52 C6
Langtoft Lincs 37 D7
Langton Durham 58 E2
Langton Lincs 46 F6
Langton Lincs 47 E7
Langton N Yorks 52 C3
Langton by Wragby Lincs 46 E5
Langton Green Kent 12 C4
Langton Green Suff 31 A8
Langton Herring Dorset 8 F5
Langton Matravers Dorset 9 G9
Langtree Devon 6 E3
Langwathby Cumb 57 C7
Langwell Ho. Highld 94 H3
Langwell Lodge Highld 92 J4
Langwith Derbys 45 F9
Langwith Junction Derbys 45 F9
Langworth Lincs 46 E4
Lanivet Corn 3 C9
Lanlivery Corn 4 F1
Lanner Corn 2 F6
Lanreath Corn 4 F2
Lansallos Corn 4 F2
Lansdown Glos 26 F6
Lanteglos Highway Corn 4 F2
Lanton Borders 62 A2
Lanton Northumb 71 G8
Lapford Devon 7 F6
Laphroaig Argyll 64 D4
Lapley Staffs 34 D4
Lapworth Warks 27 A8
Larachbeg Highld 79 G9
Larbert Falk 69 B7
Larden Green Ches E 43 G8
Largie Aberds 88 E6
Largiemore Argyll 73 E8
Largoward Fife 77 G7
Largs N Ayrs 73 H11
Largybeg N Ayrs 66 D3
Largymore N Ayrs 66 D3
Larkfield Invclyd 73 F11
Larkhall S Lanark 68 E6
Larkhill Wilts 17 G8
Larling Norf 38 G5
Larriston Borders 61 D11
Lartington Durham 58 E1
Lary Aberds 82 C5
Lasham Hants 18 G3
Lashenden Kent 13 B7
Lassington Glos 26 F4
Lassodie Fife 69 A10
Lastingham N Yorks 59 G8
Latcham Som 15 G10
Latchford Herts 29 F10
Latchford Warr 43 D9
Latchingdon Essex 20 A5
Latchley Corn 4 D5
Lately Common Warr 43 C9
Lathbury M Keynes 28 D5
Latheron Highld 94 G3
Latheronwheel Highld 94 G3
Latheronwheel Ho. Highld 94 G3
Lathones Fife 77 G7
Latimer Bucks 19 B7
Latteridge S Glos 16 C3
Lattiford Som 8 B5
Latton Wilts 17 B7
Latton Bush Essex 29 H11
Lauchintilly Aberds 83 B9
Lauder Borders 70 F4
Laugharne Carms 23 E8
Laughterton Lincs 46 E2
Laughton E Sus 12 E4
Laughton Leics 36 G2
Laughton Lincs 37 B6
Laughton Lincs 46 C2
Laughton Common S Yorks 45 D9
Laughton en le Morthen S Yorks 45 D9
Launcells Corn 6 F1
Launceston Corn 4 C4
Launton Oxon 28 F3
Laurencekirk Aberds 83 F9
Laurieston Dumfries 55 C9
Laurieston Falk 69 C8
Lavendon M Keynes 28 C6
Lavenham Suff 30 D6
Laverhay Dumfries 61 D7
Laversdale Cumb 61 G10
Laverstock Wilts 9 A10
Laverstoke Hants 17 G11
Laverton Glos 27 E7
Laverton N Yorks 51 B8
Laverton Som 16 F4
Lavister Wrex 42 G6
Law S Lanark 69 E7
Lawers Perth 75 D9
Lawers Perth 75 E10
Lawford Essex 31 E7
Lawhitton Corn 4 C4
Lawkland N Yorks 50 C3
Lawley Telford 34 E2
Lawnhead Staffs 34 C4
Lawrenny Pembs 22 F5
Lawshall Suff 30 C5
Lawton Hereford 25 C11
Laxey IoM 48 D4
Laxfield Suff 31 A9
Laxfirth Shetland 96 H6
Laxfirth Shetland 96 J6
Laxford Bridge Highld 92 E5
Laxo Shetland 96 G6
Laxobigging Shetland 96 F6
Laxton E Yorks 52 G3
Laxton Northants 36 F5
Laxton Notts 45 F11
Laycock W Yorks 50 E6
Layer Breton Essex 30 G6
Layer de la Haye Essex 30 G6
Layer Marney Essex 30 G6
Layham Suff 31 D7
Laylands Green W Berks 17 E10
Laytham E Yorks 52 F3
Layton Blackpool 49 F3
Lazenby Redcar 59 D6
Lazonby Cumb 57 C7
Le Planel Guern 11
Le Skerne Haughton Darl 58 E4
Le Villocq Guern 11
Lea Derbys 45 G7
Lea Hereford 26 F3
Lea Lincs 46 D2
Lea Shrops 33 E10
Lea Shrops 33 G9
Lea Wilts 16 C6
Lea Marston Warks 35 F8
Lea Town Lancs 49 F4
Leabrooks Derbys 45 G8
Leac a Li W Isles 90 H6
Leachkin Highld 87 G9
Leadburn Midloth 69 E11
Leaden Roding Essex 30 G2
Leadenham Lincs 46 G3
Leadgate Cumb 57 B9
Leadgate Durham 58 A2
Leadgate T&W 63 H7
Leadhills S Lanark 60 B4
Leafield Oxon 27 G10
Leagrave Luton 29 F7
Leake N Yorks 58 G5
Leake Commonside Lincs 47 G7
Lealholm N Yorks 59 F8
Lealt Argyll 72 D5
Lealt Highld 85 B10
Leamington Hastings Warks 27 B11
Leamonsley Staffs 35 E7
Leamside Durham 58 B4
Leanaig Highld 87 F8
Leargybreck Argyll 72 F4
Leasgill Cumb 49 A4
Leasingham Lincs 46 H4
Leasingthorne Durham 58 D3
Leasowe Mers 42 C5
Leatherhead Sur 19 F8
Leatherhead Common Sur 19 F8
Leathley N Yorks 51 E8
Leaton Shrops 33 D10
Leaveland Kent 21 F7
Leavening N Yorks 52 C3
Leaves Green London 19 E11
Leazes Durham 63 H7
Lebberston N Yorks 53 A6
Lechlade-on-Thames Glos 17 B9
Leck Lancs 50 B2
Leckford Hants 17 H10
Leckfurin Highld 93 D10
Leckgruinart Argyll 64 B3
Leckhampstead Bucks 28 E4
Leckhampstead W Berks 17 D11
Leckhampstead Thicket W Berks 17 D11
Leckhampton Glos 26 G6
Leckie Highld 86 E3
Leckmelm Highld 86 B4
Leckwith V Glam 15 D7
Leconfield E Yorks 52 E6
Ledaig Argyll 74 D2
Ledburn Bucks 28 F6
Ledbury Hereford 26 E4
Ledcharrie Stirling 75 E8
Ledgemoor Hereford 25 C11
Ledicot Hereford 25 B11
Ledmore Highld 92 H5
Lednagullin Highld 93 C10
Ledsham Ches W 42 E6
Ledsham W Yorks 51 G10
Ledston W Yorks 51 G10
Ledston Luck W Yorks 51 F10
Ledwell Oxon 27 F11
Lee Argyll 78 J7
Lee Devon 6 B3
Lee Hants 10 C2
Lee Lancs 50 D1
Lee Shrops 33 B10
Lee Brockhurst Shrops 33 C11
Lee Clump Bucks 18 A6
Lee Mill Devon 5 F7
Lee Moor Devon 5 E6
Lee-on-the-Solent Hants 10 D4
Leeans Shetland 96 J5
Leebotten Shetland 96 L6
Leebotwood Shrops 33 F10
Leece Cumb 49 C2
Leechpool Pembs 22 E4
Leeds Kent 20 F5
Leeds W Yorks 51 F8
Leedstown Corn 2 F5
Leek Staffs 44 G3
Leek Wootton Warks 27 B9
Leekbrook Staffs 44 G3
Leeming N Yorks 58 H3
Leeming Bar N Yorks 58 G3
Lees Derbys 35 B8
Lees Gtr Man 44 B3
Lees W Yorks 50 F6
Leeswood Flint 42 F5
Legbourne Lincs 47 D7
Legerwood Borders 70 F4
Legsby Lincs 46 D5
Leicester Leicester 36 E1
Leicester Forest East Leics 35 E11
Leigh Dorset 8 D5
Leigh Glos 26 F5
Leigh Gtr Man 43 B9
Leigh Kent 20 G2
Leigh Shrops 33 E9
Leigh Sur 19 G9
Leigh Wilts 17 B7
Leigh Worcs 26 C4
Leigh Beck Essex 20 C5
Leigh Common Som 8 B6
Leigh Delamere Wilts 16 D5
Leigh Green Kent 13 C8
Leigh on Sea Southend 20 C5
Leigh Park Hants 10 D6
Leigh Sinton Worcs 26 C4
Leigh upon Mendip Som 16 G3
Leigh Woods N Som 16 D2
Leighswood W Mid 35 E6
Leighterton Glos 16 B5
Leighton N Yorks 51 B7
Leighton Powys 33 E8
Leighton Shrops 34 E2
Leighton Som 16 G4
Leighton Bromswold Cambs 37 H7
Leighton Buzzard C Beds 28 F6
Leinthall Earls Hereford 25 B11
Leinthall Starkes Hereford 25 B11
Leintwardine Hereford 25 A11
Leire Leics 35 F11
Leirinmore Highld 92 C7
Leiston Suff 31 B11
Leitfie Perth 76 C5
Leith Edin 69 C11
Leitholm Borders 70 F6
Lelant Corn 2 F4
Lelley E Yorks 53 F8
Lem Hill Worcs 26 A4
Lemmington Hall Northumb 63 B7
Lempitlaw Borders 70 G6
Lenchwick Worcs 27 D7
Lendalfoot S Ayrs 66 H4
Lendrick Lodge Stirling 75 G8
Lenham Kent 20 F5
Lenham Heath Kent 20 G6
Lennel Borders 71 F7
Lennoxtown E Dunb 68 C5
Lenton Lincs 36 B6
Lenton Nottingham 36 B1
Lentran Highld 87 G8
Lenwade Norf 39 D6
Leny Ho. Stirling 75 G9
Lenzie E Dunb 68 C5
Leoch Angus 76 D6
Leochel-Cushnie Aberds 83 B7
Leominster Hereford 25 C11
Leonard Stanley Glos 16 A5
Leorin Argyll 64 D4
Lepe Hants 10 E3
Lephin Highld 84 D6
Lephinchapel Argyll 73 D8
Lephinmore Argyll 73 D8
Leppington N Yorks 52 C3
Lepton W Yorks 51 H8
Lerryn Corn 4 F2
Lerwick Shetland 96 J6
Lesbury Northumb 63 B8
Leslie Aberds 83 A7
Leslie Fife 76 G5
Lesmahagow S Lanark 69 G7
Lesnewth Corn 4 B2
Lessendrum Aberds 88 D5
Lessingham Norf 39 C9
Lessonhall Cumb 56 A4
Leswalt Dumfries 54 C3
Letchmore Heath Herts 19 B8
Letchworth Herts 29 E9
Letcombe Bassett Oxon 17 C10
Letcombe Regis Oxon 17 C10
Letham Angus 77 C8
Letham Falk 69 B7
Letham Fife 76 F6
Letham Perth 76 E3
Letham Grange Angus 77 C9
Lethenty Aberds 89 D8
Letheringham Suff 31 C9
Letheringsett Norf 39 B6
Lettaford Devon 5 C8
Lettan Orkney 95 D8
Letterewe Highld 86 D2
Letterfearn Highld 85 F13
Letterfinlay Highld 80 D4
Lettermorar Highld 79 C10
Lettermore Argyll 78 G7
Letters Highld 86 C4
Letterston Pembs 22 D4
Lettoch Highld 82 B2
Lettoch Highld 87 H13
Letton Hereford 25 A10
Letton Hereford 25 D10
Letton Green Norf 38 E5
Letty Green Herts 29 G9
Letwell S Yorks 45 D9
Leuchars Fife 77 E7
Leuchars Ho. Moray 88 B2
Leumrabhagh W Isles 91 F8
Levan Invclyd 73 F11
Levaneap Shetland 96 G6
Levedale Staffs 34 D4
Leven E Yorks 53 E7
Leven Fife 76 G6
Levencorroch N Ayrs 66 D3
Levens Cumb 57 H6
Levens Green Herts 29 F10
Levenshulme Gtr Man 44 C2
Levenwick Shetland 96 L6
Leverburgh = An t-Ob W Isles 90 J5
Leverington Cambs 37 D10
Leverton Lincs 47 H8
Leverton Highgate Lincs 47 H8
Leverton Lucasgate Lincs 47 H8
Leverton Outgate Lincs 47 H8
Levington Suff 31 E9
Levisham N Yorks 59 G9
Levishie Highld 80 B6
Lew Oxon 27 H10
Lewannick Corn 4 C3
Lewdown Devon 4 C5
Lewes E Sus 12 E3
Leweston Pembs 22 D4
Lewisham London 19 D10
Lewiston Highld 81 A7
Lewistown Bridgend 14 C5
Lewknor Oxon 18 B4
Leworthy Devon 6 C5
Leworthy Devon 6 F2
Lewtrenchard Devon 4 C5
Lexden Essex 30 F6
Ley Aberds 83 B7
Ley Corn 4 E2
Leybourne Kent 20 F3
Leyburn N Yorks 58 G2
Leyfields Staffs 35 E8
Leyhill Bucks 18 A6
Leyland Lancs 49 G5
Leylodge Aberds 83 B9
Leymoor W Yorks 51 H7
Leys Aberds 89 C10
Leys Perth 76 D5
Leys Castle Highld 87 G9
Leys of Cossans Angus 76 C6
Leysdown-on-Sea Kent 21 D7
Leysmill Angus 77 C9
Leysters Pole Hereford 26 B2
Leyton London 19 C10
Leytonstone London 19 C10
Lezant Corn 4 D4
Leziate Norf 38 D2
Lhanbryde Moray 88 B2
Liatrie Highld 86 H5
Libanus Powys 24 F6
Libberton S Lanark 69 F8
Liberton Edin 69 D11
Liceasto W Isles 90 H6
Lichfield Staffs 35 E7
Lickey Worcs 34 H5
Lickey End Worcs 26 A6
Lickfold W Sus 11 B8
Liddel Orkney 95 K5
Liddesdale Highld 79 F10
Liddington Swindon 17 C9
Lidgate Suff 30 C4
Lidget S Yorks 45 B10
Lidget Green W Yorks 51 F7
Lidgett Notts 45 F10
Lidlington C Beds 28 E6
Lidstone Oxon 27 F10
Lieurary Highld 94 D2
Liff Angus 76 D6
Lifton Devon 4 C4
Liftondown Devon 4 C4
Lighthorne Warks 27 C10
Lightwater Sur 18 E6
Lightwood Stoke 34 A5
Lightwood Green Ches E 34 A2
Lightwood Green Wrex 33 A9
Lilbourne Northants 36 H1
Lilburn Tower Northumb 62 A6
Lilleshall Telford 34 D3
Lilley Herts 29 F8
Lilley W Berks 17 D11
Lilliesleaf Borders 61 A11
Lillingstone Dayrell Bucks 28 E4
Lillingstone Lovell Bucks 28 D4
Lillington Dorset 8 C5
Lillington Warks 27 B10
Lilliput Poole 9 E9
Lilstock Som 7 B10
Lilyhurst Shrops 34 D3
Limbury Luton 29 F7
Limebrook Hereford 25 B10
Limefield Gtr Man 44 A2
Limekilnburn S Lanark 68 E6
Limekilns Fife 69 B9
Limerigg Falk 69 C7
Limerstone IoW 10 F3
Limington Som 8 B4
Limpenhoe Norf 39 E9
Limpley Stoke Wilts 16 E4
Limpsfield Sur 19 F11
Limpsfield Chart Sur 19 F11
Linby Notts 45 G9
Linchmere W Sus 11 A7
Lincluden Dumfries 60 F5
Lincoln Lincs 46 E3
Lincomb Worcs 26 B5
Lincombe Devon 5 F8
Lindal in Furness Cumb 49 B2
Lindale Cumb 49 A4
Lindean Borders 70 G3
Lindfield W Sus 12 D2
Lindford Hants 18 H5
Lindifferon Fife 76 F6
Lindley W Yorks 51 H7
Lindley Green N Yorks 51 E8
Lindores Fife 76 F5
Lindridge Worcs 26 B3
Lindsell Essex 30 F3
Lindsey Suff 30 D6
Linford Hants 9 D10
Linford Thurrock 20 D3
Lingague IoM 48 E2
Lingards Wood W Yorks 44 A4
Lingbob W Yorks 51 F6
Lingdale Redcar 59 E7
Lingen Hereford 25 B10
Lingfield Sur 12 B2
Lingreabhagh W Isles 90 J5
Lingwood Norf 39 E9
Linicro Highld 85 B8
Linkenholt Hants 17 F10
Linkhill Kent 13 D7
Linkinhorne Corn 4 D4
Linklater Orkney 95 K5
Linksness Orkney 95 H3
Linktown Fife 69 A11
Linley Shrops 33 F9
Linley Green Hereford 26 C3
Linlithgow W Loth 69 C9
Linlithgow Bridge W Loth 69 C8
Linshiels Northumb 62 C4
Linsiadar W Isles 90 D7
Linsidemore Highld 87 B8
Linslade C Beds 28 F6
Linstead Parva Suff 39 H9
Linstock Cumb 61 H10
Linthwaite W Yorks 44 A5
Lintlaw Borders 71 E7
Lintmill Moray 88 B5
Linton Borders 70 H6
Linton Cambs 30 D2
Linton Derbys 35 D8
Linton Hereford 26 F3
Linton Kent 20 G4
Linton N Yorks 50 C5
Linton Northumb 63 D8
Linton W Yorks 51 E9
Linton-on-Ouse N Yorks 51 C10
Linwood Hants 9 D10
Linwood Lincs 46 D5
Linwood Renfs 68 D3
Lionacleit W Isles 84 D2
Lional W Isles 91 A10
Liphook Hants 11 A7
Liscard Mers 42 C6
Liscombe Som 7 C7
Liskeard Corn 4 E3
L'Islet Guern 11
Liss Hants 11 B6
Liss Forest Hants 11 B6
Lissett E Yorks 53 D7
Lissington Lincs 46 D5
Lisvane Cardiff 15 C7
Liswerry Newport 15 C9
Litcham Norf 38 D4
Litchborough Northants 28 C3
Litchfield Hants 17 F11
Litherland Mers 42 C6
Litlington Cambs 29 D10
Litlington E Sus 12 F4
Little Abington Cambs 30 D2
Little Addington Northants 28 A6
Little Alne Warks 27 B8
Little Altcar Mers 42 B6
Little Asby Cumb 57 F8
Little Assynt Highld 92 G4
Little Aston Staffs 35 E6
Little Atherfield IoW 10 F3
Little Ayre Orkney 95 J4
Little-ayre Shetland 96 G5
Little Ayton N Yorks 59 E6
Little Baddow Essex 30 H4
Little Badminton S Glos 16 C5
Little Ballinluig Perth 76 B2
Little Bampton Cumb 61 H8
Little Bardfield Essex 30 E3
Little Barford Bedford 29 C8
Little Barningham Norf 39 B7
Little Barrington Glos 27 G9
Little Barrow Ches W 43 E7
Little Barugh N Yorks 52 B3
Little Bavington Northumb 62 F5
Little Bealings Suff 31 D9
Little Bedwyn Wilts 17 E9
Little Bentley Essex 31 F8
Little Berkhamsted Herts 29 H9
Little Billing Northants 28 B5
Little Birch Hereford 26 E2
Little Blakenham Suff 31 D8
Little Blencow Cumb 56 C6
Little Bollington Ches E 43 D10
Little Bookham Sur 19 F8
Little Bowden Leics 36 G3
Little Bradley Suff 30 C3
Little Brampton Shrops 33 G9
Little Brechin Angus 77 A8
Little Brickhill M Keynes 28 E6
Little Brington Northants 28 B3
Little Bromley Essex 31 F7
Little Broughton Cumb 56 C2
Little Budworth Ches W 43 F8
Little Burstead Essex 20 B3
Little Bytham Lincs 36 D6
Little Carlton Lincs 47 D7
Little Carlton Notts 45 G11
Little Casterton Rutland 36 E6
Little Cawthorpe Lincs 47 D7
Little Chalfont Bucks 18 B6
Little Chart Kent 20 G6
Little Chesterford Essex 30 D2
Little Cheverell Wilts 16 F6
Little Chishill Cambs 29 E11
Little Clacton Essex 31 G8
Little Clifton Cumb 56 D2
Little Colp Aberds 89 D7
Little Comberton Worcs 26 D6
Little Common E Sus 12 F6
Little Compton Warks 27 E9
Little Cornard Suff 30 E5
Little Cowarne Hereford 26 C3
Little Coxwell Oxon 17 B9
Little Crakehall N Yorks 58 G3
Little Cressingham Norf 38 F4
Little Crosby Mers 42 B6
Little Dalby Leics 36 D3
Little Dawley Telford 34 E2
Little Dens Aberds 89 D10
Little Dewchurch Hereford 26 E2
Little Downham Cambs 37 G11
Little Driffield E Yorks 52 D6
Little Dunham Norf 38 D4
Little Dunkeld Perth 76 C3
Little Dunmow Essex 30 F3
Little Easton Essex 30 F3
Little Eaton Derbys 35 A9
Little Eccleston Lancs 49 E4
Little Ellingham Norf 38 F6
Little End Essex 20 A2
Little Eversden Cambs 29 C10
Little Faringdon Oxon 17 A9
Little Fencote N Yorks 58 G3
Little Fenton N Yorks 51 F11
Little Finborough Suff 31 C7
Little Fransham Norf 38 D5
Little Gaddesden Herts 28 G6
Little Gidding Cambs 37 G7
Little Glemham Suff 31 C10
Little Glenshee Perth 76 D2
Little Gransden Cambs 29 C9
Little Green Som 16 G4
Little Grimsby Lincs 47 C7
Little Gruinard Highld 86 C2
Little Habton N Yorks 52 B3
Little Hadham Herts 29 F11
Little Hale Lincs 37 A7
Little Hallingbury Essex 29 G11
Little Hampden Bucks 18 A5
Little Harrowden Northants 28 A5
Little Haseley Oxon 18 A3
Little Hatfield E Yorks 53 E7
Little Hautbois Norf 39 C8
Little Haven Pembs 22 E3
Little Hay Staffs 35 E7
Little Hayfield Derbys 44 D4
Little Haywood Staffs 34 C6
Little Heath W Mid 35 G9
Little Hereford Hereford 26 B2
Little Horkesley Essex 30 E6
Little Horsted E Sus 12 E3
Little Horton W Yorks 51 F7
Little Horwood Bucks 28 E4
Little Houghton Northants 28 C5
Little Houghton S Yorks 45 B8
Little Hucklow Derbys 44 E5
Little Hulton Gtr Man 43 B10
Little Humber E Yorks 53 G7
Little Hungerford W Berks 18 D2
Little Irchester Northants 28 B6
Little Kimble Bucks 28 H5
Little Kineton Warks 27 C10
Little Kingshill Bucks 18 B5
Little Langdale Cumb 56 F5
Little Langford Wilts 17 H7
Little Laver Essex 30 H2
Little Leigh Ches W 43 E9
Little Leighs Essex 30 G4
Little Lever Gtr Man 43 B10
Little London Bucks 28 G3
Little London E Sus 12 E4
Little London Hants 17 G10
Little London Hants 18 F3
Little London Lincs 37 C10
Little London Lincs 37 C8
Little London Norf 39 C7
Little London Powys 32 G6
Little Longstone Derbys 44 E5
Little Lynturk Aberds 83 B7
Little Malvern Worcs 26 D4
Little Maplestead Essex 30 E5
Little Marcle Hereford 26 E3
Little Marlow Bucks 18 C5
Little Marsden Lancs 50 F4
Little Massingham Norf 38 C3
Little Melton Norf 39 E7
Little Mill Mon 15 A9
Little Milton Oxon 18 A3
Little Missenden Bucks 18 B6
Little Musgrave Cumb 57 E9
Little Ness Shrops 33 D10
Little Neston Ches W 42 E5
Little Newcastle Pembs 22 D4
Little Newsham Durham 58 E2
Little Oakley Essex 31 F9
Little Oakley Northants 36 G4
Little Orton Cumb 61 H9
Little Ouseburn N Yorks 51 C10
Little Paxton Cambs 29 B8
Little Petherick Corn 3 B8
Little Pitlurg Moray 88 D4
Little Plumpton Lancs 49 F3
Little Plumstead Norf 39 D9
Little Ponton Lincs 36 B5
Little Raveley Cambs 37 H8
Little Reedness E Yorks 52 G4
Little Ribston N Yorks 51 D9
Little Rissington Glos 27 G8
Little Ryburgh Norf 38 C5
Little Ryle Northumb 62 B6
Little Salkeld Cumb 57 C7
Little Sampford Essex 30 E3
Little Sandhurst Brack 18 E5
Little Saxham Suff 30 B4
Little Scatwell Highld 86 F6
Little Sessay N Yorks 51 B10
Little Shelford Cambs 29 C11
Little Singleton Lancs 49 F3
Little Skillymarno Aberds 89 C9
Little Smeaton N Yorks 51 H11
Little Snoring Norf 38 B5
Little Sodbury S Glos 16 C4
Little Somborne Hants 10 A2
Little Somerford Wilts 16 C6
Little Stainforth N Yorks 50 C4
Little Stainton Darl 58 D4
Little Stanney Ches W 43 E7
Little Staughton Bedford 29 B8
Little Steeping Lincs 47 F8
Little Stoke Staffs 34 B5
Little Stonham Suff 31 B8
Little Stretton Leics 36 E2
Little Stretton Shrops 33 F10
Little Strickland Cumb 57 E7
Little Stukeley Cambs 37 H8
Little Sutton Ches W 42 E6
Little Tew Oxon 27 F10
Little Thetford Cambs 37 H11
Little Thirkleby N Yorks 51 B10
Little Thurlow Suff 30 C3
Little Thurrock Thurrock 20 D3
Little Torboll Highld 87 B10
Little Torrington Devon 6 E3
Little Totham Essex 30 G5
Little Toux Aberds 88 C5
Little Town Cumb 56 E4
Little Town Lancs 50 F2
Little Urswick Cumb 49 B2
Little Wakering Essex 20 C6
Little Walden Essex 30 D2
Little Waldingfield Suff 30 D6
Little Walsingham Norf 38 B5
Little Waltham Essex 30 G4
Little Warley Essex 20 B3
Little Weighton E Yorks 52 F5
Little Weldon Northants 36 G5
Little Welnetham Suff 30 B5
Little Wenlock Telford 34 E2
Little Whittingham Green Suff 39 H8
Little Wilbraham Cambs 30 C2
Little Wishford Wilts 17 H7
Little Witley Worcs 26 B4
Little Wittenham Oxon 18 B2
Little Wolford Warks 27 E9
Little Wratting Suff 30 D3
Little Wymington Bedford 28 B6
Little Wymondley Herts 29 F9
Little Wyrley Staffs 34 E6
Little Yeldham Essex 30 E4
Littlebeck N Yorks 59 F9
Littleborough Gtr Man 50 H5
Littleborough Notts 46 D2
Littlebourne Kent 21 F9
Littlebredy Dorset 8 F4
Littlebury Essex 30 E2
Littlebury Green Essex 29 E11
Littledean Glos 26 G3
Littleferry Highld 87 B11
Littleham Devon 5 C11
Littleham Devon 6 D3
Littlehampton W Sus 11 D9
Littlehempston Devon 5 E9
Littlehoughton Northumb 63 B8
Littlemill Aberds 82 D5
Littlemill E Ayrs 67 E7
Littlemill Highld 87 F12
Littlemill Northumb 63 B8
Littlemoor Dorset 8 F5
Littlemore Oxon 18 A2
Littleover Derby 35 B9
Littleport Cambs 38 G1
Littlestone on Sea Kent 13 D9
Littlethorpe Leics 35 F11
Littlethorpe N Yorks 51 C9
Littleton Ches W 43 F7
Littleton Hants 10 A3
Littleton Perth 76 D5
Littleton Som 8 A3
Littleton Sur 18 G6
Littleton Sur 19 E7
Littleton Drew Wilts 16 C5
Littleton-on-Severn S Glos 16 C2
Littleton Pannell Wilts 17 F7
Littletown Durham 58 B4
Littlewick Green Windsor 18 D5
Littleworth Bedford 29 D7
Littleworth Glos 16 A5
Littleworth Oxon 17 B10
Littleworth Staffs 34 D6
Littleworth Worcs 26 C5
Litton Derbys 44 E5
Litton N Yorks 50 B5
Litton Som 16 F2
Litton Cheney Dorset 8 E4
Liurbost W Isles 91 E8
Liverpool Mers 42 C6
Liverpool Airport Mers 43 D7
Liversedge W Yorks 51 G8
Liverton Devon 5 D9
Liverton Redcar 59 E8
Livingston W Loth 69 D9
Livingston Village W Loth 69 D9
Lixwm Flint 42 E4
Lizard Corn 2 H6
Llaingoch Anglesey 40 B4
Llaithddu Powys 33 G6
Llan Powys 32 E4
Llan Ffestiniog Gwyn 41 F9
Llan-y-pwll Wrex 42 G6
Llanaber Gwyn 32 D2
Llanaelhaearn Gwyn 40 F5
Llanafan Ceredig 24 A3
Llanafan-fawr Powys 24 C6
Llanallgo Anglesey 40 B6
Llanandras = Presteigne Powys 25 B10
Llanarmon Gwyn 40 G6
Llanarmon Dyffryn Ceiriog Wrex 33 B7
Llanarmon-yn-Ial Denb 42 G4
Llanarth Ceredig 23 A9
Llanarth Mon 25 G10
Llanarthne Carms 23 D10
Llanasa Flint 42 D4
Llanbabo Anglesey 40 B5
Llanbadarn Fawr Ceredig 32 G2
Llanbadarn Fynydd Powys 33 H7
Llanbadarn-y-Garreg Powys 25 D8
Llanbadoc Mon 15 B9
Llanbadrig Anglesey 40 A5
Llanbeder Newport 15 B9
Llanbedr Gwyn 32 C1
Llanbedr Powys 25 D8
Llanbedr Powys 25 F9
Llanbedr-Dyffryn-Clwyd Denb 42 G4
Llanbedr Pont Steffan = Lampeter Ceredig 23 B10
Llanbedr-y-cennin Conwy 41 D9
Llanbedrgoch Anglesey 41 B7
Llanbedrog Gwyn 40 G5
Llanberis Gwyn 41 D7
Llanbethêry V Glam 14 E6
Llanbister Powys 25 A8
Llanblethian V Glam 14 D5
Llanboidy Carms 23 D7
Llanbradach Caerph 15 B7
Llanbrynmair Powys 32 E4
Llancarfan V Glam 14 D6
Llancayo Mon 15 A9
Llancloudy Hereford 25 F11
Llancynfelyn Ceredig 32 F2
Llandaff Cardiff 15 D7
Llandanwg Gwyn 32 C1
Llandarcy Neath 14 B3
Llandawke Carms 23 E7
Llanddaniel Fab Anglesey 40 C6
Llanddarog Carms 23 E10
Llanddeiniol Ceredig 24 A2
Llanddeiniolen Gwyn 41 D7
Llandderfel Gwyn 32 B5
Llanddeusant Anglesey 40 B5
Llanddeusant Carms 24 F4
Llanddew Powys 25 E7
Llanddewi Swansea 23 H9
Llanddewi-Brefi Ceredig 24 C3
Llanddewi Rhydderch Mon 25 G10
Llanddewi Velfrey Pembs 22 E6
Llanddewi'r Cwm Powys 25 D7
Llanddoged Conwy 41 D10
Llanddona Anglesey 41 C7
Llanddowror Carms 23 E7
Llanddulas Conwy 42 E2
Llanddwywe Gwyn 32 C1
Llanddyfynan Anglesey 41 C7
Llandefaelog Fach Powys 25 E7
Llandefaelog-tre'r-graig Powys 25 F8
Llandefalle Powys 25 E8
Llandegai Gwyn 41 C7
Llandegfan Anglesey 41 C7
Llandegla Denb 42 G4
Llandegley Powys 25 B8
Llandegveth Mon 15 B9
Llandegwning Gwyn 40 G4
Llandeilo Carms 24 F3
Llandeilo Graban Powys 25 D7
Llandeilo'r Fan Powys 24 E5
Llandeloy Pembs 22 D3
Llandenny Mon 15 A10
Llandevenny Mon 15 C10
Llandewednock Corn 2 H6
Llandewi Ystradenny Powys 25 B8
Llandinabo Hereford 26 F2
Llandinam Powys 32 G6
Llandissilio Pembs 22 D6
Llandogo Mon 15 A11
Llandough V Glam 14 D5
Llandough V Glam 15 D7
Llandovery = Llanymddyfri Carms 24 E4
Llandow V Glam 14 D5
Llandre Carms 24 D3
Llandre Ceredig 32 G2
Llandrillo Denb 32 B6
Llandrillo-yn-Rhos Conwy 41 B10
Llandrindod = Llandrindod Wells Powys 25 B7
Llandrindod Wells = Llandrindod Powys 25 B7
Llandrinio Powys 33 D8
Llandudno Conwy 41 B9
Llandudno Junction = Cyffordd Llandudno Conwy 41 C9
Llandwrog Gwyn 40 E6
Llandybie Carms 24 G3
Llandyfaelog Carms 23 E9
Llandyfan Carms 24 G3
Llandyfriog Ceredig 23 B8
Llandyfrydog Anglesey 40 B6
Llandygwydd Ceredig 23 B7
Llandynan Denb 42 H4
Llandyrnog Denb 42 F4
Llandysilio Powys 33 D8
Llandyssil Powys 33 F7
Llandysul Ceredig 23 B9
Llanedeyrn Cardiff 15 C8
Llanedi Carms 23 F10
Llaneglwys Powys 25 E7
Llanegryn Gwyn 32 E1
Llanegwad Carms 23 D10
Llaneilian Anglesey 40 A6
Llanelian-yn-Rhos Conwy 41 C10
Llanelidan Denb 42 G4
Llanelieu Powys 25 E8
Llanellen Mon 25 G10
Llanelli Carms 23 G10
Llanelltyd Gwyn 32 D3
Llanelly Mon 25 G9
Llanelly Hill Mon 25 G9
Llanelwedd Powys 25 C7
Llanelwy = St Asaph Denb 42 E3
Llanenddwyn Gwyn 32 C1
Llanengan Gwyn 40 H4
Llanerchymedd Anglesey 40 B6
Llanerfyl Powys 32 E6
Llanfachraeth Anglesey 40 B5
Llanfachreth Gwyn 32 C3
Llanfaelog Anglesey 40 C5
Llanfaelrhys Gwyn 40 H4
Llanfaenor Mon 25 G11
Llanfaes Anglesey 41 C8
Llanfaes Powys 25 F7
Llanfaethlu Anglesey 40 B5
Llanfaglan Gwyn 40 D6
Llanfair Gwyn 32 C1
Llanfair-ar-y-bryn Carms 24 E5
Llanfair Caereinion Powys 33 E7
Llanfair Clydogau Ceredig 24 C3
Llanfair-Dyffryn-Clwyd Denb 42 G4
Llanfair Kilgheddin Mon 25 H10
Llanfair-Nant-Gwyn Pembs 22 C6
Llanfair Talhaiarn Conwy 42 E2
Llanfair Waterdine Shrops 33 H8
Llanfair-ym-Muallt = Builth Wells Powys 25 C7
Llanfairfechan Conwy 41 C8
Llanfairpwll-gwyngyll Anglesey 41 C7
Llanfairyneubwll Anglesey 40 C5
Llanfairynghornwy Anglesey 40 A5
Llanfallteg Carms 22 E6
Llanfaredd Powys 25 C7
Llanfarian Ceredig 32 H1
Llanfechain Powys 33 C7
Llanfechan Powys 24 C6
Llanfechell Anglesey 40 A5
Llanfendigaid Gwyn 32 E1
Llanferres Denb 42 F4
Llanfflewyn Anglesey 40 B5
Llanfihangel-ar-arth Carms 23 C9
Llanfihangel-Crucorney Mon 25 F10
Llanfihangel Glyn Myfyr Conwy 42 H2
Llanfihangel Nant Bran Powys 24 E6
Llanfihangel-nant-Melan Powys 25 C8
Llanfihangel Rhydithon Powys 25 B8
Llanfihangel Rogiet Mon 15 C10
Llanfihangel Tal-y-llyn Powys 25 F8
Llanfihangel-uwch-Gwili Carms 23 D9
Llanfihangel-y-Creuddyn Ceredig 32 H2
Llanfihangel-y-pennant Gwyn 32 E2
Llanfihangel-y-pennant Gwyn 41 F7
Llanfihangel-y-traethau Gwyn 41 G7
Llanfihangel-yn-Ngwynfa Powys 33 D6
Llanfihangel yn Nhowyn Anglesey 40 C5
Llanfilo Powys 25 E8
Llanfoist Mon 25 G9
Llanfor Gwyn 32 B5
Llanfrechfa Torf 15 B9
Llanfrothen Gwyn 41 F8
Llanfrynach Powys 25 F7
Llanfwrog Anglesey 40 B5
Llanfwrog Denb 42 G4
Llanfyllin Powys 33 D7
Llanfynydd Carms 23 D10
Llanfynydd Flint 42 G5
Llanfyrnach Pembs 23 C7
Llangadfan Powys 32 D6
Llangadog Carms 24 F4
Llangadwaladr Anglesey 40 D5
Llangadwaladr Powys 33 B7
Llangaffo Anglesey 40 D6
Llangain Carms 23 E8
Llangammarch Wells Powys 24 D6
Llangan V Glam 14 D5
Llangarron Hereford 26 F2
Llangasty Talyllyn Powys 25 F8
Llangathen Carms 23 D10
Llangattock Powys 25 G9
Llangattock Lingoed Mon 25 F10
Llangattock nigh Usk Mon 25 H10
Llangattock-Vibon-Avel Mon 25 G11
Llangedwyn Powys 33 C7
Llangefni Anglesey 40 C6
Llangeinor Bridgend 14 C5
Llangeitho Ceredig 24 C3
Llangeler Carms 23 C8
Llangelynin Gwyn 32 E1
Llangendeirne Carms 23 E9
Llangennech Carms 23 F10
Llangennith Swansea 23 G9
Llangenny Powys 25 G9
Llangernyw Conwy 41 D10
Llangian Gwyn 40 H4
Llanglydwen Carms 22 D6
Llangoed Anglesey 41 C8
Llangoedmor Ceredig 22 B6
Llangollen Denb 33 A8
Llangolman Pembs 22 D6
Llangors Powys 25 F8
Llangovan Mon 25 H11
Llangower Gwyn 32 B5
Llangrannog Ceredig 23 A8
Llangristiolus Anglesey 40 C6
Llangrove Hereford 26 G2
Llangua Mon 25 F10
Llangunllo Powys 25 A9
Llangunnor Carms 23 E9
Llangurig Powys 32 H5
Llangwm Conwy 32 A5
Llangwm Mon 15 A10
Llangwm Pembs 22 F4
Llangwnnadl Gwyn 40 G4
Llangwyfan Denb 42 F4
Llangwyfan-isaf Anglesey 40 D5
Llangwyllog Anglesey 40 C6
Llangwyryfon Ceredig 24 A2
Llangybi Ceredig 24 C3
Llangybi Gwyn 40 F6
Llangybi Mon 15 B9
Llangyfelach Swansea 14 B2
Llangynhafal Denb 42 F4
Llangynidr Powys 25 G8
Llangynin Carms 23 E7
Llangynog Carms 23 E8
Llangynog Powys 33 C6
Llangynwyd Bridgend 14 C4
Llanhamlach Powys 25 F7
Llanharan Rhondda 14 C6
Llanharry Rhondda 14 C6
Llanhennock Mon 15 B9
Llanhiledd = Llanhilleth Bl Gwent 15 A8
Llanhilleth = Llanhiledd Bl Gwent 15 A8
Llanidloes Powys 32 G5
Llaniestyn Gwyn 40 G4
Llanifyny Powys 32 G4
Llanigon Powys 25 E9
Llanilar Ceredig 24 A3
Llanilid Rhondda 14 C5
Llanilltud Fawr = Llantwit Major V Glam 14 E5
Llanishen Cardiff 15 C7
Llanishen Mon 15 A10
Llanllawddog Carms 23 D9
Llanllechid Gwyn 41 D8
Llanllowell Mon 15 B9
Llanllugan Powys 33 E6
Llanllwch Carms 23 E8
Llanllwchaiarn Powys 33 F7
Llanllwni Carms 23 C9
Llanllyfni Gwyn 40 E6
Llanmadoc Swansea 23 G9
Llanmaes V Glam 14 E5
Llanmartin Newport 15 C9
Llanmihangel V Glam 14 D5
Llanmorlais Swansea 23 G10
Llannefydd Conwy 42 E2
Llannon Carms 23 F10
Llannor Gwyn 40 G5
Llanon Ceredig 24 B2
Llanover Mon 25 H10
Llanpumsaint Carms 23 D9
Llanreithan Pembs 22 D3
Llanrhaeadr Denb 42 F3
Llanrhaeadr-ym-Mochnant Powys 33 C7
Llanrhian Pembs 22 C3
Llanrhidian Swansea 23 G9
Llanrhos Conwy 41 B9
Llanrhyddlad Anglesey 40 B5
Llanrhystud Ceredig 24 B2
Llanrosser Hereford 25 E9
Llanrothal Hereford 25 G11
Llanrug Gwyn 41 D7
Llanrumney Cardiff 15 C8
Llanrwst Conwy 41 D10
Llansadurnen Carms 23 E7
Llansadwrn Anglesey 41 C7
Llansadwrn Carms 24 E3
Llansaint Carms 23 F8
Llansamlet Swansea 14 B2
Llansannan Conwy 42 F2
Llansannor V Glam 14 D5
Llansantffraed Ceredig 24 B2
Llansantffraed Powys 25 F8
Llansantffraed Cwmdeuddwr Powys 24 B6
Llansantffraed-in-Elvel Powys 25 C7
Llansantffraid-ym-Mechain Powys 33 C8
Llansawel Carms 24 E3
Llansilin Powys 33 C8
Llansoy Mon 15 A10
Llanspyddid Powys 25 F7
Llanstadwell Pembs 22 F4
Llansteffan Carms 23 E8
Llanstephan Powys 25 D8
Llantarnam Torf 15 B9
Llanteg Pembs 22 E6
Llanthony Mon 25 F9
Llantilio Crossenny Mon 25 G10
Llantilio Pertholey Mon 25 G10
Llantood Pembs 22 B6
Llantrisant Anglesey 40 B5
Llantrisant Mon 15 B9
Llantrisant Rhondda 14 C6
Llantrithyd V Glam 14 D6
Llantwit Fardre Rhondda 14 C6
Llantwit Major = Llanilltud Fawr V Glam 14 E5
Llanuwchllyn Gwyn 41 G10
Llanvaches Newport 15 B10

Llanvair Discoed Mon 15 B10
Llanvapley Mon 25 G10
Llanvetherine Mon 25 G10
Llanveynoe Hereford 25 E10
Llanvihangel Gobion Mon 25 H10
Llanvihangel-Ystern-Llewern Mon 25 G11
Llanwarne Hereford 26 F2
Llanwddyn Powys 32 D6
Llanwenog Ceredig 23 B9
Llanwern Newport 15 C9
Llanwinio Carms 23 D7
Llanwnda Gwyn 40 E6
Llanwnda Pembs 22 C4
Llanwnnen Ceredig 23 B10
Llanwnog Powys 32 F6
Llanwrda Carms 24 E4
Llanwrin Powys 32 E3
Llanwrthwl Powys 24 B6
Llanwrtud = Llanwrtyd Wells Powys 24 D5
Llanwrtyd Powys 24 D5
Llanwrtyd Wells = Llanwrtud Powys 24 D5
Llanwyddelan Powys 33 E6
Llanyblodwel Shrops 33 C8
Llanybri Carms 23 E8
Llanybydder Carms 23 B10
Llanycefn Pembs 22 D5
Llanychaer Pembs 22 C4
Llanycil Gwyn 32 B5
Llanycrwys Carms 24 D3
Llanymawddwy Gwyn 32 D5
Llanymddyfri = Llandovery Carms 24 E4
Llanymynech Powys 33 C8
Llanynghenedl Anglesey 40 B5
Llanynys Denb 42 F4
Llanyre Powys 25 B7
Llanystumdwy Gwyn 40 G6
Llanywern Powys 25 F8
Llawhaden Pembs 22 E5
Llawnt Shrops 33 B8
Llawr Dref Gwyn 40 H4
Llawryglyn Powys 32 F5
Llay Wrex 42 G6
Llechcynfarwy Anglesey 40 B5
Llecheiddior Gwyn 40 F6
Llechfaen Powys 25 F7
Llechryd Caerph 25 H8
Llechryd Ceredig 23 B7
Llechrydau Powys 33 B8
Lledrod Ceredig 24 A3
Llenmerewig Powys 33 F7
Llethrid Swansea 23 G10
Llidiad Nenog Carms 23 C10
Llidiardau Gwyn 41 G10
Llidiart-y-parc Denb 33 A7
Llithfaen Gwyn 40 F5
Llong Flint 42 F5
Llowes Powys 25 D8
Llundain-fach Ceredig 23 A10
Llwydcoed Rhondda 14 A5
Llwyn Shrops 33 G8
Llwyn-du Mon 25 G9
Llwyn-hendy Carms 23 G10
Llwyn-têg Carms 23 F10
Llwyn-y-brain Carms 22 E6
Llwyn-y-groes Ceredig 23 A10
Llwyncelyn Ceredig 23 A9
Llwyndafydd Ceredig 23 A8
Llwynderw Powys 33 E8
Llwyndyrys Gwyn 40 F5
Llwyngwril Gwyn 32 E1
Llwynmawr Wrex 33 B8
Llwynypia Rhondda 14 B5
Llynclys Shrops 33 C8
Llynfaes Anglesey 40 C6
Llys-y-frân Pembs 22 D5
Llysfaen Conwy 41 C10
Llyswen Powys 25 E8
Llysworney V Glam 14 D5
Llywel Powys 24 E5
Loan Falk 69 C8
Loanend Northumb 71 E8
Loanhead Midloth 69 D11
Loans S Ayrs 66 C6
Loans of Tullich Highld 87 D11
Lobb Devon 6 C3
Loch a Charnain W Isles 84 D3
Loch a' Ghainmhich W Isles 91 E7
Loch Baghasdail = Lochboisdale W Isles 84 G2
Loch Choire Lodge Highld 93 F9
Loch Euphoirt W Isles 84 B3
Loch Head Dumfries 54 E6
Loch Loyal Lodge Highld 93 E9
Loch nam Madadh = Lochmaddy W Isles 84 B4
Loch Sgioport W Isles 84 E3
Lochailort Highld 79 C10
Lochaline Highld 79 G9
Lochanhully Highld 81 A11
Lochans Dumfries 54 D3
Locharbriggs Dumfries 60 E5
Lochassynt Lodge Highld 92 G4
Lochavich Ho Argyll 73 B8
Lochawe Argyll 74 E4
Lochboisdale = Loch Baghasdail W Isles 84 G2
Lochbuie Argyll 79 J9
Lochcarron Highld 85 E13
Lochdhu Highld 93 E13
Lochdochart House Stirling 75 E7
Lochdon Argyll 79 H10
Lochdrum Highld 86 D5
Lochead Argyll 72 F6
Lochearnhead Stirling 75 E8
Lochee Dundee 76 D6
Lochend Highld 87 H8
Lochend Highld 94 D4
Locherben Dumfries 60 D5
Lochfoot Dumfries 60 F4
Lochgair Argyll 73 D8
Lochgarthside Highld 81 B7
Lochgelly Fife 69 A10
Lochgilphead Argyll 73 E7
Lochgoilhead Argyll 74 G5
Lochhill Moray 88 B2
Lochindorb Lodge Highld 87 H12
Lochinver Highld 92 G3
Lochlane Perth 75 E11
Lochluichart Highld 86 E6
Lochmaben Dumfries 60 E6
Lochmaddy = Loch nam Madadh W Isles 84 B4
Lochmore Cottage Highld 94 F2
Lochmore Lodge Highld 92 F5
Lochore Fife 76 H4
Lochportain W Isles 84 A4
Lochranza N Ayrs 66 A2
Lochs Crofts Moray 88 B3
Lochside Aberds 77 A10
Lochside Highld 87 F11
Lochside Highld 92 D7
Lochside Highld 93 F11
Lochslin Highld 87 C11
Lochstack Lodge Highld 92 E5
Lochton Aberds 83 D9
Lochty Angus 77 A8
Lochty Fife 77 G8
Lochty Perth 76 E3
Lochuisge Highld 79 F10
Lochurr Dumfries 60 E3
Lochwinnoch Renfs 68 E2
Lochwood Dumfries 60 D6
Lochyside Highld 80 F3
Lockengate Corn 3 C9
Lockerbie Dumfries 61 E7
Lockeridge Wilts 17 E8
Lockerley Hants 10 B1
Locking N Som 15 F9
Lockinge Oxon 17 C11
Lockington E Yorks 52 E5
Lockington Leics 35 C10
Lockleywood Shrops 34 C2
Locks Heath Hants 10 D4
Lockton N Yorks 59 G9
Lockwood W Yorks 51 H7
Loddington Leics 36 E3
Loddington Northants 36 H4
Loddiswell Devon 5 G8
Loddon Norf 39 F9
Lode Cambs 30 B2
Loders Dorset 8 E3
Lodsworth W Sus 11 B8
Lofthouse N Yorks 51 B7
Lofthouse W Yorks 51 G9
Loftus Redcar 59 E8
Logan E Ayrs 67 D8
Logan Mains Dumfries 54 E3
Loganlea W Loth 69 D8
Loggerheads Staffs 34 B3
Logie Angus 77 A9
Logie Fife 77 E7
Logie Moray 87 F13
Logie Coldstone Aberds 82 C6
Logie Hill Highld 87 D10
Logie Newton Aberds 89 E6
Logie Pert Angus 77 A9
Logiealmond Lodge Perth 76 D2
Logierait Perth 76 B2
Login Carms 22 D6
Lolworth Cambs 29 B10
Lonbain Highld 85 C11
Londesborough E Yorks 52 E4
London Colney Herts 19 A8
Londonderry N Yorks 58 H4
Londonthorpe Lincs 36 B5
Londubh Highld 91 J13
Lonemore Highld 87 C10
Long Ashton N Som 15 D11
Long Bennington Lincs 36 A4
Long Bredy Dorset 8 E4
Long Buckby Northants 28 B3
Long Clawson Leics 36 C3
Long Common Hants 10 C4
Long Compton Staffs 34 C4
Long Compton Warks 27 E9
Long Crendon Bucks 28 H3
Long Crichel Dorset 9 C8
Long Ditton Sur 19 E8
Long Drax N Yorks 52 G2
Long Duckmanton Derbys 45 E8
Long Eaton Derbys 35 B10
Long Green Worcs 26 E5
Long Hanborough Oxon 27 G11
Long Itchington Warks 27 B11
Long Lawford Warks 35 H10
Long Load Som 8 B3
Long Marston Herts 28 G5
Long Marston N Yorks 51 D11
Long Marston Warks 27 D8
Long Marton Cumb 57 D8
Long Melford Suff 30 D5
Long Newnton Glos 16 B6
Long Newton E Loth 70 D4
Long Preston N Yorks 50 D4
Long Riston E Yorks 53 E7
Long Sight Gtr Man 44 B3
Long Stratton Norf 39 F7
Long Street M Keynes 28 D4
Long Sutton Hants 18 G4
Long Sutton Lincs 37 C10
Long Sutton Som 8 B3
Long Thurlow Suff 31 B7
Long Whatton Leics 35 C10
Long Wittenham Oxon 18 B2
Longbar N Ayrs 66 A6
Longbenton T&W 63 G8
Longborough Glos 27 F8
Longbridge W Mid 34 H6
Longbridge Warks 27 B9
Longbridge Deverill Wilts 16 G5
Longburton Dorset 8 C5
Longcliffe Derbys 44 G6
Longcot Oxon 17 B9
Longcroft Falk 68 C6
Longden Shrops 33 E10
Longdon Staffs 35 D6
Longdon Worcs 26 E5
Longdon Green Staffs 35 D6
Longdon on Tern Telford 34 D2
Longdown Devon 7 G7
Longdowns Corn 2 F6
Longfield Kent 20 E3
Longfield Shetland 96 M5
Longford Derbys 35 B8
Longford Glos 26 F5
Longford London 19 D7
Longford Shrops 34 B2
Longford Telford 34 D3
Longford W Mid 35 G9
Longfordlane Derbys 35 B8
Longforgan Perth 76 E6
Longformacus Borders 70 E5
Longframlington Northumb 63 C7
Longham Dorset 9 E9
Longham Norf 38 D5
Longhaven Aberds 89 E11
Longhill Aberds 89 C9
Longhirst Northumb 63 E8
Longhope Glos 26 G3
Longhope Orkney 95 J4
Longhorsley Northumb 63 D7
Longhoughton Northumb 63 B8
Longlane Derbys 35 B8
Longlane W Berks 17 D11
Longlevens Glos 26 F5
Longley W Yorks 44 B5
Longley Green Worcs 26 C4
Longmanhill Aberds 89 B7
Longmoor Camp Hants 11 A6
Longmorn Moray 88 C2
Longnewton Borders 70 H4
Longnewton Stockton 58 E4
Longney Glos 26 G4
Longniddry E Loth 70 C3
Longnor Shrops 33 E10
Longnor Staffs 44 F4
Longparish Hants 17 G11
Longport Stoke 44 H2
Longridge Lancs 50 F2
Longridge Staffs 34 D5
Longridge W Loth 69 D8
Longriggend N Lanark 69 C7
Longsdon Staffs 44 G3
Longshaw Gtr Man 43 B8
Longside Aberds 89 D10
Longstanton Cambs 29 B10
Longstock Hants 17 H10
Longstone Pembs 22 F6
Longstowe Cambs 29 C10
Longthorpe Pboro 37 F7
Longthwaite Cumb 56 D6
Longton Lancs 49 G4
Longton Stoke 34 A5
Longtown Cumb 61 G9
Longtown Hereford 25 F10
Longview Mers 43 C7
Longville in the Dale Shrops 33 F11
Longwick Bucks 28 H4
Longwitton Northumb 62 E6
Longwood Shrops 34 E2
Longworth Oxon 17 B10
Longyester E Loth 70 D4
Lonmay Aberds 89 C10
Lonmore Highld 84 D7
Looe Corn 4 F3
Loose Kent 20 F4
Loosley Row Bucks 18 A5
Lopcombe Corner Wilts 17 H9
Lopen Som 8 C3
Loppington Shrops 33 C10
Lopwell Devon 4 E5
Lorbottle Northumb 62 C6
Lorbottle Hall Northumb 62 C6
Lornty Perth 76 C4
Loscoe Derbys 45 H8
Losgaintir W Isles 90 H5
Lossiemouth Moray 88 A2
Lossit Argyll 64 C2
Lostford Shrops 34 B2
Lostock Gralam Ches W 43 E9
Lostock Green Ches W 43 E9
Lostock Hall Lancs 49 G5
Lostock Junction Gtr Man 43 B9
Lostwithiel Corn 4 F2
Loth Orkney 95 E7
Lothbeg Highld 93 H12
Lothersdale N Yorks 50 E5
Lothmore Highld 93 H12
Loudwater Bucks 18 B6
Loughborough Leics 35 D11
Loughor Swansea 23 G10
Loughton Essex 19 B11
Loughton M Keynes 28 E5
Loughton Shrops 34 G2
Lound Lincs 37 D6
Lound Notts 45 D10
Lound Suff 39 F11
Lount Leics 35 D9
Louth Lincs 47 D7
Love Clough Lancs 50 G4
Lovedean Hants 10 C5
Lover Wilts 9 B11
Loversall S Yorks 45 C9
Loves Green Essex 20 A3
Lovesome Hill N Yorks 58 G4
Loveston Pembs 22 F5
Lovington Som 8 A4
Low Ackworth W Yorks 51 H10
Low Barlings Lincs 46 E4
Low Bentham N Yorks 50 C2
Low Bradfield S Yorks 44 C6
Low Bradley N Yorks 50 E6
Low Braithwaite Cumb 56 B6
Low Brunton Northumb 62 F5
Low Burnham N Lincs 45 B11
Low Burton N Yorks 51 A8
Low Buston Northumb 63 C8
Low Catton E Yorks 52 D3
Low Clanyard Dumfries 54 F4
Low Coniscliffe Darl 58 E3
Low Crosby Cumb 61 H10
Low Dalby N Yorks 59 H9
Low Dinsdale Darl 58 E4
Low Ellington N Yorks 51 A8
Low Etherley Durham 58 D2
Low Fell T&W 63 H8
Low Fulney Lincs 37 C8
Low Garth N Yorks 59 F8
Low Gate Northumb 62 G5
Low Grantley N Yorks 51 B8
Low Habberley Worcs 34 H4
Low Ham Som 8 B3
Low Hesket Cumb 56 B6
Low Hesleyhurst Northumb 62 D6
Low Hutton N Yorks 52 C3
Low Laithe N Yorks 51 C7
Low Leighton Derbys 44 D4
Low Lorton Cumb 56 D3
Low Marishes N Yorks 52 B4
Low Marnham Notts 46 F2
Low Mill N Yorks 59 G7
Low Moor Lancs 50 E3
Low Moor W Yorks 51 G7
Low Moorsley T&W 58 B4
Low Newton Cumb 49 A4
Low Newton-by-the-Sea Northumb 63 A8
Low Row Cumb 56 C5
Low Row Cumb 61 G11
Low Row N Yorks 57 G11
Low Salchrie Dumfries 54 C3
Low Smerby Argyll 65 F8
Low Torry Fife 69 B9
Low Worsall N Yorks 58 F4
Low Wray Cumb 56 F5
Lowbridge House Cumb 57 F7
Lowca Cumb 56 D1
Lowdham Notts 45 H10
Lowe Shrops 33 B11
Lowe Hill Staffs 44 G3
Lower Aisholt Som 7 C11
Lower Arncott Oxon 28 G3
Lower Ashton Devon 5 C9
Lower Assendon Oxon 18 C4
Lower Badcall Highld 92 E4
Lower Bartle Lancs 49 F4
Lower Basildon W Berks 18 D3
Lower Beeding W Sus 11 B11
Lower Benefield Northants 36 G5
Lower Boddington Northants 27 C11
Lower Brailes Warks 27 E10
Lower Breakish Highld 85 F11
Lower Broadheath Worcs 26 C5
Lower Bullingham Hereford 26 E2
Lower Cam Glos 16 A4
Lower Chapel Powys 25 E7
Lower Chute Wilts 17 F10
Lower Cragabus Argyll 64 D4
Lower Crossings Derbys 44 D4
Lower Cumberworth W Yorks 44 B6
Lower Cwm-twrch Powys 24 G4
Lower Darwen Blackburn 50 G2
Lower Dean Bedford 29 B7
Lower Diabaig Highld 85 B12
Lower Dicker E Sus 12 E4
Lower Dinchope Shrops 33 G10
Lower Down Shrops 33 G9
Lower Drift Corn 2 G3
Lower Dunsforth N Yorks 51 C10
Lower Egleton Hereford 26 D3
Lower Elkstone Staffs 44 G4
Lower End C Beds 28 F6
Lower Everleigh Wilts 17 F8
Lower Farringdon Hants 18 H4
Lower Foxdale IoM 48 E2
Lower Frankton Shrops 33 B9
Lower Froyle Hants 18 G4
Lower Gledfield Highld 87 B8
Lower Green Norf 38 B5
Lower Hacheston Suff 31 C10
Lower Halistra Highld 84 C7
Lower Halstow Kent 20 E5
Lower Hardres Kent 21 F8
Lower Hawthwaite Cumb 56 H4
Lower Heath Ches E 44 F2
Lower Hempriggs Moray 87 E14
Lower Hergest Hereford 25 C9
Lower Heyford Oxon 27 F11
Lower Higham Kent 20 D4
Lower Holbrook Suff 31 E8
Lower Hordley Shrops 33 C9
Lower Horsebridge E Sus 12 E4
Lower Killeyan Argyll 64 D3
Lower Kingswood Sur 19 F9
Lower Kinnerton Ches W 42 F6
Lower Langford N Som 15 E10
Lower Largo Fife 77 G7
Lower Leigh Staffs 34 B6
Lower Lemington Glos 27 E9
Lower Lenie Highld 81 A7
Lower Lydbrook Glos 26 G2
Lower Lye Hereford 25 B11
Lower Machen Newport 15 C8
Lower Maes-coed Hereford 25 E10
Lower Mayland Essex 20 A6
Lower Midway Derbys 35 C9
Lower Milovaig Highld 84 C6
Lower Moor Worcs 26 D6
Lower Nazeing Essex 29 H10
Lower Netchwood Shrops 34 F2
Lower Ollach Highld 85 E10
Lower Penarth V Glam 15 D7
Lower Penn Staffs 34 F4
Lower Pennington Hants 10 E2
Lower Peover Ches W 43 E10
Lower Pexhill Ches E 44 E2
Lower Place Gtr Man 44 A3
Lower Quinton Warks 27 D8
Lower Rochford Worcs 26 B3
Lower Seagry Wilts 16 C6
Lower Shelton C Beds 28 D6
Lower Shiplake Oxon 18 D4
Lower Shuckburgh Warks 27 B11
Lower Slaughter Glos 27 F8
Lower Stanton St Quintin Wilts 16 C6
Lower Stoke Medway 20 D5
Lower Stondon C Beds 29 E8
Lower Stow Bedon Norf 38 F5
Lower Street Norf 39 B8
Lower Street Norf 39 D9
Lower Strensham Worcs 26 D6
Lower Stretton Warr 43 D9
Lower Sundon C Beds 29 F7
Lower Swanwick Hants 10 D3
Lower Swell Glos 27 F8
Lower Tean Staffs 34 B6
Lower Thurlton Norf 39 F10
Lower Tote Highld 85 B10
Lower Town Pembs 22 C4
Lower Tysoe Warks 27 D10
Lower Upham Hants 10 C4
Lower Vexford Som 7 C10
Lower Weare Som 15 F10
Lower Welson Hereford 25 C9
Lower Whitley Ches W 43 E9
Lower Wield Hants 18 G3
Lower Winchendon Bucks 28 G4
Lower Withington Ches E 44 F2
Lower Woodend Bucks 18 C5
Lower Woodford Wilts 9 A10
Lower Wyche Worcs 26 D4
Lowesby Leics 36 E3
Lowestoft Suff 39 F11
Loweswater Cumb 56 D3
Lowford Hants 10 C3
Lowgill Cumb 57 G8
Lowgill Lancs 50 C2
Lowick Northants 36 G5
Lowick Northumb 71 G9
Lowick Bridge Cumb 56 H4
Lowick Green Cumb 56 H4
Lowlands Torf 15 B8
Lowmoor Row Cumb 57 D8
Lownie Moor Angus 77 C7
Lowsonford Warks 27 B8
Lowther Cumb 57 D7
Lowthorpe E Yorks 53 C6
Lowton Gtr Man 43 C9
Lowton Common Gtr Man 43 C9
Loxbeare Devon 7 E8
Loxhill Sur 19 H7
Loxhore Devon 6 C5
Loxley Warks 27 C9
Loxton N Som 15 F9
Loxwood W Sus 11 A9
Lubcroy Highld 92 J6
Lubenham Leics 36 G3
Luccombe Som 7 B8
Luccombe Village IoW 10 G4
Lucker Northumb 71 G10
Luckett Corn 4 D4
Luckington Wilts 16 C5
Lucklawhill Fife 77 E7
Luckwell Bridge Som 7 C8
Lucton Hereford 25 B11
Ludag W Isles 84 G2
Ludborough Lincs 46 C6
Ludchurch Pembs 22 E6
Luddenden W Yorks 50 G6
Luddenden Foot W Yorks 50 G6
Luddesdown Kent 20 E3
Luddington N Lincs 52 H4
Luddington Warks 27 C8
Luddington in the Brook Northants 37 G7
Lude House Perth 81 G10
Ludford Lincs 46 D6
Ludford Shrops 26 A2
Ludgershall Bucks 28 G3
Ludgershall Wilts 17 F9
Ludgvan Corn 2 F4
Ludham Norf 39 D9
Ludlow Shrops 26 A2
Ludwell Wilts 9 B8
Ludworth Durham 58 B4
Luffincott Devon 6 G2
Lugar E Ayrs 67 D8
Lugg Green Hereford 25 B11
Luggate Burn E Loth 70 C5
Luggiebank N Lanark 68 C6
Lugton E Ayrs 67 A7
Lugwardine Hereford 26 D2
Luib Highld 85 F10
Lulham Hereford 25 D11
Lullenden Sur 12 B3
Lullington Derbys 35 D8
Lullington Som 16 F4
Lulsgate Bottom N Som 15 E11
Lulsley Worcs 26 C4
Lumb W Yorks 50 G6
Lumby N Yorks 51 F10
Lumloch E Dunb 68 D5
Lumphanan Aberds 83 C7
Lumphinnans Fife 69 A10
Lumsdaine Borders 71 D7
Lumsden Aberds 82 A6
Lunan Angus 77 B9
Lunanhead Angus 77 B7
Luncarty Perth 76 E3
Lund E Yorks 52 E5
Lund N Yorks 52 F2
Lund Shetland 96 C7
Lunderton Aberds 89 D11
Lundie Angus 76 D5
Lundie Highld 80 B3
Lundin Links Fife 77 G7
Lunga Argyll 72 C6
Lunna Shetland 96 G6
Lunning Shetland 96 G7
Lunnon Swansea 23 H10
Lunsford's Cross E Sus 12 E6
Lunt Mers 42 B6
Luntley Hereford 25 C10
Luppitt Devon 7 F10
Lupset W Yorks 51 H9
Lupton Cumb 50 A1
Lurgashall W Sus 11 B8
Lusby Lincs 47 F7
Luson Devon 5 G7
Luss Argyll 68 A2
Lussagiven Argyll 72 E5
Lusta Highld 85 C7
Lustleigh Devon 5 C8
Luston Hereford 25 B11
Luthermuir Aberds 83 G8
Luthrie Fife 76 F6
Luton Devon 5 D10
Luton Luton 29 F7
Luton Medway 20 E4
Lutterworth Leics 35 G11
Lutton Devon 5 F6
Lutton Lincs 37 C10
Lutton Northants 37 G7
Lutworthy Devon 7 E6
Luxborough Som 7 C8
Luxulyan Corn 4 F1
Lybster Highld 94 G4
Lydbury North Shrops 33 G9
Lydcott Devon 6 C5
Lydd Kent 13 D9
Lydd on Sea Kent 13 D9
Lydden Kent 21 G9
Lyddington Rutland 36 F4
Lyde Green Hants 18 F4
Lydeard St Lawrence Som 7 C10
Lydford Devon 4 C6
Lydford-on-Fosse Som 8 A4
Lydgate W Yorks 50 G5
Lydham Shrops 33 F9
Lydiard Green Wilts 17 C7
Lydiard Millicent Wilts 17 C7
Lydiate Mers 42 B6
Lydlinch Dorset 8 C6
Lydney Glos 16 A3
Lydstep Pembs 22 G5
Lye W Mid 34 G5
Lye Green Bucks 18 A6
Lye Green E Sus 12 C4
Lyford Oxon 17 B10
Lymbridge Green Kent 13 B10
Lyme Regis Dorset 8 E2
Lyminge Kent 21 G8
Lymington Hants 10 E2
Lyminster W Sus 11 D9
Lymm Warr 43 D9
Lymore Hants 10 E1
Lympne Kent 13 C10
Lympsham Som 15 F9
Lympstone Devon 5 C10
Lynchat Highld 81 C9
Lyndale Ho. Highld 85 C8
Lyndhurst Hants 10 D2
Lyndon Rutland 36 E5
Lyne Sur 19 E7
Lyne Down Hereford 26 E3
Lyne of Gorthleck Highld 81 A7
Lyne of Skene Aberds 83 B9
Lyneal Shrops 33 B10
Lyneham Oxon 27 F9
Lyneham Wilts 17 D7
Lynemore Highld 82 A2
Lynemouth Northumb 63 D8
Lyness Orkney 95 J4
Lyng Norf 39 D6
Lyng Som 8 B2
Lynmouth Devon 7 B6
Lynsted Kent 20 E6
Lynton Devon 6 B6
Lyon's Gate Dorset 8 D5
Lyonshall Hereford 25 C10
Lytchett Matravers Dorset 9 E8
Lytchett Minster Dorset 9 E8
Lyth Highld 94 D4
Lytham Lancs 49 G3
Lytham St Anne's Lancs 49 G3
Lythe N Yorks 59 E9
Lythes Orkney 95 K5

M

Mabe Burnthouse Corn 3 F6
Mabie Dumfries 60 F5
Mablethorpe Lincs 47 D9
Macclesfield Ches E 44 E3
Macclesfield Forest Ches E 44 E3
Macduff Aberds 89 B7
Mace Green Suff 31 D8
Macharioch Argyll 65 H8
Machen Caerph 15 C8
Machrihanish Argyll 65 F7
Machynlleth Powys 32 E3
Machynys Carms 23 G10
Mackerel's Common W Sus 11 B9
Mackworth Derbys 35 B9
Macmerry E Loth 70 C3
Madderty Perth 76 E2
Maddiston Falk 69 C8
Madehurst W Sus 11 C8
Madeley Staffs 34 A3
Madeley Telford 34 E2
Madeley Heath Staffs 43 H10
Madeley Park Staffs 34 A3
Madingley Cambs 29 B10
Madley Hereford 25 E11
Madresfield Worcs 26 D5
Madron Corn 2 F3
Maen-y-groes Ceredig 23 A8
Maenaddwyn Anglesey 40 B6
Maenclochog Pembs 22 D5
Maendy V Glam 14 D6
Maentwrog Gwyn 41 F8
Maer Staffs 34 B3
Maerdy Conwy 32 A6
Maerdy Rhondda 14 B5
Maes-Treylow Powys 25 B9
Maesbrook Shrops 33 C8
Maesbury Shrops 33 C9
Maesbury Marsh Shrops 33 C9
Maesgwyn-Isaf Powys 33 D7
Maesgwynne Carms 23 D7
Maeshafn Denb 42 F5
Maesllyn Ceredig 23 B8
Maesmynis Powys 25 D7
Maesteg Bridgend 14 B4
Maestir Ceredig 23 B10
Maesy cwmmer Caerph 15 B7
Maesybont Carms 23 E10
Maesycrugiau Carms 23 B9
Maesymeillion Ceredig 23 B9
Magdalen Laver Essex 30 H2
Maggieknockater Moray 88 D3
Magham Down E Sus 12 E5
Maghull Mers 43 B6
Magor Mon 15 C10
Magpie Green Suff 39 H6
Maiden Bradley Wilts 16 H5
Maiden Law Durham 58 B2
Maiden Newton Dorset 8 E4
Maiden Wells Pembs 22 G4
Maidencombe Torbay 5 E10
Maidenhall Suff 31 D8
Maidenhead Windsor 18 C5
Maidens S Ayrs 66 F5
Maiden's Green Brack 18 D5
Maidensgrave Suff 31 D9
Maidenwell Corn 4 D2
Maidenwell Lincs 47 E7
Maidford Northants 28 C3
Maids Moreton Bucks 28 E4
Maidstone Kent 20 F4
Maidwell Northants 36 H3
Mail Shetland 96 L6
Main Powys 33 D7
Maindee Newport 15 C9
Mains of Airies Dumfries 54 C2
Mains of Allardice Aberds 83 F10
Mains of Annochie Aberds 89 D9
Mains of Ardestie Angus 77 D8
Mains of Balhall Angus 77 A8
Mains of Ballindarg Angus 77 B7
Mains of Balnakettle Aberds 83 F8
Mains of Birness Aberds 89 E9
Mains of Burgie Moray 87 F13
Mains of Clunas Highld 87 G11
Mains of Crichie Aberds 89 D9
Mains of Dalvey Highld 87 H14
Mains of Dellavaird Aberds 83 E9
Mains of Drum Aberds 83 D10
Mains of Edingight Moray 88 C5
Mains of Fedderate Aberds 89 D8
Mains of Inkhorn Aberds 89 E9
Mains of Mayen Moray 88 D5
Mains of Melgund Angus 77 B8
Mains of Thornton Aberds 83 F8
Mains of Watten Highld 94 E4
Mainsforth Durham 58 C4
Mainsriddle Dumfries 60 H5
Mainstone Shrops 33 G8
Maisemore Glos 26 F5
Malacleit W Isles 84 A2
Malborough Devon 5 H8
Malcoff Derbys 44 D4
Maldon Essex 30 H5
Malham N Yorks 50 C5
Maligar Highld 85 B9
Mallaig Highld 79 B9
Malleny Mills Edin 69 D10
Malling Stirling 75 G8
Malltraeth Anglesey 40 D6
Mallwyd Gwyn 32 D4
Malmesbury Wilts 16 C6
Malmsmead Devon 7 B6
Malpas Ches W 43 H7
Malpas Corn 3 E7
Malpas Newport 15 B9
Malswick Glos 26 F4
Maltby S Yorks 45 C9
Maltby Stockton 58 E5
Maltby le Marsh Lincs 47 D8
Malting Green Essex 30 F6
Maltman's Hill Kent 13 B8
Malton N Yorks 52 B3
Malvern Link Worcs 26 D4
Malvern Wells Worcs 26 D4
Mamble Worcs 26 A3
Man-moel Caerph 15 A7
Manaccan Corn 3 G6
Manafon Powys 33 E7
Manais W Isles 90 J6
Manar Ho. Aberds 83 A9
Manaton Devon 5 C8
Manby Lincs 47 D7
Mancetter Warks 35 F9
Manchester Gtr Man 44 C2
Manchester Airport Gtr Man 44 D2
Mancot Flint 42 F6
Mandally Highld 80 C4
Manea Cambs 37 G10
Manfield N Yorks 58 E3
Mangaster Shetland 96 F5
Mangotsfield S Glos 16 D3
Mangurstadh W Isles 90 D5
Mankinholes W Yorks 50 G5
Manley Ches W 43 E8
Mannal Argyll 78 G2
Mannerston W Loth 69 C9
Manningford Bohune Wilts 17 F8
Manningford Bruce Wilts 17 F8
Manningham W Yorks 51 F7
Mannings Heath W Sus 11 B11
Mannington Dorset 9 D9
Manningtree Essex 31 E7
Mannofield Aberdeen 83 C11
Manor London 19 C11
Manor Estate S Yorks 45 D7
Manorbier Pembs 22 G5
Manordeilo Carms 24 F3
Manorhill Borders 70 G5
Manorowen Pembs 22 C4
Mansel Lacy Hereford 25 D11
Manselfield Swansea 23 H10
Mansell Gamage Hereford 25 D10
Mansergh Cumb 50 A2
Mansfield E Ayrs 67 E9
Mansfield Notts 45 F9
Mansfield Woodhouse Notts 45 F9
Mansriggs Cumb 49 A2
Manston Dorset 9 C7
Manston Kent 21 E10
Manston W Yorks 51 F9
Manswood Dorset 9 D8
Manthorpe Lincs 36 B5
Manthorpe Lincs 37 D6
Manton N Lincs 46 B3
Manton Notts 45 E9
Manton Rutland 36 E4
Manton Wilts 17 E8
Manuden Essex 29 F11
Maperton Som 8 B5
Maple Cross Herts 19 B7
Maplebeck Notts 45 F11
Mapledurham Oxon 18 D3
Mapledurwell Hants 18 F3
Maplehurst W Sus 11 B10
Maplescombe Kent 20 E2
Mapleton Derbys 44 H5
Mapperley Derbys 35 A10
Mapperley Park Nottingham 36 A1
Mapperton Dorset 8 E4
Appleborough Green Warks 27 B7
Mappleton E Yorks 53 E8
Mappowder Dorset 8 D6
Mar Lodge Aberds 82 D2
Maraig W Isles 90 G6
Marazanvose Corn 3 D7
Marazion Corn 2 F4
Marbhig W Isles 91 F9
Marbury Ches E 43 H8
March Cambs 37 F10
March S Lanark 60 B5
Marcham Oxon 17 B11
Marchamley Shrops 34 C1
Marchington Staffs 35 B7
Marchington Woodlands Staffs 35 C7
Marchroes Gwyn 40 H5
Marchwiel Wrex 42 H6
Marchwood Hants 10 C2
Marcross V Glam 14 E5
Marden Hereford 26 D2
Marden Kent 12 B6
Marden T&W 63 F9
Marden Wilts 17 F7
Marden Beech Kent 12 B6
Marden Thorn Kent 13 B6
Mardy Mon 25 G10
Marefield Leics 36 E3
Mareham le Fen Lincs 46 F6
Mareham on the Hill Lincs 46 F6
Marehay Derbys 45 H7
Marehill W Sus 11 C9
Maresfield E Sus 12 D3
Marfleet Hull 53 G7
Marford Wrex 42 G6
Margam Neath 14 C3
Margaret Marsh Dorset 9 C7
Margaret Roding Essex 30 G2
Margaretting Essex 20 A3
Margate Kent 21 D10
Margnaheglish N Ayrs 66 C3
Margrove Park Redcar 59 E7
Marham Norf 38 D3
Marhamchurch Corn 4 A3
Marholm Pboro 37 E7
Mariandyrys Anglesey 41 B8
Marianglas Anglesey 41 B7
Mariansleigh Devon 7 D6
Marionburgh Aberds 83 C9
Marishader Highld 85 B9
Marjoriebanks Dumfries 60 E6
Mark Dumfries 54 D4
Mark S Ayrs 54 B3
Mark Som 15 G9
Mark Causeway Som 15 G9
Mark Cross E Sus 12 C4
Mark Cross E Sus 12 E3
Markbeech Kent 12 B3
Markby Lincs 47 E8
Market Bosworth Leics 35 E10
Market Deeping Lincs 37 E7
Market Drayton Shrops 34 B2
Market Harborough Leics 36 G3
Market Lavington Wilts 17 F7
Market Overton Rutland 36 D4
Market Rasen Lincs 46 D5
Market Stainton Lincs 46 E6
Market Warsop Notts 45 F9
Market Weighton E Yorks 52 E4
Market Weston Suff 38 H5
Markethill Perth 76 D5
Markfield Leics 35 D10
Markham Caerph 15 A7
Markham Moor Notts 45 E11
Markinch Fife 76 G5
Markington N Yorks 51 C8
Marks Tey Essex 30 F6
Marksbury Bath 16 E3
Markyate Herts 29 G7
Marland Gtr Man 44 A2
Marlborough Wilts 17 E8
Marlbrook Hereford 26 C2
Marlbrook Worcs 26 A6
Marlcliff Warks 27 C7
Marldon Devon 5 E9
Marlesford Suff 31 C10
Marley Green Ches E 43 H8
Marley Hill T&W 63 H8
Marley Mount Hants 10 E1
Marlingford Norf 39 E7
Marloes Pembs 22 F2
Marlow Bucks 18 C5
Marlow Hereford 33 H10
Marlow Bottom Bucks 18 C5
Marlpit Hill Kent 19 G11
Marlpool Derbys 45 H8
Marnhull Dorset 9 C6
Marnoch Aberds 88 C5
Marnock N Lanark 68 D6
Marple Gtr Man 44 D3
Marple Bridge Gtr Man 44 D3
Marr S Yorks 45 B9
Marrel Highld 93 H13
Marrick N Yorks 58 G1
Marrister Shetland 96 G7
Marros Carms 23 F7
Marsden T&W 63 G9
Marsden W Yorks 44 A4
Marsett N Yorks 57 H11
Marsh Devon 8 C1
Marsh W Yorks 50 F6
Marsh Baldon Oxon 18 B2
Marsh Gibbon Bucks 28 F3
Marsh Green Devon 7 G9
Marsh Green Kent 12 B3
Marsh Green Staffs 44 G2
Marsh Lane Derbys 45 E8
Marsh Street Som 7 B8
Marshall's Heath Herts 29 G8
Marshalsea Dorset 8 D2
Marshalswick Herts 29 H8
Marsham Norf 39 C7
Marshaw Lancs 50 D1
Marshborough Kent 21 F10
Marshbrook Shrops 33 G10
Marshchapel Lincs 47 C7
Marshfield Newport 15 C8
Marshfield S Glos 16 D4
Marshgate Corn 4 B2
Marshland St James Norf 37 E11
Marshside Mers 49 H3
Marshwood Dorset 8 E2
Marske N Yorks 58 F2
Marske-by-the-Sea Redcar 59 D7
Marston Ches W 43 E9
Marston Hereford 25 C10
Marston Lincs 36 A4
Marston Oxon 28 H2
Marston Staffs 34 C5
Marston Staffs 34 D4
Marston Warks 35 F8
Marston Wilts 16 F6
Marston Doles Warks 27 C11
Marston Green W Mid 35 G7
Marston Magna Som 8 B4
Marston Meysey Wilts 17 B8
Marston Montgomery Derbys 35 B7
Marston Moretaine C Beds 28 D6
Marston on Dove Derbys 35 C8
Marston St Lawrence Northants 28 D2
Marston Stannett Hereford 26 C2
Marston Trussell Northants 36 G2
Marstow Hereford 26 G2
Marsworth Bucks 28 G6
Marten Wilts 17 F9
Marthall Ches E 44 E2
Martham Norf 39 D10
Martin Hants 9 C9
Martin Kent 21 G10
Martin Lincs 46 F6
Martin Lincs 46 G5
Martin Dales Lincs 46 F5
Martin Drove End Hants 9 B9
Martin Hussingtree Worcs 26 B5
Martin Mill Kent 21 G10
Martinhoe Devon 6 B5
Martinhoe Cross Devon 6 B5
Martinscroft Warr 43 D9
Martinstown Dorset 8 F5
Martlesham Suff 31 D9
Martlesham Heath Suff 31 D9
Martletwy Pembs 22 E5
Martley Worcs 26 C4
Martock Som 8 C3
Marton Ches E 44 F2
Marton E Yorks 53 F7
Marton Lincs 46 D2
Marton Mbro 58 E6
Marton N Yorks 51 C10
Marton N Yorks 52 A3
Marton Shrops 33 C10
Marton Shrops 33 E8
Marton Warks 27 B11
Marton-le-Moor N Yorks 51 B9
Martyr Worthy Hants 10 A4
Martyr's Green Sur 19 F7
Marwick Orkney 95 F3
Marwood Devon 6 C4
Mary Tavy Devon 4 D6
Marybank Highld 86 F7
Maryburgh Highld 87 F8
Maryhill Glasgow 68 D4
Marykirk Aberds 83 G8
Marylebone Gtr Man 43 B8
Marypark Moray 88 E1
Maryport Cumb 56 C2
Maryport Dumfries 54 F4
Maryton Angus 77 B9
Marywell Aberds 83 D7
Marywell Aberds 83 D11
Marywell Angus 77 C9
Masham N Yorks 51 A8
Mashbury Essex 30 G3
Masongill N Yorks 50 B2
Masonhill S Ayrs 67 D6
Mastin Moor Derbys 45 E8
Mastrick Aberdeen 83 C10
Matching Essex 30 G2
Matching Green Essex 30 G2
Matching Tye Essex 30 G2
Matfen Northumb 62 F6
Matfield Kent 12 B5
Mathern Mon 15 B11
Mathon Hereford 26 D4
Mathry Pembs 22 C3
Matlaske Norf 39 B7
Matlock Derbys 44 F6
Matlock Bath Derbys 44 G6
Matson Glos 26 G5
Matterdale End Cumb 56 D5
Mattersey Notts 45 D10
Mattersey Thorpe Notts 45 D10
Mattingley Hants 18 F4
Mattishall Norf 39 D6
Mattishall Burgh Norf 39 D6
Mauchline E Ayrs 67 D7
Maud Aberds 89 D9
Maugersbury Glos 27 F9
Maughold IoM 48 C4
Mauld Highld 86 H7
Maulden C Beds 29 E7
Maulds Meaburn Cumb 57 E8
Maunby N Yorks 58 H4
Maund Bryan Hereford 26 C2
Maundown Som 7 D9
Mautby Norf 39 D10
Mavis Enderby Lincs 47 F7
Maw Green Ches E 43 G10
Mawbray Cumb 56 B2
Mawdesley Lancs 43 A7
Mawdlam Bridgend 14 C4
Mawgan Corn 2 G6
Mawla Corn 2 E6
Mawnan Corn 3 G6
Mawnan Smith Corn 3 G6
Mawsley Northants 36 H4
Maxey Pboro 37 E7
Maxstoke Warks 35 G8
Maxton Borders 70 G5
Maxton Kent 21 G10
Maxwellheugh Borders 70 G6
Maxwelltown Dumfries 60 F5
Maxworthy Corn 6 G1
May Bank Staffs 44 H2
Mayals Swansea 14 B2
Maybole S Ayrs 66 F6
Mayfield E Sus 12 D4
Mayfield Midloth 70 D2
Mayfield Staffs 44 H5
Mayfield W Loth 69 D8
Mayford Sur 18 F6
Mayland Essex 20 A6
Maynard's Green E Sus 12 E4
Maypole Mon 25 G11
Maypole Scilly 2 C3
Maypole Green Essex 30 F6
Maypole Green Norf 39 F10
Maypole Green Suff 31 B9
Maywick Shetland 96 L5
Meadle Bucks 28 H5
Meadowtown Shrops 33 E9
Meaford Staffs 34 B4
Meal Bank Cumb 57 G7
Mealabost W Isles 91 D9
Mealabost Bhuirgh W Isles 91 B9
Mealsgate Cumb 56 B4
Meanwood W Yorks 51 F8
Mearbeck N Yorks 50 C4
Meare Som 15 G10
Meare Green Som 8 B2
Mears Ashby Northants 28 B5
Measham Leics 35 D9
Meath Green Sur 12 B1
Meathop Cumb 49 A4
Meaux E Yorks 53 F6
Meavy Devon 4 E6
Medbourne Leics 36 F3
Medburn Northumb 63 F7
Meddon Devon 6 E1
Meden Vale Notts 45 F9
Medlam Lincs 47 G7
Medmenham Bucks 18 C5
Medomsley Durham 58 A2
Medstead Hants 18 H3
Meer End W Mid 27 A9
Meerbrook Staffs 44 F3
Meers Bridge Lincs 47 D8
Meesden Herts 29 E11
Meeth Devon 6 F4
Meggethead Borders 61 A7
Meidrim Carms 23 D7
Meifod Denb 42 G3
Meifod Powys 33 D7
Meigle N Ayrs 73 G10
Meigle Perth 76 C5
Meikle Earnock S Lanark 68 E6
Meikle Ferry Highld 87 C10
Meikle Forter Angus 76 A4
Meikle Gluich Highld 87 C9
Meikle Pinkerton E Loth 70 C6
Meikle Strath Aberds 83 F8
Meikle Tarty Aberds 89 F9
Meikle Wartle Aberds 89 E7
Meikleour Perth 76 D4
Meinciau Carms 23 E9
Meir Stoke 34 A5
Meir Heath Staffs 34 A5
Melbourn Cambs 29 D10
Melbourne Derbys 35 C9
Melbourne E Yorks 52 E3
Melbourne S Lanark 69 F9
Melbury Abbas Dorset 9 B7
Melbury Bubb Dorset 8 D4
Melbury Osmond Dorset 8 D4
Melbury Sampford Dorset 8 D4
Melby Shetland 96 H3
Melchbourne Bedford 29 B7
Melcombe Bingham Dorset 9 D6
Melcombe Regis Dorset 8 F5
Meldon Devon 6 G4
Meldon Northumb 63 E7
Meldreth Cambs 29 D10
Meldrum Ho. Aberds 89 F8
Melfort Argyll 73 B7
Melgarve Highld 81 D6
Meliden Denb 42 D3
Melin-y-coed Conwy 41 D10
Melin-y-ddôl Powys 33 E6
Melin-y-grug Powys 33 E6
Melin-y-Wig Denb 42 H3
Melinbyrhedyn Powys 32 F4
Melincourt Neath 14 A4
Melkinthorpe Cumb 57 D7
Melkridge Northumb 62 G3
Melksham Wilts 16 E6
Melldalloch Argyll 73 F8
Melling Lancs 50 B1
Melling Mers 43 B6
Melling Mount Mers 43 B7
Mellis Suff 31 A8
Mellon Charles Highld 91 H13
Mellon Udrigle Highld 91 H13
Mellor Gtr Man 44 D3
Mellor Lancs 50 F2
Mellor Brook Lancs 50 F2
Mells Som 16 G4
Melmerby Cumb 57 C8
Melmerby N Yorks 51 B9
Melmerby N Yorks 58 H1
Melplash Dorset 8 E3
Melrose Borders 70 G4
Melsetter Orkney 95 K3
Melsonby N Yorks 58 F2
Meltham W Yorks 44 A5
Melton Suff 31 C9
Melton Constable Norf 38 B6
Melton Mowbray Leics 36 D3
Melton Ross N Lincs 46 A4
Meltonby E Yorks 52 D3
Melvaig Highld 91 J12
Melverley Shrops 33 D9
Melverley Green Shrops 33 D9
Melvich Highld 93 C11
Membury Devon 8 D1
Memsie Aberds 89 B9
Memus Angus 77 B7
Menabilly Corn 4 F1
Menai Bridge = Porthaethwy Anglesey 41 C7
Mendham Suff 39 G8
Mendlesham Suff 31 B8
Mendlesham Green Suff 31 B7
Menheniot Corn 4 E3
Mennock Dumfries 60 C4
Menston W Yorks 51 E7
Menstrie Clack 75 H11
Menthorpe N Yorks 52 F2
Mentmore Bucks 28 G6
Meoble Highld 79 C10
Meole Brace Shrops 33 D10
Meols Mers 42 C5
Meonstoke Hants 10 C5
Meopham Kent 20 E3
Meopham Station Kent 20 E3
Mepal Cambs 37 G10
Meppershall C Beds 29 E8
Merbach Hereford 25 D10
Mere Ches E 43 D10
Mere Wilts 9 A7
Mere Brow Lancs 49 H4
Mere Grn. W Mid 35 F7
Mereclough Lancs 50 F4
Mereside Blackpool 49 F3
Mereworth Kent 20 F3
Mergie Aberds 83 E9
Meriden W Mid 35 G8
Merkadale Highld 85 E8
Merkland Dumfries 60 F3
Merkland S Ayrs 66 G5
Merkland Lodge Highld 92 G7
Merley Poole 9 E9
Merlin's Bridge Pembs 22 E4
Merrington Shrops 33 C10
Merrion Pembs 22 G4
Merriott Som 8 C3
Merrivale Devon 4 D6
Merrow Sur 19 F7
Merrymeet Corn 4 E3
Mersham Kent 13 C9
Merstham Sur 19 F9
Merston W Sus 11 D7
Merstone IoW 10 F4
Merther Corn 3 E7
Merthyr Carms 23 D8
Merthyr Cynog Powys 24 E6
Merthyr-Dyfan V Glam 15 E7
Merthyr Mawr Bridgend 14 D4
Merthyr Tudful = Merthyr Tydfil M Tydf 25 H7
Merthyr Tydfil = Merthyr Tudful M Tydf 25 H7
Merthyr Vale M Tydf 14 B6
Merton Devon 6 E4
Merton London 19 D9
Merton Norf 38 F5
Merton Oxon 28 G2
Mervinslaw Borders 62 B2
Meshaw Devon 7 E6
Messing Essex 30 G5
Messingham N Lincs 46 B2
Metfield Suff 39 G8
Metheringham Lincs 46 F4
Methil Fife 76 H6
Methlem Gwyn 40 G3
Methley W Yorks 51 G9
Methlick Aberds 89 E8
Methven Perth 76 E3
Methwold Norf 38 F3
Methwold Hythe Norf 38 F3
Mettingham Suff 39 G9
Mevagissey Corn 3 E9
Mewith Head N Yorks 50 C3
Mexborough S Yorks 45 B8
Mey Highld 94 C4
Meysey Hampton Glos 17 B8
Miabhag W Isles 90 G5
Miabhag W Isles 90 H6
Miabhig W Isles 90 D5
Michaelchurch Hereford 26 F2
Michaelchurch Escley Hereford 25 E10
Michaelchurch on Arrow Powys 25 C9
Michaelston-le-Pit V Glam 15 D7
Michaelston-y-Fedw Newport 15 C8
Michaelstow Corn 4 D1
Michealston-super-Ely Cardiff 15 D7
Micheldever Hants 18 H2
Michelmersh Hants 10 B2
Mickfield Suff 31 B8
Mickle Trafford Ches W 43 F7
Micklebring S Yorks 45 C9
Mickleby N Yorks 59 E9
Mickleham Sur 19 F8
Mickleover Derby 35 B9
Micklethwaite W Yorks 51 E7
Mickleton Durham 57 D11
Mickleton Glos 27 D8
Mickletown W Yorks 51 G9
Mickley N Yorks 51 B8
Mickley Square Northumb 62 G6
Mid Ardlaw Aberds 89 B9
Mid Auchinlech Invclyd 68 C2
Mid Beltie Aberds 83 C8
Mid Calder W Loth 69 D9
Mid Cloch Forbie Aberds 89 C7
Mid Clyth Highld 94 G4
Mid Lavant W Sus 11 D7
Mid Main Highld 86 H7
Mid Urchany Highld 87 G11
Mid Walls Shetland 96 H4
Mid Yell Shetland 96 D7
Midbea Orkney 95 D5
Middle Assendon Oxon 18 C4
Middle Aston Oxon 27 F11
Middle Barton Oxon 27 F11
Middle Cairncake Aberds 89 D8
Middle Claydon Bucks 28 F4
Middle Drums Angus 77 B8
Middle Handley Derbys 45 E8
Middle Littleton Worcs 27 D7
Middle Maes-coed Hereford 25 E10
Middle Mill Pembs 22 D3
Middle Rasen Lincs 46 D4
Middle Rigg Perth 76 G3
Middle Tysoe Warks 27 D10
Middle Wallop Hants 17 H9
Middle Winterslow Wilts 9 A11
Middle Woodford Wilts 17 H8
Middlebie Dumfries 61 F8
Middleforth Green Lancs 49 G5
Middleham N Yorks 58 H2
Middlehope Shrops 33 G10
Middlemarsh Dorset 8 D5
Middlemuir Aberds 89 F9
Middlesbrough Mbro 58 D5
Middleshaw Cumb 57 H7
Middleshaw Dumfries 61 F7
Middlesmoor N Yorks 51 B6
Middlestone Durham 58 C3
Middlestone Moor Durham 58 C3
Middlestown W Yorks 51 H8
Middlethird Borders 70 F5
Middleton Aberds 83 B10
Middleton Argyll 78 G2
Middleton Cumb 57 H8
Middleton Derbys 44 F5
Middleton Derbys 44 G6
Middleton Essex 30 E5
Middleton Gtr Man 44 B2
Middleton Hants 17 G11
Middleton Hereford 26 B2
Middleton Lancs 49 D4
Middleton Midloth 70 E2
Middleton N Yorks 51 E7
Middleton N Yorks 59 H8
Middleton Norf 38 D2
Middleton Northants 36 G4
Middleton Northumb 62 E6
Middleton Northumb 71 G10
Middleton Perth 76 C4
Middleton Perth 76 G4
Middleton Shrops 33 C9
Middleton Shrops 33 F8
Middleton Shrops 33 H11
Middleton Suff 31 B11
Middleton Swansea 23 H9
Middleton W Yorks 51 G8
Middleton Warks 35 F7
Middleton Cheney Northants 27 D11
Middleton Green Staffs 34 B5
Middleton Hall Northumb 71 H8
Middleton-in-Teesdale Durham 57 D11
Middleton Moor Suff 31 B11
Middleton-on-Leven N Yorks 58 F5
Middleton-on-Sea W Sus 11 D8
Middleton on the Hill Hereford 26 B2
Middleton-on-the-Wolds E Yorks 52 E5
Middleton One Row Darl 58 E4
Middleton Priors Shrops 34 F2
Middleton Quernham N Yorks 51 B9
Middleton St George Darl 58 E4
Middleton Scriven Shrops 34 G2
Middleton Stoney Oxon 28 F2
Middleton Tyas N Yorks 58 F3
Middletown Cumb 56 F1
Middletown Powys 33 D9
Middlewich Ches E 43 F9
Middlewood Green Suff 31 B7
Middlezoy Som 8 A2
Middridge Durham 58 D3
Midfield Highld 93 C8
Midge Hall Lancs 49 G5
Midgeholme Cumb 62 H2
Midgham W Berks 18 E2
Midgley W Yorks 44 A6
Midgley W Yorks 50 G6
Midhopestones S Yorks 44 C6
Midhurst W Sus 11 B7
Midlem Borders 70 H4
Midmar Aberds 83 C8
Midsomer Norton Bath 16 F3
Midton Invclyd 73 F11
Midtown Highld 91 J13
Midtown Highld 93 C8
Midtown of Buchromb Moray 88 D3
Midville Lincs 47 G7
Midway Ches E 44 D3
Migdale Highld 87 B9
Migvie Aberds 82 C6
Milarrochy Stirling 68 A3
Milborne Port Som 8 C5
Milborne St Andrew Dorset 9 E7
Milborne Wick Som 8 B5
Milbourne Northumb 63 F7
Milburn Cumb 57 D8
Milbury Heath S Glos 16 B3
Milcombe Oxon 27 E11
Milden Suff 30 D6
Mildenhall Suff 30 A4
Mildenhall Wilts 17 E9
Mile Cross Norf 39 D8
Mile Elm Wilts 16 E6
Mile End Essex 30 F6
Mile End Glos 26 G2
Mile Oak Brighton 11 D11
Milebrook Powys 25 A10
Milebush Kent 20 G4
Mileham Norf 38 D5
Milesmark Fife 69 B9
Milfield Northumb 71 G8
Milford Derbys 45 H7
Milford Devon 6 D1
Milford Powys 33 F6
Milford Staffs 34 C5
Milford Sur 18 G6
Milford Wilts 9 B10
Milford Haven = Aberdaugleddau Pembs 22 F4
Milford on Sea Hants 10 E1
Milkwall Glos 26 H2
Milkwell Wilts 9 B8
Mill Bank W Yorks 50 G6
Mill Common Suff 39 G10
Mill End Bucks 18 C4
Mill End Herts 29 E10
Mill Green Essex 20 A3
Mill Green Norf 39 G7
Mill Green Suff 30 D6
Mill Hill London 19 B9
Mill Lane Hants 18 F4
Mill of Kingoodie Aberds 89 F8
Mill of Muiresk Aberds 89 D6
Mill of Sterin Aberds 82 D5
Mill of Uras Aberds 83 E10
Mill Place N Lincs 46 B3
Mill Side Cumb 49 A4
Mill Street Norf 39 D6
Milland W Sus 11 B7
Millarston Renfs 68 D3
Millbank Aberds 89 D11
Millbank Highld 94 D3
Millbeck Cumb 56 D4
Millbounds Orkney 95 E6
Millbreck Aberds 89 D10
Millbridge Sur 18 G5
Millbrook C Beds 29 E7
Millbrook Corn 4 F5
Millbrook Soton 10 C2
Millburn S Ayrs 67 D7
Millcombe Devon 5 G9
Millcorner E Sus 13 D7
Milldale Staffs 44 G5
Millden Lodge Angus 83 F7
Milldens Angus 77 B8
Millerhill Midloth 70 D2
Miller's Dale Derbys 44 E5
Miller's Green Derbys 44 G6
Millgreen Shrops 34 C2
Millhalf Hereford 25 D9
Millhayes Devon 7 F11
Millhead Lancs 49 B4
Millheugh S Lanark 68 E6
Millholme Cumb 57 G7
Millhouse Argyll 73 F8
Millhouse Cumb 56 C5
Millhouse Green S Yorks 44 B6
Millhousebridge Dumfries 61 E7
Millhouses S Yorks 45 D7
Millikenpark Renfs 68 D3
Millin Cross Pembs 22 E4
Millington E Yorks 52 D4
Millmeece Staffs 34 B4
Millom Cumb 49 A1
Millook Corn 4 B2
Millpool Corn 4 D2
Millport N Ayrs 66 A4
Millquarter Dumfries 55 A9
Millthorpe Lincs 37 B7
Millthrop Cumb 57 G8
Milltimber Aberdeen 83 C10
Milltown Corn 4 F2
Milltown Derbys 45 F7
Milltown Devon 6 C4
Milltown Dumfries 61 F9
Milltown of Aberdalgie Perth 76 E3
Milltown of Auchindoun Moray 88 D3
Milltown of Craigston Aberds 89 C7
Milltown of Edinvillie Moray 88 D2
Milltown of Kildrummy Aberds 82 B6
Milltown of Rothiemay Moray 88 D5
Milltown of Towie Aberds 82 B6
Milnathort Perth 76 G4
Milner's Heath Ches W 43 F7
Milngavie E Dunb 68 C4
Milnrow Gtr Man 44 A3
Milnshaw Lancs 50 G3
Milnthorpe Cumb 49 A4
Milo Carms 23 E10
Milson Shrops 26 A3
Milstead Kent 20 F6
Milston Wilts 17 G8
Milton Angus 76 C6
Milton Cambs 29 B11
Milton Cumb 61 G11
Milton Derbys 35 C9
Milton Dumfries 54 D5
Milton Dumfries 60 E4
Milton Dumfries 60 F4
Milton Highld 86 F6
Milton Highld 86 H7
Milton Highld 87 D10
Milton Highld 87 G8
Milton Highld 94 E5
Milton Moray 88 B5
Milton N Som 15 E9
Milton Notts 45 E11
Milton Oxon 17 B11
Milton Oxon 27 E11
Milton Pembs 22 F5
Milton Perth 76 F2
Milton Ptsmth 10 E5
Milton Stirling 75 G8
Milton Stoke 44 G3
Milton W Dunb 68 C3
Milton Abbas Dorset 9 D7
Milton Abbot Devon 4 D5
Milton Bridge Midloth 69 D11
Milton Bryan C Beds 28 E6
Milton Clevedon Som 16 H3
Milton Coldwells Aberds 89 E9
Milton Combe Devon 4 E5
Milton Damerel Devon 6 E2
Milton End Glos 17 A8
Milton Ernest Bedford 29 C7
Milton Green Ches W 43 G7
Milton Hill Oxon 17 B11
Milton Keynes M Keynes 28 E5
Milton Keynes Village M Keynes 28 E5
Milton Lilbourne Wilts 17 E8
Milton Malsor Northants 28 C4
Milton Morenish Perth 75 D9
Milton of Auchinhove Aberds 83 C7
Milton of Balgonie Fife 76 G6
Milton of Buchanan Stirling 68 A3
Milton of Campfield Aberds 83 C8
Milton of Campsie E Dunb 68 C5
Milton of Corsindae Aberds 83 C8
Milton of Cushnie Aberds 83 B7
Milton of Dalcapon Perth 76 B2
Milton of Edradour Perth 76 B2
Milton of Gollanfield Highld 87 F10
Milton of Lesmore Aberds 82 A6
Milton of Logie Aberds 82 C6
Milton of Murtle Aberdeen 83 C10
Milton of Noth Aberds 83 A7
Milton of Tullich Aberds 82 D5
Milton on Stour Dorset 9 B6
Milton Regis Kent 20 E6
Milton under Wychwood Oxon 27 G9
Miltonduff Moray 88 B1
Miltonhill Moray 87 E13
Miltonise Dumfries 54 B4
Milverton Som 7 D10
Milverton Warks 27 B10
Milwich Staffs 34 B5
Minard Argyll 73 D8
Minchinhampton Glos 16 A5
Mindrum Northumb 71 G7
Minehead Som 7 B8
Minera Wrex 42 G5
Minety Wilts 17 B7
Minffordd Gwyn 32 D3
Minffordd Gwyn 41 C7
Minffordd Gwyn 41 G7
Miningsby Lincs 47 F7
Minions Corn 4 D3
Minishant S Ayrs 66 E6
Minllyn Gwyn 32 D4
Minnes Aberds 89 F9
Minngearraidh W Isles 84 F2
Minnigaff Dumfries 55 C7
Minnonie Aberds 89 B7
Minskip N Yorks 51 C9
Minstead Hants 10 C1
Minsted W Sus 11 B7
Minster Kent 20 D6
Minster Kent 21 E10
Minster Lovell Oxon 27 G10
Minsterley Shrops 33 E9
Minsterworth Glos 26 G4
Minterne Magna Dorset 8 D5
Minting Lincs 46 E5
Mintlaw Aberds 89 D10
Minto Borders 61 A11
Minton Shrops 33 F10
Minwear Pembs 22 E5
Minworth W Mid 35 F7
Mirbister Orkney 95 F4
Mirehouse Cumb 56 E1
Mireland Highld 94 D5
Mirfield W Yorks 51 H8
Miserden Glos 26 H6
Miskin Rhondda 14 C6
Misson Notts 45 C10
Misterton Leics 36 G1
Misterton Notts 45 C11
Misterton Som 8 D3
Mistley Essex 31 E8
Mitcham London 19 E9
Mitchel Troy Mon 25 G11
Mitcheldean Glos 26 G3
Mitchell Corn 3 D7
Mitcheltroy Common Mon 25 H11
Mitford Northumb 63 E7
Mithian Corn 2 D6
Mitton Staffs 34 D4
Mixbury Oxon 28 E3
Moat Cumb 61 F10
Moats Tye Suff 31 C7
Mobberley Ches E 43 E10
Mobberley Staffs 34 A6
Moccas Hereford 25 D10
Mochdre Conwy 41 C10
Mochdre Powys 33 G6
Mochrum Dumfries 54 E6
Mockbeggar Hants 9 D10
Mockerkin Cumb 56 D2
Modbury Devon 5 F7
Moddershall Staffs 34 B5
Moelfre Anglesey 41 B7
Moelfre Powys 33 C7
Moffat Dumfries 60 C6
Moggerhanger C Beds 29 D8
Moira Leics 35 D9
Mol-chlach Highld 85 G9
Molash Kent 21 F7
Mold = Yr Wyddgrug Flint 42 F5
Moldgreen W Yorks 51 H7

Molehill Green Essex 30 F2
Molescroft E Yorks 52 E6
Molesden Northumb 63 E7
Molesworth Cambs 37 H6
Moll Highld 85 E10
Molland Devon 7 D7
Mollington Ches W 43 E6
Mollington Oxon 27 D11
Mollinsburn N Lanark 68 C6
Monachty Ceredig 24 B2
Monachylemore Stirling 75 F7
Monar Lodge Highld 86 G5
Monaughty Powys 25 B9
Monboddo House Aberds 83 F9
Mondynes Aberds 83 F9
Monevechadan Argyll 74 G4
Monewden Suff 31 C9
Moneydie Perth 76 E3
Moniaive Dumfries 60 D3
Monifieth Angus 77 D7
Monikie Angus 77 D7
Monimail Fife 76 F5
Monington Pembs 22 B6
Monk Bretton S Yorks 45 B7
Monk Fryston N Yorks 51 G11
Monk Sherborne Hants 18 F3
Monk Soham Suff 31 B9
Monk Street Essex 30 F3
Monken Hadley London 19 B9
Monkhopton Shrops 34 F2
Monkland Hereford 25 C11
Monkleigh Devon 6 D3
Monknash V Glam 14 D5
Monkokehampton Devon 6 F4
Monks Eleigh Suff 30 D6
Monk's Gate W Sus 11 B11
Monks Heath Ches E 44 E2
Monks Kirby Warks 35 G10
Monks Risborough Bucks 18 A5
Monkseaton T&W 63 F9
Monkshill Aberds 89 D7
Monksilver Som 7 C9
Monkspath W Mid 35 H7
Monkswood Mon 15 A9
Monkton Devon 7 F10
Monkton Kent 21 E9
Monkton Pembs 22 F4
Monkton S Ayrs 67 D6
Monkton Combe Bath 16 E4
Monkton Deverill Wilts 16 H5
Monkton Farleigh Wilts 16 E5
Monkton Heathfield Som 8 B1
Monkton Up Wimborne Dorset 9 C9
Monkwearmouth T&W 63 H9
Monkwood Hants 10 A5
Monmouth = Trefynwy Mon 26 G2
Monmouth Cap Mon 25 F10
Monnington on Wye Hereford 25 D10
Monreith Dumfries 54 E6
Monreith Mains Dumfries 54 E6
Mont Saint Guern 11
Montacute Som 8 C3
Montcoffer Ho. Aberds 89 B6
Montford Argyll 73 G10
Montford Shrops 33 D10
Montford Bridge Shrops 33 D10
Montgarrie Aberds 83 B7
Montgomery = Trefaldwyn Powys 33 F8
Montrave Fife 76 G6
Montrose Angus 77 B10
Montsale Essex 21 B7
Monxton Hants 17 G10
Monyash Derbys 44 F5
Monymusk Aberds 83 B8
Monzie Perth 75 E11
Monzie Castle Perth 75 E11
Moodiesburn N Lanark 68 C5
Moonzie Fife 76 F6
Moor Allerton W Yorks 51 F8
Moor Crichel Dorset 9 D8
Moor End E Yorks 52 F4
Moor End York 52 D2
Moor Monkton N Yorks 51 D11
Moor of Granary Moray 87 F13
Moor of Ravenstone Dumfries 54 E6
Moor Row Cumb 56 E2
Moor Street Kent 20 E5
Moorby Lincs 46 F6
Moordown Bmouth 9 E9
Moore Halton 43 D8
Moorend Glos 16 A4
Moorends S Yorks 52 H2
Moorgate S Yorks 45 C8
Moorgreen Notts 45 H8
Moorhall Derbys 45 E7
Moorhampton Hereford 25 D10
Moorhead W Yorks 51 F7
Moorhouse Cumb 61 H9
Moorhouse Notts 45 F11
Moorlinch Som 15 H9
Moorsholm Redcar 59 E7
Moorside Gtr Man 44 B3
Moorthorpe W Yorks 45 A8
Moortown Hants 9 D10
Moortown IoW 10 F3
Moortown Lincs 46 C4
Morangie Highld 87 C10
Morar Highld 79 B9
Morborne Cambs 37 F7
Morchard Bishop Devon 7 F6
Morcombelake Dorset 8 E3
Morcott Rutland 36 E5
Morda Shrops 33 C8
Morden Dorset 9 E8
Morden London 19 E9
Mordiford Hereford 26 E2
Mordon Durham 58 D4
More Shrops 33 F9
Morebath Devon 7 D8
Morebattle Borders 62 A3
Morecambe Lancs 49 C4
Morefield Highld 86 B4
Moreleigh Devon 5 F8
Morenish Perth 75 D8
Moresby Cumb 56 D1
Moresby Parks Cumb 56 E1
Morestead Hants 10 B4
Moreton Dorset 9 F7
Moreton Essex 30 H2
Moreton Mers 42 C5
Moreton Oxon 18 A3
Moreton Staffs 34 D3
Moreton Corbet Shrops 34 C1
Moreton-in-Marsh Glos 27 E9
Moreton Jeffries Hereford 26 D3
Moreton Morrell Warks 27 C10
Moreton on Lugg Hereford 26 D2
Moreton Pinkney Northants 28 D2
Moreton Say Shrops 34 B2
Moreton Valence Glos 26 H4
Moretonhampstead Devon 5 C8
Morfa Carms 23 E10
Morfa Carms 23 G10
Morfa Bach Carms 23 E8
Morfa Bychan Gwyn 41 G7
Morfa Dinlle Gwyn 40 E6
Morfa Glas Neath 24 H5
Morfa Nefyn Gwyn 40 F4
Morfydd Denb 42 H4
Morgan's Vale Wilts 9 B10
Moriah Ceredig 32 H2
Morland Cumb 57 D7
Morley Derbys 35 A9
Morley Durham 58 D2
Morley W Yorks 51 G8
Morley Green Ches E 44 D2
Morley St Botolph Norf 39 F6
Morningside Edin 69 C11
Morningside N Lanark 69 E7
Morningthorpe Norf 39 F8
Morpeth Northumb 63 E8
Morphie Aberds 77 A10
Morrey Staffs 35 D7
Morris Green Essex 30 E4
Morriston Swansea 14 B2
Morston Norf 38 A6
Mortehoe Devon 6 B3
Mortimer W Berks 18 E3
Mortimer West End Hants 18 E3
Mortimer's Cross Hereford 25 B11
Mortlake London 19 D9
Morton Cumb 56 A5
Morton Derbys 45 F8
Morton Lincs 37 C6
Morton Lincs 46 C2
Morton Lincs 46 F2
Morton Norf 39 D7
Morton Notts 45 G11
Morton S Glos 16 B3
Morton Shrops 33 C8
Morton Bagot Warks 27 B8
Morton-on-Swale N Yorks 58 G4
Morvah Corn 2 F3
Morval Corn 4 F3
Morvich Highld 80 A1
Morvich Highld 93 J10
Morville Shrops 34 F2
Morville Heath Shrops 34 F2
Morwenstow Corn 6 E1
Mosborough S Yorks 45 D8
Moscow E Ayrs 67 B7
Mosedale Cumb 56 C5
Moseley W Mid 34 F5
Moseley W Mid 35 G6
Moseley Worcs 26 C5
Moss Argyll 78 G2
Moss Highld 79 E9
Moss S Yorks 45 A9
Moss Wrex 42 G6
Moss Bank Mers 43 C8
Moss Edge Lancs 49 E4
Moss End Brack 18 D5
Moss of Barmuckity Moray 88 B2
Moss Pit Staffs 34 C5
Moss-side Highld 87 F11
Moss Side Lancs 49 F3
Mossat Aberds 82 B6
Mossbank Shetland 96 F6
Mossbay Cumb 56 D1
Mossblown S Ayrs 67 D7
Mossbrow Gtr Man 43 D10
Mossburnford Borders 62 B2
Mossdale Dumfries 55 B9
Mossend N Lanark 68 D6
Mosser Cumb 56 D3
Mossfield Highld 87 D9
Mossgiel E Ayrs 67 D7
Mosside Angus 77 B7
Mossley Ches E 44 F2
Mossley Gtr Man 44 B3
Mossley Hill Mers 43 D6
Mosstodloch Moray 88 C3
Mosston Angus 77 C8
Mossy Lea Lancs 43 A8
Mosterton Dorset 8 D3
Moston Gtr Man 44 B2
Moston Shrops 34 C1
Moston Green Ches E 43 F10
Mostyn Flint 42 D4
Mostyn Quay Flint 42 D4
Motcombe Dorset 9 B7
Mothecombe Devon 5 G7
Motherby Cumb 56 D6
Motherwell N Lanark 68 E6
Mottingham London 19 D11
Mottisfont Hants 10 B2
Mottistone IoW 10 F3
Mottram in Longdendale Gtr Man 44 C3
Mottram St Andrew Ches E 44 E2
Mouilpied Guern 11
Mouldsworth Ches W 43 E8
Moulin Perth 76 B2
Moulsecoomb Brighton 12 F2
Moulsford Oxon 18 C2
Moulsoe M Keynes 28 D6
Moulton Ches W 43 F9
Moulton Lincs 37 C9
Moulton N Yorks 58 F3
Moulton Northants 28 B4
Moulton Suff 30 B3
Moulton V Glam 14 D6
Moulton Chapel Lincs 37 D8
Moulton Eaugate Lincs 37 D9
Moulton St Mary Norf 39 E9
Moulton Seas End Lincs 37 C9
Mounie Castle Aberds 83 A9
Mount Corn 3 D6
Mount Corn 4 E2
Mount Highld 87 G12
Mount Bures Essex 30 E6
Mount Canisp Highld 87 D10
Mount Hawke Corn 2 E6
Mount Pleasant Ches E 44 G2
Mount Pleasant Derbys 35 D8
Mount Pleasant Derbys 45 H7
Mount Pleasant Flint 42 E5
Mount Pleasant Hants 10 E1
Mount Pleasant W Yorks 51 G8
Mount Sorrel Wilts 9 B9
Mount Tabor W Yorks 51 G6
Mountain W Yorks 51 F6
Mountain Ash = Aberpennar Rhondda 14 B6
Mountain Cross Borders 69 F10
Mountain Water Pembs 22 D4
Mountbenger Borders 70 H2
Mountfield E Sus 12 D6
Mountgerald Highld 87 E8
Mountjoy Corn 3 C7
Mountnessing Essex 20 B3
Mounton Mon 15 B11
Mountsorrel Leics 36 D1
Mousehole Corn 2 G3
Mousen Northumb 71 G10
Mouswald Dumfries 60 F6
Mow Cop Ches E 44 G2
Mowhaugh Borders 62 A4
Mowsley Leics 36 G2
Moxley W Mid 34 F5
Moy Highld 80 E6
Moy Highld 87 H10
Moy Hall Highld 87 H10
Moy Ho. Moray 87 E13
Moy Lodge Highld 80 E6
Moyles Court Hants 9 D10
Moylgrove Pembs 22 B6
Muasdale Argyll 65 D7
Much Birch Hereford 26 E2
Much Cowarne Hereford 26 D3
Much Dewchurch Hereford 25 E11
Much Hadham Herts 29 G11
Much Hoole Lancs 49 G4
Much Marcle Hereford 26 E3
Much Wenlock Shrops 34 E2
Muchalls Aberds 83 D11
Muchelney Som 8 B3
Muchlarnick Corn 4 F3
Muchrachd Highld 86 H5
Muckernich Highld 87 F8
Mucking Thurrock 20 C3
Muckleford Dorset 8 E5
Mucklestone Staffs 34 B3
Muckleton Shrops 34 C1
Muckletown Aberds 83 A7
Muckley Corner Staffs 35 E6
Muckton Lincs 47 D7
Mudale Highld 93 F8
Muddiford Devon 6 C4
Mudeford Dorset 9 E10
Mudford Som 8 C4
Mudgley Som 15 G10
Mugdock Stirling 68 C4
Mugeary Highld 85 E9
Mugginton Derbys 35 A8
Muggleswick Durham 58 B1
Muie Highld 93 J9
Muir Aberds 82 E2
Muir of Fairburn Highld 86 F7
Muir of Fowlis Aberds 83 B7
Muir of Ord Highld 87 F8
Muir of Pert Angus 77 D7
Muirden Aberds 89 C7
Muirdrum Angus 77 D8
Muirhead Angus 76 D6
Muirhead Fife 76 G5
Muirhead N Lanark 68 D5
Muirhead S Ayrs 66 C6
Muirhouselaw Borders 70 H5
Muirhouses Falk 69 B9
Muirkirk E Ayrs 68 H5
Muirmill Stirling 68 B6
Muirshearlich Highld 80 E3
Muirskie Aberds 83 D10
Muirtack Aberds 89 E9
Muirton Highld 87 E10
Muirton Perth 76 E4
Muirton Perth 76 F2
Muirton Mains Highld 86 F7
Muirton of Ardblair Perth 76 C4
Muirton of Ballochy Angus 77 A9
Muiryfold Aberds 89 C7
Muker N Yorks 57 G11
Mulbarton Norf 39 E7
Mulben Moray 88 C3
Mulindry Argyll 64 C4
Mullardoch House Highld 86 H5
Mullion Corn 2 H5
Mullion Cove Corn 2 H5
Mumby Lincs 47 E9
Munderfield Row Hereford 26 C3
Munderfield Stocks Hereford 26 C3
Mundesley Norf 39 B9
Mundford Norf 38 F4
Mundham Norf 39 F9
Mundon Essex 20 A5
Mundurno Aberdeen 83 B11
Munerigie Highld 80 C4
Muness Shetland 96 C8
Mungasdale Highld 86 B2
Mungrisdale Cumb 56 C5
Munlochy Highld 87 F9
Munsley Hereford 26 D3
Munslow Shrops 33 G11
Murchington Devon 5 C7
Murcott Oxon 28 G2
Murkle Highld 94 D3
Murlaggan Highld 80 D2
Murlaggan Highld 80 E5
Murra Orkney 95 H3
Murrayfield Edin 69 C11
Murrow Cambs 37 E9
Mursley Bucks 28 F5
Murthill Angus 77 B7
Murthly Perth 76 D3
Murton Cumb 57 D9
Murton Durham 58 B4
Murton Northumb 71 F8
Murton York 52 D2
Musbury Devon 8 E1
Muscoates N Yorks 52 A2
Musdale Argyll 74 E2
Musselburgh E Loth 70 C2
Muston Leics 36 B4
Muston N Yorks 53 B6
Mustow Green Worcs 26 A5
Mutehill Dumfries 55 E9
Mutford Suff 39 G10
Muthill Perth 75 F11
Mutterton Devon 7 F9
Muxton Telford 34 D3
Mybster Highld 94 E3
Myddfai Carms 24 F4
Myddle Shrops 33 C10
Mydroilyn Ceredig 23 A9
Myerscough Lancs 49 F4
Mylor Bridge Corn 3 F7
Mynachlog-ddu Pembs 22 C6
Myndtown Shrops 33 G9
Mynydd Bach Ceredig 32 H3
Mynydd-bach Mon 15 B10
Mynydd Bodafon Anglesey 40 B6
Mynydd-isa Flint 42 F5
Mynyddygarreg Carms 23 F9
Mynytho Gwyn 40 G5
Myrebird Aberds 83 D9
Myrelandhorn Highld 94 E4
Myreside Perth 76 E5
Myrtle Hill Carms 24 E4
Mytchett Sur 18 F5
Mytholm W Yorks 50 G5
Mytholmroyd W Yorks 50 G6
Myton-on-Swale N Yorks 51 C10
Mytton Shrops 33 D10

N

Na Gearrannan W Isles 90 C6
Naast Highld 91 J13
Naburn York 52 E1
Nackington Kent 21 F8
Nacton Suff 31 D9
Nafferton E Yorks 53 D6
Nailbridge Glos 26 G3
Nailsbourne Som 7 D11
Nailsea N Som 15 D10
Nailstone Leics 35 E10
Nailsworth Glos 16 B5
Nairn Highld 87 F11
Nalderswood Sur 19 G9
Nancegollan Corn 2 F5
Nancledra Corn 2 F3
Nanhoron Gwyn 40 G4
Nannau Gwyn 32 C3
Nannerch Flint 42 F4
Nanpantan Leics 35 D11
Nanpean Corn 3 D8
Nanstallon Corn 3 C9
Nant-ddu Powys 25 G7
Nant-glas Powys 24 B6
Nant Peris Gwyn 41 E8
Nant Uchaf Denb 42 G3
Nant-y-Bai Carms 24 D4
Nant-y-cafn Neath 24 H5
Nant-y-derry Mon 25 H10
Nant-y-ffin Carms 23 C10
Nant-y-moel Bridgend 14 B5
Nant-y-pandy Conwy 41 C8
Nanternis Ceredig 23 A8
Nantgaredig Carms 23 D9
Nantgarw Rhondda 15 C7
Nantglyn Denb 42 F3
Nantgwyn Powys 32 H5
Nantlle Gwyn 41 E7
Nantmawr Shrops 33 C8
Nantmel Powys 25 B7
Nantmor Gwyn 41 F8
Nantwich Ches E 43 G9
Nantycaws Carms 23 E9
Nantyffyllon Bridgend 14 B4
Nantyglo Bl Gwent 25 G8
Naphill Bucks 18 B5
Nappa N Yorks 50 D4
Napton on the Hill Warks 27 B11
Narberth = Arberth Pembs 22 E6
Narborough Leics 35 F11
Narborough Norf 38 D3
Nasareth Gwyn 40 E6
Naseby Northants 36 H2
Nash Bucks 28 E4
Nash Hereford 25 B10
Nash Newport 15 C9
Nash Shrops 26 A3
Nash Lee Bucks 28 H5
Nassington Northants 37 F6
Nasty Herts 29 F10
Nateby Cumb 57 F9
Nateby Lancs 49 E4
Natland Cumb 57 H7
Naughton Suff 31 D7
Naunton Glos 27 F8
Naunton Worcs 26 E5
Naunton Beauchamp Worcs 26 C6
Navenby Lincs 46 G3
Navestock Heath Essex 20 B2
Navestock Side Essex 20 B2
Navidale Highld 93 H13
Nawton N Yorks 52 A2
Nayland Suff 30 E6
Nazeing Essex 29 H11
Neacroft Hants 9 E10
Neal's Green Warks 35 G9
Neap Shetland 96 H7
Near Sawrey Cumb 56 G5
Neasham Darl 58 E4
Neath = Castell-Nedd Neath 14 B3
Neath Abbey Neath 14 B3
Neatishead Norf 39 C9
Nebo Anglesey 40 A6
Nebo Ceredig 24 B2
Nebo Conwy 41 E10
Nebo Gwyn 40 E6
Necton Norf 38 E4
Nedd Highld 92 F4
Nedderton Northumb 63 E8
Nedging Tye Suff 31 D7
Needham Norf 39 G8
Needham Market Suff 31 C7
Needingworth Cambs 29 A10
Needwood Staffs 35 C7
Neen Savage Shrops 34 H2
Neen Sollars Shrops 26 A3
Neenton Shrops 34 G2
Nefyn Gwyn 40 F5
Neilston E Renf 68 E3
Neinthirion Powys 32 E5
Neithrop Oxon 27 D11
Nelly Andrews Green Powys 33 E8
Nelson Caerph 15 B7
Nelson Lancs 50 F4
Nelson Village Northumb 63 F8
Nemphlar S Lanark 69 F7
Nempnett Thrubwell N Som 15 E11
Nene Terrace Lincs 37 E8
Nenthall Cumb 57 B9
Nenthead Cumb 57 B9
Nenthorn Borders 70 G5
Nerabus Argyll 64 C3
Nercwys Flint 42 F5
Nerston S Lanark 68 E5
Nesbit Northumb 71 G8
Ness Ches W 42 E6
Nesscliffe Shrops 33 D9
Neston Ches W 42 E5
Neston Wilts 16 E5
Nether Alderley Ches E 44 E2
Nether Blainslie Borders 70 F4
Nether Booth Derbys 44 D5
Nether Broughton Leics 36 C2
Nether Burrow Lancs 50 B2
Nether Cerne Dorset 8 E5
Nether Compton Dorset 8 C4
Nether Crimond Aberds 89 F8
Nether Dalgliesh Borders 61 C8
Nether Dallachy Moray 88 B3
Nether Exe Devon 7 F8
Nether Glasslaw Aberds 89 C8
Nether Handwick Angus 76 C6
Nether Haugh S Yorks 45 C8
Nether Heage Derbys 45 G7
Nether Heyford Northants 28 C3
Nether Hindhope Borders 62 B3
Nether Howecleuch S Lanark 60 B6
Nether Kellet Lancs 49 C5
Nether Kinmundy Aberds 89 D10
Nether Langwith Notts 45 E9
Nether Leask Aberds 89 E10
Nether Lenshie Aberds 89 D6
Nether Monynut Borders 70 D6
Nether Padley Derbys 44 E6
Nether Park Aberds 89 C10
Nether Poppleton York 52 D1
Nether Silton N Yorks 58 G5
Nether Stowey Som 7 C10
Nether Urquhart Fife 76 G4
Nether Wallop Hants 17 H10
Nether Wasdale Cumb 56 F3
Nether Whitacre Warks 35 F8
Nether Worton Oxon 27 E11
Netheravon Wilts 17 G8
Netherbrae Aberds 89 C7
Netherbrough Orkney 95 G4
Netherburn S Lanark 69 F7
Netherbury Dorset 8 E3
Netherby Cumb 61 F9
Netherby N Yorks 51 E9
Nethercote Warks 28 B2
Nethercott Devon 6 C3
Netherend Glos 16 A2
Netherfield E Sus 12 E6
Netherhampton Wilts 9 B10
Netherlaw Dumfries 55 E10
Netherley Aberds 83 D10
Netherley Mers 43 D7
Nethermill Dumfries 60 E6
Nethermuir Aberds 89 D9
Netherplace E Renf 68 E4
Netherseal Derbys 35 D8
Netherthird E Ayrs 67 E8
Netherthong W Yorks 44 B5
Netherthorpe S Yorks 45 D9
Netherton Angus 77 B8
Netherton Devon 5 D9
Netherton Hants 17 F10
Netherton Mers 42 B6
Netherton Northumb 62 C5
Netherton Oxon 17 B11
Netherton Perth 76 B4
Netherton Stirling 68 C4
Netherton W Mid 34 G5
Netherton W Yorks 44 A5
Netherton W Yorks 51 H8
Netherton Worcs 26 D6
Nethertown Cumb 56 F1
Nethertown Highld 94 C5
Netherwitton Northumb 63 D7
Netherwood E Ayrs 68 H5
Nethy Bridge Highld 82 A2
Netley Hants 10 D3
Netley Marsh Hants 10 C2
Netteswell Essex 29 G11
Nettlebed Oxon 18 C4
Nettlebridge Som 16 G3
Nettlecombe Dorset 8 E4
Nettleden Herts 29 G7
Nettleham Lincs 46 E4
Nettlestead Kent 20 F3
Nettlestead Green Kent 20 F3
Nettlestone IoW 10 E5
Nettlesworth Durham 58 B3
Nettleton Lincs 46 B5
Nettleton Wilts 16 D5
Neuadd Carms 24 F3
Nevendon Essex 20 B4
Nevern Pembs 22 B5
New Abbey Dumfries 60 G5
New Aberdour Aberds 89 B8
New Addington London 19 E10
New Alresford Hants 10 A4
New Alyth Perth 76 C5
New Arley Warks 35 G8
New Ash Green Kent 20 E3
New Barn Kent 20 E3
New Barnetby N Lincs 46 A4
New Barton Northants 28 B5
New Bewick Northumb 62 A6
New-bigging Angus 76 C5
New Bilton Warks 35 H10
New Bolingbroke Lincs 47 G7
New Boultham Lincs 46 E3
New Bradwell M Keynes 28 D5
New Brancepeth Durham 58 B3
New Bridge Wrex 33 A8
New Brighton Flint 42 F5
New Brighton Mers 42 C6
New Brinsley Notts 45 G8
New Broughton Wrex 42 G6
New Buckenham Norf 39 F6
New Byth Aberds 89 C8
New Catton Norf 39 D8
New Cheriton Hants 10 B4
New Costessey Norf 39 D7
New Cowper Cumb 56 B3
New Cross Ceredig 32 H2
New Cross London 19 D10
New Cumnock E Ayrs 67 E9
New Deer Aberds 89 D8
New Delaval Northumb 63 F8
New Duston Northants 28 B4
New Earswick York 52 D2
New Edlington S Yorks 45 C9
New Elgin Moray 88 B2
New Ellerby E Yorks 53 F7
New Eltham London 19 D11
New End Worcs 27 C7
New Farnley W Yorks 51 F8
New Ferry Mers 42 D6
New Fryston W Yorks 51 G10
New Galloway Dumfries 55 B9
New Gilston Fife 77 G7
New Grimsby Scilly 2 C2
New Hainford Norf 39 D8
New Hartley Northumb 63 F9
New Haw Sur 19 E7
New Hedges Pembs 22 F6
New Herrington T&W 58 A4
New Hinksey Oxon 18 A2
New Holkham Norf 38 B4
New Holland N Lincs 53 G6
New Houghton Derbys 45 F8
New Houghton Norf 38 C3
New Houses N Yorks 50 B4
New Humberstone Leicester 36 E2
New Hutton Cumb 57 G7
New Hythe Kent 20 F4
New Inn Carms 23 C9
New Inn Mon 15 A10
New Inn Pembs 22 C5
New Inn Torf 15 B9
New Invention Shrops 33 H8
New Invention W Mid 34 E5
New Kelso Highld 86 G2
New Kingston Notts 35 C11
New Lanark S Lanark 69 F7
New Lane Lancs 43 A7
New Lane End Warr 43 C9
New Leake Lincs 47 G8
New Leeds Aberds 89 C9
New Longton Lancs 49 G5
New Luce Dumfries 54 C4
New Malden London 19 E9
New Marske Redcar 59 D7
New Marton Shrops 33 B9
New Micklefield W Yorks 51 F10
New Mill Aberds 83 E9
New Mill Herts 28 G6
New Mill W Yorks 44 B5
New Mill Wilts 17 E8
New Mills Ches E 43 D10
New Mills Corn 3 D7
New Mills Derbys 44 D3
New Mills Powys 33 E6
New Milton Hants 9 E11
New Moat Pembs 22 D5
New Ollerton Notts 45 F10
New Oscott W Mid 35 F6
New Park N Yorks 51 D8
New Pitsligo Aberds 89 C8
New Polzeath Corn 3 B8
New Quay = Ceinewydd Ceredig 23 A8
New Rackheath Norf 39 D8
New Radnor Powys 25 B9
New Rent Cumb 56 C6
New Ridley Northumb 62 H6
New Road Side N Yorks 50 E5
New Romney Kent 13 D9
New Rossington S Yorks 45 C10
New Row Ceredig 24 A4
New Row Lancs 50 F2
New Row N Yorks 59 E7
New Sarum Wilts 9 A10
New Silksworth T&W 58 A4
New Stevenston N Lanark 68 E6
New Street Staffs 44 G4
New Street Lane Shrops 34 B2
New Swanage Dorset 9 F9
New Totley S Yorks 45 E7
New Town E Loth 70 C3
New Tredegar = Tredegar Newydd Caerph 15 A7
New Trows S Lanark 69 G7
New Ulva Argyll 72 E6
New Walsoken Cambs 37 E10
New Waltham NE Lincs 46 B6
New Whittington Derbys 45 E7
New Wimpole Cambs 29 D10
New Winton E Loth 70 C3
New Yatt Oxon 27 G10
New York Lincs 46 G6
New York N Yorks 51 C7
Newall W Yorks 51 E7
Newark Orkney 95 D8
Newark Pboro 37 E8
Newark-on-Trent Notts 45 G11
Newarthill N Lanark 68 E6
Newbarns Cumb 49 B2
Newbattle Midloth 70 D2
Newbiggin Cumb 49 C2
Newbiggin Cumb 56 D6
Newbiggin Cumb 56 G2
Newbiggin Cumb 57 B7
Newbiggin Cumb 57 D8
Newbiggin Durham 57 D11
Newbiggin N Yorks 57 G11
Newbiggin N Yorks 57 H11
Newbiggin-by-the-Sea Northumb 63 E9
Newbiggin-on-Lune Cumb 57 F9
Newbigging Angus 77 D7
Newbigging Angus 77 D7
Newbigging S Lanark 69 F9
Newbold Derbys 45 E7
Newbold Leics 35 D10
Newbold on Avon Warks 35 H10
Newbold on Stour Warks 27 D9
Newbold Pacey Warks 27 C9
Newbold Verdon Leics 35 E10
Newborough Anglesey 40 D6
Newborough Pboro 37 E8
Newborough Staffs 35 C7
Newbottle Northants 28 E2
Newbottle T&W 58 A4
Newbourne Suff 31 D9
Newbridge Caerph 15 B8
Newbridge Ceredig 23 A10
Newbridge Corn 2 F3
Newbridge Corn 4 E4
Newbridge Dumfries 60 F5
Newbridge Edin 69 C10
Newbridge Hants 10 C1
Newbridge IoW 10 F3
Newbridge Pembs 22 C4
Newbridge Green Worcs 26 E5
Newbridge-on-Usk Mon 15 B9
Newbridge on Wye Powys 25 C7
Newbrough Northumb 62 G4
Newbuildings Devon 7 F6
Newburgh Aberds 89 C9
Newburgh Aberds 89 F9
Newburgh Borders 61 B9
Newburgh Fife 76 F5
Newburgh Lancs 43 A7
Newburn T&W 63 G7
Newbury W Berks 17 E11
Newbury Park London 19 C11
Newby Cumb 57 D7
Newby Lancs 50 E4
Newby N Yorks 50 B3
Newby N Yorks 58 E6
Newby N Yorks 59 G11
Newby Bridge Cumb 56 H5
Newby East Cumb 61 H10
Newby West Cumb 56 A5
Newby Wiske N Yorks 58 H4
Newcastle Mon 25 G11
Newcastle Shrops 33 G8
Newcastle Emlyn = Castell Newydd Emlyn Carms 23 B8
Newcastle-under-Lyme Staffs 44 H2
Newcastle Upon Tyne T&W 63 G8
Newcastleton or Copshaw Holm Borders 61 E10
Newchapel Pembs 23 C7
Newchapel Powys 32 G5
Newchapel Staffs 44 G2
Newchapel Sur 12 B2
Newchurch Carms 23 D8
Newchurch IoW 10 F4
Newchurch Kent 13 C9
Newchurch Lancs 50 F4
Newchurch Mon 15 B10
Newchurch Powys 25 C9
Newchurch Staffs 35 C7
Newcott Devon 7 F11
Newcraighall Edin 70 C2
Newdigate Sur 19 G8
Newell Green Brack 18 D5
Newenden Kent 13 D7
Newent Glos 26 F4
Newerne Glos 16 A3
Newfield Durham 58 C3
Newfield Highld 87 D10
Newford Scilly 2 C3
Newfound Hants 18 F2
Newgale Pembs 22 D3
Newgate Norf 39 A6
Newgate Street Herts 19 A10
Newhall Ches E 43 H9
Newhall Derbys 35 C8
Newhall House Highld 87 E9
Newhall Point Highld 87 E10
Newham Northumb 71 H10
Newham Hall Northumb 71 H10
Newhaven Derbys 44 G5
Newhaven E Sus 12 F3
Newhaven Edin 69 C11
Newhey Gtr Man 44 A3
Newholm N Yorks 59 E9
Newhouse N Lanark 68 D6
Newick E Sus 12 D3
Newingreen Kent 13 C10
Newington Kent 20 E5
Newington Kent 21 E10
Newington Kent 21 H8
Newington Notts 45 C10
Newington Oxon 18 B3
Newington Shrops 33 G10
Newland Glos 26 H2
Newland Hull 53 F6
Newland N Yorks 52 G2
Newland Worcs 26 D4
Newlandrig Midloth 70 D2
Newlands Borders 61 D11
Newlands Highld 87 G10
Newlands Moray 88 C3
Newlands Northumb 62 H6
Newland's Corner Sur 19 G7
Newlands of Geise Highld 94 D2
Newlands of Tynet Moray 88 B3
Newlands Park Anglesey 40 B4
Newlandsmuir S Lanark 68 E5
Newlot Orkney 95 G6
Newlyn Corn 2 G3
Newmachar Aberds 83 B10
Newmains N Lanark 69 E7
Newmarket Suff 30 B3
Newmarket W Isles 91 D9
Newmill Borders 61 B10
Newmill Corn 2 F3
Newmill Moray 88 C4
Newmill of Inshewan Angus 77 A7
Newmills of Boyne Aberds 88 C5
Newmiln Perth 76 D4
Newmilns E Ayrs 67 C8
Newnham Cambs 29 C11
Newnham Glos 26 G3
Newnham Hants 18 F4
Newnham Herts 29 E9
Newnham Kent 20 F6
Newnham Northants 28 C2
Newnham Bridge Worcs 26 B3
Newpark Fife 77 F7
Newport Devon 6 C4
Newport E Yorks 52 F4
Newport Essex 30 E2
Newport Highld 94 H3
Newport IoW 10 F4
Newport = Casnewydd Newport 15 C9
Newport Norf 39 D11
Newport = Trefdraeth Pembs 22 C5
Newport Telford 34 D3
Newport-on-Tay Fife 77 E7
Newport Pagnell M Keynes 28 D5
Newpound Common W Sus 11 B9
Newquay Corn 3 C7
Newsbank Ches E 44 F2
Newseat Aberds 89 D10
Newseat Aberds 89 E7
Newsham N Yorks 51 A9
Newsham N Yorks 58 E2
Newsham Northumb 63 F9
Newsholme E Yorks 52 G3
Newsholme Lancs 50 D4
Newsome W Yorks 44 A5
Newstead Borders 70 G4
Newstead Northumb 71 H10
Newstead Notts 45 G9
Newthorpe N Yorks 51 F10
Newton Argyll 73 D9
Newton Borders 62 A1
Newton Bridgend 14 D4
Newton Cambs 29 D11
Newton Cambs 37 D10
Newton Cardiff 15 D8
Newton Ches W 43 E8
Newton Ches W 43 F7
Newton Ches W 43 G8
Newton Cumb 49 B2
Newton Derbys 45 G8
Newton Dorset 9 C6
Newton Dumfries 61 D7
Newton Dumfries 61 F8
Newton Gtr Man 44 C3
Newton Hereford 25 E10
Newton Hereford 26 C2
Newton Highld 87 E10
Newton Highld 87 G10
Newton Highld 92 F5
Newton Highld 94 F5
Newton Lancs 49 F4
Newton Lancs 50 B1
Newton Lancs 50 D2
Newton Lincs 36 B6
Newton Moray 88 B1
Newton Norf 38 D4
Newton Northants 36 G4
Newton Northumb 62 G6
Newton Notts 36 A2
Newton Perth 75 D11
Newton S Lanark 68 D5
Newton S Lanark 69 G8
Newton S Yorks 45 B9
Newton Staffs 34 C6
Newton Suff 30 D6
Newton Swansea 14 C2
Newton W Loth 69 C9
Newton Warks 35 H11
Newton Wilts 9 B11
Newton Abbot Devon 5 D9
Newton Arlosh Cumb 61 H7
Newton Aycliffe Durham 58 D3
Newton Bewley Hrtlpl 58 D5
Newton Blossomville M Keynes 28 C6
Newton Bromswold Northants 28 B6
Newton Burgoland Leics 35 E9
Newton by Toft Lincs 46 D4
Newton Ferrers Devon 4 G6
Newton Flotman Norf 39 F8
Newton Hall Northumb 62 G6
Newton Harcourt Leics 36 F2
Newton Heath Gtr Man 44 B2
Newton Ho. Aberds 83 A8
Newton Kyme N Yorks 51 E10
Newton-le-Willows Mers 43 C8
Newton-le-Willows N Yorks 58 H3
Newton Longville Bucks 28 E5
Newton Mearns E Renf 68 E4
Newton Morrell N Yorks 58 F3
Newton Mulgrave N Yorks 59 E8
Newton of Ardtoe Highld 79 D9
Newton of Balcanquhal Perth 76 F4
Newton of Falkland Fife 76 G5
Newton on Ayr S Ayrs 66 D6
Newton on Ouse N Yorks 51 D11
Newton-on-Rawcliffe N Yorks 59 G9
Newton-on-the-Moor Northumb 63 C7
Newton on Trent Lincs 46 E2
Newton Park Argyll 73 G10
Newton Poppleford Devon 7 H9
Newton Purcell Oxon 28 E3
Newton Regis Warks 35 E8
Newton Reigny Cumb 57 C6
Newton St Cyres Devon 7 G7
Newton St Faith Norf 39 D8
Newton St Loe Bath 16 E4
Newton St Petrock Devon 6 E3
Newton Solney Derbys 35 C8
Newton Stacey Hants 17 G11
Newton Stewart Dumfries 55 C7
Newton Tony Wilts 17 G9
Newton Tracey Devon 6 D4
Newton under Roseberry Redcar 59 E6
Newton upon Derwent E Yorks 52 E3
Newton Valence Hants 10 A6
Newtonairds Dumfries 60 E4
Newtongrange Midloth 70 D2
Newtonhill Aberds 83 D11
Newtonhill Highld 87 G8
Newtonmill Angus 77 A9
Newtonmore Highld 81 D9
Newtown Argyll 73 C9
Newtown Ches W 43 E8
Newtown Corn 2 G6
Newtown Cumb 56 B2
Newtown Cumb 61 G11
Newtown Derbys 44 D3
Newtown Devon 7 D6
Newtown Glos 16 A3
Newtown Glos 26 E6
Newtown Hants 10 B2
Newtown Hants 10 C4
Newtown Hants 10 C1
Newtown Hants 10 C5
Newtown Hants 10 D3
Newtown Hants 17 E11
Newtown Hereford 26 D3
Newtown Highld 80 C5
Newtown IoM 48 E3
Newtown IoW 10 E3
Newtown Northumb 62 C6
Newtown Northumb 71 G8
Newtown Northumb 71 H9
Newtown Poole 9 E9
Newtown = Y Drenewydd Powys 33 F7
Newtown Shrops 33 B10
Newtown Staffs 44 F4
Newtown Staffs 44 F3
Newtown Wilts 9 B8
Newtown Linford Leics 35 E11
Newtown St Boswells Borders 70 G4
Newtown Unthank Leics 35 E10
Newtyle Angus 76 C5
Neyland Pembs 22 F4
Niarbyl IoM 48 E2
Nibley S Glos 16 C3
Nibley Green Glos 16 B4
Nibon Shetland 96 F5
Nicholashayne Devon 7 E10
Nicholaston Swansea 23 H10
Nidd N Yorks 51 C9
Nigg Aberdeen 83 C11
Nigg Highld 87 D11
Nigg Ferry Highld 87 E10
Nightcott Som 7 D7
Nilig Denb 42 G3
Nine Ashes Essex 20 A2
Nine Mile Burn Midloth 69 E10
Nine Wells Pembs 22 D2
Ninebanks Northumb 57 A9
Ninfield E Sus 12 E6
Ningwood IoW 10 F2
Nisbet Borders 70 H5
Nisthouse Orkney 95 G4
Nisthouse Shetland 96 G7
Niton IoW 10 G4
Nitshill Glasgow 68 D4
No Man's Heath Ches W 43 H8
No Man's Heath Warks 35 E8
Noak Hill London 20 B2
Noblethorpe S Yorks 44 B6
Nobottle Northants 28 B3
Nocton Lincs 46 F4
Noke Oxon 28 G2
Nolton Pembs 22 E3
Nolton Haven Pembs 22 E3
Nomansland Devon 7 E7
Nomansland Wilts 10 C1
Noneley Shrops 33 C10
Nonikiln Highld 87 D9
Nonington Kent 21 F9
Noonsbrough Shetland 96 H4
Norbreck Blackpool 49 E3
Norbridge Hereford 26 D4
Norbury Ches E 43 H8
Norbury Derbys 35 A7
Norbury Shrops 33 F9
Norbury Staffs 34 C3
Nordelph Norf 38 E1
Norden Gtr Man 44 A2
Norden Heath Dorset 9 F8
Nordley Shrops 34 F2
Norham Northumb 71 F8
Norley Ches W 43 E8
Norleywood Hants 10 E2
Norman Cross Cambs 37 F7
Normanby N Lincs 52 H4
Normanby N Yorks 52 A3
Normanby Redcar 59 E6
Normanby-by-Spital Lincs 46 D4
Normanby by Stow Lincs 46 D2
Normanby le Wold Lincs 46 C5
Normandy Sur 18 F6
Norman's Bay E Sus 12 F5
Norman's Green Devon 7 F9
Normanstone Suff 39 F11
Normanton Derby 35 B9
Normanton Leics 36 A4
Normanton Lincs 46 H3
Normanton Notts 45 G11
Normanton Rutland 36 E5
Normanton W Yorks 51 G9
Normanton le Heath Leics 35 D9
Normanton on Soar Notts 35 C11
Normanton-on-the-Wolds Notts 36 B2
Normanton on Trent Notts 45 F11
Normoss Lancs 49 F3
Norney Sur 18 G6
Norrington Common Wilts 16 E5
Norris Green Mers 43 C6
Norris Hill Leics 35 D9
North Anston S Yorks 45 D9
North Aston Oxon 27 F11
North Baddesley Hants 10 C2
North Ballachulish Highld 74 A3
North Barrow Som 8 B5
North Barsham Norf 38 B5
North Benfleet Essex 20 C4
North Bersted W Sus 11 D8
North Berwick E Loth 70 B4
North Boarhunt Hants 10 C5
North Bovey Devon 5 C8
North Bradley Wilts 16 F5
North Brentor Devon 4 C5
North Brewham Som 16 H4
North Buckland Devon 6 B3
North Burlingham Norf 39 D9
North Cadbury Som 8 B5
North Cairn Dumfries 54 B2
North Carlton Lincs 46 E3
North Carrine Argyll 65 H7
North Cave E Yorks 52 F4
North Cerney Glos 27 H7
North Charford Wilts 9 C10
North Charlton Northumb 63 A7
North Cheriton Som 8 B5
North Cliff E Yorks 53 E8
North Cliffe E Yorks 52 F4
North Clifton Notts 46 E2
North Cockerington Lincs 47 C7
North Coker Som 8 C4
North Collafirth Shetland 96 E5
North Common E Sus 12 D2
North Connel Argyll 74 D2
North Cornelly Bridgend 14 C4
North Cotes Lincs 47 B7
North Cove Suff 39 G10
North Cowton N Yorks 58 F3
North Crawley M Keynes 28 D6
North Cray London 19 D11
North Creake Norf 38 B4
North Curry Som 8 B2
North Dalton E Yorks 52 D5
North Dawn Orkney 95 H5
North Deighton N Yorks 51 D9
North Duffield N Yorks 52 F2
North Elkington Lincs 46 C6
North Elmham Norf 38 C5
North Elmshall W Yorks 45 A8
North End Bucks 28 F5
North End E Yorks 53 F8
North End Essex 30 G3
North End Hants 17 E11
North End Lincs 37 A8
North End N Som 15 E10
North End Ptsmth 10 D5
North End Som 8 B1
North End W Sus 11 D10
North Erradale Highld 91 J12
North Fambridge Essex 20 B5
North Fearns Highld 85 E10
North Featherstone W Yorks 51 G10
North Ferriby E Yorks 52 G5
North Frodingham E Yorks 53 D7
North Gluss Shetland 96 F5
North Gorley Hants 9 C10
North Green Norf 39 G8
North Green Suff 31 B10
North Greetwell Lincs 46 E4
North Grimston N Yorks 52 C4
North Halley Orkney 95 H6
North Halling Medway 20 E4
North Hayling Hants 10 D6
North Hazelrigg Northumb 71 G9
North Heasley Devon 7 C6
North Heath W Sus 11 B9
North Hill Cambs 37 H10
North Hill Corn 4 D3
North Hinksey Oxon 27 H11
North Holmwood Sur 19 G8
North Howden E Yorks 52 F3
North Huish Devon 5 F8
North Hykeham Lincs 46 F3
North Johnston Pembs 22 E4
North Kelsey Lincs 46 B4
North Kelsey Moor Lincs 46 B4
North Kessock Highld 87 G9
North Killingholme N Lincs 53 H7
North Kilvington N Yorks 58 H5
North Kilworth Leics 36 G2
North Kirkton Aberds 89 C11
North Kiscadale N Ayrs 66 D3
North Kyme Lincs 46 G5
North Lancing W Sus 11 D10
North Lee Bucks 28 H5
North Leigh Oxon 27 G10
North Leverton with Habblesthorpe Notts 45 D11
North Littleton Worcs 27 D7
North Lopham Norf 38 G6
North Luffenham Rutland 36 E5
North Marden W Sus 11 C7
North Marston Bucks 28 F4
North Middleton Midloth 70 E2
North Middleton Northumb 62 A6
North Molton Devon 7 D6
North Moreton Oxon 18 C2
North Mundham W Sus 11 D7
North Muskham Notts 45 G11
North Newbald E Yorks 52 F5
North Newington Oxon 27 E11
North Newnton Wilts 17 F8
North Newton Som 8 A1
North Nibley Glos 16 B4
North Oakley Hants 18 F2
North Ockendon London 20 C2
North Ormesby Mbro 58 D6
North Ormsby Lincs 46 C6
North Otterington N Yorks 58 H4
North Owersby Lincs 46 C4
North Perrott Som 8 D3
North Petherton Som 8 A1
North Petherwin Corn 4 C3
North Pickenham Norf 38 E4
North Piddle Worcs 26 C6
North Poorton Dorset 8 E4
North Port Argyll 74 E3
North Queensferry Fife 69 B10
North Radworthy Devon 7 C6
North Rauceby Lincs 46 H4
North Reston Lincs 47 D7
North Rigton N Yorks 51 E8
North Rode Ches E 44 F2
North Roe Shetland 96 E5
North Runcton Norf 38 D2
North Sandwick Shetland 96 D7
North Scale Cumb 49 C1
North Scarle Lincs 46 F2
North Seaton Northumb 63 E8
North Shian Argyll 74 C2
North Shields T&W 63 G9
North Shoebury Southend 20 C6
North Shore Blackpool 49 F3
North Side Cumb 56 D2
North Side Pboro 37 F8
North Skelton Redcar 59 E7
North Somercotes Lincs 47 C8
North Stainley N Yorks 51 B8
North Stainmore Cumb 57 E10
North Stifford Thurrock 20 C3
North Stoke Bath 16 E4
North Stoke Oxon 18 C3
North Stoke W Sus 11 C9
North Street Hants 10 A5
North Street Kent 21 F7
North Street Medway 20 D5
North Street W Berks 18 D3
North Sunderland Northumb 71 G11
North Tamerton Corn 6 G2
North Tawton Devon 6 F5
North Thoresby Lincs 46 C6
North Tidworth Wilts 17 G9
North Togston Northumb 63 C8
North Tuddenham Norf 38 D6
North Walbottle T&W 63 G7
North Walsham Norf 39 B8
North Waltham Hants 18 G2
North Warnborough Hants 18 F4
North Water Bridge Angus 83 G8
North Watten Highld 94 E4
North Weald Bassett Essex 19 A11
North Wheatley Notts 45 D11
North Whilborough Devon 5 E9
North Wick Bath 16 E2
North Willingham Lincs 46 D5
North Wingfield Derbys 45 F8
North Witham Lincs 36 C5
North Woolwich London 19 D11
North Wootton Dorset 8 C5
North Wootton Norf 38 C2
North Wootton Som 16 G2
North Wraxall Wilts 16 D5
North Wroughton Swindon 17 C8
Northacre Norf 38 F5
Northallerton N Yorks 58 G4
Northam Devon 6 D3
Northam Soton 10 C3
Northampton Northants 28 B4
Northaw Herts 19 A9
Northbeck Lincs 37 A6
Northborough Pboro 37 E7
Northbourne Kent 21 F10
Northbridge Street E Sus 12 D6
Northchapel W Sus 11 B8
Northchurch Herts 28 H6
Northcott Devon 6 G2
Northdown Kent 21 D10
Northdyke Orkney 95 F3
Northend Bath 16 E4
Northend Bucks 18 B4
Northend Warks 27 C10
Northenden Gtr Man 44 C2
Northfield Aberdeen 83 C11
Northfield Borders 71 D8
Northfield E Yorks 52 G6
Northfield W Mid 34 H6
Northfields Lincs 36 E6
Northfleet Kent 20 D3
Northgate Lincs 37 C7
Northhouse Borders 61 C10
Northiam E Sus 13 D7
Northill C Beds 29 D8
Northington Hants 18 H2
Northlands Lincs 47 G7
Northlea Durham 58 A5
Northleach Glos 27 G8
Northleigh Devon 7 G10
Northlew Devon 6 G4
Northmoor Oxon 17 A11
Northmoor Green or Moorland Som 8 A2
Northmuir Angus 76 B6
Northney Hants 10 D6
Northolt London 19 C8
Northop Flint 42 F5
Northop Hall Flint 42 F5
Northorpe Lincs 37 B8
Northorpe Lincs 37 D6
Northorpe Lincs 46 C2
Northover Som 8 B4
Northover Som 15 H10
Northowram W Yorks 51 G7
Northport Dorset 9 F8
Northpunds Shetland 96 L6
Northrepps Norf 39 B8
Northstowe Cambs 29 B11
Northtown Orkney 95 J5
Northway Glos 26 E6
Northwich Ches W 43 E9
Northwick S Glos 16 C2
Northwold Norf 38 F3
Northwood Derbys 44 F6
Northwood IoW 10 E3
Northwood Kent 21 E10
Northwood London 19 B7
Northwood Shrops 33 B10
Northwood Green Glos 26 G4
Norton E Sus 12 F3
Norton Glos 26 F5
Norton Halton 43 D8
Norton Herts 29 E9
Norton IoW 10 F2
Norton Mon 25 G11
Norton Northants 28 B3
Norton Notts 45 E9
Norton Powys 25 B10
Norton S Yorks 51 H11
Norton Shrops 33 G10
Norton Shrops 34 E1
Norton Shrops 34 E3
Norton Stockton 58 D5
Norton Suff 30 B6
Norton W Sus 11 D8
Norton W Sus 11 E7
Norton Wilts 16 C5
Norton Worcs 26 C5
Norton Worcs 27 D7
Norton Bavant Wilts 16 G6
Norton Bridge Staffs 34 B4
Norton Canes Staffs 34 E6
Norton Canon Hereford 25 D10
Norton Corner Norf 39 C6
Norton Disney Lincs 46 G2
Norton East Staffs 34 E6
Norton Ferris Wilts 16 H4
Norton Fitzwarren Som 7 D10
Norton Green IoW 10 F2
Norton Hawkfield Bath 16 E2
Norton Heath Essex 20 A3
Norton in Hales Shrops 34 B3
Norton-in-the-Moors Stoke 44 G2
Norton-Juxta-Twycross Leics 35 E9
Norton-le-Clay N Yorks 51 B10
Norton Lindsey Warks 27 B9
Norton Malreward Bath 16 E3
Norton Mandeville Essex 20 A2
Norton-on-Derwent N Yorks 52 B3
Norton St Philip Som 16 F4
Norton sub Hamdon Som 8 C3
Norton Woodseats S Yorks 45 D7
Norwell Notts 45 F11
Norwell Woodhouse Notts 45 F11
Norwich Norf 39 E8
Norwick Shetland 96 B8
Norwood Derbys 45 D8
Norwood Hill Sur 19 G9
Norwoodside Cambs 37 F10
Noseley Leics 36 F3
Noss Shetland 96 M5
Noss Mayo Devon 4 G6
Nosterfield N Yorks 51 A8
Nostie Highld 85 F13
Notgrove Glos 27 F8
Nottage Bridgend 14 D4
Nottingham Nottingham 36 B1
Nottington Dorset 8 F5
Notton W Yorks 45 A7
Notton Wilts 16 E6
Nounsley Essex 30 G4
Noutard's Green Worcs 26 B4
Novar House Highld 87 E9
Nox Shrops 33 D10
Nuffield Oxon 18 C3
Nun Hills Lancs 50 G4
Nun Monkton N Yorks 51 D11
Nunburnholme E Yorks 52 E4
Nuncargate Notts 45 G9
Nuneaton Warks 35 F9
Nuneham Courtenay Oxon 18 B2
Nunney Som 16 G4
Nunnington N Yorks 52 B2
Nunnykirk Northumb 62 D6
Nunsthorpe NE Lincs 46 B6
Nunthorpe Mbro 59 E6
Nunthorpe York 52 D2
Nunton Wilts 9 B10
Nunwick N Yorks 51 B9
Nupend Glos 26 H4
Nursling Hants 10 C2
Nursted Hants 11 B6
Nutbourne W Sus 11 C9
Nutbourne W Sus 11 D6
Nutfield Sur 19 F10
Nuthall Notts 35 A11
Nuthampstead Herts 29 E11
Nuthurst W Sus 11 B10
Nutley E Sus 12 D3
Nutley Hants 18 G3
Nutwell S Yorks 45 B10
Nybster Highld 94 D5
Nyetimber W Sus 11 E7
Nyewood W Sus 11 B7
Nymet Rowland Devon 6 F6
Nymet Tracey Devon 7 F6
Nympsfield Glos 16 A5
Nynehead Som 7 D10
Nyton W Sus 11 D8

O

Oad Street Kent 20 E5
Oadby Leics 36 E2
Oak Cross Devon 6 G4
Oakamoor Staffs 35 A6
Oakbank W Loth 69 D9
Oakdale Caerph 15 B7
Oake Som 7 D10
Oaken Staffs 34 E4
Oakenclough Lancs 49 E5
Oakengates Telford 34 D3
Oakenholt Flint 42 E5
Oakenshaw Durham 58 C3
Oakenshaw W Yorks 51 G7
Oakerthorpe Derbys 45 G7
Oakes W Yorks 51 H7
Oakfield Torf 15 B9
Oakford Ceredig 23 A9
Oakford Devon 7 D8
Oakfordbridge Devon 7 D8
Oakgrove Ches E 44 F3
Oakham Rutland 36 E4
Oakhanger Hants 18 H4
Oakhill Som 16 G3
Oakhurst Kent 20 F2
Oakington Cambs 29 B11
Oaklands Herts 29 G9
Oaklands Powys 25 C7
Oakle Street Glos 26 G4
Oakley Bedford 29 C7
Oakley Bucks 28 G3
Oakley Fife 69 B9
Oakley Hants 18 F2
Oakley Oxon 18 A4
Oakley Poole 9 E9
Oakley Suff 39 H7
Oakley Green Windsor 18 D6
Oakley Park Powys 32 G5
Oakmere Ches W 43 F8
Oakridge Glos 16 A6
Oakridge Hants 18 F3
Oaks Shrops 33 E10
Oaks Green Derbys 35 B7
Oaksey Wilts 16 B6
Oakthorpe Leics 35 D9
Oakwoodhill Sur 19 H8
Oakworth W Yorks 50 F6
Oape Highld 92 J7
Oare Kent 21 E7
Oare Som 7 B7
Oare W Berks 18 D2
Oare Wilts 17 E8
Oasby Lincs 36 B6
Oathlaw Angus 77 B7
Oatlands N Yorks 51 D9
Oban Argyll 79 J11
Oban Highld 79 C11
Oborne Dorset 8 C5
Obthorpe Lincs 37 D6
Occlestone Green Ches W 43 F9
Occold Suff 31 A8
Ochiltree E Ayrs 67 D8
Ochtermuthill Perth 75 F11
Ochtertyre Perth 75 E11
Ockbrook Derbys 35 B10
Ockham Sur 19 F7
Ockle Highld 79 D8
Ockley Sur 19 H8
Ocle Pychard Hereford 26 D2
Octon E Yorks 52 C6
Octon Cross Roads E Yorks 52 C6
Odcombe Som 8 C4
Odd Down Bath 16 E4
Oddendale Cumb 57 E7
Odder Lincs 46 E3
Oddingley Worcs 26 C6
Oddington Glos 27 F9
Oddington Oxon 28 G2
Odell Bedford 28 C6
Odie Orkney 95 F7
Odiham Hants 18 F4
Odstock Wilts 9 B10
Odstone Leics 35 E9
Offchurch Warks 27 B10
Offenham Worcs 27 D7
Offham E Sus 12 E2
Offham Kent 20 F3
Offham W Sus 11 D9
Offord Cluny Cambs 29 B9
Offord Darcy Cambs 29 B9
Offton Suff 31 D7
Offwell Devon 7 G10
Ogbourne Maizey Wilts 17 D8
Ogbourne St Andrew Wilts 17 D8
Ogbourne St George Wilts 17 D9
Ogil Angus 77 A7
Ogle Northumb 63 F7
Ogmore V Glam 14 D4
Ogmore-by-Sea V Glam 14 D4
Ogmore Vale Bridgend 14 B5
Okeford Fitzpaine Dorset 9 C7
Okehampton Devon 6 G4
Okehampton Camp Devon 6 G4
Okraquoy Shetland 96 K6
Old Northants 28 A4
Old Aberdeen Aberdeen 83 C11
Old Alresford Hants 10 A4
Old Arley Warks 35 F8
Old Basford Nottingham 35 A11
Old Basing Hants 18 F3
Old Bewick Northumb 62 A6
Old Bolingbroke Lincs 47 F7
Old Bramhope W Yorks 51 E8
Old Brampton Derbys 45 E7
Old Bridge of Tilt Perth 81 G10
Old Bridge of Urr Dumfries 55 C10
Old Buckenham Norf 39 F6
Old Burghclere Hants 17 F11
Old Byland N Yorks 59 H6
Old Cassop Durham 58 C4
Old Castleton Borders 61 D11
Old Catton Norf 39 D8
Old Clee NE Lincs 46 B6
Old Cleeve Som 7 B9
Old Clipstone Notts 45 F10
Old Colwyn Conwy 41 C10
Old Coulsdon London 19 F10
Old Crombie Aberds 88 C5
Old Dailly S Ayrs 66 G5
Old Dalby Leics 36 C2
Old Deer Aberds 89 D9
Old Denaby S Yorks 45 C8
Old Edlington S Yorks 45 C9
Old Eldon Durham 58 D3
Old Ellerby E Yorks 53 F7
Old Felixstowe Suff 31 E10
Old Fletton Pboro 37 F7
Old Glossop Derbys 44 C4
Old Goole E Yorks 52 G3
Old Hall Powys 32 G5
Old Heath Essex 31 F7
Old Heathfield E Sus 12 D4
Old Hill W Mid 34 G5
Old Hunstanton Norf 38 A2
Old Hurst Cambs 37 H8
Old Hutton Cumb 57 H7
Old Kea Corn 3 E7
Old Kilpatrick W Dunb 68 C3
Old Kinnernie Aberds 83 C9
Old Knebworth Herts 29 F9
Old Langho Lancs 50 F3
Old Laxey IoM 48 D4
Old Leake Lincs 47 G8
Old Malton N Yorks 52 B3
Old Micklefield W Yorks 51 F10
Old Milton Hants 9 E11
Old Milverton Warks 27 B9
Old Monkland N Lanark 68 D6
Old Netley Hants 10 D3
Old Philpstoun W Loth 69 C9
Old Quarrington Durham 58 C4
Old Radnor Powys 25 C9
Old Rattray Aberds 89 C10
Old Rayne Aberds 83 A8
Old Romney Kent 13 D9
Old Sodbury S Glos 16 C4
Old Somerby Lincs 36 B5
Old Stratford Northants 28 D4
Old Thirsk N Yorks 51 A10
Old Town Cumb 50 A1
Old Town Cumb 57 B6
Old Town Northumb 62 D4
Old Town Scilly 2 C3
Old Trafford Gtr Man 44 C2
Old Tupton Derbys 45 F7
Old Warden C Beds 29 D8
Old Weston Cambs 37 H6
Old Whittington Derbys 45 E7
Old Wick Highld 94 E5
Old Windsor Windsor 18 D6
Old Wives Lees Kent 21 F7
Old Woking Sur 19 F7
Old Woodhall Lincs 46 F6
Oldany Highld 92 F4
Oldberrow Warks 27 B8
Oldborough Devon 7 F6
Oldbury Shrops 34 F3
Oldbury W Mid 34 G5
Oldbury Warks 35 F9
Oldbury-on-Severn S Glos 16 B3
Oldbury on the Hill Glos 16 C5
Oldcastle Bridgend 14 D5
Oldcastle Mon 25 F10
Oldcotes Notts 45 D9
Oldfallow Staffs 34 D5
Oldfield Worcs 26 B5
Oldford Som 16 F4
Oldham Gtr Man 44 B3
Oldhamstocks E Loth 70 C6
Oldland S Glos 16 D3
Oldmeldrum Aberds 89 F8
Oldshore Beg Highld 92 D4
Oldshoremore Highld 92 D5
Oldstead N Yorks 51 A11
Oldtown Aberds 83 A7
Oldtown of Ord Aberds 88 C6
Oldway Swansea 23 H10
Oldways End Devon 7 D7
Oldwhat Aberds 89 C8
Olgrinmore Highld 94 E2
Oliver's Battery Hants 10 B3
Ollaberry Shetland 96 E5
Ollerton Ches E 43 E10
Ollerton Notts 45 F10

Ollerton Shrops 34 C2
Olmarch Ceredig 24 C3
Olney M Keynes 28 C5
Olrig Ho. Highld 94 D3
Olton W Mid 35 G7
Olveston S Glos 16 C3
Olwen Ceredig 23 B10
Ombersley Worcs 26 B5
Ompton Notts 45 F10
Onchan IoM 48 E3
Onecote Staffs 44 G4
Onen Mon 25 G11
Ongar Hill Norf 38 C1
Ongar Street Hereford 25 B10
Onibury Shrops 33 H10
Onich Highld 74 A3
Onllwyn Neath 24 G5
Onneley Staffs 34 A3
Onslow Village Sur 18 G6
Onthank E Ayrs 67 B7
Openwoodgate Derbys 45 H7
Opinan Highld 85 A12
Opinan Highld 91 H13
Orange Lane Borders 70 F6
Orange Row Norf 37 C11
Orasaigh W Isles 91 F8
Orbliston Moray 88 C3
Orbost Highld 84 D7
Orby Lincs 47 F8
Orchard Hill Devon 6 D3
Orchard Portman Som 8 B1
Orcheston Wilts 17 G7
Orcop Hereford 25 F11
Orcop Hill Hereford 25 F11
Ord Highld 85 G11
Ordhead Aberds 83 B8
Ordie Aberds 82 C6
Ordiequish Moray 88 C3
Ordsall Notts 45 D10
Ore E Sus 13 E7
Oreton Shrops 34 G2
Orford Suff 31 D11
Orford Warr 43 C9
Orgreave Staffs 35 D7
Orlestone Kent 13 C8
Orleton Hereford 25 B11
Orleton Worcs 26 B3
Orlingbury Northants 28 A5
Ormesby Redcar 59 E6
Ormesby St Margaret Norf 39 D10
Ormesby St Michael Norf 39 D10
Ormiclate Castle W Isles 84 E2
Ormiscaig Highld 91 H13
Ormiston E Loth 70 D3
Ormsaigbeg Highld 78 E7
Ormsaigmore Highld 78 E7
Ormsary Argyll 72 F6
Ormsgill Cumb 49 B1
Ormskirk Lancs 43 B7
Orpington London 19 E11
Orrell Gtr Man 43 B8
Orrell Mers 42 C6
Orrisdale IoM 48 C3
Orroland Dumfries 55 E10
Orsett Thurrock 20 C3
Orslow Staffs 34 D4
Orston Notts 36 A3
Orthwaite Cumb 56 C4
Ortner Lancs 49 D5
Orton Cumb 57 F8
Orton Northants 36 H4
Orton Longueville Pboro 37 F7
Orton-on-the-Hill Leics 35 E9
Orton Waterville Pboro 37 F7
Orwell Cambs 29 C10
Osbaldeston Lancs 50 F2
Osbaldwick York 52 D2
Osbaston Shrops 33 C9
Osbournby Lincs 37 B6
Oscroft Ches W 43 F8
Ose Highld 85 D8
Osgathorpe Leics 35 D10
Osgodby Lincs 46 C4
Osgodby N Yorks 52 F2
Osgodby N Yorks 53 A6
Oskaig Highld 85 E10
Oskamull Argyll 78 G7
Osmaston Derby 35 B9
Osmaston Derbys 35 A8
Osmington Dorset 8 F6
Osmington Mills Dorset 8 F6
Osmotherley N Yorks 58 G5
Ospisdale Highld 87 C10
Ospringe Kent 21 E7
Ossett W Yorks 51 G8
Ossington Notts 45 F11
Ostend Essex 20 B6
Oswaldkirk N Yorks 52 B2
Oswaldtwistle Lancs 50 G3
Oswestry Shrops 33 C8
Otford Kent 20 F2
Otham Kent 20 F4
Othery Som 8 A2
Otley Suff 31 C9
Otley W Yorks 51 E8
Otter Ferry Argyll 73 E8
Otterbourne Hants 10 B3
Otterburn N Yorks 50 D4
Otterburn Northumb 62 D4
Otterburn Camp Northumb 62 D4
Otterham Corn 4 B2
Otterhampton Som 15 G8
Ottershaw Sur 19 E7
Otterswick Shetland 96 E7
Otterton Devon 7 H9
Ottery St Mary Devon 7 G10
Ottinge Kent 21 G8
Ottringham E Yorks 53 G8
Oughterby Cumb 61 H8
Oughtershaw N Yorks 50 A4
Oughterside Cumb 56 B3
Oughtibridge S Yorks 45 C7
Oughtrington Warr 43 D9
Oulston N Yorks 51 B11
Oulton Cumb 56 A4
Oulton Norf 39 C7
Oulton Staffs 34 B5
Oulton Suff 39 F11
Oulton W Yorks 51 G9
Oulton Broad Suff 39 F11
Oulton Street Norf 39 C7
Oundle Northants 36 G6
Ousby Cumb 57 C8
Ousdale Highld 94 H2
Ousden Suff 30 C4
Ousefleet E Yorks 52 G4
Ouston Durham 58 A3
Ouston Northumb 62 F6
Out Newton E Yorks 53 G9
Out Rawcliffe Lancs 49 E4
Outertown Orkney 95 G3
Outgate Cumb 56 G5
Outhgill Cumb 57 F9
Outlane W Yorks 51 H6
Outwell Norf 37 E11
Outwick Hants 9 C10
Outwood Sur 19 G10
Outwood W Yorks 51 G9
Outwoods Staffs 34 D3
Ovenden W Yorks 51 G6
Ovenscloss Borders 70 G3
Over Cambs 29 A10
Over Ches W 43 F9
Over S Glos 16 C2
Over Compton Dorset 8 C4
Over Green W Mid 35 F7
Over Haddon Derbys 44 F6
Over Hulton Gtr Man 43 B9
Over Kellet Lancs 49 B5
Over Kiddington Oxon 27 F11
Over Knutsford Ches E 43 E10
Over Monnow Mon 26 G2
Over Norton Oxon 27 F10
Over Peover Ches E 43 E10
Over Silton N Yorks 58 G5
Over Stowey Som 7 C10
Over Stratton Som 8 C3
Over Tabley Ches E 43 D10
Over Wallop Hants 17 H9
Over Whitacre Warks 35 F8
Over Worton Oxon 27 F11
Overbister Orkney 95 D7
Overbury Worcs 26 E6
Overcombe Dorset 8 F5
Overgreen Derbys 45 E7
Overleigh Som 15 H10
Overley Green Warks 27 C7
Overpool Ches W 43 E6
Overscaig Hotel Highld 92 G7
Overseal Derbys 35 D8
Oversland Kent 21 F7
Overstone Northants 28 B5
Overstrand Norf 39 A8
Overthorpe Northants 27 D11
Overton Aberdeen 83 B10
Overton Ches W 43 E8
Overton Dumfries 60 G5
Overton Hants 18 G2
Overton Lancs 49 D4
Overton N Yorks 52 D1
Overton Shrops 26 A2
Overton Swansea 23 H9
Overton W Yorks 51 H8
Overton = Owrtyn Wrex 33 A9
Overton Bridge Wrex 33 A9
Overtown N Lanark 69 E7
Oving Bucks 28 F4
Oving W Sus 11 D8
Ovingdean Brighton 12 F2
Ovingham Northumb 62 G6
Ovington Durham 58 E2
Ovington Essex 30 D4
Ovington Hants 10 A4
Ovington Norf 38 E5
Ovington Northumb 62 G6
Ower Hants 10 C2
Owermoigne Dorset 9 F6
Owlbury Shrops 33 F9
Owler Bar Derbys 44 E6
Owlerton S Yorks 45 D7
Owl's Green Suff 31 B9
Owlswick Bucks 28 H4
Owmby Lincs 46 B4
Owmby-by-Spital Lincs 46 D4
Owrtyn = Overton Wrex 33 A9
Owslebury Hants 10 B4
Owston Leics 36 E3
Owston S Yorks 45 A9
Owston Ferry N Lincs 46 B2
Owstwick E Yorks 53 F8
Owthorne E Yorks 53 G9
Owthorpe Notts 36 B2
Oxborough Norf 38 E3
Oxcombe Lincs 47 E7
Oxen Park Cumb 56 H5
Oxenholme Cumb 57 H7
Oxenhope W Yorks 50 F6
Oxenton Glos 26 E6
Oxenwood Wilts 17 F10
Oxford Oxon 28 H2
Oxhey Herts 19 B8
Oxhill Warks 27 D10
Oxley W Mid 34 E5
Oxley Green Essex 30 G6
Oxley's Green E Sus 12 D5
Oxnam Borders 62 B3
Oxshott Sur 19 E8
Oxspring S Yorks 44 B6
Oxted Sur 19 F10
Oxton Borders 70 E3
Oxton Notts 45 G10
Oxwich Swansea 23 H9
Oxwick Norf 38 C5
Oykel Bridge Highld 92 J6
Oyne Aberds 83 A8

P

Pabail Iarach W Isles 91 D10
Pabail Uarach W Isles 91 D10
Pace Gate N Yorks 51 D7
Packington Leics 35 D9
Padanaram Angus 77 B7
Padbury Bucks 28 E4
Paddington London 19 C9
Paddlesworth Kent 21 H8
Paddock Wood Kent 12 B5
Paddockhaugh Moray 88 C2
Paddockhole Dumfries 61 E8
Padfield Derbys 44 C4
Padiham Lancs 50 F3
Padog Conwy 41 E10
Padside N Yorks 51 D7
Padstow Corn 3 B8
Padworth W Berks 18 E3
Page Bank Durham 58 C3
Pagham W Sus 11 E7
Paglesham Churchend Essex 20 B6
Paglesham Eastend Essex 20 B6
Paibeil W Isles 84 B2
Paible W Isles 90 H5
Paignton Torbay 5 E9
Pailton Warks 35 G10
Painscastle Powys 25 D8
Painshawfield Northumb 62 G6
Painsthorpe E Yorks 52 D4
Painswick Glos 26 H5
Pairc Shiaboist W Isles 90 C7
Paisley Renfs 68 D3
Pakefield Suff 39 F11
Pakenham Suff 30 B6
Pale Gwyn 32 B5
Palestine Hants 17 G9
Paley Street Windsor 18 D5
Palfrey W Mid 34 F6
Palgowan Dumfries 54 A6
Palgrave Suff 39 H7
Pallion T&W 63 H9
Palmarsh Kent 13 C10
Palnackie Dumfries 55 D11
Palnure Dumfries 55 C7
Palterton Derbys 45 F8
Pamber End Hants 18 F3
Pamber Green Hants 18 F3
Pamber Heath Hants 18 E3
Pamphill Dorset 9 D8
Pampisford Cambs 29 D11
Pan Orkney 95 J4
Panbride Angus 77 D8
Pancrasweek Devon 6 F1
Pandy Gwyn 32 E2
Pandy Mon 25 F10
Pandy Powys 32 E5
Pandy Wrex 33 B7
Pandy Tudur Conwy 41 D10
Panfield Essex 30 F4
Pangbourne W Berks 18 D3
Pannal N Yorks 51 D9
Panshanger Herts 29 G9
Pant Shrops 33 C8
Pant-glâs Powys 32 F3
Pant-glas Carms 23 D10
Pant-glas Gwyn 40 F6
Pant-glas Shrops 33 B8
Pant-lasau Swansea 14 B2
Pant Mawr Powys 32 G4
Pant-teg Carms 23 D9
Pant-y-Caws Carms 22 D6
Pant-y-dwr Powys 32 H5
Pant-y-ffridd Powys 33 E7
Pant-y-Wacco Flint 42 E4
Pant-yr-awel Bridgend 14 C5
Pantgwyn Carms 23 D10
Pantgwyn Ceredig 23 B7
Panton Lincs 46 E5
Pantperthog Gwyn 32 E3
Pantyffynnon Carms 24 G3
Pantymwyn Flint 42 F4
Panxworth Norf 39 D9
Papcastle Cumb 56 C3
Papigoe Highld 94 E5
Papil Shetland 96 K5
Papley Orkney 95 J5
Papple E Loth 70 C4
Papplewick Notts 45 G9
Papworth Everard Cambs 29 B9
Papworth St Agnes Cambs 29 B9
Par Corn 4 F1
Parbold Lancs 43 A7
Parbrook Som 16 H2
Parbrook W Sus 11 B9
Parc Gwyn 41 G10
Parc-Seymour Newport 15 B10
Parc-y-rhôs Carms 23 B10
Parcllyn Ceredig 23 A7
Pardshaw Cumb 56 D2
Parham Suff 31 B10
Park Dumfries 60 D5
Park Corner Oxon 18 C3
Park Corner Windsor 18 C5
Park End Mbro 58 E6
Park End Northumb 62 F4
Park Gate Hants 10 D4
Park Hill N Yorks 51 C9
Park Hill Notts 45 G10
Park Street W Sus 11 A10
Parkend Glos 26 H3
Parkeston Essex 31 E9
Parkgate Ches W 42 E5
Parkgate Dumfries 60 E6
Parkgate Kent 13 C7
Parkgate Sur 19 G9
Parkham Devon 6 D2
Parkham Ash Devon 6 D2
Parkhill Ho. Aberds 83 B10
Parkhouse Mon 15 A10
Parkhouse Green Derbys 45 F8
Parkhurst IoW 10 E3
Parkmill Swansea 23 H10
Parkneuk Aberds 83 F9
Parkstone Poole 9 E9
Parley Cross Dorset 9 E9
Parracombe Devon 6 B5
Parrog Pembs 22 C5
Parsley Hay Derbys 44 F5
Parson Cross S Yorks 45 C7
Parson Drove Cambs 37 E9
Parsonage Green Essex 30 H4
Parsonby Cumb 56 C3
Parson's Heath Essex 31 F7
Partick Glasgow 68 D4
Partington Gtr Man 43 C10
Partney Lincs 47 F8
Parton Cumb 56 D1
Parton Dumfries 55 B9
Parton Glos 26 F5
Partridge Green W Sus 11 C10
Parwich Derbys 44 G5
Passenham Northants 28 E4
Paston Norf 39 B9
Patchacott Devon 6 G3
Patcham Brighton 12 F2
Patching W Sus 11 D9
Patchole Devon 6 B5
Pateley Bridge N Yorks 51 C7
Paternoster Heath Essex 30 G6
Path of Condie Perth 76 F3
Pathe Som 8 A2
Pathhead Aberds 77 A10
Pathhead E Ayrs 67 E9
Pathhead Fife 69 A11
Pathhead Midloth 70 D2
Pathstruie Perth 76 F3
Patna E Ayrs 67 E7
Patney Wilts 17 F7
Patrick IoM 48 D2
Patrick Brompton N Yorks 58 G3
Patrington E Yorks 53 G9
Patrixbourne Kent 21 F8
Patterdale Cumb 56 E5
Pattingham Staffs 34 F4
Pattishall Northants 28 C3
Pattiswick Green Essex 30 F5
Patton Bridge Cumb 57 G7
Paul Corn 2 G3
Paulerspury Northants 28 D4
Paull E Yorks 53 G7
Paulton Bath 16 F3
Pavenham Bedford 28 C6
Pawlett Som 15 G9
Pawston Northumb 71 G7
Paxford Glos 27 E8
Paxton Borders 71 E8
Payhembury Devon 7 F9
Paythorne Lancs 50 D4
Peacehaven E Sus 12 F3
Peak Dale Derbys 44 E4
Peak Forest Derbys 44 E5
Peakirk Pboro 37 E7
Pearsie Angus 76 B6
Pease Pottage W Sus 12 C1
Peasedown St John Bath 16 F4
Peasemore W Berks 17 D11
Peasenhall Suff 31 B10
Peaslake Sur 19 G7
Peasley Cross Mers 43 C8
Peasmarsh E Sus 13 D7
Peaston E Loth 70 D3
Peastonbank E Loth 70 D3
Peat Inn Fife 77 G7
Peathill Aberds 89 B9
Peatling Magna Leics 36 F1
Peatling Parva Leics 36 G1
Peaton Shrops 33 G11
Peats Corner Suff 31 B8
Pebmarsh Essex 30 E5
Pebworth Worcs 27 D8
Pecket Well W Yorks 50 G5
Peckforton Ches E 43 G8
Peckham London 19 D10
Peckleton Leics 35 E10
Pedlinge Kent 13 C10
Pedmore W Mid 34 G5
Pedwell Som 15 H10
Peebles Borders 69 F11
Peel IoM 48 D2
Peel Common Hants 10 D4
Peel Park S Lanark 68 E5
Peening Quarter Kent 13 D7
Pegsdon C Beds 29 E8
Pegswood Northumb 63 E8
Pegwell Kent 21 E10
Peinchorran Highld 85 E10
Peinlich Highld 85 C9
Pelaw T&W 63 G8
Pelcomb Bridge Pembs 22 E4
Pelcomb Cross Pembs 22 E4
Peldon Essex 30 G6
Pellon W Yorks 51 G6
Pelsall W Mid 34 E6
Pelton Durham 58 A3
Pelutho Cumb 56 B3
Pelynt Corn 4 F3
Pemberton Gtr Man 43 B8
Pembrey Carms 23 F9
Pembridge Hereford 25 C10
Pembroke = Penfro Pembs 22 F4
Pembroke Dock = Doc Penfro Pembs 22 F4
Pembury Kent 12 B5
Pen-bont Rhydybeddau Ceredig 32 G2
Pen-clawdd Swansea 23 G10
Pen-ffordd Pembs 22 D5
Pen-groes-oped Mon 25 H10
Pen-llyn Anglesey 40 B5
Pen-lon Anglesey 40 D6
Pen-sarn Gwyn 32 C1
Pen-sarn Gwyn 40 F6
Pen-twyn Mon 26 H2
Pen-y-banc Carms 24 F3
Pen-y-bont Carms 23 D8
Pen-y-bont Gwyn 32 C2
Pen-y-bont Gwyn 32 E3
Pen-y-bont Powys 33 C8
Pen-y-bont ar Ogwr = Bridgend Bridgend 14 D5
Pen-y-bryn Gwyn 32 D2
Pen-y-bryn Pembs 22 B6
Pen-y-cae Powys 24 G5
Pen-y-cae-mawr Mon 15 B10
Pen-y-cefn Flint 42 E4
Pen-y-clawdd Mon 25 H11
Pen-y-coedcae Rhondda 14 C6
Pen-y-fai Bridgend 14 C4
Pen-y-garn Carms 23 C10
Pen-y-garn Ceredig 32 G2
Pen-y-garnedd Anglesey 41 C7
Pen-y-gop Conwy 32 A5
Pen-y-graig Gwyn 40 G3
Pen-y-groes Carms 23 E10
Pen-y-groeslon Gwyn 40 G4
Pen-y-Gwryd Hotel Gwyn 41 E8
Pen-y-stryt Denb 42 G4
Pen-yr-heol Mon 25 G11
Pen-yr-Heolgerrig M Tydf 25 H7
Penallt Mon 26 G2
Penally Pembs 22 G6
Penalt Hereford 26 F2
Penare Corn 3 E8
Penarlâg = Hawarden Flint 42 F6
Penarth V Glam 15 D7
Penbryn Ceredig 23 A7
Pencader Carms 23 C9
Pencaenewydd Gwyn 40 F6
Pencaitland E Loth 70 D3
Pencarnisiog Anglesey 40 C5
Pencarreg Carms 23 B10
Pencelli Powys 25 F7
Pencoed Bridgend 14 C5
Pencombe Hereford 26 C2
Pencoyd Hereford 26 F2
Pencraig Hereford 26 F2
Pencraig Powys 32 C6
Pendeen Corn 2 F2
Penderyn Rhondda 24 H6
Pendine Carms 23 F7
Pendlebury Gtr Man 43 B10
Pendleton Lancs 43 F3
Pendock Worcs 26 E4
Pendoggett Corn 3 B9
Pendomer Som 8 C4
Pendoylan V Glam 14 D6
Pendre Bridgend 14 C5
Penegoes Powys 32 E3
Penfro = Pembroke Pembs 22 F4
Pengam Caerph 15 B7
Penge London 19 D10
Pengenffordd Powys 25 E8
Pengorffwysfa Anglesey 40 A6
Pengover Green Corn 4 E3
Penhale Corn 2 H5
Penhale Corn 3 D8
Penhalvaen Corn 2 F6
Penhill Swindon 17 C8
Penhow Newport 15 B10
Penhurst E Sus 12 E5
Peniarth Gwyn 32 E2
Penicuik Midloth 69 D11
Peniel Carms 23 D9
Peniel Denb 42 F3
Penifiler Highld 85 D9
Peninver Argyll 65 F8
Penisarwaun Gwyn 41 D7
Penistone S Yorks 44 B6
Penjerrick Corn 3 F6
Penketh Warr 43 D8
Penkill S Ayrs 66 G5
Penkridge Staffs 34 D5
Penley Wrex 33 B10
Penllergaer Swansea 14 B2
Penllyn V Glam 14 D5
Penmachno Conwy 41 E9
Penmaen Swansea 23 H10
Penmaenan Conwy 41 C9
Penmaenmawr Conwy 41 C9
Penmaenpool Gwyn 32 D2
Penmark V Glam 14 E6
Penmarth Corn 2 F6
Penmon Anglesey 41 B8
Penmore Mill Argyll 78 F7
Penmorfa Ceredig 23 A8
Penmorfa Gwyn 41 F7
Penmynydd Anglesey 41 C7
Penn Bucks 18 B6
Penn W Mid 34 F4
Penn Street Bucks 18 B6
Pennal Gwyn 32 E3
Pennan Aberds 89 B8
Pennant Ceredig 24 B2
Pennant Denb 32 B6
Pennant Denb 42 G3
Pennant Powys 32 F4
Pennant Melangell Powys 32 C6
Pennar Pembs 22 F4
Pennard Swansea 23 H10
Pennerley Shrops 33 F9
Pennington Cumb 49 B2
Pennington Gtr Man 43 C9
Pennington Hants 10 E2
Penny Bridge Cumb 49 A3
Pennycross Argyll 79 J8
Pennygate Norf 39 C9
Pennygown Argyll 79 G8
Pennymoor Devon 7 E7
Pennywell T&W 63 H9
Penparc Ceredig 23 B7
Penparc Pembs 22 C3
Penparcau Ceredig 32 G1
Penperlleni Mon 15 A9
Penpillick Corn 4 F1
Penpol Corn 3 F7
Penpoll Corn 4 F2
Penpont Dumfries 60 D4
Penpont Powys 24 F6
Penrhôs Mon 25 G11
Penrherber Carms 23 C7
Penrhiw goch Carms 23 E10
Penrhiw-llan Ceredig 23 B8
Penrhiw-pâl Ceredig 23 B8
Penrhiwceiber Rhondda 14 B6
Penrhos Gwyn 40 G5
Penrhos Powys 24 G4
Penrhosfeilw Anglesey 40 B4
Penrhyn Bay Conwy 41 B10
Penrhyn-coch Ceredig 32 G2
Penrhyndeudraeth Gwyn 41 G8
Penrhynside Conwy 41 B10
Penrice Swansea 23 H9
Penrith Cumb 57 C7
Penrose Corn 3 B7
Penruddock Cumb 56 D6
Penryn Corn 3 F6
Pensarn Carms 23 E9
Pensarn Conwy 42 E2
Pensax Worcs 26 B4
Pensby Mers 42 D5
Penselwood Som 9 A6
Pensford Bath 16 E3
Penshaw T&W 58 A4
Penshurst Kent 12 B4
Pensilva Corn 4 E3
Penston E Loth 70 C3
Pentewan Corn 3 E9
Pentir Gwyn 41 D7
Pentire Corn 3 C6
Pentlow Essex 30 D5
Pentney Norf 38 D3
Penton Mewsey Hants 17 G10
Pentraeth Anglesey 41 C7
Pentre Carms 23 E10
Pentre Powys 33 F8
Pentre Powys 33 G6
Pentre Rhondda 14 B5
Pentre Shrops 33 D9
Pentre Wrex 33 A8
Pentre Wrex 33 B7
Pentre-bâch Ceredig 23 B10
Pentre-bach Powys 24 E6
Pentre Berw Anglesey 40 C6
Pentre-bont Conwy 41 E9
Pentre-celyn Denb 42 G4
Pentre-Celyn Powys 32 E4
Pentre-chwyth Swansea 14 B2
Pentre-cwrt Carms 23 C8
Pentre Dolau-Honddu Powys 24 D6
Pentre-dwr Swansea 14 B2
Pentre-galar Pembs 22 C6
Pentre-Gwenlais Carms 24 G3
Pentre Gwynfryn Gwyn 32 C1
Pentre Halkyn Flint 42 E5
Pentre-Isaf Conwy 41 D10
Pentre Llanrhaeadr Denb 42 F3
Pentre-llwyn-llŵyd Powys 24 C6
Pentre-llyn Ceredig 24 A3
Pentre-llyn cymmer Conwy 42 G2
Pentre Meyrick V Glam 14 D5
Pentre-poeth Newport 15 C8
Pentre-rhew Ceredig 24 C3
Pentre-tafarn-y-fedw Conwy 41 D10
Pentre-ty-gwyn Carms 24 E5
Pentrebach M Tydf 14 A6
Pentrebach Swansea 24 H3
Pentrebeirdd Powys 33 D7
Pentrecagal Carms 23 B8
Pentredwr Denb 42 H4
Pentrefelin Carms 23 D10
Pentrefelin Ceredig 24 D3
Pentrefelin Conwy 41 C10
Pentrefelin Gwyn 41 G7
Pentrefoelas Conwy 41 E10
Pentregat Ceredig 23 A8
Pentreheyling Shrops 33 F8
Pentre'r Felin Conwy 41 D10
Pentre'r-felin Powys 24 E6
Pentrich Derbys 45 G7
Pentridge Dorset 9 C9
Pentyrch Cardiff 15 C7
Penuchadre V Glam 14 D4
Penuwch Ceredig 24 B2
Penwithick Corn 3 D9
Penwyllt Powys 24 G5
Penybanc Carms 24 G3
Penybont Powys 25 B8
Penybontfawr Powys 33 C6
Penycae Wrex 42 H5
Penycwm Pembs 22 D3
Penyffordd Flint 42 F6
Penyffridd Gwyn 41 E7
Penygarnedd Powys 33 C7
Penygraig Rhondda 14 B5
Penygroes Gwyn 40 E6
Penygroes Pembs 22 C6
Penyrheol Caerph 15 C7
Penysarn Anglesey 40 A6
Penywaun Rhondda 14 A5
Penzance Corn 2 F3
Peopleton Worcs 26 C6
Peover Heath Ches E 43 E10
Peper Harow Sur 18 G6
Perceton N Ayrs 67 B6
Percie Aberds 83 D7
Percyhorner Aberds 89 B9
Periton Som 7 B8
Perivale London 19 C8
Perkinsville Durham 58 A3
Perlethorpe Notts 45 E10
Perranarworthal Corn 3 F6
Perranporth Corn 3 D6
Perranuthnoe Corn 2 G4
Perranzabuloe Corn 3 D6
Perry Barr W Mid 35 F6
Perry Green Herts 29 G11
Perry Green Wilts 16 C6
Perry Street Kent 20 D3
Perryfoot Derbys 44 D5
Pershall Staffs 34 B4
Pershore Worcs 26 D6
Pert Angus 83 G8
Pertenhall Bedford 29 B7
Perth Perth 76 E4
Perthy Shrops 33 B9
Perton Staffs 34 F4
Pertwood Wilts 16 H5
Peter Tavy Devon 4 D6
Peterborough Pboro 37 F7
Peterburn Highld 91 J12
Peterchurch Hereford 25 E10
Peterculter Aberdeen 83 C10
Peterhead Aberds 89 D11
Peterlee Durham 58 B5
Peter's Green Herts 29 G8
Peters Marland Devon 6 E3
Petersfield Hants 10 B6
Peterston super-Ely V Glam 14 D6
Peterstone Wentlooge Newport 15 C8
Peterstow Hereford 26 F2
Petertown Orkney 95 H4
Petham Kent 21 F8
Petrockstow Devon 6 F4
Pett E Sus 13 E7
Pettaugh Suff 31 C8
Petteridge Kent 12 B5
Pettinain S Lanark 69 F8
Pettistree Suff 31 C9
Petton Devon 7 D9
Petton Shrops 33 C10
Petts Wood London 19 E11
Petty Aberds 89 E7
Pettycur Fife 69 B11
Pettymuick Aberds 89 F9
Petworth W Sus 11 B8
Pevensey E Sus 12 F5
Pevensey Bay E Sus 12 F5
Pewsey Wilts 17 E8
Philham Devon 6 D1
Philiphaugh Borders 70 H3
Phillack Corn 2 F4
Philleigh Corn 3 F7
Philpstoun W Loth 69 C9
Phocle Green Hereford 26 F3
Phoenix Green Hants 18 F4
Pica Cumb 56 D2
Piccotts End Herts 29 H7
Pickering N Yorks 52 A3
Picket Piece Hants 17 G10
Picket Post Hants 9 D10
Pickhill N Yorks 51 A9
Picklescott Shrops 33 F10
Pickletillem Fife 77 E7
Pickmere Ches E 43 E9
Pickney Som 7 D10
Pickstock Telford 34 C3
Pickwell Devon 6 B3
Pickwell Leics 36 D3
Pickworth Lincs 36 B6
Pickworth Rutland 36 D5
Picton Ches W 43 E7
Picton Flint 42 D4
Picton N Yorks 58 F5
Piddinghoe E Sus 12 F3
Piddington Northants 28 C5
Piddington Oxon 28 G3
Piddlehinton Dorset 8 E6
Piddletrenthide Dorset 8 E6
Pidley Cambs 37 H9
Piercebridge Darl 58 E3
Pierowall Orkney 95 D5
Pigdon Northumb 63 E7
Pikehall Derbys 44 G5
Pilgrims Hatch Essex 20 B2
Pilham Lincs 46 C2
Pill N Som 15 D11
Pillaton Corn 4 E4
Pillerton Hersey Warks 27 D10
Pillerton Priors Warks 27 D9
Pilleth Powys 25 B9
Pilley Hants 10 E2
Pilley S Yorks 45 B7
Pilling Lancs 49 E4
Pilling Lane Lancs 49 E3
Pillowell Glos 26 H3
Pillwell Dorset 9 C6
Pilning S Glos 16 C2
Pilsbury Derbys 44 F5
Pilsdon Dorset 8 E3
Pilsgate Pboro 37 E6
Pilsley Derbys 44 E6
Pilsley Derbys 45 F8
Pilton Devon 6 C4
Pilton Northants 36 G6
Pilton Rutland 36 E5
Pilton Som 16 G2
Pilton Green Swansea 23 H9
Pimperne Dorset 9 D8
Pin Mill Suff 31 E9
Pinchbeck Lincs 37 C8
Pinchbeck Bars Lincs 37 C7
Pinchbeck West Lincs 37 C8
Pincheon Green S Yorks 52 H2
Pinehurst Swindon 17 C8
Pinfold Lancs 43 A6
Pinged Carms 23 F9
Pinhoe Devon 7 G8
Pinkneys Grn. Windsor 18 C5
Pinley W Mid 35 H9
Pinminnoch S Ayrs 66 G4
Pinmore S Ayrs 66 G5
Pinmore Mains S Ayrs 66 G5
Pinner London 19 C8
Pinvin Worcs 26 D6
Pinwherry S Ayrs 66 H4
Pinxton Derbys 45 G8
Pipe and Lyde Hereford 26 D2
Pipe Gate Shrops 34 A3
Piperhill Highld 87 F11
Piper's Pool Corn 4 C3
Pipewell Northants 36 G4
Pippacott Devon 6 C4
Pipton Powys 25 E8
Pirbright Sur 18 F6
Pirnmill N Ayrs 66 B1
Pirton Herts 29 E8
Pirton Worcs 26 D5
Pisgah Ceredig 32 H2
Pisgah Stirling 75 G10
Pishill Oxon 18 C4
Pistyll Gwyn 40 F5
Pitagowan Perth 81 G10
Pitblae Aberds 89 B9
Pitcairngreen Perth 76 E3
Pitcalnie Highld 87 D11
Pitcaple Aberds 83 A9
Pitch Green Bucks 18 A4
Pitch Place Sur 18 F6
Pitchcombe Glos 26 H5
Pitchcott Bucks 28 F4
Pitchford Shrops 33 E11
Pitcombe Som 8 A5
Pitcorthie Fife 77 G8
Pitcox E Loth 70 C5
Pitcur Perth 76 D5
Pitfichie Aberds 83 B8
Pitforthie Aberds 83 F10
Pitgrudy Highld 87 B10
Pitkennedy Angus 77 B8
Pitkevy Fife 76 G5
Pitkierie Fife 77 G8
Pitlessie Fife 76 G6
Pitlochry Perth 76 B2
Pitmachie Aberds 83 A8
Pitmain Highld 81 C9
Pitmedden Aberds 89 F8
Pitminster Som 7 E11
Pitmuies Angus 77 C8
Pitmunie Aberds 83 B8
Pitney Som 8 B3
Pitscottie Fife 77 F7
Pitsea Essex 20 C4
Pitsford Northants 28 B4
Pitsmoor S Yorks 45 D7
Pitstone Bucks 28 G6
Pitstone Green Bucks 28 G6
Pittendreich Moray 88 B1
Pittentrail Highld 93 J10
Pittenweem Fife 77 G8
Pittington Durham 58 B4
Pittodrie Aberds 83 A8
Pitton Wilts 9 A11
Pittswood Kent 20 G3
Pittulie Aberds 89 B9
Pity Me Durham 58 B3
Pityme Corn 3 B8
Pityoulish Highld 81 B11
Pixey Green Suff 39 H8
Pixham Sur 19 F8
Pixley Hereford 26 E3
Place Newton N Yorks 52 B4
Plaidy Aberds 89 C7
Plains N Lanark 68 D6
Plaish Shrops 33 F11
Plaistow W Sus 11 A9
Plaitford Wilts 10 C1
Plank Lane Gtr Man 43 C9
Plas-canol Gwyn 32 D1
Plas Gogerddan Ceredig 32 G2
Plas Llwyngwern Powys 32 E3
Plas Nantyr Wrex 33 B7
Plas-yn-Cefn Denb 42 E3
Plastow Green Hants 18 E2
Platt Kent 20 F3
Platt Bridge Gtr Man 43 B9
Platts Common S Yorks 45 B7
Plawsworth Durham 58 B3
Plaxtol Kent 20 F3
Play Hatch Oxon 18 D4
Playden E Sus 13 D8
Playford Suff 31 D9
Playing Place Corn 3 E7
Playley Green Glos 26 E4
Plealey Shrops 33 E10
Plean Stirling 69 B7
Pleasington Blackburn 50 G2
Pleasley Derbys 45 F9
Pleckgate Blackburn 50 F2
Plenmeller Northumb 62 G3
Pleshey Essex 30 G3
Plockton Highld 85 E13
Plocrapol W Isles 90 H6
Ploughfield Hereford 25 D10
Plowden Shrops 33 G9
Ploxgreen Shrops 33 E9
Pluckley Kent 20 G6
Pluckley Thorne Kent 13 B8
Plumbland Cumb 56 C3
Plumley Ches E 43 E10
Plumpton Cumb 57 C6
Plumpton E Sus 12 E2
Plumpton Green E Sus 12 E2
Plumpton Head Cumb 57 C7
Plumstead London 19 D11
Plumstead Norf 39 B7
Plumtree Notts 36 B2
Plungar Leics 36 B3
Plush Dorset 8 D6
Plwmp Ceredig 23 A8
Plymouth Plym 4 F5
Plympton Plym 4 F6
Plymstock Plym 4 F6
Plymtree Devon 7 F9
Pockley N Yorks 59 H7
Pocklington E Yorks 52 E4
Pode Hole Lincs 37 C8
Podimore Som 8 B4
Podington Bedford 28 B6
Podmore Staffs 34 B3
Point Clear Essex 31 G7
Pointon Lincs 37 B7
Pokesdown Bmouth 9 E10
Pol a Charra W Isles 84 G2
Polbae Dumfries 54 B5
Polbain Highld 92 H2
Polbathic Corn 4 F4
Polbeth W Loth 69 D9
Polchar Highld 81 C10
Pole Elm Worcs 26 D5
Polebrook Northants 37 G6
Polegate E Sus 12 F4
Poles Highld 87 B10
Polesworth Warks 35 E8
Polgigga Corn 2 G2
Polglass Highld 92 J3
Polgooth Corn 3 D8
Poling W Sus 11 D9
Polkerris Corn 4 F1
Polla Highld 92 D6
Pollington E Yorks 52 H2
Polloch Highld 79 E10
Pollok Glasgow 68 D4
Pollokshields Glasgow 68 D4
Polmassick Corn 3 E8
Polmont Falk 69 C8
Polnessan E Ayrs 67 E7
Polnish Highld 79 C10
Polperro Corn 4 F3
Polruan Corn 4 F2
Polsham Som 15 G11
Polstead Suff 30 E6
Poltalloch Argyll 73 D7
Poltimore Devon 7 G8
Polton Midloth 69 D11
Polwarth Borders 70 E6
Polyphant Corn 4 C3
Polzeath Corn 3 B8
Ponders End London 19 B10
Pondersbridge Cambs 37 F8
Pondtail Hants 18 F5
Ponsanooth Corn 3 F6
Ponsworthy Devon 5 D8
Pont Aber Carms 24 F4
Pont Aber-Geirw Gwyn 32 C3
Pont-ar-gothi Carms 23 D10
Pont ar Hydfer Powys 24 F5
Pont-ar-llechau Carms 24 F4
Pont Cwm Pydew Denb 32 B6
Pont Cyfyng Conwy 41 E9
Pont Cysyllte Wrex 33 A8
Pont Dolydd Prysor Gwyn 41 G9
Pont-faen Powys 24 E6
Pont Fronwydd Gwyn 32 C4
Pont-gareg Pembs 22 B6
Pont-Henri Carms 23 F9
Pont-Llogel Powys 32 D6
Pont Pen-y-benglog Gwyn 41 D8
Pont Rhyd-goch Conwy 41 D8
Pont-Rhyd-sarn Gwyn 32 C4
Pont Rhyd-y-cyff Bridgend 14 C4
Pont-rhyd-y-groes Ceredig 24 A4
Pont-rug Gwyn 41 D7
Pont Senni = Sennybridge Powys 24 F6
Pont-siân Ceredig 23 B9
Pont-y-gwaith Rhondda 14 B6
Pont-y-Pŵl = Pontypool Torf 15 A8
Pont-y-pant Conwy 41 E9
Pont y Pennant Gwyn 32 C5
Pont yr Afon-Gam Gwyn 41 F9
Pont-yr-hafod Pembs 22 D4
Pontamman Carms 24 G3
Pontantwn Carms 23 E9
Pontardawe Neath 14 A3
Pontarddulais Swansea 23 F10
Pontarsais Carms 23 D9
Pontblyddyn Flint 42 F5
Pontbren Araeth Carms 24 F3
Pontbren Llwyd Rhondda 24 H6
Pontefract W Yorks 51 G10
Ponteland Northumb 63 F7
Ponterwyd Ceredig 32 G3
Pontesbury Shrops 33 E9
Pontfadog Wrex 33 B8
Pontfaen Pembs 22 C5
Pontgarreg Ceredig 23 A8
Ponthir Torf 15 B9
Ponthirwaun Ceredig 23 B7
Pontllanfraith Caerph 15 B7
Pontlliw Swansea 14 A2
Pontllyfni Gwyn 40 E6
Pontlottyn Caerph 25 H8
Pontneddfechan Powys 24 H6
Pontnewydd Torf 15 B8
Pontrhydfendigaid Ceredig 24 B4
Pontrhydyfen Neath 14 B3
Pontrilas Hereford 25 F10
Pontrobert Powys 33 D7
Ponts Green E Sus 12 E5
Pontshill Hereford 26 F3
Pontsticill M Tydf 25 G7
Pontwgan Conwy 41 C9
Pontyates Carms 23 F9
Pontyberem Carms 23 E10
Pontyclun Rhondda 14 C6
Pontycymer Bridgend 14 B5
Pontyglasier Pembs 22 C6
Pontypool = Pont-y-Pŵl Torf 15 A8
Pontypridd Rhondda 14 C6
Pontywaun Caerph 15 B8
Pooksgreen Hants 10 C2
Pool Corn 2 E5
Pool W Yorks 51 E8
Pool o' Muckhart Clack 76 G3
Pool Quay Powys 33 D8
Poole Poole 9 E9
Poole Keynes Glos 16 B6
Poolend Staffs 44 G3
Poolewe Highld 91 J13
Pooley Bridge Cumb 56 D6
Poolfold Staffs 44 G2
Poolhill Glos 26 F4
Poolsbrook Derbys 45 E8
Pootings Kent 19 G11
Pope Hill Pembs 22 E4
Popeswood Brack 18 E5
Popham Hants 18 G2
Poplar London 19 C10
Popley Hants 18 F3
Porchester Nottingham 36 A1
Porchfield IoW 10 E3
Porin Highld 86 F6
Poringland Norf 39 E8
Porkellis Corn 2 F5
Porlock Som 7 B7
Porlock Weir Som 7 B7
Port Ann Argyll 73 E8
Port Appin Argyll 74 C2
Port Arthur Shetland 96 K5
Port Askaig Argyll 64 B5
Port Bannatyne Argyll 73 G9
Port Carlisle Cumb 61 G8
Port Charlotte Argyll 64 C3
Port Clarence Stockton 58 D5
Port Driseach Argyll 73 F8
Port e Vullen IoM 48 C4
Port Ellen Argyll 64 D4
Port Elphinstone Aberds 83 B9
Port Erin IoM 48 F1
Port Erroll Aberds 89 E10
Port-Eynon Swansea 23 H9
Port Gaverne Corn 3 A9
Port Glasgow Invclyd 68 C2
Port Henderson Highld 85 A12
Port Isaac Corn 3 A8
Port Lamont Argyll 73 F9
Port Lion Pembs 22 F4
Port Logan Dumfries 54 E3
Port Mholair W Isles 91 D10
Port Mor Highld 78 D7
Port Mulgrave N Yorks 59 E8
Port Nan Giùran W Isles 91 D10
Port nan Long W Isles 84 A3
Port Nis W Isles 91 A10
Port of Menteith Stirling 75 G8
Port Quin Corn 3 A8
Port Ramsay Argyll 79 G11
Port St Mary IoM 48 F2
Port Sunlight Mers 42 D6
Port Talbot Neath 14 B3
Port Tennant Swansea 14 B2
Port Wemyss Argyll 64 C2
Port William Dumfries 54 E6
Portachoillan Argyll 72 H6
Portavadie Argyll 73 G8
Portbury N Som 15 D11
Portchester Hants 10 D5
Portclair Highld 80 B6
Portencalzie Dumfries 54 B3
Portencross N Ayrs 66 B4
Portesham Dorset 8 F5
Portessie Moray 88 B4
Portfield Gate Pembs 22 E4
Portgate Devon 4 C5
Portgordon Moray 88 B3
Portgower Highld 93 H13
Porth Corn 3 C7
Porth Rhondda 14 B6
Porth Navas Corn 3 G6
Porth Tywyn = Burry Port Carms 23 F9
Porth-y-waen Shrops 33 C8
Porthaethwy = Menai Bridge Anglesey 41 C7
Porthallow Corn 3 G6
Porthallow Corn 4 F3
Porthcawl Bridgend 14 D4
Porthcothan Corn 3 B7
Porthcurno Corn 2 G2
Porthgain Pembs 22 C3
Porthill Shrops 33 D10
Porthkerry V Glam 14 E6
Porthleven Corn 2 G5
Porthllechog Anglesey 40 A6
Porthmadog Gwyn 41 G7
Porthmeor Corn 2 F3
Portholland Corn 3 E8
Porthoustock Corn 3 G7
Porthpean Corn 3 D9
Porthtowan Corn 2 E5
Porthyrhyd Carms 23 E10
Porthyrhyd Carms 24 E4
Portincaple Argyll 73 D11
Portington E Yorks 52 F3
Portinnisherrich Argyll 73 B8
Portinscale Cumb 56 D4
Portishead N Som 15 D10
Portkil Argyll 73 E11
Portknockie Moray 88 B4
Portlethen Aberds 83 D11
Portling Dumfries 55 D11
Portloe Corn 3 F8
Portmahomack Highld 87 C12
Portmeirion Gwyn 41 G7
Portmellon Corn 3 E9
Portmore Hants 10 E2
Portnacroish Argyll 74 C2
Portnahaven Argyll 64 C2
Portnalong Highld 85 E8
Portnaluchaig Highld 79 C9
Portnancon Highld 92 C7
Portnellan Stirling 75 E7
Portobello Edin 70 C2
Porton Wilts 17 H8
Portpatrick Dumfries 54 D3
Portreath Corn 2 E5
Portree Highld 85 D9
Portscatho Corn 3 F7
Portsea Ptsmth 10 D5
Portskerra Highld 93 C11
Portskewett Mon 15 C11
Portslade Brighton 12 F1
Portslade-by-Sea Brighton 12 F1
Portsmouth Ptsmth 10 D5
Portsmouth W Yorks 50 G5
Portsonachan Argyll 74 E3
Portsoy Aberds 88 B5
Portswood Soton 10 C3
Porttanachy Moray 88 B3
Portuairk Highld 78 E7
Portway Hereford 25 E11
Portway Worcs 27 A7
Portwrinkle Corn 4 F4
Poslingford Suff 30 D4
Postbridge Devon 5 D7
Postcombe Oxon 18 B4
Postling Kent 13 C10
Postwick Norf 39 E8
Potholm Dumfries 61 E9
Potsgrove C Beds 28 F6
Pott Row Norf 38 C3
Pott Shrigley Ches E 44 E3
Potten End Herts 29 H7
Potter Brompton N Yorks 52 B5
Potter Heigham Norf 39 D10
Potter Street Essex 29 H11
Potterhanworth Lincs 46 F4
Potterhanworth Booths Lincs 46 F4
Potterne Wilts 16 F6
Potterne Wick Wilts 17 F7
Potternewton W Yorks 51 F9
Potters Bar Herts 19 A9
Potter's Cross Staffs 34 G4
Potterspury Northants 28 D4
Potterton Aberds 83 B11
Potterton W Yorks 51 F10
Potto N Yorks 58 F5
Potton C Beds 29 D9
Poughill Corn 6 F1
Poughill Devon 7 F7
Poulshot Wilts 16 F6
Poulton Glos 17 A8
Poulton Mers 42 C6
Poulton-le-Fylde Lancs 49 F3
Pound Bank Worcs 26 A4
Pound Green E Sus 12 D4
Pound Green IoW 10 F2
Pound Green Worcs 34 H3
Pound Hill W Sus 12 C1
Poundbury Dorset 8 E5
Poundfield E Sus 12 C4
Poundland S Ayrs 66 H4
Poundon Bucks 28 F3
Poundsgate Devon 5 D8
Poundstock Corn 4 B3
Powburn Northumb 62 B6
Powderham Devon 5 C10
Powerstock Dorset 8 E4
Powfoot Dumfries 61 G7
Powick Worcs 26 C5
Powmill Perth 76 H3
Poxwell Dorset 8 F6
Poyle Slough 19 D7
Poynings W Sus 12 E1
Poyntington Dorset 8 C5
Poynton Ches E 44 D3
Poynton Green Telford 34 D1
Poystreet Green Suff 30 C6
Praa Sands Corn 2 G4
Pratt's Bottom London 19 E11
Praze Corn 2 F4
Praze-an-Beeble Corn 2 F5
Predannack Wollas Corn 2 H5
Prees Shrops 34 B1
Prees Green Shrops 34 B1
Prees Heath Shrops 34 B1
Prees Higher Heath Shrops 34 B1
Prees Lower Heath Shrops 34 B1
Preesall Lancs 49 E3
Preesgweene Shrops 33 B8
Prenderguest Borders 71 E8
Prendwick Northumb 62 B6
Prengwyn Ceredig 23 B9
Prenteg Gwyn 41 F7
Prenton Mers 42 D6
Prescot Mers 43 C7
Prescott Shrops 33 C10
Pressen Northumb 71 G7
Prestatyn Denb 42 D3
Prestbury Ches E 44 E3
Prestbury Glos 26 F6
Presteigne = Llanandras Powys 25 B10
Presthope Shrops 34 F1
Prestleigh Som 16 G3
Preston Borders 70 E6
Preston Brighton 12 F2
Preston Devon 5 D9
Preston Dorset 8 F6
Preston E Loth 70 C4
Preston E Yorks 53 F7
Preston Glos 17 A7
Preston Glos 26 E3
Preston Herts 29 F8
Preston Kent 21 E9
Preston Kent 21 E7
Preston Lancs 49 G5
Preston Northumb 71 H10
Preston Rutland 36 E4
Preston Shrops 33 D11
Preston Wilts 17 D7
Preston Wilts 17 D9
Preston Bagot Warks 27 B8
Preston Bissett Bucks 28 F3
Preston Bowyer Som 7 D10
Preston Brockhurst Shrops 33 C11
Preston Brook Halton 43 D8
Preston Candover Hants 18 G3
Preston Capes Northants 28 C2
Preston Crowmarsh Oxon 18 B3
Preston Gubbals Shrops 33 D10
Preston on Stour Warks 27 C9
Preston on the Hill Halton 43 D8
Preston on Wye Hereford 25 D10
Preston Plucknett Som 8 C4
Preston St Mary Suff 30 C6
Preston-under-Scar N Yorks 58 G1
Preston upon the Weald Moors Telford 34 D2
Preston Wynne Hereford 26 D2
Prestonmill Dumfries 60 H5
Prestonpans E Loth 70 C2
Prestwich Gtr Man 44 B2
Prestwick Northumb 63 F7
Prestwick S Ayrs 67 D6
Prestwood Bucks 18 A5
Price Town Bridgend 14 B5
Prickwillow Cambs 38 G1
Priddy Som 15 F11
Priest Hutton Lancs 49 B5
Priest Weston Shrops 33 F8
Priesthaugh Borders 61 C10
Primethorpe Leics 35 F11
Primrose Green Norf 39 D6
Primrose Valley N Yorks 53 B7
Primrosehill Herts 19 A7
Princes Gate Pembs 22 E6
Princes Risborough Bucks 18 A5
Princethorpe Warks 27 A11
Princetown Caerph 25 G8
Princetown Devon 5 D6
Prion Denb 42 F3
Prior Muir Fife 77 F8
Prior Park Northumb 71 E8
Priors Frome Hereford 26 E2
Priors Hardwick Warks 27 C11
Priors Marston Warks 27 C11
Priorslee Telford 34 D3
Priory Wood Hereford 25 D9
Priston Bath 16 E3
Pristow Green Norf 39 G7
Prittlewell Southend 20 C5
Privett Hants 10 B5
Prixford Devon 6 C4
Probus Corn 3 E7
Proncy Highld 87 B10
Prospect Cumb 56 B3
Prudhoe Northumb 62 G6
Ptarmigan Lodge Stirling 74 G6
Pubil Perth 75 C7
Puckeridge Herts 29 F10
Puckington Som 8 C2
Pucklechurch S Glos 16 D3
Pucknall Hants 10 B2
Puckrup Glos 26 E5
Puddinglake Ches W 43 F10
Puddington Ches W 42 E6
Puddington Devon 7 E7
Puddledock Norf 39 F6
Puddletown Dorset 9 E6
Pudleston Hereford 26 C2
Pudsey W Yorks 51 F8
Pulborough W Sus 11 C9
Puleston Telford 34 C3
Pulford Ches W 43 G6
Pulham Dorset 8 D6
Pulham Market Norf 39 G7
Pulham St Mary Norf 39 G8
Pulloxhill C Beds 29 E7
Pumpherston W Loth 69 D9
Pumsaint Carms 24 D3
Puncheston Pembs 22 D5
Puncknowle Dorset 8 F4
Punnett's Town E Sus 12 D5
Purbrook Hants 10 D5
Purewell Dorset 9 E10
Purfleet Thurrock 20 D2
Puriton Som 15 G9
Purleigh Essex 20 A5
Purley London 19 E10
Purley W Berks 18 D3
Purlogue Shrops 33 H8
Purls Bridge Cambs 37 G10
Purse Caundle Dorset 8 C5
Purslow Shrops 33 G9
Purston Jaglin W Yorks 51 H10
Purton Glos 16 A3
Purton Glos 16 A3
Purton Wilts 17 C7
Purton Stoke Wilts 17 B7
Pury End Northants 28 D4
Pusey Oxon 17 B10
Putley Hereford 26 E3
Putney London 19 D9
Putsborough Devon 6 B3
Puttenham Herts 28 G5
Puttenham Sur 18 G6
Puxton N Som 15 E10
Pwll Carms 23 F9
Pwll-glas Denb 42 G4
Pwll-trap Carms 23 E7
Pwll-y-glaw Neath 14 B3
Pwllcrochan Pembs 22 F4
Pwllgloyw Powys 25 E7
Pwllheli Gwyn 40 G5
Pwllmeyric Mon 15 B11
Pye Corner Newport 15 C9
Pye Green Staffs 34 D5
Pyecombe W Sus 12 E1
Pyewipe NE Lincs 46 A6
Pyle = Y Pîl Bridgend 14 C4
Pyle IoW 10 G3
Pylle Som 16 H3
Pymoor Cambs 37 G10
Pyrford Sur 19 F7
Pyrton Oxon 18 B3
Pytchley Northants 28 A5
Pyworthy Devon 6 F2

Q

Quabbs Shrops 33 G8
Quadring Lincs 37 B8
Quainton Bucks 28 G4
Quarley Hants 17 G9
Quarndon Derbys 35 A9
Quarrier's Homes Invclyd 68 D2
Quarrington Lincs 37 A6
Quarrington Hill Durham 58 C4
Quarry Bank W Mid 34 G5
Quarryford E Loth 70 D4
Quarryhill Highld 87 C10
Quarrywood Moray 88 B1
Quarter S Lanark 68 E6
Quatford Shrops 34 F3
Quatt Shrops 34 G3
Quebec Durham 58 B2
Quedgeley Glos 26 G5
Queen Adelaide Cambs 38 G1
Queen Camel Som 8 B4
Queen Charlton Bath 16 E3
Queen Dart Devon 7 E7
Queen Oak Dorset 9 A6
Queen Street Kent 20 G3
Queen Street Wilts 17 C7
Queenborough Kent 20 D6
Queenhill Worcs 26 E5
Queen's Head Shrops 33 C9
Queen's Park Bedford 29 D7
Queen's Park Northants 28 B4
Queensbury W Yorks 51 F7
Queensferry Edin 69 C10
Queensferry Flint 42 F6
Queensferry Crossing Edin 69 C10
Queenstown Blackpool 49 F3
Queenzieburn N Lanark 68 C5
Quemerford Wilts 17 E7
Quendale Shetland 96 M5
Quendon Essex 30 E2
Queniborough Leics 36 D2
Quenington Glos 17 A8
Quernmore Lancs 49 D5
Quethiock Corn 4 E4
Quholm Orkney 95 G3
Quicks Green W Berks 18 D2
Quidenham Norf 38 G6
Quidhampton Hants 18 F2
Quidhampton Wilts 9 A10
Quilquox Aberds 89 E9
Quina Brook Shrops 33 B11
Quindry Orkney 95 J5
Quinton Northants 28 C4
Quinton W Mid 34 G5
Quintrell Downs Corn 3 C7
Quixhill Staffs 35 A7
Quoditch Devon 6 G3
Quoig Perth 75 E11
Quorndon Leics 36 D1
Quothquan S Lanark 69 G8
Quoyloo Orkney 95 F3
Quoyness Orkney 95 H3
Quoys Shetland 96 B8
Quoys Shetland 96 G6

R

Raasay Ho. Highld 85 E10
Rabbit's Cross Kent 20 G4
Raby Mers 42 E6
Rachan Mill Borders 69 G10
Rachub Gwyn 41 D8
Rackenford Devon 7 E7
Rackham W Sus 11 C9
Rackheath Norf 39 D8
Racks Dumfries 60 F6
Rackwick Orkney 95 D5
Rackwick Orkney 95 J3
Radbourne Derbys 35 B8
Radcliffe Gtr Man 43 B10
Radcliffe Northumb 63 C8
Radcliffe on Trent Notts 36 B2
Radclive Bucks 28 E3
Radcot Oxon 17 B9
Raddery Highld 87 F10
Radernie Fife 77 G7
Radford Semele Warks 27 B10
Radipole Dorset 8 F5
Radlett Herts 19 B8
Radley Oxon 18 B2
Radmanthwaite Notts 45 F9
Radmoor Shrops 34 C2
Radmore Green Ches E 43 G8
Radnage Bucks 18 B4
Radstock Bath 16 F3
Radstone Northants 28 D2
Radway Warks 27 D10
Radway Green Ches E 43 G10
Radwell Bedford 29 C7
Radwell Herts 29 E9
Radwinter Essex 30 E3
Radyr Cardiff 15 C7
Rafford Moray 87 F13
Ragdale Leics 36 D2
Raglan Mon 25 H11
Ragnall Notts 46 E2
Rahane Argyll 73 E11
Rainford Mers 43 B7
Rainford Junction Mers 43 B7
Rainham London 20 C2
Rainham Medway 20 E5
Rainhill Mers 43 C7
Rainhill Stoops Mers 43 C8
Rainow Ches E 44 E3
Rainton N Yorks 51 B9
Rainworth Notts 45 G9
Raisbeck Cumb 57 F8
Raise Cumb 57 B9
Rait Perth 76 E5
Raithby Lincs 47 D7
Raithby Lincs 47 F7
Rake W Sus 11 B7
Rakewood Gtr Man 44 A3
Ram Carms 23 B10
Ram Lane Kent 20 G6
Ramasaig Highld 84 D6
Rame Corn 2 F6
Rame Corn 4 G5
Rameldry Mill Bank Fife 76 G6
Ramnageo Shetland 96 C8
Rampisham Dorset 8 D4
Rampside Cumb 49 C2
Rampton Cambs 29 B11
Rampton Notts 45 E11
Ramsbottom Gtr Man 50 H3
Ramsbury Wilts 17 D9
Ramscraigs Highld 94 H3
Ramsdean Hants 10 B6
Ramsdell Hants 18 F2
Ramsden Oxon 27 G10
Ramsden Bellhouse Essex 20 B4
Ramsden Heath Essex 20 B4
Ramsey Cambs 37 G8
Ramsey Essex 31 E9
Ramsey IoM 48 C4
Ramsey Forty Foot Cambs 37 G9
Ramsey Heights Cambs 37 G8
Ramsey Island Essex 30 H6
Ramsey Mereside Cambs 37 G8
Ramsey St Mary's Cambs 37 G8
Ramseycleuch Borders 61 B8
Ramsgate Kent 21 E10
Ramsgill N Yorks 51 B7
Ramshorn Staffs 44 H4
Ramsnest Common Sur 11 A8
Ranais W Isles 91 E9
Ranby Lincs 46 E6
Ranby Notts 45 D10
Rand Lincs 46 E5
Randwick Glos 26 H5
Ranfurly Renfs 68 D2
Rangag Highld 94 F3
Rangemore Staffs 35 C7
Rangeworthy S Glos 16 C3
Rankinston E Ayrs 67 E7
Ranmoor S Yorks 45 D7
Ranmore Common Sur 19 F8
Rannerdale Cumb 56 E3
Rannoch Station Perth 75 B7
Ranochan Highld 79 C11
Ranskill Notts 45 D10
Ranton Staffs 34 C4
Ranworth Norf 39 D9
Raploch Stirling 68 A6
Rapness Orkney 95 D6
Rascal Moor E Yorks 52 F4
Rascarrel Dumfries 55 E10
Rashiereive Aberds 89 F9
Raskelf N Yorks 51 B10
Rassau Bl Gwent 25 G8
Rastrick W Yorks 51 G7
Ratagan Highld 85 G14
Ratby Leics 35 E11
Ratcliffe Culey Leics 35 F9
Ratcliffe on Soar Leics 35 C10
Ratcliffe on the Wreake Leics 36 D2
Rathen Aberds 89 B10
Rathillet Fife 76 E6
Rathmell N Yorks 50 D4
Ratho Edin 69 C10
Ratho Station Edin 69 C10
Rathven Moray 88 B4
Ratley Warks 27 D10
Ratlinghope Shrops 33 F10
Rattar Highld 94 C4
Ratten Row Lancs 49 E4
Rattery Devon 5 E8
Rattlesden Suff 30 C6
Rattray Perth 76 C4
Raughton Head Cumb 56 B5
Raunds Northants 28 A6
Ravenfield S Yorks 45 C8
Ravenglass Cumb 56 G2
Raveningham Norf 39 F9
Ravenscar N Yorks 59 F10
Ravenscraig Invclyd 73 F11
Ravensdale IoM 48 C3
Ravensden Bedford 29 C7
Ravenseat N Yorks 57 F10
Ravenshead Notts 45 G9
Ravensmoor Ches E 43 G9
Ravensthorpe Northants 28 A3
Ravensthorpe W Yorks 51 G8
Ravenstone Leics 35 D10
Ravenstone M Keynes 28 C5
Ravenstonedale Cumb 57 F9
Ravenstown Cumb 49 B3
Ravenstruther S Lanark 69 F8
Ravensworth N Yorks 58 F2
Raw N Yorks 59 F10
Rawcliffe E Yorks 52 G2
Rawcliffe York 52 D1
Rawcliffe Bridge E Yorks 52 G2
Rawdon W Yorks 51 F8
Rawmarsh S Yorks 45 C8
Rawreth Essex 20 B4
Rawridge Devon 7 F11
Rawtenstall Lancs 50 G4
Raxton Aberds 89 E8
Raydon Suff 31 E7
Raylees Northumb 62 D5
Rayleigh Essex 20 B5
Rayne Essex 30 F4
Rayners Lane London 19 C8
Raynes Park London 19 E9
Reach Cambs 30 B2
Read Lancs 50 F3
Reading Reading 18 D4
Reading Street Kent 13 C8
Reagill Cumb 57 E8
Rearquhar Highld 87 B10
Rearsby Leics 36 D2
Reaster Highld 94 D4
Reawick Shetland 96 J5
Reay Highld 93 C12
Rechullin Highld 85 C13
Reculver Kent 21 E9
Red Dial Cumb 56 B4
Red Hill Worcs 26 C5
Red Houses Jersey 11
Red Lodge Suff 30 A3
Red Rail Hereford 26 F2
Red Rock Gtr Man 43 B8
Red Roses Carms 23 E7
Red Row Northumb 63 D8
Red Street Staffs 44 G2
Red Wharf Bay Anglesey 41 B7
Redberth Pembs 22 F5
Redbourn Herts 29 G8
Redbourne N Lincs 46 C3
Redbrook Mon 26 G2
Redbrook Wrex 33 A11
Redburn Highld 87 E8
Redburn Highld 87 G12
Redburn Northumb 62 G3
Redcar Redcar 59 D7
Redcastle Angus 77 B9
Redcastle Highld 87 G8
Redcliff Bay N Som 15 D10
Redding Falk 69 C8
Reddingmuirhead Falk 69 C8
Reddish Gtr Man 44 C2
Redditch Worcs 27 B7
Rede Suff 30 C5
Redenhall Norf 39 G8
Redesdale Camp Northumb 62 D4
Redesmouth Northumb 62 E4
Redford Aberds 83 F9
Redford Angus 77 C8
Redford Durham 58 C1
Redfordgreen Borders 61 B9
Redgorton Perth 76 E3
Redgrave Suff 38 H6
Redhill Aberds 83 C9
Redhill Aberds 89 E6
Redhill N Som 15 E11
Redhill Sur 19 F9
Redhouse Argyll 73 G7
Redhouses Argyll 64 B4
Redisham Suff 39 G10
Redland Bristol 16 D2
Redland Orkney 95 F4
Redlingfield Suff 31 A8
Redlynch Som 8 A6
Redlynch Wilts 9 B11
Redmarley D'Abitot Glos 26 E4
Redmarshall Stockton 58 D4
Redmile Leics 36 B3
Redmire N Yorks 58 G1
Redmoor Corn 4 E1
Rednal Shrops 33 C9
Redpath Borders 70 G4
Redpoint Highld 85 B12
Redruth Corn 2 E5
Redvales Gtr Man 44 B2
Redwick Newport 15 C10
Redwick S Glos 15 C11
Redworth Darl 58 D3
Reed Herts 29 E10
Reedham Norf 39 E10
Reedness E Yorks 52 G3
Reeds Beck Lincs 46 F6
Reepham Lincs 46 E4
Reepham Norf 39 C6
Reeth N Yorks 58 G1
Regaby IoM 48 C4
Regoul Highld 87 F11
Reiff Highld 92 H2
Reigate Sur 19 F9
Reighton N Yorks 53 B7
Reighton Gap N Yorks 53 B7
Reinigeadal W Isles 90 G7
Reiss Highld 94 E5
Rejerrah Corn 3 D6
Releath Corn 2 F5
Relubbus Corn 2 F4
Relugas Moray 87 G12
Remenham Wokingham 18 C4
Remenham Hill Wokingham 18 C4
Remony Perth 75 C10
Rempstone Notts 36 C1
Rendcomb Glos 27 H7
Rendham Suff 31 B10
Rendlesham Suff 31 C10
Renfrew Renfs 68 D4
Renhold Bedford 29 C7
Renishaw Derbys 45 E8
Rennington Northumb 63 B8
Renton W Dunb 68 C2
Renwick Cumb 57 B7
Repps Norf 39 D10
Repton Derbys 35 C9
Reraig Highld 85 F13
Rescobie Angus 77 B8
Resipole Highld 79 E10
Resolis Highld 87 E9
Resolven Neath 14 A4
Reston Borders 71 D7
Reswallie Angus 77 B8
Retew Corn 3 D8
Retford Notts 45 D11
Rettendon Essex 20 B4
Rettendon Place Essex 20 B4
Revesby Lincs 46 F6
Revesby Bridge Lincs 47 F7
Rew Street IoW 10 E3
Rewe Devon 7 G8
Reydon Suff 39 H10
Reydon Smear Suff 39 H10
Reymerston Norf 38 E6
Reynalton Pembs 22 F5
Reynoldston Swansea 23 G9
Rezare Corn 4 D4
Rhôs Carms 23 C8
Rhôs Neath 14 A3
Rhŷd-y-foel Conwy 42 E2
Rhaeadr Gwy = Rhayader Powys 24 B6
Rhandirmwyn Carms 24 D4
Rhayader = Rhaeadr Gwy Powys 24 B6
Rhedyn Gwyn 40 G4
Rhemore Highld 79 F8
Rhencullen IoM 48 C3
Rhes-y-cae Flint 42 E4
Rhewl Denb 42 F4
Rhewl Denb 42 H4
Rhian Highld 93 H8
Rhicarn Highld 92 G3
Rhiconich Highld 92 D5
Rhicullen Highld 87 D9
Rhidorroch Ho. Highld 86 B4
Rhifail Highld 93 E10
Rhigos Rhondda 24 H6
Rhilochan Highld 93 J10
Rhiroy Highld 86 C4
Rhisga = Risca Caerph 15 B8
Rhiw Gwyn 40 H4
Rhiwabon = Ruabon Wrex 33 A9
Rhiwbina Cardiff 15 C7
Rhiwbryfdir Gwyn 41 F8
Rhiwderin Newport 15 C8
Rhiwlas Gwyn 32 B5
Rhiwlas Gwyn 41 D7
Rhiwlas Powys 33 B7
Rhodes Gtr Man 44 B2
Rhodes Minnis Kent 21 G8
Rhodesia Notts 45 E9

Rhodiad Pembs 22 D2
Rhondda Rhondda 14 B5
Rhonehouse or Kelton Hill Dumfries 55 D10
Rhoose = Y Rhws V Glam 14 E6
Rhos-fawr Gwyn 40 G5
Rhos-goch Powys 25 D8
Rhos-hill Pembs 22 B6
Rhos-on-Sea Conwy 41 B10
Rhos-y-brithdir Powys 33 C7
Rhos-y-garth Ceredig 24 A3
Rhos-y-gwaliau Gwyn 32 B5
Rhos-y-llan Gwyn 40 G4
Rhos-y-Madoc Wrex 33 A9
Rhos-y-meirch Powys 25 B9
Rhosaman Carms 24 G4
Rhosbeirio Anglesey 40 A5
Rhoscefnhir Anglesey 41 C7
Rhoscolyn Anglesey 40 C4
Rhoscrowther Pembs 22 F4
Rhosesmor Flint 42 F5
Rhosgadfan Gwyn 41 E7
Rhosgoch Anglesey 40 B6
Rhoshirwaun Gwyn 40 H3
Rhoslan Gwyn 40 F6
Rhoslefain Gwyn 32 E1
Rhosllanerchrugog Wrex 42 H5
Rhosmaen Carms 24 F3
Rhosmeirch Anglesey 40 C6
Rhosneigr Anglesey 40 C5
Rhosnesni Wrex 42 G6
Rhosrobin Wrex 42 G6
Rhossili Swansea 23 H9
Rhosson Pembs 22 D2
Rhostryfan Gwyn 40 E6
Rhostyllen Wrex 42 H6
Rhosybol Anglesey 40 B6
Rhu Argyll 73 E11
Rhu Argyll 73 G7
Rhuallt Denb 42 E3
Rhuddall Heath Ches W 43 F8
Rhuddlan Ceredig 23 B9
Rhuddlan Denb 42 E3
Rhue Highld 86 B3
Rhulen Powys 25 D8
Rhunahaorine Argyll 65 D8
Rhuthun = Ruthin Denb 42 G4
Rhyd Gwyn 41 F8
Rhyd Powys 32 E5
Rhyd-Ddu Gwyn 41 E7
Rhyd-moel-ddu Powys 33 H6
Rhyd-Rosser Ceredig 24 B2
Rhyd-uchaf Gwyn 32 B5
Rhyd-wen Gwyn 32 D3
Rhyd-y-clafdy Gwyn 40 G5
Rhyd-y-fro Neath 24 H4
Rhyd-y-gwin Swansea 14 A2
Rhyd-y-meirch Mon 25 H10
Rhyd-y-meudwy Denb 42 G4
Rhyd-y-pandy Swansea 14 A2
Rhyd-y-sarn Gwyn 41 F8
Rhyd-yr-onen Gwyn 32 E2
Rhydaman = Ammanford Carms 24 G3
Rhydargaeau Carms 23 D9
Rhydcymerau Carms 23 C10
Rhydd Worcs 26 D5
Rhydding Neath 14 B3
Rhydfudr Ceredig 24 B2
Rhydlewis Ceredig 23 B8
Rhydlios Gwyn 40 G3
Rhydlydan Conwy 41 E10
Rhydness Powys 25 D8
Rhydowen Ceredig 23 B9
Rhydspence Hereford 25 D9
Rhydtalog Flint 42 G5
Rhydwyn Anglesey 40 B5
Rhydycroesau Powys 33 B8
Rhydyfelin Ceredig 32 H1
Rhydyfelin Rhondda 14 C6
Rhydymain Gwyn 32 C4
Rhydymwyn Flint 42 F5
Rhyl = Y Rhyl Denb 42 D3
Rhymney = Rhymni Caerph 25 H8
Rhymni = Rhymney Caerph 25 H8
Rhynd Fife 77 E7
Rhynd Perth 76 E4
Rhynie Aberds 82 A6
Rhynie Highld 87 D11
Ribbesford Worcs 26 A4
Ribblehead N Yorks 50 B3
Ribbleton Lancs 50 F1
Ribchester Lancs 50 F2
Ribigill Highld 93 D8
Riby Lincs 46 B5
Riby Cross Roads Lincs 46 B5
Riccall N Yorks 52 F2
Riccarton E Ayrs 67 C7
Richards Castle Hereford 25 B11
Richings Park Bucks 19 D7
Richmond London 19 D8
Richmond N Yorks 58 F2
Rickarton Aberds 83 E10
Rickinghall Suff 38 H6
Rickleton T&W 58 A3
Rickling Essex 29 E11
Rickmansworth Herts 19 B7
Riddings Cumb 61 F10
Riddings Derbys 45 G8
Riddlecombe Devon 6 E5
Riddlesden W Yorks 51 E6
Riddrie Glasgow 68 D5
Ridge Dorset 9 F8
Ridge Hants 10 C2
Ridge Wilts 9 A8
Ridge Green Sur 19 G10
Ridge Lane Warks 35 F8
Ridgebourne Powys 25 B7
Ridgehill N Som 15 E11
Ridgeway Cross Hereford 26 D4
Ridgewell Essex 30 D4
Ridgewood E Sus 12 E3
Ridgmont C Beds 28 E6
Riding Mill Northumb 62 G6
Ridleywood Wrex 43 G7
Ridlington Norf 39 B9
Ridlington Rutland 36 E4
Ridsdale Northumb 62 E5
Riechip Perth 76 C3
Riemore Perth 76 C3
Rienachait Highld 92 F3
Rievaulx N Yorks 59 H6
Rift House Hrtlpl 58 C5
Rigg Dumfries 61 G8
Riggend N Lanark 68 C6
Rigsby Lincs 47 E8
Rigside S Lanark 69 G7
Riley Green Lancs 50 G2
Rileyhill Staffs 35 D7
Rilla Mill Corn 4 D3
Rillington N Yorks 52 B4
Rimington Lancs 50 E4
Rimpton Som 8 B5
Rimswell E Yorks 53 G9
Rinaston Pembs 22 D4
Ringasta Shetland 96 M5
Ringford Dumfries 55 D9
Ringinglow S Yorks 44 D6
Ringland Norf 39 D7
Ringles Cross E Sus 12 D3
Ringmer E Sus 12 E3
Ringmore Devon 5 G7
Ringorm Moray 88 D2
Ring's End Cambs 37 E9
Ringsfield Suff 39 G10
Ringsfield Corner Suff 39 G10
Ringshall Herts 28 G6
Ringshall Suff 31 C7
Ringshall Stocks Suff 31 C7
Ringstead Norf 38 A3
Ringstead Northants 36 H5
Ringwood Hants 9 D10
Ringwould Kent 21 G10
Rinmore Aberds 82 B6
Rinnigill Orkney 95 J4
Rinsey Corn 2 G4
Riof W Isles 90 D6
Ripe E Sus 12 E4
Ripley Derbys 45 G7
Ripley Hants 9 E10
Ripley N Yorks 51 C8
Ripley Sur 19 F7
Riplingham E Yorks 52 F5
Ripon N Yorks 51 B9
Rippingale Lincs 37 C6
Ripple Kent 21 G10
Ripple Worcs 26 E5
Ripponden W Yorks 50 H6
Rireavach Highld 86 B3
Risabus Argyll 64 D4
Risbury Hereford 26 C2
Risby Suff 30 B4
Risca = Rhisga Caerph 15 B8
Rise E Yorks 53 E7
Riseden E Sus 12 C5
Risegate Lincs 37 C8
Riseholme Lincs 46 E3
Riseley Bedford 29 B7
Riseley Wokingham 18 E4
Rishangles Suff 31 B8
Rishton Lancs 50 F3
Rishworth W Yorks 50 H6
Rising Bridge Lancs 50 G3
Risley Derbys 35 B10
Risley Warr 43 C9
Risplith N Yorks 51 C8
Rispond Highld 92 C7
Rivar Wilts 17 E10
Rivenhall End Essex 30 G5
River Bank Cambs 30 B2
Riverhead Kent 20 F2
Rivington Lancs 43 A9
Roa Island Cumb 49 C2
Roachill Devon 7 D7
Road Green Norf 39 F8
Roade Northants 28 C4
Roadhead Cumb 61 F11
Roadmeetings S Lanark 69 F7
Roadside Highld 94 D3
Roadside of Catterline Aberds 83 F10
Roadside of Kinneff Aberds 83 F10
Roadwater Som 7 C9
Roag Highld 85 D7
Roath Cardiff 15 D7
Roberton Borders 61 B10
Roberton S Lanark 69 H8
Robertsbridge E Sus 12 D6
Roberttown W Yorks 51 G7
Robeston Cross Pembs 22 F3
Robeston Wathen Pembs 22 E5
Robin Hood W Yorks 51 G9
Robin Hood's Bay N Yorks 59 F10
Roborough Devon 4 E6
Roborough Devon 6 E4
Roby Mers 43 C7
Roby Mill Lancs 43 B8
Rocester Staffs 35 B7
Roch Pembs 22 D3
Roch Gate Pembs 22 D3
Rochdale Gtr Man 44 A2
Roche Corn 3 C8
Rochester Medway 20 E4
Rochester Northumb 62 D4
Rochford Essex 20 B5
Rock Corn 3 B8
Rock Northumb 63 A8
Rock W Sus 11 C10
Rock Worcs 26 A4
Rock Ferry Mers 42 D6
Rockbeare Devon 7 G9
Rockbourne Hants 9 C10
Rockcliffe Cumb 61 G9
Rockcliffe Dumfries 55 D11
Rockfield Highld 87 C12
Rockfield Mon 25 G11
Rockford Hants 9 D10
Rockhampton S Glos 16 B3
Rockingham Northants 36 F4
Rockland All Saints Norf 38 F5
Rockland St Mary Norf 39 E9
Rockland St Peter Norf 38 F5
Rockley Wilts 17 D8
Rockwell End Bucks 18 C4
Rockwell Green Som 7 D10
Rodborough Glos 16 A5
Rodbourne Swindon 17 C8
Rodbourne Wilts 16 C6
Rodbourne Cheney Swindon 17 C8
Rodd Hereford 25 B10
Roddam Northumb 62 A6
Rodden Dorset 8 F5
Rode Som 16 F5
Rode Heath Ches E 44 G2
Rodeheath Ches E 44 F2
Roden Telford 34 D1
Rodhuish Som 7 C9
Rodington Telford 34 D1
Rodley Glos 26 G4
Rodley W Yorks 51 F8
Rodmarton Glos 16 B6
Rodmell E Sus 12 F3
Rodmersham Kent 20 E6
Rodney Stoke Som 15 F10
Rodsley Derbys 35 A8
Rodway Som 15 H8
Rodwell Dorset 8 G5
Roe Green Herts 29 E10
Roecliffe N Yorks 51 C9
Roehampton London 19 D9
Roesound Shetland 96 G5
Roffey W Sus 11 A10
Rogart Highld 93 J10
Rogart Station Highld 93 J10
Rogate W Sus 11 B7
Rogerstone Newport 15 C8
Roghadal W Isles 90 J5
Rogiet Mon 15 C10
Rogue's Alley Cambs 37 E9
Roke Oxon 18 B3
Roker T&W 63 H10
Rollesby Norf 39 D10
Rolleston Leics 36 E3
Rolleston Notts 45 G11
Rolleston-on-Dove Staffs 35 C8
Rolston E Yorks 53 E8
Rolvenden Kent 13 C7
Rolvenden Layne Kent 13 C7
Romaldkirk Durham 57 D11
Romanby N Yorks 58 G4
Romannobridge Borders 69 F10
Romansleigh Devon 7 D6
Romford London 20 C2
Romiley Gtr Man 44 C3
Romsey Hants 10 B2
Romsey Town Cambs 29 C11
Romsley Shrops 34 G3
Romsley Worcs 34 H5
Ronague IoM 48 E2
Rookhope Durham 57 B11
Rookley IoW 10 F4
Rooks Bridge Som 15 F9
Roos E Yorks 53 F8
Roosebeck Cumb 49 C2
Rootham's Green Bedford 29 C8
Rootpark S Lanark 69 E8
Ropley Hants 10 A5
Ropley Dean Hants 10 A5
Ropsley Lincs 36 B5
Rora Aberds 89 C10
Rorandle Aberds 83 B8
Rorrington Shrops 33 E9
Roscroggan Corn 2 E5
Rose Corn 3 D6
Rose Ash Devon 7 D6
Rose Green W Sus 11 E8
Rose Grove Lancs 50 F4
Rose Hill E Sus 12 E3
Rose Hill Lancs 50 F4
Rose Hill Suff 31 D8
Roseacre Kent 20 F4
Roseacre Lancs 49 F4
Rosebank S Lanark 69 F7
Rosebrough Northumb 71 H10
Rosebush Pembs 22 D5
Rosecare Corn 4 B2
Rosedale Abbey N Yorks 59 G8
Roseden Northumb 62 A6
Rosefield Highld 87 F11
Rosehall Highld 92 J7
Rosehaugh Mains Highld 87 F9
Rosehearty Aberds 89 B9
Rosehill Shrops 34 B2
Roseisle Moray 88 B1
Roselands E Sus 12 F5
Rosemarket Pembs 22 F4
Rosemarkie Highld 87 F10
Rosemary Lane Devon 7 E10
Rosemount Perth 76 C4
Rosenannon Corn 3 C8
Rosewell Midloth 69 D11
Roseworth Stockton 58 D5
Roseworthy Corn 2 F5
Rosgill Cumb 57 E7
Roshven Highld 79 D10
Roskhill Highld 85 D7
Roskill House Highld 87 F9
Rosley Cumb 56 B5
Roslin Midloth 69 D11
Rosliston Derbys 35 D8
Rosneath Argyll 73 E11
Ross Dumfries 55 E9
Ross Northumb 71 G10
Ross Perth 75 E10
Ross-on-Wye Hereford 26 F3
Rossett Wrex 42 G6
Rossett Green N Yorks 51 D9
Rossie Ochill Perth 76 F3
Rossie Priory Perth 76 D5
Rossington S Yorks 45 C10
Rosskeen Highld 87 E9
Rossland Renfs 68 C3
Roster Highld 94 G4
Rostherne Ches E 43 D10
Rosthwaite Cumb 56 E4
Roston Derbys 35 A7
Rosyth Fife 69 B10
Rothbury Northumb 62 C6
Rotherby Leics 36 D2
Rotherfield E Sus 12 D4
Rotherfield Greys Oxon 18 C4
Rotherfield Peppard Oxon 18 C4
Rotherham S Yorks 45 C8
Rothersthorpe Northants 28 C4
Rotherwick Hants 18 F4
Rothes Moray 88 D2
Rothesay Argyll 73 G9
Rothiebrisbane Aberds 89 E7
Rothienorman Aberds 89 E7
Rothiesholm Orkney 95 F7
Rothley Leics 36 D1
Rothley Northumb 62 E6
Rothley Shield East Northumb 62 D6
Rothmaise Aberds 89 E6
Rothwell Lincs 46 C5
Rothwell Northants 36 G4
Rothwell W Yorks 51 G9
Rothwell Haigh W Yorks 51 G9
Rotsea E Yorks 53 D6
Rottal Angus 82 G5
Rotten End Suff 31 B10
Rottingdean Brighton 12 F2
Rottington Cumb 56 E1
Roud IoW 10 F4
Rough Close Staffs 34 B5
Rough Common Kent 21 F8
Rougham Norf 38 C4
Rougham Suff 30 B6
Rougham Green Suff 30 B6
Roughburn Highld 80 E5
Roughlee Lancs 50 E4
Roughley W Mid 35 F7
Roughsike Cumb 61 F11
Roughton Lincs 46 F6
Roughton Norf 39 B8
Roughton Shrops 34 F3
Roughton Moor Lincs 46 F6
Roundhay W Yorks 51 F9
Roundstonefoot Dumfries 61 C7
Roundstreet Common W Sus 11 B9
Roundway Wilts 17 E7
Rous Lench Worcs 27 C7
Rousdon Devon 8 E1
Routenburn N Ayrs 73 G10
Routh E Yorks 53 E6
Row Corn 4 D1
Row Cumb 56 H6
Row Heath Essex 31 G8
Rowanburn Dumfries 61 F10
Rowardennan Stirling 74 H6
Rowde Wilts 16 E6
Rowen Conwy 41 C9
Rowfoot Northumb 62 G2
Rowhedge Essex 31 F7
Rowhook W Sus 11 A10
Rowington Warks 27 B9
Rowland Derbys 44 E6
Rowlands Castle Hants 10 C6
Rowlands Gill T&W 63 H7
Rowledge Sur 18 G5
Rowlestone Hereford 25 F10
Rowley E Yorks 52 F5
Rowley Shrops 33 E9
Rowley Hill W Yorks 44 A5
Rowley Regis W Mid 34 G5
Rowly Sur 19 G7
Rowney Green Worcs 27 A7
Rownhams Hants 10 C2
Rowrah Cumb 56 E2
Rowsham Bucks 28 G5
Rowsley Derbys 44 F6
Rowstock Oxon 17 C11
Rowston Lincs 46 G4
Rowton Ches W 43 F7
Rowton Shrops 33 D9
Rowton Telford 34 D2
Roxburgh Borders 70 G6
Roxby N Lincs 52 H5
Roxby N Yorks 59 E8
Roxton Bedford 29 C8
Roxwell Essex 30 H3
Royal Leamington Spa Warks 27 B10
Royal Oak Darl 58 D3
Royal Oak Lancs 43 B7
Royal Tunbridge Wells Kent 12 C4
Royal Wootton Bassett Wilts 17 C7
Roybridge Highld 80 E4
Roydhouse W Yorks 44 A6
Roydon Essex 29 H11
Roydon Norf 38 C3
Roydon Norf 39 G6
Roydon Hamlet Essex 29 H11
Royston Herts 29 D10
Royston S Yorks 45 A7
Royton Gtr Man 44 B3
Rozel Jersey 11
Ruabon = Rhiwabon Wrex 33 A9
Ruaig Argyll 78 G3
Ruan Lanihorne Corn 3 E7
Ruan Minor Corn 2 H6
Ruarach Highld 80 A1
Ruardean Glos 26 G3
Ruardean Woodside Glos 26 G3
Rubery Worcs 34 H5
Ruckcroft Cumb 57 B7
Ruckhall Hereford 25 E11
Ruckinge Kent 13 C9
Ruckland Lincs 47 E7
Ruckley Shrops 33 E11
Rudbaxton Pembs 22 D4
Rudby N Yorks 58 F5
Ruddington Notts 36 B1
Rudford Glos 26 F4
Rudge Shrops 34 F4
Rudge Som 16 F5
Rudgeway S Glos 16 C3
Rudgwick W Sus 11 A9
Rudhall Hereford 26 F3
Rudheath Ches W 43 E9
Rudley Green Essex 20 A5
Rudry Caerph 15 C7
Rudston E Yorks 53 C6
Rudyard Staffs 44 G3
Rufford Lancs 49 H4
Rufforth York 51 D11
Rugby Warks 35 H11
Rugeley Staffs 34 D6
Ruglen S Ayrs 66 F5
Ruilick Highld 87 G8
Ruishton Som 8 B1
Ruisigearraidh W Isles 90 J4
Ruislip London 19 C7
Ruislip Common London 19 C7
Rumbling Bridge Perth 76 H3
Rumburgh Suff 39 G9
Rumford Corn 3 B7
Rumney Cardiff 15 D8
Runcorn Halton 43 D8
Runcton W Sus 11 D7
Runcton Holme Norf 38 E2
Rundlestone Devon 5 D6
Runfold Sur 18 G5
Runhall Norf 39 E6
Runham Norf 39 D10
Runham Norf 39 E11
Runnington Som 7 D10
Runsell Green Essex 30 H4
Runswick Bay N Yorks 59 E9
Runwell Essex 20 B4
Ruscombe Wokingham 18 D4
Rush Green London 20 C2
Rush-head Aberds 89 D8
Rushall Hereford 26 E3
Rushall Norf 39 G7
Rushall W Mid 34 E6
Rushall Wilts 17 F8
Rushbrooke Suff 30 B5
Rushbury Shrops 33 F11
Rushden Herts 29 E10
Rushden Northants 28 B6
Rushenden Kent 20 D6
Rushford Norf 38 G5
Rushlake Green E Sus 12 E5
Rushmere Suff 39 G10
Rushmere St Andrew Suff 31 D9
Rushmoor Sur 18 G5
Rushock Worcs 26 A5
Rusholme Gtr Man 44 C2
Rushton Ches W 43 F8
Rushton Northants 36 G4
Rushton Shrops 34 E2
Rushton Spencer Staffs 44 F3
Rushwick Worcs 26 C5
Rushyford Durham 58 D3
Ruskie Stirling 75 G9
Ruskington Lincs 46 G4
Rusland Cumb 56 H5
Rusper W Sus 19 H9
Ruspidge Glos 26 G3
Russell's Water Oxon 18 C4
Russel's Green Suff 31 A9
Rusthall Kent 12 C4
Rustington W Sus 11 D9
Ruston N Yorks 52 A5
Ruston Parva E Yorks 53 C6
Ruswarp N Yorks 59 F9
Rutherford Borders 70 G5
Rutherglen S Lanark 68 D5
Ruthernbridge Corn 3 C9
Ruthin = Rhuthun Denb 42 G4
Ruthrieston Aberdeen 83 C11
Ruthven Aberds 88 D5
Ruthven Angus 76 C5
Ruthven Highld 81 D9
Ruthven Highld 87 H11
Ruthven House Angus 76 C6
Ruthvoes Corn 3 C8
Ruthwell Dumfries 60 G6
Ruyton-XI-Towns Shrops 33 C9
Ryal Northumb 62 F6
Ryal Fold Blackburn 50 G2
Ryall Dorset 8 E3
Ryarsh Kent 20 F3
Rydal Cumb 56 F5
Ryde IoW 10 E4
Rye E Sus 13 D8
Rye Foreign E Sus 13 D7
Rye Harbour E Sus 13 E8
Rye Park Herts 29 G10
Rye Street Worcs 26 E4
Ryecroft Gate Staffs 44 F3
Ryehill E Yorks 53 G8
Ryhall Rutland 36 D6
Ryhill W Yorks 45 A7
Ryhope T&W 58 A5
Rylstone N Yorks 50 D5
Ryme Intrinseca Dorset 8 C4
Ryther N Yorks 52 F1
Ryton Glos 26 E4
Ryton N Yorks 52 B3
Ryton Shrops 34 E3
Ryton T&W 63 G7
Ryton-on-Dunsmore Warks 27 A10

S

Sabden Lancs 50 F3
Sacombe Herts 29 G10
Sacriston Durham 58 B3
Sadberge Darl 58 E4
Saddell Argyll 65 E8
Saddington Leics 36 F2
Saddle Bow Norf 38 D2
Saddlescombe W Sus 12 E1
Sadgill Cumb 57 F6
Saffron Walden Essex 30 E2
Sageston Pembs 22 F5
Saham Hills Norf 38 E5
Saham Toney Norf 38 E5
Saighdinis W Isles 84 B3
Saighton Ches W 43 F7
St Abbs Borders 71 D8
St. Abb's Haven Borders 71 D8
St Agnes Corn 2 D6
St Agnes Scilly 2 D2
St Albans Herts 29 H8
St Allen Corn 3 D7
St Andrews Fife 77 F8
St Andrew's Major V Glam 15 D7
St Anne Ald 11
St Annes Lancs 49 G3
St Ann's Dumfries 60 D6
St Ann's Chapel Corn 4 D5
St Ann's Chapel Devon 5 G7
St Anthony-in-Meneage Corn 3 G6
St Anthony's Hill E Sus 12 F5
St Arvans Mon 15 B11
St Asaph = Llanelwy Denb 42 E3
St Athan V Glam 14 E6
St Aubin Jersey 11
St Austell Corn 3 D9
St Bees Cumb 56 E1
St Blazey Corn 4 F1
St Boswells Borders 70 G4
St Brelade Jersey 11
St Breock Corn 3 B8
St Breward Corn 4 D1
St Briavels Glos 16 A2
St Bride's Pembs 22 E3
St Brides Major V Glam 14 D4
St Bride's Netherwent Mon 15 C10
St Brides super Ely V Glam 14 D6
St Brides Wentlooge Newport 15 C8
St Budeaux Plym 4 F5
St Buryan Corn 2 G3
St Catherine Bath 16 D4
St Catherine's Argyll 73 C10
St Clears = Sanclêr Carms 23 E7
St Cleer Corn 4 E3
St Clement Corn 3 E7
St Clements Jersey 11
St Clether Corn 4 C3
St Colmac Argyll 73 G9
St Columb Major Corn 3 C8
St Columb Minor Corn 3 C7
St Columb Road Corn 3 D8
St Combs Aberds 89 B10
St Cross South Elmham Suff 39 G8
St Cyrus Aberds 77 A10
St David's = Tyddewi Pembs 22 D2
St David's Perth 76 E2
St Day Corn 2 E6
St Dennis Corn 3 D8
St Devereux Hereford 25 E11
St Dogmaels Pembs 22 B6
St Dogwells Pembs 22 D4
St Dominick Corn 4 E5
St Donat's V Glam 14 E5
St Edith's Wilts 16 E6
St Endellion Corn 3 B8
St Enoder Corn 3 D7
St Erme Corn 3 D7
St Erney Corn 4 F4
St Erth Corn 2 F4
St Ervan Corn 3 B7
St Eval Corn 3 C7
St Ewe Corn 3 E8
St Fagans Cardiff 15 D7
St Fergus Aberds 89 C10
St Fillans Perth 75 E9
St Florence Pembs 22 F5
St Genny's Corn 4 B2
St George Conwy 42 E2
St George's V Glam 14 D6
St Germans Corn 4 F4
St Giles Lincs 46 E3
St Giles in the Wood Devon 6 E4
St Giles on the Hth. Devon 6 G2
St Harmon Powys 24 A6
St Helen Auckland Durham 58 D2
St Helena Warks 35 E8
St Helen's E Sus 13 E7
St Helens IoW 10 F5
St Helens Mers 43 C8
St Helier Jersey 11
St Helier London 19 E9
St Hilary Corn 2 F4
St Hilary V Glam 14 D6
Saint Hill W Sus 12 C2
St Illtyd Bl Gwent 15 A8
St Ippollytts Herts 29 F8
St Ishmael's Pembs 22 F3
St Issey Corn 3 B8
St Ive Corn 4 E4
St Ives Cambs 29 A10
St Ives Corn 2 E4
St Ives Dorset 9 D10
St James South Elmham Suff 39 G9
St Jidgey Corn 3 C8
St John Corn 4 F5
St John's IoM 48 D2
St John's Jersey 11
St John's Sur 18 F6
St John's Worcs 26 C5
St John's Chapel Durham 57 C10
St John's Fen End Norf 37 D11
St John's Highway Norf 37 D11
St John's Town of Dalry Dumfries 55 A9
St Judes IoM 48 C3
St Just in Roseland Corn 3 F7
St Just Corn 2 F2
St Katherine's Aberds 89 E7
St Keverne Corn 3 G6
St Kew Corn 3 B9
St Kew Highway Corn 3 B9
St Keyne Corn 4 E3
St Lawrence Corn 3 C9
St Lawrence Essex 20 A6
St Lawrence IoW 10 G4
St Leonard's Bucks 28 H6
St Leonards Dorset 9 D10
St Leonards E Sus 13 F6
Saint Leonards S Lanark 68 E5
St Levan Corn 2 G2
St Lythans V Glam 15 D7
St Mabyn Corn 3 B9
St Madoes Perth 76 E4
St Margaret South Elmham Suff 39 G9
St Margaret's Hereford 25 E10
St Margarets Herts 29 G10
St Margaret's at Cliffe Kent 21 G10
St. Margaret's Hope Orkney 95 J5
St Mark's IoM 48 E2
St Martin Corn 4 F3
St Martins Corn 2 G6
St Martin's Jersey 11
St Martins Perth 76 D4
St Martin's Shrops 33 B9
St Mary Bourne Hants 17 F11
St Mary Church V Glam 14 D6
St Mary Cray London 19 E11
St Mary Hill V Glam 14 D5
St Mary Hoo Medway 20 D5
St Mary in the Marsh Kent 13 D9
St Mary's Jersey 11
St Mary's Orkney 95 H5
St Mary's Bay Kent 13 D9
St Maughans Mon 25 G11
St Mawes Corn 3 F7
St Mawgan Corn 3 C7
St Mellion Corn 4 E4
St Mellons Cardiff 15 C8
St Merryn Corn 3 B7
St Mewan Corn 3 D8
St Michael Caerhays Corn 3 E8
St Michael Penkevil Corn 3 E7
St Michael South Elmham Suff 39 G9
St Michael's Kent 13 C7
St Michaels Worcs 26 B2
St Michael's on Wyre Lancs 49 E4
St Minver Corn 3 B8
St Monans Fife 77 G8
St Neot Corn 4 E2
St Neots Cambs 29 B8
St Newlyn East Corn 3 D7
St Nicholas Pembs 22 C3
St Nicholas V Glam 14 D6
St Nicholas at Wade Kent 21 E9
St Ninians Stirling 68 A6
St Osyth Essex 31 G8
St Osyth Heath Essex 31 G8
St Ouens Jersey 11
St Owens Cross Hereford 26 F2
St Paul's Cray London 19 E11
St Paul's Walden Herts 29 F8
St Peter Port Guern 11
St Peter's Jersey 11
St Peter's Kent 21 E10
St Petrox Pembs 22 G4
St Pinnock Corn 4 E3
St Quivox S Ayrs 67 D6
St Ruan Corn 2 H6
St Sampson Guern 11
St Stephen Corn 3 D8
St Stephen's Corn 4 C4
St Stephens Corn 4 F5
St Stephens Herts 29 H8
St Teath Corn 4 C1
St Thomas Devon 7 G8
St Tudy Corn 4 D1
St Twynnells Pembs 22 G4
St Veep Corn 4 F2
St Vigeans Angus 77 C9
St Wenn Corn 3 C8
St Weonards Hereford 25 F11
Saintbury Glos 27 E8
Salcombe Devon 5 H8
Salcombe Regis Devon 7 H10
Salcott Essex 30 G6
Sale Gtr Man 43 C10
Sale Green Worcs 26 C6
Saleby Lincs 47 E8
Salehurst E Sus 12 D6
Salem Carms 24 F3
Salem Ceredig 32 G2
Salen Argyll 79 G8
Salen Highld 79 E9
Salesbury Lancs 50 F2
Salford C Beds 28 E6
Salford Gtr Man 44 C2
Salford Oxon 27 F9
Salford Priors Warks 27 C7
Salfords Sur 19 G9
Salhouse Norf 39 D9
Saline Fife 69 A9
Salisbury Wilts 9 B10
Sallachan Highld 74 A2
Sallachy Highld 86 H2
Sallachy Highld 93 J8
Salle Norf 39 C7
Salmonby Lincs 47 E7
Salmond's Muir Angus 77 D8
Salperton Glos 27 F7
Salph End Bedford 29 C7
Salsburgh N Lanark 69 D7
Salt Staffs 34 C5
Salt End E Yorks 53 G7
Saltaire W Yorks 51 F7
Saltash Corn 4 F5
Saltburn Highld 87 E10
Saltburn-by-the-Sea Redcar 59 D7
Saltby Leics 36 C4
Saltcoats Cumb 56 G2
Saltcoats N Ayrs 66 B5
Saltdean Brighton 12 F2
Salter Lancs 50 C2
Salterforth Lancs 50 E4
Salterswall Ches W 43 F9
Saltfleet Lincs 47 C8
Saltfleetby All Saints Lincs 47 C8
Saltfleetby St Clements Lincs 47 C8
Saltfleetby St Peter Lincs 47 D8
Saltford Bath 16 E3
Salthouse Norf 39 A6
Saltmarshe E Yorks 52 G3
Saltney Flint 43 F6
Salton N Yorks 52 B3
Saltwick Northumb 63 F7
Saltwood Kent 21 H8
Salum Argyll 78 G3
Salvington W Sus 11 D10
Salwarpe Worcs 26 B5
Salwayash Dorset 8 E3
Sambourne Warks 27 B7
Sambrook Telford 34 C3
Samhla W Isles 84 B2
Samlesbury Lancs 50 F1
Samlesbury Bottoms Lancs 50 G2
Sampford Arundel Som 7 E10
Sampford Brett Som 7 B9
Sampford Courtenay Devon 6 F5
Sampford Peverell Devon 7 E9
Sampford Spiney Devon 4 D6
Sampool Bridge Cumb 56 H6
Samuelston E Loth 70 C3
Sanachan Highld 85 D13
Sanaigmore Argyll 64 A3
Sanclêr = St Clears Carms 23 E7
Sancreed Corn 2 G3
Sancton E Yorks 52 F5
Sand Highld 86 B2
Sand Shetland 96 J5
Sand Hole E Yorks 52 F4
Sand Hutton N Yorks 52 D2
Sandaig Highld 85 H12
Sandal Magna W Yorks 51 H9
Sandale Cumb 56 B4
Sandbach Ches E 43 F10
Sandbank Argyll 73 E10
Sandbanks Poole 9 F9
Sandend Aberds 88 B5
Sanderstead London 19 E10
Sandfields Glos 26 F6
Sandford Cumb 57 E9
Sandford Devon 7 F7
Sandford Dorset 9 F8
Sandford IoW 10 F4
Sandford N Som 15 F10
Sandford S Lanark 68 F6
Sandford Shrops 34 B1
Sandford on Thames Oxon 18 A2
Sandford Orcas Dorset 8 B5
Sandford St Martin Oxon 27 F11
Sandfordhill Aberds 89 D11
Sandgate Kent 21 H8
Sandgreen Dumfries 55 D8
Sandhaven Aberds 89 B9
Sandhead Dumfries 54 E3
Sandhills Sur 18 H6
Sandhoe Northumb 62 G5
Sandholme E Yorks 52 F4
Sandholme Lincs 37 B9
Sandhurst Brack 18 E5
Sandhurst Glos 26 F5
Sandhurst Kent 13 D6
Sandhurst Cross Kent 13 D6
Sandhutton N Yorks 51 A9
Sandiacre Derbys 35 B10
Sandilands Lincs 47 D9
Sandilands S Lanark 69 G7
Sandiway Ches W 43 E9
Sandleheath Hants 9 C10
Sandling Kent 20 F4
Sandlow Green Ches E 43 F10
Sandness Shetland 96 H3
Sandon Essex 20 A4
Sandon Herts 29 E10
Sandon Staffs 34 B5
Sandown IoW 10 F4
Sandplace Corn 4 F3
Sandridge Herts 29 G8
Sandridge Wilts 16 E6
Sandringham Norf 38 C2
Sandsend N Yorks 59 E9
Sandside Ho. Highld 93 C12
Sandsound Shetland 96 J5
Sandtoft N Lincs 45 B11
Sandway Kent 20 F5
Sandwell W Mid 34 G6
Sandwich Kent 21 F10
Sandwick Cumb 56 E6
Sandwick Orkney 95 K5
Sandwick Shetland 96 L6
Sandwith Cumb 56 E1
Sandy C Beds 29 D8
Sandy Carms 23 F9
Sandy Bank Lincs 46 G6
Sandy Haven Pembs 22 F3
Sandy Lane Wilts 16 E6
Sandy Lane Wrex 33 A9
Sandycroft Flint 42 F6
Sandyford Dumfries 61 D8
Sandyford Stoke 44 G2
Sandygate IoM 48 C3
Sandyhills Dumfries 55 D11
Sandylands Lancs 49 C4
Sandypark Devon 5 C8
Sandysike Cumb 61 G9
Sangobeg Highld 92 C7
Sangomore Highld 92 C7
Sanna Highld 78 E7
Sanndabhaig W Isles 84 D3
Sanndabhaig W Isles 91 D9
Sannox N Ayrs 66 B3
Sanquhar Dumfries 60 C3
Santon N Lincs 46 A3
Santon Bridge Cumb 56 F3
Santon Downham Suff 38 G4
Sapcote Leics 35 F10
Sapey Common Hereford 26 B4
Sapiston Suff 38 H5
Sapley Cambs 29 A9
Sapperton Glos 16 A6
Sapperton Lincs 36 B6
Saracen's Head Lincs 37 C9
Sarclet Highld 94 F5
Sardis Carms 23 F10
Sarn Bridgend 14 C5
Sarn Powys 33 F8
Sarn Bach Gwyn 40 H5
Sarn Meyllteyrn Gwyn 40 G4
Sarnau Carms 23 E8
Sarnau Ceredig 23 A8
Sarnau Gwyn 32 B5
Sarnau Powys 25 E7
Sarnau Powys 33 D8
Sarnesfield Hereford 25 C10
Saron Carms 23 C8
Saron Carms 24 G3
Saron Denb 42 F3
Saron Gwyn 40 E6
Saron Gwyn 41 D7
Sarratt Herts 19 B7
Sarre Kent 21 E9
Sarsden Oxon 27 F9
Sarsgrum Highld 92 C6
Satley Durham 58 B2
Satron N Yorks 57 G11
Satterleigh Devon 6 D5
Satterthwaite Cumb 56 G5
Satwell Oxon 18 C4
Sauchen Aberds 83 B8
Saucher Perth 76 D4
Sauchie Clack 69 A7
Sauchieburn Aberds 83 G8
Saughall Ches W 42 E6
Saughtree Borders 61 D11
Saul Glos 26 H4
Saundby Notts 45 D11
Saundersfoot Pembs 22 F6
Saunderton Bucks 18 A4
Saunton Devon 6 C3
Sausthorpe Lincs 47 F7
Saval Highld 93 J8
Savary Highld 79 G9
Savile Park W Yorks 51 G6
Sawbridge Warks 28 B2
Sawbridgeworth Herts 29 G11
Sawdon N Yorks 59 H10
Sawley Derbys 35 B10
Sawley Lancs 50 E3
Sawley N Yorks 51 C8
Sawston Cambs 29 D11
Sawtry Cambs 37 G7
Saxby Leics 36 D4
Saxby Lincs 46 D4
Saxby All Saints N Lincs 52 H5
Saxelbye Leics 36 C3
Saxham Street Suff 31 B7
Saxilby Lincs 46 E2
Saxlingham Norf 38 B6
Saxlingham Green Norf 39 F8
Saxlingham Nethergate Norf 39 F8
Saxlingham Thorpe Norf 39 F8
Saxmundham Suff 31 B10
Saxon Street Cambs 30 C3
Saxondale Notts 36 B2
Saxtead Suff 31 B9
Saxtead Green Suff 31 B9
Saxthorpe Norf 39 B7
Saxton N Yorks 51 F10
Sayers Common W Sus 12 E1
Scackleton N Yorks 52 B2
Scadabhagh W Isles 90 H6
Scaftworth Notts 45 C10
Scagglethorpe N Yorks 52 B4
Scaitcliffe Lancs 50 G3
Scalasaig Argyll 72 D2
Scalby E Yorks 52 G4
Scalby N Yorks 59 G11
Scaldwell Northants 28 A4
Scale Houses Cumb 57 B7
Scaleby Cumb 61 G10
Scaleby Hill Cumb 61 G10
Scales Cumb 49 B2
Scales Cumb 56 D5
Scales Lancs 49 F4
Scalford Leics 36 C3
Scaling Redcar 59 E8
Scallastle Argyll 79 H9
Scalloway Shetland 96 K6
Scalpay W Isles 90 H7
Scalpay Ho. Highld 85 F11
Scalpsie Argyll 73 H9
Scamadale Highld 79 B10
Scamblesby Lincs 46 E6
Scamodale Highld 79 D11
Scampston N Yorks 52 B4
Scampton Lincs 46 E3
Scapa Orkney 95 H5
Scapegoat Hill W Yorks 51 H6
Scar Orkney 95 D7
Scarborough N Yorks 59 H11
Scarcliffe Derbys 45 F8
Scarcroft W Yorks 51 E9
Scarcroft Hill W Yorks 51 E9
Scardroy Highld 86 F5
Scarff Shetland 96 E4
Scarfskerry Highld 94 C4
Scargill Durham 58 E1
Scarinish Argyll 78 G3
Scarisbrick Lancs 43 A6
Scarning Norf 38 D5
Scarrington Notts 36 A3
Scartho NE Lincs 46 B6
Scarwell Orkney 95 F3
Scatness Shetland 96 M5
Scatraig Highld 87 H10
Scawby N Lincs 46 B3
Scawsby S Yorks 45 B9
Scawton N Yorks 51 A11
Scayne's Hill W Sus 12 D2
Scethrog Powys 25 F8
Scholar Green Ches E 44 G2
Scholes W Yorks 44 B5
Scholes W Yorks 51 F9
Scholes W Yorks 51 G7
School Green Ches W 43 F9
Scleddau Pembs 22 C4
Sco Ruston Norf 39 C8
Scofton Notts 45 D10
Scole Norf 39 H7
Scolpaig W Isles 84 A2
Scone Perth 76 E4
Sconser Highld 85 E10
Scoonie Fife 76 G6
Scoor Argyll 78 K7
Scopwick Lincs 46 G4
Scoraig Highld 86 B3
Scorborough E Yorks 52 E6
Scorrier Corn 2 E6
Scorton Lancs 49 E5
Scorton N Yorks 58 F3
Scotbheinn W Isles 84 C3
Scotby Cumb 61 H10
Scotch Corner N Yorks 58 F3
Scotforth Lancs 49 D4
Scothern Lincs 46 E4
Scotland Gate Northumb 63 E8
Scotlandwell Perth 76 G4
Scots' Gap Northumb 62 E6
Scotsburn Highld 87 D10
Scotscalder Station Highld 94 E2
Scotscraig Fife 77 E7
Scotston Aberds 83 F9
Scotston Perth 76 C2
Scotstoun Glasgow 68 D4
Scotstown Highld 79 E11
Scotswood T&W 63 G7
Scottas Highld 85 H12
Scotter Lincs 46 B2
Scotterthorpe Lincs 46 B2
Scottlethorpe Lincs 37 C6
Scotton Lincs 46 C2
Scotton N Yorks 51 D9
Scotton N Yorks 58 G2
Scottow Norf 39 C8
Scoughall E Loth 70 B5
Scoulag Argyll 73 H10
Scoulton Norf 38 E5
Scourie Highld 92 E4
Scourie More Highld 92 E4
Scousburgh Shetland 96 M5
Scrabster Highld 94 C2
Scrafield Lincs 47 F7
Scrainwood Northumb 62 C5
Scrane End Lincs 37 A9
Scraptoft Leics 36 E2
Scratby Norf 39 D11
Scrayingham N Yorks 52 C3
Scredington Lincs 37 A6
Scremby Lincs 47 F8
Scremerston Northumb 71 F9
Screveton Notts 36 A3
Scrivelsby Lincs 46 F6
Scriven N Yorks 51 D9
Scrooby Notts 45 C10
Scropton Derbys 35 B7
Scrub Hill Lincs 46 G6
Scruton N Yorks 58 G3
Sculcoates Hull 53 F6
Sculthorpe Norf 38 B4
Scunthorpe N Lincs 46 A2
Scurlage Swansea 23 H9
Sea Palling Norf 39 C10
Seaborough Dorset 8 D3
Seacombe Mers 42 C6
Seacroft Lincs 47 F9
Seacroft W Yorks 51 F9
Seadyke Lincs 37 B9
Seafield S Ayrs 66 D6
Seafield W Loth 69 D9
Seaford E Sus 12 G3
Seaforth Mers 42 C6
Seagrave Leics 36 D2
Seaham Durham 58 B5
Seahouses Northumb 71 G11
Seal Kent 20 F2
Sealand Flint 42 F6
Seale Sur 18 G5
Seamer N Yorks 52 A6
Seamer N Yorks 58 E5
Seamill N Ayrs 66 B5
Searby Lincs 46 B4
Seasalter Kent 21 E7
Seascale Cumb 56 F2
Seathorne Lincs 47 F9
Seathwaite Cumb 56 E4
Seathwaite Cumb 56 G4
Seatoller Cumb 56 E4
Seaton Corn 4 F4
Seaton Cumb 56 C2
Seaton Devon 8 F1
Seaton Durham 58 A4
Seaton E Yorks 53 E7
Seaton Northumb 63 F9
Seaton Rutland 36 F5
Seaton Burn T&W 63 F8
Seaton Carew Hrtlpl 58 D6
Seaton Delaval Northumb 63 F9
Seaton Ross E Yorks 52 E3
Seaton Sluice Northumb 63 F9
Seatown Aberds 88 B5
Seatown Dorset 8 E3
Seave Green N Yorks 59 F6
Seaview IoW 10 E5
Seaville Cumb 56 A3
Seavington St Mary Som 8 C3
Seavington St Michael Som 8 C3
Sebergham Cumb 56 B5
Seckington Warks 35 E8
Second Coast Highld 86 B2
Sedbergh Cumb 57 G8
Sedbury Glos 15 B11
Sedbusk N Yorks 57 G10
Sedgeberrow Worcs 27 E7
Sedgebrook Lincs 36 B4
Sedgefield Durham 58 D4
Sedgeford Norf 38 B3
Sedgehill Wilts 9 B7
Sedgley W Mid 34 F5
Sedgwick Cumb 57 H7
Sedlescombe E Sus 13 E6
Sedlescombe Street E Sus 13 E6
Seend Wilts 16 E6
Seend Cleeve Wilts 16 E6
Seer Green Bucks 18 B6
Seething Norf 39 F9
Sefton Mers 42 B6
Seghill Northumb 63 F8
Seifton Shrops 33 G10
Seighford Staffs 34 C4
Seilebost W Isles 90 H5
Seion Gwyn 41 D7
Seisdon Staffs 34 F4
Seisiadar W Isles 91 D10
Selattyn Shrops 33 B8
Selborne Hants 10 A6
Selby N Yorks 52 F2
Selham W Sus 11 B8
Selhurst London 19 E10
Selkirk Borders 70 H3
Sellack Hereford 26 F2
Sellafirth Shetland 96 D7
Sellibister Orkney 95 D8
Sellindge Kent 13 C9
Sellindge Lees Kent 13 C10
Selling Kent 21 F7
Sells Green Wilts 16 E6
Selly Oak W Mid 34 G6
Selmeston E Sus 12 F4
Selsdon London 19 E10
Selsey W Sus 11 E7
Selsfield Common W Sus 12 C2
Selsted Kent 21 G9
Selston Notts 45 G8
Selworthy Som 7 B8
Semblister Shetland 96 H5
Semer Suff 30 D6
Semington Wilts 16 E5
Semley Wilts 9 B7
Send Sur 19 F7
Send Marsh Sur 19 F7
Senghenydd Caerph 15 B7
Sennen Corn 2 G2
Sennen Cove Corn 2 G2
Sennybridge = Pont Senni Powys 24 F6
Serlby Notts 45 D10
Sessay N Yorks 51 B10
Setchey Norf 38 D2
Setley Hants 10 D2
Setter Shetland 96 E6
Setter Shetland 96 H5
Setter Shetland 96 J7
Settiscarth Orkney 95 G4
Settle N Yorks 50 C4
Settrington N Yorks 52 B4
Seven Kings London 19 C11
Seven Sisters Neath 24 H5
Sevenhampton Glos 27 F7
Sevenoaks Kent 20 F2
Sevenoaks Weald Kent 20 F2
Severn Beach S Glos 15 C11
Severn Stoke Worcs 26 D5
Severnhampton Swindon 17 B9
Sevington Kent 13 B9
Sewards End Essex 30 E2
Sewardstone Essex 19 B10
Sewardstonebury Essex 19 B10
Sewerby E Yorks 53 C7
Seworgan Corn 2 F6
Sewstern Leics 36 C4
Sezincote Glos 27 E8
Sgarasta Mhor W Isles 90 H5
Sgiogarstaigh W Isles 91 A10
Shabbington Bucks 28 H3
Shackerstone Leics 35 E9
Shackleford Sur 18 G6
Shade W Yorks 50 G5
Shadforth Durham 58 B4
Shadingfield Suff 39 G10
Shadoxhurst Kent 13 C8
Shadsworth Blackburn 50 G3
Shadwell Norf 38 G5
Shadwell W Yorks 51 F9
Shaftesbury Dorset 9 B7
Shafton S Yorks 45 A7
Shalbourne Wilts 17 E10
Shalcombe IoW 10 F2
Shalden Hants 18 G3
Shaldon Devon 5 D10
Shalfleet IoW 10 F3
Shalford Essex 30 F4
Shalford Sur 19 G7
Shalford Green Essex 30 F4
Shallowford Devon 6 B6
Shalmsford Street Kent 21 F7
Shalstone Bucks 28 E3
Shamley Green Sur 19 G7
Shandon Argyll 73 E11
Shandwick Highld 87 D11
Shangton Leics 36 F3
Shankhouse Northumb 63 F8
Shanklin IoW 10 F4
Shanquhar Aberds 88 E5
Shanzie Perth 76 B5
Shap Cumb 57 E7
Shapwick Dorset 9 D8
Shapwick Som 15 H10
Shardlow Derbys 35 B10
Shareshill Staffs 34 E5
Sharlston W Yorks 51 H9
Sharlston Common W Yorks 51 H9
Sharnbrook Bedford 28 C6
Sharnford Leics 35 F10
Sharoe Green Lancs 49 F5
Sharow N Yorks 51 B9
Sharp Street Norf 39 C9
Sharpenhoe C Beds 29 E7
Sharperton Northumb 62 C5
Sharpness Glos 16 A3
Sharpthorne W Sus 12 C2
Sharrington Norf 38 B6
Shatterford Worcs 34 G3
Shaugh Prior Devon 4 E6
Shavington Ches E 43 G10
Shaw Gtr Man 44 B3
Shaw W Berks 17 E11
Shaw Wilts 16 E5
Shaw Green Lancs 49 H5
Shaw Mills N Yorks 51 C8
Shawbury Shrops 34 C1
Shawdon Hall Northumb 62 B6
Shawell Leics 35 G11
Shawford Hants 10 B3
Shawforth Lancs 50 G4
Shawhead Dumfries 60 F4
Shawhill Dumfries 61 G8
Shawton S Lanark 68 F5
Shawtonhill S Lanark 68 F5
Shear Cross Wilts 16 G5
Shearington Dumfries 60 G6
Shearsby Leics 36 F2
Shebbear Devon 6 F3
Shebdon Staffs 34 C3
Shebster Highld 93 C13
Sheddens E Renf 68 E4
Shedfield Hants 10 C4
Sheen Staffs 44 F5
Sheepscar W Yorks 51 F9
Sheepscombe Glos 26 G5
Sheepstor Devon 5 E6
Sheepwash Devon 6 F3
Sheepway N Som 15 D10
Sheepy Magna Leics 35 E9
Sheepy Parva Leics 35 E9
Sheering Essex 30 G2
Sheerness Kent 20 D6
Sheet Hants 11 B6
Sheffield S Yorks 45 D7
Sheffield Bottom W Berks 18 E3
Sheffield Green E Sus 12 D3
Shefford C Beds 29 E8
Shefford Woodlands W Berks 17 D10
Sheigra Highld 92 C4
Sheinton Shrops 34 E2
Shelderton Shrops 33 H10
Sheldon Derbys 44 F5
Sheldon Devon 7 F10
Sheldon W Mid 35 G7
Sheldwich Kent 21 F7
Shelf W Yorks 51 G7
Shelfanger Norf 39 G7
Shelfield W Mid 34 E6
Shelfield Warks 27 B8
Shelford Notts 36 A2
Shellacres Northumb 71 F7
Shelley Essex 20 A2
Shelley Suff 31 E7
Shelley W Yorks 44 A6
Shellingford Oxon 17 B10
Shellow Bowells Essex 30 H3
Shelsley Beauchamp Worcs 26 B4
Shelsley Walsh Worcs 26 B4
Shelthorpe Leics 35 D11
Shelton Bedford 29 B7
Shelton Norf 39 F8
Shelton Notts 36 A3
Shelton Shrops 33 D10
Shelton Green Norf 39 F8
Shelve Shrops 33 F9
Shelwick Hereford 26 D2
Shenfield Essex 20 B3
Shenington Oxon 27 D10
Shenley Herts 19 A8
Shenley Brook End M Keynes 28 E5
Shenley Church End M Keynes 28 E5
Shenleybury Herts 19 A8
Shenmore Hereford 25 E10
Shennanton Dumfries 54 C6
Shenstone Staffs 35 E7
Shenstone Worcs 26 A5
Shenton Leics 35 E9
Shenval Highld 80 A6
Shenval Moray 82 A4
Shepeau Stow Lincs 37 D9
Shephall Herts 29 F9
Shepherd's Green Oxon 18 C4
Shepherd's Port Norf 38 B2
Shepherdswell Kent 21 G9
Shepley W Yorks 44 B5
Shepperdine S Glos 16 B3
Shepperton Sur 19 E7
Shepreth Cambs 29 D10
Shepshed Leics 35 D10
Shepton Beauchamp Som 8 C3
Shepton Mallet Som 16 G3
Shepton Montague Som 8 A5
Shepway Kent 20 F4
Sheraton Durham 58 C5
Sherborne Dorset 8 C5
Sherborne Glos 27 G8
Sherborne St John Hants 18 F3
Sherbourne Warks 27 B9
Sherburn Durham 58 B4
Sherburn N Yorks 52 B5
Sherburn Hill Durham 58 B4
Sherburn in Elmet N Yorks 51 F10
Shere Sur 19 G7
Shereford Norf 38 C4
Sherfield English Hants 10 B1
Sherfield on Loddon Hants 18 F3
Sherford Devon 5 G8
Sheriff Hutton N Yorks 52 C2
Sheriffhales Shrops 34 D3
Sheringham Norf 39 A7
Sherington M Keynes 28 D5
Shernal Green Worcs 26 B6
Shernborne Norf 38 B3
Sherrington Wilts 16 H6
Sherston Wilts 16 C5
Sherwood Green Devon 6 D4
Shettleston Glasgow 68 D5
Shevington Gtr Man 43 B8
Shevington Moor Gtr Man 43 A8
Shevington Vale Gtr Man 43 B8
Sheviock Corn 4 F4
Shide IoW 10 F3
Shiel Bridge Highld 80 B1
Shieldaig Highld 85 A13
Shieldaig Highld 85 C13
Shieldhill Dumfries 60 E6
Shieldhill Falk 69 C7
Shieldhill S Lanark 69 F9
Shielfoot Highld 79 E9
Shielhill Angus 77 B7
Shielhill Invclyd 73 F11
Shifford Oxon 17 A10
Shifnal Shrops 34 E3
Shilbottle Northumb 63 C7
Shildon Durham 58 D3
Shillingford Devon 7 D8
Shillingford Oxon 18 B2
Shillingford St George Devon 5 C10
Shillingstone Dorset 9 C7
Shillington C Beds 29 E8
Shillmoor Northumb 62 C4
Shilton Oxon 27 H9
Shilton Warks 35 G10
Shilvington Northumb 63 E7
Shimpling Norf 39 G7
Shimpling Suff 30 C5
Shimpling Street Suff 30 C5
Shincliffe Durham 58 B3
Shiney Row T&W 58 A4
Shinfield Wokingham 18 E4
Shingham Norf 38 E3
Shingle Street Suff 31 D10
Shinner's Bridge Devon 5 E8
Shinness Highld 93 H8
Shipbourne Kent 20 F2
Shipdham Norf 38 E5
Shipham Som 15 F10
Shiphay Torbay 5 E9
Shiplake Oxon 18 D4
Shipley Derbys 35 A10
Shipley Northumb 63 B7
Shipley Shrops 34 F4
Shipley W Sus 11 B10
Shipley W Yorks 51 F7
Shipley Shiels Northumb 62 D3
Shipmeadow Suff 39 G9
Shippea Hill Sta. Cambs 38 G2
Shippon Oxon 17 B11
Shipston-on-Stour Warks 27 D9
Shipton Glos 27 G7
Shipton N Yorks 52 D1
Shipton Shrops 34 F1
Shipton Bellinger Hants 17 G9
Shipton Gorge Dorset 8 E3
Shipton Green W Sus 11 D7
Shipton Moyne Glos 16 C5
Shipton on Cherwell Oxon 27 G11
Shipton Solers Glos 27 G7
Shipton-under-Wychwood Oxon 27 G9
Shiptonthorpe E Yorks 52 E4
Shirburn Oxon 18 B3
Shirdley Hill Lancs 42 A6
Shirebrook Derbys 45 F9
Shiregreen S Yorks 45 C7
Shirehampton Bristol 15 D11
Shiremoor T&W 63 F9
Shirenewton Mon 15 B10
Shireoaks Notts 45 D9
Shirkoak Kent 13 C8
Shirl Heath Hereford 25 C11
Shirland Derbys 45 G7
Shirley Derbys 35 A8
Shirley London 19 E10
Shirley Soton 10 C3
Shirley W Mid 35 H7
Shirrell Heath Hants 10 C4
Shirwell Devon 6 C4
Shirwell Cross Devon 6 C4
Shiskine N Ayrs 66 D2
Shobdon Hereford 25 B11
Shobnall Staffs 35 C8
Shobrooke Devon 7 F7
Shoby Leics 36 D2
Shocklach Ches W 43 H7
Shoeburyness Southend 20 C6
Sholden Kent 21 F10
Sholing Soton 10 C3
Shoot Hill Shrops 33 D10
Shop Corn 3 B7
Shop Corn 6 E1
Shop Corner Suff 31 E9
Shore Mill Highld 87 E10
Shoreditch London 19 C10
Shoreham Kent 20 E2
Shoreham-By-Sea W Sus 11 D11
Shoresdean Northumb 71 F8
Shoreswood Northumb 71 F8
Shoreton Highld 87 E9
Shorncote Glos 17 B7
Shorne Kent 20 D3
Short Heath W Mid 34 E5
Shortacombe Devon 4 C6
Shortgate E Sus 12 E3
Shortlanesend Corn 3 E7
Shortlees E Ayrs 67 C7
Shortstown Bedford 29 D7
Shorwell IoW 10 F3
Shoscombe Bath 16 F4
Shotatton Shrops 33 C9
Shotesham Norf 39 F8
Shotgate Essex 20 B4
Shotley Suff 31 E9
Shotley Bridge Durham 58 A1
Shotley Gate Suff 31 E9
Shotleyfield Northumb 58 A1
Shottenden Kent 21 F7
Shottermill Sur 11 A7
Shottery Warks 27 C8
Shotteswell Warks 27 D11
Shottisham Suff 31 D10
Shottle Derbys 45 H7
Shottlegate Derbys 45 H7
Shotton Durham 58 C5
Shotton Flint 42 F6
Shotton Northumb 71 G7
Shotton Colliery Durham 58 B4
Shotts N Lanark 69 D7
Shotwick Ches W 42 E6
Shouldham Norf 38 E2
Shouldham Thorpe Norf 38 E2
Shoulton Worcs 26 C5
Shover's Green E Sus 12 C5
Shrawardine Shrops 33 D10
Shrawley Worcs 26 B5
Shrewley Common Warks 27 B9
Shrewsbury Shrops 33 D10
Shrewton Wilts 17 G7
Shripney W Sus 11 D8
Shrivenham Oxon 17 C9
Shropham Norf 38 F5
Shrub End Essex 30 F6
Shucknall Hereford 26 D2
Shudy Camps Cambs 30 D3
Shulishadermor Highld 85 D9
Shurdington Glos 26 G6
Shurlock Row Windsor 18 D5
Shurrery Highld 93 D13
Shurrery Lodge Highld 93 D13
Shurton Som 7 B11
Shustoke Warks 35 F8
Shute Devon 7 F7
Shute Devon 8 E1
Shutford Oxon 27 D10
Shuthonger Glos 26 E5
Shutlanger Northants 28 C4
Shuttington Warks 35 E8
Shuttlewood Derbys 45 E8
Siabost bho Dheas W Isles 90 C7
Siabost bho Thuath W Isles 90 C7
Siadar W Isles 91 B8
Siadar Iarach W Isles 91 B8
Siadar Uarach W Isles 91 B8
Sibbaldbie Dumfries 61 E7
Sibbertoft Northants 36 G2
Sibdon Carwood Shrops 33 G10
Sibford Ferris Oxon 27 E10
Sibford Gower Oxon 27 E10
Sible Hedingham Essex 30 E4
Sibsey Lincs 47 G7
Sibson Cambs 37 F6
Sibson Leics 35 E9
Sibthorpe Notts 45 H11
Sibton Suff 31 B10
Sibton Green Suff 31 A10
Sicklesmere Suff 30 B5
Sicklinghall N Yorks 51 E9
Sid Devon 7 H10
Sidbury Devon 7 G10
Sidbury Shrops 34 G2
Sidcot N Som 15 F10
Sidcup London 19 D11
Siddick Cumb 56 C2
Siddington Ches E 44 E2
Siddington Glos 17 B7
Sidemoor Worcs 26 A6
Sidestrand Norf 39 B8
Sidford Devon 7 G10
Sidlesham W Sus 11 E7
Sidley E Sus 12 F6
Sidlow Sur 19 G9
Sidmouth Devon 7 H10
Sigford Devon 5 D8
Sigglesthorne E Yorks 53 E7
Sighthill Edin 69 C10
Sigingstone V Glam 14 D5
Signet Oxon 27 G9
Silchester Hants 18 E3
Sildinis W Isles 91 F7
Sileby Leics 36 D1
Silecroft Cumb 49 A1
Silfield Norf 39 F7
Silian Ceredig 23 A10
Silk Willoughby Lincs 37 A6
Silkstone S Yorks 44 B6
Silkstone Common S Yorks 44 B6
Silloth Cumb 56 A3
Sills Northumb 62 C4
Sillyearn Moray 88 C5
Siloh Carms 24 E4
Silpho N Yorks 59 G10
Silsden W Yorks 50 E6
Silsoe C Beds 29 E7
Silver End Essex 30 G5
Silverburn Midloth 69 D11
Silverdale Lancs 49 B4
Silverdale Staffs 44 H2
Silvergate Norf 39 C7
Silverhill E Sus 13 E6
Silverley's Green Suff 39 H8
Silverstone Northants 28 D3
Silverton Devon 7 F8
Silvington Shrops 34 H2
Silwick Shetland 96 J4
Simmondley Derbys 44 C4
Simonburn Northumb 62 F4
Simonsbath Som 7 C6
Simonstone Lancs 50 F3
Simprim Borders 71 F7
Simpson M Keynes 28 E5
Simpson Cross Pembs 22 E3
Sinclair's Hill Borders 71 E7
Sinclairston E Ayrs 67 E7
Sinderby N Yorks 51 A9
Sinderhope Northumb 57 A10
Sindlesham Wokingham 18 E4
Singdean Borders 61 C11
Singleborough Bucks 28 E4
Singleton Lancs 49 F3
Singleton W Sus 11 C7
Singlewell Kent 20 D3
Sinkhurst Green Kent 13 B7
Sinnahard Aberds 82 B6
Sinnington N Yorks 59 H8
Sinton Green Worcs 26 B5
Sipson London 19 D7
Sirhowy Bl Gwent 25 G8
Sisland Norf 39 F9
Sissinghurst Kent 13 C6
Sisterpath Borders 70 F6
Siston S Glos 16 D3
Sithney Corn 2 G5
Sittingbourne Kent 20 E5
Six Ashes Staffs 34 G3
Six Hills Leics 36 C2
Six Mile Bottom Cambs 30 C2
Sixhills Lincs 46 D5
Sixpenny Handley Dorset 9 C8
Sizewell Suff 31 B11
Skail Highld 93 E10
Skaill Orkney 95 E5
Skaill Orkney 95 G3
Skaill Orkney 95 H6
Skares E Ayrs 67 E8
Skateraw E Loth 70 C6
Skaw Shetland 96 G7
Skeabost Highld 85 D9
Skeabrae Orkney 95 F3
Skeeby N Yorks 58 F3
Skeffington Leics 36 E3
Skeffling E Yorks 53 H9
Skegby Notts 45 F8
Skegness Lincs 47 F9
Skelberry Shetland 96 M5
Skelbo Highld 87 B10
Skelbrooke S Yorks 45 A9
Skeldyke Lincs 37 B9
Skellingthorpe Lincs 46 E3
Skellister Shetland 96 H6
Skellow S Yorks 45 A9
Skelmanthorpe W Yorks 44 A6
Skelmersdale Lancs 43 B7
Skelmonae Aberds 89 E8
Skelmorlie N Ayrs 73 G10
Skelmuir Aberds 89 D9
Skelpick Highld 93 D10
Skelton Cumb 56 C6
Skelton E Yorks 52 G3
Skelton N Yorks 58 F1
Skelton Redcar 59 E7
Skelton York 52 D1
Skelton-on-Ure N Yorks 51 C9
Skelwick Orkney 95 D5
Skelwith Bridge Cumb 56 F5
Skendleby Lincs 47 F8
Skene Ho. Aberds 83 C9
Skenfrith Mon 25 F11
Skerne E Yorks 52 D6
Skeroblingarry Argyll 65 F8
Skerray Highld 93 C9
Skerton Lancs 49 C4
Sketchley Leics 35 F10
Sketty Swansea 14 B2
Skewen Neath 14 B3
Skewsby N Yorks 52 B2
Skeyton Norf 39 C8
Skiag Bridge Highld 92 G5
Skibo Castle Highld 87 C10
Skidbrooke Lincs 47 C8
Skidbrooke North End Lincs 47 C8
Skidby E Yorks 52 F6
Skilgate Som 7 D8
Skillington Lincs 36 C4
Skinburness Cumb 61 H7
Skinflats Falk 69 B8
Skinidin Highld 84 D7
Skinnet Highld 93 C8
Skinningrove Redcar 59 D8
Skipness Argyll 73 H7
Skippool Lancs 49 E3
Skipsea E Yorks 53 D7
Skipsea Brough E Yorks 53 D7
Skipton N Yorks 50 D5
Skipton-on-Swale N Yorks 51 B9
Skipwith N Yorks 52 F2
Skirbeck Lincs 37 A9
Skirbeck Quarter Lincs 37 A9
Skirlaugh E Yorks 53 F7
Skirling Borders 69 G9
Skirmett Bucks 18 C4
Skirpenbeck E Yorks 52 D3
Skirwith Cumb 57 C8
Skirza Highld 94 D5
Skulamus Highld 85 F11
Skullomie Highld 93 C9
Skyborry Green Shrops 25 A9
Skye of Curr Highld 82 A1
Skyreholme N Yorks 51 C6
Slackhall Derbys 44 D4
Slackhead Moray 88 B4
Slad Glos 26 H5
Slade Devon 6 B4
Slade Pembs 22 E4
Slade Green London 20 D2
Slaggyford Northumb 57 A8
Slaidburn Lancs 50 D3
Slaithwaite W Yorks 44 A4
Slaley Northumb 62 H5
Slamannan Falk 69 C7
Slapton Bucks 28 F6
Slapton Devon 5 G9
Slapton Northants 28 D3
Slatepit Dale Derbys 45 F7
Slattocks Gtr Man 44 B2
Slaugham W Sus 12 D1
Slaughterford Wilts 16 D5
Slawston Leics 36 F3
Sleaford Hants 18 H5
Sleaford Lincs 46 H4
Sleagill Cumb 57 E7
Sleapford Telford 34 D2
Sledge Green Worcs 26 E5
Sledmere E Yorks 52 C5
Sleightholme Durham 57 E11
Sleights N Yorks 59 F9
Slepe Dorset 9 E8
Slickly Highld 94 D4
Sliddery N Ayrs 66 D2
Sligachan Hotel Highld 85 F9
Slimbridge Glos 16 A4
Slindon Staffs 34 B4
Slindon W Sus 11 D8
Slinfold W Sus 11 A10
Sling Gwyn 41 D8
Slingsby N Yorks 52 B2
Slioch Aberds 88 E5
Slip End C Beds 29 G7
Slip End Herts 29 E9
Slipton Northants 36 H5
Slitting Mill Staffs 34 D6
Slochd Highld 81 A10
Slockavullin Argyll 73 D7
Sloley Norf 39 C8
Sloothby Lincs 47 E8
Slough Slough 18 D6
Slough Green W Sus 12 D1
Sluggan Highld 81 A10
Slumbay Highld 85 E13
Slyfield Sur 18 F6

Slyne Lancs 49 C4
Smailholm Borders 70 G5
Small Dole W Sus 11 C11
Small Hythe Kent 13 C7
Smallbridge Gtr Man 50 H5
Smallburgh Norf 39 C9
Smallburn Aberds 89 D10
Smallburn E Ayrs 68 H5
Smalley Derbys 35 A10
Smallfield Sur 12 B2
Smallridge Devon 8 D2
Smannell Hants 17 G10
Smardale Cumb 57 F9
Smarden Kent 13 B7
Smarden Bell Kent 13 B7
Smeatharpe Devon 7 E10
Smeeth Kent 13 C9
Smeeton Westerby Leics 36 F2
Smercleit W Isles 84 G2
Smerral Highld 94 G3
Smethwick W Mid 34 G6
Smirisary Highld 79 D9
Smisby Derbys 35 D9
Smith Green Lancs 49 D4
Smithfield Cumb 61 G10
Smithincott Devon 7 E9
Smith's Green Essex 30 F2
Smithstown Highld 85 A12
Smithton Highld 87 G10
Smithy Green Ches E 43 E10
Smockington Leics 35 G10
Smoogro Orkney 95 H4
Smythe's Green Essex 30 G6
Snaigow House Perth 76 C3
Snailbeach Shrops 33 E9
Snailwell Cambs 30 B3
Snainton N Yorks 52 A5
Snaith E Yorks 52 G2
Snape N Yorks 51 A8
Snape Suff 31 C10
Snape Green Lancs 43 A6
Snarestone Leics 35 E9
Snarford Lincs 46 D4
Snargate Kent 13 D8
Snave Kent 13 D9
Snead Powys 33 F9
Sneath Common Norf 39 G7
Sneaton N Yorks 59 F9
Sneatonthorpe N Yorks 59 F10
Snelland Lincs 46 D4
Snelston Derbys 35 A7
Snettisham Norf 38 B2
Sniseabhal W Isles 84 E2
Snitter Northumb 62 C6
Snitterby Lincs 46 C3
Snitterfield Warks 27 C9
Snitton Shrops 34 H1
Snodhill Hereford 25 D10
Snodland Kent 20 E3
Snowden Hill S Yorks 44 B6
Snowdown Kent 21 F9
Snowshill Glos 27 E7
Snydale W Yorks 51 H10
Soar Anglesey 40 C5
Soar Carms 24 F3
Soar Devon 5 H8
Soar-y-Mynydd Ceredig 24 C4
Soberton Hants 10 C5
Soberton Heath Hants 10 C5
Sockbridge Cumb 57 D7
Sockburn Darl 58 F4
Soham Cambs 30 A2
Soham Cotes Cambs 38 H1
Solas W Isles 84 A3
Soldon Cross Devon 6 E2
Soldridge Hants 10 A5
Sole Street Kent 20 E3
Sole Street Kent 21 G7
Solihull W Mid 35 H7
Sollers Dilwyn Hereford 25 C11
Sollers Hope Hereford 26 E3
Sollom Lancs 49 H4
Solva Pembs 22 D2
Somerby Leics 36 D3
Somerby Lincs 46 B4
Somercotes Derbys 45 G8
Somerford Dorset 9 E10
Somerford Keynes Glos 17 B7
Somerley W Sus 11 E7
Somerleyton Suff 39 F10
Somersal Herbert Derbys 35 B7
Somersby Lincs 47 E7
Somersham Cambs 37 H9
Somersham Suff 31 D7
Somerton Oxon 27 F11
Somerton Som 8 B3
Sompting W Sus 11 D10
Sonning Wokingham 18 D4
Sonning Common Oxon 18 C4
Sonning Eye Oxon 18 D4
Sontley Wrex 42 H6
Sopley Hants 9 E10
Sopwell Herts 29 H8
Sopworth Wilts 16 C5
Sorbie Dumfries 55 E7
Sordale Highld 94 D3
Sorisdale Argyll 78 E5
Sorn E Ayrs 68 H4
Sornhill E Ayrs 67 C8
Sortat Highld 94 D4
Sotby Lincs 46 E6
Sots Hole Lincs 46 F5
Sotterley Suff 39 G10
Soudley Shrops 34 C3
Soughton Flint 42 F5
Soulbury Bucks 28 F5
Soulby Cumb 57 E9
Souldern Oxon 28 E2
Souldrop Bedford 28 B6
Sound Ches E 43 H9
Sound Shetland 96 H5
Sound Shetland 96 J6
Sound Heath Ches E 43 H9
Soundwell S Glos 16 D3
Sourhope Borders 62 A4
Sourin Orkney 95 E5
Sourton Devon 6 G4
Soutergate Cumb 49 A2
South Acre Norf 38 D4
South Allington Devon 5 H8
South Alloa Falk 69 A7
South Ambersham W Sus 11 B8
South Anston S Yorks 45 D9
South Ascot Windsor 18 E6
South Ballachulish Highld 74 B3
South Balloch S Ayrs 66 G6
South Bank Redcar 59 D6
South Barrow Som 8 B5
South Beach Gwyn 40 G5
South Benfleet Essex 20 C4
South Bersted W Sus 11 D8
South Brent Devon 5 E7
South Brewham Som 16 H4
South Broomhill Northumb 63 D8
South Burlingham Norf 39 E9
South Cadbury Som 8 B5
South Cairn Dumfries 54 C2
South Carlton Lincs 46 E3
South Cave E Yorks 52 F5
South Cerney Glos 17 B7
South Chard Som 8 D2
South Charlton Northumb 63 A7
South Cheriton Som 8 B5
South Cliffe E Yorks 52 F4
South Clifton Notts 46 E2
South Cockerington Lincs 47 D7
South Cornelly Bridgend 14 C4
South Cove Suff 39 G10
South Creagan Argyll 74 C2
South Creake Norf 38 B4
South Croxton Leics 36 D2
South Croydon London 19 E10
South Dalton E Yorks 52 E5
South Darenth Kent 20 E2
South Duffield N Yorks 52 F2
South Elkington Lincs 46 D6
South Elmsall W Yorks 45 A8
South End Bucks 28 F5
South End Cumb 49 C2
South End N Lincs 53 G7
South Erradale Highld 85 A12
South Fambridge Essex 20 B5
South Fawley W Berks 17 C10
South Ferriby N Lincs 52 G5
South Garth Shetland 96 D7
South Garvan Highld 80 F1
South Glendale W Isles 84 G2
South Godstone Sur 19 G10
South Gorley Hants 9 C10
South Green Essex 20 B3
South Green Kent 20 E5
South-haa Shetland 96 E5
South Ham Hants 18 F3
South Hanningfield Essex 20 B4
South Harting W Sus 11 C6
South Hatfield Herts 29 H9
South Hayling Hants 10 E6
South Hazelrigg Northumb 71 G9
South Heath Bucks 18 A6
South Heighton E Sus 12 F3
South Hetton Durham 58 B4
South Hiendley W Yorks 45 A7
South Hill Corn 4 D4
South Hinksey Oxon 18 A2
South Hole Devon 6 D1
South Holme N Yorks 52 B2
South Holmwood Sur 19 G8
South Hornchurch London 20 C2
South Hykeham Lincs 46 F3
South Hylton T&W 63 H9
South Kelsey Lincs 46 C4
South Kessock Highld 87 G9
South Killingholme N Lincs 53 H7
South Kilvington N Yorks 51 A10
South Kilworth Leics 36 G2
South Kirkby W Yorks 45 A8
South Kirkton Aberds 83 C9
South Kiscadale N Ayrs 66 D3
South Kyme Lincs 46 H5
South Lancing W Sus 11 D10
South Leigh Oxon 27 H10
South Leverton Notts 45 D11
South Littleton Worcs 27 D7
South Lopham Norf 38 G6
South Luffenham Rutland 36 E5
South Malling E Sus 12 E3
South Marston Swindon 17 C8
South Middleton Northumb 62 A5
South Milford N Yorks 51 F10
South Millbrex Aberds 89 D8
South Milton Devon 5 G8
South Mimms Herts 19 A9
South Molton Devon 7 D6
South Moreton Oxon 18 C2
South Mundham W Sus 11 D7
South Muskham Notts 45 G11
South Newbald E Yorks 52 F5
South Newington Oxon 27 E11
South Newton Wilts 9 A9
South Normanton Derbys 45 G8
South Norwood London 19 E10
South Nutfield Sur 19 G10
South Ockendon Thurrock 20 C2
South Ormsby Lincs 47 E7
South Otterington N Yorks 58 H4
South Owersby Lincs 46 C4
South Oxhey Herts 19 B8
South Perrott Dorset 8 D3
South Petherton Som 8 C3
South Petherwin Corn 4 C4
South Pickenham Norf 38 E4
South Pool Devon 5 G8
South Port Argyll 74 E3
South Radworthy Devon 7 C6
South Rauceby Lincs 46 H4
South Raynham Norf 38 C4
South Reston Lincs 47 D8
South Runcton Norf 38 E2
South Scarle Notts 46 F2
South Shian Argyll 74 C2
South Shields T&W 63 G9
South Shore Blackpool 49 F3
South Somercotes Lincs 47 C8
South Stainley N Yorks 51 C9
South Stainmore Cumb 57 E10
South Stifford Thurrock 20 D3
South Stoke Oxon 18 C2
South Stoke W Sus 11 D9
South Street E Sus 12 E2
South Street Kent 21 E8
South Street Kent 21 F7
South Street London 19 F11
South Tawton Devon 6 G5
South Thoresby Lincs 47 E8
South Tidworth Wilts 17 G9
South Town Hants 18 H3
South View Hants 18 F3
South Walsham Norf 39 D9
South Warnborough Hants 18 G4
South Weald Essex 20 B2
South Weston Oxon 18 B4
South Wheatley Corn 4 B3
South Wheatley Notts 45 D11
South Whiteness Shetland 96 J5
South Widcombe Bath 16 F2
South Wigston Leics 36 F1
South Willingham Lincs 46 D5
South Wingfield Derbys 45 G7
South Witham Lincs 36 D5
South Wonston Hants 17 H11
South Woodham Ferrers Essex 20 B5
South Wootton Norf 38 C2
South Wraxall Wilts 16 E5
South Zeal Devon 6 G5
Southall London 19 C8
Southam Glos 26 F6
Southam Warks 27 B11
Southampton Soton 10 C3
Southborough Kent 12 B4
Southbourne Bmouth 9 E10
Southbourne W Sus 11 D6
Southburgh Norf 38 E5
Southburn E Yorks 52 D5
Southchurch Southend 20 C6
Southcott Wilts 17 F8
Southcourt Bucks 28 G5
Southdean Borders 62 C2
Southdene Mers 43 C7
Southease E Sus 12 F3
Southend Argyll 65 H7
Southend W Berks 18 D2
Southend Wilts 17 D8
Southend-on-Sea Southend 20 C5
Southernden Kent 20 G5
Southerndown V Glam 14 D4
Southerness Dumfries 60 H5
Southery Norf 38 F2
Southfield Northumb 63 F8
Southfleet Kent 20 D3
Southgate Ceredig 32 H1
Southgate London 19 B9
Southgate Norf 39 C7
Southgate Swansea 23 H10
Southill C Beds 29 D8
Southleigh Devon 7 G11
Southminster Essex 20 B6
Southmoor Oxon 17 B10
Southoe Cambs 29 B8
Southolt Suff 31 B8
Southorpe Pboro 37 E6
Southowram W Yorks 51 G7
Southport Mers 49 H3
Southpunds Shetland 96 L6
Southrepps Norf 39 B8
Southrey Lincs 46 F5
Southrop Glos 17 A8
Southrope Hants 18 G3
Southsea Ptsmth 10 E5
Southstoke Bath 16 E4
Southtown Norf 39 E11
Southtown Orkney 95 J5
Southwaite Cumb 56 B6
Southwark London 19 D10
Southwater W Sus 11 B10
Southwater Street W Sus 11 B10
Southway Som 15 G11
Southwell Dorset 8 G5
Southwell Notts 45 G10
Southwick Hants 10 D5
Southwick Northants 36 F6
Southwick T&W 63 H9
Southwick W Sus 11 D11
Southwick Wilts 16 F5
Southwold Suff 39 H11
Southwood Norf 39 E9
Southwood Som 8 A4
Soval Lodge W Isles 91 E8
Sowber Gate N Yorks 58 H4
Sowerby N Yorks 51 A10
Sowerby W Yorks 50 G6
Sowerby Bridge W Yorks 51 G6
Sowerby Row Cumb 56 C5
Sowood W Yorks 51 H6
Sowton Devon 7 G8
Soyal Highld 87 B8
Spa Common Norf 39 B8
Spacey Houses N Yorks 51 D9
Spadeadam Farm Cumb 61 F11
Spalding Lincs 37 C8
Spaldington E Yorks 52 F3
Spaldwick Cambs 29 A8
Spalford Notts 46 F2
Spanby Lincs 37 B6
Sparham Norf 39 D6
Spark Bridge Cumb 49 A3
Sparkford Som 8 B5
Sparkhill W Mid 35 G6
Sparkwell Devon 5 F6
Sparrow Green Norf 38 D5
Sparrowpit Derbys 44 D4
Sparsholt Hants 10 A3
Sparsholt Oxon 17 C10
Spartylea Northumb 57 B10
Spaunton N Yorks 59 H8
Spaxton Som 7 C11
Spean Bridge Highld 80 E4
Spear Hill W Sus 11 C10
Speen Bucks 18 B5
Speen W Berks 17 E11
Speeton N Yorks 53 B7
Speke Mers 43 D7
Speldhurst Kent 12 B4
Spellbrook Herts 29 G11
Spelsbury Oxon 27 F10
Spelter Bridgend 14 B4
Spencers Wood Wokingham 18 E4
Spennithorne N Yorks 58 H2
Spennymoor Durham 58 C3
Spetchley Worcs 26 C5
Spetisbury Dorset 9 D8
Spexhall Suff 39 G9
Spey Bay Moray 88 B3
Speybridge Highld 82 A2
Speyview Moray 88 D2
Spilsby Lincs 47 F8
Spindlestone Northumb 71 G10
Spinkhill Derbys 45 E8
Spinningdale Highld 87 C9
Spirthill Wilts 16 D6
Spital Hill S Yorks 45 C10
Spital in the Street Lincs 46 D3
Spithurst E Sus 12 E3
Spittal Dumfries 54 D6
Spittal E Loth 70 C3
Spittal Highld 94 E3
Spittal Northumb 71 E9
Spittal Pembs 22 D4
Spittal Stirling 68 B4
Spittal of Glenmuick Aberds 82 E5
Spittal of Glenshee Perth 82 F3
Spittalfield Perth 76 C4
Spixworth Norf 39 D8
Splayne's Green E Sus 12 D3
Spofforth N Yorks 51 D9
Spon End W Mid 35 H9
Spon Green Flint 42 F5
Spondon Derby 35 B10
Spooner Row Norf 39 F6
Sporle Norf 38 D4
Spott E Loth 70 C5
Spratton Northants 28 A4
Spreakley Sur 18 G5
Spreyton Devon 6 G5
Spridlington Lincs 46 D4
Spring Vale S Yorks 44 B6
Spring Valley IoM 48 E3
Springburn Glasgow 68 D5
Springfield Dumfries 61 G9
Springfield Essex 30 H4
Springfield Fife 76 F6
Springfield Moray 87 F13
Springfield W Mid 35 G6
Springhill Staffs 34 E5
Springholm Dumfries 55 C11
Springkell Dumfries 61 F8
Springside N Ayrs 67 C6
Springthorpe Lincs 46 D2
Springwell T&W 63 H8
Sproatley E Yorks 53 F7
Sproston Green Ches W 43 F10
Sprotbrough S Yorks 45 B9
Sproughton Suff 31 D8
Sprouston Borders 70 G6
Sprowston Norf 39 D8
Sproxton Leics 36 C4
Sproxton N Yorks 52 A2
Spurstow Ches E 43 G8
Spynie Moray 88 B2
Squires Gate Blackpool 49 F3
Srannda W Isles 90 J5
Sronphadruig Lodge Perth 81 F9
Stableford Shrops 34 F3
Stableford Staffs 34 B4
Stacey Bank S Yorks 44 C6
Stackhouse N Yorks 50 C4
Stackpole Pembs 22 G4
Staddiscombe Plym 4 F6
Staddlethorpe E Yorks 52 G4
Stadhampton Oxon 18 B3
Stadhlaigearraidh W Isles 84 E2
Staffield Cumb 57 B7
Staffin Highld 85 B9
Stafford Staffs 34 C5
Stagsden Bedford 28 D6
Stainburn Cumb 56 D2
Stainburn N Yorks 51 E8
Stainby Lincs 36 C5
Staincross S Yorks 45 A7
Staindrop Durham 58 D2
Staines-upon-Thames Sur 19 D7
Stainfield Lincs 37 C6
Stainfield Lincs 46 E5
Stainforth N Yorks 50 C4
Stainforth S Yorks 45 A10
Staining Lancs 49 F3
Stainland W Yorks 51 H6
Stainsacre N Yorks 59 F10
Stainsby Derbys 45 F8
Stainton Cumb 57 D6
Stainton Cumb 57 H7
Stainton Durham 58 E1
Stainton Mbro 58 E5
Stainton N Yorks 58 G2
Stainton S Yorks 45 C9
Stainton by Langworth Lincs 46 E4
Stainton le Vale Lincs 46 C5
Stainton with Adgarley Cumb 49 B2
Staintondale N Yorks 59 G10
Stair Cumb 56 D4
Stair E Ayrs 67 D7
Stairhaven Dumfries 54 D5
Staithes N Yorks 59 E8
Stake Pool Lancs 49 E4
Stakeford Northumb 63 E8
Stalbridge Dorset 8 C6
Stalbridge Weston Dorset 8 C6
Stalham Norf 39 C9
Stalham Green Norf 39 C9
Stalisfield Green Kent 20 F6
Stalling Busk N Yorks 57 H11
Stallingborough NE Lincs 46 A5
Stalmine Lancs 49 E3
Stalybridge Gtr Man 44 C3
Stambourne Essex 30 E4
Stambourne Green Essex 30 E4
Stamford Lincs 36 E6
Stamford Bridge Ches W 43 F7
Stamford Bridge E Yorks 52 D3
Stamfordham Northumb 62 F6
Stanah Cumb 56 E5
Stanborough Herts 29 G9
Stanbridge C Beds 28 F6
Stanbridge Dorset 9 D9
Stanbrook Worcs 26 D5
Stanbury W Yorks 50 F6
Stand Gtr Man 43 B10
Stand N Lanark 68 D6
Standburn Falk 69 C8
Standeford Staffs 34 E5
Standen Kent 13 B7
Standford Hants 11 A7
Standingstone Cumb 56 C2
Standish Gtr Man 43 A8
Standlake Oxon 17 A10
Standon Hants 10 B3
Standon Herts 29 F10
Standon Staffs 34 B4
Stane N Lanark 69 E7
Stanfield Norf 38 C5
Stanford C Beds 29 D8
Stanford Kent 13 C10
Stanford Bishop Hereford 26 C3
Stanford Bridge Worcs 26 B4
Stanford Dingley W Berks 18 D2
Stanford in the Vale Oxon 17 B10
Stanford-le-Hope Thurrock 20 C3
Stanford on Avon Northants 36 H1
Stanford on Soar Notts 35 C11
Stanford on Teme Worcs 26 B4
Stanford Rivers Essex 20 A2
Stanfree Derbys 45 E8
Stanghow Redcar 59 E7
Stanground Pboro 37 F8
Stanhoe Norf 38 B4
Stanhope Borders 69 H10
Stanhope Durham 57 C11
Stanion Northants 36 G5
Stanley Derbys 35 A10
Stanley Durham 58 A2
Stanley Lancs 43 B7
Stanley Perth 76 D4
Stanley Staffs 44 G3
Stanley W Yorks 51 G9
Stanley Common Derbys 35 A10
Stanley Gate Lancs 43 B7
Stanley Hill Hereford 26 D3
Stanlow Ches W 43 E7
Stanmer Brighton 12 F2
Stanmore Hants 10 B3
Stanmore London 19 B8
Stanmore W Berks 17 D11
Stannergate Dundee 77 D7
Stanningley W Yorks 51 F8
Stannington Northumb 63 F8
Stannington S Yorks 45 D7
Stansbatch Hereford 25 B10
Stansfield Suff 30 C4
Stanstead Suff 30 D5
Stanstead Abbotts Herts 29 G10
Stansted Kent 20 E3
Stansted Airport Essex 30 F2
Stansted Mountfitchet Essex 30 F2
Stanton Glos 27 E7
Stanton Mon 25 F10
Stanton Northumb 63 E7
Stanton Staffs 44 H5
Stanton Suff 30 A6
Stanton by Bridge Derbys 35 C9
Stanton-by-Dale Derbys 35 B10
Stanton Drew Bath 16 E2
Stanton Fitzwarren Swindon 17 B8
Stanton Harcourt Oxon 27 H11
Stanton Hill Notts 45 F8
Stanton in Peak Derbys 44 F6
Stanton Lacy Shrops 33 H10
Stanton Long Shrops 34 F1
Stanton-on-the-Wolds Notts 36 B2
Stanton Prior Bath 16 E3
Stanton St Bernard Wilts 17 E7
Stanton St John Oxon 28 H2
Stanton St Quintin Wilts 16 D6
Stanton Street Suff 30 B6
Stanton under Bardon Leics 35 D10
Stanton upon Hine Heath Shrops 34 C1
Stanton Wick Bath 16 E3
Stanwardine in the Fields Shrops 33 C10
Stanwardine in the Wood Shrops 33 C10
Stanway Essex 30 F6
Stanway Glos 27 E7
Stanway Green Suff 31 A9
Stanwell Sur 19 D7
Stanwell Moor Sur 19 D7
Stanwick Northants 28 A6
Stanwick-St-John N Yorks 58 E2
Stanwix Cumb 61 H10
Stanydale Shetland 96 H4
Staoinebrig W Isles 84 E2
Stape N Yorks 59 G8
Stapehill Dorset 9 D9
Stapeley Ches E 43 H9
Stapenhill Staffs 35 C8
Staple Kent 21 F9
Staple Som 7 B10
Staple Cross E Sus 13 D6
Staple Fitzpaine Som 8 C1
Staplefield W Sus 12 D1
Stapleford Cambs 29 C11
Stapleford Herts 29 G10
Stapleford Leics 36 D4
Stapleford Lincs 46 G2
Stapleford Notts 35 B10
Stapleford Wilts 17 H7
Stapleford Abbotts Essex 20 B2
Stapleford Tawney Essex 20 B2
Staplegrove Som 7 D11
Staplehay Som 7 D11
Staplehurst Kent 13 B6
Staplers IoW 10 F4
Stapleton Bristol 16 D3
Stapleton Cumb 61 F11
Stapleton Hereford 25 B10
Stapleton Leics 35 F10
Stapleton N Yorks 58 E3
Stapleton Shrops 33 E10
Stapleton Som 8 B3
Stapley Som 7 E10
Staploe Bedford 29 B8
Staplow Hereford 26 D3
Star Fife 76 G6
Star Pembs 23 C7
Star Som 15 F10
Stara Orkney 95 F3
Starbeck N Yorks 51 D9
Starbotton N Yorks 50 B5
Starcross Devon 5 C10
Stareton Warks 27 A10
Starkholmes Derbys 45 G7
Starlings Green Essex 29 E11
Starston Norf 39 G8
Startforth Durham 58 E1
Startley Wilts 16 C6
Stathe Som 8 B2
Stathern Leics 36 B3
Station Town Durham 58 C5
Staughton Green Cambs 29 B8
Staughton Highway Cambs 29 B8
Staunton Glos 26 F4
Staunton Glos 26 G2
Staunton in the Vale Notts 36 A4
Staunton on Arrow Hereford 25 B10
Staunton on Wye Hereford 25 D10
Staveley Cumb 56 G6
Staveley Cumb 56 H5
Staveley Derbys 45 E8
Staveley N Yorks 51 C9
Staverton Devon 5 E8
Staverton Glos 26 F5
Staverton Northants 28 B2
Staverton Wilts 16 E5
Staverton Bridge Glos 26 F5
Stawell Som 15 H9
Staxigoe Highld 94 E5
Staxton N Yorks 52 B6
Staylittle Powys 32 F4
Staynall Lancs 49 E3
Staythorpe Notts 45 G11
Stean N Yorks 51 B6
Stearsby N Yorks 52 B2
Steart Som 15 G8
Stebbing Essex 30 F3
Stebbing Green Essex 30 F3
Stedham W Sus 11 B7
Steele Road Borders 61 D11
Steen's Bridge Hereford 26 C2
Steep Hants 10 B6
Steep Marsh Hants 11 B6
Steeple Dorset 9 F8
Steeple Essex 20 A6
Steeple Ashton Wilts 16 F6
Steeple Aston Oxon 27 F11
Steeple Barton Oxon 27 F11
Steeple Bumpstead Essex 30 D3
Steeple Claydon Bucks 28 F3
Steeple Gidding Cambs 37 G7
Steeple Langford Wilts 17 H7
Steeple Morden Cambs 29 D9
Steeton W Yorks 50 E6
Stein Highld 84 C7
Steinmanhill Aberds 89 D7
Stelling Minnis Kent 21 G8
Stemster Highld 94 D3
Stemster Ho. Highld 94 D3
Stenalees Corn 3 D9
Stenhousemuir Falk 69 B7
Stenigot Lincs 46 D6
Stenness Shetland 96 F4
Stenscholl Highld 85 B9
Stenso Orkney 95 F4
Stenson Derbys 35 C9
Stenton E Loth 70 C5
Stenton Fife 76 H5
Stenwith Lincs 36 B4
Stepaside Pembs 22 F6
Stepping Hill Gtr Man 44 D3
Steppingley C Beds 29 E7
Stepps N Lanark 68 D5
Sterndale Moor Derbys 44 F5
Sternfield Suff 31 B10
Sterridge Devon 6 B4
Stert Wilts 17 F7
Stetchworth Cambs 30 C3
Stevenage Herts 29 F9
Stevenston N Ayrs 66 B5
Steventon Hants 18 G2
Steventon Oxon 17 B11
Stevington Bedford 28 C6
Stewartby Bedford 29 D7
Stewarton Argyll 65 G7
Stewarton E Ayrs 67 B7
Stewkley Bucks 28 F5
Stewton Lincs 47 D7
Steyne Cross IoW 10 F5
Steyning W Sus 11 C10
Steynton Pembs 22 F4
Stibb Corn 6 E1
Stibb Cross Devon 6 E3
Stibb Green Wilts 17 E9
Stibbard Norf 38 C5
Stibbington Cambs 37 F6
Stichill Borders 70 G6
Sticker Corn 3 D8
Stickford Lincs 47 G7
Sticklepath Devon 6 G5
Stickney Lincs 47 G7
Stiffkey Norf 38 A5
Stifford's Bridge Hereford 26 D4
Stillingfleet N Yorks 52 E1
Stillington N Yorks 52 C1
Stillington Stockton 58 D4
Stilton Cambs 37 G7
Stinchcombe Glos 16 B4
Stinsford Dorset 8 E6
Stirchley Telford 34 E3
Stirkoke Ho. Highld 94 E5
Stirling Aberds 89 D11
Stirling Stirling 68 A6
Stisted Essex 30 F4
Stithians Corn 2 F6
Stittenham Highld 87 D9
Stivichall W Mid 35 H9
Stixwould Lincs 46 F5
Stoak Ches W 43 E7
Stobieside S Lanark 68 G5
Stobo Borders 69 G10
Stoborough Dorset 9 F8
Stoborough Green Dorset 9 F8
Stobshiel E Loth 70 D3
Stobswood Northumb 63 D8
Stock Essex 20 B3
Stock Green Worcs 26 C6
Stock Wood Worcs 27 C7
Stockbridge Hants 10 A2
Stockbury Kent 20 E5
Stockcross W Berks 17 E11
Stockdalewath Cumb 56 B5
Stockerston Leics 36 F4
Stockheath Hants 10 D6
Stockiemuir Stirling 68 B4
Stocking Pelham Herts 29 F11
Stockingford Warks 35 F9
Stockland Devon 8 D1
Stockland Bristol Som 15 G8
Stockleigh English Devon 7 F7
Stockleigh Pomeroy Devon 7 F7
Stockley Wilts 17 E7
Stocklinch Som 8 C2
Stockport Gtr Man 44 C2
Stocksbridge S Yorks 44 C6
Stocksfield Northumb 62 G6
Stockton Hereford 26 B2
Stockton Norf 39 F9
Stockton Shrops 33 E8
Stockton Shrops 34 F3
Stockton Warks 27 B11
Stockton Wilts 16 H6
Stockton Heath Warr 43 D9
Stockton-on-Tees Stockton 58 E5
Stockton on Teme Worcs 26 B4
Stockton on the Forest York 52 D2
Stodmarsh Kent 21 E9
Stody Norf 39 B6
Stoer Highld 92 G3
Stoford Som 8 C4
Stoford Wilts 17 H7
Stogumber Som 7 C9
Stogursey Som 7 B11
Stoke Devon 6 D1
Stoke Hants 10 D6
Stoke Hants 17 F11
Stoke Medway 20 D5
Stoke Suff 31 D8
Stoke Abbott Dorset 8 D3
Stoke Albany Northants 36 G4
Stoke Ash Suff 31 A8
Stoke Bardolph Notts 36 A2
Stoke Bliss Worcs 26 B3
Stoke Bruerne Northants 28 D4
Stoke by Clare Suff 30 D4
Stoke-by-Nayland Suff 30 E6
Stoke Canon Devon 7 G8
Stoke Charity Hants 17 H11
Stoke Climsland Corn 4 D4
Stoke D'Abernon Sur 19 F8
Stoke Doyle Northants 36 G6
Stoke Dry Rutland 36 F4
Stoke Farthing Wilts 9 B9
Stoke Ferry Norf 38 F3
Stoke Fleming Devon 5 G9
Stoke Gabriel Devon 5 F9
Stoke Gifford S Glos 16 D3
Stoke Golding Leics 35 F9
Stoke Goldington M Keynes 28 D5
Stoke Green Bucks 18 C6
Stoke Hammond Bucks 28 F5
Stoke Heath Shrops 34 C2
Stoke Holy Cross Norf 39 E8
Stoke Lacy Hereford 26 D3
Stoke Lyne Oxon 28 F2
Stoke Mandeville Bucks 28 G5
Stoke Newington London 19 C10
Stoke on Tern Shrops 34 C2
Stoke-on-Trent Stoke 44 H2
Stoke Orchard Glos 26 F6
Stoke Poges Bucks 18 C6
Stoke Prior Hereford 26 C2
Stoke Prior Worcs 26 B6
Stoke Rivers Devon 6 C5
Stoke Rochford Lincs 36 C5
Stoke Row Oxon 18 C3
Stoke St Gregory Som 8 B2
Stoke St Mary Som 8 B1
Stoke St Michael Som 16 G3
Stoke St Milborough Shrops 34 G1
Stoke sub Hamdon Som 8 C3
Stoke Talmage Oxon 18 B3
Stoke Trister Som 8 B6
Stoke Wake Dorset 9 D6
Stokeford Dorset 9 F7
Stokeham Notts 45 E11
Stokeinteignhead Devon 5 D10
Stokenchurch Bucks 18 B4
Stokenham Devon 5 G9
Stokesay Shrops 33 G10
Stokesby Norf 39 D10
Stokesley N Yorks 59 F6
Stolford Som 15 G8
Ston Easton Som 16 F3
Stondon Massey Essex 20 A2
Stone Bucks 28 G4
Stone Glos 16 B3
Stone Kent 13 D8
Stone Kent 20 D2
Stone S Yorks 45 D9
Stone Staffs 34 B5
Stone Worcs 34 H4
Stone Allerton Som 15 F10
Stone Bridge Corner Pboro 37 E8
Stone Chair W Yorks 51 G7
Stone Cross E Sus 12 F5
Stone Cross Kent 21 F10
Stone-edge Batch N Som 15 D10
Stone House Cumb 57 H9
Stone Street Kent 20 F2
Stone Street Suff 30 E6
Stone Street Suff 39 G9
Stonebroom Derbys 45 G8
Stoneferry Hull 53 F7
Stonefield S Lanark 68 E5
Stonegate E Sus 12 D5
Stonegate N Yorks 59 F8
Stonegrave N Yorks 52 B2
Stonehaugh Northumb 62 F3
Stonehaven Aberds 83 E10
Stonehouse Glos 26 H5
Stonehouse Northumb 62 H2
Stonehouse S Lanark 68 F6
Stoneleigh Warks 27 A10
Stonely Cambs 29 B8
Stoner Hill Hants 10 B6
Stone's Green Essex 31 F8
Stonesby Leics 36 C4
Stonesfield Oxon 27 G10
Stonethwaite Cumb 56 E4
Stoney Cross Hants 10 C1
Stoney Middleton Derbys 44 E6
Stoney Stanton Leics 35 F10
Stoney Stoke Som 8 A6
Stoney Stratton Som 16 H3
Stoney Stretton Shrops 33 E9
Stoneybreck Shetland 96 N8
Stoneyburn W Loth 69 D8
Stoneygate Aberds 89 E10
Stoneygate Leicester 36 E2
Stoneyhills Essex 20 B6
Stoneykirk Dumfries 54 D3
Stoneywood Aberdeen 83 B10
Stoneywood Falk 68 B6
Stonganess Shetland 96 C7
Stonham Aspal Suff 31 C8
Stonnall Staffs 35 E6
Stonor Oxon 18 C4
Stonton Wyville Leics 36 F3
Stony Cross Hereford 26 D4
Stony Stratford M Keynes 28 D4
Stonyfield Highld 87 D9
Stoodleigh Devon 7 E8
Stopes S Yorks 44 D6
Stopham W Sus 11 C9
Stopsley Luton 29 F8
Stores Corner Suff 31 D10
Storeton Mers 42 D6
Stornoway W Isles 91 D9
Storridge Hereford 26 D4
Storrington W Sus 11 C9
Storrs Cumb 56 G5
Storth Cumb 49 A4
Storwood E Yorks 52 E3
Stotfield Moray 88 A2
Stotfold C Beds 29 E9
Stottesdon Shrops 34 G2
Stoughton Leics 36 E2
Stoughton Sur 18 F6
Stoughton W Sus 11 C7
Stoul Highld 79 B10
Stoulton Worcs 26 D6
Stour Provost Dorset 9 B6
Stour Row Dorset 9 B7
Stourbridge W Mid 34 G5
Stourpaine Dorset 9 D7
Stourport on Severn Worcs 26 A5
Stourton Staffs 34 G4
Stourton Warks 27 E9
Stourton Wilts 9 A6
Stourton Caundle Dorset 8 C6
Stove Orkney 95 E7
Stove Shetland 96 L6
Stoven Suff 39 G10
Stow Borders 70 F3
Stow Lincs 37 B6
Stow Lincs 46 D2
Stow Bardolph Norf 38 E2
Stow Bedon Norf 38 F5
Stow cum Quy Cambs 30 B2
Stow Longa Cambs 29 A8
Stow Maries Essex 20 B5
Stow-on-the-Wold Glos 27 F8
Stowbridge Norf 38 E2
Stowe Shrops 25 A10
Stowe-by-Chartley Staffs 34 C6
Stowe Green Glos 26 H2
Stowell Som 8 B5
Stowford Devon 4 C5
Stowlangtoft Suff 30 B6
Stowmarket Suff 31 C7
Stowting Kent 13 B10
Stowupland Suff 31 C7
Straad Argyll 73 G9
Strachan Aberds 83 D8
Stradbroke Suff 31 A9
Stradishall Suff 30 C4
Stradsett Norf 38 E2
Stragglethorpe Lincs 46 G3
Straid S Ayrs 66 G4
Straith Dumfries 60 E4
Straiton Edin 69 D11
Straiton S Ayrs 67 F6
Straloch Aberds 89 F8
Straloch Perth 76 A3
Stramshall Staffs 35 B6
Strang IoM 48 E3
Stranraer Dumfries 54 C3
Stratfield Mortimer W Berks 18 E3
Stratfield Saye Hants 18 E3
Stratfield Turgis Hants 18 F3
Stratford London 19 C10
Stratford St Andrew Suff 31 B10
Stratford St Mary Suff 31 E7
Stratford Sub Castle Wilts 9 A10
Stratford Tony Wilts 9 B9
Stratford-upon-Avon Warks 27 C8
Strath Highld 85 A12
Strath Highld 94 E4
Strathan Highld 80 D1
Strathan Highld 92 G3
Strathan Highld 93 C8
Strathaven S Lanark 68 F6
Strathblane Stirling 68 C4
Strathcanaird Highld 92 J4
Strathcarron Highld 86 G2
Strathcoil Argyll 79 H9
Strathdon Aberds 82 B5
Strathellie Aberds 89 B10
Strathkinness Fife 77 F7
Strathmashie House Highld 81 D7
Strathmiglo Fife 76 F5
Strathmore Lodge Highld 94 F3
Strathpeffer Highld 86 F7
Strathrannoch Highld 86 D6
Strathtay Perth 76 B2
Strathvaich Lodge Highld 86 D6
Strathwhillan N Ayrs 66 C3
Strathy Highld 93 C11
Strathyre Stirling 75 F8
Stratton Corn 6 F1
Stratton Dorset 8 E5
Stratton Glos 17 A7
Stratton Audley Oxon 28 F3
Stratton on the Fosse Som 16 F3
Stratton St Margaret Swindon 17 C8
Stratton St Michael Norf 39 F8
Stratton Strawless Norf 39 C8
Stravithie Fife 77 F8
Streat E Sus 12 E2
Streatham London 19 D10
Streatley C Beds 29 F7
Streatley W Berks 18 C2
Street Lancs 49 D5
Street N Yorks 59 F8
Street Som 15 H10
Street Dinas Shrops 33 B9
Street End Kent 21 F8
Street End W Sus 11 E7
Street Gate T&W 63 H8
Street Lydan Wrex 33 B10
Streethay Staffs 35 D7
Streetlam N Yorks 58 G4
Streetly W Mid 35 F6
Streetly End Cambs 30 D3
Strefford Shrops 33 G10
Strelley Notts 35 A11
Strensall York 52 C2
Stretcholt Som 15 G8
Strete Devon 5 G9
Stretford Gtr Man 44 C2
Strethall Essex 29 E11
Stretham Cambs 30 A2
Strettington W Sus 11 D7
Stretton Ches W 43 G7
Stretton Derbys 45 F7
Stretton Rutland 36 D5
Stretton Staffs 34 D4
Stretton Staffs 35 C8
Stretton Warr 43 D9
Stretton Grandison Hereford 26 D3
Stretton-on-Dunsmore Warks 27 A11
Stretton-on-Fosse Warks 27 E9
Stretton Sugwas Hereford 25 D11
Stretton under Fosse Warks 35 G10
Stretton Westwood Shrops 34 F1
Strichen Aberds 89 C9
Strines Gtr Man 44 D3
Stringston Som 7 B10
Strixton Northants 28 B6
Stroat Glos 16 B2
Stromeferry Highld 85 E13
Stromemore Highld 85 E13
Stromness Orkney 95 H3
Stronaba Highld 80 E4
Stronachlachar Stirling 75 F7
Stronchreggan Highld 80 F2
Stronchrubie Highld 92 H5
Strone Argyll 73 E10
Strone Highld 80 E3
Strone Highld 81 A7
Strone Invclyd 73 F11
Stronmilchan Argyll 74 E4
Strontian Highld 79 E11
Strood Medway 20 E4
Strood Green Sur 19 G9
Strood Green W Sus 11 A10
Strood Green W Sus 11 B9
Stroud Glos 26 H5
Stroud Hants 10 B6
Stroud Green Essex 20 B5
Stroxton Lincs 36 B5
Struan Highld 85 E8
Struan Perth 81 G10
Strubby Lincs 47 D8
Strumpshaw Norf 39 E9
Strutherhill S Lanark 68 F6
Struy Highld 86 H6
Stryt-issa Wrex 42 H5
Stuartfield Aberds 89 D9
Stub Place Cumb 56 G2
Stubbington Hants 10 D4
Stubbins Lancs 50 H3
Stubbs Cross Kent 13 C8
Stubbs Green Norf 39 F9
Stubb's Green Norf 39 F8
Stubhampton Dorset 9 C8
Stubton Lincs 46 H2
Stuckgowan Argyll 74 G6
Stuckton Hants 9 C10
Stud Grn. Windsor 18 D5
Studham C Beds 29 G7
Studland Dorset 9 F9
Studley Warks 27 B7
Studley Wilts 16 D6
Studley Roger N Yorks 51 B8
Stump Cross Essex 30 D2
Stuntney Cambs 38 H1
Sturbridge Staffs 34 B4
Sturmer Essex 30 D3
Sturminster Marshall Dorset 9 D8
Sturminster Newton Dorset 9 C6
Sturry Kent 21 E8
Sturton N Lincs 46 B3
Sturton by Stow Lincs 46 D2
Sturton le Steeple Notts 45 D11
Stuston Suff 39 H7
Stutton N Yorks 51 E10
Stutton Suff 31 E8
Styal Ches E 44 D2
Styrrup Notts 45 C10
Suainebost W Isles 91 A10
Suardail W Isles 91 D9
Succoth Aberds 88 E4
Succoth Argyll 74 G5
Suckley Worcs 26 C4
Suckquoy Orkney 95 K5
Sudborough Northants 36 G5
Sudbourne Suff 31 C11
Sudbrook Lincs 36 A5
Sudbrook Mon 15 C11
Sudbrooke Lincs 46 E4
Sudbury Derbys 35 B7
Sudbury London 19 C8
Sudbury Suff 30 D5
Suddie Highld 87 F9
Sudgrove Glos 26 H6
Suffield N Yorks 59 G10
Suffield Norf 39 B8
Sugnall Staffs 34 B3
Suladale Highld 85 C8
Sulaisiadar W Isles 91 D10
Sulby IoM 48 C3
Sulgrave Northants 28 D2
Sulham W Berks 18 D3
Sulhamstead W Berks 18 E3
Sulland Orkney 95 D6
Sullington W Sus 11 C9
Sullom Shetland 96 F5
Sullom Voe Oil Terminal Shetland 96 F5
Sully V Glam 15 E7
Sumburgh Shetland 96 N6
Summer Bridge N Yorks 51 C8
Summer-house Darl 58 E3
Summercourt Corn 3 D7
Summerfield Norf 38 B3
Summergangs Hull 53 F7
Summerleaze Mon 15 C10
Summersdale W Sus 11 D7
Summerseat Gtr Man 43 A10
Summertown Oxon 28 H2
Summit Gtr Man 44 B3
Sunbury-on-Thames Sur 19 E8
Sundaywell Dumfries 60 E4
Sunderland Argyll 64 B3
Sunderland Cumb 56 C3
Sunderland T&W 63 H9
Sunderland Bridge Durham 58 C3
Sundhope Borders 70 H2
Sundon Park Luton 29 F7
Sundridge Kent 19 F11
Sunipol Argyll 78 F6
Sunk Island E Yorks 53 H8
Sunningdale Windsor 18 E6
Sunninghill Windsor 18 E6
Sunningwell Oxon 17 A11
Sunniside Durham 58 C2
Sunniside T&W 63 H8
Sunnyhurst Blackburn 50 G2
Sunnylaw Stirling 75 H10
Sunnyside W Sus 12 C2
Sunton Wilts 17 F9
Surbiton London 19 E8
Surby IoM 48 E2
Surfleet Lincs 37 C8
Surfleet Seas End Lincs 37 C8
Surlingham Norf 39 E9
Sustead Norf 39 B7
Susworth Lincs 46 B2
Sutcombe Devon 6 E2
Suton Norf 39 F6
Sutors of Cromarty Highld 87 E11
Sutterby Lincs 47 E7
Sutterton Lincs 37 B8
Sutton C Beds 29 D9
Sutton Cambs 37 H10
Sutton Kent 21 G10
Sutton London 19 E9
Sutton Mers 43 C8
Sutton N Yorks 51 G10
Sutton Norf 39 C9
Sutton Notts 36 B3
Sutton Notts 45 D10
Sutton Oxon 27 H11
Sutton Pboro 37 F6
Sutton S Yorks 45 A9
Sutton Shrops 34 B2
Sutton Shrops 34 G3
Sutton Som 8 A5
Sutton Staffs 34 C3
Sutton Suff 31 D10
Sutton Sur 19 G7
Sutton W Sus 11 C8
Sutton at Hone Kent 20 D2
Sutton Bassett Northants 36 F3
Sutton Benger Wilts 16 D6
Sutton Bonington Notts 35 C11
Sutton Bridge Lincs 37 C10
Sutton Cheney Leics 35 E10
Sutton Coldfield W Mid 35 F7
Sutton Courtenay Oxon 18 B2
Sutton Crosses Lincs 37 C10
Sutton Grange N Yorks 51 B8
Sutton Green Sur 19 F7
Sutton Howgrave N Yorks 51 B9
Sutton In Ashfield Notts 45 G8
Sutton-in-Craven N Yorks 50 E6
Sutton in the Elms Leics 35 F11
Sutton Ings Hull 53 F7
Sutton Lane Ends Ches E 44 E3
Sutton Leach Mers 43 C8
Sutton Maddock Shrops 34 E3
Sutton Mallet Som 15 H9
Sutton Mandeville Wilts 9 B8
Sutton Manor Mers 43 C8
Sutton Montis Som 8 B5
Sutton on Hull Hull 53 F7
Sutton on Sea Lincs 47 D9
Sutton-on-the-Forest N Yorks 52 C1
Sutton on the Hill Derbys 35 B8
Sutton on Trent Notts 45 F11
Sutton St Edmund Lincs 37 D9
Sutton St James Lincs 37 D9
Sutton St Nicholas Hereford 26 D2
Sutton Scarsdale Derbys 45 F8
Sutton Scotney Hants 17 H11
Sutton under Brailes Warks 27 E10
Sutton-under-Whitestonecliffe N Yorks 51 A10
Sutton upon Derwent E Yorks 52 E3
Sutton Valence Kent 20 G5
Sutton Veny Wilts 16 G5
Sutton Waldron Dorset 9 C7
Sutton Weaver Ches W 43 E8
Sutton Wick Bath 16 F2
Swaby Lincs 47 E7
Swadlincote Derbys 35 D9
Swaffham Norf 38 E4
Swaffham Bulbeck Cambs 30 B2
Swaffham Prior Cambs 30 B2
Swafield Norf 39 B8
Swainby N Yorks 58 F5
Swainshill Hereford 25 D11
Swainsthorpe Norf 39 E8
Swainswick Bath 16 E4
Swalcliffe Oxon 27 E10
Swalecliffe Kent 21 E8
Swallow Lincs 46 B5
Swallowcliffe Wilts 9 B8
Swallowfield Wokingham 18 E4
Swallownest S Yorks 45 D8
Swallows Cross Essex 20 B3
Swan Green Ches W 43 E10
Swan Green Suff 31 A9
Swanage Dorset 9 G9
Swanbister Orkney 95 H4
Swanbourne Bucks 28 F5
Swanland E Yorks 52 G5
Swanley Kent 20 E2
Swanley Village Kent 20 E2
Swanmore Hants 10 C4
Swannington Leics 35 D10
Swannington Norf 39 D7
Swanscombe Kent 20 D3
Swansea = Abertawe Swansea 14 B2
Swanton Abbott Norf 39 C8
Swanton Morley Norf 38 D6
Swanton Novers Norf 38 B6
Swanton Street Kent 20 F5
Swanwick Derbys 45 G8
Swanwick Hants 10 D4
Swarby Lincs 36 A6
Swardeston Norf 39 E8
Swarister Shetland 96 E7
Swarkestone Derbys 35 C9
Swarland Northumb 63 C7
Swarland Estate Northumb 63 C7
Swarthmoor Cumb 49 B2
Swathwick Derbys 45 F7
Swaton Lincs 37 B7
Swavesey Cambs 29 B10
Sway Hants 10 E1
Swayfield Lincs 36 C5
Swaythling Soton 10 C3
Sweet Green Worcs 26 B3
Sweetham Devon 7 G7
Sweethouse Corn 4 E1
Sweffling Suff 31 B10
Swepstone Leics 35 D9
Swerford Oxon 27 E10
Swettenham Ches E 44 F2
Swetton N Yorks 51 B7
Swffryd Caerph 15 B8
Swiftsden E Sus 12 D6
Swilland Suff 31 C8
Swillington W Yorks 51 F9
Swimbridge Devon 6 D5
Swimbridge Newland Devon 6 C5
Swinbrook Oxon 27 G9
Swinderby Lincs 46 F2
Swindon Glos 26 F6
Swindon Staffs 34 F4
Swindon Swindon 17 C8
Swine E Yorks 53 F7
Swinefleet E Yorks 52 G3
Swineshead Bedford 29 B7
Swineshead Lincs 37 A8
Swineshead Bridge Lincs 37 A8
Swiney Highld 94 G4
Swinford Leics 36 H1
Swinford Oxon 27 H11
Swingate Notts 35 A11
Swingfield Minnis Kent 21 G9
Swingfield Street Kent 21 G9
Swinhoe Northumb 71 H11
Swinhope Lincs 46 C6
Swining Shetland 96 G6
Swinithwaite N Yorks 58 H1
Swinnow Moor W Yorks 51 F8
Swinscoe Staffs 44 H5
Swinside Hall Borders 62 B3
Swinstead Lincs 36 C6
Swinton Borders 71 F7
Swinton Gtr Man 43 B10
Swinton N Yorks 51 B8
Swinton N Yorks 52 B3
Swinton S Yorks 45 C8
Swintonmill Borders 71 F7
Swithland Leics 35 D11
Swordale Highld 87 E8
Swordland Highld 79 B10
Swordly Highld 93 C10
Sworton Heath Ches E 43 D9
Swydd-ffynnon Ceredig 24 B3
Swynnerton Staffs 34 B4
Swyre Dorset 8 F4
Sychtyn Powys 32 E5
Syde Glos 26 G6
Sydenham London 19 D10
Sydenham Oxon 18 A4
Sydenham Damerel Devon 4 D5
Syderstone Norf 38 B4
Sydling St Nicholas Dorset 8 E5
Sydmonton Hants 17 F11
Syerston Notts 45 H11
Syke Gtr Man 50 H4
Sykehouse S Yorks 52 H2
Sykes Lancs 50 D2
Syleham Suff 39 H8
Sylen Carms 23 F10
Symbister Shetland 96 G7
Symington S Ayrs 67 C6
Symington S Lanark 69 G8
Symonds Yat Hereford 26 G2
Symondsbury Dorset 8 E3
Synod Inn Ceredig 23 A9
Syre Highld 93 E9
Syreford Glos 27 F7
Syresham Northants 28 D3
Syston Leics 36 D2
Syston Lincs 36 A5
Sytchampton Worcs 26 B5
Sywell Northants 28 B5

T

Taagan Highld 86 E3
Tabost W Isles 91 F8
Tabost W Isles 91 A10
Tackley Oxon 27 F11
Tacleit W Isles 90 D6
Tacolneston Norf 39 F7
Tadcaster N Yorks 51 E10
Taddington Derbys 44 E5
Taddiport Devon 6 E3
Tadley Hants 18 E3
Tadlow C Beds 29 D9
Tadmarton Oxon 27 E10
Tadworth Sur 19 F9
Tafarn-y-gelyn Denb 42 F4
Tafarnau-bach Bl Gwent 25 G8
Taff's Well Rhondda 15 C7
Tafolwern Powys 32 E4
Tai Conwy 41 D9
Tai-bach Powys 33 C7
Tai-mawr Conwy 32 A5
Tai-Ucha Denb 42 G3
Taibach Neath 14 C3
Taigh a Ghearraidh W Isles 84 A2
Tain Highld 87 C10
Tain Highld 94 D4
Tainant Wrex 42 H5
Tainlon Gwyn 40 E6
Tai'r-Bull Powys 24 F6
Tairbeart = Tarbert W Isles 90 G6
Tairgwaith Neath 24 G4
Takeley Essex 30 F2
Takeley Street Essex 30 F2
Tal-sarn Ceredig 23 A10
Tal-y-bont Ceredig 32 G2
Tal-y-Bont Conwy 41 D9
Tal-y-bont Gwyn 32 C1
Tal-y-bont Gwyn 41 C8
Tal-y-cafn Conwy 41 C9
Tal-y-llyn Gwyn 32 E3
Tal-y-wern Powys 32 E4
Talachddu Powys 25 E7
Talacre Flint 42 D4
Talardd Gwyn 32 C4
Talaton Devon 7 G9
Talbenny Pembs 22 E3
Talbot Green Rhondda 14 C6
Talbot Village Poole 9 E9
Tale Devon 7 F9
Talerddig Powys 32 E5
Talgarreg Ceredig 23 A9
Talgarth Powys 25 E8
Talisker Highld 85 E8
Talke Staffs 44 G2
Talkin Cumb 61 H11
Talla Linnfoots Borders 61 A7
Talladale Highld 86 D2
Tallarn Green Wrex 33 A10
Tallentire Cumb 56 C3
Talley Carms 24 E3
Tallington Lincs 37 E6
Talmine Highld 93 C8
Talog Carms 23 D8
Talsarn Carms 24 F4
Talsarnau Gwyn 41 G8
Talskiddy Corn 3 C8
Talwrn Anglesey 40 C6
Talwrn Wrex 42 H5
Talybont-on-Usk Powys 25 F8
Talygarn Rhondda 14 C6
Talyllyn Powys 25 F8
Talysarn Gwyn 40 E6
Talywain Torf 15 A8
Tame Bridge N Yorks 58 F6
Tamerton Foliot Plym 4 E5
Tamworth Staffs 35 E8
Tan Hinon Powys 32 G4
Tan-lan Conwy 41 D9
Tan-lan Gwyn 41 F8
Tan-y-bwlch Gwyn 41 F8
Tan-y-fron Conwy 42 F2
Tan-y-graig Anglesey 41 C7
Tan-y-graig Gwyn 40 G5
Tan-y-groes Ceredig 23 B7
Tan-y-pistyll Powys 33 C6
Tan-yr-allt Gwyn 40 E6
Tandem W Yorks 51 H7
Tanden Kent 13 C8
Tandridge Sur 19 F10
Tanerdy Carms 23 D9
Tanfield Durham 63 H7
Tanfield Lea Durham 58 A2
Tangasdal W Isles 84 J1
Tangiers Pembs 22 E4
Tangley Hants 17 F10
Tanglwst Carms 23 C8
Tangmere W Sus 11 D8
Tangwick Shetland 96 F4
Tankersley S Yorks 45 B7
Tankerton Kent 21 E8
Tannach Highld 94 F5
Tannachie Aberds 83 E9
Tannadice Angus 77 B7
Tannington Suff 31 B9
Tansley Derbys 45 G7
Tansley Knoll Derbys 45 F7
Tansor Northants 37 F6
Tantobie Durham 58 A2
Tanton N Yorks 58 E6
Tanworth-in-Arden Warks 27 A8
Tanygrisiau Gwyn 41 F8
Tanyrhydiau Ceredig 24 B4
Taobh a Chaolais W Isles 84 G2
Taobh a' Ghlinne W Isles 91 F8
Taobh a Thuath Loch Aineort W Isles 84 F2
Taobh a Tuath Loch Baghasdail W Isles 84 F2
Taobh Tuath W Isles 90 J4
Taplow Bucks 18 C6
Tapton Derbys 45 E7
Tarbat Ho. Highld 87 D10
Tarbert Argyll 65 C7
Tarbert Argyll 72 E5
Tarbert Argyll 73 G7
Tarbert = Tairbeart W Isles 90 G6
Tarbet Argyll 74 G6
Tarbet Highld 79 B10
Tarbet Highld 92 E4
Tarbock Green Mers 43 D7
Tarbolton S Ayrs 67 D7
Tarbrax S Lanark 69 E9
Tardebigge Worcs 27 B7
Tarfside Angus 82 F6
Tarland Aberds 82 C6
Tarleton Lancs 49 G4
Tarlogie Highld 87 C10
Tarlscough Lancs 43 A7
Tarlton Glos 16 B6
Tarnbrook Lancs 50 D1
Tarporley Ches W 43 F8
Tarr Som 7 C10
Tarrant Crawford Dorset 9 D8
Tarrant Gunville Dorset 9 C8
Tarrant Hinton Dorset 9 C8
Tarrant Keyneston Dorset 9 D8
Tarrant Launceston Dorset 9 D8
Tarrant Monkton Dorset 9 D8
Tarrant Rawston Dorset 9 D8
Tarrant Rushton Dorset 9 D8
Tarrel Highld 87 C11
Tarring Neville E Sus 12 F3
Tarrington Hereford 26 D3
Tarsappie Perth 76 E4
Tarskavaig Highld 85 H10
Tarves Aberds 89 E8
Tarvie Highld 86 F7
Tarvie Perth 76 A3
Tarvin Ches W 43 F7
Tasburgh Norf 39 F8
Tasley Shrops 34 F2
Taston Oxon 27 F10
Tatenhill Staffs 35 C8
Tathall End M Keynes 28 D5
Tatham Lancs 50 C2
Tathwell Lincs 47 D7
Tatling End Bucks 19 C7
Tatsfield Sur 19 F11
Tattenhall Ches W 43 G7
Tattenhoe M Keynes 28 E5
Tatterford Norf 38 C4
Tattersett Norf 38 B4
Tattershall Lincs 46 G6
Tattershall Bridge Lincs 46 G5
Tattershall Thorpe Lincs 46 G6
Tattingstone Suff 31 E8
Tatworth Som 8 D2
Taunton Som 7 D11
Taverham Norf 39 D7
Tavernspite Pembs 22 E6
Tavistock Devon 4 D5
Taw Green Devon 6 G5
Tawstock Devon 6 D4
Taxal Derbys 44 E4
Tay Bridge Dundee 77 E7
Tayinloan Argyll 65 D7
Taymouth Castle Perth 75 C10
Taynish Argyll 72 E6
Taynton Glos 26 F4
Taynton Oxon 27 G9
Taynuilt Argyll 74 D3
Tayport Fife 77 E7
Tayvallich Argyll 72 E6
Tealby Lincs 46 C5
Tealing Angus 77 D7
Teangue Highld 85 H11
Teanna Mhachair W Isles 84 B2
Tebay Cumb 57 F8
Tebworth C Beds 28 F6
Tedburn St Mary Devon 7 G7
Teddington Glos 26 E6
Teddington London 19 D8
Tedstone Delamere Hereford 26 C3
Tedstone Wafre Hereford 26 C3
Teeton Northants 28 A3
Teffont Evias Wilts 9 A8
Teffont Magna Wilts 9 A8
Tegryn Pembs 23 C7
Teigh Rutland 36 D4
Teigncombe Devon 5 C7
Teigngrace Devon 5 D9
Teignmouth Devon 5 D10
Telford Telford 34 E2
Telham E Sus 13 E6
Tellisford Som 16 F5
Telscombe E Sus 12 F3
Telscombe Cliffs E Sus 12 F2
Templand Dumfries 60 E6
Temple Corn 4 D2
Temple Glasgow 68 D4
Temple Midloth 70 E2
Temple Balsall W Mid 35 H8
Temple Bar Carms 23 E10
Temple Bar Ceredig 23 A10
Temple Cloud Bath 16 F3
Temple Combe Som 8 B6
Temple Ewell Kent 21 G9
Temple Grafton Warks 27 C8
Temple Guiting Glos 27 F7
Temple Herdewyke Warks 27 C10
Temple Hirst N Yorks 52 G2
Temple Normanton Derbys 45 F8
Temple Sowerby Cumb 57 D8
Templehall Fife 69 A11
Templeton Devon 7 E7
Templeton Pembs 22 E6
Templeton Bridge Devon 7 E7
Templetown Durham 58 A2
Tempsford C Beds 29 C8
Ten Mile Bank Norf 38 F2
Tenbury Wells Worcs 26 B2
Tenby = Dinbych-y-Pysgod Pembs 22 F6
Tendring Essex 31 F8
Tendring Green Essex 31 F8
Tenston Orkney 95 G3
Tenterden Kent 13 C7
Terling Essex 30 G4
Ternhill Shrops 34 B2
Terregles Banks Dumfries 60 F5
Terrick Bucks 28 H5
Terrington N Yorks 52 B2
Terrington St Clement Norf 37 D11
Terrington St John Norf 37 D11
Teston Kent 20 F4
Testwood Hants 10 C2
Tetbury Glos 16 B5
Tetbury Upton Glos 16 B5
Tetchill Shrops 33 B9
Tetcott Devon 6 G2
Tetford Lincs 47 E7
Tetney Lincs 47 B7
Tetney Lock Lincs 47 B7
Tetsworth Oxon 18 A3
Tettenhall W Mid 34 E4
Teuchan Aberds 89 E10
Teversal Notts 45 F8
Teversham Cambs 29 C11
Teviothead Borders 61 C10
Tewel Aberds 83 E10
Tewin Herts 29 G9
Tewkesbury Glos 26 E5
Teynham Kent 20 E6
Thackthwaite Cumb 56 D3
Thainston Aberds 83 F8
Thakeham W Sus 11 C10
Thame Oxon 28 H4
Thames Ditton Sur 19 E8
Thames Haven Thurrock 20 C4
Thamesmead London 19 C11
Thanington Kent 21 F8
Thankerton S Lanark 69 G8
Tharston Norf 39 F7
Thatcham W Berks 18 E2
Thatto Heath Mers 43 C8
Thaxted Essex 30 E3
The Aird Highld 85 C9
The Arms Norf 38 F4
The Bage Hereford 25 D9
The Balloch Perth 75 F11
The Barony Orkney 95 F3
The Bog Shrops 33 F9
The Bourne Sur 18 G5
The Braes Highld 85 E10
The Broad Hereford 25 B11
The Butts Som 16 G4
The Camp Glos 26 H6
The Camp Herts 29 H8
The Chequer Wrex 33 A10
The City Bucks 18 B4
The Common Wilts 9 A11
The Craigs Highld 86 B7
The Cronk IoM 48 C3
The Dell Suff 39 F10
The Den N Ayrs 66 A6
The Eals Northumb 62 E3
The Eaves Glos 26 H3
The Flatt Cumb 61 F11
The Four Alls Shrops 34 B2
The Garths Shetland 96 B8
The Green Cumb 49 A1
The Green Wilts 9 A7
The Grove Dumfries 60 F5
The Hall Shetland 96 D8
The Haven W Sus 11 A9
The Heath Norf 39 C7
The Heath Suff 31 E8
The Hill Cumb 49 A1
The Howe Cumb 56 H6
The Howe IoM 48 F1
The Hundred Hereford 26 B2
The Lee Bucks 18 A6
The Lhen IoM 48 B3
The Marsh Powys 33 F9
The Marsh Wilts 17 C7
The Middles Durham 58 A3
The Moor Kent 13 D6
The Mumbles = Y Mwmbwls Swansea 14 C2
The Murray S Lanark 68 E5
The Neuk Aberds 83 D9
The Oval Bath 16 E4
The Pole of Itlaw Aberds 89 C6
The Quarry Glos 16 B4
The Rhos Pembs 22 E5
The Rock Telford 34 E2
The Ryde Herts 29 H9
The Sands Sur 18 G5
The Stocks Kent 13 D8
The Throat Wokingham 18 E5
The Vauld Hereford 26 D2
The Wyke Shrops 34 E3
Theakston N Yorks 58 H4
Thealby N Lincs 52 H4
Theale Som 15 G10
Theale W Berks 18 D3
Thearne E Yorks 53 F6
Theberton Suff 31 B11
Theddingworth Leics 36 G2
Theddlethorpe All Saints Lincs 47 D8
Theddlethorpe St Helen Lincs 47 D8
Thelbridge Barton Devon 7 E6
Thelnetham Suff 38 H6
Thelveton Norf 39 G7
Thelwall Warr 43 D9
Themelthorpe Norf 39 C6
Thenford Northants 28 D2
Therfield Herts 29 E10
Thetford Lincs 37 D7
Thetford Norf 38 G4
Theydon Bois Essex 19 B11
Thickwood Wilts 16 D5
Thimbleby Lincs 46 F6
Thimbleby N Yorks 58 G5
Thingwall Mers 42 D5
Thirdpart N Ayrs 66 B4
Thirlby N Yorks 51 A10
Thirlestane Borders 70 F4
Thirn N Yorks 58 H3
Thirsk N Yorks 51 A10
Thirtleby E Yorks 53 F7
Thistleton Lancs 49 F4

Thistleton Rutland 36 D5
Thistley Green Suff 38 H2
Thixendale N Yorks 52 C4
Thockrington Northumb 62 F5
Tholomas Drove Cambs 37 E9
Tholthorpe N Yorks 51 C10
Thomas Chapel Pembs 22 F6
Thomas Close Cumb 56 B6
Thomastown Aberds 88 E5
Thompson Norf 38 F5
Thomshill Moray 88 C2
Thong Kent 20 D3
Thongsbridge W Yorks 44 B5
Thoralby N Yorks 58 H1
Thoresway Lincs 46 C5
Thorganby Lincs 46 C6
Thorganby N Yorks 52 E2
Thorgill N Yorks 59 G8
Thorington Suff 31 A11
Thorington Street Suff 31 E7
Thorlby N Yorks 50 D5
Thorley Herts 29 G11
Thorley Street Herts 29 G11
Thorley Street IoW 10 F2
Thormanby N Yorks 51 B10
Thornaby-on-Tees Stockton 58 E5
Thornage Norf 38 B6
Thornborough Bucks 28 E4
Thornborough N Yorks 51 B8
Thornbury Devon 6 F3
Thornbury Hereford 26 C3
Thornbury S Glos 16 B3
Thornbury W Yorks 51 F7
Thornby Northants 36 H2
Thorncliffe Staffs 44 G4
Thorncombe Dorset 8 D2
Thorncombe Dorset 9 D7
Thorncombe Street Sur 19 G7
Thorncote Green C Beds 29 D8
Thorncross IoW 10 F3
Thorndon Suff 31 B8
Thorndon Cross Devon 6 G4
Thorne S Yorks 45 A10
Thorne St Margaret Som 7 D9
Thorner W Yorks 51 E9
Thorney Notts 46 E2
Thorney Pboro 37 E8
Thorney Crofts E Yorks 53 G8
Thorney Green Suff 31 B7
Thorney Hill Hants 9 E10
Thorney Toll Pboro 37 E9
Thornfalcon Som 8 B1
Thornford Dorset 8 C5
Thorngumbald E Yorks 53 G8
Thornham Norf 38 A3
Thornham Magna Suff 31 A8
Thornham Parva Suff 31 A8
Thornhaugh Pboro 37 E6
Thornhill Cardiff 15 C7
Thornhill Cumb 56 E2
Thornhill Derbys 44 D5
Thornhill Dumfries 60 D4
Thornhill Soton 10 C3
Thornhill Stirling 75 H9
Thornhill W Yorks 51 H8
Thornhill Edge W Yorks 51 H8
Thornhill Lees W Yorks 51 H8
Thornholme E Yorks 53 C7
Thornley Durham 58 C4
Thornley Durham 58 C2
Thornliebank E Renf 68 E4
Thorns Suff 30 C4
Thorns Green Ches E 43 D10
Thornsett Derbys 44 D4
Thornthwaite Cumb 56 D4
Thornthwaite N Yorks 51 D7
Thornton Angus 76 C6
Thornton Bucks 28 E4
Thornton E Yorks 52 E3
Thornton Fife 76 H5
Thornton Lancs 49 E3
Thornton Leics 35 E10
Thornton Lincs 46 F6
Thornton Mbro 58 E5
Thornton Mers 42 B6
Thornton Northumb 71 F8
Thornton Pembs 22 F4
Thornton W Yorks 51 F6
Thornton Curtis N Lincs 53 H6
Thornton Heath London 19 E10
Thornton Hough Mers 42 D6
Thornton in Craven N Yorks 50 E5
Thornton-le-Beans N Yorks 58 G4
Thornton-le-Clay N Yorks 52 C2
Thornton-le-Dale N Yorks 52 A4
Thornton le Moor Lincs 46 C4
Thornton-le-Moor N Yorks 58 H4
Thornton-le-Moors Ches W 43 E7
Thornton-le-Street N Yorks 58 H5
Thornton Rust N Yorks 57 H11
Thornton Steward N Yorks 58 H2
Thornton Watlass N Yorks 58 H3
Thorntonhall S Lanark 68 E4
Thorntonloch E Loth 70 C6
Thorntonpark Northumb 71 F8
Thornwood Common Essex 19 A11
Thornydykes Borders 70 F5
Thoroton Notts 36 A3
Thorp Arch W Yorks 51 E10
Thorpe Derbys 44 G5
Thorpe E Yorks 52 E5
Thorpe Lincs 47 D8
Thorpe N Yorks 50 C6
Thorpe Norf 39 F10
Thorpe Notts 45 H11
Thorpe Sur 19 E7
Thorpe Abbotts Norf 39 H7
Thorpe Acre Leics 35 C11
Thorpe Arnold Leics 36 C3
Thorpe Audlin W Yorks 51 H10
Thorpe Bassett N Yorks 52 B4
Thorpe Bay Southend 20 C6
Thorpe by Water Rutland 36 F4
Thorpe Common Suff 31 E9
Thorpe Constantine Staffs 35 E8
Thorpe Culvert Lincs 47 F8
Thorpe End Norf 39 D8
Thorpe Fendykes Lincs 47 F8
Thorpe Green Essex 31 F8
Thorpe Green Suff 30 C6
Thorpe Hesley S Yorks 45 C7
Thorpe in Balne S Yorks 45 A9
Thorpe in the Fallows Lincs 46 D3
Thorpe Langton Leics 36 F3
Thorpe Larches Durham 58 D4
Thorpe-le-Soken Essex 31 F8
Thorpe le Street E Yorks 52 E4
Thorpe Malsor Northants 36 H4
Thorpe Mandeville Northants 28 D2
Thorpe Market Norf 39 B8
Thorpe Marriot Norf 39 D7
Thorpe Morieux Suff 30 C6
Thorpe on the Hill Lincs 46 F3
Thorpe St Andrew Norf 39 E8
Thorpe St Peter Lincs 47 F8
Thorpe Salvin S Yorks 45 D9
Thorpe Satchville Leics 36 D3
Thorpe Thewles Stockton 58 D5
Thorpe Tilney Lincs 46 G5
Thorpe Underwood N Yorks 51 D10
Thorpe Waterville Northants 36 G6
Thorpe Willoughby N Yorks 52 F1
Thorpeness Suff 31 C11
Thorrington Essex 31 F7
Thorverton Devon 7 F8
Thrandeston Suff 39 H7
Thrapston Northants 36 H5
Thrashbush N Lanark 68 D6
Threapland Cumb 56 C3
Threapland N Yorks 50 C5
Threapwood Ches W 43 H7
Threapwood Staffs 34 A6
Three Ashes Hereford 26 F2
Three Bridges W Sus 12 C1
Three Burrows Corn 2 E6
Three Chimneys Kent 13 C7
Three Cocks Powys 25 E8
Three Crosses Swansea 23 G10
Three Cups Corner E Sus 12 D5
Three Holes Norf 37 E11
Three Leg Cross E Sus 12 C5
Three Legged Cross Dorset 9 D9
Three Oaks E Sus 13 E7
Threehammer Common Norf 39 D9
Threekingham Lincs 37 B6
Threemile Cross Wokingham 18 E4
Threemilestone Corn 3 E6
Threemiletown W Loth 69 C9
Threlkeld Cumb 56 D5
Threshfield N Yorks 50 C5
Thrigby Norf 39 D10
Thringarth Durham 57 D11
Thringstone Leics 35 D10
Thrintoft N Yorks 58 G4
Thriplow Cambs 29 D11
Throckenholt Lincs 37 E9
Throcking Herts 29 E10
Throckley T&W 63 G7
Throckmorton Worcs 26 D6
Throphill Northumb 63 E7
Thropton Northumb 62 C6
Throsk Stirling 69 A7
Throwleigh Devon 6 G5
Throwley Kent 20 F6
Thrumpton Notts 35 B11
Thrumster Highld 94 F5
Thrunton Northumb 62 B6
Thrupp Glos 16 A5
Thrupp Oxon 27 G11
Thrushelton Devon 4 C5
Thrussington Leics 36 D2
Thruxton Hants 17 G9
Thruxton Hereford 25 E11
Thrybergh S Yorks 45 C8
Thulston Derbys 35 B10
Thundergay N Ayrs 66 B1
Thundersley Essex 20 C4
Thundridge Herts 29 G10
Thurcaston Leics 36 D1
Thurcroft S Yorks 45 D8
Thurgarton Norf 39 B7
Thurgarton Notts 45 H10
Thurgoland S Yorks 44 B6
Thurlaston Leics 35 F11
Thurlaston Warks 27 A11
Thurlbear Som 8 B1
Thurlby Lincs 37 D7
Thurlby Lincs 46 F3
Thurleigh Bedford 29 C7
Thurlestone Devon 5 G7
Thurloxton Som 8 A1
Thurlstone S Yorks 44 B6
Thurlton Norf 39 F10
Thurlwood Ches E 44 G2
Thurmaston Leics 36 E2
Thurnby Leics 36 E2
Thurne Norf 39 D10
Thurnham Kent 20 F5
Thurnham Lancs 49 D4
Thurning Norf 39 C6
Thurning Northants 37 G6
Thurnscoe S Yorks 45 B8
Thurnscoe East S Yorks 45 B8
Thursby Cumb 56 A5
Thursford Norf 38 B5
Thursley Sur 18 H6
Thurso Highld 94 D3
Thurso East Highld 94 D3
Thurstaston Mers 42 D5
Thurston Suff 30 B6
Thurstonfield Cumb 61 H9
Thurstonland W Yorks 44 A5
Thurton Norf 39 E9
Thurvaston Derbys 35 B8
Thuxton Norf 38 E6
Thwaite N Yorks 57 G10
Thwaite Suff 31 B8
Thwaite St Mary Norf 39 F9
Thwaites W Yorks 51 E6
Thwaites Brow W Yorks 51 E6
Thwing E Yorks 53 B6
Tibbermore Perth 76 E3
Tibberton Glos 26 F4
Tibberton Telford 34 C2
Tibberton Worcs 26 C6
Tibenham Norf 39 G7
Tibshelf Derbys 45 F8
Tibthorpe E Yorks 52 D5
Ticehurst E Sus 12 C5
Tichborne Hants 10 A4
Tickencote Rutland 36 E5
Tickenham N Som 15 D10
Tickhill S Yorks 45 C9
Ticklerton Shrops 33 F10
Ticknall Derbys 35 C9
Tickton E Yorks 53 E6
Tidcombe Wilts 17 F9
Tiddington Oxon 18 A3
Tiddington Warks 27 C9
Tidebrook E Sus 12 D5
Tideford Corn 4 F4
Tideford Cross Corn 4 E4
Tidenham Glos 16 B2
Tideswell Derbys 44 E5
Tidmarsh W Berks 18 D3
Tidmington Warks 27 E9
Tidpit Hants 9 C9
Tidworth Wilts 17 G9
Tiers Cross Pembs 22 E4
Tiffield Northants 28 C3
Tifty Aberds 89 D7
Tigerton Angus 77 A8
Tigh-na-Blair Perth 75 F10
Tighnabruaich Argyll 73 F8
Tighnafiline Highld 91 J13
Tigley Devon 5 E8
Tilbrook Cambs 29 B7
Tilbury Thurrock 20 D3
Tilbury Juxta Clare Essex 30 D4
Tile Cross W Mid 35 G7
Tile Hill W Mid 35 H8
Tilehurst Reading 18 D3
Tilford Sur 18 G5
Tilgate W Sus 12 C1
Tilgate Forest Row W Sus 12 C1
Tillathrowie Aberds 88 E4
Tilley Shrops 33 C11
Tillicoultry Clack 76 H2
Tillingham Essex 20 A6
Tillington Hereford 25 D11
Tillington W Sus 11 B8
Tillington Common Hereford 25 D11
Tillyarblet Angus 83 G7
Tillybirloch Aberds 83 C8
Tillycorthie Aberds 89 F9
Tillydrine Aberds 83 D8
Tillyfour Aberds 83 B8
Tillyfourie Aberds 83 B8
Tillygarmond Aberds 83 D8
Tillygreig Aberds 89 F8
Tillykerrie Aberds 89 F8
Tilmanstone Kent 21 F10
Tilney All Saints Norf 38 D1
Tilney High End Norf 38 D1
Tilney St Lawrence Norf 37 D11
Tilshead Wilts 17 G7
Tilstock Shrops 33 B11
Tilston Ches W 43 G7
Tilstone Fearnall Ches W 43 F8
Tilsworth C Beds 28 F6
Tilton on the Hill Leics 36 E3
Timberland Lincs 46 G5
Timbersbrook Ches E 44 F2
Timberscombe Som 7 B8
Timble N Yorks 51 D7
Timperley Gtr Man 43 D10
Timsbury Bath 16 F3
Timsbury Hants 10 B2
Timsgearraidh W Isles 90 D5
Timworth Green Suff 30 B5
Tincleton Dorset 9 E6
Tindale Cumb 62 H2
Tingewick Bucks 28 E3
Tingley W Yorks 51 G8
Tingrith C Beds 29 E7
Tingwall Orkney 95 F4
Tinhay Devon 4 C4
Tinshill W Yorks 51 F8
Tinsley S Yorks 45 C8
Tintagel Corn 4 C1
Tintern Parva Mon 15 A11
Tintinhull Som 8 C4
Tintwistle Derbys 44 C4
Tinwald Dumfries 60 E6
Tinwell Rutland 36 E6
Tipperty Aberds 89 F9
Tipsend Norf 37 F11
Tiptoe Hants 9 E11
Tipton W Mid 34 F5
Tipton St John Devon 7 G9
Tiptree Essex 30 G5
Tir-y-dail Carms 24 G3
Tirabad Powys 24 D5
Tiraghoil Argyll 78 J6
Tirley Glos 26 F5
Tirphil Caerph 15 A7
Tirril Cumb 57 D7
Tisbury Wilts 9 B8
Tisman's Common W Sus 11 A9
Tissington Derbys 44 G5
Titchberry Devon 6 D1
Titchfield Hants 10 D4
Titchmarsh Northants 36 H6
Titchwell Norf 38 A3
Tithby Notts 36 B2
Titley Hereford 25 B10
Titlington Northumb 63 B7
Titsey Sur 19 F11
Tittensor Staffs 34 B4
Tittleshall Norf 38 C4
Tiverton Ches W 43 F8
Tiverton Devon 7 E8
Tivetshall St Margaret Norf 39 G7
Tivetshall St Mary Norf 39 G7
Tividale W Mid 34 F5
Tivy Dale S Yorks 44 B6
Tixall Staffs 34 C5
Tixover Rutland 36 E5
Toab Orkney 95 H6
Toab Shetland 96 M5
Toadmoor Derbys 45 G7
Tobermory Argyll 79 F8
Toberonochy Argyll 72 C6
Tobha Mor W Isles 84 E2
Tobhtarol W Isles 90 D6
Tobson W Isles 90 D6
Tocher Aberds 89 E6
Tockenham Wilts 17 D7
Tockenham Wick Wilts 17 C7
Tockholes Blackburn 50 G2
Tockington S Glos 16 C3
Tockwith N Yorks 51 D10
Todber Dorset 9 B7
Todding Hereford 33 H10
Toddington C Beds 29 F7
Toddington Glos 27 E7
Todenham Glos 27 E9
Todhills Cumb 61 G9
Todlachie Aberds 83 B8
Todmorden W Yorks 50 G5
Todrig Borders 61 B10
Todwick S Yorks 45 D8
Toft Cambs 29 C10
Toft Lincs 37 D6
Toft Hill Durham 58 D2
Toft Hill Lincs 46 F6
Toft Monks Norf 39 F10
Toft next Newton Lincs 46 D4
Toftrees Norf 38 C4
Tofts Highld 94 D5
Toftwood Norf 38 D5
Togston Northumb 63 C8
Tokavaig Highld 85 G11
Tokers Green Oxon 18 D4
Tolastadh a Chaolais W Isles 90 D6
Tolastadh bho Thuath W Isles 91 C10
Toll Bar S Yorks 45 B9
Toll End W Mid 34 F5
Toll of Birness Aberds 89 E10
Tolland Som 7 C10
Tollard Royal Wilts 9 C8
Tollbar End W Mid 35 H9
Toller Fratrum Dorset 8 E4
Toller Porcorum Dorset 8 E4
Tollerton N Yorks 51 C11
Tollerton Notts 36 B2
Tollesbury Essex 30 G6
Tolleshunt D'Arcy Essex 30 G6
Tolleshunt Major Essex 30 G6
Tolm W Isles 91 D9
Tolpuddle Dorset 9 E6
Tolvah Highld 81 D10
Tolworth London 19 E8
Tomatin Highld 81 A10
Tombreck Highld 87 H9
Tomchrasky Highld 80 B4
Tomdoun Highld 80 C3
Tomich Highld 80 A5
Tomich Highld 87 D9
Tomich House Highld 87 G8
Tomintoul Aberds 82 D3
Tomintoul Moray 82 B3
Tomnaven Moray 88 E4
Tomnavoulin Moray 82 A4
Ton-Pentre Rhondda 14 B5
Tonbridge Kent 20 G2
Tondu Bridgend 14 C4
Tonfanau Gwyn 32 E1
Tong Shrops 34 E3
Tong W Yorks 51 F8
Tong Norton Shrops 34 E3
Tonge Leics 35 C10
Tongham Sur 18 G5
Tongland Dumfries 55 D9
Tongue Highld 93 D8
Tongue End Lincs 37 D7
Tongwynlais Cardiff 15 C7
Tonna Neath 14 B3
Tonwell Herts 29 G10
Tonypandy Rhondda 14 B5
Tonyrefail Rhondda 14 C6
Toot Baldon Oxon 18 A2
Toot Hill Essex 20 A2
Toothill Hants 10 C2
Top of Hebers Gtr Man 44 B2
Topcliffe N Yorks 51 B10
Topcroft Norf 39 F8
Topcroft Street Norf 39 F8
Toppesfield Essex 30 E4
Toppings Gtr Man 43 A10
Topsham Devon 5 C10
Torbay Torbay 5 F10
Torbeg N Ayrs 66 D2
Torboll Farm Highld 87 B10
Torbrex Stirling 68 A6
Torbryan Devon 5 E9
Torcross Devon 5 G9
Tore Highld 87 F9
Torinturk Argyll 73 G7
Torksey Lincs 46 E2
Torlum W Isles 84 C2
Torlundy Highld 80 F3
Tormarton S Glos 16 D4
Tormisdale Argyll 64 C2
Tormitchell S Ayrs 66 G5
Tormore N Ayrs 66 C1
Tornagrain Highld 87 G10
Tornahaish Aberds 82 C4
Tornaveen Aberds 83 C8
Torness Highld 81 A7
Toronto Durham 58 C2
Torpenhow Cumb 56 C4
Torphichen W Loth 69 C8
Torphins Aberds 83 C8
Torpoint Corn 4 F5
Torquay Torbay 5 E10
Torquhan Borders 70 F3
Torran Argyll 73 C7
Torran Highld 85 D10
Torran Highld 87 D10
Torrance E Dunb 68 C5
Torrans Argyll 78 J7
Torranyard N Ayrs 67 B6
Torre Torbay 5 E10
Torridon Highld 86 F2
Torridon Ho. Highld 85 C13
Torrin Highld 85 F10
Torrisdale Highld 93 C9
Torrisdale-Square Argyll 65 E8
Torrish Highld 93 H12
Torrisholme Lancs 49 C4
Torroble Highld 93 J8
Torry Aberdeen 83 C11
Torry Aberds 88 E4
Torryburn Fife 69 B9
Torterston Aberds 89 D10
Torthorwald Dumfries 60 F6
Tortington W Sus 11 D9
Tortworth S Glos 16 B4
Torvaig Highld 85 D9
Torver Cumb 56 G4
Torwood Falk 69 B7
Torworth Notts 45 D10
Tosberry Devon 6 D1
Toscaig Highld 85 E12
Toseland Cambs 29 B9
Tosside N Yorks 50 D3
Tostock Suff 30 B6
Totaig Highld 84 C7
Totaig Highld 85 F13
Tote Highld 85 D9
Totegan Highld 93 C11
Tothill Lincs 47 D8
Totland IoW 10 F2
Totnes Devon 5 E9
Toton Notts 35 B11
Totronald Argyll 78 F4
Totscore Highld 85 B8
Tottenham London 19 B10
Tottenhill Norf 38 D2
Tottenhill Row Norf 38 D2
Totteridge London 19 B9
Totternhoe C Beds 28 F6
Tottington Gtr Man 43 A10
Totton Hants 10 C2
Touchen End Windsor 18 D5
Tournaig Highld 91 J13
Toux Aberds 89 C9
Tovil Kent 20 F4
Tow Law Durham 58 C2
Toward Argyll 73 G10
Towcester Northants 28 D3
Towednack Corn 2 F3
Tower End Norf 38 D2
Towersey Oxon 28 H4
Towie Aberds 82 B6
Towie Aberds 89 B8
Towiemore Moray 88 D3
Town End Cambs 37 F10
Town End Cumb 49 A4
Town Row E Sus 12 C4
Town Yetholm Borders 71 H7
Townend W Dunb 68 C3
Towngate Lincs 37 D7
Townhead Cumb 57 C7
Townhead Dumfries 55 E9
Townhead S Ayrs 66 F5
Townhead S Yorks 44 B5
Townhead of Greenlaw Dumfries 55 C10
Townhill Fife 69 B10
Townsend Bucks 28 H4
Townsend Herts 29 H8
Townshend Corn 2 F4
Towthorpe York 52 D2
Towton N Yorks 51 F10
Towyn Conwy 42 E2
Toxteth Mers 42 D6
Toynton All Saints Lincs 47 F7
Toynton Fen Side Lincs 47 F7
Toynton St Peter Lincs 47 F8
Toy's Hill Kent 19 F11
Trabboch E Ayrs 67 D7
Traboe Corn 2 G6
Tradespark Highld 87 F11
Tradespark Orkney 95 H5
Trafford Park Gtr Man 43 C10
Trallong Powys 24 F6
Tranent E Loth 70 C3
Tranmere Mers 42 D6
Trantlebeg Highld 93 D11
Trantlemore Highld 93 D11
Tranwell Northumb 63 E7
Trapp Carms 24 G3
Traprain E Loth 70 C4
Traquair Borders 70 G2
Trawden Lancs 50 F5
Trawsfynydd Gwyn 41 G9
Tre-Gibbon Rhondda 14 A5
Tre-Taliesin Ceredig 32 F2
Tre-vaughan Carms 23 D9
Tre-wyn Mon 25 F10
Trealaw Rhondda 14 B6
Treales Lancs 49 F4
Trearddur Anglesey 40 C4
Treaslane Highld 85 C8
Trebanog Rhondda 14 B6
Trebanos Neath 14 A3
Trebartha Corn 4 D3
Trebarwith Corn 4 C1
Trebetherick Corn 3 B8
Treborough Som 7 C9
Trebudannon Corn 3 C7
Trebullett Corn 4 D4
Treburley Corn 4 D4
Trebyan Corn 4 E1
Trecastle Powys 24 F5
Trecenydd Caerph 15 C7
Trecwn Pembs 22 C4
Trecynon Rhondda 14 A5
Tredavoe Corn 2 G3
Treddiog Pembs 22 D3
Tredegar Bl Gwent 25 H8
Tredegar Newydd = New Tredegar Caerph 15 A7
Tredington Glos 26 F6
Tredington Warks 27 D9
Tredinnick Corn 3 B8
Tredomen Powys 25 E8
Tredunnock Mon 15 B9
Tredustan Powys 25 E8
Treen Corn 2 G2
Treeton S Yorks 45 D8
Tref-y-Clawdd = Knighton Powys 25 A9
Trefaldwyn = Montgomery Powys 33 F8
Trefasser Pembs 22 C3
Trefdraeth Anglesey 40 C6
Trefdraeth = Newport Pembs 22 C5
Trefecca Powys 25 E8
Trefechan Ceredig 32 G1
Trefeglwys Powys 32 F5
Trefenter Ceredig 24 B3
Treffgarne Pembs 22 D4
Treffynnon Pembs 22 D3
Treffynnon = Holywell Flint 42 E4
Trefgarn Owen Pembs 22 D3
Trefil Bl Gwent 25 G8
Trefilan Ceredig 23 A10
Trefin Pembs 22 C3
Treflach Shrops 33 C8
Trefnanney Powys 33 D8
Trefnant Denb 42 E3
Trefonen Shrops 33 C8
Trefor Anglesey 40 B5
Trefor Gwyn 40 F5
Treforest Rhondda 14 C6
Trefriw Conwy 41 D9
Trefynwy = Monmouth Mon 26 G2
Tregadillett Corn 4 C3
Tregaian Anglesey 40 C6
Tregare Mon 25 G11
Tregaron Ceredig 24 C3
Tregarth Gwyn 41 D8
Tregeare Corn 4 C3
Tregeiriog Wrex 33 B7
Tregele Anglesey 40 A5
Tregidden Corn 3 G6
Treglemais Pembs 22 D3
Tregole Corn 4 B2
Tregonetha Corn 3 C8
Tregony Corn 3 E8
Tregoss Corn 3 C8
Tregoyd Powys 25 E9
Tregroes Ceredig 23 B9
Tregurrian Corn 3 C7
Tregynon Powys 33 F6
Trehafod Rhondda 14 B6
Treharris M Tydf 14 B6
Treherbert Rhondda 14 B5
Trekenner Corn 4 D4
Treknow Corn 4 C1
Trelan Corn 2 H6
Trelash Corn 4 B2
Trelassick Corn 3 D7
Trelawnyd Flint 42 E3
Trelech Carms 23 C7
Treleddyd-fawr Pembs 22 D2
Trelewis M Tydf 15 B7
Treligga Corn 4 C1
Trelights Corn 3 B8
Trelill Corn 3 B9
Trelissick Corn 3 F7
Trellech Mon 26 H2
Trelleck Grange Mon 15 A10
Trelogan Flint 42 D4
Trelystan Powys 33 E8
Tremadog Gwyn 41 F7
Tremail Corn 4 C2
Tremain Ceredig 23 B7
Tremaine Corn 4 C3
Tremar Corn 4 E3
Trematon Corn 4 F4
Tremeirchion Denb 42 E3
Trenance Corn 3 C7
Trenarren Corn 3 E9
Trench Telford 34 D2
Treneglos Corn 4 C3
Trenewan Corn 4 F2
Trent Dorset 8 C4
Trent Vale Stoke 34 A4
Trentham Stoke 34 A4
Trentishoe Devon 6 B5
Treoes V Glam 14 D5
Treorchy = Treorci Rhondda 14 B5
Treorci = Treorchy Rhondda 14 B5
Tre'r-ddôl Ceredig 32 F2
Trerulefoot Corn 4 F4
Tresaith Ceredig 23 A7
Tresawle Corn 3 E7
Trescott Staffs 34 F4
Trescowe Corn 2 F4
Tresham Glos 16 B4
Tresillian Corn 3 E7
Tresinwen Pembs 22 B4
Treskinnick Cross Corn 4 B3
Tresmeer Corn 4 C3
Tresparrett Corn 4 B2
Tresparrett Posts Corn 4 B2
Tressait Perth 75 A11
Tresta Shetland 96 D8
Tresta Shetland 96 H5
Treswell Notts 45 E11
Trethosa Corn 3 D8
Trethurgy Corn 3 D9
Tretio Pembs 22 D2
Tretire Hereford 26 F2
Tretower Powys 25 F8
Treuddyn Flint 42 G5
Trevalga Corn 4 C1
Trevalyn Wrex 43 G6
Trevanson Corn 3 B8
Trevarren Corn 3 C8
Trevarrian Corn 3 C7
Trevarrick Corn 3 E8
Trevaughan Carms 22 E6
Treveighan Corn 4 D1
Trevellas Corn 2 D6
Treverva Corn 3 F6
Trevethin Torf 15 A8
Trevigro Corn 4 E4
Treviscoe Corn 3 D8
Trevone Corn 3 B7
Trewarmett Corn 4 C1
Trewassa Corn 4 C2
Trewellard Corn 2 F2
Trewen Corn 4 C3
Trewennack Corn 2 G5
Trewern Powys 33 D8
Trewethern Corn 3 B9
Trewidland Corn 4 F3
Trewint Corn 4 B2
Trewint Corn 4 C3
Trewithian Corn 3 F7
Trewoofe Corn 2 G3
Trewoon Corn 3 D8
Treworga Corn 3 E7
Treworlas Corn 3 F7
Treyarnon Corn 3 B7
Treyford W Sus 11 C7
Trezaise Corn 3 D8
Triangle W Yorks 50 G6
Trickett's Cross Dorset 9 D9
Triffleton Pembs 22 D4
Trimdon Durham 58 C4
Trimdon Colliery Durham 58 C4
Trimdon Grange Durham 58 C4
Trimingham Norf 39 B8
Trimley Lower Street Suff 31 E9
Trimley St Martin Suff 31 E9
Trimley St Mary Suff 31 E9
Trimpley Worcs 34 H3
Trimsaran Carms 23 F9
Trimstone Devon 6 B3
Trinafour Perth 75 A10
Trinant Caerph 15 A8
Tring Herts 28 G6
Tring Wharf Herts 28 G6
Trinity Angus 77 A9
Trinity Jersey 11
Trisant Ceredig 32 H3
Trislaig Highld 80 F2
Trispen Corn 3 D7
Tritlington Northumb 63 D8
Trochry Perth 76 C2
Trodigal Argyll 65 F7
Troed-rhiwdalar Powys 24 C6
Troedyraur Ceredig 23 B8
Troedyrhiw M Tydf 14 A6
Tromode IoM 48 E3
Trondavoe Shetland 96 F5
Troon Corn 2 F5
Troon S Ayrs 67 C6
Trosaraidh W Isles 84 G2
Trossachs Hotel Stirling 75 G8
Troston Suff 30 A5
Trottiscliffe Kent 20 E3
Trotton W Sus 11 B7
Troutbeck Cumb 56 B5
Troutbeck Cumb 56 F6
Troutbeck Bridge Cumb 56 F6
Trow Green Glos 26 H2
Trowbridge Wilts 16 F5
Trowell Notts 35 B10
Trowle Common Wilts 16 F5
Trowley Bottom Herts 29 G7
Trows Borders 70 G5
Trowse Newton Norf 39 E8
Trudoxhill Som 16 G4
Trull Som 7 D11
Trumaisgearraidh W Isles 84 A3
Trumpan Highld 84 B7
Trumpet Hereford 26 E3
Trumpington Cambs 29 C11
Trunch Norf 39 B8
Trunnah Lancs 49 E3
Truro Corn 3 E7
Trusham Devon 5 C9
Trusley Derbys 35 B8
Trusthorpe Lincs 47 D9
Trysull Staffs 34 F4
Tubney Oxon 17 B11
Tuckenhay Devon 5 F9
Tuckhill Shrops 34 G3
Tuckingmill Corn 2 E5
Tuddenham Suff 30 A4
Tuddenham St Martin Suff 31 D8
Tudeley Kent 20 G3
Tudhoe Durham 58 C3
Tudorville Hereford 26 F2
Tudweiliog Gwyn 40 G4
Tuesley Sur 18 G6
Tuffley Glos 26 G5
Tufton Hants 17 G11
Tufton Pembs 22 D5
Tugby Leics 36 E3
Tugford Shrops 34 G1
Tullibardine Perth 76 F2
Tullibody Clack 75 H11
Tullich Argyll 73 B9
Tullich Highld 81 A8
Tullich Muir Highld 87 D10
Tulliemet Perth 76 B2
Tulloch Aberds 83 F9
Tulloch Aberds 89 E8
Tulloch Perth 76 E3
Tulloch Castle Highld 87 E8
Tullochgorm Argyll 73 D8
Tulloes Angus 77 C8
Tullybannocher Perth 75 E10
Tullybelton Perth 76 D3
Tullyfergus Perth 76 C5
Tullymurdoch Perth 76 B4
Tullynessle Aberds 83 B7
Tumble Carms 23 E10
Tumby Woodside Lincs 46 G6
Tummel Bridge Perth 75 B10
Tunga W Isles 91 D9
Tunstall E Yorks 53 F9
Tunstall Kent 20 E5
Tunstall Lancs 50 B2
Tunstall N Yorks 58 G3
Tunstall Norf 39 E10
Tunstall Stoke 44 G2
Tunstall Suff 31 C10
Tunstall T&W 58 A4
Tunstead Derbys 44 E5
Tunstead Gtr Man 44 B4
Tunstead Norf 39 C8
Tunworth Hants 18 G3
Tupsley Hereford 26 D2
Tupton Derbys 45 F7
Tur Langton Leics 36 F3
Turgis Green Hants 18 F3
Turin Angus 77 B8
Turkdean Glos 27 G8
Turleigh Wilts 16 E5
Turn Lancs 50 H4
Turnastone Hereford 25 E10
Turnberry S Ayrs 66 F5
Turnditch Derbys 44 H6
Turners Hill W Sus 12 C2
Turners Puddle Dorset 9 E7
Turnford Herts 19 A10
Turnhouse Edin 69 C10
Turnworth Dorset 9 D7
Turriff Aberds 89 C7
Turton Bottoms Blackburn 50 H3
Turves Cambs 37 F9
Turvey Bedford 28 C6
Turville Bucks 18 B4
Turville Heath Bucks 18 B4
Turweston Bucks 28 E3
Tushielaw Borders 61 B9
Tutbury Staffs 35 C8
Tutnall Worcs 26 A6
Tutshill Glos 15 B11
Tuttington Norf 39 C8
Tutts Clump W Berks 18 D2
Tuxford Notts 45 E11
Twatt Orkney 95 F3
Twatt Shetland 96 H5
Twechar E Dunb 68 C6
Tweedmouth Northumb 71 E8
Tweedsmuir Borders 60 A6
Twelve Heads Corn 3 E6
Twemlow Green Ches E 43 F10
Twenty Lincs 37 C7
Twerton Bath 16 E4
Twickenham London 19 D8
Twigworth Glos 26 F5
Twineham W Sus 12 E1
Twinhoe Bath 16 F4
Twinstead Essex 30 E5
Twinstead Green Essex 30 E5
Twiss Green Warr 43 C9
Twiston Lancs 50 E4
Twitchen Devon 7 C6
Twitchen Shrops 33 H9
Two Bridges Devon 5 D7
Two Dales Derbys 44 F6
Two Mills Ches W 42 E6
Twycross Leics 35 E9
Twyford Bucks 28 F3
Twyford Derbys 35 C9
Twyford Hants 10 B3
Twyford Leics 36 D3
Twyford Lincs 36 C5
Twyford Norf 38 C6
Twyford Wokingham 18 D4
Twyford Common Hereford 26 E2
Twyn-y-Sheriff Mon 25 H11
Twynholm Dumfries 55 D9
Twyning Glos 26 E5
Twyning Green Glos 26 E6
Twynllanan Carms 24 F4
Twynmynydd Carms 24 G3
Twywell Northants 36 H5
Ty-draw Conwy 41 E10
Ty-hen Carms 23 D8
Ty-hen Gwyn 40 G3
Ty-mawr Anglesey 40 B6
Ty Mawr Carms 23 B10
Ty Mawr Cwm Conwy 42 H2
Ty-nant Conwy 32 A5
Ty-nant Gwyn 32 C5
Ty-uchaf Powys 32 C5
Tyberton Hereford 25 E10
Tyburn W Mid 35 F7
Tycroes Carms 24 G3
Tycrwyn Powys 33 D7
Tydd Gote Lincs 37 D10
Tydd St Giles Cambs 37 D10
Tydd St Mary Lincs 37 D10
Tyddewi = St David's Pembs 22 D2
Tyddyn-mawr Gwyn 41 F7
Tye Green Essex 29 H11
Tye Green Essex 30 E2
Tye Green Essex 30 F4
Tyldesley Gtr Man 43 B9
Tyler Hill Kent 21 E8
Tylers Green Bucks 18 B6
Tylorstown Rhondda 14 B6
Tylwch Powys 32 G5
Tyn-y-celyn Wrex 33 B7
Tyn-y-coed Shrops 33 C8
Tyn-y-fedwen Powys 33 B7
Tyn-y-ffridd Powys 33 B7
Tyn-y-graig Powys 25 C7
Ty'n-y-groes Conwy 41 C9
Ty'n-y-maes Gwyn 41 D8
Tyn-y-pwll Anglesey 40 B6
Ty'n-yr-eithin Ceredig 24 B3
Tyncelyn Ceredig 24 B3
Tyndrum Stirling 74 D6
Tyne Tunnel T&W 63 G9
Tyneham Dorset 9 F7
Tynehead Midloth 70 E2
Tynemouth T&W 63 G9
Tynewydd Rhondda 14 B5
Tyninghame E Loth 70 C5
Tynron Dumfries 60 D4
Tynygongl Anglesey 40 B6
Tynygraig Ceredig 24 B3
Tŷ'r-felin-isaf Conwy 41 D10
Tyrie Aberds 89 B9
Tyringham M Keynes 28 D5
Tythecott Devon 6 E3
Tythegston Bridgend 14 D4
Tytherington Ches E 44 E3
Tytherington S Glos 16 C3
Tytherington Som 16 G4
Tytherington Wilts 16 G6
Tytherleigh Devon 8 D2
Tywardreath Corn 4 F1
Tywyn Conwy 41 C9
Tywyn Gwyn 32 E1

U

Uachdar W Isles 84 C2
Uags Highld 85 E12
Ubbeston Green Suff 31 A10
Ubley Bath 16 F2
Uckerby N Yorks 58 F3
Uckfield E Sus 12 D3
Uckington Glos 26 F6
Uddingston S Lanark 68 D5
Uddington S Lanark 69 G7
Udimore E Sus 13 E7
Udny Green Aberds 89 F8
Udny Station Aberds 89 F9
Udston S Lanark 68 E5
Udstonhead S Lanark 68 F6
Uffcott Wilts 17 D8
Uffculme Devon 7 E9
Uffington Lincs 37 E6
Uffington Oxon 17 C10
Uffington Shrops 33 D11
Ufford Pboro 37 E6
Ufford Suff 31 C9
Ufton Warks 27 B10
Ufton Nervet W Berks 18 E3
Ugadale Argyll 65 F8
Ugborough Devon 5 F7
Uggeshall Suff 39 G10
Ugglebarnby N Yorks 59 F9
Ughill S Yorks 44 C6
Ugley Essex 30 F2
Ugley Green Essex 30 F2
Ugthorpe N Yorks 59 E8
Uidh W Isles 84 J1
Uig Argyll 73 E10
Uig Highld 84 C6
Uig Highld 85 B8
Uigen W Isles 90 D5
Uigshader Highld 85 D9
Uisken Argyll 78 K6
Ulbster Highld 94 F5
Ulceby Lincs 47 E8
Ulceby N Lincs 46 A5
Ulceby Skitter N Lincs 46 A5
Ulcombe Kent 20 G5
Uldale Cumb 56 C4
Uley Glos 16 B4
Ulgham Northumb 63 D8
Ullapool Highld 86 B4
Ullenhall Warks 27 B8
Ullenwood Glos 26 G6
Ulleskelf N Yorks 51 E11
Ullesthorpe Leics 35 G11
Ulley S Yorks 45 D8
Ullingswick Hereford 26 D2
Ullinish Highld 85 E8
Ullock Cumb 56 D2
Ulnes Walton Lancs 49 H5
Ulpha Cumb 56 G3
Ulrome E Yorks 53 D7
Ulsta Shetland 96 E6
Ulva House Argyll 78 H7
Ulverston Cumb 49 B2
Ulwell Dorset 9 F9
Umberleigh Devon 6 D5
Unapool Highld 92 F5
Unasary W Isles 84 F2
Underbarrow Cumb 56 G6
Undercliffe W Yorks 51 F7
Underhoull Shetland 96 C7
Underriver Kent 20 F2
Underwood Notts 45 G8
Undy Mon 15 C10
Unifirth Shetland 96 H4
Union Cottage Aberds 83 D10
Union Mills IoM 48 E3
Union Street E Sus 12 C6
Unstone Derbys 45 E7
Unstone Green Derbys 45 E7
Unthank Cumb 56 C6
Unthank Cumb 57 B8
Unthank Cumb 57 C7
Unthank End Cumb 56 C6
Up Cerne Dorset 8 D5
Up Exe Devon 7 F8
Up Hatherley Glos 26 F6
Up Holland Lancs 43 B8
Up Marden W Sus 11 C6
Up Nately Hants 18 F3
Up Somborne Hants 10 A2
Up Sydling Dorset 8 D5
Upavon Wilts 17 F8
Upchurch Kent 20 E5
Upcott Hereford 25 C10
Upend Cambs 30 C3
Upgate Norf 39 D7
Uphall W Loth 69 C9
Uphall Station W Loth 69 C9
Upham Devon 7 F7
Upham Hants 10 B4
Uphampton Worcs 26 B5
Uphill N Som 15 F9
Uplawmoor E Renf 68 E3
Upleadon Glos 26 F4
Upleatham Redcar 59 E7
Uplees Kent 20 E6
Uploders Dorset 8 E4
Uplowman Devon 7 E9
Uplyme Devon 8 E2
Upminster London 20 C2
Upnor Medway 20 D4
Upottery Devon 7 F11
Upper Affcot Shrops 33 G10
Upper Ardchronie Highld 87 C9
Upper Arley Worcs 34 G3
Upper Arncott Oxon 28 G3
Upper Astrop Northants 28 E2
Upper Badcall Highld 92 E4
Upper Basildon W Berks 18 D2
Upper Beeding W Sus 11 C10
Upper Benefield Northants 36 G5
Upper Bighouse Highld 93 D11
Upper Boddington Northants 27 C11
Upper Borth Ceredig 32 G2
Upper Boyndlie Aberds 89 B9
Upper Brailes Warks 27 E10
Upper Breakish Highld 85 F11
Upper Breinton Hereford 25 D11
Upper Broadheath Worcs 26 C5
Upper Broughton Notts 36 C2
Upper Bucklebury W Berks 18 E2
Upper Burnhaugh Aberds 83 D10
Upper Caldecote C Beds 29 D8
Upper Catesby Northants 28 C2
Upper Chapel Powys 25 D7
Upper Church Village Rhondda 14 C6
Upper Chute Wilts 17 F9
Upper Clatford Hants 17 G10
Upper Clynnog Gwyn 40 F6
Upper Cumberworth W Yorks 44 B6
Upper Cwm-twrch Powys 24 G4
Upper Cwmbran Torf 15 B8
Upper Dallachy Moray 88 B3
Upper Dean Bedford 29 B7
Upper Denby W Yorks 44 B6
Upper Denton Cumb 62 G2
Upper Derraid Highld 87 H13
Upper Dicker E Sus 12 F4
Upper Dovercourt Essex 31 E9
Upper Druimfin Argyll 79 F8
Upper Dunsforth N Yorks 51 C10
Upper Eathie Highld 87 E10
Upper Elkstone Staffs 44 G4
Upper End Derbys 44 E4
Upper Farringdon Hants 18 H4
Upper Framilode Glos 26 G4
Upper Glenfintaig Highld 80 E4
Upper Gornal W Mid 34 F5
Upper Gravenhurst C Beds 29 E8
Upper Green Mon 25 G10
Upper Green W Berks 17 E10
Upper Grove Common Hereford 26 F2
Upper Hackney Derbys 44 F6
Upper Hale Sur 18 G5
Upper Halistra Highld 84 C7
Upper Halling Medway 20 E3
Upper Hambleton Rutland 36 E5
Upper Hardres Court Kent 21 F8
Upper Hartfield E Sus 12 C3
Upper Haugh S Yorks 45 C8
Upper Heath Shrops 34 G1
Upper Hellesdon Norf 39 D8
Upper Helmsley N Yorks 52 D2
Upper Hergest Hereford 25 C9
Upper Heyford Northants 28 C3
Upper Heyford Oxon 27 F11
Upper Hill Hereford 25 C11
Upper Hopton W Yorks 51 H7
Upper Horsebridge E Sus 12 E4
Upper Hulme Staffs 44 F4
Upper Inglesham Swindon 17 B9
Upper Inverbrough Highld 87 H11
Upper Killay Swansea 23 G10
Upper Knockando Moray 88 D1
Upper Lambourn W Berks 17 C10
Upper Leigh Staffs 34 B6
Upper Lenie Highld 81 A7
Upper Lochton Aberds 83 D8
Upper Longdon Staffs 35 D6
Upper Lybster Highld 94 G4
Upper Lydbrook Glos 26 G3
Upper Maes-coed Hereford 25 E10
Upper Midway Derbys 35 C8
Upper Milovaig Highld 84 D6
Upper Minety Wilts 17 B7
Upper Mitton Worcs 26 A5
Upper North Dean Bucks 18 B5
Upper Obney Perth 76 D3
Upper Ollach Highld 85 E10
Upper Padley Derbys 44 E6
Upper Pollicott Bucks 28 G4
Upper Poppleton York 52 D1
Upper Quinton Warks 27 D8
Upper Ratley Hants 10 B2
Upper Rissington Glos 27 G9
Upper Rochford Worcs 26 B3
Upper Sandaig Highld 85 G12
Upper Sanday Orkney 95 H6
Upper Sapey Hereford 26 B3
Upper Saxondale Notts 36 B2
Upper Seagry Wilts 16 C6
Upper Shelton C Beds 28 D6
Upper Sheringham Norf 39 A7
Upper Skelmorlie N Ayrs 73 G11
Upper Slaughter Glos 27 F8
Upper Soudley Glos 26 G3
Upper Stondon C Beds 29 E8
Upper Stowe Northants 28 C3
Upper Stratton Swindon 17 C8
Upper Street Hants 9 C10
Upper Street Norf 39 D9
Upper Street Norf 39 D9
Upper Street Suff 31 E8
Upper Strensham Worcs 26 E6
Upper Sundon C Beds 29 F7
Upper Swell Glos 27 F8
Upper Tean Staffs 34 B6
Upper Tillyrie Perth 76 G4
Upper Tooting London 19 D9
Upper Tote Highld 85 C10
Upper Town N Som 15 E11
Upper Treverward Shrops 33 H8
Upper Tysoe Warks 27 D10
Upper Upham Wilts 17 D9
Upper Wardington Oxon 27 D11
Upper Weald M Keynes 28 E4
Upper Weedon Northants 28 C3
Upper Wield Hants 18 H3
Upper Winchendon Bucks 28 G4
Upper Witton W Mid 35 F6
Upper Woodend Aberds 83 B8
Upper Woodford Wilts 17 H8
Upper Wootton Hants 18 F2
Upper Wyche Hereford 26 D4
Upperby Cumb 56 A6
Uppermill Gtr Man 44 B3
Uppersound Shetland 96 J6
Upperthong W Yorks 44 B5
Upperthorpe N Lincs 45 B11
Upperton W Sus 11 B8
Uppertown Derbys 45 F7
Uppertown Highld 94 C5
Uppertown Orkney 95 J5
Uppingham Rutland 36 F4
Uppington Shrops 34 E1
Upsall N Yorks 58 H5
Upshire Essex 19 A11
Upstreet Kent 21 E9
Upthorpe Suff 30 A6
Upton Cambs 37 H7
Upton Ches W 43 F7
Upton Corn 4 D3
Upton Dorset 8 F6
Upton Dorset 9 E8
Upton Hants 10 C2
Upton Hants 17 F10
Upton Leics 35 F9
Upton Lincs 46 D2
Upton Mers 42 D5
Upton Norf 39 D9
Upton Northants 28 B4
Upton Notts 45 E11
Upton Notts 45 G11
Upton Oxon 18 C2
Upton Pboro 37 E7
Upton Slough 18 D6
Upton Som 7 D8
Upton W Yorks 45 A8
Upton Bishop Hereford 26 F3
Upton Cheyney S Glos 16 E3
Upton Cressett Shrops 34 F2
Upton Cross Corn 4 D3
Upton Grey Hants 18 G3
Upton Hellions Devon 7 F7
Upton Lovell Wilts 16 G6
Upton Magna Shrops 34 D1
Upton Noble Som 16 H4
Upton Pyne Devon 7 G8
Upton St Leonard's Glos 26 G5
Upton Scudamore Wilts 16 G5
Upton Snodsbury Worcs 26 C6
Upton upon Severn Worcs 26 D5
Upton Warren Worcs 26 B6
Upwaltham W Sus 11 C8
Upware Cambs 30 A2
Upwell Norf 37 E10
Upwey Dorset 8 F5
Upwood Cambs 37 G8
Uradale Shetland 96 K6
Urafirth Shetland 96 F5
Urchfont Wilts 17 F7
Urdimarsh Hereford 26 D2
Ure Shetland 96 F4
Ure Bank N Yorks 51 B9
Urgha W Isles 90 H6
Urishay Common Hereford 25 E10
Urlay Nook Stockton 58 E4
Urmston Gtr Man 43 C10
Urpeth Durham 58 A3
Urquhart Highld 87 F8
Urquhart Moray 88 B2
Urra N Yorks 59 F6
Urray Highld 87 F8
Ushaw Moor Durham 58 B3
Usk = Brynbuga Mon 15 A9
Usselby Lincs 46 C4
Usworth T&W 63 H9
Utkinton Ches W 43 F8
Utley W Yorks 50 E6
Uton Devon 7 G7
Utterby Lincs 47 C7
Uttoxeter Staffs 35 B6
Uwchmynydd Gwyn 40 H3
Uxbridge London 19 C7
Uyeasound Shetland 96 C7
Uzmaston Pembs 22 E4

V

Valley Anglesey 40 C4
Valley Truckle Corn 4 C1
Valleyfield Dumfries 55 D9
Valsgarth Shetland 96 B8
Valtos Highld 85 B10
Van Powys 32 G5
Vange Essex 20 C4
Varteg Torf 25 H9
Vatten Highld 85 D7
Vaul Argyll 78 G3
Vaynor M Tydf 25 G7
Veensgarth Shetland 96 J6
Velindre Powys 25 E8
Vellow Som 7 C9
Veness Orkney 95 F6
Venn Green Devon 6 E2
Venn Ottery Devon 7 G9
Vennington Shrops 33 E9
Venny Tedburn Devon 7 G7
Ventnor IoW 10 G4
Vernham Dean Hants 17 F10
Vernham Street Hants 17 F10
Vernolds Common Shrops 33 G10
Verwood Dorset 9 D9
Veryan Corn 3 F8
Vicarage Devon 7 H11
Vickerstown Cumb 49 C1
Victoria Corn 3 C8
Victoria S Yorks 44 B5
Vidlin Shetland 96 G6
Viewpark N Lanark 68 D6
Vigo Village Kent 20 E3
Vinehall Street E Sus 13 D6
Vine's Cross E Sus 12 E4
Viney Hill Glos 26 H3
Virginia Water Sur 19 E7
Virginstow Devon 6 G2
Vobster Som 16 G4
Voe Shetland 96 E5
Voe Shetland 96 G6
Vowchurch Hereford 25 E10
Voxter Shetland 96 F5
Voy Orkney 95 G3

W

Wackerfield Durham 58 D2
Wacton Norf 39 F7
Wadbister Shetland 96 J6
Wadborough Worcs 26 D6
Waddesdon Bucks 28 G4
Waddingham Lincs 46 C3
Waddington Lancs 50 E3
Waddington Lincs 46 F3
Wadebridge Corn 3 B8
Wadeford Som 8 C2
Wadenhoe Northants 36 G6
Wadesmill Herts 29 G10
Wadhurst E Sus 12 C5
Wadshelf Derbys 45 E7
Wadsley S Yorks 45 C7
Wadsley Bridge S Yorks 45 C7
Wadworth S Yorks 45 C9
Waen Denb 42 F2
Waen Denb 42 F4
Waen Fach Powys 33 D8
Waen Goleugoed Denb 42 E3
Wag Highld 93 G13
Wainfleet All Saints Lincs 47 G8
Wainfleet Bank Lincs 47 G8
Wainfleet St Mary Lincs 47 G9
Wainfleet Tofts Lincs 47 G8
Wainhouse Corner Corn 4 B2
Wainscott Medway 20 D4
Wainstalls W Yorks 50 G6
Waitby Cumb 57 F9
Waithe Lincs 46 B6
Wake Lady Green N Yorks 59 G7
Wakefield W Yorks 51 G9
Wakerley Northants 36 F5
Wakes Colne Essex 30 F5
Walberswick Suff 31 A11
Walberton W Sus 11 D8
Walbottle T&W 63 G7
Walcot Lincs 37 B6
Walcot N Lincs 52 G4
Walcot Shrops 33 G9
Walcot Swindon 17 C8
Walcot Telford 34 D1
Walcot Green Norf 39 G7
Walcote Leics 36 G1
Walcote Warks 27 C8
Walcott Lincs 46 G5
Walcott Norf 39 B9
Walden N Yorks 50 A6
Walden Head N Yorks 50 A5
Walden Stubbs N Yorks 52 H1
Waldersey Cambs 37 E10
Walderslade Medway 20 E4
Walderton W Sus 11 C6
Walditch Dorset 8 E3
Waldley Derbys 35 B7
Waldridge Durham 58 A3
Waldringfield Suff 31 D9
Waldringfield Heath Suff 31 D9
Waldron E Sus 12 E4
Wales S Yorks 45 D8
Walesby Lincs 46 C5
Walesby Notts 45 E10
Walford Hereford 25 A10
Walford Hereford 26 F2
Walford Shrops 33 C10
Walford Heath Shrops 33 D10
Walgherton Ches E 43 H9
Walgrave Northants 28 A5
Walhampton Hants 10 E2
Walk Mill Lancs 50 F4
Walkden Gtr Man 43 B10
Walker T&W 63 G8
Walker Barn Ches E 44 E3
Walker Fold Lancs 50 E2
Walkerburn Borders 70 G3
Walkeringham Notts 45 C11
Walkerith Lincs 45 C11
Walkern Herts 29 F9
Walker's Green Hereford 26 D2
Walkhampton Devon 4 E6
Walkington E Yorks 52 F5
Walkley S Yorks 45 D7
Wall Northumb 62 G5
Wall Staffs 35 E7
Wall Bank Shrops 33 F11
Wall Heath W Mid 34 G4
Wall under Heywood Shrops 33 F11
Wallaceton Dumfries 60 E4
Wallacetown S Ayrs 66 E6
Wallacetown S Ayrs 67 D6
Wallands Park E Sus 12 E3
Wallasey Mers 42 C6
Wallcrouch E Sus 12 C5
Wallingford Oxon 18 C3
Wallington Hants 10 D4
Wallington Herts 29 E9
Wallington London 19 E9
Wallis Pembs 22 D5
Walliswood Sur 19 H8
Walls Shetland 96 J4
Wallsend T&W 63 G9
Wallston V Glam 15 D7
Wallyford E Loth 70 C2
Walmer Kent 21 F10
Walmer Bridge Lancs 49 G4
Walmersley Gtr Man 44 A2
Walmley W Mid 35 F7
Walpole Suff 31 A10
Walpole Cross Keys Norf 37 D11
Walpole Highway Norf 37 D11
Walpole Marsh Norf 37 D10
Walpole St Andrew Norf 37 D11
Walpole St Peter Norf 37 D11
Walsall W Mid 34 F6
Walsall Wood W Mid 34 E6
Walsden W Yorks 50 G5
Walsgrave on Sowe W Mid 35 G9
Walsham le Willows Suff 30 A6
Walshaw Gtr Man 43 A10
Walshford N Yorks 51 D10
Walsoken Cambs 37 D10
Walston S Lanark 69 F9
Walsworth Herts 29 E8
Walters Ash Bucks 18 B5
Walterston V Glam 14 D6
Walterstone Hereford 25 F10
Waltham Kent 21 G8
Waltham NE Lincs 46 B6
Waltham Abbey Essex 19 A10
Waltham Chase Hants 10 C4
Waltham Cross Herts 19 A10
Waltham on the Wolds Leics 36 C4
Waltham St Lawrence Windsor 18 D5
Walthamstow London 19 C10
Walton Cumb 61 G11
Walton Derbys 45 F7
Walton Leics 36 G1
Walton M Keynes 28 E5
Walton Mers 42 C6
Walton Pboro 37 E7
Walton Powys 25 C9
Walton Som 15 H10
Walton Staffs 34 B4
Walton Suff 31 E9
Walton Telford 34 D1
Walton W Yorks 51 E10
Walton W Yorks 51 H9
Walton Warks 27 C9
Walton Cardiff Glos 26 E6
Walton East Pembs 22 D5
Walton-in-Gordano N Som 15 D10
Walton-le-Dale Lancs 50 G1
Walton-on-Thames Sur 19 E8
Walton on the Hill Staffs 34 C5
Walton on the Hill Sur 19 F9
Walton-on-the-Naze Essex 31 F9
Walton on the Wolds Leics 36 D1
Walton-on-Trent Derbys 35 D8
Walton West Pembs 22 E3
Walwen Flint 42 E5
Walwick Northumb 62 F5
Walworth Darl 58 E3
Walworth Gate Darl 58 D3
Walwyn's Castle Pembs 22 E3
Wambrook Som 8 D1
Wanborough Sur 18 G6
Wanborough Swindon 17 C9
Wandsworth London 19 D9
Wangford Suff 39 H10
Wanlockhead Dumfries 60 B4
Wansford E Yorks 52 D6
Wansford Pboro 37 F6
Wanstead London 19 C11
Wanstrow Som 16 G4
Wanswell Glos 16 A3
Wantage Oxon 17 C10
Wapley S Glos 16 D4
Wappenbury Warks 27 B10
Wappenham Northants 28 D3
Warbleton E Sus 12 E5
Warblington Hants 10 D6
Warborough Oxon 18 B2
Warboys Cambs 37 G9
Warbreck Blackpool 49 F3
Warbstow Corn 4 B3
Warburton Gtr Man 43 D10
Warcop Cumb 57 E9
Ward End W Mid 35 G7
Ward Green Suff 31 B7
Warden Kent 21 D7
Warden Northumb 62 G5
Wardhill Orkney 95 F7
Wardington Oxon 27 D11
Wardlaw Borders 61 B8
Wardle Ches E 43 G9
Wardle Gtr Man 50 H5
Wardley Rutland 36 E4
Wardlow Derbys 44 E5
Wardy Hill Cambs 37 G10
Ware Herts 29 G10
Ware Kent 21 E9
Wareham Dorset 9 F8
Warehorne Kent 13 C8
Waren Mill Northumb 71 G10
Warenford Northumb 71 H10
Warenton Northumb 71 G10
Wareside Herts 29 G11
Waresley Cambs 29 C9
Waresley Worcs 26 A5
Warfield Brack 18 D5
Warfleet Devon 5 F9
Wargrave Wokingham 18 D4
Warham Norf 38 A5
Warhill Gtr Man 44 C3
Wark Northumb 62 F4
Wark Northumb 71 G7
Warkleigh Devon 6 D5
Warkton Northants 36 H4
Warkworth Northants 27 D11
Warkworth Northumb 63 C8
Warlaby N Yorks 58 G4
Warland W Yorks 50 G5
Warleggan Corn 4 E2
Warlingham Sur 19 F10
Warmfield W Yorks 51 G9
Warmingham Ches E 43 F10
Warmington Northants 37 F6
Warmington Warks 27 D11
Warminster Wilts 16 G5
Warmlake Kent 20 F5
Warmley S Glos 16 D3
Warmley Tower S Glos 16 D3
Warmonds Hill Northants 28 B6
Warmsworth S Yorks 45 B9
Warmwell Dorset 9 F6
Warndon Worcs 26 C5
Warnford Hants 10 B5
Warnham W Sus 11 A10
Warninglid W Sus 11 B11
Warren Ches E 44 E2
Warren Pembs 22 G4
Warren Heath Suff 31 D9
Warren Row Windsor 18 C5
Warren Street Kent 20 F6
Warrington M Keynes 28 C5
Warrington Warr 43 D9
Warsash Hants 10 D3
Warslow Staffs 44 G4
Warter E Yorks 52 D4
Warthermarske N Yorks 51 B8
Warthill N Yorks 52 D2
Wartling E Sus 12 F5
Wartnaby Leics 36 C3
Warton Lancs 49 B4
Warton Lancs 49 G4
Warton Northumb 62 C6
Warton Warks 35 E8
Warwick Warks 27 B9
Warwick Bridge Cumb 61 H10
Warwick on Eden Cumb 61 H10
Wasbister Orkney 95 E4
Wasdale Head Cumb 56 F3
Wash Common W Berks 17 E11
Washaway Corn 3 C9
Washbourne Devon 5 F8
Washfield Devon 7 E8
Washfold N Yorks 58 F1
Washford Som 7 B9
Washford Pyne Devon 7 E7
Washingborough Lincs 46 E4
Washington T&W 63 H9
Washington W Sus 11 C10
Wasing W Berks 18 E2
Waskerley Durham 58 B1
Wasperton Warks 27 C9
Wasps Nest Lincs 46 F4
Wass N Yorks 52 B1
Watchet Som 7 B9
Watchfield Oxon 17 B9
Watchfield Som 15 G9
Watchgate Cumb 57 G7
Watchhill Cumb 56 B3
Watcombe Torbay 5 E10
Watendlath Cumb 56 E4
Water Devon 5 C8
Water Lancs 50 G4
Water End E Yorks 52 F3
Water End Herts 19 A9
Water End Herts 29 G7
Water Newton Cambs 37 F7
Water Orton Warks 35 F7
Water Stratford Bucks 28 E3
Water Yeat Cumb 56 H4
Waterbeach Cambs 29 B11
Waterbeck Dumfries 61 F8
Waterden Norf 38 B4
Waterfall Staffs 44 G4
Waterfoot E Renf 68 E4
Waterfoot Lancs 50 G4
Waterford Herts 29 G10
Waterhead Cumb 56 F5
Waterhead Dumfries 61 D7
Waterheads Borders 69 E11
Waterhouses Durham 58 B2
Waterhouses Staffs 44 G4
Wateringbury Kent 20 F3
Waterloo Gtr Man 44 B3
Waterloo Highld 85 F11
Waterloo Mers 42 C6
Waterloo N Lanark 69 E7
Waterloo Norf 39 D8
Waterloo Perth 76 D3
Waterloo Poole 9 E9
Waterloo Shrops 33 B11
Waterloo Port Gwyn 40 D6
Waterlooville Hants 10 D5
Watermeetings S Lanark 60 B5
Watermillock Cumb 56 D6
Waterperry Oxon 28 H3
Waterrow Som 7 D9
Water's Nook Gtr Man 43 B9
Waters Upton Telford 34 D2
Watersfield W Sus 11 C9
Waterside Aberds 89 F10
Waterside Blackburn 50 G3
Waterside Cumb 56 B4
Waterside E Ayrs 67 F7
Waterside E Ayrs 67 B7
Waterside E Dunb 68 C5
Waterside E Renf 68 E4
Waterstock Oxon 28 H3
Waterston Pembs 22 F4
Watford Herts 19 B8
Watford Northants 28 B3
Watford Gap Staffs 35 E7
Wath N Yorks 51 B9
Wath N Yorks 51 C7
Wath N Yorks 52 B2
Wath Brow Cumb 56 E2
Wath upon Dearne S Yorks 45 B8
Watlington Norf 38 D2
Watlington Oxon 18 B3
Watnall Notts 45 H9
Watten Highld 94 E4
Wattisfield Suff 31 A7
Wattisham Suff 31 C7
Wattlesborough Heath Shrops 33 D9
Watton E Yorks 52 D6
Watton Norf 38 E5
Watton at Stone Herts 29 G10
Wattston N Lanark 68 C6
Wattstown Rhondda 14 B6
Wauchan Highld 80 E1
Waulkmill Lodge Orkney 95 H4
Waun Powys 32 E4
Waun-y-clyn Carms 23 F9
Waunarlwydd Swansea 14 B2
Waunclunda Carms 24 E3
Waunfawr Gwyn 41 E7
Waungron Swansea 23 F10
Waunlwyd Bl Gwent 25 H8
Wavendon M Keynes 28 E6
Waverbridge Cumb 56 B4
Waverton Ches W 43 F7
Waverton Cumb 56 B4
Wavertree Mers 43 D6
Wawne E Yorks 53 F6
Waxham Norf 39 C10
Waxholme E Yorks 53 G9
Way Kent 21 E10
Way Village Devon 7 E7
Wayfield Medway 20 E4
Wayford Som 8 D3
Waymills Shrops 34 A1
Wayne Green Mon 25 G11
Wdig = Goodwick Pembs 22 C4
Weachyburn Aberds 89 C6
Weald Oxon 17 A10
Wealdstone London 19 C8
Weardley W Yorks 51 E8
Weare Som 15 F10
Weare Giffard Devon 6 D3
Wearhead Durham 57 C10
Weasdale Cumb 57 F8
Weasenham All Saints Norf 38 C4
Weasenham St Peter Norf 38 C4
Weatherhill Sur 12 B2
Weaverham Ches W 43 E9
Weaverthorpe N Yorks 52 B5
Webheath Worcs 27 B7
Wedderlairs Aberds 89 E8
Wedderlie Borders 70 E5
Weddington Warks 35 F9
Wedhampton Wilts 17 F7
Wedmore Som 15 G10
Wednesbury W Mid 34 F5
Wednesfield W Mid 34 E5
Weedon Bucks 28 G5
Weedon Bec Northants 28 C3
Weedon Lois Northants 28 D3
Weeford Staffs 35 E7
Week Devon 7 E6
Week St Mary Corn 4 B3
Weeke Hants 10 A3
Weekley Northants 36 G4
Weel E Yorks 53 F6
Weeley Essex 31 F8
Weeley Heath Essex 31 F8
Weem Perth 75 C11
Weeping Cross Staffs 34 C5
Weethley Gate Warks 27 C7
Weeting Norf 38 G3
Weeton E Yorks 53 G9
Weeton Lancs 49 F3

Weeton N Yorks 51 E8
Weetwood Hall Northumb 71 H9
Weir Lancs 50 G4
Weir Quay Devon 4 E5
Welborne Norf 39 E6
Welbourn Lincs 46 G3
Welburn N Yorks 52 A2
Welburn N Yorks 52 C3
Welbury N Yorks 58 F4
Welby Lincs 36 B5
Welches Dam Cambs 37 G10
Welcombe Devon 6 E1
Weld Bank Lancs 50 H1
Weldon Northumb 63 D7
Welford Northants 36 G2
Welford W Berks 17 D11
Welford-on-Avon Warks 27 C8
Welham Leics 36 F3
Welham Notts 45 D11
Welham Green Herts 29 H9
Well Hants 18 G4
Well Lincs 47 E8
Well N Yorks 51 A8
Well End Bucks 18 C5
Well Heads W Yorks 51 F6
Well Hill Kent 19 E11
Well Town Devon 7 F8
Welland Worcs 26 D4
Wellbank Angus 77 D7
Welldale Dumfries 61 G7
Wellesbourne Warks 27 C9
Welling London 19 D11
Wellingborough Northants 28 B5
Wellingham Norf 38 C4
Wellingore Lincs 46 G3
Wellington Cumb 56 F2
Wellington Hereford 25 D11
Wellington Som 7 D10
Wellington Telford 34 D2
Wellington Heath Hereford 26 D4
Wellington Hill W Yorks 51 F9
Wellow Bath 16 F4
Wellow IoW 10 F2
Wellow Notts 45 F10
Wellpond Green Herts 29 F11
Wells Som 15 G11
Wells Green Ches E 43 G9
Wells-Next-The-Sea Norf 38 A5
Wellsborough Leics 35 E9
Wellswood Torbay 5 E10
Wellwood Fife 69 B9
Welney Norf 37 F11
Welsh Bicknor Hereford 26 G2
Welsh End Shrops 33 B11
Welsh Frankton Shrops 33 B9
Welsh Hook Pembs 22 D4
Welsh Newton Hereford 25 G11
Welsh St Donats V Glam 14 D6
Welshampton Shrops 33 B10
Welshpool = Y Trallwng Powys 33 E8
Welton Cumb 56 B5
Welton E Yorks 52 G5
Welton Lincs 46 E4
Welton Northants 28 B2
Welton Hill Lincs 46 D4
Welton le Marsh Lincs 47 F8
Welton le Wold Lincs 46 D6
Welwick E Yorks 53 G9
Welwyn Herts 29 G9
Welwyn Garden City Herts 29 G9
Wem Shrops 33 C11
Wembdon Som 15 H8
Wembley London 19 C8
Wembury Devon 4 G6
Wembworthy Devon 6 F5
Wemyss Bay Invclyd 73 G10
Wenallt Ceredig 24 A3
Wenallt Gwyn 32 A5
Wendens Ambo Essex 30 E2
Wendlebury Oxon 28 G2
Wendling Norf 38 D5
Wendover Bucks 28 H5
Wendron Corn 2 F5
Wendy Cambs 29 D10
Wenfordbridge Corn 4 D1
Wenhaston Suff 39 H10
Wennington Cambs 37 H8
Wennington Lancs 50 B2
Wennington London 20 C2
Wensley Derbys 44 F6
Wensley N Yorks 58 H1
Wentbridge W Yorks 51 H10
Wentnor Shrops 33 F9
Wentworth Cambs 37 H10
Wentworth S Yorks 45 C7
Wenvoe V Glam 15 D7
Weobley Hereford 25 C11
Weobley Marsh Hereford 25 C11
Wereham Norf 38 E2
Wergs W Mid 34 E4
Wern Powys 32 D5
Wern Powys 33 D8
Wernffrwd Swansea 23 G10
Wernyrheolydd Mon 25 G10
Werrington Corn 4 C4
Werrington Pboro 37 E7
Werrington Staffs 44 H3
Wervin Ches W 43 E7
Wesham Lancs 49 F4
Wessington Derbys 45 G7
West Acre Norf 38 D3
West Adderbury Oxon 27 E11
West Allerdean Northumb 71 F8
West Alvington Devon 5 G8
West Amesbury Wilts 17 G8
West Anstey Devon 7 D7
West Ashby Lincs 46 E6
West Ashling W Sus 11 D7
West Ashton Wilts 16 F5
West Auckland Durham 58 D2
West Ayton N Yorks 52 A5
West Bagborough Som 7 C10
West Barkwith Lincs 46 D5
West Barnby N Yorks 59 E9
West Barns E Loth 70 C5
West Barsham Norf 38 B5
West Bay Dorset 8 E3
West Beckham Norf 39 B7
West Bedfont Sur 19 D7
West Benhar N Lanark 69 D7
West Bergholt Essex 30 F6
West Bexington Dorset 8 F4
West Bilney Norf 38 D3
West Blatchington Brighton 12 F1
West Bowling W Yorks 51 F7
West Bradford Lancs 50 E3
West Bradley Som 16 H2
West Bretton W Yorks 44 A6
West Bridgford Notts 36 B1
West Bromwich W Mid 34 F6
West Buckland Devon 6 C5
West Buckland Som 7 D10
West Burrafirth Shetland 96 H4
West Burton N Yorks 58 H1
West Burton W Sus 11 C8
West Butterwick N Lincs 46 B2
West Byfleet Sur 19 E7
West Caister Norf 39 D11
West Calder W Loth 69 D9
West Camel Som 8 B4
West Challow Oxon 17 C10
West Chelborough Dorset 8 D4
West Chevington Northumb 63 D8
West Chiltington W Sus 11 C9
West Chiltington Common W Sus 11 C9
West Chinnock Som 8 C3
West Chisenbury Wilts 17 F8
West Clandon Sur 19 F7
West Cliffe Kent 21 G10
West Clyne Highld 93 J11
West Clyth Highld 94 G4
West Coker Som 8 C4
West Compton Dorset 8 E4
West Compton Som 16 G2
West Cowick E Yorks 52 G2
West Cranmore Som 16 G3
West Cross Swansea 14 C2
West Cullery Aberds 83 C9
West Curry Corn 6 G1
West Curthwaite Cumb 56 B5
West Darlochan Argyll 65 F7
West Dean W Sus 11 C7
West Dean Wilts 10 B1
West Deeping Lincs 37 E7
West Derby Mers 43 C6
West Dereham Norf 38 E2
West Didsbury Gtr Man 44 C2
West Ditchburn Northumb 63 A7
West Down Devon 6 B4
West Drayton London 19 D7
West Drayton Notts 45 E11
West Ella E Yorks 52 G6
West End Bedford 28 C6
West End E Yorks 52 F5
West End E Yorks 53 F7
West End Hants 10 C3
West End Lancs 50 G3
West End N Som 15 E10
West End N Yorks 51 D7
West End Norf 38 E5
West End Norf 39 D11
West End Oxon 17 A11
West End S Lanark 69 F8
West End S Yorks 45 B10
West End Suff 39 G10
West End Sur 18 E6
West End W Sus 11 C11
West End Wilts 9 B8
West End Wilts 16 D6
West End Green Hants 18 E3
West Farleigh Kent 20 F4
West Felton Shrops 33 C9
West Fenton E Loth 70 B3
West Ferry Dundee 77 D7
West Firle E Sus 12 F3
West Ginge Oxon 17 C11
West Grafton Wilts 17 E9
West Green Hants 18 F4
West Greenskares Aberds 89 B7
West Grimstead Wilts 9 B11
West Grinstead W Sus 11 B10
West Haddlesey N Yorks 52 G1
West Haddon Northants 28 A3
West Hagbourne Oxon 18 C2
West Hagley Worcs 34 G5
West Hall Cumb 61 G11
West Hallam Derbys 35 A10
West Halton N Lincs 52 G5
West Ham London 19 C11
West Handley Derbys 45 E7
West Hanney Oxon 17 B11
West Hanningfield Essex 20 B4
West Hardwick W Yorks 51 H10
West Harnham Wilts 9 B10
West Harptree Bath 16 F2
West Hatch Som 8 B1
West Head Norf 38 E1
West Heath Ches E 44 F2
West Heath Hants 18 F2
West Heath Hants 18 F5
West Helmsdale Highld 93 H13
West Hendred Oxon 17 C11
West Heslerton N Yorks 52 B5
West Hill Devon 7 G9
West Hill E Yorks 53 C7
West Hill N Som 15 D10
West Hoathly W Sus 12 C2
West Holme Dorset 9 F7
West Horndon Essex 20 C3
West Horrington Som 16 G2
West Horsley Sur 19 F7
West Horton Northumb 71 G9
West Hougham Kent 21 G9
West Houlland Shetland 96 H4
West-houses Derbys 45 G8
West Huntington York 52 D2
West Hythe Kent 13 C10
West Ilsley W Berks 17 C11
West Itchenor W Sus 11 D6
West Keal Lincs 47 F7
West Kennett Wilts 17 E8
West Kilbride N Ayrs 66 B5
West Kingsdown Kent 20 E2
West Kington Wilts 16 D5
West Kinharrachie Aberds 89 E9
West Kirby Mers 42 D5
West Knapton N Yorks 52 B4
West Knighton Dorset 8 F6
West Knoyle Wilts 9 A7
West Kyloe Northumb 71 F9
West Lambrook Som 8 C3
West Langdon Kent 21 G10
West Langwell Highld 93 J9
West Lavington W Sus 11 B7
West Lavington Wilts 17 F7
West Layton N Yorks 58 F2
West Lea Durham 58 B5
West Leake Notts 35 C11
West Learmouth Northumb 71 G7
West Leigh Devon 6 F5
West Lexham Norf 38 D4
West Lilling N Yorks 52 C2
West Linton Borders 69 E10
West Liss Hants 11 B6
West Littleton S Glos 16 D4
West Looe Corn 4 F3
West Luccombe Som 7 B7
West Lulworth Dorset 9 F7
West Lutton N Yorks 52 C5
West Lydford Som 8 A4
West Lyng Som 8 B2
West Lynn Norf 38 C2
West Malling Kent 20 F3
West Malvern Worcs 26 D4
West Marden W Sus 11 C6
West Marina E Sus 13 F6
West Markham Notts 45 E11
West Marsh NE Lincs 46 A6
West Marton N Yorks 50 D4
West Meon Hants 10 B5
West Mersea Essex 31 G7
West Milton Dorset 8 E4
West Minster Kent 20 D6
West Molesey Sur 19 E8
West Monkton Som 8 B1
West Moors Dorset 9 D9
West Morriston Borders 70 F5
West Muir Angus 77 A8
West Ness N Yorks 52 B2
West Newham Northumb 62 F6
West Newton E Yorks 53 F7
West Newton Norf 38 C2
West Norwood London 19 D10
West Ogwell Devon 5 D9
West Orchard Dorset 9 C7
West Overton Wilts 17 E8
West Park Hrtlpl 58 C5
West Parley Dorset 9 E9
West Peckham Kent 20 F3
West Pelton Durham 58 A3
West Pennard Som 15 H11
West Pentire Corn 3 C6
West Perry Cambs 29 B8
West Putford Devon 6 E2
West Quantoxhead Som 7 B10
West Rainton Durham 58 B4
West Rasen Lincs 46 D4
West Raynham Norf 38 C4
West Retford Notts 45 D10
West Rounton N Yorks 58 F5
West Row Suff 38 H2
West Rudham Norf 38 C4
West Runton Norf 39 A7
West Saltoun E Loth 70 D3
West Sandwick Shetland 96 E6
West Scrafton N Yorks 51 A6
West Sleekburn Northumb 63 E8
West Somerton Norf 39 D10
West Stafford Dorset 8 F6
West Stockwith Notts 45 C11
West Stoke W Sus 11 D7
West Stonesdale N Yorks 57 F10
West Stoughton Som 15 G10
West Stour Dorset 9 B6
West Stourmouth Kent 21 E9
West Stow Suff 30 A5
West Stowell Wilts 17 E8
West Strathan Highld 93 C8
West Stratton Hants 18 G2
West Street Kent 20 F6
West Tanfield N Yorks 51 B8
West Taphouse Corn 4 E2
West Tarbert Argyll 73 G7
West Thirston Northumb 63 D7
West Thorney W Sus 11 D6
West Thurrock Thurrock 20 D2
West Tilbury Thurrock 20 D3
West Tisted Hants 10 B5
West Tofts Norf 38 F4
West Tofts Perth 76 D4
West Torrington Lincs 46 D5
West Town Hants 10 E6
West Town N Som 15 E10
West Tytherley Hants 10 B1
West Tytherton Wilts 16 D6
West Walton Norf 37 D10
West Walton Highway Norf 37 D10
West Wellow Hants 10 C1
West Wemyss Fife 70 A2
West Wick N Som 15 E9
West Wickham Cambs 30 D3
West Wickham London 19 E10
West Williamston Pembs 22 F5
West Willoughby Lincs 36 A5
West Winch Norf 38 D2
West Winterslow Wilts 9 A11
West Wittering W Sus 11 E6
West Witton N Yorks 58 H1
West Woodburn Northumb 62 E4
West Woodhay W Berks 17 E10
West Woodlands Som 16 G4
West Worldham Hants 18 H4
West Worlington Devon 7 E6
West Worthing W Sus 11 D10
West Wratting Cambs 30 C3
West Wycombe Bucks 18 B5
West Wylam Northumb 63 G7
West Yell Shetland 96 E6
Westacott Devon 6 C4
Westbere Kent 21 E8
Westborough Lincs 36 A4
Westbourne Bmouth 9 E9
Westbourne Suff 31 D8
Westbourne W Sus 11 D6
Westbrook W Berks 17 D11
Westbury Bucks 28 E3
Westbury Shrops 33 E9
Westbury Wilts 16 F5
Westbury Leigh Wilts 16 F5
Westbury-on-Severn Glos 26 G4
Westbury on Trym Bristol 16 D2
Westbury-sub-Mendip Som 15 G11
Westby Lancs 49 F3
Westcliff-on-Sea Southend 20 C5
Westcombe Som 16 H3
Westcote Glos 27 F9
Westcott Bucks 28 G4
Westcott Devon 7 F9
Westcott Sur 19 G8
Westcott Barton Oxon 27 F11
Westdean E Sus 12 G4
Westdene Brighton 12 F1
Wester Aberchalder Highld 81 A7
Wester Balgedie Perth 76 G4
Wester Culbeuchly Aberds 89 B6
Wester Dechmont W Loth 69 D9
Wester Denoon Angus 76 C6
Wester Fintray Aberds 83 B10
Wester Gruinards Highld 87 B8
Wester Lealty Highld 87 D9
Wester Milton Highld 87 F12
Wester Newburn Fife 77 G7
Wester Quarff Shetland 96 K6
Wester Skeld Shetland 96 J4
Westerdale Highld 94 E3
Westerdale N Yorks 59 F7
Westerfield Shetland 96 H5
Westerfield Suff 31 D8
Westergate W Sus 11 D8
Westerham Kent 19 F11
Westerhope T&W 63 G7
Westerleigh S Glos 16 D4
Westerton Angus 77 B9
Westerton Durham 58 C3
Westerton W Sus 11 D7
Westerwick Shetland 96 J4
Westfield Cumb 56 D1
Westfield E Sus 13 E7
Westfield Hereford 26 D4
Westfield Highld 94 D2
Westfield N Lanark 68 C6
Westfield Norf 38 E5
Westfield W Loth 69 C8
Westfields Dorset 8 D6
Westfields of Rattray Perth 76 C4
Westgate Durham 57 C11
Westgate N Lincs 45 B11
Westgate Norf 38 A4
Westgate Norf 38 A5
Westgate on Sea Kent 21 D10
Westhall Aberds 83 A8
Westhall Suff 39 G10
Westham Dorset 8 G5
Westham E Sus 12 F5
Westham Som 15 G10
Westhampnett W Sus 11 D7
Westhay Som 15 G10
Westhead Lancs 43 B7
Westhide Hereford 26 D2
Westhill Aberds 83 C10
Westhill Highld 87 G10
Westhope Hereford 25 C11
Westhope Shrops 33 G10
Westhorpe Lincs 37 B8
Westhorpe Suff 31 B7
Westhoughton Gtr Man 43 B9
Westhouse N Yorks 50 B2
Westhumble Sur 19 F8
Westing Shetland 96 C7
Westlake Devon 5 F7
Westleigh Devon 6 D3
Westleigh Devon 7 E9
Westleigh Gtr Man 43 B9
Westleton Suff 31 B11
Westley Shrops 33 E9
Westley Suff 30 B5
Westley Waterless Cambs 30 C3
Westlington Bucks 28 G4
Westlinton Cumb 61 G9
Westmarsh Kent 21 E9
Westmeston E Sus 12 E2
Westmill Herts 29 F10
Westminster London 19 D10
Westmuir Angus 76 B6
Westness Orkney 95 F4
Westnewton Cumb 56 B3
Westnewton Northumb 71 G8
Westoe T&W 63 G9
Weston Bath 16 E4
Weston Ches E 43 G10
Weston Devon 7 H10
Weston Dorset 8 G5
Weston Halton 43 D8
Weston Hants 10 B6
Weston Herts 29 E9
Weston Lincs 37 C8
Weston N Yorks 51 E7
Weston Northants 28 D2
Weston Notts 45 F11
Weston Shrops 34 C1
Weston Shrops 34 F1
Weston Staffs 34 C5
Weston W Berks 17 D10
Weston Beggard Hereford 26 D2
Weston by Welland Northants 36 F3
Weston Colville Cambs 30 C3
Weston Coyney Stoke 34 A5
Weston Favell Northants 28 B4
Weston Green Cambs 30 C3
Weston Green Norf 39 D7
Weston Heath Shrops 34 D3
Weston Hills Lincs 37 C8
Weston-in-Gordano N Som 15 D10
Weston Jones Staffs 34 C3
Weston Longville Norf 39 D7
Weston Lullingfields Shrops 33 C10
Weston-on-the-Green Oxon 28 G2
Weston-on-Trent Derbys 35 C10
Weston Patrick Hants 18 G3
Weston Rhyn Shrops 33 B8
Weston-Sub-Edge Glos 27 D8
Weston-super-Mare N Som 15 E9
Weston Turville Bucks 28 G5
Weston under Lizard Staffs 34 D4
Weston under Penyard Hereford 26 F3
Weston under Wetherley Warks 27 B10
Weston Underwood Derbys 35 A8
Weston Underwood M Keynes 28 C5
Westonbirt Glos 16 C5
Westoncommon Shrops 33 C10
Westoning C Beds 29 E7
Westonzoyland Som 8 A2
Westow N Yorks 52 C3
Westport Argyll 65 F7
Westport Som 8 C2
Westrigg W Loth 69 D8
Westruther Borders 70 F5
Westry Cambs 37 F9
Westville Notts 45 H9
Westward Cumb 56 B4
Westward Ho! Devon 6 D3
Westwell Kent 20 G6
Westwell Oxon 27 H9
Westwell Leacon Kent 20 G6
Westwick Cambs 29 B11
Westwick Durham 58 E1
Westwick Norf 39 C8
Westwood Devon 7 G9
Westwood Wilts 16 F5
Westwoodside N Lincs 45 C11
Wetheral Cumb 56 A6
Wetherby W Yorks 51 E10
Wetherden Suff 31 B7
Wetheringsett Suff 31 B8
Wethersfield Essex 30 E4
Wethersta Shetland 96 G5
Wetherup Street Suff 31 B8
Wetley Rocks Staffs 44 H3
Wettenhall Ches E 43 F9
Wetton Staffs 44 G5
Wetwang E Yorks 52 D5
Wetwood Staffs 34 B3
Wexcombe Wilts 17 F9
Wexham Street Bucks 18 C6
Weybourne Norf 39 A7
Weybread Suff 39 G8
Weybridge Sur 19 E7
Weycroft Devon 8 E2
Weydale Highld 94 D3
Weyhill Hants 17 G10
Weymouth Dorset 8 G5
Whaddon Bucks 28 E5
Whaddon Cambs 29 D10
Whaddon Glos 26 G5
Whaddon Wilts 9 B10
Whale Cumb 57 D7
Whaley Derbys 45 E9
Whaley Bridge Derbys 44 D4
Whaley Thorns Derbys 45 E9
Whaligoe Highld 94 F5
Whalley Lancs 50 F3
Whalton Northumb 63 E7
Wham N Yorks 50 C3
Whaplode Lincs 37 C9
Whaplode Drove Lincs 37 D9
Whaplode St Catherine Lincs 37 C9
Wharfe N Yorks 50 C3
Wharles Lancs 49 F4
Wharncliffe Side S Yorks 44 C6
Wharram le Street N Yorks 52 C4
Wharton Ches W 43 F9
Wharton Green Ches W 43 F9
Whashton N Yorks 58 F2
Whatcombe Dorset 9 D7
Whatcote Warks 27 D10
Whatfield Suff 31 D7
Whatley Som 8 D2
Whatley Som 16 G4
Whatlington E Sus 13 E6
Whatstandwell Derbys 45 G7
Whatton Notts 36 B3
Whauphill Dumfries 55 E7
Whaw N Yorks 57 F11
Wheatacre Norf 39 F10
Wheatcroft Derbys 45 G7
Wheathampstead Herts 29 G8
Wheathill Shrops 34 G2
Wheatley Devon 7 G8
Wheatley Hants 18 G4
Wheatley Oxon 28 H2
Wheatley S Yorks 45 B9
Wheatley W Yorks 51 G6
Wheatley Hill Durham 58 C4
Wheaton Aston Staffs 34 D4
Wheddon Cross Som 7 C8
Wheedlemont Aberds 82 A6
Wheelerstreet Sur 18 G6
Wheelock Ches E 43 G10
Wheelock Heath Ches E 43 G10
Wheelton Lancs 50 G2
Wheen Angus 82 F5
Wheldrake York 52 E2
Whelford Glos 17 B8
Whelpley Hill Herts 18 A6
Whempstead Herts 29 F10
Whenby N Yorks 52 C2
Whepstead Suff 30 C5
Wherstead Suff 31 D8
Wherwell Hants 17 G10
Wheston Derbys 44 E5
Whetsted Kent 20 G3
Whetstone Leics 36 F1
Whicham Cumb 49 A1
Whichford Warks 27 E10
Whickham T&W 63 G8
Whiddon Down Devon 6 G5
Whigstreet Angus 77 C7
Whilton Northants 28 B3
Whim Farm Borders 69 E11
Whimble Devon 6 F2
Whimple Devon 7 G9
Whimpwell Green Norf 39 C9
Whinburgh Norf 38 E6
Whinnieliggate Dumfries 55 D10
Whinnyfold Aberds 89 E10
Whippingham IoW 10 E4
Whipsnade C Beds 29 G7
Whipton Devon 7 G8
Whirlow S Yorks 45 D7
Whisby Lincs 46 F3
Whissendine Rutland 36 D4
Whissonsett Norf 38 C5
Whistlefield Argyll 73 D10
Whistlefield Argyll 73 D11
Whistley Green Wokingham 18 D4
Whiston Mers 43 C7
Whiston Northants 28 B5
Whiston S Yorks 45 D8
Whiston Staffs 34 D4
Whiston Staffs 44 H4
Whitbeck Cumb 49 A1
Whitbourne Hereford 26 C4
Whitburn T&W 63 G10
Whitburn W Loth 69 D8
Whitburn Colliery T&W 63 G10
Whitby Ches W 43 E6
Whitby N Yorks 59 E9
Whitbyheath Ches W 43 E6
Whitchurch Bath 16 E3
Whitchurch Bucks 28 F4
Whitchurch Cardiff 15 C7
Whitchurch Devon 4 D5
Whitchurch Hants 17 G11
Whitchurch Hereford 26 G2
Whitchurch Oxon 18 D3
Whitchurch Pembs 22 D2
Whitchurch Shrops 33 A11
Whitchurch Canonicorum Dorset 8 E2
Whitchurch Hill Oxon 18 D3
Whitcombe Dorset 8 F6
Whitcott Keysett Shrops 33 G8
White Coppice Lancs 50 H2
White Lackington Dorset 8 E6
White Ladies Aston Worcs 26 C6
White Lund Lancs 49 C4
White Mill Carms 23 D9
White Ness Shetland 96 J5
White Notley Essex 30 G4
White Pit Lincs 47 E7
White Post Notts 45 G10
White Rocks Hereford 25 F11
White Roding Essex 30 G2
White Waltham Windsor 18 D5
Whiteacen Moray 88 D2
Whiteacre Heath Warks 35 F8
Whitebridge Highld 81 B6
Whitebrook Mon 26 H2
Whiteburn Borders 70 F4
Whitecairn Dumfries 54 D5
Whitecairns Aberds 83 B11
Whitecastle S Lanark 69 F9
Whitechapel Lancs 50 E1
Whitecleat Orkney 95 H6
Whitecraig E Loth 70 C2
Whitecroft Glos 26 H3
Whitecross Corn 3 B8
Whitecross Falk 69 C8
Whitecross Staffs 34 C4
Whiteface Highld 87 C10
Whitefarland N Ayrs 66 B1
Whitefaulds S Ayrs 66 F5
Whitefield Gtr Man 44 B2
Whitefield Perth 76 D4
Whiteford Aberds 83 A9
Whitegate Ches W 43 F9
Whitehall Blackburn 50 G2
Whitehall W Sus 11 B10
Whitehall Village Orkney 95 F7
Whitehaven Cumb 56 E1
Whitehill Hants 11 A6
Whitehills Aberds 89 B6
Whitehills S Lanark 68 E5
Whitehough Derbys 44 D4
Whitehouse Aberds 83 B8
Whitehouse Argyll 73 G7
Whiteinch Glasgow 68 D4
Whitekirk E Loth 70 B4
Whitelaw S Lanark 68 F5
Whiteleas T&W 63 G9
Whiteley Bank IoW 10 F4
Whiteley Green Ches E 44 E3
Whiteley Village Sur 19 E7
Whitemans Green W Sus 12 D2
Whitemire Moray 87 F12
Whitemoor Corn 3 D8
Whitemore Staffs 44 F2
Whitenap Hants 10 B2
Whiteoak Green Oxon 27 G10
Whiteparish Wilts 9 B11
Whiterashes Aberds 89 F8
Whiterow Highld 94 F5
Whiteshill Glos 26 H5
Whiteside Northumb 62 G3
Whiteside W Loth 69 D8
Whitesmith E Sus 12 E4
Whitestaunton Som 8 C1
Whitestone Devon 6 B3
Whitestone Devon 7 G7
Whitestone Warks 35 G9
Whitestones Aberds 89 C8
Whitestreet Green Suff 30 E6
Whitewall Corner N Yorks 52 B3
Whiteway Glos 16 B5
Whiteway Glos 26 G6
Whitewell Aberds 89 B9
Whitewell Lancs 50 E2
Whitewell Bottom Lancs 50 G4
Whiteworks Devon 5 D7
Whitfield Kent 21 G10
Whitfield Northants 28 E3
Whitfield Northumb 62 H3
Whitfield S Glos 16 B3
Whitford Devon 8 E1
Whitford Flint 42 E4
Whitgift E Yorks 52 G4
Whitgreave Staffs 34 C4
Whithorn Dumfries 55 E7
Whiting Bay N Ayrs 66 D3
Whitkirk W Yorks 51 F9
Whitland Carms 22 E6
Whitletts S Ayrs 67 D6
Whitley N Yorks 52 G1
Whitley Reading 18 D4
Whitley Wilts 16 E5
Whitley Bay T&W 63 F9
Whitley Chapel Northumb 62 H5
Whitley Lower W Yorks 51 H8
Whitley Row Kent 19 F11
Whitlock's End W Mid 35 H7
Whitminster Glos 26 H4
Whitmore Staffs 34 A4
Whitnage Devon 7 E9
Whitnash Warks 27 B10
Whitney-on-Wye Hereford 25 D9
Whitrigg Cumb 56 C4
Whitrigg Cumb 61 H8
Whitsbury Hants 9 C10
Whitsome Borders 71 E7
Whitson Newport 15 C9
Whitstable Kent 21 E8
Whitstone Corn 6 G1
Whittingham Northumb 62 B6
Whittingslow Shrops 33 G10
Whittington Glos 27 F7
Whittington Lancs 50 B2
Whittington Norf 38 F3
Whittington Shrops 33 B9
Whittington Staffs 34 G4
Whittington Staffs 35 E7
Whittington Worcs 26 C5
Whittle-le-Woods Lancs 50 G1
Whittlebury Northants 28 D3
Whittlesey Cambs 37 F8
Whittlesford Cambs 29 D11
Whittlestone Head Blackburn 50 H3
Whitton Borders 62 A3
Whitton N Lincs 52 G5
Whitton Northumb 62 C6
Whitton Powys 25 B9
Whitton Shrops 26 A2
Whitton Stockton 58 D4
Whitton Suff 31 D8
Whittonditch Wilts 17 D9
Whittonstall Northumb 62 H6
Whitway Hants 17 F11
Whitwell Derbys 45 E9
Whitwell Herts 29 F8
Whitwell IoW 10 G4
Whitwell N Yorks 58 G3
Whitwell Rutland 36 E5
Whitwell-on-the-Hill N Yorks 52 C3
Whitwell Street Norf 39 C7
Whitwick Leics 35 D10
Whitwood W Yorks 51 G10
Whitworth Lancs 50 H4
Whixall Shrops 33 B11
Whixley N Yorks 51 D10
Whoberley W Mid 35 H9
Whorlton Durham 58 E2
Whorlton N Yorks 58 F5
Whygate Northumb 62 F3
Whyle Hereford 26 B2
Whyteleafe Sur 19 F10
Wibdon Glos 16 B2
Wibsey W Yorks 51 F7
Wibtoft Leics 35 G10
Wichenford Worcs 26 B4
Wichling Kent 20 F6
Wick Bmouth 9 E10
Wick Devon 7 F10
Wick Highld 94 E5
Wick S Glos 16 D4
Wick Shetland 96 K6
Wick V Glam 14 D5
Wick W Sus 11 D9
Wick Wilts 9 B10
Wick Worcs 26 D6
Wick Hill Wokingham 18 E4
Wick St Lawrence N Som 15 E9
Wicken Cambs 30 A2
Wicken Northants 28 E4
Wicken Bonhunt Essex 29 E11
Wicken Green Village Norf 38 B4
Wickenby Lincs 46 D4
Wickersley S Yorks 45 C8
Wickford Essex 20 B4
Wickham Hants 10 C4
Wickham W Berks 17 D10
Wickham Bishops Essex 30 G5
Wickham Market Suff 31 C10
Wickham Skeith Suff 31 B7
Wickham St Paul Essex 30 E5
Wickham Street Suff 30 C4
Wickham Street Suff 31 B7
Wickhambreux Kent 21 F9
Wickhambrook Suff 30 C4
Wickhamford Worcs 27 D7
Wickhampton Norf 39 E10
Wicklewood Norf 39 E6
Wickmere Norf 39 B7
Wickwar S Glos 16 C4
Widdington Essex 30 E2
Widdrington Northumb 63 D8
Widdrington Station Northumb 63 D8
Wide Open T&W 63 F8
Widecombe in the Moor Devon 5 D8
Widegates Corn 4 F3
Widemouth Bay Corn 4 A3
Widewall Orkney 95 J5
Widford Essex 30 H3
Widford Herts 29 G11
Widham Wilts 17 C7
Widmer End Bucks 18 B5
Widmerpool Notts 36 C2
Widnes Halton 43 D8
Wigan Gtr Man 43 B8
Wiggaton Devon 7 G10
Wiggenhall St Germans Norf 38 D1
Wiggenhall St Mary Magdalen Norf 38 D1
Wiggenhall St Mary the Virgin Norf 38 D1
Wigginton Herts 28 G6
Wigginton Oxon 27 E10
Wigginton Staffs 35 E8
Wigginton York 52 D1
Wigglesworth N Yorks 50 D4
Wiggonby Cumb 56 A4
Wiggonholt W Sus 11 C9
Wighill N Yorks 51 E10
Wighton Norf 38 B5
Wigley Hants 10 C2
Wigmore Hereford 25 B11
Wigmore Medway 20 E5
Wigsley Notts 46 E2
Wigsthorpe Northants 36 G6
Wigston Leics 36 F2
Wigthorpe Notts 45 D9
Wigtoft Lincs 37 B8
Wigton Cumb 56 B4
Wigtown Dumfries 55 D7
Wigtwizzle S Yorks 44 C6
Wike W Yorks 51 E9
Wike Well End S Yorks 45 A10
Wilbarston Northants 36 G4
Wilberfoss E Yorks 52 D3
Wilberlee W Yorks 44 A4
Wilburton Cambs 29 A11
Wilby Norf 38 G6
Wilby Northants 28 B5
Wilby Suff 31 A9
Wilcot Wilts 17 E8
Wilcott Shrops 33 D9
Wilcrick Newport 15 C10
Wilday Green Derbys 45 E7
Wildboarclough Ches E 44 F3
Wilden Bedford 29 C7
Wilden Worcs 26 A5
Wildhern Hants 17 F10
Wildhill Herts 29 H9
Wildmoor Worcs 34 H5
Wildsworth Lincs 46 C2
Wilford Nottingham 36 B1
Wilkesley Ches E 34 A2
Wilkhaven Highld 87 C12
Wilkieston W Loth 69 D10
Willand Devon 7 E9
Willaston Ches E 43 G9
Willaston Ches W 42 E6
Willen M Keynes 28 D5
Willenhall W Mid 34 F5
Willenhall W Mid 35 H9
Willerby E Yorks 52 F6
Willerby N Yorks 52 B6
Willersey Glos 27 E8
Willersley Hereford 25 D10
Willesborough Kent 13 B9
Willesborough Lees Kent 13 B9
Willesden London 19 C9
Willett Som 7 C10
Willey Shrops 34 F2
Willey Warks 35 G10
Willey Green Sur 18 F6
Williamscott Oxon 27 D11
Willian Herts 29 E9
Willingale Essex 30 H2
Willingdon E Sus 12 F4
Willingham Cambs 29 A11
Willingham by Stow Lincs 46 D2
Willington Bedford 29 D8
Willington Derbys 35 C8
Willington Durham 58 C2
Willington T&W 63 G9
Willington Warks 27 E9
Willington Corner Ches W 43 F8
Willisham Tye Suff 31 C7
Willitoft E Yorks 52 F3
Williton Som 7 B9
Willoughbridge Staffs 34 A3
Willoughby Lincs 47 E8
Willoughby Warks 28 B2
Willoughby-on-the-Wolds Notts 36 C2
Willoughby Waterleys Leics 36 F1
Willoughton Lincs 46 C3
Willows Grn. Essex 30 G4
Willsbridge S Glos 16 D3
Willsworthy Devon 4 C6
Wilmcote Warks 27 C8
Wilmington Devon 7 G11
Wilmington E Sus 12 F4
Wilmington Kent 20 D2
Wilminstone Devon 4 D5
Wilmslow Ches E 44 D2
Wilnecote Staffs 35 E8
Wilpshire Lancs 50 F2
Wilsden W Yorks 51 F6
Wilsford Lincs 36 A6
Wilsford Wilts 17 F8
Wilsford Wilts 17 H8
Wilsill N Yorks 51 C7
Wilsley Pound Kent 13 C6
Wilsom Hants 18 H4
Wilson Leics 35 C10
Wilsontown S Lanark 69 E8
Wilstead Bedford 29 D7
Wilsthorpe Lincs 37 D6
Wilstone Herts 28 G6
Wilton Borders 61 B10
Wilton Cumb 56 E2
Wilton N Yorks 52 A4
Wilton Redcar 59 E6
Wilton Wilts 9 A9
Wilton Wilts 17 E9
Wimbish Essex 30 E2
Wimbish Green Essex 30 E3
Wimblebury Staffs 34 D6
Wimbledon London 19 D9
Wimblington Cambs 37 F10
Wimborne Minster Dorset 9 E9
Wimborne St Giles Dorset 9 C9
Wimbotsham Norf 38 E2
Wimpson Soton 10 C2
Wimpstone Warks 27 D9
Wincanton Som 8 B6
Wincham Ches W 43 E9
Winchburgh W Loth 69 C9
Winchcombe Glos 27 F7
Winchelsea E Sus 13 E8
Winchelsea Beach E Sus 13 E8
Winchester Hants 10 B3
Winchet Hill Kent 12 B6
Winchfield Hants 18 F4
Winchmore Hill Bucks 18 B6
Winchmore Hill London 19 B10
Wincle Ches E 44 F3
Wincobank S Yorks 45 C7
Windermere Cumb 56 G6
Winderton Warks 27 D10
Windhill Highld 87 G8
Windhouse Shetland 96 D6
Windlehurst Gtr Man 44 D3
Windlesham Sur 18 E6
Windley Derbys 35 A9
Windmill Hill E Sus 12 E5
Windmill Hill Som 8 C2
Windrush Glos 27 G8
Windsor N Lincs 45 A11
Windsor Windsor 18 D6
Windsoredge Glos 16 A5
Windygates Fife 76 G6
Windyknowe W Loth 69 D8
Windywalls Borders 70 G6
Wineham W Sus 11 B11
Winestead E Yorks 53 G8
Winewall Lancs 50 E5
Winfarthing Norf 39 G7
Winford IoW 10 F4
Winford N Som 15 E11
Winforton Hereford 25 D9
Winfrith Newburgh Dorset 9 F7
Wing Bucks 28 F5
Wing Rutland 36 E4
Wingate Durham 58 C5
Wingates Gtr Man 43 B9
Wingates Northumb 63 D7
Wingerworth Derbys 45 F7
Wingfield C Beds 29 F7
Wingfield Suff 39 H8
Wingfield Wilts 16 F5
Wingham Kent 21 F9
Wingmore Kent 21 G8
Wingrave Bucks 28 G5
Winkburn Notts 45 G11
Winkfield Brack 18 D6
Winkfield Row Brack 18 D5
Winkhill Staffs 44 G4
Winklebury Hants 18 F3
Winkleigh Devon 6 F5
Winksley N Yorks 51 B8
Winkton Dorset 9 E10
Winlaton T&W 63 G7
Winless Highld 94 E5
Winmarleigh Lancs 49 E4
Winnal Hereford 25 E11
Winnall Hants 10 B3
Winnersh Wokingham 18 D4
Winscales Cumb 56 D2
Winscombe N Som 15 F10
Winsford Ches W 43 F9
Winsford Som 7 C8
Winsham Som 8 D2
Winshill Staffs 35 C8
Winskill Cumb 57 C7
Winslade Hants 18 G3
Winsley Wilts 16 E5
Winslow Bucks 28 F4
Winson Glos 27 H7
Winson Grn. W Mid 34 G6
Winsor Hants 10 C2
Winster Cumb 56 G6
Winster Derbys 44 F6
Winston Durham 58 E2
Winston Suff 31 B8
Winston Green Suff 31 B8
Winstone Glos 26 H6
Winswell Devon 6 E3
Winter Gardens Essex 20 C4
Winterborne Clenston Dorset 9 D7
Winterborne Herringston Dorset 8 F5
Winterborne Houghton Dorset 9 D7
Winterborne Kingston Dorset 9 E7
Winterborne Monkton Dorset 8 F5
Winterborne Stickland Dorset 9 D7
Winterborne Whitechurch Dorset 9 D7
Winterborne Zelston Dorset 9 E7
Winterbourne S Glos 16 C3
Winterbourne W Berks 17 D11
Winterbourne Abbas Dorset 8 E5
Winterbourne Bassett Wilts 17 D8
Winterbourne Dauntsey Wilts 9 A10
Winterbourne Down S Glos 16 D3
Winterbourne Earls Wilts 9 A10
Winterbourne Gunner Wilts 17 H8
Winterbourne Monkton Wilts 17 D8
Winterbourne Steepleton Dorset 8 F5
Winterbourne Stoke Wilts 17 G7
Winterburn N Yorks 50 D5
Winteringham N Lincs 52 G5
Winterley Ches E 43 G10
Wintersett W Yorks 51 H9
Wintershill Hants 10 C4
Winterton N Lincs 52 H5
Winterton-on-Sea Norf 39 D10
Winthorpe Lincs 47 F9
Winthorpe Notts 46 G2
Winton Bmouth 9 E9
Winton Cumb 57 E9
Winton N Yorks 58 G5
Wintringham N Yorks 52 B4
Winwick Cambs 37 G7
Winwick Northants 28 A3
Winwick Warr 43 C9
Wirksworth Derbys 44 G6
Wirksworth Moor Derbys 45 G7
Wirswall Ches E 33 A11
Wisbech Cambs 37 E10
Wisbech St Mary Cambs 37 E10
Wisborough Green W Sus 11 B9
Wiseton Notts 45 D11
Wishaw N Lanark 68 E6
Wishaw Warks 35 F7
Wisley Sur 19 F7
Wispington Lincs 46 E6
Wissenden Kent 13 B8
Wissett Suff 39 H9
Wistanstow Shrops 33 G10
Wistanswick Shrops 34 C2
Wistaston Ches E 43 G9
Wistaston Green Ches E 43 G9
Wiston Pembs 22 E5
Wiston S Lanark 69 G8
Wiston W Sus 11 C10
Wistow Cambs 37 G8
Wistow N Yorks 52 F1
Wiswell Lancs 50 F3
Witcham Cambs 37 G10
Witchampton Dorset 9 D8
Witchford Cambs 37 H11
Witham Essex 30 G5
Witham Friary Som 16 G4
Witham on the Hill Lincs 37 D6
Withcall Lincs 46 D6
Withdean Brighton 12 F2
Witherenden Hill E Sus 12 D5
Witheridge Devon 7 E7
Witherley Leics 35 F9
Withern Lincs 47 D8
Withernsea E Yorks 53 G9
Withernwick E Yorks 53 E7
Withersdale Street Suff 39 G8
Withersfield Suff 30 D3
Witherslack Cumb 49 A4
Withiel Corn 3 C8
Withiel Florey Som 7 C8
Withington Glos 27 G7
Withington Gtr Man 44 C2
Withington Hereford 26 D2
Withington Shrops 34 D1
Withington Staffs 34 B6
Withington Green Ches E 44 E2
Withleigh Devon 7 E8
Withnell Lancs 50 G2
Withybrook Warks 35 G10
Withycombe Som 7 B9
Withycombe Raleigh Devon 5 C11
Withyham E Sus 12 C3
Withypool Som 7 C7
Witley Sur 18 H6
Witnesham Suff 31 C8
Witney Oxon 27 G10
Wittering Pboro 37 E6
Wittersham Kent 13 D7
Witton Angus 83 F7
Witton Worcs 26 B5
Witton Bridge Norf 39 B9
Witton Gilbert Durham 58 B3
Witton-le-Wear Durham 58 C2
Witton Park Durham 58 C2
Wiveliscombe Som 7 D9
Wivelrod Hants 18 H3
Wivelsfield E Sus 12 D2
Wivelsfield Green E Sus 12 D2
Wivenhoe Essex 31 F7
Wivenhoe Cross Essex 31 F7
Wiveton Norf 38 A6
Wix Essex 31 F8
Wixford Warks 27 C7
Wixhill Shrops 34 C1
Wixoe Suff 30 D4
Woburn C Beds 28 E6
Woburn Sands M Keynes 28 E6
Wokefield Park W Berks 18 E3
Woking Sur 19 F7
Wokingham Wokingham 18 E5
Wolborough Devon 5 D9
Wold Newton E Yorks 52 B6
Wold Newton NE Lincs 46 C6
Woldingham Sur 19 F10
Wolfclyde S Lanark 69 G9
Wolferton Norf 38 C2
Wolfhill Perth 76 D4
Wolf's Castle Pembs 22 D4
Wolfsdale Pembs 22 D4
Woll Borders 61 A10
Wollaston Northants 28 B6
Wollaston Shrops 33 D9
Wollaton Nottingham 35 B11
Wollerton Shrops 34 B2
Wollescote W Mid 34 G5
Wolsingham Durham 58 C1
Wolstanton Staffs 44 H2
Wolston Warks 35 H10
Wolvercote Oxon 27 H11
Wolverhampton W Mid 34 F5
Wolverley Shrops 33 B10
Wolverley Worcs 34 H4
Wolverton Hants 18 F2
Wolverton M Keynes 28 D5
Wolverton Warks 27 B9
Wolverton Common Hants 18 F2
Wolvesnewton Mon 15 B10
Wolvey Warks 35 G10
Wolviston Stockton 58 D5
Wombleton N Yorks 52 A2
Wombourne Staffs 34 F4
Wombwell S Yorks 45 B7
Womenswold Kent 21 F9
Womersley N Yorks 51 H11
Wonastow Mon 25 G11
Wonersh Sur 19 G7
Wonson Devon 5 C7
Wonston Hants 17 H11
Wooburn Bucks 18 C6
Wooburn Green Bucks 18 C6
Wood Dalling Norf 39 C6
Wood End Herts 29 F10
Wood End Warks 27 A8
Wood End Warks 35 F8
Wood Enderby Lincs 46 F6
Wood Field Sur 19 F8
Wood Green London 19 B10
Wood Hayes W Mid 34 E5
Wood Lanes Ches E 44 D3
Wood Norton Norf 38 C6
Wood Street Norf 39 C9
Wood Street Sur 18 F6
Wood Walton Cambs 37 G8
Woodacott Devon 6 F2
Woodale N Yorks 50 B6
Woodbank Argyll 65 G7
Woodbastwick Norf 39 D9
Woodbeck Notts 45 E11
Woodborough Notts 45 H10
Woodborough Wilts 17 F8
Woodbridge Dorset 8 C6
Woodbridge Suff 31 D9
Woodbury Devon 5 C11
Woodbury Salterton Devon 5 C11
Woodchester Glos 16 A5
Woodchurch Kent 13 C8
Woodchurch Mers 42 D5
Woodcombe Som 7 B8
Woodcote Oxon 18 C3
Woodcott Hants 17 F11
Woodcroft Glos 15 B11
Woodcutts Dorset 9 C8
Woodditton Cambs 30 C3
Woodeaton Oxon 28 G2
Woodend Cumb 56 G3
Woodend Northants 28 D3
Woodend W Sus 11 D7
Woodend Green Northants 28 D3
Woodfalls Wilts 9 B10
Woodfield Oxon 28 F2
Woodfield S Ayrs 66 D6
Woodford Corn 6 E1
Woodford Devon 5 F8
Woodford Glos 16 B3
Woodford Gtr Man 44 D2
Woodford London 19 B11
Woodford Northants 36 H5
Woodford Bridge London 19 B11
Woodford Halse Northants 28 C2
Woodgate Norf 38 D6
Woodgate W Mid 34 G5
Woodgate W Sus 11 D8
Woodgate Worcs 26 B6
Woodgreen Hants 9 C10
Woodhall Herts 29 G9
Woodhall Invclyd 68 C2
Woodhall N Yorks 57 G11
Woodhall Spa Lincs 46 F5
Woodham Sur 19 E7
Woodham Ferrers Essex 20 B4
Woodham Mortimer Essex 20 A5
Woodham Walter Essex 30 H5
Woodhaven Fife 77 E7
Woodhead Aberds 89 E7
Woodhey Gtr Man 50 H3
Woodhill Shrops 34 G3
Woodhorn Northumb 63 E8
Woodhouse Leics 35 D11
Woodhouse N Lincs 45 B11
Woodhouse S Yorks 45 D8
Woodhouse W Yorks 51 F8
Woodhouse W Yorks 51 G9
Woodhouse Eaves Leics 35 D11
Woodhouse Park Gtr Man 44 D2
Woodhouselee Midloth 69 D11
Woodhouselees Dumfries 61 F9
Woodhouses Staffs 35 D7
Woodhurst Cambs 37 H9
Woodingdean Brighton 12 F2
Woodkirk W Yorks 51 G8
Woodland Devon 5 E8
Woodland Durham 58 D1
Woodlands Aberds 83 D9
Woodlands Dorset 9 D9
Woodlands Hants 10 C2
Woodlands Highld 87 E8
Woodlands N Yorks 51 D9
Woodlands S Yorks 45 B9
Woodlands Park Windsor 18 D5
Woodlands St Mary W Berks 17 D10
Woodlane Staffs 35 C7
Woodleigh Devon 5 G8
Woodlesford W Yorks 51 G9
Woodley Gtr Man 44 C3
Woodley Wokingham 18 D4
Woodmancote Glos 16 B4
Woodmancote Glos 26 F6
Woodmancote Glos 27 H7
Woodmancote W Sus 11 C11
Woodmancote W Sus 11 D6
Woodmancott Hants 18 G2
Woodmansey E Yorks 53 F6
Woodmansterne Sur 19 F9
Woodminton Wilts 9 B9
Woodnesborough Kent 21 F10
Woodnewton Northants 36 F6
Woodplumpton Lancs 49 F5
Woodrising Norf 38 E5
Wood's Green E Sus 12 C5
Woodseaves Shrops 34 B2
Woodseaves Staffs 34 C3
Woodsend Wilts 17 D9
Woodsetts S Yorks 45 D9
Woodsford Dorset 9 E6
Woodside Aberdeen 83 C11
Woodside Aberds 89 D10
Woodside Brack 18 D6
Woodside Fife 77 G7
Woodside Hants 10 E2
Woodside Herts 29 H9
Woodside Perth 76 D5
Woodside of Arbeadie Aberds 83 D9
Woodstock Oxon 27 G11
Woodstock Pembs 22 D5
Woodthorpe Derbys 45 E8
Woodthorpe Leics 35 D11
Woodthorpe Lincs 47 D8
Woodthorpe York 52 E1
Woodton Norf 39 F8
Woodtown Devon 6 D3
Woodtown Devon 6 D3
Woodvale Mers 42 A6
Woodville Derbys 35 D9
Woodyates Dorset 9 C9
Woofferton Shrops 26 B2
Wookey Som 15 G11
Wookey Hole Som 15 G11
Wool Dorset 9 F7
Woolacombe Devon 6 B3
Woolage Green Kent 21 G9
Woolaston Glos 16 B2
Woolavington Som 15 G9
Woolbeding W Sus 11 B7
Wooldale W Yorks 44 B5
Wooler Northumb 71 H8
Woolfardisworthy Devon 6 D2
Woolfardisworthy Devon 7 F7
Woolfords Cottages S Lanark 69 E9
Woolhampton W Berks 18 E2
Woolhope Hereford 26 E3
Woolhope Cockshoot Hereford 26 E3
Woolland Dorset 9 D6
Woollaton Devon 6 E3
Woolley Bath 16 E4
Woolley Cambs 29 A8
Woolley Corn 6 E1
Woolley Derbys 45 F7
Woolley W Yorks 45 A7
Woolmer Green Herts 29 G9
Woolmere Green Worcs 26 B6
Woolpit Suff 30 B6
Woolscott Warks 27 B11
Woolsington T&W 63 G7
Woolstanwood Ches E 43 G9
Woolstaston Shrops 33 F10
Woolsthorpe Lincs 36 B4
Woolsthorpe Lincs 36 C5
Woolston Devon 5 G8
Woolston Shrops 33 C9
Woolston Shrops 33 G10
Woolston Soton 10 C3
Woolston Warr 43 D9
Woolstone Keynes 28 E5
Woolstone Oxon 17 C9
Woolton Mers 43 D7
Woolton Hill Hants 17 E11
Woolverstone Suff 31 E8
Woolverton Som 16 F4
Woolwich London 19 D11
Woolwich Ferry London 19 D11
Woonton Hereford 25 C10
Wooperton Northumb 62 A6
Woore Shrops 34 A3
Wootten Green Suff 31 A9
Wootton Bedford 29 D7
Wootton Hants 9 E11
Wootton Hereford 25 C10
Wootton Kent 21 G9
Wootton N Lincs 53 H6
Wootton Northants 28 C4
Wootton Oxon 17 A11
Wootton Oxon 27 G11
Wootton Shrops 33 C9
Wootton Shrops 33 H10
Wootton Staffs 34 C4
Wootton Staffs 44 H5
Wootton Bridge IoW 10 E4
Wootton Common IoW 10 E4
Wootton Courtenay Som 7 B8
Wootton Fitzpaine Dorset 8 E2
Wootton Rivers Wilts 17 E8
Wootton St Lawrence Hants 18 F2
Wootton Wawen Warks 27 B8
Worcester Worcs 26 C5
Worcester Park London 19 E9
Wordsley W Mid 34 G4
Worfield Shrops 34 F3
Work Orkney 95 G5
Workington Cumb 56 D1
Worksop Notts 45 E9
Worlaby N Lincs 46 A4
World's End W Berks 17 D11
Worle N Som 15 E9
Worleston Ches E 43 G9
Worlingham Suff 39 G10
Worlington Suff 30 A3
Worlingworth Suff 31 B9
Wormald Green N Yorks 51 C9
Wormbridge Hereford 25 E11
Wormegay Norf 38 D2
Wormelow Tump Hereford 25 E11
Wormhill Derbys 44 E5
Wormingford Essex 30 E6
Worminghall Bucks 28 H3
Wormington Glos 27 E7
Worminster Som 16 G2
Wormit Fife 76 E6
Wormleighton Warks 27 C11
Wormley Herts 29 H10
Wormley Sur 18 H6
Wormley West End Herts 29 H10
Wormshill Kent 20 F5
Wormsley Hereford 25 D11
Worplesdon Sur 18 F6
Worrall S Yorks 45 C7
Worsbrough S Yorks 45 B7
Worsbrough Common S Yorks 45 B7
Worsley Gtr Man 43 B10
Worstead Norf 39 C9
Worsthorne Lancs 50 F4
Worston Lancs 50 E3
Worswell Devon 4 G6
Worth Kent 21 F10
Worth W Sus 12 C2
Worth Matravers Dorset 9 G8
Wortham Suff 39 H6
Worthen Shrops 33 E9
Worthenbury Wrex 43 H7
Worthing Norf 38 D5
Worthing W Sus 11 D10
Worthington Leics 35 C10
Worting Hants 18 F3
Wortley S Yorks 45 C7
Wortley W Yorks 51 F8
Worton N Yorks 57 G11
Worton Wilts 16 F6
Wortwell Norf 39 G8
Wotherton Shrops 33 E8
Wotter Devon 5 E6
Wotton Sur 19 G8
Wotton-under-Edge Glos 16 B4
Wotton Underwood Bucks 28 G3
Woughton on the Green M Keynes 28 E5
Wouldham Kent 20 E4
Wrabness Essex 31 E8
Wrafton Devon 6 C3
Wragby Lincs 46 E5
Wragby W Yorks 51 H10
Wragholme Lincs 47 C7
Wramplingham Norf 39 E7
Wrangbrook W Yorks 45 A8
Wrangham Aberds 89 E6
Wrangle Lincs 47 G8
Wrangle Bank Lincs 47 G8
Wrangle Lowgate Lincs 47 G8
Wrangway Som 7 E10
Wrantage Som 8 B2
Wrawby N Lincs 46 B4
Wraxall Dorset 8 D4
Wraxall N Som 15 D10
Wraxall Som 16 H3
Wray Lancs 50 C2
Wraysbury Windsor 19 D7
Wrayton Lancs 50 B2
Wrea Green Lancs 49 F3
Wreay Cumb 56 B6
Wreay Cumb 56 D6
Wrecclesham Sur 18 G5
Wrecsam = Wrexham Wrex 42 G6
Wrekenton T&W 63 H8
Wrelton N Yorks 59 H8
Wrenbury Ches E 43 H8
Wrench Green N Yorks 59 H10
Wreningham Norf 39 F7
Wrentham Suff 39 G10
Wrenthorpe W Yorks 51 G9
Wrentnall Shrops 33 E10
Wressle E Yorks 52 F3
Wressle N Lincs 46 B3
Wrestlingworth C Beds 29 D9
Wretham Norf 38 G5
Wretton Norf 38 F2
Wrexham = Wrecsam Wrex 42 G6
Wrexham Industrial Estate Wrex 43 H6
Wribbenhall Worcs 34 H3
Wrightington Bar Lancs 43 A8
Wrinehill Staffs 43 H10
Wrington N Som 15 E10
Writhlington Bath 16 F4
Writtle Essex 30 H3
Wrockwardine Telford 34 D2
Wroot N Lincs 45 B11
Wrotham Kent 20 F3
Wrotham Heath Kent 20 F3
Wroughton Swindon 17 C8
Wroxall IoW 10 G4
Wroxall Warks 27 A9
Wroxeter Shrops 34 E1
Wroxham Norf 39 D9
Wroxton Oxon 27 D11
Wyaston Derbys 35 A7
Wyberton Lincs 37 A9
Wyboston Bedford 29 C8
Wybunbury Ches E 43 H10
Wych Cross E Sus 12 C3
Wychbold Worcs 26 B6
Wyck Hants 18 H4
Wyck Rissington Glos 27 F8
Wycoller Lancs 50 F5
Wycomb Leics 36 C3
Wycombe Marsh Bucks 18 B5
Wyddial Herts 29 E10
Wye Kent 21 G7
Wyesham Mon 26 G2
Wyfordby Leics 36 D3
Wyke Dorset 9 B6
Wyke Shrops 34 E2
Wyke Sur 18 F6
Wyke W Yorks 51 G7
Wyke Regis Dorset 8 G5
Wykeham N Yorks 52 A5
Wykeham N Yorks 52 B4
Wyken W Mid 35 G9
Wykey Shrops 33 C9
Wylam Northumb 63 G7
Wylde Green W Mid 35 F7
Wyllie Caerph 15 B7
Wylye Wilts 17 H7
Wymering Ptsmth 10 D5
Wymeswold Leics 36 C2
Wymington Bedford 28 B6
Wymondham Leics 36 D4
Wymondham Norf 39 E7
Wyndham Bridgend 14 B5
Wynford Eagle Dorset 8 E4
Wyng Orkney 95 J4
Wynyard Village Stockton 58 D5
Wyre Piddle Worcs 26 D6
Wysall Notts 36 C2
Wythall Worcs 35 H6
Wytham Oxon 27 H11
Wythburn Cumb 56 E5
Wythenshawe Gtr Man 44 D2
Wythop Mill Cumb 56 D3
Wyton Cambs 29 A9
Wyverstone Suff 31 B7
Wyverstone Street Suff 31 B7
Wyville Lincs 36 C4
Wyvis Lodge Highld 86 D7

Y

Y Bala = Bala Gwyn 32 B5
Y Barri = Barry V Glam 15 E7
Y Bont-Faen = Cowbridge V Glam 14 D5
Y Drenewydd = Newtown Powys 33 F7
Y Felinheli Gwyn 41 D7
Y Fenni = Abergavenny Mon 25 G9
Y Ffôr Gwyn 40 G5
Y Fflint = Flint Flint 42 E5
Y-Ffrith Denb 42 D3
Y Gelli Gandryll = Hay-on-Wye Powys 25 D9
Y Mwmbwls = The Mumbles Swansea 14 C2
Y Pîl = Pyle Bridgend 14 C4
Y Rhws = Rhoose V Glam 14 E6
Y Rhyl = Rhyl Denb 42 D3
Y Trallwng = Welshpool Powys 33 E8
Y Waun = Chirk Wrex 33 B8
Yaddlethorpe N Lincs 46 B2
Yafford IoW 10 F3
Yafforth N Yorks 58 G4
Yalding Kent 20 F3
Yanworth Glos 27 G7
Yapham E Yorks 52 D3
Yapton W Sus 11 D8
Yarburgh Lincs 47 C7
Yarcombe Devon 8 D1
Yard Som 7 C9
Yardley W Mid 35 G7
Yardley Gobion Northants 28 D4
Yardley Hastings Northants 28 C5
Yardro Powys 25 C9
Yarkhill Hereford 26 D3
Yarlet Staffs 34 C5
Yarlington Som 8 B5
Yarlside Cumb 49 C2
Yarm Stockton 58 E5
Yarmouth IoW 10 F2
Yarnbrook Wilts 16 F5
Yarnfield Staffs 34 B4
Yarnscombe Devon 6 D4
Yarnton Oxon 27 G11
Yarpole Hereford 25 B11
Yarrow Borders 70 H2
Yarrow Feus Borders 70 H2
Yarsop Hereford 25 D11
Yarwell Northants 37 F6
Yate S Glos 16 C4
Yateley Hants 18 E5
Yatesbury Wilts 17 D7
Yattendon W Berks 18 D2
Yatton Hereford 25 B11
Yatton N Som 15 E10
Yatton Keynell Wilts 16 D5
Yaverland IoW 10 F5
Yaxham Norf 38 D6
Yaxley Cambs 37 F7
Yaxley Suff 31 A8
Yazor Hereford 25 D11
Yeading London 19 C8
Yeadon W Yorks 51 E8
Yealand Conyers Lancs 49 B5
Yealand Redmayne Lancs 49 B5
Yealmpton Devon 5 F6
Yearby Redcar 59 D7
Yearsley N Yorks 52 B1
Yeaton Shrops 33 D10
Yeaveley Derbys 35 A7
Yedingham N Yorks 52 B4
Yeldon Bedford 29 B7
Yelford Oxon 17 A10
Yelland Devon 6 C3
Yelling Cambs 29 B9
Yelvertoft Northants 36 H1
Yelverton Devon 4 E6
Yelverton Norf 39 E8
Yenston Som 8 B6
Yeo Mill Devon 7 D7
Yeoford Devon 7 G6
Yeolmbridge Corn 4 C4
Yeovil Som 8 C4
Yeovil Marsh Som 8 C4
Yeovilton Som 8 B4
Yerbeston Pembs 22 F5
Yesnaby Orkney 95 G3
Yetlington Northumb 62 C6
Yetminster Dorset 8 C4
Yettington Devon 7 H9
Yetts o' Muckhart Clack 76 G3
Yieldshields S Lanark 69 E7
Yiewsley London 19 C7
Ynys-meudwy Neath 24 H4
Ynysboeth Rhondda 14 B6
Ynysddu Caerph 15 B7
Ynysgyfflog Gwyn 32 D2
Ynyshir Rhondda 14 B6
Ynyslas Ceredig 32 F2
Ynystawe Swansea 14 A2
Ynysybwl Rhondda 14 B6
Yockenthwaite N Yorks 50 B5
Yockleton Shrops 33 D9
Yokefleet E Yorks 52 G4
Yoker W Dunb 68 D4
Yonder Bognie Aberds 88 D5
York York 52 D1
York Town Sur 18 E5
Yorkletts Kent 21 E7
Yorkley Glos 26 H3
Yorton Shrops 33 C11
Youlgreave Derbys 44 F6
Youlstone Devon 6 E1
Youlthorpe E Yorks 52 D3
Youlton N Yorks 51 C10
Young Wood Lincs 46 E5
Young's End Essex 30 G4
Yoxall Staffs 35 D7
Yoxford Suff 31 B10
Yr Hôb = Hope Flint 42 G6
Yr Wyddgrug = Mold Flint 42 F5
Ysbyty-Cynfyn Ceredig 32 H3
Ysbyty Ifan Conwy 41 F10
Ysbyty Ystwyth Ceredig 24 A4
Ysceifiog Flint 42 E4
Yspitty Carms 23 G10
Ystalyfera Neath 24 H4
Ystrad Rhondda 14 B5
Ystrad Aeron Ceredig 23 A10
Ystrad-mynach Caerph 15 B7
Ystradfellte Powys 24 G6
Ystradffin Carms 24 D4
Ystradgynlais Powys 24 G4
Ystradmeurig Ceredig 24 B4
Ystradowen Carms 24 G4
Ystradowen V Glam 14 D6
Ystumtuen Ceredig 32 H3
Ythanbank Aberds 89 E9
Ythanwells Aberds 89 E6
Ythsie Aberds 89 E8

Z

Zeal Monachorum Devon 6 F6
Zeals Wilts 9 A6
Zelah Corn 3 D7
Zennor Corn 2 F3